COLLECTED CRITICA

CW00821294

GEOFFREY H

The *Collected Critical Writings* gathers more than forty years of Hill's published criticism, in a revised final form, and also adds much new work. It will serve as the canonical volume of criticism by Hill, the pre-eminent poet-critic whom A. N. Wilson has called 'probably the best writer alive, in verse or in prose'. In his criticism Hill ranges widely, investigating both poets (including Jonson, Dryden, Hopkins, Whitman, Eliot, and Yeats) and prose writers (such as Tyndale, Clarendon, Hobbes, Burton, Emerson, and F. H. Bradley). He is also steeped in the historical context – political, poetic, and religious – of the writers he studies. Most importantly, he brings texts and contexts into new and telling relations, neither reducing texts to the circumstances of their utterance nor imagining that they can float free of them. A number of the essays have already established themselves as essential reading on particular subjects, such as his analysis of Vaughan's 'The Night', his discussion of Gurney's poetry, and his critical account of *The Oxford English Dictionary*. Others confront the problems of language and the nature of value directly, as in 'Our Word is Our Bond', 'Language, Suffering, and Silence', and 'Poetry and Value'. In all his criticism, Hill reveals literature to be an essential arena of civic intelligence.

Born in Bromsgrove, Worcestershire in 1932, Geoffrey Hill is the author of a dozen books of poetry. From 1988 to 2006 he taught as a University Professor and Professor of Literature and Religion at Boston University. He is also Honorary Fellow of Keble College, Oxford; Honorary Fellow of Emmanuel College, Cambridge; Fellow of the Royal Society of Literature; and Fellow of the American Academy of Arts and Sciences. He currently lives in Cambridge, England.

Kenneth Haynes is Associate Professor of Comparative Literature and Classics at Brown University.

COLLECTED CRITICAL WRITINGS

GEOFFREY HILL

EDITED BY

KENNETH HAYNES

OXFORD
UNIVERSITY PRESS

OXFORD
UNIVERSITY PRESS

Great Clarendon Street, Oxford OX2 6DP

Oxford University Press is a department of the University of Oxford.
It furthers the University's objective of excellence in research, scholarship,
and education by publishing worldwide in

Oxford New York

Auckland Cape Town Dar es Salaam Hong Kong Karachi
Kuala Lumpur Madrid Melbourne Mexico City Nairobi
New Delhi Shanghai Taipei Toronto

With offices in

Argentina Austria Brazil Chile Czech Republic France Greece
Guatemala Hungary Italy Japan Poland Portugal Singapore
South Korea Switzerland Thailand Turkey Ukraine Vietnam

Oxford is a registered trade mark of Oxford University Press
in the UK and in certain other countries

Published in the United States
by Oxford University Press Inc., New York

British Library Cataloguing in Publication Data

Data available

Library of Congress Cataloging in Publication Data

Data available

Typeset by SPI Publisher Services, Pondicherry, India
Printed in Great Britain
on acid-free paper by
CPI Group (UK) Ltd, Croydon, CR0 4YY

ISBN   978-0-19-920847-0 (Hbk.)
       978-0-19-923448-6 (Pbk.)

4 6 8 10 9 7 5 3

TO THE UNIVERSITY OF LEEDS
IN MEMORY OF
EDWARD BOYLE
1923–1981

Criticism is now left fronting the material, to recreate which it possesses and feels both the mission and the strength. And this may be considered an artificial position, in so far as the individual critic never does actually separate himself from the whole of his historical knowledge, but invariably brings with him to the work a portion of the traditional object, already rationalized and made part of his present and critical world. Nor is this apparent anticipation of his result unjustified in the individual, if that which he brings as a canon to criticism has been itself already confronted with criticism and rationalized by virtue of it—i.e. has been concluded to be actual fact from a critical standpoint which is essentially the same as the critic's own. For the true world is continually growing, and when part of history has been made real it at once becomes a means for the realization of the remainder. Artificial then as the complete separation of criticism from its material appears and moreover is, when we regard the individual alone, yet it is far from being so as soon as we consider the process of criticism in itself.

F. H. Bradley

Just Criticism is a stern but laudable prophet & time & truth are the only disciples who can discern & appreciate his predictions & these touchstones fashionable pretentions with all her mob of public applause cannot pass but shrinketh into insignificance & silent nothingness from their just derision like shadows from a sunbeam & true merit at its eulogys 'grows with its grow[th] strengthens with his strength' & meets at last the honours & glorys of a protracted renown like the unexpected fulfilment of a prophecy.

John Clare

A rather different two-sidedness appears in the scene where the court-popinjay at Plashey offers [Thomas of] Woodstock sixpence to hold the horse he has ridden into the castle because he dare not foul his lovely boots. On the surface this is the age-old farce of mistaken identity: the supposed groom is only a Duke. . . . But there is a sense in which the laugh is on Plain Thomas. He and his sober mind are so much out of fashion that the fool can never know the standards by which he is being derided . . . It is ironical that [Woodstock's] contempt is only irony, impenetrable by its nominal victim: it measures the solid man's defeat that the coxcomb passes unscathed. The episode bears far less weighty implications, yet *au fond* it is like Hamlet fooling Osric—bitterly, because he is defeated by him. Thus right-mind-edness, impotent in a rotting world, is driven to cynicism or self-pity; for what else is the appeal to past tradition, when the lords of the present never understand, but ideal self-commiseration in the glasses of dead eyes?

A. P. Rossiter

Contents

The Lords of Limit

O Lords of Limit, training dark and light
W. H. Auden

Quintilian calls him [Horace] 'felicissime audax', and Petronius refers to his 'curiosa felicitas' or 'studied felicity'.

Oxford Companion to Classical Literature

And for this reason we call the doctrine of *the things that can be and go wrong* on the occasion of such utterances, the doctrine of the *Infelicities*.

J. L. Austin, *How to Do Things with Words*

It is always a significant question to ask about any philosopher: what is he afraid of?

Iris Murdoch, *On 'God' and 'Good'*

... the Igbo believe that when a man says yes his chi will also agree; but not always. Sometimes a man may struggle with all his power and say yes most emphatically and yet nothing he attempts will succeed. Quite simply the Igbo say of such a man: *Chie ekwero.* (His chi does not agree.) Now, this could mean one of two things; either the man has a particularly intransigent chi or else it is the man himself attempting too late to alter that primordial bargain he had willingly struck with his chi, saying yes now when his first unalterable word had been no, forgetting that 'the first word gets to Chukwu's house'.

Chinua Achebe, *Morning Yet on Creation Day*

I

Poetry as 'Menace'
and 'Atonement'

Thus my noblest capacity becomes my deepest perplexity; my noblest opportunity, my uttermost distress; my noblest gift, my darkest menace.

The quotation-marks around 'menace' and 'atonement' look a bit like raised eyebrows. 'Menace' from what, and to whom? 'Atonement' by whom, and for what? Is one perhaps offering to atone for the menace of one's own jargon? In fact, though this title may appear 'challenging', it presents little more than a conflation of two modernist clichés. That it does so is an act of choice but the choice is exercised in order to demonstrate the closeness of constraint. Behind the façade of challenge is the real challenge: that of resisting the attraction of terminology itself, a power at once supportive and coercive.

Language, the element in which a poet works, is also the medium through which judgements upon his work are made. That commonplace image, founded upon the unfinished statues of Michelangelo, 'mighty figures straining to free themselves from the imprisoning marble', has never struck me as being an ideal image for sculpture itself; it seems more to embody the nature and condition of those arts which are composed of words. The arts which use language are the most impure of arts, though I do not deny that those who speak of 'pure poetry' are attempting, however inadequately, to record the impact of a real effect. The poet will occasionally, in the act of writing a poem, experience a sense of pure fulfilment which might too easily and too subjectively be misconstrued as the attainment of objective perfection. It seems less fanciful to maintain that, however much a poem is shaped and finished, it remains to some extent within the 'imprisoning marble' of a quotidian shapelessness and imperfection. At the same time I would claim the utmost significance for matters of technique and I take no cynical view of those rare moments in which the inertia of language, which is also the coercive force of language, seems to have been overcome.

Ideally, as I have already implied, my theme would be simple; simply this: that the technical perfecting of a poem is an act of atonement, in the radical etymological sense—an act of at-one-ment, a setting at one, a bringing into concord, a reconciling, a uniting in harmony; and that this act of atonement is described with beautiful finality by two modern poets: by W. B. Yeats when he writes in a letter of September 1935, to Dorothy Wellesley, that 'a poem comes right with a click like a closing box' and by T. S. Eliot in his essay of 1953, 'The Three Voices of Poetry':

> when the words are finally arranged in the right way—or in what he comes to accept as the best arrangement he can find—[the poet] may experience a moment of exhaustion, of appeasement, of absolution, and of something very near annihilation, which is in itself indescribable.

Anyone who has experienced that moment in which a poem 'comes right' must, I believe, give instinctive assent to such statements. And yet, in admitting this word 'instinctive', do I not put my argument in jeopardy and betray my deepest conviction? For it is not my intention to say anything which could either excite or placate those who associate creativity with random spontaneity and who regard form and structure as instruments of repression and constraint. It is as well to be reminded that my phrase was 'instinctive *assent*'; and if 'instinct' is a 'natural or spontaneous tendency or inclination', 'assent' is 'agreement with a statement . . . or proposal that does not concern oneself'. From the depths of the self we rise to a concurrence with that which is not-self. For so I read those words of Pound: 'The poet's job is to *define* and yet again define till the detail of surface is in accord with the root in justice.'

I am attempting to convey, through these preliminary remarks, my belief that a debate of this nature is committed to a form of mimesis. The speaker must submit to an exemplary ordeal, analogous to that ordeal which Empson disarmingly calls 'the effort of writing a good bit of verse'. 'Mimesis', though, is an alluring term and exemplary ordeals are supposed to be ascetic. Define and yet again define. When Auerbach, in his book *Mimesis*, refers to a 'method of posing the problem so that the desired solution is contained in the very way in which the problem is posed' he acknowledges a pattern which is both austere and seductive. In posing the problem we 'show what it is like' to come up against rawness and contingency but not for a moment do we seriously put our mastery in hazard. When D. M. MacKinnon, on the other hand, remarks that Plato may have recognized, in the life and death of Socrates, 'a concretion, one might say a *mimesis*, of the way in which things ultimately are' we are possibly shaken out of our self-containment, our passionate attachment to those forms of hermetic mastery which must be so rebuked by life. But Romantic art is thoroughly familiar with the reproaches of life. Accusation, self-accusation, are the very life-blood of its most assured rhetoric: As Yeats puts it, in his poem 'The Circus Animals' Desertion':

> Those masterful images because complete
> Grew in pure mind but out of what began?
> A mound of refuse or the sweepings of a street,
> Old kettles, old bottles, and a broken can,
> Old iron, old bones, old rags, that raving slut
> Who keeps the till. Now that my ladder's gone
> I must lie down where all the ladders start
> In the foul rag and bone shop of the heart.

How it is possible, though, to revoke 'masterful images' in images that are themselves masterful? Can one renounce 'completion' with epithets and rhyme-patterns that in themselves retain a certain repleteness? T. S. Eliot's 'Marina' has been described as a 'poem that stammers into the hardly sayable' but I do not understand this remark. Though Eliot advocates humility and surrender, I do not think that he ever consciously surrenders rhetorical mastery. 'And why should he?' would be a fair question; but if I observe that 'Marina' seems to me to be an extremely eloquent poem and eminently 'sayable', I do so in the context of that obsessive self-critical Romantic monologue in which eloquence and guilt are intertwined, and for which the appropriate epigraph would be one abrupt entry in Coleridge's 1796 Notebook: 'Poetry—excites us to artificial feelings—makes us callous to real ones'.

There is a striking paragraph in Hannah Arendt's essay on Walter Benjamin in which she argues that to describe him and his work at all adequately 'one would have to make a great many negative statements'; as, for example, 'his erudition was great, but he was no scholar . . . he was greatly attracted . . . by theology . . . but he was no theologian and he was not particularly interested in the Bible . . . he thought poetically, but he was neither a poet nor a philosopher'. This quotation is central, indeed crucial, to the presentation of my argument. I have already conceded that, however challenging my title may appear, it nonetheless conforms. It is a not unfamiliar modernist theory which 'requires art to be destructive', which 'takes the violence of novelty as essential to success'. I may choose to ignore this theory, but I can't seem to be ignorant of it. I have to say, therefore, that the 'menace' to which I propose to refer is not that species of anti-bourgeois terrorism with which the names of Baudelaire, the Surrealists, and Antonin Artaud have been indiscriminately linked. Nor is it the menace of the poetry of Négritude as polemically invoked by Sartre in writing of Césaire: 'Surrealism, a European poetic movement, is stolen from the Europeans by a Negro who turns it against them.' Nor is it that menace to which Hugh Kenner alludes in his epitaph for the American poet H. D.: 'Her grown life was a series of self-destructions, her poetic discipline one of these.'

As for 'atonement', the modern age is not unfamiliar with a literature of penitence; there is even, one may add, a literature of penitential literature. Thomas Mann is on record as saying that his novel *Doctor Faustus* is 'confession and sacrifice through and through'. The sin of Mann's protagonist, the composer Adrian Leverkühn, is in some respects similar to that which Maritain termed ' "angelism", the refusal of the creature to submit to or be ruled by any of the exigencies of the created natural order'. And yet, of course, such a refusal to submit to these exigencies has itself been seen as the crime of capitalism, imperialism, modern technology, and technological warfare. So there is a sense in which the modern artist is called upon to atone for his own illiberal pride and a sense in which he is engaged in vicarious expiation for the pride of the culture which itself rejects him. He can't win; but, you might say, he can't lose either; for in the words of Grotowski, in his book *Towards a Poor Theatre*, the actor 'does not sell his body but sacrifices it. He repeats the atonement; he is close to [secular] holiness'. It is, you may well feel, the sort of testimonial at which one looks twice.

Hannah Arendt, on the other hand, is reluctant to 'recommend' Walter Benjamin to our attention, to adjust his solitary witness to any of our recommended categories. One respects her scruple and her strategy. The 'negative statements' through which she vindicates, against the current of assumption, the man she believes Benjamin to be, themselves constitute a form of Romantic mimesis. Readers of the *Biographia Literaria* may note that Coleridge's concern is not so much with thought as with 'the mind's self-experience in the act of thinking' and that this 'self-experience' is most clearly realized by the process of '*win*[*ning* one's] way up against the stream' or of observing how 'human nature itself [fights] up against [the] wilful resignation of intellect' to the dominion of common assumption and mechanical categorization. For Matthew Arnold, in his essay 'The Function of Criticism at the Present Time', the crucial vindication of Burke's integrity is his capacity to 'return . . . upon himself'; and a recent critic has described the Odes of Keats in precisely these terms: 'There was for Keats a certain justness, perhaps even a necessity, in beginning the first of the Odes [of 1819: the "Ode to Psyche"] by a return upon himself'. It is, of course, a frequently observed fact that the first word of the final stanza of Keats's 'Ode to a Nightingale' ('Forlorn! the very word is like a bell') echoes the last word of the preceding stanza ('Of perilous seas, in faery lands forlorn'). The echo is not so much a recollection as a revocation; and what is revoked is an attitude towards art and within art. The menace that is flinched from is certainly mortality ('Where youth grows pale, and spectre-thin, and dies') but it is also the menace of the high claims of poetry itself. 'Faery lands forlorn' reads like an exquisite pastiche of Spenserian idiom and Miltonic cadence: 'Stygian cave forlorn' ('L'Allegro', 1. 3); 'these wilde Woods forlorn' (*Paradise Lost*, IX. 910). We perhaps too readily assume that the characteristic Romantic mode is an expansive gesture ('Hail to thee, blithe Spirit! Bird thou never wert'). That which MacKinnon has described, in speaking of Kant, as a 'tortuous and strenuous argument, whose structure torments the reader' is equally a paradigm of these lines:

> Not, I'll not, carrion comfort, Despair, not feast on thee;
> Not untwist—slack they may be—these last strands of man
> In me ór, more weary, cry *I can no more*. I can;
> Can something, hope, wish day come, not choose not to be.

Hopkins may be said to embody here the positive virtue of negative statements, which I have already remarked in Hannah Arendt's essay.

As I have also previously remarked, we are not unfamiliar with a modern literature of penitence, nor indeed with that required secondary reading which is at times, and not inappropriately, a penance in itself. One is, so to speak, 'winning one's way up against the stream'. In both Europe and North America, there has been a proliferation of studies devoted to aspects of the interrelationship of theology and literature, or 'the coinherence of religion and culture', to use the wider terms which some prefer. Nathan A. Scott and

his colleagues in the Divinity School of the University of Chicago have
produced, and have inspired others to produce, a considerable body of
criticism and exegesis which may fairly be described as being ecumenically
nourished by the work of the Catholic Maritain and the Protestants Tillich
and Bonhoeffer. It would seem unreasonable not to concur with Scott's
précis of the situation; his suggestion that among 'the principal motives that
underlie the general movement of [literary] criticism in our period' is the
attempt 'to offer some resistance to the reductionist tendency of modern
scientism', and that such 'resistance' is vulnerable to its own reductionist
tendency whereby the precious autonomy of the poem may appear as no
more than a structure of grammar and syntax. Scott is opposed to both
'reductionist scientism' and aesthetic hermeticism. He quotes with approval
Vivas's view of the aesthetic experience as 'intransitive attention' and de
Rougemont's definition of the work of art as a 'calculated trap for meditation'. The key terms for Scott's argument are 'attention' and 'meditation'
because both words suggest not only an active contemplation of minute
particulars and a resistance to sentimental substitution but also an 'ultimate
concern' for 'the world of existence that transcends the work'. My reservations, I have already implied, relate not so much to principle as to
practice. Although he recognizes that the artist only 'makes good his
vocational claim . . . by the extent of the success with which he shapes the
substance of experience', Scott's interpretation of what constitutes 'substance of experience' strikes me as being more simply discursive and more
tenuous than his endorsement of such terms as 'intransitive attention' leads
one to expect. Having been told, in the course of a single essay on Saul
Bellow, that *Henderson the Rain King* is an 'adventure in atonement', that
'the comedy of *Herzog* is a comedy of redemption', that 'the drama [in the
late books] becomes explicitly a drama of reconciliation', it is with peculiar
urgency of assent that one recalls MacKinnon's remark: 'the language of
repentance is not a kind of bubble on the surface of things' or encounters
Henry Rago's proper insistence that 'when the language is that of the
imagination, we can be grateful enough to read that language as it asks to
be read: in the very density of the medium, without the violence of
interpolation or reduction'.

   It is, I think, crucial at this point to draw a distinction between, on the
one hand, a formal acknowledgement of the human condition of anxiety or
guilt and, on the other, 'the empirical guilty conscience'. It is one thing to
talk of literature as a medium through which we convey our awareness, or

indeed our conviction, of an inveterate human condition of guilt or anxiety; it is another to be possessed by a sense of language itself as a manifestation of empirical guilt. In G. K. Chesterton's study, *Charles Dickens*, he remarks that 'a saint after repentance will forgive himself for a sin; a man about town will never forgive himself for a *faux pas*. There are ways of getting absolved for murder; there are no ways of getting absolved for upsetting the soup'. In Helen Waddell's novel *Peter Abelard*, we encounter the thought again, shorn of its risible bathos and delivered with a becoming genial ironic *gravitas* by Gilles de Vannes, Canon of Notre Dame:

> For one can repent and be absolved of a sin, but there is no canonical repentance for a mistake.

Out of context this has just the right weight and edge to enhance the thesis and the occasion. But it may be that Chesterton grasped the truth of the matter. Under scrutiny, this is the essence to which my term 'empirical guilt' is reduced: to an anxiety about *faux pas*, the perpetration of 'howlers', grammatical solecisms, misstatements of fact, misquotations, improper attributions. It is an anxiety only transiently appeased by the thought that misquotation may be a form of re-creation.

'No man but a blockhead ever wrote, except for money.' Like Boswell, I feel a little distress at Johnson's blunt remark and like Boswell I hasten to add that 'numerous instances to refute this will occur to all who are versed in the history of literature'. If, however, we choose to take Johnson's words as a figure of speech implying that everyone writes from impure motives, whether from that 'necessity' which he himself cites, or from a desire for 'wreaths of fame and interest', or for 'erotic honey', or whatever, Johnson's cynicism may seem more sustainable. If that is so, let us postulate yet another impure motive, remorse, and let us suggest that one may continue to write and to publish in a vain and self-defeating effort to appease one's own sense of empirical guilt. It is ludicrous, of course. 'A knitting editor once said "if I make a mistake there are jerseys all over England with one arm longer than the other." ' Set that beside Nadezhda Mandelstam's account of the life and death of her husband, the Russian poet Osip Mandelstam, and one can scarcely hope to be taken seriously. People are imprisoned and tortured and executed for the strength of their beliefs and their ideas, not for upsetting the soup. And yet one must, however barely, hope to be taken seriously. It seems to me one of the indubitable signs of Simone Weil's greatness as an ethical writer that she associates the act of writing not with a generalized awareness of sin but with specific crime, and proposes a system whereby 'anybody, no matter who, discovering an avoidable error in a printed text or radio broadcast, would be entitled to bring an action before [special] courts' empowered to condemn a convicted offender to prison or hard labour. It may well strike others as unassailable evidence that the woman was merely an obsessional neurotic. Perhaps one could phrase the matter more moderately and say that one does not regard it as at all eccentric to endorse the view that grammar is a 'social and public institution', or to share W. K. Wimsatt's belief in 'the fullness of [the poet's] responsibility as public performer in a complex and treacherous medium'.

Stephen Spender, in his useful little book on Eliot, raises the question of the distinction between 'legal crime' and 'sin' in Eliot's thought. In *The Elder Statesman*, Lord Claverton declares:

> It's harder to confess the sin that no one believes in
> Than the crime that everyone can appreciate.
> For the crime is in relation to the law
> And the sin is in relation to the sinner.

Spender says that 'the point Eliot is trying to make is of course that "sin" is worse than "crime"'. The logic, if it is logic, underlying Claverton's words is that it is made more objectively difficult to confess if no one apart from oneself believes that there is anything which needs to be confessed. Spender is sceptical of the manner in which Eliot demonstrates his distinction and his priorities; and I would agree that some scepticism is justified. In *The Family Reunion* and *The Elder Statesman* 'sin' is more important than 'crime' partly because the criminal act is ultimately revealed to be either non-existent or very much less than one had been led to imagine. Reflecting upon his last play *The Elder Statesman*, one is inclined to wonder how far Eliot has succeeded in distinguishing 'sin' from those other mental or psychic states which solipsists might confuse with it. As Harry Guntrip once suggested:

> It may be that the practical and relevant approach to the problem of sin for this age is by the study of the devastations, personal, social, and spiritual, which are the product of anxiety.

Doubtless he has a very strong case; but to Eliot, despite the portrayal of 'pathological despondency', 'psychic impotence', in *The Waste Land* and other poems, it would seem, possibly, a blurring of categories, an abdication of priorities. Yet that which Claverton retrospectively describes, and what he immediately undergoes when accosted by Gomez and Mrs Carghill, seems very like one aspect of that condition which Guntrip calls 'anxiety'. But that is precisely Eliot's point, you will fairly remonstrate. In a secular age we experience anxiety until we learn to read ourselves aright and know that we act and suffer as creatures of sin. Even so, I still maintain that something has eluded Eliot, eluded him in 'the very density of the medium'. Grover Smith, in his essay on *The Elder Statesman*, says that 'Claverton, troubled by his role in [the past lives of Gomez and Mrs Carghill], is indifferent to their future, though neither has wronged him so much as he has wronged them. He makes no atoning gesture'; but Smith seems to imply that this is an ironic profundity of Eliot's making. It seems to me, however, that in determining the order of priority between 'sin' and 'anxiety' 'the kind of pleasure that poetry gives' is to be experienced through contact with the force-fields of these conflicting yet colluding entities. To control such forces demands an *askesis* rather different from the 'ascetic rule' which Eliot laid down for himself in the writing of dramatic verse:

> the ascetic rule to avoid poetry which could not stand the test of strict dramatic utility.

That 'poetry' which is excluded on utilitarian grounds is, I would argue, that very element which could master the violence of the conflict and collusion between the sacramental and the secular, between the dogmatic exclusiveness of 'sin' and the rich solipsistic possibilities of 'anxiety'. I would further suggest that Eliot's asceticism in the three post-war verse plays is too often a kind of resignation, or what W. W. Robson, in an acute criticism of the later essays, calls 'abstention'. He is left with a language that is at once aloof and ingratiating, unambiguous yet ambivalent. In the essay 'Poetry and Drama' Eliot speaks of 'a fringe of indefinite extent, of feeling which we can only detect, so to speak, out of the corner of the eye and can never completely focus ... At such moments, we touch the border of those feelings which only music can express'. As Eliot well knew, however, a poet must also turn back, with whatever weariness, disgust, love barely distinguishable from hate, to confront 'the indefinite extent' of language itself and seek his 'focus' there. In certain contexts the expansive, outward gesture towards the condition of music is a helpless gesture of surrender, oddly analogous to that stylish aesthetic of despair, that desire for the ultimate integrity of silence, to which so much eloquence has been so frequently and indefatigably devoted.

Edward Mendelson, the editor of the posthumous *Collected Poems* of W. H. Auden, has said that 'as he grew older Auden became increasingly distrustful of vivid assertions, increasingly determined to write poems that were not breathtaking but truthtelling' and has endorsed the poet's motives and actions with his own suggestion that 'the local vividness of a line or passage can blind a reader into missing a poem's overall shape'. I would suggest, however, that the proof of a poet's craft is precisely the ability to effect an at-one-ment between the 'local vividness' and the 'overall shape', and that this is his truthtelling. When the poem 'comes right with a click like a closing box', what is there effected is the atonement of aesthetics with rectitude of judgement. The suggestion that the proof of a poet's integrity is a conviction that he must sacrifice 'vividness' to 'shape' seems to me to stem from a very dubious philosophy of authorial responsibility to the 'reader'. My argument is thus obliged to distinguish between this matter of 'empirical guilt' which is involved with 'the density of the medium' and the principles of Christian penitence and humility which were, it seems reasonable to suggest, the disciplines of conscience within which Eliot and Auden increasingly worked. One is left with the awkward observation that the acceptance of a principle of penitential humility in the conduct of life does not necessarily inhibit a readiness to accept the status of 'maestro' conferred by a supportive yet coercive public. Fashionable adulation of the 'maestro' when there is so little recognition of the 'fabbro' is one aspect of what C. K. Stead mordantly but not unfairly calls the 'struggle between poets and "poetry-lovers"', except that the very word 'struggle' suggests purpose and engagement. As Jon Silkin has remarked, 'it is not disagreement we have now but deafness'. Deafness, yes; and arbitrary assumption. To 'assume' is literally 'to take unto (oneself)', 'adopt', 'usurp'; and the fashion in which society can 'take up' and 'drop' the poet (as John Clare was taken up, and dropped) is a form of usurpation which has little or no connection with intrinsic value. 'Where are our war poets?', and all that.

In April 1915, six months before he himself was killed in action, aged twenty, the poet Charles Sorley wrote, in a letter home:

> [Rupert Brooke] is far too obsessed with his own sacrifice, regarding the going to war of himself (and others) as a highly intense, remarkable and sacrificial exploit, whereas it is merely the conduct demanded of him (and others) by the turn of circumstances, where non-compliance with this demand would have made life intolerable . . . He has clothed his attitude in fine words: but he has taken the sentimental attitude.

Sorley's criticism of Brooke is at once brilliant in its economy and far-reaching in its adumbration. I even suggest that it atones for Brooke's 'sentimental attitude'; that is, it brings together details and perceptions which the 'sentimental attitude' has arbitrarily set apart and at odds. When Sorley turns upon the nub of the question it is with a turn of phrase precisely evoking the supportive yet coercive role of militant cliché. Two days before Sorley wrote this letter, Churchill's obituary on Brooke had appeared in *The Times*:

> A voice had become audible, a note had been struck, more true, more thrilling, more able to do justice to the nobility of our youth in arms engaged in this present war, than any other.

Within the ambience of Churchill's rhetoric, however, it was Sorley rather than Brooke who died the exemplary death. It is, of course, open to suggestion that, in so dying, he abjured the witness of his own poetic intelligence, the intelligence that could so illuminate his brief but trenchant comment on Brooke's lyrical 'compliance with a demand'; and that, in so doing, he became a passive accessory to rampantly jingoistic pseudo-poetry. But I see it differently. It is not that public rhetoric degrades Sorley's acute perception but that Sorley's perceptive statement redresses and redeems the rhetoric of the *Times* obituary and establishes a sounder basis for judging the nature of exemplary conduct.

It may well seem that, at this point, my argument vacillates. Having persistently stressed that we encounter both the 'menace' and the atoning power of poetry within the 'indefinite extent' of language itself, I now make my appeal to something else. In seeking to present Sorley as an atoning agent, I support my appeal to the 'poet's intelligence' with a gesture towards something beyond words. To this objection I would respond that 'utterance' and 'act' are not distinct entities. The philosopher Rush Rhees puts the case well:

> For we speak as others have spoken before us. And a sense of language is also a feeling for ways of living that have meant something.

Sorley, we may say, 'saw it through' even as he 'saw through it'; and I cannot believe that this could be regarded as the abjuring of 'thought' by 'deed'. I can see it only as an exemplary instance of the at-one-ment of the 'sense of language' with the feeling for the ways of life.

Charles Sorley's brief life was remarkably at unity with itself; and one must inevitably ask to what extent 'exemplary atonement' is possible when the life is otherwise. A student of Coleridge has recently written:

it is precisely through [the] perpetual dialectic between ideal and sinful reality that Coleridge is able to introduce his particular fusion of intellectual and *moral* qualities. In his experience as a ruined man, moral awareness, and even wisdom, were encountered through failure rather than success.

And one would add that what is especially noteworthy is the quality of disinterested stoicism with which this habitually self-pitying man was able to bring his own broken life and aspirations into the focus of meditation.

> In silence listening, like a devout child,
> My soul lay passive, by thy various strain
> Driven as in surges now beneath the stars,
> With momentary Stars of my own birth,
> Fair constellated Foam, still darting off
> Into the darkness; now a tranquil sea,
> Outspread and bright, yet swelling to the Moon.

That is from the poem 'To William Wordsworth, Composed on the Night after his Recitation of a Poem on the Growth of an Individual Mind' (1807). The beauty of the image of 'fair constellated foam' does not conceal the nature of the experience which Coleridge is evoking. The brightness is ephemeral, it moves outward from the centre into the darkness where it is quenched or lost. But we note also that there are other stars; and, bearing in mind the broodingly complex nature of Coleridge's inspiration, it may be legitimate to relate the first reference to the 'stars' to those of the prose gloss (virtually a marginal prose poem) added to the 1817 edition of 'The Ancient Mariner': in particular to a passage which Humphry House rightly calls 'that one long sentence of astounding beauty' and which I would call an out-standingly beautiful image of the attainability of atonement:

> In his loneliness and fixedness he yearneth towards the journeying Moon, and the stars that still sojourn, yet still move onward; and every where the blue sky belongs to them, and is their appointed rest, and their native country and their own natural homes, which they enter unannounced, as lords that are certainly expected and yet there is a silent joy at their arrival.

Flux is redrawn as harmonious motion towards rest; and rest is seen as active contemplation, not as stagnation. The mariner knows enough of stagnation; the stars are of another order. And in the poem 'To William Wordsworth', the private utterance of highly organized art can for a while stabilize the self-dissipating brilliance of the listener's mind, that is, Coleridge's mind, the mind that is concentrating upon that very diffusion. It is a transfiguring of weakness into strength, a subsuming, which Kathleen Coburn effectively characterizes in a note concerning the title of her 1973 Riddell Lectures on Coleridge, *The Self Conscious Imagination*:

> The two senses of the word are thus antithetical, *self-conscious* (1) as being realistically accurate about one's identity, and *self-conscious* (2) as being anything but clear, in fact painfully in doubt.

One must try to balance the accounts. I have argued, with MacKinnon, that 'the language of repentance is not a kind of bubble on the surface of things' and I have endorsed Rago's suggestion that we comprehend such language 'in the very density of the medium'. But from that point I sustain two views of the matter, divergent views, you may well think, which threaten to tear my argument apart. In speaking of Charles Sorley, and the *Times* obituary on Brooke, I have seriously proposed that one writer can make vicarious atonement for other writers' sins of commission and omission. In speaking of Coleridge's poem 'To William Wordsworth' I have suggested that a poet can transfigure his own dissipation by a metaphor that perfectly comprehends it. But I have added a comic sub-plot, this business of 'empirical guilt' which, as I seem to have conceded, appears to be nothing more than a trivial anxiety about upsetting the soup. What credence can be given to remorse over a *faux pas* in a world of actual terror, in which poetry is increasingly asked to be 'prophetic, menacing, terrorist, violent, protesting'?

In his diary for the years 1935–50, *Il mestiere di vivere* (translated into English as *This Business of Living*), Cesare Pavese comments that 'the political body does not die and so does not have to answer for itself before any God'. It is the entry for 14 June 1940. Was Pavese, perhaps, aware of Benedetto Croce's comment on Machiavelli's *Il principe*: that it shows 'a clear recognition of the necessity and autonomy of politics, of politics which is beyond, or rather, below moral good and evil, of politics which has its own laws against which it is useless to rebel'? In the second of his 1969 T. S. Eliot Memorial Lectures, Conor Cruise O'Brien gives a sharply critical account of those whom he calls 'American neo-Burkeans' and their belief that Burke's central achievement was 'to close the Machiavellian schism between politics and morality'. O'Brien considers this belief to be false. In his view 'the famous schism was not closed at all but was simply one of those distressing matters, abounding in the Burkean universe, for which some arrangement of veils was normally appropriate'. If O'Brien is right, and I cannot see that he is wrong, he is nonetheless correct to concede, in the same lecture, that Burke 'understood the density of the human medium in which change occurs, and the cost of change'. I do not overlook my own caveat about the need to resist the attraction of terminology itself, when I remark the affinity of phrase that connects O'Brien's allusion to the nature of society ('the density of the human medium'), Wimsatt's reference to 'a complex and treacherous medium' and Rago's suggestion that we read the language of the imagination 'as it asks to be read: in the very density of the medium'. You may say that I am merely proving susceptible to the influence of random association; but in answer I would say that these three 'densities' are more than mutually attractive correlatives. We are involved here with something other than a 'conceptual elaboration of the similarity between literary and moral judgment'. It is rather a recognition that in the act of 'making' we are necessarily delivered up to judgement. Among contemporary theologians it is D. M. MacKinnon who, unless I grievously misread him, most acutely perceives and articulates the matter which I am here struggling to express. In the course of a discussion of Butler's ethics, he refers to a suggestion which, as he says, perhaps 'strikes us as ill-conceived and old-fashioned': the 'suggestion of an "ought" somehow imposing itself upon us out of the matter of the actual'. Such would be a way of closing the 'schism' not only between politics and morality but also between 'literary and moral judgment', a 'schism' which the very word 'similarity' only serves to emphasize.

Equally, however, O'Brien's 'the study of literature is a social science' does not adequately take the strain of his own argument. That 'is' is itself schismatic. The cogency of his criticism is perhaps more truly appreciated if we sense a continuity between the Coleridgean 'self-conscious imagination' and O'Brien's own 'suspecting glance'. If the socio-political 'scene' in recent years has been characterized by an unsuspecting allegiance to 'slogans [and] sages', by the worship of charisma, instant wizardry, and all that is 'technically sweet', we may ask to what extent literary aesthetics have colluded with such sentimentality and cynicism. In such an epoch, the sense of 'empirical guilt' involved with what can be termed 'culpably careless proof-reading' has an intrinsic value, for, in such a context (to quote MacKinnon once more), 'one can never be quite at ease in the presence of the suggestion that . . . a teleological ethic need not have the slightest truck with utilitarianism'.

Claude Lévi-Strauss has said that 'the poet behaves with regard to language like an engineer trying to form heavier atoms from lighter ones'.

Karl Barth remarked that sin is the 'specific gravity of human nature as such'. I am suggesting that it is at the heart of this 'heaviness' that poetry must do its atoning work, this heaviness which is simultaneously the 'density' of language and the 'specific gravity of human nature'. There is perhaps no need for me to point out that my thesis is as much symptomatic as diagnostic, that in its account of certain aspects and effects of Romanticism it is itself a part of that which it describes; in some respects its tendency to 'swim up against the stream' of much current thinking about the nature and function of poetry is itself a minor Romantic trait. The major Romanticism of our time, or that which some propound as the major Romanticism, sees the poet's vocation as a 'searching for a way of reconciling human vision with the energies, powers, presences, of the non-human cosmos'. Charles Olson has described the poem as a 'high energy-construct and, at all points, an energy-discharge'. In such cases the 'menace' of poetry may be taken as referring not only to the 'energy' which is to be released, at whatever cost, but also to the inevitable fatalities occurring in any high-risk occupation. In my thesis, however, the idea of 'menace' is entirely devoid of sublimity: it is meanly experiential rather than grandly mythical. The poet as I envisage him is quite unlike the Baudelaire of Eliot's celebrated panegyric ('Baudelaire was man enough for damnation'); whereas the craft of poetry itself, as I describe it, comes close to resembling that 'frightful discovery of morality' to which Eliot alludes in one of his finest passages, the account of the nature of Beatrice in Middleton and Rowley's play *The Changeling*:

> In every age and in every civilization there are instances of the same thing: the unmoral nature, suddenly trapped in the inexorable toils of morality—of morality not made by man but by Nature—and forced to take the consequences of an act which it had planned light-heartedly. Beatrice is not a moral creature; she becomes moral only by becoming damned.

But even though I choose to regard that vision of 'the unmoral nature suddenly trapped in the inexorable toils of morality' as an oblique yet penetrating insight into the nature of the creative act, the resemblance is imperfect; and in that imperfection lies our ambiguous hope. The reason why the poet's 'discovery' is finally not to be confused with Beatrice's 'discovery' is perhaps implied by my reference to that *vision* of 'the unmoral nature' by which I attempt to set at one the piercing insight and the carnal blundering, in which I intentionally recollect Coleridge's capacity to 'transfigure his own dissipation by a metaphor that perfectly comprehends it'. It has been said that 'real poets often predict their own future in verse'. One may choose to glean from this what optimism one can. Julian Green is 'somewhat of the opinion' that the poet Charles Péguy 'was providentially influenced by his own work' and H. A. Williams has said 'the academic study of prayer may lead a man to pray'. Or one may choose to read it in a darker light. The seventeenth-century divine, Jeremy Taylor, drew a significant distinction between 'attrition' and 'contrition'. '*Attrition* begins with fear, *Contrition* hath hope and love in it; the first is a good beginning, but it is no more.' And Jarrett-Kerr writes that 'repentance is an attitude of mind which implies readiness to have the mind changed (*metanoia*)'. It is therefore conceivable that a man could refuse to accept the evident signs of grace in his own work; that he himself could never move beyond that 'sorrow not mingled with the love of God' even though his own poems might speak to others with the voice of hope and love.

If only as a formality one should perhaps make explicit what has been implicit throughout this discussion. It is evident that my argument is attracted, almost despite itself, towards an idea by which it would much prefer to be repelled. But surely, one may be asked to concede, it is more than attraction. Is it not a passionate adherence; a positive identification with the agnosticism—some might wish to call it the magnificent agnostic faith—whose summation is in the 'Adagia' of Wallace Stevens?

> After one has abandoned a belief in god, poetry is that essence which takes its place as life's redemption.

Stevens is here in the tradition of Arnold and the Symbolists. Vincent Buckley has suggested that Arnold 'explicitly associates the notion of mastering a hostile world with the interpretative power of poetry' and Arthur Symons in *The Symbolist Movement in Literature*, a minor work which had a major influence on Eliot and Yeats, celebrates the making of poetry as a sacred task. We may note how persistently Symons's book dwells upon the concept of 'mastery', whether 'laboriously acquired', as with Huysmans, practised with 'supreme disinterestedness' by Mallarmé, or sensually-instinctual in the genius of Rimbaud. According to Symons, Rimbaud 'brought into French verse something of that "gipsy way of going with nature, as with a woman"; a very young, very crude, very defiant and sometimes very masterly sense of just those real things which are too close to us to be seen by most people with any clearness'. The major caveat which I would enter against a theological view of literature is that, too often, it is not theology at all, but merely a restatement of the neo-Symbolist mystique celebrating verbal mastery; an expansive gesture conveying the broad sense that Joyce's *Ulysses* or Rilke's *Duino Elegies* 'must, in the splendor of its art, evoke astonishment at the sheer magnificence of its lordship over language'. If an argument for the theological interpretation of literature is to be sustained, it needs other sustenance than this.

P. T. Forsyth writes that 'the effect on us of the moral ideal is not simply admiration; it is confusion; it is accusation; it is judgment... Its very grandeur fills us with a sense of weakness, nay, of blame, shame and despair'. And yet through this very blame, shame and despair, we rise to a discovery of true personality. 'The man who does not rise to be a person', says Forsyth, 'becomes an item... He knows nothing of action, only of incident... He knows nothing of responsibility, of guilt, of sin; and his only goodness is goodness of heart, because he is built that way, and that is the way of least resistance, and is always popular.' It seems not unreasonable to draw from these two statements one's own conclusion: that in the constraint of shame the poet is free to discover both the 'menace' and the atoning power of his own art. However much and however rightly we protest against the vanity of supposing it to be merely the 'spontaneous overflow of powerful feelings', poetic utterance is nonetheless an utterance of the self, the self demanding to be loved, demanding love in the form of recognition and 'absolution'. The poet is perhaps the first to be dismayed by such a discovery and to seek the conversion of his 'daemon' to a belief in altruistic responsibility. But this dismay is as nothing compared to the shocking encounter with 'empirical guilt', not as a manageable hypothesis, but as irredeemable error in the very substance and texture of one's craft and pride. It is here that the poet knows the affliction of 'being fallen into the "they"' and yet it is here that selfhood may be made at-one with itself. He may learn to live in his affliction, not with the cynical indifference of the reprobate but with the renewed sense of a vocation: that of necessarily bearing his peculiar unnecessary shame in a world growing ever more shameless. He may 'rise to be a person' in a society of aggregates and items; he may even transfigure and redeem that 'word-helotry' to which George Steiner sees the merely literate man ultimately condemned in a culture divided between electronic data-processing and music. 'Attrition begins with fear.' True; but perhaps, as William Empson has said, in his verse-meditation after Bunyan:

To take fear as the measure
May be a measure of self-respect. Indeed
As the operative clue in seeking treasure

Is normally trivial and the urgent creed
To balance enough possibles; as both bard
And hack must blur or peg lest you misread;

As to be hurt is petty, and to be hard
Stupidity; as the economists raise
Bafflement to a boast we all take as guard;

As the flat patience of England is a gaze
Over the drop, and 'high' policy means clinging;
There is not much else that we dare to praise.

2

The Absolute Reasonableness
of Robert Southwell

When Robert Southwell wrote of the 'inhuman ferocity' with which Catholic recusants were treated in Elizabethan England he was not toying with hyperbole. 'Grinding in the Mill, being beaten like slaves, and other outragious vsages' were, again in his own words, but 'ordinary punishments'; and from the extraordinary, the 'more fierce and cruell' penal torments inflicted upon certain priests and laymen, our powers of contemplation recoil. Ours, but not his. Southwell's prose writings, with the exception of the brief but crucial *Spiritual Exercises and Devotions*, were not intended primarily for his own ascetic meditational practice; they were, as the title of his major prose work makes explicit, epistles of comfort 'to the Reverend Priestes, & to the Honorable, Worshipful, & other of the Laye sort restrayned in Durance for the Catholicke Fayth'; but they are not without indications that by such means he was able to apply Ignatian practice to a double purpose, 'seeing in imagination the material place where the object is that we wish to contemplate'. The 'object contemplated' was most frequently and formally the Passion of Christ; but there can be little doubt that for Southwell it was also his own 'almost inevitable martyrdom'. A. O. Meyer remarks that a 'yearning for martyrdom' was 'the only fault that can be found with the priests of the Elizabethan age'; but in adding that 'the death of the martyrs ever remained the catholic mission's most effective means for achieving its purpose' he may be thought to have annulled the force of the criticism and to have provided, albeit obliquely, a means for understanding the quality of mystical pragmatism which illuminates much of Southwell's work. The dangerous term 'mystical' may be tagged with J. R. Roberts's precise observation that in Southwell's poem, 'The Burning Babe', 'there is a note . . . of his having lost himself in ecstatic delight, the goal of Ignatian methodology', although I would not wish to claim this as the keynote for Southwell's work as a whole, or even as the prime characteristic of the Ignatian method practised by the Jesuit missionaries in Elizabethan England. Southwell, as his letters to Aquaviva, Agazzari, and Robert Persons reveal, was minutely and meticulously practical in his conduct of missionary matters, seeking permission, for instance, to 'bless 2,000 rosaries and 6,000 grains, for here all are asking for such objects'. Southwell's predecessor in the field, Edmund Campion, had 'particularly recommended . . . that such of the Society as should be sent upon the *English Mission*, should be able Preachers'; and Southwell's own suggestions were fully in accord with this precedent. He wrote to Fr Agazzari in Rome: 'Every priest here is useful, especially those who are well skilled in moral theology and controversy . . . Preachers are here in great request: hence it is most important that the students should practise themselves, so as to acquire readiness of speech and a plentiful supply of matter.' The editors of the Clarendon Press text of his poems remind us that 'English was for him the language of his apostolate'. After years of exile he needed to apply himself 'with much diligence to the study of his native tongue'.

Southwell does not shirk the word 'controversy'; and neither should we. Louis L. Martz has written of 'an England shaken by a threefold controversy, Catholic against Anglican against Puritan'; but Meyer refers to 'the internal divisions within the catholic camp'; and more recent studies confirm this view. John Bossy has drawn attention to the 'mutual recrimination' and 'stress between [recusant] clergy and laity'; and his assessment is endorsed by J. C. H. Aveling's suggestion that 'amongst English Catholics' in general there existed an 'anti-Jesuit opposition of a powerful and virulent kind'. 'Threefold' must therefore become 'fourfold' and the statement rephrased to read 'Catholic against Catholic against Anglican against Puritan'.

Such statements must, at the least, be allowed as caveats against the 'special pleading' of the 'English Catholic legend', as Aveling calls it. Pierre Janelle's *Robert Southwell the Writer* (1935) associates certain admirable qualities— 'a cheerful and loving patience, a gentle and restrained manliness'—too exclusively with pre-Reformation Englishness and with Elizabethan recusant Englishness in particular. That such tones are manifestly present, in the key-works of Edmund Campion and Robert Southwell, one would not for a moment dispute. What is disputable is the contention that these qualities are simply attributable to heredity or national characteristics. Martz is on surer ground in associating that 'mild, moderate, and cheerful temper', which characterizes some of Southwell's finest work, with Franciscan tradition and practice. Janelle himself is aware that Franciscan ascetical writings were 'in great favour among the early Jesuits. Southwell was at one with his order in this respect'. If we adopt Janelle's terms, we might call 'a cheerful and loving patience' Franciscan, a 'gentle and restrained manliness' Ignatian; and say that both strands are united in the prose and verse of Southwell and in Campion's brief masterpiece, his 'Challenge' or 'Letter to the Council', vulgarly known as 'Campion's Brag'.

Southwell composed his *Humble Supplication* 'rapidly and vehemently'; Campion's 'Challenge' was 'written without preparation, and in the hurry of a journey', but one would hesitate to call such works 'spontaneous effusions'. They have nothing in common with that facile self-expression which so debases much modern acceptance of spontaneity. Such ease and rapidity as they manifest are the issue of years of arduous rhetorical and meditational discipline, both classical and Ignatian. They are, moreover, the fruit of a 'well-ordered will'; impulse and effect are at one. Christopher Devlin has written that 'the deliberate refusal to allow desire and choice to be separated was the main inspiration of seventeenth-century religious art and poetry' and his words might be justly applied to the work of these two sixteenth-century Jesuits. 'Cheerful . . . patience' and 'restrained manliness' have to be seen as, at one and the same time, the expression of 'desire' and the choice of a 'suitable controversial means of expression'.

The Proclamation of 1591, 'A declaration of great troubles pretended against the Realme by a number of Seminarie Priests and Iesuists', demonstrated the prescience of Campion's 'Challenge', written some ten years earlier, before the full spate of persecutions, in anticipation of just such accusations and slanders. 'Brag' was itself a term of abuse foisted by the opposition on Campion's apologia. The 1591 Proclamation, to which Southwell made an immediate reply, attacked the missionary priests as 'dissolute yong men' disguised in a variety of 'apparell', 'many as gallants, yea in all colours, and with feathers . . . and many of them in their behauior as Ruffians'. Campion, after his capture, had been addressed by his Anglican adversaries in public disputation as '*miles gloriosus*', that is, as the strutting and braggart mercenary of Plautine and Renaissance comedy. It is in such a context that one must interpret the truism that 'the most important weapons for mission work were casuistry and controversy'. Southwell's controversialist skill, like Campion's, took effect in appearing non-controversial. They abstained from what Helen C. White has pithily termed 'the creative art of denigration' and practised instead a polemic of rapprochement. It was possible, of course, to be master of both styles. In the preface to the 1585 edition of his *Christian Directorie guiding Men to their Salvation*, Robert Persons complained that 'a spirite of contradiction and contention ... for the most parte hindereth devotion' but between 1592 and 1594 he was directing what have been called 'uncompromising and inflammatory writings', some of them against his co-religionists. It was possible, also, for a particular rhetorical gesture to be the mask of a quite contrary intent. The title-page of the 'Rhemes' New Testament (1582), reads like an epitome of this method. 'Translated faithfvlly into English', the work claims to have been undertaken 'for cleering the Controversies in religion, of these daies'; but in the light of the quotation from St Augustine, which serves as one of its two epigraphs, 'cleering ... Controversies' means confounding 'Heretikes: vvhose deceites cease not to circumuent and beguile ... the more negligent persons'. The 'Rhemes' 'annotations' are also thoroughly contentious.

'Controversy', says Meyer, 'had its poets too.' One of these, the 'witty and courageous martyr' Richard Gwynne, wrote a number of so-called 'carols' in Welsh. Of Gwynne's song of triumph at the assassination of the Protestant Prince William of Orange, J. H. Pollen remarks that 'it is plainly wanting both in forbearance and in good feeling'. Meyer calls it 'a terrible example of the lengths to which religious excitement can drive a man' but presents it as 'a solitary case, an ugly discord breaking in upon the pure harmony of the poetry of English catholics'. The 'carol' is in fact far less 'terrible' in tone and content than Meyer suggests and, as an example of controversialist rhetoric, seems scarcely remarkable. Even so, those apologetical arguments which attribute fanatical enthusiasm to none but Puritan extremists and 'caddish' behaviour only to Erastian deans and time-serving judges and magistrates are notably unfair; and that vision of the pre-dissolution Church, movingly evoked by a modern Catholic historian ('the intimate religion of the little shrines ... God's Presence in tranquillity in the fields'), is a beautiful but nostalgic image for which some Englishmen already possibly 'hankered' as early as the mid-sixteenth century, and which perhaps bore, and bears, little resemblance to late medieval and early Tudor reality. As Christopher Haigh has cogently detailed, in pre-Reformation Lancashire 'local communities met together only in the churches' and, 'violence was even more likely [there] than elsewhere'. There is a violence of morbid religious excitement, and Haigh gives instances of this. There is also something that Wordsworth called 'savage torpor', concomitant with 'sluggishness of spirit', 'spissa ignorantia'. Elizabethan and Jacobean Catholicism not only endured both kinds, it also perpetuated them, or sank into them, and it is a fair inference that Southwell recognized that the contest to which he had been summoned was to be fought upon a number of fronts.

Paradoxically, one of these fronts was that of excessive zeal. Richard Simpson, in his *Edmund Campion: A Biography* (1867), names the members of an 'association' of 'young gentlemen of great zeal and forwardness in religion' who acted as guides and 'lay assistants' to the first generation of Jesuit missionaries on their journeys around England. Numbered among this ardent and appealing company were Anthony Babington and the young poet Chidiock Tichborne. It is significant that one of Babington's harshest critics was to be Robert Southwell. In a letter to Aquaviva he wrote of 'that wicked and ill-fated conspiracy, which did to the Catholic cause so great mischief'; and in the *Humble Supplication* he referred, with a more aloof contempt, to 'greene witts . . . easily . . . ouerwrought by Master Secretaries subtill and sifting witt'.

It must be acknowledged that the 1591 Proclamation, in its mocking use of the word 'feathers', though false in tone is probably correct on a point of fact. Southwell was by no means the only missionary priest to concede, uneasily, that it was frequently necessary to appear in 'apparell' quite at odds with 'the graue attire that best suteth our Calling'. To the reasonable question how a turn of phrase can be at once false and true, there is the answer that it is a matter of context; that equity requires a respect for context. It was one thing for Fr Gerard, in hourly peril of arrest, torture, and a protracted death, to go about 'garnished with gold or silver lace, satin doublets, and velvet hose of all colours'; it was quite another to be numbered among the courtly and versifying desperadoes of the Babington Plot.

Southwell's necessary choice, therefore, was the achievement of a style ardent yet equable, eloquent and assured yet without 'panache', that is, not tricked out with 'feathers'. It is worth saying again that he was no less a controversialist for sounding non-controversial. Dr William Allen, founder and president of the English College at Douay, had written that, since 'heretics', Protestant controversialists, were wont to 'plume themselves' on their mastery of the vulgar tongue, the future missionaries should practise to 'acquire greater power and grace' in the vernacular. Janelle suggests, a little tendentiously, that in the penultimate chapter of *An Epistle of Comfort* 'Southwell carefully avoids the threatening tone that was so common a

feature in the polemical writings of contemporary Puritans'. Ernst Cassirer, it is
true, once called puritanism 'a thoroughly quarrelsome and quarrel-seeking
religion'; but Christopher Morris fairly reminds us that Archbishop Whitgift's
chaplain 'the "saintly" Lancelot Andrewes could make a cruel joke in execrable taste' at the expense of the imprisoned Puritan separatist Henry Barrow,
whose response was 'you speak philosophically but not Christianly'. Catholic
and Puritan alike fell victim to Elizabeth's penal laws and Anglicanism was 'as
Erastian as Elizabeth herself'. Meyer has remarked that 'no puritan could have
surpassed in bitterness and hatred' the vituperation of the 1591 Proclamation
whose 'contumelious termes' occasioned from Fr Robert Persons 'a reply full
of bitterness, hatred and scorn' and from Fr Robert Southwell the courteous
protest of *An Humble Supplication.*

   In confronting the strategy of the Proclamation Southwell undertook a
double defence. Edmund Campion, in his great 'Challenge' of 1580, had
appealed for 'fair light', 'good method', and 'plain dealing' to be 'cast upon
these controversies, that possibly her zeal of truth and love of her people
shall incline her noble Grace to disfavour some proceedings hurtful to the
Realm, and procure towards us oppressed more equitie'. The Proclamation
lards its threats and vilifications with well-timed cynical gestures of mock
reasonableness and tolerance, appealing in the name of all that is 'naturall'
and 'honorable' against that which is 'wilfull' and 'monstrous', 'the slander-
ous speeches and Libelles of the Fugitiues abroad'. In the England of
Elizabeth, say the authors of the Proclamation, those 'professing contrary
religio[n]' who 'refuse to come to Church' 'are knowen not to be impeached for the same ... but onely by payment of a pecuniary summe'.
Answered even in its own terms, without reference to executions and
incarcerations, this is cant. Such travesties of 'fair light', 'good method',
and 'plain dealing' are of course far more numbing than the most savage
vituperation. Southwell's double defence required him to ensure not only
that Campion's pedal-note 'equitie' continued to resonate freely but also
that the Proclamation's speciously equable tone was refuted by a 'power and
grace' able to judge such a travesty, not so much by attack as by being simply
yet manifestly on the level. Southwell appeals, in the manner of Campion,
directly to Elizabeth herself, to 'measure [her] Censure with reason and
Equity' and to weigh a 'sound beliefe' against a 'shadow of likelihoode':

> For to say we doe [the allegede treasons] vpon hope to be enritched with
> those possessions that others now enjoy hath but very small semblance of

probability, considering how much likelyer we are to Inherit your Racks and
possesse your places of Execution, then to surviue the present Incumbents of
spirituall livings, or live to see any dignities at the King of Spaines disposition.

In its poise and resolution, phrase taking the measure of phrase, this passage
both seeks and obtains satisfaction for the injury received; but it is a sign of
Southwell's unflaunted mastery that the satisfaction does not seem to be the
effect of a rhetorical 'turn' or the consummation of a mere *reductio ad*
absurdum. We are persuaded that Southwell, in every sense, delivers a just
sentence. 'Let it be scanned with Equity, how little seeming of truth [the
Proclamation's charge of sedition] carrieth.'

It is noteworthy to what extent Southwell, across the range of the prose
and verse composed during his six years' active apostolate, sounds and
resounds the simple clear note of Campion's 'Challenge' calling for 'more
equitie' towards the oppressed recusant minority. Time and again the word
is spoken with direct, unaffected eloquence; and yet, ironically, involved in
the term there remains a virtually insoluble ambiguity both of primary
definition and of circumstantial application. 'For a long time', F. W. Maitland observes, 'English equity seem[ed] to live from hand to mouth.' He
also says that 'no one was prepared to define by legislation what its place
should be'. The *OED* article on 'equity' defines it as 'the recourse to general
principles of justice (the *naturalis aequitas* of Roman jurists) to correct or
supplement the provisions of the law'; but it remains a moot point whether
such 'recourse' signifies an attainable legal process or a hypothetical 'notion
of an appeal to "higher law" '. There is a particular passage in Southwell's
work where the citing of 'equitie' strikes one with the full force of a parable,
an exemplary figure bearing witness to a sustainable reality. In the beautiful
prose meditation, printed in 1591, *Marie Magdalens Funeral Teares*, the
weeping penitent standing before the empty tomb is supposed, for the
argument's sake, to consider it an 'impeachment' of her 'right' for Christ
thus to 'conuey himselfe away without thy consent'. Since it is a 'rule in the
lawe of nature' that a donor cannot 'dispose of his gift without the possessors
priuitie', 'thou maiest imagine it a breach of equitie', 'if he hath take[n] a
way himself'. In 'The Author to the Reader', introducing his long poem
'Saint Peters Complaynt' (from *Moeoniae*, 1595), there are, again, lines
which have an emblematic containment:

> *If equities even-hand the balance held,*
> *Where* Peters *sinnes and ours were made the weightes:*

Elsewhere, however, in other sections of *Marie Magdalens Funeral Teares*, in the *Humble Supplication*, also of 1591, in the 'Letter to Sir Robert Cecil', of 6 April 1593, and in the *Short Rules of a Good Life* (1595) Southwell employs the term 'equity' in what we may refer to as an 'appealing' pattern: 'Thogh I were to sue to the greatest tyrant, yet the equitie of my sute is more then halfe a grant'; 'And as the equity of the cause, doth breath courage into the defendors'; 'might in equity Challenge all mens penns to warne you of soe perilous Courses'; 'and incline you to measure your Censure with reason and Equity'; 'so far as with justice and equity they can demand'; 'For though an indifferent arbiter ... could not in equity disprove my courses'.

According to Hugh Trevor-Roper, the 'great age of the recusants was ... the age of their greatest dilemma'. The Papal Bull of 1570, *Regnans in Excelsis*, pronouncing sentence of excommunication upon Elizabeth, was sufficiently hasty in conception and 'uncanonical' in its terminology to permit some seeming latitude in the matter of negotiation and compromise. The 'declaration of allegiance' of 1585, submitted by the wealthy and influential Catholic layman Sir Thomas Tresham, was 'an attempt to work out some kind of acceptable division between the spheres of influence which might be covered by a Catholic gentleman's relation to his queen and his relation to his priest'. And for the next twenty years, during which well over a hundred Catholic priests and laymen went to the scaffold and while his own feelings grew increasingly hostile towards the Jesuit mission, Tresham, with exemplary patience or remarkable obtuseness, persisted in his attempts to effect a compromise between conscience and 'acceptability'. Such a compromise was, in fact, unattainable because the government, in Machiavellian fashion, proceeded 'in accordance with "reason of state", which was somehow different from normal reason'.

When Robert Southwell, having already been tortured several times, was brought for interrogation before the Privy Council, he was complimented on the courtesy of his demeanour and was asked why he had not behaved with equal reasonableness to his tormentor Topcliffe. 'Because,' he answered, 'I have found *by experience* that the man is not open to reason.' The mission-priests faced a situation in which the 'normal reason' of men like Tresham was compromised at every turn by 'reason of state'. Southwell's retort, in an instant, both judges the travesty and redeems the word. Equity was, indeed, forced to live 'from hand to mouth'. Where it chiefly endured, sustained and sustaining, was in printed 'supplication' and 'challenge', in the extempore but nonetheless deeply meditated speeches in court, in enforced 'conferences' and on the scaffold; and, of course, in Southwell's poems. Maitland has said that 'after the brilliant thirteenth century . . . Law was . . . divorced from literature'. Through the nature of a paradox, a glimpse of reunification was made possible, in the age of Elizabeth, by the work of those whose lives were forfeit to a more savage kind of divorce. It has been argued that 'during Shakespeare's lifetime equity was both an important ethical principle and, through the Court of Chancery, an increasingly strong legal force'. *Measure for Measure* has been called a 'masterpiece of comedy on the theme of administering the law with justice and equity'. But for the arraigned priests and laymen there was no Court of Chancery and the only theatre in which they could enact their 'theme' of the weighing of justice with equity was the public arena of controversy, trial, and execution. The strength of the creative paradox turns, then, upon the legal helplessness of the petitioners. As Paul Vinogradoff has shown, there was a forensic precedent in Roman Law, going back at least as far as the Bologna law school of the late eleventh century, in which Irnerius defined 'equity' as 'the mere enunciation of a principle of justice'. 'Mere enunciation' in the work of Campion and Southwell had not only to proclaim the inviolability of an ethical principle but also to appear invested in the authority of 'strong legal force', even though its only court of appeal was the appeal of its own eloquence. It is our recognition of this fact which justifies Janelle's allusion to Southwell's conduct at his trial and execution as being 'a work of art of supreme beauty'.

Our concern is with the style of Robert Southwell, a poet in both verse and prose. Style is not simply the manner in which a writer 'says what he has to say'; it is also the manner of his choosing not to say. There is a distinction to be drawn here between the manner of not-saying and the demeanour of silence. At his trial in 1535 Sir Thomas More had made what R. W. Chambers calls his 'great plea for the liberty of silence'. The Elizabethan missionaries were, in all humility, proud of their silence under torture. The seminary-priest John Ingram, soon to be executed at Newcastle upon Tyne, reported that Topcliffe had called him a 'monster' of 'strange taciturnity'. Robert Cecil told how he had seen Southwell, subjected to a 'new kind of torture', 'remain as dumb as a tree-stump; and it had not been possible to make him utter one word'. This very 'taciturnity' and 'dumbness' are in themselves powerful coadjutors to the eloquence of the polemical and meditative writings. But 'choosing not-to-say', just as much as a choice of words, presupposes a 'hinterland' of style, a 'back-country' of

what might, for better or worse, have been said. In our necessary exploration of the 'back-country' of Southwell's eloquence we encounter violence and coarse preciosity and disgust, and what he himself significantly
referred to as 'wittye crueltye'.

There is a passage in Thomas Nashe's *The Unfortunate Traveller* (1594)
describing a public execution:

> The executioner needed no exhortation herevnto, for of his owne nature was
> he hackster good inough ... At the first chop with his wood-knife would he
> fish for a mans heart, and fetch it out as easily as a plum from the bottome of a
> porredge pot.

A modern scholar has written that 'the pleasure in a job well done palliates
some of the unpleasantness of the description'; which seems a cruelly inept
comment on Nashe's 'witty cruelty'. At the execution of Fr Edmund
Gennings in 1591, 'the martyr crying upon St Gregory his patron to assist
him, the hangman astonished said with a loud voice, "God's wounds! His
heart is in my hand and yet Gregory is in his mouth" '. There is a world of
difference between talk of pleasure palliating unpleasantness and Janelle's
suggestion that Southwell made of his own execution 'a work of art of
supreme beauty'; it is the difference between collusion and transfiguration.
It has already been remarked that the Ignatian exercise of 'seeing in imagination the material place where the object is that we wish to contemplate'
must, for Southwell, have involved the 'seeing' of his own almost inevitable
martyrdom. In the *Epistle of Comfort* he writes:

> And as a cunninge imbroderer hauinge a peece of torne or fretted veluet for
> his ground, so contryueth and draweth his worke, that the fretted places being
> wroughte ouer with curious knottes or flowers, they farr excel in shew the
> other whole partes of the veluet: So God being to worke vpon the grou[n]de
> of our bodyes, by you so rente & dismembred, will couer the ruptures,
> breaches, & wounds, which you haue made, with so vnspeakable glory,
> that the whole partes which you lefte shalbe highlye beautifyed by them.

An immediate objection would be that Southwell is too much the 'cunning
embroiderer', that he 'contriveth and draweth' too 'curiously'; but a more
patient consideration would have to concede that the 'ground' upon which
he weaves his variations could not be more plainly stated: 'our bodyes ...
rente & dismembred'. Southwell is foresuffering his own agony even as he
rises serenely above the fear and the violence: 'Our teares shalbe turned into
triumphe, our disgrace into glorye, all our miseryes into perfect felicitye.'

Violence of one kind Southwell not only allows but approves. In his Latin *Spiritual Exercises and Devotions*, which belong to the years of his novitiate, he writes:

> It is a great hindrance to refrain from using violence to oneself, to offer but a feeble resistance to the passions and other obstacles, or to adopt remedies which are almost useless. 'For the kingdom of heaven suffers violence and the violent bear it away.' Moreover experience shows that even the most powerful means are scarcely sufficient for our cure.

This reflection turns upon a scriptural text, Matthew 11: 12, which 'had particular significance for Southwell': *Regnum coelorum vim patitur, et violenti rapiunt illud.* This is a text which is recognized by modern commentators to be notoriously 'difficult', 'enigmatic'. Who are 'the men of violence'? The modern 'consensus' agrees that the term must be glossed in a pejorative sense: they are the men of 'hostile intent': Herod, the Pharisees, 'official Israel', the persecutors of both John the Baptist and Christ. This reading would have been apposite at a time when 'official England' seemed bent on out-Heroding Herod; nonetheless, Nashe, in *The Unfortunate Traveller*, glosses it as 'the violence of good works, the violence of patient suffering'; and Southwell, who quotes the text several times, everywhere takes it in a favourable allegorizing sense. In the *Epistle of Comfort*, where the text is also used as the epigraph on the title-page, he writes 'and though our champions, be of more courage, and our foes more enfeebled, since our redemption, yet doth *the Kingdome of heauen still suffer violence, and the violent beare it awaye*'. If there is a touch of ambiguity here, Southwell resolves it by adding a phrase from 2 Timothy 2: 5, '*and none shall be crowned, but they that haue lawfullye foughte for it*'. The second stanza of the lyric 'At home in heaven' also turns upon the Matthean text. Addressing the aspiring soul Southwell writes:

> Thy ghostly beautie offred force to god,
> It cheynd him in the linckes of tender love.

He is in no way at odds here with the reading established by the early Church Fathers or with the scriptural exegesis of his time, whether Catholic or Protestant. Luther had written, quoting this text, 'in my judgment, prayer is indeed a continuous violent action of the spirit as it is lifted up to God'. The so-called 'Evangelical Catholic' Juan de Valdés commented on the text thus: 'if you wish to take the Kingdom of Heaven, do violence to yourself, and so you will fear nothing'. The 'Rhemes' New Testament of 1582 does not annotate the text; but the Jesuit commentator, Cornelius à Lapide, provides a detailed allegorizing gloss. Though only six years younger than Southwell, he cannot truly be considered as being of the same 'generation'. He became Professor of Exegesis at Louvain in 1596, the year after the martyr–poet's death, and his New Testament *Commentaries*, begun in 1616, were not published until 1639. It is not unreasonable to suppose, however, that Lapide's seventeenth-century *Commentaries* drew upon the kind of biblical exegesis prevalent in Jesuit circles in the closing years of the previous century. Lapide's interpretation states that 'for the Kingdom of Heaven's sake worldly men do violence to themselves by the cultivation of repentance, poverty, continence, mortification'. He further interprets 'violence' as the heroism necessary to endure the sufferings of martyrdom: 'Thus let each believer consider that with his utmost energy he must struggle up to Heaven by means of a ladder hedged about with knives'.

   Although Southwell's, like Nashe's, gloss on 'violence' in Matthew 11: 12 is at odds with some modern New Testament criticism, in other contexts he clearly associates the word with Herodian savagery and with the disorders of the private will. He writes, in one passage, of 'tiranical persecution . . . most violentlye bent' against Catholics, in another of 'violent tortures', and, in a third, of those who 'haue with violence martyred and oppressed vs'. He depicts the 'violence' of Mary Magdalen's grief as well as her 'violent' love. There is indeed a suggestion that he associates 'violence' with the temptation to do wrong in a good cause: 'if thy Lord might be recouered by violence . . . wouldest thou aduenture a theft to obtaine thy desire'. When, in the brief but most beautiful 'A prayer in temptation', he writes, 'I am urged against my will and violently drawn to think that which from my heart I detest' it is as though we have found the focus upon which these different lines of emphasis converge. One might risk the suggestion that in these radical changes of connotation, Southwell is instinctively probing, more keenly than he would consciously recognize, his own conformity with doctrine and the limits of his own rhetoric; as though in matters theological his poetic vision had a prescient advantage over his theology. But the contrary suggestion is equally tenable: that the range of possibility in 'violence' in no way eludes him; that his method is simply and profoundly eloquent, 'speaking out', 'making clear', the complex hazards of equity:

   as not to feel sorrow in sorrowful chances is to want sense, so not to bear it with
   moderation is to want understanding; the one brutish, the other effeminate.

Janelle is quite right, however, to suggest that here 'mere reasonableness [is] raised to a divinely spiritual plane'. Southwell's style is equity made palpable; it is also, as has already been implied, an art of 'transfiguration'. The term connotes both 'metamorphosis' and 'elevation'. What, one may ask, is to be transfigured? And one may answer; the violence, the preciosity and disgust, the 'witty cruelty', the 'hinterland' of Elizabethan mannerism and atrocity. In a significant sense, for the devout recusant the medium of 'transfigura-tion' already existed in the form of the reliquary: 'Of the venerable martyr [Thomas] Bolliquer...a little piece of his heart...some of his praecor-dia...some papers greased with his fat'. Richard Simpson commented in 1857—and Bede Camm quotes him with approval—'these relics were not the less venerable on account of the disgusting processes they had gone through; the horror does not attach to them, but to the brutes who presided over the butchery'. The very strength of Simpson's emphasis registers the intensity of the 'horror' and the 'disgust' which are there to be overcome. A manuscript 'Catalogue of Martyrs', written c.1594, probably in the hand of Southwell's friend and co-worker John Gerard, records the martyrdom of Fr Thomas Pilchard, 'quartered' in 1587. The 'officers retorninge home, many of them died presently crying out they were poisoned with the smell of his bowells ... A laye man was executed there some 4 years after ... whoe beinge asked at his deathe, [what] had moved him to that resolution, etc., he saide, "Nothinge but the smell of a pilcharde" '. This is the kind of thing that Southwell 'lived with' in every sense. In 1584, while still at the English College in Rome, he received, from a friend who had been standing 'under the gibbet', a detailed account of the martyrdom of George Haydock. For Southwell the 'ladder hedged about with knives' could never have been a mere emblem; and, in this, I believe, is one of the sources of his rhetorical strength. To speak of his 'fastidiousness' in the face of such atrocious business might seem to imply a wincing kind of sensitivity. What he attains is rather an eloquent moderation, neither 'brutish' nor 'effeminate'. He too could contrive a 'conceit' out of disembowelling but his witty exercise differs markedly from that of Nashe and has little in common with the 'Catalogue of Martyrs', the rhetoric of which is the equivalent of a typo-grapher's manicule. In a letter of December 1586 to Fr Agazzari, he writes: 'You have "fishes" there [i.e. in Rome] greatly wanted here, which, "when disemboweled, are good for anointing to the eyes and drive the devils away," while, if they live, "they are necessary for useful medicines" '. Southwell's letters from England were sometimes written in a 'veiled style' for reasons of security; but these words are not so much like a 'code' as like a serenely witty form of tact. They resemble what an Elizabethan musician would have called a 'division upon a ground', a variation upon some verses from chapter 6 of the Apocryphal Book of Tobias:

> Then sayd the Angel to him: Take out the entralles of this fishe, and his hart, and gal, and liuer, keepe to thee: for these are necessarie and profitable for medecines...If thou put a little peece of his hart vpon coales, the smoke therof driueth out al kinde of diuels, either from man or from woman, so that it cometh no more vnto them.

A recusant martyr's 'entralles' were, of course, 'taken out', his heart was burned, fragments of his body were kept by the faithful as 'necessarie... medecines'. Southwell, significantly, adapts his source to suggest the virtues of the living priest as well as those of the 'embowelled' martyr. It is noteworthy too that both the minatory 'exemplum' of Pilchard's bowels and Southwell's 'conceit' of ministration and martyrdom must surely refer to the same scriptural source. The first, however, is pitched at the level of Tudor chapbook or even jest-book; it is, literally, a 'vulgar spectacle'. I have said that Southwell 'lived with' this kind of thing in every sense; and he was also capable of exploiting vulgar spectacle. His *Epistle of Comfort* contains 'a warning to the persecutors' as blatantly *ad hominem* as anything in the 'Catalogue of Martyrs' or Bunyan's *Grace Abounding*:

> Remember the sodayne and horrible deathe of one Yonge an Apostata and Pourswivaunt who pursuing a Catholike at Lambeth fell doune on the sodayne, ere he could laye handes on him that he persecuted and foming at the mouthe presentlye dyed.

Even though, as is well known, Southwell worked mainly among the nobility and gentry, and though Arundel House must have provided an exceptionally cultured spiritual environment, he was nonetheless 'hedged round' with sordid violence; he knew that his own execution would be a 'vulgar spectacle' too. I do not imply that he was 'sceptical' of these popular marvels (indeed, he challenges anyone who might doubt that the Thames stood still on the day of Campion's martyrdom). I do suggest, however, that one of the achievements of his own polemical style is its ability to turn both injustice and 'revenge' in the direction of equity; towards 'the reparation of wrongs rather than the punishment of offences'.

More than one authority has described Southwell's characteristic method as that of 'transformation', and it is a word which matches the terminology of biblical scholars discussing another of Southwell's texts: Philippians 3: 21. 'Transformation' can be read both as an acknowledgement that a significant amount of Southwell's work comprises 'translations, adaptations . . . imitations' and 'parodies' and as a recognition of a process that he himself called 'wonderful alteratio[n]'. Strictly interpreted, this means the radical change in 'mens maners' engendered by the blood of martyrs. Figuratively applied, it could be said to describe a crucial 'turn' which is a feature of his style:

> And this is that which Saint *Paule* sayd: *Reformabit corpus humilitatis nostrae, configuratum corpori claritatis suae*: He shall reforme the body of our humility confygured vnto the bodye of his brightnesse. Whiche phrase of speache argueth, that the more the body for him is humbled in torments, the more shall yt be partaker of hys brightnesse in glorye.

'Reform' is the 1582 'Rhemes' reading of the text which a modern scholar paraphrases as '[He] will refashion our body of lowliness to share the form of his body of glory'. The doctrinal point which is currently stressed—'that Paul does not think of his eternal blessedness in terms of the separation of the soul from the body'—is not the matter upon which Southwell concentrates. His concern is to affirm both that the 'scattered parts' of the martyrs will be 'reformed', restored, put together again; and that in due proportion as the body is disfigured for His sake on earth so it shall partake of 'transformation' at Christ's Parousia. Southwell's 'phrase of speech' is one that 'argues' for ultimate equity. But again, it is a sense of equity which turns upon a meticulous attention to sequence and context. As he is at pains to make clear, the transfiguration upon Mount Tabor preceded the Passion. It was more a sign of an initiation to extremity of suffering than a reward for suffering endured and transcended. The word 'reason' itself becomes part of the sinew of Southwell's argument here:

> There is no reason, that Christe shoulde shew him selfe more fauorable to vs, that haue bene his enemyes, then to his owne bodye, neyther can we iustlye complayne, if ere we find him, he giue vs a sipp of that bitter chalice, of which for our sakes he was contente to drincke so full a draught. Yea we may be hartelye glad, if after long teares and deepe syghes, we maye in the ende fynde him at all, whether it be in the pouertye of the cribb and maunger, or in the agonyes of his bloodye sweate in the gardeyne, or in the middest of blasphemyes, reproches, and false accusations at the tribunals, or in the tormentes of a shamefull death vpon the Crosse.

Christ 'transfigured in *Mounte Thabor*...was also at the same time, heard talkinge *de excessu* of his bitter passion'. Christ 'transfigured', therefore, is not the Christ-in-glory of the Parousia. What Yeats was to call 'Calvary's turbulence' was perhaps better understood by Southwell. His 'turns' are models of, and ways of mastering, the turbulence in 'the air around him' and in his own spirit: 'For Thy sake allow me to be tortured, mutilated, scourged, slain and butchered' he had written in his early *Spiritual Exercises and Devotions*, adding 'I refuse nothing'. These three words are of radical significance: they are the 'wonderful alteration' of a hovering morbidity into a positive oblation.

Reference has already been made to the 'hinterland' of Southwell's style and to the violence and preciosity and disgust which we encounter there. There was also, in Elizabethan as in modern literature, a disgustingly violent preciosity. We are assured that Southwell knew a fair amount of Ovid by heart; and in the *Metamorphoses* the Elizabethan student could find the flaying alive of Marsyas by Apollo. In Seneca's *Thyestes*, 'faythfully Englished' in 1560 by Jasper Heywood, the future Jesuit Provincial: 'From bosomes yet aliue out drawne the trembling bowels shake'. In John Studley's translation of the same dramatist's *Hippolytus*, the protagonist is trampled and torn to pieces amid the wreckage of his chariot:

> From bursten Paunch on heapes his bloudy bowells tumble thick.

In the Elizabethan 'hinterland', where spectacular 'closet' horror can at any time become the routine hideousness of public spectacle, how can one say where metaphor ends and reality begins?

This weak rhetorical question is out of keeping, however, with Southwell's power to distinguish and affirm. At the heart of his own eloquent style stands a patristic text which, in the *Epistle of Comfort*, he attributes to St Cyprian confronting his persecutors:

> Whye doest thou turne thee to the fraylty of our bodyes? Why stryuest thou with the weakenesse of our fleshe? Encounter with the force of our minde; impugne the stoutnesse of our reasonable portion; disproue our faythe; ouercome vs by disputation if thou canst, ouercome vs by reason.

It is here that we encounter the paradigm for the 'absolute reasonableness' to which my argument alludes. The 'force of our minde' is a key-term for Southwell's form of argument as Donne's 'masculine perswasive force' is a key-term for his; but the differences of implication between the two phrases are greater than any apparent similarities. For Southwell, 'force of . . . minde' is manifested in the power to remain unseduced and unterrified, whereas Donne's words relish their own seductive strength. Helen Gardner has fairly remarked that Donne forbids us to 'make any simple equation between the truth of the imagination and the truth of experience'. If that is so we may regard Southwell as Donne's antithesis, for his constant practice is to show 'how well Verse and Vertue suite together' and the 'simple equation' which Donne precludes is the 'equity' to which Southwell appeals in phrases which are like emblems of his faithful reason: 'Whose measure best with measured wordes doth sitt'; 'Where vertewes starres god sonne of justice is'; 'And though ech one as much as all receive | Not one too much, nor all too little have'.

The correlative of equity is sacrifice and Southwell sacrifices a great deal, even the poet's delight in self-sustaining, self-supporting wit. Helen C. White has written of his predilection for 'Baroque . . . transformation' but perhaps the matter turns more upon his sensitivity to a secular domain of 'baroque' inequity, of 'uneven account', which he seeks, in his poetry as in his prose, to 'reform' to a 'just measure': 'the affections ordinate, and measurable, all the passions gouerned by reason, and settled in a perfecte calme' and 'in the syghte of God'. It is entirely characteristic of Southwell's art, however, that, 'ordinate and measurable' though it is, it brings us face to face with violent contradictions. We are bound to assent both to its mediocrity and its monotony, for 'mediocrity' is essentially nothing more nor less than 'measured conduct or behaviour' and 'monotony' is 'sameness of tone or pitch'. If, however, we take this latter term to mean 'wearisome sameness of effect, tedious recurrence of the same objects, actions, etc.', we give our assent to Southwell's indictment of our carnal world. In his eyes it is a world vacuously full of 'loathed pleasures', 'disordred order', 'pleasing horrour', 'balefull blisse', 'Cruell Comforts'. The existence of the carnal sinners is an oxymoronic treadmill; and their only means of redemption is by way of the divine paradox. St Ignatius, it has been said, was particularly 'awestruck' 'by the fact that the Creator had become man' and Southwell is in this, as in all things else, Ignatian. God disadvantaged himself for man's advantage, and this priest who is also a poet is concerned to stress both sides of the redemptive equation:

> This little Babe so fewe daies olde
> Is come to ryfle Satans folde

> All hell doth at his presence quake
> Though he himselfe for cold doe shake
> For in this weake unarmed wise
> The gates of hell he will surprise.

Jeffrey Wainwright draws attention to the 'naïve though winning concession' which he finds in one of Southwell's turns of phrase ('Passions I allow,
and loues I approue'). 'Winning' is exquisitely apt. 'Naive' calls for more
care; but is justifiable. We are hereby directed to the crux of Southwell's
circumstance and achievement. Southwell is 'naive', if 'witty cruelty' is the
world's alternative; but if he is so, it is by choice; and the choice is doubly
purposeful. His 'naivety' is to some extent penitential, submitting the
upstart creative 'will' to 'bonds' of humility; and it is, to a further extent,
evangelistic. His Nativity Poems, wholly in keeping with Ignatian precept,
as Roberts has shown, weigh the harshness and the tenderness of the scene at
Bethlehem in order to win men to repentance and love.

    One cannot choose 'naivety', however, if one has no sophistication from
which to turn. Southwell was a highly sophisticated master both of classical
rhetoric and of the modern Euphuistic style. In 'New heaven, new warre'
such words as 'ryfle' and 'surprise' are placed with a beautiful tact; and
though the rhyme 'quake' / 'shake' may sound naive we should not assume
that naivety is the cause. That 'complexity of association' detected elsewhere in Southwell's writings is here the 'ground' upon which he 'works',
instead of 'curious knots and flowers', the lilt of a child's catechism. The
paradox of the naked new-born babe, the shivering child who shivers the
gates of hell, is at the heart of his vision. It is ultimately a vision of great
serenity, but that serenity is achieved in the full awareness of the realities of
spiritual and legal violence.

    There is a sad irony in the fact that Antonin Artaud, godfather of the
'theatre of cruelty', translated Southwell's 'The Burning Babe' ['Le Bébé de
feu'] during his incarceration in the asylum at Rodez. Southwell would not
grudge him that grace; but it would be a matter for regret if the violent
preciosities of extremism were to set their seal of approval on Southwell's
profoundly different understanding of the condition of both the tormented and the ecstatic soul. 'Christe was . . . heard talkinge *de excessu* of his
bitter passion.' 'Excessus' signifies 'ecstasy'. The word was so used by St
Bernard, the author closest perhaps to Southwell's heart, whose works he
cited in *An Epistle of Comfort*; which were also his 'solace' during his
imprisonment in the Tower. We may seem here to have returned to that

suggestion with which we began, that Southwell, in 'The Burning Babe', appears to have 'lost himself in ecstatic delight'. The circle is not quite closed, however. The 'pretty babe all burninge bright', the Christ Child, is 'scorched with excessive heate' which emanates from his own 'faultles brest'. There is certainly 'complexity of association' here, which cannot be dismissed as 'the most hackneyed of all conceits', nor finally defended as a parody of the Petrarchan tradition. One would read 'excessive' heat simply in the *OED*'s 'neutral' sense, i.e. 'exceeding what is usual' not 'exceeding what is right', if one were not already aware of the striking parallels between this poem and such contemporary Jesuit devotional exercises as Puente's *Meditations*. The Christ Child may indeed be talking 'de excessu' from amid a fiery ecstasy of sacrificial love; but I am unable to share the view that Southwell himself is 'lost . . . in ecstatic delight'. There is a note of deliberate naivety in the poem which may be read as a 'variation . . . on the medieval nativity-ballad, done after the Jesuit manner'. This fact would in no way preclude a sensitive apprehension of the nature of ecstatic experience. St Ignatius himself was much influenced by mystical tradition. But deeply versed though Southwell may have been in the methodology of 'excessus', he was alert to the dangerous implications of excessive behaviour. 'Excesse of minde' is the 'Rhemes' translation of the term in Acts 10: 10, which the Bishops' Bible (1568) renders as 'traunce'. Even so, Southwell, in his *Short Rules of a Good Life*, wrote that 'excess in the voice and immoderate loudness are always certain signs of passion and therefore ought to be used but upon some extraordinary necessity'. For Southwell to have 'lost himself' merely in a poem would have required more self-centredness than he was capable of. This keenly witty man who was so properly sceptical of 'phancy' and 'self delite' employed all the resources of his wit to moderate between grace and peril in this most dangerous area of the religious life. 'Let vs but consider, the last tragicall pageant of [Christ's] Passion, wherein he wone vs, and lost him selfe. And marke the excessiue loue shewed therin', he wrote in *An Epistle of Comfort*. 'Excess', 'excessive', 'de excessu', 'Passion', 'passion', 'violence', 'equitie': these are all cruces, the little crosses upon which the passion of his reasonableness is enacted for us. We have it on the authority of Christopher Devlin that 'the Jesuit discipline, in the design of St Ignatius, sets up an interior tension which can only be resolved by crucifixion. At the heart of it there is an element of supernatural wildness'. In the words 'discipline' and 'wildness' we confront that paradox which Southwell perfectly understood, as I believe he also understood the fulcrum of Ignatian 'design'. I would further suggest that the radical pun perceivable in 'ecstasy', in being 'beside oneself', either with a frenzy of egoistic inclinations or with a disciplined indifference to them, would not be lost on him. When he was brought out to endure 'the torments of a shameful death' Southwell could speak, with perfect calm and tact, in the idiom of his own *Epistle of Comfort*: 'I am come hither to play out the last act of this poor life'. Even at that moment he could retain his grasp on 'complexity' and yet speak with absolute simplicity. And it was such complex simplicity, I would finally claim, that enabled this man of discipline to concede, in *Marie Magdalens Funeral Teares*, the 'wonderful alteration' of 'wildness' itself: 'Loue is not ruled with reason, but with loue'.

3

'The World's Proportion': Jonson's Dramatic Poetry in *Sejanus* and *Catiline*

> The worlds proportion disfigur'd is,
> That those two legges whereon it doth relie,
> Reward and punishment are bent awrie.

J onson's two Roman tragedies have seemed to many readers to be harsh, intractable and unrewarding. From time to time accusations of soulless pedantry have been made against their author. According to John Sandys:

> Jonson is constantly hampered by his learning . . . In his *Catiline* and his *Sejanus* we find elaborate notes from Sallust and from Tacitus respectively, to prove he had good authority for every detail in his drama, and to make it perfectly plain that 'Fancy had no part in his work'. While Jonson thus preserves the outer garb of the Roman world and allows the soul to escape him, Shakespeare makes his men true Romans.

Both Coleridge and Swinburne, however, have intelligent notes on the relationship of these plays to the Jacobean political dilemma. They are at least prepared to accept that Jonson's choice, and treatment, of his themes may have been governed by something other than scholarly perverseness.

In both *Sejanus* and *Catiline*, Jonson manages to blend a forthright dogmatism with an astute trimming. This makes him, in a way, an epitome of the disturbed decades preceding the outbreak of the Civil War. This was the time of Selden, the troubled parliamentarian; and of Falkland, the troubled

Royalist; and Jonson knew them both. And, at a period when the tensions between Court and City were becoming increasingly felt, Jonson abandoned the public theatres for ten years to become a writer and producer of masques for royalty and aristocracy. A despiser of the crowd, he yet said 'Words are the Peoples' and captured in his comedies the idioms and inflexions of common speech. And modern critics have, of course, sufficiently appraised Jonson's 'accurate eye for... oddities', his 'quick ear for the turns of ordinary speech'. Nevertheless, this very admiration produces its own kind of danger. To suggest that art, to be significant, must grow from vernacular roots is so much a contemporary necessity that it becomes, almost, a required cliché. And to say that, in Jonson,

> the tricks of shysters and crooks, mountebanks, lawyers, news-vendors, and monopoly-hunters are transferred to the stage with all the relish of one who sees for himself what is under his nose

is to make his satire seem more indulgent than it is. 'Relish' and 'under his nose' suggest a slightly myopic gourmand.

The thorough evaluation that the comedies have received from various hands appears to leave a residual implication: that compared to the tough contact with life in plays like *The Alchemist* or *Bartholomew Fair,* the world of the Roman tragedies is an abstraction, a retreat into formulas and commonplaces. The cadences and imagery of these plays are certainly at a remove from those of Busy or Dol Common; but it could be argued that the grand commonplaces—even those that refer back to Latin originals—are as much part of the seventeenth-century climate as are the idioms of the great comic characters. It seems to be a modern fallacy that 'living speech' can be heard only in naked privacy; in fact the clichés and equivocations of propaganda or of 'public relations' are also part of the living speech of a society. Character writers of the seventeenth century used Roman allusions, as modern political cartoonists employ a kind of visual shorthand, to elicit a required stock response. It could be argued that the high-pitched invective that runs through *Sejanus* and *Catiline* is superb 'cartoon' language, with all the serious overstatement and polemic relevance of that art:

> CICERO. What domesticke note
>   Of priuate filthinesse, but is burnt in
>   Into thy life? What close, and secret shame,
>   But is growne one, with thy knowne infamy?

The vituperative 'filthinesse', 'shame', 'infamy' could, perhaps, be taken too easily as a mere stage-anger, as an abstraction from the tensions, the 'humanity', of real experience. The stresses of Jacobean and Caroline society, culminating in the Civil War, were real enough; yet men declared their living angers, their immediate and pressing problems, in a language comparable to that of *Catiline*. The *Declaration of the County of Dorset, June 1648* was framed in the following terms:

> We demand ...
>
> (iv) That our Liberties (purchase of our ancestors' blood) may be redeemed from all former infringements, and preserved henceforth inviolable; and that our ancient liberties may not lie at the mercy of those that have none, nor enlarged and repealed by votes and revotes of those that have taken too much liberty to destroy the Subjects ...
>
> (vii) That we may no longer subjugate our necks to the boundless lusts and unlimited power of beggarly and broken Committees, consisting generally of the tail of the gentry, men of ruinous fortunes and despicable estates, whose insatiate desires prompt them to continual projects of pilling and stripping us.

The 'boundless lusts' and 'ruinous fortunes' anathematized in the *Declaration* may be set against Cicero's denunciation of Catiline and his fellows, their 'filthinesse', their 'shipwrack'd mindes and fortunes'.

Jonson shares with the authors of the *Declaration* a dual attitude towards the name and nature of liberty. The 1648 petition puts liberty in two poses: the first respectable; the second disreputable. 'Liberty' in the first case is plainly involved with property and heredity ('purchase of our ancestors' blood'). Opposed to this is a second, destructive 'liberty', synonymous with licence ('boundless lusts', 'insatiate desires'). In Jonson's moral world, also, a stress and counter-stress is evoked from the conflicting connotations of words such as 'liberty' or 'freedom'. In the Roman tragedies 'liberty' seems frequently equated with irresponsible power:

> CAT[ILINE]. Wake, wake braue friends,
> And meet the libertie you oft haue wish'd for.
> Behold, renowne, riches, and glory court you ...
> And, being *Consul*, I not doubt t'effect,
> All that you wish, if trust not flatter me,
> And you'd not rather still be slaues, then free.
> CET[HEGUS]. Free, free. LON[GINUS]. 'Tis freedom.
> CVR[IVS]. Freedom we all stand for.

As parallel to this grotesque shout there is, in *Sejanus*, the 'Senates flatterie'
of the new favourite Macro; their weak cries of 'Liberty, liberty, liberty' as
he takes Sejanus' place. The irony here is that the Senators cry out to
celebrate the return of that liberty which is a concomitant of property and
stability; but we know that 'liberty', under Macro, will still be only
'licence'—a renewal of 'pilling and stripping'.

The civic alternatives to such dissolute, destroying forces are 'industrie',
'vigilance' and a proper reverence for the gods. The Second Chorus in
Catiline speaks of the need 'to make a free, and worthy choice'; and the
good soldier, Petreius, instructs his army in the fundamentals for which it is
fighting:

> PETREIVS. The quarrell is not, now, of fame, of tribute,
> ... but for your owne republique,
> For the rais'd temples of th' immortall gods,
> For all your fortunes, altars, and your fires,
> For the deare soules of your lou'd wiues, and children,
> Your parents tombes, your rites, lawes, libertie,
> And, briefly, for the safety of the world.

It is clear from this that the word 'liberty' regains, in the oratory of Petreius,
its respectable associations, being securely anchored next to 'lawes' and
preceded by the pietist sequence: 'gods', 'altars', 'wiues', 'children'. There
is danger in the handling of such deliberately emotive catalogues. At worst,
such rhetoric can become a confusion of apparent humility and actual
hectoring. William Wordsworth, a late democrat beginning the drift back
to conservative orthodoxy, employs a similar imagery in his sonnets of 1802:

> altar, sword and pen,
> Fireside, the heroic wealth of hall and bower.

Wordsworth's invocation is more burdened by the self-imposed Romantic
role of poet-as-prophet. Jonson, exploiting the dramatic medium, is able to
distance his orthodox eloquence by projecting it through the mouth of a
persona.

Elsewhere, too, the essentially conservative rhetoric is handled with
persuasive charm, as in the *Catiline* dedication to the Earl of Pembroke:

> MY LORD, In so thick, and darke an ignorance, as now almost couers the age,
> J craue leaue to stand neare your light: and, by that, to bee read. Posteritie
> may pay your benefit the honor, & thanks: when it shall know, that you dare,

in these Iig-giuen times, to countenance a legitimate Poeme. J must call it so, against all noise of opinion: from whose crude, and ayrie reports, J appeale, to that great and singular faculty of iudgement in your Lordship, able to vindicate truth from error. It is the first (of this race) that euer J dedicated to any person, and had J not thought it the best, it should haue beene taught a lesse ambition. Now, it approcheth your censure cheerefully, and with the same assurance, that innocency would appeare before a magistrate.

This is a well-contrived amalgam of religious, political, and literary connotations. The key-words embody dual associations of order, authority, and harmony in more than one field. 'To vindicate truth from error' sounds like Hooker; and 'iudgement' and 'innocency' have theological overtones, even though Jonson's prime application is in secular self-vindication. 'Innocency' thus serves to fuse the ideas of divine order and human law. 'Censure' is the province of priest and magistrate and satirist; it is also the privilege of master-patron to servant-poet as Jonson suggests. The dedication is not only an extremely bland and suasive piece of self-defence; it is also a testament to conservative legitimist order; within the bounds of such prose the tenure of kings and magistrates is unquestionably secure. The very 'assurance', the intuitive rightness of Jonson's usage, stems from a familiar rhetoric, a vision of order typified by Sir Thomas Wilson:

> I thinke meete to speake of framing, and placing an Oration in order, that the matter beeing aptly setled and couched together: might better please the hearers, & with more ease be learned of al men. And the rather I am earnest in this behalf, because I knowe that al things stande by order, and without order nothing can be.

Again, in Jonson's own 'Epistle to Selden', the statesman is praised for his 'manly elocution', a phrase in which a way of speaking and a way of living become one and the same.

Such evocative vindications of wholeness exist, of course, in a social and dramatic context where the unity of ethic and action is a rarity. For the world of Jonson's Roman tragedies is a world 'bent awrie', distorted chiefly by the perverted lust for private gain at the expense of public good. Against all the evidence of tawdry chaos Jonson poses the orthodoxy of Cicero and Cato: rather as Pope, in the *Epistles to Several Persons*, celebrates the decency of agrarian Order in the face of the Whig financiers; and as Yeats sets the 'great melody' of Burke against all manifestations of 'Whiggery'.

In both Roman plays Jonson's vision of moral and civic disorder—though embodied in several forms—is most immediately presented as a reversal of

roles in man and woman; as an abdication of power and choice by the
former, a usurpation of private and public control by the latter. In *Catiline*
the perverted natures of the protagonists are stressed. Sempronia has a very
'masculine' wit; she is 'a great states-woman', a 'shee-*Critick*' who can also
play 'the orator'. And, in her conversation with Fulvia she acts and sounds
like Brutus in his tent:

> SEM[PRONIA]. I ha' beene writing all this night (and am
>   So very weary) vnto all the *tribes*,
>   And *centuries*, for their voyces, to helpe CATILINE
>   In his election. We shall make him *Consul*,
>   I hope, amongst vs ...   FVL[VIA]. Who stands beside?
>   (Giue me some wine, and poulder for my teeth.
> SEM. Here's a good pearle in troth!   FVL. A pretty one.
> SEM. A very orient one!) There are competitors.

The derangement is here stressed by the abrupt parenthesis of womanish
trivia, chatter about pearls and dentifrice. Sempronia's strength is an errant
thing, a matter of coarse presumption and gesturing.

As moral and dramatic corollary to this 'roaring girl' is the sharp depiction, throughout the play, of lasciviousness and hysteria in the men of
Catiline's party. There is the incident of the homosexual attempt on one
of Catiline's pages, an episode which so disturbed Coleridge that he suggested emending it out of existence; he called it 'an outrage to probability'.
This is precisely its point. The nineteenth century preferred a half-remorse-
ful majesty in its great apostates, a power which Jonson is not prepared to
depict in the Catiline conspiracy. His rebellion *is* an outrage to probability
where 'probability' is more or less synonymous with 'Nature' and the
'moral law'. What Jonson does give is a dramatic relevance to outrage and
abnormality; and where the actions of the protagonists seem most to elude
the patterns of reason, that is the point of Jonson's attack. These opponents
of Cicero are 'men turn'd *furies*', whose 'wishings tast of woman'; into
whose mouths Jonson puts a deliberately grotesque hyperbole:

> CET[HEGUS]. Enquire not. He shall die.
>   Shall, was too slowly said. He'is dying. That
>   Is, yet, too slow. He'is dead.

In this projection of a world of spiritual and physical disorder the Roman
tragedies are close to certain of the comedies. In *Epicoene* (1609), varied
strata of imagery and action are explored, to discover intricate evidence of

ethical and sexual abnormality; of dangerous (even if trivial) perversion in the private and public functioning of human natures. Sejanus, too, was once

> the noted *pathick* of the time . . .
> And, now, the second face of the whole world.

And here the theme of sexual inversion is absorbed into that of broken status, debauched hierarchy. It was by trading his body that Sejanus rose from serving-boy to be potential master of Rome.

In *Catiline,* the play of action and imagery, though less intricate than the machinations of *Epicoene,* has its own manner of involvement. Apart from the logical balancing of illogical sexual conditions in men and women, there is a recurring pattern of significant epithets. The conspirators are described (even self-described) as 'needy' and 'desperate', 'wild', 'lost'. But they are also shown to be possessed by 'sleep' and 'sloth'. At moments of crisis they shout like excited women, or make passes at boys. To be both 'wild' and 'sleepy', 'desperate' yet 'slothful', is gross indecorum, even in rebellion's own terms. It is a double inconsistency, a double irony.

In fact Jonson's method, in both the Roman plays, might be termed an anatomy of self-abuse. It is clear that the *Catiline* conspirators are destroyed as much by their own grotesque self-contradictions as by the bourgeois virtue of Cicero. And in both plays a dangerous apathy or rashness on the part of the body-politic is a contributor to the tragedy. Rome, 'bothe her owne spoiler, and owne prey', is always as much sinning as sinned against. Jonson has Sejanus say:

> All *Rome* hath beene my slaue;
> The *Senate* sate an idle looker on,
> And witnesse of my power; when I haue blush'd,
> More, to command, then it to suffer.

At first sight this might appear an inappropriate hyperbole, since Sejanus is presented throughout as a blushless villain. It is certainly no sign of regeneration on the part of the evil-doer; but rather a late outcropping of the morality-technique. Sejanus, though villain, is allowed an objective condemnation of the ills of the State, is even, for a moment, permitted a Ciceronian touch. Compare:

> CIC[ERO]. O *Rome,* in what a sicknesse art thou fall'n!
> How dangerous, and deadly! when thy head
> Is drown'd in sleepe, and all thy body feu'ry!
> No noise, no pulling, no vexation wakes thee,
> Thy *lethargie* is such.

In some respects Jonson has Sejanus fill a dual role. He blends some of the characteristics of 'Scourge'—bringing torment to a corrupt world—with all the attributes of the *arriviste*, the supposedly amoral disrupter of society's settled decency. As *Sejanus* progresses, Jonson's moral scathing is directed more and more against the blushless dereliction of Senate and people; their abandonment of moral choice. Rome displays the vice of apathy rather than the virtue of patience. This deliberate duality is again stressed at the end. Although it would be quite inappropriate to speak of Jonson's 'sympathy' for Sejanus, nevertheless the drive of the satire is here against society at large rather than against the solitary villain. There is dramatic pity for Sejanus and his children at this point; not because, as human being, Sejanus deserves it, but because his immediate role as mob-victim makes such treatment necessary.

Jonson's dramatic rhetoric, in these two Roman tragedies, is so constructed as to work on two levels, yet to a single end, a comprehensive moral effect. The hyperbole of the protagonists is often so excessive as to be a parable of the spiritual and physical debauchery. At the same time, varied sequences of key-words signal the ethical truth of the action, like spots of bright marker-dye in a greasy flood. In Catiline's wooing of Aurelia, the satiric method is one of profound parody:

> CAT[ILINE]. Wherefore frownes my sweet?
>   Haue I too long beene absent from these lips,
>   This cheeke, these eyes? What is my trespasse? speake.
> AVR[ELIA]. It seemes, you know, that can accuse your selfe.
> CAT. I will redeeme it...
> AVR. You court me, now.   CAT. As I would alwayes, Loue,
>   By this *ambrosiack* kisse, and this of *nectar*.

Here is an epicene savouring, a ludicrous distinction between flavours in the kisses, each one mincingly appropriated by the demonstrative. It is the absurdity of over-meticulousness. A Spenserian–Petrarchan sexual reverence is employed in a context which makes Catiline's euphuism obscene. Marvell adapts the method in 'To his Coy Mistress':

> Two hundred to adore each Breast

where the point is to satirize the idea of virginity as good bargaining-material. In Marvell, as in Jonson, the perspective requires the utterance of deliberate cliché, but cliché rinsed and restored to function as responsible speech. As the lover in *Amoretti* asks for 'pardon' and 'grace' from the beloved and fears lest he 'offend', so Catiline and his paramour toy with a sacramental idiom ('trespasse', 'accuse', 'redeeme'). The suggestive rhetoric is finely used. Catiline is made to utter an effective *mélange* of portentousness and offhand cynicism. We know that he takes himself too seriously and humanity too lightly (his Petrarchan 'fidelity' is pasted nicely upon a cynical confession of wife-disposal). The total irony of this scene, of course, depends on the fact that this tiny Petrarchan mock-trial is the nearest Catiline ever gets to an understanding of trespass, or of redemption. He and Aurelia utter, unknowingly, a Punch-and-Judy burlesque of the play's great meanings. It is significant that this evocative scene should be an act of courtship. It is through such sexual attitudinizing and mutual titillation, through such an exposé of the mechanics of allurement, that Jonson presents his broader commentary on the corrupt practices of self-seeking and preferment. The forwardness of the female, the decorative word-spinning of the male, are far from being dramatically inconsistent. And though the gaudy Petrarchan is elsewhere seen as a cold destroyer it is, in fact, the pervading odour of blood that gives a poignant ruthlessness to Catiline's dalliance, his calling Aurelia 'sweet'.

As in Marvell's 'To his Coy Mistress', or Pope's *An Epistle to Dr. Arbuthnot*, Jonson's language is frequently literary in the best sense of the term. That is, its method requires that certain words and phrases, by constant repetition in popular literary modes, shall have been reduced to easy, unquestioned connotations. These connotations are then disturbingly scrutinized. Pope's:

> Oblig'd by hunger and Request of friends

requires for its effect the common formula of gentlemanly apologia on the part of coy amateurs bringing out verse. It is 'hunger' that blasts the cliché into a new perspective. Marvell's wit feeds off Suckling's 'Love's Feast' as much as it does off Marlowe's 'Passionate Shepherd'. Jonson needs the Petrarchan mask even while, in the Catiline–Aurelia scene, he tears it apart. And, in the following soliloquy from *Sejanus,* Jonson is able to blend the authoritarian tones of Hall-like satire with suggestions of tongue-in-cheek duplicity on the part of the speaker. Sejanus has just concluded his scene of apparently forthright discussion with Tiberius and is alone:

> SEIANVS. Sleepe,
>   Voluptuous CAESAR, and securitie
>   Seize on thy stupide powers, and leaue them dead
>   To publique cares, awake but to thy lusts.

This holds good on two levels. Tiberius *is* voluptuous and does neglect public affairs (though not nearly so much as Sejanus imagines). So far, Sejanus' words may be taken as choric, as in a morality or a satire, setting the scene for the imminent fall of princes. The difference is that Sejanus is gleeful rather than sorrowing or indignant, and that the 'prince' whose fall is imminent is not Tiberius. Tiberius is, in fact, far from stupefied, and succeeds in shepherding Sejanus to the slaughter. Hence, Sejanus' choric comment (still true in its essential commentary on an evil prince) becomes also a statement, by implication, of the fatal blindness of hubris, of Sejanus' own recklessness and greed. In the light of what the audience knows but Sejanus does not, the imperatives of the confident puppet-master ('Sleepe, voluptuous Caesar') slide into the subjunctives of a wishful-thinker ('and [may] securitie seize on thy stupide powers').

From a study of such examples one would conclude that Jonson is able to employ ambiguity—of word, phrase, or situation—to give what is ultimately a quite unambivalent expression to moral preference or decision. There is, however, a secondary form of ambiguity at work in both plays—more subjective, more cunning even; and with roots in the Janus-like situation of the professional moralist in Jacobean England.

In *Sejanus,* for instance, crucial political implications are guided into a kind of dramatic cul-de-sac; as in the scene where Sabinus is tempted into self-betrayal by Sejanus' hirelings:

> SAB[INUS]. No ill should force the subiect vndertake
> Against the soueraigne, more then hell should make
> The gods doe wrong. A good man should, and must
> Sit rather downe with losse, then rise vniust.
> Though, when the *Romanes* first did yeeld themselues
> To one mans power, they did not meane their liues,
> Their fortunes, and their liberties, should be
> His absolute spoile, as purchas'd by the sword.
> LAT[IARIS]. Why we are worse, if to be slaues, and bond
> To CAESARS slaue, be such, the proud SEIANVS!
> He that is all, do's all, giues CAESAR leaue
> To hide his vlcerous, and anointed face,
> With his bald crowne at *Rhodes*.

The opening of Sabinus' argument is orthodox, reflecting Tudor statecraft as expressed in the Tenth Homily (1547), and anticipating the Canons of 1606 and the Laudian Canons of 1640. James I's considered opinion that 'it was unfit for a subject to speak disrespectfully of any "anointed king", "though at hostility with us" ', gives the orthodox viewpoint succinctly enough. Sabinus' acceptance of the official dogmas comes out even in the pithiness of the trotting couplets with which his speech opens. The thought clicks neatly into place together with the rhyme. Then, as a kind of conditional afterthought, Sabinus suggests that very scrutiny of the tenure of kings which he appears to reject at the beginning. The Tudor apologist suddenly begins to speak like a moderate post-Restoration Whig, one to whom: 'government exists, not for the governors, but for the benefit of the governed, and its legitimacy is to be judged accordingly'. Compare, too, the tone of the opening three lines ('hell', 'the gods') with the ironic use of 'absolute' to qualify, not 'kingship', but 'spoile'. Dramatically speaking, this argument (absolutist dogma and Whig qualification) is delivered with the appeal of a Lost Cause. Sabinus is innocently speaking his own doom; his 'fault' is predetermined; his stage audience is wholly composed of *agents provocateurs* and concealed spies, so that his appeals to civic rectitude are sealed off from directly influencing the outcome of the tragedy. It is the theatre audience or the reader ('invisible' witnesses) who are exposed to the full vision of the noble conservative humiliated and betrayed by exponents of corrupt power, of cynical *realpolitik*. And it is arguable that the line:

> To hide his vlcerous, and anointed face

gains much of its power through a suspension (rather than a union) of opposites. It is at once a well-turned translation of Tacitus' Latin, and an ambiguous metaphor juxtaposing two hostile connotations. These are: 'anointed' in the sense of 'smeared with (ointment or cosmetic)' and 'anointed', meaning 'marked with sacramental authority' (compare 'The Lord's anointed'). Hence, the phrase pivots Jonson's two most powerful social attitudes—disgust at corruption and reverence for consecrated power—thus: 'Tiberius is corrupt; nevertheless, he is the anointed of the gods'. 'Face' continues the deliberate ambivalence; it is both physiognomy and 'cheek' (one is reminded of the character called 'Face' in *The Alchemist*); 'bald crown' signifies both 'hairless head' (a private impotence) and 'stripped authority' (a public impotence). As these words are spoken by Latiaris, the hireling, only in order to trap Sabinus they cannot, therefore, be taken as active radicalism. The image is securely bedded down in a web of tangential implication.

This scene in particular makes nonsense of the view of Jonson's 'originally non-dramatic' nature. He so deploys his conservative philosophy as to give it the attraction of Resistance idealism. He commits himself less deeply than, say, Marvell, who, in 'An Horatian Ode Upon Cromwel's Return from Ireland', speaks—in his own voice, and without dramatic distancing—of Charles's 'helpless Right' and of the 'bloody hands' of the 'armed Bands' round the scaffold. And Jonson's dramatic cunning is also in significant contrast to the procedure of 'Variety', a poem by John Donne or one of his contemporaries:

> The golden laws of nature are repeald,
> Which our first Fathers in such reverence held;
> Our liberty's revers'd, our Charter's gone,
> And we made servants to opinion,
> A monster in no certain shape attir'd,
> And whose originall is much desir'd,
> Formlesse at first, but growing on it fashions,
> And doth prescribe manners and laws to nations.
> Here love receiv'd immedicable harmes,
> And was dispoiled of his daring armes ...
> Onely some few strong in themselves and free
> Retain the seeds of antient liberty,
> Following that part of Love although deprest,
> And make a throne for him within their brest,
> In spight of modern censures him avowing
> Their Soveraigne, all service him allowing.

The key-words here are like those in Jonson's Roman plays: 'Liberty', 'free'. But it is clear that their significance is far from the 'Ciceronian' ideal. This poet's 'liberty' is not the state of civic wisdom based on 'industry and vigilance', nor is it a concomitant of inherited property. 'Strong in themselves and free' smells more of the dangerous anarchism that, in *Catiline,* yearns to use the 'free sword'. The implications of 'Our liberty's revers'd' and 'Retain the seeds of antient liberty' sing out much more sharply and defiantly in 'Variety' than do the equivalent but well-buffered iconoclasms in Jonson. And, at the crux of his argument, the poet, in offering fealty to a 'Soveraigne' clearly not 'anointed of the Lord', commits a kind of witty high treason. In his own voice he pays homage to 'libertine' nature in terms that Shakespeare preferred to put into the mouth of a branded villain, the bastard Edmund in *Lear.* And, in Jonson, this kind of 'freedom' belongs to degenerate conspirators, rather than to Cecil-like 'new men' such as Cicero. Both Jonson and Shakespeare, though prepared to give an airing to subversive statements in their work, tend to contract out of direct commitment; whereas the author of 'Variety' pursues, with a cynical faithfulness, the conclusions made inevitable by his accepted premises. It could be argued that such distinctions are the product of the time; distinctions between 'revolutionary' ideas circulating in manuscript verses among a small, cultured élite and ideas handled in the drama, a medium struggling against official censorship, and always in the blast of public scrutiny and comment. The ambivalence is certainly there. It was noted by Coleridge, when he said of *Sejanus*:

> This *anachronic* mixture of the Roman Republican, to whom Tiberius must have appeared as much a Tyrant as Sejanus, with the *James-and-Charles-the-1st* zeal for legitimacy of Descent, is amusing.

In *Catiline*, Jonson's treatment of the 'Ciceronian' virtues, and his attitude to the Cicero–Catiline struggle provide a working example of the dramatist's capacity for suspended judgement. Sempronia describes Cicero as:

> A meere vpstart,
> That has no pedigree, no house, no coate,
> No ensignes of a family? FVL. He'has vertue.
> SEM. Hang vertue, where there is no bloud: 'tis vice,
> And, in him, sawcinesse. Why should he presume
> To be more learned, or more eloquent,
> Then the nobilitie? or boast any qualitie
> Worthy of a noble man, himselfe not noble?
> FUL. 'Twas vertue onely, at first, made all men noble.
> SEM. I yeeld you, it might, at first, in *Romes* poore age;
> When both her Kings, and *Consuls* held the plough,
> Or garden'd well: But, now, we ha' no need,
> To digge, or loose our sweat for't.

Jonson so places the virtue of old Rome in the mouth of a 'modern' degenerate that he gets away with a good deal. To dig or to lose one's sweat honestly at the plough becomes the sweet untainted antithesis to the 'sloth', 'fatness', 'lethargy' of the present. Any scepticism we might have had regarding the tireless virtue of simple poverty is ruled out of court together with Sempronia's gibes. All that she sees as laughable or contemptible we are to receive as serious and worthy. 'Romes poore age' is unquestionably Rome's great age. Similarly, in *Cynthias Reuells* (1600):

> the ladie ARETE, or *vertue,* a poore *Nymph* of CYNTHIAS traine, that's scarce able to buy her selfe a gowne

is, in fact, a powerful chastiser of prodigality and corruption. By a connotative slide, therefore, 'poor' is made synonymous with 'pure'.

Jonson is noted for the hard precision of his images; and justly. He builds magnificently so that he may destroy:

> we will eate our mullets,
> Sous'd in high-countrey wines, sup phesants egges,
> And haue our cockles, boild in siluer shells,
> Our shrimps to swim againe, as when they liu'd,
> In a rare butter, made of dolphins milke,
> Whose creame do's looke like opalls.

The moral pleasure here stems from Mammon's lavishing of such imaginative effort on shrimps; and 'rare butter' is a good, serious joke. Jonson's recreation of the bulk and weight of corruption, of criminal–farcical expenditure, is superb. On the other hand, the persuasive weight of such imagery is sufficient to commit the listener to the acceptance of a good deal of simple and evocative language, as part of Jonson's vision of the good life. In the First Chorus of *Catiline*, the pejorative vision of the effeminate men of new Rome (a terse set of epithets: 'kemb'd', 'bath'd', 'rub'd', 'trim'd', 'sleek'd') works into a passage of much more tenuous verbal gesturing when old Rome is evoked:

> Hence comes that wild, and vast expence,
> That hath enforc'd *Romes* vertue, thence,
> Which simple pouerty first made.

And Fulvia's reply to Sempronia is also a case in point. Her:

> 'Twas vertue onely, at first, made all men noble

is plainly on the right side of the moral fence. 'All men' sounds very liberal and fine; so does the easy juxtaposition of 'vertue' and 'noble'. In practice, though, Jonson's social vision is as far from a Leveller's dream as it is from any real faith in a natural aristocracy. Phrases like 'all men' merely make gestures towards a proper definition.

Such evasions are to be distinguished from the valid workings of dramatic and rhetorical persuasion. Take, for contrast, this sequence from *Catiline*:

> CHOR[US]. The voice of CATO is the voice of *Rome*.
> CATO. The voice of *Rome* is the consent of heauen!
> And that hath plac'd thee, CICERO, at the helme.

Here, the anadiplosis, linking Cato's word to the authority of heaven, appears as a legitimate rhetorical parable of the great chain of Being. And, in this context, the commonplace of ship-of-state (as, elsewhere, the commonplace for body-politic) appears as an authentic, even though limited, statement of civic faith. Jonson *is* pedantic, but his pedantry has little or nothing in common with the supposedly neurotic crabbedness of the unworldly scholar. He is pedantic as Fulke Greville in his *Life of Sidney* is pedantic: each is prepared to risk appearing over-scrupulous in the attempt to define true goodness:

> he piercing into mens counsels, and ends, not by their words, oathes, or complements, all barren in that age, but by fathoming their hearts, and powers, by their deeds, and found no wisdome where he found no courage, nor courage without wisdome, nor either without honesty and truth.

In Jonson, too, the insistent comparison, qualification and paradox—sometimes appearing in-grown—are made to sound as an uncomplicated defiance of a labyrinthine age. The world of the Roman plays, like that of many of the comedies, is a world full of false witness:

> We haue wealth,
> Fortune and ease, and then their stock, to spend on,
> Of name, for vertue.

If 'name' is a mere commodity, an advertisement without relation to substance or property or ethic, how can 'name' alone be trusted? 'Name' must be demonstrated as belonging or not-belonging to 'thing'; its properties plainly discussed. Hence, in Jonson's dramatic rhetoric, antithetical pairings are frequent: 'inward' opposes 'outward'; 'justice', 'law'; 'private gain' is won by 'public spoil'. In the world of the Roman plays, this degree of moral scrutiny is painful, but necessary. This is the celebration of a good man, the dead Germanicus, in *Sejanus:*

> He was a man most like to vertue'; In all,
> And euery action, neerer to the gods,
> Then men, in nature; of a body' as faire
> As was his mind; and no lesse reuerend
> In face, then fame: He could so vse his state,
> Temp'ring his greatnesse, with his grauitie,
> As it auoyded all selfe-loue in him,
> And spight in others.

Here, the heavy antitheses are wrenched across the line, with considerable moral and muscular effort. They do not fall harmoniously within the line-period—and within the limits of their own predetermined world—as do Dryden's fluent couplets to the good man, Barzillai:

> In this short File *Barzillai* first appears;
> *Barzillai* crown'd with Honour and with Years . . .
> In Exile with his Godlike Prince he Mourn'd;
> For him he Suffer'd, and with him Return'd.
> The Court he practis'd, not the Courtier's art:
> Large was his Wealth, but larger was his Heart:
> Which, well the Noblest Objects knew to choose,
> The Fighting Warriour, and Recording Muse.

Dryden has everything off pat and, in terms of his bland wit, Charles is unquestionably 'godlike'. This is the very point that Jonson labours to verify in the portrait of Germanicus: 'In all, | And every action, neerer to the gods, | Then men'. Jonson's qualifications worry the verse into dogs-teeth of virtuous self-mistrust. If this passage is painfully spiky, Dryden's approaches fatty degeneration. 'For him . . . with him', 'Large was . . . larger was' are syntactically flabby, embodying the complacent elevation of the thought. The repeated '*Barzillai* . . . *Barzillai*' gestures in the general direction of virtue and goodwill. The overall tone of the Barzillai panegyric, it can be argued, has much to do with Dryden's thoroughgoing acceptance of his lot as laureate of the Tory oligarchy. The famously smooth irony of the opening of *Absalom and Achitophel* is, ultimately, an indulgent cherishing irony, making such a smiling gentlemanly thing of equivocation that only a puritan cit could object.

Jonson's sense of the complexity of Order is very different, both poetic-ally and politically, from Dryden's practical political attack and defence. Jonson's awareness can produce both the richly suggestive ambiguities of the Catiline–Aurelia courtship, or Latiaris' speech about Tiberius, and the fine assurance of the Pembroke Dedication. But there are occasions when, it seems, Jonson succumbs to the contradictions of the age; when he is unable, even reluctant, to tie down and tame the airy, floating connotations in words such as 'noble', or 'vertue', or 'poverty'. The *Catiline* Chorus, for example, speaks of 'simple poverty' as though this, and this alone, accounted for the 'vertue' of Old Rome. Such a moral slogan is as blandly shallow as anything produced by Dryden's political partisanship. And in *The New Inne* (1631) there is this, equally emotive, exchange:

NUR[SE]. Is pouerty a vice? BEA[UFORT]. Th'age counts it so.
NUR. God helpe your Lordship, and your peeres that think so,
  If any be: if not, God blesse them all,
  And helpe the number o'the vertuous,
  If pouerty be a crime.

Yet, in *Catiline* it is made explicit that 'need' is the reason that so many flock to the conspirators' support. And Volturtius, a turncoat and minor villain, is contemptuously dismissed by Cato without punishment; is even promised:

> money, thou need'st it.
> 'Twill keep thee honest: want made thee a knaue.

Poverty, then, is a virtue only when it is associated with a remote, lyrically evoked agrarian order, a world so distant that it appears static; or when it provides a temporary refuge for missing persons of good family. The poverty that really preoccupies Jonson is the reverse of simple and is far from static; is, in fact, a prime mover in that constant flux of demand and supply; the seventeenth-century urban predicament.

This world of savage indecorum, which, like Tiberius, 'acts its tragedies with a comic face', which to Donne appears 'bent awrie', is a world that Jonson struggles to subdue. It may be true that:

> In *Catiline* as in *Sejanus,* Jonson appears wholly inaccessible to the attraction of
> the profound 'humanity' and psychology of Shakespearian tragedy

but it is equally true that he is inaccessible to that periodic debauching which the Shakespearian 'humanity' suffered at the hands of, say, Beaumont and Fletcher. Jonson redeems what he can:

> It is not manly to take ioy, or pride
> In humane errours (wee doe all ill things,
> They doe 'hem worst that loue 'hem, and dwell there,
> Till the plague comes) The few that haue the seeds
> Of goodnesse left, will sooner make their way
> To a true life, by shame, then punishment.

4

'The True Conduct of Human Judgment': Some Observations on *Cymbeline*

When Queen Elizabeth was dead they cut up her best clothes to make costumes for Anne of Denmark's masques. These performances,

especially after the advent of Inigo Jones in 1607, became the rage of Jacobean London. The Vision in *Cymbeline* was clearly designed in response to this taste.

Shakespeare's actual working brief is unfortunately not so clear. One cannot conclude that *Cymbeline* was created for the Court or even specifically for the Blackfriars. Evidence, which is extremely tenuous, seems to indicate a performance at the Globe, *c.*1611. It is of course true that, even if the play was designed primarily for the public stage, its author was a servant of the royal household 'taking rank between the Gentlemen and Yeomen'. The king, though not a niggardly patron, was easily bored and preferred hunting. On the other hand, if the King's Men were employed as purveyors of *divertimenti*, they were no worse off than, say, Monteverdi at Mantua and probably more highly favoured. In terms of the dignity of art this is not saying much but 'since Princes will have such Things' it is possible for serious artists to elicit a private freedom from the fact of not being received as they deserve.

It has been suggested that *Cymbeline* was a 'dual purpose' play, adaptable to either public or private production. It may, in that case, have said different things to different audiences. A Court or Blackfriars audience could have seen what it expected, 'an unlikely story...an exhibition of tricks'. In daylight, at the Globe, the 'tricks' just might have appeared as critiques, oblique metaphors, or moral emblems. The supposition that a private audience was necessarily more sophisticated than a public one is questionable. There is an edgy watchfulness to the play's virtuosity which might indicate Shakespeare's reluctance 'to commit himself wholly to the claims of his material'. No such reluctance need be deduced. Even so, an element of reserve about the claims of orthodox mystique, or about the eloquence of current political mythology, might be demonstrable. Imogen sees Britain's relation to the world's volume as being 'of it, but not in't' (III. iv. 141), an enigmatic phrase which might equally well describe *Cymbeline*'s capacity for private nuance in its unfolding of the supreme theme of national regeneration and destiny.

Myths were things of utility to Tudor and Stuart politicians. They were also, though more sensitively, things of utility to the dramatist. The thought of Shakespeare hamstrung and humiliated by his own sycophancy is obtrusive but not inescapable. In the light of Emrys Jones's persuasive essay it would be unwise to ignore the relevance of Stuart myth to our understanding of this play. Henry VII was the saviour of his people; his great-great-grandson James VI and I, the unifier and pacifier, was 'the fulfilment of the oldest prophecies of the British people'. To the medieval chroniclers Kymbeline was a man of peace whose reign coincided with the birth of Christ. Shakespeare could have read this in Holinshed and sensed the connotations. Milford Haven, where the secular redeemer had landed in 1485, was a hallowed place celebrated in Tudor and Stuart patriotic verse. Such numinous power is not unknown even in the twentieth century:

> I felt that Stalingrad was in the middle of the world, a place where the final conflict between good and evil was fought out.

Holy and awesome places do exist, and there is propriety in Imogen's being 'magnetized to this, enchanted, spot', 'this same blessed Milford' (III. ii. 60), and in the contrivance of the play's denouement there. It is less easy to concede, however, that the political myth provides

> a kind of interpretative key to events on the stage which, without such a key, appear insufficiently motivated, almost incoherent.

To suggest this while concluding that the play is finally guilty of 'a central fumbling, a betrayal of logic' is to say in effect that one still finds it incoherent. The symptoms have merely been associated with a different cause, with over-caution induced by its 'being too close to its royal audience'.

One's own case would be put rather differently. It would be that Shakespeare's involvement with the claims of his material is full and unqualified while, in his view of extraneous and imposed value-judgements, he remains singularly open-minded. The play's virtuosity is manifested in the association of committed technique with uncommitted observation. It is aware of the fact of compromise but it is in no sense compromised. Recognizing the aims and expectations of such a company as the King's Men, who were undoubtedly popular at the Jacobean Court, one also admits the reasonableness of the suggestion that Shakespeare may have had James in mind when writing *Cymbeline*. Scepticism should be directed not so much against an extremely plausible hypothesis as against a number of moral and aesthetic conclusions which have been drawn from it. Even if it were an established fact that a royal audience actually attended a performance of this play, the proposition that Shakespeare therefore 'officiously' protected his royal protagonist from 'the consequences of his weak nature and ill-judged actions' would still be open to debate. It could be argued that *Cymbeline* is more subtly and sensitively handled than the objection allows and that the play shows considerable openness in places where its metaphysics have been assumed to be nothing if not transcendental. One of these is the love of those 'two supremely excellent human beings' Imogen and Posthumus; the other is the theme of the king's peace. Since one accepts that the strands of personal and national destiny are interwoven, to debate these elements is to study the crucial implications of the play. In each case, one would suggest, Shakespeare stands back not through timidity or unconcern but in order to obtain focus. His concern is with nearness and distance, with adjustment of perspective; in his handling of character and situation he makes a proper demonstration of that concern.

Imogen must be understood in terms proper to the dramatic context. For so long, and for so many admirers, she had been simply 'one of the great women of Shakespeare or the world'. There were, of course, dissenting voices. Shaw's reaction to the adulatory tradition was rough but not impertinent:

> All I can extract from the artificialities of the play is a double image—a real woman *divined* by Shakespear without his knowing it clearly ... and an idiotic paragon of virtue produced by Shakespear's *views* of what a woman ought to be.

The antithesis is arbitrary, the premise invalid, the naturalistic criterion misleading. Shaw supposes the dramatist to be merely intuitive when he is, in fact, quite deliberate. Shakespeare has shaped his play to procure the reality of the woman from the romance of her setting. Shaw's perception of a dichotomy and his suggestion of a double image nonetheless have considerable value. It could be said that *Cymbeline* involves the realization of double images, not as Donne's visualization of the spirit of mutual regard ('My face in thine eye, thine in mine appeares') but as we might refer to double exposures in photography: accidental or contrived palimpsests that come from one view having been superimposed on another. Does the supremely excellent Imogen commit a breach of natural propriety when she speaks of Posthumus, after his departure, to his servant Pisanio? She wishes that she had made him

>   sweare
> The Shees of Italy should not betray
> Mine interest, and his Honour.   (I. iv. 28–30)

These words are said to be 'quite out of character' but the objection rests on a preconceived notion of what this character comprises. Imogen's remark is not a happy one and it is difficult to see how, in the circumstances, it could be. Shakespeare's interest is in certain kinds of immaturity and in the inaccuracy and imbalance affecting relationships. Imogen wishes, when she meets 'Polydore' and 'Cadwal', that

>   they
> Had bin my Fathers Sonnes, then had my prize
> Bin lesse, and so more equall ballasting
> To thee, *Posthumus*.   (III. vi. 76–8)

'Ballasting' could mean 'freight' or 'stabilizing weight'. Imogen seems to mean that a male heir to the throne would have reduced her own status to a level nearer that of Posthumus. Her words acknowledge how Posthumus' conquest of her must have appeared to some observers—as a piratical act—and imply a fear that those who foresaw disaster in such inequality may have been right. In the play's opening scenes the breach of convention and the strained court relations create the original milieu for inflationary panegyric and protestation. The love-cries of Posthumus and Imogen are a lyrical defiance of circumstance and a breeding-ground of error. The courtiers involve themselves in partisan polemic. A 'perfect' Posthumus is necessary to their own self-respect. What they say of him is bound to seem 'too good to be true' but to suppose that Shakespeare is himself off-balance is to miss

the point of the situation. It has been suggested that 'Shakespeare intends us
to accept the First Gentleman's estimate of [Posthumus'] virtue'. That
Shakespeare intends nothing of the kind has been argued just as strongly.
The wager-plot reveals

> beneath Posthumus' apparently perfect gestures an essential meanness in the
> man himself and in the conventional virtue that he embodies.

This is perhaps overstressed. Meanness is not intrinsic to Posthumus' nature
and can be eradicated. Nevertheless, the point is taken. He survives and
matures in grace, but from a condition in which he was possibly more like
Iachimo or the despised Cloten than his admirers could have credited.
Iachimo, at least in the wager-scene, is not so much a villain as a catalyst
for Posthumus' own arrogance and folly. At the end of the play both men
express personal remorse in terms that bear comparison. Iachimo feels that
guilt 'takes off [his] manhood', the air of Imogen's homeland 'enfeebles'
him (v. ii. 2–4). Posthumus' conscience is 'fetter'd' (v. iv. 8). One man
regards his honours as but 'scorne' (v. ii. 7), the other thinks of himself as
debased coin (v. iv. 25). Posthumus, in forgiving Iachimo, is in a sense
forgiving himself. Implied comparisons between Posthumus and Cloten are
also to be discerned. The suggestion has indeed been made that 'the two
characters, never on stage together, should be played by a single actor' and
the significant visual pun, whereby Imogen is convinced that Cloten's body
is her husband's, has frequently been noted. It is more significant that
Posthumus is finally not Cloten and one sees that the irony reflects as
strongly upon Imogen as upon her husband. What kind of man did she
imagine him to be? Did she truly know him at all? The double irony is
beautifully released in her mistaken tears.

At such points Shakespeare is treating ideas of false assumption, false
connection. The objection that Posthumus' jealousy 'has no significance
in relation to any radical theme, or total effect, of the play' seems without
real foundation. When the husband recoils from his wife's supposed infide-
lity the play focuses, not in any simple way upon character, but upon the
experience of relationship:

> Me of my lawfull pleasure she restrain'd,
> And pray'd me oft forbearance: did it with
> A pudencie so Rosie, the sweet view on't
> Might well haue warm'd olde Saturne; that I thought her
> As Chaste as vn-Sunn'd Snow.   (II. v. 9–13)

It is right to point to the 'sensual poison' at work here. Are we, though, to regard this merely as the extravagance of Posthumus' contaminated imagination? The paragon of romantic love now sees his marital function, somewhat obtusely, as the taking of 'lawfull pleasure', yet his words, unlike those of Claudio in *Much Ado* or of Leontes, do seem to imply a degree of genuine recollection rather than of purely fanciful diatribe. The recollection is of a somewhat vulnerable awkwardness on both sides. These are, after all, wedded lovers and not two virginal puppets from *The Faithful Shepherdess*, to whose theoretical exacerbations phrases like 'A pudencie so Rosie' and 'As Chaste as vn-Sunn'd snow' seem more properly to belong. In spite of what has been called 'the puritanical emphasis on pre-nuptial purity in *The Winter's Tale* and *The Tempest*' the tone of Perdita's 'But quicke, and in mine armes' seems the real heart of innocence whereas this admittedly second-hand description of Imogen's nuptial modesty does not. Conversely, Imogen and Posthumus have, from the opening of the plot, a grim actuality of separation to contend with; a matter that other young lovers in the Romances do not have to face so blankly. The very fact that they are already married when the play begins is what makes them exceptional. They are even then beyond the conventional romantic consummation. As Imogen imagines her husband's ship sailing further and further away and the figure of Posthumus becoming smaller and smaller, the language with which she tries to grasp her loss has a touch of that extravagance displayed by the courtiers who try to force Posthumus into attitudes of perfection. We are not unmoved by the human credibility of this but we should recognize that, between such over-refinement of invention and the bitter grossness later displayed by Posthumus, there is a moral and emotional hiatus. There is no 'deep centre' here but rather a loss or failure of contact. This, I would argue, is evidence of Shakespeare's psychological accuracy.

The state of the relationship here is a state of tactlessness, meaning 'the absence of the keen faculty of perception or discrimination' or, more simply, 'being out of touch'. There is a vice which, according to Bacon,

> brauncheth it selfe into two sorts; delight in deceiuing, and aptnesse to be deceiued, imposture and Credulitie: which although they appeare to be of a diuers nature, the one seeming to proceede of cunning, and the other of simplicitie; yet certainely, they doe for the most part concurre . . . as we see it in fame, that hee that will easily beleeue rumors, will as easily augment rumors.

A feasible corollary might be that there is a kind of naivety which asks to be devoured and a natural and partly unconscious collusion between the deceived and the deceiver: between, for instance, Posthumus and Iachimo, Imogen and Iachimo, Cymbeline and the Queen. There is a language surrounding this collusion, a twofold idiom of inflation, on the one hand fairly innocent and spontaneous, on the other a matter of policy. Of the First Gentleman's gush of praise for Posthumus' qualities it could be said, in a phrase used of Shakespeare's royal master, that 'the sums he gave away so easily were not his to give'. This adds some point to Posthumus' later reference to himself as 'light' coin. As though sensing the folly of former inflation, he recoils to the other extreme of debasement.

The question of the play's rhetorical patriotism is more problematical. Cloten's 'tactlessness', the juxtaposition in him of oafish petulant inadequacy and outspoken nationalistic fervour, has been discussed by Wilson Knight. There is possibly a slight oversimplification in the description of Cloten's rudeness to the Roman envoy as 'British toughness' and 'integrity':

> Cloten . . . is for once in his element without being obnoxious.

One would suggest that, on the contrary, Cloten is obnoxious, and so is the Queen; their patriotism is an exacerbation rather than an amelioration of this. It is somewhat reminiscent of the old ranting of *Locrine*. The fact that a proportion of Shakespeare's audience would undoubtedly identify itself with Cloten's xenophobia and thus be trapped in an emotional cul-de-sac makes for an interesting piece of dramatic ambivalence.

> The Britons defy Troglodytes, Aethiopians, Amazons and 'all the hosts of Barbarian lands', if these 'should dare to enter in our little world'.

Finally, Cymbeline admits that his resistance to Rome had been instigated by his 'wicked Queene' (v. v. 463). In view of James's self-appointed task as European peacemaker, Shakespeare's portrayal of such erroneous and ferocious insularity might be regarded as a tenable risk; but the question is boldly treated and taken further than mere diplomacy would have required.

There is, in fact, little indication of any desire on the part of the dramatist to make discreet alignments with official Jacobean policy, and the suggestion that 'the character of Cymbeline . . . has a direct reference to James I', insofar as this implies a commitment to eulogy, is not convincing. One would accept, however, that Shakespeare caught, accurately and retentively, a certain tone of Jacobean mystique and that an oblique awareness of royalist views and demands can be detected. It is as though, in the play's finale, we were presented with a completely open situation. A British king is seen for what he is: uxorious, irrational, violent when prodded, indulgent, of absolute status, and ultimately invulnerable. This might be taken as a disinterested view of the 'law' of Prerogative. The concluding atmosphere of transcendental peace has been found appealing. The king reiterates the word 'peace' three times in eight lines (v. v. 478–85) and also speaks of 'my peace' (v. v. 459). One is reminded that

> some earlier editors were so offended by the apparent megalomania of '*my* peace' that they emended to 'by'.

The editorial procedure may have been questionable but the original suspicion may not have been entirely groundless. Cymbeline's evocation of peace is a happy combination of the cursory and the opulent. To his daughter he admits his 'folly' (v. v. 67); politically, the guilt is laid upon a defunct secondary cause. There is a passage in *The Trew Law of Free Monarchies* (1603) which simultaneously concedes and vetoes possible monarchical deficiencies. The people, writes James, should look to the king:

> fearing him as their Iudge, louing him as their father; praying for him as their protectour; for his continuance, if he be good; for his amendement, if he be wicked; following and obeying his lawfull commands, eschewing and flying his fury in his vnlawfull, without resistance, but by sobbes and teares to God.

Such a thesis, many-faceted and unanswerable, destroys objections by assimilation. Critics who object to the plodding inadequacy of the verse spoken by the 'poore Ghosts' of the Leonati (v. iv) may not have considered that the play needs an element of formal pleading which is quite distinct from the eloquent magnanimity of confirmed majesty. Their wooden, archaic clichés are like an emblem of old and rather weary sincerity, whereas Cymbeline's concluding oratory is the reaffirmation of the mystique of status.

Shakespeare is in accord with the *Trew Law* to the extent that he brings the play to an end 'without resistance'. It is neither adulatory nor satiric, but observes what is there. Altogether, one feels that *Cymbeline* betrays nothing, is eminently logical and does not fumble. To be left, at the end, with things inexplicable and intractable is a perennial hazard for all artists; but in Shakespeare's last plays an acceptance of this seems to be at the heart of his dramatic vision. It is hardly scepticism, rather a kind of pragmatism, a necessary counterpoise to the thoroughly pragmatic 'myths' of the Stuarts. It has been said that 'the ending of *The Tempest* is very moving, not least because it is so reticent'. Reticence about things that cannot be reconciled is a characteristic of the last plays. In *Henry VIII* this tacit recognition is itself reduced to a formula as the two conflicting obituaries of Wolsey are presented in sequence by Queen Katherine and Griffith. The play sounds a note of political quietism while in *Cymbeline* the tension of paradox is persistently felt. In each case, however, we are involved in a dualistic acceptance of things as they are. Such dualisms seem to avoid the chain of cause and effect which drives the tragedies. They avoid, also, the formal concept of Tragedy in which hamartia indicates the irreparable severing of tragic experience from the normal conduct of life; the start of the irreversible slide down the scale of act and consequence. In the late plays hamartia appears as something integral to the human condition, innate, to be lived with.

Admittedly, this observation might be little more than a truism stretched awkwardly between time-serving cynicism, lazy nostalgia, and altruistic resilience. There are comments of a relatively simple kind, spanning the range of Elizabethan–Jacobean chronology, which would qualify as any one of these. John Lyly argued, sometime in the 1580s, that

> If wee present a mingle-mangle, our fault is to be excused, because the whole worlde is become an Hodge-podge.

One finds a reminiscent explanation prefaced by the composer Thomas Tomkins to his *Songs* of 1622. These, he hopes, are

> sutable to the people of the world, wherein the rich and the poore, sound and lame, sad and fantasticall, dwell together.

Uncomplicated observations of this nature are possibly imitated in Hamlet's

> the Age is growne so picked, that the toe of the Pesant comes so neere the heeles of our Courtier, hee galls his Kibe.   (v. i. 151–3)

Such an aphorism is far from representing the mood caught in Shakespeare's so-called Romances. Their spirit is altogether more complex and has been excellently described. Even so, Lyly and Tomkins are not alone in their persuasion that the world of common observation is one which disobeys at every turn the world of overriding mythology and that such contradictions affect the nature of art and the ways in which people respond to it. A sense of mundane fallibility is stated with characteristic authority by Bacon. Of the false appearance imposed by words he writes:

it must be confessed, that it is not possible to diuorce our selues from these fallacies and false appearances, because they are inseparable from our Nature and Condition of life.

He adds, however, that 'the Caution of them . . . doth extreamely importe the true conducte of Humane Iudgement', thereby converting what might have been a merely passive acceptance into something active and therapeutic. The last act of *Cymbeline* reveals a possibly analogous attitude, particularly as the play's major dilemma has been brought about largely by false appearances imposed by words. Just how far Shakespeare is from an indulgence in flaccid geniality is shown by the summary disposal of Cloten and the crazed death of the Queen. One might say of the final gallimaufry, mirroring in so many ways the sad and fantastical, that it avoids instruction, whether comic or tragic, but is, in Bacon's sense of the term, 'cautionary'.

It has been suggested that 'there is more Baconism in late Shakespeare than is normally recognized'. This is clearly a challenging suggestion; it would perhaps not be possible to establish 'Shakespeare's Bacon' on the same basis of documentary evidence as is available for Shakespeare's Plutarch or Shakespeare's Montaigne. It is arguable, however, that *Cymbeline* turns on an awareness of experiment or experiential knowledge. Imogen's cry:

> Experience, oh thou disproou'st Report   (IV. ii. 34)

which is, in some senses, the leitmotiv of the play, is uttered at a point where the threads of the action are interwoven: the marriage story with that of the lost children and the theme of Britain. Its facets illuminate all areas. 'Experimentation had long had its connections with magic', and the Queen who possesses, or imagines she possesses, 'strange ling'ring poysons' (I. v. 34), 'mortall Minerall' (V. v. 50), is a practitioner of Bacon's 'degenerate Naturall Magicke'. Shakespeare twists and exaggerates one side of Bacon's casuistical dichotomy between lawful and unlawful investigation. Wilson Knight speaks of the Queen's 'instinctive' support of her son, a perceptive epithet suggesting that element of unregenerate energy which also inspires her murderous cunning and her evil exploitation of natural resources. The two lost princes are also seen, in some of their acts, as housing 'primal nature in its ferocious . . . aspect'. There is, however, a major difference between the Queen's nature and theirs. Guiderius kills Cloten with what seems an untroubled animal reflex but the princes' moral intelligence partakes of 'rehabilitated nature'. They are moved by that sense of proportion which is a requirement of true relationship. When Arviragus says:

> We haue seene nothing:
> We are beastly: subtle as the Fox for prey,
> Like warlike as the Wolfe, for what we eate:
> Our Valour is to chace what flyes.   (III. iii. 39–42)

this is not, as it might seem, emblematic fatalism. It was a Renaissance understanding that 'Man had learned about his own nature from his observance of animals' and Arviragus' self-reproach has an experiential emphasis. The scene provides a significant departure from orthodox commonplace. Belarius' truisms about Court *v.* Country are a point of departure rather than a place of rest and have dramatic relevance as revealing the force of an obsession rather than the truth of an ideal. His values, are questioned by the two princes who argue, in effect, that *a priori* value must be submitted to, and substantiated by, experience.

Cymbeline has been called an experimental drama mainly because of its competitive awareness of the new Jacobean stage-fashion for Romance. The term could be applied in other ways, since the play is significantly experimental with its characters, values, and situations. One simple essential in an experiment is time. Philario says of Posthumus, with unintentional irony:

> How Worthy he is I will leaue to appeare hereafter, rather then story him in his owne hearing.   (I. iv. 33–5)

The events of the play perform what the First Gentleman admitted he could not: they 'delue' Posthumus 'to the roote' (I. i. 28). To say that the realization of character involves the realization of situation is to proclaim the obvious. Such an emphasis is necessary, however, for *Cymbeline* is above all a study of situation, relationship, environment, and climate of opinion. If we are 'on occasion . . . content to forget the play and concentrate on its heroine' very great harm is in fact done. Again, the question of possible dramatic bias may be raised. If Cymbeline himself, who is both character and 'climate', seems to elude the extremes of scrutiny one need not infer evasiveness on the dramatist's part. The king's decision, though victorious, to pay his 'wonted Tribute' after all (v. v. 462) invites us to take it seriously, as a gesture of deep humility and the play's moment of truth. It might be taken more appropriately as a token of considerable ambivalence. Its solemnity exists for the participants in the immediate situation while the play itself contains a reserve of irony. Cymbeline's magnanimous gesture is also one of Shakespeare's supremely comic moments. If it is a moment of truth this is because it lays bare the absurdity of the original mouthing and posturing and pointless antagonism.

> Laud we the gods,
> And let our crooked Smoakes climbe to their Nostrils
> From our blest Altars.   (v. v. 476–8)

The poetry is both plangent and jagged. 'Should not the smoke of an acceptable sacrifice rise undeviously to the heavens?' It is a proper question. Cymbeline's command makes an uncontrollable element appear deliberate, converting the accidental and the thwart into a myth of order and direction. Such a myth reflects a royal sense of occasion and the mystique of status but one recognizes that the phrase has the kind of resonance which could bring more distant connotations into sympathetic vibration. This evocation of majestic aplomb belongs, as it were, partly to Cymbeline the 'character', partly to Shakespeare the dramatist: on the one hand 'business as usual', on the other 'this is what the reality of Prerogative is like'. Such a double-take would be quite in accord with the play's feeling for compromise. *Cymbeline*'s sense of finality, seen in this light, resides in its capacity to annul, through time, exhaustion and sleep, the business of the wicked and arrogant and the impetuosity of the immature. 'Crooked Smoakes', considered as the dramatist's 'own' metaphor, is like silent music, a visual rendering of the favourite Jacobean musical device known as 'chromatic tunes'. What this means is embodied in a line of Pisanio's:

> Wherein I am false, I am honest: not true, to be true.   (IV. iii. 42)

This is the taming of 'false relation' to a new constructive purpose. Dissonance is the servant preparing the return of harmony. In the words of John Danyel's lute-song of 1606:

> Vncertaine certaine turnes, of thoughts forecast,
> Bring backe the same, then dye and dying last.

Cymbeline, which 'aims at effecting the gratification of expectancy rather than the shock of surprise', brings back the same in both grace and mediocrity. It brings back husband to wife and tribute to Rome. It also reaffirms the king in the dualism of his selfhood and his prerogative. Shakespeare is perhaps ready to accept a vision of actual power at cross-purposes with the vision of power-in-grace; 'the real world', in fact, 'in which the life of the spirit is at all points compromised'. To make such a suggestion is not to push

Shakespeare into placid cynicism or angry satire but it is to feel that he at least knew the difference between acceptance and indulgence. *Cymbeline* has been called 'enchanted ground'. If it is, then that ground is

> drenched in flesh and blood, *Ciuile Historie*, *Moralitie*, *Policie*, about the which mens affections, praises, fortunes doe turn and are conuersant

—steeped, that is, in those knowledges which men generally 'taste well'.

5

Jonathan Swift: The Poetry
of 'Reaction'

In general, when we use the word 'reaction', we may be referring to a supposedly 'retrograde tendency' in politics or to a 'revulsion' of feeling. Since the political and pathological aspects of Swift's work have been amply debated, the purpose of the present exercise may appear open to question. It should be emphasized that, in proposing the term 'reaction' for this discussion, my chief endeavour is to define and describe an essential quality of Swift's creative intelligence: the capacity to be at once resistant and reciprocating.

I am aware that, in the consideration of Augustan poetry in general and Swift's poetry in particular, arbitrary assumptions as to the irreconcilability of wit and feeling still carry weight; and Swift is especially vulnerable to those distortions of interpretation which occur when ideas are extracted from the texture of language. To state my own case in its most basic terms is to say that if, as a moralist, Swift's concern is with the ordering of acceptance and rejection, as a moral artist he can transfigure his patterns. We may readily perceive that this demands from the poet a most sensitive awareness of the things which are being reacted against and that at his finest this sensitivity works as a catalyst to transform, say, autocratic disdain into a cherishing particularity. We recognize just as readily that this awareness can be fully realized only in the medium of language itself, the true marriage, in words, of wit and feeling.

It is no longer possible to explain Swift's genius in terms of convenient myth. That he was not 'mad' is attested by eminent medical and scholarly authority; that he suffered, in 1742, a brain-lesion followed by senile decay seems probable and, in view of his advanced age, unremarkable. Nevertheless, for a considerable part of his life he was certainly ill and demonstrably eccentric, concerned to the point of obsession with manifestations of the absurd and irrational in himself, in particular enemies and friends, and in society at large. Certain episodes in his career would have justified such concern, among them his fruitless efforts to reconcile the quarrel between Bolingbroke and Oxford, the oppressive infatuation of Esther Van Homrigh, the threat of arrest by the Walpole administration, and of physical assault by Richard Bettesworth. These were matters of more than clinical observation, but such observations, in the form of philosophical and political theory, were not overlooked. Swift read and annotated his volumes of Machiavelli, Bacon, Harrington, and Hobbes. Sir William Temple had been attracted by the truism that events in history could be largely explained by noting the 'passions and personal dispositions' which rule the private lives of public men; and the master's fondness for the commonplace seems to have been shared by his pupil. One may feel, therefore, that to view the intimate eccentricities of Swift in their larger context is in accord with his own creative disposition. Such poems as 'An Apology to the Lady Carteret', 'Lady Acheson Weary of the Dean', and 'Verses on the Death of Dr. Swift' suggest that, as a poet, he could represent personal predicaments emblematically and turn private crisis into public example. W. B. Yeats, whose view was understandably influenced by the prevailing myth of Swift as *poète maudit*, to some extent justified his acceptance of the legendary figure by making it representative of the destruction of an epoch. The final silencing of Swift was the silencing of the voice of moral authority in his place and time: 'more than the "great Ministers" had gone'.

In Swift a sense of tradition and community is challenged by a strong feeling for the anarchic and the predatory. A necessary qualification is that the appeal of Community exists not as a fine Platonic idea but as something soberly lived, taken into the daily pattern of conduct and work. A reader of his correspondence, as of the *Journal* and birthday poems to Stella, comes to accept the real presence, as well as the ritual, of his friendships. This affects the poetry, in particular its power to move with fluent rapidity from private to public utterance and from the formal to the intimate in the space of a few lines. At times, in the letters to Bolingbroke and Oxford, what is private is simultaneously public in its implications. It is of course true that when one has a few good friends and those friends happen to be the most important men in England, E. M. Forster's injunction 'only connect' has a particularly happy significance. It might be objected that such ideal conditions hardly existed for Swift after the debacle of 1714; it might also be remarked that the familiar verse which, we are told, 'occupied so much of Dean Swift's leisure' in Ireland became a half-defensive exaggeration of the sudden failure to connect, a play on the vicissitudes of being 'in' or 'out':

> When I saw you to-day, as I went with Lord Anglesey,
> Lord! said I, who's that parson? how awkwardly dangles he!
> When whip you trot up, without minding your betters,
> To the very coach side, and threaten your letters.

This is the conversion to familiar nuance of the public admonitory tone of seventeenth-century satire, but for the intimate joke to have bite it still needs the public contact, an edge of hard fact. In a letter to Pope, years afterwards, Swift wrote that:

> I was t'other day reckoning twenty Seven great Ministers or men of Wit and Learning, who are all dead, and all of my Acquaintance within twenty years past.

He continued, as though trying to balance his account, with the names of nineteen 'men of distinction and my friends who are yet alive'. Primarily an ageing man's game of patience, it is still a suggestive catalogue both for the timbre of the voice and for the data it provides. Several of those named, including Lord Berkeley, Lord Carteret, the Duke of Ormonde, and the Earl of Pembroke had held high office as Lord Justice or Lord Lieutenant in Ireland. The younger Swift, 'taking his ease at the Castle', had enjoyed friendly acquaintance with Berkeley and Pembroke. Carteret's term of office (1724–30) enabled the old and celebrated writer to exercise a nice intricacy of formal yet familiar association with a man whose intellect was at once engaged and frustrated in the practicalities of government. However daunting the periods of Irish reclusion may have seemed, they were far from bringing total eclipse.

Swift has been called 'a practical politician in everything he wrote'; he was, in a variety of senses, a born administrator. Dr Johnson, who was not over-indulgent towards Swift's memory, admitted his capability as Dean of St Patrick's. It has been remarked that, in Ireland, the administrative class to which Swift's family belonged could be 'numbered in the hundreds' yet formed 'a kind of social capital on which he drew interest for the rest of his life'. It was necessarily a self-contained society. Ireland's ruling caste, as the historian William Lecky pointed out, was 'planted in the midst of a hostile and subjugated population'.

Among the coterie of Swift's Dublin years were a number of people, active in their public lives, who wrote occasional verses and sometimes took part in humorous rhyming contests with the Dean and other friends. His literary acquaintance included Dr Patrick Delany, Dr Richard Helsham, George Rochfort, William Dunkin, and the Earl of Orrery. Stella also wrote, and a character in Yeats's *The Words upon the Window-pane* claims that she was a better poet than Swift; though on the evidence of the three pieces which are attributed to her the argument is untenable. These verses are less impressive than some by Swift's other close friend, Dr Thomas Sheridan. 'Tom Punsibi's Letter to Dean Swift' (*c.*1727) is an immaculate example of that style of familiar naturalism in which Swift himself excelled:

> When to my House you come dear Dean,
> Your humble Friend to entertain,
> Thro' Dirt and Mire, along the Street,
> You find no Scraper for your Feet:
> At this, you storm, and stamp, and swell,
> Which serves to clean your Feet as well:
> By steps ascending to the Hall,
> All torn to rags with Boys and Ball.
> Fragments of Lime about the Floor,
> A sad uneasy Parlor Door.

Sheridan's description of the miry street may be an admiring echo of Swift's earlier 'A Description of a City Shower' (1710) but it is clear from the accuracy of his writing that Swift had found a reciprocating talent. Apparently:

> so successful was Sheridan in imitating Swift's style that even Delany found it difficult to distinguish the work of one from that of the other.

But if 'Tom Punsibi's Letter' is imitation, it is so in the good neo-classical sense and is distinct from simple mimicry or mere plagiarism. Familiarity with Sheridan's work may have given Swift a much-needed incentive for his own familiar verse, a more racy and immediate contact than the admired Pope and a disciple and confederate in the 'Hudibrastic' line.

Swift, in his old age, is reputed to have had the whole of Butler's *Hudibras* by heart and it is somewhat surprising to find no mention of this work in the catalogue of his library. Swift's library was admittedly not widely representative of the achievements of modern English poetry. He had Spenser, Milton, Pope, Prior, Gay, and Parnell but not, apparently, those two predecessors with whom, as a satirist, he is now most often associated. Of these, Butler is one, and for the absence of Rochester there may have been sufficient reason since even the libertine Earl's return to Christianity had been made under the aegis of the detested latitudinarian Bishop Burnet. Although Swift 'never was one of his Admirers' it is difficult not to be in sympathy with those critics who cite the 'agony and indignation' of Rochester's major satires as a precedent for Swift's own work in the genre and hard not to suppose that the Dean had read them, perhaps with mixed feelings about their 'Hobbesian' views but with a professional attention to detail. Compare Rochester's

> With mouth screw'd up, conceited winking eyes,
> And breasts thrust forward; Lord! sir, she replyes,
> It is your goodness and not my deserts
> Which makes you show this learning, witt, and parts.
> Hee puzled bites his nailes, both to display
> The sparkling ring, and think what next to say,
> And thus breakes forth afresh; Madam I Gad,
> Your luck att Cards last night was very bad:
> Att Cribbage fifty-nine, and the next Show
> To make the Game and yet to want those two!

with Swift's

> 'Stand further Girl, or get you gone,
> 'I always lose when you look on.
> Lord, Madam, you have lost Codill;
> I never saw you play so ill.
> 'Nay, Madam, give me leave to say
> 'Twas you that threw the Game away;
> 'When Lady *Tricksy* play'd a Four,
> 'You took it with a Matadore.

That the advantage of this comparison appears to be with Rochester is not wholly due to the exigencies of arbitrary selection. He is a lyric dramatist: the 'mouth screwed up', the gesture with the ring, seem to occur in a sequence of human cause and effect. Rochester peoples a situation with actors who themselves grasp that they are 'situated' and must therefore act to live. Swift, it might seem, though often praised for his sense of situation, shows less concern for human predicament than for the more obvious tones of social behaviour. He converts manners into mannerism; or he presents a formal setting which serves as a *pied-à-terre* for punitive excursions:

> My female Friends, whose tender Hearts
> Have better learn'd to act their Parts
> Receive the News in *doleful Dumps*,
> 'The Dean is dead, (*and what is Trumps?*)'

Here, though, the rhyming wit itself works like a 'trump' or triumph to snatch brilliant personal success from a position of elected disadvantage. A constant preoccupation with verbal routines is a characteristic of Swift, as may be seen in *A Proposal for Correcting, Improving and Ascertaining the English Tongue* (1712) or *A Compleat Collection of Genteel and Ingenious Conversation* (1738), and his satiric art in 'Verses on the Death of Dr Swift' depends on a seemingly perfect rapport between clichés. The effect does not merely require the bathos of the move from 'dead' to 'Trumps'; it also needs a constant frisson or sympathetic vibration between truisms, 'Friends', 'tender', 'doleful'. There is even a reverse thread of ironic suggestion linking 'News' and 'Friends'. The very solidity of Rochester's characterization is itself releasing. Swift's nuance-haunted repartee puts the burden of correct or incorrect response on the reader and is capable of employing pathos as a trap for obtuse decency:

> 'The Dean, if we believe Report,
> 'Was never ill receiv'd at Court:
> 'As for his Works in Verse and Prose,
> 'I own my self no Judge of those:
> 'Nor, can I tell what Cricks thought 'em;
> 'But, this I know, all People bought 'em;
> 'As with a moral View design'd
> 'To cure the Vices of Mankind:
> 'His Vein, ironically grave,
> 'Expos'd the Fool, and lash'd the Knave:

In order to isolate and describe Swift's own idiom it is necessary to recognize contacts, both those which excite and those which inhibit the growth of idiosyncratic art. If Swift's friendship with Thomas Sheridan stands at one pole of the creative field, Addison's influence possibly represents the opposite extreme. It is known that Addison drastically edited two of Swift's poems, 'Vanbrug's House' and 'Baucis and Philemon', by 'cutting out many strokes that gave vigour and force to the description'. Although Swift always referred to Addison in terms of personal respect it is clear that Swift's creative tact was a very different thing from Addison's literary taste.

Nor was there always a perfect understanding with such close acquaintances as Delany and Orrery, who were sometimes disturbed by Swift's breaches of etiquette. It is not altogether astonishing to find in Swift's poetic satire a certain amount of irritation at the spurious proscriptions of false delicacy and a clear distinction between squeamishness and decorum. The question of 'reaction' implies more than a manipulation of antitheses. With many aspects of the consensus of taste Swift was undoubtedly able to agree, and it would be patronizing to suppose that he necessarily regarded himself as sacrificing original liberty on the altar of caste. Despite the possibly inhibiting surveillance of Addison or Temple and the sympathetic reservations of Delany and Orrery, Swift's poetry gained more than it lost by his overall adherence to the major canons of his class. 'The Journal of a Modern Lady' (1729) contains a scathing account of the trivial malice of social gossip:

> Nor do they trust their Tongue alone,
> To speak a Language of their own;
> But read a Nod, a Shrug, a Look,
> Far better than a printed Book;
> Convey a Libel in a Frown,
> And wink a Reputation down;
> Or by the tossing of the Fan,
> Describe the Lady and the Man.

But, setting ethics aside, this 'language' is no mean achievement in quick, economical mimicry. Swift never did leave ethics aside but it is still true that his poems have a good deal of the gadding energy and, at times, something of the spleen and complacency of the society which they inhabit.

It may be that close-knit communities need to evolve sophisticated weapons of control. Eighteenth-century verse sometimes aims to 'disarm'. *The Rape of the Lock* is such a poem; Swift's 'Cadenus and Vanessa' (1713) is another. This work originated in the Esther Van Homrigh affair; Swift was 'embarrassed but unwilling to end the situation'. Ostensibly a tale in verse, 'Cadenus and Vanessa' is a working blueprint for the kind of poem which it then discovers itself to be; its task is to test various techniques against varying situations and successfully reduce a dangerous immediacy to a more remote hypothesis:

> She railly'd well, he always knew,
> Her Manner now was something new;
> And what she spoke was in an Air,

> As serious as a Tragick Play'r.
> But those who aim at Ridicule
> Shou'd fix upon some certain Rule,
> Which fairly hints they are in jest,
> Else he must enter his Protest:
> For, let a Man be ne'er so wise,
> He may be caught with sober Lies;
> A Science which he never taught,
> And, to be free, was dearly bought:
> For, take it in its proper Light,
> 'Tis just what Coxcombs call, *a Bite*.

Given the situation between Swift and Vanessa, such terms as 'in an Air', 'As serious as', 'may be caught', 'a Tragick Play'r' are a breath-taking defiance of gravity. The passage turns on the words 'railly'd' and '*Bite*', two technical terms out of the social rhetoric of the time. The requirements for a successful 'bite' were specified by Swift himself:

> You must ask a bantering question, or tell some damned lie in a serious manner, and then she will answer or speak as if you were in earnest: and then cry you, 'Madam, there's a *bite*'.

Receiving an answer 'as if you were in earnest' suggests, in the Swift–Vanessa relationship, a denouement more far-reaching than the crisis of a rhetorical game; yet the whole point of the rhetoric is to defuse the emotional charge.

The somewhat complex question of raillery as an eighteenth-century social and literary phenomenon has been the subject of much able and detailed discussion. In terms of pure theory it is possible to distinguish two major types: 'ironical praise that is really satire or reproof' and its opposite, 'something that at first appeared a Reproach, or Reflection; but, by some Turn of Wit unexpected and surprising, ended always in a Compliment, and to the Advantage of the Person it was addressed to'. Swift favoured, in principle, the second type and was particularly careful to make the distinction between constructive raillery and mere abuse:

> So, the pert Dunces of Mankind
> Whene're they would be thought refin'd,
> Because the Diff'rence lyes abstruse
> 'Twixt Raillery and gross Abuse,
> To show their Parts, will scold and rail,
> Like Porters o'er a Pot of Ale.

In the light of these meticulous distinctions and the insistence on the social and ethical advantages of the art, one recognizes all the more sharply those occasions when it is bungled or simply set aside. When Swift was at Market Hill, 'the neighbouring Ladies', according to Faulkner, 'were no great Understanders of Raillery'. Market Hill was a rural estate and the implication here may be that country cousins are no match for urban wit. But it seems that these same urbanities frequently wore thin. Sheridan angered Delany and, in the end, lost Swift's friendship with raw remarks that were ill-taken. Participants in the humorous verse 'battles', which were a feature of the intellectual circle, not infrequently lost their tempers; Swift was at various times culprit, victim, and peacemaker. His own poem 'The Journal' (1721), describing in terms of affectionate raillery the household activities of the Rochforts and their guests, led to his being criticized for abusing the hospitality of friends. The casualty rate could, admittedly, have been higher; but the point would seem to be that, notwithstanding the precise distinctions between fine raillery and coarse insult, mistakes were frequently made, even by such skilled practitioners. It may seem that infringements occurred through the necessity to turn in small tight circles of mutual exacerbation and the obligation to demonstrate superior skill. Despite accidents this high-strung technique had its value in a close community, permitting the reiteration of such real or imagined values as accuracy, tact, and feeling. It offered a way of beating the bounds between the permissible and the unspeakable, of driving out the drones and instructing the rest. In a letter to William Pulteney of 7 March 1736/7 Swift acclaimed his recipient's 'more than an old Roman Spirit' which had been 'the constant Subject of Discourse and of Praise among the whole few of what unprostituted people have remain[ed] among us'. Swift had a tendency to count heads. 'Few' and 'unprostituted' is what the drama of unity required, in the teeth of human limitation, for the sake of the *manes*. He wrote to the Earl of Oxford, 3 July 1714:

> For in your publick Capacity you have often angred me to the Heart, but, as a private man, never once. So that if I only lookd towards my self I could wish you a private Man to morrow.

In one sense this is telling praise; in another, it is a courteous and restrained lament for the failure to achieve unity of Being. In one important respect, the mutual regard of two 'unprostituted' people is everything; but at the same time, given the ideal integrity of public life, it is not enough. Perhaps this is the value for Swift, emotionally and philosophically, of the defeated

man and it may be the truly creative thing that he received from the ideas
and example of Sir William Temple. Defeat restores Unity of Being, if only
hermetically and in isolation. Although critics quite properly stress the
manifest differences between the early Pindarics and the mature verse, it is
possible to detect a thread of continuity, a line of development starting with
the Pindaric celebration of the defeated man (Temple; Sancroft), continuing
through the 1716 poem to Oxford, 'How blest is he, who for his Country
dies', and culminating in the comic exorcisms of Swift's own defeat.
His political and ecclesiastical embarrassment, his 'exile', were factors to
which he personally refused to succumb, but which, as a poet, he provoked
into a series of difficult encounters. The situation of 'An Apology to
the Lady Carteret' (1725) and 'Verses on the Death of Dr. Swift' (1731) is
defeat, either by bodily humiliation or the trivia of daily encounters or
the triumph of philistine life, but wit converts the necessary failure into
moral and rhetorical victory. The prime significance of Swift's 'sin of wit' is
that it challenges and reverses in terms of metaphor the world's routine of
power and, within safe parentheses, considers all alternatives including
anarchy.

Swift's attitude towards the anarchic was significantly ambiguous. In
principle he abhorred all its aspects, from lexical and grammatical to social
and political; pragmatically he played along with it to some extent; poetic-
ally he reacted to it with a kindling of creative delight. While, in the main,
anarchy was a mob-attribute, it is open to suggestion that Swift also
recognized a Jonsonian sense of disorder, an imbalance of humours in
those who governed policy or money. Viewed in this light, great bad
men like Marlborough or Walpole were a threat to the body politic.
Although Swift, in common with other contemporaries, offered analyses
of raillery and although a subsequent process of scholarly abstraction has
tended to give such discussions an apparent universality in Augustan literary
and social debate, his work is noteworthy for its so-called 'ungenerous' and
'inexcusable' attacks on Marlborough and somewhat lesser figures like
Baron Cutts and Archbishop Hort, poems in which he abandons the salon
of raillery for the pillory of invective. There seems little to distinguish the
tone of 'The Character of Sir Robert Walpole' or the anti-Marlborough
piece 'On the Death of a Late Famous General' from the kind of procedure
that Swift, in 'To Mr. Delany', purported to despise. It should be stressed
that in considering the poems themselves, when one notes the distinction
between raillery and invective one is describing the difference between two

equal forces rather than between superior and inferior kinds. If 'Verses on the Death of Dr. Swift' is the apotheosis of raillery it is equally apparent that 'The Legion Club' (1736) is Swift's masterpiece of invective:

> KEEPER, shew me where to fix
> On the Puppy Pair of *Dicks*;
> By their lanthorn Jaws and Leathern,
> You might swear they both are Brethren:
> *Dick Fitz-Baker*, *Dick* the Player,
> Old Acquaintance, are you there?
> Dear Companions hug and kiss,
> Toast *old Glorious* in your Piss.
> Tye them Keeper in a Tether,
> Let them stare and stink together;
> Both are apt to be unruly,
> Lash them daily, lash them duly.

Invective is a touchy subject. 'The Legion Club' has been criticized for being an 'uncontrolled outburst' but in these lines Swift, with manifest control, describes the vicious as being also, in a sense, helpless. 'Stare' perfectly expresses fixated energy. 'Old Acquaintance' seems equally well judged: the two 'Companions', Richard Tighe and Richard Bettesworth, were well-known opponents of Swift, participants in lengthy feuds. In the poem he makes them 'old' in the sense that the devil is 'old' Nick; that is, their sinful madness is inveterate. This is the fusion of familiar and formal in a word. Or consider:

> Bless us, *Morgan*! Art thou there Man?
> Bless mine Eyes! Art thou the Chairman?
> Chairman to yon damn'd Committee!
> Yet I look on thee with Pity.

Here an 'impossible' rhyme ('there Man' / 'Chairman') toys with the 'impossibility' of finding a decent man like Morgan in such a place, while its thumping obviousness simultaneously confirms his presence. The magisterial tone quite transcends the real source of Swift's outrage, a pot-and-kettle dispute between the Irish clergy and the landowner-dominated Irish Parliament over the question of pasturage tithes. It is poetically convincing and technically invulnerable; not an 'uncontrolled outburst' but in places a deft simulation of one. Because it is so convincing it could even be said to react upon its source. While admitting the parochial nature of the original feud, one is prepared to accept that universal principles of human conduct—

justice, dignity and right dealing—are here involved and that Swift's protest is uttered on behalf of common honesty and freedom.

Supposedly 'uncontrolled' outbursts also affect that most sensitive area of Swiftian research, what used to be known as the 'unprintable' poems. There is a line of defence on these which laudably aims to explode the pathological fallacy but requires careful qualification. It has been said that Swift 'is hardly more scatological than others of his contemporaries'. Attention has been drawn to possible parallels in Dryden's version of Juvenal's 'Tenth Satire', in a burlesque (dated 1702) of L'Estrange's *Quevedo's Visions* and in *Le Diable boiteux* of Lesage. Parts of Smollett's *Humphry Clinker* and *Adventures of an Atom* also constitute admissible evidence. But when all has been allowed Swift still remains more comprehensively and concentratedly scatological than his English contemporaries. One cannot seriously compare such squibs as the anonymous 'On a F[ar]t Let in the House of Commons' with 'Cassinus and Peter', or 'Strephon and Chloe' with the mild and modish pornography of Prior:

> At last, I wish, said She, my Dear—
> (And whisper'd something in his Ear.)

'Whisper'd something' is truly symptomatic of the mode and perhaps helps to explain by contrast the nature of Swift's verse, which cuts through that barrier of shame and coquetry where it is only too easy to excite a snigger with gestures of mock reticence. The best of Swift's scatological poems can therefore be called 'harrowing' in the true sense of that word. It is open to argument that the best are those which are most susceptible to accusations, on the part of hostile critics, of violent morbid obsession.

It may be proper, as a preliminary step, to establish the robustness of Swift's scatological humour:

> My Lord, on Fire amidst the Dames,
> F[art]s like a Laurel in the Flames.

Here it subsists in the comedy of 'on Fire' and 'like a Laurel', in the suggestion of genial heat and sparkling Olympian success. It occurs in later work such as 'Strephon and Chloe' (1731):

> He found her, while the Scent increas'd,
> As *mortal* as himself at least.
> But, soon with like Occasions prest,

> He boldly sent his Hand in quest,
> (Inspir'd with Courage from his Bride,)
> To reach the Pot on t'other Side.
> And as he fill'd the reeking Vase,
> Let fly a Rouzer in her Face.

'He boldly sent his Hand in quest' is the language of lyrical pornography applied to an unlyrical situation. The catharsis of the episode has been well described as effected by 'the surprise of the line in which that word [Rouzer] appears, startling the reader to laughter or at least to exclamation'. It would be difficult to find a word that blends the outrageous and the festive more effectively than this. Swift is capable of outrage at the world of spontaneous reflexes but he is equally offended by the false notions of 'divinity' previously entertained by Strephon about women and by Chloe about men; hence the real importance of the perception in '*mortal*'. In a basic sense these anarchic explosions are more real than the sublimities of attenuated fancy but they are still grotesque, Swift suggests, when contrasted with the proper decencies and restraints of life:

> On Sense and Wit your Passion found,
> By Decency cemented round.

But the very fact that these basic functions do have this element of truth in the situation, and come with a mixture of unexpectedness and inevitability, produces something of the festive energy of farce. However deliberately the retrenching moralist may stand at guard (e.g. the routine phraseology of the concluding lines) the poetic imagination still cherishes the creatures of its invention.

To return upon our opening argument: if it is a mistake to reject Swift's major scatological work as the reflex of an aberrant psychology, it is equally inadequate to defend Swift on the basis of 'healthy laughter', an evasive term that fails to cover the dominant characteristics of his verse. D. H. Lawrence wrote of the 'mad, maddened refrain' of the 'Celia shits' verses. Irvin Ehrenpreis's contrary and, one might say, prevailing view—that 'the complainants' case would be best proved if Swift were *not* intense on such subjects'—is arguably as simplistic as Lawrence's condemnation.

Consider two passages, the first from 'A Panegyrick on the Dean, in the Person of a Lady in the North' (1730). Composed as a contribution to the mirth of the Achesons at Market Hill, it is cast in the form of an address of commendation to the Dean by Lady Acheson herself. Its topic is the erection of two latrines on the estate and the reluctance of the menials to make full use of the amenities:

> Yet, some Devotion still remains
> Among our harmless Northern Swains;
> Whose Off'rings plac't in golden Ranks,
> Adorn our chrystal River's Banks:
> Nor seldom grace the flow'ry downs,
> With spiral Tops, and Copple-Crowns:
> Or gilding in a sunny Morn
> The humble branches of a Thorn.

'Devotion', 'Off'rings', 'chrystal', 'gilding', use pastoral idealization like a joke about having to step carefully. 'Perfectly calculated' it may be, a teasing of mock fastidiousness and salon refinement, in which the details are fancifully arranged, but it does not rise above a comedy of manners.

Set against this the end of 'A Beautiful Young Nymph Going to Bed' (1731):

> The Nymph, tho' in this mangled Plight,
> Must ev'ry Morn her Limbs unite.
> But how shall I describe her Arts
> To recollect the scatter'd Parts?
> Or shew the Anguish, Toil, and Pain,
> Of gath'ring up herself again?
> The bashful Muse will never bear
> In such a Scene to interfere.
> *Corinna* in the Morning dizen'd,
> Who sees, will spew; who smells, be poison'd.

The perfect dryness of 'recollect', the peremptory burlesque of the eighteenth-century colloquial rhyme 'dizen'd' / 'poison'd', have complete control over the plangencies of 'Anguish, Toil, and Pain'. Though not compassionate in a modern altruistic sense, Swift nonetheless recognizes the sanctity of the human image even in its horridly fallen condition.

However, if this is not the 'gnashing insanity' that Lawrence thinks he sees, neither is it the unflinching vision of *A Modest Proposal*, where Swift can overlay the small circle of a mean intelligence (his persona) with the ample radius of the intellect itself and make his tacit reservations tense with humane implication. The intelligence of 'A Beautiful Young Nymph Going to Bed' can be asserted only by rhetorical closure. We are not here selecting good from bad taste but trying to describe differences of imaginative grasp in situations where certain kinds of raw human material are common to all.

It is possible that 'perfectly calculated' could, in some instances, be better expressed as 'predetermined' or even 'academic'. The academic Swift is a significant figure, notably in *A Proposal for Correcting, Improving and Ascertaining the English Tongue*, an attempt to predetermine the future shape of the language in accordance with his overriding political convictions and apprehensions. Swift's linguistic attitude is a kind of Tory stoicism, a rather simpler form of resistance than that of the poems. Its limitations are perhaps best described by Dr Johnson, in the Preface to his *Dictionary*, where he remarks on the futility of trying to secure language from corruption and decay and of imagining that one has the 'power to change sublunary nature, and clear the world at once from folly, vanity, and affectation'. One recalls Yeats's saying that Swift 'foresaw' Democracy as 'the ruin to come'. If this is so, it only intensifies the creative paradox of his poetry whose energy seems at times to emerge from the destructive element itself. In his own copy of Dr Gibbs's paraphrase of the Psalms Swift scribbled unflattering comments alongside examples of slovenly rhyming. Of 'more-pow'r' he commented: 'Pronounce this like my Lady's woman'. Yet in Swift's own poetry this lexical and grammatical arrogance is transfigured in such a work as 'The Humble Petition of Frances Harris' (1701). Mrs Harris was one of Lady Berkeley's gentlewomen:

> Yes, says the *Steward,* I remember when I was at my Lady *Shrewsbury's,*
> Such a thing as this happen'd, just about the time of *Goosberries* ...
>
> The *Devil* take me, said she, (blessing her self,) if I ever saw't!
> So she roar'd like a *Bedlam,* as tho' I had call'd her all to naught.

Some years later, in 1718, Swift wrote a further poem, 'Mary the Cook-Maid's Letter to Dr. Sheridan', along similar lines of character and idiom. A number of his polemical pieces adopt, or affect, the form and phrasing of the popular street-ballads of the day: 'Peace and Dunkirk: Being an Excellent New Song upon the Surrender of Dunkirk' (1712); 'An Elegy upon the Much-Lamented Death of Mr. Demar, the Famous Rich Man' (1720); 'An Excellent New Song Upon His Grace Our Good Lord Archbishop of Dublin' (1724); 'Clever Tom Clinch Going to be Hang'd' (1726); 'The Yahoo's Overthrow; or the Kevan Bayl's New Ballad ... to the tune of "Derry down"' (1734). The Bagford, Pepys, and Roxburghe Collections contain possible precedents and analogues, such as the anonymous 'South

Sea Ballad' of 1720, which could be compared and contrasted with Swift's poem, 'The Bubble', of the same year. If we refer to the confrontation of two distinct kinds of poetic tradition and method, a popular and an aristocratic, and if we relate Swift's Pindaric 'aberration' to the kind of sublimity invoked by Sir William Temple in his *Essay on Heroick Virtue* (1690) there will be a temptation to claim that a timely encounter with popular colloquial verse 'redeemed' Swift as a poet. But there is no simple and obvious way in which this could be affirmed. Some of Swift's poems may have achieved immediate popular success, but one still has reservations about calling him a 'popular' poet; he did not so much use as demonstrate the colloquial; the very kind of accuracy he achieved was the result of a certain aloofness. He was able to fix his perspectives:

> And so say I told you so, and you may go tell my Master; what care I?
> And I don't care who knows it, 'tis all one to *Mary*.
> Every body knows, that I love to tell Truth and shame the Devil,
> I am but a poor Servant, but I think Gentle folks should be civil.

If one is conscious, throughout, of the dualistic nature of Swift's genius and achievement, it is not inappropriate that so much of his energy should have been expended upon, and re-charged from, the dualistic nature of Irish life and politics, or that one should be able to find both the cold disdain and the fervent identification of the poems coexisting in the style of *The Drapier's Letters,* whose effect on the Irish people is happily evoked by Lecky's general encomium on Swift:

> He braced their energies; he breathed into them something of his own lofty
> and defiant spirit; he made them sensible at once of the wrongs they endured,
> of the rights they might claim, and of the forces they possessed.

Given the current English political attitude, to be in Ireland, the 'depending kingdom', as a member of the so-called governing class was to be in a 'situation' of considerable difficulty. Swift polemically rejected the situation as a principle in the fourth *Drapier's Letter* but encountered it daily as a fact. His sensitive reaction to this situation, both personal and national, resulted in a release of creative energy which could not have been produced by the application of principle alone. Swift had little sympathy with Shaftesbury; but the crowning paradox is that his own poetry is one of the most powerful expressions in eighteenth-century English literature, prior to

Blake, of that kind of resistance which the Whig philosopher so eloquently described:

> And thus the natural free Spirits of ingenious Men, if imprisoned and controul'd, will find out other ways of Motion to relieve themselves in their *Constraint*... 'Tis the persecuting Spirit has rais'd the *bantering* one ... The greater the Weight is, the bitterer will be the Satir. The higher the Slavery, the more exquisite the Buffoonery.

6

Redeeming the Time

In her cogent and illuminating *Sartre*, Iris Murdoch claims that:

> The smaller, expanding world of the nineteenth century, where the disruptive forces were not only dispossessed and weak, but incoherent, disunited, and speechless, could think itself a single world wherein rational communication on every topic was a possibility.

One looks nervously for a hidden language-game: e.g. the century could think itself a single world, could cherish the hypothesis; but probably it did not; or, if it did, perhaps it deceived itself. Some major questions are begged, not only as to the area of possibility but also as to the limits of metaphor in 'speechless'. Henry Adams, it is true, remarked that 'Beyond a doubt, silence is best' but Adams, in his several substantial volumes, was the patentee of one of the most obliquely cautious of modern styles; and in any case he was dispossessed only in an acutely specialized sense of the term. Those who were dispossessed in the more mundane demotic fashion, deprived of rightful franchise, income, and leisure, tended to be vociferous rather than speechless. E. P. Thompson, a scholar whom one may fairly call left of centre, has drawn attention to 'that demagogic element, inevitable in a popular movement excluded from power or hope of power, which encouraged the wholly unconstructive rhetoric of denunciation'. R. H. Tawney, equally sympathetic towards the principles of democratic progress, wrote of 'the orgy of mob oratory in which Chartism finally collapsed'. Anything less like a 'single world' than the nineteenth century it would be hard to discover; and without moving outside the circumference of Iris Murdoch's model arena one encounters the violent clashing of contradictions. It is at least open to suggestion that the epoch was marked by a drastic breaking of tempo and by an equally severe disturbance of the supposedly normative patterns of speech.

It should not be thought, however, that in referring to the possibility of a 'language-game' one is being lightly dismissive, or underrating those implicit and explicit tactics whereby a class or faction might contrive to project itself as 'the world'. Ethical definitions have been said to 'involve a wedding of descriptive and emotive meaning, and accordingly have a frequent use in redirecting and intensifying attitudes'. The confines of a determined world 'give' so as not to give; tropes are predestined to free election; the larger determinism allows for the smaller voluntarism. It has been said that Locke, in his presentation of the institution of 'lawful government', appeals to his readers

> by the use of a compelling *image*—the image of a body which cannot move except in the direction in which 'the greater force' carries it. The image is clearly drawn from dynamics, and would have had a special appeal in the age of Newton.

Even in this pseudo-Newtonian world, the by-products of entropy may be expected: among them the trivia of decayed good taste and the 'demagogic . . . rhetoric of denunciation':

> Here I stand the Factory King, declared King by the most contemptible enemies of the Cause. Yorkshire is mine! (*Cheers.*) Lancashire is mine! (*Cheers.*) Scotland is mine! (*Cheers.*) All Christendom is mine! (*Cheers.*) WE WILL HAVE THE BILL.

These words are Richard Oastler's, 'feverish' they have been called, and such utterance has been attributed to:

> the striking change of disposition that had come over Oastler in the months since he had first discovered his platform powers . . . [T]hat at least a part of his personality found a dangerous delight in the thunders of the multitude it was now too obvious to doubt.

'Disposition' and 'personality' are insecure bases upon which to build speculation, whereas the nature of a man's occupation, the range of his expectations and the limits of his security might well be influential in forming not only the terms in his vocabulary but also the rhythms and cadences of his speech. Richard Oastler, like the father of George Eliot, was a land-agent; he was an agrarian ultra-Tory and a devout Anglican; he was also resident in the West Riding of Yorkshire at the time of its greatest social upheaval. To allude to the range of his expectations and the limits of his security is neither to impugn the disinterested courage of his actions nor to bring the discussion round in a full circle to speculation about individual disposition and personality. England has been described, in a congested metaphor, as 'the classic soil of... transformation' from a largely agrarian to an urban proletarian society, and whether one chooses to let the phrase stand, with all its thronging connotations, or to isolate the three terms 'classic', 'soil', and 'transformation', Engels's words are not inappropriate to the fortunes and misfortunes of nineteenth-century English styles. Oastler's words are decidedly unfortunate. When allowance has been made for the effect of partisan enthusiasm or prejudice upon the style of contemporary reporting, Oastler remains caught in the involuntary comedy of his voluntary stance. Phrases redolent of heroic Protestantism ('here I stand', 'enemies of the Cause') and presumably chosen for that reason, are degraded into a mummer's rant. The 'classic' oration of a tribune of the people suffers a grotesque 'transformation', 'soiled' by the outflow of a fractured tradition. A rooted man, faced by the uprooted, by a floating population of the new proletariat, is unable to prevent his own words floating. Their hectic nature has possibly less to do with any personal fever than with the contagion of circumstance. Elsewhere in radical utterance a more circumstantial manner of address is itself an acknowledgement of determinism, as in the declaration of the Nottingham branch of the United Committee of Framework-Knitters, *c.*1812:

> It is true that Government has interfered in the regulation of wages in times long since gone by; but the writings of Dr. Adam Smith have altered the opinion, of the polished part of society, on this subject. Therefore, to attempt to advance wages by parliamentary influence, would be as absurd as an attempt to regulate the winds.

By 'circumstantial' one means that the authors of this passage try to account for circumstances and also that they 'go about' their direct task with language that is itself enclosed, 'fenced round' by idioms of the society which determines the realities of the situation. They are writing up, and writing up to, the subject; and writing up involves the acceptance of terms that have come down. The canting locution 'polished' had been thoroughly drubbed by Johnson as early as the middle years of the eighteenth century. Johnson was familiar with the brutality and drudgery underlying the polished life but he was also his own master and capable of exerting mastery. His sardonic stoicism resurfaces, in the working-class Nottingham of 1812, as an intelligent but etiolated fatalism. In his view 'the polished part of society' seemed vain and foolish; the framework-knitters of 1812 know that the polish is that of adamant.

An enquiry into the nature of rhythm must first attempt to account for the inertial drag of speech. Language gravitates and exerts a gravitational pull. Oastler is not 'compelling' but compelled. Social locutions which to others might be scarcely more than half-comic irritants impose upon the Nottingham framework-knitters a force as shiftless as that of nature itself. In Wordsworth's 'Ode: Intimations of Immortality', published in 1807, the line

> Heavy as frost, and deep almost as life!

is a weighed acknowledgement of custom's pressure; stanza eight is allowed to settle onto this line. However, the poet immediately breaks continuity, thrusts against the arrangement, the settlement, with a fresh time-signature

> O joy! that in our embers
> Is something that doth live.

It has been pointed out that in this poem 'the prevailing rhythm is merely iambic' and the Ode has been further described as 'broken-backed'. Saintsbury may be technically correct; but Wordsworth's strategy of combining a pause with a change of time-signature within the 'merely iambic' prevailing rhythm overrides both the propriety and the pressure. The Ode is indeed broken but the break, far from being an injury sustained, is a resistance proclaimed. If language is more than a vehicle for the transmission of axioms and concepts, rhythm is correspondingly more than a physiological motor. It is capable of registering, mimetically, deep shocks of recognition. This quality in Wordsworth's Ode was finely perceived by Gerard Hopkins and explained in his letter of 23 October 1886 to Canon Dixon:

> There have been in all history a few, a very few men, whom common repute, even where it did not trust them, has treated as having had something happen to them that does not happen to other men, as having *seen something*, whatever that really was ... [H]uman nature in these men saw something, got a shock ... [I]n Wordsworth when he wrote that ode human nature got another of those shocks ... [H]is insight was at its very deepest ... The rhymes are so musically interlaced, the rhythms so happily succeed (surely it is a magical change 'O joy that in our embers').

Hopkins's praise is to my mind in no way extravagant and his remarks constitute a major contribution to the study of rhythm. Wordsworth's 'insight was at its very deepest' and he 'saw' rhythmically. To do justice to the quality of his seeing one must refer again to Richard Oastler and to the Nottingham framework-knitters. Writers on linguistics employ a term 'stress-pitch-juncture'. '"Juncture" is that particular configuration of pause and pitch characteristics by which the voice connects linguistic units to each other or to silence.' In this case one requires a modified term, 'stress-pitch-disjuncture'. Oastler, instead of being able to subsume the satirical attacks of his opponents, is made, through his own verbosity, an accessory to their mockery. The Nottingham men are made to mouth the vulgarisms of their betters and to repine half-heartedly for 'times long since gone by'. Energy and perception have been driven apart. Perception has turned to fatalism, energy has flung into frenzy. If Wordsworth has indeed 'seen something' he has seen, or foreseen, the developing life-crisis of the nineteenth century. In the Ode the shock to be suffered by Oastler and the Nottingham men, among many others, is redeemed by the silence between stanzas eight and nine and by the immediate, abrupt surge with which the 'joy' of nine's opening lines resists, pulls away from, the gravitational field of the closing lines of stanza eight. Wordsworth transfigures a fractured world. As Hopkins truly said 'surely it is a magical change "O joy that in our embers"'. This is one of the rare contexts in which the debased word 'magical' regains some of its pristine power. Yet although 'magical' is allowable, 'change' is the key-word and should take precedence. To show why this is so, some comparison is necessary.

George Eliot is a writer with a fine sense of traditional rhythmic life, as is shown by chapter 18, 'Church', of *Adam Bede*:

> But Adam's thoughts of Hetty did not deafen him to the service; they rather blended with all the other deep feelings for which the church service was a channel to him this afternoon, as a certain consciousness of our entire past and our imagined future blends itself with all our moments of keen sensibility. And to Adam the church service was the best channel he could have found for his mingled regret, yearning, and resignation; its interchange of beseeching cries for help, with outbursts of faith and praise—its recurrent responses and the familiar rhythm of its collects, seemed to speak for him as no other form of worship could have done.

Here, 'recurrent responses' is a wide-ranging term. The responses are to be understood both as recurring within the limited time-span of a particular Anglican evensong, following the established pattern of the rubric, and as recurring over an implied and indefinite number of years, Sunday by Sunday, season by season. It is by such means that 'channels' are created;

by the joint working of abrasion and continuity. 'Responses' is the correct term for the established form of congregational participation in the liturgy. At the same time, over and below this literal meaning, the word connotes the continuity of human response in general to an ancient process of parochial and national life. The collects of the Anglican Church are composed of liturgical prose; they could properly be said to possess rhythm, though not metre. Here again, however, 'familiar rhythm' is both liturgical and extra-liturgical, telling of a rhythm of social duties, rites, ties, and obligations from which an individual severs himself or herself at great cost and peril, but implying also the natural sequences of stresses and slacks in the thoughts and acts of a representative human being. In George Eliot's last book, *Impressions of Theophrastus Such* (1879), there is an essay called 'Looking Backward' in which the fictitious narrator is the son of a country parson in the Midlands. In this essay George Eliot writes significantly of 'the speech of the landscape'. It is as though, at the end of her creative span, the author could compress into a phrase of five words the essence of paragraphs and chapters of earlier work such as *Adam Bede* (1859). The ethics are right—whether or not one happens to share them is immaterial—she is happy with the theme and the theme is happy with her. It is of course 'organic' and half-feudal, imbued with 'affectionate joy in our native landscape, which is one deep root of our national life and language'. Such a style can unite the strength of the 'deep root' with an evocation of the concomitant torpor of 'fat central England'. To praise the quintessential mastery of this late essay is not to abandon, nor even to qualify, one's praise of chapter 18 of *Adam Bede*, which could fairly be discussed under the general heading of 'poetics'.

It is instructive and saddening to set alongside these passages of masterly conflation such an example of blatant, disingenuous compounding as is the 1868 pamphlet *Address to Working Men by Felix Holt*:

> But I come back to this: that, in our old society, there are old institutions, and among them the various distinctions and inherited advantages of classes, which have shaped themselves along with all the wonderful slow-growing system of things made up of our laws, our commerce, and our stores of all sorts, whether in material objects, such as buildings and machinery, or in knowledge, such as scientific thought and professional skill...After the Reform Bill of 1832 I was in an election riot, which showed me clearly, on a small scale, what public disorder must always be; and I have never forgotten that the riot was brought about chiefly by the agency of dishonest men who professed to be on the people's side.

The source of one's objection must be clearly defined: it is in an area where misunderstanding is all too easy. An early critic of the piece protested that 'Felix Holt the Radical is rather Felix Holt the Conservative; he is not even a Tory-Democrat'. It would not be within our area of debate to attack the pamphlet on *a priori* political grounds. If George Eliot is a conservative here she is equally so in the beautiful essay 'Looking Backward'. The falsity of the pamphlet lies in its rhythmic gerrymandering and not in its basic code of beliefs. George Eliot has denied us the cross-rhythms and counterpointings which ought, for the sake of proper strategy and of good faith, to be part of the structure of such writing. In short, she has excluded the antiphonal voice of the heckler. Felix's argument is fair enough but it ought to be fairly heckled, as for instance: 'in our old society, there are old institutions . . . which have shaped themselves' (antiphonal voice of heckler: 'Shaped themselves? how? as naturally and as easily as leaves on the tree?'). Or: 'I have never forgotten that the riot was brought about chiefly by the agency of dishonest men' (heckler: 'Name three.'). George Eliot has denied us 'the drama of reason'.

The phrase is Coleridge's. On 28 January 1810 he wrote to Thomas Poole. He noted that he had been studying *The Spectator* 'with increasing pleasure & admiration' but immediately qualified this praise with the suggestion that Addison's paper had 'innocently contributed to the general taste for unconnected writing'. 'Innocently' seems in every sense a judicious emphasis. Coleridge's suggestion seems to be that a style which, around the year 1710, issued from and upheld a genuinely humane sensibility had, by 1810, been run down into the 'fixities and definites' of a mere 'law of association', into the inert 'general taste' and cliché-ridden fancy that served to gloss over the barbarous prejudice of 'the polished part of society'. In the same letter of 1810 Coleridge defends his own style by anticipating likely objections:

> Of Parentheses I may be too fond—and will be on my guard in this respect—. But I am certain that no work of empassioned & eloquent reasoning ever did or could subsist without them—They are the *drama* of Reason—& present the thought growing, instead of a mere Hortus siccus.

For one whose 'thought' has been popularly presented as fetching 'wide circuits' and as coming 'to no visible end' Coleridge maintained a striking continuity and consistency in his meditation of many years upon the drama of reason. Of crucial significance is his desiderated 'moral copula' which would, he believed, 'take from History its accidentality—and from Science its fatalism'. His sense of the moral copula, though not exclusively grammatical, was attuned to the minute particulars of grammar and etymology:

> For if words are not THINGS, they are LIVING POWERS, by which the things of most importance to mankind are actuated, combined, and humanized.

The words 'actuated, combined, and humanized' take the strain against 'the general taste for unconnected writing':

> On some future occasion, more especially demanding such disquisition, I shall attempt to prove the close connection between veracity and habits of mental accuracy; the beneficial after-effects of verbal precision in the preclusion of fanaticism, which masters the feelings more especially by indistinct watch-words.

At this point the question might well be raised as to what precisely we have in mind when approving Coleridge's disapproval of 'unconnected writing'. It would be a fair question and one hopes that it could be fairly answered. As Coleridge's reserved praise, or laudatory reservations, about Addison's style serve to indicate, the issue cannot be reduced to a simplistic quarrel between epochs. On the contrary, some lessons on the right conduct of the moral copula might be drawn from an author whose style Coleridge considered 'detestable', from Gibbon's use of the conjunction 'but':

> The architecture and government of Turin presented the same aspect of tame and tiresome uniformity; but the court was regulated with decent and splendid economy.
>
> By fencing with so skilful a master, I acquired some dexterity in the use of my philosophic weapons; but I was still the slave of education and prejudice.

Of the first of these examples it might be said that it is a bland modulation of the 'trimming' style. If that is so, it must be conceded that the trimming is so openly and palpably effected as to preclude objection. Exception cannot be taken, because exemption has not been claimed. The style which pronounces judgement is open to receive it. In the second example Gibbon achieves a plain style which, in a basic and necessary sense, establishes empirical connectives. As such it is to be fairly distinguished from persuasion by means of 'tendentious equivocation' or 'compelling...image' or by means of 'wit', as in Chesterfield:

[Chesterfield is] best satisfied when he has reduced his idea to the *atom* of prose, the 'detached thought,' which is the natural medium of wit.

As Coleridge's 'copula' could be said to have been anticipated in Swift or Johnson or Gibbon, so his own criteria are frequently reminiscent of Augustan ideals. His definition of prose as 'words in their best order', the emphasis upon 'Good Sense' and 'very plain language' have obvious precedents. It is the very strength with which he endorses such qualities that underlines the merit of his readiness to risk convolution and incommunicability in the effort to draw men '*thro*'... words into the power of reading Books in general'. It was apparent, even later, in Victorian England, that the eighteenth-century patrimony of speech remained a source of mixed blessings and embarrassments:

> [Newman's] language is that of the ordinary educated persons of his day. [His terms] are drawn from the tradition of British empiricism. They had become so much a part of educated speech that it is a nice question whether they ought to be considered technical terms at all.

These comments are intended to apply only to Newman's Anglican period. That his later style was a more complex procedure is suggested by Walter E. Houghton. Referring to Newman's method of argument in two sentences of the *Apologia* Houghton remarks:

> The structure here is so intricate and involved, the meaning so hard to follow at first reading, that one is tempted not to praise the style but to charge it with unnecessary awkwardness and obscurity... And yet, in return for that sacrifice (and it is a deliberate sacrifice: he could, of course, write with perfect clarity of form when he chose), Newman's structure has caught and projected the very sense of wavering, of being pulled back and forth and forth and back, which he was undergoing.

Houghton's analysis is well glossed by John Beer who notes that, at this specific point, Newman's writing 'diverges from the normal pattern of Victorian prose by the undertow of reluctance in its arguments'. This is excellently said, provided that we do not lose sight of the fact that the words are immediately applicable to two sentences and that Houghton's own footnotes refer us to, at most, another half-dozen brief passages of comparable pattern. To point to the sparsity of examples is not to imply a reproach. Newman's proper economy is admirable and one may see it anticipated by Coleridge in the letter of 1810:

> I shall endeavor to pitch my note to the Idea of a common well-educated thoughtful man, of ordinary talents; and the exceptions to this rule shall not form more than one fifth of the work—. If with all this it will not do, well! And *well* it will be, in its noblest sense: for *I* shall have done my best.

Houghton's 'deliberate sacrifice' which has particular sacramental relevance in the case of Newman is by no means irrelevant to a consideration of Coleridge, whose passages of self-criticism, which claim precedent and authority from the example of Hooker, strike the reader as being diagnostically resolute rather than symptomatically irresolute. He writes in *Biographia Literaria*:

> If I may dare once more adopt the words of Hooker, 'they, unto whom we shall seem tedious, are in no wise injured by us, because it is in their own hands to spare that labor, which they are not willing to endure'.

And *Table Talk* records that:

> All that metaphysical disquisition at the end of the first volume of the Biographia Literaria is unformed and immature; it contains the fragments of the truth, but it is not full, nor thought out. It is wonderful to myself to think, how infinitely more profound my views now are, and yet how much clearer they are. The circle is completing; the idea is coming round to, and to be, the common sense.

However much irony and reservation is directed towards Coleridge's real and hypothetical neuroses as the source of his convolutions and hesitancies, the rectitude of his decision seems unassailable. He surely foresaw the obligation to enact the drama of reason within the texture of one's own work, since nothing else would serve. His parentheses are antiphons of vital challenge.

The value of the antiphonal style was perceived by Matthew Arnold in 'The Function of Criticism at the Present Time':

> Mr Roebuck will have a poor opinion of an adversary who replies to his defiant songs of triumph only by murmuring under his breath, *Wragg is in custody*; but in no other way will these songs of triumph be induced gradually to moderate themselves.

Arnold's sentence is a little scenario and *Wragg is in custody* is abruptly expressive within the scenario. 'Defiant' is an epithet ironically accorded Mr Roebuck, whose 'triumph' is then defied by Arnold 'under his breath'.

It is a brief comic masterstroke in counterpoint. Its effectiveness exposes all
the more drastically the failure of an adjacent passage:

> has any one reflected what a touch of grossness in our race, what an original
> shortcoming in the more delicate spiritual perceptions, is shown by the
> natural growth amongst us of such hideous names,—Higginbottom, Stiggins,
> Bugg! . . . by the Ilissus there was no Wragg, poor thing!

The indignation has glided aside into something much less. One can plot
the swerve, the graph of descent. 'Wragg is in custody' appals Arnold, and
rightly, because it speaks with the voice of the beadle, the complacent
harshness of the penal code lopping off 'the superfluous Christian name', a
process endorsed by the jubilant tribunes of the vox populi. However, the
name Wragg itself strikes Arnold's sensitive ear as horridly vulgar; the critic
who has warned against catch-words is caught by a word and, in an
unguarded moment, righteous anger and unrighteous taste become compounded. The indignation of a just and compassionate man is degraded
into a whinny of petty revulsion. Is she 'poor thing' because of her hideous
life or because of her 'hideous' name? In 1836 a factory inspector had
discovered a Rochdale weaver 'passionately fond of ancient history' who
had named his daughters in accordance with his passion. 'But only think',
wrote the inspector, 'what a word was added to each, a word which the
poor weaver could neither change nor modify; Barraclough—Pandora
Barraclough!'

The issue would seem to be between two forms of sacrifice: sacrifice *of*
or sacrifice *to*. The first involves making a burnt offering of a powerful and
decent desire, the desire to be immediately understood by 'a common
well-educated thoughtful man, of ordinary talents'. Its structure is a recognition and a resistance; it is parenthetical, antiphonal, it turns upon itself;
its most consistent practitioners, in the nineteenth century, are Coleridge,
in the prose works, and Hopkins; isolated, significant examples are to be
found in Newman and T. H. Green. Its text might be taken equally from
Coleridge, Green, or Hopkins. Hopkins wrote to Bridges on 6 November
1887:

> Plainly if it is possible to express a sub[t]le and recondite thought on a subtle
> and recondite subject in a subtle and recondite way and with great felicity and
> perfection, in the end, something must be sacrificed, with so trying a task, in
> the process, and this may be the being at once, nay perhaps even the being
> without explanation at all, intelligible.

Hopkins wrote elsewhere to Bridges 'it is true this Victorian English is a bad business' and his remark may be interpreted in two interrelated ways. His own syntax, in the letter of 6 November 1887, is a bad business; it is, to apply one of his own terms, 'jaded'. If we were to enquire why, apart from the commonly invoked private neurasthenic reasons, Hopkins's style should be so near the end of its tether, we might well find the answer in a different form of bad business. In 1832, John Stuart Mill observed that 'a certain laxity in the use of language must be borne with, if a writer makes himself understood'. He added the important rider that 'to understand a writer who uses the same words as a vehicle for different ideas, requires a vigorous effort of co-operation on the part of the reader'. If Mill may be regarded as speaking here for a dualistic mode of acceptance, Hopkins may be considered as standing for the minority mode of non-acceptance. The 'general taste' of which Coleridge wrote is, as he knew, no innocent datum but something vicious, even if 'innocent'; to an extent the innocence compounds the vice. This much was evident as early as Burney's review of the 1798 *Lyrical Ballads,* and Burney's tonality may have been haunting Wordsworth's mind when he complained, in the 1802 additions to the Preface, of

> men who speak of what they do not understand; who talk of Poetry as of a matter of amusement and idle pleasure; who will converse with us as gravely about a *taste* for Poetry, as they express it, as if it were a thing as indifferent as a taste for rope-dancing, or Frontiniac or Sherry.

George Eliot was aware of the detrition of general taste. Mrs Transome, in *Felix Holt,* was one of those who, in youth, 'had laughed at the Lyrical Ballads and admired Southey's Thalaba' and her laughter is certainly meant, in retrospect, to ring hollow.

It is the difference, essentially, between vital and inert structures. If these terms appear portentous and suggestive of a 'certain laxity', they may be partly redeemed by close illustration. The 'magical change' between stanzas eight and nine of the 'Immortality' Ode is vital; Oastler's speech and Arnold's 'has anyone reflected' are inert. To these categories one must add a third: where a malign activity is made possible by the very inertia of general taste:

> It is, in fact, the constant aim and tendency of every improvement in machinery to supersede human labour altogether, or to diminish its cost, by substituting the industry of women and children for that of men; or that of ordinary labourers, for trained artisans.

The *OED* defines 'or' as 'a particle co-ordinating two (or more) words, phrases, or clauses, between which there is an alternative'. Scarcely ever can a 'particle' have been employed with such brutal power as in Dr Ure's suave persuasion. Suavity of this nature casts its silvery filaments around those virtues which nineteenth-century artisans were permitted to cherish. George Howell visited the Great Exhibition of 1851:

> I cannot express my feelings as I entered that vast palace of iron and as I glanced around the multifarious and magnificent collection of the products of the world there represented. All dreams of fairy land were eclipsed in a moment.

If one takes issue with this it is because one can look beyond Howell's 'dreams of fairy land' to Dr Ure's hive of industry.

If Fancy deals, as Coleridge says, with 'fixities and definites', then Howell's delight at the Crystal Palace is fanciful, not imaginative. One's protest is directed not so much against as on behalf of Howell's dream. It is the blatant coexistence in nineteenth-century England of his 'I cannot express' and Dr Ure's 'or' that distresses. Howell's words may be juxtaposed with a radical statement of some twenty years earlier:

> How strange that machinery should have an inverted and continually diverging effect upon society, rendering the condition of those attendant upon it worse and worse while others are reaping its amazing productiveness in pernicious luxury.

The two passages are in some respects strikingly complementary: 'amazing productiveness' correlates with 'multifarious and magnificent' but far more noteworthy than any similarity is the antithetical and divergent nature of what is argued. The Huddersfield men are perceptive ('diverging' is their word, and it is right) but they are also overborne, and know it. They are angry yet half-numbed by the monstrous nature of the world. It is in the syntax: 'How strange' introduces a sequence that ought, in justice, to be far-fetched but is in fact the glacial drift of their lives. George Howell, in contrast, is not overborne but rather borne up on the warmth of his astonishment and delight. Historians may point to a relative easing of conditions in the 1850s, as contrasted with the 1830s. When that much has been conceded we are left with Howell's ballooning platitudes, further symptoms of a diremption between perception and utterance, energy and effect. It is as though an iron wedge had been driven between the two passages.

There is some justification here for Coleridge's stress upon the 'moral copula' to 'take from History its accidentality—and from Science its fatalism'. It might perhaps be added that the significance of Coleridge's distinction between primary and secondary imagination, particularly when read in the light of later pronouncements in *Table Talk*, is that the first represents an ideal democratic birthright, a light that ought to light every person coming into the world. In the event, the majority is deprived of this birthright in exchange for a mess of euphoric trivia and, if half-aware of its loss, is instructed to look for freedom in an isolated and competitive search for possessions and opportunity. Therefore the secondary imagination, the formal creative faculty, must awaken the minds of men to their lost heritage, not of possession but of perception. Within certain contexts, such as that of Ure's *Philosophy of Manufactures*, even such virtues as 'rigorous self-improvement' might be fanciful rather than imaginative. F. M. Leventhal, describing the influence of Methodist teaching on the young George Howell, remarks that:

> the prescription of obedience and industry concealed an underlying ambiguity. Without denying that moral indiscipline could lead to social rebelliousness, it was equally clear that moral rectitude encouraged self-reliance. The logical outcome of education and perseverance was ambition for self-betterment, not a humble acceptance of inferior status.

It could be said, however, that 'ambition', like 'humble acceptance', is more than a matter of belief or attitude; it is a matter of what is available or allowed. Even so, Leventhal's choice of terms is helpful. It is at least open to suggestion that each of the terms or concepts, 'obedience', 'industry', 'indiscipline', 'logical outcome', adumbrates its own distinctive rhythm, or rhythmic disjuncture, and that an 'underlying ambiguity' governs the nature of rhythm as much as it does the nature of ethics.

Hopkins wrote that he employed sprung rhythm as being 'nearest to the rhythm of prose, that is the native and natural rhythm of speech'. In the context which this present discussion has attempted to establish it could be argued that the citation of a uniquely 'native and natural rhythm of speech' is itself highly selective, even ideological. This is not said in reproof. A study of the underlying ambiguity of nineteenth-century society enhances rather than detracts from one's respect for Hopkins's achievement. If asked to explain in more detail the nature of this alleged ambiguity, one would turn for support to authoritative discussions of 'the commodity status of time' and of 'mechanical time versus organic time'. The opportunity to refer to

such extensive, complex and subtle arguments permits one's own suggestion to be made much more simplistically. Crudely stated, the difference is
between being 'in' stride and 'out of' stride. The 'magical change' in the
'Immortality' Ode is perhaps the greatest moment in nineteenth-century
English poetry; but in choosing this term one is suggesting restriction as well
as potency. The recognition and the strategy to match the recognition—the
cessation of 'stride', the moment of disjuncture, the picking up of fresh
'stride'—were of their very nature inimitable; they were of, and for, that
moment. It could be said, however, that in his choice of themes and
methods, Hopkins is attempting a correlative pattern. The achievement of
sprung rhythm is its being 'out of stride' if judged by the standards of
common (or running) rhythm, while remaining 'in stride' if considered as
procession, as pointed liturgical chant or as shanty. In 'Harry Ploughman'
the man is in stride, his craft requires it; and the poem itself, in its rhythm
and 'burden lines', is the model of a work song. In the companion-piece,
'Tom's Garland', the dispossessed are thrown out of work and out of stride
and the piece is, both discursively and rhythmically, perhaps the harshest,
most crabbed, of all Hopkins's poems. It is as though the poet is implying
that, because the men cannot work, therefore the poem itself cannot.
Hopkins's persistent sense of being 'jaded' may, as has already been conceded, have neurasthenic causes; but this concession does not diminish the
respect that is due to him for encompassing in his rhythm not only 'the
achieve of, the mastery of the thing' but also 'the jading and jar of the cart'.
'Tom's Garland' is a failure, but it fails to some purpose; it is a test to
breaking point of the sustaining power of language.

In arguing for Hopkins's vital perception of the underlying ambiguities in
nineteenth-century speech rhythms one comes to recognize the central
importance of two phrases in particular. They are 'abrupt self', in 'Henry
Purcell', and '(my God!) my God', in '[Carrion Comfort]'. For Hopkins
man is revealed in his intense selfhood and in his most frightful splintering.
In the contemporary *Times* reports of the 1875 wreck of the *Deutschland*
Hopkins could have read of a desperate man hacking at his wrist with a
penknife in the hope of a comparatively painless death by bleeding, of
another hanging himself behind the wheelhouse, of a last message placed
in a bottle, even as he read of a gaunt nun calling out 'O Christ, come
quickly!' and 'My God, my God, make haste, make haste' till the end came.

The power of short prayer is discussed in chapter 37 of the *Cloud of
Unknowing*:

> A ma*n* or a wo*m*man, affraied wiþ any sodeyn chau*n*ce of fiir, or of mans
> deeþ, or what ell*es* þat it be, sodenly in þe hei3t of his speryt he is dreuyn upon
> hast & upon nede for to cr*i*e or for to prey after help. 3e, how? Sekirly not in
> many woordes, ne 3it in o woorde of two silabes. & whi is þat? For hym
> þi*n*keþ to longe tariing, for to declare þe nede & þe werk of his spirit. & þ*er*fore
> he brestiþ up hidously wiþ a grete spirit, & cryeþ bot a litil worde of o silable,
> as is þis worde FIIR or þis worde OUTE.

Helen Gardner in her essay 'Walter Hilton and the Mystical Tradition in
England' glosses the essential meaning of the author of the *Cloud*:

> the mind must be emptied of all thought, save that which is contained in the
> short words 'God' and 'Love', and by this unknowing alone can God be
> known and loved, not God in His goodness or in His mercy, but the 'nakid
> beyng of him'.

If we remove the phrase 'nakid beyng' from its immediate and proper
theological context and apply it somewhat impressionistically, we may
consider that it has a strong connotative impact, and, further, that the
connotations aid our study of Hopkins. 'Aid our study' is tentative; one
could not legitimately go beyond it. The following remarks proceed by
analogy, not by evidence. Man, as well as God, could be a 'nakid beyng':
man destitute; essential man. Wordsworth uses 'naked' in this double sense.

In a letter to his mother, written from Stonyhurst, 2 March 1871,
Hopkins devotes half the available space to a demonstration of the characteristic Lancashire intonation 'Ay!' The letter is designed to entertain and
divert the recipient but the overt intention does not conceal the close
attention paid to the phonology and physiology of the utterance. Hopkins
describes the conversation of two gardeners:

> What the one says the other assents to by the roots and upwards from the level
> of the sea. He makes a kind of Etna of assent, without effort but with a long
> fervent breathing out of all the breath there is in him. The word runs through
> the whole scale of the vowels beginning broad in the barrel of the waist and
> ending fine on the drop of the lip. For this reason I believe it is a natural sign
> of agreement and not conventional . . . It is always intoned.

Intonation can refer to the 'manner of utterance of the tones of the voice in
speaking' as in 'that unfortunate intonation of Aberdeenshire'. 'An "intonation pattern" is the amalgam of features of stress, pitch, and juncture which
occur as part of a spoken phrase.' It is also a technical term in church music:
'The opening phrase of a plain-song melody, preceding the Reciting-note,

and usually sung either by the priest alone, or by one or a few of the choristers.' The range of the two words 'scale' and 'intoned' in Hopkins's letter is potentially that of the two words 'responses' and 'rhythm' in chapter 18 of *Adam Bede*.

Here again, however, the differences are as significant as the resemblances. A rhythm of 'interchange' was available to George Eliot as it was not to Hopkins. To say this is not to ignore either her self-excommunication from the Church of England or the social ostracism endured by Lewes and herself. In 1859, the year of *Adam Bede*, she wrote in a letter of 'a sympathy...that predominates over all argumentative tendencies. I have not returned to dogmatic Christianity...but I see in it the highest expression of the religious sentiment that has yet found its place in the history of mankind'. Being able to think in these terms—Hopkins would have considered it a sloppy form of idealism—enabled her to stay imaginatively, if not actually, 'in stride' with Anglican parochial and national life. The power of this Anglican 'rhythm' should not be underrated:

> The medieval cathedrals and churches, the rich ceremonies that surround the monarchy, the historic titles of Canterbury and York, the social organization of the country parishes, the traditional culture of Oxford and Cambridge, the liturgy composed in the heyday of English prose style—all these are the property of the Church of England.

These are not the words of an Anglican apologist; they are those of Evelyn Waugh, explaining the initial sense of loss sometimes experienced by English converts to Rome. Hopkins wrote to his father, 16 October 1866:

> I am surprised you shd. say fancy and aesthetic tastes have led me to my present state of mind: these wd. be better satisfied in the Church of England, for bad taste is always meeting one in the accessories of Catholicism.

Michael Trappes-Lomax had pointed out that in the mid-1830s, at about the time of Pugin's conversion, the Mass, 'except for the private chapels of rare wealthy Catholics and a few other places, was said in garrets, in tawdry assembly-rooms, in lofts over stables'. It would be wrong to suggest that the tawdriness was the sole prerogative of Catholics. Before his submission to Rome Pugin had been disgusted by the damage done to English churches either by neglect or by the 'folly and arrogance' of misguided restorers. He had been equally horrified by the manners of some of the Anglican clergy: he complained that 'the Rev.—— goes to perform the service in *top boots* and *white cord breeches*' and that the son of a bishop had 'lost £7,000 at the last Lincoln races'. I do not think that such evidence alters the basic fact that Anglicanism, however debased and abused, could offer a 'rhythm' of responses and that the English convert to Rome, however much he might gain, nonetheless suffered an abruption of this familiar rhythm. George Eliot, in *Adam Bede,* as in the late essay 'Looking Backward', establishes a pattern of inherited living, in which the interchange of expectation and limitation constitutes the private drama. In Hopkins virtually the reverse is true: he begins with 'nakid beyng' and proceeds to build up a 'scale'. Walter J. Ong has commented:

> If Hopkins' claims for his rhythm are acceptable, he must have been, con-
> sciously or unconsciously, hearing it everywhere...the rhythms of a lan-
> guage are already rooted when the poet arrives, and the real question to be
> answered concerning Hopkins' sprung rhythm is, What was this thing he was
> discovering all around him?

One of the aims of this present discussion has been to question, albeit tentatively and inadequately, the premise of 'rooted' speech-rhythms. This may seem an astonishing suggestion in the light of the phrase 'assents to by the roots' in the Stonyhurst letter of 2 March 1871. My opinion, which is of course open to challenge, is that the essential word is the reiterated 'assents ... assent'. To assent by the roots is to become an entire embodiment of *assent.* What seems to have delighted Hopkins was the simple coherence of spirit, voice and body: a humorous corollary to his most intense concern. When D. P. McGuire states that Hopkins 'comprehended...the characteristic features of the oncoming world: the still increasing tempo...of modern life' his terms merit serious consideration. One answer to Ong's question 'what was this thing [Hopkins] was discovering all around him?' could be 'increasing tempo'; another answer could be 'the ambivalent power of the "short words"'. The short words are neither rooted nor uprooted, graced nor ungraced; they may go with the 'tempo' or they may be made to react against it. They are the most elemental material, and they are the abrupt selving of prayer: 'We lash with the best or worst | Word last!'

The task of the Catholic poem, at least as practised by Hopkins, could be seen as corresponding to the task of the tall nun who 'christens her wild-worst Best'. The poet, who made sensitive reference in his letters to the gifts and sacrifice of the Elizabethan Jesuits Campion and Southwell and who

must have known also of the staunchness and death-agonies of the Carthu-
sians martyred at Tyburn in 1535, must have sensed also how the mor-
phemes of demotic speech, the irreducible 'Ay!' of subsistence, could be
reconciled both with the mystic discipline of 'short prayer', with the significance of the Corpus Christi procession, and with the sustained melody
of Gregorian chant. In the death-cry of Prior Houghton there is for us a
dreadful mingling of physical agony and willing oblation, of helplessness and
horror struggling to transmute themselves into a voluntary sacrifice. To one
with Hopkins's theological and poetic discipline the cries could be more
meaningfully (it would be offensive to say more easily) assimilated into the
liturgy and emblems of martyrdom:

> The copy of the *Summa* which Campion was using...survives at Manresa
> College, Roehampton; it is annotated in his own hand and opposite an
> argument on baptism by blood occurs the single *mot prophète et radieux,*
> 'Martyrium'.

The 'short word', 'mot prophète et radieux' ('ah! bright wings'; 'ah my
dear'), tackles the brutality, buffoonery, and mere obtuseness of English and
transfigures it. 'Wragg, poor thing' or 'WE WILL HAVE THE BILL' are there in
' "Some find me a sword; some | The flange and the rail; flame, | Fang, or
flood", goes Death on drum', 'They fought with God's cold—', 'And wears
man's smudge and shares man's smell'; and they are answered by 'I did say
yes' and by 'Christ, King, Head'. What we have termed the ambivalent
power of the short words is most eloquently realized in the final line of
'Carrion Comfort': '(my God!) my God'. The abrupted experiences once
more commune with each other: the expletive of a potentially filthy bare
forked animal ('I wretch', 'carrion') and the bare word of faith.

 'Extremes meet': the appropriate term is Hopkins's own. He is writing of
his own art, and of Whitman:

> Extremes meet...this savagery of [Whitman's] art, this rhythm in its last
> ruggedness and decomposition into common prose, comes near the last
> elaboration of mine ['The Leaden Echo and the Golden Echo'].

This may not be good Whitman criticism but it is good Hopkins criticism.
In suggesting that our 'rhythm' enacts our life-process, or that life-process
involves rhythm ('you cannot eat your cake and keep it: he eats his off-hand,
I keep mine. It makes a very great difference'), he verges upon a symbolism
of society and of history as pertinent and as vulnerable to challenge as those

of Henry Adams and W. B. Yeats. Unlike them he had no need to extend his perception into a formula. It was his gain but in some respects, possibly, our loss. The tension between 'off-hand' and 'keep', and between 'eat' and 'keep' is an essential tension, particularly when the partaking of the elements at Mass is borne in mind. There is a consuming which is part of the process of 'organic' dissolution, and there is an absorption which is not. In a letter written some time afterwards, Hopkins noted:

> The only good and truly beautiful recitative is that of plain chant...It is a natural development of the speaking, reading, or declaiming voice.

'Decomposition' (explicit) is poised against 'composition' (implicit); we break down into 'common prose', we build, we scale up from, common prose. Taking the two letters together one can see that the pattern is too fluid to be 'rooted'; at the same time one recognizes that 'fluid' is suggestively approximate to those processes of dissolution which the theologian Hopkins rejected. One senses again that the letter to his mother on the morpheme of Lancashire speech and the letter to Bridges on the Corpus Christi procession may be more significant to a study of his poetry than has perhaps been realized. 'Ay!' could be simply inclusive of passion and belief; the Corpus Christi procession was sacramentally inclusive of passion and belief. Highly popular as well as richly liturgical, it did not spill over into the demotic but drew the demotic in. Possibly the best description of Hopkins's poetic method would be his own 'recurb' and 'recovery'.

All this could legitimately be termed 'paternalistic', 'conservative', even 'reactionary'. Such descriptions would not be value-judgements on the poetry itself. One word which, in my opinion, ought not to be applied is the word 'decadent', yet it figures prominently in a distinguished and widely known essay on Hopkins:

> Hopkins wrote in a decadent age, and if he is its greatest poet, he may be so because he cultivates his hysteria and pushes his sickness to the limit. Certainly he displays, along with the frantic ingenuity, another decadent symptom more easily recognized, the refinement and manipulation of sensuous appetite...Much of his work, in criticism and poetry alike, is concerned with restoring to a jaded palate the capacity for enjoyment.

Donald Davie's critical diction is here richly allusive rather than 'pure'. The phrase 'cultivates his hysteria' is an allusion to the entry in Baudelaire's Journal, 'I have cultivated my hysteria with delight and terror'. If one wishes to imply decadent 'sensuous appetite', would it not be more accurate to speak of a 'sated' rather than of a 'jaded' palate? Hopkins referred to himself as 'jaded'—exhausted by overwork and by nervous stress. To use this word and to suggest that it is precisely synonymous with satiety seems to me just a little tendentious.

That Hopkins wrote in a decadent age is unarguable; but to see him as quintessential of that condition is to fail to comprehend what decadence truly is. In contrast to Coleridge and Hopkins, it was 'decadent' of Mill to concede 'a certain laxity' for the sake of ease of communication: acquiescence requires quiescence. Ure's *Philosophy of Manufactures* is a degrading work. It was 'decadent' of Arnold to stoop to the indulgence of his more delicate spiritual perceptions: with all his intelligence and compassion he could not stop himself falling for the sneer, and such 'falling' is 'decadence'. It was decadent of George Eliot to write two separate essays, 'Address to Working Men' and 'Debasing the Moral Currency', the first of which betrays the priorities implied in the second, with no sense of contact or coherence between them. To fall for these things or to conspire so that others fall for them is decadence. Against all this Hopkins's poetry established a dogged resistance. Both ethically and rhythmically, his vocation was to redeem the time.

7

'Perplexed Persistence':
The Exemplary Failure
of T. H. Green

T. H. Green could be said to have provided an epigraph for his own work when he wrote of Butler that 'his value as an ethical writer is due to the same cause which makes his speculation perplexed and self-contradictory'. Praise of Green is not infrequently accompanied by major reservation, and when it is unqualified it is of dubious value, as for instance, he 'sent us out once again on the high pilgrimage towards Ideal Truth', where the symptomatic 'high', as in 'high idealism', strikes a tone which Green for the most part avoided in his own work. 'He would not have liked high language such as this to be applied to himself' wrote Nettleship, of the obituary tributes; though, in a significant concession, he added 'but it is true'. Insofar as Nettleship's comments demonstrate a confrontation between Green's respect for concreteness and his immediate admirers' zeal for abstraction, they may be taken as a marginal indication of the central issues in Green's metaphysical and ethical debate. 'Abstract the many relations from the one thing, and there is nothing' he wrote in *Prolegomena to Ethics*, as elsewhere he argued that Burke revealed 'true philosophic insight' when he opposed the 'attempt to abstract the individual from . . . the relations embodied in habitudes and institutions which make him what he is'. The phrase 'concrete experience' is to be found in Green before it is found in I. A. Richards.

That Nettleship should find the concession necessary is indicative of the strained relations between intention and reception which prompted some of Green's best writing and speaking but which also rendered him liable to those blurrings and evasions which detract from the power of his ethical style.

He criticized Butler for being 'content to leave the moral nature a cross of unreconciled principles' while, as a corollary, he argued that 'Man reads back into himself, so to speak, the distinctions which have issued from him, and which he finds in language' and that, in this 'retranslation', he 'changes the fluidity which belongs to them in language, where they represent ever-shifting attitudes of thought and perpetually cross each other, for the fixedness of separate things'. Green shares here a prevalent ethical emphasis of his time, the recognition that while we are 'unconditionally bound', 'necessarily belonging to such a world', being so bound is not necessarily the same as being in a fix and is most certainly not the same as being a fixer. In his dual application of the word 'cross', once as noun and once as verb, in two consecutive paragraphs, Green finds words for an essentially Kantian crux. The nature of the world is such as we are constrained to recognize, the ineluctable fact, but to be content with the rich discrepancies which this offers is nonetheless dangerous and is sometimes treacherous. If, in making this emphasis, Green is equal to the strength of such contemporary ethical art as George Eliot's, he also shows symptoms of contemporary weakness and rigidity. Both aspects may be examined in relation to an observation by Coleridge which stands as a paradigm for some of the most significant Romantic and post-Romantic debate on the supposed 'formal engagement' between literature and society. Coleridge takes a passage from one of Donne's sermons which, he argues, 'sways & oscillates', in its use of the word 'blood', between a 'spiritual interpretation' and a physical sense: 'Yea, it is most affecting', Coleridge writes, 'to see the Struggles of so great a mind to preserve its inborn fealty to the Reason under the servitude to an accepted article of *Belief*'. There are times when it seems that Green himself is marked by some such discrepancy between 'fealty' and 'servitude'. This is not to argue that he was uniquely deficient but rather to suggest how the common struggles of the time took a particular form in his work. In *Prolegomena* he claims that we apprehend knowledge as we 'apprehend the import of a sentence...In reading the sentence we see the words successively...[but] throughout that succession there must be present continuously the consciousness that the sentence has a meaning as a whole'. He further contends that we need to make 'constant reference to the expression of that experience which is embodied, so to speak, in the habitual phraseology of men, in literature, and in the institutions of family and political life'. It could be argued that Coleridge's objection is applicable here and that Green's 'so to speak' and 'phraseology of men' oscillate between a literal and a metaphoric sense.

Pragmatic obedience to the structure of the sentence, in order to apprehend a part of that sentence, is not the same as adherence to a metaphor of grammar, the 'habitual phraseology' of men, unless it is decreed that it shall seem so. 'So to speak', in this context, enables him to accept the decree without necessarily promulgating it.

Though the cast of his ethical thought was opposed to the currently dominant forms of adherence and coercion, Green himself too often wrote in those 'vague but insistent' terms which Whitehead has justly categorized as 'social symbolism': 'Thus the "Treatise of Human Nature" and the "Critic of Pure Reason", taken together, form the real bridge between the old world of philosophy and the new'. Although, as Green noted elsewhere, 'every explanation ... involves a metaphor', 'real bridge' here pre-empts its own verification. It lacks the resonance of those 'hypnotizing' terms to which Whitehead draws attention, but its tacit premise is still the 'response of action to symbol' which is at the centre of that strategy. And this strategy is itself crucial in certain forms of nineteenth-century Liberal bridge-building. In the words of J. S. Mill: 'We hold that these two sorts of men [Benthamites and Coleridgeans], who seem to be, and believe themselves to be, enemies, are in reality allies'. Although 'we hold that' and 'in reality' are set obliquely to each other, Mill's phrasing is designed to conceal the angularity of his proposition. It is 'in reality' which exerts the greater persuasive rhetoric and effectively overrides the proviso in 'we hold'. Later in the century than either Mill or Green, the economist Alfred Marshall wrote that economic studies 'call for and develop the faculty of sympathy, and especially that rare sympathy which enables people to put themselves in the place, not only of their comrades, but also of other classes'. Here again it could be said that such phrasing is so much a part of innocuous common parlance that to object is a sign only of hermetic irritability. And it is true that we have no good reason to dissent from MacKinnon's recognition of 'the language of ethics' as a 'language of prescription, exhortation, persuasion, moral tradition' with 'its own texture and laws'. But of even greater significance is his caveat that we must 'recognise in the authority [of the moral law] which ... unconditionally constrains us the voice of our own nature as rational beings, and not the brusque, sheerly unintelligible dictate of a despot'. Green's 'real bridge', Mill's 'in reality' and Marshall's 'in the place of' seem attempts at an illicit bridging of 'the chasm which the Kantian analysis of judgment left between subject and object'. And there is, in this form of illicit persuasiveness, a hint of the despotic. In such instances we are not so much 'unconditionally constrained' as constrained to be conditioned; it is less a matter of language living in usage than of usage perching and hatching parasitically upon the surface of language. It would be unjust to argue that such devices are the product of cynicism. At the same time it would be naive to contend that sincerity confers absolution. Towards the end of his life Green sincerely anticipated a time 'when every Oxford citizen will have open to him at least the precious companionship of the best books in his own language'. 'At least' betrays a desperation that the overt optimism will not concede. 'Best' by whose judgement, or according to what criteria? Does it mean of incontestable formal excellence, even though shocking to some susceptibilities (e.g. *Les Fleurs du mal*), or does it mean incontestably good-hearted, like Mrs Humphry Ward's *Robert Elsmere,* which was dedicated to Green's memory? There can be little doubt that his allegiance was to that 'compound of optimism and humanism', a typically mid-Victorian variety of what William James called 'the religion of healthy-mindedness'. Green was a Liberal who objected to the more materialistic forms in which ideas of Liberal progress took shape during his lifetime. He deplored, in *Prolegomena,* a state of society in which so many were 'left to sink or swim in the stream of unrelenting competition, in which we admit that the weaker has not a chance'. In the words of H. J. Laski, 'Green and his followers emphasized not the individual over against the process of government, but the individual in the significant totality of his relations with it'.

There is a case to be made for the suggestion that one of the major discoveries of modern criticism has been the method of transferring 'significant totality of relations' to a contextual plane and of conferring a consequent distinction upon those authors or individual works which fulfil most completely that kind of expectation: Keats, in the Odes, George Eliot in *Middlemarch,* or the poems of Green's sometime pupil Gerard Hopkins. If that is indeed the case, then modern criticism is ratifying an inclination which has been present in ethical writing since at least the time of Arnold. When Arnold praised a paragraph in Burke's 'Thoughts on French Affairs' as 'one of the finest things in English Literature' he reversed significantly an order of precedence. Burke's concern was not with 'literature' in that hypostatically pure form. In Arnold's statement the 'literature' is central, the politics a catalyst in the creation of the integral substance. This is not to suggest that Arnold was unconcerned with the politics but rather that he saw literature as containing politics within a sphere of more precisely adjusted anxieties. Green is both better and worse than Arnold. On the whole he refuses Arnold's trim formulas and offers a closer reading of the patterns of relationship. But even if it is now widely customary to read a text in the way that Laski suggests that Green's ideal state could be 'read', Green's own work is not amenable to this form of approach. It could be left an open question whether on this issue he rebukes modern criticism or modern criticism rebukes him, since there is a proper reluctance to bestow on any one critical position the power of seemingly absolute arbitration. Even so there is in Green a confused thinness analogous to, though not identical with, the superficiality of secular evangelism, from Mill to J. M. Keynes, which encouraged what the latter called 'the civilising arts of life' while largely disregarding their stubborn textures. In 1889 the theologian P. T. Forsyth commented that 'the best preaching analyses its text, and even discusses points of its grammar' but what sometimes passed for the best preaching in the nineteenth century was in some respects deficient in that kind of analysis. Since Green and Sidgwick were celebrated for the fervency of their utterance, their own failure to meet the terms of Forsyth's criterion merits some examination. In a letter written in 1868 Sidgwick said: 'Oh, how I sympathise with Kant! with his passionate yearning for synthesis and condemned by his reason to criticism', a sentence which speaks more for the moodiness of mid-Victorian intellectualism than for the mood of Kant. The manner in which it yearns over the dichotomy tells us a good deal about the characteristic gestures of Sidgwick and of Green also. It is open to suggestion that in a deep sense they soften Kant's rigour while, at a superficial level, they accommodate his rigorous tone. The difference between Kant and the Victorian students of Kant in England may well turn on a difference of emphasis concerning that which 'points beyond the data'. In Kant this is a 'common element' existing as 'a logical presupposition, a purely formal implication'; in Sidgwick and Green that which points beyond the data is more often a pious wish. Pious wishes are of course wholly valid, unless they are presented as logical presuppositions and purely formal implications. It is then that they cease to be 'that which points beyond the data' and become the 'vague ultimate reasons' which Whitehead has so precisely described. These slight yet massive differences oblige us to draw yet again upon the Coleridgean distinction between fealty and servitude and to say that Sidgwick and Green, while appreciating the distinction in principle, confused its obligations in practice.

It must be said again that to discuss the shortcomings of Green and Sidgwick is to be caught up with ' "*Bona fide* perplexity", as having its

origin really in intellectual difficulties, not in any selfish interest'. And in this
sense the virtues of Green in particular are difficult to extricate from his
shortcomings. At his best he is sufficiently acute as a moral analyst to
encourage the suggestion that his self-thwartings and bafflings are acts of
homage and abnegation to the Wordsworthian principle. Richter speaks of a
'Wordsworthian sentiment' to be found in him and suggests that the poet
was one of the influences disposing Green to 'a pantheistic conception of
God as manifest in nature as a spiritual principle'. Green described the 'Ode
to Duty' as 'the high-water-mark of modern poetry'. It could be said,
however, that there is something more dourly fundamental than 'sentiment',
something more stubbornly empirical than even the most high-minded
spiritual principle, in Green's Wordsworthian strain. In his essay 'Popular
Philosophy in its Relation to Life' (1868) Green proves himself to be a critic
of insight and cogency. That quality in Wordsworth which evidently holds
Green's critical imagination is one which might be described as the capacity
to go against one's own apparent drift:

> In England, it was specially Wordsworth who delivered literature from
> bondage to the philosophy that had naturalised man. This may at first sight
> seem a paradoxical statement of the relation between one known popularly as
> the 'poet of nature' and a system which had magnified 'artifice'. It is not so
> really.

'It is not so really.' Seemingly laconic, to the verge of inelegance, this phrase
offers its own rebuke to the afflatus of 'real bridge' and 'best books', gives
the rebuff of imaginative scepticism to fanciful idealism. 'It is not so really'
because as Green strongly implies, here and elsewhere, the dogmatic spasms
of 'I like' and 'I don't like' can claim no sanction from Wordsworth's
popularly misconstrued 'spontaneous overflow of powerful feelings'. 'The
natural man is the passive man.' Green's observation is closely followed by
his friend and editor, A. C. Bradley, in his own essay on Wordsworth,
printed in *Oxford Lectures On Poetry* (1909). At the heart of Bradley's vision
of Wordsworth is a sense that the poet comprehended a bi-fold authority:
both an acceptance of 'the fixed limits of our habitual view' and a dogged
experiential working towards what MacKinnon has called 'the voice of our
own nature'. Bradley speaks of 'that perplexed persistence, and that helpless
reiteration of a question' which he sees as characteristic of Wordsworth's
'Resolution and Independence'. It is evident, however, that Bradley has
some reservations about this 'perplexed persistence' and fears that it may

verge on the 'ludicrous' in ways that Wordsworth's 'intimation[s] of boundlessness' do not. We here touch upon a contradiction that affects Green as
much as it affects Bradley. Keenly perceptive of the 'data' which form the
texture of a work, each still yearns for the 'vague ultimate reasons' which
poetry such as Wordsworth's may seem to provide. Each is inclined to treat
weakness as strength and strength as weakness and to override his own
shrewdest judgements upon the work. Bradley's words are nonetheless a
fine description of a critical perception and a critical method which are in
the poem's own structure. It is worth noting that the line 'Perplexed, and
longing to be comforted' does not appear in the original 1807 text; we could
say that the poem took time to realize the voice of its own nature in this line.
The fact remains that Bradley is asking Wordsworth to de-fuse the source of
the ludicrous, as being un-ideal, whereas the poet accommodates the
possibility of the ludicrous into the situation and the dialogue. The narrator's final pious couplet, though morally worthy, is certainly not the
intimation of boundlessness that some readers expect; it has been considered
anticlimactic and naive. In a general observation on Wordsworth, Leslie
Stephen said that he 'speaks as from inspiration, not as the builder of a logical
system . . . When he tried to argue, he got, as he admits with his usual *naïveté*,
"endlessly perplexed"'. But Wordsworth, as the opening stanzas of 'Resolution and Independence' reveal, perceived the perils of 'inspiration'; and in
his poem he built a logical system to embody a meditation upon the true and
false natures of that state of being. His creative gift was to transform the
helpless reiterations of raw encounter into the 'obstinate questionings' of his
meditated art without losing the sense of rawness. And Bradley is admirable
in his own perplexed insight into what Wordsworth had to do: 'Yet with all
this, and by dint of all this, we read with bated breath'.

Green has something of this positive quality which Stephen idly termed
'*naïveté*'. Hastings Rashdall, a critic who nevertheless dedicated a major
work to Green's memory, stated that:

> The ethical system of Kant (assisted in England by the influence of Butler and
> his followers) has produced a hopeless confusion between the question
> whether Morality consists in promoting an end and the question what that
> end is.

It could be argued that as Wordsworth transformed helpless reiteration into
obstinate questioning so Green, working directly from Kant and Butler and
indirectly from Wordsworth and Coleridge, transformed what Rashdall calls

'hopeless confusion' into something more closely resembling perplexed persistence. It had the nature of a physical shock:

> I had the privilege of taking a few essays to Mr. Green . . . I went to his home with my work, and he used to sit over the fire, 'tying himself into knots'. He beat out his music with some difficulty, and the music itself was not an ordinary melody.

Richter says that Green was a bad speaker and cites the opinion of one of Green's admirers, Henry Scott Holland, that he was 'cruelly inarticulate'. Such a view is strongly modified by testimony from those who knew him as well and admired him as much as did Holland. Nettleship wrote: 'Few, I think, can have been more successful in avoiding conversational inadvertence, and the saying of things which had better not have been said'. J. H. Muirhead has described Green's Lay Sermon of 1877 as conveying his ideas 'with singular clearness and with a telling application to the intellectual difficulties of the time'. If Green appeared to some as 'cruelly inarticulate' it can only have been through a form of vocational renunciation, an 'almost confounding humility', a decision as personal yet as formal as that of Hopkins to burn his early poems. Another student has recalled:

> I . . . followed his remarkable lectures with enthusiasm and tense strain . . . I can remember that I did not understand a single word as I wrote down the perplexing tangle of phrases furiously and at lightning-speed: then in the quiet of my rooms I brooded over them till light seemed to gleam from the written word.

Among the words that figure prominently in this and the previously quoted student-memoir are 'music', 'perplexing', and 'gleam', three key-words in 'Tintern Abbey'. There is a sense in which Green's students seem to have responded to his words as Wordsworth responded to his own primary experience. It is also worth remarking that 'music' is a term which can be exploited both ideally and empirically. It is the 'still, sad music of humanity' and it is the precise detail of articulation, the 'difficult music' of communication. Coleridge commenced the second essay of *The Friend* by stating that 'an author's harp must be tuned in the hearing of those, who are to understand its after harmonies'. The image of the harper is apt. He is simultaneously a hireling without privacy and a master of pitch and cadence. His concern with tuning is attributable both to his own professional conscience and to his servitude to those who can call the tune. Some of Green's own most cogent objections are to 'the charlatanry of common sense', and to the citing of 'agreeable sensations and reflections' as supposed criteria for determining the value of literature. He regarded 'cultivated opinion' as 'confused' as well as being guilty of 'wilfulness' and shallowness. It could be said that the working alternative to the spasmodic 'I like' and 'I don't like' was embodied in his own seemingly 'inarticulate' utterance. As a tutor to Oxford gentlemen he shared some of Mark Pattison's doubts about the examination system and some of his suspicions that it might encourage a specious fluency. In *Prolegomena* he wrote of the scholar's or artist's 'temptation to be showy instead of thorough'. At the same time, as an educational reformer, Green seems to have sensed that he had a duty to reveal the freedom of the word to those who were, in Wordsworth's term, 'Shy, and unpractis'd in the strife of phrase'. It is possible to see an inevitable strain and thwarting in this dual situation: discouraging the wrong sort of fluency and self-display at one level while encouraging the right sort of fluency and self-realization at another.

Graham Hough has suggested that 'the oral channel was probably the one through which most of the Coleridgean influence originally worked' and he has drawn an illuminating analogy between the power and effect of the Highgate table talk and the influence, at once intimate and far-reaching, of Oxford and Cambridge tutorials conducted by such men as Newman, Jowett, Green, and Hare, some of whom were Coleridgeans by direct inheritance, some of whom were not. A necessary proviso is that such access and influence testify not only to intellectual calibre—formidable though that undoubtedly was—but also to the intimate prerogatives of a social élite. At the same time such tutors, Green in particular, were fully aware that they addressed the privileged and they drew such an awareness into their forms of moral instruction. In certain ways, therefore, Green may be regarded as a protagonist in the Coleridgean 'drama of reason' and his speech may be understood as an extension of the original author–reader scenario sketched with much grim humour in the pages of *The Friend*.

In saying this one is perhaps in danger of overstating Green's achievement. Richard Chenevix Trench's *On the Study of Words* (1851) is as steeped in the notion of pastoral care as is Green's fragmentary address 'The Word is Nigh Thee' and Trench was far more orthodox than Green in his religious belief. If we consider 'impulse' alone, then Trench's book could be simply described as an attempt to provide 'valuable warnings...against subtle temptations and sins'. And yet the book he wrote was far more radical

than anything by the 'radical' Green. It was Trench who learned from
Coleridge, via Emerson, 'how deep an insight into the failings of the
human heart lies at the root of many words'. The difference is both slight
and deep. One of Green's prime aims was to resist any tendency towards
that fatalism which he saw as the dark side of utilitarian hedonism, towards a
condition in which 'there is no alternative but to let the world have its way,
and my own inclinations have their way'. He could be regarded, however,
as an example of how the anti–utilitarian, anti-hedonist, may yet be held in
the gravitational field created by those forces. An acute critic of impulse,
Green could counter it only in terms of superior impulse: 'It may very well
happen that the desire which *affects* a man most strongly is one which he
decides on resisting.' In so doing he endorsed his opponents' standards in
the act of challenging them. The very terms he chose called the tune. As
a sentence from his testimony before the 1877 Oxford University Commission suggests, he equated 'literary skill' with skilful superficiality:
'Success... naturally falls to the man of most literary skill, who can bring
his mind to bear most promptly and neatly on any subject that may be set
before him.' There is therefore an air of frustration, of wasted labour, in
Green's attempts to get under the skin of verbal acceptance. Nettleship's
'Memoir' puts on record that 'Those who have ever heard it will remember
the peculiar smack of his utterance of the word *tilth*'; and ' "Swing" was a
favourite word with him to describe the movement of native eloquence,
and he would express his dissatisfaction with much contemporary English
poetry by saying, with a characteristic gesture of the hand, "There is no
swing in it" '. This is of course a seductive example because we cannot fail to
be aware of the use made of the word 'swing' by Green's occasional pupil
Hopkins, in the early poem 'Heaven-Haven' ('And out of the swing of the
sea'). But freed from these associations we see that Green's words are merely
impulsive, verging on the kind of bluster so effectively parodied by Hopkins
when he evoked a manner that 'came in with Kingsley and the Broad
Church School', 'the air and spirit of a man bouncing up from table with
his mouth full of bread and cheese and saying that he meant to stand no
blasted nonsense'.

There is one other haunting fragment of unrealized possibility. Nettleship
also records that Green:

> had a theory in composing... that all superfluous words should be extirpated,
> the fewest and most compressed used: that, if possible, an essay should consist

of one indivisible paragraph, the connected expression of a single proposition
or a single syllogism.

But it remains an early 'theory'. Here again it is in the work of his pupil
Hopkins, a pupil with whom his relations seem to have been fairly edgy,
that we find Green's ideals realized: in the 'indivisible . . . connected expression' of 'Spelt from Sibyl's Leaves' or, perhaps more arguably, in the syntax
of the final stanza of 'The Wreck of the Deutschland', with its culminating
line which, in Elisabeth Schneider's words, is 'locked together in the hook-
and-eye grip of the possessive case':

> Our hearts' charity's hearth's fire, our thoughts' chivalry's throng's lord.

Schneider gives a striking description, although one recalls that when
Coleridge referred to 'all the *hooks-and-eyes* of the memory' he apologized
for using 'so trivial a metaphor', sensing perhaps that it might suggest
something more simply and mechanistically associative than he intended.
Hopkins seems rather to be stressing, against the linear process, an enfolding
of possessives, in order, as Schneider rightly says, 'to create the closest unity
of all human values in Christ'. I cannot entirely agree with her suggestion
that 'the effect is arbitrary and labored'. The method, I would accept, is
arbitrary and laboured but the effect is one of hard-won affirmation.

It seems to me that there is some analogy between the method and effect
of Hopkins's poem and the method and effect of Green's lectures. Green's
method was repeatedly called 'difficult', but the effect of his words, as we
have heard, was likened to 'music' or to a 'gleam'. Admittedly, one is
dealing here with subjective impressions. Many of Green's lectures have
survived and are printed in the *Works*. The series on 'The English Commonwealth' brings out the 'earnestness' and 'exhilaration of energy' which
Green found in the period. For him there appears to have been a 'swing' in
it. Elsewhere, his lectures now seem heavy with the diffuseness of paraphrase rather than tense with the bafflements of communication. But the
subjective evidence cannot be set aside; it exists in its own right:

> Though he had great difficulty in expressing himself at that time . . . Everyone
> saw that there was great substantial value and originality in the work; and the
> very difficulty of his utterance gave one the feeling that he was working the
> thing out, and not repeating other people's phrases or ideas . . . The men in
> fact took a sort of pride in the difficult process which he went through before
> he got things clear, as if it were in some way the joint action of us all.

Even if it is conceded that young men, chasing after charisma, will always hunt down what they seek, through these outmoded Victorian locutions there shines an act of recognition which is stronger than the commerce of mere egotisms. In part, though only in part, 'the joint action of us all' is the burden of the concluding lines of 'The Wreck of the Deutschland', the creation of 'the closest unity of all human values in Christ'. Rather than transaction or projection, a Green lecture appears as an act of atonement, in the arena of communication, between the 'unconscious social insolence' of the listener and what Coleridge termed the seeming 'assumption of superiority' on the part of the speaker.

It has been said that, for Green, 'the characteristic thing about human experience is that it is thinking experience'. It is a token both of his achievement and of his relative failure that so much of the 'exhilaration of energy', which he manifestly aroused, should be conveyed to us in the form of reminiscence. He himself wrote of the 'weakness . . . which belongs to all ideas not actualised, to all forms not filled up' and several reasons could be advanced for Green's naggingly persistent failure to actualize his own ideas. It could be attributed to the 'hopeless confusion' about means and ends that Rashdall saw as characteristic of English paraphrases of Kantian ethics. Or it could be traced to the overriding confusion as to the nature of the 'formal engagement' in public discourse, a debate in which Wordsworth and Coleridge stand as heroic protagonists. Richter detects, throughout Green's ethics, 'signs of the strain produced by his merger of conservative concepts with liberal and even radical values' and he is, I think, correct in this major respect: the reasons for Green's relative failure are not separate and distinct but manifold. Green, as much as Mill or Sidgwick, was writing to be received, and, at the same time, was conducting a running battle with the premises of current receptivity. Newman wrote that 'where there is no common measure of minds, there is no common measure of arguments'. Of the nineteenth-century 'Liberal' writers it could be said that they sought a 'common measure' to set 'against mere impulse and mere convention alike', but were left too often with immoderate commonplace. Sidgwick's 'law infinitely constraining and yet infinitely flexible' is no 'law' at all, but a rather shifty rationalization of a condition of servitude. The efforts of Mill, Sidgwick, and Green are too easily reducible to the terms of Mill's own assumption that it was good 'to enlighten . . . practice by philosophical meditation', a procedure which leaves pragmatism and idealism as two separate floating entities. It may be that Mill, to use Bagehot's chilling phrase, is feeling the minds of his readers 'like a good rider feels the mouth of his horse', but if that is so it is revealed as a self-defeating exercise. There is some irony in the fact that Mill introduces his essay on Coleridge with such a proposal. 'Meditation' is here regarded as being on a par with 'opinions' and 'mental tendencies'. If practice can be so 'enlightened' by meditation, then meditation can also be forbidden access to the pragmatic domain. What Coleridge gives, however, is a constant demonstration that meditation is central to practice, whereas 'opinion', 'tendency', and 'enlightenment' are peripheral and non-resistant. It has been suggested that one of the dominant philosophical tenets against which Coleridge contended was 'the dogmatic assumption of the principle of *dichotomy*'. If, as Richter has claimed, Coleridge was one of the several exemplars upon whom Green based his own 'faith', it could likewise be suggested that this faith is set out in Green's essay on Aristotle. He writes there of the 'unfused antithesis of the "necessary" and the "contingent"' as manifesting the 'Aristotelian dualism [at its] most conspicuous'; and he ponders upon Aristotle's thesis in such a way as to bring out those elements which are susceptible to a belief in interchange rather than separation: 'The account of the form or essence, then, as a "substance dematerialised" may be replaced by an account of it as a "potentiality actualised"'. There remains in Green's discursive faith, however, a fundamental separation which no amount of theoretical application can bridge. This failure may be termed a failure of imagination because there seems to be no connection in Green's mind between his recognition of an 'account of form' on the one hand and his suppositions about the workings of the poetic mind on the other. Admittedly, he is intent on warning the poet against the perils of euphoria and his words might be taken as a parody of the euphoric state. But there cannot be a parody where there has been no perception of the real condition. We receive no hint from this that Green knew what he was talking about: 'As the poet, traversing the world of sense, which he spiritualises by the aid of forms of beauty, finds himself ever at home, yet never in the same place.'

The question 'how the moral intelligence gets into poetry' is of course quite distinct from the question 'how morality gets into poetry' or 'how moral is poetry?' If Green so often disappoints us it is because his critical insights are too frequently dissolved, dissipated, without being re-created. But even this is far from being a simple matter of mere personal vacillation. It could be said that a study of Kant, while encouraging an emphasis upon contextual relationships in general, could nevertheless inspire incompatible applications of the idea of context. 'The new students of Kant in England' drew from their study, among other inferences, the suggestion that '[one] could not, for instance, distinguish even particular items unless [one] were also aware of the context or series in which the items appear'; and it is this sense of 'context or series' which, arguably, is of prime importance in Green's pattern of thinking. The thesis that context distinguishes the items, significant though it might be in projecting an idea of reciprocity between the state and the individual, is nevertheless a definition more at the service of empirical application than of creative imagination. At the same time, 'the form by which spatial and temporal data are apprehended as elements in a whole that points beyond the data' was one which made possible an indifference towards, and even a contempt for, context in anything other than a serial, spatial sense:

> Not as to the sensual ear, nor necessarily through the stinted expression of verbal signs, but as a man communes with his own heart, you may speak to God . . . Prayer indeed, if of the right sort, is already incipient action; or, more properly, it is a moral action which has not yet made its outward sign.

It is possible that 'sensual ear' is an echo from 'Ode on a Grecian Urn'; if so, the phrase is not uncharacteristic of Green's habit of demanding poetry's support while effectively denying it the power to act. When Green directs his attention to the 'stinted expression of verbal signs' he stints the whole question too, by deploying gobbets of Shakespeare, Keats, and Tennyson as simple emotional referents. It could be contended, in his defence, that, in stressing a dichotomy between 'heart' and 'sign', Green is most essentially Wordsworthian and that if we praise the scruple of Wordsworth's distinction between a 'mechanical' art and 'real and substantial' suffering we can scarcely deny our tribute to Green. It could also be observed that the question whether our 'feeling', i.e. 'faith', is more trustworthy than our reason, was raised by Sidgwick, who wrote of Tennyson's *In Memoriam* that he felt there 'the indestructible and inalienable minimum of faith which humanity cannot give up because it is necessary for life'. A pioneering study, in English, of Karl Barth's theology states that Sidgwick's gloss on Tennyson 'admirably catches Barth's tone' and that it also anticipates Barth's stress on 'the intolerable crisis which is felt when life is viewed "existentially"'. I would say that the comparison is too generous and that the citation of Barth makes one only too acutely aware of what is deficient in Sidgwick, and in Green also. The distinction between rigorous abnegation and easy abdication, so keenly asserted by them in principle, is not always marked in their own practice. When Wordsworth says, of the female vagrant, that:

> She ceased, and weeping turned away,
> As if because her tale was at an end
> She wept;—because she had no more to say
> Of that perpetual weight which on her spirit lay

he is indeed implying that words are 'in some degree mechanical' compared to the woman's action and suffering. But in order to bring out the difference Wordsworth puts in a collateral weight of technical concentration that releases the sense of separateness: the drag of the long phrasing across the formalities of the verse, as if the pain would drag itself free from the constraint. In 'as if' and 'because', pedantically isolating her, we glimpse the remoteness of words from suffering and yet are made to recognize that these words are totally committed to her existence. They are her existence. Language here is not 'the outward sign' of a moral action; it is the moral action.

In Green's work we may find an approximate understanding of the nature of such action, but we are indebted to his pupil, friend and biographer R. L. Nettleship for a precise formulation. Nettleship perceived that:

> the consciousness which we express when we have found the 'right word' is not the same as our consciousness before we found it; so that it is not strictly correct to call the word the expression of what we meant before we found it.

A. C. Bradley recalls that it was Green who suggested to Nettleship that he might 'approach philosophy from the side of language'. One cannot readily determine from the context whether 'from the side of' is a direct quotation from Green rather than Bradley's paraphrase. It is perhaps fair to say that either Green or Bradley, or both, regarded the matter as one of optional angles rather than as a necessary belonging to such a world. Green's comparative diffuseness on this issue is made all the more noticeable by his otherwise strong emphasis on necessary belonging, on 'the "I" that has felt as well as thought, and has thought in its feeling'. It is in a passage concerning the 'relation of each to the other' that Green comes closest, if not to a realization, at least to an adumbration, of Nettleship's perception:

> As has been pointed out, the sensible 'here' has, while I write it, become a 'there', the sensible 'now' a 'then'. We may call the sensible 'heres' and 'nows' an 'indistinguishable succession of points or moments', 'each changing place

with that which goes before'; but in the very act of naming, *i.e.* of knowing
them, we transmute them.

If it were possible to isolate the final statement ('but in the very act of
naming...') from the overriding context it would also be possible to argue
that Green is moving towards Nettleship's position; but such a plea cannot
be entered. For Green, the transmutation is into 'categories' and 'general
attribute[s]' whereby we 'who are within the process' experience a form of
'placing ourselves outside the process by which our knowledge is developed'. Green stresses two major issues of this dualism: the knowledge so
gained is 'imperfect, and, through its imperfection, progressive'; it 'implies
the undivided presence of the thinking self'. It could be said that, while the
pattern of Green's ideas about the thinking self is centripetal, the pattern of
his thinking about ideas is centrifugal. There is therefore a dualism within
the texture of what he makes, and this dualism divides what he does from
what his admirers say that he does.

'[Green] gave us back the language of self-sacrifice', wrote Henry Scott
Holland. That Green gave to his readers crucial ideas of self-sacrifice is
beyond dispute:

> He may 'find no place for repentance' in the sense of cancelling or getting rid
> of the evil which his act has caused; but in another sense the recognition of
> himself as the author of the evil is, in promise and potency, itself repentance.

That these ideas were taken up and put into practice, to the benefit of the
community, is again an incontestable fact. It seems to me, however, that
Holland's words must be qualified. Green gave ideas but he did not give a
'language'; and in failing to give a 'language' he closed off one dimension of
moral intelligence. The importance of Nettleship's perception is that it does
not seal off the moral action from the linguistic action. Indeed it is the
positive coalescence of these forms of action that is manifested in the
cogency of his statement.

In the course of a valuable discussion of the traditions of moral thought,
Dorothea Krook has drawn attention 'to the significant common ground
that may be seen to exist between poetry and philosophy when both are
viewed as products of the creative imagination'. It is in this domain that
Green, who had so much to say, has so little to give. And this realization
strikes with a particular irony. It was an Anglican priest, Dean Inge, who
quite properly discerned that 'From Coleridge to von Hügel... the deepest
and the most forceful [moral and religious] teaching has come from lay

writers'. He included in his list the names of Green, Sidgwick, and Nettleship. If 'deep seriousness and earnest desire to know the truth and make the
world a better place' were the sum of the moral imagination, Green would
be above criticism. But it is not; and, as one who, albeit unwittingly, divided
morality from the moral intelligence, Green must, I think, be vulnerable to
attack. His perorations are ominous, looking upwards and outwards to times
'when the poet shall idealise life without making abstraction of any of its
elements'. Yet even while warning against abstraction Green failed in one
necessary act of concentration. The 'element' was there and he could not
see it. The extent of his loss, and ours, becomes clear when we turn, not
only to Nettleship's statement, but also to a discussion which his own
argument seems, in some respects, to anticipate: Donald MacKinnon on
'introspection and the language of freedom':

> 'I could have done otherwise'. Such a phrase might express not simply a
> retrospective glance at what might have been, but *an act of repentance* which it
> makes concrete. When the prodigal said that he would 'arise and go to his
> father', he was no doubt, from one point of view, recording the fruit of
> inward communing with himself. But at the same time he was making that
> communing something more than a mere daydream, and he made it so by
> linguistic action. He said something to himself, and, by saying, he did
> something.

We may perhaps say that, viewed in the light of this suggestion, Green's
work is both a summons to activity (including a summons to acts of sacrifice
and atonement) and also the outward sign of fruitful inward communing;
but not 'at the same time'. It is not a doing-by-saying. Consequently,
although he asserts the significance of the poetic act as a moral act, his
assertions are 'mere daydream'.

If Green, despite these several reservations, still attracts one's prolonged
and intensive meditation, it is chiefly because he bears witness, as in the
characteristic 'An Answer to Mr. Hodgson', to that central and inescapable
conflict in which all who engage in public discourse become involved.
The original subscribers to Coleridge's *The Friend* numbered just under
four hundred. He was satisfied, we are told, 'to direct his remarks to the
"learned class" he was later to call the "clerisy"'. He required 'the
attention of my reader to become my fellow-labourer' but from the
surviving comments of several self-assured readers—Josiah Wedgwood,
the Lloyds, and others—it is evident that some of them considered that
he asked too much. His readers, with few exceptions, rebuffed his

attempts, finding him 'abstruse and laboured' as others, later, found Green 'cruelly inarticulate'.

As Blake said, the accuser is god of this world. It is possible to find in this recognition a necessary resilience, such as is present in the poetry and prose of Wordsworth, especially in the 'Preface' to *Lyrical Ballads*, in the poetry and marginalia of Blake and in the flashes of grotesque comedy, the interpolated cries and groans, of *Biographia Literaria* and *The Friend*. Green's lectures, as we know them in the expressive re-enactments of those who attended them, make their own restricted but valid discovery of the 'formal engagement'. Green was, in an immediate sense, requiring his audience to become his fellow-labourer. Even if we say that he does little more than demonstrate the pitch of attention at which the true (as opposed to the spectral) Coleridgean 'clerisy' might be expected to work, that is ample praise and makes a proper rebuke to the gods of this world. In the sacrificial nature of his perplexed persistence and in his vulnerability to the accusation which his servitude draws upon itself, Green achieves his own substantial freedom and power and remains as one of the most crucial writers in nineteenth-century Britain. There are triumphs that entrap and defeats that liberate. Green is creative in his distress. To speak of his exemplary failure is to see him in the light of a noble phrase borrowed from Forsyth; it is to say that he 'passed through negative stages to his positive rest'.

8

What Devil Has Got into John Ransom?

The question, as it stands, is rhetorical and contentious. To Donald Davidson, who raised it, the answer was clear enough. It was a devil of a betrayal, as Ransom had accurately predicted. 'It will seem', he wrote, 'like treason and unfriendship' to Davidson's die-hard Southern Agrarianism not merely to recant from those once-shared principles and policies but also to flourish one's recantations in print. To Allen Tate, working a later tack and writing in a different vein, Ransom was not so much possessed of a devil as gripped by a 'mania' which drove him in later years to the ruinous rewriting, the 'compulsive revisions' of poems written in early middle age. Those who know their Ransom will justly observe that not all his revisions were in effect 'ruinous', though the impulse may have been; and his admirers will be inclined to add that 'devil' and 'mania' are weirdly ill-fitting masks for a poet whose favoured stance was a compounding of stoic ceremony and stoic laughter. It is true of course that laughter need not always be pleasant nor ceremony what it seems. Davidson once called Ransom's epistolary style 'meaty and flavorsome' and Tate with equal relish remarked that 'John throws a very wicked style, indeed'. Those were early days. Some years later Davidson would take exception to his 'cruelly polite snobbishness'. Would we be justified, then, in saying that Ransom possessed a devil of a style, in keeping with his own premise that 'if we were better men we might do with less of art'? This would be the customary half-truth. Even so shrewd a stylist as Ransom does not entirely possess his style, self-possessed as he may seem; but neither is he wholly possessed by it. There was more than a mere tactical diffidence in his remark that 'it is common for critics to assume that a good poet is in complete control of his argument'; implying, of course, that he may well not be. In the writing of a poem, he

says, 'argument fights to displace...meter' while 'meter fights to displace...argument'.

Here, though, my thesis may appear vulnerable, not merely to the
stringent logic which Ransom preached and on frequent occasions practised, but to any barely audible murmur of dissent. When I speak of
Ransom's style, I gather allusions randomly from poetry and prose. Judged
by one of his own formal distinctions, this will not do. The author of 'a
good poem', he once suggested, is in its making 'freed from his juridical or
prose self'. In a late essay, however, he suggests an affinity between the
'vocalism' of the poem and that of 'meditative and imaginative prose'. I do
not think that he makes his point at all well; but it is a concession and
I intend to exploit it. One might add, with more fairness perhaps, that
the 'juridical or prose self' can be taken as a figure of speech referring to the
empirical, quotidian self which is to be distinguished from the 'I' of the
'poem' (whether in verse or prose). In saying this I knowingly allude to his
celebrated definition of the poem as 'nothing short of a desperate ontological or metaphysical manoeuvre'. If it is permissible to define a poem in
this way—and it does seem, I concede, a formula at once all-embracing and
exclusive—then Ransom's essays can be defined as poems, since 'desperate
ontological...manoeuvres' is what they are. Allen Tate declared that
Ransom's critical essays 'have the formal felicities of his poetry' but this,
though a crucial perception, remains a half-truth unless we add that they
show the concomitant infelicities of clearing one's meanings at an extreme
pitch of concentration and in circumstances of complex difficulty. If Ransom's essays are prose-poems they are so in a particular dimension; and it is a
dimension not of freedom but of constraint. One could argue that there is
a characteristic poetic crisis where rhetoric is ontologically determined
(which is tolerable, even desirable) and where ontology is rhetorically
fixed (which is intolerable but possibly unavoidable).

Ransom's definition, embracing 'agony' as well as desperation, occurs in
the closing pages of a book which begins by rebuking the young poets for
their neglect of the craftsmanlike qualities: 'wit and playfulness, dramatic
sense, detachment'. Are we to see Ransom's art as a measure of these
extremes? Some would say yes. A phrase—'torture of equilibrium'—from
one of his best-known poems is taken as an appropriate epigraph for his life's
work. Miller Williams calls him 'the supreme equilibrist' and remarks that
'balance is the word which will probably surface most frequently in any
discussion of Ransom's poetry'. Despite the consensus we may better

appreciate Ransom's final achievement by not shirking the occasions when he is thrown off balance. In his fine dialogue-poem 'Eclogue' one of the characters declares 'We are one part love | And nine parts bitter thought'; and the nine:one ratio seems to me no less emblematic of Ransom's consciousness and craft than is the five:five equilibrium to which our attention is most often directed. Of course, one might be happier to express it as an equation and, indeed, Ransom, with his emphasis on such terms as 'playfulness', 'dramatic sense', 'detachment', seems to recommend that we should. The particular acidity of his 'playfulness' on the subject of Romantic suffering is characterized in the poem 'Survey of Literature' by his rhyming the name Shelley with the phrase 'pale lemon jelly', but he does not come off from the confrontation with much credit. Shelley is Shelley and Ransom is silly. What is it that persuades a poet of such intelligence to think so highly of so shallow a poem and to cling to it so obstinately while renouncing work of much greater quality? Why compound impertinence by injustice to oneself?

Impertinence is often a symptom of nervous strain; and 'nervous strain', according to Ransom, who credits I. A. Richards with the thought, is the 'peculiar plight of the moderns'. All commentators on Ransom's life and work have exhibited an understandable and proper reluctance to show the scars of the private man. Allen Tate wrote, after his death, that he carried 'an intolerable burden of conflict that only occasionally, and even then indirectly, came to the surface'; and Ransom himself, in old age, conceded 'an intense sympathy' for T. S. Eliot, 'that tortured soul who achieved serenity'. But what is this 'privacy' of ours, whether of the intellect or of the passions? George Eliot's dictum is well known: 'there is no private life which has not been determined by a wider public life'; and though the main drift of Ransom's metaphysics could be called anti-deterministic he was enough of a Calvinist to find a number of painful conclusions inescapable. A poet of his calibre makes himself unique through 'an act of will' which is primarily an act of critical 'attention' and it would be doing him a disservice to imply a quality of uniqueness to any of his raw apprehensions as such: they are the Anglo-American cultural commonplaces of the last hundred years, from Henry James to the Lost Generation and beyond. 'The plight of a religious poet in an age of reason is desperate'; 'I am an Anglophile . . . But I am not so Anglophile as I am American'; these are the not-unfamiliar signals of the post-Romantic lost traveller. One of Ransom's poems, 'Old Mansion', is subtitled 'after Henry James' and another is called 'Man Without Sense of

Direction'. It should be added that, in Ransom as in every writer of significance, context is everything and that he takes care not only to purge and
enrich clichés by exactness and resonance but also to abrogate, by contextual means, that pathos which certain words and phrases might excite in
isolation.

Donald Davidson once remarked that 'John isn't a balance wheel, he is a
mystery', but 'mystery' itself is perhaps a term too much steeped in pathos. It
is arguable that Davidson might more happily have kept the mechanistic
bite of the metaphor if he had said: not a balance wheel but an eccentric.
That which is eccentric is not concentric; it does not share a common
centre; and phrases of absence, of exclusion, are a recurrent theme in
Ransom's work, in the polemical and critical prose as well as in the
poems. He broods deliberately, though, in terms of a lost focus: an idea
which usefully involves the hazards of psychic distress with those of technical maladjustment. Of explicators and explications he remarks that 're-
spect ceases | For centers lost in so absurd circumference'. In 'Winter
Remembered', the 'I' of the lyric narrative finds himself 'Far from my
cause, my proper heat and center'. For the eponymous protagonist of
another poem, '[Robert] Crocodile': 'It is too too possible he has wandered
far | From the simple center of his rugged nature'. An 'eccentric', it may be
noted, is also a mechanical device which can convert rotary into rectilinear
motion; and we could remark that, whereas the characters in Ransom's
poems tend to go round in circles, he has acknowledged a liking for the
'workmanlike poetic line carrying forward the argument'. But, as we said,
context is everything; and Ransom's 'liking', *in situ*, is a confession of some
embarrassment, as he feels that a relish in the carrying forward of argument
can be indulged at the expense of characters, who matter more. This is one
check upon free-ranging hypothesis; and there are others, for example,
his own sceptical playfulness with the term 'eccentric' itself. Commenting
on Donne's 'Valediction Forbidding Mourning' he suggests that the
'metaphysical figure ... tries to endear [the lovers] to us, by making them
slightly ... eccentric'. 'Old Man Playing With Children' is indeed a celebration of eccentricity and an indictment of 'middling ways'. There is a further
complication in Robert Buffington's insistence that 'the three careers of
Ransom—as poet, as critic, and as *Kulturkritiker*—run their courses about [a]
common center'. If we follow Buffington's argument, the 'center' is itself a
kind of denial: the determination to 'keep ... reason and emotion separate'.
This feat, I would have thought, is impossible—for anyone other than the

victim of some form of psychosis, and certainly for the poet engaged in what Ransom calls 'the agony of composition'. One could conceive, however, that the desire could well be there, as the devil of a temptation.

Allen Tate, as scrupulous in his weighing of sympathies as of antipathies, traced back the 'mania' which, in his view, afflicted Ransom in his dotage, to an excessive 'reliance on *logic* as the ultimate standard of judgment'. 'Logic' is, like 'balance', a word which tends to recur in discussions of Ransom's work. In Rubin's recent study it is successively described as 'calm', 'inexorable', and 'remorseless'. It becomes increasingly difficult, though, to see how this 'logic' really works, for, as Rubin demonstrates effectively enough, when circumstances arose which made a 'system' imperative, practical 'logic' was in fact deficient. In the Agrarian symposium, *I'll Take My Stand*, published in 1930, not only the intrinsic coherence of the argument but also the effectiveness of its dissemination were vitiated by conceptual confusions and by errors of tactics and policy; and for these Ransom seems to have been in considerable measure responsible. To this evidence might be added Graham Hough's observation that Ransom's critical writings are by no means free from solecisms, 'eccentricities of nomenclature and description and history . . . that would certainly merit censure in . . . a Ph.D. thesis'. I do not think it unfair to suggest that, if by 'logical' we mean 'capable of reasoning correctly', then Allen Tate is more consistently cogent than Ransom; and if we mean 'sticking to the facts', then Donald Davidson has the more literal mind.

It is ironic to find words such as 'inexorable' and 'remorseless' featuring so emphatically in appraisals of Ransom's work because there is a sense in which he is deficient in straightforward conceptual rigour. He wrote, in 1924, that 'no art and no religion is possible until we make allowances, until we manage to keep quiet the *enfant terrible* of logic that plays havoc with the other faculties'. This 'logic', of which he is fairly sceptical, may with some appropriateness be termed a 'spectral' logic since Blake's Spectre is 'the rational power . . . [which] is anything but reasonable . . . of the divided man'. 'Anything in which reason and heart are separated has its Spectre.' This 'spectral' logic approximates to the logic of 'abstraction' which Ransom consistently opposed, arguing with a particular and detailed irony against that which he regarded as an arrogant 'Platonism' in aesthetics and science. In any account of his thinking it is necessary to distinguish abstract 'logic', which he did not admire, from 'logical structure', which he did— which indeed he saw as essential to the attainment of the 'beautiful

poem'—as well as from that characteristic virtù which T. D. Young has
called his 'natural inclination toward honest (and sometimes severe) judgments'. Yet while the intention of exegetes is, quite properly, to praise
Ransom's honest severity and command of formal structure, they finally
assert the perfection of a 'logical' strategy which is in fact far from flawless
and which is, in any case, of doubtful efficacy in the making of poems or
of that 'meditative . . . prose' which Ransom admits into the ambience of
poetic effect. When a critic is able, without discernible irony, to praise the
'remorseless' logic with which Ransom attacks the 'ruthless' nature of
modern science and industry it may be taken as a symptom of some
confusion. If the one is 'predatory' why not the other? There may be
some way of explaining this, but the matter is not even noticed as something
to be explained. Ransom has said that 'we may hardly deny to a word its
common usage, and poetry is an experience so various as to be entertained
by everybody'. This remark cannot be wholly devoid of pessimistic irony.
What at first glance seems a moral imperative ('we can hardly deny') may in
fact be only a resigned acceptance of the coercive force of 'common usage'
and the solipsistic free-for-all. These nuances, rich in themselves, do not sit
easily with Ransom's unambiguous affirmation that 'the kind of poetry
which interests us is . . . the act of an adult mind'. There is a disjunction
too abrupt to be resolved by such terms as 'tortured equilibrium'. 'Desperate' is a word to which Ransom sometimes resorts; and he permits himself
crucial statements which communicate a sense of vertigo rather than of
balance. 'Images are clouds of glory for the man who has discovered that
ideas are a sort of darkness' he writes, and there is nothing 'balanced' about
this: it is a perception, and endorsement, of extremes. As he presents it, the
ontological world (he took Kant as his mentor) is one in which we ought to
prepare our minds to be 'perpetually disquieted'. He suggests that 'a man is
impelled to take action when he finds himself uncomfortable, or in need, or
lost, in some given "situation"'; and if he has any reservation about his
mentor it is that Kant finally 'takes comfort' in the idea of the mind's
existing 'wholly in the barren and simple world of the quantities'. To
hope for this, Ransom argues, is 'to hope for a peace that is hardly to be
distinguished from suicide, and not at all from mutilation'.

Ransom's word 'situation' is a revealing term. 'Piazza Piece', 'Lady Lost',
'Janet Waking', 'Two in August', 'Moments of Minnie', 'Parting at Dawn',
'Parting without a Sequel', '*Fait Accompli*', 'Conrad Sits in Twilight', 'Prel-
ude to an Evening', are poems of 'situation' where the nuances range from

simple 'setting' to the fullest implications of being in a devil of a fix. 'The Equilibrists' ('Predicament indeed!') and 'Captain Carpenter' ('he fell in with ladies in a rout') narrate fatal games of consequences. The title 'Prometheus in Straits' ironically narrows the convention, limits expectation: Prometheus, not 'bound', but in 'awkward or straitened circumstances, a difficulty or fix'. The irony or ambiguity in these poems turns indifferently upon the outcome of decision or indecision. Whether the protagonists act or do not act, they appear equally maimed by bitter circumstance. 'Situation' is inescapable; 'stance' or 'attitude' is vital. Ransom clearly favours a ceremonious stoicism, the capacity, perhaps, to 'learn a style from a despair'. The phrase is William Empson's, and there is a degree of reciprocity, of qualified rapport, between these two poet-critics. *The Kenyon Critics*, a volume which Ransom edited in 1951, includes an essay by Empson, who had visited Kenyon College as a Fellow in 1948. T. D. Young's biography of Ransom reproduces a photograph of Empson taken in the company of Allen Tate, Cleanth Brooks, F. O. Matthiessen, and Ransom himself. The words 'qualified rapport' must be emphasized. Ransom published a piece in the *Southern Review* (vol. 4: 1938–9) with the title 'Mr. Empson's Muddles' and, as late as 1969, his approach, though broadly admiring, was still critical. As Christopher Norris has pointed out, the later study reveals that it was mainly the 'character of logical explicitness' which Ransom had come to mistrust in Empson's criticism, 'the reading of the poet's muddled mind by some later, freer and more self-conscious mind'. This is by no means the only occasion on which Ransom's 'wicked style' is directed against critical exegetes, whose activities provoke him, in 'Prometheus in Straits', to 'gestures not of deference'. The Prometheus in this poem is, by implication, the long-suffering fire-bringer, the divine spirit, the Paraclete, at best embarrassed and at worst betrayed by the activities of the exegete; a circumstance depicted in the subsequent poem 'Our Two Worthies' as a near-blasphemous travesty of the Christian apostolic succession. Primary sources are compromised by secondary material.

It is scarcely conceivable that Ransom could have been unaffected by his own 'straits' or have felt entirely unembarrassed by his own criticism. Hough suggests that a subdued but persistent hostility to academe prompted Ransom's bouts of 'obstinate intellectual waywardness'. One must distinguish between waywardness and error. I cannot think that any writer perpetrates an actual solecism in order to show his defiance, least of all Ransom, who had his proper share of *amour propre* and who valued the

'beautiful thing' too highly to get factual details 'oddly wrong' on purpose. I concede the probability of emotional discomfort, however, and
the likelihood of its being exacerbated in a man to whom 'academic
standing' was 'his bread and meat', who was always 'seriously concerned
about his prospects in the academic world' and who was never less than
insistent that 'he must have full credit for all of his efforts'. Ransom's
claims for the 'anonymity' of achieved art make it seem tantamount to a
breach of etiquette to refer to these things. Nevertheless I would accept
Rubin's suggestion that, in the essay on 'Lycidas' with its title 'A Poem
Nearly Anonymous', 'Ransom on Milton . . . is also Ransom *as* Milton, or
Ransom on Ransom'. In such passages Ransom's criticism is neither 'pure'
nor 'impure'. That is to say, it attends meticulously to its own procedures;
its self-elected argument is not marred by palpable illogic; and yet, if set
in a broader, more 'historical' perspective, its lines of approach appear
both wilfully determined and 'oddly wrong'. His hypothesis that Milton
wrote 'Lycidas' 'smooth' and rewrote it 'rough' thereby demonstrating his
'lordly contempt' for the traditional restraints of his art and exposing 'the
ravage of his modernity' is a view that cannot be sustained against the
evidence of historical scholarship. The 'lordly contempt' is not Milton's
but Ransom's; and this arrogance of speculation is as substantial a part of
his creative being as is the amiable unpretentiousness, the 'serenity' and
'gentleness' to which tribute is so often and so rightly paid. There is, of
course, no blatant self-expression in Ransom's work. Allen Tate once said
that 'self-expression' is a term that ought to be 'tarred and feathered', and
I know of nothing in Ransom that would dissociate him from that view.
But self-affirmation may be very different from self-expression, and
can take anonymity as one of its forms. This distinction is drawn by implication in a passage in *The World's Body* where Ransom differentiates between
'two kinds of individualism', the one 'greedy and bogus . . . egoism', the other
'contemplative, genuine and philosophical'. But this is a contrariety which
cannot be established by mere assertion. It must be maintained, heuristically,
by an exemplary vigilance and distinction of tone which ideally cannot be
faulted but which, in actuality, falters and errs at times, as it must. This in
itself is enough to account for the 'nervous strain' to which both Richards
and Ransom allude. The contemplative, which is akin to Schopenhauer's
'knowledge without desire', annuls or transcends, and thereby redeems,
'predatory and acquisitive interest' and possibly 'nervous strain' as well.

It is certainly open to suggestion that Ransom's particular technical achievement has been the conversion of 'strain' into 'pitch'. To be 'contemplative' is to achieve 'pitch of attention'. Like the lover in an early poem by Robert Graves, whose work he admired and who was, in turn, one of his first champions in England, Ransom hears 'the groan of ants who undertake | Gigantic loads for honour's sake'; but he can also hear the 'minute whispering, mumbling, sighs' of language itself. As Vivienne Koch has perceived, Ransom's alteration of the line 'two immaculate angels fallen on earth' to 'angels lost in each other and fallen to earth' not only 'enriches the denotative content'; it also strengthens the poem's logical structure. In their first appearance in the magazine *The Fugitive* (March 1925) two lines of 'Eclogue' are both mannered and fey ('They run to the fields, and apprehend the thrushes, | And print the fairy dew'). 'Apprehend' is conceitedly stiff and 'fairy dew' is tawdry. In *Selected Poems* (1945) this becomes 'They run to the fields, and beautiful the thrushes, | Fabulous the dew'. In changing 'apprehend' to 'beautiful' Ransom exchanges a self-assertive intellectualism for an undemanding banality. But, in the end, the banality is not there; it has been dissolved in the uncanny lightness of the word 'fabulous'. This is a dangerously volatile word but Ransom has tamed and tuned this very susceptibility, allowing the halftones of 'not really there' and 'miraculously *there*' to blend most 'beautifully'. Ten years later, in *Poems and Essays* (1955), the lines read 'And listen! are those not the doves, the thrushes? | Look there! the golden dew'. The 'golden dew' of 1955 is no less a cliché than was the 'fairy dew' of 1925. It is not revision but reversion; not renunciation but ruin. What has 'impelled' Ransom; or what has led him on? In the three versions under consideration, Jane Sneed's vision of the fields of dew is immediately challenged by her lover John Black, who has the 'last say': 'O innocent dove, | This is a dream.' Does Ransom believe that he has made the 'dream' so 'fabulous', so miraculously 'there', that we might be too dazed to attend to John Black's reproof unless he turns syntax itself into a kind of travesty? Or is he going against his own best advice in ignoring the 'disparity' between a poem's 'grammar' and its 'real logic'? The 'grammar' of the dialogue between Jane Sneed and John Black is more deliberately spelt out in 1955 but the 'real logic' may belong more to the 1945 reading where miraculous simple truth is a 'dream' far worthier of John Black's renunciatory cry than are the fussy expostulations of 1955. The battle is not yet over, however. The third edition of *Selected Poems* (1969) contains a further variant; and the analysis which I have so far offered is substantially qualified by this. The whole of the stanza in question is now omitted, the antepenultimate stanza moves into the penultimate position, and John Black's 'This is a dream' now refers to the previously unconsidered claim that lovers' eyes 'are almost torches good as day, | And one flame to the other flame cries Courage, | When heart to heart slide they.' And in the light of this we look again at the lovely stanza of 1945 and find that it is a succession of lyrical arabesques around the keynote 'unafraid' (which is itself a close variant of 'courage' two lines before. Ransom may have felt it was too close). F. O. Matthiessen suggested that Ransom, in the act of revising, 'felt his way back into the meaning' of a poem. This may now seem a truism perhaps; but it is originally perceived and sensitively phrased and stands up well to an empirical test. There will be legitimate differences of opinion about these things; but I am persuaded that Ransom, through a process of apparently marginal tinkering and trimming, discovered a long-concealed central disproportion in the poem and finally, after something like forty years, found it possible to clear his meaning. If his own phrase, 'torture of equilibrium', can be said to apply to his own work (an application which I would strongly qualify but not wholly discount) then its validity is surely tried here, in the 1969 text. The hurt and the poise are exacerbated and enhanced where the 'dream' to be revoked is of 'courage' and tenderness rather than of 'thrushes' and 'fabulous...dew'. The 'real logic' of the poem belongs, after all, not to the 1945 version but to the text of 1969.

Ransom once remarked that poets have to 'consider technique as a charge upon their conscience' and this is burden enough; it is a devil of a conscience. To write at Ransom's pitch of attention is to be in ontological and semantic 'straits'. Acute sensitivity to the richness of 'denotative content' is also vulnerability to acoustical din, a situation in which the very finesse of the poet's perceptions becomes a source of bafflement and panic and, at worst, of self-destruction. In his chapter on I. A. Richards in *The New Criticism* Ransom wrote that 'the confusion of our language is a testimony to the confusion of the world. The density or connotativeness of poetic language reflects the world's density'. This statement could fairly be said to come from the heart of Ransom's metaphysics and to go to the heart of his poetics. It can scarcely be denied, however, that if 'world's density' is a metaphor, 'confusion of...language' is a fact. Though syntax may shape an antithesis, imbalance will not melt into equilibrium. In attending to this, however, we give attention to the 'crucial' Ransom: to the method and the 'madness'. My justification for this last piece of impertinence is a recollection of his own observation that

'Platonic . . . idealists . . . who worship universals, laws . . . reason . . . are simply
monsters'. His own idiom is not devoid of Platonism, as his recourse to such
terms as 'good poet', 'good poem', and 'beautiful poem' may sufficiently
indicate. To insist on a 'grammar' of total prohibition when the 'real logic' of
the situation points to relative acceptances is itself a 'monstrous' idealism or, as
Allen Tate said, a 'mania'. This is not simply a word which is being turned
upon Ransom. Whether or not Tate recalled the fact, the word already
belonged to Ransom's weaponry of wisdom and satire. He once described
'an absorbing speciality' as 'a small mania' and quoted, in a different context,
T. S. Eliot's definition of a sub-species of Jonsonian 'humour': 'a simplified
and somewhat distorted individual with a typical mania'. If we ask
whether Ransom's infelicities signify a 'humour' or a 'negative capability' it
is a question which we are bound to try to resolve in due course. It may be
observed, in the interim, that the irony of Tate's trapping Ransom inside his
own armour is not particularly unhappy. It is a timely reminder of the
closeness, in agreement and dispute, between friends and colleagues who
formed the 'Fugitive' group, later the nucleus of the 'Agrarian' movement.
Donald Davidson's terse evocation of 'great mutual attraction, with perhaps
some repulsion here and there' will serve admirably. In the 'Acknowledge-
ments' to *The World's Body* (1938) Ransom writes of his 'obligations' to Tate
and of observations surfacing 'in a manner to illustrate the theory of anonymous or communal authorship'. And it is from a poem published in 1969 by
another former student and life-long friend of Ransom, Robert Penn Warren,
that I take the injunction: 'In this century, and moment, of mania | Tell me a
story'. If, going against the grain of Ransom's principles, we were to generalize upon his work and make abstraction from his dense particularity, we
might say that his poems are indeed 'stories' and that some of his best deal
with 'moments of mania', extraordinary delusions about the nature of love or
wisdom or the capacity for endurance. If constrained to synthesize the
diversity of his aesthetic and polemical pieces, we could argue that, from
the first volume *God Without Thunder* (1930) to the last collection of occasional pieces, *Beating the Bushes* (1970), he testifies against a 'century of mania',
the epidemic excitement of the 'naturalistic rabble' and the 'aggressions', the
'cold fury' of science. But however strongly and however rightly we maintain
that Ransom's poems are not 'confessions' but 'stories' and that his essays are
forensic speeches of prosecution and defence in which admission is, by
convention, oblique, we must still concede that the double consequence of
a poet's involvement with language is complicity and revelation. Exegesis,

which is a kind of science, is in a continual 'cold fury' of appetite for proof of
absolute 'mastery', but the poet's 'agony' is more likely to be an empirical
involvement with that process whereby 'confusion' becomes 'density'. But is
it, perhaps, only 'empirical' in theory? If Ransom's 'equation' is in fact unreal,
'transformation' is a leap of metaphor not a process of reasoning. Ransom,
I think, concedes as much. 'Poetic metaphor' is a 'loose analogical technique', he says; and, once we have conceded analogy, we can 'approve' the
conclusion that the 'ritual of the public occasions' is a style of poetry and
encourage the idea of 'ceremony' as an interchangeable term. Yet here again
logic is baffled. Public occasions may be poetry but the poem, or, more
precisely, the modern poem, is not a public occasion. 'It is not about "res
publica," the public thing.' We seem to detect here a tincture of irony, the
mild private travesty of a gross public indifference. Allen Tate puts it more
candidly when he numbers poetry among those 'discredited forms' which
have been 'defeated by the popular vote'. Ransom's observation is, in
contrast, a 'kind of obliquity' which, in his view, art so often is. One
might say that art is 'oblique' because other things are 'unequal': 'We are
creatures of a knowledge which is hopelessly unequal in its features' he wrote
in 1930, a statement which the young Allen Tate had anticipated by five
years in one of his pioneering informal appraisals of Eliot. Modern poetry,
Tate said, is not 'intrinsically difficult' but poet and audience are trying
to effect an exchange in a 'currency of two different languages'. Ransom
greatly admired 'strong-minded' Tate. He admired creative and critical
tough-mindedness generally, though preferably disciplined by the traditional
courtesies, and was himself inclined to stoicism. If he was 'shaken' it was
assuredly 'not as a leaf'.

Since 'irony', together with 'logic' and 'equilibrium', is a term consistently favoured by Ransom's critics we should heed his own caveats. Irony is
acceptable in the particular circumstance; it is 'objectionable only when it is
made poetic staple'. If we found that works of art 'were agreed in never
exhibiting moral aspirations ... or human efforts triumphant ... it would
occur to us that artists were professionally mean and misanthropic, and
fixed their evidences'. In his own work Ransom displays a decent modicum
of 'human efforts triumphant', not only as matter for narrative (in the
poems) or demonstration (in the critical prose) but also as a staple quality
of the rhetorical tone. Poetry's relation to 'res publica' can never be other
than tangential; but this can be seen as but one aspect of a more profound
and far-reaching 'contingency' which it is man's glory, as well as his fate, to

encounter. There can be no question but that the term 'contingent' and its cognates have formed a constant ingredient in his verbal stock for more than forty years, making his style of metaphysics 'meaty and flavorsome'. In *God Without Thunder*, 'nature still waits, unconquerable, unintelligible and contingent'; in his second prose book, *The World's Body* (1938), he points to 'things as they are in their rich and contingent materiality', 'the world populated by the stubborn and contingent objects'. In an essay of 1945, later collected in *Beating the Bushes* (1970), we read of 'the vast depths of . . . natural contingency'. Closely correlative idioms include 'the stubborn "manifold" of this world', 'marvelling, and revelling in the thick *dinglich* substance', 'the denser and more refractory original world', 'ontological density', 'the dense and brilliant yet obscure world of the modern poets', 'stubborn substance', 'dense natural context'. This terminological congress, this feast of concepts, this 'thick *dinglich*' spread, should be sufficient to dull the edge of anyone's anxiety about the perils of 'abstraction'.

F. P. Jarvis has argued for the influence of F. H. Bradley on Ransom's critical theory, but, leaving influence aside, I am more struck by affinities with the other Bradley, the author of *Shakespearean Tragedy*, whose thinking, like Ransom's, was considerably directed by his reading of Kant and Hegel. I am even inclined to suggest that Ransom unlocked his metaphysics of poetry with the same key that Bradley used to unlock his metaphysics of tragedy: both moving Hegel's term 'ethical substance' backwards and forwards until it 'clicked' with their own thought. Bradley embodied it in his definition of 'the essentially tragic fact'; Ransom quotes it in a late essay. In 'Hegel's Theory of Tragedy', a chapter in his *Oxford Lectures on Poetry* (1909), Bradley writes of the 'self-division and intestinal warfare of the ethical substance, not so much the war of good with evil as the war of good with good'. Ransom's first publication, at other than a parochial level, an article called 'The Question of Justice', appeared in the July 1915 issue of the *Yale Review*. Ransom argues here for the 'right' and 'moral dignity' of both Britain and Germany and claims that the tragedy of the situation is that 'two good ideals should prove so irreconcilable'. It almost seems as if the accident of 'intestinal warfare' in the 'denser and more refractory . . . world' of 1914 enabled Ransom to make a literal translation of Bradley's Hegelian metaphor of 1909. But if we are sufficiently tempted by the approximation to allow ourselves the supposition that Ransom was acquainted with the Oxford Lectures, the logic of the hypothesis requires his knowledge of Bradley's other statement: '[Poetry's] nature is to be not a part, nor yet a copy, of the real world (as we commonly understand that phrase), but to be a world by itself, independent, complete, autonomous.' There is a footnote to *The World's Body* which states that 'the artist resorts to the imitation because it is inviolable, and it is inviolable because it is not real'. Bradley's 'as we commonly understand that phrase' is a timely reminder that our perplexity is caused less by ontological definitions *per se* than by the 'currency of two different languages' which, regrettably, happen to share the same vernacular. But Ransom also says, in the same note, 'As science more and more completely reduces the world to its types and forms, art, replying, must invest it again with body.' How an art that is 'not real' can invest the real world with 'body' is a matter which Ransom never resolves, in its juridical or prose sense, though he is at pains to do so by 'sly analogy' (the epithet is his) 'taking advantage of the hazard of language'. As a type of pseudo-logic, 'sly analogy' is more dubious than the typical metaphysical conceit, which plays the game properly: but we must accept Ransom's attachment to it because, five years later, he is still in its grip. 'A poem', he notes in 1943, 'densifying itself with content . . . is about the dense, actual world.' We in turn are bound to observe that Ransom's verbal substance is at its thickest and most suggestive where its 'logic' is thinnest. 'Is about' is a pathetically frail locution to act as the ontological membrane between two such '*dinglich*' clauses. If we are to have pseudo-logic, Marvell's 'A Definition of Love' is preferable. The argument presented there, that the more 'truly parallel' things are, the less likely it is that they will ever meet, is in effect saying 'don't design "perfect" analogies as a substitute for "identity" because, in the end, they won't "come across"'.

Ransom once pertinently remarked that 'the seventeenth century had the courage of its metaphors' and this stands as one of his most telling appraisals. At his best he is himself a metaphysical poet in this sense, deriving the proper power of his tropes from one of the most traditional of all metaphors, the Hebraic *ruah*, the rushing of a mighty wind, the Holy Spirit, the creative voice which, in one of his last essays, he affirms is also the voice of the poet. In 1930, in his first prose book, Ransom said that 'ruah' appropriately represented 'majesty combined with contingency' and I believe that he demonstrates the courage of his own metaphors when he allows the old conflict of form and substance to be just that. 'Trope' is a term possibly over-resorted to in recent years. I use it because it means 'turn', and it is a particular kind of turn that I have in mind. Ransom's own definition of 'trope' is apposite. 'Figures of speech twist accidence away from the straight course' is a precise description of the little swirl, or gyre, of stubborn reiterative outcry, disturbing but not halting the ceremonial procedure of his traditional verse-forms: 'Why should two lovers be frozen apart in fear? | And yet they were, they were'; 'And heard the clock that clanged: Remember, Remember'; 'No, No, she answered in the extreme of fear'; 'A cry of Absence, Absence, in the heart'; 'Honor, Honor, they came crying. | Importunate her doves'; 'Whose ministers post and cry, "Thus saith, Thus saith"'; 'until I knew | That I was loved again, again'; 'Conrad, Conrad, aren't you old | To sit so late in a mouldy garden? | ...Anchovy toast, Conrad!' These little irruptions of outcry may be encouraging or censorious, summoning to tea or laying down the law in some other way; or they may be passionate protests at enforced obedience or desperate affirmations of disobedience; but they are so human in their ring (even if given to 'doves' or a 'clock') that the sound of the kites, in Ransom's most celebrated poem, repeatedly whetting their beaks 'clack clack' over the poor remnants of Captain Carpenter, is like a disgusting parody of the human activity. In itself, of course, there is nothing unique in such repetitive exclamations. In lyric poetry instances from Sidney, Keats, and Hopkins spring to mind; but the particular interest of Ransom's reiterations is threefold. First, they are, as he says, 'importunate'; they irrupt into preordained ceremonies (i.e. the 'forms') or into reverie or dull habitude (i.e. the narrative occasions) which would be easier to conduct, or to bear, if they did not. Or they speak remorselessly, in moments of crisis, of the normative, the 'code', that has been outraged or forfeited. Secondly, they occur often enough and in such a manner for us to call the pattern 'characteristic'. Thirdly, this 'characteristic' trope in turn characterizes Ransom's feeling for 'the stubborn "manifold" of this world'. In an essay of 1942 he projects a notion of laughter which, 'if it could be articulate, would be found reiterating, Substance, Substance' at the 'ingenuous idealist' and his 'program'. So laughter shouts 'substance substance' at the abstract with exactly the same cadence as the heart cries 'Absence, Absence' or the importunate doves their 'Honor, Honor'. And cadence itself, at this pitch of intensity, becomes a form of substance, a monad. Giordano Bruno, from whom Leibniz may have derived the term, conceived of the 'monad' as being at once a 'material atom' and an 'irreducible metaphysical element of being'; and it is such a twofold sense which pertains here. It has a core of pragmatic truth applicable to the work of good poets in general and to Ransom's work in particular. The word 'cry' and its derivatives form what is perhaps the most frequently recurring group

of words in his poetry; and the 'cry' is peculiarly a 'monad' in which the
physiological 'speaks out' for the ontological. It is the minimal utterance
which, paradoxically, is expressive of a multiplicity of psychic nuance:
abandonment, affirmation, solitude, communion; as the medieval mystics
perceived in their teaching on the efficacy of monosyllabic prayer. The
particular characteristic of the reiterated cry is arguably its power to transform pure spontaneous reflex into an act of will. It is not without significance that the passage from *Hamlet* which Ransom chooses for analysis is
Claudius' speech in which he breaks into his own instructions for the 'close
following' of Ophelia with the reiterated 'O Gertrude, Gertrude!' It may
fairly be inferred that Ransom's interest is caught by the sudden compounding of guilt, anxiety, grief, and love in the most elemental utterance as it
seeks to make desperate affirmation out of mere recoil. Ransom wrote with
discriminating admiration, in *God Without Thunder*, of Psalm 88, praising its
'realism', its 'sense of hard—very hard—fact' that is yet 'not quite submissive to the fact'. If we were to seek a method whereby an ontological
principle is to be transformed into an idiomatic monad, this requirement
might be met by the idiosyncratic 'cry' of a Ransom poem, since a cry is
simultaneously a 'fact' and the resistance to a fact, a 'reaction' and a
reaching-out. Despite his avowed allegiance to 'classical' criteria, Ransom
is not surprisingly re-enacting a typical Romantic 'situation': one that had
been confronted by Keats in his Letters where, in February 1818, he
appeared satisfied to cite 'a few Axioms' concerning poetry and, three
months later, felt bound to declare that 'axioms in philosophy are not
axioms until they are proved upon our pulses'.

When we read C. H. Sisson's finely judged appreciation of Thomas
Hardy's so-called 'awkwardnesses'—'The rhythm of the verse, with its
hesitations, sudden speeds, and pauses which are almost silences, is the
very rhythm of thought'—we understand how the implications of the
Keatsian 'pulse' can be comprehended as 'rhythm'. When we read Ransom,
between whose work and Hardy's several critics have suggested close
affinities, the technical issues are a little different. Technically he is one of
the least 'awkward' of poets and yet his formal grace is in a constant state of
alertness against 'awkwardnesses' which, even so, contrive to irrupt into the
manners and measures of the verse. I shall call this the 'trope of infelicity'; it
is not infelicitous. It is, moreover, Ransom's characteristic development of
the Keatsian 'negative capability'; characteristic in that its frequent burden is
the articulation of some 'mania' in men and women, some intense solipsistic

passion, in themselves the very opposite of the Keatsian virtù. Such an appraisal of the poems, however, leaves unchallenged Tate's description of the old Ransom's persistent interference with his own poems as 'mania'. What I have tried to show is that the 'mania' is the dark side of that coexistence of 'majesty' and 'contingency' which, in its other aspect, produces the masterly fables of the poems. It is a radical miscalculation, which Ransom obliquely concedes in his note to his most ruinously reconstructed poem, 'Prelude to an Evening', when he wryly remarks that 'the social issue is saved, but I, like some of my friends, am not sure whether an expiation is always in the interest of a fiction'. And I would say that Robert Buffington is correct in his suggestion that the error stems from Ransom's confusion of theology and morality. 'Theology' in this instance equates with 'fiction' of course, and the 'devil' that has got into John Ransom at this late stage is a decent little devil whose highly moral whisper is that one can genuinely make amends for some actual or supposed betrayal in 'real life' by tampering years later with the evidence of the fiction. Whatever Ransom may have thought or said, the revised 'Prelude to an Evening' is a 'weakened and trivial form'.

That last phrase is from Raymond Williams's acute analysis of the failures of later Eliot. And when Williams goes on to suggest that 'it is part of the real complexity of this extraordinary man [Eliot] that he could repeatedly and genuinely mistake...compromise for communication', I am inclined to note how effectively these words describe Ransom's own mistakes. The causes are not precisely the same, perhaps. Eliot could genuinely mistake 'the fashionable requirements' of Shaftesbury Avenue or the Edinburgh Festival for the needs of 'a wider audience'. Ransom did not have to endure that degree of worldly temptation, but I do not think that there was any great difference in kind, despite the gross inequality of their respective worldly rewards. In each case the error is traceable to a root cause in the 'currency of two different languages' circulating within the same vernacular. It is at the same time a simple confusion and a deep intractable problem. One could say that Ransom diagnosed it perfectly well when he wrote that 'behind poetry is the whole loosely articulated body of the language'. The 'literal sense' of 'language' is 'the whole body of words and of methods of combination of words used by a nation, people, or race'. It is the 'loose articulation' of its figurative senses which, I believe, increasingly betrays Ransom. It may be agreed that in such locutions as, say, 'the language of polite letters' more is implied than 'the methods of combination of words'. Such a 'language' is in fact a 'code' of acceptances, a consensus of taste or prejudice. I would suggest that, in his later writings, Ransom is inclined to confuse 'consensus' with 'language' and the consensus is increasingly that of the 'dull readers—with whom I concede my own affiliations'. If this is not serious it is cynical, and, at the risk of sounding like Matthew Arnold's little niece, I cannot see that it is 'wholly serious'. More and more frequently, from *The New Criticism* (1941) onwards, Ransom is provoked into the writing of scenarios in which 'those Yale professors' absurdly confront 'the common barbarian reader'. The provocation is understandable enough. He testified, in *The World's Body*, to 'that terrible problem . . . of poetic strategy' and again, in *The New Criticism*, to his belief that 'poetic strategy' is 'the last and rarest gift given to poets'; and it is arguably a chastening experience for any innovatory writer to find his arduous strategy become the fluent tactics of his disciples. Ransom had attempted in 1938 to demonstrate a crucial 'paradox': how 'the possibility of poetry depended on an event that carried also the possibility of its destruction'. It is not unreasonable that in 1952, reviewing a new book by Cleanth Brooks, he should remark that paradoxes 'are easy to find once you are searching for them'. He is endeavouring, we may say, to disembarrass the 'real logic' of poetic strategy from the 'grammar' of methodology. We may say also that this is 'the essentially tragic fact': the 'self-divisions and intestinal warfare' within a body of critical writing 'more intense than a language has ever known'.

I have suggested that the double-consequence of a poet's involvement with language is complicity and revelation. I have also suggested that Ransom's essays are, like his poems, 'desperate ontological . . . manoeuvres'. There is a thrill of 'mastery' in the tropes; but it is possible for a poet to serve the integrity of thought and language in the exemplary nature of his constraint. The particular interest of Ransom is in the achievement (the revelation) and in the price he paid for it (the complicity). 'The bad artists', he writes, 'are cruelly judged . . . and the good artists may be humorously regarded, as persons strangely possessed.' This is Ransom being slightly 'mischievous'. His colleagues seem to have liked this streak in him; but I would suggest that his somewhat coy indulgence of the 'humble reader' does the integrity of his criticism a mischief. In *A Survey of Modernist Poetry* (1927), Laura Riding and Robert Graves had championed Ransom's 'Captain Carpenter' against the demands and prejudices of the 'plain reader' who 'does not want a critical attitude' but rather 'poetical feelings of simple pleasure or pain'. Nothing has happened in the intervening years to make one wish these words unsaid; and Ransom's sorry wit can be distinctly inferior to his grasp of infelicity. He has been led, like Eliot, genuinely to mistake compromise for communication. It is not only the 'bad artists' who are cruelly judged. The good are too. I do not think that Ransom would have wished it otherwise.

9

Our Word Is Our Bond

> And I might mention that, quite differently again, we could be issuing any of these utterances, as we can issue an utterance of any kind whatsoever, in the course, for example, of acting a play or making a joke or writing a poem—in which case of course it would not be seriously meant and we shall not be able to say that we seriously performed the act concerned.
>
> J. L. Austin

Sir Philip Sidney, as shrewd as he was magnanimous, evidently had it in mind to keep poetry out of the courts: 'Now for the *Poet*, he nothing affirmeth, and therefore never lieth'. Since his time poets, with more vision than apprehension, have been endeavouring to thrust it back into the theatre of litigation. 'The Imagination may be compared to Adam's dream—he awoke and found it truth.' 'The poem is the cry of its occasion, | Part of the res itself and not about it.' Ezra Pound, who wrote magisterially on behalf of poets 'All values ultimately come from our judicial sentences', in the end found himself cruelly and impotently at odds with the US judiciary. Seeking to attribute causes, or even reasons, for this savage contretemps one is presented with several possibilities. It may be that Pound misjudged a critical matter of status or perhaps he misconstrued a fine point of semantics. A further complicating factor is that legal distinctions may themselves be classifiable as 'fictions' or 'peculiar paradoxes'. Pound's sense of 'justice' and 'value', we may feel, accords with an antique hierarchy of ideal ontological principles and agencies formerly defined in such terms as *intellectus agens* or *recta ratio factibilium*, whereas his indictment for alleged treason took place in the domain of *mens rea* and *actus reus*, the world of common law. He is vulnerable to accusations that he naively or wilfully regarded his wartime broadcasts as being in some way traditionally privileged and protected by his status as poet, 'boasting of the sanctity of what [he] carried'; an attitude at best archaic and at worst arrogantly idiosyncratic; oblivious of, or indifferent to, the 'real world' which lies 'out there', where things (and people) regularly 'get done'. This 'real world' of current documentary appeal reminds one in its simplicity of the 'substratum' of the early empiricists. Other forms of empiricism, however, are rather more formidable. 'If you are a judge and say "I hold that . . ." then to say you hold is to hold; with less official persons it is not so clearly so; it may be merely descriptive of a state of mind.' Tested against this distinction Pound's 'judicial sentences' begin to appear less magisterial. J. L. Austin remarks that 'a performative utterance will . . . be *in a peculiar way* hollow or void if said by an actor on the stage, or if introduced in a poem, or spoken in soliloquy'. In his sense of the term, 'ordinary language' is 'rich and subtle' in certain kinds of 'pressingly practical matter' but these matters exclude such 'parasitic uses of language' as 'Goe, and catche a falling starre' which are 'not serious', not the 'full normal use' of the medium.

Isaiah Berlin notes that Austin was 'determined to try to reduce whatever could be so reduced to plain prose'. Austin himself stated that 'accuracy and morality alike are on the side of the plain saying that *our word is our bond*', nonetheless making play with the motto of the Stock Exchange as he did so. Observation will incline us to feel that the timbre of 'plain prose' is unlike that of 'plain saying'. The former is simply reductive ('reduce . . . reduced'), the latter amply assertive ('alike . . . on the side of'). If we stir the soil about the roots of either of these locutions we unearth seventeenth-century shards. The plain intention of both statements to be directly functional does not obliterate such discoveries. The crucial questions are how much 'play' remains in language after the logical excisions have been performed and whether this play is definable as 'controlled interplay' or as that 'play' which means that something designed for precise mechanical utility is showing signs of malfunction. Austin's belief that the expression 'I do' occurs in the Anglican marriage service is manifestly of some significance in a work entitled *How to Do Things with Words* even though the mistake may be, as J. O. Urmson avers, 'philosophically unimportant'. It at least provides a point of contact between two observations which would other-wise be hard to reconcile. The first is that in Austin's teaching 'there appeared to be nothing between him and the subject of his criticism or exposition'; the second attributes to him an awareness of 'the complex and recalcitrant nature of things'. The first is a bright memorable impression of a transparent success; yet, as the second implies, the very idea of a 'transparent' verbal medium is itself an inherited and inherent opacity. Where there is 'semantic content' it is most likely that there will be semantic 'refraction', 'infection' of various kinds; for example 'even "ordinary" language will often have become infected with the jargon of extinct theories' or 'considerations . . . may infect statements'. Once you have released such a word as 'infect' how is it to be contained? Systems that appear 'perfectly neat and easy', as T. H. Green said of Hume, have a way of raising 'awkward questions'. Empiricism admitted complexity. Locke, for instance, 'distinguished clearly between simple ideas and complex ideas'; but to allude to the 'complex and recalcitrant nature of things' is to hit upon a timbre quite different from the tone in which one refers to the aggregates and compounds of Empiricism which, though it did not entirely reserve such a phrase as 'manifold inextricable labyrinths' to the errors and disputes of the old Schoolmen, nonetheless regarded the 'inflexible natures . . . of things' as amenable to rational understanding and analysis. Locke's opinion was that 'things themselves', if approached without 'preconceived notions', 'will shew us in what way they are to be understood'. That there is a marked difference in weight between 'natures' and 'nature' in these citations is itself a ponderable suggestion. The 'natures of things' are their compounded properties, the 'nature of things' seems to take on a metaphysical denseness.

Empiricism, we may remind ourselves, regards words as being 'of excellent use' when rightly understood and as powers only in a dark and negative sense when they 'impose on the understanding'. Berkeley's eschewing of 'all controversies purely verbal' is, in part, a caveat against mistaking empty words for legitimate concepts, but it is also, in part, a verbal gambit, a bid to score in a controversy. The empiricists are in at least one respect heirs of the Cambridge Platonists. 'If it were not for Sin, *we* should converse together as *Angels* do' said Whichcote. The empiricists, too, would in theory be happier with forms of sensuous or conceptual communion, 'naked, undisguised ideas' 'stripped of words'. In practice, of course, their own words have pith and spice. Santayana's reference to Locke's 'controversial relish' is apposite, and Berkeley has something of this 'relish' too. Locke, in his *Conduct of the Understanding* (published posthumously, 1706), refers to a 'jejune and dry way of writing . . . a sour and blunt stiffness tolerable in mathematicians only'. In Berkeley's *Commonplace Book*, kept between 1705 and 1708, we read: 'the short jejune way in mathematiques will not do in metaphysiques & ethiques'. Here Berkeley's use of 'jejune', despite a first impression of affinity and concord, makes, I would conjecture, a 'retort' upon Locke, and essays raillery. The bite of the raillery is more strongly appreciated if we know that Locke's 'sour and blunt stiffness' is itself a wry tribute to that manner of writing, not a denigration of it. He distinctly prefers 'plain unsophisticated arguments' to 'plausible discourses'. Yet this paragraph of oblique regard is itself in no sense plain and unsophisticated. It manifests a plausible urbane wit that is pleased to appear dry and dour. In Locke's own style, and in Berkeley's rallying to his style, there is a briskly nuanced play which, slight as it is, is nonetheless in excess of the empiricist desideratum that words should excite only the 'proper sentiments', that, in the 'ordinary affairs of life', they should be received as no more and no less than acceptable tokens of exchange, 'signs or counters', 'fiduciary symbols'.

Seventeenth-century philosophical antagonists, such as Hobbes and the Cambridge Platonists, were united in arguing that plain speech had a status superior to that of metaphor or carefully elaborated discourse, though it is necessary to add that Whichcote's 'candor' does not plainly equal Hobbes's 'Perspicuous Words' and that, at the heart of the matter where Hobbes and the Platonists pursue their most immediate concerns, plain speech has scarcely more status than has figurative speech. If it is preferred it is because it is supposed to get in the way less. The focus of Hobbes's attention is not words but power. The Platonists' concern is less with 'fiduciary symbols' than with faith, conceived of as human reason directly intuiting the Divine Reason. There is not, in either case, a neglect of the serviceable parts of language. Whichcote is always concerned to 'speak accurately' and Hobbes's audacity is as much a matter of style as of thought; but these immediate concerns are subject to overriding considerations and objectives; in the one case a keenness of withdrawal from the 'troublesome multiplicity' of the things of this world and in the other a demonstration of the world's ineluctable necessity. This, then, is the direction in which impetus, or entropy, impels us. Wordsworth's 'real language of men' is, like his 'native and naked dignity of man', still a fiction, still one of those 'airy useless notions' that Locke contrasts with 'real and substantial knowledge'. To employ another Lockean idiom, real and substantial knowledge 'bottoms' on real estate and common law, the basis of what T. H. Green sums up as 'the wisdom of the world'. Or, to choose a form of words less tinctured or 'infected' by one's own preconceived notions, we could perhaps say that neither Hobbes nor Cudworth would dispute unduly Austin's statement that we use 'a sharpened awareness of words to sharpen our perception of, though not as the final arbiter of, the phenomena'.

If 'real' is opposed to 'ideal', Austin, who admired the methodology of the natural sciences, the 'patient accumulation of data about actual usage', is a realist, drawing numerous examples from law reports, relating others to 'the conduct of meetings and business'. His work on 'descriptive fallacies' has been of particular utility to jurists and, as Passmore has indicated, to moral and legal philosophers ('see particularly the distinction between "description" and "ascription" in H. L. Hart'). He requires that we study '*actual* languages, *not* ideal ones' and one can all too readily envisage the contempt with which he would dismiss Santayana's assertion that 'mind is incorrigibly poetical' in its transmutations of material facts and practical exigencies into 'many-coloured ideas'. If such etiolations were the truth of poetry one would be bound to favour Austin's prosaic method, 'taking the sentences *one at a time,* thoroughly settling the sense (or hash) of each before proceeding to the next one'. Performative utterances that are '*in a peculiar way* hollow or void', that cannot be said to enact, contrive to avoid taking the rap for their own claims. In this respect the *MHRA Style Book* is basically Austinian:

> Avoid the practice of using quotation marks as an oblique excuse for a loose, slang, or imprecise (and possibly inaccurate) word or phrase. Quotation marks should normally be reserved to indicate direct quotation from other writers.

One must avoid casuistry; and quotation marks, except as an indication of direct quotation, are a casuistically ideal language masquerading as an actual one. On consideration, however, this proscriptive view appears too simplistically exclusive. In Pound's use of quotation marks in *Homage to Sextus Propertius* and *Hugh Selwyn Mauberley* ('"Wherefrom father Ennius, sitting before I came, hath drunk"'; 'The "age demanded" chiefly a mould in plaster') the effect is not that of avoiding the rap but rather of recording the rapping noise made by those things which the world throws at us in the form of prejudice and opinion, 'egocentric naïveties' and 'obtuse assurance'. The *MHRA Style Book* inculcates one excellent kind of fidelity, to the patient accumulation of data about actual usage, but it also suggests, by tacit implication and even while urging upon us a strict acceptance of personal responsibility, that not only the data contained in 'direct quotation from other writers' but also the medium of language itself are more transparent, more innocent, than we have any right to expect. It does not forewarn us that, when we quote, we are necessarily engrafting, together with scrupulously accurate formulations, much loose, slang, or imprecise matter and many 'compacted doctrines'. Nor does it indicate how these obliquities are to be registered, except by some ideal scientific neutrality of tone. Yet when Austin states that 'philosophers often seem to think that they can just "assign" any meaning whatever to any word', his own use of quotation marks indicates the limitations of the basically utilitarian approach to 'the innumerable and unforeseeable demands of the world upon language' and concedes that a touch of miming may be a proper part of the process of assessment. When G. H. Lewes admired Jane Austen for, among other things, her lack of sentiment, Charlotte Brontë retorted 'you scornfully enclose the word ["sentiment"] in inverted commas'. Here the demands of the world upon language are being mutually though incompatibly registered. And when we read how the First World War soldier, in his disillusionment, 'turned and picked up some of the fine phrases which had stirred his heart' so that ' "Remember Belgium!" was heard with ironic and bitter intonations in the muddy wastes of the Salient' we encounter the same phenomenon in a more extreme manifestation. As Coleridge said, 'our chains rattle, even while we are complaining of them'. 'Inverted commas' are a way of bringing pressure to bear and are also a form of 'ironic and bitter' intonation acknowledging that pressure is being exerted. They have a satiric function, can be used as tweezers lifting a commonplace term out of its format of habitual connection. That which the *MHRA Style Book* sees as 'oblique excuse' may in fact be direct or oblique rebuke. 'Our word is our bond' is an exemplary premise, but if we take it in the positivist sense alone we take only part of its mass and weight. 'Our chains rattle...' is the inescapable corollary for any writer who takes up Austin's stringent sentiment. At the same time, the necessary consequence of admiring Austin's logic would seem to be that there is nothing to take up. 'If said by an actor on the stage, or if introduced in a poem, or spoken in soliloquy' our ideal terms can have no actual consequences. Does it not necessarily follow, therefore, that the audacity of Pound's 'all values ultimately come from our judicial sentences' is achieved at the expense of a missed connection, precisely the one which Austin picks up in his caveat about 'the final arbiter of... the phenomena'? In claiming 'ultimate' sanction Pound is merely 'surveying the invisible depths of ethical space', a practice which, in Austin's view, permits a variety of moral 'welshing'. Poetry has no 'phenomena', in Austin's sense, only 'noumena' or perhaps 'nous', that 'act of mind' which is also the 'sense or meaning' of its own statements.

There would seem to be, as we have said, much cherishing prescience as well as shrewdness in Sidney's contention that the poet 'nothing affirmeth, and therefore never lieth'. It appears at least to offer a compromise whereby the fiction can be given its proper status precisely because it does not claim that it could be 'seriously performed': 'it is that faining notable images of vertues, vices, or what els...which must be the right describing note to know a Poet by'. The thought occurs to us that the poet is here being generously propositioned. If he will accept that his art is a miniature emblem or analogy of res publica rather than a bit of real matter lodged in the body politic there is much scope for the exercise of serious and refined example. Sidney certainly invites a high degree of imaginative responsibility, of the kind and order that is manifested in Sonnet LXVIII of Spenser's *Amoretti*:

> This ioyous day, deare Lord, with ioy begin,
>   and grant that we for whom thou diddest dye
>   being with thy deare blood clene washt from sin,
>   may liue for euer in felicity.
> And that thy loue we weighing worthily,
>   may likewise loue thee for the same againe:
>   and for thy sake that all lyke deare didst buy,
>   with loue may one another entertayne.
> So let vs loue, deare loue, lyke as we ought,
>   loue is the lesson which the Lord vs taught.

Within limits, this exercise of semantic judgement is exemplary. Christ's blood is 'deare' because it is precious; it is precious because it was the price of man's ransom and it cost Christ dear in terms of dire suffering. The tenderness between betrothed lovers ('deare loue'), the fealty of servant to master ('deare Lord'), are only possible because of the hard, grievous sacrifice of Christ. What happens here is more solemn than a play of wit; it is a form of troth-plight between denotation and connotation. Spenser's text is also wedded to the text of 1 Corinthians: 'ye are dearly bought'. The 'felicissime audax', the 'curiosa felicitas', of pagan rhetoric are reborn and baptized in Spenser's 'felicity'. But it is a felicitousness which knows its place and which achieves its directness by not being presumptuous, by respecting priority and status. The intelligence may be consummate but the consummation is elsewhere, as the stance of the final couplet suggests. 'So let vs loue, deare loue, lyke as we ought' is already leaving the poem behind; the 'lesson' to which the poet directs us is, as the Austinians would say, 'extra-linguistic'. It must also be said that, when we read *Amoretti* in its entirety, the felicity of LXVIII appears uncharacteristic of the sequence, which terminates in quarrel and separation. The Pauline cadences of this sonnet are unheralded by the Petrarchan cadences of LXVII and leave no posterity in the twenty-one sonnets which succeed, for these fluctuate between clichés of loss, absence, mortality, on the one hand, and, on the other, appeals to the superior virtues of 'contemplation', of 'beholding the Idaea playne'. It is not possible to determine precisely in what proportion this sense of relapse is due to artistic impatience, the 'haste and botching' at the time of publication or to Spenser's desire to embody a Sidneian awareness of the gulf between 'erected wit' that 'maketh us know what perfectio[n] is' and 'infected wil' that 'keepeth us fro[m] reaching unto it'.

Theodore Spencer observed that Sidney 'extolled poetry as greater than either of its rivals, philosophy and history, for it combined the wisdom of the one with the concrete examples of the other'; but this is an observation that calls for some modification. Sidney writes on occasion as though recognizing that the poet is in reality forced to compound his '*Idea*' of wisdom with the 'particular truth of things', that, like the historian, he is 'captived to the trueth of a foolish world'. The likeness of these phrases exacerbates the degree of their unlikeness. Sidney, even while composing a 'Defence', is resisting two possible defensive postures: one, that the coercive power of the 'particular truth of things' makes all 'truth' merely contingent and relative; the other, that the status of the 'idea' provides the poet with an Archimedean ec-stasis, a station above and beyond the world's gravity and folly, a place of serenely measured hypotheses. Fulke Greville offers a simpler gloss on his friend's beautifully guarded but honest involvements and returns: 'For my own part, I found my creeping Genius more fixed upon the Images of Life, than the Images of Wit.' 'Creeping Genius' has a blunt 'foolishness' which Sidney eschews in his treatise though not in such poems as Sonnet 71 of *Astrophil and Stella* where 'erected wit', pursuing the 'idea' of a Platonic Stella, is, by the truth of a foolish world, moved by carnal impulses: ' "But ah," Desire still cries: "give me some food" '. 'Erected wit' has, after all, inspired merely what a contemporary treatise called 'an erection of those engendring parts'. This ironic realization comes as a perfectly calculated surprise and one has to distinguish between such effects, where the poet is winningly in command of his own perplexity and weakness, and passages within which, or between which, there lies an area of real perplexity, 'dark and disputed matter', problems which the writer 'unconsciously' raises.

We return here upon an ineluctable problem: that those for whom
writing is like 'bearing a part in the conversation' must regard with incomprehension those for whom it is 'blindness' and 'perplexity' and that those
for whom 'composition' is a struggle with dark and disputed matter will
inevitably dismiss as mere worldliness the ability to push on pragmatically
with the matter in hand. The theologian D. M. MacKinnon is scrupulous in
his observation that 'rich possibilities' may depend upon 'quick practical
perception' and justly chastening when he notes that 'the most intimate self-
interrogation' can quickly assume 'the highly questionable status of the
subjective and capricious'. At the same time, T. H. Green's 'there is that
in us which is the negation of each of our acts, yet relative to each of them,
and making them what they are' takes account of the highly questionable
nature of 'objective status', if this is seen as some Archimedean platform for
'naked undisguised ideas' 'stripped of words'. To restrict MacKinnon's
'quick practical perception' to this kind of functional immediacy would
be to misconstrue him as gravely as one would misrepresent Austin by
implying that 'transparent' means anything like 'rudimentary' or is even
directly equatable with Sprat's 'primitive purity and shortness'.

In referring to ineluctable problems, therefore, we would do well to
consider Austin's warning that 'we can know the facts and yet look at them
mistakenly or perversely' and, in that light, to take up the question whether,
in arguments of this kind, certain transcendental explanations are preferred
because they appeal merely to temperamental proclivities which incline one
to favour either a comic or a melodramatic view of such matters. The
comedians, according to this theory, would favour notions of 'felicity',
the 'providence of wit'; the melodramatists, searching the same facts,
would apply a more sombre tincture: 'infected wil', 'concupiscence of
witt', 'anarchy of witt'. We could emblematize the possibilities in the
following way. Cudworth, in his *Sermon Preached Before the House of Commons*, 1647, warns against 'shaping . . . out' God 'according to the Model of
our selves, when we make him nothing but a *blind, dark, impetuous Self will*,
running through the world; such as we our selves are furiously acted with'.
We feel at once how the density, the weight, of this statement manifests
itself in the very concept to which, Cudworth says, we should not give
weight. To maintain that the italicized words are the most ponderable is to
suggest no more than that Cudworth, while declaring that God is not the
image of our solipsism, mimics our solipsistic furor. To take '*blind, dark,
impetuous Self will*', out of context, as motto or epigraph (and the printer's

italics offer us that temptation) is melodramatic and perversely stimulating. This sermon anticipates by a few years Vaughan's 'But living where the Sun | Doth all things wake, and where all mix and tyre | Themselves and others, I consent and run | To ev'ry myre'. It is true that Vaughan is speaking of sin, not language; but one might insist, subjectively and capriciously, that precisely because one can refer so readily and properly to 'the run of the verse' or the run of a sentence, the writer's vocation is the one which 'consents' most readily, which 'runs' most directly, to its own confusion. It is, in a peculiar way, the most oxymoronic art: its very making is its undoing. In a poet's involvement with language, above all, there is, one would darkly and impetuously claim, an element of helplessness, of being at the mercy of accidents, the prey of one's own presumptuous energy. The salutary pithiness of Thomas Hobbes springs from his unlamenting, sardonic observation of this affliction, in the brusque 'for if he would not have his words so be understood, he should not have let them runne'. And the comedians, from Nashe to Beckett, could also insist that the undoing of language is, as often as not, the making of it. J. L. Austin is himself a writer in the comic tradition. His radical 'doctrine of the *Infelicities*' could not be more happily expressed.

'Comic tradition' is, however, an infected term. The system within which Austin exercises his discriminations is not quite a comedy of manners and not quite a line of wit. When a man named Austin entitles his lectures 'Sense and Sensibilia' he is simultaneously being precise and asserting something; he is accepting the gift, the aptness of the thing given, and he is displaying his own 'gift', his aptitude for making the most of the *donnée,* in a pleasing way, to himself and to us, though the pleasure is of a minor kind. We are tickled and suspect that our feeling coincides exactly with the author's. G. J. Warnock remarks, with unnecessary diffidence, that 'not everyone, I imagine, found Austin's jokes—including the really silly ones— as funny as I did'. In *How to Do Things with Words* the conclusions are embodied in a final series of comparative word-lists. Nonetheless, the advocate of patient accumulation also 'liked authority' and enjoyed a keen 'sense of his own position'. He minutely and accurately discriminates the senses of English words and phrases, and instructs us how we may 'learn from the distinctions encapsulated in their ordinary uses'. To drive with attention may not be the same as to drive 'with care'; 'clumsily he trod on the snail' is to be distinguished from 'he trod on the snail clumsily'; 'without effect' does not (in a particular circumstance) mean 'without consequences, results, effects'. He is at the same time a polemicist of distinctive irony. A reference to the jurists' 'timorous fiction, that a statement of "the law" is a statement of fact' contains a crucial distinction but is distinctly different from the 'patient accumulation of data'. There is a pleasurable impatience in 'timorous'. 'Clumsily he trod on the snail' is at once a discrimination of meaning and a nuance about the heavy-footedness 'out there'. One might feel, however, that it is entirely just for Austin's method to hover between manners and wit since, as we have observed, one of his epistemological cruces is the necessity to meet the innumerable and unforeseeable demands of the world upon language. The world and the word are equipoised and Austin's sense of occasion is as strong as his sense of semantic propriety. The disposition of his Harvard seminars ('In these discussions the physical and dialectical centre of gravity located itself, predictably, in the person of Austin') can be taken as a paradigm of language's connection with the 'world'. But how is the 'world' to be reckoned in this instance? Primarily it is the 'magic circle' of the philosophers, described in Berlin's memoir, with a larger circumference than David Hume's but held together by similar ideals and expectations. It is a 'World', the attention of which one seeks to attract by 'Elegance & Neatness' of address, the indifference of which condemns one to calamitous 'Obscurity'. Yet, at the same time, that which the Austin seminar concentrates upon is nothing less than the 'world', epistemologically and ethically conceived, ranging from the implications of Sidney's 'most excelle[n]t resting place for al worldly learning' to those of Hopkins's ambiguous, ungraspable 'world-wielding' force ('something that makes, builds up and breeds . . . something that unmakes or pulls to pieces'). The world of which Austin takes account in his quips and parables is basically cheerful, hedonistic, preoccupied with business, professional conduct, and games-playing but it is also shot through with anger, infelicity, blank incomprehension:

> The man himself, such is the overriding power of the pattern, will sometimes accept corrections from outsiders about his own emotions, i.e. about the correct description of them. He may be got to agree that he was not really angry so much as, rather, indignant or jealous, and even that he was not in pain, but only fancied he was.

If we take the full force of 'overriding', the 'pattern' will appear to be coercive, proscriptive. However, 'working the dictionary' as Austin prescribes, we note that historical usage infects the word with a variety of 'considerations'. It may be 'unconstitutional' to override but constitutions themselves have the power to do so. There is a worldly ambivalence in Austin too: a brusque rebuttal of '*insouciant* latitude' on the one hand; on the other a tolerance, though not necessarily an acceptance, of routine. The world wags vigorously in his work and he is also a bit of a wag. The man who 'only fancied' he was in pain belongs to the same comic order as the faith-healer of Deal. Austin, we are told, 'could not bear histrionics', 'gaudy pronouncements', 'escape into metaphor or rhetoric or jargon or metaphysical fantasy'. It is itself a philosophical irony that a mind which strove for accuracy of definition while registering most acutely the quotidian duplicities, which sought 'decent and comely order' as fervently as did the authors of the antique tropes, felt free to regard poetry as one of the non-serious '*parasitic*' '*etiolations* of language', as a kind of 'joking'.

One's perplexity in this matter is compounded by the recognition that, notwithstanding the force of his slighting asides, there is a 'poetic' quality in Austin's writing at its best, as, for example, in the finesse with which, in successive paragraphs, he moves from the ironic negative 'spiritual assumption of a spiritual shackle' to the 'plain saying that *our word is our bond*'. In this sequence the prescriptive sense of 'arbitrary constraint' and the affirmative sense of 'covenant' are firmly and reciprocally adjusted. By 'poetic' in this context one means no more than that the richness and subtlety of 'ordinary language' have been amply realized, not simply run into or stumbled over by someone who is 'flurried' or 'anxious to get off' as Austin would say; but it remains a quality to be noted, and one which he himself might have noted more. At one point he justifies the use of 'jargon' to explain varieties of behaviour 'which have not been...hallowed by ordinary language'; at another he writes that 'superstition and error and fantasy of all kinds do become incorporated in ordinary language'. Here again we may note that the way in which 'hallowed' and 'superstition' jar slightly against each other's grain constitutes Austin's way of setting a 'plot'. Though his prevailing thesis is that our function is to 'clear up...usage', 'arrive at...meanings', a counterpointed idea is that 'the word snares us' and that we may 'cheerfully subscribe to, or have the grace to be torn between, simply disparate ideals'. One can see precisely why a parenthetical clause is as far as he can go towards desperation, since any further move in this direction would be deplorably towards 'the old Berkeleian, Kantian ontology of the "sensible manifold"'. So far, we may say, Austin's ethical toughness is nothing less than admirable; and, so far, his feel for the tension between 'cheerfully', 'grace', and 'torn' has the fineness of poetic tact. But only so far. When Austin's cheerfulness veers towards contempt he seems to care less: 'a_2 ["clumsily he trod on the snail"] might be a poetic inversion for b_2 ["he trod on the snail clumsily"]'. 'Poetic' exists to cause offence. It is a parody, the limits of which are not precisely drawn and which are therefore variable according to Austin's particular whim. Iris Murdoch suggests that 'in a way' he ' "saves" . . . the old impersonal atom-world of Hume and Russell' 'by substituting an impersonal language-world'. This describes the intention or the effect fairly enough; but his own language is not really 'impersonal' at all. The one 'infection' that he fails to realize (in the semantic fullness of that word) is the infection of wit by manners; the one 'superstition' he does not wholly eradicate is the mystique of his own superior intelligence.

Things seem, and perhaps are, tougher now than they were, or appeared to be, when R. L. Nettleship wrote in 'Language and its Function in Knowledge': 'The only proof that language really *is* communication, and that there *is* a mutual understanding (συνθήκη) is that we act on the belief that there is, and that this belief is justified by the results'. Taken out of context, however, this sentence makes Nettleship appear more of an un-perturbed utilitarian than in fact he is. He is closer to the Coleridgean 'drama of reason' than that:

> Words are symbols made by us, but we come to look upon them as mysteri-ous agencies, under whose power we are . . . If we all tend to become the 'victims of words,' the corollary is that we should mean something by our words, and know what we mean. We cannot get over the difficulty by blaming language or declining to use it.

The impetus of Nettleship's argument seems to require him to take the Coleridgean sense of words as 'LIVING POWERS' and to re-express it as a negative fallacy; but he does not quite do that, even though 'mysterious' is used critically not mystically. By working with the 'we' and 'if' clauses the critic chooses to remain 'within the process'. If we follow T. H. Green's argument, as put forward in his paper 'The Philosophy of Aristotle', to place ourselves 'outside the process by which our knowledge is developed' is to conceive of an untenable 'ecstasy', whereas to recognize our being within the process is to accept our true condition. It must nonetheless be accepted that, in the work of the so-called British Idealists, there remains a residuum of words which, while appearing weighty and stubborn, are in fact fluid and amenable. In this respect the work of Austin and his followers, who are suspicious of 'ideal' languages and who desiderate the 'transparency' of description, may be seen to be a radical departure and to attempt a radical criticism. Green's use of the Kantian 'manifold' is in part a technical gloss and in part an impressionistic tincture. Much the same could be said, however, of certain remarks by Austin which fall into a semantic hiatus between two individually distinct tones: one of empirical description, the other of 'malicious pleasure'. With 'J. L. Austin / *Sense and Sensibilia*' we know precisely where we are; with 'if the poet says "Go and catch a falling star" or whatever it may be, he doesn't seriously issue an order' we suspect raillery.

Coleridge observed that 'to a youth led from his first boyhood to investigate the meaning of every word and the reason of its choice and position, Logic presents itself as an old acquaintance under new names'. In post-Coleridgean chronology these 'names' include poetry and 'linguistic phenomenology'. By 'poetry' one means, in the context of this discussion, 'troped' utterance, 'ontological manoeuvre', sometimes 'desperate', some-times felicitous, occasionally marked by that strain of desperate felicity which R. P. Blackmur noted as a characteristic of 'the classical mode in the arts' in modern times. It is 'as if order *required* distress'. 'Required' is, in the circumstances, well judged, hovering as it does between questions of temperament and technique. Kenneth Burke has described 'workmanship' as 'a trait in which the ethical and the esthetic are one'. The appeal of this statement rests in the conviction that a formula exists for achieving a consummation of technique which simultaneously 'satisfies the desire of a moral agent' and, in so doing, resolves the 'old difficulty', as it has been called, 'of conceiving . . . *an activity with end attained*'. Both the New Criti-cism and Austinian verbal analysis are in this respect scions of that passage from *Biographia Literaria* in which Coleridge aligns 'verbal precision' and 'mental accuracy', at once prescribing 'modes of intellectual energy' and proscribing 'fanaticism', 'indistinct watch-words'. There is here no division to be inferred between 'energy' and 'precision'. Austin's objection to this might be that Coleridge's own terms constitute nothing more than indis-tinct watchwords, metaphysical fantasy, pretence. '*Praetendere* in Latin', he writes, 'never strays far from the literal meaning of holding or stretching one thing in front of another in order to protect or conceal or disguise it: even in such a figurative use as that in Ovid's "praetendens culpae splendida verba tuae", the words are still a façade to hide the crime'. Austin's reference is to the *Remedia amoris,* lines 239–40, 'Nec te Lar patrius, sed amor revocabit amicae | Praetendens culpae splendida verba tuae', and 'crime' is, in fact, a shade too portentous a rendering of the 'weakness' involved in letting oneself be lured back by sexual desire and in disguising that motive in brave words about home and country. There is indeed a range of ironic implication in Ovid's use of 'culpa' and 'splendida verba' ('the grand name without the grand thing'), his realization of the manner in which 'holding forth' can be a way of withholding, which Austin chooses not to point out, either because he takes it to be self-evident or because he is excluding from consideration anything to do with 'that rather woolly word "imply" '. A poem, in his opinion, is not 'issued in ordinary circumstances'. This makes sense. What also makes sense is Ransom's 'the density or connota-tiveness of poetic language reflects the world's density', an observation which Austin might also dismiss as metaphysical fantasy. Those invocations at the heart of Hopkins's 'The Wreck of the Deutschland'—'O Deutsch-land, double a desperate name!', 'Double-naturèd name,' 'O unteachably after evil, but uttering truth'—would be, from that angle of vision, incor-rigibly self-stultifying. Notwithstanding such logical objections it must be affirmed that it is at such points, or nodes, where 'stultification' might seem the most reasonable verdict, that poetry encounters its own possibilities. The word 'blind' upon which Wordsworth homes in so often is itself a compounding of blankness and intuition: at one time 'Dim sadness, and blind thoughts I knew not nor could name', at another 'A pleasurable feeling of blind love'. Those other Wordsworthian key-words 'gleam' and 'perplexity' gather their reciprocating force from this blank recognition: from the sense that without the perplexity there would be no gleam and that the 'blindness' embodies them both. When Hopkins writes 'dogged in den' he does not mean what he means by 'dear and dogged man'. Yet his early fathoming of words as 'heavy bodies' bears most fully on this matter. He is drawn down to a double nature within the etymological stratum, where *dǫgd* (hounded) and *dǫ·gèd* (tenacious) lie like shards or bones of 'most recondite and difficult' matter within the simple hereditary accruals of the vernacular. It is 'man's malice' that is 'dogged in den', a sense at once opposed to the 'dear and dogged' and yet inextricably tied to it. *Dǫ·gèd* itself once meant 'currish', 'sullenly obstinate'; that it came gradually to signify something more 'dear' than this is due among other things to Dr Johnson's decision, in 1779, to refer to 'a dogged veracity'.

We are therefore driven to look again at Nettleship's unwillingness to accept the idea of words as 'mysterious agencies, under whose power we are' and to insist, despite having sympathy with this admirable form of common sense, that there *is* something 'mysterious', some 'dark and disputed matter' implicated in the nature of language itself. But the mystery is nothing more nor less than 'ordinary circumstances', 'habitudes and institutions', 'cultivated opinion', 'traditional pieties and naïve beliefs', what Locke termed 'the audible discourse of the company' and Austin designated as 'the conduct of meetings and business'. 'Our word is our bond' (shackle, arbitrary constraint, closure of possibility) is correlative to 'our word is our bond' (reciprocity, covenant, fiduciary symbol). 'Mastery' is as much as is not servitude. The 'ineluctable problem' is therefore, as might reasonably be expected, elementary and empirical. To encounter it, however, is like encountering a blank in one's own thinking where '*bona fide* perplexity' is hardly distinguishable from obtuseness, and instinctive flinching from disingenuous evasion. Donne, for example, freely invents 'paradoxes and problems' but he also has problems that are not paradoxes, that cannot be 'impudently' troped but must be rawly acknowledged. 'I did best when I had least truth for my subject' is aware that it calls 'best' into question; though this observation is more oblique than those statements, in *Devotions upon Emergent Occasions*, which bind the erected wit into the mortal sickness of man's engendering parts ('to lay him sicke in his owne bed of wantonnesse') or which, still more blankly, set the foundations of our helplessness even deeper than the region of the 'infected wil':

> Or if these occasions of this selfe-destruction, had any contribution from our owne *wils* . . . wee might divide the rebuke, & chide our selves as much as them . . . But what have I done, either to *breed,* or to *breath* these *vapors*? They tell me it is m*y Melancholy*: Did I infuse, did I drinke in *Melancholly* into my selfe? It is my *thoughtfulnesse*; was I not made to *thinke*? It is my *study*; doth not my *Calling* call for that?

If we were to thrash this matter out, either with him or against him, we could argue that Donne, while conceiving of a passivity which he strives to separate from malignant intention, precludes, in that very conceiving and striving, the completeness of the distinction. He argues that in '*Fevers* upon wilful distempers of drinke, and surfets, *Consumptions* upon intemperances, & licentiousnes' and the like 'our selves are in the plot, and wee are not onely *passive,* but *active* too, to our owne destruction'. This is not, we may say, like having one's proper 'calling', one's ordained faculties, turned into the very accessories of destruction. Some thirty years before Donne's *Devotions* were printed, the public stage had exhibited Marlowe's Faustus

wilfully and perversely confounding licentiousness with study. There
remained sound reasons for Donne's desire to draw a moral distinction
between them. Even so, one might still quibble with his apparent inference
that the metaphor 'our selves are in the plot' in some way ceases to apply
when we abandon 'distempers', 'intemperances, and licentiousness' in
favour of 'thoughtfulnesse' and 'study'. It could be contended that what
T. H. Green calls being 'within the process' and Donne calls being 'in the
plot' is the peculiar nature and burden of that activity we are accustomed to
call 'thinking experience'. It is within the process of such experience that we
are not only active but passive too, exhibiting the symptom at the very
moment that we diagnose the condition. But this is something more openly
empirical, less amenable to the simple revenge cliché of the libertine sinner
laid sick in the bed of his own 'wantonnesse'. It is more the recognition that
our '*Noble* parts . . . for all their priviledges . . . are not priviledged from our
misery'. Donne has not, after all, missed or evaded the point. Nygren says
that 'in Augustine, the sinful soul is "*bent down*" to earth; in Luther, it is "*bent
upon itself*"'. Whether we ourselves cling to the Augustinian or to the
Lutheran emphasis our conclusion must be that the language a writer uses
and the writer who uses the language are inextricably involved and implicated. If Hopkins's words are 'heavy bodies' they are 'bent down to earth'; if
the creative spirit is necessarily 'bent upon itself', then its deepest intuitions
are ineluctably compounded with its most inveterate stubbornness and
incapacity. This is the perplexity upon which Donne briefly but searchingly
touches when he alludes to our being in some sense vocationally compromised, condemned by the very nature of our 'calling'.

To the reasonable retort that one is 'vocationally compromised' only by
being temperamentally predisposed to view matters in this dark light, by an
inclination to the melodramatic, one may reasonably concede that the
'hazardous course', the 'partial surrender', the 'adjustment for practical
purposes', are unavoidable and unarguable ('our word is our bond') but
that one is not bound by anything other than temperament and indoctrin-
ation to the manner in which the exigencies are viewed. But even here one
might be conceding too much, simply to oblige. There have always been
rich opportunities for confusing temperament with technique and it may be
inequitable to wish the confusion upon some chosen author. Dryden, for
instance, who in one place celebrates 'the providence of wit', in another
deplores its 'anarchy'. It would be unwise to suppose some violent change
of mood on his part, but reasonable to assume his customary pragmatic

acceptance of the need for an altered mode. 'Infections' are 'ordinary circumstances' and the dyer's hand, steeped in etymology if nothing else, is, by that commonplace craftsmanlike immersion, an infected hand. One can say with Augustine 'curva voluntas' or with Peirce 'Actuality is something *brute*. There is no reason in it. I instance putting your shoulder against a door and trying to force it open against an unseen, silent, and unknown resistance.' Either way this is the gravamen of the matter, but the matter may of course be an occasion for levity.

Austin himself has remarked that 'we must consider the total situation in which the utterance is issued—the total speech-act'. If one accepts the paradigm of the warning notice which in 'saying that customers are warned *is* warning the customers' one is not finally annulling the extra-linguistic sanction of convention. As Warnock notes, such a warning contains, either explicitly or implicitly, the word 'hereby'. ' "Hereby" is an indication that the utterance *itself* is doing the job that it says is done.' This is, by general consent, one of the most compelling instances in which to *say* something is to *do* something; and yet the inescapable correlative seems to be that 'hereby' can do what it says only because there exists some idea of sanction (real or fictional) to back it up. Romantic and modern poetry, we may suggest, yearns for this sense of identity between saying and doing—'all values ultimately come from our judicial sentences'—but to Pound's embarrassment and ours it discovers itself to possess no equivalent for 'hereby'. It does not seem possible to call into court, on poetry's behalf, those other 'necessary circumstances' which would establish its claim to be a juridical agent, except in a grotesquely negative form. For anyone predisposed to regard Pound's statement as mere 'holding forth', 'splendida verba' cloaking self-delusion, inane 'culpa', the Faustian catastrophe would have been enacted outside the Washington courtroom in 1945: 'When I asked him whether he wanted to stand mute or would prefer to enter a plea, he was unable to answer me. His mouth opened once or twice as if to speak, but no words came out.' But the silence is here too eloquent a rebuke to the 'inviolable voice'. If, in Pound's humiliation, we have an exemplary instance of 'idea' brought face to face with 'the particular truth of things', we have equally a parable of the due process of law enmeshed in various 'self-stultifying procedures' ('A ... he comes back to them [i.e. "fixed" ideas] all the time, but none of them is clear. It is all vague ... Q. You mean vague to the examiner? A. Yes, of course'). MacKinnon is right: 'rich possibilities' do depend upon 'quick practical perception' and the distinctions between the absolutes and partialities of justice are a matter of quick practical perception too. 'All four experts ... attested a prevailing "grandiosity" in the poet, which they said indicated his abnormal mental state.' It may be grandiose or 'delusional' to claim that one possesses 'the key to the peace of the world through the writings of Confucius' since so unworldly a sense of the world must be, by that definition, self-stultifying, oxymoronic, impotent enactment, 'hollow or void' as though introduced in a poem or spoken in soliloquy. At the same time, the 'peculiar legal paradox' that, as a result of the court's verdict, 'Pound found himself, in effect, under a sentence of life imprisonment despite the fact that he was innocent in the eyes of the law' is in itself more oxymoronic than paradoxical.

This is not said to let Pound off the hook, or to spare him the rap. Cornell's suggestion that he 'was imprisoned despite the fact that he is one of the great literary figures of our time, perhaps in part because of that fact' is 'incorrigibly poetical' in Santayana's dubious sense. Pound, in his *Paris Review* interview, said that 'there is the struggle not to sign on the dotted line for the opposition'. His own idiom implicates itself in 'the conduct of meetings and business'. Our chains rattle, even while we are complaining of them. The moral offence of his vicious anti-semitism does not call into question the integrity of his struggle; neither does the integrity of the struggle absolve him of responsibility for the vulgar cruelty. The essential culpability of his wartime broadcasts was not their eruption into 'that stupid suburban prejudice', as he self-indulgently called it, but their 'insufficient desperation', as Richard Reid has observed. The more important word here is 'insufficient'. 'Saeva indignatio' is no guarantee of verdictive accuracy, or even of perception; and it is lack of attention, or 'care', which brings Pound to the point of 'signing on the dotted line' for the rulers of the darkness of this world—not in spite of, but through, the mundane struggle, the 'being bound' to push on with the matter in hand, no matter what, where the matter is the 'heavy bodies', the 'solid entities', the 'compacted doctrines'.

T. H. Green argued that, in revolutionary Jacobinism, Hume's 'philosophy of feeling ... had by a necessary process recoiled upon itself'. He had in mind that inert compound of 'wilfulness' and acquiescence to 'necessity' which he regarded as the negative side of hedonistic materialism. 'Recoil' upon the self should therefore, I believe, be distinguished from that 'return upon the self' which may be defined as the transformation of mere reflex into an 'act of attention', a 'disinterested concentration of purpose' upon one's own preconceived notions, prejudices, self-contradictions and errors. Viewed in this light Pound's ultimate remorse ('I guess I was off base all along'), though not baseless, was unbalanced; a recoil rather than a return. In a note scribbled to his defence lawyer from St Elizabeth's Hospital he wrote:

enormous work / to be / done. / & no driving / force / & everyone's / inexactitude / very / fatiguing

'Everyone's inexactitude' (if, against the run of that bias, we include his own) comes closer to the heart of the matter than 'off base all along'. 'All values ultimately come from our judicial sentences' sounds magisterially Shelleyan but in fact does less than justice to Pound's grasp of *logopoeia*. Christopher Ricks's redefinition, 'all values ultimately go into our judicial sentences', stands the perception in its rightful place, at the receiving end of 'the innumerable and unforeseeable demands of the world upon language', rather than in a position of vatic privilege. Since Pound places such emphasis upon definition ('The poet's job is to *define* and yet again define till the detail of surface is in accord with the root in justice') it is not unjust to take him up precisely on this point, on this disjunction of the aesthetic and the ethical. Coleridge observed that 'the cultivation of the judgement is a positive command of the moral law'. In such pronouncements as 'all values ultimately come . . . ', 'positive command' detaches itself from 'cultivation of the judgement'. The resultant tone strikes one as being nothing more than the assertion of status; and 'I guess I was off base all along' becomes complicitously egocentric.

The usefulness of Ricks's redefinition is that it both assuages and aggravates one's awareness of the obligation to judge definitively those matters which one is arbitrarily stuck with. To take a stand upon such questions is one thing; mere vatic 'status' is another. 'Fact is richer than diction' as Austin says, but there seems no just cause to infer from this a parasitic role for poetic statement. Of *Homage to Sextus Propertius* Pound wrote 'I certainly omitted no means of definition that I saw open to me'. The final line of the sequence:

And now Propertius of Cynthia, taking his stand among these

conflates two lines of Propertius' Latin: 'Cynthia quin etiam versu laudata Properti | hos inter si me ponere Fama volet'. The passive ('hos inter si me ponere') becomes the active 'taking his stand'. The major implications of the change certainly involve a claim to status, to be 'among' the true poets.

The minor nuances include a hint of proud vulnerability (having to stand up for oneself in such a world) and the fleeting glimpse of a cocksure literary flâneur ('Near Q. H. Flaccus' book-stall'). The status fought for, and accomplished, within the comedy and melodrama of this sequence, is, therefore, that of standing by one's words in a variety of tricky situations and is a different matter from abstractedly surveying the depths of ethical space ('all values ultimately come ... '). The pitch of the last line is stubborn, jaunty, and yet elegiacally aware of the tragic farce of being bound to maintain standards against such odds. Each of these tonalities is appropriate in its impropriety, given the 'imbecility' against which it is pitched. It is true that 'imbecility' is Pound's prejudice, but *Homage* is aware of prejudice and other coarsenesses, as it allows that 'fact is richer than diction' in the very process of evolving a means of defining its response to matters of such perplexity.

Contemporary aesthetics, when they are being ethical (as in the exegetical work of Nathan A. Scott), seek 'exemplary instances of the literary imagination supervising its project'. This leads, all too often, to a style of appraisal which is little better than a series of exclamation marks: 'extraordinary adroitness', 'wonderfully nuanced and deeply affecting', 'astounding range of ... vocabulary', a form of that Orphic afflatus which the critic elsewhere views with some unease. Yet we are required to take inflationary adjectives as a true evocation of the poet's 'redeeming work' in face of 'the world's absurdity'. There is therefore an inherent irony in meditating, as Scott does, upon 'absolute closures of possibility' in terms so effusive and grandiose. Such 'closures' are consistently seen, by practitioners of this mode, as thematic data, as matter for discursive explication; but it is the modish style itself which, with its simplistic affirmations, most drastically forecloses on other possibilities. The vigorous pursuit of misery, degradation and guilt thus appears in a peculiar way ebulliently heartless and obtuse. In itself, however, 'absolute closures of possibility' is a phrase worth pondering. It merits being taken, not in Scott's style of defining a superficial sense of the 'Absurd', but as something more closely approximate to that 'foundational' thinking, that grasp of 'primal reality', which he elsewhere wishes upon his hypothetical figure of 'the poet'. The approximation would be closer to Greville's 'creeping Genius' or to Sidney's historian who 'wanting the precept, is so tied, not to what should be, but to what is' than to Scott's Heideggerean adept; but such humiliation would be Scott's 'foundational thinking' with a vengeance.

To return upon ourselves. When Hopkins writes of 'dark and disputed matter' he is not, in the first instance, thinking of linguistic manifolds. He is meditating primarily upon the nature of voluntary and involuntary acts, the 'active' and 'passive' will, the 'free' and the 'constrained'; upon the distinctions between these which must be drawn and observed, and upon the numerous cross-thwartings which make the maintaining of such distinctions an arduous and perilous task. There is an essential 'freedom of pitch' (which is when 'I instress my will to so-and-so') and there is 'accident[al]' 'freedom of field'. If, however, language as medium is a prime manifestation of 'freedom of field' and the right-keeping of will manifests 'freedom of pitch', Hopkins's theological crux is necessarily a linguistic crux. The abrupt and ugly phrasings ('*the doing* be, *the doing* choose, *the doing* so-and-so') excessively, even absurdly, concentrate the sense of pitch. It is a consciousness which accepts that the determining of grace necessitates at times a graceless articulation: we are reminded that Hopkins was, albeit briefly, a pupil of T. H. Green. But he was also a student of Plato. As a number of his poems reveal, he would regard it as more desirable that grace should be gracefully embodied and declared. Felicity, always to be desired, is met with in unlikely places, even in a 'hantle of howlers' scattered across the broad expanse of freedom of field: 'Caesar is proud and pompeous', 'The Wife of Bath was a real woman's man', 'Swift's misagony'. As Edwin Morgan remarks, these 'are hardly "errors" except to a niggardly imagination'. Morgan's essay, like Austin's felicitous account of the 'infelicities', is a demonstration in the comic mode: 'It may seem extraordinary that such brilliant compressions of relevant meaning . . . should all start up unbidden out of mere confusion and hastiness of mind.' It is also, despite the philosophical irony motivating its patient accumulation of data about actual usage, basically optimistic in its view of the workings of spontaneity, the 'self unqualified in volition', and the complex and recalcitrant nature of things. 'Brilliant' is of course the travesty of a felicity, a cleverly planted self-stultifying oxymoron. A brilliant self-betrayal must be in a peculiar way hollow or void, a kind of joking in which the agent fails to see the joke through which our 'murky thought willy-nilly comes clean', is 'betrayed into actuality'. The 'first-grade or classic pun' is parenthetically insulated by the imbecile context and it gives 'pleasure to the reader' somewhat in the way that Sir Fopling Flutter and Mrs Malaprop gave pleasure to the polite audiences of their times. It is not unlike our relish of the fine distinction between 'clumsily he trod on the snail' and 'he trod on the snail clumsily', where it would be disproportionate to consider the feelings of the snail. Actuality is something brute; but romantic pessimism and melodramatic addiction to culpability are still subject to Iris Murdoch's caveat: 'ideas of guilt and punishment can be the most subtle tool of the ingenious self... and the unworthiness of one's motives is interesting.' Yet here again distinctions may validly be drawn. 'Motives', in Murdoch's critical usage, are transcendental, are part of the solipsistic 'interestingness of existence' and do not necessarily equate with vocational, technical intent. Greville's 'creeping Genius' is something other than the melancholy poor cousin of Murdoch's 'ingenious self' and Sidney's distinction between 'erected wit' and 'infected wil' is not overly concerned with 'ideas of guilt and punishment'. The essential question is whether one can properly talk of an 'irreproachable skill'. Pound thought that one could. 'Verbalism demands a set form used with irreproachable skill.' And Kenneth Burke's 'workmanship . . . in which the ethical and the esthetic are one' presupposes that the 'faultless' is in all senses practicable. The ethical and the aesthetic come together at those points where 'freedom of pitch' and 'freedom of field' perfectly intersect or perfectly coincide. And when the conjunction is bungled we discover the complicity between a solecism and 'a sloppy and slobbering world'. The charge that the 'transition from generalization to practice completely eluded' Pound, though excessive, at least takes with a proper seriousness the idea that 'rhetoric' is a part of the ontology of moral action. The desperation of 'I never did believe in Fascism, God damn it', the angry bewilderment of 'everyone's inexactitude very fatiguing', are both pre-judged by 'the tyro can not play about with such things, the game is too dangerous'. Pound had written this, in 1917, in an essay on Laforgue, 'the finest wrought' of modern French satirists. 'Finest wrought' and 'everyone's inexactitude' are mutually uncomprehending and Pound stands condemned by his own best judgement, the 'tyro' to his own mastery. The transcript of the Washington hearing preserves a number of solemn and vacuous pronouncements by advocates and experts on both sides, but the observation that 'the crime with which he is charged is closely tied up with his profession of writing' has an ineluctability that is not diminished by its banal obviousness. Austin's principles are vindicated, though his prejudices and self-satisfactions are not. The word-monger, word-wielder, is brought to judgement *by his being the person who does* the uttering... In written utterances (or "inscriptions"), *by his appending his signature*'. Our word is our bond.

I suggested, at the start of this discussion, that Pound may have miscon-strued a fine point of semantics. In *How to Do Things with Words* Austin writes that 'a verdictive is a judicial act as distinct from legislative or executive acts, which are both exercitives'. Pound's error was to confuse the two, to fancy that poets' 'judicial sentences' are, in mysterious actuality, legislative or executive acts. But poets are not legislators, unless they happen to be so employed, in government or law; and '*recta ratio factibilium*' is not '*mens rea*' or '*actus reus*'. The 'world's' revenge, during his court-hearing and its aftermath, was unwittingly to pay him back, confusion for confusion, with legislative or executive acts presuming to be true verdictives: 'Now comes Dorothy Pound, as Committee of the person and estate of Ezra Pound, an incompetent person.' If we seek the *mot juste*, it was no more and no less than poetic justice. 'And when one has the mot juste', as Pound observed, 'one is finished with the subject.'

The Enemy's Country

Deeds, it seems, may be Justified by Arbitrary Power, when words are question'd in a Poet.

John Dryden

You cannot call a man an artist until he shows himself capable of reticence and of restraint, until he shows himself in some degree master of the forces which beat upon him.

Ezra Pound

The Enemy's Country

A Note on the Title

I have taken my title from Thomas Nashe and from William Davenant. In 'The Epistle Dedicatorie' of *Strange Newes*, an attack on the Cambridge pedant *G.H.*, Nashe commends the work to his 'verie friend' Apis lapis (Beeston) with this flourish: 'Thou art a good fellow I know, and hadst rather spend ieasts than monie. Let it be the taske of thy best tearmes, to safeconduct this booke through the enemies countrey'. Davenant, in the 'Author's Preface' to *Gondibert*, has his conceit of 'the vast field of Learning, where the Learned . . . lye . . . maliciously in Ambush' and where one must 'travail . . .' as 'through the Enemy's country'. Since I follow MacDiarmid in desiring 'A learned poetry wholly free | From the brutal love of ignorance' and hold, with John Berryman, that 'all the artists who have ever survived were intellectuals—sometimes intellectuals *also*, but intellectuals', my choice of these sallies against learning may appear self-stultifyingly perverse. I will not stoop to the defensive innuendo that learning is antipathetic to 'true' intellect or that genius may be estimated by the depth of its immersion in 'meer Nature'. Nashe plied his anti-pedantic learning with comic grace and Yeats's contrast between young poets 'tossing' in lyric anguish and aged impotent scholars who 'edit and annotate' such gems of youthful suffering is a piece of sentimental cant. To 'think what other people think' is as likely to be the province of 'the popular boys'. If for 'vast field of Learning' we substitute 'vast apparatus of Opinion' we may be nearer the mark. Intellect will always be learned, albeit at times idiosyncratically. Of 'culture' and 'education' as currently understood and practised, one feels less confident.

Davenant elected as his guide through the enemy's country 'his much honor'd friend M. Hobbes' as one who went 'not by common Mapps' but 'painefully made [his] own Prospect'. My book's subtitle is wrenched out of Hobbes. 'Words, contexture, and other circumstances of Language' I take to signify the relation of word to word and of the body of words to those contingencies and accommodations marginally glossed among the 'Lawes of Nature' in *Leviathan*: 'covenants of mutuall trust', 'covenants extorted by feare', 'justice of manners and justice of actions', 'submission to arbitrement', etc.

A Note on References in the Text

Although the bulk of the reference material is reserved to the last section of the book, I have, wherever practicable, given page-references immediately after quotations in the text. This has proved possible only in those cases where I have made recurrent reference to a particular volume or to a run of volumes. Citations within the text are as follows:

Chapter 10. *The Poems of John Dryden*, ed. James Kinsley, 4 vols. (Oxford: Oxford University Press, 1958); page-numbers run consecutively through the four volumes. *The Works of John Dryden*, ed. Edward Niles Hooker, H. T. Swedenberg, Jr., and Vinton A. Dearing, 20 vols. (Berkeley, CA: University of California Press, 1956–2000); reference to this edition is by volume and page, e.g. '13: 49'. *The Letters of John Dryden*, ed. Charles E. Ward (Durham, NC: Duke University Press, 1942); references are prefaced by 'Ls'.

Chapter 11. HUMANE NATURE: | Or, | The fundamental Elements | OF | POLICIE | . . . By THO. HOBBS of *Malmesbury*. | *London* . . . 1650; references to this edition are preceded by 'H'. OF | LIBERTIE | AND | NECESSITY. | A TREATISE, | . . . by *Thomas Hobs*. | . . . LONDON, | . . . 1654; references preceded by 'L'. *Reliquiae Wottonianae*: the editions of 1651 (A), 1654 (B), and 1672 (C). References to Dryden's letters and to the Oxford and Berkeley editions of his *Poems* and *Works* are indicated as in Chapter 10.

Chapter 12. John Donne, *The Satires, Epigrams and Verse Letters*, ed. W. Milgate (Oxford: Clarendon Press, 1967); reference by page-number. Izaac Walton, *The Compleat Angler 1653–1676*, ed. Jonquil Bevan (Oxford: Clarendon Press, 1983); reference by page-number. The context should make it clear whether the numbers refer to Donne or to Walton. References to *Reliquiae Wottonianae* as in Chapter 11.

Chapter 13. References for Dryden's poetry and prose are to the Oxford and Berkeley editions cited in Chapter 10.

Chapter 14. All notes and references will be found in the last section of the book (pp. 659–68).

10

Unhappy Circumstances

Aubrey records that the philosopher Thomas Hobbes, although 'marvellous happy and ready in his replies' when baited by the 'witts at Court', was reluctant to 'conclude hastily' in questions of weight and import: 'he turned and winded and compounded in philosophy, politiques, etc. as if he had been at Analyticall worke.' This distinction between the particular virtues of instant repartee and of protracted and complex deliberation merits some remark at the present time when, it could fairly be said, the force of the distinction has been largely forgotten and when to 'turn' and 'wind' and 'compound' in one's arguments is to be taken as being contemptuously self-regarding, as holding oneself wilfully aloof from the proper business of discourse and communication.

When Hobbes defined his 'fifth Law of Nature' as 'compleasance', that is to say '*That every man strive to accommodate himselfe to the rest*', he established a mode of conduct and discourse for those who perhaps only partly understood him. Some twenty years after *Leviathan* appeared, an entire handbook, or 'conduct book' was devoted to *The Art of Complaisance or the Means to Oblige in Conversation*; and scholars of Restoration Comedy have shown how the 'double nature' of a society's dedication to ruthless self-gratification and to 'civility and affability' is accommodated in the word 'compleasance' itself. The very difficulty one has in defining the relationship between self-seeking and civility exemplifies the shifty utility of the term. It was observed of Mary Rich, Countess of Warwick, a good and charitable lady, that she was 'the foundress and inventress, of a new science—the art of obliging', and it would be unjust to assume that her way of 'obliging' was equatable with the way 'to oblige in Conversation'.

One could perhaps say that self-gratification was sought and attained through the practice of civility or one could argue that 'patience, humility, civility and affability' were forms of humane reproof to the lust for selfish

domination. In Etherege's *The Man of Mode* Harriet rebukes Dorimant: 'I am
sorry my face does not please you as it is, but I shall not be complaisant and
change it'. In Hobbes's terms she is playing at being '*Stubborn, Insociable,
Froward, Intractable*' but as she acts out the frowardness she is all the more
eloquently revealed as being beautiful, desirable, marvellous happy, and
ready in her replies. Beauty and status, in such theatre fictions, give every
appearance of resolving the intractabilities of judgement and circumstance
which the authors of those stage-fictions encountered not only outside the
domain of the theatre but also within the contractual obligations and
financial constraints of the business. Car Scroope's 'Prologue' and Dryden's
'Epilogue' to Etherege's play force the concept of 'Arbitrary Power' (178;
cf. 1020) out of the charmed circle of the fiction, where it is taken care of in
the spectacle of youthful and attractive ingenuity outwitting the twin
tyrannies of crabbed age and commodity, into the immediate circumstances
of the author's resentful dependence on a fickle and ignorant public which
he mirrors to itself, aped and reflected in the least attractive humours and
business of the stage. In Dryden's theatre prologues and epilogues the
didactic satire of Jonsonian comedy and the bitter self-vindication of Jonson's 'An Ode. To himselfe' are compounded, though in the compounding
a quite distinct timbre is realized. Jonson's 'Ode' proclaims the virtue of a
'high and aloofe' lyric *otium*. Dryden's most characteristic theatre work
acknowledges that drudgery, *nec-otium*, is to be the medium of his achievement, its stultification and its paradoxical release. In this respect he is more
'Hobbesian' than is Rochester. The implications of '*That every man strive to
accommodate himselfe to the rest*' are grained and cross-grained into the body of
his work, as the incompatibilities of 'strive' and 'accommodate' are themselves wedged together in Hobbes's phrase. I would agree that, in the
concluding moments of Etherege's play, Harriet's depiction of the 'great
rambling lone house' of her rural exile has 'poignancy'; it is a brief but
intensely memorable speech. 'Poignancy' will accommodate either pleasure
or pain, rather as the heroine's own words move with elusive grace between
ennui and *otium*. What she feels is ennui, or the prospect of it. Of the
exquisite manner in which she diverts her sorrow one may say, as Dr
Johnson said of one of Cowley's conceits, 'the mind must be thought
sufficiently at ease' that can attend to the minute particulars of the fancy.
Etherege's characters, even when unhappily circumstanced, retain an edge
of advantage over the author of the 'Epilogue' who, at the time of the play's
first performance in 1676, had recently incurred the enmity of the Earl of

Rochester and who increasingly came to feel, in his dealings with the public
world, the pressure of 'my unhappy Circumstances, that ... have confin'd
me to a narrow choice' (869).

These words were carefully rather than cautiously framed. The 'unhappy
Circumstances' by 1697 were the social and economic consequences of his
refusal to abjure the faith and practice of Roman Catholicism in the years
following the abdication of James II. A member of a proscribed religion,
Dryden was deprived of his public offices and had reason to anticipate
difficulty in obtaining patronage. The 'Pastorals' were dedicated to the
Roman Catholic nobleman Lord Clifford (869–73), the 'Georgics' in the
same 1697 volume carried a dedication to the second earl of Chesterfield
(912–18), an adherent of the Stuart cause who had retired from public life
when William of Orange took the throne. John Sheffield, third earl of
Mulgrave and Marquis of Normanby, 'Sharp judging *Adriel* the Muses
friend' (239), to whom Dryden dedicated his translation of the *Aeneis*
(1003 ff.) as well as the earlier *Aureng-Zebe*, was, though not a Catholic, a
staunch supporter of the Duke of York, later James II. It is true that he
managed his political accommodations with fair success under William III,
but the exceptional constancy of his patronage, transcending political and
religious factionalism, earned tributes not only from Dryden himself but also
from John Dennis. As the judgement of these individual members of the
'Learned Nobility' (869) resists and transforms unhappy circumstance so
Dryden in his own more humiliating straits contrives a style which will give
due emphasis to the sharpness of the affliction and to the fact that he is 'not
dispirited with [his] Afflictions' (1424). To be narrowly confined is to be in
straitened circumstances but to be confined to a narrow choice places the
final emphasis on the limited freedom to choose. The word is not without
spirit. Dryden can still contrive a touch of resonance from a flat recital.

The matter of how to relate *otium* to *negotium* (etymologically impacted,
separable by means of paronomasia), the question of how to obtain, amid
the world's circumstances, that 'vacation from other busines', the 'intervalls
and ease' in which to think and write, are problems that have proved
recurrently ponderable since Seneca composed his *De brevitate vitae* and *De
otio*. Francis Meres, in 1598, lamented the absence of any support for the
'famous and learned Lawreat masters of England' comparable to that which
'the Emperor Augustus, or Octauia his sister, or noble Mecaenas' lavished
upon Virgil and Horace. Milton, keenly sensing how much he owed to his
father's support, acknowledged the debt, both in the 'Ad Patrem' of *c*.1632

('Aoniae iucunda per otia ripae') and, ten years later, in *The Reason of Church-Government* ('Yet ease and leasure was given thee for thy retired thoughts out of the sweat of other men'). Dryden's letters and prefaces often revert to such matters, as do his 'Oxford' prologues and epilogues. John Locke refers to the problem in 'the Epistle to the Reader' introducing his *Essay Concerning Humane Understanding*, a work written, as he says, 'by incoherent parcels' and with 'long intervals of neglect'. The issues are succinctly stated by Ezra Pound in private letters and public tracts at the time of his attempt to raise funds sufficient to enable both Eliot and Joyce to devote their whole time and energy to writing: 'The only thing one can give an artist is leisure in which to work.' That was in 1922. Years later, in 1959, he added a footnote: 'Leisure is time plus money, or at any rate time without monetary worry.' As Dryden remarked in the last year of his life 'they who beare the purse will rule' (Ls 135). Dryden and Pound are indeed comparable in their awareness of the political and economic realities of circumstance, of the ways in which the writer's judgement of word-values both affects and is affected by his understanding of, or his failure to comprehend, the current reckonings of value in the society of his day. It is an irony to be briefly noted that Pound, unlike Eliot, was not an admirer of Dryden; he curtly dismissed the 'platitude and verbosity', 'that outstanding aridity'. Even so I would maintain that, judged by Pound's standard of measure ('you cannot call a man an artist until . . . he shows himself in some degree master of the forces which beat upon him'), Dryden's work manifests, albeit with varying degrees of finality, his command of the essential facts: that a poet's words and rhythms are not his utterance so much as his resistance. His 'choice of *Words*, and Harmony of Numbers' as Dryden would say, his 'technic' as Yeats and Pound called it, must resist the pressure of circumstances or be inundated by the tide of 'compleasance'. To the caveat that Pound's observation—an early one, from the *Patria Mia* of 1912—refers to a specific stage in a writer's development, the point at which the raw tyro becomes a genuine apprentice, a potential master capable of making his prize-song, I would respond that with every new work the true poet reverts to that condition. He cannot have a 'career' but as a lifelong apprentice-master he may well compose more than one masterpiece.

To suggest that Dryden accepted Hobbes's definition of value—'The *Value*, or WORTH of a man, is as of all other things, his Price', 'a mans Labour also, is a commodity exchangeable for benefit, as well as any other thing'—is to say only that he accepted it as an unhappy circumstance, especially in the case of his sometimes acrimonious dealings with Jacob Tonson, publisher in 1697 of *The Works of Virgil Translated into English Verse*. Dryden's value for the book-trade was equivalent to quantity of production and Tonson argued the price of the Ovid translations in a letter of 1692 accusing the poet of short-changing him: 'that makes for 40 guyneas . . . 1518 lines; And all that I have for fifty guyneas are but 1446' (Ls 51). Dryden in turn, in two letters of 1695, complained that Tonson had passed him base money: 'besides the clipd money, there were at least forty shillings brass' (Ls 75). The state of the English currency at that time was 'deplorable'. There was a recoining of the silver money in 1696 but even this reformation left 'the poorer and more ignorant folk . . . with clipped money on their hands'.

It is not inappropriate that some of these contentious exchanges arose out of negotiations for the publishing of Dryden's *Virgil*. Dryden himself, I believe, is entirely aware of the poetic justice, the exemplary ironies, of labouring in his circumstances over the *Eclogues* and the *Georgics*. This latter work, particularly, is a sustained invocation to the virtues of '*labor*', hard work, the necessity for incessant vigilant toil in order to make Nature yield her richness. On the evidence of his own critical writings and autobiographical allusions it appears that Dryden bears in mind two kinds of '*labor*': the tenacity of the craftsman and the drudgery of the hack. It is a matter of angry pride with him to redeem the circumstances of the second by exercising the skill and judgement of the first. He suggests that in the *Eclogues*, an early work, Virgil's 'Pinions were not harden'd to maintain a long laborious flight' (870). His main criticism of Ovid is that 'as his Verse came easily, he wanted the toyl of Application to amend it' (795). The poet, like the rural craftsman, the husbandman, must expend time, knowledge, and effort in cutting back the over-luxuriant and in coaxing the stubbornly unproductive to yield. There is, however, a bleaker aspect to the Virgilian '*labor*', a harsher emphasis concentrated in the word '*improbus*' which is crucial to our understanding of the way Virgil has grasped the realities of agrarian circumstance. This is '*labor*' seen as a bare and bitter subsistence, 'endless Labour urg'd by need' (924) in Dryden's rendering, a phrase which even as he hit upon its clinching felicity must have struck home with infelicitous force of circumstance.

In his letters the word 'drudgery' is the one he most often applies, as if it were the wry appropriation of one of Shadwell's gibes (1919), to the circumstances of his working life: 'goeing to drudge for the winter' (Ls 13), 'my business heere is to unweary my selfe, after my studyes, not to drudge' (Ls 23), 'I am still drudging on: always a Poet, and never a good one' (Ls 109), 'I am still drudgeing at a Book of Miscellanyes' (Ls 113). In Book XV of the *Metamorphoses*, a translation of which appeared in Dryden's last book, Ovid writes, in a passage devoted to sacrificial beasts, 'quid meruere boves, animal sine fraude dolisque, | innocuum, simplex, natum tolerare labores?' Dryden's version of these lines, 'How did the toiling Oxe his Death deserve, | A downright simple Drudge, and born to serve?' (1722), imbues the close rendering with a particular resonance. 'Downright' is the operative word, containing as it does the double sense of 'plainly' and 'merely'. Dryden contains in a clause that ambivalent feeling about innocence, guilelessness, which the word 'silly' also carried for a time; the suspicion that to be pious, holy, and good, in this world, is to be simple-minded.

His thinking is therefore complicated, in a way that directly affects the timbre of his style, by the fact that when he writes, as he not infrequently does, of his own 'labour' the word, basic as it sounds, has more than one connotation. It may mean a commissioned undertaking ('enjoin'd a fresh Labour' 1425) or it may connote those things which exhaust the mind and distract it from the tasks to which it is most suited ('when I labour'd under such Discouragements' 1424). It may also suggest, in Dryden as in Davenant, the 'Vigilance and labour' of one who must be constantly alert to those 'malitiously in Ambush', of one who 'travails through the Enemy's country'. Those are Davenant's phrases. Dryden writes of enemies too; the malice of the 'heavy gross-witted Fellows' (796) and their kind: 'What labour wou'd it cost them to put in a better Line, than the worst of those which they expunge in a True Poet?' (791–2). If in such emphasis on the inveterate hostilities both Davenant and Dryden may be called 'Hobbesian', that affinity depends less on paraphrasable philosophy than on tincture, 'as streams through Mines bear tinctures of their Ore' (30).

There is evidence of such tincture in Dryden's version of the *Georgics*. The 'Ploughman' and 'the lab'ring Steer' (923) are downright English for 'hominumque boumque labores' but in 'lab'ring Husband' (927), 'lab'ring Swain' (928), 'lab'ring Hand' (929), 'lab'ring Hind' (931), Dryden is picking up from Virgil's text contingent implications, such as the 'durum genus' which he translates as 'hard laborious Kind' (921), and is concentrating them in the English participle-adjective. Though not excluding all reference to 'sweet Vicissitudes of Rest and Toyl' that 'Make easy Labour' (921), Dryden places considerable emphasis upon the bare and bitter subsistence. Where Virgil writes that Winter, the farmer's lazy time, 'loosens the weight of care' ('hiems curasque resolvit') Dryden reworks it as 'Forget their Hardships, and recruit for more' (929). In the interpolated 'and recruit for more' genial relaxation becomes recuperation for yet 'more' hard labour; *otium* recharges the *negotium*; the remission is only a part of an unremitting pattern and Dryden labours to drive that irony home. In Virgil 'sightless moles dig out chambers' ('aut oculis capti fodere cubilia talpae'); in the English version 'the blind laborious Mole, | In winding Mazes works her hidden Hole' (925). The Latin 'fodere', 'to dig, or delve', is ponderously duplicated in the English by an adjective 'laborious' and by a verb 'works'.

   It is exactly at this point, however, in the midst of this busyness, that we unearth a hidden oxymoron from the winding mazes of English poetry; for what Dryden's verse has idly discovered is that 'Mole' rhymes with 'Hole'. There is at times in the digging and delving of the craft a blind complicity between '*labor*' and '*otium*'. That which is 'laboured' may at the same time be 'otiose' for the 'laboured' may not, in fact, have been worked on enough. One may fairly ask of Dryden's 'lab'ring Husband', 'lab'ring Swain', 'lab'ring Hand', 'lab'ring Hind', and 'toiling Swain' (929) whether they are, after all, local intensifications of Virgil's counter-theme, '*labor*' as bare and bitter subsistence, or whether they are time-saving prefabrications that ease the verse along.

   If this is indeed the case it demonstrates little more than that a major writer may be beset by the same minor problems which embarrass and confuse his lesser contemporaries. A minor problem left unmastered, how-ever, comes to exercise a disproportionate advantage, and in the art of poetry it is so often the effortless that impedes. Mildmay Fane, second earl of Westmorland, in his *Otia Sacra* of 1648, praises what his modern editor calls 'the virtues of contemplative quiet' and the withdrawal from the 'competitive *negotium*' of courtly and urban life. But even if his 'Rimes' are, as Fane says his were, 'beguilers of spare times', and even while he is propounding a doctrine of contemplative withdrawal, the poet is necessarily engaged in a competitive *negotium*; he is competing with the strengths and resistances and enticements of the English language. To fail to effect the essential negotiations with its fecund recalcitrance, its seeming complai-sance, is to labour into otiosity ('Bidding me be of comfort, but not griev'd'; 'So should our frozen hearts be thaw'd, and Melt'; 'Thus then rows'd up and wak'ned, I began'; 'How's that attain'd? By heat, not cold'; 'Grant, with his Dayes, thy Grace increase, and fill | His Heart, nor leave there room to harbour ill'; 'But over-fed, we surfet'). When Dr Johnson wrote that in Cowley's poem on the death of Hervey there is 'a very just and ample delineation of such virtues as a studious privacy admits, and such intellectual excellence as a mind not yet called forth to action can display' the collocation of 'studious privacy' and 'not yet called forth to action' suggests that what he desiderates is an active involvement in the daily business of the world's affairs. As he wrote to the Reverend Dr Wetherell in 1776, 'Few things are more unpleasant than the transaction of business with men who are above knowing or caring what they have to do'. We need to make a clear distinction between this indictment of patronizing untroubled carelessness and the mood of 'frigid tranquillity' with which, he claims, he dismisses his English Dictionary to the world; though a sense of the world's bland heedless power connects both statements. 'I have protracted my work till most of those whom I wished to please have sunk into the grave, and success and miscarriage are empty sounds.' Johnsonian sonority is here attuned to a hollow echo of itself and one cannot unperplex a philosophy of language from an aesthetic of style, an aesthetic of style from the unhappy circumstances.

It would be a just though simple abstract of such directly involved power to say that the *negotium* of language is inextricably a part of the world's business or that, in Laurence Binyon's words, 'just as a man's language is an unerring index of his nature, so the actual strokes of his brush in writing or painting betray him and announce either the freedom and nobility of his soul or its meanness and limitation'. Mildmay Fane's sentiments, his philosophical programme, the paraphrasable content of his work, are above reproach; his brush-strokes are inept. One must therefore conclude that there is yet another oxymoron embedded in the inmost texture of English writing: the viciousness of virtue when virtue is not called forth to action in the *negotium* of language itself.

The example of the 'brush-stroke', which deeply influenced Ezra Pound's thinking, Binyon took from the ancient Chinese. The stress on the brush-stroke itself as the factive energy by which the 'subjective element', individual personality, is made one, for good or ill, with circumstance, contiguity, enables Pound to argue cogently for the ethical and aesthetic identity of the active intelligence and the public activity: 'the "statesman cannot govern, the scientist cannot participate his discoveries, men cannot agree on wise action without language", and all their deeds and conditions

are affected by the defects or virtues of idiom.' I do not claim that in making
this emphasis Pound has advanced beyond the position maintained by
Samuel Johnson, who understood the clash and complicity between the
self and circumstance and whose sardonic emphasis on 'above', in his
indictment of those who engage in business while conceiving themselves
superior to it, endorses his indignation that Gray in 'The Bard' was above
knowing or caring about the actual mechanics of weaving a piece of cloth.

It is of course a matter of common observation that the actual mechanics of
quotidian life, whether in the seventeenth or the present century, are inevitably a matter of ambivalent regard. 'Business' is at once a necessary desirable
activity furthering the proper concerns of the common weal and an arbitrary,
tyrannical, distracting power preventing some other desirable activity or
condition from reaching fulfilment. That such observations appear to gravi-
tate so naturally to the oxymoronic is perhaps owing to an original Senecan
artifice: the 'desidiosa occupatio' and 'iners negotium' of *De brevitate vitae*.
The author of *Hudibras* wrote in his commonplace book 'Although the
Management of almost all the Busnesse in the world may appeare very
extravagant and Ridiculous, yet whosoever consider's it Rightly will finde
that it cannot be avoyded, nor possibly be don any other way'. Butler's
observation not only confronts an ambiguity, it also poses one. The question
turns on what is meant by 'consider's it Rightly'. Does it imply 'with a shrewd
appraisal of the going-rate of things' or 'according to justice and equity as in
the old rightwiseness'? English poetry and prose, certainly since Chaucer,
have registered many varied attempts to match the arts of language to the
tough integument of 'Busnesse' by proposing various fictions in which the
creative will can be imagined as operative above or below the middle ground
of circumstance, the field of brokerage, negotiation, and compromise. The
manner in which Andrew Marvell conceives of Cromwell as the '*Amphion*' of
the English nation, 'Learning a Musique in the Region clear, | To tune this
lower to that higher Sphere', or hymns the triumph of 'Choice' over
'Necessity' in Admiral Blake's victory over the Spaniards, is similar to the
style in which Dryden celebrates the resistless genius of the newly dead,
apotheosized Henry Purcell: 'Struck dumb they all admir'd the God-like
Man' (863). 'Resistless genious' is Marvell's phrase; the panegyric to triumphant selfhood is common to both.

Students of seventeenth-century literature are told that when Dryden
and his contemporaries speak of 'genius' they mean something less romantic
than Coleridge's 'royal prerogative of Genius' or Santayana's 'barbaric

genius'; something more sober and reputable than 'Genius in the rôle of Caliban'. According to the usual caveats 'genius', to Dryden, would signify not the '*daimon*', not the 'strange and powerful *numen*' which, possessing the artist, marks him out as 'different and superior in kind', but a strong natural aptitude, the technical and temperamental affinity of the born craftsman for the raw materials of the *métier*. 'I find [Homer] a Poet more according to my Genius than Virgil' (Ls 121) is evidently temperamental affinity. 'Shakespear had a Genius for [Tragedy]' (Ls 71) just as evidently signifies a most forceful natural aptitude, as in 'A happy *Genius* is the gift of Nature'. But when Dryden observes that the 'distinguishing Character' of Lucretius' 'Soul and Genius' is 'a certain kind of noble pride, and positive assertion of his Opinions' (395), this is something other than a matter of temperamental affinity, inherent gifts. 'He is every where confident of his own reason, and assuming an absolute command not only over his vulgar Reader, but even his Patron' (ibid.). When Charles Blount writes to the Earl of Rochester 'No, my Lord, your mighty genius is a most sufficient argument of its own immortality', the implication 'different and superior in kind' is palpable. Rochester is being flattered by a social inferior as Dorset, Roscommon, Radcliffe, or Mulgrave are flattered by their social inferior Dryden and as the Earl of Pembroke is flattered by John Locke in the 'Epistle Dedicatory' to *An Essay Concerning Humane Understanding*. The historical accident that Rochester is a poet of great power does not annul the force of an original circumstance or of the expediency which it called forth into action. Dorset and Roscommon were mediocrities extravagantly praised by the professionals who depended on them. 'Genius' was evidently awarded *jure natalium* to men of high social standing, and lowborn professionals were sometimes favoured by patrons for political reasons that had nothing to do with intrinsic merit. There are various shifts in the word 'genius' itself which suggest that it is 'combating betwixt two different Passions' as, in the essay *Of Dramatic Poesie*, the genius of Ovidian poetry is said to 'show the various movements of the soul' (17: 30). The root of the matter is perhaps to be found in Hobbes's distinction between natural and instrumental power. '*Naturall Power*, is the eminence of the Faculties of Body, or Mind: as extraordinary Strength, Forme, Prudence, Arts, Eloquence, Liberality, Nobility. *Instrumentall* are those Powers, which acquired by these, or by fortune, are means and Instruments to acquire more: as Riches, Reputation, Friends, and the secret working of God, which men call Good Luck.' The mixed feelings, then as now, about the nature and quality of 'genius' arise

from the complex system of brokerage and bargaining between reciprocating groups of 'haves' and 'have-nots', a pattern discreetly sketched more
than once in Dryden's letters to the aristocracy. The tone of seventeenth-
century dedications strongly suggests that those who possess 'instrumentall'
power are to be credited with 'naturall' power as a perquisite of status ('the
secret working of God, which men call Good Luck') and that those who do
not are liable to find their 'naturall' power slighted or denied. When Dryden
depicts himself 'strugling with Wants, oppress'd with Sickness, curb'd in
my Genius, lyable to be misconstrued in all I write' (1424), 'curb'd in my
Genius' may mean 'when I laboured under such discouragements at my
honest trade of versing' and it may also mean 'denied the true and just return
for my "naturall" power, my "extraordinary strength" of "eloquence",
through the "instrumentall" fiat of men of riches and reputation'. Flattery
of the patron is embedded in the same stratum of speech and expectation as
is the self-justification of the patronized.

In writing as he did of 'naturall' and 'instrumentall' power Hobbes
codified certain perceptions about human nature and conduct. He would
not have claimed credit for initiating them. The brief and fated equipoise, in
Shakespeare's Richard III, of natural and instrumental power is made
manifest in the curt swagger of 'whom I (some three monthes since) |
Stab'd in my angry mood, at Tewkesbury', the phrase indifferently conceding superior self-knowledge and base self-exposure, the preening *otium*
of tyrannical power which will be forced to acknowledge, by the end of the
play, the pageant-like *negotium* of traditional moral law in the procession of
ghosts. There is hierarchy even in this. In Marlowe's *Edward II* the professional hanger-on Spencer says to his fellow practitioner Balduck 'You must
be proud, bold, pleasant, resolute, | And now and then stab, as occasion
serues'. 'Now and then stab' is a servile popinjay version of a real tyrant's
amoral *otium* of 'mood'. The utterance of naked will, as much below the
level of prescriptive and proscriptive terms like 'moral' and 'immoral' as
'resistless genious' is above the sordid brokerage of this world, is one that
haunts the 'just city', 'res publica', poets and philosophers—the 'Qual io fui
vivo, tal son morto' of Capaneus or Richard of Gloucester's 'I am my selfe
alone', with which Dante and Shakespeare dealt so comprehensively and
comprehendingly. The ambivalent power of 'What I was living, that am
I dead' is felt in Pound's 'E. P. Ode Pour L'Election de Son Sepulchre' and
in drafts of the 'Malatesta Cantos'. Pound translates Clytemnestra's words
after the murder of Agamemnon as 'I did it. That's how it is'. We hear this

pitch of voice in Mosca's cry in Canto XXVIII of the *Inferno*: 'Capo ha cosa fatta' ('A thing done makes an end'). In 1917 Pound claimed that the Renaissance enlightenment 'still gleams in the common Italian's "Così son io!" when asked for the cause of his acts'. Six years later he had modified his opinion: 'The Italian "*Così son io*," is a priceless heritage from the renaissance, but it is egocentric and possibly inferior to my grandmother's recognition of the demarcation and rights of personality.' The 'possibly' and 'my grand-mother's' both concede and resist a worldly attitude to quaint old-fashioned scruple and certitude. Even if the energy declaring itself in 'That's how it is' or 'Capo ha cosa fatta' or 'Così son io' or 'Stone Dead hath no Fellow' or '*We have donne our businesse*' or 'stab as occasion serues' is conceived as being an irreducible monad of the assertive rebellious will, the judging imagination still persists in 'reducing' it, that is, 'bringing it into proper order', 'making it conformable or agreeable to a standard'. It is observable in this context that Dryden's lyric and discursive eloquence, in either of the two 'harmonies' of verse and prose can be associated with that observation about Ovid: his capacity to 'show the various movements of a Soul combating betwixt two different Passions' (17: 30). Although it would be rash to attribute the opinions of a speaker in a dialogue simply or naively to the author of that dialogue, these words of Eugenius may be applied to Dryden's own work. It is a characteristic traceable in the critical and polemical prose as well as in the reserved eloquence of 'To the Memory of Mr. Oldham'.

The suggestion that English poetry and prose, in the latter part of the seventeenth century, retained mass, density, gravity, that it did not reduce itself *instanter* to a compliance with those edicts about 'vicious abundance of *Phrase*', 'the ambitious obscurity of expressing more then is perfectly con-ceaved', is one that strikes less oddly on the scholarly ear today than it perhaps once did. Carew's admiring witness of achievement in the exemplary con-frontation of genius with 'our stubborne language', as he phrased it in his elegy on Donne, persists in Davenant's conception of 'Poesy, which (like contracted *Essences* seemes the utmost strength and activity of Nature)'; and even Dryden's patron the Earl of Roscommon, in *An Essay on Translated Verse* (1684), esteems 'The comprehensive *English Energy* ... The weighty *Bullion* of One Sterling Line'. Dryden's acquaintance Richard Swan, a 'notorious pun-ster', wrote, some time in the 1690s, a letter in an elaborately punning style, revelling in its own innocently vicious abundance of phrase, accusing the poet in wordy jest of not being a man of his word (Ls 137, 189). To go beyond such evidence, however, and to suggest that the 'stubborne language', the

'comprehensive *English Energy*', so thrives upon the unavoidable 'Busnesse' of
the world as to become an equal '*daimon*' to that of 'genius' itself, a real
'strength and activity of Nature', is to hazard accusations of lexical mysticism.
It is at such points, nonetheless, that we are bound to recognize the way in
which the formal creative or critical judgement and the inchoate force of
circumstance become awkwardly implicated or stand in irreducible confrontation. 'Meaning' itself either strives to accommodate, or strives to free itself
from an accommodation which it feels as curb and compromise upon the
integrity of utterance. One is reminded that the 'vultum clausum' attributed
by Clarendon to Henry Vane the Younger and the '*viso sciolto*' recommended
by 'an old Roman courtier' to Sir Henry Wotton, and by Wotton to the
young John Milton, although seemingly antithetical, are alternative masks
for venturing into the world of 'Busnesse', where the different shades of
meaning tend to pass into or include each other. They are formal expressions
of the same essential policy, for being as Izaac Walton put it 'as free and open-
hearted, as discretion will warrant me to be with a stranger' or, as Marvell
reportedly put it more bluntly: 'not play[ing] the good-fellow in any man's
company in whose hands he would not trust his life'.

The more gifted the writer the more alert he is to the gifts, the things
given or given up, the *données*, of language itself. Conversely, the otiosity
and vacuity of formal language occur when the writer's energy of judgement is not equal to the force of circumstance, to the strength and activity or
to the resistant inertia of 'our stubborne language'. The writer may be
simply inept or he may fancy himself above the gravitational field of the
negotium; or he may feel under some contractual or other obligation to
descant fancifully upon a suggestion that he knows to be in fact a gross yet
tenuous hyperbole. The fatuous poetry and prose of the late seventeenth
century are often fatuous because of their readiness to oblige. 'To be
admitted your *Menial* is, in effect, a Maintainance for Life: And what may
the good Servant expect when even the bad (such as my self) meet with
Rewards so unproportion'd to any Merit they can pretend by their Service.'
Even as Robert Gould balances his clauses he recognizes that what he is
about is unbalanced, 'unproportion'd'. His poems, indeed, show some
bitterness towards the '*Quality*', 'The Fools of *Title* and *Estate*'. A seemingly
infinite obligingness of language may indicate an onerous burden of obligation, though the obligation may be only that of accommodating oneself to
expectation. The work of Gould's friend John Oldham was immortalized
by Dryden as 'harsh' and 'rugged' (389) but those epithets are themselves

under some constraint, judiciously poising the alternatives of censure and praise. Oldham laboured to achieve decorum and smoothness, succeeding well enough for Ezra Pound, in the *ABC of Reading*, to praise the 'sustained' 'melody' of his elegy on Rochester, an imitation of Moschus' *Epitaphios Bionos*. And Oldham's faults, elsewhere in his work, were as much those of vacuity and otiosity as of roughness or lameness. His praise of 'holy Prodigality' is itself prodigal of fancy, and when he likens his subject to the 'All-great Creator, who | Can only by diffusing greater grow' he is both effusive and diffuse. A line such as 'The boundless Stock can never be exhausted quite' shows all too clearly how bounded and exhausted the invention is. This is language addressing itself to the topic as Gould addresses himself to the Earl of Abingdon; it finds itself situated like the 'Poor' in Dryden's 'Eleanora' (his elegy for Abingdon's wife), who have become accustomed to take her wondrous bounty for granted: 'So sure the Dole, so ready at their call, | They stood prepar'd to see the Manna fall' (586). 'Prepar'd' here means 'in a posture to receive' and it also means complacent in expectation. To be so 'prepar'd' is to be ill prepared, redeless. When 'inspiration', which Davenant fairly calls 'a dangerous word' and which Hobbes likens to the workings of a 'Bagpipe', is taken, as it commonly is, to mean going along with the prevailing windy cant, with whatever currently passes for divine *afflatus*, it becomes indistinguishable from the tamest *bienséance*. 'Poetique Rage' is reduced to a convenient tag rhyming with 'frantick Age', 'guilty Age', and so on. The manna of inspiration is nothing more than an inspired manner.

Dryden himself is by no means free from tags, such as the easily 'shining Share' (927) where Virgil has the 'durum . . . dentem', the 'hard tooth' of the 'blunted share'. 'Eleanora', a commissioned elegy for a woman 'whom he had never seen', endeavours to 'fix' 'Virtue's Image' in imitation of Eleanora's own resolute qualities and to stress 'th'Impressions of her Mind' (591) by the particularly emphatic return upon this rhyme-word ('so large a Mind', 'rare Endowments of the Mind', 'glimpses of her glorious Mind' 591–2). Such routine offerings as 'Look on thy tender Pledges left behind' or 'And shed a beam of Comfort from above' (594) or 'One sigh, did her eternal Bliss assure' (593) are the merest 'bye-writing' of panegyric. However, when Keats employed this term, perhaps by analogy with 'by-talk', he was remarking how, in *King Lear*, Shakespeare can transform the routine, the commonplace, the 'uninspired', into something 'more marvellous than the whole ripped up contents of Pernambuca'. In 'They stood prepar'd to see the Manna fall' Dryden meets their idle expectation that it always will with his knowledge that in due course their servile complacency will be disappointed. Charity has its laudable place, as has laudatory verse; at the same time this language takes the measure of those common vices which habitually tag themselves to uncommon virtue.

Dryden is able to involve, to creative ends, the stubborn linguistic strength and complaisant activity of the English tongue with the wilfulness and ignorance of the English people, the crowd's 'gross instinct, of what pleases or displeases them' (13: 13). 'For, we are fallen into an Age of Illiterate, Censorious, and Detracting people.' So Dryden wrote in the essay prefixed to *The State of Innocence and Fall of Man*, his 'tagged' version of *Paradise Lost*. 'For, we are fallen' carries a sense both of fortuitous occurrence and of guilty consequence: 'it is our chance misfortune to be so circumstanced' or, 'inveterate depravity wills that it shall be so'. Doctrinal theology has here reduced itself to a more accommodating turn of phrase but there is no simple distinction between Hobbesian secularism and Miltonic theology. As might be expected of those whose 'Interests and Tenets did run counter to each other', Hobbes and Milton have created complementary worlds; and insofar as Dryden is working a Hobbesian vein he is to a correlative extent Miltonic. The stratum of deliberation into which, and out of which, he works with his most characteristic energy is one which the author of *Paradise Lost* would have regarded as theologically and ethically dubious: I mean that rich and dangerous vein of proud, resentful, yet stoical consciousness of injured merit which provides a distinctive tincture in the 'Preface' to *All for Love*, the epistle to Sir Godfrey Kneller, numerous theatre prologues and epilogues, and in the 'Postscript' to the translation of *Virgil's Aeneis* ('curb'd in my Genius . . . not dispirited with my Afflictions' 1424). The tone here approaches that which in Milton is the expression of the archetypal rebellious will. It is equally the case that Dryden places a strong emphasis upon the virtue of the 'Legislative style' ('Plain and Natural, and yet Majestick . . . A Man is to be cheated into Passion, but to be reason'd into Truth' 311). The legislative style is Dryden's equivalent to the Seraph Abdiel.

It is therefore all the more worthy of remark that so much of his distinctive energy springs from his openness to 'passion', understood both as the effect of cheating eloquence and as the source of 'noble eagerness' (13: 38):

> How I lov'd
> Witness ye Dayes and Nights, and all your hours,
> That Danc'd away with Down upon your Feet,
> As all your bus'ness were to count my passion.   (13: 49)

The power of these words stems from the fact that they simultaneously excite and appease contradictory forces of emotions, powers which, brought into such contact, ought to be self-stultifying but which, mysteriously, we feel, are not. Antony has a genius for love and a genius for being fated, and his words illuminate the 'secret working of God, which men call Good Luck' in more than one way. They have something of the dolphin-like bounty and largess of genius and something of the arrogance of privileged *otium* that can so make a hyperbole of itself, as though in taking liberties with rhetoric one were actually making oneself free of fate. This speech is the summation of the bitter reproach heaped upon Antony by his own remorse and by the indignation of his devoted followers, accusations of 'desperate sloth' (13: 35) and 'inglorious ease' (13: 33), but it is also crossed with a weft which maintains that Cleopatra's remembrance of 'transcendent passion' (13: 40) is equally true. It is both retrospective and prescient. Gathering up all that can be said by way of recrimination it yet anticipates the Hobbesian apotheosis of the lovers in which culpable lust is transfigured as a lustre appropriate to 'Princes, and men of conspicuous power (anciently called *Heroes*)'. For Dryden, the maker and arbiter of Antony's eloquence, the 'conspicuous power' manifests itself in the magisterial trope 'As all your bus'ness were to count my passion' in which the 'bus'ness of the World' (13: 49), 'the bus'ness of Mankind to part us' (13: 48), has its narrow moral triumph snatched away into the power of its beleaguered adversary. The destructive business of time, attrition, misjudgement, folly, the vacuous, otiose hyperbole of bad Restoration 'heroique', all the 'unhappy circumstances' of life and art, turned at one stroke of defiant judgement into infinite leisure.

The Tartar's Bow and
the Bow of Ulysses

'Tuneful and well measur'd Song', as Milton praised it in his tribute to Henry Lawes's word-setting, is not exclusively a matter of technique. It also involves a recognition and acceptance of one's place in the scheme of things. The musician, spanning words 'with just note and accent', shows his mastery in acknowledging that the poet is master. It is the composer's duty and privilege to 'humor' the English tongue, to 'comply with [its] peculiar nature and exigencies' and perhaps to confer, by so doing, 'a particular character or style'. The distinction between advocating technical compliance and maintaining the civil 'Arts of Complacency and good behaviour' (645) is not always easily drawn; and our literature might be less rich and resonant if things were otherwise. Milton's sonnet pays its own tribute to reciprocity, and not merely in a phrase or two of stately cant ('Thou honour'st Verse, and Verse must lend her wing | To honour thee, the Priest of *Phoebus* Quire'). The poem did not achieve its final form without trial and error and is, even now, not impeccable. Against the exemplary handling of enjambment, 'span | Words', where the phrasing does what it says, reaching across the bar-line to place its 'Words' on the right spot with just the right emphasis, one has to set an infelicity in the matching of lines two and three ('how to span . . . not to scan . . .'). It is not the rhyme itself that produces this effect but the syntax: the little jingle of 'how to . . . not to'. Milton's drafts show him worrying at his phrasing, here and elsewhere in the sonnet. In line three he first wrote 'words with just notes, wch till then usd to scan' and then tried 'when most were wont to scan'. In line eight he changed 'that didst reform thy art, the cheif among' to 'That with smooth aire couldst humor best our tongue'. One senses that Milton, in 1646, is a little troubled by a matter that has continued to vex musical scholarship: the question of how far the claim that Lawes 'first taught' the 'declamatory' *stilo recitativo* to English song-writers is fair to his contemporaries. Lawes himself, in words that closely resemble Milton's, said that it was John Wilson who 'taught . . . our Language, first, to speak in Tone'. Modern scholarship cites the names of Coperario and Lanier, and one is reminded that Ferrabosco had experimented with recitative. But equally good authority holds that Milton's praise is not excessive, that Lawes was the first to practise the art with consistent excellence, and that the sonnet intends no more than this.

Notwithstanding such caveats it seems fair to say that, as he drafted, Milton could scarcely avoid pondering, phrase by phrase, the nature of truthfulness and equity and the possibility that, in a sonnet praising propor- tion, his praise might be disproportionate. The little vacuity of 'how to . . . not to' creeps in as the more perplexedly judicious 'wch till then usd to' and 'when most were wont to' are successively eased out. Milton is also 'humoring' several 'exigencies'; he too is composing a 'smooth aire', yet the smoothness is affected by a perplexity which, even as it is being erased, leaves its mark on the syntax of the *textus receptus*.

It does not seem to me that, in making this emphasis, one is unduly imposing one's own perplexities. Thomas Hobbes stated, in his treatise of *Humane Nature*, that 'there is scarce any word that is not made *equivocal* by divers contextures of speech, or by diversity of pronunciation and gesture' (H 50–1). Milton's sonnet is a 'gesture' that takes as its topos 'diversity of pronunciation' ('Words with just note and accent', 'committing short and long'). Nor is it wholly without equivocation. It is not absolutely invulner- able to Hobbes's charge that '*Ratio* now is but *Oratio*' (H 56). It will be objected that Hobbes, like Bacon, regarded equivocation, all forms of ambiguity in language, as 'intolerable' and worked for their eradication; and, from that, it may be concluded that he and Bacon were at liberty to stand aloof from the 'intolerable wrestle | With words and meanings'. Empirical observation confirms that this is not so. Bacon, in *The Advance- ment of Learning*, argues that 'wordes, as a *Tartars* Bowe, doe shoote backe vppon the vnderstanding of the wisest, and mightily entangle, and peruert the Iudgement'. He is not offering an aloof analysis for, as he says, 'it is not possible to diuorce our selues from these fallacies and false appearances, because they are inseparable from our Nature and Condition of life'. His thesis moves forward in the direction of 'the wisedome of the *Mathemat- icians*' and the 'definitions of our wordes and termes' but his gaze is also retrospective, looking towards Plato's 'fayned supposition . . . of the Caue' ('our spirites are included in the Caues of our owne complexions and Customes'). It may be a 'fayned supposition', but the inseparability of 'fallacies and false appearances' from our progressive endeavours is not treated as a mere '*fiction* of the Minde' (H 24). Bacon may be compromising with an equivocation (Hobbes would say that 'all *metaphors* are by profession *equivocal*', H 50) but that is a different matter. In translating this passage into Latin Bacon found himself engaged upon the clearance of his own meaning. Where he had originally seemed to suggest that the defining of our words precludes confusion of judgement he now inserted 'attamen haec omnia non sufficiunt' and his analogy of the Tartar bowman reads more cogently here than in the original English: 'retro in intellectum (unde profecta sint) retorqueant'.

Meaning, for Hobbes, is implicated with intent. For example, 'it is *necessary* . . . to *trace* and *finde out*, by many Experiences, what men do mean by calling things just and unjust' (H 41). 'What men do mean . . . ' stands here both for the sense in which we are to take men's words and for the sense which they contrive to impose upon their words. When we ask of someone 'What do you mean by it?' we are not implying that a literal translation will suffice. We are objecting to an imposition, to an intent that we suspect we discern; we are letting it be known that we wish to trace and find out the whole '*drift*, and *occasion*, and *contexture* of the speech, as well as the *words* themselves' (H 51). The use of names is 'imposed arbitrarily by men' (H 40) partly through politic deliberation, partly because such im-positions are 'inseparable from our Nature and Condition of life' and because, as Hobbes says, '*Deliberation* is nothing else but . . . alternate *hope* and *fear*' (L 68). Thus, in arguing that we must find out by experience 'what men do mean', he himself compounds with an equivocation, not in order to evade a question but to intensify the sense of a necessary perplexity ('*free from Necessitation* I say, no man can be' L 45).

If what a writer 'means' is what he advocates, or may be supposed to advocate, his 'thesis' or programme, Hobbes's meaning is not unrecogniz-able in that 'collective body of assumptions' which the minor literature of an age makes current. Sir Robert Howard's notion, resolutely challenged by Dryden, that in questions of aesthetic judgement one cannot 'infringe the Liberty of Opinion' or 'censure the satisfaction of others' and that the author's, or spectator's 'taste', that is to say his unregulated fancy and prejudice, is the sole and rightful arbiter, may possibly derive from Hobbes's observation that 'the *Smell* and *Taste* of the *same thing*, are *not* the *same* to *every man*, and therefore are *not* in the thing *smelt* or *tasted*, but in the *men*' (H 17). Howard's complaisant assumption is merely another idol of the market-place. Hobbes wrote that 'by *Spontanity* is meant *inconsiderate action*' (L 74); he also said that a thing may be 'easie and plain . . . but withal false' (L 46).

Hobbes's 'meaning', therefore, comprises an argument, a thesis which is unequivocal, which looks 'prouidently towards the *Future*', and a counter-argument, realized within the texture of his writing, which grasps that the equivocal and the ambiguous are intrinsic to human nature and civic history. One is so impeded by custom, opinion, circumstance, and all other forms of 'tyrannizing' (L 50), by appetite, passion, a density of 'inconsiderate action', 'too *hasty* concluding' (H 2), 'the rash embracing of wrong principles' (L 35), 'hard sayings' (L 64), that 'the *contrary* must needs appear a great Paradox' (H 8). 'Paradox' is itself 'intrinsecal' to Hobbes's work and coexists with a didactic incisiveness which would be glad to see it erased from human discourse. On the one hand 'Colour is not inherent in the Object, but an effect thereof upon us' (H 16); on the other, there are impediments which are 'intrinsecal', 'in the nature' of things (L 70). '*Liberty*', he writes '*is the absence of all the impediments to Action that are not contained in the nature and intrinsecal qualitie of the Agent*' (L 69–70). This return upon the 'intrinsecal' from the non-inherent is one of several epitomes of stylistic method that may be perilously abstracted from the texture of his work. Intrinsic quality of style is the simultaneous recognition of strength and impediment which, as it declares itself triumphantly possessed of such knowledge, suffers the ignominious consequences of that possession. Even the most unequivocal utterance is affected by the circumstantial and contingent matter implicated in our discourse, 'which being derived from the custom and common use of speech, representeth unto us not our own conceptions' (H 51). As with his contemporaries, Hobbes's word both for the continuity or contiguity of things and for the structure and composition of artefacts is 'contexture'. One might, in the seventeenth century, have 'certain fortuitous Concretions and Contextures of Atoms', 'a regular Contexture of continued Policy', and 'The Contexture of sentence with sentence'. When Hobbes writes that 'we are to consider the *drift*, and *occasion*, and *contexture* of the speech, as well as the *words* themselves', it is 'drift' and 'contexture' that tune the sentence. 'Contexture' here is close to 'circumstance' understood as 'the totality of surrounding things'. In the next sentence he adds 'It is therefore a great ability in a man, out of the words, contexture, and other circumstances of Language, to deliver himself from

Equivocation, and to finde out the true meaning of what is said' (H 51). Here the 'words' precede and partly subsume the 'contexture', and the 'circumstances' appear less as 'the totality of surrounding things' than as the 'material adjuncts', the 'things belonging' to language. Extrinsic and intrinsic 'contexture' are related but the nature and extent of that relationship are indeterminate. We may feel that such implications are largely substantiated by our experience, our understanding, but they remain implications, gathered from 'the Contexture of sentence with sentence'. We are uncertain whether the body of a text is a real embodiment or merely the idea of one. Our most effective words, which, Puttenham says, 'make yeelding and flexible' 'the minde of man', encounter in Hobbes a 'necessitie' against which they are of 'no effect' (L 55). Language, even as it takes the measure of things, falls short. Its various formalities, syntax, prosody, etc., are enacted partly within the domain of a paradox: that its limitations and inadequacies are defined by its own cogency and eloquence; but there remain circumstances which baffle all attempts at definition. Poetic measure (metre and cadence), like other adjuncts of 'Oratio', is a manifestation of 'Custom' which 'hath so great a power, that the Minde suggesteth onely the first word; the rest follow *habitually*' (H 56) while, at the same time, it is the power to override, with its ever-renewing capacity for springing and counterpointing, the habitual and the customary.

It would be an absurdity, however, to suggest that English writers required the sanction of Bacon and Hobbes before engaging with these intrinsic perplexities. When Chaucer employs the identical line 'Allone, withouten any compaignye', once, in 'The Knight's Tale', in a plangent threnody, and once, soon afterwards, in 'The Miller's Tale', describing the 'chambre' of 'hende Nicholas', he shows himself not unaware of the necessity for considering 'the *drift*, and *occasion*, and *contexture* of the speech, as well as the *words* themselves'. The measures of Skelton and Wyatt anticipate the perception that 'our discourse... being derived from the custom and common use of speech, representeth unto us not our own conceptions'.

'Measure' in *The Arte of English Poesie* 'is but the quantitie of a verse, either long or short'. In Skelton's *Magnyfycence* 'Measure' is a moral idea ranged against the 'wylde Insolence' of 'Lyberte': 'I ponder by nomber; by Measure all thynge is wrought'. 'Nomber' here signifies order and aggregation in all their forms, but the particular sense of 'conformity, in verse or music, to a certain regular beat or measure' was also current at that time.

Skelton, in *Magnyfycence*, makes his metrical variations, from rime royal to macaronic hexameter or to the so-called tumbling verse, embody and enact his ethical priorities. It is a commonplace to say that the play is deficient in 'character-drawing'. This is to overlook the evidence that in such passages as the soliloquy of Clokyd Colusyon, who employs, because he is a courtly hypocrite, the magisterial Chaucerian rime royal already adopted by Meas-ure and Felycyte, the character is in the measure:

> To passe the tyme and order whyle a man may talke
> Of one thynge and other to occupy the place,
> Then for the season that I here shall walke,
> As good to be occupied as vp and downe to trace
> And do nothynge; how be it, full lytell grace
> There cometh and groweth of my comynge;
> For Clokyd Colusyon is a perylous thynge.

'Measure' here is both the gravity of the form and Clokyd Colusyon's taking its measure with perverse and meditative relish. He takes the measure of his situation physically ('*Hic deambulat*') and metaphysically ('And craftely can I grope how euery man is mynded'). This recital of his own motives and actions is simultaneously an enactment of the ways in which such evil genius is disseminated among mankind. Idle people desire to be entertained; Clokyd Colusyon is entertaining them. *Magnyfycence* is an entertainment, 'A goodly interlude and a merry'. Clokyd Colusyon is rightly estimating his place in the world's business; that is his *métier*; but Skelton is also considering him rightly, according to the measure of righteousness. The rectitude of such verse is manifested in its capacity to measure up to the demands of active vice and to the authority of active virtue; it is a brooding third force in which the magisterial rime royal and the cynical travesty of the magisterial style are balanced but not equated.

Wyatt's 'They fle from me that sometyme did me seke' is at one with, while it is at odds with, the aristocratic Chaucerian idioms, like those in 'The Squire's Tale'. The formalities of Wyatt's poem are reminiscent of the courtly love-complaint of an earlier generation; its intimate procedures are not. '[H]er armes long & small' sounds like Charles d'Orleans; 'meke', 'fortune', 'gentilnes', 'new fangilnes' all have a Chaucerian tincture. But though intensely evocative of older styles of conduct and expectation, 'gentil', 'gentilness', are still part of Wyatt's own speech and have not been artificially resurrected. '[G]ood and gentill fashons', 'gentill wordes and fashon', 'gentill and good answer', are phrases found in his diplomatic correspondence. 'And I have leve to goo of her goodenes' is a barbed variant of such 'good and gentill fashons'. As a diplomat, and an author of careful dispatches, he was well placed to observe and assess occasions of disadvantage, ill-suitedness, and perilous 'variance'; and it is variance with which 'They fle from me' is engaged. The strength of a word like 'gentil' is also its weakness; its weakness is its strength. 'Good and gentill fashons' are powerful enough to be called upon, even by those who have no intention of acting upon the principles which sustain them. They are derided, yet they defy derision:

> It was no dreme I lay brode waking
>> but all is torned thorough my gentilnes
>> into a straunge fasshion of forsaking
>> and I have leve to goo of her goodenes
>> and she also to vse new fangilnes
>> but syns that I so kyndely am serued
> I would fain knowe what she hath deserued.

Chaucer himself precludes our saying that Wyatt's poem takes to the point of parody the irrelevance of 'Chaucerian' courtly values at the Court of Henry VIII or in the various diplomatic milieux of Europe. The inherent contradiction in 'gentilnesse', 'curteisie', is that, while being adjuncts of worldly privilege and spiritual authority, they are susceptible to parody and worse forms of insult, rendering their possessors liable to humiliation and servitude. Chaucer knew this. So, for that matter, did the author of *The Ancrene Riwle*, who instructed his gentle-born anchoresses to offer up as a form of penitential oblation their endurance of 'haughty behaviour at the hands of those who might once have been [their] serfs'. 'Curteisie' may be no more than nervous over-refinement expressing itself in unwitting self-parody. On the other hand some forms of affronted fastidiousness may appear naive and comical only when viewed from a prejudiced standpoint which is itself nothing but a mode, which Chaucer and Wyatt both call 'newfangleness'. But if it is true that Wyatt consolidates Chaucer's findings it is also true that he fragments Chaucer's certitudes. In Arcite's death-speech in 'The Knight's Tale' there is an atonement between sexuality and 'gentilesse'. Wyatt's inventiveness in 'They fle from me' is shown in the way he stresses the divisiveness, the division between them. He has, however, charged his verse with the task of rendering even this accountable. He has embodied the abruptness, astonishment, flat dejection, in the pace and pause of the line: 'But syns that I so kyndely ame serued | I would fain knowe what she hath deserued.' Accountability is rendered through paronomasia.

Paronomasia, according to Henry Peacham in *The Garden of Eloquence*, is 'a figure which declineth into a contrarie by a likelihood of letters, either added, changed, or taken away'. Puttenham writes of 'prosonomasia' whereby words 'do pleasantly encounter and (as it were) mock one another by their much resemblance', as in 'proue' and 'reproue'. Wyatt's 'kyndely' tacitly declines into a contrary as the ingenuous compiler of *Tottel's Miscellany* conceded and confirmed in changing it to 'vnkyndly'. 'Serued' and 'deserued' encounter and mock one another by their much resemblance, but not 'pleasantly'. The seventh chapter of the third book ('Of Ornament') of *The Arte of English Poesie* reveals that its author, perhaps more than some other Elizabethan instructors in eloquence, gave attention to those figures which 'passe the ordinary limits of common vtterance', drawing the mind 'from plainnesse and simplicitie to a certaine doublenesse', but it also reveals that, for him, 'keeping measure' was pre-eminently 'pleasant conueyance', the poet being 'appointed not for a iudge, but rather for a pleader, and that of pleasant & louely causes and nothing perilous, such as be those for the triall of life, limme, or liuelyhood'. Puttenham's chapter is itself a 'figuratiue speach', a mild form of 'merry skoffe', ensuring that, after all, figures which pass the ordinary limits of common utterance do not pass the ordinary limits of proper amusement provided for 'princely dames, yong ladies, gentle-women and courtiers' in Elizabethan England.

One is not arguing, either ingenuously or disingenuously, that a moun-tebank spontaneity of self-expression should usurp the role of studied 'ornament poeticall'. There remains, nonetheless, a proximity between Wyatt's 'kyndely' and Puttenham's 'pleasantly' that is also Shakespeare's 'spacious bredth of [a] diuision'. In the 'Defence' prepared by Wyatt for his trial in 1541 one finds a figure precisely anticipating one of Puttenham's examples of prosonomasia: 'proue and reproue'. Wyatt writes 'I doute not but the reste of there proffes wilbe but reproffes in euerie honeste mans iudgmente'. For Wyatt, in these circumstances, the matter of 'but one smale syllable chaynged' is not a 'pretty' optional embellishment but the nub of his predicament. '[W]hat thynge is that that these mene wolde not wreste for there purpose that wreste suche thynges?' One is not arguing, either, for the status of 'circumstance' as an arbiter or for the moral superiority of some notional 'experience of real life' over the unrealities of bookish rhetoric.

Puttenham himself, faced with certain charges in 1570, poised his defence on the precise interpretation of the word 'goodnesse' and in another work attributed to him, the *Justificacion*, a defence of Elizabeth's policy in 'the Affaire of Mary Queene of Scottes', he shows some casuistical skill in the choice and interpretation of words. The question is not one of quantitative differential in 'real and substantial action and suffering' nor of the supposed marginal status of 'ornament poeticall', 'figures rhethoricall', in the 'practisis' and 'trafiques' of the world. The question is rather one of a qualitative difference in realization. Wyatt, in his 'Defence', masters his fear and focuses his indignation through bookish rhetoric, not in spite of it. One's case for the outstanding merit of 'They fle from me' is based on the recognition that some writers, more than others, realize (understand and establish as contextual fact) that the 'figures' do not run in pleasant and lovely parallel to 'practisis' and 'trafiques' but are inextricably a part of the world's figuring and trafficking, and that this is a circumstance which the 'figures' are bound at once to suffer and to judge. Donne's Verse Letters to Sir Henry Wotton or Nashe's *Pierce Penilesse His Svpplication to the Diuell* are metaphysical in the way that Troilus' speech on the defection of Cressida is metaphysical: in the realization that their conceits, however strained, are less fantastic than the common effects of custom and habit and the everyday 'wrestings' of accident or of deliberate cruelty and malice. Wotton, when he died in 1639, left this 'prudent, pious Sentence' (as his biographer Walton calls it) to be placed on his tombstone: 'DISPUTANDI PRURITUS FIT ECCLE-SIARUM SCABIES . . . THE ITCH OF DISPUTATION WIL PROVE THE SCAB OF THE CHURCH'. There is a place for such 'morall Images, and Examples' and Puttenham's knack, much admired by his modern editors, of demonstrating how 'the "fleering frumpe" is accompanied by "drawing the lippe awry, or shrinking vp the nose"' does not in itself constitute a superior form of observation. It is Nashe who, in 1592, wrests out of rhetoric, common speech, and common observation a style in which the 'fain[ing]' of 'Poets' both judges and is judged by the feigning of those who are not 'poets'. 'Ovt vpon it, how long is Pride a dressing her selfe?' is as clear to the eye as is Puttenham's 'fleering frumpe'; more than that, it enlivens sententiousness with a pretty pun to make an oblique judgement on rhetorical style itself. Nashe is presciently translating Wotton's 'pruritus' and 'scabies' from axiom into activity. His writing closely ruminates upon the world's itch, its unending contumacious prurience, and the recurrent exclamations of his style involve the angry cries of the bewildered people with his own 'iesting' anger that things are so. In such writing we are at least given some ground for suggesting that words, even when they 'bend' or 'twist back' upon the progress of the argument, are not bound to do so destructively, as Bacon's figure of the Tartar bowman would suggest; it is not inevitable that words rebel against all attempts at better distinction, even when rebellion and loss of distinction are the matter of their contemplation.

It could be argued that in saying 'we are at least given some ground for' I concede the weakness of my position. I have never supposed that I was arguing from a position of strength. My concern is with 'words, contexture, and other circumstances of Language', with language, judgement, and circumstance; not only the ways in which judgement is conveyed through language but also the difficulty of clearing the terms of judgement amid the mass of circumstance, the pressures of contingency. 'Cum autem intellectus acutior aut observatio diligentior res melius distinguere velit, verba obstrepunt' ('and where a more acute intellect or a more diligent observation tries to introduce a better distinction, words rebel'). But 'obstrepere' is literally 'to make noise against', 'to shout down'. Against Bacon's exemplum of the Tartar's bow one may set the metaphor of the writer as a player upon an instrument: 'You have got to know exactly where you are going, aurally and physically[,] and then you have got to make exactly the right movement to take you there at the right time'.

> Two Paradises 'twere in one
> To live in Paradise alone.

This begins as paronomasia, according to Peacham's definition: 'Two' / 'to', 'Paradises' / 'Paradise', 'in one' / 'alone'. But the energy of Marvell's figure is in direct opposition to the notion of 'declining into a contrary'; it is more an ascension into the positive. The particular beauty of these lines is their reconciling of the ephemeral, the elusive, with the 'knowing'. The strained metaphysical fancy which supposes that an inclusive exclusiveness is at one with an exclusive inclusiveness is made to sound so simply right, with such a singing felicity, that 'a more diligent observation' and 'a better distinction' appear to have been made, and made against the odds. The words do 'twist back' upon the understanding from which they proceeded but the imagination has already actively reconciled itself to this.

In referring to the 'strained metaphysical fancy' I intend both 'pushed beyond what is natural and reasonable' and 'purified' from grosser elements. The grossness is not merely the bulk, weight, density of contingent circumstance; it is also the palpable awkwardness of method: the negative, threatening paradox at the heart of 'Metaphysical' poetics is that the process of refining may itself be a gross piece of mechanics. 'Cribrate', meaning 'to sift', 'cribration', meaning 'sifting', are not words that have filtered through into common usage. Their meaning is not only that matters can be successfully refined and reduced but also that they obstruct their own claim. It is true that Donne more than once succeeds in turning the obstruction to advantage, as when he evokes the needful but awkward 'dissections, & cribrations, and examinings of Hereticall adventures upon' God's Word, or alerts his auditors to 'this examination, this agitation, this cribration, this pursuit of thy *conscience* to *sift* it, to follow it from the *sinnes* of thy *youth* to thy *present sinnes*', adding 'That's *time spent* like thy *Saviours*'. In a letter of April 1627 to Sir Robert Ker he discusses a sermon which has caused him much trouble. The trouble arose less from any theological perplexity (though the sermon has its grimly controversial moments) than from Donne's being drawn, against his own volition, into a quarrel between the Archbishop of Canterbury and William Laud, at that time Bishop of Bath and Wells; a quarrel in which the king strongly favoured Laud while Donne, on no good evidence, was suspected of supporting the Archbishop. Despite his acute intellect and diligent observation this sermon did cause offence and Donne wrote urgently to request Ker's mediation at Court, ruefully observing 'as Card. *Cusanus* wrote a book *Cribratio Alchorani*, I have cribrated, and re-cribrated, and post-cribrated the Sermon'. Donne's overemphasis of the already obtrusive term, clogging the process in the very effort to sift more finely, reads as a distressed parody of the perplexed circumstance, a travesty of his own anxious scholarship—its powerless exercise of powerful diligence and scruple, confronted by the 'prejudice' and 'displeasure' of the men of power.

If I say that all writers are bound to work with relative proportions of 'hefting' words to 'tuning' words I must immediately add that Hobbes's caveat 'all *metaphors* are by profession *equivocal*' still applies and that the same word may satisfy either attribute at one time or another: it is a matter of the drift and occasion and contexture of the speech. Words, generally, may be taken as hefting words 'such . . . as may serve for the upholding common Conversation and Commerce, about the ordinary Affairs and Conveniencies of civil Life', the approximate meanings, the jargon, that 'Men make a shift with, in the ordinary Occurrences of Life, where they find it necessary to be understood, and therefore they make signs till they are so'. John

Locke's way of putting it, particularly apposite to this matter, is itself more than a mere shifting; it is a judicious weighing of an effect. Men do weigh their words pragmatically, albeit with more 'unsteady and confused Notions' than Locke's, in the furtherance of their 'Conveniencies', and his phrases settle themselves comfortably enough into the medium which they effectively describe and assess. By 'tuning' I mean to suggest something more than the Lockean ability to put words in their place. It has more affinity, as I understand it, with George Herbert's 'being true to [the] businesse'. His exemplary priest 'hath exactly sifted the definitions of all vertues, and vices; especially canvasing those, whose natures are most stealing, and beginnings uncertaine'. Herbert's 'hath exactly sifted' is of a different temper from Donne's 'cribrated, and re-cribrated, and post-cribrated' and is equally distinct from Locke's civil empirical precision. The Parson's eye establishes 'just occasion', mortifies covetousness, gluttony. Donne, in his letter to Ker, expresses mortification of a different kind; it is not Herbert's 'divine vertue' but an unhappy circumstance. He deliberately tunes in to the harshness, makes comically wretched 'business' out of a bad business. In 'Hymne to God, my God, in my sicknesse', on the other hand, when he writes 'Since I am comming to that Holy roome, | Where, with thy Quire of Saints for evermore, | I shall be made thy Musique', he is retuning and reconciling the afflicted man's angry, humiliated cry, in Lamentations, for divine retribution and restitution: 'Behold, their sitting downe, and their rising vp; I *am* their musicke', words which he himself glosses, in his verse-paraphrase 'The Lamentations of Jeremy', 'I am their song, whether they rise or sit'. From 'their musicke', 'their song', to 'thy Musique'; the tone of one who laments his sojourn in the enemy's country transposed to the melody of one who journeys to the celestial city.

The 'tuning' faculty involves tuning out as well as tuning in. The extent to which any writer is, or is not, aware of 'overtones', 'harmonics', in the language, the degree to which it is possible, necessary, or desirable for a reader to 'hear' the harmonics, are matters of nice speculation. Should I, or should I not, for instance, in my own choices of 'hefting', try to tune out all recollection of Leontes' 'violent Hefts' in Act II, scene i, of *The Winter's Tale*? I would agree that a judicious weighing of one's words might find intolerable such a grotesque eruption. On the other hand, an image of violent psychic and physical nausea is not inappropriate to an account of the always exhausting, at times mortifying and ignominious, struggle with language: 'verba obstrepunt'. 'I have cribrated, and re-cribrated, and post-cribrated'. What is this if not a series of violent hefts?

In Donne's Verse Letters to Sir Henry Wotton, in Marvell's parliamentary correspondence, the reciprocating stressfulness of what Hobbes calls 'the custom and common use of speech', at once ours and not ours, is encountered as a sense of persistent attrition. In the Verse Letters the harassment of the enduring images of worth, the moral images and examples, by the perversity and absurdity of 'habituall vice', 'egregious gests' (73–4), is engineered into a rhetoric that succeeds in retorting upon the perversity. It would be unjust to ask as much of Marvell's hastily written letters. 'I returned the civillest words that I could coyne at the present & renderd him your humble thanks for his continuall patronage of you.' So Marvell wrote to the Mayor of Hull, in November 1668, of his meeting with one of the king's generals. 'Coyne' is two-sided though not two-faced. It means, I take it, 'I made a genuine representation of your wishes out of the words that I was expected to utter, that it was expedient to say.' Words are simultaneously true specie and specious. Marvell writes with candour rather than with cynicism of an occasion on which both parties had weighed the business that demands our civillest words. In the lyric dialogues and soliloquies, mostly assumed to date from no later than the early 1650s, Marvell's finesse shows in his tuning in to the possibility of tuning out from this kind of 'business'. In those poems the word 'business' itself, to which he resorts so many times in his letters, does not feature except as the shadowy 'busie Companies of Men', somewhere out there, beyond the happy confines of 'The Garden'. The quick-wittedness needed to coin the civillest words one can contrive is still not the wit of 'Two Paradises 'twere in one | To live in Paradise alone'. There are two sentences in particular, from the letters of this period, which epitomize the attrition of circumstance upon judgement. In October 1666 he writes to the Mayor of Hull 'really busynesse dos so multiply of late that I can scarce snatch time to write to you'. Barely adumbrated in this hasty phrase is that Horatian theme which Marvell, a poet acutely aware of the perils and ecstasies of 'snatching time', had found so appealing. But now there is no time, no *otium* amid the grinding parliamentary *negotium*, for anything other than expedient coining, no place for the gratuitous word-play which is at the same time a considered judgement upon the world of business. We do hear a brief wry reprise of that sense of 'precious Time' some years later, in the letter 'To A Friend in Persia' of August 1671: 'Now, after my usual Method, leaving to others what relates to Busyness, I address myself, which is all I am good for, to be your Gazettier.' The friend was with the East India Company and the letter is replete with business, though the news is rattled through *alla burlesca* ('the *Bishop of Cullen* is attacking the City of *Colen*' etc.).

In seventeenth-century English the word 'business' itself is both hefted and tuned. It may have the function of shorthand: '*Civill* or *Ecclesiasticall* businesse', 'office-business', 'publicke businesse', 'law businesse', 'the businesse of the House'. It may be a form of code. 'The Ballast businesse' and 'the French Merchants businesse' briefly summarize lengthy parliamentary investigations into malpractices. This usage shades imperceptibly, through the matching of circumstance by circumspection, into euphemism. There are matters best conveyed, as Sir Henry Wotton observes, in the Venetian manner, '*sotto parole tacite*', and 'business' is at times as good as a nod or a wink. 'My L: Mordants businesse' alludes to an impeachment; 'the businesse of Chatham' is parliament's enquiry into the national humiliation suffered when the Dutch burnt the English fleet at anchor. There is a further form of euphemism implicated in terror and cruelty. 'You are not ignorant of our Business with you' in Dryden's *Amboyna* means 'I will not speak of the tortures to which we are about to subject you, for they are, as you are aware, unspeakable.' This is perhaps a particular 'aesthetic' application. In the affairs and business of the world the word usefully compounds the direct and oblique. When Pepys writes 'my Tanger=Boates business' it is both a money-making venture and a euphemism for the knowledge of his own bribe-taking, for the uneasy negotiation between conscience and opportunism, greed and fear. 'Business' can mean one's specific function, *métier*, a commitment and obligation born of a particular aptitude—'For the *Moral* (as *Bossu* observes) is the first business of the *Poet*'. This can flick into mockery when a Restoration theatre audience is informed ''tis your business to be couz'ned here'. The word's spectrum has, at one extreme, Clarendon's valediction to Falkland, at the other, Cromwell's words on hearing of the death of the Royalist Charles Cavendish '*We have donne our businesse*'. Clarendon writes of Falkland 'Thus fell, that incomparable younge man . . . havinge so much dispatched the businesse of life, that the oldest rarely attayne to that immense knowledge, and the youngest enter not into the world with more innocence'. 'Businesse' here comprehends the wise management of a great patrimony, the exemplary conduct of public affairs, the acquisition of a moral education through classical reading, and the practice of the established religion. It excludes the possibility that 'business' itself may be a word of curt dispatch, whereas Cromwell's '*businesse*' takes pleasure in the fact that it is so. Clarendon succeeds very well in what he is after: a conflation of the Virgilian '*mortalia*' ('For, this life, is ... a businesse, and a perplext businesse', as Donne said) with Pauline exhortation ('Make you perfect in euery good worke to doe his will').

It may be objected that much of what I have to say ingenuously presumes that poets' apprehensions are what weigh and govern common daily experience and practice. My answer must be that 'Domestique affaires', in the sixteenth and seventeenth centuries, could comprehend such public matters as the day-to-day survival of the common weal, a 'Princely wakefulnesse', as Greville called it, in face of 'the dangerous temptations of power, wealth, and practice'. A further objection would make the point that, whether in Greville's *The Life of the Renowned Sr Philip Sidney* or in Dryden's letters, 'poetry' and 'Poetical' may be used to mean not 'reall', not genuine. Dryden assures the Earl of Chesterfield that the translation of the *Georgics* was dedicated to him 'from the bottom of my heart, and without poetry' (Ls 91). Such caveats were axiomatic. It was equally axiomatic, however, that the axioms themselves, the 'safe precepts of divine, and moral duty', were not, in fact, safe at all but were continually threatened by those agencies which the diplomatic Wotton epitomized as 'buisinesses and other accidents'. That 'all *metaphors* are by profession *equivocal*' can be taken as strengthening the opinion of those who understand 'Poetical' to mean fictitious or as supporting the view that the equivocal is, in any case, that which constitutes the reality of poetry's grasp upon protean matter.

Dryden remarks, in the first sentence of the 'Preface' to *All for Love*, that 'the death of *Anthony* and *Cleopatra*, is a Subject which has been treated by the greatest Wits of our Nation, after *Shakespeare*; and by all so variously, that their example has given me the confidence to try myself in this Bowe of *Ulysses* amongst the Crowd of Sutors; and, withal, to take my own measures, in aiming at the Mark' (13: 10). Dryden is equivocal. If Shakespeare is the one true master of the 'Bowe' then Dryden is one of the 'insolent' suitors, the 'devourers' of the Shakespearian patrimony. But, in Homer, none of the suitors can string the bow; the possession of that requisite strength is what sets Ulysses apart. Homer describes him trying the bow as another might tune a lyre. Dryden presents himself as if with the strung bow in his grasp, stepping forward, 'aiming at the Mark', taking his own 'measures'. With this phrase he comprehends the necessary expertise (like the 'aptnesse' and 'cunnynge' that Ascham's *Toxophilus* dilates upon) and the need to weigh and gauge his own abilities with a view to what he may expect of himself. One is true to one's aim by taking one's true aim in the measures of a craft that is at once intimately one's own and not one's own. It is gratifying to observe that *All for Love* was written *con amore*. He would say of it 'I never writ any thing for my self but *Anthony and Cleopatra*'. In *The Elements of Architecture* Wotton remarks that '*Con Amore*' is one of 'three notable *Phrases*' in use 'among *Italian* Artizans'; he says that it means something is done with 'a *loving diligence*' as distinct from 'a bare and *ordinary diligence*' or even 'a *learned diligence*'. 'They mean not with love to the *Bespeaker* of the *Worke*, but with a love and delight in the *Worke* it selfe.' Dryden and his fellow professionals wrote, for the most part, as 'Artizans' and most of the time, of necessity, with an eye 'to the *Bespeaker* of the *Worke*'. The wonder is that, with Dryden, again and again, the three modes of diligence 'concurre' as Wotton suggests that, 'in an eminent *Authour*', they should. In the 'Preface' to *All for Love* Dryden so handles the prescribed formalities that, within the space of a sentence, he moves from being an upstart competitor to one who feels that he has come home. The equivocation, therefore, does not preclude a proud certainty. It is a cursory formal nod in the direction of 'compleasance', the obligatory accommodation of critical opinion and of the rabble of one's so-called peers. It is also the necessary sense of occasion, the measuring of the moment when genius will step forward and declare itself. It is, too, the recognition that 'business' is not only the arbitrariness and attrition of the 'usuall traffique' but is also the firm grasp of common things. When the tuning and the hefting 'concurre' we know it, it is self-evident. To this extent we may say that Emerson is vindicated in his grand claim: 'Instantly we know whose words are loaded with life, and whose not'.

12

Caveats Enough in
their Own Walks

An apophthegm of Cicero claims that it is an error of judgement for statesmen to think and act as if they were living 'in Platonis πολιτείᾳ' and not 'in Romuli faece'. Bacon, in *The Advancement of Learning,* and Clarendon in his portrayal of Lord Falkland find it apposite to their didactic purposes, as does Pound in his sixty-fifth Canto. Bacon concedes that it may be a fault of 'learned men' to 'contend sometimes too farre, to bring thinges to perfection; and to reduce the corruption of manners, to honestie of precepts, or examples of too great height'. Yet, as he says, 'they haue Caueats ynough in their owne walkes'. Clarendon records that Falkland's friends 'did believe that he was of a temper and composition fitter to lyve in Republica Platonis then in faece Romuli; but this rigidnesse was only exercised towards himselfe, towards his frends infirmityes no man was more indulgent'. Between the self-imposed sanctions of a vulnerable 'rigidnesse' and the magnanimous tolerance for what Clarendon terms 'the common practice of men' the ethical terrain is ill defined but negotiable. One may distinguish broadly between those authors who, while concurring with Bacon's 'Caueats ynough in their owne walkes', nonetheless treat the caveat itself as one of many pertinent commonplaces and those whose concurrence is embodied in the contexture of the style itself.

Between 1597/8 and 1604 Donne addressed four 'Verse Letters' to his lifelong friend Henry Wotton. The last of these, 'To Sir Henry Wotton, at his going Ambassador to Venice' (75–6), is a poem of ten quatrains making what appears to be an easy progress through the familiar formalities, formal familiarities, of Jacobean compliment. It claims and celebrates courteous acquaintance and advances the orthodox proposition that the king himself 'derives' (i.e. imparts, transmits) his 'soule', his 'vertue', to the obedient and grateful subject through the rites, the instruments, of hieratic fealty: in Wotton's case, the letters patent of his brand-new knighthood, and of his recent appointment, the credential letters which he duly presented to the Doge in September 1604. The poem acts as the diligent secretary to its own moral images and examples, referring in order of status, as though at some cabinet of privileged responsibility, to the 'reverend papers' bearing 'Our good and great Kings lov'd hand and fear'd name', the 'learned papers' of the scholar-diplomat himself, the 'loving papers', the farewell letters of friends and well-wishers, and finally the 'honest paper' of Donne's own valedictory, which both serves and subsumes the rest.

The conduct of the public estate, since it invests and has invested in it so much of one's own private state or condition, is, as Donne implies in his poems to Wotton, a 'knottie riddle' (71). Wotton was soon to discover the fitness of similar expressions. His dispatches from Venice, even while they furthered with exemplary devotion the interests of his 'Most Dear and Dread Soveraign' James I (A 384), were threaded with caveat and deploration concerning the politic entanglements of his 'ambassage'. He wrote frequently of 'this intricat buisinesse', 'the bowels of this perplexed buisinesse', 'the principall knott of the whole Businesse', 'one maine knott in the whole businesse'. Donne's 'knottie riddle' says compactly what several of his contemporaries had said, or were about to say, at greater length: it evokes the real labour of 'nosce teipsum'. Such a knot is a perplexing of several strands: lines of axiomatic prescription and proscription, sinews of present policy; there is, as Wotton advised, a proper 'tyme to knit knotts'. Greville's *Life of the Renowned Sr Philip Sidney* upholds the ideal which, he argues, Sidney upheld: the attainment of a difficult 'ballance' between 'ambition' and the 'safe precepts of divine, and moral duty'. Wotton, in 1622, writes of the Prince of Condé and Paolo Sarpi in conference, of the Prince's pressing questions on certain difficult and delicate matters, and of Sarpi's answers 'holding a meane betweene confession and denyall, and yet w[it]hout equiuocation'. It is evident that Sarpi's dexterity in holding a mean between confession and denial is to be distinguished from Sidney's 'ballance' between ambition and precept though it is equally evident that they are comparable instances of '*Policie*', Bacon's 'most immersed' of knowledges. The apparently clear distinction between Wotton's desire 'to reduce ... irregularities ... to constant principles' (C 413) and Bacon's expressed dislike of 'that which taketh the way, to reduce Learning to certaine emptie and barren Generalities' is deceptive. There are reserves of irony in Wotton's

manner when he contemplates the ethics of the Jacobean Court. Bacon, who
reservedly admired Machiavelli's up-to-date grasp of the 'cose del mondo',
resembled the Italian theorist in his command of the ancient maxims and
exempla. He seems no less 'beholden' to Cicero than he is to '*Macciauell &
others that write what men doe and not what they ought to do*'. If 'doe' is the
'common practice of men' then 'ought' is the 'rigidnesse' which was to bring
the gentle Falkland to such distress.

Once the idea of 'rigidnesse' has been accommodated it may become
malleable. One may have an ironic stoicism of style in which a 'seueare' love
of justice and a 'praecise' love of truth, the 'examples of too great height',
seem conscious of their marginal status. In May 1613 Wotton wrote from
London to Sir Edmund Bacon in the country with news of an action before
the Star Chamber. He remarked that the Lord Privy Seal, believing himself
defamed in a private letter, 'hath been moved besides his own nature, and
(as some think also) besides his wisdom, to call these things into publick
discourse; *quae spreta exolescunt*, if ancient grave Sentences do not deceive us'
(C 411). The gist of this, both in the Latin and in Wotton's gloss, is that if
you disdain contumely it will be quickly forgotten; if you react angrily it
will stick. The ancient grave sentences heard wryly exclaiming from the
wings of this worldly theatre appear to be those of Tacitus' *Annals*, iv. 34:
a rehearsing of some words from the apologia of the doomed historian
Cremutius Cordus, impeached by Sejanus' minions and condemned by
Tiberius. This rhetorical set piece argues that despotic attempts to destroy
truth-telling books succeed only in heaping the tyrants with ignominy and
their victims with renown. Seneca wrote *Ad Marciam de consolatione* for the
daughter of Cordus, a piece in which the rigidness of her father's virtue is
grasped by a brief implacable phrase: 'proscribentes in aeternum ipse proscripsit'. There is no room for negotiation in that grammatical lock. Yet in
Wotton's 'if ancient grave Sentences do not deceive us' such austere
rectitude, to which undoubtedly he gave entire assent, receives the tincture
of some quaint and harmless pedantry: 'I take pleasure (speaking to a
Philosopher) to reduce (as near as I can) the irregularities of Court to
constant principles' (C 413). This suggestion that attention to 'constant
principles' is to be equated with private 'pleasure', even with amateurishness
('as near as I can'), may appear a gesture of wry helplessness. It is rather a
steely diffidence, which will not accede to indifference, which accepts the
fact that judgement may be disadvantaged by circumstance, and which trusts
to style to have the last word—literally, one may say, for in his last will and

testament Wotton requested, in a series of sharply civil phrases, 'the solici-
tation of my Arrears' (A c11), indicating that his outstanding debts should be
paid by his executors out of the salary that was still owing to him. His
biographer Izaac Walton catches the nuance in his comment that 'a doubt
still remains, whether it discovered more *holy wit*, or *conscionable policy*' (A c7
verso), though it is to be noted that in the following sentence he feels
obliged to reduce that equivocation to an unambiguously pious sentiment.
Virtually in the same breath he vindicates Wotton's judgement and compromises with the circumstance.

  Bacon wrote that 'the wit and minde of man, if it worke vpon matter,
which is the contemplation of the creatures of God worketh according to
the stuffe, and is limited thereby'. Walton's own art, in *The Compleat Angler*,
constitutes a *via media* between the 'wit' of man and the 'matter', between
axiom and experiment, between virtue-in-contemplation and virtue-in-
action. It is Bacon's 'diligent and exquisite . . . Historie of liuing creatures'
made manifest in the spinning of a pleasant yarn. But experiment here
substantiates Ecclesiastes' axiom that '*Every thing is beautifull in his season*'.
Bacon, in *The Advancement of Learning*, had quoted the words with equal
pleasure. At their finest, as well as at their most fidgety, the Anglican
Royalists manipulate a responsive thread between the wit and mind of
their sentiments and that matter, of which language is a part, contemplated
in its most minute particulars. Clarendon precisely qualifies the 'flowinge
delightfulnesse' of Falkland's language with the 'chast[ness]' of his 'tounge
and eare'. Walton prefers 'doing that natural office' (295) for acts of copu-
lation between the creatures which Aubrey cheerily calls 'bussinesse'. For
Walton the communion of nature with man is itself like that 'convivium
philosophicum' or 'convivium theologicum' to which Clarendon compared the conversation of Falkland.

> *Aldrovandus* says . . . all fish that live in clear and sharp streames, are made by
> nature their mother of such exact shape and pleasant colours, purposely to
> invite us to a joy and contentednesse in feasting with her . . . *Salvian* [takes the
> Umber to be so called] from his swift swimming or gliding out of sight, more
> like a shadow or a Ghoste then a fish. Much more might be said both of the
> smell and taste, but I shal only tell you, that Saint *Ambrose* the glorious Bishop
> of *Millan* (who liv'd when the Church kept Fasting dayes) calls him the *flowre
> fish*, or flowre of fishes.

Walton's finesse is shown here in his keeping a due respect between the
connotations of 'sharp' and 'pleasant'. A natural 'joy and contentednesse' is

sanctified by the pronouncing of Saint Ambrose's name; our appetite for the
'feast' is both chastened and whetted by the salutary proximity of the 'fast'.
An admirer of Herbert's 'Sweet day, so cool, so calm, so bright', Walton
writes as if he takes it for a paradigm. That poem's generous and obsequious
compliance is introduced by Piscator's words to his scholar Viator ('nay and
the earth smels as sweetly too') and, the song-recital completed, Viator
speaks in the aural afterglow of Herbert's words ('I thank you, good
Master . . . for the sweet enjoyment of the pleasant day'; 111–12).

When this book first appeared, however, it was far from being a pleasant
day for Royalist Anglicans. That condition of felicity to which both Walton
and Clarendon appeal is retrospective and pre-emptive. Clarendon is a
special pleader and Walton's angling is at times the *via media* between
ingenuousness and the disingenuous. That which Walton successfully re-
trieves in passages of *The Compleat Angler* and the *Lives* is the Jacobean and
Caroline Anglican comeliness. That spirit, itself at odds with the frequent
dereliction of ecclesiastical duties and fabrics, is epitomized by George
Wither's 'Song XIII' ('Oh my *Loue*, how comely now') of *The Hymnes
and Songs of the Church*, 'plainely and briefly express[ing] in *Lyrick-verse*' the
exuberant equivocal metaphors of The Song of Solomon, which Orlando
Gibbons provided with 'Musicke agreeable to the matter'. 'Comeliness' is a
quality pre-eminently celebrated in Donne's tribute to the memory of
Magdalen Herbert, Lady Danvers, George Herbert's mother: 'To this
consideration of her *person* then, belongs this, that *God* gave her such a
comelinesse, as, though shee were not *proud* of it, yet she was so content with
it, as not to goe about to mend it, by any *Art* . . . Her *rule* was *mediocrity*'. Its
pervasiveness is traceable in Wotton's favouring 'apt *Coherence*, without
distraction, without *confusion*', an architecture that keeps 'a due *Respect*
between the *Inhabitant* and the *Habitation*' (A 259, 304), in Clarendon's
praise of Falkland's 'generous and obsequious complyance with all good
men', together with Walton's love of 'choice Song, and sweetly sung' (90),
of the 'good, plain, unperplext Catechism, that is printed with the old
Service Book' (76), and of what he calls 'the most honest, ingenious,
harmless Art of Angling' (69). The tactical paradox self-evidently turns on
the notion of 'art', on the attainment of a skilled artlessness which, while not
'contemptible to men of best vnderstandings', is ideally 'what the Common
apprehension can best admit'. Wither is at pains to stress not only that he
and Gibbons have eschewed 'the curious Fancies of the Time' but also that
to have kept to the 'curious' mode would have been the easier way.

Walton's own 'ingenious' art, like the word itself in seventeenth-century English, is not always what it may seem.

The Life of Sir Henry Wotton appeared in 1651 as the preface to the first edition of *Reliquiae Wottonianae*. *The Compleat Angler* was published two years later. The exemplary figure to whom tribute is offered in both books is the man who has fought his way through defeats and pyrrhic victories to achieve, at last, a felicitous mediocrity between contemplation and action, conscience and policy; a felicity for which the art of angling provides at once the mystical ideal and the practical exercise. It is as if Walton, in tuning and tempering his own style, has chosen to identify with the persona of Wotton's late, retired meditations. In 1651 he depicts Wotton daily praising God for a 'particular *Mercy*' (A c5 verso); in 1654 the record is more precise and more expansive; it is the 'particular mercy, of an exemption from busines' (B 60). *The Compleat Angler* is wholly in sympathy with this mood of 'exemption'. It pleases Walton to appear as a stubbornly conservative poetry-lover. 'Old fashioned Poetry, but choicely good' he observes of songs by the once brilliantly threatening libertine 'atheists' Marlowe and Ralegh (89). Donne, the subject of one of Walton's *Lives*, appears in *The Compleat Angler* merely as the author of that pert parody 'The Baite', cited to show that 'hee could make soft and smooth Verses, when he thought them fit and worth his labour' (137–8). In the first and second editions Walton claims that Marlowe's and Ralegh's verse was 'much better then that now in fashion in this Critical age' (89). In the third edition of 1661 this becomes 'much better then the strong lines that are now in fashion in this criticall age'. But 'strong lines', a Jacobean 'metaphysical' predilection persisting in the 'strong Expressions' of Cleveland and his imitators, were even less in favour in 1661 than they had been in 1653 or 1655. Old-fashioned Walton is not so stubborn as to be out of step with shifting prejudice, a new strength of opinion which dismisses 'strong lines' as 'no better then Riddles' and deplores all ventures into 'palpable darknesse' and 'ambitious obscurity'.

There are, nonetheless, intimations in *The Compleat Angler* that Walton is not unaware that his 'ingenious Art' lets down a thread from the bright day into a 'palpable darkness' 'where the water is deep, and runs quietly' (146). Wotton certainly thought of diplomacy as angling. 'At this the Fish did not bite' he noted, of some rejected political feeler. Among the authors of 'Commendatory Verses' added to the second edition of Walton's book were those who pondered the reciprocal connection: 'Vagos honesta fraude pisces decipis' (432). To practise on 'these creatures' the arts of ensnarement is an innocent form of policy: 'Fish from your arts do rescue men' (429). When you have spliced the live frog on your line, Piscator advises, as though floating one of Machiavelli's maxims, 'use him as though you loved him... that he may live longer' (126). It is as if Walton's awareness of the duplicitous world is itself divided, partly into the practical manage-ment of his line, partly into the security of well-tried commonplace: 'you will find angling to be like the vertue of Humility, which has a calmness of spirit, and a world of other blessings attending upon it' (205–6). It is reminiscent of Greville's 'reciprocall Paradise of mutuall humane duties' or Wotton's, or Donne's, tributes to 'mediocrity' and 'due Respect'. There is, however, another kind of middle way which Walton is less inclined to admit into the contemplation of English poetry or the advocacy of English virtue: the 'betwixt' of constraint, enforcement, or perplexity, heard in Lear's 'To come betwixt our sentence and our power', or the 'Epitaph on the Earl of Strafford' ('Huddled up 'twixt Fit and Just... 'Twixt Treason and Convenience'), in Marvell's 'But Fate does Iron wedges drive, | And always crouds it self betwixt', and in Eugenius' opinion that Ovid excelled in showing 'the various movements of a Soul combating betwixt two different Passions'. This is a region into which Walton dips, from time to time, with equivocal metaphors but refrains from taking up into the domain of 'reason... worthy the consideration of a wise man' (82).

In a letter from Venice to a friend in England Wotton wrote 'In the mean while till his Majestie shall resolve me again into mine own plaine and simple elements, I have abroad done my poor endeavour according to these occasions which God hath opened' (A 406). The way of life of the later Wotton is that of one who has happily returned upon his own prescience, who has had the resolution to be resolved into 'plaine and simple elements', finding his happiness in the dissolution of worldly prom-ises and hopes. It is this spirit that Walton, in *The Life of Sir Henry Wotton* and *The Compleat Angler*, offers to his readers as the essence of the moral life. In Wotton's testament, as in his recorded *bons mots*, eloquence and readiness of conceit, previously whetted on dangerous circumstance, have been largely exempted from such business, either by Walton's tact in associating 'holy' and 'conscionable' with 'wit' and 'policy' or by their own withdrawal into a self-sustaining reflective mannerism: 'Nor did he forget his innate pleasure of *Angling*; which he would usually call, his idle time not idly spent' (A c6).

Walton enhances the felicities of exempted wit by demonstrating what it has been exempted from: for instance, that 'accident' at the outset of

Wotton's diplomatic career when his wit placed him in jeopardy and 'much clouded' his prospects of royal favour; that 'pleasant definition' '*Legatus est vir bonus peregrè missus ad mentiendum Reipublicae causa*' which he 'could have been content should have been thus Englished. *An Embassadour is an honest man sent to lie abroad for the good of his Countrey*'. However, 'the word for *lie* (being the hinge upon which the Conceit was to turn) was not so express'd in Latin as would admit (in the hands of an enemy especially) so fair a Construction as Sir *Henry* thought in *English*' (A cɪ verso). Wotton's and Walton's discovery of an inoperative 'hinge' anticipates Pound's remark that '*logopoeia*' is a 'tricky and undependable mode' which 'does not translate' and it is not out of sympathy with Bacon's caveat about 'delicacies and affectations', vanity of style, the ambition to make things seem more ingenious than they really are. In *The Life of Wotton*, as in *The Compleat Angler*, Walton is reluctant to appear over-ingenious or to 'break the rules of Civility' (183) or of 'discretion' (63). Familiar as he is with the conventional workings of the line of wit ('I have made a recreation, of a recreation' 59), there are a number of semantic hazards and opportunities with which he does not engage, a particular box of tricks which he itemizes but does not take up. Although, in 1661, he dismisses the 'strong lines' of the suspect Metaphysicals, he continues to urge the value of strong lines to his own ingenious-ingenuous Art: 'And you must Fish for him with a strong Line', 'take a strong small hook tied to a strong line' (318). He is either not aware of, or not interested in, the ironic possibilities of the collocation. Herbert's 'box where sweets compacted lie' means much to him but the suggestiveness of another box is left where he found it, with Wotton's holy wit or conscionable policy: that '*Chest, or* Cabinet *of Instruments and Engines of all kinds of uses*' bequeathed by Wotton to a close friend, 'in the lower box whereof, are some fit to be bequeathed to none but so entire an honest man as he is'. According to Walton's marginal note: 'In it were *Italian* locks, pick-locks, screws to force open doors; and things of worth and rarity, that he had gathered in his forrain Travell' (A c10 verso). Even 'holy Mr *Herbert*' (111), who was not shy of matching the strings of his lute to the 'stretched sinews' of his crucified Lord, would have sensed something ponderable there. For Walton, 'the very sinews of vertue' are not strong lines or the lute's 'struggle' for its 'part' with all its 'art'; they are, as he says, 'good company and good discourse' (214). That safe platitude marks the extent of the 'exemption' which he permits himself and those on whose behalf he writes.

In Donne's four verse letters to Wotton one finds, even more than 'crabbed and ambiguous syntax' and the stretched sinews of conceit, a recognition of the simple rightness of things of virtue, which nonetheless has to be grasped through 'incongruity' (74), by way of the 'crooked' (74), the 'adverse' (71), the 'extremes' (71). In the third letter, 'H. W. in Hiber[nia] Belligeranti' (74–5), Donne engineers a conceit out of the curve-necked alchemical vessels, the 'crooked lymbecks', to argue that the morally crooked world may be made to retort upon itself, may be the means of the soul's self-purification. In the second letter he names the 'seely honesty' and 'neat integritie' of those who, 'in this worlds warfare', are doomed as 'Indians 'gainst Spanish hosts' (73). The epithets both mock and commiserate with the ill-fated petitioners, comprehending their ingenuousness and the world's ingenuities. Donne perceives that the medium of language must itself be conceived as a 'crooked lymbeck'. To claim that his particular poetic virtue leaves not a hair's-breadth between moral principle and poetic practice is a half-truth unless one adds that his practice is to find fit expression for the unfittedness of 'Countries, Courts, Towns' (71) to lives of rectitude. He writes, in the first of the set, that we are unavoidably stained by the things 'wee must touch' (71); in the last he adds 'Wee must for others vices care' (76). What is 'care'? To care is 'to take thought for' and 'to know sorrow for' and 'to be of service to'. Are we to serve the vices of others, or to suffer pain for them, or to be wounded by the knowledge of our servitude?

In 'To Sir Henry Wotton, at his going Ambassador to Venice' the celebration of a plain virtue seems a plain audacity:

> But though she [Fortune] part us, to heare my oft prayers
>   For your increase, God is as neere me here;
> And to send you what I shall begge, his staires
>   In length and ease are alike every where.   (76)

Such audacity is to be distinguished from the pleasant effrontery of Wotton's unlucky *jeu d'esprit*. 'God is as neere me here' strikes the note of that direct steadfastness which we are to believe the author found in his departing friend. Yet simple power has not been simply achieved. To reach this point Donne has had to take the measure of a political jargon ('derives', 'command', 'admit', 'audience', 'your honour', 'businesse', 'Courts and Warres', 'Spies' (vb.), 'staires') as well as of his own wounded ambition. As Walton observed, years later, when he inserted this poem into the second (1654) edition of *Reliquiae Wottonianae*, 'his dear friend Dr *Donne*, (then a private Gentleman) was not one of that number that did personally accompany him in this voyage' (B 36). To compare and contrast Walton's brisk parenthetical tact with Donne's scarcely tactful parentheses—'For mee (if there be such a thing as I) | Fortune (if there be such a thing as shee)'—is to remark how the individual poetic voice can, and must, realize its own power amid, and indeed out of, that worldly business which makes certain desires and ambitions unrealizable. Donne addresses Wotton, about to embark on the further hazards of the world, as a man who has already creditably encountered a number of the world's hazards '(Schooles and Courts and Warres o'rpast)', ''Tis therefore well your spirits are now plac'd | In their last Furnace, in activity'. Compare and contrast Wotton's own 'it is now too late to put me in a new Furnace' (A 392). The 'furnace' of alchemical 'activity' which is also the 'furnace of aduersitie' in Ecclesiasticus (chapter 2, verse 5) where 'acceptable menne' show their worth like gold, will further purify qualities in Wotton that are already well tried and that, in turn, will prove the metal of those with whom he comes in contact. It is what Davenant will later call 'the painfull activenesse of Vertue'. To claim that what is to be purified is already sufficiently pure through the exercise of learned discipline ('From which rich treasury you may command | Fit matter whether you will write, or doe') is to risk labouring the matter to the point where labour becomes otiosity. In the 'activity' of the poem, however, we are convinced that the nature of the moral life is an integrated process and that such retrospection is no less active than is Wotton's imminent diplomatic itinerary:

> To sweare much love, not to be chang'd before
>   Honour alone will to your fortune fit;
> Nor shall I then honour your fortune, more
>   Then I have done your honour wanting it.   (76)

Although Donne's poem presents his friend as a man whose integrity fully justifies the tribute, the strenuous play of such argument is something from which Wotton's own style gently unperplexes itself, as in the letter from Venice some six years later. 'In the mean while till his Majestie shall resolve me again into mine own plaine and simple elements' makes a diplomatic gesture out of the old scholastic physics that Marlowe's Faustus, in his last agony, so frantically clawed at; and contrives to imply that the 'plain and simple' are fated to appear pedantic and outmoded in a world devoted to other matters. Such words reflect the style of guarded amateurism which astute professionals, wishing to appear harmless, find desirable to cultivate in certain circumstances. It is a form of self-containment under duress. While Wotton in his own practice of this ingeniously ingenuous art is superior to his later belletristic admirers who seem unable to take seriously the relation of judgement to circumstance, he is nonetheless, in his elaborate self-exemptions, his apparently 'plain and simple' gestures, particularly vulnerable to their naive or insouciant patronage. The Rt Hon. H. H. Asquith, in his presidential address to the English Association in 1919, offers himself as a 'somewhat threadbare amateur' yet pronounces magisterially on what he calls 'the sovereign quality of Style'. 'Style', which is 'incommunicable, almost indefinable, never mistakable', is epitomized for Asquith by Wotton's 'incomparable lines "On his Mistress, the Queen of Bohemia"'. Logan Pearsall Smith, in 1907, observes of the same poem:

> written by an ambassador in an idle moment at Court, to a princess in whose service he was about to start on an impossible mission, [this] ... bit of verse ... takes its place among the most lovely of English lyrics ... Neither Queen nor ambassador probably gave, amid the cares of state, a second thought to the little poem. Yet, such is the magic of art, these verses have done more than anything else, perhaps, to make both of them remembered.

'Such is the magic of art', 'among the most lovely of English lyrics', embody two contradictory ideals which the patron finds equally appealing and would be pleased to reconcile to his personal satisfaction. The first is that poetry is essentially non-negotiable, it issues from 'idle moments' parenthetically enjoyed 'amid the cares of state' and to them it returns. It speaks from and to the '*otium*' not the '*negotium*'. The second is that, when all the worldly damage has been done, when cynicism and opportunism have had free reign, the 'magic' will be rediscovered wonderfully undiminished, parenthetically preserved, as though in some trust-fund of privileged continuity, 'incommunicable, almost indefinable, never mistakable'. 'Such is the magic of art', 'among the most lovely of English lyrics', presume, through otiosity, to confer a mystical status and authority on an art which is, through the agency of such cant, retained on the margins of the 'ordinary Affairs and Conveniences of civil Life'.

It is necessary, and necessarily chastening, to have to return upon the undeniable fact that neither Wotton nor his biographer Walton shows himself over-concerned with questions of poetic authority or status. Wotton affects to regard poetry either as a servant of the 'wanton cries' of 'Youth' or as ineffectual 'Plaints' barely audible above the real cries of loss:

> But is He gon? and live I Ryming here,
> As if some Muse would listen to my Lay.   (A 528)

He writes to Sir Edmund Bacon that 'Surprizal' by political 'businesses' 'hath disturbed my Muses so' (C414) and even *The Elements of Architecture* is called 'these vacant Observations' (A 297). This show of diffidence was required of a gentleman; but in Wotton's case the mannerism has been chosen with some forethought. 'On his Mistris, the Queen of Bohemia', written in 1619 or 1620 and suggested by some phrases of Petrarch, catches a reflection from the world of Wotton's 'forraign imployments in the service of this Nation', in particular, from 'the *Bohemian* businesse', 'the *Bohemian* Motions' (A 367–8), which so marred the happiness and fortune of his beloved Elizabeth, daughter of James I and wife to the Elector Palatine. It does not, however, reflect back upon those 'imployments', that 'businesse', those 'Motions', but upon something else:

> You meaner *Beauties* of the *Night* . . .
> You *Common people* of the *Skies*;
>   What are you when the *Moon* shall rise?

The rhetorical question is a defiant affirmation, in tune with his customary style of address to her: '*Most Resplendent Queen, even in the Darknesse of Fortune*' (A 494), '*Of cleer and resplendent vertues through the clouds of her Fortune*' (A c10), 'and even by her obscurity the more resplendent' (A 156). The poem is therefore a cameo, a miniature, of an apotheosis: his exaltation of that 'Image of [her] excellent Vertues' which, as he confessed to her, he had long since taken 'into [his] heart' (A 494). This form of exaltation is itself an exemption. When Milton addresses Henry Lawes— 'Thy worth and skill exempts thee from the throng'—that worth, that skill, are not an incommunicable '*Eclypse* and *Glory*'. Wotton's lyric adoration is held reserved from the matter that surrounds it, the harsh circumstances of 'the *Bohemian* businesse', as he clearly believed the subject of his address was to be held inviolably aloof from the sordid and bitter intrigues that had plunged her into the '*Darknesse of Fortune*'. In being so preferred above the '*Common people* of the *Skies*' the object of adoration is also raised above the common practice of men and above the routine idioms of Wotton's own diplomatic correspondence ('the businesse of *Bohemia*', A 372).

Shortly after completing this poem Wotton was engaged, as James's ambassador extraordinary to Vienna, in the hopeless task of attempting to reconcile the Elector Palatine to the Emperor Ferdinand. At the conclusion of the negotiations the emperor presented him with a 'Jewell of Diamonds of more worth then a thousand pounds'. Though Wotton received it 'with all tearms of honour' (which in subsequent revisions became 'all Circumstances and Terms of Honour') he nonetheless gave it away the next morning, declaring 'an indisposition to be the better for any gift that came from an enemy to his Royall Mistress; for so the Queen of *Bohemia* was pleas'd he should call her'. In so turning an honour received into a rebuke delivered Wotton was perhaps guided by the diplomatic practice of the time, but he also drew upon those qualities which he praised exemplary statesmen for possessing and which he himself possessed in good measure: 'great dexteritie in the conduct of affayres a cleere and extemporal iudgment much eloquence, and reddinesse of conceyte'. In 'On His Mistris, the Queen of Bohemia' it is as if the poet has elected to forgo the 'great dexterity', the 'clear and extemporal judgement', the active 'eloquence and readiness of conceit' appropriate to the *negotium*, the 'Motions', while retaining 'all outward Circumstances and Terms of Honour' in the beautifully set but conventional imagery of exaltation. The trope from which it derives is typified by the 'rich Iewel in an Æthiops eare: | Beauty too rich for vse, for earth too deare' of *Romeo and Juliet*. Wotton's poem is the equivalent of the 'Jewell of Diamonds of more worth then a thousand pounds' if that jewel had been simply retained and displayed, if it had not been put to 'use', in an instance of 'clear and extemporal judgement', made the 'hinge' upon which an effective diplomatic 'conceit' was to 'turn'.

Wotton, who knew what it was to suffer the forgetfulness and withdrawal of those in high places, emulates the art of courtly, masque-like self-withdrawal in the self-referential rhetorical questions of the poem: 'Tell me, if *she* were not design'd | Th' *Eclypse* and *Glory* of her kind?', questions to which there is no effectual answer. Assent would be otiose, dissent *lèse-majesté*. It is a lyricism contrasting sharply with the unlyrical tone of the verse letters addressed to him by John Donne. In these the language is awkwardly self-alerting to the nature of moral and linguistic circumstance, where the 'state' of the individual touches 'points of conuenience, and accommodating for the present' which, says Bacon, 'the Italians call *Ragioni di stato*'; in Machiavelli's terms, 'l'ordine delle cose', 'le cose del mondo', 'i tempi e le cose'. It is from such 'affayres of the world' that Wotton's lyricism, both by personal choice and by proxy, is exempted. 'To exempt' is etymologically 'to take out' and, in *The Compleat Angler*, he is indeed taken out and set down 'quietly in a Summers evening on a bank a fishing' (76). Walton here repeats some of Wotton's verse 'because it glides as soft and sweetly from his pen, as that River does now by which it was then made' (ibid.). It is, as we have observed, a characteristic of Walton's own style to glide softly and sweetly away from the proximity of too curious confrontations: 'I might say more of this, but it might be thought curiosity or worse' (124). 'A peece of meritoriouse curiositie' is Wotton's bland allusion to his own work in intercepting and deciphering the correspondence of Jesuits and other disaffected Catholics. 'Honest industrie' is another smoothly unhappy term for the practice ('I call that honest which tendeth to the discouerie of such as are not so by what meanes soeuer while I am upon the present occupation'). This sentence is enough to refute Logan Pearsall Smith's claim that Wotton's diplomatic correspondence reveals 'how wholeheartedly, in becoming a diplomatist, he had adopted the morality of that profession'. A 'whole-hearted' man would not need to gloss 'honest' so wryly. He is reported as observing, in his last days, *'though I have been and am a man compass'd about with humane frailties, Almighty God hath by his grace prevented me from making shipwrack of faith and a good Conscience'* (C e4). Such sentiments run parallel to poetic commonplace as to 'the safe precepts of divine and moral duty'. But Wotton, who so equivocated with the word 'honest', would know that language is more than a discreet courier between *de facto* circumstance and *de jure* commitments. As much as a man himself, a man's language is 'enter'd into very intrinsecal Familiarity' with 'dangerous matter'.

Among Plutarch's *Moralia* there is an essay of which Henry Vaughan published a translation, in 1651, with the title *Of the Benefit Wee May Get by Our Enemies*. We benefit, according to Plutarch, from being reviled and traduced by those who hate us, for by such harsh means one comes to know oneself. 'Where our wellwishers will give us no Councell, wee must make use of our Enemies words, and by a discreet application advantage our selves.' Equally, we are to guard against that 'vitious unfolding of our selves, extenuated with an Apologie of *a word escaped from me*, or, *I slipt a word unawares*' which 'never happens but to lavish, irresolute persons who by reason of their infirmitie of judgment, or loose Custome of life, stick alwaies in the same errours'. Walton recounts Wotton's misfortune as if it were an addendum to Plutarch's essay, emphasizing the readiness with which 'the hands of an Enemy' will distort one's fair constructions. The witticism, we are told, 'slept quietly . . . almost *eight years*' until 'by accident' it fell into the hands of a 'Romanist', a controversialist who used it in polemic against King James and the English Church (A c2). The *Life* further records that Wotton

eventually righted himself with his royal master by an apology 'so ingenuous, so cleer, so choicely eloquent' that the king declared him to have
'commuted sufficiently for a greater offence' (A c2). Such whimsical largess
is one of the innumerable perquisites of real power. Wotton writes as one
who knows, by experience, the savage indifference that cohabits with
occasional magnanimity and who is attuned, by faith and learning, to the
'ancient grave sentences' that do not deceive us. In *The Elements of Architecture*, acknowledging Pliny the Elder's discourse on Greek and Roman
statuary, he writes 'And true it is indeed, that the *Marble Monuments &
Memories* of wel deserving Men, wherewith the very high ways were *strewed*
on each side, was not a bare and transitory Entertainment of the *Eye*, or only
a gentle deception of *Time* to the *Traveller.* But had also a secret and strong
Influence, even into the advancement of the *Monarchy*, by continuall representation of vertuous Examples; so as in that point, ART became a piece of
State' (A 292–3). The tone here is smoother than the circumstances which it
accommodates. 'Continual' implies unbroken succession, a civic consensus
stretching from republican times well into the period of the Caesars ('even
into the advancement of the *Monarchy*'). But Wotton, who had alluded
to that passage in Tacitus' *Annals* where Cremutius Cordus accuses his
accusers, would know that in the same speech Cordus pointedly refers to
the venerated statues of the dead Brutus and Cassius 'quas ne victor quidem
abolevit'. Various passages in Tacitus and others suggest that Augustus, and
later Trajan, showed a politic limited tolerance of such veneration, which
was, for the most part, exercised in discreet privacy. The careful Latin
distinctions between public proscription and private exemption are elided,
in Wotton's historical synopsis, to a 'secret' influence exerted in public
places. Those Romans who retained republican sentiments 'even into the
advancement of the *Monarchy*' kept a sense of 'vertue' different from that
currently in vogue, and dismissed Augustan modes of conduct as 'adulatio'
and 'avaritia'. What, then, is Wotton's 'continuall representation of vertuous Examples'? And how does he envisage art as 'a piece of State'? In its
most apparent sense it is to be seen as an ancillary of civic didacticism, a
piece of the consensus; but when Cremutius Cordus, facing his unjust
judges, honours the memory of Brutus and Cassius by speaking of their
revered effigies his speech, like those statues, is a piece of state in a different
sense. It is a piece of unassimilated matter lodged in the body politic and
Wotton, in 1613, lodges a fragment of it in his own observation on current
flagitia. His particular quality is to have annexed, for 'vertuous examples',

a style which the *Annals* associate with the enigmatic pronouncements of a tyrant. Like Tiberius he uses 'verba . . . pauca et sensu permodesto', though to the end of undercutting and outwitting 'Tiberius'. It is in more than one sense, however, a modest achievement and Hobbes's recommendation that we should take 'the *drift*, and *occasion*, and *contexture*' (H 51) of a speech seems particularly apposite. Wotton turns 'drift' into a form of stylistic exemption and there is a limit to what can be done with 'gentle deception'. Ben Jonson, who, in Act III of *Sejanus*, closely paraphrases Cordus' speech from the *Annals*, is full and direct where Wotton is laconic and oblique. On the other hand, drama, with its formal denouement, is a medium especially well suited to dealing with the just and unjust types of humanity represented in the writings of Tacitus and Plutarch, that 'vitious unfolding of our selves' which Jacobean and Restoration dramatists excelled in depicting. A word 'slipt . . . unawares' in a letter, a dispatch, or a treatise, or in the course of an evening's entertainment among those in whose hands one could not trust one's life, is a different matter from the theatrical presentation of 'lavish, irresolute persons' or 'words with words reueng'd'.

Literary handbooks encourage the assumption that Donne's poetry was not considered 'metaphysical' until Dryden, in 1692, used the phrase 'affects the Metaphysicks' (604) to conjure up an old-fashioned, quaintly intricate mode of writing. This assumption ignores the fact that, in the *Essayes in Divinity*, Donne had coined the term 'meta-theology' to denote 'a profounder theology than that recognized by divines'. The analogy here is palpable; self-evidently affecting the metaphysics, conscious that it is 'misinterpretable; since to some palates it may taste of Ostentation'. The knotty riddling of Donne's verse and prose moves from, and through, rhetorical bravado and 'alarums' (he himself enters that caveat) to an engagement with meta-poetics, a profounder poetry than that recognized by conventional instructors in rhetoric and conduct. There is a letter of *c.*1600, attributed to him, which is taken as referring to his early 'Paradoxes': 'they are but swaggerers: quiet enough if you resist them'. It is no simple matter to describe and celebrate honour, constancy, or even a mere life-and-death seriousness of mind, in figures notoriously associated with the impertinent, the irreverent, the parodic ('When thou hast done, thou hast not done'). There is nonetheless an irreducible paradox or oxymoron in the mundane constitution, and the literary paradox is a formal submission that 'things' are so: 'they have beene written in an age when any thing is strong enough to overthrow [truth]'. Such a discovery had itself been anticipated by Wyatt

('But what thynge is that that these mene wolde not wreste for there purpose that wreste suche thynges') and by Nashe ('There is nothing that if a man list he may not wrest or peruert'). Wyatt's 'what thynge', Nashe's 'nothing', Donne's 'any thing', are phrases of the most menial hefting recognized for what they are: tokens and agents of protean callousness. Tyrannical cunning and tyrannized intelligence are accommodated equally, though without equity, in such terms. 'Meta-poetry', as I labour to define it, challenges Bacon's 'Policie' as the most 'immersed' of crafts or 'knowledges' while resisting the cynical fatalism that may accompany the 'logical' liberation of the mind. Meta-poetry is immersed in the knowledge that it is so immersed. To be thus immersed in knowledge is not the same as to be steeped in axiomatic wisdom and experience of the world, as Donne recognizes that Wotton is ('you may command | Fit matter whether you will write, or doe' (75)). To infold, to perplex, the word 'honour' with itself, as in the sixth stanza of 'To Sir Henry Wotton, at his going Ambassador to Venice', is to enact virtue's struggle to clear and maintain its own meaning amid the commonplace approximations, the common practice of men.

If Wotton himself remains a minor poet it is partly because, when he chooses lyric expression, his 'intrinsecal Familiarity' with what men do is not immersed in, is not infused by, the practice of an uncommon alertness to the common practices of speech. In entering even this diffident caveat against the comely verse of 'On his Mistris, the Queen of Bohemia' or the comely prose of Walton's *The Compleat Angler* and *The Life of Sir Henry Wotton* one is liable to be dismissed as some kind of latter-day Ranter or Muggletonian. A style at once so ingenuous and so ingenious appears, indeed, to have taken certain pre-emptive measures against this kind of clownish truculence. Just so, one infers from Asquith's presidential style the solecism that would be committed if one were to so take him at his word ('threadbare amateur') as to treat with scorn his trifling and patronizing 'reflections'. Asquith shows what the tensile seventeenth-century comeliness has been reduced to by 1919, after some three hundred years of drift and occasion and contexture. Wotton's 'You *Common people* of the *Skies*' balances very prettily between political fact and poetical fancy. Nonetheless, viewed in the light of Donne's poem to him, it may appear like an 'example . . . of too great height', self-exempted from Donne's importunate yet humble caveats.

'Fitness', a word of discretion and dispatch ('habilitas'), allowing 'ableness', 'handsomeness', to rub along with compleasance and special pleading, also stands for the maintaining of rectitude. Donne's argument tunes itself into, and against, the word ('Fit matter', 'will to your fortune fit', 'Which fits them', 'nothing else so fit for mee'). These four verse letters show respect not only for Wotton the man but also for the tradition of learned morals, active virtue, which he exemplifies. In addressing his friend Donne undertakes, at a deeper level than convention requires, a rehearsal of the traditional understanding that, by a study of 'the short and sure precepts of good example', a wise man prepared himself to face, unperplexed, the manifold perplexities of state affairs. He goes over what must presently be said and done by going over again what has many times been said and done, and puts himself to school in the very phrases with which he commends ethical scholarship and well-versed moral action:

> But, Sir, I' advise not you, I rather doe
> Say o'er those lessons, which I learn'd of you.   (73)

13

Dryden's Prize-Song

Dryden's lofty contempt for 'common Libellers' (605), his depiction of the 'just' satirist as one 'arm'd with the power of Verse, to Punish and make Examples of the bad' (606), might fairly attract the epithet 'magisterial', compounding as it does the idea of authority and mastery, if it were not for the fact that the poet in his own use of the word hedged it about with various caveats. The 'sublime and daring Genius' of Lucretius, which he likened to that of Hobbes, seemed to him 'Magisterial' in its 'positive assertion' of 'Opinions', its 'disdain' for 'all manner of Replies' (395). He protested that Sir Robert Howard, in his hasty retort upon the essay *Of Dramatick Poesie*, had overlooked the fact that the piece was 'a Dialogue sustain'd by Persons of several Opinions' and had been 'pleased to charge me with being Magisterial' (9: 15). Dryden was concerned that the judicious author, for all his care to establish right meanings, is fated to be misconstrued. 'Many men', he wrote, 'are shock'd at the name of Rules, as if they were a kinde of Magisterial prescription upon Poets' (13: 248). That sentence itself is a confrontation between the hasty 'prejudicate Opinions' (658) of 'many men', those whose 'judgment is a meer Lottery' (17: 73), and his own resolute opinion. Our obligation as informed readers is to take into account both the special pleading and the circumstantial facts, a task made all the more necessary and difficult since Dryden himself draws circumstance ('many men') not only into his critical strategy but also into the timbre of his writing. 'I will first see how this will relish with the Age' (13: 247): he marks down in a word the fickleness of public taste and adds a relish to his own controversial style.

Dr Johnson wrote in his essay on Dryden that to 'judge rightly of an author, we must transport ourselves to his time, and examine what were the wants of his contemporaries, and what were his means of supplying them'. He added, however, that in such works as the essay *Of Dramatick Poesie* 'the

author proves his right of judgement, by his power of performance'. In such
a context 'our' capacity to 'judge rightly' of circumstance adumbrates, but is
not made equivalent to, the exercise of an author's creative judgement,
which is a 'power' that circumstantial considerations neither enhance nor
excuse. We have here the makings of an antithesis but Johnson sees that it is
a more oblique and complex business than that. Dryden anticipates Johnson's perception. With 'pleased to charge' and 'many men' and 'relish' he
'proves his right of judgement' over the prejudicate and the circumstantial.
The dangerous volatile element, present here as it is absent from Johnson's
argument, is the contentious special pleading. A sense of injured merit, of
what Pound would term the 'intelligence at bay', is strong in Dryden but,
like Pound in *The Pisan Cantos*, he seems able to view his own *amour propre*
as one among the other competing forces in the mundane business;
demanding and meriting utterance but also in need of chastening and
restraint. Again like Pound he perceives how the thwartness of these things
is to be registered 'according to the Etymology of the word' (662). This
recognition is manifested not only in the scrupulous anxiety over niceties of
translation ('The word *Rejicit* I know will admit of both senses' 1051), but
also in the sharpness with which he turns upon one of Howard's solecisms
('*delectus verborum* is no more *Latine* for the Placing of Words, than *Reserate* is
Latine for shut the Door' 9: 8). In much the same spirit he handles Casau-
bon's defence of Persius' learning ('he did *ostendere*, but not *ostentare*'),
considering that this 'turns it handsomly, upon that supercilious Critick'
Scaliger who had accused the Latin poet of ostentatious pedantry (641).
'Turns it handsomly' has its own relish. It sounds like the 'Well done!' that
acclaims something at once finely achieved and morally just, where the
'right of judgement' is indeed at one with the 'power of performance'
though, in fact, it congratulates one despotic scholar for savaging another.
This is a relish which we are to distinguish from the superciliousness of
'taste'. Dryden's brother-in-law Sir Robert Howard, in taking issue with *Of
Dramatick Poesie*, had claimed that "tis not necessary for Poets to study strict
reason' and that 'in the difference of *Tragedy* and *Comedy*, and of *Fars* it self,
there can be no determination but by the Taste'. Dryden would have none
of this. Such appeals to 'taste' were gestures of surrender not only to the
indiscriminate rabble but also to the chaos in the individual mind, 'a
confus'd Mass of Thoughts, tumbling over one another in the Dark',
which is what inspiration is before its elements are 'either chosen or rejected
by the Judgment' (8: 95). 'The liking or disliking of the people gives the

Play the denomination of good or bad, but does not really make, or constitute it such' (9:11). 'Constitute' relates both to the consistency of the thing in itself and to its formal establishment in the public domain. Dryden here differentiates 'denomination' from constitution as emphatically as Ruskin would distinguish between extrinsic and intrinsic value or Pound insist that 'technique is the only gauge and test of a man's lasting sincerity', the instrument by which we distinguish the 'serious artist' from 'the disagreeable young person expressing its haedinus egotism'.

Dryden makes his own concessions, it is true; even in matters of taste and judgement, half-assenting to the polite fiction that on such questions the 'Noblesse' do not share the confusions of 'the multitude, the οἱ πολλοί' (17: 73). But that which is conceded may have been constrained, at best by a sense of obligation, at worst by exaction. The edge of Dryden's arguments is whetted upon this fact. There are 'rules' which are more equitable than 'taste' and there are the requirements of 'compleasance', of 'prejudicate opinions', which confound rules with taste and turn judgement into a parody of itself. When Dryden stresses the necessity for a right 'choice of words' he is, like Pound, emphasizing eloquent cogency ('Our language is noble, full, and significant'; 17: 78, 9: 8) as well as 'propriety of sound' (15: 9). Again like Pound he is opposing the 'graded and measured word' to haedinus egotism; but when Pound claims that 'literature is language charged with meaning' his meaning is more than a little diffused. Quotidian language, both casual and curial, is itself highly charged, but charged with the enormous power of the contingent and circumstantial, a 'confused mass of thoughts', a multitudinous meaning amid which the creative judgement must labour to choose and reject. There are 'meanings' which are self-evidently wrong ('reserate' is not Latin for 'shut the door') but the 'meaning' of a poem, its constitution, the composition of its elements, is not so readily abstractable from the constituted opinions and solecisms of the age; and though the grading and measuring of words presupposes the ability to recognize ambiguities, there are some ambiguities so deeply impacted with habit, custom, procedure, that the 'recognition' is in effect the acknowledgement of irreducible bafflement. Dryden and Pound are alike in their feeling for a language that is as expressive of the labour and bafflement as it is of the perfected judgement. Sir Robert Howard's kind of 'taste', on the other hand, is the prerogative of a particular kind of confidence, it goes with power and status; and Dryden shares with Montaigne and Bacon a relish for the wry *bon mot* of the philosopher Favorinus chided by his friends for giving way in a dispute with the emperor on a point of etymology: 'voudriez vous qu'il ne fut pas plus sçavant que moy, luy qui commande à trente legions?'

Bacon alludes to this anecdote in *The Advancement of Learning*: 'Neither was it accounted weakenesse, but discretion in him that would not dispute his best with *Adrianus Caesar*, excusing himselfe, *That it was reason to yield to him, that commaunded thirtie Legions*. These and the like applications and stooping to points of necessitie and conuenience cannot bee disallowed'. The way the question is put, both in Montaigne's French and in Florio's English version of it, the curt confrontation of 'you', 'him', and 'I' discreetly rendered in the routine civility of 'voudriez vous', '*would you not have him to be much wiser then I*', is only partly glossed by Bacon's 'stooping to . . . necessitie and conuenience'. The sardonic conflation of the fiction of free choice with the fact of *force majeure* is not precisely the same as an equation in Machiavellian diplomacy. One may indeed state with exemplary frankness the 'reasons' for an unavoidable avoidance of absolute frankness in dealings with the world of power and prerogative. Dryden, who was well acquainted with Montaigne's essays, alludes to the same riposte, both in *A Defence of an Essay of Dramatick Poesy* and in his preface to *All for Love*. What Bacon calls 'discretion' Dryden dubs 'good grace' in those who had 'Wit enough to yield the Prize . . . and not contend with him who had thirty Legions: They were sure to be rewarded if they confess'd themselves bad Writers, and that was somewhat better than to be Martyrs for their reputation' (13: 15). Dryden's irony is the more strained and the words 'wit enough' and 'good grace' exacerbate that tone. In the preface to his translation of Ovid's *Epistles* he writes 'But Deeds, it seems, may be Justified by Arbitrary Power, when words are question'd in a Poet' (178). Taken together, Dryden's 'justified by Arbitrary Power' and Johnson's 'proves his right of judgement, by his power of performance', statements too much at odds to be resolved by a formal oxymoron or paradox, mark out an area of bafflement, stultification, which the creative intelligence is forced to encounter as though it possessed the 'brute' force that Charles S. Peirce imputes to 'actuality'. 'Style', whether regarded as a series of tactical accommodations along the lines of Boileau's *L'Art poétique* or as 'nothing short of a desperate ontological or metaphysical manœuvre', must in some form admit the contrary of that which it affirms. It is undoubtedly true that the French seventeenth-century neo-classicists propounded 'the necessity for rendering the action [of a play] conformable to the particular taste of the audience' but even in that critical description the words 'necessity', 'conformable', 'particular taste' bristle with Hobbesian contradictions. Behind Boileau's trim prescriptive questions ('Voulez-vous du public meriter les amours?', 'Voulez-vous sur la scene étaler des ouvrages . . . ?', 'Voulez-vous longtemps plaire, et jamais ne lasser?', 'Voulez-vous faire aimer vos riches fictions?') stands the question of Montaigne's Favorinus 'voudriez vous qu'il ne fut pas plus sçavant que moy, luy qui commande à trente legions?'

To the suggestion that such a conclusion is merely impressionistic I would answer that the actual writings of the French theorists strongly qualify Joel Spingarn's notion of the 'single point of view' which, in his estimation, particularly recommended them to English authors and audiences 'eager for the results rather than the processes of such discussion'. There may be, in Boileau, d'Aubignac, and others, a final emphasis but that is not at all the same thing as a single point of view. D'Aubignac's emphasis, in his *Pratique du théâtre*, is in fact divided between imperative advice that the poet–dramatist should render his work 'admirable aux Spectateurs: car il ne travaille que pour leur plaire' and the equal imperative to contrive everything 'comme s'il n'y avoit point de Spectateurs'. So too Dryden divides his emphasis when in *The Dedication of the Aeneis* he writes 'A Poet cannot speak too plainly on the Stage: for *Volat irrevocabile verbum*; the sense is lost if it be not taken flying: but what we read alone we have leisure to digest. There an Author may beautifie his Sense by the boldness of his Expression, which if we understand not fully at the first, we may dwell upon it, 'till we find the secret force and excellence' (1010). Such statements excite awkward questions. Of what purpose or value is it to arouse the admiration and goodwill of your audience if, in the act of catering to their tastes and prejudice, you must forgo 'the secret force and excellence' of the work? We seem here to brush against the prejudice that stage business is too conversant with mundane opinion, 'complesance', '*negotium*', a more superficial exercise than is that 'dwelling upon' the matter which only solitary 'leisure' can give.

Such an emphasis would not be alien to the aloof humanism of Montaigne, admired by English writers of the period from Bacon to Dryden and by none more keenly than by those whose circumstances forced them to confront the tyranny of the market-place: Montaigne's 'La tourbe, mere d'ignorance, d'injustice et d'inconstance'. Those lines in Dryden's 'The Medall' beginning 'Almighty Crowd, thou shorten'st all dispute' (256) read like a close paraphrase of Montaigne's opinion. Viewed from a different angle, Montaigne's disdainful emphasis on 'facile' in 'au people, juge peu exacte, facile à piper, facile à contenter' satirically pre-empts the advice of

Boileau and others as to the desirability of ease and facility in one's striving for public success: 'N'offrez rien au Lecteur que ce qui peut luy plaire'.

Montaigne, it must be added, had, from the age of 38 when he took possession of his little castle, the library on the third floor of the round tower, sufficient means to hold himself aloof, physically and spiritually, from 'la tourbe'. Dryden, despite the fact that he came of a landowning family and had married an earl's daughter, did not enjoy such freedom. In the idiom of the day both Montaigne and he could be said to 'drive' their 'studies' to the end of private and public improvement; but Dryden was also driven by what he called 'the Vocation of Poverty to scribble' (13: 14). Montaigne, contemplating his own position of vantage, mused on 'le monde' and 'moy': 'Les autres vont tousjours ailleurs, s'ils y pensent bien; ils vont tousjours avant ... moy je me roulle en moy mesme'. Dryden was one who had necessarily to go 'tousjours avant'; there was no option. He contracted with the Theatre Royal, c.1668, 'to write three plays annually in return for one and a quarter shares', a contract which he never managed fully to honour. In the last years of his life his business dealings with the publisher Tonson, closely calculated on both sides, which certainly promised profitable returns, rendered him accountable to his partner for every line; and that is a rather different thing from making oneself accountable for every word. Montaigne, from the age of 38, was at liberty to meditate at his choice and desire. Dryden knew that there were liberties which he could not afford to take or would take at his peril. We weigh ''tis dangerous to offend an Arbitrary Master' (1020) against 'When a Poet is throughly provok'd, he will do himself Justice, however dear it cost him' (1016) and conclude that Dryden's own style is a matter of constant vigilant negotiation among and between 'danger', 'justice', and 'cost'. It may be added that it is one of the virtues of his style to transform a driven condition into a cadenced vehemence and that 'however dear it cost him' strikes one as having earned its place in the syntax of his conviction as Montaigne's 's'ils y pensent bien' does not. On the other hand, when Dryden in a letter of 1673 compliments the Earl of Rochester on possessing 'all the happinesse of an idle life, join'd with the good Nature of an Active' (Ls 9), he is, by implication, acknowledging the weight and import of Montaigne's 'moy je me roulle en moy mesme'. Even for the most public, the most 'occasional', of poets his outgoing energy must reciprocally depend on the degree to which he can roll him into himself; and Dryden shows that he is not unaware of the extent to which 'a flood of little businesses, which yet are necessary to . . . Subsistance' (Ls 123) imposes a ceaseless attrition upon this intimate creative selfhood. The fact that, year in year out, he transcended his circumstances in his art does not diminish the force of the observation. In the end he sent the publisher of the *Fables* more than eleven thousand lines instead of the ten thousand for which he had contracted. This is what is referred to, rather too easily, as his giving 'good measure'. Dryden gave good measure in the structure and cadence of his lines and paragraphs where '*otium*' and '*nec-otium*' come together in the only way that counts. There is nothing in his own theorizing to suggest that he would dissent from Boileau's 'Que toûjours le Bon sens s'accorde avec la Rime' but in his practice he contrives his 'harmony' ('Verse . . . or . . . the other Harmony of Prose' 1446) not only out of the 'natural disadvantages', the 'Monosyllables' of English 'clog'd with consonants' (15: 7 and 13: 223; see also 1053), the laborious negotiating of 'le bon sens' amid the heavy-laden language of 'custom and common use' (17: 29), but also out of a reconciling of circumstance and judgement not unlike that 'daily practice in the World' of a statesman whom he admired and praised: his capacity 'to work and bend [men's] stubborn Minds, which go not all after the same Grain, but each of them so particular a way, that the same common Humours, in several Persons, must be wrought upon by several Means' (8: 97). One hears from time to time of Dryden's 'duplicity', 'ambivalence', 'doubletalk', and 'shuffling'. I do not think one can so describe a man at bay without observing an ambivalence within the term 'at bay' itself. It is both 'the chorus of barking raised by hounds in immediate conflict with a hunted animal' and the 'position of a hunted animal when, unable to flee farther, it turns, faces the hounds, and defends itself at close quarters'. The 'chorus' determines the 'position' but the creature in that position manifests its own determination and may well force the chorus back upon an urgent and surprising redefinition.

When Dryden, in the preface to *All for Love*, refers contemptuously to 'this Rhyming Judge of the Twelvepenny Gallery' (13: 17) he is retorting upon an attack by the Earl of Rochester. He affects to believe that his assailant is one of the '*Petits Esprits*' rather than someone whose status as one 'of the highest Rank, and truest Understanding' (1052–3) it would be dangerous to deny; Dryden dismisses a man whose social prerogative is to dismiss others. With a throw-away colloquialism he precisely infringes a set of aesthetic distinctions based on social hierarchy. Jean Segrais divided literary critics into three classes and Dryden followed his lead in the

Dedication of the Aeneis: beginning with the 'Mobb-Readers', moving to 'a middle sort' unable to discern the difference between 'ostentatious Sentences, and the true sublime', and ending with 'the Highest Court of Judicature, like that of the Peers', of which, Dryden adds, his dedicatee the Earl of Mulgrave 'is so great an Ornament' (1052–3). Our contemporary scepticism fastens upon Dryden's own ostentatious and placatory sentences in his addresses to patrons; his own scepticism, working a more dangerous track, implies that 'Mobb-Readers' are to be found at all levels, including that of the patrons. In his *Discourse Concerning the Original and Progress of Satire* he concedes that one of the reasons for the obscurity of Aulus Persius Flaccus in his satires may have been that 'the fear of his safety under *Nero*, compell'd him to this darkness in some places' (639). It is reasonable to suppose that anything written as code will be 'obscure'. Dryden's insult to Rochester, though in code, could not be more clear. For 'rhyming judge of the twelvepenny gallery' we are to read 'one who purports to belong to "the highest court of judicature"' and, further, 'one who commands thirty legions'. The deliberated insult has the quality of impenetrable transparency. In the dedication of *Examen Poeticum* Dryden sketches the circumstances that require and provoke this kind of disingenuous ingenuousness: 'If I am the Man, as I have Reason to believe, who am seemingly Courted, and secretly Undermin'd: I think I shall be able to defend my self, when I am openly Attacqu'd' (793). To be 'seemingly courted', 'secretly undermined', implies that 'strife' is cynically accommodated to 'the Politeness of *Rome*' (661). It also means that courtship and treachery are accommodated to each other. The 'openness' of 'I think I shall be able to defend my self, when I am openly Attacqu'd' suggests that the massive plainness of Dryden is a very different thing from 'the plain style' as it is commonly conceived and that it has more in common with Davenant's argument when, directly calling upon the tutelary spirit of Hobbes, he likens the poet's progress amid 'the Learned' to one who 'travails through the Enemy's country' and the 'wise Poet' to 'a wise Generall' who 'will not shew his strengths till they are in exact government and order; which are not the postures of chance, but proceed from Vigilance and labour'.

> What *Virgil* wrote in the vigour of his Age, in Plenty and at Ease, I have undertaken to *Translate* in my Declining Years: strugling with Wants, oppress'd with Sickness, curb'd in my Genius, lyable to be misconstrued in all I write; and my Judges, if they are not very equitable, already prejudic'd against me, by the *Lying Character* which has been given them of my Morals.

> Yet steady to my Principles, and not dispirited with my Afflictions, I have, by
> the Blessing of God on my Endeavours, overcome all difficulties; and, in some
> measure, acquitted my self of the Debt which I ow'd the Publick, when
> I undertook this Work.   (1424)

The strength of Dryden's own argument stems here from its being at
once ingenuous and at bay. While genuinely striving to accommodate itself
to a style of compleasant address (it is from the 'Postscript to the Reader' of
the *Aeneis* translation) it is imbued with resentment against those 'curbs' and
'misconstructions' which are the inevitable dark side of 'civility' and 'affability'. Dryden is careful to establish and confirm an unambitious contractual tone
with 'undertaken', 'undertook', 'Endeavours', 'acquitted'. The more ambitiously emotive words, 'strugling', 'oppress'd', 'curb'd', are both restrained and
justified by the unemotional. The unemotional is part of the emotive, as
plainness has its part to play in eloquence. We are not able, we are not invited,
to distinguish precisely between the elements of sober factual recital, bitter
special pleading, righteous indignation, wounded *amour propre*. Dryden's tone
persuades us that though the injustices may be cogently summarized they are
not to be summarily passed over. The 'Publick' is in debt to him for all those
injuries received, even though with overt modesty he acknowledges that
'Debt which I ow'd the Publick, when I undertook this Work'. This passage,
written near the end of his life, is a summation of those several utterances of
endurance, indignation, and honest doubt heard at intervals throughout his
work: the theatre prologues and epilogues, the critical essays, the dedications.
''Tis not that I am mortified to all ambition, but I scorn as much to take it from
half-witted Judges, as I shou'd to raise an Estate by cheating of Bubbles'; 'For
the Reputation . . . of my Poetry, it shall either stand by its own Merit; or fall
for want of it' (791). It is also, by implication, the résumé of a long history of
'prejudic'd' 'misconstruing'; of Rochester's accusations of arrogance and
Shadwell's sneers. In such passages of self-vindication style itself turns 'at
bay'. When, in the *Discourse Concerning Satire*, Dryden rehearses the real and
alleged defects of style in the work of Aulus Persius Flaccus, its metrical
lameness, the crowded obscurity of its diction, one senses not only his own
constrained adherence to compleasance—it is 'stubborn, insociable, froward,
intractable' to write like that—but also the strong pull of sympathy towards
that very stubbornness and intractability. I am here thinking less of the
appeals to mitigating circumstances (Persius wrote in the days of Nero, he
died before he had arrived at maturity of judgement) than of the qualified

but distinct admiration for the exacerbated, as well as the exacerbating, spirit of such work. Dryden the theorist would no doubt urge a distinction between raw power and a deliberated 'boldness of . . . Expression' that may be dwelt upon at leisure ''till we find the secret force and excellence'; in practice, as in the elegy 'To the Memory of Mr. Oldham', he comes close to compounding the two. There is something secreted in his praise of such 'secret force', a judgement that eludes and transcends the immediate circumstance. It is the 'prevailing character or spirit', the 'characteristic method or procedure', of the work, its 'genius' according to contemporary terminology; but it is also a superior power bestowed, as though by 'the Blessing of God', on the 'Endeavour' itself, on that creative spirit which turns at bay upon the compleasant maxims of the age; it becomes that 'Genius' which enables a poem to 'force its own reception in the World' (215). Eliot is quite wrong in his contention that Dryden's words 'state immensely, but their suggestiveness is almost nothing', that they lack 'overtone' or 'nebula'; and Auden is, to say the least, rash when he claims that 'they mean exactly what, on first reading, they seem to say'.

> Farewel, too little and too lately known,
> Whom I began to think and call my own;
> For sure our Souls were near ally'd; and thine
> Cast in the same Poetick mould with mine.
> One common Note on either Lyre did strike,
> And Knaves and Fools we both abhorr'd alike:
> To the same Goal did both our Studies drive,
> The last set out the soonest did arrive.
> Thus *Nisus* fell upon the slippery place,
> While his young Friend perform'd and won the Race.
> O early ripe! to thy abundant store
> What could advancing Age have added more?
> It might (what Nature never gives the young)
> Have taught the numbers of thy native Tongue.
> But Satyr needs not those, and Wit will shine
> Through the harsh cadence of a rugged line.
> A noble Error, and but seldom made,
> When Poets are by too much force betray'd.
> Thy generous fruits, though gather'd ere their prime ⎫
> Still shew'd a quickness; and maturing time   ⎬
> But mellows what we write to the dull sweets of Rime. ⎭
> Once more, hail and farewel; farewel thou young,
> But ah too short, *Marcellus* of our Tongue;

> Thy Brows with Ivy, and with Laurels bound;
> But Fate and gloomy Night encompass thee around.   (389)

'To the Memory of Mr. Oldham' was Dryden's contribution to a set of memorial verses prefacing the *Remains of Mr. John Oldham in Verse and Prose*, 1684. It is a poem that contrives to be harmonious and generous in recollection while exercising discernment in its weighing of virtues and limitations and of what, in the circumstances, one is free to say of these. It harmonizes with the general tenor of lament and tribute. One of Dryden's fellow memorialists, in an anonymous contribution, also likens Oldham to Marcellus. Dryden's piece recollects in style, and the style is judiciously reminiscent of the spirit in which Oldham himself had composed 'To the Memory... of Mr. Charles Morwent', 'To the Memory of...Mr. Harman Atwood', 'Upon the Works of Ben Johnson', and 'A Satyr Touching Nobility: Out of Monsieur Boileau'. In Oldham's elegies for friends, a 'blooming Ripeness' and 'full ripe Vertues' are fancied as eternized even in their untimely cropping, in the fashion of Horatian paradox; and the dead man is spared 'dull Habitude'. Ben Jonson is lauded by Oldham as 'Rich in thy self, to whose unbounded store | Exhausted Nature could vouchsafe no more', and the words 'A Fool, or Knave' occur in the 'Satyr Touching Nobility'.

In November 1684, when 'To the Memory of Mr. Oldham' first appeared, Dryden was in his fifty-fourth year and had been Poet Laureate for well over a decade. Oldham had died in 1683, aged 30. His life had been the common career of impecunious drudgery until, shortly before his death, 'he was taken into [the] Patronage' of the Earl of Kingston and 'lived with him in great respect at *Holme-Pierpont* in *Nottinghamshire*'. He had also attracted, and unlike Dryden had not lost, the favour of the Earl of Rochester. It has been suggested that 1684 was a 'relatively serene' year in Dryden's life. Compared with the previous two years it may have been relatively free from vituperation and libel but to suppose it in any way 'serene' is to underrate the power of memory and its capacity to affect current thoughts and emotions. 'Memory' was for Dryden a creative faculty. Sixteen years later, in the Preface to the *Fables*, he would speak of himself as being 'as vigorous as ever in the Faculties of my Soul, excepting only my Memory, which is not impair'd to any great degree' (1446). The poem to Oldham is an 'in memoriam' where the formal commitment to recollection, embodied in the virtually seamless texture of literary echoes, touches upon actual and urgent memories, both overt and tacit; the overt being taken up with the commemoration of a common cause against 'Knaves and Fools' and the tacit, not unrelated to that cause, gravitating to thoughts of ill luck and ill usage: thoughts with which the remembrance of Oldham is perplexingly implicated.

It has been said that Rochester's 'capricious patronage of poets brought in its train envy, backbiting and hatred'. Dryden had fallen from favour around the year 1675 and Rochester's attack on him was circulating, anonymously, shortly afterwards. At about the same time Oldham was received into favour. Not only did the younger man supplant Dryden in the esteem of a powerful and dangerous coterie; he may also be said to have pre-empted the elder poet's claim to be regarded as the innovator of heroic satire. Oldham's *Satyrs upon the Jesuits*, which established his celebrity, was published in 1680–1, the year before *Absalom and Achitophel*, but Dryden's *MacFlecknoe*, which is a strange hybrid, an heroic lampoon, was circulating in manuscript probably some three years before Oldham's satires were written and five years before they appeared in print. 'A transcript of part of [*MacFlecknoe*] in Oldham's hand . . . is dated "A° 1678"' (1914) and other poets borrowed from it before it was published in 1682. Dryden's succinct adaptation, in the 'Oldham' elegy, of the foot-race episode from Book V of the *Aeneid* reads like an open verdict on these circumstances. In Virgil's rendering of the scene the Trojan contest is scarcely an exercise in simple-hearted virtue and magnanimity. It is marred by several instances of un-sportsmanlike behaviour and complaint, like 'disagreeable young person[s] expressing [their] haedinus egotism', and terminates in the wholesale distribution of handsome consolation-prizes that take the edge off victory and the sting from defeat. None of this is lost in Dryden's version. Euryalus, the victor, is awarded 'a stately Steed' (1182) but Nisus comes off very handsomely with 'an ample Shield; | Of wond'rous Art by *Didymaon* wrought' (1184). One wonders whether this is a display of civic equity, 'equal Justice', or of aesthetic anarchy: 'Then thus the Prince; let no Disputes arise: | Where Fortune plac'd it, I award the Prize. | But Fortune's Errors give me leave to mend, | At least to pity my deserving Friend' (1183). This may be the 'indulgent' face of patronage, a master-stroke of magisterial aplomb; but Aeneas still reminds one of Sir Robert Howard proclaiming that 'in the difference of *Tragedy* and *Comedy*, and of *Fars* it self, there can be no determination but by the *Taste*'. 'To the Memory of Mr. Oldham' is Dryden's 'Shield' and 'wond'rous Art', his consolation, his own prize-song. Its art is demonstrated by the stylishness with which it both maintains the decorum of 'indulgence' and implies the cost that decorum extorts from 'curb'd' genius. 'Thus *Nisus* fell . . .' The Latin of Book V has 'sed . . .'. Dryden contrives to blend into the echoes of Book V the heartfelt panegyric ('venerande puer', 'fortunati ambo') and the heroic sorrow of Book IX, in which Euryalus and Nisus fall in battle, race together into death. Such a tone is much more appropriate for a funeral elegy, as is the last line's invocation of Book VI ('sed nox atra caput tristi circumvolat umbra'). The 'wonder' is that, beneath it, runs a contrary thread, as though Dryden were sardonically taking Howard at his word and as though there were indeed '*no difference betwixt* Comedy *and* Tragedy *but what is made by the taste only*' (9: 11). 'Thus *Nisus* fell upon the slippery place': 'slippery place' suggests a Senecan sententiousness but is discreetly adapting 'sed pronus in ipso | concidit immundoque fimo sacroque cruore'. 'Fimus' is animal excrement. Nisus slips in the dung and blood of the freshly sacrificed animals. Our own coarse colloquialism 'in the shit', apparently not current before the mid-nineteenth century, might fairly describe Dryden's feeling about the general run of his worldly luck; but 'Thus *Nisus* fell upon the slippery place', which slides together some five lines of the source, manages to be both euphemistic and decently 'classical'. 'His Heels flew up; and on the grassy Floor, | He fell, besmear'd with Filth, and Holy Gore' (1182) is how Dryden pitches it in his *Aeneis*. 'His Heels flew up' could be from a ballad of low life. The cleaned-up phrasing of the 'Oldham' elegy does not completely disguise, however, the indecencies of the world's ill luck, inequitable, 'indulgent' judgements, and outrageous juxtapositions. The *victor ludorum* prize for which, through the ludicrous collapse of Nisus, Euryalus unexpectedly qualifies is at once the 'stately Steed' of poetic acclaim and an early death.

One senses, at the same time, that Dryden disdains to write for Oldham an 'Insolent, Sparing, and Invidious Panegyrick' (603) and that this refusal is as much a matter of self-respect as of respect for the subject. Sincerity is a complex, not a simple, state. If poetry were simply plain statement, discourse, one would conclude that Dryden is several times unjust not only to his own superior qualities as a poet but also to the power and accuracy of his own critical judgement. 'A noble Error, and but seldom made, | When Poets are by too much force betray'd.' Oldham himself is something of a special pleader on the matter, acknowledging that 'some persons found fault with the roughness of my Satyrs formerly publisht' but contending that 'the way I took, was out of choice, not want of judgment' and that 'I did not so much mind the Cadence, as the Sense and expressiveness of my words, and therefore chose not those, which were best dispos'd to placing themselves in

Rhyme, but rather the most keen, and tuant, being the suitablest to my Argument'. Robert Gould, in 'To the Memory of Mr. John Oldham', follows suit with 'How wide shoot they, that strive to blast thy Fame, | By saying, that thy Verse was rough and lame?' and with the further suggestion that such critics misconstrue the function and style of satire by asking it to produce the same effect as 'plyant' and 'smooth' love verses. Gould's tribute was not included in the first edition of the *Remains*; it was added in 1687, the same year in which his attack on Dryden—*The Laureat . . . Jack Squob's History*—appeared in print. It is possible, therefore, that Gould is 'shooting' at Dryden in his defence of Oldham, bridling at those graciously measured reservations as if they had been attempts to 'blast' Oldham's reputation. Such pleas beg the question that Dryden would be least inclined to indulge or overlook: the question of how far 'Sense and expressiveness' can be accomplished where 'Cadence' is not minded. I concur with the view that Dryden's poem, while demonstrating magnanimity of judgement in this matter of opinion, teaches a strict lesson in how to master sense and expressiveness through cadence and rhyme. The main burden of his statement is critical and prosodic but there is sufficient 'nebula' to blur criticism into notions of high vocation and salutary sternness. It is helpful, in the circumstances, that both 'rugged' and 'harsh' permit a latitude of interpretation. They could be taken to mean either technical inadequacy, or the possession of a stalwart, independent virtue, or the 'true end of Satyre . . . the amendment of Vices by correction' (216). Dryden referred at various times to a 'rugged, and unharmonious' verse of ten monosyllables (1054), of which there are numerous instances in Oldham's work, to 'the plainness, fierceness, rugged virtue | Of an old true-stamp *Roman*' (13: 27), and to the need for satire to prescribe 'harsh Remedies to an inveterate Disease' (216). When he claims on Oldham's behalf that 'Wit will shine | Through the harsh cadence of a rugged line' the sonorities of plain statement are diffused into a number of overtones. Such words do not directly consent to the special pleading but neither do they directly rebuke it. Dryden is engaged not only with the combined weight of social expectation and literary convention, and with his genuine liking and sympathy for the younger man, but also with the knowledge of his own extreme vulnerability to the kind of partisan misconstruing that men like Robert Gould were so ready to make.

In the *Discourse Concerning the Original and Progress of Satire*, published some eight years after the 'Oldham' elegy, Dryden commemorates the achievement,

and observes the faults, of the Roman poets Lucan and Persius. His reluctance
to charge them with 'Faults, from which Humane Nature, and more especially
in Youth, can never possibly be exempted' is matched by his readiness to
'wonder how they, who Dyed before the Thirtieth Year of their Age, cou'd
write so well, and think so strongly' (640). Oldham was just 30 when he died:

> Thy generous fruits, though gather'd ere their prime
> Still shew'd a quickness; and maturing time
> But mellows what we write to the dull sweets of Rime.

'We' is again concessionary; it condescends, in the sense then prevailing: it
stoops voluntarily and graciously; but condescension and compleasance are
bound into the same nexus. 'Rime', like cadence, is for Dryden the means
whereby the poet achieves 'sense and expressiveness'. 'Dull sweets of Rime'
submits judgement to circumstance rather as Dryden exempts noble patrons
from 'Faults, from which Humane Nature', one might reasonably think,
'can never possibly be exempted'. In verses written at about the same time as
the 'Oldham' elegy and addressed 'To the Earl of *Roscomon*, on his Excellent
Essay on *Translated Verse*', rhyme as 'Manly Sweetness' in the right hands
(e.g. Roscommon's) is contrasted with its debasing effect in the wrong hands
(the French): 'At best a pleasing Sound, and fair barbarity' (387). The
personal note in 'To the Memory of Mr. Oldham' is intense, but not so
simplistically that we are obliged to see Dryden fearing his own inevitable
decline into mellifluous etiolation. The triple rhyme and alexandrine,
enforcing our awareness of 'rime' even as he condescends to dismiss its
'dull sweets', make a triple *congé* to language, judgement, and circumstance;
to the various enforcements and agreements of 'Civil Conversation' (648)
and to what 'wond'rous Art' can make of them.

Bunyan's Mr By-ends makes 'a very low *Conje*, and they also gave him a
Complement', 'they' being Mr *Hold-the-World*, Mr *Mony-love*, and Mr *Save-
all*. Dryden anticipates Bunyan in a poem of 1677: 'For ill Men, conscious of
their inward guilt, | Think the best Actions on By-ends are built' (162).
We are some way towards appreciating the genius with which Dryden drives
his trade when we recognize that, for him, those acquaintances of Bunyan's
By-ends, and other cruel and meretricious figures of striving Restoration
'compleasance'—'my Lord *Turn-about*, my Lord *Time-server*, my Lord
Fair-speech... Also Mr. *Smooth-man*, Mr. *Facing-bothways*, Mr. *Any-thing*—
are to be encountered in the *otium* and *negotium*, the self-elected exemptions
and the 'little businesses... necessary to... Subsistance', that constitute the

art itself and the criticism which attends, patronizes, and reduces it to order: ''tis dangerous to offend an Arbitrary Master.' Good writing is a contributor to 'Civil Conversation', yet at the same time it is not; it 'travails through the Enemy's country' along the paths of civil conversation and 'the common Track of Business, which is not always clean' (915). That common track is less a cheerily nid-nodding consensus than a treadmill of progress ('ils vont tousjours avant') where many incompatibles are obliged to keep some semblance of common time and order. What we call the writer's 'distinctive voice' is a registering of different voices. It is because those exemplary names in *The Pilgrim's Progress* ('Mr. *Smooth-man*'; 'Mr. *Any-thing*') combine both the fierceness of Bunyan's contempt and the relish of his well-rewarded vigilance, and because he urges them forward upon the 'track of business' by his innate sense of rhythm and cadence, that they lodge themselves so in our minds, coming up out of the common stock and yet newly created with a fresh distinction.

'Distinction' may also be conferred as a matter of status by public fiat, *force majeure*, corporate obtuseness, or political expediency, like the laureateships conferred on Thomas Shadwell, Henry James Pye, and Alfred Austin, or like the accolade 'good writing' itself. Such absurdities may with some justice be recorded by an expletive (*'merde alors!'*) because such an expletive doubly satisfies our sense of the arbitrary. At a primitive level it too is an expression of 'intelligence at bay'. The 'prosaic' strength that poetry must have, that sense of being 'loaded with life', the virtue of being 'good sense, at all events', requires, I would say, that the implications of 'at all events' are not readily separable from the implications of '... *alors*' ('at that time', 'in that case', 'well, then', 'so what'). Even in those sentences that sound most at bay (Wyatt's 'what thynge is that that these mene wolde not wreste for there purpose that wreste suche thynges', Whitman's 'And often to me they are alive after what custom has served them, but nothing more') there is the particular force and relish of an 'exact government and order; which are not the postures of chance, but proceed from Vigilance and labour'. Style is a seamless contexture of energy and order which, time after time, the effete and the crass somehow contrive to part between them; either paying tremulous lip-service to the 'incomparable' and the 'incommunicable' or else toadying to some current notion of the demotic.

Pound observed in a late interview that 'a great deal of literature is born of hate and ... whatever is sound in it emerges from the ruins'; and Dryden's contemporary, Samuel Butler, noted in his commonplace book that 'Malice' has 'Power...above all other Passions, to highten Wit and Fancy', adding that 'Panegyriques' are 'commonly as Dull as they are false'. 'To the Memory of Mr. Oldham' is a 'panegyrique' which seeks to be lively and true and to associate with magnanimity those qualities of wit and fancy which Butler saw as the prerogative of malice. Dryden's strength and integrity manifest themselves in his running the difficult middle course between the impositions and implications of 'Voulez-vous du public meriter les amours?' and 'voudriez vous qu'il ne fut pas plus sçavant que moy, luy qui commande à trente legions?' One does not break decorum, or even syntax, in shifting from the *bienséance* of the first to the cynical stoicism of the second. Dryden does not break decorum either; for decorum becomes magnanimity, while magnanimity does not annul the force of his own feelings. 'When a Poet is throughly provok'd, he will do himself Justice, however dear it cost him.' When the poet has been 'provok'd' into magnanimity we should not, in justice, underrate the cost of that.

14

'Envoi (1919)'

'Envoi (1919)' recalls in its title the form of the alba (e.g. 'Alba Innominata', a version of which Pound had included in his *Exultations* of 1909) and in its opening lines the melody of Waller's 'Goe lovely rose' which had been set by Milton's friend and collaborator, the Royalist musician Henry Lawes. From the time of his first discovery of Lawes's music Pound held it in the highest esteem. 'To Thomas Campion his ghost, and to the ghost of Henry Lawes, as prayer for the revival of music': so runs the dedication to the translation of Cavalcanti's 'Donna mi prega' which Pound published in 1928. It is equally the case that Pound held the theory and practice of the nineteenth-century French poet Théophile Gautier, particularly his *Émaux et Camées*, in comparably high esteem and that Gautier's prescriptive 'Chaque pièce devait être un médaillon' can be seen as anticipating the title of 'Medallion', the final poem in *Hugh Selwyn Mauberley*. At the same time, as Pound suggested in an essay of February 1918, 'On the Hard and Soft in French Poetry', to view 'hardness' itself as 'a virtue in the poetic' is an error; the hardness must be a virtue in the 'intent'; the poet should be 'intent on conveying a certain verity of feeling'. Gautier, according to Pound, understood this; Heredia, 'perhaps the best' of his followers, did not. Among the English poets of the generation immediately preceding his own Pound singled out Lionel Johnson as one with 'similar ambitions' to Gautier, adding that 'if Gautier had not written, Johnson's work might even take its place in Welt-literatur . . . might stand for this clearness and neatness'. Those careful locutions ('if Gautier had not written', 'might even take its place') sufficiently temper the enthusiasm and provide circumstantial evidence for those who would retain 'Medallion' as a poem by the fictional Hugh Selwyn Mauberley rather than as a lyric by E.P. The principles are 'hard' but the practice, which shapes the final cameo, celebrates a 'virtue in the poetic' rather than in the intent. 'The eyes turn topaz.'

We are invited to observe a quality where we might have expected to receive 'a certain verity of feeling'.

All this adds up to what anxious scholarship describes as an 'interpretative crisis'. Up to a point the scholar's desire for terra firma is analogous, though not equivalent, to the poet's search for a 'strategic position' and Pound, the scholar-poet, would not be unsympathetic to a desire for precise definition hard-won from those perplexities of circumstance which Henry Gaudier had called 'the incessant struggle in the complex city'. But it would be sentimental to claim too close a rapport on this basis. To complain that a critical reading which differs from one's own 'destroys the only planned structure discernible in *HSM*' is to sound like someone whose fractious child has just knocked the jigsaw off the table; and to argue that 'Part II of *Mauberley* is in general more satisfactory than Part I: we are surer of the object that Pound has his eye on' is in effect, if not in intention, to reverse the order of priorities upon which he always insisted. When Pound wrote, in 1910, 'Villon is no theorist, he is an objective fact' he was not encouraging us to impose critical theories about the primacy of objective fact upon our reading of poetic artefacts. Criticism which is, on many occasions, the faculty and instrument of judgement is on other occasions, possibly more numerous, part of the body of circumstance out of which and against which the single voice of creative intelligence must be made articulate. Modern criticism in this guise is one of the shapes of protean Opinion, one of the petty 'lords of the temporal world', something quite other than that 'sublimity of the critical sense' which Pound associated with Henry James at his strongest. *Homage to Sextus Propertius* and *Hugh Selwyn Mauberley* are noteworthy for the manner in which Opinion, not only as the prejudiced voice but also as the prejudging ear, figures among the dramatis personae of the work, and for the way in which 'sublimity of the critical sense' is kept resolutely in view amid the clamour and the 'gross silence'. Pound suggested as much when he remarked that 'Mauberley is . . . an attempt to condense the James novel' since he was contending in 1918 that though James at his weakest offers a mere '*étude* in ephemera' at his best 'he does, nevertheless, treat of major forces, even of epic forces, and in a way all his own'. To any one inclined to suggest that emphasis on 'the body of circumstance' is ludicrously out of proportion to Pound's 'major forces' I would respond that, in 'the domination of modern life', it is the 'ephemera', 'all sorts of intangible bondage', that have usurped the role of the ancient epic forces and that Pound is at least the equal of Ben Jonson and Dryden, both in recognizing this factor and in discovering how to treat of it 'in a way all his own'.

Pound's criticism, particularly of those he most admired, concentrates attention upon the forces of attrition, upon the resistant virtues of morale and style, and upon those flaws, even in the best, which helplessly collude with the ruling imbecilities. He said 'I am tired of hearing pettiness talked about Henry James's style'. His own view and sense of style are 'epic'. Subsumed in this, 'pettiness', 'ephemera', have their ponderable mass and weight. Whitman, he says, 'goes bail for the nation': an epic tribute; yet he argued that Whitman was badly flawed and hampered by his 'catalogues and flounderings', his 'crudity'. Indebted as Pound was to Laurence Binyon's *The Flight of the Dragon* (1911), and to his conversation, he nonetheless deplored Binyon's 'disgusting attitude of respect toward predecessors whose intellect is vastly inferior to his own'. Influenced in his own thinking by Allen Upward's *The Divine Mystery*, which, in 1913, he described as 'the most fascinating book on folk-lore that I have ever opened', and by the same author's *The New Word*, he could bring himself to suggest, after Upward's suicide, that he had 'shot himself in discouragement on reading of [the Nobel] award to Shaw. Feeling of utter hopelessness in struggle for values'. Such a timbre is not unlike Upward's own in his autobiography, which has been defined as one of 'forced levity and grim desperation . . . betraying the lacerated spirit'. Even so, Upward remained for Pound 'the old combattant' and is so commemorated in the first of *The Pisan Cantos*. Such sweeping disparities in fact stem from a coherent emphasis: that the self-same writer may become the helpless and hopeless victim of those circumstances which he has acutely diagnosed and assayed. This is to view the matter in its most negative aspect. One can concede the perplexity more positively in the words which Pound used when reviewing the life's work, the interlocked strengths and weaknesses, of A. R. Orage: 'you could call [him] a damn fool *and* respect him'. There remains an arguable distinction between a style that is largely symptomatic of 'forced levity and grim desperation' and one in which such tones are part of a polemical spectrum that also includes examples of art's power to transcend circumstance, its capacity 'to free the intellect from the tyranny of the affects'. It is certainly possible to see both 'Envoi (1919)' and 'Medallion' as lyrics diversely maintaining that belief, if not that capacity; each modified by, and modifying, the clamour of the 'affects' within the sequence; the various voices of 'demand', 'censure', hysteria, exaggeration, mendacity, with which it reverberates.

The 'function of an art', so expressed, is an invocation not an Archimedean 'proof'; it is essentially one's feeling that things are so (an emphasis

somewhat different from, and more vulnerable than, Hardy's poignant
'Hoping it might be so' yet pitched against not dissimilar 'affects' of common
sense). It is a state of mind which Pound, in 1912, had the ingenuousness to
admit: 'This difference, this dignity . . . must be conveyed . . . by the art of the
verse structure, by something which exalts the reader, making him feel that he
is in contact with something arranged more finely than the commonplace'.
That reiterated 'something', which does not strike one as deliberate, or much
deliberated, concedes the intense subjectivism with which objectivity may be
proclaimed, and naively approximates to the resonances of 'Envoi (1919)'
rather than to the nuances of 'Medallion'.

James's significance for Pound, in the early years, is registered in the
emphasis which the younger man placed on the capacity for intense feeling
matched by a 'capacious intelligence' and the 'incessant labour of minute
observation'. 'The passion of it, the continual passion of it in this man who,
fools said, didn't "feel". I have never yet found a man of emotion against whom
idiots didn't raise this cry.' This sentence stands as a characteristic gesture of
Pound's conviction. The world's obtuseness, imperviousness, its active or
passive hostility to valour and vision, is not only the object of his denunciation;
it is also the necessary circumstance, the context in which and against which
valour and vision define themselves: 'In the gloom, the gold gathers the light
against it'. If it were not for the darkness and the enemies' torches the beauty of
factive *virtù* would not shine out so in defiance of that circumstance which the
'gathering' has in part transformed. The difference between 'Feeling of utter
hopelessness in struggle for values', in Pound's comment on Upward's
suicide, and 'In the gloom, the gold gathers the light against it', from Canto
11, the last of the 'Malatesta' Cantos, is all in the definition; the raw material is
the same: the detritus of the Dantean *Malebolge* which Pound had begun to sift
and assay in his first prose book *The Spirit of Romance*, compounded with 'the
ἀνάγκη of modernity, cash necessity', 'the aimless turmoil and restlessness
of humanity' in general; in particular, 'the violent against art, and the usurers',
'the devil-driven pandars', 'the still malignity of the traitor's wallow'. Malatesta,
'famous condottiere, military engineer, and patron of the arts', defines himself
by resistant achievement: 'against the power that was . . . Sigismundo cut
his notch'; '*templum aedificavit*'. The suicide of an 'old combattant' such as
Allen Upward seemed a hopeless surrender of self-defining, self-vindicating
virtù. 'The suicide is not serious   from conviction', Pound wrote, years later in
Canto 93, but 'from sheer physical depression'.

If you affirm that 'the function of an art is to free the intellect from the tyranny of the affects' the statement nonetheless remains embedded in affects; requires, indeed, those dispositions or predispositions to effect its freedom from them. Exacerbation and enhancement are to some extent correlative. In 'Envoi (1919)' the concept of 'time' is, as it remains for Pound, also a complex emotion simply stated. It is the inescapable natural attrition lamented by the Roman and Renaissance love-poets whom he greatly admired: Propertius ('nox tibi longa venit nec reditura dies') and Campion imitating Propertius ('When thou must home to shades of vnder ground') and Waller in that song which acts as Pound's point of departure and remonstrance ('The common fate of all things rare'); it is also the domain of the temporal, of 'the lords of the temporal world'. One of the several inter-involved ways in which 'Time is the evil' is that it is the continuum in which the lords of the temporal world manifest their cruelty and their contempt. Pound is not such a fool as to suppose that the continuum is describable only in negative terms. Malatesta was a lord of the temporal world and 'Rhythm is a form cut into TIME'. But Pound, at times, grounds himself on treacherous axioms as though they were indeed truths of first inscription. The stubbornness of one's dogmatism, the force of one's own hubris, are themselves factors in the world's general arbitrariness, 'coercions', 'personal tyranny'; and 'anyone can run to excesses . . . It is hard to stand firm in the middle'. It is worth recalling that Pound had begun to read Confucius and Mencius, in French translations, as early as 1913, under the guidance of Allen Upward ('Law of MOU is law of the middle, the pivot'; 'Kung employed the right word neither in excess nor less than his meaning').

It is one thing to maintain the principle of the 'just middle' and the *mot juste*; it is another to find, in the articulation of one's 'life-long, unchangeable passion', all the crucial terms pre-empted by the very powers one most deplores: the 'prominent or protuberant public figures', the 'gargoyles', that is, poets 'with high reputation, most of whose work has gone since into the discard', by that 'Provincialism' which is 'ignorance plus a lust after uniformity'. Instead of the 'just middle' one has 'a soft terminology . . . an endless series of indefinite middles', 'the pimps' paradise of indefinite verbiage'. In theory and principle Pound was always entirely clear about the necessary counter-measures. From at least the time of *The Spirit of Romance*, in 1910, and probably before, he had no doubt that the study and imitation of Provençal and Tuscan poetry and poetic theory was the focal point of a truly resistant and reformative virtuous craft. His simultaneous and subsequent discoveries—Kung, Flaubert, Gautier, the art of

Arnold Dolmetsch in reviving seventeenth-century instrumental music and
song—did not contradict or override the Provençal–Tuscan *paideuma*
but arranged themselves in correlative order around that focus. Arnaut
Daniel, Guido Cavalcanti: in these men 'the preciseness of the description
denotes . . . a clarity of imaginative vision'; 'it is in the spirit of this period
to be precise'. Pound was clearly moved, and considered himself instructed
(as who would not?), by the luminous implications of those lines in the
thirty-third canto of the *Paradiso* in which 'substance and accidents and their
customs' are bound together by love 'in such wise that that which I speak
is a simple light'. It seems to have been Pound's lifelong endeavour to
find the means whereby that Dantean conception could be registered in
the demonstrable technicalities of English verse. It was, one may add, the
intuition that, at the highest level of technical accomplishment, the 'simple'
embraces and is embraced by 'substance and accidents' that, in the first and
second decades of the twentieth century, suggested to Pound an alternative
to the arrogant provincialism of American opinion on literary matters, its
assumption that, as he sardonically reported, 'The style of 1870 is the final
and divine revelation'. At the same time Provençal and Tuscan clarity of
intelligence is equally a rebuke to the 'new, nickel-plated, triumphant'
social mechanisms in America and Europe (epitomized in *Hugh Selwyn
Mauberley* by 'pianola', 'kinema', 'steam yacht') which were rapidly ousting
the 'courteous, tawdry, quiet old'. 'The traditional methods are not antiquated, nor are poets necessarily the atavisms which they seem', he declared
in 1912. They are not antiquated, not atavisms, if one has in mind Dante's
idea that you can bind the complex into a simple light or assents to the
sensuous intellect of Cavalcanti's 'Donna mi prega'. Nonetheless the statement presupposes that 'the traditional methods are not antiquated' will be
understood in precisely those terms that the proposer had in mind and will
not be welcomed as a piece of sympathetic Luddism by upholders of the
'courteous, tawdry, quiet old'. When Pound writes 'traditional methods' he
does not mean 'derivative convention'. In 1912, no less than at the present
day, this was a distinction not easily impressed upon the consensus.

When, in the first line of 'Envoi (1919)', the poet addresses his 'dumb-born
book' he is echoing 'still-born' from the sixth poem of the sequence, an
allusion to the unacclaimed achievement of Edward FitzGerald, author of *The
Rubáiyát of Omar Khayyám*, a work which Pound admired, one of those
master-craftsmen born out of their due time, a genus with which Pound
to some extent aligned himself: 'The English Rubaiyat was still-born | In

those days'. But 'dumb-born' is not 'still-born' after all. Pound's 'book', the twelve poems of the sequence which precede 'Envoi (1919)', is 'dumb-born' because the tradition of '*motz el son*', the art of perfectly matching words and melody, mastered by the Provençal poet-singers and practised for the last time in England by Campion and Lawes, has in its passing left lyric speech bereft of its truest *melopoeia*. Men like Gautier and Laforgue and Landor have reintroduced other virtues, 'hardness' and '*logopoeia*', and much may be done with these, as *Homage to Sextus Propertius* and the twelve poems of *Hugh Selwyn Mauberley* (Part I) manifestly demonstrate; even so 'Envoi (1919)' recognizes in its opening phrase that the music of its own unfolding will be the only *melopoeia* the 'book' will have. The book may be 'dumb-born' in the further sense that its audience must be assumed to be deaf to its language: its *logopoeia* as much as its *melopoeia*. In 1919, criticizing some poems sent to him by Natalie Barney, Pound observed 'you use words that are not archaic but simply dead.—The archaism has its use but the dead word can only serve in Laforguian irony'. The average poetry-reader of the *lustrum* 1915–20, secure enough in his ignorance of, or contempt for, Laforguian ironies, would be much less secure with the distinction that Pound was drawing between 'archaic' and 'dead'. At such periods, much of the attrition experienced by a writer in Pound's situation comes from the general muzziness of things, the immense labour of picking one's way, as he said, between the 'not quite it' and the 'not quite not it'. Incompatibility is not some peculiar act of bad faith; it is in the nature of circumstance itself; and that vulnerable archaic 'beauty', to the ardent and arduous defence of which Pound committed all his energies, would not, at first encounter, in any way disturb his esteemed great aunt under whose tutelage he had first visited Europe at the age of twelve and for whom 'the one adjective, beautiful', sufficed, albeit 'with apologies', for everything European 'from Alps to San Marco and Titians . . . and to the glass filagrees of Murano'. And 'that song of Lawes', if we take it as token of the high achievement of seventeenth-century English song, would have been entirely sympathetic to the ears of those minor American lyrists of the late nineteenth and early twentieth centuries represented in the influential anthologies of Jessie B. Rittenhouse.

The first issues of Harriet Monroe's magazine *Poetry*, founded in 1912, do not appear wholly unlike Rittenhouse's *The Little Book of Modern Verse* which appeared in the following year. Ridgely Torrence and Madison Cawein, whose poem 'Waste Land' was included in the fourth issue, had been featured in Rittenhouse's *The Younger American Poets* of 1904, which also gave attention to the work of Louise Imogen Guiney, now best remembered for her devoted research into the life of Henry Vaughan; Mary McNeil Fenollosa who, some years later, entrusted Pound with the editing of her late husband's papers on the Chinese Written Character and the Japanese Noh; Lizette Woodworth Reese, author of *A Handful of Lavender*; and Arthur Upson, whose posthumous *Collected Poems* of 1909 included 'After a Dolmetsch Concert' and 'A Viola D'Amore, XVIth Century', dedicated 'to Arnold Dolmetsch'. The first of these poems by Upson was reprinted in *The Little Book of Modern Verse*. Pound met Dolmetsch in 1913 and published tributes to his work in 1915 and 1917. Dolmetsch became for Pound one of several mentors in the different arts who showed that, rightly understood, the 'archaic' disciplines were the key to 'mak[ing] it new'. Pound also concluded that the massive ignorance concerning the old music which Dolmetsch was endeavouring to make known, music that had 'once been the pleasure of the many', amounted to 'a judgment on democracy'. For Pound the old music starts with 'the vortex of pattern' and is radically distinct from 'impressionist or "emotional" music'. 'This old music was not theatrical. You played it yourself as you read a book of precision . . . It was not an interruption but a concentration.' The significance, such as it is, of Upson's 'After a Dolmetsch Concert' is that it is 'impressionist or "emotional" ', a theatrical interruption of concentration on precise and more enduring patterns ('Out of the conquered Past | Unravishable Beauty; | Hearts that are dew and dust | Rebuking the dream of Death'). To the ignorant ear, conscious of theme but not of timbre or nuance, Upson and Pound would be speaking the same language, since they were discoursing upon the same subject and since the difference between Upson's derivative Keatsian 'Unravishable Beauty' and Pound's new-made Waller ('Go, dumb-born book | Tell her that sang me once that song of Lawes') is precisely the kind of distinction that the '*lustrum*' could not attune to. As Rittenhouse wrote of Lizette Woodworth Reese, her work showed 'constant affinity with Herrick, though it is rarely so blithe' or again 'She would recapture the blitheness of Herrick, the valor of Lovelace'. Lovelace's 'To Althea, from Prison' merits an allusion in *The Pisan Cantos* ('at my grates no Althea') but 'lavender', a word cultivated by Reese, was for Pound a term of denigration, as in the 'olde lavender' of the 'perfumed writers' or in 'the "sweet dim faded lavender" tone' of James at his most etiolated. As we have observed, the opposition is clear enough in principle, persuading one that the necessary distinctions can be communicated in practice. In practice, however, the matter appears more complex and more elusive. In 1938 Pound would be praising Chaucer's sense of inherited song modes 'worn smooth in the mind, so that the words take the quality for singing'. The crux here is 'worn smooth'. It is one thing to treat of smoothness as a factive adjunct within the tradition of '*motz el son*'; it is another to encounter the anodyne smoothness, 'the "sweet dim faded lavender" tone', of the effete neo-Cavaliers. Pound's problem in 'Envoi (1919)' is that, in seeking to restore the quality of *melopoeia* as he understood it to be inherent in the craft of seventeenth-century English song, he comes perilously close to being thought to endorse the 'blitheness', etc. that Rittenhouse associated with the Cavalier lyric. It is an extreme form of the problem that all poets face: in making a choice one is also drawing down, as though by natural gravity, that which one has not chosen but which is an inextricable part of the 'circumstance'. Pound said 'you cannot call a man an artist until he shows himself capable of reticence and of restraint, until he shows himself in some degree master of the forces which beat upon him'. It *is* a question of 'degree': if 'Envoi' behaves cavalierly towards reticence, 'Medallion' modifies what we think of the value of 'restraint'. This caveat makes all the more urgent and poignant those claims to absolute judgement which Pound from time to time puts forward on behalf of poets and poetry. In these congeries, however, Rittenhouse, for all her masterful brokerage of the extrinsic and ephemeral, is finally shown to be a tyro in matters of intrinsic value.

Pound, from his juvenilia through to *The Pisan Cantos* and *Drafts and Fragments* steadily emphasized the qualities of affirmation, love, praise, veneration: 'By what characteristic may we know the divine forms? | By beauty'. In his imaginary conversation with Rabelais, 'An Anachronism at Chinon', first published in 1917, he has the modern 'student' observe that the spirit of the Renaissance humanist's classroom is now found only 'among a few scattered enthusiasts, men half ignorant in the present "scholarly" sense, but alive with the spirit of learning, avid of truth, avid of beauty, avid of strange and out of the way bits of knowledge'. The dangerously rhetorical 'avid of', thrice repeated, the seemingly unguarded 'beauty', are protected, though only in part, by the irony of the title, 'An Anachronism'. In his autobiographical fragment *Indiscretions* (1920) Pound remarked that his father was 'the naivest man who ever possessed sound sense' and throughout his own work, from the early *The Spirit of Romance* and *Patria Mia* to the last fragments, he remains convinced that one ought to be able to proclaim the virtues and values simply, directly, even 'naively', if that is how it is fated to appear in the world's eyes: 'Till change hath broken down | All things save Beauty alone'; 'What thou lov'st well shall not be reft from thee'. At the same time he is, in his critical writings, breaking down the simple coherence of 'Beauty' as it stands proclaimed in 'Envoi (1919)' into a number of facets: 'Beauty is a brief gasp between one cliché and another'; 'Beauty *is* an accusation'; or (in *The Pisan Cantos*) ' "beauty is difficult" sd/ Mr Beardsley'. The matter is further perplexed by Pound's awareness of 'conflicts in himself between modernism and passéism', his need to move away from the 'archaizing Wardour Street of his first collections'. In a letter to James Joyce, in July 1917, he referred to the 'mellifluous archaism' of a version from Horace on which he was currently engaged. In his first prose book *The Spirit of Romance* one encounters such belletrisms as 'sheer poetic magic', 'infinitely more beautiful', 'the noblest love lyric in the world', 'nothing more or less than the magical quality of poetry'; and in the later tributes to the music-making of the Dolmetsch family his evocation of the old music ('tones clear as brown amber') is precious rather than precise. With such phrases it is not easy to determine whether we are picking up a few pieces of parochial detritus or whether Pound, grimly aware that he is proselytizing in the enemy's country, is pragmatically trading a few catch-words in the 'provincial' tongue as the necessary price for being given any sort of hearing, even the most cursory and indifferent. Parallel with this runs a zealous attempt at definition, begun early and persisted in for many years, in which 'the beautiful' is equated with 'τὸ καλόν'. It is likely that Pound first encountered the concept when reading Coleridge in 1907: the proposal that the Greek words for 'the beautiful' embody the sense of like calling to like, a sense reflected in the (false) etymology. When, in the third lyric of *Hugh Selwyn Mauberley*, he writes 'We see τὸ καλόν | Decreed in the market place' the irony scarcely needs glossing, though one recollects a letter of William James recording 'To Kalon' in 1900 as the label on an American claret.

The kind of ironic enjambment in 'τὸ καλόν | Decreed in the market place', the conflation, in the last line of the same poem, of the Olympian victory-wreath with the tin *cache-sexe* for nude statues cited in the brusque note to his nervous publisher Elkin Mathews, is a style designed to mime and master a particular ambience. He describes such circumstances, in his obituary on A. R. Orage, as the 'quicksand of obfuscation, the ignorance, the non-correlation, the irritation of the jostled, the gross silence of hired concealers'. One of the discoveries of 'modernist' poetry has been the technique of transposing the hopeless 'irritation of the jostled', 'the gross silence of hired concealers', into the kind of rapid juxtapositions and violent lacunae that one finds in the third and fourth poems of *Hugh Selwyn Mauberley*—phrase callously jostling with phrase, implication merging into implication ('pli selon pli'), sententiae curtly abandoned. These become key instruments of the 'intelligence at bay'. This too is a phrase of Pound's. It occurs in a memorial tribute of 1915 to Rémy de Gourmont celebrating, among other virtues, his beneficent influence on writers younger than himself, 'a vortex of twenty men, and among them five or six of the most intelligent young men in Paris... These men were plotting a gigantic blague. A "blague" when it is a fine blague is a satire upon stupidity, an attack. It is the weapon of intelligence at bay; of intelligence fighting against an alignment of odds'. That 'blague' was a particular piece of tactics, a farcical mock election parodying a journalistic penchant for titling nonentities 'Prince des Penseurs', 'Prince des Poètes' or 'Prince des Conteurs'. By 1918 Pound was using the term of Henry James, calling him 'the great blagueur', referring, in the same essay, to his 'blague and benignity'. *Homage to Sextus Propertius*, that '*collage* of poker-faced misreadings', contains strong elements of blague; so does the third poem in the *Mauberley* sequence. But 'Envoi (1919)' seems, on first acquaintance, to hold itself aloof from such tactics:

> Tell her that sheds
> Such treasure in the air,
> Recking naught else but that her graces give
> Life to the moment,
> I would bid them live
> As roses might, in magic amber laid,
> Red overwrought with orange and all made
> One substance and one colour
> Braving time.

What is 'braving time'? It is to challenge, to defy, with a tincture of 'bravura', the 'display of daring or defiance; brilliancy of execution', as in 'a passage or piece of music requiring great skill and spirit in its execution, written to task the artist's powers'. 'Envoi (1919)' is a bravura performance. In such lines Pound is, perhaps, seeking to answer one of his own earlier questions. In 1913, quoting some lines of Beddoes, he had asked 'Can a man write poetry in a purely archaic dialect?' and had answered 'Presumably he can, and Beddoes has done so'. In the year of this poem's composition he remarked to Natalie Barney 'The archaism has its use.' We should ask ourselves what 'use' the archaism may be thought to have in 'Envoi (1919)'. For one thing, it takes the various facets and possibilities of 'Beauty' as Pound tried to define it or as he had heard it defined ('Beauty *is* an accusation', ' "beauty is difficult" sd/ Mr Beardsley') and concentrates them in something that, in 1912, he had called the 'beauty of the means'. 'Labour on the TECHNIQUE of singable words is honourable labour', he would write in 1938, adding 'God knows I worked in the dark from 1905 onwards, and the light has come very slowly'. Pound also reminded Binyon that, years previously, he had heard him say 'Slowness is beauty', which 'struck me as very odd in 1908 (when I certainly did not believe it) and has stayed with me ever since'. Those who have left accounts of Pound's manner of reading aloud his own and others' work have recorded the 'strongly marked time', the slow pace of his delivery: 'He reads it that slow. It's stately, majestical'; 'Rhythm extremely exact and tempo very slow'. It would seem that a number of things slowly came together, from the technical and ethical peripheries, all focused upon a sense of tempo and all understood as the necessary basis for accurate judgement and for any genuine act of swift intuition. Pound's theory of the 'great bass' in music is that 'down below the lowest note synthesized by the ear and "heard" there are slower vibrations ... The whole question of tempo, and of a main base in all musical structure resides in use of these frequencies'.

Such words as 'tempo', 'structure', and 'frequencies' brought here into arbitrary collocation with reminiscences of the slow pace of his delivery may suggest a claim on my part that 'Envoi (1919)' converts the idea 'Slowness is beauty' into a pattern of metrics that can be mathematically demonstrated. I make no such claim. Pound reads 'that slow' because it feels right; and it feels right because 'slow pace' is an ethos before it is anything else. In his reading of *The Divine Comedy* Pound's eye and ear were attracted by those episodes in the *Inferno* and the *Purgatorio* describing Dante's encounters with Sordello and other worthy albeit flawed and troubled spirits 'delli occhi onesta e tarda', 'con occhi tardi e gravi'. He emphatically associated these phrases with Henry James, 'The massive head, the slow uplift of the hand *gli occhi onesti e tardi* ... the lightning incision'. It is to be observed that 'slowness' is the necessary ethical and physical preparative for that 'quality of a sudden vision of intuition or glimpse into things', that 'inevitable swiftness and rightness in a given field' which, for Pound, was the essential *virtù* of 'genius'. Here too he is in accord with Allen Upward, who noted in his autobiography 'I wrote *The New Word* in a fortnight. I had been composing it for twenty-five years'.

The factive 'swiftness', whatever might be supposed to the contrary, has nothing in common with the rapidity of access and communication found desirable by contemporary civilization: the 'kinetic' ('prose kinema'). In Febrary 1916, in an essay on 'Mr James Joyce and the Modern Stage', Pound wrote 'Professionals tell us: "Oh, they have quickened the tempo. Ibsen is too slow," and the like. So we have Shaw; that is to say, Ibsen with the sombre reality taken out'. Slowness seems to be concomitant, therefore, with a certain kind of integrity of the imagination, 'full of certitude and implacable, and unswerving', the kind that tends to be rejected by the 'compleasant', the accommodating, as 'naive' or 'reactionary' or 'archaic' or slow on the uptake and that finds itself punished in some way, 'at bay', set about by malice and misunderstanding, branded by its own purgatorial suffering, and yet imbued perhaps with a 'sombre reality', perhaps with 'something which exalts the reader, making him feel that he is in contact with something arranged more finely than the commonplace'. One would claim no more for Pound's performance of his own work, as on the 1939 disc which includes a reading of 'Envoi (1919)', than that it sounds 'full of certitude and implacable, and unswerving' and might 'exalt' the listener, making him feel that he is in contact with something arranged more finely than the commonplace. The pace and pitch of the voice do not solve the 'whole question of tempo' as it affects one's understanding of this and other poems; but they emphatically confirm an attitude of mind and must, of course, be susceptible to the charge of vocal attitudinizing and moral portentousness. If, however, one were asked, on such grounds, to concede that 'Envoi (1919)' reads as 'impressionistically' as Arthur Upson's 'After a Dolmetsch Concert' the concession should not be made. It confuses the accidental with the intrinsic. When Upson writes 'Hearts that are dew and dust | Rebuking the dream of death' the statement is otiose, the verb collapses into its own vacuity. When Pound recites what he has written— 'One substance and one colour | Braving time'—his word 'braving' is already so placed, so cunningly circumstanced, that it can sustain not only the intermingled, interacting portentousness and irony of the poem itself but also the overweening, gratuitous sonorities of Pound's recital.

'Envoi (1919)' is required to carry a weightier and more complex syntax than is Waller's 'Goe lovely rose', upon which it is based. The laboured conditionals ('Hadst thou but...', 'Then were there...', 'I would...',

'As roses might . . . ', 'May be as fair . . . ', 'Might, in new ages . . . ') admit the
power of the 'accidentals and imperfections'. At the same time the verse
insists on the melopoeic quality of rhythm and cadence, as though this were
indivisible from 'a certain verity of feeling'. In an essay on the sculptor
Brancusi, published some two years after *Mauberley*, Pound suggested that
'perhaps every artist at one time or another believes in a sort of elixir or
philosopher's stone produced by the sheer perfection of his art; by the
alchemical sublimation of the medium; the elimination of accidentals and
imperfections'. 'Sheer perfection' is one of those usages, like Asquith's
'almost indefinable, never mistakable' essence of 'style', which, while salut-
ing a lyric sublimation, succeed only in perpetuating a sense of poetical
redundancy. The concluding words of 'Envoi (1919)', 'Till change hath
broken down | All things save Beauty alone', maintain the idea of 'sheer
perfection' though at some remove from the complacent aplomb with
which that phrase is commonly uttered. Beauty, which for Pound included
the 'consummation of métier', a crafted entity, the 'melody which most in-
centres the soul', or an ' "absolute rhythm", a rhythm . . . which corresponds
exactly to the emotion or shade of emotion to be expressed', is, in the drift
and occasion and contexture of things, hardly to be wrested from the
subjective impressions of Herbert Asquith or Jessie B. Rittenhouse promul-
gated as matters of public acceptance and judgement.

Rittenhouse had met Pound in New York early in 1911 'on his one and
only visit' to the Poetry Society of America. Seven years later, in the January
1918 issue of *The Bookman*, she reviewed the American edition of *Lustra . . . with Earlier Poems*. Though she found 'much beauty' in 'the Chinese
section, *Cathay*' and welcomed the reappearance, among the earlier poems,
of the 1912 collection *Ripostes*, particularly its 'haunting and lovely poem'
'Δώρια', her review as a whole was unfavourable, expressing strong disapproval of Pound's 'bewildering medley of tongues and styles' and asking
'What is his own voice, his own style, his own individuality?' Though she
conceded that, out of this 'poetic scrap-bag' of languages and cultures,
Pound 'weaves for himself a fabric of song which might be beautiful had
[he] the art to make it so' the qualification was tendentious. In praising
Pound's earlier work she had already acknowledged his artistry. Her present
objection was rather to the moral flaw, as she conceived it, in his recent
intentions. Demanding 'something worthy of the inspiration' and finding
that Pound had 'repudiated his earlier manner', the style which she had been
pleased to approve, Rittenhouse accused him of setting 'a trap for his critics'.

The meaning and implications of 'something of beauty and value', 'something worthy of the inspiration', and suchlike phrases must be teased out from among the lyric congeries of Lizette Woodworth Reese, Arthur Upson, Madison Cawein, Clinton Scollard, Orrick Johns, and others, who gave 'charm and romance to the immediate thing'. While not claiming that 'Go, dumb-born book' stands as a direct riposte to the prejudicate opinions of the *Bookman* review, one may fairly regard it as a poem 'at bay', confronting not only the fragile appeal but also the heavy proscriptions of the Rittenhouse ethos.

It is as much the strength as the weakness of 'Envoi (1919)' that its melopoeic certitude does not annul the numerous uncertainties. If we set this poem alongside 'The Return', composed some seven years earlier ('See, they return; ah, see the tentative | Movements, and the slow feet, | The trouble in the pace and the uncertain | Wavering!'), where the rhythm is 'reflective', composed 'to the feel of the thing', or if one thinks of 'The Coming of War: Actaeon', which had appeared in *Lustra*, the later poem seems in some respects retrograde. Pound was to say, reflecting upon the early period many years later, in *The Pisan Cantos*, 'To break the pentameter, that was the first heave'; and this is indeed what 'The Return' and 'The Coming of War: Actaeon' succeed in doing. But in the second stanza of 'Envoi (1919)' the nine irregular lines are six regular pentameters in disguise. The 'detail of surface' is not quite 'in accord with the root in justice'. One may surmise, therefore, that Pound has his attention focused on something other than that '[bringing] forth from the inner nature' to which his concept of 'absolute rhythm' was devoted. 'Rhythm' here is not easily separated from metrical subterfuge; it is not absolute but relative, reminiscent, an adjunct to something else; and that something else is not entirely divorced from 'blague'. But whereas blague, as Pound seems to envisage it, begins with pomp and ends in derision, this poem emerges from circumstances of derision ('Wrong from the start', 'Bent resolutely on wringing lilies from the acorn') into its defiant, self-conscious *melopoeia*: 'poetry which moves by its music, whether it be a music in the words or an aptitude for, or suggestion of, accompanying music'.

This 'self-consciousness' is a crux which I have, perhaps contentiously, introduced. Though one is not obliged to think of it as a Prufrockian nervous inhibition, it undeniably implies a sharp apprehension, a shade more vulnerable than self-awareness, of the circumstances in which the self speaks and acts. The actual, historical protagonist of *Homage to Sextus*

Propertius had been, in Pound's estimation, both keenly aware and intensely self-conscious, Laforgue's precursor in the discovery and practice of 'good verbalism', the deployment of 'the word in some special relation to "usage" '. *Homage* itself is an exercise in this mode, as are the first and third poems of the *Mauberley* sequence. 'E. P. Ode pour l'Election de Son Sepulchre' is cast as a deriding of E.P. by the triumphalism of current 'usage', the rhetoric of the political and literary *imperium*. Yet even as he was preparing his logopoeic *Homage* for publication Pound suggested that, in certain cases, logopoeia may be 'the utterance of clever people in despair'. Work on *Homage* and *Mauberley* proceeded concurrently with the composition of the earliest *Cantos*. Versions of the first three were printed at the end of the first American edition of *Lustra*, where Rittenhouse found them incoherent but preferable to 'Contemporiana'. In December 1919 Pound wrote to his father that he had 'done cantos 5, 6, 7, each is more incomprehensible than the one preceding it; I don't know what's to be done about it'. 'Incomprehensible', used like this, makes a mockery of despair; it is a word at bay.

'Envoi (1919)', defying the incomprehensible and the despairing in its 'canorous lyric measures', yet embarrassingly placed in relation, or disrelation, to the sequence as a whole, stands for 'what's to be done about it' and for what cannot be 'done' about it: 'it' in this case being fairly typified (I would argue) by the kind of canorous lyric measures that Rittenhouse preferred to the measures of *Lustra* or by ex-Prime Minister Asquith's 1919 tribute to 'the sovereign quality of Style'. Pound's melopoeia is itself drawn into 'a dance of the intelligence among words and ideas and modification of ideas and characters' since what is 'modified' in 'Envoi (1919)' is by implication the question 'What is his own voice, his own style, his own individuality?' The absolute is brought back to become a part of the relative and the conditional, the not quite it and the not quite not it; but, so circumstanced, is all the more fully and directly affirmed. Lyric utterance stands as witness to a faith in 'sheer perfection' even while it is standing scrutiny as a piece of evidence in the natural history of such belief. ' "[B]eauty is difficult" sd/ Mr Beardsley.' When Pound put that phrase into *The Pisan Cantos*, his source, one supposes, was Yeats, the sixteenth chapter of 'The Tragic Generation': 'I said to [Beardsley] once, "You have never done anything to equal your Salome with the head of John the Baptist." I think that for the moment he was sincere when he replied, "Yes, yes; but beauty is so difficult" '. Yeats was in two minds about Beardsley; divided between admiration for his 'noble courage' and despair at the 'spirit of mockery' which he saw as more and more withering in its effect. 'Yes, yes; but beauty is so difficult' is therefore to be taken both as an act of witness, a testimony, and as an abdication of responsibility. 'For the moment', Yeats thinks, 'he was sincere'. The difference between the pitch of Yeats's concession, or caveat, and the cadence of 'Envoi (1919)' is marked by a proximity of phrase: 'Recking naught else but that her graces give | Life to the moment'. As I see it, Pound sets himself the task, as much in this poem as in *The Pisan Cantos* some twenty-five years later, of transposing 'bravery' from the domain of the merely 'sincere' (which is ephemeral and solipsistic) into a form of 'substance' and 'colour' successfully detached from the ephemeral. The strength and weakness of 'Envoi (1919)' is that we are given a not wholly satisfactory process in the guise of a satisfyingly finished piece. Integrity is in the mood (largely the moods of the verb), otiosity is in the mode (those lyrical affirmatives scarcely to be distinguished from the school of Rittenhouse). Integrity, so circumstanced, relapses into the merely sincere; and beauty—against the grain of the argument—remains 'a brief gasp between one cliché and another'.

Style and Faith

Knowledge cannot save us, but we cannot be saved without Knowledge;
Faith is not on this side Knowledge, but beyond it; we must necessarily
come to *Knowledge* first, though we must not stay at it, when we are come
thither.

John Donne

If it were not for Sin, *we* should converse together as *Angels* do.

Benjamin Whichcote

Preface

In his exegesis of Psalm 11—and his approach here is applied equally to the other psalms—John Calvin asks whether the translation from the Hebrew is correct in point of detail. Of verse 5, 'Jehovah approves the righteous man', Calvin notes: 'The Hebrew word *bachan*, which we have rendered *to approve*, often signifies *to examine* or *try*. But in this passage I explain it as simply meaning, that God so inquires into the cause of every man as to distinguish the righteous from the wicked . . . God distinguishes between the righteous and the unrighteous, and in such a way as shows that he is not an idle spectator.'

I am prepared to argue, and indeed this book is an attempt at such an argument, that it is a characteristic of the best English writing of the early sixteenth to late seventeenth centuries that authors were prepared and able to imitate the original authorship, the *auctoritas*, of God, at least to the extent that forbade them to be idle spectators of their own writing.

As a generalization such implications of authority are also true of the best writing of later periods, though I would contend that here such excellence is more isolated and more beleaguered. In saying this I have no desire to add my voice to the chorus of contemporary cultural lament, a centrifugal movement in which immense generalizations are produced out of solipsistic rancour.

It strikes me that the sentences from Calvin with which I began could stand as an epigraph to John Donne's several presentations of an essential theme throughout his devotional writing: that of God's grammar. It is a question whether we now understand, let alone receive, this grammar as Donne intended us to grasp it:

> The Holy Ghost is an eloquent Author, a vehement, and an abundant Author, but yet not luxuriant; he is far from a penurious, but as far from a superfluous style too.

With Donne, style *is* faith: a measure of delivery that confesses his own inordinacy while remaining in all things ordinate. To state this is to affirm

one's recognition of his particular authority in having achieved the equation; one recognizes also such authority in Milton and Herbert. They are
not, generally, otherwise to be equated.

   In most instances style and faith remain obdurately apart. In some cases,
despite the presence of well-intentioned labour, style betrays a fundamental
idleness which it is impossible to reconcile with the workings of good faith.

15

Common Weal, Common Woe

It is touching, as well as contingent, that the publication of the Second Edition of the *Oxford English Dictionary* (*OED*) should have taken place in the centenary year of Gerard Hopkins's death.[1] Though Hopkins was not formally associated with the great enterprise—as he was with Joseph Wright's *English Dialect Dictionary*—his lifetime (1844–89) coincided, as James Milroy has pointed out, 'with the heyday of English philology'. He was in his fourteenth year when the proposal to inaugurate a New Dictionary of the English Language was carried at a meeting of the Philological Society; when the first section (A–ANT) appeared from the Clarendon Press in February 1884, *The Wreck of the Deutschland* had been in existence eight years. When the final sheets of the *Dictionary* went to press in January 1928, 'almost exactly seventy years from the date' of the Philological Society's resolution, *Poems of Gerard Manley Hopkins* had been before the public for a decade. Its small first printing, sponsored by Robert Bridges, friend both of Hopkins and of the *Dictionary* and memorialist of James Murray's chief associate, Henry Bradley, sold its last copies in the year of the *OED*'s completion.

Although, as these collocations indicate, Hopkins cannot have drawn in any significant way on the *Dictionary* itself, few would dispute his indebtedness to its forerunners and their sometimes inaccurate etymologies; particularly to Richard Chenevix Trench, by whom, as the *Dictionary of National Biography* recorded in 1899, 'the Oxford English dictionary, at present proceeding under Dr Murray's editorship, was originally suggested and its characteristics indicated'. Two of Trench's books, *On the Study of Words* (1851) and *English Past and Present* (1855), gained a wide readership, and each went into numerous editions during Hopkins's lifetime.

---

[1] *The Oxford English Dictionary*, 2nd edn., prepared by J. A. Simpson and E. S. C. Weiner, 20 vols., 21,728 pages (Oxford: Clarendon Press, 1989).

Disremember Trench noted as 'still common in Ireland', and Hopkins may have discovered it there: 'Spelt from Sibyl's Leaves', in which the word appears, is a Dublin sonnet of 1884–6. He was not the first author to adopt *disremember*. It occurs in Mrs Gaskell's *Mary Barton* (1848), and Ouida anticipated Hopkins by a few years. The original *Dictionary* cited Gaskell, Ouida, and three other examples spanning the years 1836–80. Although the *Supplement* of 1933 found two further citations, one from 1815, the other from 1928, it overlooked or ignored Hopkins, whose *Poems* had gone into a second edition in 1930. The 1972 *Supplement* added three more quotations, this time including '*c* 1885 G. M. Hopkins *Poems* (1918) 52'. The new Second Edition incorporates the findings of both *Supplements* into the original record.

Such details are worth attention because they exemplify the *Dictionary*'s strengths and limitations. On the one hand they bear witness to an initial vigilance of such generous scope that it can take up an out-of-the-way word, furnished with five instances of its usage, and to a pertinacity of revision that does not grudge time and labour spent in adding a further five citations. On the other hand they make a public exhibition of the contri- butors', or editors', inability, over half a century, to recognize the one usage which significantly changes the pitch of the word ('qúite | Disremembering, dísmémbering áll now'). The Second Edition heads its entry '*v*. Chiefly *dial.* [f. DIS 6 + REMEMBER *v*.] To fail to remember; to forget. (*trans.* and *absol.*)'. If this may be thought sufficient for the nine other citations, it patently fails to register the metamorphic power of Hopkins's context. 'Disremembering', in 'Spelt from Sibyl's Leaves', is not, as the *Dictionary* presumes, 'failing to remember', 'forgetting'; it is 'dismembering the memory'.

It may be thought that, in arguing the case in these terms, one has confused an English Dictionary on Historical Principles with a mere Dictionary of Quotations and is raising an outcry over some missing gem. This is not so. K. M. Elisabeth Murray remarks (in *Caught in the Web of Words: James A. H. Murray and the 'Oxford English Dictionary'* [1977], to which I am in debt for a number of facts and quotations) that her grandfather 'accepted ... as axiomatic' the Philological Society's opinion that 'the literary merit or demerit of any particular writer, like the comparative elegance or inelegance of any given word, is a subject upon which the Lexicographer is bound to be almost indifferent', and with this working principle one is in broad agreement. If I say, therefore, that I consider the *OED*'s treatment of Hopkins's language inadequate, I am raising a practical, not a sentimental, objection. My concern is with what the editors originally termed 'The

Signification (*Sematology*)' and now call 'The Signification, or *senses*'. For *self-being* the Second Edition adds Hopkins (retreat-notes of August 1880) to the original citations from Golding (1587), Fotherby (*ante* 1619), and Bishop Hall (*a* 1656), and the same meditation also serves to illustrate *selve / selving* (unknown to the original editors and overlooked or rejected by the 1933 *Supplement*). The signification of the word *pitch*, in the same set of notes, remains undefined, nor is the sematology of 'Pitched past pitch of grief' (in the sonnet 'No worst, there is none') adduced at any point in the entries on *pitch* and *pitched*.

Murray had conceded, in his original Preface (later retitled 'General Explanations'), that to 'discover and exhibit' the order in which a word has acquired 'a long and sometimes intricate series of significations...are among the most difficult duties' of a dictionary such as this. One would be sympathetic to the suggestion that Hopkins, in his uses of *pitch / pitched*, has pitched its significations beyond the range of the *OED*'s reductive method if it were not for the fact that, in his notes 'On Personality, Grace and Free Will', he has himself offered a model reduction: 'So also *pitch* is ultimately simple positiveness, that by which being differs from and is more than nothing and not-being.' In recent years there have been scholarly glosses on 'the peculiar meaning Hopkins gives to the word' (for example, in Peter Milward's *A Commentary on... 'The Wreck of the Deutschland'* [1968]), which the compilers of the O–SCZ *Supplement* (1982) appear not to have considered. Those responsible for the H–N *Supplement* (1976) drew on twentieth-century attempts at definition in their entries for *inscape* and *instress*. The latter word is described there, and in the new edition, as 'the force or energy which sustains an inscape'. Norman H. MacKenzie writes in *A Reader's Guide to Gerard Manley Hopkins* (1981) that, 'though this scarcely covers all his examples, it seems impossible to find a simple definition which will'. I do not think that 'simple definition' is necessarily what one needs or what the founders of the enterprise had principally in mind when they spoke of the need to make 'a Dictionary worthy of the English language'. As William Empson remarked, 'short dictionaries should be improved, because they are intended for people who actually need help'; the *OED* is not for those who 'actually need help' in that sense. Empson's 'general proposal' was that 'the interactions of the senses of a word should be included'; he also referred to words which 'straddle' the logical distinctions. In Hopkins's *pitch* several otherwise distinct senses can be felt as 'going together', as Empson would say.

The *Dictionary*'s first editors sometimes dealt firmly with blurred or uncertain significations in cases which involved chronological descent or collocation of various authors. Thus, 'From *c* 1550 to *c* 1675 *silly* was very extensively used in senses 1–3, and in a number of examples it is difficult to decide which shade of meaning was intended by the writer'; or, 'Ingenious II. Used by confusion for INGENUOUS or L. *ingenuus*'; and 'Ingenuous 6. In 17th c. frequently misused for *ingenious*: see INGENIOUS 1–3. *Obs*'. They edit less authoritatively those cases, equally characteristic of the seventeenth century, in which distinct, even opposed, senses of a word alternate in the work of a single author, changing that 'long and sometimes intricate series of significations' into a stylistic field where the compounding of language with political or religious commitment may be either a matter of deliberate display or a case of unwitting revelation. In the entry on *dexterity* ('2. Mental adroitness or skill ... cleverness, address, ready tact') the reader is apprised that Sense 2 occurs 'sometimes in a bad sense: cleverness in taking an advantage, sharpness'. The citation from Clarendon's *History of the Rebellion* ('The dexterity that is universally practised in those parts') is ambivalently placed and, in its brief citation, elusive in tone. Read in context (towards the end of Book Eight) the phrase still holds a good deal in reserve. Clarendon is alluding to the manners and morals of Antrim's Irish and Montrose's Scottish highlanders, from whose ranks it was planned to raise an army 'that was not to depend upon any supplies of money, or arms, or victual, but what they could easily provide for themselves, by the dexterity that is universally practised in those parts'. How far, if at all, does Clarendon's sense of his word conform to the editorial definition? This is not a case to be explained by 'sometimes in a bad sense'. Whatever is happening to the 'good' and 'bad' connotations is happening within the space of eighteen words, where what is 'good' is determined by the necessities of the 'good' cause and what is 'bad' by the unexplored hinterland of 'what they could easily provide for themselves'.

No one reading the *OED* entry would be able to deduce that *dexterity* was one of the rhetorical janus-words of seventeenth-century politics or that Clarendon was a master in his style of deployment. One may compare his characterization of the constitutionalist Royalist Falkland, whom he admired, with his treatment of the republican Sir Henry Vane the Younger, whom he hated. Of the former Clarendon writes, 'he had a memory retentive of all that he had ever reade, and an understandinge and judgement to apply it, seasonably and appositely, with the most dexterity and addresse';

and of the latter, 'Ther neede no more be sayd of his ability, then that he was chosen to cozen and deceave a whole nation, which excelled in craft and dissemblinge, which he did with notable pregnancy and dexterity'. When I say that Clarendon was a master of his style I mean that *dexterity* is a word embedded by the usage of the time in what Clarendon terms 'the common practice of men', the 'temper and spirit' of the age, the 'posture of affairs', and that his partiality and animus are notably successful when they are contriving their own exceptions in the midst of this common medium.

One misses, in the *OED*'s treatment of this word, the kind of succinct annotation which accompanies the definition of 'common weal, commonweal 2. The whole body of the people, the body politic; a state, community. = COMMONWEALTH 2'. The editorial note reads, 'This use was adversely criticized by Elyot: see quot. 1531'. And indeed the quotation from *The Boke Named the Gouernour* proves to be one of those exemplary citations in which the quality of a mind at work in its domain, a compounding of discursive plainness and hauteur, at once comely and ungainly, is conveyed in a few characteristic clauses: 'hit semeth that men haue ben longe abused in calling *Rempublican* a commune weale . . . there may appere lyke diuersitie to be in englisshe betwene a publike weale and a commune weale, as shulde be in latin betwene *Res* publica and Res *plebeia*'. In the original text the phrases here strung together by the editorial ellipses are divided by five sentences. The trimming is self-evidently at one with the editorial principles and practices reviewed by the February 1928 issue of the *Periodical*, the house publication of the Clarendon Press, in its salute to 'The Completion of the Oxford English Dictionary 1884–1928':

> Some quotations [on the 'slips' submitted by contributors] have been excerpted with such brevity as to be obscure and need filling up from the original source. More often they are too long to print as they stand—a sagacious worker is careful to copy out ample context, where the meaning might otherwise be uncertain—and need cutting down; the quotable portion is indicated to the printer by underlining in coloured ink or pencil.

Murray, in a series of photographs (reproduced in *Caught in the Web of Words*) taken in the Oxford Scriptorium, immersed in, or looking up from, his labours, white-bearded, wearing his velvet cater-cap, resembles a memorial portrait of some immolated biblical scholar of the Reformation. The resemblance was not wholly accidental (*Caught in the Web of Words*, Index, page 382: 'martyrdom, sense of'; page 383: 'opinions on: academic robes').

The imperative to 'discover and exhibit' a 'long and sometimes intricate series of significations' appears morally correlative to, if not derivative from, theological disputations at the time of the Reformation, when the fate of souls could be determined by a point of etymology or grammar. It is no disparagement to suggest that the labours of successive editors and associate editors between 1879 and 1928 seem more akin to the 'diligence' of Tyndale or of Ascham's *Scholemaster* than to the visionary philology of Trench's spiritual mentors Coleridge ('For if words are not THINGS, they are LIVING POWERS') and Emerson ('Parts of speech are metaphors, because the whole of nature is a metaphor of the human mind'). Murray's editorial stamina, his 'iron determination and capacity for unremitting work', may be preferred to Coleridge's spasmodic, though intense, labours. One cannot, however, dismiss Coleridge's words. The man who wrote that, in Shakespeare's poems, 'the creative power, and the intellectual energy wrestle as in a war embrace' and who thought of images in poetry as 'diverging and contracting with the . . . activity of the assimilative and of the modifying faculties' was making sense in a way that bears upon the nature and function of such a work as the *OED*. In the original argument between Murray and the Delegates of the Clarendon Press there was a mistaken premise, or false equation, and the implications of this continue to confuse debate. The contention quickly became a self-parody in which 'famous quotations' were set in judgment over 'crack-jaw medical and surgical words' and language taken from the newspapers. At this level of absurdity one has no hesitation in declaring for Murray; his acerbic reference to the Delegates' apparent inability to 'acknowledge contemporary facts and read the signs of the times' was fully justified. But on both sides of the argument one is aware of a polite blank gaze turned upon those elements in language which Coleridge and Trench constantly endeavoured to bring to the attention of a national readership.

In his 'General Explanations' to the *OED*, Murray wrote that 'to every man the domain of "common words" widens out in the direction of his own reading, research, business, provincial or foreign residence, and contracts in the direction with which he has no practical connexion: no one man's English is *all* English'. Murray edited four texts for the Early English Text Society before his acceptance of responsibility for the *Dictionary* foreclosed upon every other 'practical connexion', a restriction which he bitterly regretted. One cannot doubt Murray's selflessness 'in the interest of English Literature'. At the same time, as his granddaughter's biography reveals, his trust in the rectitude of his own literary judgement was magisterial: 'He held all his life to the opinion that novel reading was a waste of time'. Under constant pressure from the Delegates to save space and money by cutting 'superfluous quotations', he conceded grudgingly, recording in the 'General Explanations' that

> the need to keep the Dictionary within practicable limits has ... rendered it necessary to give only a minimum of quotations selected from the material available, and to make those given as brief as possible. It is to be observed that in their abridged form they simply illustrate the word, phrase, or construction, for which they are given, and do not necessarily express the sentiments of their authors.

One notes the characteristic scrupulousness; one notes further that 'express the sentiments of their authors' consorts oddly with such phrases as 'a long and sometimes intricate series of significations'. One is inclined to question how closely, in instances of crucial decision, the kind of judgement implied by 'express the sentiments' can apply itself to 'intricate ... significations'.

One feels a similar unease in reading Robert Bridges's memoir of Henry Bradley, the *Dictionary*'s second editor, whose philological knowledge has been fairly described as 'of an unusually wide and accurate nature'. Bridges sought Bradley's opinion, during the compilation of the anthology *The Spirit of Man* (1916), regarding quotations from Shelley. 'Bradley knew Shelley, but not so well as I did, and he was surprised by the accumulated force of the chosen passages, and by the true insight that underlay the rich poetry.' I accept that we are seeing Bradley through Bridges's eyes, but, judging by opinions quoted elsewhere in the memoir, I do not think that Bradley's literary sentiments are misrepresented. As in the case of Murray, one senses a sharp discrepancy between the remarkable accuracy of Bradley's philological knowledge and the postprandial murmurings of literary 'taste': 'the sentiments of their authors', 'true insight', 'rich poetry', 'the author can *write*, which few Germans can'. Was Bridges more at ease with such condescending tattle than with Hopkins's poetry, of which he had been the loyal, though at times obtuse, guardian? His memoir of Bradley first appeared in 1926, eight years after his edition of Hopkins's *Poems*. For almost twenty years, *c.*1871–89, he had been the recipient of letters, from Stonyhurst, Liverpool, Dublin, and elsewhere, containing some of the toughest yet most tactful literary criticism of the nineteenth century. That Bridges should cherish Hopkins's work while remaining impervious to its

discoveries is strange yet not uncommon. In this he seems entirely representative of that long and unbroken succession in English letters which,
while always ready to embrace 'sentiments', is itself without feeling; which is
oblivious, most of all when in its presence, to the creative 'tact' that Coleridge
describes in his July 1802 letter to William Sotheby. When *The Times*, in
support of Murray's editorial policy, stated that for the illustration of verbal
nuance, 'any respectable and recognized publication ... may very likely be
more apt for the lexicographer's purpose than a literary masterpiece' it was
untroubled by its own nuance. 'Literary masterpiece' here looks complacently
down—to adapt T. H. Green's phrase—on that which it belittles by the
imposition of such a compliment. It seems to me no real answer to say, 'Well,
the principle is perfectly sound' since, in the work undertaken by Murray and
his colleagues, the principle is inseparable from the nuance, as the wording of
the *Times* piece simultaneously argues and betrays.

Hopkins, who so revered common speech, was the one writer of the
'heyday of English philology' fully to comprehend that principle is inseparable from nuance. The main burden of his poetic argument, both in
theory and in practice, was to guard the essential against the inessential,
the redundant, the merely decorative. There was a price to be paid, as Eric
Griffiths has demonstrated, in effects of 'willed contrivance', in 'those
declarations [which] often ring with a worried exaggeration because [Hop-
kins] feels himself so misapprehended by his readers'. 'Feeling', in this kind
of context, is not readily separable from what Hopkins's fellow Scotist
Charles Peirce called 'the Brute Actuality of things and facts'. What
Griffiths calls, with a slight but significant shift, 'a simultaneous character
of independent life and of willed contrivance' and 'this double character of
independent life and willed contrivance in the words' is to be judged against
other manifestations of 'doubleness' and simultaneity. One might fairly ask:
What was Murray, if not simultaneously a dedicated 'man of science', as he
describes himself, 'interested in that branch of Anthropology which deals
with the history of human speech', and a reader who professed indifference
to a significant part of that literature on which his science relied? 'I am not
a literary man.... I am not specially interested in Arthur & his knights,
nor in the development of the modern newspaper.' As with those other
terms of brokerage and taste—'famous quotations', 'literary masterpiece',
'true insight that underlay the rich poetry'—it makes no difference
whether the words are uttered in homage or contempt. In either case
it is, as Wordsworth said, the language of 'men who speak of what they

do not understand'; it is the 'sciolism', as Coleridge named it, the 'pretentious superficiality of knowledge' (*OED*) of the literary amateur, indivisible in Murray's case from philological knowledge and lexicographical ability of the highest order. It is a fact at once perplexing and illuminating that, while the making of the *Dictionary* disclosed a vast semantic field in which the brute actuality of English misapprehension could be charted as never before, some of the most telling evidence failed to lodge itself in these pages. One does not find, in the entries for *undiscerned*, *undiscerning*, any recognition of Hobbes's tribute to Sidney Godophin, 'unfortunately slain in the beginning of the late Civill warre, in the Publique quarrell, by an undiscerned, and an undiscerning hand'. *Leviathan* is cited in the 'List of Books Quoted in the Oxford English Dictionary'. Murray in 1879 had asked his team of voluntary readers to 'give us, not only all the *extraordinary* words or constructions in their books, but also as many *good*, *apt*, *pithy* quotations for ordinary words as their time and patience permit'. In which category would *undiscerned*, *undiscerning* find their niche? I would say that in Hobbes's use of them they are ordinary words raised to an extraordinary pitch of signification. How is it possible that a reader of *Leviathan*, specifically briefed to pick out both extraordinary and ordinary usage, could fail to register the reciprocating force of these words? Or how is it possible for an editor, with the *Leviathan* citation before him, to believe that it is less apt, less pithy, than the two seventeenth-century examples he finally sends forward for printing?

In attempting an answer one is bound to meditate on the application of the word 'reduce' to a variety of editorial activities. The *Periodical* (February 1928) acknowledged 'the volunteer sub-editors . . . by whom the millions of slips were reduced to a form in which the various staffs could readily handle them without loss of time'; in the 'Historical Introduction' to the 1933 edition this became 'handling and reducing to alphabetic order . . . three and a half millions of slips'. Murray, in his 'General Explanations', wrote that 'practical utility has some bounds, and a Dictionary has definite limits: the lexicographer must, like the naturalist, "draw the line somewhere", in each diverging direction'. In his dealings with the Delegates he was constantly resisting demands that the scope of the *Dictionary* should be drastically reduced. The entry for the word *reduce* (in the July 1904 fascicule, edited by W. A. Craigie and his assistants) is an exemplary 'reducing' (as in: 'reduce, 14a–c') of its own 'series of significations', running to just under seven columns of print. It may justly be added, however, that among the many consequences and effects of such 'reduction' one is as likely to encounter those which 'break down' and 'lessen' as those which 'refer (a thing) to its origin' or 'bring to a certain order or arrangement'. Murray and his colleagues strike one as being finely attuned to English usages which are themselves reductive, collocative, analytical (as in the notes on Elyot's 'publike weal' vs 'commune weale', or on *sensuous*, 'Apparently invented by Milton, to avoid certain associations of the existing word *sensual*'). When they are presented with 'the assimilative and . . . the modifying faculties' at work in language, when they encounter reciprocity or simultaneity, the outcome is sometimes less happy.

The entry for *private* is inadequate to the protean energy of that word in seventeenth-century English. At the level of practical utility, Milton's 'hee unobserv'd | Home to his Mothers house privat returnd' is markedly more 'apt' and 'pithy' an illustration of the quasi-adverbial use than is the quotation from Pepys which the editors preferred. At the same time one notes that the play between 'unobserv'd' and 'privat' so modifies the pitch of the latter word that, while fulfilling the terms of the *OED*'s simple definition ('privately, secretly'), it holds something of its signification in reserve. This 'reserve' has to do in part with Christ's nature, as envisaged by Milton, in part with his circumstances (having conquered the temptation to make himself world-famous and immensely relevant) and in part with the capacity of the imagination to be at once constrained and inviolable. As usual, the *Dictionary* copes well with the reductive uses of *private*: for example, its occurrences in liturgical rubrics and legal clauses dealing with rights of property. It notes (*private 5c*) 'Private judgement' and (under *privy* III.8) 'privy verdict, a verdict given to the judge out of court'. It does not record, under 'private' or under 'verdict', Bunyan's 'who every one gave in his private Verdict against [Faithful] among themselves, and afterwards unanimously concluded to bring him in guilty before the Judge'. Is Bunyan's 'private Verdict' omitted because the citations for 'privy verdict' and 'private judgement' are deemed to have precluded any action by the modifying faculties? It would be hard to find a use of 'private' with more pith than this; 'private verdict' is not a synonym for 'private judgement' or for 'privy verdict'. Bunyan depicts collusion between private malice and public sanction and suggests that legal procedures and terminology may be entirely subsumed by a monstrous unlawfulness of self-will.

One is discovered, at this point, returning upon the proposition that the lexicographer's responsibility is to the genius of the language (*genius*, '3c. Prevailing character or spirit, general drift, characteristic method or procedure') rather than to the 'literary masterpiece' or to any associated notion of individual 'genius' (the sematology of that term in the eighteenth and nineteenth centuries is cogently reduced in the introductory note to Sense 5). After the introduction of such caveats, however, one remains open to persuasion that the genius of the language is peculiarly determined by, and is correlatively a determinant of, 'the special endowments which fit a man for his peculiar work' (Sense 4). When Hobbes writes of 'the knavery of such persons, as make use of... superstitious feare; to passe disguised in the night, to places they would not be known to haunt', he allows his own language to be visited by a shade of Caroline fancy. The irony at the expense of the 'timorous, and supperstitious' who are so deceived is modified by a recognition, embodied in the syntax and cadence, that he is himself much taken with the modifying notion 'haunt' and with his own ability to give it the last word. This touch of stylistic self-delight does not precisely match Hobbes's views on 'exact definitions first snuffed, and purged from ambiguity' which, like the pronouncements of the Philological Society, are generally 'taken as axiomatic'. In such instances language appears sharply conscious both of its own workings and of the 'general drift' of assumption, the 'prevailing character' of human nature in the mass, against which the words of special endowment, such as *haunt*, appear as if illuminated from within. It is arguable that Hobbes regarded even a model discourse composed of 'Perspicuous Words' as being potentially chargeable with 'juggling and confederate knavery' and that it is the equivocal nature of his regard that gives the style its particular edge.

In an undergraduate essay of 1867, Hopkins maintained that 'the run of thought in the age braces up and carries out what lies its own way and discourages and minimises what is constitutionally against its set: different times like a shifted light give prominence by turns to different things'. Throughout the seventy years from inception to 'completion', the *OED* drew upon an inheritance of two such opposing energies. Coleridge, constitutionally against the 'set' of the age, whose style, in prose argument, is characterized by phrases descriptive of resisting the current, became, through the influence of the *Lay Sermons*, *Aids to Reflection*, and the book *On the Constitution of the Church and State*, the source of a powerful 'run of thought' during the remainder of the nineteenth century. Philosophically speaking, the *OED* developed, at several removes, from Coleridgean ideas of organic unity; practically speaking, its methods of compilation were bound to expose the limitations of second-hand philosophical doctrines and the myths of nationhood. The Philological Society's call for a dictionary worthy of the English language was committed to a form of words apparently succinct but dissolving into infinite suggestiveness. As a directive it compares poorly with Tyndale's injunction 'that the scripture oughte to be in the english tonge'. Any mythic power that Tyndale's words might transmit to nationalists of later generations would be a romanticizing of his plain practicalities. In the making of the *OED*, the protracted arduous procedures were an elaborate scientific descant on a simple theme: from Trench's flourish of 1855, 'The love of our native language, what is it in fact, but the love of our native land expressing itself in one particular direction?' to Bridges's 1926 valediction to Henry Bradley, who had 'devoted forty years of his life to the Oxford Dictionary. He recognized the national importance of that work. He understood thoroughly the actual conditions of our time, and the power of the disruptive forces that threaten to break with our literary tradition'. Such statements return us once more upon Murray's separation of the signification of words from the 'sentiments' of authors. If one distrusts Bridges's general sentiment about 'disruptive forces' in the 1920s it is because one has reason to distrust the particular signification that 'our' and 'literary' and 'tradition' had acquired in his keeping. If sentiments could be treated as volatile essences one would be rid of these perplexities; one would be free to concur with Bridges 'wholeheartedly', as they say. Coleridge claimed, in the first chapter of *Church and State*, that 'it is the privilege of the few to possess an idea: of the generality of men, it might be more truly affirmed, that they are possessed by it'. John Colmer, in his edition of *Church and State*, glosses this as 'an interesting recognition of the largely unconscious ideas that "possess" ordinary men and that partly account for consensus, social cohesion, and the continuous life of institutions'. Empirical observation suggests that in the making of the *OED*, the possessors were at once, and indistinguishably, the possessed. One might observe that the *OED* began as an 'idea' and ended as an 'institution', a 'consensus'. One might add that it began as an 'idea' and became, through scientific application, a 'conception' ('bringing any given object or impression into the same class with any number of other objects, or impressions, by means of some character or characters common to them all'). Such application, whether in etymological science or in the mere toil of writing English, constrains, and may even destroy, the 'privilege' of the 'idea'. It is a blessing, both for the genius of the language, and for the 'peculiar work' of the writer, that this is so. Melville, in 'The March into Virginia', one of his *Battle-Pieces* of 1866, evokes the young Union soldiers, in their untried blitheness, who will 'die experienced ere three days are spent— | Perish, enlightened by the vollied glare'. We 'see' the silhouettes of the soldiers as they are simultaneously illuminated and extinguished in the blaze of musketry; we 'feel' the shock of their recognition as they are 'instructed' in the 'Brute Actuality of things and facts', their blithe ignorance erased in an 'illuminated' instant, together with their lives. The verb *to enlighten* has both physical and metaphysical significations; Melville achieves a shocking coincidence in sematology. The *OED* recognizes, under Sense 2 ('Now chiefly *poet.* or *rhetorical*'), some words by Longfellow: 'Thou moon...all night long enlighten my sweet lady-love!' Such 'sentiments'—they were published in 1843—may be thought of as furnishing in a small way the blithe inexperience that stumbled into the enlightenment of the vollied glare. Melville redeems the lexicographer's tag 'now chiefly *poet.* or *rhetorical*' in the instant that he renders it void.

James Murray argued, in his 1910 'Lecture on Dictionaries', that 'Every fact faithfully recorded, and every inference correctly drawn from the facts, becomes a permanent accession to human knowledge...part of eternal truth, which will never cease to be true'. Here as elsewhere in the history of the making of the *OED*, one becomes aware of the discrepancy between a lexicographer's 'inference correctly drawn from the facts' and the kind of correct inference which is drawn—for example—in Melville's poem. 'Perish, enlightened by the vollied glare' is an accession to human knowledge of the distinction between fancy and imagination as 'enlighten my sweet lady-love' or 'Cannon behind them | Volley'd and thunder'd', or even 'part of the eternal truth, which will never cease to be true' are not. When a lexicographer commits himself to the idea of a sublime communion between his science and 'eternal truth' is he able, scientifically, to draw the correct inference from his own platitude? One remembers Johnson's sardonic allusion, in the Preface to the *English Dictionary*, to 'the elixir that promises to prolong life to a thousand years'.

Considered pragmatically, Murray's desperate optimism was a splendid quality. Without it he could not have withstood the manifold burdens: unremitting drudgery, financial insecurity, constant attrition in his dealings with the Delegates of the Clarendon Press. One may question whether the hyperbole of the 'Lecture on Dictionaries' is itself an effect of attrition, of necessary compromise. His biographer has noted that 'the recognition of the Dictionary as a national asset was sealed when James Murray suggested

that the whole work should be dedicated to Queen Victoria'. K. M. Elisabeth
Murray is never less than judicious in her use of words: 'was sealed' is both pact
and fate, or pact *as* fate; an 'asset' is 'a single item appearing on the debit side'.
It is not what Coleridge had in mind in his reference to 'national benefits'.

   That the great work of Murray, his associates and his successors is a matter
of immeasurable national indebtedness should be a proposal not subject to
debate. That the very nobility of its achievement is inseparable from the
stubbornness of its flaws is possibly a more contentious suggestion. As I have
attempted to indicate, there are particular intensities of signification—
indicated by Coleridge's 'activity of the assimilative and of the modifying
faculties' and by Empson's 'interactions'—which nonetheless seem inessential to 'consensus, social cohesion, and the continuous life of institutions'.
The *OED* is an institution with its own 'continuous life', and the computer
is now operating in the interests of cohesion: '*Data capture by ICC, Fort
Washington, PA*' (see imprint page). If there had been an original bias or
imperception (the suggestion is, I have conceded, contentious) I would not
now expect it to be reconsidered. Where the quality of an entry can be
improved by the simple fact of being brought up to date, the new edition is
excellent. *Populism, populist*, had been so overtaken by political circumstance
that the 1933 entries were virtually unusable. They are now much improved. The entries under 'private, *a.*' have been extended (see, for example, additions to 'private enterprise'), and significations unknown in 1933
are now recorded. In place of *7a–b* we have *7a–l*, of which *7k* is 'private
language: a language which can be understood by the speaker only'. The
first citation if from Anscombe's 1953 translation of Wittgenstein; I choose
to make of this an instance of exemplary irony. The sixteenth- and
seventeenth-century entries for 'private, *a.*' have been slightly retouched.
There is a new—and I would have to say unnecessary—citation (for 1673)
under *2a*. What I have called 'the protean energy of that word in seventeenth-century English' is still off the record. It might well appear to the
consensus as 'a language which can be understood by the speaker only'.
Hopkins's coinage *unchancelling* of 1875–6 is ignored ('Thy unchancelling
poising palms were weighing the worth', *Deutschland*, stanza 21). There is
difficulty about the meaning, as Peter Milward says, though he and others
have committed their conjectures to print. I think one might have a quarrel
with the *Dictionary* people over this. Is it (as by their silence they imply) a
nonce-word, a sliver of private language, 'understood by the speaker only',
or is it, by virtue of its particular belonging, a word of real, though 'difficult',

signification? *Tofu*, picked up by the 1933 *Supplement*, with citations going back to 1880, receives further samplings (1981, *Guardian:* 'In the United States . . . tofu has become an "in" food'). Is the name of an easily analysable substance that has appeared on a million menus more real than a word, peculiarly resistant to analysis, which has lodged itself in a few thousands of minds?

Most of what one wants to know, including much that it hurts to know, about the English language is held within these twenty volumes. To brood over them and in them is to be finally persuaded that sematology is a theological dimension: the use of language is inseparable from that 'terrible aboriginal calamity' in which, according to Newman, the human race is implicated. Murray, in 1884, missed that use of 'aboriginal'; it would have added a distinctly separate signification to the recorded examples. In 1989 it remains unacknowledged.

In what sense or senses is the computer acquainted with original sin?

16

Of Diligence and Jeopardy

Tyndale's translation of the New Testament was first printed in 1525–6. A revised version appeared in 1534, and it is upon this later text that David Daniell's new edition is based.[1] N. Hardy Wallis, in the publication undertaken for the Royal Society of Literature in 1938, also preferred Tyndale's revised text. *Tyndale's New Testament*, as now published by Yale University Press, is a 'modern-spelling edition'. The decision to modernize is to be regretted, and one regrets also that the opportunity was not taken to reissue and put into wider circulation the Wallis edition.

The modernizers appear to have a strong common-sense case for proceeding as they do. Those who plead for the retention of old spelling are perhaps sentimentalists, dilettanti of 'forme and pressure', self-deluded in their passion since the pristine orthography may in fact be the flourishes of a secretary or an amanuensis rather than the marks of the maker; other details may represent nothing more than the conventions and aberrations of a particular printing house. Variants, eccentric even by the standards of the time, in a 1535 New Testament were once received as pious imitations of rustic speech, in the spirit of Tyndale's Erasmian reply to 'a certeyne deuine': that 'ere many yeares, hee would cause a boy that driueth the plough to know more of the Scripture than hee did'. They are now attributed either to the uncertainties of Flemish compositors or, as A. W. Pollard argues, to the phonetic enthusiasm of a 'bookish' English press-corrector working for the Antwerp printers.

It must also be conceded that whereas Francis Fry's 1862 reprint of Tyndale's first New Testament, like his reprint in the following year of the same translator's *The Prophete Jonas*, is a true facsimile, reproducing not

---

[1] *Tyndale's New Testament, translated from the Greek by William Tyndale in 1534*. A modern-spelling edition, with an introduction by David Daniell, 429 pages (New Haven, CT: Yale University Press, 1989).

only the black-letter typeface but also the spellings, contractions, and
virgules of the original, several of the most valuable modern old-spelling
editions of Tyndale (for example, J. I. Mombert's 1884 reprint of the Lenox
Library Pentateuch and the Wallis New Testament of 1938) are 'verbatim'
rather than 'facsimile' texts. As he himself makes clear, Mombert's edition
'does not give the *letter* in facsimile'. He emphasizes that he had in mind 'the
ready use of the volume by a large number of readers' and that the 'first
intention of reproducing the Original ... in the same type ... had to be
abandoned as incompatible with the ends to be served' by his edition.
Wallis's 'alterations', such as the substitution of roman for black-letter and
the removal of contractions, were undertaken 'in order to clarify the text'
for the benefit of that 'large body of readers and Bible students' envisaged by
Isaac Foot when he proposed the edition.

There is a superficial similarity between such ideal motives and those of
the new Yale 'modern-spelling' edition 'dedicated to showing the accessibility of Tyndale's New Testament even after 450 years'. In matters of
speech and writing, however, we cannot regard motive as something
which lies outside the contextual frame; it is through 'the processe, ordre
and meaninge' of the 'texte' that motive declares or betrays itself. There is in
fact an incompatibility between the Mombert and Yale editions which
could be characterized as the difference between an old humility, not
unworthy of Tyndale, and a newer spirit of accommodation. Mombert, in
his Preface, alerts his reader to 'the imperfection which marks all human
effort, especially where it aims to avoid it', and which, despite the 'great
pains ... taken to secure accuracy', may have left inaccuracies undetected in
his edition. The pains of the Yale edition are different: 'It is uncomfortable ... when a late Middle-English word, long ago defunct, suddenly jars
the reader and needs glossing'.

For Mombert, the jarring (labour, diligence, anxiety, the anticipation of
self-reproach) is inherent in that vocational 'effort' to which he is dedicated.
The Yale editor's dedication to the task of revealing the 'accessibility' of his
client seems paramount and self-descriptive: 'There is ... a powerful case for
a modern-spelling Tyndale. In the clangour of the market-place of modern
popular translations, Tyndale's ravishing solo should be heard across the
world'. Yale University Press, in common with its rivals in academic
publishing, has, doubtless, a fair understanding of the 'clangour of the
marketplace', and one would be a little surprised if any reader, apart from
a few valetudinary conservatives, were to feel in any degree 'uncomfortable'

with, or 'jarred' by, the striking inappositeness of such promotional lyricism. A sense of jarring, of discomfort, as things naturally inherent in the common processes of endurance and endeavour, belongs to a different, outmoded, order of understanding; the understanding in which Tyndale added his colophon 'To the Reder' at the end of his first New Testament ('Count it as a thynge not havynge his full shape / but as it were borne afore hys tyme / even as a thi[n]g begunne rather then fynnesshed') or in which Luther composed—and Tyndale translated and amplified—the 'Prologe to the Epistle of Paule to the Romayns' ('Lyke as a sicke man cannot suffer that a man shulde desire of him to runne to lepe and to doo other dedes of an whole man').

Increasingly during the last fifty years commentators on Augustine have been willing to concede that 'the doctrine of original sin has become for modern men and women unintelligible and unbelievable' and that, in consequence, 'there is ... to the modern mind, a certain unreality' in such discussions. Original sin may be described not only in terms of concupiscence and wilfulness, our nature 'gredie to do euell', as Tyndale declares in his marginal gloss on Romans 5: 25, but also as that imperfection which stamps all activity of the graceless flesh, a category from which much achievement of a high order, much scrupulous and indeed noble endeavour, cannot be excluded, if the work is done 'without faith', 'with oute the sprite of God'. This sense of natural inborn helplessness, 'when a man wills to act rightly and cannot', is a significant thread, yet no more than a thread, in the Pauline Epistles and in Augustine, and has been cogently summarized, albeit as a 'pseudo-concept', in Ricoeur's 'le mal est une sorte d'involontaire au sein même du volontaire, non plus en face de lui, mais en lui, et c'est cela le serf-arbitre'. I have called it no more than a thread. In the Epistles the prevailing pattern is one of 'grace and apostleshyppe' (Romans 1: 5), and both Luther and Tyndale affirm this faith. My capacity to make any judgement on these matters is confined to the field of semantics, and one must therefore face the prospect that what Luther, in his *Lectures on Romans*, calls the 'terrible curving in on itself' of the life of mere nature is apparent even within the small compass of these words. I am not indifferent to Ricoeur's warning: 'We never have the right to speculate on either the evil that we inaugurate, or on the evil that we find, without reference to the history of salvation' (Peter McCormick's translation), nor am I oblivious to the danger and responsibility which may be incurred when, for whatever reason, one is unable to give real assent to the terms of Ricoeur's caveat. In such a circumstance it is possible, or even probable, that criticism, committed to examine 'the involuntariness at the very heart of the voluntary', is revealed as a symptom of that which it claims to diagnose.

It should not be too promptly concluded, however, that criticism, in such straits, becomes a mere travesty of itself. Criticism lives with travesty as its natural condition, that condition of 'ioperdy', 'ieopardye' or 'ieopardie', as Tyndale or his printers variously spell it, by which mankind is variously threatened and distressed. Jeopardy, we could say by way of summary from Tyndale, compounds 'all the synne which we doo by chaunce of frailte', 'ouermoch busyenge and vnquyetynge thy self a[n]d drounynge thy self in worldly busynesse vnchristenlye', 'the dampnacion of the lawe and captiuite of ceremonies', the 'Idolatrie of...imaginacion', a condition from which only those that 'dyed in the faith' are assuredly exempt. Even so, it is far from evident that Tyndale's, and others', belief in such mortal jeopardy marked either their lives or their writings with ineluctable gloom. Erasmus's *Enchiridion* (1503), which impressed Tyndale and which he is known to have translated (though the anonymous English version first published in 1533 may not be his), argued that 'some affections [passions] be so nygh neygh-bours to virtue / that it is ieopardous leest we sholde be deceyued, the diuersitye is so daungerous and doutfull', but the tenor of the argument at this point is one of cheerful instruction: 'These affections are to be corrected and amended / and may be turned very well to that virtue whiche they most nygh resemble'. Tyndale, in *The Obedience of a Christen Man*, is tougher than this. Despite Tyndale's early interest in the *Enchiridion*, the Florentine Neoplatonism which informs Erasmus's book seems remote from the work of the English reformer. Yet even Tyndale's charge that Christ's closest followers 'after so lo[n]ge hearinge of Christes doctrine were yet ready to fight for Christ cleane age[n]st Christes teachi[n]ge' is free from any tincture of fatalism. Such betrayal, such restoration, is seen as in all senses exemplary: 'yf christes disciples were so lo[n]ge carnal what wo[n]der is it / yf we be not all perfecte ye first daye'.

I take issue with the manner in which the argument is stressed on page xxiv of the introduction to the Yale edition: 'at pro-Establishment moments...as in Titus 3, where Tyndale has "Warn them that they submit themselves to rule and power, to obey the officers..." the Authorized Version has (and the capitals appear in 1611 and many following editions) "Put them in mind to be subject to Principalities and Powers, to obey magistrates..." '. If the editor wishes to associate 'the ring of Establishment

authority' with the shift from 'rule and power' to 'Principalities and Powers'
it is disingenuous to suggest, as he clearly does, that the 1611 translators
shoulder the blame for 'distancing' Tyndale. The change was effected by
those who revised the Geneva New Testament between 1557 and 1560.
'Warne them that they submit them selues to Rule and Power to obey, that
they be ready vnto all good workes' (1557) became, in the Geneva Bible of
1560, 'Pvt them in remembrance that they be subject to the Principalities
[&] Powers, [&] that they be obedient, [&] readie to euerie good worke'.
The OED shows an identical shift, between 1557 and 1560, in Ephesians
6: 12 (1560 'For we wrestle not against flesh and blood, but against principalities [1557 Rulers], against powers') and in Colossians 1: 16 (1560 'whether
they be Thrones, or Dominions, or Principalities, or Powers [1534 TINDALE
to 1557 Geneva, maieste or lordshippe, ether rule or power]').

To dispute the direction, or bias, of a polemical argument is a rather
different matter from challenging the occasional point of fact. One is moving
from matters of scholarly detail to tenebrous questions of power and purpose.
By 'polemical' I refer to the Yale editor's militant claim that 'in their new
allegiance to "relevance", publishers and the public have been allowed to
forget the man who laid the foundation of the Bible in English' and to his
tone of 'aggressive controversy' when considering translators' 'committees',
whether of 1611 or of 1970 ('Tyndale was not a committee'). Indifference and
forgetfulness are lamentable characteristics of our time, but his introduction
does not really resist such trends. Despite a brief token listing of books for
further reading, it has, in the presentation of its case ('Tyndale's Bible translations have been the best-kept secrets in English Bible history', etc.), its own
manner of forgetting. Such a coyness as 'best-kept secrets' slights the memory
of those earlier scholars who dedicated themselves to the just recognition of
Tyndale's achievement: Francis Fry, James Isidor Mombert, A. W. Pollard,
Henry Guppy, R. W. Chambers, and Isaac Foot, among numerous others. The
Work of William Tindale by S. L. Greenslade (1938), cited in the Yale edition's
'Further Reading', not only 'has a short selection of his works', it also contains
an essay, 'Tindale and the English language' by Gavin Bone, which anticipates
by fifty years the present editor's praise of Tyndale as a writer who can sound
strikingly 'modern', whose short sentences hit home, whose simplicity is an
adjunct of conscious craftsmanship. If 'the significance of Tyndale as a highly
conscious craftsman' remains unestablished, as the new introduction insists,
one can only respond that, in the domain of the review-fed intelligentsia, the
power of established fact is scarcely distinguishable from the potency of

transient reputation. Norman Davis (*William Tyndale's English of Controversy*, 1971) states, by no means rashly, that 'the excellence of Tyndale's translations has been recognized almost from the time they appeared, and has often been analysed and justly praised', but in the world of amnesia and commodity this kind of established fact is no longer thought sufficient. 'Tyndale's ravishing solo' must now be 'heard across the world' as if he were some dissident poet in line for the Nobel Prize.

Mombert, in the 1884 Preface to his edition of Tyndale's Pentateuch, alludes to the recent unveiling, by the Earl of Shaftesbury, of the monument on the Thames Embankment to 'the Apostle of Liberty, who, at the cost of his life, gave to the people of English tongue much of the English Bible'. This simple equation of Tyndale's apostleship with the emancipatory ethos of, say, William Wilberforce or Abraham Lincoln goes happily enough with the century's run of thought but is theologically anachronistic, as is the Yale editor's 'Tyndale spoke for all humanity'. It is true that in *The Obedience of a Christen Man* he attacked the 'bloudy' doctrine of Rome 'in as moch as we be taught euen of very babes / to kyll a turke / to slee a Jewe / to burne an heritike' and that, in the 'Prologe' to his translation of Exodus, he showed how God, 'when all is past remedye a[n]d brought into desperacion', 'then fulfilleth his promises, and that by an abiecte and a castawaye, a despised and a refused person'. Even so, it now takes as much innocent ingenuity to suppose that such eloquence anticipates the 'Family of Man' culture as it formerly took to believe that Tyndale shared the spirit of Shaftesburyan philanthropy. For all its insistence on the 'goodly lawes of loue', Tyndale's doctrine is one of election through faith: in the New Testament colophon 'To the Reder' he writes of 'the edyfyi[n]ge of Christis body (which is the co[n]gregacion of them that believe)', and this is a far cry from notions of secular 'egalitarian' openness and availability.

It may be objected that I am wilfully reading this nonsense about the 'egalitarian' 'caring' society into the Yale editor's remarks and that, in context, what he claims is no more and no less than that Tyndale created an English style which was eloquent, cogent, and free from the 1611 Bible's 'Latin-inspired' cadences framed by and for the 'mandarin classes'.

The *OED*'s first record of 'mandarin class' is 1947—John Hayward's British Council pamphlet *Prose Literature since 1939*: 'If literature is to extend its civilising mission among the literate masses; if it is not to become the arcane cult of a mandarin class; it must impose its values, and insist on their supreme importance'. The Yale editor writes, 'The Authorised Version panel, Latin-inspired, spoke for the mandarin classes in the unforgettable "Sufficient unto the day is the evil thereof". But Tyndale spoke for all humanity in his, even more memorable, "For the day present hath ever enough of his own trouble" '. So to present Tyndale partly recalls Dean Milman, Gosse, Logan Pearsall Smith, and others, on Donne's preaching style, his 'incomparable eloquence' before this or that 'great concourse' of Jacobean 'noblemen and gentlemen'; it also partly recalls a thinner style of semi-official high-mindedness ('The opinions expressed...are...not necessarily those of the British Council'). Hayward had critical integrity and did the best he could with his otiose brief; it could fairly be said, however, that his 'civilising mission among the literate masses' is almost certainly more 'mandarin' than the opinions entertained by Laurence Chaderton or those members of the 1611 committee who thought like him.

The Yale editor would probably argue, and with some justice, that he does not see himself as an ingenuous disciple of the half-hearted British Council style of 'civilising' mission and that the introduction makes clear his dislike of applying any kind of diffusive wash to the clear intent of Tyndale's work. 'Cleaue vnto the texte and playne storye' and 'The litterall sense is spirituall' are injunctions, claims, of a somewhat different kind from the assumption that 'literature' must 'impose its values', and the Yale Introduction is sharp enough with those whose main justification for the 1611 Bible is its status as 'Sublime English Literature', 'a particular glory of English letters', 'the acme of achievable literary perfection'. But it is also regrettably the case that if one cleaves to the text and plain story of the introduction one finds it a sad jumble of stylistic solecisms and illogical conclusions. You cannot, with equity, sneer at 'Sublime English Literature' or pass judgement on 'committees of people with no ears' if your own 'hearing' permits the use of such phrases as 'best-kept secrets in English Bible History', 'Tyndale's ravishing solo', 'the vivid, powerful, desert-wind intensity of much of Hebrew prophecy', 'enormous and popular tome' (cf. 'smothered under tomes of what amounted to free association'), 'epoch-making', 'the bad press that Tyndale has had', 'give us Tyndale any day', 'yet Tyndale can do equally well what Sir Walter Scott, in another context, called "the Big Bow-Wow Strain"', as the Pauline Epistles and Hebrews show'. I anticipate the common-sense retort: that all these instances are entirely adequate to their expository purpose and that for such a purpose the stylistic finesse of Henry James is not required. It is shocking, nonetheless, that this gesture of mediation between Tyndale's 'solitary music' and 'today's reader' so markedly lacks every quality and characteristic sustained by the original work; the 'wonderful ear', the 'trenchant reasoning'.

When the various concessions to common sense have been made (for example, the amount of editorial discretion in the old 'verbatim' editions which even purists are willing to accept; the current availability of exact photographic reproductions of black-letter texts), it is here that one's case against this modern-spelling edition of Tyndale finally rests. A tractable 'English' project ('accessible Tyndale') has insinuated itself into Tyndale's intractable purpose (to make the New and Old Testaments accessible, in English, to 'the laye people'). This is not so much transmission as a kind of contamination. It is commonly supposed that mediation calls for mediocrity, as though for a guarantee of sincerity and good faith. The Yale editor writes in the apparent belief that there is little to distinguish 'today's reader' from Tyndale's 'laye people' whom it was 'impossible to stablysh . . . in any truth, excepte yᵉ scripture were plainly layde before their eyes in their mother tonge'. He appears to work on the assumption that ignorance at the end of the twentieth century is not to be distinguished from ignorance in the first quarter of the sixteenth. Our ignorance, however, results from methods of communication and education which have destroyed memory and dissipated attention. Tyndale, who constantly laments and rebukes common ignorance, nonetheless follows Luther in his emphasis on memory and attention. His 'Prologe in to . . . Deuteronomye' calls it 'a boke worthye to be rede in daye and nyghte and neuer to be oute of handes'; in the translation-adaptation of the 'Prologe to . . . Romayns' he writes, of Paul's Epistle, 'I thynke it mete, that euery Christen man not only knowe it by rote and with oute the boke, but also exercise him selfe therin euermore continually, as with the dayly brede of the soule'. Gavin Bone noted how, in such writing, sense and rhythm, and 'the old punctuation of bars drawn across at the end of the rhythmical clause', go together (today's reader of the Yale edition may compare and contrast page 62 of the text with the photographed page from the 1534 volume used as frontispiece). Luther and Tyndale encouraged rumination ('the moare it is chewed the plesander it is'); modern reinterpretation of their design is at once excitable and inert: 'Tyndale understood how to get variety of secondary stresses to make an even flow that pulls the reader along'. To be 'pull[ed] along' is to be passive, helpless; St Augustine, with whose thought Tyndale, like Luther, was well acquainted, depicted (in *Enchiridion*, VIII, 26) mankind's involvement in the consequences of original sin 'quo traheretur per errores doloresque diuersos ad illud extremum . . . sine fine supplicium' (Ernest Evans translates, 'dragged through divers errors and sorrows'; Albert C. Outler gives 'led, through divers errors and sufferings').

If I am here implying that the Yale editor seems not fully to comprehend the semantic implications of his theology, my suggestion is not without a trace of fellow-feeling. An invitation—to make Tyndale accessible to to-day's reader, or to write a review article—is accepted, and the trap is sprung. One is from that moment committed to suffer the 'involuntary' at the heart of the 'voluntary' undertaking. The Yale introduction claims that Tyndale's work is 'uncovered' by the modernized spelling: an extraordinary choice of word if one thinks of Leviticus 18 in the 1611 version, though the aston-ishment is muted for the reader of that chapter in Tyndale's Pentateuch, which has 'discouer' in almost every instance. One wishes that the invol-untary comminatory power of the curious usage had been attended to even as the sentence volunteered its speciousness and absurdity to the editorial gaze: 'With modernised spelling, and no other changes at all, that translation is here uncovered to show it as the modern book it once was'. This claim, I am bound to say, is an impertinence. To make Tyndale's revised New Testament of 1534 'accessible' to 'today's reader' is not to discover it as the modern book it once was. The modern book it *once* was remains in the sufficiency and jeopardy of 'its difficult early-sixteenth-century spelling': 'The ne- | we Testament | dyly | gently corrected and | compared with the | Greke by Willyam | Tindale: and fynes- | shed in the yere of ou | re Lorde God | A.M.D. [&] xxxiiij. | in the moneth of | Nouember'.

The Yale editor, I have already observed, objects to those who cherish the Bible, particularly the 1611 version, in an exclusively secular fashion as 'the acme of achievable literary perfection'. Such protest is not new. Gavin Bone flustered the cogency of his admirable essay of 1938 with such exclamations as 'There is no vestige of literariness in [Tyndale's] writings' and 'think of a Bible written by Pater'. Norman Davis retorted, in his 1971 lecture, that 'writing for purely literary effect perhaps there is not, or not much; but effect in the sense of getting results was what Tyndale wanted'. Such conclusions appear, in principle, faithful to Tyndale's own priorities ('though we read the scripture [&] bable of it never so moch, yet if we know not... wherfore it was geven... it profiteth vs nothinge at all'), but the arguments on which they depend are in fact simplistic and inequitable. The underlying assumption, betrayed by such phrases as 'no vestige of literari-ness' and 'purely literary effect', is that those who cannot give real assent to Tyndale's intentions and 'results' ('It is not ynough therfore to read and talke of it only, but we must also desyre god daye and night instantly to open oure eyes') are perforce mere parodists and self-parodists, 'ydle disputers, and braulers aboute vayne wordes'. It seems to me, however, that those who coin, or adopt, dismissive phrases which pivot on the words 'literature', 'literary', 'literariness', are themselves in thrall to the very negligencies and sentimentalities which they condemn. 'Pater' is brought into the quarrel because, though they are justly angered by the confusing of grace with refinement, election with elitism, their terms of judgement are still dictated by the stereotypes which their arguments reject.

This kind of self-impacting, the oxymoron of prejudicate opinion, is not uncommon even among those students and editors of Tyndale who might be expected to have taken his precepts to heart. In 'W. T. Vnto the Reader' (1545) Tyndale declares that 'in manye places, where the text semeth at the fyrst choppe harde to be vnderstonde, yet the circumstances before and after, and often readinge together, maketh it playne ynough etc'. Tyndale has his own style of equity, though he dispenses it somewhat differently from the Elizabethan Jesuits Campion and Southwell, for whom the word 'equitie' itself is a keynote in their polemic eloquence of 'reason', 'good method', and 'plain dealing'. Tyndale's sense of equity is characterized by the gait of his clauses from 'at the fyrst choppe harde' to 'playne ynough etc' and by the stress on the final words, in which the impression of a diligent constancy and the impression of some urgent extempore business are shrewdly maintained. Tyndale's grammar, the 'litterall', conceives of the 'spirituall' as though within a heart-sense of the verb 'apply': 'to put a thing into practical contact with another' (his 'that we maye applye the medicyne of the scripture, every ma[n] to his awne sorcs' antedates by some eleven years the *OED*'s earliest citation for Sense 3 *trans*). I would say that he required intense application from his 'brethren and felowes of one fayth': 'diligence' is one of the characteristic words by which we know him. And his solicitude for 'the weake stomackes' defies translation into the market-research idioms of his latest advocates and successors, the 'team' responsible for the Revised English Bible (REB) (1989), who feel 'that since the Bible is the ultimate guide to the Christian faith, then it must respond to the changing demands of the times we live in'.[2] There is no end to the 'demands' which the 'times' will make. The 'Age', in this, is like any other moral or emotional blackmailer. Why must it be left to a distressed

---

[2] *The Revised English Bible with the Apocrypha*. A revised edition of the New English Bible of 1970, with a preface by Donald Coggan, Chairman of the Joint Committee on the Revision (Oxford and Cambridge: Oxford University Press and Cambridge University Press, 1989).

and errant lay person to instruct trained theologians, or those who act and
speak for them, in such elementary truths? For Tyndale, as for Luther, the
'demands' issued, at one and the same time, from the 'bloudy' hierarchy of
Rome and from the tyranny of original sin. The old partisan savagery may
have sunk from sight, together with much else of historical remembrance, in
the latest ecumenical 'think tank', but I find it hard to accept that the
immanence of 'corrupt nature' is now supposed an archaic concept or that
such words as Tyndale's 'even as a man wold obtayne ye fauoure of wordely
tirantes' can be treated as merely the utterance of some irrelevant ancient
prejudice. The Yale editor appears to dislike the merchants of 'relevance' as
much as I do. But it must be added that, although he is with me in spirit, in
the 'process, order and meaning of the text' he is with them. What has the
Luther–Tyndale 'Prologe to . . . Romayns' to do with the kind of 'powerful
case' assumed by him and by the puffers of the Revised English Bible except
to judge it across a void? The law and the faith proclaimed by Luther and
Tyndale are not user-friendly; they are 'terreble . . . a[n]d to be tre[m]bled at',
as Tyndale wrote of Deuteronomy 28 and 29. The paragraph on predestin-
ation in 'Prologe to . . . Romayns' is likewise 'terrible'. There are those who
find the words, in the 1549 Communion Service, about unworthily receiving
the sacrament ('for then wee become gyltie of the body and bloud of Christ
our sauior, we eate and drinke our owne damnacion') equally terrible and to
be trembled at. This I understand. I do not 'understand' this comment of
Lord Coggan's, published in an REB press release: 'When my wife and
I celebrated our 40th wedding anniversary I bought her a piece of jewellery
and I did *not* wrap it in newspaper. So it is with the Bible—the greatest
treasure of all must likewise be presented worthily'. 'Presented worthily' must
mean something apart from 'leatherex boards, with attractive gilt blocking',
though it calls for charity (not, I think, love) to allow the point. The First
Prayer Book's 'yf wee receyue the same unworthely' is recognizably of the
same spiritual and temporal world as Tyndale's 'yf they . . . runne at ryotte
beyonde his lawes and ordinaunces'. It is a world so beyond comprehension
that the ambition to render it 'accessible', 'available to today's reader', is in
every sense vain. The doctrine, the faith, of Luther and Tyndale are an alien
tongue; it was an element of Barth's greatness, in *Der Römerbrief*, to recognize
this foreignness: 'The Kingdom of God is a foreign country'. He also wrote
that 'The Gospel . . . does not negotiate or plead'. Those responsible for
programming what the REB's press materials call 'A "New Look" for the
Good Book' are committed to negotiation and pleading before all else: 'If the

Bible's language becomes too difficult, then the Churches run the risk of losing touch with their congregations'.

I anticipate the protest that in so emphasizing the promotional material I overlook the achievement which is thus promoted; that I am confusing the accidental with the essential and substantial, the contingent with the necessary. My answer would apply Tyndale's remark about grammar to these other 'circumstances before and after'. The language of the REB scholars, in setting out their premises and principles, is hardly to be distinguished from the idioms of the hired publicist: 'The revision has been concerned to avoid archaisms, technical terms, and pretentious language as far as possible'. This is specious syntax. An archaism can be historically determined and described by lexicography; a technical term can be defined; 'pretentious language', as used here, is a small balloon of prejudice and ignorant self-approval. The statement may indeed betray 'the involuntariness at the very heart of the voluntary', but it is no accident. It is intimately and palpably of the same substance as 'the times we live in'.

The times we live in justly demand and approve proficiency, meticulousness, in laboratory work. Provided one asks no more than this the scholarship of 'the REB team' can be duly acknowledged. 'The translators and revisers have taken into consideration not only the evidence presented in recent editions of the Greek text, but also the work of exegetical and literary scholarship, which is continuing all the time' (REB: NT, iii). I do not question the scope and precision of their data-processing. I would further acknowledge that where 'process' is itself the theme of the biblical narrative, as, for example, in Jeremiah 32, the account of the prophet's purchase of a piece of land, the new translators can supply an idiom wholly in keeping with the requirements of the age: 'Fields will be bought and sold, deeds signed, sealed, and witnessed, in Benjamin' (verse 44, REB; New English Bible reads 'shall'). Contrasted with this, the sixteenth-century Bibles pay their words out, slowly, on the nail: 'yee londe shalbe bought for money, [&] euyde[n]ces made ther vpon [&] sealed before witnesses in the countre of Ben Jamin'. One is reminded of Bone's observation that 'each sentence of the old prose is a monument . . . It is not a facet of truth, to be merged with another quick facet as that falls uppermost'. I am not sure about 'monument', but it is true that the ordonnance of the 'old prose' seems able to work in complete harmony with the injunction, in Leviticus, to 'kepe myne ordinaunces' (19: 19; Tyndale's English). The new style ('deeds signed, sealed, and witnessed') is that of the quick turnover; it has its own brusque cogency; it is untouched by that sense of the travail of knowledge, the knowledge of travail, which can whet the eloquence of the 'old prose' but which can also sound repetitious and burdensome. It has been the 'guiding principle' of the REB team 'to seek a fluent and idiomatic way of expressing biblical writing in contemporary English'. Jeremiah 32: 44, in the new style, is undeniably fluent. But Jeremiah, in the narrative, had nowhere to go; in Gordon Rupp's words, 'He was a prisoner in Jerusalem which was completely encircled by the armies of Babylon and his field was in enemy-occupied territory'; its purchase 'was a great gesture of faith, that those formidable enemies would melt away'. The ordinant Tudor prose ('Me[n] shal bye fields for siluer, and make writings, and seale them, and take witnesses in the land of Beniamin') endorses the 'great gesture' and seals the 'faith' with the witness of its conjunctions. Conversely, the faith of the REB appears to be that its 'fluent and idiomatic...English' will cause its own formidable enemies ('archaisms', 'pretentious language', 'complex or technical terms') to melt away; its 'field at Anathoth' is the patronage of the Book-of-the-Month Club.

One's objection to the Revised English Bible and to the Yale modern-spelling New Testament is not that they are modern. Joyce, in exile, thought about Dublin properties and the properties of English as Jeremiah thought about his field and as Tyndale thought about 'the processe, ordre and meaninge of the texte'. The quarrel turns, as it usually does, on matters of perception and imperception. It probably did not occur to 'the REB team' that the Delegates and the Syndics of the two University Presses would entrust the work of its lifetime to press agents whose natural locutions include 'it is read out loud in church' and 'the predominant aim behind the revision being to produce a work that could be read out loud', who cannot perceive the awful risibility of describing the Bible as 'a living tool'. But as Bible scholars they ought to have foreseen this; the obligation to do so is inherent in those teachings about grammar, 'diligence' and the 'flesh' which have come down to them from Tyndale ('the circumstances before and after') and ultimately from Augustine ('quo traheretur per errores dolor-esque diuersos', etc.).

The moral attitudes of the REB 'team', or of those who address the world on its behalf, resemble those of the 'group' responsible for the Second Edition of the *Oxford English Dictionary* (1989). 'Conscientious Bible translators' are 'sensitive' to occurrences of 'sexism in the Bible', says one REB press release. The *OED* group recently emasculated (Sense *2b esp*)

James Murray's century-old 'General Explanations'. Where he wrote, 'For
to every man the domain of "common words" widens out in the direction
of his own reading, research, business', it silently emends, 'For the domain
of "common words" widens out in the direction of one's own reading,
research, business'. I am not the first to point out that it takes a lot of nerve
(Sense 10b *colloq*) to interfere in this way with the prefatory matter of a work
devoted to 'historical principles'.

The purpose of that apparent digression is to lay the ground of my
contention. The English Bible and the English Dictionary, the two great
recorders of our memory, conscience, travail, and diligence, have been
given over to those whose 'law' is derived less from Tyndale than from
Wemmick ('the office is one thing, and private life is another'). In the
mechanics of their office they are meticulous collators and scrutineers. In
'private life' their taste in reading appears to conform to the unexacting
standards of the professional middle class. But since Wemmick's Law is a
fallacy, 'private' taste recoils upon public function: 'The Joint Committee
was concerned that *The Revised English Bible* should be written in a fluent
style, and advice was sought from prominent literary figures such as the late
Philip Larkin, the poet, and the novelist Mary Stewart' (press release). This
self-sanctioning of one's own limited capacities and predilections is not the
'due humility' for which Lord Coggan vouches in his preface; it is a serene
imperception.

Those who read my objection as an unjust elitist contempt for what Lord
Coggan terms 'intelligibility', or for the needs of worshippers drawn from 'a
wide range of ages and backgrounds', might ask themselves how it was that
in 1910, Everyman's Library could bring out its edition of *The First and
Second Prayer Books of Edward VI* with a scholarly introduction by the Bishop
of Gloucester and with the original Tudor spelling unchanged. J. M. Dent,
the founder of the series, and Ernest Rhys, its first editor, were not insensi-
tive to the needs of 'the weak stomachs' among their wide readership, but,
like some other men of letters at that time, they showed respect for the
intelligence of 'ordinary' people by occasionally making demands upon it.
To set the old Everyman text and introduction against the introduction and
text of the Yale New Testament, or to read Lord Coggan's preface to the
REB after the Bishop of Gloucester, is to begin to understand the irreparable
damage inflicted, during the past ninety years or so, on the common life of
the nation. 'Intelligibility', 'accessibility', do not make sense, do not cohere,
without 'diligence', as Tyndale defines it.

Does he 'define' it, though? 'Diligently', it must immediately be said, is a jeopardous adverb in his writings. It stands on the title page of *The Obedience of a Christen Man* (1528) and of the 1534 New Testament, as if he were impressing his own literal and spiritual imprimatur for the elect. It is the word that he gives to Herod's practices in Matthew 2: 7, 8, and 16 ('dyligently enquyred of them'; 'Goo and searche dyligently'; 'which he had diligently searched oute of the wyse men'). In the 'Prologe' to *Jonas* it is associated with 'ypocrites'. Within the space of a few pages in the 'Prologe in to . . . Numeri [Numbers]' it is used to condemn the Pharisees' excessive concern with details of the ritual laws and to commend the reading of 'gods word . . . with a good herte'. Pre-eminently, 'diligence', 'diligent', 'diligently' remain words of covenant, constancy, and constant application: 'Yf thou shalt herken diligently vnto the voyce of the Lorde thy God' (Deuteronomy 28: 1): 'to preache the Gospell with all diligence' (Tyndale's 'Prologe' to 2 Timothy). Tyndale, in the same passage, observes that 'Paul exhorteth Timothe to goo forwarde as he had begonne . . . as it nede was, seinge many were fallen awaye'. The phrase 'as it nede was' admits jeopardy: so does a clause in the anonymous English version of the *Enchiridion* of Erasmus: 'bycause they can not chose but of necessite be occupied, and besyed'; but the two contexts, though in one sense complementary, are also contrary to one another. Each is cognizant of what Tyndale elsewhere calls 'the worlde of weake people' (Pentateuch 1530: 'a prologe shewinge the vse of the scripture'). Tyndale's words on 2 Timothy draw close to Paul's 'No man that warreth, entanglith him silfe with worldely busynes'; the English *Enchiridion* considers the best intentions and endeavours of 'temporall . . . princes' to be necessarily entangled with 'the besynesse of the worlde'. One's understanding of 'diligence', 'diligent', 'diligently', would be that they trace the barely distinguishable spiritual boundary between that which is immersed in and that which is detached from the world's business. In doing so they undertake their own proper business within the grammar of the covenant. 'Diligence' is in part defined by that 'jeopardy' which its task is to resist and endure.

It is clear from Lord Coggan's preface to the REB, and from the several sheets of accompanying press release, as it is from the Yale New Testament's reference to 'accessibility' and 'difficult early-sixteenth-century spelling', that significant numbers of contemporary theologians and textual scholars accept, as one of their major duties, the protection of 'today's reader', tomorrow's worshipper, from the jeopardy of cultural embarrassment or the faintest possibility of mental or emotional strain. This is altogether a different issue from the attainment of increased accuracy, a principle with which one is not in dispute and which Tyndale himself established on his 1534 title page: 'dylygently corrected and compared with the Greke'. One objects to the conflation of textual accuracy with current hygienic fads and fancies ('fluent style', 'best possible page appearance', etc.). The press release, on the 'team''s sensitivity to gender-words, claims that it 'has been careful to use inclusive or unspecific words whenever it judged that that sense belonged to the ancient texts'. Revision of this kind is, in itself, not new. The REB, Job 1: 19, reads 'which fell on the young people' where the 1611 Bible had 'it fell vpon the yong men'. As the Hebrew word means 'youths and maidens', the change to the 'inclusive' term is entirely justified. But in making this alteration the REB is merely following the example set by the NEB and, before that, by the Revised Standard Version. What is new is the opportunistic pitch of the REB's press agents in compounding a well-established scholarly procedure with the 'concerned' jargon of the trade. The 'Joint Committee' and the 'team' may throw up their hands and declare (in all good faith) that they had not thought to become entangled with worldly business. It seems to me, nonetheless, that they have been confused in their diligence. There are signs that the word 'diligence' itself is an embarrassment to them. Although not obsolete or archaic, it is scarcely 'contemporary . . . idiomatic' (the latest citations, in the new *OED*, for 'diligence' are 1871 and 1875 [*Law*], for 'diligent' 1887, for 'diligently' 1894). One might suppose that an 'attempt . . . to use consistently the idiom of contemporary English' (REB: NT, iv; cf. REB: OT, xvii) would apply itself to a thorough revision of this word which so evokes sixteenth- and seventeenth-century moral energy and scruple. But I can find no consistency in the REB's practice. When Tyndale, in Deuteronomy 28: 1, uses 'diligently' (1611: 'diligently'), REB retains it (see also Deuteronomy 13: 14). In Deuteronomy 6: 17, where the 1611 Bible reads, 'You shall diligently keepe the Commandements' ('diligently' is not in Tyndale's version), REB gives, 'You must diligently keep the commandments'; in 2 Peter 1: 5, 10, Tyndale's 'And hervnto geve all diligence' and 'brethren, geve the moare diligence' (1611 'give diligence') become, in the REB, 'You should make every effort' (NEB, 'you should try your hardest') and 'do your utmost to establish (NEB, 'exert yourselves to clinch').

When Tyndale, in *The Obedience of a Christen Man*, argued that 'it is better to suffer one tyraunte th[an] mani [&] to sofre wronge of one the[n] of every ma[n]', he was, as the lesser evil, compounding with political necessity, to which he gave a kind of credence but which was nonetheless contributory to 'yᵉ stro[n]ge fyre of tribulation and purgatorye of oure flesh' (*Pentateuch*, 1530: 'A Prologe shewinge the vse of the scripture'). In such 'business', the diligence of grammatical understanding ('the circumstances before and after') was made both a reflection of and a means of looking upon the contest between the circumstances of the world and of the spirit. The best one can say of the REB translators and revisers is that, though they are masters of the apparatus of scholarship, they lack diligence of the imagination. One can hardly distinguish, as they go their 'fluent and idiomatic' way, the word of scholarly discrimination from the euphemism of the letter of reference. The worst that one can say of them is that they have surrendered without a qualm to 'the worlde of weake people' which they have dreadfully confused with that of 'a boy that driueth the plough'. Their work is consequently in thrall to the 'many tyrants' of commerce and society. The crassness and imperviousness of the publishing jargon seem so perilously close to Tyndale's 'bondage of their awne ymaginacions and inuencions', so inimical to Barth's 'The Gospel does not expound or recommend itself. It does not negotiate or plead, threaten, or make promises. It withdraws itself always when it is not listened to for its own sake' (Edwyn C. Hoskyns's translation).

I had intended to say that the Word of God in English could now withdraw from the clamour of its 'promotion' into the 'inaccessibility' of Mombert's edition of Tyndale's Pentateuch or Wallis's edition of the 1534 New Testament or, best of all perhaps, the old Everyman edition of *The First and Second Prayer Books of Edward VI*. But maybe that is too tempting to be right. The alternative conjecture would be that the Word diligently withdraws *into* the modern world's jeopardy, the 'captiuite of ceremonies', to make there its 'affirmation of resurrection'.

17

Keeping to the Middle Way

Robert Burton projected several attributes of his persona Democritus Junior, eminent among them his collateral vocations as 'Divine' and as 'schollar'. There is not always, with writers, complete reciprocity between what is projected and what is felt and expressed, but in Democritus Junior there is a more complete interrelationship and exchange than one might in reason expect from the author of a post-Ramist anatomy:

> It is most true, *stylus virum arguit*, our style bewraies us, and as Hunters find their game by the trace, so is a mans *Genius* descried by his workes.

Burton's translation of the tag is not wilful: 'bewraie' fairly represents the several implications of *arguere*; so much for the 'schollar'. The 'Divine' (I parody anatomy) hears the phrase within the contexture of English scriptural renderings (Tyndale to King James): 'Surely thou also art one of them, for thy speech bewrayeth thee'—Matthew 26: 73—Peter's accent gives him away, and in truth he denies the truth. It is not scriptural truth that Burton is here defending but a form of verity that may exist chiefly in contexts of declaration that are also occasions of self-revelation, self-exposure. Although 'descried' is an innocuous retracing of 'arguit', even to leave such a trace can be dangerous, if not fatal. Who among the most ordinary of Protestant readers—exercising the retentive memory prescribed by Tyndale—would forget the scriptural paradigm? But because Burton so places it, the further suggestion that a writer's essential character stands forth in his 'stile' is self-evidently nothing to be ashamed of. The emphases are held in apposition, not felt as confrontation. The effect more closely resembles William Empson's 'tug between two interests', except that in this case 'two' is restrictive: if one retains the idea of pairs, there must be several pairings—fecundity and measure, diligence and folly, unity and variety, plenitude and the void. What is traced or followed here is not—or not evidently—a matter of rhetorical formalities. Burton in the guise of Democritus Junior appears to scorn paradoxes, rating them with the 'unrighteous subtleties' of papists, the 'mad pranks' of atheists and anabaptists. He moves, more tactfully than formal rhetoric might allow, and yet with a hunter's instinct, through resonances that are themselves part of the accumulating memory of post-Reformation written and spoken English. And this particular 'genius', at this particular time, is not Burton's property alone. Shakespeare has it in superabundance, but he is richly anticipated by Nashe, and quarries him. Even Hobbes, who would clamp down on this kind of contextual memory as on a lode of well-buried abstruseness, knows perfectly well how to work its seams.

What I am here adumbrating seems more inclined to Erasmian *copia* than to Ramist anatomy; I find Walter J. Ong's instructive *Ramus, Method, and the Decay of Dialogue* (1959) too abrupt in its ascription of Burton's work simply to a Ramist 'fad', together with Nashe's *Anatomie of Absurditie* and Lyly's *Anatomy of Wit*. Though Burton professes that he was unmethodical in his reading, he claims 'method' for the work itself, although Ramus figures only once among the many whom he elects, by quotation and marginal citation, as names to dress his story. 'Divines use *Austins* words *verbatim* still, and our Storie-dressers doe as much, hee that comes last is commonly best': Burton 'does best' because in an important sense he too 'comes last'. He writes in commanding knowledge of ancient and modern predecessors—'the composition and method is ours onely, and shewes a Schollar'—and in the sharp awareness that priorities and circumstances are in process of change ('is ours onely' could be read as 'my sole contribution is the method' or as 'my mastery of synthesis is unique'). A sense of authorial pride and a sense of massive and grateful indebtedness seem to hold together in Burton as they do in Nashe and, with significant differences of emphasis, in Donne. One misses such gratitude in *Leviathan* (except for the noble tribute, first and last, to Sidney Godolphin). Burton, Nashe, and Donne are memorialists as well as innovators, but, with Godolphin dead, it remains for Hobbes to conclude, as it remained for John of Patmos to prophesy, that the former things are passed away.

Burton was pre-eminently what he declared himself to be: a scholar. He was, less evidently to readers of a future time but evidently to himself and for the congregation to which he conscientiously ministered, a man in holy orders, a priest of the Ecclesia Anglicana. He suggests, here and there, that he has no taste for 'controversie' and for that reason, though not exclusively for that reason, he may be seen as keeping largely (rather than narrowly) to his rooms in Christ Church. I would suggest that he follows, as closely as Donne, though tracing a somewhat different game, the diligent mediocrity of Jewel's *Apologie*, Whitgift's *Answer to the Admonition* and Hooker's *Ecclesiasticall Politie*. 'The *medium* is best' is Burton, as is 'sobriety and contemplation joyne our soules to God' and, from Proverbs, 'keepe thine heart with all diligence'.

I do not say that one must submit to *Ecclesiasticall Politie*, as though its 'laws' had the status in Christian history of Tertullian's *regula quidem fidei una omnio est, sola immobilis et irreformabilis*. Though Hooker incorporates this same 'rule' into his Third Booke, he does so in order to establish a crucial distinction between the 'rule of faith', which is 'immoueable', and the 'lawe of outwarde order and politie', which may be 'varied by times places persons and other the like circumstances'. Behind his powerful and elusive arguments stand other tacit and explicit forms of appeal, which it is his purpose to reconcile by sweetness of presentation, as if, though demonstrably recalcitrant, they were yet open to reason. What I here call 'sweetness' is not mellifluousness but rather a quality to be understood through Donne's 'oftentimes Judgement signifies not *meer Justice*, but as it is attempred and sweetned with Mercy'. Those elements of dispute, to which Hooker thus tempers his sentence, I would take to include the recusant witness ennobled by William Rastell's 1557 folio of *The Workes of Sir Thomas More* and the Protestant martyrology gathered and perpetuated by John Foxe's *Actes and Monumentes* of 1563. The publication of Rastell's edition during the Marian reaction, with its dedication to the Catholic queen, and the regular appearance during Elizabeth's reign of augmented editions of Foxe's book give sufficient evidence that Hooker, as champion of the *via media*, was not fighting straw men or empty air. The case of Foxe presented complications, as *Actes and Monumentes* celebrated not only the founding martyrs, the presiding saints and confessors, of the reformed English Church but also those from whom the most radical and acrimonious of Calvinist Puritans and separatists drew their inspiration. In matters of style and faith, which are the main burden of the present discussion, the post-Henrician conditions of church and state politics determined that Burton's analysis of religious melancholy had been preceded by 'Roman' and Genevan forms of the practice: forms which Burton was not fully at liberty to recognize. His work has a number of substantial citations from More's Latin *Utopia* but none, it seems, from *A Dialoge of Comfort Agaynst Trybulacion*, in which More submits to self-examination on such questions as an individual's ability to endure penal solitary confinement as 'an horrour enhaunced of our own fantasye' and confronts his immediate 'terrour of shamfull & paynfull deth'. J. R. Knott, in his *Discourses of Martyrdom* (1993), footnotes a modern psychoanalytical urge to read Foxe as a mere record of 'compulsive neurotic and pathological behavior' but rightly points out that Foxe himself took some account of the psychology of fear, the occasions of faltering, and agrees with Warren Wooden that the flaws are part of Foxe's portrayal of the full humanity of witness among those whose sufferings he relates in reiterative harrowing detail.

The crux that unites the incompatibilities of More and Foxe is the acceptance of 'persecucion for the fayth' as inevitable, even necessary. Although such persecution was to continue in England throughout the seventeenth century, Burton's professed attitude to such things is that they are among a myriad horrors born of human superstition and fantasy: 'No greater hate, more continuate, bitter faction, warres, persecution in all ages, then for matters of religion'; 'It is incredible to relate, did not our dayly experience evince it, what factions...have beene of late for matters of Religion in France, and what hurlie burlies all over *Europe*, for these many yeares'. The phrase 'did not our dayly experience evince it' exemplifies the manner in which Burton's style itself evinces precisely why, and how, it is as it is. It must set itself to record, like a day-book, the minutiae of monstrous confusion; it must perforce run and reel with the dreadful European 'hurlie burlies', and yet reduce all to the idea of a quotidian Christian life as it might be: a sanative commitment to honest charity ('even all those vertuous habits...which no man can well performe, but he that is a Christian, a true regenerate man'). The inherent danger with such an unremittingly busy style is that it will become, or will be understood as having become, mere cynical worldly prattle. I have a sense that Burton would take the French *politiques* as a model if he were not constrained to present them as 'loose Atheisticall spirits...too predominant in all kingdomes'.

I do not say that Burton wrote either directly or indirectly in the full comprehension of Hooker's achievement that we, with the benefit of hindsight, believe we possess. As various scholars have observed, *Ecclesiasticall Politie* caused no great stir when the first four books appeared in 1593, and its reputation remained (perhaps deliberately) shrouded during the early decades of the next century. Nevertheless Helen Gardner has claimed (and I accept) that Donne 'absorbed Hooker's conception of the *via media* so deeply that it [became] the basis of his own thinking'. I suggest only that to know Hooker on the need to free 'our mindes...from all distempered affections' and to read Donne on 'inordinate melancholies, and irreligious dejections of spirit' (and on the resorting to 'fooles' and 'comedies' as vain antidotes) is to comprehend Burton on the 'immoderate' nature of carnal and religious melancholy, and the inanities with which men seek to divert it. As Hooker says, 'we are naturally induced to seeke communion and fellowship with others' and 'All men desire to leade in this world a happie life. That life is led most happily, wherein all virtue is exercised without impediment or let'. Burton anatomizes melancholy in its hydra-headed forms; he dissects its monstrous capacity to hinder communion and fellowship.

When Burton writes that 'our stile bewraies us' or that 'the method is ours onely' the pronoun hovers in its senses between the proud singular ('a mans *Genius* descried by his workes') and the penitential collective of *The Book of Common Prayer* ('our manifolde sinnes and wickednes'). The English 'common prayer' itself derives from ancient Latin usage, the *Publica est nobis et communis oratio* of the Church Fathers to whom both Rome and Lambeth appealed in their contentions. It is to be noted that Hooker's English retains the Latin order ('the love of publique devotion...the verie forme and reverende solemnitie of common prayer dulie ordered'), but, while that is strictly the case, to read the Anglicans is to be aware of a particular strength of resonance in their use of the word 'common' itself. It is resonant because it is ambiguous, and Hooker, Donne, and Burton (and Nashe also) play it across the full range of its ambiguities. I receive the impression, from Jewel's *Apologia Ecclesiae Anglicanae* (first English translation 1562), that 'common' signifies an English reformed 'Catholike' order of charity ('to thintent that the people, as Paule doth admonish vs, by ye co[m]mon praier may receaue a co[m]mon profit') and that such forms of common observance are to be distinguished from 'ye multitude of idle cerimones' which now signify the public worship of Rome. I do not claim that one could safely generalize from such particulars; I say only that the suggestion appears to hold for a particular context and may do so in others. Hooker names 'common advise' as that body of right counsel which validates and rectifies 'whatsoeuer is herein publiquely don' and blames sectaries who judge 'anie blinde and secret corner' to be 'a fit house of common prayer'. 'Common advise' seems to me to take up Jewel's 'all the good fathers & catholike byshops, not only in the old testament, but also in the new' and excludes as usual, therefore, all that is covered by Hooker's *'the vulgar sort amongst you'* or Burton's 'the gullish commonalty'.

Some evidence to support my suggestion may be found in that common stand-by, Elyot's *Boke Named the Governour*: his contention that there 'may appere lyke diuersitie to be in englisshe betwene a publike weale and a commune weale, as shulde be in latin, betwene *Res publica, & Res plebeia'*. There is no doubt here as to Elyot's pitch, and he strikes me as being isolated in the certitude of his definition. In contrast, the Anglican apologists are masters of tonal indeterminacy and ring changes on 'the common good'. My reference is in part retrospective: to a semantic opportunity (or possibly opportunism) that had accompanied the small grammatical shift from the Church in England to the Church of England; and to the apparently slight difference of grammatical opinion which, between 1555 and 1558, had sent members of the reforming party (or schismatic faction) to their excruciating deaths. To this I would add a sense of the continuance, into the late years of the century, of that formal reasonableness established in the preface to the 1549 *Booke of the Common Prayer*, to 'appease all suche diuersitie (if any arise), and for the resolucion of all doubtes . . . for the quietyng and appeasyng of the same'.

The doubts to be resolved, however, do not encompass matters of papistical conscience but matters of reformed practice. The people may require assistance in coming to terms with the new language of authority. The authority itself is now to stand unquestioned. Hooker is magisterially persuasive in ranging across the senses of the word 'common', but none of his uses would make good case-law. He moves us to the affective equivalent of a reasoned conviction, or a proof, that we have been given a secure intermediary, even intercessory, term between the alien, and alienating, power of the Bishop of Rome and the alienated private interpretations of Puritan enthusiasts. When common supplications are made to God out of the midst of common sufferings, we forget the 'gullish commonalty', and the sufferings themselves are reduced (in comely theory) from extortionate private musings to the comfortable words of common confession and absolution. Burton again:

> I [the melancholic] am a contemptible and forlorne wretch, forsaken of God, and left to the mercilesse fury of evill spirits. I cannot hope, pray, repent, &c. How often shall I [Burton] say it, thou maist performe all these duties, Christian offices, & be restored in good time.

In citing such arguments and examples, however, I am also anticipating the major differences of emphasis that make *The Anatomy of Melancholy* a radically different work from *Ecclesiasticall Politie*. Burton quotes massively and with marked equity from the pieties of pagan as well as Christian authors; Hooker too gives judicious attention to the axioms and precepts, the *loci communes*, of Plato, Aristotle, and Cicero. From neither Hooker nor Burton does one gather any sense of disdain for that common inheritance of experience and wisdom, and in this they are true heirs of Calvin's magnanimity. But Hooker puts the 'pouertie' of modern 'Ramystry' firmly in its place: 'Of marveilous quicke dispatch it is, and doth shewe them that have it as much almost in three dayes, as if it dwell threescore yeares with them'. One can see how a question of rhetoric might well be construed as a matter of spiritual fidelity and how 'stile' might indeed 'bewraie' the author.

Burton could pass, or even stand, for one of Hooker's 'diligent observers of circumstances, the loose regarde whereof is the nurce of vulgar follie', but where Hooker places law and reason at the centre of comprehension and Christian offices at the heart of polity, Burton, like Nashe, is a parodist of 'loose regarde' and a hunter of vulgar folly: 'It is a wonder to read of that infinite superstition ... as he that walkes by Moonshine in a wood, they groped in the darke ... which the Divell perceaving, ledde them farther out [that is, out of the right way, further into the dark]'. This passage, though I have given it piecemeal, is worth pondering as a whole. One recognizes how Burton stands halfway between two other great comedians: Shakespeare, of *A Midsummer Night's Dream*, and Hobbes, of 'Apparitions or Visions' and 'The Kingdome of Darknesse'. 'It is a wonder to read of ...': philosophically and morally the words adjure us to keep our hearts with all diligence; tactically, they catch the excitement of the romances and voyages, of the theatrical opportunism that Sidney deplores and Nashe appropriates. Burton, like Nashe and unlike Hooker, exposes his own method of diligent observation to the dangerous forces of circumstance; in doing so he is at least in part an adventurer, an ambivalent faculty which again he shares with Nashe.

But they are all Romans 13 and 'Litany and Suffrages' men, really. They are also, by diverse ways of inheritance and in differing forms, spiritual heirs of the moderate reformers in the first half of the sixteenth century: as strongly against enclosure, engrossing, and brokage as they are opposed to levelling and 'mu[n]grel *Democratia*'. Burton's 'For that which is common, and every mans, is no mans' is the same commonplace as Nashe's 'That which is disperst, of all is despised'. Burton's 'Sheepe demolish Townes, devoure men, &c' repeats More's protest in *Utopia*. Nashe's 'vnder-hand cloaking of bad actions with Common-wealth pretences' (1592) closely recalls charges of double-dealing during Somerset's Protectorate (1547–9) and as closely anticipates Donne, in his Christmas Day sermon of 1621: 'pretences of *publique good*, with which men of power and authority apparell their oppressions of the poore'. To proceed by analogy: it is as if the authorial voice in Nashe's *Christs Teares over Iervsalem*, in Burton's declaration of his 'Utopia', and in Donne's Christmas sermon, inherits the public responsibility of those 'censorys' or 'conseruaterys of the commyn wele', as Erasmian humanists in the 1530s had envisaged such positions of justice (though with little if any discernible influence on actual Henrician legislation). To analogize further, it is as if the effort 'to translate wisdom into political action' which baffled humanists like Elyot and Starkey translates itself, in the prose of Nashe and Burton, into the praxis of an individual style. The energy has to go somewhere; since it cannot realize itself as a legislative act, it turns back into the authority and eccentricity of style itself. When Burton writes of the universality of human folly that 'to insist in every particular were one of Hercules labours, there's so many ridiculous instances, as motes in the Sun', his sentence is simultaneously a ridiculing dismissive hyperbole and a ridiculous 'mote' in a huge, dogged, half-comic endeavour to perform what the author is, by this very token, saying cannot be done. Nashe, and Burton also, are like the 'artificers' described in 'Democritus to the Reader': 'that as *Salust* long since gave out of the like, *Sedem animae in extremis digitis habent*, their Soule, or *intellectus agens*, was placed in their fingers ends': the pen moves with erudite instinct—*stylus virum arguit*—and their 'curious Workes' are their books, evidence of genius and industry in a land where 'only industry is wanting'. W. R. Mueller observes that Burton's concern is 'not only...the melancholy person but also...the melancholy kingdom, particularly England. He sees a definite relationship between the two, and is seeking national, as well as individual, salvation'. We have, in any case, Burton's own words on the matter; but Mueller is right to stress its significance.

   Donne, who would have questioned Mueller as to the exact meaning of 'salvation', stands more than a little apart on the status of *intellectus agens*, closer to Hooker yet not wholly with him. He redefines the *Commune bonum*, to which Nashe refers, as the *Bonum simplex* of Augustine and submits the curious works of his profane making to the divinely reasonable order of *Ecclesiasticall Politie*:

When I behold with mine eyes some small and scarce discerneable graine or seede whereof nature maketh promise that a tree shall come; and when afterwardes of that tree any skilfull artificer undertaketh to frame some exquisite and curious worke, I looke for the event, I move no question about performance either of the one or of the other.

The first part of Hooker's sentence is the methodical opposite of Burton's 'To insist in every particular . . . '; its conclusion stands as though in opposition to Burton's endorsement of *Sedem animae in extremis digitis habent*. Hooker's crucial phrase is 'I moue no question about performance'; Burton's method is to move such questions repeatedly *in extremis digitis*; Nashe's moral and verbal curiosity works well *in extremis*. Hooker simply (as it appears) relegates 'any skilfull artificer' and 'some exquisite and curious worke' to stand as exemplary details in the pattern of a greater whole, a final unity. And yet, of course, Hooker and Burton reprove the same kinds of vain curiosity. Donne, in his funeral sermon for Sir William Cokayne, 12 December 1626, described the mid-1620s as 'our narrow and contracted times, in which every man determines himselfe in himselfe, and scarce looks farther'. He would be in two minds, I think, about Burton's Herculean labours, understanding them to a great extent as Burton himself comprehended his own intelligence and industry but also judging them as complicitous with '*spiritus vertiginis*, the spirit of deviation, and vaine repetition', failings for which Donne drew upon himself as a perverse example to his own congregation: 'I pray giddily, and circularly, and returne againe and againe to that I have said before, and perceive not that I do so'. But here, finally, they would concur: on the unremitting vigilance needed if the diagnosis is not to become one more addition to the list of symptoms of that which Donne calls 'spirituall wantonnesse'; a state which he, like Burton, would wish to see precisely distinguished from 'a spirituall drunkennesse in the Saints of God themselves'.

Burton, like Nashe, read in and quoted from Erasmus, and both authors have a grasp of 'abundance' and of its dissipated twin, redundancy. Erasmus observes particularly of the English that they are not 'frugal' and, in dedicating the first version of *De copia verborum* to John Colet, praises the 'great fruitfulness' of Colet's educational reforms. Nashe, who cites the *Copia* and *Moriae encomium*, celebrates 'increase', 'liberalitie', 'bounty', even the 'sumptuous', though he does so in a book dedicated to the red herring and titled *Lenten Stuffe*. There is a strong counter-turn running among Nashe's abundant figures; it stresses 'profligated labour' and 'bounty' made 'bankerupt'. He contrives to show the 'generous high-mindedness', for which Erasmus praised Colet, travestied by the social climber and academic careerist Gabriel Harvey: 'how affluent and copious thy name is in all places, though *Erasmus* in his *Copia verborum* neuer mentions it.'

Erasmus, in amiable disputation with Colet, associates fecundity with multiplicity in scriptural interpretation, while his respondent argues that 'it is the function of that very fertility to bear not several things but some one thing, and that very thing the truest'. Speaking emblematically, I see Colet presiding in spirit over Donne's sermons and Erasmus as abetting the style of Nashe and Burton. Donne, naturally attracted by what Colet calls 'exuberant fertility and abundance', dedicates his sacred art to their reduction. Nashe and Burton, by inclination and vocation 'adamantine persequutor[s] of superstition' (as Burton said of Lucian), in practice derive a method from the literal meaning of '*persequor*': they give superstition and 'ferall vices' of all kinds the run of the field so as to 'find their game by the trace'. The *OED* is in no doubt that Burton's 'ferall' is from the Latin *feralis* and means 'deadly', 'fatal'; I do not question the correctness of that derivation. It also cites a work that Burton consulted, Thomas Wright's *The Passions of the Minde* (1601), for 'ferall' from the Latin *fera*, a wild beast: 'Some ... arrive at a certayne ferall or savage brutishnesse'. Though Burton, despite some local appearances to the contrary, would not prescribe or encourage the fancy to run wild, I cannot think that his imagination was shut against the suggestiveness of this particular semantic overtone.

For Erasmus, multiplicity is intellectual and spiritual bounty, and I believe that Nashe and Burton think so too. If they had thought otherwise, we would not have their books (or not the books that we have); but knowing bounty as they do, they also know the voraciousness and sterility of ignorance, ambition, and ingratitude—Nashe's 'whole catalogue of wast authours', his 'greedy seagull ignorance ... apt to deuoure any thing', Burton's 'gallantry and misery of the world', 'wise men degraded, fooles preferred'. Democritus Junior, like the other pleaders of the 'common good', has scarcely a good word for clamant and crowding Demos: his 'boiles of the common-wealth', Donne's 'expert beggars' (as distinct from 'them who are truley poore'), Nashe's 'rubbish menialty', Hobbes's 'the more ignorant sort, (that is to say, the most part, or generality of the people)', Clarendon's 'dirty people of no name'. What he has, in common with others who are here discussed, is an attitude of challenge towards questions of social origin. He is less direct than either Hobbes ('I am one of the Common People') or Bunyan ('my father's house being of that rank that is meanest, and most despised of all the families in the Land'). Burton, a scion of the minor gentry, uses philosophical personae and syllogistic sophistry to balance a point of mockery where all pretension to wisdom is reduced to a common baseness, a 'commonalty' in which, by an ambiguous grammatical sequence, he appears willing to include himself. He is neither like Hobbes, the pleb matching himself with the best that Great Tew has to offer, nor like Bunyan, exaggerating the baseness of his origin in order to prove all the more emphatically his election to a domain of 'Grace and Life' denied to those of 'high-born state according to the flesh'. Burton finds himself where he has put himself, betwixt-and-between, as a slightly trucu-lent Bergamask to the serious pace of his *via media*.

Wyndham Lewis, who is like Nashe's belated twin, strangely miscon-strued 'the brilliant rattle of that Elizabethan's high-spirited ingenuity, stupefying monotony ... empty energy'. I would say that Nashe, like Bur-ton, understands that sphere of action, which the Gospels and Epistles call 'this world', to be '*Mundus furiosus*', the domain of stupefying monotony and purposeless energy. The 'high-spirited ingenuity', which Lewis allows, is the verbal strength and adventurousness which Nashe brings to the investigation of torpor and satiety. Burton's word for this domain is *ataxia* (the English form 'ataxy' got into print in 1615, six years before the first appearance of Burton's book). The 'empty energy' that motivates 'this world' is, in the macrocosm, the force of Democritus' atoms colliding in the void; within the microcosm, it is 'so many heades so many whirlegigs' and, as Nashe most directly and empirically knew, the endless wear and tear of—and on—inventiveness itself, subject to the ever-increasing demands of the public press.

If 'Democritus to the Reader' has any advantage over Nashe's *Pierce Penilesse*, it is because Burton's persona, which he may well have taken from Erasmus's *Moriae encomium*, so perfectly matches microcosm to macro-cosm, the minutely tactical to the grandly conceptual, a once-for-all stroke of luck and genius. Nashe's own self-fulfilling, comprehensive discovery is the red herring, the 'king of fishes' to all of good faith and stinking fish for papists and other infidels. I sense more sharply in Nashe's 'light friskin of ... witte' than in Burton's 'extemporean stile' (as he is pleased to name it) a strain of what Pound calls the 'intelligence at bay'. 'Caveat' is a term that Nashe regenerates from the jargon of the day: 'may wee not then haue recourse to that caueat of Christ in the Gospell, *Cauete ab hipocritis*'; 'I cannot forbid anie to thinke villainously, *Sed caueat emptor*. Let the interpreter beware; for none euer hard me make Allegories of an idle text'. The suggestion that 'emptor' means 'interpreter' springs from the same animus that interprets 'carnifex' as 'schollar' or even as 'meat-eater' (a red herring taken with due acknowledgement from the jest of a certain Dr Watson). Democritus Junior in his turn forewarns 'melancholy men...warily to peruse that Tract...& *caveant Lectores ne cerebrum iis excutiat*', while his next-to-last words are 'CAVETE FAELICES'.

If Burton's motto is 'expertus loquor' or 'experto crede roberto' or even 'sed de his satis', Nashe's must be '*sed caueat emptor*'. He has been terribly misread by his purchasers, desirous of a further purchase on him, even by those such as Wyndham Lewis (and the present author, *mea maxima culpa*) who greatly admire him. That we do so misconstrue him is partly his own devising. He deals with the reader, as the witty Dr Watson dealt with his 'fleshly minded' acquaintance, by 'retorting very merily his owne licentious figures vpon him'. In their sense of what 'licentious figures' do, and where and what they lead to—Hell—Burton and Nashe have marked similarities. Compare them on the final straits of wit: 'We [devils], that to our terror and griefe do know their [Poets', Philosophers'] dotage by our sufferings, reioyce to thinke how these sillie flyes plaie with the fire that must burne them'; 'Their [pagan philosophers'] wittie workes are admired here on earth, whilst their Soules are tormented in Hell fire'. Each sees the damned as suffering in a redaction of this world's cruelties. A phrase of Burton in particular—'naked to the worlds mercy'—springs from that common synthetic philosophical marl (Pauline, Augustinian, Senecan, Erasmian, etc.) upon which 'Democritus Junior' grows his wit. Hobbes writes 'Of Man' and 'Of the Kingdome of Darknesse', as if in felicitous memory of such 'reliques' that, at the same time, he wishes to consign, together with those 'senselesse and ambiguous words' which he works so felicitously, to the oblivion of their own darkness ('wandering amongst innumerable absurdities').

There is a particular phrase in *Leviathan* which links it to an earlier mode of moral observation (as represented, let us say, by Cornwallis's *Discourses upon Seneca the Tragedian* of 1601). In Cornwallis, it is a maxim: 'Patience is founded in the true discourse of the minde'; in Hobbes, an anatomy summarized: 'In summe, the Discourse of the Mind, when it is governed by designe, is nothing but *Seeking*, or the faculty of Invention, which the Latines call *Sagacitas*, and *Solertia*; a hunting out of the causes, of some effect

present or past; or of the effects, of some present or past cause'. The nature
of the true discourse of the mind seems to me to be the central issue of *The
Anatomy of Melancholy* and to be much more than a marginal concern in
Nashe. For Nashe, the true discourse of the mind is to be found in the
faculty of invention, 'hellish' as this may be. With Burton, it is finally made
clear that he does not wish to rest in invention, nor are we finally scorned
and baffled purchasers of his activity as we are of Nashe's. Paradoxically, that
which establishes the ultimate difference between writers drawing on such
common Christian humanist stock is movement. 'It is most true, *stylus virum
arguit*', and the factor which distinguishes Burton from Nashe, Burton and
Nashe from Hooker, and Hobbes from all of them, is pace. They pace
themselves differently. Democritus Junior's anatomy of his own style—
'*effudi quicquid dictavit Genius meus*'—reappears as Hobbes's laconic scorn,
dismissive of logorrhoea: 'For if he would not have his words so be
understood, he should not have let them runne'.

In one of his Lincoln's Inn sermons, Donne writes that 'God speaks to us
in oratione stricta, in a limited, in a diligent form: Let us [not] speak to him *in
oratione soluta*'. Judged by this criterion, as much as by the later priorities of
Hobbes, Burton is likely to appear 'loose'. There are repetitions which can
scarcely be read as accidents; for example, the account of Democritus
surrounded by dissected animal carcasses which appears twice within thirty
pages; others, such as the adage 'For he that cares not for his owne is master
of another mans life' repeated a dozen pages on, read like trifling oversights.
Far from trifling is the manner in which, throughout 'Democritus to the
Reader', Burton runs a marginal inventory of a particular word which has
clearly snagged his mind in the course of his scholarly reading: *stultus* and its
cognates; in this section he supplies some forty to fifty entries for the word.
There are precedents for the deployment of words as moral focuses: R. S.
Sylvester shows how More, in the Latin text of his *Richard III*, adopts
Tacitean words—*pavor, adulatio, accusatores, delatores*—to suggest the likeness
of 'close & couert dealing' in Roman and contemporary tyranny. For
Burton, even so, *stultus / stultitia* has an exceptionally powerful attraction,
and the style which it influences and affects is English, not Latin.

Burton could perhaps be said to have invented, to suit his own sense of
decorum (which is strong), an English form of *stultiloquium* (= a foolish
babbling) and of the Plautine *stultiloquentia*, several years before 'stultiloquy'
appeared in English usage (and, even then, in a pejorative sense: Jeremy
Taylor's 'What they call facetiousnesse and pleasant wit, is indeed to all wise

persons a meer Stultiloquy, or talking like a foole', 1653). I would hazard the
further suggestion that Hooker's sense of 'loose regarde' and Donne's '*in
oratione soluta*' here encounter Burton's different order, or range. If 'encounter' sounds too deliberate, let us say that they are brushed aside, in
passing, by such locutions as 'We must make the best construction of it',
'Mixt diseases must have mixt remedies', 'Great care and choice, much
discretion is required in this kinde'. The last of these quotations is noteworthy: it can be taken—by analogy—to indicate how Burton's 'extem-
poranean stile' does not run counter to 'discretion' and is indeed, as he says,
'partly affected'. Hobbes's feigning, in the dedication of *Leviathan*, that he is
ready to be taken for an opinionated old goose (but a Capitoline goose, no
less) is reminiscent of Burton's tactical affectation, though with a forensic
edge that Burton does not claim.

If Hooker's assiduous citing of 'reason', in senses that are both definitive
and highly allusive, derives from Aquinas; if Donne's public oratory for-
malizes private traits which may strike us as close to Pauline yearning for
exemption from the flesh (*cupio dissolvi*), Burton's method openly declares
its debt to Hippocrates and Galen and to modern physicians, while its
theology of healing remains Augustinian. *Be not solitary, be not idle*, the
urgent affirmative grammatically placed as a negative, which, so far as I
can gather, is Burton's compact enrichment of things said by Hippocrates
and by the Portuguese physician Fonseca (d. 1622), concludes the vast
argument at 3.4.2.6. The close proximity, as a doubly moral–medicinal
colophon, of Hippocrates and Augustine indicates an evenness of regard
towards Greek sanity (Hippocrates' pupil Galen is cited even more than
his master) and Christian teaching on sin and grace:

> This likewise should we now have done, had not our will beene corrupted,
> and as we are enjoyned to love God with all our heart, and all our soule: for to
> that end were we borne, to love this object, as *Melancthon* discourseth, and to
> enjoy it.

The feral openness of our time may detect a pun in the sharing of an element
between Burton's title and the Graecized name of the Lutheran humanist
Philipp Schwarzerdt, but I think that on this point at least Burton would
reiterate *Sed de his satis*. Where we pluck out 'found poems', Burton, in the
Augustinian mode which he shared with Nashe and Donne, would find
restlessness, or a treadmill of wit, 'endlesse argument of speech' which, as
Nashe concluded, must be broken off 'abruptlie'. The injunction *Be not*

solitary, be not idle is not meant to urge self-dissipation amid infinite variety of business, in any 'praecipitate, ambitious age'. Hippocrates' advice has somehow to be reconciled with the Psalmist's 'Be styll then, and knowe that I am God'. In undertaking to anatomize eloquence such as this, one is exhibiting fragments of a synthesis which, though composed of minute particulars, transcends all Ramist itemizing. Consider in this light one sentence from the final section, 'Cure of Despaire':

> If any man, saith *Lemnius*, will attempt such a thing [exorcism], without all those jugling circumstances, Astrologicall Elections, of time, place, prodigious habits, fustian, big, sesquipedall words, spells, crosses, characters, which Exorcists ordinarily use, let him follow the example of *Peter* and *John*, that without any ambitious swelling tearmes, cured a lame man, *Acts 3. In the name of Christ Jesus rise and walke.*

The manner in which the huge, 'loose', referential edifice of *The Anatomy of Melancholy*, the 'confused company of notes ... writ with as small deliberation, as I doe ordinarily speake', can yet be so tellingly pointed and cadenced by one sentence—the simple authority of 'In the name of Christ Jesus rise and walke'—is wonderful almost beyond words. As Burton was not the prolix 'smatterer' carefully presented in the 1621 postlude, I have little doubt that he fully appreciated the quality of what he had achieved and considered his labours well spent.

It is as if, in his capacity for such fine tuning, Burton realizes the equivalent in words of that 'accurate musicke' which he records as being used against 'agitation of spirits', 'vaine feare and crased phantasie'. 'Accurate musicke' is, and is not, like Donne's 'equall musick' in the peroration to his Whitehall sermon of 29 February 1627–8: 'where there shall be no ... darknesse nor dazling, but one equall light, no noyse nor silence, but one equall musick, no fears nor hopes, but one equall possession'. The order of Donne's words is analogous to that of Hooker's Christian reason: 'by ... steppes and degrees it ryseth unto perfection of knowledge', where perfection is the confirmation of ultimate equity of redemption in the elect: yet Donne's text, out of which the sublime knowledge arises, is Acts 7: 60, the prayer of the dying protomartyr Stephen that the criminal ignorance of his slayers be not imputed to them. Donne's words elsewhere in the sermon are virtually identical with Hooker's; he proposes that 'the name of *Stephen* hath enough in it to serve not only the vehementest affection, but the highest ambition'. Hooker had urged Cartwright, Travers, Whitaker, and their fellow Puritans to ask themselves 'whether it be force of reason or vehemencie of affection, which hath bread, and still doth feede these opinions in you'. 'Vehemencie of affection' / 'vehementest affection': in Anglican apologia of this period the line drawn between the inordinate and the ordinate can be as fine as this. Circumstance commands it, but individual genius turns circumstance into an approximate free will. 'Accurate musicke' is a figure that plucks on a variety of strings, and Burton's 'We must make the best construction of it' (by which he means 'if a man put desperat hands upon himselfe, by occasion of madnesse or melancholy...as *ex vi morbi*') could have marked him as injudicious, even libertine, in the eyes of Hooker, who would regard him as arguing loosely from 'things doubtfull'. However, this is a principle which Hooker partly concedes, if only to shift his polemical grip on Cartwright, in the 'Preface' to *Ecclesiasticall Politie*. Donne, who left *Biathanatos* unpublished, writes of 'a rule that ordinates and regulates our faith': 'inordinate' is his characteristic pejorative ('inordinate melancholies', 'inordinate sadnesse', 'inordinate love', 'inordinateness of affections', 'inordinate lamentation', 'inordinate sorrow growes into sinfull melancholy'); yet he himself inclines to the inordinate.

There is a body of exegesis which—influenced by Freud—sees Donne so strongly possessed not only by the 'death wish' but also by a lifetime's struggle against it that this consideration should powerfully, even finally, determine our sense of the overall direction and significance of his work. He confesses the temptation on at least one occasion and I cannot disprove the claim that he suffered from a lifelong suicidal tendency, but even those who urge this hypothesis would agree that '*Cupio dissolvi*, To have a desire that we might be dissolved, and be with Christ' is Pauline theology, notwithstanding the vehement affection which Donne may reasonably be supposed to bring to it.

What I have principally in mind is not so much a broad question of morbid psychology as a minute particular of inaccurate music. I instance the last two words of one of Donne's greatest poems, the 'Hymne to Christ, at the Authors last going into Germany' (1619):

> Seale then this bill of my Divorce to All,
> On whom those fainter beames of love did fall;
> Marry those loves, which in youth scattered bee
> On Fame, Wit, Hopes (false mistresses) to thee.
> Churches are best for Prayer, that have least light:
> To see God only, I goe out of sight:

> And to scape stormy dayes, I chuse
> An Everlasting night.

It is perhaps unnecessary to our sense of this stanza that the fifth line should be recognized as a commonplace found in More's *Utopia*. It is, however, necessary, here as elsewhere in Donne and his contemporaries, to accept that each of those authors could take for granted his readers' intimacy with the Scriptures, either in the Vulgate or in one of several English translations.

From whatever point of witness a seventeenth-century reader might approach Donne's words, 'everlasting night' would surely strike eye and ear as a shocking spiritual oxymoron or wild aural pun: it retorts upon 'The Anniversarie', the celebration of love's 'first, last, everlasting day', but inordinately so. We seem too close in spirit to that 'most fearefull and most irrevocable Malediction' in the fifteenth expostulation of *Devotions* (1624). There is little point in appealing to the mystics. If the night is 'everlasting', it cannot be either the dark night of the soul or the cloud of unknowing.

But of course Donne glosses his own darkness—in the funeral sermon for Sir William Cokayne:

> The Gentils, and their Poets, describe the sad state of Death so, *Nox una obeunda*, That it is one everlasting Night; To them, a Night; but to a Christian, it is *Dies Mortis*, and *Dies Resurrectionis*, The day of Death, and The day of Resurrection; We die in the light, in the sight of Gods presence, and we rise in the light, in the sight of his very Essence.

Not the Scriptures, then, or the mystics, but possibly Catullus (*Nox est perpetua una dormienda*) and Propertius (*Nox tibi longa venit nec reditura dies*). E. M. Simpson writes that Donne 'turns from the Old Testament to Catullus for his associative magic'. 'Associative magic' would perhaps suffice if the poets in question were Thomas Campion and Campion's Catullus or Propertius, but it does not take the measure of Donne's allusiveness, either in the sermon or in the 'Hymne to Christ'. In the sermon, the measure is *in oratione stricta*, in the poem *in oratione soluta*. Compared to the last stanza of 'A Nocturnall upon S. Lucies Day', in which Donne, albeit with pronounced difficulty, offers up the sensuality of *Songs and Sonets* as the sensuousness of rectified affection, 'A Hymne to Christ' ends with an enigma. I would find it hard to accept that an echo of the Latin elegists is a sufficient counter-weight to the alienated New Testament phrase; and though I still regard the 'Hymne' as the greater of these two great poems, it seems nonetheless that a price was paid and continues to be paid for its particular kind of power. The complicity of elegiac sophistry with spiritual equivocation has a touch of the 'ferall' about it, *ex vi morbi*, as it might be. My reference to 'inaccurate' music must be set directly against Burton's 'Others commend accurate musicke, so *Saul* was helped by *Davids* harpe', as it is my contention that Donne here eludes Burton's progress *ad sanam mentem* and returns his own music to perturbation. Even so I have to concede that rational objection scarcely touches the ultimate power of poetry such as this, and that the quality of the finest seventeenth-century metaphysical writing transforms Bacon's derogation of the scholastics—'fierce with darke keeping'—to claim tribute even from the grudging inventiveness of Bacon's animosity and to reclaim such 'keeping' to the light of spiritual eloquence, as to Hooker's 'The power of the ministerie of God translateth out of darknes into glorie'. Part of that darkness for Donne—who understood that 'darke texts need notes'—would be the Neoplatonic mysticism of Pico della Mirandola, which he admired and which, in Edgar Wind's telling phrase, he 'rescu[ed] from degradation'.

I have observed that in the contextures of this writing the inordinate and the ordinate are at times finely separated. The standard rhetorical figures merely trace the outline of such characteristics and, even then, in a relatively crude style. There is, however, a particular complicity of actives and passives invoked by these writers which may take its bearings from Calvin's interpretation of Augustine on free will and the bondage of the will. I have particularly in mind 'Man receaued in deede to be able if he would, but he hadde not to will yt he might be able'. The figures most closely aligned with this doctrinal–grammatical dilemma are perhaps *paronomasia* and *traductio* (I do not find it easy, in particular cases, to distinguish one usage from the other). Nashe, in *Christs Teares over Iervsalem*, engages with *traductio* so intensely as to mimic reprobate treachery. Insofar as the nature of women is here being traduced, Nashe is himself subject to reprobation; he carries the infection in his own style: and I am convinced that he knows this:

> Euer since *Euah* was tempted, and the Serpent preuailed with her, weomen haue tooke vpon them both the person of the tempted and the tempter. They tempt to be tempted, and not one of them, except she be tempted, but thinkes herselfe contemptible. Vnto the greatenesse of theyr great Grand-mother *Euah*, they seeke to aspire, in being tempted and tempting.

The pattern 'being tempted and tempting'—passive and active—is repeated in Donne's sermons and *Devotions* ('I am a reciprocall plague; passively and actively contagious'; 'our selves are in the plot, and wee are not onely *passive*, but *active* too, to our owne destruction'). With Burton, as I understand him, the passive is made up of the vast common heap of 'melancholy [taken] in what sense you will, properly or improperly, in disposition or habit, for pleasure or for paine, dotage, discontent, feare, sorrow, madnesse, for part, or all, truly, or metaphorically, 'tis all one'. That ''tis all one' elides a Shakespearian sense of clowning insouciance and fool's comeuppance with a seemingly endless *sorites* of mental and spiritual suffering ('the whole must needs followe by...induction'), so minutely recorded that all sufferings appear reduced to a voluminous monotone. With Burton—again, as I understand him—the active declares itself in plain, even severe, statements of faith and practice that stand out from the tragic–comic welter like inspirations of 'God's grammar':

> Thy soule is Eclipsed for a time, I yeeld, as the Sunne is shadowed by a clowd, no doubt but those gratious beames of Gods mercy will shine upon thee againe, as they have formerly done, those embers of Faith, Hope and Repentance, now buried in ashes, will flame out afresh, and be fully revived. Want of faith, no feeling of grace for the present, are not fit directions, we must live by faith not by feeling, 'tis the beginning of grace to wish for grace: we must expect and tarry.

'We must live by faith, not by feeling': this at the heart of several hundred thousand words dedicated to an 'anatomy' of diseased feeling. *In the name of Christ Jesus rise and walke.*

In an undated sermon (1622?) delivered at St Paul's, Donne attends to an unnamed scholar's act of *paronomasia*; 'depart[ing] from the ordinary reading [of the Booke of Psalmes], which is *Sepher Tehillim*, The booke of Praise, and to read it, *Sepher Telim*, which is *Acervorum*, The book of Heapes, where all assistances to our salvation are heaped and treasured up'. It is fitting, I think, to end here; for it was not beyond the wit of the author of *The Anatomy of Melancholy* to conceive his own work as a book of heaps out of a heap of books: a mere *sorites* to set his name to, even while Bacon was showing forth to a new age the 'harmonie of a science supporting each part the other'. Yet in that heap the makings of a finer anatomy, a grander organum, a richer treasure, a nobler volume of praise.

18

A Pharisee to Pharisees

Henry Vaughan provided texts for several of his poems, as a priest would for a sermon. 'The Night' has John 3.[1]

> There was a man of the Pharisees, named Nicodemus, a ruler of ye Iewes: The same came to Iesus by night, and said vnto him, Rabbi, wee know that thou art a teacher come from God: for no man can doe these miracles that thou doest, except God be with him. Iesus answered, and said vnto him, Verily, verily, I say vnto thee, except a man be borne againe, he cannot see the kingdome of God. (John 3: 1–3)

At what point did Nicodemus see the light? Did he see it because he had come, or did he come because he had seen it? Jesus gently chides him for his questions: 'Art thou a master of Israel, and knowest not these things?' (10).

The narrative makes Nicodemus seem a mixture of inoffensive ignorance, genuine perplexity, and chop-logic: 'How can a man be borne when he is old? can he enter the second time into his mothers wombe, and be borne?' (4). But Vaughan calls him 'wise' Nicodemus. In making the decision to seek Christ, he was, according to the Scripture, 'doing truth' or 'coming to the light'. Nicodemus was a Pharisee, a leading member of the ruling ecclesiastical party. Coming to Jesus at all was a dangerous thing to do. Therefore he came under cover of darkness. Jesus makes a primary act of conversion, from the literal to the figurative, in seeing this darkling venture as the stumbling of ignorance away from reprobation and towards truth: 'And this is the condemnation, that light is come into the world, and men loued darknesse rather then light, because their deedes were euill' (19). But Nicodemus, although a Pharisee, did not love the darkness rather than the light; in coming to Jesus by night he was declaring his innate love of the light.

---

[1] The full text of 'The Night' can be found in the notes, on pp. 683–4.

We are as yet only being drawn towards the poem; we are to see how the poem stands in the presence of the scriptural episode and its hints of sympathetic pre-cognition, of intuition overcoming rational antipathy (it would have been reasonable for Nicodemus in those circumstances to have felt hostility towards Jesus). Vaughan's feelings towards the scriptural event are intensely sympathetic; he is drawn to it; his rhyme, as we shall discover, will attempt to chime with the theme, as his figures of speech will descant upon the basic measure, night : light.

The narrative of John 3 discovers two men taking each other's measure: 'Nicodemus answered, and said vnto him, How can these things be? Iesus answered, and saide vnto him, Art thou a master of Israel, and knowest not these things?' (9–10). Since a poet's concern is with both metre and rhyme we may expect Vaughan to be drawn to demonstrations of measure in its several senses. He must measure up to the task of imagining these natural and supernatural beings as they take the measure of each other and of destiny, of time and eternity, of knowledge and ignorance, faith and doubt; and his own words must be measured against, must chime faithfully with, the received words of Scripture.

Somewhere along the way we have begun to read the poem. Like representatives of Nicodemus, who represented us, we are strongly drawn to it, but drawn also to exercise our chop-logic upon it. In speaking of Vaughan's words chiming faithfully with the received words of Scripture we also beg questions of faith and conformity. His inventive imagination adheres 'to words and rhythms' picked up in his meditative reading, but his brusque departures and rapid conflations are as emphatic as his adherences. The citing of the text and the initial naming of 'wise Nicodemus' provide a focus for manifold soundings and radiations. Throughout the poem, recollections of Exodus 39–40, 1 Kings 6, The Song of Solomon 5: 2, Malachi 4: 2, and Hebrews 9: 14 are as strong as, or stronger than, those of John 3, and there are further darkling allusions which may bring to mind Genesis 18, Boehme, Paracelsus, and Vaughan's own prose. I do not think, however, that these allusions necessarily restrict the poem to the communing of initiates. Biblical exegetes from Augustine to Calvin took the view that 'wise Nicodemus' was in some respects rather dim, and Vaughan seems to have 'his own, similar understanding of Nicodemus' limited wisdom'. But the limited wisdom does not preclude 'blest' belief, and the blessing does not exclude human limitations. Once we have turned to the setting, the situation, of John 3, it becomes pervasive, unforgettable, and the relationship of Nicodemus' perplexed desire to the 'sacred leafs', the 'fulness of the Deity', the 'deep, but dazling darkness' of the manifest truth, is unmistakable. I have suggested that Jesus, in taking the physical darkness to be spiritual darkness, performs an initial act of poetic conversion; yet the figure of speech is intended to be literally true. Poetic metaphor is a means of converting the actual into the real. To see the reader of 'The Night' as a lay figure for Nicodemus may be only a late and dusky impertinence. Nicodemus, for all his exemplary academic dimness, was truly 'wise' and truly 'blest'; the reality of Scripture attests to that. The blessing, or the wisdom, involved in any other individual case can be nothing more than conjectural radiations emanating from, or directed upon, that focus. One cannot rule out the possibility, however, that Vaughan, a 'bookish poet', would concur with H. A. Williams's suggestion that 'the academic study of prayer may lead a man to pray'. I would further agree that 'The Night' 'refuses to make any easy divisions between the poet and his corrupt times'. The 'land of darkness and blinde eyes' is Palestine *c.*30 CE, the 'late and dusky' environment may be Wales and England under the Commonwealth, the 'loud, evil days' are, according to Vaughan, his own; but it is to his purpose that we should sense a miry compounding of implication. I concur with those who hesitate to call 'The Night' a visionary poem, since 'vision' is too commonly taken to mean effortless, unimpeded rapture. Vaughan's embroilment in national and personal distress makes him doubly conscious: of impetus and impediment; of a world hastening to catastrophe; of humanity fearfully laggard in its recognition of the apocalyptic signs.

The impetus and the impediment are equally registered in the poem. It 'quickens to a palpable ecstasy', but that ecstasy, in stanza six, is also markedly derivative; and in stanza seven ecstasy itself is narrowed and compacted to an urgent desire:

> Were all my loud, evil days
> Calm and unhaunted as is thy dark Tent,
> Whose peace but by some *Angels* wing or voice
> Is seldom rent.

These lines especially in their involvement of annunciation with violence and breaking are, like the visitation they describe, serene yet troubling. 'Rend' and 'rent', in the Scriptures, occur most often in contexts of lamentation, punishment and dread: 'I wil surely rend the kingdome from thee' (1 Kings 11: 11), 'and [I] will rent the kall of their heart' (Hosea 13: 8). In Matthew 27: 51, the veil of the Temple is 'rent', and so are the rocks. Exodus 39: 23 describes how the robe of the ephod was bound 'that it should not rent'. Indeed, if there is a direct source for stanzas four and seven it is most likely to be found in the concluding chapters of Exodus, which narrate and describe the building of the 'Tabernacle of the Tent of the Congregation' with its 'Mercie seat of . . . gold' and 'Vaile of the couering', and its covering of cloud. In noting the probable source we note also how Vaughan at once assents to and dissents from that which inspires him. The 'dark Tent', 'calm and unhaunted', is one of his most intense affirmations; the 'mercy-seat of gold', together with 'dead and dusty *Cherub*' and 'carv'd stone', is rejected as a piece of edifying (and possibly Pharisaical) clutter. It is 'living works' that are to be treasured. If it is possible to be faithful both to letter and spirit and yet stand solitary and heterodox in one's conflations or diffusions of letter and spirit, Vaughan's 'The Night' is the autocratic manifestation of that possibility. It makes a mosaic out of Mosaic (and many other) echoes, but the mosaic is a 'living work', like that 'blest Mosaic thorn' celebrated by Christopher Smart. The creative mystery dwells in Vaughan's capacity to vivify a method that might so easily have produced second-rate *appliqué*. 'Others might expound the letter; Vaughan lived the text.'

We would be 'ill-guiding' and ill-guided, however, if we were to suppose that 'living the text' is, for Vaughan, much like that spontaneous overflow of divine immanence which Christ's 'own living works' declare. The poem is acutely aware of immanence, as it is of imminence; there are serene celebrations of indwelling; even so, something remains within and withdrawn when all has been quantified and qualified. The troubling power of the '*Angels* wing or voice' is still unaccountable:

> And the Cherubims spread out their wings on high, *and* couered with their wings ouer the Mercie seat, with their faces one to another; *euen* to the Mercie seat ward were the faces of the Cherubims.   (Exodus 37: 9)

But these serene and noble beings are compounded in the 'dead and dusty *Cherub*' of stanza four. It is true that 'the Lord called vnto Moses, and spake vnto him out of the Tabernacle of the Congregation' (Leviticus 1: 1), but that recollection does not entirely contain the 'fulness' which I believe Vaughan is summoning to, and from, his own indwelling imagination. Pedantry not only spells constraint; it is also freedom; and 'bookish' Vaughan had anticipated Alexander Cruden in his knowledge that 'tent' signifies 'an apartment or lodging-place made of canvas or other cloth on poles' (Genesis 4: 20) as well as 'the covering of the tabernacle' (Exodus 26: 11).

> In *Abr'hams* Tent the winged guests
> (O how familiar then was heaven!)
> Eate, drinke, discourse, sit downe, and rest
> Untill the Coole, and shady *Even*.

Though 'Religion' brings angels' wings and voices into a tent it is without
any suggestion of the calm being 'rent'. Even so it is possible that in 'The
Night' Vaughan is echoing his own poetry as much as he is echoing his own
prose. 'Religion' had appeared in the first edition of *Silex Scintillans* (1650);
'The Night' was included in the second, enlarged, edition of 1655. 'Religion' itself has its clear source in Genesis 18: 1–3:

> And the LORD appeared vnto [Abraham] in the plaines of Mamre: and he sate in
> the tent doore, in the heat of the day. And he lift vp his eyes and looked, and,
> loe, three men stood by him: and when he saw *them*, he ranne to meete them
> from the tent doore, and bowed himselfe toward the ground, And said, My
> Lord, If now I haue found fauour in thy sight, passe not away, I pray thee, fro
> thy seruant.

The three men, who are at once angels and the voice of the Lord (it is
Vaughan who sees them as 'winged'), bring blessing and assurance to
Abraham and Sarah but the threat of imminent destruction to Sodom.
Abraham risks the Lord's wrath by speaking up for the 'righteous' who
may dwell there. But 'earely in the morning' he sees the smoke rising from
the cities of the plain. In 'Religion' Vaughan excludes the wrath and
retribution that are a part of the angels' bearing. In 'The Night' it is as
though he elliptically concedes these attributes in the brusquely disproportionate 'rent' which seems to intrude from the margins of his recollection.

We may question, however, whether such connotations 'intrude' or are
'drawn in'. 'One of the largest and most recurrent' of Vaughan's image-
clusters 'has, for common factor, the idea of magnetism', and he may have
been drawn or impelled towards this interest by the hermetical studies of
his brother Thomas. The stanza from 'Religion' makes clear that his ideal of
an 'active commerce' between 'the various planes of existence', between
angels and men, would be a 'familiar' 'discourse', a quotidian but holy
communing, a matter of calm and untroubled daily practice rather than of
clandestine nocturnal comings and goings. Vaughan, as Royalist and Anglican, was the adherent of twin causes, both defeated. 'By 1650 Vaughan's
earthly Church of England had in fact vanished.' Two of his prose works
published in 1652 and 1654, during the interregnum, bear upon the study of

his poetry, of 'The Night' in particular. 'The logical prose content [of "The Night"] is to be found in *The Mount of Olives*.' Vaughan composed that work, one section of which bears the title 'Man in Darkness', to encourage the practice of solitary devotion among his readers 'in these times of persecution and triall'. In the dedicatory epistle to Sir Charles Egerton, Vaughan writes: 'The *Sonne* of *God* himself (when *he* was *here*) had no place to put his head in; And his *Servants* must not think the *present measure* too hard, seeing their *Master* himself took up his *nights-lodging* in the cold *Mount* of *Olives*'. In the preface to *Flores Solitudinis . . . Collected in his Sicknesse and Retirement*, 1654, he declares:

> *I write unto thee out of a land of darknesse, out of that unfortunate region, where the Inhabitants sit in the shadow of death: where destruction passeth for propagation, and a thick black night for the glorious day-spring. If this discourage thee, be pleased to remember, that there are bright starrs under the most palpable clouds, and light is never so beautifull as in the presence of darknes.*

If we regard 'The Night' and its several darknesses in the light of such evidence we discover how the sympathetic attraction of otherwise disparate images and echoes from the Old and New Testaments, from a variety of non-scriptural sources and from Vaughan's own writings creates a positive embracing of abnegation, a transferring of potentiality from the darkness of a stricken soul, a stricken cause and a stricken church into a visionary intensity. The ecstatic night of The Song of Solomon, the night of Christ's several cold and solitary vigils (as recounted in Vaughan's other 'texts' for this poem, Mark 1: 35 and Luke 21: 37), possibly that night, also, in which 'an horrour of great darknesse' fell upon Abraham and a voice prophesied that his seed should be a stranger in a land that was not theirs (Genesis 15: 12–13), all these attractive and repellent nocturnal associations are synthesized, transfigured, converted by the dominating metaphor of the darkness which saw the conversion of the Pharisee Nicodemus. 'Conversion' is the key to the metaphysics of *Silex Scintillans* and to the poetics of 'The Night'. Coldness, destitution, deprivation (as in *The Mount of Olives*), darkness, blindness, deadness, silence are made the magnetic points of contact with the Divine Grace. Night is heaven, and heaven takes on some of the qualities of visionary darkness:

> Gods silent, searching flight:
> When my Lords head is fill'd with dew, and all
> His locks are wet with the clear drops of night;
> His still, soft call;
> His knocking time; The souls dumb watch,
> When Spirits their fair kinred catch.

This is Vaughan being 'bookish' again, plagiarizing The Song of Solomon 5: 2 and Revelation 3: 20 with magnetic originality, as though he were simply catching 'fair kinred' of his thought. There seems no reason to dispute S. L. Bethell's claim that in this stanza the poet 'recreates through sensory material an intuition of eternal reality'. It is significant that Bethell refers to 'sensory material' rather than to 'sensuous experience'. Sensuous experience is what is evoked; the sensory material I take to be language itself.

It would perhaps be generally agreed that a 'poetic' use of language involves a release and control of the magnetic attraction and repulsion which words reciprocally exert. One is impelled, or drawn, to enquire whether that meta-physical rapport felt to exist between certain English rhyme-pairings is the effect of commonplace rumination or the cause of it. Auden, in New Year Letter, makes 'womb' : 'tomb' a trick in his 'Devil's' sophistry, implying that the easy availability of the rhyme is complicitous with our trite melancholy and angst. Sir Thomas Browne, meditating in 1658 on funeral urns 'making our last bed like our first; nor much unlike the Urnes of our Nativity', may cause one to suppose that speculative pseudo-logic works independently of the gravitational pull of words; yet he too is 'rhyming' in a sense, only with shapes, not sounds. Sigurd Burckhardt suggests that a pun is 'the creation of a semantic identity between words whose phonetic identity is, for ordinary language, the merest coincidence'. Heard in this way, all rhyming is punning; as, seen in the light of hermetical philosophy, all creation is a form of rhyming, or 'union of elemental extremes', and would be especially so to Vaughan, 'committed as he was to a belief in the validity of the specialized microcosmism of hermeticism'. That which Milton disdains as 'the troublesom and modern bondage of Rimeing' is troublesomely binding as much because it is easy as because it is hard: an imputation endorsed by Aubrey's report of Milton's lofty permission for Dryden to 'tagge his Verses'. The troublesome ease may be inferred too from the work of Thomas Campion, whose Observations in the Art of English Poesie, with its reference to 'the childish titillation of riming', anticipates Milton's dismissive tone. His own lyrics from the four books of ayres, in which 'loue' rhymes with either 'moue' or 'proue', or their moods and cognates, in song after song, obligingly demonstrate his contention. Such rhymes are evidently easy for the singing voice; they are also 'tags', that is to say, they show a 'pretty knack', they 'buttonhole' attention, but they are not 'like cleare springs renu'd by flowing', not 'voluble', as is 'Rose-cheekt Lawra', Campion's own masterly 'example' of unrhymed verse. At the same time one might be bound to accept, for it would be hard to deny, the way in which a modish metaphysics of love's oxymoronic power accrues from the mellifluous repetitiveness of these rhymes, as Donne appears independently to have noted: his hyperbolic rhyming in 'The Canonization' seems designed to draw attention to the discovery. The impulse of 'loue', at once fixed and flighty, to 'moue' and 'remoue' is an incitement for Campion's singer to 'proue' its falseness or its truth:

> Changing shapes like full-fed *Ioue*
> In the sweet pursuit of loue.

It is fitting that this lordly rhyme should consummate *The Ayres that Were Svng and Played at Brougham Castle* since both change and permanence are in Jove's protean gift.

In Vaughan's poetry a rhyme which occurs with striking frequency is 'light : night', or 'night : light'. Here, too, basic mechanics assume ontological dimensions. S. L. Bethell has remarked on 'the light–darkness opposition in Vaughan', but such a rhyme embodies more than an opposition. It is a twinning: a separation which is simultaneously an atonement ('Wise *Nicodemus* saw such light | As made him know his God by night') and a conjunction which exacerbates the sense of divorce ('And by this worlds ill-guiding light, | Erre more then I can do by night'). In the pairing 'light' : 'night' and 'night' : 'light' itself, there is nothing remarkable except its bookish obviousness. Campion is drawn to it several times, notably in the refrain of 'My Sweetest Lesbia'; so is Herbert. Wotton proffers it handsomely ('On his Mistris, the Queen of Bohemia') and Jonson makes it sound both securely traditional ('A Hymne on the Nativitie of My Saviour') and sententiously challenging (in the third 'turne' of 'To the Immortal Memorie . . . '). But in Vaughan the eye and ear are dogged with a particularly dogged tenacity: 'In the first birth of light, | And death of Night' ('To Amoret, Walking in a Starry Evening'); 'I'le leave behind me such a *large, kind light*, | As shall *redeem* thee from *oblivious night*' ('To the River *Isca*'); 'The first (pray marke,) as quick as light | Danc'd through the floud, | But, th'last more heavy then the night | Nail'd to the Center stood' ('Regeneration'); '(*for at night* | *Who can have commerce with the light?*)' ('Vanity of Spirit'); 'But these all night | Like Candles, shed | Their beams, and light | Us into Bed' ('Joy of my life!'); 'As he that in some Caves thick damp | Lockt from the light, | Fixeth a solitary lamp | To brave the night'; 'Yet I have one *Pearle* by whose light | All things I see, | And in the heart of Earth, and night | Find Heaven, and thee' ('Silence, and stealth of days!'); 'Call in thy *Powers*; run, and reach | Home with the light, | Be there, before the shadows stretch, | And *Span* up night' ('The Resolve'); 'Above are restles *motions*, running *Lights*, | Vast Circling *Azure*, giddy *Clouds*, days, nights'; 'O lose it not! look up, wilt Change those *Lights* | For *Chains* of *Darknes*, and *Eternal Nights?*' ('Rules and Lessons'); 'The Dew thy herbs drink up by night, | The beams they warm them at i'th' light' ('Repentance'); 'Or wil thy all-surprizing light | Break at midnight?'; 'The whole Creation shakes off night, | And for thy shadow looks the light' ('The Dawning'); 'I saw Eternity the other night | Like a great *Ring* of pure and endless light | All calm, as it was bright' ('The World'); 'The first glad tidings of thy early light, | And resurrection from the earth and night' ('Ascension-day'); 'Their magnetisme works all night, | And dreams of Paradise and light'; 'Their little grain expelling night | So shines and sings, as if it knew | The path unto the house of light' ('Cock-Crowing'); 'Dear feast of Palms, of Flowers and Dew! | Whose fruitful dawn sheds hopes and lights, | Thy bright solemnities did shew, | The third glad day through two sad nights' ('Palm-Sunday'); 'Tempests and windes, and winter-nights, | Vex not, that but one sees thee grow, | That *One* made all these lesser lights' ('The Seed growing secretly'); 'Were not thy word (dear Lord!) my light. | How would I run to endless night' ('The Men of War'); 'Who shews me but one grain of sincere light? | False stars and fire-drakes, the deceits of night' ('The Hidden Treasure'); 'And onely see through a long night | Thy edges, and thy bordering light!' ('Childe-hood'); 'To thy bright arm, which was my light | And leader through thick death and night!' ('Abels blood'); 'This litle *Goshen*, in the midst of night, | And Satans seat, in all her Coasts hath light' ('Jacobs Pillow, and Pillar'); 'O beamy book! O my mid-day | Exterminating fears and night! | The mount, whose white Ascendents may | Be in conjunction with true light!' ('The Agreement'); 'Should poor souls fear a shade or night, | Who came (sure) from a sea of light?' ('The Water-fall').

It is reasonable to ponder what it is that draws or impels Vaughan towards this rhyme. Is it an instinctual gravitation, or a conscious application to the sensory material of his brother's and other hermetical writers' theories about magnetism and sympathetic attraction? Or is it that Vaughan has so concentrated his mind on the abstract eschatology of 'light–darkness opposition' that he is relatively or even totally indifferent to the monotonous uninventiveness of his word-finding? Such addiction is indeed vulnerable to suggestions that it renders null and void a poet's unique claim to whatever prestige his craft may have: his capacity to invent, to 'compose', to 'find out in the way of original contrivance'; to 'create, produce, or construct by original thought or ingenuity'; to 'devise first, originate', to 'bring into use formally, or by authority'. It could be argued, of course, that the word 'invent' itself contains contradictory implications and that to 'come upon', which suggests chance discovery, is to be distinguished from 'devise' or 'bring into use', which imply forethought and manufacture.

'The Night' itself, it is true, contains powerful contradictory energies, but it must be said that our own readings of the poem are themselves liable to disabling contradictions because, for a variety of contemporary cultural reasons, we 'see not all clear' when we try to calculate the ratios of vision to craft. E. C. Pettet finds the final stanza over-inventive, merely ingenious, 'manufactured', as though 'something of the organic impulse and life of the poem, its intensity and seriousness, has gone'. J. F. S. Post has argued that 'despite the achievement of a timeless vision, no poem of Vaughan's shows better his reluctance to dissolve into rapture'. 'Shows better' and 'reluctance' suggest a fuller understanding both of Vaughan's vision and his perplexities and of his way of 'bringing into use formally, or by authority' the envisioning of perplexity itself:

> There is in God (some say)
> A deep, but dazling darkness; As men here
> Say it is late and dusky, because they
>   See not all clear;
>   O for that night! Where I in him
>   Might live invisible and dim.

'Lux est umbra Dei', according to Ficino. Vaughan's contemporary Sir Thomas Browne quoted the phrase in support of his own preference for 'adumbration'. 'Some say' confirms the validity of the poem's perplexed meditation; it does not, in my view, dissipate its 'mystical awareness'. If awareness is to have any value at all as a critical term, it must be allowed to retain that innate sense of being 'on one's guard'. This is surely what the poem's 'full intensity' rejoices in: that Nicodemus came warily but nonetheless came upon the truth and that, as he did so, nature kept vigil and was no less wary than it was entranced ('did watch and peep | And wonder'). Though we too should be wary of reading Vaughan, a 'thorough-going intellectual', as if he were a childlike precursor of Romanticism, our sense of 'awareness' is enhanced when, in stanza six, the God of The Song of Solomon 5: 2 and of Revelation 3: 20 comes like a mousing owl over the fields by the Usk, with 'silent, searching flight' and 'still, soft call'. To be the 'catch' of Spirits is a fearful rapture.

'The Night' celebrates the absoluteness of 'blest' belief while it asserts
a mortal 'consent' to mundane 'darkness' and 'myre'. It is the supposed
discrepancy between celebration and assertion that has troubled some
readers. But I suspect that Vaughan himself has spotted the catch: he writes
of himself as one who is doubly caught. He is both possessed by God and
gripped by a sense of his own unworthiness ('*Servus inutilis: peccator maximus*'
as he was to remain, in his own mind) and of his own and others' subjection
to Cromwellian republican tyranny. If we are persuaded of the validity of
Vaughan as poet of the absolute, it is because he has validity as poet of
'contingency', a term which covers 'close connexion or affinity of nature'
(1612), an 'event conceived as of possible occurrence in the future' (*a*1626)
and mere 'chance', 'fortuitousness' (1623).

> O for that night! where I in him
> Might live invisible and dim.

'Might' is conditional, but so are stanza seven's 'Were all my loud, evil days'
and 'Then I in Heaven all the long year | Would keep'. Contingency
surrounds, in the form of grammar, syntax, and verse-structure, the 'Dionysian' absolute, the 'deep, but dazling darkness'. As Post has observed,
'detached yet "possessed"', the final stanza 'seems to shuttle between two
realms . . . without relinquishing touch with either'.

In the light of this observation one may add that Vaughan's metaphysics,
his bookish but spontaneous and sincere paradox of 'deep, but dazling
darkness', or his persistent 'light-darkness opposition', working through
the rhyme-pattern, poem after poem, transforms contingency itself into a
density, an essential 'myre', though without the accidents of language
thereby being denied or tamed. Each time the words 'light' : 'night',
'night' : 'light' chime they reassert 'merest coincidence' even while they
are affirming a theological or hermetic theorem as clear and absolute in
Vaughan's mind as 'the square of the hypotenuse'. One is drawn towards
the invention of a term—'metaphysical phonetics'—to try to define what is
happening through this reiterative pattern. But this would merely create a
further 'theorem', and I am far from convinced that the relationship between
vision and language in poetry, or at least in Vaughan's kind of poetry, works
according to theorems, particularly hermetic ones.

Frank Kermode has been taken to task for suggesting that Vaughan's
'conversion' 'was rather a poetic than a religious experience'. This claim,
though extreme, has the considerable virtue of conceiving language as

something other than a mere ancillary of 'vision' or 'experience'. Language is a vital factor of experience, and, as 'sensory material', may be religiously apprehended. Post has written at some length on Vaughan's 'poetics of conversion', meaning principally his transformation of *The Temple* into *Silex Scintillans*: 'No one read Herbert with greater benefit or imagination'. I believe that one could go further and say that Vaughan fashioned regeneration by regenerating fashion. E. C. Pettet has noted how the 'shining ring of eternity' to be found in the great opening lines of 'The World' is 'already intimated' in the pretty secular verses 'To Amoret, Walking in a Starry Evening'. He could have added that the 'light' : 'night' rhyme of 'To Amoret' 'intimates' its own regeneration in the light–darkness eschatology of Vaughan's religious poems, and of 'The Night' in particular.

Walter J. Ong, deep in the dazzling darkness of his brilliant essay 'Wit and Mystery', tells us that, for Aquinas, 'Christian theology and poetry are indeed not the same thing, but lie at opposite poles of human knowledge. However, the very fact that they are opposite extremes gives them something of a common relation to that which lies between them: they both operate on the periphery of human intellection. A poem dips below the range of the human process of understanding-by-reason as the subject of theology sweeps above it'. The 'awareness' of Vaughan's religious poetry is an awareness of such extremes. That which lies between these extremes, in his beautiful poem 'The Night', is the conversion-conversation of Jesus and Nicodemus in which that which is above understanding-by-reason (theology) and that which dips below the process of understanding-by-reason (the contingent nature of sensory material) are briefly made to chime.

19

The Eloquence of Sober Truth

It is fortunate for the estate of humane letters, as we have received it from the writers represented in *Early Responses to Hobbes*, that a sense of overall and general truth may be gained as a real effect of such writings, irrespective of whether sincerity or authenticity (as we are inclined to understand them) can be discovered at the source.[1] The formal admixture of the plain and the florid, of openness and cunning ('wresting', deliberated misreading), of magnanimity and malice, of public application and private referral, of empiricism and ideology, that is to say, the quotidian practical eloquence of controversy evident in these works, finds little or no answering resonance among a specialist or a general readership of our own time. Understandably so. Rightly to evaluate John Bramhall and the first earl of Clarendon would be to recognize ourselves as barely having moved from under the shadow of their contentions. And such recognition would, for millennial idealists and cynics alike, be asking too much.

Of the authors here represented, it can be said that, although not always knowing where they stood, they knew in general how they stood, from what and from whom they were descended and how they wished to be seen to have stood: in relation not only to authority and precedent but also to posterity. The awareness of providence, agency, and delegation, of being required by conscience and circumstance to act as intercessor between flawed past, uncertain present, and unsecured future, is suggested most powerfully by the exordium to Clarendon's *History of the Rebellion and*

[1] *Early Responses to Hobbes*, edited by G. A. J. Rogers. Six volumes, boxed (New York and London: Routledge: Thoemmes Press, 1996), 1,699 pages. The volumes discussed in this essay are *A Defence of True Liberty*, by John Bramhall, Bishop of Derry (1655); *Observations, Censures, and Confutations of Notorious Errours in Mr Hobbs his Leviathan*, by William Lucy, Bishop of St David's (1663); and *A Brief View and Survey of the . . . Errors . . . in Mr. Hobbes's Leviathan*, by Edward Hyde (Edward, Earl of Clarendon) (1676).

Civil Wars in England, which he began to draft on 18 March 1646: an opening sentence, 'a mighty period of nearly five hundred words', in which details of syntax and word-choice significantly invoke the emphatic cadence of Richard Hooker's exordium to *The Lawes of Ecclesiasticall Politie* (1593). In so committing himself, Edward Hyde (as he then was) eloquently recalled to life a definitive voice of the Elizabethan Church and State, but a voice considerably changed, strained, by the circumstances of the intervening half-century. It was a purposed eloquence which, already under attack when Hooker adopted it and made it his own, had, in less than fifty years, been rendered obsolete. For Clarendon, however, situated as he was, to be, or to sound, obsolete was to be, or to sound, legitimate.

Legitimacy is not sincerity, nor is it the personalist authenticity of Emerson and the Emersonians. The significance of *Early Responses to Hobbes*, for us as much as for seventeenth-century thought and polity, is the preponderance of discourse. The authors argue, often tendentiously, sometimes crudely, very much in their own interest, but they are not, with the possible exception of Robert Filmer, monologuists, nor are they determinists or mechanistic dialecticians; they engage with the (hostile) other as a contending voice among others. They recognize their own contentiousness, their own partiality, and thereby acknowledge, in a sense, their parity, their common partaking in that condition, that innate incompetence, which Hooker had called 'this our imbecillitie'.

Clarendon's own debt to Hooker evidently comprehends more than the matter of a grandiose but mismanaged exordium. The fluent magnanimity of the *Lawes*, its 'peaceful and lofty sentences' (as A. P. D'Entrèves called them), is authentic but not unambiguous. There is a polity to declare and defend, and this is a politic style. It is scarcely conceivable that Hooker believed it possible to disarm by peaceful means the Presbyterian aggression: in a disadvantageous position he sees the advantage to be gained from using words with a marked courtesy towards the quality of reciprocal discourse or, at least, towards a fiction of the desired reciprocity. Such usage represents or affects to represent the writer's 'diligent and distinct consideration', the neglect of which, Hooker implies, is a key failing in his opponents. That Clarendon commences his *History* with an imitation of Hooker's opening paragraph is due mainly, I suggest, to his politic grasp of associational pitch-values. His representation of the issues is frequently neither diligent nor distinct nor considerate, but to arouse the memory—and when it serves, the hollow memory—of peaceful and lofty sentences is eminently worth his time and labour.

There is a semantic doubleness, a double valency, in English public writing of the sixteenth and seventeenth centuries that constitutes its own form of minor tradition, and here also one can see that Clarendon is working in a mode which derives from Hooker. To what extent, beyond the opening tribute, this is always a conscious derivation I would find it harder to decide. To take one characteristic example: in Hooker, 'dexterity' is a word of ambivalent tone, an ambivalence which is even more pronounced when Clarendon adopts it. In one instance in Hooker, it applies to the 'subtiltie of Satan'; in another it affirms the 'works of nature' as they are seen to be 'exact' and 'by divine arte performed'. The 'admirable dexteritie of wit' which Hooker attributes to the original reforming inspiration of Calvin cannot be taken as a term of unqualified respect, though, when Hooker found a theory or practice abhorrent, as he did 'Ramistry', he was not one to mince words. Egil Grislis's observation that '[his] attitude toward Calvin ... may reflect both respect and censure' is appropriately judicious, and confirms my sense that 'dexterity' was a word typically resorted to, in cases of suspended judgement, by those conscientiously desiring to maintain equity but that it characterized also those whose disabling perplexity of mind gradually works through to the reader and may also have become apparent to the author himself during the process of composition.

Conscious as Hyde must have been, in 1646, that the *History*, as critical of Stuart mismanagement as it was laudatory of Charles I's private virtues, could not be made public in the foreseeable future, its style, in part recollected for an immediate audience of one—his own reflective self— and in part projected for an unfathomable posterity, betrays his divided attention, if not his confusion. The 'mighty' opening period of the *History* is unwieldy; it is also ungrammatical. For 'may loose the recompense dew to their virtue' read 'may [not] loose the recompense dew to their virtue'. Clarendon aimed to write with a persuasive frankness while being not entirely scrupulous in his handling of debatable matters which, as they were in themselves formidable and complex, also on occasion eluded his otherwise formidable style of elegiac–forensic 'vindication'. It is revealing that he too allows a considerable amount of slack in his use of the word 'dexterity'. When he approves the whole constitution of the man, as he does with Lord Falkland, it signifies the ability to apply one's understanding and judgement with celerity, 'seasonably and appositely'. Where he detests his subject, as he does Henry Vane the younger and William Waller, it points to a celerity in self-promotion, a talent to 'cozen and deceave'. The Earl of

Strafford, whose 'passions', especially that of 'pride', Clarendon presents as in part responsible for the national catastrophe, 'the late woful calamities in *England*', 'the late execrable Rebellion', but whose inherent strength of character raised him above his accusers, 'made his Defence with all imaginable Dexterity; answering this, and evading that, with all possible skill and eloquence'. The range of implication is perhaps wider in Clarendon than in Hooker; necessity of circumstance, strongly sensed in the *Lawes*, is even more pressingly evident in the *History* and the autobiographical *Life*. In each case, we are simultaneously aware of a particular kind of grammatical structure and a particular theory of moral virtue: dexterity is at once the proper credential of a serious writer and a craft potentially sinister; a cunning spring-trap as likely to catch the magisterial author as it is to deal with the miscreant object of his censure.

Virtually without exception, the various authors represented in *Early Responses to Hobbes* leave little room to doubt that language, in relation to private and public practice, is at the heart of the matter: the matter being principally that of the instauration, destruction, and restoration of a true national identity and doctrine. Bishop Bramhall of Derry would be glad enough to stand by the authority of moral axioms—for example, 'deceitfull men do not love to descend to particulars'—but his style is transitional: we see axiom in process of its translation into working exemplar:

> a precedent generall deliberation how to do any act, as for instance, how to write, is not sufficient to make a particular act, as my writing this individuall reply[,] to be freely done, without a particular and subsequent deliberation.

In William Lucy's *Observations, Censures and Confutations of . . . Leviathan* (1663), the empirical shifts even further, into satire:

> When he writ his *Leviathan*, there was *motion*, but this *Leviathan*, I hope, is not *motion*; it may, perhaps, in heedlesse Readers, cause *motion* and *commotion*, but certainly it lies still under my paper at this time, and will do all this night.

In Bramhall's *Defence of True Liberty* (1655), the distinction between necessity and freedom is pointed by the availability of the verb forms 'must write' and 'may write' and is affirmed by the judiciousness with which an author chooses between them. The burden of his charge is that Thomas Hobbes constantly 'changeth shapes in . . . one particular' and that such shape-shifting implicates etymology, logic, and common honesty. Moreover (according to Bramhall), Hobbes misconstrues as often as he intentionally misleads; his errors stem from simple incompetence as much as from a perverted will; or, rather, the common errors as much as the sophisms are the outward and visible sign of a radical inward desperation. For Bramhall to 'descend to particulars', to 'strike ... at the root of [the] question', is both to anatomize deceitfulness and self-deception and to establish the ground of right dealing. Lucy, exercised as much by Socinian errors as by Hobbes's waywardness with Scriptural texts, proposes to 'take every word apart, and vindicate it from their several Objections'.

In numerous instances which these authors present, to 'strike ... at the root' is the same as to clear the 'genuine sense' of a word from Hobbes's specious application of it, or to 'rip up the bottom of [a] business', as in the several pages which Bramhall devotes to eradicating the senses of 'voluntary' and 'spontaneous' planted by his antagonist and to nurturing a genuine sense of them, in keeping with his—Bramhall's—understanding of sense and reason. If I take this to imply that Bramhall and Lucy are more open to Ramist method than was Hooker, my suggestion hangs by a slender thread—that of the term 'anatomy' in English literary usage during the sixteenth and seventeenth centuries—and is also strongly attached to Walter J. Ong's observation that Petrus Ramus's *Commentary on the Christian Religion* sets itself 'explicitly the task of illustrating the theological loci'. The early responders, to the Hobbes of the original *De cive* of 1642 as well as of the later *Leviathan*, are strong advocates and assailants of the loci, but they are primarily turning an emphasis which they may have drawn from a knowledge of Ramus into forms of argument strongly opposed to Ramist tendencies in general, a modification which one also recognizes in Robert Burton's *Anatomy of Melancholy*. This first appeared in 1621 and, together with Philip Sidney's *Arcadia* (1590), commits, but does not abandon, its discourse to that debatable ground where, in the corrupt state of man, private and public interests are determined—but not irretrievably—by the indeterminate.

Bramhall seeks to establish his moral ground against the author of *De cive* by submitting, at the very outset of the debate, a basic question concerning the scope and limits of self-knowledge in contexts of such contentiousness: whether those 'affections' which 'betray our understandings' may 'produce an implicite adhaerence in the one [person] more than in the other'.

If one could legitimately elide chronological sequence, it would be possible to claim that Bramhall desires to expose 'implicite adhaerence' as the graceless twin of that 'inhaerent' 'vertue' which Hobbes celebrates in his recollections of Sidney Godolphin. Further, it is as if Bramhall enters the tacit caveat that true magnanimity calls for more than a magnificent ingenuity of phrase. As he says elsewhere in *A Defence of True Liberty*, 'this controversy . . . is not about Words, but about Things; not what the words Voluntary or Free do or may signifie but whether all things be extrinsecally praedetermined to one'. In so saying, of course, he focuses attention—his and ours—all the more urgently on questions of language, the nature of meaning. The unarguable circumstances telling against my chronological elision is that the private disputation between Bramhall and Hobbes took place six years before the tribute to Godolphin was made public in 1651; the source of the dispute, as we have noted, was not *Leviathan* but the *De cive* of 1642. A more persuasive response would be that the later Hobbes is everywhere implicit—and often explicit—in the earlier writings, and that Bramhall's original objection to his opponent's 'meer Logomachy' in *De cive* would have been reinforced by a subsequent reading of *Leviathan*. He would not, in 1651, have seen any cause to retract.

Chronology and its intractabilities notwithstanding, the contention over disparate elements to which I have alluded in the phrase 'true national identity and doctrine' manifestly traces and retraces the likeness and unlikeness between 'implicite adhaerence' and 'inhaerent' 'vertue'. Although the root cause of Bramhall's objections to *De cive* is the apparent inability of Hobbes's argument to grasp the nature of that 'true morall liberty, which is in question between us', Hobbes's summoning of the spectre of blind necessity, near the end of *Leviathan*, in his second reflection on Godolphin's untimely death, 'unfortunately slain in the beginning of the late Civill warre . . . by an undiscerned, and an undiscerning hand', challenges all other examples of contemporary *laus et vituperatio* to approach anywhere near its tragic resonance, let alone take its measure. Hobbes's nearest rivals in rhetorical power, in such deploration, are Sidney in the *Arcadia*, Walter Ralegh and, in certain instances, Clarendon.

So to elevate into exemplary maxims, epigrammatic conclusiveness, as I do here, those turns of phrase which the original contestants would have considered mere examples of 'tautology' and 'wresting', the issue of 'meer animosity', 'antipathy', 'melancholy', 'desperate imaginations' (imaginings), on one side or the other, is to risk being taken as assuming a dictatorial privilege of hindsight. The issue remains, even so. If Hobbes's theory of the Passions is 'very far from being *the true Key to open the cipher of other mens thoughts*', as Clarendon avers, and if the caveat is honestly entered (and it

may not be), where and how is the 'key' to be obtained? Clarendon chides
Hobbes for his 'mirth' at the expense of the 'Schole-men' who, the
barrenness of their speculation notwithstanding, at least contributed 'terms
of Art . . . which in truth are a cipher to which all men of moderate Learning
have the key'. It is apparent, however, that 'cipher' in Clarendon's second
sense is not exactly conformable to his earlier use of the term. In the second
instance the key is application; in the first it is construal. We are therefore
returned to the original point at issue: How are statements to be read? How
are they *meant* to be read? It is on this point, or question, that all those who
felt themselves called to make 'Animadversions upon' either *De cive* or the
later *Leviathan* appear, on the face of it, to be in agreement. This state of
accord, or its simulacrum, derives in no inconsiderable part from Hooker's
tactics of politic concord, judicious censure, gestures of magnanimity: a style
which he had already established some years prior to the appearance in print
of the first four books of *Ecclesiasticall Politie*: 'Conster his [St Paul's] wordes,
and ye cannot misconster myne. I speake no otherwise. I ment no otherwise.'

The standard procedure is that of the 'necessary requisite', even though
ideas as to what constituted the requisite mean standard differed from author
to author. Ong stresses the inherent force of the 'commonplace' in the
textures of even the most individual style and argument. One would add
only that the *idea* of the body of commonplace was itself not only convenient but also powerfully suggestive to writers of this period, as a kind of
secular *adiaphora*, indifferent matter which should figure either as an unfailing reservoir of tried and tested human wisdom and experience or as an
immovable bulk of *pseudodoxia*, rumour, and common report, supposedly
justifying any given author's reasonable contempt for, and distrust of, 'this
present age full of tongue and weake of braine', the 'Sophisters and seditious
Oratours apply[ing] themselves to the many headed multitude'.

Struck here by Bramhall's choice of words, our automatic response is
'Shakespeare'. But how far, if at all, was *Coriolanus* regarded as essential, or
advisable, or prudent matter by the 1640s? The phrase 'many-headed multitude' is in Sidney's *Arcadia* and was taken by him and by others from Horace's
first *Epistle*. The root question with regard to the use of commonplace at that
time relates less to genealogy than to genius, the 'natural ability or capacity' to
render significant that which is given; to 'form . . . and model' (Hyde, on
William Chillingworth) an individual contribution to the shared discourse.
I infer that among the many reasons for a consensus against Hobbes, as

represented by this set of *Early Responses* and by other writings not represented, was a suspicion—or a recognition—that, in his work, style becomes a different kind of individual attestation: an attestation to singular power. Although Hobbes is at pains to assert that laughing to scorn, the 'Sudden glory' of self-applause when 'observing the imperfections of other men', is itself 'a signe of Pusillanimity', his own negative attributes were pre-eminently, as his foes insisted, pettiness of spirit, cowardliness, and timidity (that is, 'pusillanimity'). His genius is that he does not write in accordance with his own prescription. 'The Light of humane minds is Perspicuous Words, but by exact definitions first snuffed, and purged from ambiguity': yet he is a master of nuance and innuendo, tactics absolutely requiring that our language retains, and is directed so as to retain, a good deal of partly consumed matter, the stuff of contrary feelings and perplexed experience, even a certain amount of bad odour. (See further in Part One, chapter 2, his play on 'haunt', meaning the malign activity attributed by the credulous to ghosts and apparitions but meaning also the malign activity of 'crafty ambitious persons' who spread 'fearful tales' about a particular location—for instance, a churchyard—so that they themselves may 'haunt' or frequent it for their own nefarious purposes.) And what kind of business does Hobbes conduct with faith and works, meaning and usage, in the following excerpt? He declares 'our Senses, and Experience, [and] our naturall Reason' to be

> the talents which [God] hath put into our hands to negotiate, till the coming again of our blessed Saviour; and therefore not to be folded up in the Napkin of an Implicate Faith, but employed in the purchase of Justice, Peace, and true Religion.

From Tyndale (1526) through to the King James Bible (1611), 'napkin' renders the Greek σουδάριον (Latin *sudarium*), literally 'sweat-cloth', in Luke 19: 20, John 11: 44 and 20: 7, and Acts 19: 12. In Luke, it is the piece of cloth in which the bad servant has 'kept' (Tyndale) or 'layd up' (King James) the one talent with which he had been entrusted. In John 20: 7, it is the face-covering left in the empty tomb, 'not lying with the linnen clothes, but wrapped together in a place by it selfe' (1611). Hobbes appears to have implicated a secondary sense with the primary sense of his words. In paraphrase, his emphasis is plainly on 'good works', the investing, not the hoarding, of God's gifts. But his secondary sense—the linen 'wrapped together', folded up—happens to be the primary meaning of an essential tenet of Christian belief. The meaning of the resurrection is implicit in the sign of the folded σουδάριον, but an 'implicate faith', a faith that will not come forth into declaration at the very site of the mystery, that remains folded in on itself, set aside, is no faith at all: the heart of doctrine is here mute witness rather than redemptive and eloquent mystery.

It could be argued that in saying 'Hobbes appears to have implicated...', I overstate the case, attributing intention, deliberation, where there may be only misapplication; and that Hobbes is simply hoist with the petard of his contempt for the solecisms of others, 'for if he would not have his words so be understood, he should not have let them runne'. I take it as a crux, a test of interpretative judgement, here. If Hobbes has failed to estimate, allow for, or otherwise register, the weight and power of John 20: 7, its capacity to distort with implication the familiar admonition of Luke 19: 20, the moral is that, as Donne claims, 'the Holy Ghost in penning the Scriptures delights himself... with a propriety... of language' and that someone who thinks barbarously and gracelessly will overreach into self-revelation and submission. God is not mocked; nor, finally, is his language. On the contrary, however, I find that sentences such as we have here testify to Hobbes's leaps of imaginative power, and, further, that the clue to the particular quality of his mind is given by another characteristic turn, in Part One, chapter 4. There, ostensibly, he is simply categorizing particular applications ('speciall uses of Speech') within the 'generall use of Speech'. The fourth of these special uses is exemplified by our ability 'to please and delight our selves, and others, by playing with our words, for pleasure or ornament, innocently'.

Let us consider for a moment 'our selves, and others'. Henry Vaughan wrote, probably in the same lustrum that saw the publication of *Leviathan*:

> But living where the Sun
> Doth all things wake, and where all mix and tyre
> Themselves and others, I consent and run
> To ev'ry myre.
>
> ('The Night', 1655)

And—earlier—Donne had written, c.1628:

> Wilt thou forgive that sinne by which I wonne
> Others to sinne? and, made my sinne their doore?
>
> ('A Hymne to God the Father')

Behind the *I / other* tenor in both Donne and Vaughan, we may find that of the earliest prayers and collects of the Church of England, 'Catholic but reformed', under Cranmer; as in the prayer for mercifulness from the Edwardian *Primer* of 1553: 'even as thou our heavenly Father art merciful, and promisest that if we be merciful to other, we shall obtain mercy of thee'. Hobbes has a way of playing the stern old formalities into a state of suspended animation, for that is what 'pleasure and ornament' amount to here. I can think of no seventeenth-century usage outside Shakespeare, for instance in Iago's 'honest', that is less innocent than Hobbes's 'innocently', and the comma immediately preceding it is as wicked as it is perfect.

If, as Ong maintains, one 'result of the opportunity offered by print' was that thousands of copies of 'commonplace books in various guises...flooded the market for some two hundred years after the invention of alphabetic typography', then opportunism evidently becomes a factor of style, and style itself, since 'commonplace' is the datum, or base, shifts markedly towards implications of register. By 'register' I intend to suggest—balancing between verb and substantive—a (precise) manner of setting down; an entitlement to set down; a device for admitting or excluding, for example, air, heat, smoke (the first recorded use of this sense is in Ben Jonson's *The Alchemist*, 1610).

The third suggestion, as it will appear the most far-fetched, needs to be tackled at once. 'Heat', as a reading of Clarendon, Milton, and others of their contemporaries makes evident, is a term of seventeenth-century ethical polity. Clarendon presents himself as learning to 'subdue...that pride, and suppress...that heat and passion he was naturally inclined to be transported with'; 'heat', for him, means appetite, 'uncharitableness', and 'ignorance'; he associates it with the political and ecclesiastical agitation of the 1630s: 'heat and animosity' on the one side challenged by 'heat and passion' on the other. With Milton, in *Areopagitica*, the sense of the word is held at the other extreme of the spectrum: 'where that immortall garland is to be run for, not without dust and heat'.

One has to differentiate, even so, between this and the other forms of registration which were becoming more widely established. The mode I have in mind is not the international state-law of 'the incomparable *Grotius*' (as Clarendon addressed him); it is not contracted according to the principles of Comenius's *Analytical Didactic*, wherein 'all the general and particular activities that meet in the act of teaching, learning, and knowing' are examined; it does not proceed by those 'exquisite reasons and theorems almost mathematically demonstrative' which Milton attributed to John Selden's method in *De jure naturali*. Clarendon, in fact, contentiously associates the 'Rules of Arithmetic and Geometry' with the 'imaginary Government . . . of which no Nation hath ever yet had the experiment', that phantom issuing from the seditious brain of Hobbes of Malmesbury.

The fundamental pattern of registration in the present set of *Responses* is more conservative; a modulation rather than a modification of already existing forms of ratiocination and eloquence. There is a marked willingness to defend the Scholastic Philosophers against the brutishness—as they read it—of Hobbes's contempt. Both Clarendon and Bishop Lucy, however, refer to 'Etymologie'; Bramhall claims that Hobbes exploits double meanings ('the ambiguous acceptions of the word, free'); Clarendon objects to the 'mist of words' which obscures the 'Fallacies upon which [Hobbes] raises his Structure'.

It is evident, however, that their own arguments are aided—and indeed, abetted—by the contemporary interchangeability of the terms 'proprietie' and 'property'. Clarendon, for example, refers to 'the Liberty and propriety of the Subject' and, on the following page, salutes 'the precious terms of Property and Liberty' which must not be perverted into 'absurd and insignificant words, to be blown away by the least breath of [Hobbes's] monstrous Soveraign'. 'Property', for Clarendon, is a 'precious term', as 'Occupancy' is 'a sacred title' to Lucy. In these three instances, as elsewhere, 'property', 'propriety', and 'occupancy' represent private tenure with secure enjoyment of 'Lands and Goods' but also, by a slight degree of extension, they indicate qualities of intellectual and civic deportment which may be claimed and possessed as self-evident right of title. 'Propriety' is, on this basis, self-possession (a quality of character) stemming from an assurance of inalienable right to property, together with the free acceptance of all duties and obligations pertaining thereto:

> the Copies and Transcripts of antient Landmarks, making the Characters more plain and legible of what had bin practic'd and understood in the preceding Ages, and the observation whereof are of the same profit and convenience to King and People.

My sense of the matter is that if Clarendon were abruptly required to vindicate (a verb he favoured) in under fifty words his conception of the role of author in the second half of the seventeenth century, he could hardly do better (always supposing he deigned to answer) than to take these, his own words from *A Brief View and Survey*, which appeared posthumously in 1676. And if he were further obliged to defend, at equally short notice, his conception of the just work of polity, he could—with propriety—direct his interrogator to the same manuscript source.

That Clarendon could so—and so incidentally, as it must seem—focus a double vocation, an ethical twinning which he himself would not have stooped to comment on, is a necessary caveat against overconfidence in broad comparison and conjecture. Having said that, I would say also that Clarendon writes with a sense of authority and that he clearly requires a sufficient competence in his reader to distinguish between such authority and the stylistic 'exercise ... [of] an absolute Dictatorship', 'imperious averment', a presumption of 'having the Soveraign power over all definitions', absolute confidence in the 'Sovereignty ... of [one's] own capricious brain, and haughty understanding', all of which indicate vices of theory and practice characterizing the arch-seducer Hobbes. Clarendon takes for granted that there is a legitimate distinction to be drawn between Hobbes's imperiousness and his own forms of hauteur ('such inestimable Treasure ... ventur'd against dirty people of no name'), though the dividing line is much less obvious to us now than it was to him.

It is equally the case that Clarendon points us in the general direction of a systematic alternative code of procedure. Contrary to Hobbes's 'imperious averment', there is 'a proper and devout custom of speaking', which the Hobbists deride but which still has power to 'vindicate ... the Truth from the malice that would oppress it'. As I have suggested, Clarendon's style is intended to maintain and display that proper and devout custom of speaking; an exhibition of standards in direct opposition to the improper and impious and aggressive new way of Hobbes. It is meant to exemplify 'reflexion, without which there can be no thinking to [any good] purpose'. As I have also suggested, the 'devout custom' is evoked by an imitation of Hooker (an imitation that comes perilously close to travesty, nonetheless). Clarendon's propriety has a double root; it is partly the acknowledged excellence of Anglican custom and partly the lordly self-possession of one who is wholly untroubled by his contempt for dirty people of no name, the illiterate and dispossessed, and who at the heart of the matter writes as if he were deaf to the radical discrepancies among these allegiances and attitudes, between Anglican religious polity on the one hand and, on the other, the vision of the suffering servant prophesied by Isaiah and manifested in Christ.

Clarendon's style, therefore, however firmly it adheres to the principle of integrity and comeliness, in practice is bound to show signs of strain, of badly resolved perplexity, partly realized contradiction, and implicit self-contradiction. The strain is felt in some usages more than others; it appears particularly as the manner in which certain words are recurrently placed: for example 'custom', 'tradition', 'integrity', 'desperate', and—above all—'private'. Clarendon writes, 'ordain'd and constituted by custom and acceptation' (of the signification of words), and, again, 'that common practice of circumspection and providence, which custom and discretion hath introduced into human life'. But he notes also 'all the customes of the Nations' as proscribed by God to the Israelites, and classifies among the 'enormities of the Roman Church' its 'errors of Tradition'. Bramhall equates 'custome' with 'proclivity' and proclivity with 'vitious habits'; yet his 'old truth derived by inheritance or succession from mine ancestors' is surely also a form of custom. For Lucy, the 'natural' capacity shown by 'Beasts or Dogs' to 'love' what is 'profitable' for them and to detest that which is 'hurtful', can also be called *natural appetite*, which, in turn, can be viewed as *custome*. In his *Observations upon H. Grotius, 'De Jure Belli, & Pacis'* (1657), Robert Filmer argues that

> it is not the being of a custome that makes it lawfull, for then all customes, even evil customes, would be lawfull; but it is the approbation of the supreame power that gives a legality to the Custome: where there is no supream power over many nations, their Customes cannot be made legall.

As I understand the business, the authors of these early responses to *De cive* and *Leviathan* are fully competent to negotiate, for the best terms each can get, among a compact body of ambiguities: ambiguities which are in part ethical, part civil, part etymological. Reading them, I again lose confidence in my ability to name the benefits and improvements which John Locke conferred on English philosophy, religion, polity, and language when he set himself to nullify the capacity of words to excite 'Disputes' and to 'reduce' 'all . . . Terms of Ambiguity and Obscurity' to 'determined Collections of the simple *Ideas* they do or should stand for'. The rubric to the *OED*'s entry on the verb 'to reduce', that most characteristic term of seventeenth- and eighteenth-century ratiocination, is exemplary of the matter as it stood then and stands now:

> The original sense of the word, 'to bring back', has now almost entirely disappeared, the prominent modern sense being 'to bring down' or 'to diminish'. A clear arrangement of the various uses (many of them found only in the language of the 15–17th centuries) is rendered difficult by the

extent to which the different shades of meaning tend to pass into or include each other.

It now strikes me that there is very little in Locke's programme of remedial analysis that has not been anticipated by Bramhall; and, further, that Bramhall is no less concerned than is Locke at the moral and emotional attrition which is the toll exacted by ambiguity, obscurity, and all forms of disputation. The difference between them is, in part, that Bramhall's moral theology is taken deeply into the body of his 'Etymologie' and that Locke's is not. To the blunt retort 'Then Locke has achieved with perfect finesse the task he set himself: and religion, philosophy and the English language are the better for it', I would respond that the perplexed matter of tradition, or custom, as we have received it, gives evidence that to legislate as 'the end of Speech' 'that those Sounds, as Marks may make known [our] *Ideas* to the Hearer' is to presume to disconnect language from the consequences of our common imbecility. The Lockean prescription names a legitimate function of language; but its tacit proscriptions turn legitimacy into tyranny. As with other patrimonies, our language is both a blessing and a curse, but in the right hands it can mediate within itself, thereby transforming blessing into curse, curse into blessing. I note W. D. J. Cargill Thompson's insistence that Locke is not Hooker's heir, and that the supposed derivation is largely the issue of Whig myth-making. Hooker's theology is also involved with etymology; and Bramhall, who in theory anticipates Locke, is in practice closer to Hooker and, even, to Calvin.

I draw to this conclusion through my sense of the emphasis placed by Bramhall, as by Hooker before him, and by Calvin before that, on the nature of contingency, circumstance: 'For as much as actions are often altered and varied by the circumstances of Time, Place and Person'; 'of such questions they cannot determine without rashnes, in as much as a great part of them consisteth in speciall circumstances'; 'And also the same could not be simply determined without rashness, forasmuch as a great parte of the order of this question consisteth in circumstances'.

Though Hooker appears to be copying Thomas Norton virtually word for word, it is probable that he is working directly from Calvin's Latin, to which his marginal annotation ('*Cal. instit.li.4.cap 20, Sect 8.*') refers. This is a telling instance of the manner in which the hypothetical apprehension of contingency and circumstance can be—and, especially at this period, is— a most immediate realization, and a working through, of the contingent and circumstantial in which one is caught up or, all too often, merely caught. Hooker's 'Preface' is not, in the first instance, addressed to interested general readers (as we construe 'interest' and 'reader') but to a compact, interested, and inward body of English Presbyterian controversialists: inward, I mean, with every word and phrase of Calvin's Latin *Institutes*. Hooker so engages the cause, the men, the books, that it is always with renewed surprise that one discovers, or is reminded, that the foundation-works of that cause were twenty years old by the time the first four books of *Ecclesiasticall Politie* were put into print. Archbishop Whitgift, still at that time Dean of Lincoln and Master of Trinity College, Cambridge, had hotly contested the Presbyterian case on the spot in 1572–3. More recently, the Anglican apologist Richard Bancroft had taken on the Marprelates in terms as acridly mocking as those of the pamphlets themselves.

It is generally accepted that Hooker was delegated, and in part self-delegated, to the writing of his great apologia armed with a distinct working brief. As V. J. K. Brook observes:

> The *Ecclesiastical Polity* represents the crowning victory of Whitgift's campaign, raising the issues out of a mire of petty querulousness to a high level of reverence, toleration, humility.

Reverence, toleration, and humility are not necessarily qualities of the delegated stylist's personality. It should be understood, moreover, that Hooker was able to flex and direct a style of reverence, toleration, and humility because there were others—like Whitgift—able and prepared to turn the screws of suspension, deprivation, imprisonment and, in a few cases (William Hackett, John Penry, John Greenwood, and Henry Barrow), execution. Hooker's delegated, arduous procedure is to make official doctrine and formal eloquence not seem but be reciprocally 'proportionable': 'The Church of Christ is a bodie mysticall. A bodie cannot stand, unlesse the partes thereof be proportionable'. Bramhall, in 1645 (published 1651), contends that

> where *T.H.* demands how it is possible for the liberty of doing, or not doing this or that good or evil, to consist in God and Angels, without a liberty of doing or not doing good or evill. The answer is obvious and easy, *referendo singula singulis* rendering every act to its right object respectively.

It may be worth repeating here that, on the evidence of this set of *Early Responses*, one engrained idea, of Hobbes's completing Francis Bacon's work for the eradication of Scholastic Philosophy from seventeenth-century intellectual life, must be strongly qualified. The 'Schole-men' are no more and no less agencies in Bramhall's argument than is the theory and practice of etymology. To the Bishop of St David's (William Lucy), in his *Observations* of 1663, the question of faith may be resolved by subsequent empirical consideration of initial dogmatic statements concerning, for example, duty ('afterward, upon experience, or examination, they find it congruent to the *will* of God; then they practice it accordingly with *confidence*').

All three instances could ultimately derive from a common Scholastic source. But I must here qualify my own claim. In terms of theory and general topos, it is possible to align Hooker's 'proportionable' with Lucy's '*Congruence*' and Bramhall's 'rendering every act to its right object respectively' and conclude that, over the span of seventy most turbulent years, they manifest a remarkable continuity and coherence. Such paraphrase, however, gives false readings by cancelling out individual pitch, and, in context, Bishop Lucy's pitch is markedly different from that of Hooker. In the light of my earlier comments on Hooker's style, it would be difficult to claim that we move from his *mystique* to Lucy's *politique*. The 'body mystical' of the *Lawes* itself is a feature of polity. Even so, one could say with some justice that it is of real concern to Hooker that the 'parts ... proportionable' should be adducible both to Christian doctrine and to the eloquent structures of his defence of that doctrine. If we add that, in Lucy's 'find it congruent', the author is concerned to give as much emphasis to the activity of confirming as to the status of congruence, a change of pitch must be conceded to that. Bramhall in turn gives weight to his verb, 'rendering', from the Latin gerund '*referendo*'. Could one show that the Bishops of Derry and of St David's accommodate Hobbes in such details and that the post-Restoration cast of the Church of England will be a slow but progressive secularization intermitted by bouts of reactionary 'enthusiasm'? While the liturgical Service of Confirmation is retained throughout as the Anglican *rite de passage*, more is increasingly claimed by, and bitterly conceded to, the soteriological activity of confirming oneself in the faith, until the mystical pragmatism of the search itself becomes the validating activity of evangelical belief, both within the Church (for instance, John Newton of Olney) and among the several categories of separated brethren. The confrontation, in August 1739, between Bishop Butler and John Wesley provides an exemplary indication:

B[ishop Butler]. And Mr. Whitefield says in his Journal: 'There are promises
still to be fulfilled in me.' Sir, the pretending to extraordinary revelations and
gifts of the Holy Ghost is a horrid thing—a very horrid thing!

There is, I believe, an unbroken continuity from the arguments feeding
into, and arising out of, the Elizabethan 'Settlement' (less a settlement than a
redistribution of weight and bias) to this disputation between two powerfully conservative Anglicans who were alike in their opposition to deism
and the Deists. Wesley claimed to be empowered, by the terms of his
Oxford Fellowship, to an 'indeterminate commission to preach the word
of God in any part of the Church of England', or, failing that, by 'my
business on earth...to do what good I can'. To Butler, Wesley was a
trespasser on the property of the diocese of Bristol and on the propriety of
behaviour deemed congruent with and within the limits of salvation.
Wesley's 'business' was to endeavour to save the ignorant and depraved
masses from the natural desperation of their lives and from the supernatural
consequences of their despair. To Butler, I would conclude, Wesley's
activities made him no better than a desperado.

Such observations may be dismissed as mere wordplay. My position here
is that, with the 1559 Acts of Supremacy and of Uniformity, if not before, an
element of wordplay was taken into the official language of state. Having
restored—after the Marian abeyance—her father's title of 'Supreme Head'
of the English Church, Elizabeth compounded with vociferous Puritan
protest and gave royal assent to the substituted words 'Supreme Governor'.
Gerald Bray calls it 'a change of form, but not of substance'. Christopher
Morris has noted that, among other 'Elizabethan assumptions', ' "reason of
state" ...was somehow different from normal reason'. The Acts of 1559
recapitulated and reinforced the fiction that a crisis of soteriology could be
identified as latent and active sedition, as lèse-majesté, and as conduct threatening the common weal, the well-being of the state. Despairing men are
desperate men; desperate men are instant and armed desperadoes. At times,
as one reads, life-and-death decisions of state appear to be projections of the
rhetorical figure traductio.

The Elizabethan Injunctions—also of 1559, but closely following those of
Edward VI, of 1547—enjoined the parish clergy to stock up on 'comfortable places and sentences of Scripture' against the 'vice of damnable despair'
if and when they were apprised of its presence among their parishioners—an
anarchic flock very readily equated with 'ridiculous men and bewitched'

(Bancroft), 'common persons and private men' (Whitgift), 'the common sort of men', 'the vulgar sort', 'the multitude' (all Hooker), 'the many headed multitude' (Bramhall, after Horace, Sidney, et al.), 'dirty people of no name' (Clarendon), 'secret corner-meetings and assemblies in the night' (Hooker again, though it could easily be mistaken for Hobbes).

Just as some kind of mental *membrana* (as Ben Jonson might say) rendered these fine scholars and spiritual wrestlers incapable of recognizing, in such 'secret corner-meetings and assemblies in the night', the origins of the Christian Church in Jewish discipleship (Nicodemus visiting Jesus 'by night', John 3: 2; the disciples at evening in the locked room, John 21: 19), so something in the pitch of contingency and circumstance rendered them all too fluent in a kind of theatrical 'tragic' bombast and fustian: 'desperate cause', 'more desperately rebellious', 'innovators and seditious orators', 'Sophisters and seditious Oratours' (all Bramhall); 'acts of rage and despair', 'melancholy', 'desperate imaginations', 'seditious and erroneous Doctrines' (all Clarendon). It is like recovering phrases from a failed and discarded Tragedy of State. One can sense an affinity between such phrases and the language of Sidney's *Arcadia* (1590) or of Jonson's *Sejanus* (1603–5) and *Catiline* (1611), but Sidney's and Jonson's critical intelligence is fully aware of cause and effect, and of the pathology of the humours for which a strident euphuism, interspersed with episodes of the laconically outrageous, offers an effective range of expression. Bramhall and Clarendon are at once magisterial and imbecile (to recall Hooker's word), but the proverbial 'Stone Dead hath no Fellow' nonetheless stands plumb with its uncanny power of register at the heart of Clarendon's account of the impeachment of Strafford.

Torquato Tasso, in his *Discourses on the Heroic Poem*, commented that 'Extremely beautiful and ornate . . . are additions that imply opposition and contradiction'; he cites, from Petrarch's *Trionfo d'Amore* 4, 143–7: '*chiaro disnore e gloria oscura e nigra, | perfida lealtate e fido inganno*'. At some indeterminate date, possibly 1536–7, the Henrician scholar-diplomat Henry Parker, Lord Morley, translated the *Trionfi*, rendering the lines remarked by Tasso as:

> Cleare dishonoure, and glory obscure and darke;
> False lealtie lefte not there to warke.

If we consider what is held 'tacitly' (yet another word of their conjuring) when Tasso remarks on the high ornamental value of certain rhetorical figures, figures which nonetheless turn upon moral negations, annulments, cynical flauntings of the incongruent, it is possible to perceive compromises and compromisings as forms of eloquence and forms of eloquence as compromised. Hobbes seems to hold this commonplace as his patent. To put the issue in a slightly different form: *traductio* is the figure whereby you 'turne and tranlace a word into many sundry shapes'; it is also traduction: 'the act of traducing or defaming, calumny, slander, traducement'. The *OED* marks this sense as '*rare*' and not before 1656, but as I have attempted to show elsewhere, Sir Thomas Wyatt—to cite one striking example—was clearly on to the essential connection between speech-turns and malpractice, 'safe' convention and malicious invention, in the late 1530s. There are, of course, instances of 'traduction' which are both eloquent and morally congruent. Hooker shows a particular felicity in 'The prophet Abacuk remained faithfull in weaknes though weake in faith', but Hooker would not have dissented from Sidney's trope of worldly sweetness turned to

> poysonous sugar of flatterie: which some vsed, out of the innate basenesse of their hart, straight like dogges fawning vppon the greatest... But his minde (being an apt matter to receiue what forme their amplifying speeches woulde lay vpon it) daunced so prettie a musicke to their false measure, that he thought himselfe the wisest, the woorthyest, and best beloued, that euer gaue honour to a royall tytle.

There is a sense in which, half a century to a century later, the authors here reviewed—Clarendon in particular—have not noticeably extended the perimeter of Sidney's axiomatic ethical polity. Thus Clarendon, from the Introduction to *A Brief View and Survey*:

> That saying of *Nosce teipsum*, in the sense of *Solon* who prescribed it, was a sober truth, but was never intended as an expedient to discover the similitude of the thoughts of other men by what he found in himself, but as the best means to suppress and destroy that pride and self-conceit, which might temt him to undervalue other men, and to plant that modesty and humility in himself, as would preserve him from such presumption.

Clarendon is, of course, contending that Hobbes has radically misconstrued the basic Humanist prescription for self-recovery; he is much as 'Antiphilus his base-borne pride borne high by flatterie' is to the author of the *Arcadia*; though Hobbes is chiefly the recipient of self-flattery. He is both tyrant and false prophet.

The type of exemplary figure represented by Solon, particularly as memorialized by Isocrates (and further memorialized by Clarendon and Swift), stood in relation to issues of English polity in a manner which is simply incomprehensible to the modern educator and policy-maker. We return once more to the nature—or definition—of the 'necessary requisite'. For Clarendon, Bramhall, and, I will hazard, even for the Milton of *Areopagitica* and the *Tractate of Education*, it is not a question of progress so much as of 'resuscitation' (as C. A. Patrides discerned with characteristic acumen): 'The end then of Learning is to *repair* the ruins of our first Parents by *regaining* to know God aright' (my italics). It is even more, in the understanding of Clarendon's pregnant phrase, the necessary 'sober truth'. Clarendon detested Bramhall; Thomas Tenison revered and defended him. All three would have seen in Milton's republicanism and mortalism, if they were even aware of it, the groundwork for a godless tyranny. The one common aspiration among these violently disunited spirits, otherwise united only in their opposition to Hobbes, was a belief in, a working towards, the eloquence of 'sober truth': an eloquence which, in Bramhall, is something other than the cult of 'plain dealing', and which for Clarendon is something other than the affectation of plain speaking. In the *Brief View and Survey*, Hobbes is seen as 'pretending to so much plainness and perspicuity'.

If we are to understand from this that Hobbes is a false claimant to such qualities, we are obliged to adjust our sense of the word, some thirty pages on in Clarendon's book, when we read that Sidney Godolphin's early death in the Civil War was 'an irreparable loss . . . lamented by all men living who pretended to Virtue, how much divided soever in the prosecution of that quarrel'. Godolphin is mourned by persons of integrity, whether Royalist or Parliamentarian, who can recognize sober truth when they see it: persons whose claim to recognize true virtue can, for the most part, be taken on trust.

When Bramhall maintains that his controversy with Hobbes 'is not about Words, but about Things', he makes the point somewhat elliptically. The things do not anticipate Locke's 'Substances'; they read like the metaphysical elements required by speculation, the nature of things as conceived, or misconceived, by the understanding or misunderstanding of fallible human minds: 'not what the words Voluntary or Free do or may signifie, but whether all things be extrinsecally praedetermined to one'. The case that these ill-assorted, frequently incompatible, variously gifted antagonists bring against Hobbes is one that is grounded in matters of claim and entitlement. Such questions of entitlement are fundamentally political; Bramhall's Aristotelian observation that 'man...is a politicall creature' runs like a seventeenth-century thorough bass under the variety of opinions and counter-opinions presented in these six volumes. For each of them, the intersection of politics and language occurs in certain word-usages, as in property / propriety, private / public, but the crux, for them, is not etymology (present though that word is in their vocabulary) but *intention*. And with intention we find that they, and we, have re-engaged with the matter of English polity.

The question of polity is, at its most basic level as also in the most elevated language of response, that of entitlement to speak, one's right to claim authority, albeit as a private person contending in—and with—a public matter. The implications of 'They who to States and Governours of the Commonwealth direct their Speech . . . or wanting such accesse in a private condition, write that which they foresee may advance the publick good', reach back through Hooker to such early Reform writings as Tyndale's *Obedience of a Christen Man* and anticipate the situation of both Bramhall when he wrote *A Defence of True Liberty* (deprived of his see and in exile with the remnant of the House of Stuart) and Clarendon.

Clarendon's situation as an exile, from 1646 until 1660 and again from 1667 until his death in 1674, was one of enforced privacy. He was private chiefly because deprived of office; there were nonetheless matters of state to which he was still privy. Reflections on the private as a condition of deprivation are less prominent in these arguments than are considerations of the private as an entitlement to property and a just claim to be treated with propriety. Clarendon's 'Epistle Dedicatory to the King's Most Excellent Majesty' is a strategic exception, but here the policy is counterpoised by a sense of the author's being sincerely (as they would say) cast down, dejected, wretched. There is a quality of political chiaroscuro in the sincere interplay of public polemic and private sorrow in Clarendon's last work.

20

The Weight of the Word

The critical limitations of *Reason, Grace and Sentiment* are (as such limitations generally are) inseparable from a general limitation of insight and imagination.[1] Intellectually confident in its documentation of cant words when these are a part of the seventeenth- and eighteenth-century detritus, the book is oblivious to its own compliance with the prevailing jargon of modern communication. Attempts to discriminate and evaluate repeatedly collapse upon the words 'interesting', 'interestingly' or 'of more interest than': and this in a work that labours to define and distinguish the various senses which the word 'interest' carried during the period 1660–1780 ('the Interest of *Sects*', 'the interest of virtue', 'the true Interest of the Christian Religion', etc.). Such a tic ('very interesting', 'particularly interesting', 'extraordinarily interesting') is the kind of stylistic solecism which is reducible to a philosophy that some will find laudable. The author has 'not taken the reader's knowledge of the period for granted' and hopes that 'this method of presentation will make the book accessible to undergraduates as well as scholars'.

Questions of accessibility turn upon matters of context. In both sacred and secular writings we may receive, at any instant, a sense of things inaccessible suddenly made accessible, where grammar and desire are miraculously at one. The effect may appear to be studied (as in Milton or Hopkins) or spontaneous (as in the Wesleys or Wordsworth); what delights and silences us is the sustained moment of communion between the two kinds of eloquence and apprehension, whether in Cranmer's collects or Campion's 'Brag' or the great hymns of Watts and Charles Wesley.

---

[1] Isabel Rivers, *Reason, Grace and Sentiment: A Study of the Language of Religion and Ethics in England 1660–1780. Volume I: Whichcote to Wesley*, 277 pages (Cambridge: Cambridge University Press, 1991).

I am not suggesting that consent to my paradigm would be widespread, either then or now: a variety of opinions on the matter characterized the period covered by *Reason, Grace and Sentiment*; the majority of them appear at first sight more consonant with Professor Isabel Rivers's method of presentation than with my mode of dissent (for example, Gilbert Burnet's 'a *Preacher* is to fancy himself, as in the Room of the most unlearned Man in his whole Parish'; John Wesley's 'I design plain truth for plain people. . . . I labour to avoid all words which are not easy to be understood'). In fairly stating her own adherence to the principle of accessibility, Rivers implicitly associates herself with one of the main strands in her thesis: that of the 'plain and natural Method' praised by Burnet in his *Pastoral Care*. Burnet acknowledged, with more fairness than some of his contemporaries, the just demands of more difficult forms of writing which 'require a good deal of previous Study' and ought not to be attempted before one is 'ready'. Rivers fails to perceive that when all things are 'interesting' there is not 'readiness' but stasis; that authorial 'accessibility' is now no more than a commodity cry; and that her book, like its readership, is consequent upon the very forces and circumstances which it describes. Even if she is able to acknowledge this rationally, I do not think that she is moved by it affectively. If she were, the temper of her style would be other than it is:

> My subject is the language of religious and moral prose, and my methods are those of the literary historian of ideas. I have concentrated on language because I am interested in the history of religious and moral thought for its own sake, not in relation to another subject, such as science or politics, and because I believe that it is only through the careful study of language that meaning can be ascertained.

These sentences stand as an epitome of the book's larger failure to connect. The author's gratitude to her general editor and her publishers for 'agreeing' to a two-volume format is misplaced. You do not 'do justice to a very complex subject' by simply reduplicating an original misconstruction. Concentration, in Rivers's 'I have concentrated on language', must be understood as heavy accumulation of data and not as intensity of perception. When 'concentration' means 'mass', it can also mean dissipation of perceptual and structural cogency, as I think is the case here.

I do not grasp, for instance, Rivers's motive for proposing to discuss Locke's civil and religious thought as if she were considering two distinct philosophical entities ('For Locke's religious views see . . . Volume II') when, throughout the present volume, *Whichcote to Wesley*, she is at pains to show how his thought is implicated in arguments for and against a view of religion as 'fitted to man in his worldly state' and how Anglican latitudin-arians and dissenters alike employed terms drawn from the *Essay Concerning Human Understanding* as well as from *The Reasonableness of Christianity*. I cannot accept that those who pondered 'Degrees of Assent' (Book IV, chapter xvi of the *Essay*) would have concluded that Locke had distinct 'religious views':

> This only may be said in general. That as the Arguments and Proofs, *pro* and *con*, upon due Examination, nicely weighing every particular Circumstance, shall to any one appear, upon the whole matter, in a greater or less degree, to preponderate on either side, so they are fitted to produce in the Mind such different Entertainment, as we call *Belief, Conjecture, Guess, Doubt, Wavering, Distrust, Disbelief,* etc.

I accept that Locke speaks elsewhere of 'Propositions (especially about Matters of Religion)', but he is there making a case that in 'unwary, as well as unbiass'd Understandings', such propositions may be 'riveted...by long Custom and Education beyond all possibility of being pull'd out again'. The rational and affective tempers of his thinking are mutually secured in that 'riveted'. Lumpish words like 'religious views' belong more to the mechanics of subediting than to the entertainments of Locke's prose.

Of the three moral and affective qualities named in the title of this study, 'sentiment' remains the most elusive; the inherent difficulties are compounded by the fact that Rivers proposes to reserve its full discussion to Volume II, which will 'essentially explore the tension between the languages of reason and sentiment' as Volume I 'essentially explores the tension between the languages of reason and grace'. If her feeling for words and their implications were more consonant with the capacities of her chosen authors, she would have thought twice before reducing them to the level of that bit of etiolated jargon. The quality of 'sentiment' is itself a factor in the debate between 'grace' and 'reason'; it is, moreover, a quality which reveals itself mainly in grammar: vocabulary, syntactical order, and affective device. As locution we hear it in Edward Stillingfleet's 'Without perplexing our minds about those more nice and subtile specu-lations', in Benjamin Whichcote's 'To stand upon nice and accurate Distinctions of [words], is needless; useless', in Burnet's 'I have ever thought, that the true Interest of the Christian Religion was best consulted,

when nice disputing about Mysteries was laid aside and forgotten' and in
William Law's 'It is not a Doctrine that requires learned or nice Speculations, in order to be rightly apprehended by us'.

The common factor in these emphases is the term 'nice', implying a
finicky, over-subtle, 'scholastic' concern with minutiae and suggesting, in
each of these authors, an assumption of a close agreement of common
sense between writer and reader. 'Assumption' may here be understood as
legitimate 'postulate' and as 'unwarrantable claim'; and I would argue that
in the four citations given above, 'nice' is an assumption situated between
those two senses of that term. In the seventeenth century, as the *Oxford
English Dictionary* (*OED*) article states, 'it is difficult to say in what
particular sense the writer intended ['nice'] to be taken'. A few years
earlier than Stillingfleet, Jeremy Taylor argued that 'the way to destruction
is broad and plausible, the way to heaven nice and austere'; some thirty
years later than Stillingfleet, Dryden deployed the word with coarse
refinement to dismiss the quaint, outmoded style of Donne: 'He ... perplexes the Minds of the Fair Sex with nice Speculations of Philosophy,
when he shou'd ingage their hearts, and entertain them with the softnesses
of Love.' I do not think that Stillingfleet, Whichcote or Burnet would
balk at the word 'broad', since latitude is what they desired, though they
would be pained by Taylor's collocations. In attempting to describe their
several styles of rational persuasion, one is touching on symptomatic
elision of the deliberated and the unwitting. To call the issue 'complacency' is not to insinuate a term that is unknown in seventeenth-century
theological writings; it is not even to turn their own idiom against them.
Richard Baxter writes of 'the love of Complacencie and Acceptation' as a
Divine gesture; Isaac Barrow warns against the 'arbitrary opinion and
fickle humour of the people; complacence in which is vain'. There is,
even so, in the work of Whichcote, Barrow, and even Law, an indifference to contextual 'otherness' which is too simple a corollary of their
moral objection to the 'obstinate and contumacious'.

Whichcote wrote that 'by wickedness [a man] passes into a *Nature*
contrary to his own'. I am willing to claim as an empirical fact that when
you write at any serious pitch of obligation you enter into the nature of
grammar and etymology, which is a nature contrary to your own. You
cannot extricate yourself from this 'contrary nature' by some kind of
philosophical fiat or gesture of spiritual withdrawal. Hobbes categorized
'Compleasance' as a 'Law of Nature': '*That every man strive to accommodate*

himselfe to the rest'. In the palpable contrariness of '*strive*' / '*accommodate*' one recognizes the working of intelligence at a more than conceptual level; it is like Locke's 'riveted', where a word is struck into the body of a sentence in such a way that a 'particular sense' of the mind is at one with the particular sensuousness of an instinctual choice.

I anticipate two main objections to these ideas. The first is that the 'accommodation', the 'particular sense', which I derive from Hobbes and Locke appeals to the satirical *frisson* almost exclusively; it anticipates Pope ('familiar Toad') but not Watts or Charles Wesley. The second is that Whichcote and, especially, Law established clear theological reasons why the attraction of 'contrary' Nature is alien to a life of Christian discipline. There is arguably something obstinate and contumacious in an attempt to force their quality of spiritual desire ('the silent Longing of the Heart') into an unacceptable fashion of contextual sensuousness, a mere 'Accomplishment . . . of the lettered World' which Law would have dismissed as '*Form*, and *Fiction*, and empty beating of the Air'.

George Herbert is ruled out of Rivers's discussion. Without his example we are inclined to assume spiritual initiatives in proposals which ought rather to be seen as derivations and attenuations. Burnet's remarks on the inappropriateness of learned sermons for rural congregations had been anticipated by Herbert's first Bemerton sermon of 1630 ('*since Almighty God does not intend to lead men to heaven by hard Questions*'). That this Laudian observant of the Canonical Hours could be so revered by the 'mere Nonconformist' Baxter, that his paraphrase of 'The 23d Psalme' should have been set, first by Henry Lawes as a courtly solo to the lute, then by John Playford in the plainest four-part harmony (perfectly matching the spirit of the Bemerton sermon and perfectly attuned to Nonconformist practice), is eloquent testimony to his reconciling of 'grace' and 'reason'. As Barnabas Oley observed when noting Herbert's '*singular Dexterity*' in administering reproof with gentleness, the quality of his reconciling art is embodied in the '*Garb and phrase*' of his writing.

It is this sense of 'garb and phrase' which is missing from Rivers's 'careful study of language', and I do not see how, without it, 'meaning' can be rightly 'ascertained'. The diligent listing of Barrow's use of the 'co-prefix' is an 'interesting' abstraction, not a 'concentration'. Meaning is not 'established', even in those writers who greatly desire to see it so; it is concatenation, ellipsis, lacuna: as much in those who speak 'pertinently, plainly, piercingly, and somewhat properly' as in those who strain after far-fetched conceits. Watts's 'meaning', as an apologist, is not determined, in 1707, by

'If any Expressions occur to the Reader that savour of an Opinion different from his own, yet he may observe these are generally such as are capable of an extensive Sense, and may be used with a charitable Latitude'. Nor is it determined, in 1747, by 'I hope I have kept the middle way between a libertinism of principles, and a narrow uncharitable spirit'. Watts's 'capable of an extensive Sense' in no way resembles Rivers's 'I take "language" in a broad sense to include . . . '. She simply assumes the concurrence of language with one's expectations; his 'Sense' is a deliberated sentiment; an 'extensive Sense' is what, in fact, his sentence is. Such meaning is not to be 'ascertained'; it must be entertained, as we entertain, with our sense of the circumstantial shifts of forty years, the difference of implication between 'charitable Latitude' and 'libertinism of principles'. That passage from Locke's *Essay* ('This only may be said in general . . . '), to which I have previously referred, epitomizes the 'sensible pleasure', or the entertaining haziness, of philosophical latitude: the 'nice . . . weighing' of 'every particular Circumstance' turns into a syntactical comedy of manners, though one is not precisely sure what Locke's own manners are in this case. The grammar, nice yet licentious, is comparable to Barrow's description of the charitable man as 'virtuously voluptuous' and a 'laudable epicure'.

Coleridge's opinion was that Barrow wrote '*pertly* . . . at times, while his Thoughts are always grave, & fortunate'. There is nothing 'fortunate' in the citations which Rivers gives from Barrow's sermon 'The Duty and Reward of Bounty to the Poor'; in these Barrow shows himself, as Taylor would say, 'broad and plausible'. But 'particular Circumstance' can no more be overlooked in matters of style that it can in 'due Examination' of the mind's entertainment or in questions of equity. We may take one sentence from Barrow's sermon 'Of Resignation to the Divine Will', speaking of Christ's submission to the details of his Passion: 'He was to stand (as it were) before the Mouth of Hell, belching Fire and Brimstone on his Face'. Set against Foxe, this appears as sentiment; there is no 'as it were' in his accounts of the protracted sufferings of such martyrs as John Lambert, John Hooper, and Nicholas Ridley. Foxe has been termed a 'sensationalist', and even though, on the evidence of the *OED*, 'sensation' did not exist in any of its forms or senses during the period when *Actes and Monuments* was being compiled, one must concede that it is all here: the 'physical sensibility', the 'mental apprehension', the 'strong impression (e.g. of horror, admiration . . .) produced in a . . . body of spectators', the 'production of violent emotion as an aim in works of literature or art'.

Rivers, who rightly emphasizes Foxe's significance for Bunyan ('to confirm the Truth by way of Suffering'), also observes that language 'was recognised at the outset as a dividing point between the latitude-men and the puritans' and that latitudinarians were eager to make 'corrections to the sixteenth-century theology that now seemed wrong-headed'. To glance again at the passages from Barrow and Locke is to acknowledge a small part of the cost of those corrections. On the other hand, one can set that sentence of Barrow against two from Burke's *Enquiry* of 1757:

> All *general* privations are great, because they are all terrible; *Vacuity, Darkness, Solitude* and *Silence*. With what a fire of imagination, yet with what severity of judgment, has Virgil amassed all these circumstances where he knows that all the images of a tremendous dignity ought to be united, at the mouth of hell!

In Barrow there is at least no 'tremendous dignity'; sentiment has not yet descended to aesthetic trifling. But of course there *is* descent (both in the sense of lineage and of deterioration) from Barrow's 'to stand (as it were) before the Mouth of Hell' to Burke's 'what a fire of imagination . . . !' This is what gravity (of sentiment) descends to when it lacks 'temper'.

It is an irony of sorts that this missing 'temper' is in fact a term prominently employed by writers of latitudinarian sympathy; by Whichcote especially: 'When the Principles of our Religion become the *Temper* of our Spirits, then we are truly religious'; 'The *State* of Religion consists in a divine Frame and *Temper* of mind: and shews it self in a *Life* and Actions, conformable to the divine Will'; 'There is no Happiness, or Peace; but in the Compliance of the *Temper* of our Minds with the Reason of things: which is a Conformity with the Everlasting Law of Righteousness'. Of 'temper' in this sense there is ample evidence in Law: in the prescript for 'an exact and frequent method of devotion' which made him John Wesley's early spiritual mentor and in the pitch of a '*lively, zealous, watchful, self-denying spirit*'—the syntax itself a prescription for the soul's rebuttal of idle enthusiasm.

This is still within the bounds of ascetic theory: part of Law's 'relentless consistency in applying spiritual principles'. But as I have elsewhere suggested, one cannot simply assume consistency of insight and imagination from consistency of principle.

> To proceed; if you was to use yourself (as far as you can) to pray always in the *same* place . . . if any *little room*, (or if that cannot be) if any particular *part* of a room was thus used, this kind of consecration of it, as a place *holy* unto God,

would have an effect upon your mind, and dispose you to such tempers, as
would very much assist your devotion.

You could argue from this Law's high qualities as a spiritual director,
tempering 'relentless consistency' with an acknowledgement of particular
circumstance. Even so, the line between principle and sentiment is so fine
here that the slippage of one word—'a kind of consecration' for Law's 'this
kind of consecration'—would suffice to tip the fineness into boudoir
mawkishness, would have 'an effect upon [the] mind' very different from
that which Law intended. And yet any attempt to apply, reduce, or otherwise paraphrase Law's instruction inevitably (I believe) dissipates his particular grammar and leaves the 'kind' of consecration an open or indifferent
question, susceptible to any ephemeral mood, disposition or 'temper'. I am
not convinced that, at a time when 'nice' distinctions were considered
tedious, Law's distinctions could be received with a concomitant finesse.
Dr Johnson and John Wesley were spiritually strengthened by reading
him, but the witness of those two exceptional spirits does not negate the
force of the caveat: that the distance between grace and sentiment may be
the breath of a syllable, dissolved in an instant, rather than that slow-motion
relay race of trend and tendency depicted by literary historians of ideas.

The question returns upon the nature of 'temper' and on Whichcote's, or
his editors', latitude in reading the term. Its sense is firm enough when the
target is mere temperament: 'To live after *Temper*, is below Reason, and
short of Virtue.' My sense of Whichcote's characteristic usage (so far as one
can accurately judge a reduced text like the *Aphorisms*) is that 'temper' is
itself inclined towards 'inclination'—'mental condition', 'habitual disposition', 'frame of mind', 'humour'—and that statements which appear to
offer an 'extant' medium (to adapt Baxter's phrase) in which inclination
might be checked are in fact little more than gestures in that direction: 'Our
Happiness depends upon Temper within, and Object without.' Even this
falls short of the sense of 'temper' as 'due or proportionate mixture or
combination of elements or qualities'. Whichcote's style, therefore, tends
to follow inclination even where inclination is rebuked: 'A *wise* Man is more
than Temper; a *good* Man much more.' It smacks of table-talk, though one is
once more reminded that edited 'aphorisms' may have been picked out by a
mind predisposed to relish the taste of 'opinion'.

The question was, even then, to some extent academic. George Herbert
had already committed the matter to the 'garb and phrase' of his poetry and

prose, verbal contextures which happily resolved the perplexities by which
his successors were to be troubled a century later.

> In vain we tune our formal Songs,
>   In vain we strive to rise;
> *Hosannas* languish on our Tongues,
>   And our Devotion dies.

Watts's 'formal Songs' are, in his conviction of spiritual coldness, further off
from him than Whichcote's 'Object without'. I have already suggested that it
may be a limitation of Whichcote's theological idiom that makes him
attribute an encounter with 'contrary' Nature to 'wickedness' rather than to
experiential profession, as Donne does in the *Devotions*: 'But what have
I done, either to *breed*, or to *breath* these *vapors*? They tell me it is … my
thoughtfulnesse; was I not made to *thinke*? It is my study; doth not my *Calling*
call for that?' Neither Whichcote nor Law (with his *Serious Call*) nor Watts
seems to clinch original sin in relation to the formalities, the constraints, and
opportunities, of 'calling' in quite this way. Once you begin to thin the matter
down to 'inward Sentiments' versus '*arbitrary signs*', sentiment calls the tune to
such effect that modern theologians are still in thrall to it. Owen Chadwick's
life of Michael Ramsey records, or interprets, an early stage in Ramsey's
spiritual way: 'He saw that the intellectual side of him could not be wrong,
somehow he must baptize it'. One can understand the appeal of the metaphor
(Chadwick is not the only contemporary theological writer to use it), but
'intellectual side' is an arbitrary distinction, and 'somehow' is itself, in this
context, an 'arbitrary sign'. George Herbert had already, by the early 1630s,
healed (presciently) the lesions of late seventeenth- and eighteenth-century
sentiment and its 'intellectual' side, the residues of which still trouble Ramsey
and his biographer. In 'Affliction (IV)', particularly, Herbert is not only more
severe than the latitude-men and scientists in the detail of self-scrutiny; he
recognizes the 'detail' for what it simultaneously is: a depressive sentiment,
not an exclusive spiritual concept or a mystical hypothesis, however eloquent.
If we recall Watts's 'In vain we tune our formal Songs' in the light of
Herbert's poem, written some seventy years earlier, we recognize that Watts's
anxiety has been rendered otiose by the words of the older poet:

> Then shall those powers, which work for grief
>   Enter thy pay,
>   And day by day
> Labour thy praise, and my relief.

This is Whichcote's 'by wickedness [a man] passes into a *Nature* contrary to his own' put into reverse process. 'Contrary' Nature, which we do not doubt Herbert has experienced by direct suffering as much as by intuition, is set to redemptive 'labour' in a way that reduces Watts's line to a plaintive bleat and offers Chadwick (whose attention is elsewhere) a real logic of sacramental grammar in place of an etiolated 'somehow'. In Chadwick's book, not altogether surprisingly, it is Herbert's admiring imitator Walton who is given the penultimate valediction—'Of this blest man, let his just praise be given, | Heaven was in him, before he was in heaven'—an amiable style-book couplet with an attenuated Anglican 'metaphysical' cadence, but without the sense of theological discovery that Herbert's poem awakens line by line. It is not that one is confusing technical felicity with a theological category like 'sufficient grace': the theologians would be justified in coming down hard on that solecism. It is that no other English poet can convince us, as Herbert can, that the 'otherness' of figurative language is, even as we meet it, instantly turned upon itself 'in a sense most true'. Though poetry for Herbert does not enjoy a privileged place in the daily round, his poems have the dignity of any common task that is sufficient to offer up ordinariness to the life of grace.

Rivers may object to my poetic excursus (as it must seem to her), since she clearly states at the commencement of her discussion that her 'subject is the language of religious and moral prose'. My answer must be that, in undertaking a study of the language of 'Reason, Grace and Sentiment' in England from 1660 to 1780, she had no choice but to consider the language of poetry together with that of prose. How, for instance, is one to follow the trace of eighteenth-century sentiment without the evidence of Addison's two *Spectator* papers of August 1712? If Addison's prose in these essays is what you would expect ('There is not a more pleasing exercise of the mind than gratitude'; 'In our retirements every thing disposes us to be serious'), the hymn concluding each paper is a modulation which relates to the question raised by Watts in his anxiety about 'formal songs'. The 'piece...of divine poetry' for Saturday, 9 August ('When all thy mercies, O my God'), is perhaps little more than a verse paraphrase of the latitudinarian psalm that is *The Spectator* no. 453 ('If gratitude is due from man to man, how much more from man to his Maker?' etc.). It proves the diffusive strength of the 'very pleasing sensation in the mind of a grateful man' in several ways: for instance, by 'doubling' the 'store' of platitude already present in the essay and by 'gently clear[ing]' the word 'transported' of any slight penal associations it has carried since 1666. The major qualification to all this mild success is one's sense that Addison is not equal to the terms of his own question 'O how shall words with equal warmth | The gratitude declare . . . ?' In Herbert as in Wesley we are convinced either that words do constitute a worthy correlative to the sensations of 'wonder, love, and praise' or that to the poet, in a particular circumstance, words are indeed cold and remote from the incommunicable longing of the heart. Addison's language weakly conciliates both possibilities with the result that a 'piece of divine poetry' is also (I think half-consciously so) a divine piece of poetry.

The second piece, the 'ode', as Addison calls it, from *Spectator* 465 ('*The spacious Firmament on high*'), is a different matter. Its relation to Addison's other divine meditations in prose and verse is comparable with Burnet's distinction between 'a right notion of style' and 'a false pitch of a wrong sublime'. It is not exactly comparable because Burnet, in context, begs the question whether there is a true pitch of a right sublime. It is as if, in his ode, Addison intuitively perceives the 'rhetorick' of a right sublime which corrects the pitch of his own effusions but is not to be reduced to the level of Burnet's 'right notion of style'. This is the kind of resolution, it seems to me, which closely pertains to the 'very complex subject' that Rivers seeks to address.

Her presentation of 'complexity' requires us to consider 'states of mind' and 'senses . . . natural and spiritual', with their commingled affects and effects ('disagreement . . . over . . . meaning', 'recurrent emphasis', 'disclaimer', and innumerable other modulations and modifications). At the same time, we are to note, as if in passing, any individual characteristics of eloquence, such as the 'peculiar edge' which Calamy praised in Richard Baxter's delivery of his 'thoughts'. The main weakness of Rivers's thesis is her failure to recognize that a 'peculiar edge' can be something other than an attractive 'mettle' or even an exemplary cogency; that it can mark, stylistically, the ethical line between compliance and resistance, sentiment and reason, enthusiasm and meditative attention. Quoting as she does, both extensively and minutely, she nonetheless fails to 'read' the grammar that she has so painstakingly accumulated, like Baxter's 'consideration awakeneth our reason from its sleep, till it rouse up itself, as Sampson', or 'meditation produceth reason into act'. The grammar of 'consideration awakeneth our reason from its sleep' and 'meditation produceth reason into act' is like a template of the spiritual grammar of Herbert's poems or Law's prose or Charles Wesley's hymns. I do not think that language which moves with such a natural mimesis can be adequately translated into, or represented by, the parataxis 'Reason, Grace and Sentiment', which is uncommitted either to collocation or consequence.

What I have termed 'natural mimesis' is, in Charles Wesley, the 'spontaneous' movement of a creative spirit at once submissive to revealed authority and hard-pressed by brute fact. In his case, the 'peculiar edge' of the writing is the line which reason draws between enthusiasm and grace. The theme of Wesley's hymns is recurrently that of 'taste'; taste is also his 'temper', his instrument for endowing hard distinctions with a real effect of ease and freedom. Isaac Barrow had written, to encourage the practice of Charity, that 'the communication of benefits to others [is] accompanied with a very delicious relish upon the mind of him that practises it'. Richard Baxter had declared that 'it is a sign of a distempered heart that loseth the relish of Scripture excellency'. Barrow makes 'relish' resemble the word of a sybarite; for Baxter it remains the seal of self-knowledge. The word is impacted with the self-contradictions and manifold abuse of 'the language of religion and ethics', a language which was Wesley's inescapable patrimony. That 'temper' which Rivers cites, frequently yet inconsequentially, is concluded in Wesley as he concludes upon it. His greatest hymns are the key to the arch of 'Reason, Grace and Sentiment'.

If 'temper' in Wesley is also taste, and if taste is also the eucharistic 'taste', his rhetoric and 'inward Sentiments' would seem, in principle, so remarkably interfused that, as in Herbert, the one is transformed within the other. In practice, of Wesley's several thousand hymns, a few score at most have this effect of perfect balance, of 'peculiar edge', which separates the 'delicious relish' of spiritual self-regard from the experiential relish of the awakened heart discovering, or recovering, its true temper. If he is less consistent than Herbert, and less fine in his spirituality, he is not unworthy of the comparison. It might further be argued that the run-up against brute actuality, harsh though it was for Herbert, was harsher still for the Wesleys, and that this caused an excess of strain, an infusion of gall, which the hymns were bound to take and taste. Herbert had condescended, in the decent sense that then applied, to his unlettered flock; but seventeenth-century Bemerton was not eighteenth-century Wednesbury, or Olney, or the Kingswood collieries. The Anglican, high Tory Wesleys were in daily contact with circumstances which, among a vast number of greater and lesser effects, swept away the old style of condescension (it can still be heard in the isolated, reclusive William Law, who died in 1761) and with it much of the old language of grace as it had been known in Herbert's 'Redemption'.

'Condescension' is subject to the same circumstantial pressures as 'complacency'. The Wesleys had not foreseen the strength of antinomian complacency which their own eloquence largely excited and which took against them from the midst of their own following. Charles Wesley's language of 'grace' and 'taste' was, from an early stage, controversial in ways that Herbert's had less need to accommodate, though controversy, in the hymns, frequently appears as a pre-emptive note of accurate surprise ('Blest with this Antepast of Heaven!'). In moving, with the force of its exclamation, to embrace affirmations like John Owen's 'tasting how gracious the Lord is', in withdrawing upon the dry, bookish alertness of 'antepast', this line epitomizes Wesley's nervous vigilance towards his own style of faith. The Wesleys aroused enthusiasm and, at the same time, deprecated certain of its consequences.

Rivers suggests that John Wesley's 'appeal to feeling is solipsistic' and that 'contemporaries were justified in their criticism'. I would rather say that both Wesleys grew increasingly aware of the two-natured power of their evangelical oratory: how it awakened many into a redemptive, spiritual, common life and drove some into an anarchic emotional solitude. I question Whaling's statement that 'the philosophical or theological nature of the [eucharistic] sacrifice is not [Charles Wesley's] concern; he is joyfully aware that Christ has died sacrificially for all men'. The emphasis on 'all men' *was* 'philosophical and theological'; that is to say, it was an Arminian reading of the nature of the Atonement, a reading deliberately pitched against the Calvinist interpretation of Whitefield and his supporters. There was, in addition, a persistent philosophical or theological difference between the Wesleys themselves, with John entering frequent caveats against his brother's doctrinal language, as in this characteristic warning to a correspondent: 'Take care you are not hurt by anything in the *Short Hymns* contrary to the doctrines you have long received'.

I think it entirely possible for a hymn to be, at one and the same time, joyful and 'unhappy'; that kind of oxymoron is inherent in the creative matter, the ganglion of language and circumstance from which the piece of divine poetry is created:

> Now, even now, we all plunge in,
> And drink the purple wave.

This is wretched because it is 'gushing' ('Gushing streams of life' are found in the preceding stanza). It is gushing because, at the crux of his theological imagination, Wesley is finally unable to dispose and reconcile the protean fluctuations of that extreme sentiment known to admirers and detractors alike as religious 'enthusiasm'. Cowper, in 'The Cast-away', working at the cold negative pole of the same emotion, is desperately laconic ('For then, by toil subdued, he drank | The stifling wave, and then he sank'), but one is not offering such stylistic resolution as an answer to Wesley's problem. Cowper and Wesley, at this point, standing on opposite sides of the same central flaw or fault, are strikingly complementary in their felicity and wretchedness.

Such oxymoronic constructions find themselves awkwardly placed between the technical and the spiritual. The awkwardness, however, is entirely appropriate to the subject of Rivers's thesis and to the spirit of my contention. 'Original sin, in Wesley's view, is the essential underpinning of Christianity.' This, the crucial statement in her book, affects throughout, implicitly if not explicitly, the temper of her argument, even when it is concerned with those latitude-men who appear, at first sight, to be paddling away from the unpleasant proximity of the thought. I could have wished Rivers to have 'felt', in a variety of practical applications, the all-pervading relevance of Wesley's affirmation, as I could have wished her to recognize the close practical applicability of several other citations, like Baxter's argument for the 'natural "pondus"', or necessitating principle' or his belief that 'good books are a very great mercy to the world'.

In order to keep the terms of this discussion 'open', I would allow that the commitment to an unqualified belief in original sin need not be the absolute prerequisite for taking seriously a 'natural "pondus"', or necessitating principle' of English style. One could try to restrict the question to Hobbesian mechanics, his 'certain impulsion of nature' comparable to 'that whereby a stone moves downward', but a Calvinist like Jonathan Edwards adapted natural impulsion to sustain his conviction of a human nature 'as it were heavy as lead', and Hobbes himself asserted, in *De corpore politico*, that '*the Divine Moral Law, and the Law of Nature, is the Same*'. One could of course elect to read Hobbes's equation as metaphor, but I cannot myself see any way of escaping complete assent to the doctrine of original sin, which, in the contexture of this argument, may be understood as no more and no less than 'the imperfection which marks all human effort, especially where it aims to avoid it'. The 'human effort' in Rivers's book cannot be gainsaid; her scholarship is arduous and scrupulous but is finally vitiated by the radical imperfections, the errors of premise and inference, which I have endeavoured to describe in detail. Painful though it is to say so, I believe that her desire to conciliate 'accessibility' is the equivalent of Baxter's 'idle heart in hearing'; it is an 'idleness' of the critical, historical, and, indeed, the scholarly imagination that annuls so much of the formidable business of her research. Her introduction to *Reason, Grace and Sentiment* assumes the inescapable public contexture of our personal responsibility to the word while, at the same time, her inescapable personal idiom subordinates the public significance to a different priority which Jonathan Edwards called '*private interest*' ('interest' is her poor substitute for Ruskin's 'intrinsic value').

The contrast between a 'cold rational language of philosophical argument' and a 'warm affectionate language of evangelical preaching' which Rivers associates with Watts (a distinction modified rather than confirmed by his lines about 'formal songs') has had, in the long term, deleterious effects. So has the widespread emphasis, among theologians as well as scientists, on words as 'arbitrary signs'. From the seventeenth century to the present day it has led to false conclusions, such as Rivers's own suggestion that Watts's 'tone and method of arguing are of more interest than his doctrinal solutions'. Literary historians of ideas justify their condescension by such 'signs' without registering how emphatically they are contradicted within the texture of, say, Baxter's own writings. Language, especially in the authors discussed here, *is* a doctrinal solution, in which 'solution' acts or suffers what it describes: *OED* sense 1.1*a* fusing with senses 11.5*a* & *c* (*transf.*) and 6*a*; with finesse or not, as the case may be; with or without direct authorial agency. This caveat is required in the case of Whichcote's *Aphorisms*, where, as has been suggested, the 'fusing' is less complete than the author's regard for 'temper' would lead one to expect. There is more gravity, in the sense that Hobbes and Jonathan Edwards would stress, more feeling for 'intrinsic Malignity', than the weight of an aphorism can sustain. One suggests here a distinction between aplomb (*à plomb*, 'according to the plummet') and Hobbes's 'certain impulsion of nature' or Edwards's 'internal mutual attraction . . . whereby the whole becomes one solid coherent body'. There is even a sense in which 'aplomb' works to defy, or deny, the Hobbesian gravity, persistently bobbing up in a Galsworthian sort of way: 'There is nothing so intrinsically Rational, as *Religion* is: nothing, that can so Justify itself: nothing, that hath so pure Reason to recommend itself; as Religion hath'. What is 'Rational' here is chiefly the concept: the grammar betrays a strong sentiment regarding the concept. However, as Rivers observes, 'there are special, perhaps insoluble' textual problems with Whichcote's writings. She expertly notes these details (she is at her best on such points), though without drawing the most obvious conclusion from her own scrutiny.

The extent to which John Wesley interfered with the doctrinal solutions of his brother's hymns is well known and well documented. His editing was entirely 'reasonable', in that high-minded eighteenth-century way, which means that a good deal of 'sentiment' was also involved: sentiment, in the main, about the nature of 'grace'. But with Wesley we are spared, for decent high Tory, Anglican reasons, subjective impressions about the egalitarian rough house of words and ideas (an absurd reach-me-down version of seventeenth-century elitist 'taste'). Such impressions, on the impulse or inclination of scholars less diligent and less textually disciplined than Rivers, bear us down into one solid coherent body of anarchy; a brute actuality with which to confront the Wesleys, who so feared and resisted the anarchic in all its religious and political manifestations.

Charles Wesley: A Reader, edited by an American Methodist scholar of some standing, was published by the Oxford University Press in 1989. There was need for such a compilation, bringing together 'hymns, sermons, letters, and journal materials—many rare and hitherto unknown'—from the scattered works of this great devotional poet. The reader who does not have the sources at his or her elbow recognizes slowly (and with some natural reluctance) the extent of what is amiss with the edition. The hymns are imprinted with gross errors of transcription which anyone with even an elementary grasp of metre and rhyme ought to have picked up, by educated intuition, at proof-stage if not before. With certain exceptions, misreadings of the manuscripts can be corrected by collation with *The Unpublished Poetry of Charles Wesley*, volume II (1990); among the exceptions are pieces from 'MS John', for which recourse must be had to the Methodist Church Archives in the John Rylands University Library of Manchester. Among exemplary details we may record the following cluster: 'And Satan lays the lunacy and waste', page 387 ('And Satan lays the vineyard waste', *Unpublished Poetry*, page 23); 'Purge all our faith and blood away', page 386 ('Purge all our filth and blood away', MS John); 'Which reaches for the when and now', page 387 ('Which teaches God the when and how', *Unpublished Poetry*, page 28); 'That wicked one rival consume [our nature?]', page 385 ('That wicked One reveal, consume', MS John). These errors strike me as being qualitatively different from the general run of typographical mishap ('*for* wordly *read* worldly', etc.) with which all who tempt print are habitually afflicted. When 'filth' becomes 'faith' and the 'vineyard' 'lunacy', we have fallen into an inverse theological dimension where Wesley's doctrinal art is pitched back into anarchy and where a good book is no longer a very great mercy to the world. The most charitable view of the matter is a 'philosophical' one, leading to the conclusion that the editor of *Charles Wesley: A Reader* believes so absolutely in the primacy of 'concept' that words, to him, actually are 'arbitrary' and can be thus abandoned to their own natures. It is a type of literary antinomianism, extreme but not unique.

The 'obvious conclusion' which Rivers has failed to draw from her own most useful remarks on the textual problems in Whichcote is the recognition of a misconceived *métier*. In the present undertaking, I believe, she has been ill-advised. A 'study' of the language of religion and ethics which cannot push itself beyond a repetitious 'interest' is merely adding weight to the 'stone' that 'moves downward'. There is, however, a present need for good critical editions of (among others) Baxter, Whichcote, and Law, and Rivers's manifest qualities would best be devoted to such an end. Against the odds and a good deal of evidence, I still regard the effort to bring secular scholarship (and poetics and the 'fine arts') into the field of the theological judgement as something other than a search for the philosopher's stone. At the same time, one recognizes that the general drift of the tendency has been towards an effusive post-Symbolism (e.g. 'Images of Atonement in the Novels and Short Stories of William Faulkner') which coy and prurient exercises in the 'confessional' mode have further dissipated. The writings considered in *Reason, Grace and Sentiment*, at once more reserved and more of a revelation, form the nexus of a different order of theological understanding, inherent in etymology and the contextures of grammar and syntax, clamped to a paradox that the 'one solid coherent body' of the work may be its 'Intrinsic Goodness', its reconciling of style and faith, or an abandoned finality of mind and soul, an intrinsic malignity 'as it were heavy as lead'.

21

Dividing Legacies

T. S. Eliot's Clark Lectures, delivered at Trinity College, Cambridge, in 1926, were a distinguished contribution to a series which has not always received such good returns on its modest investment. Ronald Schuchard's meticulously annotated edition makes *The Varieties of Metaphysical Poetry* an indispensable work of reference, and not only for professional readers of Eliot.[1] The lecturer was evidently dissatisfied with what he had achieved in these papers and in the subsequent Turnbull Lectures of 1933, a second shot, no less inconclusive, at the same topic. He withheld the typescripts of both sets from publication, and one can see why, even though by the standards that now prevail his reluctance may seem excessively fastidious.

To adapt one of Eliot's own figures to the purpose of my argument, I would say that the proper weight of any formal topic is related to its centre of gravity and that this centre, not surprisingly, is the most difficult element to establish in the composition of any lecture or essay. The true centre of *The Varieties of Metaphysical Poetry* is not easy to ascertain, in part because Eliot has seen, but not fully addressed, the problem; his anxious shifts and reservations complicate rather than clarify the issue. He observes that 'we have ... to consider the centre of gravity of metaphysical poetry to lie somewhere between Donne and Crashaw, but nearer the former than the latter'. Subsequently he backs away from 'what many of you will have expected, a neat and comprehensive definition', because in order to satisfy expectation 'I should have had to draw in the background much

---

[1] T. S. Eliot, *The Varieties of Metaphysical Poetry: The Clark Lectures at Trinity College, Cambridge, 1926, and the Turnbull Lectures at the Johns Hopkins University, 1933*, edited and introduced by Ronald Schuchard (London: Faber & Faber, 1993; New York: Harcourt Brace Jovanovich, 1994).

more completely, with the figures of James, and Charles, and Hooker, and Laud, and Hyde and Strafford'. It was a misjudgement not to bring these 'figures' under review, as it was to suggest that in any case they could be regarded as 'background'. It was a further miscalculation not to let go of the 'hypothetical' project, the comparison and contrast with 'Dante and his School' to which he had referred in his letter of thanks to J. Middleton Murry. (Murry, editor of *The Athenaeum*, had successfully nominated him for the Cambridge appointment after A. E. Housman had declined it.)

As is usually the case in such circumstances, the electors pressed Eliot hard for a theme and title; his nomination having been confirmed on 6 March 1925, his topic was 'approved' on 14 April. It also appears probable that two studies, M. P. Ramsay's *Les Doctrines médiévales chez Donne* (1917) and Mario Praz's recently published *Secentismo e marinismo in Inghilterra*, which, at the time, appeared to point to the centre of gravity for his own discourse, in the event directed his thought away from its true centre. Schuchard observes that Eliot, soon after the conclusion of his Clark Lectures, moved to a consideration of the author of *The Lawes of Ecclesiasticall Politie* in the essay on Lancelot Andrewes, of September 1926, and that he returned to Hooker three years later in a contribution to *The Listener*. Though Schuchard does not say that Eliot's way of making up the arrears is equivalent to a properly developed discussion at the time, his footnote on this, a half-page of small, dense print, implies a weight and cogency which is not evident in any of Eliot's own references to the author of *The Lawes of Ecclesiasticall Politie*. Schuchard quotes from the *Listener* piece—'The style of Hooker, and the style of Bacon, have a stiffness due to their intellectual antecedents being Latin and not English prose'—and I must draw my own conclusions from what he cites. It has to be said that in proposing the three periods—'the *trecento* in Italy and the seventeenth century in England', together with the period 1870–90 in France—as equivalently, if not interchangeably, 'metaphysical' for the purposes of his Cambridge lectures, Eliot irrecoverably misdirected his own argument away from its centre of gravity. It was a disciple of Eliot, the late Helen Gardner, who eventually made the necessary conjunction in her edition of Donne's *Divine Poems* (1951): 'To read the *Essays in Divinity* or the Sermons ... is to feel at once that Donne has absorbed Hooker's conception of the *via media* so deeply that it has become the basis of his own thinking'. This is of course a particularly happy discovery for a disciple of Eliot to have made since it was through his example, after 1927, that the *via media* once more came into acceptable critical parlance.

As we have seen, the metaphor 'centre of gravity' is Eliot's own, as is the equally suggestive 'points of triangulation'. These figures are useful, even essential, in helping to establish Eliot's necessary tone of tentative authority, perhaps the most attractive of his various *personae* and one which, as he thought, derived in part from the manner of F. H. Bradley, that 'curious blend of humility and irony, an attitude of extreme diffidence about his own work'.

It was Bradley who, in 1914, expressed gratification at 'the increasing devotion amongst us to metaphysical inquiry'. Twelve years later, at the commencement of the Clark Lectures, Eliot, though much indebted to Bradley, can less afford his relaxed amplitude of phrase. Where Bradley contrives to suggest a gratified disengagement from unnecessary particulars ('there has been, I think, a rise in the general level of English philosophical thought such as fifty years ago might well have seemed incredible'), Eliot contrives at the start to suggest a pursuit and scrutiny of the '*echt metaphysisch*' more close and stringent than any subsequent detail can match. While arguing to disengage the peculiar qualities of seventeenth-century meta-physical poetry in England from the broad connotations of philosophical metaphysics, he presents significant aspects of his case still from within the circuit of Bradley's comprehension, drawing his own terms of assessment, as Schuchard demonstrates, from such Bradleian passages as 'On our Know-ledge of Immediate Experience' or 'Floating Ideas and the Imaginary'. In his preface (1964) to *Knowledge and Experience in the Philosophy of F. H. Bradley*, Eliot recalls how it was 'as a pupil of Harold Joachim, the disciple of Bradley who was closest to the master', that he came to 'an understanding of what I wanted to say and of how to say it'. He means—more certainly—the understanding of the philosopher than the saying of the poet, though it is not futile to consider *Marina*, at least, in the context of Bradley's critique of floating ideas ('ideas may be recognized as merely imaginary, and, taken in this character, they float suspended above the real world').

It is not, however, as a pupil of a disciple of Bradley that Eliot considers 'the style of Hooker, and the style of Bacon'. It is difficult to name the mask he has here chosen to assume: one is inclined to say 'protégé of George Saintsbury' except that Saintsbury was probably more solidly bottomed in his knowledge of that period. It is nonetheless apparent that when Eliot is wearied by 'the most arduous, the most concentrated critical labour of which detailed record exists' he slips, not into incoherence but into a mechanical alternative mode of discourse exemplified by, if not imitated from, Saintsbury, to whom *Homage to John Dryden* (1924) is dedicated, or Charles Whibley, to whose memory *The Use of Poetry and the Use of Criticism* (1933) is inscribed. I mean by this that Eliot, who, in the correspondence pages of *The Athenaeum* (27 February 1920), attacked the 'apathy' of 'the so-called cultivated and civilized class', was to some extent a practitioner of its modes and to a further extent their beneficiary. Schuchard notes that Eliot's review of Housman's 1933 Leslie Stephen lecture, *The Name and Nature of Poetry*, was far from hostile; that an advance copy of *Journey of the Magi* was inscribed to Housman with the author's 'respectful homage'; and that Housman evidently appreciated and to some extent reciprocated the sympathy. It is germane to our sense of *A Shropshire Lad* and *Last Poems* to understand that Housman can invoke, as a rhetorical tribute to precedent, the classical *apatheia* and at the same moment appeal to a less elevated form of apathy, that indolence of 'cultivated' taste, which Eliot deplores in his letter to *The Athenaeum*. What is most, and what is least, admirable in Housman and in those who value him is contained within the tacit qualifications of that word. Eliot has more facets than this, but his singleness of purpose within his divided conditions and unhappy circumstances is more clearly, more ambitiously, stated than are Housman's own professions and demurrals. Again I refer to a particular source, Eliot's letter of April 1919 to one of his former teachers at Harvard, J. H. Woods:

> There are only two ways in which a writer can become important—to write a great deal, and have his writings appear everywhere, or to write very little. It is a question of temperament. I write very little and I should not become more powerful by increasing my output. My reputation in London is built upon one small volume of verse, and is kept up by printing two or three more poems in a year. The only thing that matters is that these should be perfect in their kind, so that each should be an event.

It is of course true that in writing to Woods at that time Eliot had a particularly difficult case to make on his own behalf. The professor thought very highly of Eliot's potential and prospects as an academic philosopher and had concerned himself about the practicalities of Eliot's return to Harvard to take up a teaching post in Philosophy. 'Please let us be reassured that your interest in Philosophy is as strong as before', Woods had written in June 1916, in the same letter which reported that Eliot's doctoral dissertation on F. H. Bradley had been accepted in partial fulfilment of the requirements for

that degree. In the next few years Eliot's main task in writing not only to the
Harvard philosophers but also to his parents would be to persuade them, and
perhaps in a sense himself, that by remaining in London to write poetry and to
pick up a living from various kinds of literary journeyman-work he had not
irretrievably ruined his life and unforgivably blighted their expectations. Even
with this concession to circumstance, however, I find that the letter places
a remarkably heavy stress on the particulars of career-making. Eliot's self-
evaluation is in terms of a calculating idealism; the effect is gratingly oxymoronic: 'important', 'powerful', 'reputation', 'event'; the commitment
suggested by 'perfect in their kind' is abraded in the surrounding context.

   Four years after the delivery of the Clark Lectures he had achieved an
'extraordinary power' (the words are G. Wilson Knight's) to influence literary
opinion. In Peter Ackroyd's words, Eliot was always 'shrewd enough to make
his peace with an age to which he did not truly belong'. Richard Wollheim's
conjecture is that it was 'only after he had made some kind of initial
submission to a force, felt in itself to be uncongenial or external, that he
possessed the liberty to do something for himself or on his own account'.
Eliot himself observed, having in mind Donne's Catholic patrimony and
apostasy, 'Conflict is contact'; and immediately added, 'The air which Donne
breathed was infused with Jesuitism'. But I should have supposed that
'contact', as argued here, is an entirely different state or process from infusion
as he here conceives it. Eliot's scholarly intuition is acute: he anticipates the
speculations of Martz, Gardner, Raspa, and others who emphasize Donne's
critical and creative involvement with Jesuit spirituality. His deductions are
less effectively conveyed: 'For you can hardly fight anyone for very long
without employing his weapons and using his methods; and to fight a man
with ideas means adapting your ideas to his mind.' Not necessarily, though it
may have been necessary for Eliot to convert a vulnerability into a truism.
The tone of his delivery throughout both sets of lectures shows him acting, at
least in part, on his own dubious maxim. He urges the significance of what
he terms the 'psychologism' of Jesuit practice and believes that he has established its influence on Donne's style of thought. The *Oxford English Dictionary*
(1989) gives two principal senses of 'psychologism'; neither of them strikes me
as apposite to Eliot's purpose. 'Psychologism' is either a form of 'idealism as
opposed to sensationalism' or 'the tendency to explain in psychological terms
matters which are considered to be more properly explained in other ways'. The
deficiency may be that of the compilers—it is possible that Eliot's usage significantly modifies the given senses, but on balance I doubt it. If it is in any

way appropriate to employ a term not current before the nineteenth century, I would suggest that the Ignatian method seeks to move the exercitant by an edited sensationalism, e.g.: 'The fourth point is to use in imagination the sense of touch, for example, by embracing and kissing the place where the persons walk or sit, always endeavouring to draw some spiritual fruit from this'. And if, alternatively, we attempt to apply OED sense 2 we arrive at conclusions directly opposed to Ignatian proprieties of explanation.

It is worth repeating that Eliot's instinct for spotting the significant detail in a line of thought or nexus of circumstance is that of a true scholar-critic. The conclusions which he derives from his scholarly and critical *aperçus* nevertheless strike me as being anachronistic, broadly impressionistic. I would accept that 'psychologism' in the OED sense 2, even if inadmissible as a description of Ignatian method, illuminates the poems of the period 1926–30, in particular *Marina*, which has been called 'Eliot's most elusive poem'. In Denis Donoghue's judgement this poem 'makes sense' as being about 'waking up to find yourself a Christian, not knowing quite what to make of it all'. It is within this particular area of suggestion, at once contracted and expansive, that the second definition of 'psychologism' indeed makes sense. The voice of the poem is acutely conscious of attempting to explain, to itself and others, matters more properly explained in other ways. These other ways may reasonably be understood as those of Anglo-Catholic doctrine and practice; the way in which that understanding moves, and moves us, in the poem remains, at least as I understand it, essentially Bradleian. I note here the organization of *Essays on Truth and Reality* (1914), where the chapter on 'Faith' is immediately succeeded by the discussion of 'Floating Ideas and the Imaginary', a chapter to which Eliot made frequent reference in his doctoral dissertation. Bradley argues that 'the origin of faith, it seems to me clear, may be what we call emotional; and, even perhaps apart from emotion, faith can arise through what may be termed a non-active suggestion'. The rhythm and syntax of *Marina* seem scarcely to rise out of the non-active (this is their achievement) while possessing sufficient resilience to pull away from the static horror of Hercules' cry of recognition (the Senecan epigraph).

I am far from suggesting that the final incoherence of the Clark Lectures is mysteriously vindicated in the coherences, the coherent elusiveness, of *Marina*. The difficult economy of invention can do without that kind of condescension. That which misdirects itself in the academic context is not vicarious, not in payment for the subliminal self-discoveries of a Baudelairean

Christian poet. The source of the error is in part, I believe, the scholarly oversight to which I have referred: Eliot's failure to take rightly the measure of Hooker. That Eliot himself apprehended the extent to which he had missed Hooker's significance is indicated by the proliferation of his successive returns upon the matter: in the essay on Andrewes later that year, in 'The Genesis of Philosophic Prose: Bacon and Hooker' (1929), in 'The Prose of the Preacher' (1929), and again in the Turnbull Lectures of January 1933. To say that 'the subject of Hooker's book is a very interesting one, and indeed very pertinent to some modern problems' is to be as far from the quick of the matter as when he says that Hooker's prose has a stiffness due to its intellectual antecedents being Latin and not English.

I had better explain what I mean in this instance by the quick of the matter. In April 1921 Eliot gave a BBC talk in the course of which he drew attention to the fineness of Shakespeare's dramatic sense; he focused on the words of the dying Charmian, in *Antony and Cleopatra*, spoken over the dead body of her mistress:

> It is well done, and fitting for a Princesse
> Descended of so many Royall Kings.
> Ah Souldier.

Eliot pointed out that Shakespeare added to the text of North's *Plutarch*, from which he was working, 'the two plain words, *ah, soldier*'. Eliot continued, 'I could not myself put into words the difference I feel between the passage if these two words *ah, soldier* were omitted and with them. But I know there is a difference, and that only Shakespeare could have made it.' In stating the issue as he does Eliot *has* of course put into words, very finely, the difference that he says he cannot explain. Christopher Ricks comments, 'If in some game I had to instance one paragraph from Eliot to show that he was a great critic, I should choose this, from a radio talk which he never himself reprinted. For it is an act of genius in the critic to see that the act of genius in the artist was the cry "Ah, Souldier"'. From this, as from other sources, I draw my conclusion that within the semantic field, felicities and infelicities are herded indiscriminately together and that it requires a particular quality of aural sensitivity, a vigilance at once intuitive and disciplined, to make sense of one or the other or both. This we may call 'recognition', a term doubly applicable to Eliot's mind and art, for he is one who—psychologically and spiritually—commits himself to, and requires a very great deal from, evocations of rediscovery and redemption.

In the light of such affirmations it is at first bewildering to discover the frequency with which Schuchard is obliged to correct misquotations and 'minor mistranscriptions' in these lectures. One can go only so far in arguing that Eliot prepared the text under great pressure of various kinds; so does everyone, in one way or another; so did Péguy, famed for his impeccable proof-reading. It is of course true that, unlike the majority of Clark Lectures, Eliot's were not subsequently prepared by the author for the press. But his misquotations and minor mistranscriptions are also strongly instinctual; for example, his recollection that the butcher and the beaver marched shoulder to shoulder 'from necessity' and not 'merely from nervousness', as Lewis Carroll had imagined, or that Shakespeare's 'gnomic utterance' in *King Lear* (v. ii. 9–11) reads:

> Man must abide
> His going hence, even as his coming hither;
> Ripeness is all.

When I say 'instinctual' I mean instinctively metaphysical, and I suggest also that Eliot's metaphysics sometimes require the exquisite pointing of a word or two, as in 'Ah, soldier', and at other times do not. Bradley famously observed that metaphysics is 'the finding of bad reasons for what we believe upon instinct', and one might place 'Tradition and the Individual Talent', 'The Function of Criticism', 'Hamlet', and 'The Metaphysical Poets' in that category. But Bradley was also a 'rigorous metaphysician', permitted or self-permitted his relish of insouciance, and Eliot's doctoral dissertation upon him is not merely the 'painfully obscure work' that Wollheim declares it to be. Its argument resolves into clarity, particularly at points where a chord in Eliot's mind resonates to a note in Bradley or to something recalled (possibly) from Josiah Royce's seminar of 1913–14. At one of these meetings Royce introduced to the discussion Charles Peirce's belief 'that there is a mysterious harmony between the mind of the scientist and the order of nature; for otherwise, supposing it were a mere matter of chance as to what hypotheses he should devise, he would rarely hit upon any true and adequate explanations'. Eliot needs words, in a metaphysical sense, as a manifestation of that 'mysterious harmony' by which the mind not only reconciles itself with the 'order of nature' but also prefigures that reconciliation. Eliot states, in his treatise on Bradley:

> In really great imaginative work the connections are felt to be bound by as logical necessity as any connections to be found anywhere; the apparent irrelevance is due to the fact that terms are used with more or other than

their normal meaning, and to those who do not thoroughly penetrate their significance the relation between the aesthetic expansion and the objects expressed is not visible.

The key to our understanding here, as in much else concerning Eliot, is Bradley's 'My Station and Its Duties'. John Passmore, with what I take to be genial asperity, observes that 'My Station and Its Duties' also shows us what Bradley 'believed upon instinct'. The possibility of picking up the wrong key, for us as for Eliot, is present throughout a reading of Bradley. Take, for example, 'On Our Knowledge of Immediate Experience':

> We ... have experience in which there is no distinction between my aware-ness and that of which it is aware. There is an immediate feeling, a knowing and being in one, with which knowledge begins; and, though this in a manner is transcended, it nevertheless remains throughout as the present foundation of my known world.

If we proceed no further we appear to be in that region of atonement ('there is an immediate feeling, a knowing and being in one') which is the focal point of desire in *Marina* and *Ash-Wednesday* and is intended to be heard as the proclaimed consummation of *Little Gidding*. For Bradley, however, as I understand it, this is not the blessed finality but the necessary point of unavoidable departure. The attempt to stay or to recover will be regressive or retrograde. It is possible to understand how, given the Roycean–Brad-leian inheritance, Eliot's discovery of Dante is inevitable, at one with 'the mysterious harmony between the mind of the scientist and the order of nature', and not only inevitable but foreordained, so that Bradley's primal 'knowing and being in one' is at the same time the final '*sì come rota ch'igualmente è mossa*' of the *Paradiso*. In accordance with this paradigm— Dante does not declare that he is paraphrasing Aquinas—one's words can take up another's; nor is it essential that the words so taken up should be exactly quoted. One is not, in fact, quoting but recognizing. I infer that the 'psychologism' runs somewhat in this manner. Indeed it could be said that the psychologism is unanswerably proved and justified by 'Ah Souldier', the two plain words which wholly transform with genius the dutiful words from North and which, three hundred years later, are formally recognized, by the reciprocating genius of Eliot, as great imaginative work.

It is equally the case, however, that if one accepts the metaphysical profile which I have drawn, it must be accepted—or conceded—that the obtrusion of Dante and exclusion of Hooker damage the structure of these lectures beyond immediate recovery. The necessary connection which Eliot failed to make was not that 'Hooker's philosophy was much more "mediaeval" than Donne's', true as that is, or that 'the intellectual achievement and the prose style of Hooker and Andrewes came to complete the structure of the English Church as the philosophy of the thirteenth century crowns the Catholic Church': these are fair points well within the competence of a decent man of letters such as Charles Whibley. Eliot's encounter with language, in the making of *Prufrock and Other Observations* and *Ara Vos Prec*, was already at a pitch above and beyond the range of such minor settlements. His sense of this is uncomfortably conveyed in small tonal irritants and irritations throughout the lectures: 'what many of you will have expected; a neat and comprehensive definition', 'But I think that I warned you', 'You will perhaps think it unjust of me'. The distinction to be emphasized here is between pitch and tone. The style of Eliot's address to his audience is a matter of tone; the burden of his analytical criticism is, or ought to be, the question of pitch. To meet with Hooker in significant engagement is to encounter questions of pitch: to take note that the word 'reason' as Hooker deploys it throughout *The Lawes of Ecclesiasticall Politie* has at least seven distinct senses. It signifies God's great original purpose and design and also mankind's highest capacity to recognize God's proposed design and to imitate it; it signifies a decent common sense as well as opinion and prejudice; it is necessity and determinism and certain causes of certain effects; it is also used to suggest formal ratiocination. Hooker's 'style' is to a large extent his semantic ingenuity, his ability to make these senses merge and part with equanimity, though not always with equity. Of similar significance to our grasp of *Ecclesiasticall Politie* is the skill with which Hooker can alter the pitch of the word 'common': 'common received error', 'common sense or phancy', 'a common opinion held by the Scribes', 'the common sorte of men', 'common discretion, and judgement', 'in every action of common life', 'the common good', 'common miserie', 'the mindes of the common sorte', 'for common utilities sake'. Clearly, 'common discretion, and judgement' is pitched differently from 'a common opinion held by the Scribes', which is itself at a different pitch than 'the minds of the common sort'. Hooker's *belief*, we may say, is that each separate pitch is justified by an equivalent degree on a scale determined by chapter 13 of St Paul's Epistle to the Romans. Hooker's *equivocation*, we may decide, is in the tacit invitation to his readers to accept that hierarchical distinctions and brute natural obduracies are alike resolved into equity by fiat of the commonweal and the administrations of the 1559 *Book of Common Prayer.*

If, as Eliot claims, 'the centre of gravity of metaphysical poetry [lies] somewhere between Donne and Crashaw, but nearer the former than the latter', it is incumbent upon him to demonstrate that 'centre of gravity' is, critically speaking, a term of common utility. I am not persuaded that he does so. The pitch of the argument can to an extent be determined by the empirical judgement that one brings to Eliot's use of the words 'thought', 'idea', 'figure', 'image', 'conceit'. In terms of thought, notion, idea, Eliot appears anti-Cartesian insofar as he dismisses the sixth *Meditation* as an 'extraordinarily crude and stupid piece of reasoning' at the point where Descartes denies that one can deduce the existence of the body from the 'distinct idea of corporeal nature, which I have in my imagination'. It further appears, at an initial acquaintance, that Eliot values the pre-Cartesian elements in Donne's poetics that are at the same time Cartesianism turned upon itself: 'the sensuous interest of Donne in his own thoughts as objects'. 'I attempted to show', Eliot announced at the end of the fourth lecture, 'that this interest naturally led [Donne] to expression by conceits'. What is missing from Eliot's appraisal, however, is a convincing presentation of 'sensuous interest'; he gives us an idea, a notion, an indication, of sensuous interest. I am clear in my own mind that what I have called the pitch of Hooker's prose is also the sensuous interest of that prose; I am equally convinced that a discovery of the pitch of Donne's language in, say, 'A Nocturnall upon S. Lucies Day' or 'A Hymne to Christ, at the Authors last going into Germany' would also be a recognition of the sensuous interest of those poems. I do not detect that awareness in what Eliot finds to say in praise of Donne's figures felicitously 'teasing the idea', even 'creat[ing] the idea'; or in what he has to say, a shade less sympathetically, of our having (parenthetically) to 'swallow the idea of the indeterminability of time in the future state, and then pass on at once to the difficult idea, startlingly expressed, of the namelessness of the soul, of its distinction from the breathing composite of soul and body which we knew'. I find in this sentence no sensuous interest, that is to say, no sense of pitch, no centre of gravity; one is again reminded how much critical description is in fact tautologous. Eliot concludes that 'the only thing that holds [Donne's] poems, or any one poem, together, is what we call unsatisfactorily the personality of Donne'. I believe that he is mistaken in this conclusion, and it is evident that he himself senses that something is wrong. He is forced to take up extrinsic 'personality', 'unsatisfactorily', as he admits, precisely because intrinsic pitch has not been attended to. 'Personality' has to stand as a substitute centre of gravity.

Schuchard foresees a happy likelihood that 'the publication of Eliot's Clark Lectures on metaphysical poetry will have as much impact on our revaluation of his critical mind as did the facsimile edition of *The Waste Land* (1971) on our comprehension of his poetic mind'; I will end with a few observations on this speculation, though not with the enthusiasm of assent which its tone of *pietas* invites. Three years before he delivered the Clark Lectures Eliot had suggested, in 'The Function of Criticism' (1923), that 'probably . . . the larger part of the labour of an author in composing his work is critical labour', and he would rightly object to this belated editorial presumption that one can so neatly divide the 'critical' from the 'poetic' mind.

That, however, is not the most important issue arising from the publication of these lectures. I have attempted to show that throughout his argument Eliot aims at pitch but, for the most part, succeeds only in tone. I say 'succeeds' because tone is what people expect and suppose themselves familiar with. It was the pitch of *Prufrock and Other Observations* that disturbed and alienated readers; it was the tone of *Four Quartets* that assuaged and consoled them. That is to say, Eliot's poetry declines over thirty years from pitch into tone, and these late-published papers contribute significant evidence to the history of that decline.

In 'The Love Song of J. Alfred Prufrock' (1910–11) the distinction between I, me, my, we, us, our, you, your, his, her, they, them, one, it, its, is a proper distinction in pitch; in *Little Gidding* (1942) communication is by tone:

> You are not here to verify,
> Instruct yourself, or inform curiosity
> Or carry report. You are here to kneel
> Where prayer has been valid. And prayer is more
> Than an order of words, the conscious occupation
> Of the praying mind, or the sound of the voice praying.

How is the repeated 'you' to be understood? Is it the modern second person singular or the second person plural, or is it the emphatic demotic substitute for what the *OED* terms a 'quite toneless, proclitic or enclitic, use of "one"'? Is Eliot instructing himself, self-confessor to self-penitent, taking upon himself penitentially the burden of common trespass, or is he haranguing the uninitiated,

some indeterminate other—or others—caught trespassing on his spiritual property? Do these lines contain, even, a redundant echo from *The Waste Land*, the
exclamatory 'You' of line 76, the closest Eliot could get, in the grammar of
modern English, to the pitch of Baudelaire's 'Tu' in line 39 of 'Au Lecteur'?
Whatever it is, it is no match for the quality of pitch which Eliot caught in just
two words, two just words, in *Antony and Cleopatra*. Ricks, in his fine appraisal to
which I have referred, says that we cannot be sure of the 'posture proper to the
cry' and that the 'responsibility for settling upon the best response has been
manifestly delegated' to us by Shakespeare. My argument does not require that
we should be relieved of the office proper to our intelligence. My objection to
the lines from *Little Gidding* has nothing to do with deliberated indeterminacy of
pitch; I hear in them the semantic equivalent of *tinnitus aurium*, and I say that one
cannot rightly be expected, as reader, to take responsibility for this condition.

Juxtapose the passage from *Little Gidding* with the following sentence
from Wordsworth's 'Preface' (1800) to *Lyrical Ballads*:

> It is supposed, that by the act of writing in verse an Author makes a formal
> engagement that he will gratify certain known habits of association, that he
> not only thus apprizes the Reader that certain classes of ideas and expressions
> will be found in his book, but that others will be carefully excluded.

Reading lines from *Little Gidding* in the light of Wordsworth's argument
I find that Eliot stands in relation to Wordsworth's sense of pitch ('It is
supposed, that') not as one similarly situated but as a commentator on the
general tone or tonelessness of things. Certain classes of ideas and expressions will be found at Little Gidding—subsequently in *Little Gidding*—rich
in known habits of association, and others will be carefully excluded. If I add
that of course I am not impugning the sincerity of Eliot's Anglo-Catholic
devotion I fall into the same error which Eliot fell into when he was forced
to address—'unsatisfactorily'—'the personality of Donne'. And I have to
disagree with Christopher Ricks when he finds that, in *Little Gidding*,
'antagonism to clichés—like the expression of antagonism through
clichés—has been succeeded by confidence in their good sense, in their
generous common humanity'. I do not claim that it is impossible for clichés
in poetry to correspond to, or represent, a generous common humanity.
Whitman, for instance, uses them in a vital and comradely way in *Drum-
Taps*. I do say, however, that the 'apathy ... more flagitious than abuse' to
which Eliot acutely drew attention in 1920 is a determining factor in the
tonality of his own later poetry and in its public reception, and that Ricks is

uncharacteristically imperceptive in his response to this factor. I would ask him to place his 'generous common humanity' within the field of Hooker's common equivocation and to determine how much weight and pressure that generous humanity can sustain.

The residual beneficiaries of *Four Quartets* have been Larkin and Anglican literary 'spirituality', two seeming incompatibles fostered by a common species of torpor. If I were to ask Ricks how it is that, against all the evidence his own unrivalled critical intelligence could bring to the process, he is pleased to be numbered among Larkin's advocates, I anticipate that he might answer, 'Because he speaks to the human condition'.

Inventions of Value

22

Translating Value:
Marginal Observations on a
Central Question

A. C. Bradley, in 'Poetry for Poetry's Sake' (1901), posited an 'intrinsic', as opposed to an 'ulterior', value for poetry; the latter being, for instance, the poem's utility as 'a means to culture or religion'. He insisted that the 'ulterior worth' of a work cannot 'directly determine its poetic worth'. I. A. Richards took issue with this, arguing in *Principles of Literary Criticism* (1924) that certain of Bradley's ulterior values 'may be directly concerned in our judgements of the poetic values of experiences. Otherwise ... the word "poetic" becomes a useless sound'. To resolve this critical stand-off requires us to determine what is meant by the term 'directly'. Put somewhat differently, questions of value are inseparable from matters of translation; and translation itself involves more than the matching up of equivalent verbal signs. Even so, it took rather longer than I care to admit before I was prepared to concede that Ruskin's 'intrinsic value' does not guarantee, or even have a direct relation to, the presence of intrinsic value. The phrase is at best a promissory note, at worst a semantic relic to ward off the evil eye of commodity.

It would be less than honest not to acknowledge that there is a personal edge to my academic concern with the nature of the intrinsic. It is not always easy to maintain, on questions that press harshly upon the self, that disinterestedness of observation which many would understand—and justly—to be an essential prerequisite for any description of value, or indeed for any honest attempt to arrive at such a description. Among the requisites for true criticism, according to Hume, are a 'mind free from all *prejudice*', 'a delicate taste of wit or beauty', 'a due attention to the object'; but this admirable prescription, and an honest endeavour to put it into practice, were ineffective against Hume's own prejudicate opinion that Bunyan is inferior to Addison and that any attempt to claim otherwise would be 'absurd and ridiculous'.

One cannot, however, argue *ex hypothesi* that such quaint prejudicates have been replaced, two and a half centuries later, by the self-evidently superior practices of what we are to call *science de la littérature*. Christopher Ricks is right to argue that an objectivity which elides 'personal values' to personal 'preferences' and which, having further equated the false compound with 'interest' and 'prejudice', proposes its elimination in the best interests of mental hygiene, is itself interested and prejudiced and 'implacably hostile to literature'.

In saying that questions of value are inseparable from matters of translation, I do not propose to limit that suggestion to the problems of translating from, say, Pascal's French into late seventeenth-century or modern English. Translation, conventionally understood, presents in a sustainedly demanding form matters which require vigilance of all users of language. To make an assessment at the present time of the vocabulary of David Hume's two essays 'Of the Delicacy of Taste and Passion' (1741) and 'Of the Standard of Taste' (1757) is to face issues arising from his use of the term 'delicacy' which scarcely differ in degree from those which relate to questions of how best, in 1688 or 1950, to render Pascal's '*esprit de finesse*'. I have particularly in mind a recent observation that 'the taste model, even in Hume's sensitive hands, must be too simple'. There is a difficulty with 'Hume's sensitive hands' if I may so express it; I cannot hear the semantic pitch of the word 'sensitive', even while I recognize that this word is intended as a succinct equivalent to Hume's own range of sense in his repeated use of the word 'delicacy' and its cognates. 'Delicacy' and 'delicate' in Hume's essays mean different things at different moments and 'Hume's sensitive hands' relates to Hume's language (for example, 'Those finer emotions of the mind are of a very tender and delicate nature') about as closely as 'the Polite Wit', 'the refin'd wit', or 'the nimbly discerning mind' relate to '*esprit de finesse*'.

I find particularly noteworthy in Hume's thinking—as represented by the two essays under discussion—his readiness to take contingency into account ('The good or ill accidents of life are very little at our disposal') and his ability to bring it into semantic play ('Philosophers have endeavored to render happiness entirely independent of every thing external. That degree of perfection is impossible to be *attained*'). One is aware of the pressure of collective opinion upon individual judgement but aware also that an original cast of mind can be attained even when the subject of debate is, in several senses, the subjection of the particular to the general, the ideal to the actual:

> It is natural for us to seek a *Standard of Taste*; a rule, by which the various sentiments of men may be reconciled; at least, a decision, afforded, confirming one sentiment, and condemning another.

If this sentence simply declared that it is necessary, within the social milieu, to determine a literary *sensus communis* of value whereby prescription and proscription may be generally agreed, I would accept without reservation that 'the taste model, even in Hume's sensitive hands, must be too simple'. What we term Hume's sensitivity of grasp and touch is largely revealed in the care with which he shows that the model cannot be simple: 'It is natural for us' is placed so as to be slightly outside, or a shade obliquely on to, the prejudicates which it presents. The phrase attains a position with respect to the idea. Hobbes's depiction of beliefs 'wrought into' human nature by custom and laws requires that we give due attention to the pitch of 'wrought into'; the phrase itself, its self attained in context. Demonstrative vocabulary is not exempt from the contingencies which affect that which is demonstrated. Hobbes sometimes appears to think otherwise, but he does not write like one who takes exemption for granted. The significance of Hume on Taste is that he sees it partly as 'wrought', a matter of prejudicates, and in part arrived at through a mental discipline, a self-knowledgeable understanding of how deeply prejudiced we are, even—or especially—in our common agreements. In this respect at least, Hume recalls Hobbes and anticipates Wordsworth's attack on prejudicates in the 'Preface' to *Lyrical Ballads* and the 'Essay, Supplementary to the Preface' of 1815.

Although Wordsworth esteemed Hume among the very worst of critics, beaten into lowest place only by Adam Smith, his two major critical pieces comprehend the nature and power of contingent circumstance in a way that could well be thought to derive from Hume's two papers:

> It is supposed, that by the act of writing in verse an Author makes a formal engagement that he will gratify certain known habits of association, that he not only thus apprizes the Reader that certain classes of ideas and expressions will be found in his book, but that others will be carefully excluded.

The point at issue with 'It is supposed' is whether it indicates the acceptance or the rejection of majority opinion. According to my reading, Wordsworth does more than neutrally take note of the supposition; he is not so much taking as giving notice that certain required literary dues and social *congés* will not be offered in and by his work. It is true that in general usage the grammatical pitch of 'It is supposed' can be variable; herein is its particular usefulness: in the way it evades precise translation from, or into, mood and intention. In the 'Preface' to *Lyrical Ballads* he is more discreet than in the 'Essay Supplementary' of 1815 where he shows himself vulnerable to his own disappointment and anger: 'But the ignorance of those who have chosen to stand forth as my enemies'; 'opponents whom I internally despise', etc. Even in the earlier essay, however, the angry scorn is intermittently vented: those 'who talk of Poetry as a matter of amusement and idle pleasure'.

Wordsworth's vulnerability bears upon my own approach to questions and issues of value. My strong prejudice in his favour being particularly marked at such points, we must consider the possibility that I overestimate here through sympathy as I may undervalue elsewhere because of antipathy. One may say, adapting Hume, that such forms of reaction 'transport' the speaker 'beyond all bounds of prudence and discretion', render the work valueless as an instrument of general social intelligence. Drawing on the same authority one might plead the opposite case as a vindication of Wordsworth. Where Hume's require- ment for this species of integrity is that 'the perfection of the man, and the perfection of the sense or feeling, are found to be united', the defence might enter the plea that, where the imperfection of the man is nakedly realized in the speech, integrity and value are affirmed. It could be added that 'naked', for Wordsworth, is a term with ethical weight. Even then one would not have strong cause for complaint if the plea were rejected on the grounds of mere sentiment. One would perhaps be on firmer ground in making clear the significance to one's own thinking of the term 'realized'. I mean by 'realized' basically what Hume means by 'to fix and ascertain', but with semantic resonances that he might reject; and I illustrate my Humean definition from an author whose realizations were outside Hume's range of hearing, acute though that was across the spectrum of 'the common sentiments of human nature'. Bunyan's question, which for Hume would have been intrinsically absurd and ridiculous, is: how do you teach yourself to distinguish the treacherous common sense of the reprobate from the faithful knowledge of the elect; the answer is, you work at it:

> Then [*Christian*] went to the outward door, that leads into the *Castle yard*, and with his Key opened the door also. After he went to the *Iron* Gate, for that must be opened too, but that Lock went *damnable* hard, yet the Key did open it.

Bunyan's ability is to make a passage of emblematic discourse suddenly become the mind's activity: 'but that Lock went *damnable* hard'. The word is caught at the precise moment of translation from imprecation to recognition.

It so happens that this particular, and in context exemplary, instance of recognition takes the form of a pun; and it is a fact that, as numerous commentators have noted, 'many meanings can have *one word*' and that 'Donne is really the kind of being to whom the word *done* can be applied'. But that which unites the pun with other types of semantic recognition is the common factor of attention (which, in its time, has been the 'diligence' which the first Lutheran and Calvinist translators of the Bible attributed—rightfully for the most part— to themselves and, in its time, has been the phrase *sedem animae in extremis digitis habent* which commended itself to Robert Burton, 'their Soule, or *intellectus agens*, was placed in their fingers ends'). Emerson is therefore well within my range of understanding when he observes that Coleridge excels 'in the fineness of distinctions he could indicate, touching his mark with a needle's point'; so also is Housman's praise of his great predecessor in the emendation of Latin texts: that 'when one has halted at some stubborn perplexity of reading or interpretation . . . [one] turns to Bentley and sees Bentley strike his finger on the place and say *thou ailest here, and here*'.

If moral discourse required no further justification than force of sentiment, strength of commitment; if ethical premise had a happily uncomplicated relationship to language, and language to value, there would be scarcely anything of significance in Ruskin's massive *oeuvre* to which '*thou ailest here, and here*' would not apply as his most telling motto. The text implicit in his major writings, though, so far as I know, it is made explicit only once, is Deuteronomy 27: 17. In a letter to the *Manchester City News* (April 1884), he charges the proposed railway through the Derbyshire dales with a planned destruction of the peasants' landmarks:

> 'A landmark only!'—and Heaven bless the mark—what better should they be? And who is he, and what is his guilt, who removes his neighbour's landmark?

The Deuteronomic 'land-marke' of 1611 is set against the later 'scenic' sense acceptable to 'the tripper from Manchester or Birmingham' whom the proposed railway will make free of the Dales, effectively disenfranchising the time-hallowed liberties of the peasantry. 'Cursed *be* he that remooueth his neighbours land-marke: and all the people shall say, Amen.' 'Amen', so uttered, would be, for the theological moralist, whether Jewish or Christian, the absolute, clinching, recognition and assertion of value. Inevitably, Ruskinian secular attestations of value are tinged with the sardonic and elegiac.

This letter appeared one month later than *The Storm Cloud of the Nineteenth Century*, a volume comprising two lectures delivered in February 1884. It is a book about a curse, a curse incurred when England, together with her industrial neighbours and rivals, 'blasphemed the name of God deliberately and openly'. The 'plague-wind' and the accompanying 'plague-cloud' are at once the miasma of vast industrial desecration and a divine retribution visited upon ill-gotten wealth. Nature itself is now poisonously, blightingly, implicated in the evil reversal of natural process brought about by human greed and ingratitude: the wind drives a smoke cloud that looks 'as if it were made of dead men's souls'. There is an element of somber punning here if one comprehends Ruskin's visionary sense of 'illth', the neologism he coined for *Unto This Last* (1860–2).

When *Unto This Last* was reissued in the Everyman Library in 1907, Oliver Lodge observed in his introduction that 'Mr Ruskin is always very precise in his use of language; every word employed by him is employed with due thought given to its meaning and history and uttermost significance'. It is true that Ruskin is always definite—I choose this word as standing indeterminately between 'precise' and 'emphatic'—but I would question Lodge's terms. 'Intrinsic value', as Ruskin uses it, is emphatic but not precise; though its power of emphasis is due in great part to its capacity to *suggest* precision. Ruskin devotes many pages throughout his collected writings to establishing a density of evidence to justify his neologism 'illth'; by contrast 'intrinsic value' is, I would have said, *not* rooted in its 'meaning and history and uttermost significance'. It is whatever we desire shall stand as the moral opposite of illth and collective national bad faith.

When Hobbes, on the dedication page of *Leviathan*, celebrates the 'inhaerent' virtue of the dead Godolphin and when, several hundred pages later, he returns to mourn the extinction of that inherency, in a Civil War skirmish, by 'an undiscerned, and an undiscerning hand'; when Hume appeals to the 'durable admiration, which attends those works, that have survived all the caprices of mode and fashion, all the mistakes of ignorance and envy', 'inhaerent' virtue and 'durable admiration' directly anticipate Ruskin's 'intrinsic value'. Hume is not saying that the value is conferred by the admiration, but that society will in the end be brought to recognize the value that has always been there. In Ruskin's words, 'Used or not, their own power is in them and that particular power is in nothing else', or 'Everything costs its own Cost, and one of our best virtues is a just desire to pay it.'

The basis of 'intrinsic value' lies in seventeenth-century monetary debate, in which it carried several conflicting senses. The monetarists in turn had drawn their term out of the language of the despised Scholastics. Any study of the early fiscal terminology will demonstrate the historical inaccuracy of taking Ruskin's adoption of it in any absolute sense. His own rhetorical mannerism, in Letter 12 of *Fors Clavigera*, is its own caveat:

> And you will find that the essence of the mis-teaching, of your day, concerning wealth of any kind, is in this denial of intrinsic value. What anything is worth, or not worth, it cannot tell you: all that it can tell is the exchange value. What Judas, in the present state of Demand and Supply, can get for the article he has to sell, in a given market, that is the value of his article:—Yet you do not find that Judas had joy of his bargain.

This—and with sorrow I say it—is rant. R. W. Dixon's remark, in a letter to Hopkins, that Carlyle 'spoiled Ruskin's style for him' does not go unsupported; and *Fors Clavigera: Letters to the Workmen and Labourers of Great Britain* (1871–84), contains more than one eloquent tribute to the writer he called 'master'. His closest approach to what Lodge calls 'due thought given to [the] meaning and history' of intrinsic value is in Letter 37 of *Fors* (January 1874); and here he seems to be, intentionally or unintentionally, in the line of Locke's thinking on this subject in the *Second Treatise of Government*. Locke argues that although two pieces of land may have 'the same natural, intrinsick Value', it is 'Husbandry', '*Labour . . . which puts the greatest part of Value upon land*, without which it would scarcely be worth any thing'. Intrinsic value, when considered in terms of an improved and improving husbandry, is that which, left simply to itself, will remain unrealized. Is it, then, anything more than a formal figure given as the basis for a set of estimates? In the January 1874 *Fors*, Ruskin uses not dissimilar terms: 'I should best like a bit of marsh land of small value'; 'I will make the best of it that I can, at once, by wage-labour, under the best agricultural advice'. I cannot see how these ideals are essentially different from Locke's estimates. It is in the moral approach that they differ. Locke's attitude to the labourers engaged in the schemes of improved husbandry was 'unusually harsh' even by the standards of that time. Ruskin's views are paternalistically benevolent. But this exists in his social writings as an aura, rather than a realization, of language; and 'intrinsic value', which appears to carry precise meaning, is part of that 'aura'.

Christopher Ricks has observed that 'the longing for something indispensable, for a *sine qua non*, is part of the long history of being misguided not only about literary studies but about literature itself'. I do not myself see that a longing for something indispensable is *per se* misguided; though I concede the dangers and would accept that most attempts to embody the 'longing' create metaphysical wraiths. Ruskin's 'intrinsic value' is, in and of itself, such a wraith; but, according to my argument, it remains a term which points in the right direction, towards semantic realizations that have some substance.

The question for Wordsworth is: how to confer 'moral existence' on those 'who, according to the classical morality', as Trilling reminds us, 'should have no moral life at all'. The answer is, again, that you work at it. There is language and there is character, of which intelligence is a part and what we call 'personality' a part; and each is subjected to a considerable range of contingent forces:

> There is a comfort in the strength of love;
> 'Twill make a thing endurable, which else
> Would break the heart:—Old Michael found it so.

To some extent the strength and endurance that the poem records are composed of elements which can equally bring about weakness and torpor. The gift which ensures the right reading subsists in the strength and endurance of the language, which itself contains elements that could easily be left to drift into a significantly different, Humean, acceptance of 'good sense, that directs men in the ordinary occurrences of life'. Since I do not believe that 'texts' write themselves, I am here considering a quality of Wordsworth's intelligence and personality. The particular qualities which he values in human nature correspond to language, 'a thing subject to endless fluctuations and arbitrary associations'. I do not propose that Wordsworth 'masters' the arbitrariness: that is something which Hobbes achieves in his own rich, enigmatic, and arbitrary style which shuts out most of what Wordsworth desires to include. Wordsworth, as in the three lines here quoted from 'Michael', feels intelligently through language, with its endless fluctuations and arbitrary associations in such a way that in recording how 'love . . . will make a thing endurable' he makes out of language an entity able to endure. I would conclude from this particular instance, not as a general rule, that language is love's correlate; and that Wordsworth is here translating ethos into activity, an exchange which had eluded Hume, though I suspect that he would claim this aspect of translation to be a quibble for which he did not choose to stoop aside. Endurance is one of the great words which lie directly on the active–passive divide, subject to the fluctuations and arbitrariness that Wordsworth cites; and it is here, on the line, that, through language, value is to be realized, provided that the writer can 'touch . . . his mark with a needle's point', 'strike his finger on the place'.

In the course of this discussion I several times employ the term 'pitch', which elsewhere I have distinguished from 'tone'. I was first drawn to consider its appositeness to these questions when reading, many years ago, Jon Stallworthy's observation that 'where words are concerned [Yeats] has almost perfect pitch'. In an uncollected essay I subsequently glossed Stallworthy's observation with a couple of sentences which may perhaps be usefully repeated here:

> A poet who possesses such near-perfect pitch is able to sound out his own conceptual discursive intelligence . . . [He] is hearing words in depth and is therefore hearing, or sounding, history and morality in depth.

Subsequently I added to this sense of pitch ideas drawn from Hopkins's spiritual writings, for example, 'Nothing else in nature comes near this unspeakable stress of pitch, distinctiveness, and selving, this selfbeing of my own.' Hopkins's editor enters the caveat that Hopkins 'does not distinguish sufficiently between his "*pitch*" (which seems to be Scotus's *gradus*) and Scotus's *haecceitas* [this-ness]'. Technically speaking (which, as I follow through the argument, is simultaneously ethically speaking) two matters principally concern me in my own study of Hopkins's writings: (1) how he achieves the 'this' (the finished poem) which can properly be said to be the correlative of his 'this-ness' of self-being; (2) how he understands and resolves the technical paradox implied by his use of the colloquial 'unspeakable'; it is evident that his poems do 'speak' the 'unspeakable' at a pitch that simultaneously represents intense formality and idiomatic immediacy.

One other word has more recently become of particular significance to me as indicating that instantaneous realization of the correlative within the contingent, a realization which is the 'something indispensable', the '*sine qua non*', of working justly in words; of working justice into and through and out of language. The word first struck me (that I think is the entirely apposite verb) when, a couple of years ago, I was rereading Burke's *Reflections on the Revolution in France*: 'A politician, to do great things, looks for a *power*, what our workmen call a *purchase*'. The statement is itself an epitome of the close contraries within a seemingly uncomplicated utterance. Despite the *Oxford English Dictionary*'s entry which gives this as the earliest recorded use of sense III.15 *fig.* ('A "hold", "fulcrum", or position of advantage for accomplishing something; a means by which one's own power or influence is increased') I do not recognize a parity between, on the one hand, 'politician' / '*power*' and, on the other, 'workmen' / '*purchase*'. Burke has effected a takeover of the workman's term and the *OED* regularizes the coup. 'Politician' / '*power*' is expansive; 'workmen' / '*purchase*' contracts in to the particular and the contractual. The viciousness of Burke goes with the expansive; the good in him speaks through the contractual.

Hobbes, in *Leviathan* (1651), provides the *OED*'s earliest citation for the use of purchase, sense I.7 *fig.* ('Acquisition at the cost of something immaterial, as effort, suffering, or sacrifice'): 'Our Senses and Experience . . . are the Talents . . . to be . . . employed in the purchase of Justice, Peace, and true Religion'. In the work of words, the immaterial (senses, experience, talents) must take a purchase on the material, i.e. language-as-medium. In theory and principle this is a factor that Ruskin effectively comprehends. I have in mind not only 'Everything costs its own Cost, and one of our best virtues is a just desire to pay it' but also several of his observations on the art of Turner. It was one of these that Hopkins—among the greatest English workers of purchase—took purchase on. Ruskin had praised an apparent incongruity in Turner's 'Pass of Faido', the insertion of a distant coach-and-horses in an otherwise empty landscape of majestic desolation. Ruskin dismissed the objection of Taste and Sensibility—that the intrusion of the quotidian and commonplace destroyed the sense of the Sublime—with a sublime practicality of his own: 'The dream insisted particularly on the great fact of its having come by the road'. That is to say that the *value* of the 'dream' is authenticated, validated, by the recognition of the difficulty with which purchase is obtained: you work at it, work it through. Hopkins's recognition of the particular quality, the quality of the particular, not only in Turner's purchase on significant detail but also in Ruskin's purchase on the method by which Turner separates true from false vision, enables him to grasp and articulate one of his own most searching realizations of instress: 'Not imposed outwards from the mind as for instance by melancholy or strong feeling':

> I see
> The lost are like this, and their scourge to be
> As I am mine, their sweating selves; but worse.

Here, the entire personal and doctrinal issue—the matter at debate is that of the proximity to damnation—requires a syntactical membrane as thin as the semi-colon that separates the two final words 'but worse' from the preceding phrases. The speaker of the poem cries out from the midst of a purgatorial desolation so intense that it is hellish; but finally it is not hell. I know that the damned suffer, the speaker declares; but I know also that I am not damned. It is, in a sense, a doctrinal formality, a matter of status; there is a touch of forensic dryness in the placing of that semi-colon; a dryness which is as significant as the extremity of suffering. The semi-colon, here, is at once recognition, fact, and value.

To preclude a final misunderstanding which could vitiate, retroactively, the entire course of my argument, I will say here that the issues of language and value under discussion in this chapter are not to be mistaken for that *ignis fatuus* known to the philosophers as 'value-rich vocabulary'.

23

Language, Suffering, and Silence

Questions of silence are essentially questions of value. In Europe between 1939 and 1945 the value of silence was twenty-four hours: the estimated maximum period that a person could be expected to endure Gestapo interrogation before breaking down and giving away names and secrets. In sixteenth-century England the value of silence, in legal terms, was equal to the value of a particular patrimony. If arraigned for treason or felony a man of property could, by refusing to plead, ensure the non-forfeiture of his estate. The price he paid was condemnation to the slow process of execution known as *peine forte et dure*.

In 1586, Margaret Clitheroe, a Catholic laywoman, was put to death by *peine forte et dure*. Her crime was to have sheltered recusant priests and to have had Mass celebrated in her house. She chose not to plead so that, it has been suggested, her children and household servants would not be called to give evidence; or in order, as has also been suggested, 'to save the jury from convicting her against their consciences.'

During this period the Jesuit Robert Southwell 'remain[ed] as dumb as a tree-stump' under interrogation by torture; and the seminary-priest John Ingram was called a 'monster' of 'strange taciturny' by his baffled inquisitor.

It is open to conjecture that the word 'taciturny'—and the frame of mind or spirit to which it is attached in these closely-related instances—was a recusant usage deriving from accounts or recollections of the arraignment of Thomas More in 1535. His defence was that 'for this my taciturnitie and silence [on the matter and question of the imposed Oath of Supremacy] neyther your lawe nor any lawe in the world is able iustly and rightly to punishe me'. A further conjecture is that More's sense of the word may have derived from its use in the anonymous mid-fifteenth-century English translation of the *Imitatio Christi*. In the chapter headed '*Ayenis veyne iugementes of menne*', St Paul is described as having suffered slanders for the most part 'with pacience and mekenesse', though on occasion he spoke out 'leste by his taciturnite occasion of offendinge myght haue been yiuen to the feble in feithe'. The *Oxford English Dictionary* (*OED*) cites this as the earliest recorded use of the word. The editor of the recent Early English Text Society edition of this translation suggests, no doubt correctly, that the author of the *Imitatio* has here in mind 'Paul's defence of himself before Agrippa in Acts 26'.

Taciturnity in these citations does not have an absolute value, any more than suffering itself has or any more than the words 'absolute value' have. R. W. Chambers, in his biography of More, writes of the martyr's 'great plea for the liberty of silence'. Chambers modulates that air of expansiveness inseparable from the hallowed commonplace 'freedom of speech', words which, for citizens of democracies, lie somewhat lightly upon the tongue. When More at his trial turned witheringly upon Richard Rich for his damning act of perjury—though of course the man was not *seen* to wither—he marked him as one long 'esteemed very light of your tonge, a common lyer, a great dycer, and of no commendable fame'. For More's generation and its immediate successors, questions of taciturnity versus loquacity were themselves more tight-lipped than R. W. Chambers's 'great plea' is able to suggest. 'Great plea' belongs in the same ideal category of conventional eloquence as 'Man's Unconquerable Mind,' the title which Chambers chose for another of his books from Wordsworth's sonnet to Toussaint L'Ouverture.

The *Imitatio Christi*, glossing Acts 26, shows that taciturnity, as much as speech, must be used with a sense of moderation. Otherwise it belongs with the passions. Two sermons by John Donne bear particularly on this point. 'Christ did not absolutely forbid teares, but regulate and order their teares, that they might weepe in the right place' and again:

> So whosoever thou be, that canst not readily pray, at least pray, that thou mayst pray. For, as in bodily, so in spirituall diseases, it is a desperate state, to be speechlesse.

If we weep, it is to be in the right place; when we speak we are to speak advisedly; our taciturnity, or silence, must be able to moderate itself. Weigh More's 'esteemed very light of your tonge' against 'it is a desperate state, to be speechlesse'. Both are true.

We would be advised to weigh Paul's words to Agrippa, and the *Imitatio*'s gloss on Paul, against their kenotic paradigm—Christ before the High Priest ('But Iesus held his Peace', Matthew 26: 63), before the chief priests and elders ('he answered nothing', Matthew 27: 12), and before Pilate ('And he answered him to neuer a word', Matthew 27: 14).

The unknown poets and musicians who composed the African-American spiritual 'They crucified my Lord ... An' he never said a mumbalin' word', appear to have conflated the several silences of Christ's Passion and, further, to have shifted the theological centre of gravity. In St Matthew's Gospel, chapters 26 and 27, the setting is discourse, even though Jesus 'held his peace'. In the words of the spiritual, discourse has been overwhelmed by projection and identification. 'He never said a mumbalin' word' can be taken to mean 'He uttered no word *of complaint*'. In concert arrangement, for solo voice with piano accompaniment, as sung by Marian Anderson or Roland Hayes, the repeated 'Not a word, not a word' introduces an ambiguity. The musical and grammatical cadence sounds as if it is saying 'He uttered no word *at all*'. To what extent, if to any extent, the original poet-musicians *willed* an ambiguity cannot be established with final certainty.

Christa K. Dixon in her gloss on the spiritual observes that 'Jesus not only refused to speak in his own defense; he didn't even mumble a subdued curse: "An' he never said a mumbalin' word" '. She continues, 'Jesus' silence at his trial so impressed the slaves—who themselves had to be silent in the face of trials and executions—that it was transposed into a major theological statement'. In the assessment of Arthur C. Jones, 'The story, strictly taken, is altered, of course; Jesus is reported in the Bible to have uttered at least a few words ... In this particular case, the most important symbolism is embodied in *Jesus the stoic*, paralleling the ability of African people to endure stoically the physical and emotional agony of slavery ... Although they could not control the outward circumstances of their abuse, they could control ... the extent to which they acknowledged their pain. To be silent was one powerful form of resistance'. To James H. Cone, this refrain 'An' he never said a mumbalin' word', a refrain which recurs in various of these songs, conveys the meaning that 'black folks ... were impressed by the Passion because they too had been rejected, beaten, and shot without a chance to say a word in defense of their humanity'.

These three descriptions—of the grammar or the rhetoric of this one crucial phrase—are asymmetrically related, even though they are not directly and mutually opposed. Jesus the *stoic* is a thought to conjure with. It is entirely appropriate that this should be so. It is a phrase, a cadence, which intersects with direct meanings obliquely, yet cogently, in a way that is characteristic of significant poetic statement. It means *both* 'He never uttered a word of complaint' *and* 'He uttered no word at all'.

Even doctrinal poetry is finally made meaningful, is finally made to be understood, by something other than the doctrine. That at least is my understanding of the matter. That 'something other' is a gift of *technē*, which itself becomes something other in the process of making the gift. When Wittgenstein in the *Tractatus* says that 'the silent adjustments to understand colloquial language are enormously complicated', he is neither more nor less essential to my meaning than is the response of an anonymous slave when asked 'where black people got their songs':

> I'll tell you; it's dis way. My master call me up and order me a short peck of corn and a hundred lash. My friends see it and is sorry for me. When dey come to de praise meetin' dat night dey sing about it. Some's very good singers and know how; and dey work it in, work it in, you know; till dey get it right; and dat's de way.

This is how 'it' is done when 'it' is done right, by some (who are very good singers): 'and dey work it in, work it in, you know'. 'It' is the subject, the matter to be added, and 'it' is the imagination's kneading process, the theme identifying itself with and in the language; the language identifying itself with and in the theme.

There is a particular concentration of the burden of the 'Kenotic Hymn' preserved in some verses of the second chapter of Paul's Letter to the Philippians, '[Christ] made himselfe of no reputation, and tooke vpon him the forme of a seruant, and was made in the likenesse of men'. In the Greek, the word which the King James translators render as 'of a seruant,' is δούλου, *of a slave*. In the light of the spiritual, the force in *of a slave* is piercing. 'He never said a mumbalin' word' is not simply silence; it is what a slave-owner or field overseer would call 'dumb insolence'.

But if the intrusion of 'never . . . a mumblin'' concentrates and resonates, it also diffuses. Donne, like Burton in *The Anatomy of Melancholy*, commands us to speak for our salvation: 'it is a desperate state, to be speechlesse'. But the slave-Christ of the spiritual, flogged and nailed, cannot speak. That is to say, he cannot in terms of 'working it in', be allowed to speak, so that the overwhelming force of the pathos—Christ as insulted and injured field-worker—shall not be deflected.

Christian religious language has, over the past three or four hundred years, moved between doctrine and sentiment, at best like a shuttle, at worst like the Bishop of Llandaff whom Wordsworth likened to a drunk man having 'business on both sides of the road'. In English, the reciprocal pull on the thread of doctrine with sentiment has never been more finely and more consistently worked than by George Herbert. A little over seventy years later than Herbert, in Isaac Watts's 'Preface' to his *Horae Lyricae* of 1709, there is a marked change of emphasis: 'The wonders of our religion, in a plain narration, and a simple dress, have a native grandeur, a dignity and a beauty in them, though they do not utterly disdain all methods of ornament'.

The first collectors and editors of the 'Cabin and Plantation Songs', as spirituals were first called, Thomas P. Fenner (1874), Helen W. Ludlow (1891), R. Nathaniel Dett (1926), write as heirs of Watts who have found, among the freed slaves, evidence that Watts's trope—'The wonders of our religion, in a plain narration, and a simple dress, have a native grandeur, a dignity and a beauty in them'—is a matter of social fact throughout the Cotton Belt. 'Native grandeur'—as Keats said of Adam's Dream, they 'awoke and found it truth'.

It may not be possible to say precisely when, or how, the sense of 'silence' as a forensic equivocation—a position that is neither assent nor refusal of assent, a strategy for assuring personal salvation, even though it cannot save one's life (More, Clitheroe, Southwell)—became the silence of human potentiality: by the time of Wordsworth's *Prelude* (1805 edn., Book 12, ll. 266–72) it is already presented with authority:

> men for contemplation framed,
> Shy, and unpractis'd in the strife of phrase,
> Meek men, whose very souls perhaps would sink
> Beneath them, summon'd to such intercourse:
> Theirs is the language of the heavens, the power,
> The thought, the image, and the silent joy;
> Words are but under-agents in their souls.

These are a type of contemplative found, as Wordsworth emphasizes, 'among the walks of homely life': there is an implication that 'silent joy' is sacrally dependent upon the public inarticulacy and disregardedness. Clearly, if in the 1939–45 *Résistance* silence had a value, estimated but practically accurate, and if, in 1535 or 1586, silence conferred a legal benefit matched by an exact and terrible legal penalty, it seems equally clear that the value of silence in 'silent joy' is beyond computation, as it is in Nathaniel T. Dett's description of the singing of a small group of old black women at a 'backwoods "afterservice" ':

> looking into the faces of the singers, I was struck by evidences of spiritual elevation, and I realized that in some mysterious way these unlettered people, by a common consent, were mutually enjoying a communion with eternal forces by a method of evocation beyond the reach of the uninitiated.

The public resonance and availability of ethical poetics, from Words-worth to Wilfred Owen, requires that the value *shall*, in terms of strict computation, be beyond measure. Consider the sense of dedication with which Owen on sick-leave in England declares, on 31 December 1917, that in order to describe the suffering of the common soldiers he 'must go back and be with them' or, having returned to the Front, writes:

> I came out to help these boys—directly by leading them as well as an officer can; indirectly, by watching their sufferings that I may speak of them as well as a pleader can. I have done the first.

The disarming confession of limitation (in the final clause—'I have done the first') is offset by the imbalance of the premise. Owen's sense of his own value as 'pleader' for the inarticulate common soldier presupposes his unawareness or inability to comprehend that at least three of the finest British poets of that war, Isaac Rosenberg, Ivor Gurney, and David Jones, had gone, or were still going, as 'common soldiers' through all that he describes—none of them rose above the rank of private.

As the velocity of regression has increased since 1933, the language of silence (such oxymorons are unavoidable and, when insisted on, cultic) has shifted yet again. The silence of the Shoah is the silence of total obliteration, the eradication of history, nothingness. The Iraqi writer in exile, Kanan Makiya, affirms in the final section of his book *Cruelty and Silence* that to the inevitable question 'Who do you write for?' the only answer he can come up with is 'I write for myself, like everyone else'—a 'confusing answer', as he concedes. Makiya's 'I write for myself' is so close to the kind of tag we have come to expect of the American or British product of creative writing courses that one must insist here on its major unlikeness. A Jew of the Shoah, an Iraqi opponent of Saddam Hussein, must elect to write and to speak on the same plane at which Thomas More and Margaret Clitheroe elected to be silent. This may be the source of Makiya's 'confus[ion]': that the utterance of a covenant against degradation is grammatically indistinguishable from the braggart 'creativity' of the un-creative. It is a desperate state to be speechless, but as was observed at the beginning of the chapter, 'questions of silence are essentially questions of value'.

We are hereby committed to the critical view that shades of distinction—in sensibility, imagination, and ethical position—can be semantically 'placed' and assessed. Further, it may be possible to comprehend an ethical distinction grammatically, as when we place a brief observation by William Tyndale (*c.*1477–1536) alongside one by Ezra Pound (1885–1972). Tyndale: 'Though we be sinners, yet is the cause right'; Pound: 'To confess wrong without losing rightness'. Tyndale's grammar conforms to the model noted by the *OED*: '*Though*, sense II.i a [*conjunction* or *conjunctive adverb*]: Introducing a subordinate clause expressing a fact: Notwithstanding that; in spite of the fact that, although'. It adds that *Though* in this usage formerly took the subjunctive 'where the indicative is now used'. And we see that Tyndale's verb is indeed in the subjunctive ('Though we be sinners'). What is remarkable in the syntax of these nine plain words is the capacity to present a crux of Lutheran soteriology in simple idiomatic English. By 'crux' is meant the reformer's—indeed the Reformation's—emphasis on *cor corvum in se ipsum*, the heart bent inwards upon itself, a trope perhaps derived from Augustine's *detortae in infima voluntatis*. Tyndale's introductory subordinate clause stoops to confess the fact of our innate sinfulness, a turn which, introducing the direct affirmation of faith, is immediately rectified by it. The words are scrupulous but avoid scrupulosity. By contrast, the Pound—'To confess wrong without losing rightness'—is grammatically self-serving and metrically glib. It sounds superficially right, but it is not right; it is like a travesty of a profound spiritual recognition, *semper peccator, semper penitens, semper justus*.

And yet Tyndale himself had recently slipped on this very place—'Thus we are synners and no synners'—and More, in the second part of *The Confutacyon of Tyndale's Answer* (early 1533) mocked his spiritual impertinence. There may just have been time between the publication of More's gibe and the writing of Tyndale's second letter to Frith (late spring 1533) for the rebuke to have been taken to heart. Whether Tyndale's 'Though we be sinners, yet is the cause right' represents a conscious act of self-correction is a matter that cannot now be confirmed.

I can at least reconfirm my own conviction that the 'terrible aboriginal calamity' in the contexture of human life constantly implicates, and is implicated by, the textures of our uttered thought, though it is no less a force in the presence of the unuttered and the unutterable.

If the historical contextures are attended to, our search for an absolute standard of value takes on a complexion of relativity. I find this difficult to admit as a Christian; but it is by no means the only difficulty which, as a Christian, I find myself confronting. The contemporary pseudo-dogma which maintains that the degree of suffering experienced by persons of an artistic or a literary bent shall constitute an accurate register of the quality of their work is one which requires close scrutiny. This particular gnosis is especially vulnerable to the test of historical relevance. There is no genuine parity between, say, Wordsworth's sense, in and around 1800, that he had an obligation to engage social injustice in such poems as 'The Female Vagrant' or 'Resolution and Independence' and Robert Lowell's compulsion to batten on the suffering of his wife and daughter for *Notebooks* and *The Dolphin* or Sylvia Plath's urge to fantasize a cruel psychopathology for her dead father.

Wordsworth's early readership was comparatively small and relatively homogeneous. He himself characterized it as having a comparable social status to his own, adding 'People in our rank in life are perpetually falling into one sad mistake, namely, that of supposing that human nature and the persons they associate with are one and the same thing'. As the early reviews of *Lyrical Ballads* (1798) made evident, such readers—or at any rate the tribunes of that reading public—did not wish their prejudices thus confronted by narrative and metaphor detailing the innate worthiness, and inequitable burdens, of exemplary characters drawn from the English rural poor. Wordsworth suffered, in a not too drastic way, for his temerity and effrontery: the small first edition of *Lyrical Ballads* was effectively ostracized by reviewers and readers, and the poet's reputation was established with difficulty against heavy opposition. There is no true comparison between the English aristocratic and upper middle class culture of 1798 which was, with some notable exceptions, angrily unprepared for Wordsworth's early style, and the pluralistic, pseudo-egalitarian global commodity culture two hundred years later. When a publisher, or a publicity person announces, in the late 1990s that a new volume of poems 'expresses solidarity with the poor and the oppressed' what is being offered, essentially, is 'more of the same'. 'Suffering', within this wide contemporary literary perimeter, is the equivalent of minor Elizabethan pastoral or eighteenth-century poetic diction.

Those who find such a conclusion inimical to their preferences have tried, and will try again, to associate it with politico-philosophical positions which are in fact inimical to me also. Consider four literary statements on art in relation to suffering. In 1853, in the 'Preface' to the first edition of his *Poems*, Matthew Arnold explained why he had decided to exclude from that collection one of his major works, the lyrical drama *Empedocles on Etna*. He had come to realize, he wrote, that the work dealt with a species of human situation 'in which the suffering finds no vent in action . . . in which there is everything to be endured, nothing to be done'. Though this might accurately represent a significant aspect of the human condition, it was not 'a representation from which men can derive enjoyment'. In 1936 W. B. Yeats, in his editorial introduction to *The Oxford Book of Modern Verse: 1892–1935*, defended his decision to exclude from the anthology, with relatively minor exceptions, the poets of the First World War: 'I have rejected these poems for the same reason that made Arnold withdraw his *Empedocles on Etna* from circulation; passive suffering is not a theme for poetry'. In 1940 W. H. Auden's new volume of poems, *Another Time*, included 'Musée des Beaux Arts' ('About suffering they were never wrong, | The Old Masters') and 'In Memory of W. B. Yeats', with its claim that although 'poetry makes nothing happen', it is nonetheless 'A way of happening, a mouth'. In 1953 there appeared the first English edition of a book by a Polish author at that time little known in Western Europe or the USA: this was *The Captive Mind* by Czesław Miłosz. In his second chapter, Miłosz presents this parable for our instruction:

> The work of human thought *should* withstand the test of brutal, naked reality. If it cannot, it is worthless. Probably only those things are worth while which can preserve their validity in the eyes of a man threatened with instant death.
>
> A man is lying under machine-gun fire on a street in an embattled city. He looks at the pavement and sees a very amusing sight: the cobblestones are standing upright like the quills of a porcupine. The bullets hitting against their edges displace and tilt them. Such moments in the consciousness of a man *judge* all poets and philosophers.

To the reasonable question 'what, in your judgement, is the common factor in all these quotations?' one could fairly respond: they are all aesthetic valuations. Given the climate of our culture in a number of respects, the word 'aesthetic' is more difficult to demonstrate in the Miłosz than in the quotations which precede it. Nonetheless, if the cant word 'elitist' can now be applied anywhere, it should be placed against this passage. Miłosz, in the opening sentence here quoted, purports to establish new terms of the utmost purity: the existential finality of things and moments; and with the apparent equity of 'work of human thought' he gestures towards the inclusive; a general redemption of the imagination through the witness of extreme experience, of survived extremity. What the quoted passage actually communicates is something different: the elitism of the man-of-the-moment. It excludes from aesthetic regeneration those works unbaptized by an arbitrary extreme experience of 'brutal, naked reality'. The kind of work Miłosz appears to have dismissively in mind is that of a typical 1930s Warsaw café intellectual, an inadequate base for a dogma as exclusive as Miłosz attempts here. It is possible that, if pressed, he would say that Shakespeare's sonnets or Emily Dickinson's poems can be recalled, recited *sotto voce*, by someone in extreme peril without losing their validity, but he doesn't actually say that. If he *had* said that, his own criterion would better withstand objection. Miłosz actually says that the work of 'all' poets and philosophers is to stand or fall, in terms of its relevance to 'human thought', and the crux of the matter is an experience, a few moments of extreme tension and heightened sense-perception. The criteria here draw eclectically from the curt mannerisms of Hemingway and from the Proustian '*moments privilégiés*'. There is at once something hectoring and self-congratulatory here; and I would contrast with it Sections 33–6 of 'Song of Myself', those verse-paragraphs of the shipwreck, the Alamo, the fight of the *Bonhomme Richard*, to consider how Whitman, far from excluding generality and commonality by the sharply particular, intensifies it by such means, making the extremity a revelation of human suffering and of an endurance both exceptional and to be expected of humankind in its great diversity of natures and capacities. Or contrast with Miłosz Wordsworth's broadly unthreatening use of 'naked' throughout his writings. It is as though Miłosz were coming forward, out of the dreadful sufferings of Warsaw in the years 1939–45, claiming to validate Arnold's dictum from a position aloof, superior, condescending, possibly threatening.

It is strange to see so much subsequent work tied either directly or indirectly to Arnold's critical misjudgement and self-misreading. There is no good reason to accept Arnold's premise, as Yeats of course does even while he struts and preens around it like a D'Annunzio in Irish tweeds. The true key-word in Arnold's self-sentencing is not 'action', as one initially takes it, and as—perhaps—the author intends it, but 'enjoyment'. What this is saying is that art cannot be tolerated if it does not issue in enjoyment. One can see, in the overall context of the 1853 'Preface', that

Arnold is being drawn into a false position by Schiller, whom he quotes: 'The right art is that alone, which creates the highest enjoyment'. Add, as you imagine yourself watching the machine-gun bullets striking the stones, 'and the highest enjoyment is the experience of the extreme' and you have the whole post-Nietzschean panorama suddenly before you, the cultic 'Theatre of Cruelty', the apotheosis of the Marquis de Sade.

There is a quality in Yeats's auditory faculty, auditory imagination, which saves his poetry, at its best, from the worst excesses of Nietzschean doctrinal sentiment. The closing lines of 'The Second Coming', when contrasted with the mystical affectation of that poem's source-ideas, are a case in point. Yeats's introduction to *The Oxford Book of Modern Verse* does not have the benefit of a strenuous mediating factor. Language under the kind of extreme pressure which the making of poetry requires, can, on occasion, push the maker beyond the barrier of his or her own limited intelligence. If I were to consider undertaking a theology of language, this would be one of a number of possible points of departure for such an exploration: the abrupt, unlooked-for semantic recognition understood as corresponding to an act of mercy or grace. As it stands, however, the Arnold–Yeats 'passive suffering is not a theme for poetry' is, in terms of the moral imagination, on a par with Pound's 'To confess wrong without losing rightness'.

It is perhaps a further mistake to try to answer the Poundian–Yeatsian apothegm with yet another, as Auden does in his elegy on the death of Yeats:

> For poetry makes nothing happen: it survives
> In the valley of its saying where executives
> Would never want to tamper.

This is clearly intended as a rebuke of sorts to the old maestro's 'passive suffering is not a theme for poetry'. Even so, it only partially solves the futile conundrum set by Arnold's confusion of the semantics of 'action'. For Arnold, 'action' is confusedly both the topos which a poet 'selects' for the particular poem and also the activity of the world, a sphere of contingency into which the unsuccessful work of art fails, in some indeterminate way, to 'vent' itself. The implied correlative to this, though Arnold does not quite say so, would be that the successful work does effect the existential leap from topos to commitment. Auden shifts the emphasis slightly: 'it survives | In the valley of its saying' intends a riposte to, not a paraphrase of, the opinion that understands 'poetry makes nothing happen' as a confession of incapacity, rather than as a tribute to its intrinsic value. But the addition of 'where

executives | Would never want to tamper' is an error. It trivializes not only
the activities of the world of commerce and commodity, which is a power
to be reckoned with even in its phases of aberrant weakness, but also the
various ways in which the overreachings and shortcomings of business
values might be met in justice. Auden's 'valley of...saying' is just over
the hill from the one in which Tennyson sets his brook to 'bicker' its way.
Auden perhaps meant to say that the achieved work of art is its own
sufficient act of witness. If that is what he meant, I agree with him, but
I think there are more competent ways of putting it.

I would seriously propose a theology of language; and a primary exercise
to be undertaken towards its establishment. This would comprise a critical
examination of the grounds for claiming (a) that the shock of semantic
recognition must be also a shock of ethical recognition; and that this is the
action of grace in one of its minor, but far from trivial, types; (b) that the art
and literature of the late twentieth century require a memorializing, a
memorizing, of the dead as much as, or even more than, expressions of
'solidarity with the poor and the oppressed'. Suffering is real, but 'suffering'
is a sing-song, that is to say, cant. If a poet or painter were to inquire of such
a theology how, in this case, 'solidarity' could still be shown, the answer
which I should hope to hear would be 'give alms'. This response to that
particular inquiry does not originate with me but with the Catholic priest
who was also a poet, Fr Gerard Hopkins of the Society of Jesus. It can be
found in two successive letters, of 19 and 29 January 1879, to his great friend
Robert Bridges, physician and poet. Having, somewhat indirectly, recommended his friend—a nominal Church of England man—to try prayer,
Hopkins adds:

> I have another counsel open to no objection and yet I think it will be
> unexpected. I lay great stress on it. It is to give alms...that is, for instance,
> you might know of someone needing and deserving an alms to give which
> would require you in prudence to buy no books till next quarter day or to
> make some equivalent sacrifice of time.

One sees how Hopkins brings the point home to the place where this
particular recipient, a book-lover, will be galled: give till it hurts, and in
your special case this may involve the sacrifice of your treasured monthly
book-allowance.

These are matters which, rightly, affect the minutiae of one's own critical
and descriptive vocabulary. Why, for instance, did I feel constrained to use

the awkward periphrasis 'Catholic priest who was also a poet' rather than the succinct 'priest and poet' or even 'priest-poet'? It is because such forms imply a parity between the two vocations; a parity that Hopkins steadily refused to his own poetic gifts, gifts which he must have recognized as being outstanding. Except when directed by his superiors to provide celebratory offerings for a Church festival, as he occasionally was, Hopkins believed himself barely entitled, if entitled at all, to withdraw his attention from his duty to the work of Christ in the world in order that it might be bestowed on the lesser practice of literary composition. He repeatedly stressed the value of humble unlettered faithfulness: 'The moral of this is, brethren, that God's work is first to be done, then ours'. And again:

> To lift up the hands in prayer gives God glory, but a man with a dungfork in his hand, a woman with a sloppail, give him glory too. He is so great that all things give him glory if you mean they should. So then, my brethren, live.

Hopkins, with Victorian aesthetics at his fingertips, sometime pupil of Walter Pater, leans away from the aesthetic equation, takes the weight of the more awkward stresses of a world which, in justice, contains aesthetics as a good, but is not to be either ruled or saved by them.

24

Tacit Pledges

It is no mere extravagance when a poet talks of a nation's soul. It is the
objective mind which is subjective and self-conscious in its citizens: it feels
and knows itself in the heart of each.

If this chapter honours the work of Housman—and I hope that it does—it
does so obliquely and in accordance with the terms of its epigraph which
is taken, not from Housman, but from F. H. Bradley. Our main concern
here is with matters of style: with particulars of syntax, rhythm, and cadence,
and with the problems of pitch. Considered in its negative aspect, a writer's
style is what he or she is left with after the various contingent forces of
attrition have taken their toll. Considered more positively, style marks the
success an author may have in forging a personal utterance between the
hammer of self-being and the anvil of those impersonal forces that a given
time possesses. Hammer and anvil together distort as well as shape. None
of this, I agree, bears much resemblance to Housman's own description of
making, as given in the 1933 Leslie Stephen Lecture, *The Name and Nature of
Poetry*. It does bear some resemblance, however, to isolated observations
found variously in Housman's correspondence and scholarly and critical
writings: 'What Balfour did in his premiership was to prevent Chamberlain
from quite ruining the party. Outside Parliament, Chamberlain was much
the stronger of the two'; 'Class is a real thing: we may wish that it were not,
and we may pretend that it is not, but I find that it is'; 'we . . . usually fit our
judgments not to the truth of things nor even to our own impressions of
things, true or false, but to the standard of convention'; 'the amount of sub-
conscious dishonesty which pervades the textual criticism of the Greek and
Latin classics is little suspected except by those who have had occasion to
analyse it'; 'There is something novel to me not only in Mr. Stone's dealings

with his native tongue but in his attitude towards his customers: it opens a vista of new relations between the producers and consumers of commodities'.

So to isolate these observations may be to render Housman's mind and art a disservice by seeming to imply that something finally fails to cohere. In fact his remarks on contingency and circumstance are altogether firm and coherent although they do not exactly cohere with his poetry. The absence of correlative which we sense in other poets of those years is at least in part the legacy of John Stuart Mill—the aplomb of this logician's conclusion that, whereas 'eloquence is *heard*, poetry is *over*heard.' Mill's disservice to the critical imagination, as to the civic imagination, is in no way rectified by his persistent harping on the therapeutic value of poetry's presentation of the emotions. He marginalizes authenticity of feeling as he pushes away the critical element of the imagination; these qualities are given over, in Mill's commonweal, to the licensed eccentricities that in some unspecified way check and balance the potential tyranny of the democratic majority.

One may be able to suggest the pervasiveness of the difficulty, as well as Housman's significant but limited success in negotiating it, by a comparison with a much younger poet, Charles Sorley (1895–1915), who admired Housman despite the 'somewhat self-satisfied dislike of life' betrayed by *A Shropshire Lad* and who recognized as the particular strength of Hardy's *Jude the Obscure* that 'it was [Jude's] conscientiousness that did for him'. On 28 April 1915, already in the army and writing home to his mother, Sorley took note of the public eulogies for Rupert Brooke who had died five days previously en route to Gallipoli: 'He is far too obsessed with his own sacrifice, regarding the going to war of himself (and others) as a highly intense, remarkable and sacrificial exploit, whereas it is merely the conduct demanded of him (and others) by the turn of circumstances, where non-compliance with this demand would have made life intolerable'. Less than six months after writing this, Sorley too was dead, killed at Loos.

When Housman declared, in his autobiographical résumé of 1933, that 'the Great War cannot have made much change in \the/ opinions of any man of imagination', he spoke within his rights as a man of imagination whose opinions had not changed, though 'any' is open to challenge. I see in this no grounds for radical indignation but I do claim it as admissible evidence in a debate which draws in public and private forces and restraints.

Housman's sister, Katharine E. Symons, recalled in her memorial tribute to him that he had enclosed a copy of his poem 'Illic Jacet', originally published in 1900, with a letter of condolence in 1915 'when one of my sons was killed in Flanders'. These nine words are set as though by a spirit level; what they both gauge and embody is a ground of assent, publicly sustained and privately contained, to what Sorley called 'conduct demanded', to that which F. H. Bradley named 'the universal maintaining medium'. Clement Symons was not the first member of the family to die in battle. George Herbert Housman, beloved youngest brother of Katharine and Alfred, had been killed in October 1901 while serving with the rank of sergeant in the King's Royal Rifles, a casualty of the latter stages of the Boer War. Certain of Housman's poems are, in a proper sense, the aftermath of that bitter loss: 'The Olive', published in 1902 'on the conclusion of the peace' with the Boers, 'Astronomy', published in 1904, and—presumably—'Farewell to a name and a number', unpublished prior to the posthumous *More Poems* of 1936. They have a pitch of utterance which sets them apart from the idealized elegiac militarisms of *A Shropshire Lad*. There is nothing else in Housman that is quite comparable to the precisely held, stark, and simple complexity (anger, grief, pride, love, disillusionment) in the second quatrain of 'Farewell to a name and a number'; this is the closest Housman gets to Sorley's 'it was his conscientiousness that did for him':

> So ceases and turns to the thing
> He was born to be
> A soldier cheap to the King
> And dear to me.

To say that this quatrain achieves a verbal edge unique in Housman's poetry is to contend against a range of particular felicities which have been noted many times: 'And trains all night groan on the rail', 'Where I lodge a little while', 'The lover of the grave', 'the strengthless dead', 'the coloured counties', 'the truceless armies', 'Sleepy with the flow of streams', 'The moon stands blank above', 'cloud-led shadows', 'The felon-quarried stone', 'All desired and timely things', 'The pine lets fall its cone', 'The upshot beam would fade', 'lying about the world', 'silent hills indenting | The orange band of eve', 'When the bells justle in the tower'. The quality of such phrases arises from three forms of sensuous apprehension: first the capacity to present the particular in such a way that it appears to rise spontaneously from direct observation: 'And trains all night groan on the rail', 'cloud-led shadows', 'The upshot beam would fade'; secondly the ability to choose what Yeats called 'the intellectually surprising word which is also the correct word': 'When the bells justle in the tower'. The two qualities are interrelated: 'The upshot beam' is at once topographically accurate and accurate by Yeats's criterion of the sensuous intellect. A third form of apprehension arises from a logopoeic form of grammar and syntax—'The lover of the grave, the lover | That hanged himself for love', 'in the fields where cuckoo-flowers | Are lying about the world'. You could say that, contrasted to the finesse of these instances, there is a touch of the obvious in 'A soldier cheap to the King | And dear to me'. In order to touch the quick of the obvious in just this way, however, Housman's imagination had to retort upon deeply established characteristics of civic and spiritual patrimony, the essence and substance of Midlands Tory patriotism, such as he had acquired from his own family and its surroundings and which he never deserted: the tacit pledges made, from time to time, ceremonious and vocal, such as Bromsgrove's celebrations of Queen Victoria's Golden and Diamond Jubilees in 1887 and 1897, recorded in the columns of *The Bromsgrove Weekly Messenger* and by such local historians as Alfred Palmer. To reduce joyous expenditure ('the town was tastefully decorated, and the display of flags and buntings was almost universal') to an actual reckoning, and to bring it down to the level of such blunt speaking as 'cheap to the King | And dear to me' is to go against the *mores* which display their premises in 'tastefully decorated' and which find their proper eloquence in Katharine Symons's exemplary reticence. That such bluntness was not made public until 1936 is as significant as its having been uttered in the first place. By the time the posthumous *More Poems* appeared, several more turns of circumstance had occurred, ensuring that the odd, brusque pertinence of 'cheap to the King' (Victoria having died in January 1901, nine months before Sergeant Housman fell at Bakenlaagte) is perforce returned to the marginal private domain from which it can scarcely be said to have emerged. Would one be justified in saying that, in Housman's poetry, tacit pledges frequently become taciturn?

The term 'tacit pledges' is taken from Henry James's novel *The Tragic Muse* (1890), where it is observed of the elderly English *haut bourgeois*, Charles Carteret, that in his presence the much younger man Nick Dormer 'found himself immersed in an atmosphere of tacit pledges which constituted the very medium of intercourse and yet made him draw his breath a little in pain when, for a moment, he measured them'. So much alertness of intelligence and sensibility, so much that strikes one as somehow *distrait*, in the writing of the period, has to do with the conduct of life in such an atmosphere, such an 'intercourse', the consideration of which moves us, as it moved them, to a style in which measure can be, if only momentarily, affirmed. One way of describing Housman's particular grammar of lyric poetry would be to say that it attempts what James's syntax attempts in that sentence from *The Tragic Muse*: it seeks primarily to 'measure' and what it seeks to measure are the 'tacit pledges' and the 'pain'; and it seeks to do so with a measure of decorum. There is an additional force of irony in that the 'tacit' must further contain, for Housman as for James, the presence of that which 'dare not speak its name' and the pain of accommodating the forbidden within lives which, even without that element, had given and were to continue to give emotional and moral hostages to fortune. When, soon after Wilde's release from Reading Gaol, Housman sent him a copy of *A Shropshire Lad*, that too was a tacit pledge.

'Because I liked you better | Than suits a man to say'—Housman's restrained and strained characteristic as a poet is epitomized, in its negative aspect, by these 'stiff and dry' verses from *More Poems*. 'We parted, stiff and dry'—the pitch of the grammar is faithful to the hurt of the occasion; the words are formal and frank, though one cannot use the latter word without recognizing the myriad social prescriptions and proscriptions, the botched diplomacies, which have, over many decades, required its special tone of euphemism. If I call *More Poems* XXXI 'frank' I mean that it says about as much as it refrains from saying and that it is so openly unrecognizant of its hostages to Freudian ribaldry.

'Freudian', possibly, one may find the reaction of the receiver who was called in when Grant Richards, Housman's publisher, went bankrupt. As Housman reported to his brother Laurence in 1929: 'The financial expert . . . thought that he would like to read *A Shropshire Lad*. He did, or as much as he could; then, in his own words, "I put it behind the fire. Filthiest book I ever read: all about rogering girls under hedges"'. Or one may find, in this extravagant response, if it took place as Housman describes it, a brutish but not incomprehensible denial, a disabling of the book's oblique formalities and mannered remote intimacies. The century-long chronicle of the varied fortunes of *A Shropshire Lad* is not without its *grotesqueries*, with Laurence, A. E. Housman's younger brother and literary executor, as guardian of the grotto. It was he who cut as 'unprintable' the financial expert's last four words and it was he who, late in life, with characteristic prurient frankness, observed that his brother, having invented in Terence Hearsay the 'fig-leaf of a fictitious character', was able to 'let himself go'. The ambivalence in 'let himself go' exemplifies the difficult relationship that can exist between a body of work, which is by common repute instantly accessible, and the prejudicate opinions and predilections of the reading public, a body which palpably exists, which can be measured in gross terms of royalty returns, which imposes, albeit passively, an undeniable power of sanction, but which is, even so, a non-entity. The salaciously judgemental 'let himself go'—tally ho, to his true disreputable nature, to vicarious unnatural debauch, along the fancied road to moral ruin—dissolves into 'letting go', that other tenuous sense of self-loss, at once dereliction and consolation, which is the benison we sparingly receive from the most muted of Housman's valedictory cadences:

> We'll to the woods no more,
> The laurels all are cut,
> The bowers are bare of bay
> That once the Muses wore;
> The year draws in the day
> And soon will evening shut:
> The laurels all are cut,
> We'll to the woods no more.
> Oh we'll no more, no more
> To the leafy woods away,
> To the high wild woods of laurel
> And the bowers of bay no more.

This lyric, the epigraph of *Last Poems* (1922), dedicates itself to letting go: letting go, by way of not going; by accepting, in the sense that metre and rhyme may imply acceptance even against the grammar of the thing, that some early promise of happiness and fulfilment has irretrievably gone. The word 'go' itself, which has its place in Housman's source, the French folk-song 'Nous n'irons plus au bois', is here tacit, eased out by the faintly archaic grammar of the first, eighth, and ninth lines. Housman, moreover, lets go, or partly lets go, in the pattern of monorhyme: lines 1, 8, 9, and 12 form a pattern unique in his verse. There is a full rhyme in lines 10 and 12 (*away / bay*) but it is half hidden, half heard.

The effect here is obliquely contrary to that which Housman, in *The Name and Nature of Poetry*, attributed to one of Blake's early lyrics, 'Memory, hither come' from *Poetical Sketches*: 'the stanza does but entangle the reader in a net of thoughtless delight'. As is the way with contraries, each is bound to the other by implication. Blake's lyric is not thoughtless: the thoughtlessness lies in Housman's complacent description. There is 'thought' in

A Shropshire Lad and in *Last Poems* but it is not taken through the turn of circumstances as even the most spontaneous of Blake's songs are.

And, in a sense, thoughtlessness is the desired consummation:

> When I shall lie below them,
> A dead man out of mind.

Or:

> For nature, heartless, witless nature,
>   Will neither care nor know
> What stranger's feet may find the meadow
>   And trespass there and go,
> Nor ask amid the dews of morning
>   If they are mine or no.

This is still the poetry of amusement, according to the sense in which Addison wrote in an early *Spectator*, that he had spent an afternoon 'amusing my self with the Tomb-stones and Inscriptions' in Westminster Abbey; and Housman's style could be found acceptable, after a brief acclimatization, by the more sceptical readers of that paper, as necessarily consequent upon the bold but tastefully sublime hypotheses of Addison's 'Ode':

> *What though, in solemn Silence, all*
> *Move round the dark terrestrial Ball?*
> *What tho' nor real Voice nor Sound*
> *Amidst their radiant Orbs be found?*
> *In Reason's Ear they all rejoice,*
> *And utter forth a glorious Voice,*
> *For ever singing, as they shine,*
> *'The hand that made us is divine'.*

It is as if Blake's genius leaps from Addison's final line to create, by law of contraries, 'The Tyger'; and it is equally as if the rational piety of the 'Ode' continues to run down, of its own inertia, for some considerable time, just over two hundred years, to issue in Housman's 'For nature, heartless, witless nature, | Will neither care nor know'. These words seem drawn from the tacit recesses of Addison's formal optimism, and the 'eternal shade', the 'peace and darkness', of the poem that Housman titled 'For My Funeral' (and which was sung at the collegiate service for him in 1936), mitigate the cosmic witlessness only by the resigned wit, the Cyrenaic casuistry, of its own final line: 'And wilt cast forth no more', 'more' rhyming with 'restore'.

For a period during the 1930s Ludwig Wittgenstein, then Fellow of
Trinity College, Cambridge, was near neighbour to Housman, a resident
Fellow of the same college; an anecdote recalls the occasion on which
Housman refused Wittgenstein's urgent request to use his lavatory. That
these two men should have enjoyed such testy proximity is like a charade
in which radical incompatibilities of intellect and sensibility—of intellects
which nonetheless divide between them some of the most illustrious tro-
phies of their century—are reduced to yet another clash of stereotypical
minor eccentricities. In claiming here a form of parity I have in mind
Housman's incontestable greatness as a classical scholar while admitting
that the particular nature of his achievement and fame as a poet cannot be
divorced from the body of his intellectual being or from the private and
public circumstances of his life, greatly though he desired that this should be
so. Housman and Wittgenstein, in common with F. H. Bradley, Bertrand
Russell, and T. S. Eliot, were drawn from several directions and in several
ways to consider the name and nature of solipsism. It would be appropriate
to say that there are as many definitions of solipsism as there are individuals
who wish to waste time over a self-inflicted task. Wittgenstein sets 'Idealists,
Solipsists and Realists' a-sparring 'as if they were stating facts recognized by
every reasonable human being'. The *OED* (*Oxford English Dictionary*, 2nd
edn., 1989) is succinct: 'The view or theory that the self is the only object of
real knowledge or the only thing really existent. Also, = EGOISM 1, and in
weakened sense'. In this context Housman presents the most marked,
because the most divided, example. In his capacity as a textual critic he
indicted bad scholarship as a form of aggressive or torpid egoism, editorial
'self-complacency' as he termed it; and he defined its moral antithesis in
clear practical terms: 'to read attentively, think correctly, omit no relevant
consideration, and repress self-will'. Taking a phrase from Arnold, he paid
his great predecessor Bentley this cogent tribute:

> *Lucida tela diei*: these are the words that come into one's mind when one has
> halted at some stubborn perplexity of reading or interpretation, has witnessed
> Scaliger and Gronouius and Huetius fumble at it one after another, and then
> turns to Bentley and sees Bentley strike his finger on the place and say *thou
> ailest here, and here.*

In *A Shropshire Lad*, *Last Poems*, and the posthumous *More Poems*, on
the other hand, his poetry is imbued with solipsism and seems passively
to reflect, rather than actively to reflect upon, the prevailing modes of

philosophical parlance. In 1893, three years before the publication of *A Shropshire Lad*, F. H. Bradley stated, in *Appearance and Reality*, that 'it is by the same kind of argument [i.e., that I arrive at other souls by means of other bodies, and the argument starts from the ground of my own body] that we reach our own past and future. And here Solipsism, in objecting to the existence of other selves, is unawares attempting to commit suicide'. In May 1895—which marked the end of 'the most prolific period' of Housman's lyric writing, a period of five months in which he had written 'twenty-five of the poems destined for his Terence Hearsay collection'—an article in the Jesuit periodical *The Month* referred to our being under spiritual penalty, 'under pain of "solipsism", of being shut up within our own subjectivity'. I do not suggest that when Housman was engaged upon the 'Hearsay' poems he had necessarily heard talk of this term, introduced, according to the *OED*, in 1874 by A. C. Fraser in his *Selections from Berkeley*, or of its cognate 'solipsistic' taken up by William James; I suggest merely that one can use the word without fear of anachronism. We have Housman's observation that, in matters of perception, 'Our bodies are much superior to our minds'. And when Sorley noted 'a remarkable feature of [Housman's] poetry—its earthiness'—he was perhaps finding in *A Shropshire Lad* something more akin to Bradley's 'I arrive at other souls by means of other bodies, and the argument starts from the ground of my own body' than to the verdict of the reader who found it 'the filthiest book' he had ever read.

My own application of the word 'body' would relate rather more to the body of the work than to that of the disappointed eponymist Terence Hearsay. While keeping somewhat closer to the Bradleian sense of 'suicide' than to that of Durkheim (1897), I would nonetheless argue that, even in the most objectively formal sense, Housman's theory of poetry, as advanced in the Leslie Stephen Lecture of 1933, could be considered as the summation of an attempt to commit suicide (in Bradley's sense, 'unawares'). Housman's poetic self objects to the existence of 'other selves'—for example, to the other self of Blake. To say of Blake's work that it 'answers to nothing real' is to project upon its significant body of meaning the tyranny of one's own ethical solipsism. I would add that, in the twenty-six years between the appearance of *A Shropshire Lad* and the publication of *Last Poems*, Housman's exquisite lyrical gift was balanced upon the possibility of Bradleian dissolution; that it survived, tenuously, was due in great part to his own form of *insouciance*. In this he seems the disinherited heir of Mill. If Bradley is correct in his critical description of Mill's philosophy, the relation to Housman is through 'philosophical' or 'practical' hedonism since this clearly is the light in which Housman desires his mind to be read. For Mill 'the one unpardonable sin in a versified composition, next to the absence of meaning, and of true meaning, is diffuseness' and, in that sense, Housman is an ideally compact poet. Equally for Mill 'Poetry is feeling, confessing itself to itself in moments of solitude, and embodying itself in symbols, which are the nearest possible representations of the feeling in the exact shape in which it exists in the poet's mind'. In that sense Housman is ideally confessional. But these qualities reduce themselves to a solipsism, an oxymoron enjoined by Mill's sentimental rationalism. The sardonic prose of Housman's *Manilius* prefaces is truly forensic: it is public capacity and accountability, in a significant aspect or sector, that are on trial in these essays and Housman's eloquence is aware that it will be heard. The verse, on the other hand, is to be 'overheard' and when, finally, badgered and driven to expatiate on the nature of 'this stuff'—as if it were ectoplasm or a nocturnal emission—he reacts with coy anger: 'I take no pride in it [*The Name and Nature of Poetry*]. I would rather forget it, and have my friends forget. I don't wish it to be associated with me'. His instinctive judgement, at the heart of this denial, is entirely correct. The situation of the poet, as one of the licensed eccentrics exalted and belittled by the inheritors of Mill's dicta, is ultimately futile—especially when the lyric talent is itself circumscribed by those perimeters of self-knowledge and cultural judgement. In this Housman is diametrically opposed by the poetry of Thomas Hardy, an obsessed and obsessive being who began at the age of fifty-eight, two years after the appearance of *A Shropshire Lad*, to publish those volumes of poetry which are great lyrical dramas of sexual—particularly marital—solipsism and suicidal introversion.

That quality which distinguishes Hardy's poetry from Housman's is technical rather than philosophical; or let us say that certain characteristics of 'depth'—as we might think of calling it—can be realized in terms of 'thought' only by the reach and grasp of technical perception and accomplishment. Take as our correlative an entry in Wittgenstein's *Notebooks 1914–1916* which became formulation 5.64 of the *Tractatus Logico-Philosophicus* of 1922, the year in which Housman brought out *Last Poems* and Eliot published *The Waste Land*:

> Here we see that solipsism strictly carried out [*streng durchgeführt*] coincides with pure realism.

> The I in solipsism shrinks to an extensionless point and there remains the
> reality co-ordinated with it.

The grammar of modernism in its closest matching of Wittgenstein's
statement appears as the semantic and syntactical catalepsis of the last
poems of Paul Celan and the final plays of Beckett. But the great precursors
are to be found at various points along this grammatical spectrum—Eliot,
from 'The Love-Song of J. Alfred Prufrock' to, at least, *Marina*; even the
Hardy of 'Concerning Agnes'.

> I could not, though I should wish, have over again,
>   That old romance . . .
>
> I could not. And you do not ask me why.
>   Hence you infer
> That what may chance to the fairest under the sky
>   Has chanced to her.
> Yes. She lies white, straight, features marble-keen,
> Unapproachable, mute, in a nook I have never seen.

The reason for claiming that even this acknowledges, by inference, the force
of Wittgenstein's perception is that the abrupt phrases show at once the
narrator's mind lapsing into solipsistic reverie and tugging free of the lapse in
the self-same grammatical placement: 'I could not', 'I could not', 'Hence
you infer', 'Yes'. The coincidence is that the texture of the verse which
speaks for the 'solipsism' finally remains as the reality coordinated with it.
For Hardy the proximate condition to solipsism is an ever-present contingent circumstance, to be squinnied at, regarded askance, ruggedly contested. In Housman's poems of subjective projection, 'Her strong
enchantments failing' and 'When the eye of day is shut', the metrical-
grammatical pattern is itself solipsistic, so that the voice which sounds
with allurement or menace and the voice which defies the allurement or
menace are finally indistinguishable in the pitch and cadence of the chant. It
is as if that which is spoken in a Housman poem remains in thrall to that
which is unspoken: in this respect defiance is not the same as resistance—

> Her strong enchantments failing,
>   Her towers of fear in wreck,
> Her limbecks dried of poisons
>   And the knife at her neck,
>
> The Queen of air and darkness
>   Begins to shrill and cry,

> 'O young man, O my slayer,
>   To-morrow you shall die.'
>
> O Queen of air and darkness,
>   I think 'tis truth you say,
> And I shall die to-morrow;
>   But you will die to-day.

Housman told an enquirer that 'The queen of air and darkness comes from a line of Coventry Patmore's "the powers of darkness and the air", which in its turn is a reference to "the prince of the power of the air" in Ephesians II 2; and the meaning is Evil'. It was understood by Housman's nephew Clement Symons (killed in 1915) as 'the portrayal of conflict in which cowardly fear was vanquished'. If this is so, the antagonists sing an identical melody. This may eventually tell us something of significance not only with respect to Housman but also in relation to a gifted reader of Housman, Wilfred Owen (1893–1918), and his ambivalent struggle with the spirit of high Victorian 'Poetry'; it may tell us something of the power of English tacit pledges; but one cannot conclude from this that Housman works at the pitch of creative understanding which we recognize in Hardy, Gurney, or Rosenberg. As I have suggested, Housman's poems are full of defiance but they do not resist.

In the chapter on 'Solipsism' in *Appearance and Reality* Bradley wrote of a 'truth to which Solipsism has blindly borne witness':

> My way of contact with Reality is through a limited aperture. For I cannot get at it directly except through the felt 'this', and our immediate interchange and transfluence takes place through one small opening. Everything beyond, though not less real, is an expansion of the common essence which we feel burningly in this one focus.

My suggestion would be that much minor 'lyrical' writing is minor because it is the equivalent of Bradley's 'limited aperture' and that this is particularly so with the poetry of Housman. That it is equally so of the poetry of Owen is a suggestion likely to meet much resistance, but I believe it to be the case: as much as with Housman, everything in Owen is got at through the 'felt "this"'. The 'felt "this"' must be understood as including much that James termed 'tacit pledges'; and that which is 'felt' can be interpreted in radically different ways: Owen feels things very much as Housman feels things but brings those feelings to conclusions antagonistic to Housman. Owen's 'Disabled' parodies the kind of public lyrical sentiment which, among other forms of public seduction, it is implied, brought the legless and armless soldier to his plight; the poem by Housman which Owen has chiefly in mind is 'To an Athlete Dying Young':

> And round that early-laurelled head
> Will flock to gaze the strengthless dead,
> And find unwithered on its curls
> The garland briefer than a girl's.

It is no mitigation, in this kind of confrontation, that the word which gives its peculiar logopoeic strength to the quatrain is the word 'strengthless', the word which, in the original Greek (ἀμενηνός), in the eleventh book of the *Odyssey*, describes the ghosts who flock to drink the blood of the ditch in order that they may speak. One recognizes both knowledge and judgement in the rightness of Housman's word; to place one's words in such a way shows distinction. Drawing upon the same episode Bradley remarks, in one of his *Aphorisms*, that 'The shades nowhere speak without blood, and the ghosts of Metaphysic accept no substitute. They reveal themselves only to that victim whose life they have drained, and, to converse with shadows, he himself must become a shade'. Some sense of a metaphysical or existential penalty being its own just price, its own tacit pledge, seems to have been in the intellectual climate, for the German classical scholar Ulrich von Wila-mowitz-Moellendorf wrote, in 1908, in very similar terms:

> We know that ghosts cannot speak until they have drunk blood; and the spirits which we evoke demand the blood of our hearts. We give it to them gladly; but if they then abide our question, something from us has entered into them; something alien, that must be cast out in the name of truth.

The 'something alien' that Owen desired to cast out in the name of truth was in part this metaphysical patrimony; it comprised 'many books' and much 'Poetry'. To pledge the heart's blood in any figurative sense became for him an inexpiable moral betrayal:

> Heart, you were never hot
> Nor large, nor full like hearts made great with shot.

Because Owen faced the machine-guns with unflinching courage we may fancy that his opinions were carefully objective and his aesthetics ethically superior to those of poets who, like Tennyson and Housman, eulogized the fallen from a safe distance; but this is not actually the case. The sensibility-in-action of 'Greater Love' is in fact no different from the sensibility-in-repose of 'To an Athlete Dying Young'. Owen wrote, in August 1917:

> I have just been reading Siegfried Sassoon, and am feeling at a very
> high pitch of emotion. Nothing like his trench life sketches has ever been
> written or ever will be written. Shakespere reads vapid after these. Not
> of course because Sassoon is a greater artist, but because of the subjects,
> I mean.

This is not qualitatively different from Housman's 'I think that to transfuse
emotion—not to transmit thought but to set up in the reader's sense a
vibration corresponding to what was felt by the writer—is the peculiar
function of poetry'. It is rather that the 'turn of circumstances' has turned
Owen's subjectivism to face a destructive force approaching from an entirely different direction. If 'the peculiar function of poetry' is to be
established in relation to the century, it must be understood in the sense
of Wittgenstein's coordinate or in the sense in which one might envisage an
alternative to Bradley's 'limited aperture'.

It was Housman's ill-luck, though not a mischance peculiarly reserved to
him, that, having in part succeeded in transferring a style of decorum from
the magisterium of scholarship to the domain of the supposedly 'spontaneous' Romantic lyric—by way of Bridges's *Shorter Poems* and the *Odes* of
Horace—the very decorum should have been indicted by Owen, in the
name of his 'expressionless' men, as if it were no less despicable than an
editorial in Horatio Bottomley's *John Bull*:

> If you could hear, at every jolt, the blood
> Come gargling from the froth-corrupted lungs,
> Obscene as cancer, bitter as the cud
> Of vile, incurable sores on innocent tongues,—
> My friend, you would not tell with such high zest
> To children ardent for some desperate glory,
> The old Lie: Dulce et decorum est
> Pro patria mori.

This 'famous Latin tag' (it is actually a Greek tag Latinized) belongs, in its
Horatian context (*Ode* 3.2), to a poem marked by 'abrupt' and unsettling
changes of emphasis, which has been described as 'the most difficult,
perhaps the only difficult ode, in the cycle of [Horace's] Roman Odes', a
poem which could be said presciently to acknowledge, both in its abrupt-
ness and 'mysterious avoidance', the force of Sorley's objections to Brooke's
sonnet sequence '1914'. 'Mysterious avoidance', among other elements of
making, has been part of the burden of this chapter: mysterious avoidances
are to be accounted correlatives of tacit pledges.

My decision to consider, under one heading, Housman in confrontation with a number of his contemporaries must itself abide the reader's question. I would hope that it is possible to show how a seemingly arbitrary collocation of authors can illuminate not only the direct and oblique features of their work but also something of the nature of tacit pledges and of the force for good or ill which this can exert, in a particular society, upon the supposedly 'individual' and 'original' voice. Our proper desire and true aim in the critical examination of a body of work that has moved us, whether to assent or to dissent, is to satisfy ourselves, to be satisfied in our selves, that we have justly recognized the achievement of a 'particular sought pitch and accent'. In the contrary mode, when we admit that we have failed to take the 'straight measure' of the work, it is an appropriate discipline to determine, as precisely as we are able, whether the fault lies in us, in our predilections, presuppositions, prejudicate opinions, our tacit pledges, or in the fact of some '*usurping* consciousness' within the work itself, its 'displacement', for whatever rhyme or reason, from its 'indispensable centre'.

Each of these phrases—'particular sought pitch and accent', 'straight measure', '*usurping* consciousness', 'indispensable centre', 'displacement'—I owe to the one source: the 'Preface' which Henry James wrote to *The Tragic Muse* when it was reprinted in the New York 'Definitive' Edition in 1908. If Housman's poetry is itself displaced from an indispensable centre, this does not displace respect or deny accomplishment. Nor does it claim to have discovered an unprecedented dilemma or plight. I return for the last time upon the matter of John Stuart Mill, to the *Autobiography* and the essays on poetry where he slights poetry even as he stoops to praise its timely contribution to the recovery of his spirits; and to the essay *On Liberty*, in which 'genius', which he purports to honour and which he sees, with some justice, as being perennially vulnerable to 'the general tendency of things throughout the world . . . to render mediocrity the ascendant power among mankind', is nonetheless brought down to the level of his own mediocrity. Mill's conception of the context for genius diffuses into an '*atmosphere* of freedom' in which alone 'Genius can . . . breathe freely'.

In chapter XVI of *Essays on Truth and Reality* F. H. Bradley footnotes an allusion to Shelley's 'The Sensitive Plant': 'I do not know whether this in my case is a mark of senility, but I find myself now taking more and more as literal fact what I used in my youth to admire and love as poetry'. Bradley's emphasis on 'literal fact' is hardly an improvement on Mill's 'atmosphere', although we are perhaps intended to understand the words

as somehow putting Mill's kind of sensibility firmly in its place, in acknowledgement of an inescapable 'turn of circumstance'. Housman's poetry,
unlike his scholarship, his textual emendations, is caught between Mill's
'atmosphere' and Bradley's 'literal fact'. What T. S. Eliot concluded, in
the course of his study of Bradley, was that 'Solipsism has been one
of the dramatic properties of most philosophical entertainers. Yet we cannot
discard it without recognizing that it rests upon a truth'. The thought
here is Bradley's, from chapter XXI of *Appearance and Reality*; the entertainment is Eliot's: he seems too easily pleased here by his powers of
detachment though his tone does not exactly represent his conclusions on
the question.

James argues, in the New York 'Preface' to *The Tragic Muse*, that 'no
character in a play (any play not a mere monologue) has, for the right
expression of the thing, a *usurping* consciousness; the consciousness of others
is exhibited exactly in the same way as that of the "hero" '.

Transposing James's concern with drama to my own concern with
poetry, I would claim that the poet in the poem is bound to take on
the challenge of the 'usurping consciousness'; either he accepts it or he is
the ignorant recipient of a destructive burden. There is rarely an unambiguous issue to this contest. To be wholly defeated by the challenge is to be
drawn down into 'mere monologue'. Many poems move us with their
knowledge of what is being exacted by such a confrontation: in this sense
there can be a difficult beauty of imperfection; but it is not, in such cases, a
beauty of thought. It is a manifest beauty of intelligence—by which I mean,
as the *Oxford English Dictionary* means, in one of its several senses of
'intelligence': 'understanding as a quality of admitting of degree'. Eliot
conceded that solipsism rests upon a truth; but one would add that, if
solipsism is to be redeemed from mere monologue, the intelligence which
is brought to bear upon it cannot be simply conceptual. What James called
the 'indispensable centre' of such work must be realized within the many
dimensions of language itself (though language is never, in actuality, language itself):

> A worm fed on the heart of Corinth,
> Babylon and Rome.
> Not Paris raped tall Helen,
> But this incestuous worm
> Who lured her vivid beauty
> To his amorphous sleep.

England! famous as Helen
Is thy betrothal sung
To him the shadowless,
More amorous than Solomon.

Housman's 'strengthless dead' is good; Isaac Rosenberg's 'amorphous sleep'
is better. The strength of 'strengthless' momentarily holds back from the
epigram 'find unwithered on its curls | The garland briefer than a girl's';
'amorphous' is what 'vivid beauty' comes to; it is the ultimate dissolution of
'fame'; and it is the necessary condition of fame; the fame to which, in 1916,
England is incestuously betrothed. 'Amorphous sleep' draws down the
solipsistic beauties of English poetry into itself, the 'amorphous' transflu-
ently becomes 'amorous'. This is not so much Blake's 'rose' that is 'sick' or
his 'invisible worm | That flies in the night'—though for Rosenberg that
poem is evidently more than thoughtless delight—as the amorphous idea of
English poetry, which 'answers to nothing real' yet is 'packed with material
to set nostalgic imagination to work'.

James Russell Lowell, in *Among My Books* (1870), desiderated a 'quality in
man which . . . gives classic shape to our own amorphous imaginings'.
Housman's poems, in their several gatherings, from *A Shropshire Lad*
(1896) to *Additional Poems* (1937), famously bring classic shape to amorphous
imaginings. To say that they 'bring' is not to say that they 'give'. Giving, as I
would understand it—particularly in the work of Housman's much younger
contemporaries Gurney and Rosenberg—presupposes 'understanding as a
quality of admitting of degree': the intelligence made manifest in Gurney's
'Tewkesbury' ('What is best of England, going quick from beauty, | Is
manifest, the slow spirit going straight on') and in every phrase of Rosenberg's brief poem, in the perceived sensual plighting of 'amorphous' /
'amorous' that is England's fatal love for herself. But intelligence, such as
we find in Rosenberg, is a quality that 'England' has never been over-
disposed to acknowledge, for it has never 'delighted and inspired generations of readers'.

25

Gurney's 'Hobby'

From an Edinburgh hospital in October 1917, awaiting the reviews of his first book *Severn & Somme*, Gurney wrote to his friend Marion Scott: 'they will not say much to affect me, for the sight of the whole thing in proof convinced me that humility should be my proper mood, and gratitude for a hobby found when one was needed'. It is hard to accept that a poet who had already written 'Strange Service', 'Pain', and 'Servitude' could, at the heart of his intelligence, suppose that what he practised was 'pursued merely for the amusement or interest that it affords', or with a devotion 'out of proportion to its real importance'.

A brusque but reasonable retort would be that 'hobby' is the *mot juste* and that when Gurney, later in the same letter, writes of having a 'larger and finer string to my bow' he pre-empts one's objection. As a musician he trained to professional standards though not, in the end, to the satisfaction of his examiners, at the Royal College of Music. As early as 1912 he had composed 'Sleep', a setting of words by John Fletcher, which some musicians regard as one of the finest English songs of the twentieth century. As a poet, however, he had to get by without formal instruction and his letters are a record of predilections and prejudices, discoveries and disenchantments. As his autodidact's rage of discovery turned into a discovery of rage, he drew sustenance and example from the political philosophy of Belloc and the poetry of Whitman. In a letter to Marion Scott, on New Year's Day, 1916, he wrote that he had ordered a copy of Belloc's *The Servile State*, clearly approving its anti-Socialist, anti-Collectivist, thesis. Whitman's poetry, he wrote, had taken him 'like a flood'. Among his late asylum poems there is verse not only 'in the manner of Walt Whitman' but also possessed by, or purporting to be possessed by, the spirit of the American poet who is credited, gnomically, with co-authorship: 'Walt Whitman. / (Ivor Gurney here. / probably all-altering / F W Harvey's *Ironical* work)'.

The editor of the *Collected Poems of Ivor Gurney* advises us to take due note of '*Ironical*'. He warns that Gurney 'detested irony'. If that is true then this is a way of confusing 'them', the daemonic Ironies that interfere with mortal destinies, or the human persecutors, the enemy, those who engineered and directed the 'electrical waves' which were tormenting him. There is some evidence to suggest that Gurney had a depressive's gift for clowning. He, like others, relished the collocations of subsistence-level English and French ('Compree no grub?') and improved on the donnée: 'Bide a wee, s'il vous plait'. He cherished daft puns, nicknames, and flat-footed witticisms. Herbert Howells, addressed as 'My dear Howler' or as 'Erbert Owls', was provided with a curriculum vitae and list of publications including 'the great (Sanscrit) Te Deum, for the opening of the new lavatory in the Dead Language Section of the British Museum'; his friend Mrs Chapman became La Comptesse Tilda; and a revered poetic invocation was made to face about: 'Dear houses, the very God does seem asleep'.

On 3 November 1917 he wrote: 'There's a bit of luck: owing to slight indigestion (presumably due to gas; wink, wink!) I am to go to Command Depot for two months'. He had endured over a year's front-line existence with patient courage and had already been wounded; nevertheless he seems overscrupulously to have felt some remorse at having escaped the trenches. Expecting 'No more than a week's sick', he found that he had got 'Blighty', and 'wink, wink!' hints at doctored evidence, mimes a skiver's self-congratulation. Marion Scott is made both confidante and spectator of a comic turn, a send-up of confessions and self-betrayal which is nonetheless a genuine attempt to appease the Accuser, who, as Blake said, is the God of this World. It is the uneasy jauntiness of the cornered man. Donald Davie has praised Gurney's 'mastery of decorum', his command, in the poems, of 'any number of distinct styles'. I do not question this knack but believe it may be less important than Gurney's other decorous mastery, his grasp of the way words and tones sit within our lives and the way they situate the life of one man in relation, or disrelation, to his comrades and his superiors. P. J. Kavanagh considers that 'the intricacies of human relations are not his subject'. It is true that he is not a story-teller, as Browning and Frost are; but 'wink, wink!' is no less aware of 'intricacies' and contingencies than are 'My Last Duchess' or 'Snow'. One's 'subject' may be one's theme; but it can equally be the substance that we subject to our disinterested possessive contemplation—the texture of the material in which we work. 'Texture' is a word that Gurney weaves into his theories and ideals: Schubert's

C Major Quintet 'looks to have | Very good texture', there is a 'true |
Texture of rare living | Azure'. 'The Artist respects his materials, loves their
peculiarities of texture and management, and deals with them gently as with
his own flesh and blood.' He anticipates by several years Brophy and
Partridge's published work on the songs and slang of the British soldier,
'little bits of jargon', 'grub, Fritz, and Blighty', 'poor bare jests . . . "On the
wire, at Loos" . . . "Gassed at Mons" . . . "My numbers up" '. He notes
abrupt thoughts and sayings that have the 'intricacies of human relations'
still clinging to them: 'When on a sudden, "Crickley" he said. How I started
| At that old darling name of home!' Or:

> I saw a scrawl on a barn door a few days ago. It will interest you, I think.
>   'Where is my wandering Boy tonight?
>   Neuve Chapelle' (and date.)
> That's all, and pretty grim at that.

His hearing of these snatched and shaken things is not random, though it
may sound so. He plainly intended his five 'Sonnets 1917' as a riposte to
Brooke's '1914' sonnets which, he said, 'were written before the grind of
the war and by an officer (or one who would have been an officer)'. This
'protest', the assertion of 'the accumulative weight of small facts against the
one large', reminds us of his admiration for Belloc and Chesterton. Belloc
argued that the Socialist, or Collectivist, reformer is 'disturbed by multitudinous things'; 'all that human and organic complexity which is the colour
of any vital society offends him by its infinite differentiation'. Those details
in Gurney to which Kavanagh and Davie justly attend, 'the silhouettes of
certain trees in certain lights', 'all the beauties of his beloved Gloucestershire', are not degraded by the political collocation. 'Infinite', 'infinitely',
like all words that make gestures towards the 'exalted spiritual', is to be used
with caution. Belloc's 'infinite differentiation' compounds it with the
quotidian, the intricacies of human relations; and Gurney, who on occasion
uses the word as convention prescribes ('And infinitely far that star Capella'), more often rams it against the human and organic, as in his poem
about Canadian troops returning from the trenches, 'Faces infinitely grimed
in'. The first two words anticipate a commonplace of long-suffering, or a
long-suffering commonplace ('infinitely patient, cheerful, resourceful,
weary'), the third and fourth repel the truism, though without wholly
annulling it or the decent traditional sentiments that go with it. 'Infinitely',
having been situated within the technology of the line, doesn't know where

to put itself, though Gurney, who has here embarrassed it, is elsewhere considerate enough in the duties he places on it ('Infinite lovely chatter of Bucks accent'; 'Everyday things the mind | Infinitely delighted'; 'one of my infinite dead generations of brothers'). Kavanagh claims that Gurney's 'occasional bathetic contrasts ... are ... intentional'. I would question whether 'bathos' is precisely the right word; I see the contrast as being deliberately, even aggressively, oxymoronic: 'nothing | But loathing and fine beauty', 'England, terrible | And dear taskmistress'.

That invocation is from the final poem in *Severn & Somme*, proofs of which, recently read, had triggered his remark about poetry being a 'hobby'.

> The unnoticed nations praise us, but we turn
> Firstly, only to thee—'Have we done well?
> Say, are you pleased?'

The sense of formal petition in these lines, intensely conscious of twin consecrations, patriotism and poetic vocation, sits as oddly with his self-humbling 'gratitude for a hobby found' as does a friend's recollection of his 'astonishing creative pride'. From the opening pages of *Severn & Somme* to the asylum poem, 'Chance to Work' with its prefix 'For the English Police / For Scotland Yard', he insistently pleads 'the great honour of song', the seriousness, the high significance of the poet's duty to his craft and to England, the distinction of the craft, the recognition that is its due.

'Hobby' does not do justice, then, to Gurney's dedication or to his position. Brooding on the word may nevertheless help us to appreciate what that position was and to see that justice is done. 'A favourite occupation or topic, pursued merely for the amusement or interest that it affords ... an individual pursuit to which a person is devoted (in the speaker's opinion) out of proportion to its real importance.' Once we allow the *Oxford English Dictionary*'s caveat 'in the speaker's opinion' we find that we are dealing with a shifty status-word. A 'hobby' may be pursued in the intervals of employment; it lacks public utility, status, or prestige. The word can parody and dwarf the value of human activity, and is ready to hand for complicitous bouts of self-deprecation or self-therapy. It is also susceptible to mystical enfranchisement and elevation. A hobby may be whatever is not 'competitive or bureaucratic toil'. It may even take on the aura of 'universal duty': 'Woman ... should have not one trade but twenty hobbies'. In context, Chesterton's observation is less patronizing than it sounds. He is urging, so he says, 'The Emancipation of Domesticity', an emancipation envisaged in accordance with his crypto-Catholic sociology, stressing the central importance of family life and private property in the creation and preservation of democracy. He is obliged to contend with an already-prejudiced usage, seeking to show that these so-called 'hobbies' are in fact true professions, untainted by commodity. 'Hobby', a word in which solipsism and public bias are compacted, is, in effect, itself oxymoronic: eccentric yet central, peripheral but focal, an 'amusement' attended by devotion and sacrifice. Of amateur status it may be pursued with a degree of emotional and technical concentration more intense than that bestowed upon day-labour or a salaried profession.

As one might expect, given the various contingencies, we find Gurney, in his poems and letters, vacillating between two notions. On the one hand poetry is a spontaneous though imperative way of relieving the feelings ('Out of the heart's sickness the spirit wrote | For delight, or to escape hunger, or of war's worst anger'). On the other it is a craft, a discipline to be acquired with difficulty and by way of laborious trial and error. 'Do as you please', 'punctuate as you please', he writes to his amanuensis Marion Scott in late 1916 and early 1917. 'The grammar of my book is, technically speaking, often shaky. Never poetically. I say what I want to say.' 'Poetic-ally' here signifies an essence, independent of, uninhibited by, 'shaky' grammar, uncertain punctuation. This is a dangerously volatile notion. For a young man in Gurney's circumstances—and he is always insistent that particular circumstances are acknowledged—the necessity to make something of oneself, to proclaim one's identity by expressing oneself, strongly felt by any artist, is experienced with particular intensity: 'There is no time to revise here [in the trenches], and if the first impulse will not carry the thing through, then what is written gets destroyed'. 'Neither he [F. W. Harvey] nor I have lived in the proper atmosphere to write much yet—the company of men who are trying for the same end and prize of a modern technique.' These observations, eight months apart, place a com-mon stress on circumstance, but the first speaks of 'impulse', the second of 'technique'. It would be wrong, however, to see an irreversible process of definition in Gurney's thinking at this period. It remained, during the war years, intermittently self-contradictory, expressing a perplexity not wholly of his own making. In the midst of his recurrent references to what he calls 'craft', 'method', 'scrupulousness', 'care', 'respect...[for]...materials', he will appear abruptly to go against the grain of this growing concern. 'It seems to me', he remarks on 3 August 1917, 'a work of Art never should be greatly praised for its perfection; for that should set off its beauty, and its beauty or truth should be the chief impression on the mind. To praise a thing for its faultlessness is to damn it with faint praise'. This, however, is less a contradiction than a synthesis. It is not that technical mastery precludes creative mystery; it is that the greatest craft is one which is transfigured into the most telling simplicity: 'I say, I would like to get hold of some of Verhaeren. He seems to have hold of an artistic dogma that is my foundation stone, and perpetual starting point—that simplicity is most powerful and to be desired above all things whatsoever'.

'Foundation-stone' is a four-square civic word with which to commemorate a private sense of dedication. Gurney is not unique in finding that he has encountered an oxymoronic circumstance in which a derisory hobby is nonetheless born of common experience and speaks not only to our common humanity but also to the 'corporate life and mutual obligations'. The uniqueness is always a matter of texture. 'Common' is one of his value-words, as it is for Belloc, who writes of England's vanquished 'common life which once nourished [the] social sense'. Gurney has 'the dearness of common things', 'beauty | Of common living', 'the common goodness of those soldiers shown day after day', 'the day's | Common wonder'. But against this wondrous and dear commonness we have to set those other occurrences in his poetry, where 'common' is as common parlance would have it, a word that imposes extrinsic 'standards' upon the intrinsic qualities of the thing described: 'the commonness of the tale', 'To be signallers and to be relieved two hours | Before the common infantry', 'Casual and common is the wonder grown—', 'a Common Private makes but little show', 'How England should take as common their vast endurance'. What is the precise difference, we may fairly ask, between 'the day's | Common wonder' and the 'wonder' that has grown 'common'? The attempt to answer one's own question is a slow and perplexing business but through it we may reach to the crux of Gurney's perplexity and achievement. A reader of Belloc's *The Servile State* is soundly instructed in that distinction between 'inertia and custom' and 'instinct' and 'tradition' which lies at the heart of the 'Distributist' philosophy. Gurney endures a process of self-discovery and self-loss where that distinction, though still applicable, is for a time far less clear. It is not so much that there is an impassable gulf between the precious 'common wonder' and the indifferent curiosity of the world. It is rather that our truths of first inscription, the objects of our love and fealty, are at the

same time slighted, marginal to the world's mart and focus of interest, and
further, that we have no privilege of remaining aloof from the crassest
misjudgement, the cruellest slight.

When Gurney arranges the title-page of his first book: '*Severn & Somme* /
by / Ivor Gurney / Private, of the Gloucesters' he briefly holds in balance
what Lionel Trilling would later call 'the reality of self' and 'the reality of
circumstance'. 'Private' is at once bluntly descriptive and elliptically challenging. The five 'Sonnets 1917' which end the volume, were, we recall,
'intended to be a sort of counterblast against' Brooke's '1914' yet they are
dedicated 'To the Memory of Rupert Brooke'. Does this rebut Kavanagh's
assertion that Gurney 'detested irony', or does it show not only a readiness
to compromise with public sentiment but also an eagerness to be seen as
Brooke's rightful heir? Gurney was not alone in criticizing Brooke's sequence. Rosenberg, who dismissed those 'begloried sonnets', gives the
impression of quietly pushing them aside as items of no concern or challenge to his own search for a poetry that is complex yet 'as simple as ordinary
talk'. *Severn & Somme*, published by Sidgwick and Jackson, Brooke's publishers, is much more 'after the English manner', as consecrated by Brooke,
Binyon, and the general consensus. The 'radiant shining' of 'Requiem'
recollects the largess of Brooke's 'The Dead': 'a gathered radiance, | A
width, a shining peace, under the night'. However, Gurney's book also
makes a determined bid to wrest the 'English manner' from the hands of the
officer class and to bestow it upon comrades in 'heavy servitude', 'The boys
who laughed and jested with me but yesterday, | So fit for kings to speak to'.

'Mind you take care of him. His loss would be a national loss.' General Sir
Ian Hamilton's instructions to Brooke's commanding officer, on the eve of
departure for the Aegean and the Dardanelles, define by stark antithesis the
national status of Gurney's 'hobby', of his 'great honour of song', devoted to
'England's royal grace and dignity'. 'These sonnets are personal—never
were sonnets more personal since Sidney died—and yet the very blood
and youth of England seem to find expression in them.' That encomium
which appeared on 11 March 1915, more than a month before Brooke's
death, anticipates the tone of Churchill's myth-making *Times* obituary of 26
April. It cannot be claimed that Gurney's 'Preface' to *Severn & Somme*, dated
'Spring, 1917', intentionally echoes the tone of that 1915 press notice, but
neither does it positively exclude such resonances: 'Most of the book is
concerned with a person named Myself, and the rest with my county,
Gloucester, that whether I die or live stays always with me'. Gurney's

tone here is both derivative and uncertain: 'I never was famous, and a Common Private makes but little show' tries for a plain man's self-reliant jocularity but like one or two other phrases in the 'Preface', sounds merely gauche. There can be little doubt that with *Severn & Somme* Gurney aimed to set to rights certain matters of social prerogative and privilege. A 'Common Private' would be seen to have made a considerable showing and would therefore be accorded his rightful place in the English pantheon. The book was amiably received and after twelve months went into a second impression. By 1917, however, Harvey's *A Gloucestershire Lad* had reached its fourth impression, Brooke's *1914 and Other Poems*, its twenty-first. Gurney's second volume, *War's Embers* (1919) was less successful than *Severn & Somme* and a third collection, *Rewards of Wonder*, was rejected in the same year. I see no reason to dispute Edmund Blunden's claim that, as the evidence of rejection accumulated, Gurney was 'aflame with anger' or Michael Hurd's suggestion that 'he began to feel that he had been betrayed by the country he loved and whose cause his art and his life had served'. Statements from the later poems confirm these opinions: '(I was a war poet, England bound to honour by Her blood)'; 'Who, first war poet, am under three Hells and lie | (Sinned against desperately by all English high-sworn to Duty)'. It may be thought that I have misconstrued Gurney's intention in these phrases and that the indignation is less wounded literary *amour-propre* than exemplary rage on behalf of 'boys bemocked at'. I do not say that the disinterested indignation is excluded. Even so, an acute personal disappointment is subsumed. Gurney, at once ambitious and innocent, remained unreconciled to the discovery that acclaim is not commensurate with achievement.

Jon Silkin, in an eloquent and just appreciation of Gurney, argues that the minute particulars of word-choice may be ultimately traceable to 'enormous social forces'. Turning for substantiation to some lines from *War's Embers* ('But still he died | Nobly, so cover him over | With violets of pride'), he observes that ' "Nobly" is not merely the individual soldier's attribute; it is the propagandistic aura that the state awards the dead ... After hesitating between these conflicting attitudes, Gurney, disappointingly, moves the stanza in the aureate direction'. 'Aureate' is ponderable in the circumstances. In one of his last letters, to Abercrombie (Edward Marsh quotes it in his 'Memoir'), Brooke remarked 'I've been collecting ... one or two of the golden phrases that a certain wind blows from (will the Censor let me say?) Olympus, across these purple seas'. Marsh consecrates the self-consciousness more solemnly than Brooke perhaps intends. 'Of the "golden phrases" only the merest fragments remain.'

In such circumstances the cliché may briefly appear to be vivified by 'reality of self'. Rosenberg, Gurney, and Sorley were all privately sceptical of Brooke's publicly acclaimed qualities. It is one's recognition of the hiatus between private intelligence and public sentiment that vindicates Silkin's reference to enormous social forces. It was Gurney's own recognition of this hiatus which concentrated his creative insight as it drained his psychic resilience. Brooke, with his 'red-gold waves of hair' and his 'golden phrases' was, and for some evidently remains, the '*embodiment* of poetry'. How is it possible, one asks, for superficial verbal glister to be accepted as the outward sign of 'some inner, spiritual, reality'? The *Collected Poems* of 1918 is lavishly 'aureate': 'golden hours', 'misty gold', 'golden glory', 'Golden Stair', 'golden dream', 'golden height', 'golden sea', 'gold air', 'golden space', 'Golden forever, eagles, crying flames'.

W. W. Gibson's slim volume *Friends* (1916), dedicated 'To the Memory of Rupert Brooke', was described by Gurney in the preface to *Severn & Somme* as 'a great little book'. Its language attempts to embody that original 'simple act of presence and of direct communication' to which Brooke's admirers paid homage, but succeeds merely in reduplicating cliché: 'golden sky', 'golden head', 'golden words', 'golden rhyme', 'pure gold', 'gold casket', 'terrible golden fury', 'golden height', 'golden glow', 'golden peace', 'golden light', 'burnished gold', 'gold wings', 'gold glow'. Whether such inane repetitiousness is to be characterized as ineptitude or as a self-restricting minor aptitude may seem to be a question defying analysis. Judgement in these matters should not, however, depend on the toss of a half-sovereign. One seeks a word. The word is perhaps 'absorption'. Gibson has successfully absorbed Brooke's influence; he is in that sense an opportunist and a *pasticheur*, yet, at the same time, he is sincerely absorbed in his zealous homage to the 'inner, spiritual, reality' of Brooke's 'presence' and 'direct communication'. He is sufficiently doting to overlook the kind of cynical frisson which Brooke occasionally favours, as in 'Menelaus and Helen': 'her golden voice | Got shrill as he grew deafer'. As F. W. Bateson acutely perceived, Brooke occasionally 'carried off' the artificiality of his Pre-Raphaelite diction 'by half-laughing at it'.

There is also a strong 'aureate' vein in Gurney, however; a 'golden room' bard immured in his isolation: 'Bask in the warm, dream poetry of the gold flame', 'Let me but have a room | Of golden night quiet—', 'homely songs of gold', 'O warmth! O golden light!', 'lamp shadows | Golden and black on gold', 'lit with gold firelight thrown | Lovely about the room', 'dark with firelight's gold power'. It is the complicity between received opinion and personal expectation that is rebuffed by his spasmodically bitter and violent conjunctions: 'Golden firelight or racked frost hurt me to the nerve'. Belloc had written, in *The Servile State*, of 'every form of touting and cozening which competitive Capitalism carries with it'. Gurney's painful discovery is that this 'touting and cozening' involves and compromises not only the most highly valued poetic idiom of the day but also his own ambition which had rejoiced in the sincerest emulation. When he writes of post-war 'disappointed men | Who looked for the golden Age to come friendly again', it is the particular quality of his imagination to seize on that word of Georgian largess and to place it in all its cozening power. At the same time it is as though he takes the bankrupted stock into the receivership of his own idiom; in more than one sense he is going to make it pay:

> O for some force to swing us back there to some
> Natural moving towards life's love, or that glow
> In the word to be glow in the State, that golden age come
> Again, men working freely as nature might show,
> And a people honouring stage-scenes lit bright with fine sound
> On a free soil, England happy, honoured and joy-crowned.

The 'men working freely', 'England happy', are with difficulty enfranchised from a syntax that is far from free. 'That glow | In the word to be glow in the State' is at once over-deliberate and under-defined. The ungainly thrust of the word 'glow' athwart the slowed-down gabble of the metre is an effort to wrest activity from inertia, a concept from a cliché, to affirm what the 'golden age come | Again', the unity of poetic and political vision, might be in England if it could only be brought into being. This is one of those instances, however, where the raw etymology of a word contains more energy than is released in the poetic context by which it is constrained. Such verbal bafflement is at the root of Gurney's undeniable failings and failures but also of his incontestable grandeur. According to *The Servile State* the 'moral strain . . . arising from the divergence between what our laws and moral phrases pretend, and what our society actually is, makes of that society an utterly unstable thing'. There is, nonetheless, a condition of equilibrium, or suspension, where craft and expediency meet and where minor talents are well able to secure themselves. Gurney's 'curious originality', his 'peculiar unconventionality...not hostile to traditions', is, in large part, a refusal to adjust craft-logic to reasons of expediency. He, like other poets, draws upon the common dole, the distributed received opinions, but increasingly in his work these take on the weight of the circumstantial, the contingent. This capacity to comprehend that words exist by some other law than that of one's own fancy, even while subjecting them to the discipline of imagination, increasingly distinguishes Gurney's poetry from that of the more successful Georgians whom he admired. The jolt of his phrases, at times disabling, at other times releasing, is a recognition not only that goodness and sincerity may be other names for humiliation and bewilderment, but also that simplicity is most powerful and to be desired above all things whatsoever, and that 'We shall enter unsurprised into our own'.

In 'The Homelessness of Jones', the eleventh chapter of the first part of *What's Wrong With the World* (1910), Chesterton envisages a man who 'has always desired the divinely ordinary things', who 'has chosen or built a small house that fits like a coat...And just as he is moving in, something goes wrong. Some tyranny, personal or political, suddenly debars him from the home.' Gurney observed in a letter to Marion Scott that she had 'a great house in London, but I doubt whether it can be to you what a tiny house may be, even if...the piano leaves little room for free movement'. Hurd notes that 'at one point, in May 1920', Gurney believed 'that he had found the cottage he had dreamed of in the trenches...though [it] proved an impossibility'. In the asylum poem 'Chance to Work' he is perhaps reliving that period of concentrated hope and disappointment: 'Many songs...then a good farm | Took me...Yet it is difficult | In a house not one's own to work'. This 'work' was not the farm-work, which he enjoyed ('Hedging, plough-helping, stone shifting, Labour was good'); it was merely what he was supremely gifted to do ('Working in strict discipline, music, or strict rhyme'), his 'hobby' in other words. One's hobby is not necessarily what one chooses, it may be one's lot; that which is by tacit decree one's hobby since it cannot be seen to be work. 'Did they look for a book of wrought art's perfection, | Who promised no reading, nor praise, nor publication?' Or:

> The pages fill with black notes, the paper-bill goes
> Up and up, till the musician is left staring
> At a String Quartet nobody in the world will do...
> And what Schumann would say there's no one to be caring.
> Now, had it been a joke, or some wordy, windy poem
> About Destiny or Fatal-Way or Weltmüth or Sarsparilla,
> London would have hugged to it like a glad gorilla...

This churlish lampooning of poetry as a metropolitan raree-show compounds a dislike of modernism with a reminder that poetry has sometimes been a profitable commodity; had, indeed, proved recently to be so, under the auspices of Edward Marsh. Frank Swinnerton has described how 'this remarkable character was apparently destined by Nature to be Private Secretary to innumerable Cabinet Ministers, and in his spare time to be one of the greatest encouragers of young poets that the world had seen'. The ludicrous disproportion of the last phrase (Marsh's hobby, indeed) should not cause us to underestimate the real power of social cachet, of the semi-official stamp of approval, or to overlook the professional zeal with which Marsh conducted his hobby of literary patronage. Statements such as Swinnerton's are in fact a form of floatation; they procure a ready assent by simply taking for granted that it will not be withheld. General Hamilton's absolute confidence in Brooke as a major national asset has a similar aplomb, and Gibson's *Friends* easily buys into the same serious and thoughtful complacency. In his *Commonplace Book* for 8 January 1914, R. H. Tawney wrote that 'the economic conditions of the unprivileged classes are determined not by consent, but by *force majeure*'. It may seem perverse to claim that the gentle overabundance of Gibson's 'Rupert Brooke' is itself a manifestation of '*force majeure*' but the perversity, like the pressure, is already there, in what Whitman called 'words of routine' as in that nexus of expectation and accolade which Owen came to recognize and condemn as 'Poetry': 'Above all I am not concerned with Poetry', '(That's for your poetry book)'. It would be unjust to deny Marsh's several acts of generosity to both Rosenberg and Gurney; it would be sentimental to claim that he valued them as he valued Brooke, or even Gibson, or Abercrombie. Tawney added that 'in modern society the individual is not face to face with nature. Between him and nature stands a human superior'. In much Georgian verse the 'human superior' is Marsh, or Hamilton, or Gosse 'like a king . . . with favourites, his chosen heirs, young men and women of promise', or the 'red-gold' apparition of Brooke himself. Poetry, in this ambience, is hardly to be distinguished from Patrimony. The significance of Gurney and Rosenberg is not that they were 'unprivileged' men, nor even that they were unprivileged men of genius, but that their poetic intelligences proved able to take that strain arising from the divergence between what phrases pretend and what society actually is. To say this is not to underrate the severity of the strain or, in Gurney's case, the denseness of the perplexity. It is, after all, a perplexing matter to receive an inheritance that is at the same time an imposition, an ancient right that is also a deprivation.

Gurney found himself possessed of a dual heritage, a double burden, a twofold deprivation: *Patria* and Patrimony. In the earlier poems the two are spiritually, as well as etymologically, entwined: 'Ere he has scorned his Father's patrimony'. In the later work, the patrimony becomes more and more the question of an unhonoured draft, and the unfailing love of the *patria* (Gloucestershire and England) becomes a separate thing from the hatred of a ruling caste, 'the Prussians of England':

> We'll have a word there too, and forge a knife,
> Will cut the cancer threatens England's life.

Belloc had seen the growth of the servile state exemplified 'in Prussia and in England'. Though Lord Milner had 'sincerely attempted to introduce German efficiency' into British administration, Chesterton did not commend his efforts. Gurney acknowledged the patrimony of his own political thought: 'My dear lady your eagle eye will detect Belloc here; and why not?' Reading between the lines of his letters it is evident that he had been brave, in atrocious conditions, in the way he most admired, with 'that half cynical nobility and clearness of eye that forbid men to complain much', that 'stoical fatalism' which Hardy regarded as characteristically English. Such qualities Gurney saw epitomized, simply and profoundly, in the comrades of his own regiment, the 2nd / 5th Gloucesters, of whom he spoke in the 'Preface' to *Severn & Somme*, and to whom he dedicated three poems in *War's Embers*.

But Gurney was not a simple man; and for a complex mind and spirit, I would guess, even to be comradely is not a simple act. Its own form of consciousness, even self-consciousness, is a palimpsest: knowing one's worth while knowing that one is expected to know one's place. Gurney wrote to Edward Marsh early in 1922, sending his '5 Songs of Rupert Brooke', 'of which I do not think very much, but they are probably better than those of most folk'. Hurd says that 'Marsh did not reply. Nor did he return the manuscript'. Gurney's tone, at once incisive and unsure, self-affirming and fatalistic, recurs in the letters and poems: 'Some men have to form themselves, to control their every tiniest movement of spirit, and indeed to create their own world'. 'This dumbness would not matter, only that it makes distrust in oneself.' Or:

> Till the politest voice—a finicking accent, said:
> 'Do you think you might crawl through, there: there's a hole?' In the afraid

Darkness, shot at; I smiled, as politely replied—
'I'm afraid not, Sir.' There was no hole no way to be seen.

This, while sounding unpremeditated, is exquisitely balanced ('exquisitely' keeps its distance from 'finicking', I hope). 'As politely' both matches and counters 'the politest' and 'There was no hole no way to be seen' puts the kibosh on 'there's a hole'. The perfect good manners of the episode are simultaneously a tone-poem of the class-system, and a parody of what it is that brings two men through the exercise of traditional discipline and reason, into a situation of unpremeditated terror and absurdity. It may be that on this subject Gurney is not quite the equal of Charles Sorley at his best. He does not match the cogency and economy of Sorley's perception that the loud, public acclaim for Brooke's '1914' sonnets is consonant with the poetry's eloquent, innocent complicity in 'conduct demanded by the turn of circumstances, where non-compliance with this demand would have made life intolerable'. It is necessary to add, therefore, that the strength and finesse of Sorley's intelligence, so manifest in the letters, is sacrificed in the poems to a noble but constricting patrimony. It is not that Sorley's phrases lack stoical or even sceptical irony ('So be merry, so be dead'; 'And the blind fight the blind'; 'Who sent us forth? Who brings us home again?'; 'It is easy to be dead') but that the pitch and rhythm of the voice are subject to a predetermined rule of measurement and value that is stronger than the solitary dissentient intelligence. W. R. Sorley dedicated *Moral Values and the Idea of God* (1918) to his son's memory and the memory of 'many thousands who gave their lives freely in a great cause'. The volume also carries a two-page advertisement for *Marlborough and Other Poems*, quoting extracts from sixteen press-notices. Those words and that gesture publicly immolate the personal pride and grief. Quiet grief and dignity themselves draw upon a patrimony in which national identity and Idealism are compounded. W. R. Sorley cites the poets in his treatise, Goethe, Keats, and Donne among them, but though he recognizes what Gurney calls 'texture' he evades its implications, here preferring 'higher vision' and there rebuking 'the licence of a poet'. The charge that in the last stanza of 'Ode on a Grecian Urn' there is 'a confusion of values' might be sustainable if Keats were simply taking a 'message' or reading a 'lesson', as Sorley supposes. It was presumably he who re-grouped his son's poems in the 'definitive' edition of 1919, titling the four sections 'Of the Downs', 'Of School', 'Of Life and Thought', 'Of War and Death'. The most generous sentiment does not equal the justice attained by accuracy of thought, since sentiment is already entailed and accuracy of thought starts afresh with each new context and texture.

That which at times stands between Gurney and his own nature is something more overt, more violently remarked on. The 'finicking accent' is the voice that calls the tune ('as politely replied'). The Marsh–Gurney episode is instructive. To speak out, in certain ways, is a solecism to be rebuked by silence. And 'silence' itself is both active and passive: either punitively imposed or self-inflicted. 'Dumb' recurs in Gurney like the negation of 'The beauty | Of common living', and like the substantiation of 'a Common Private makes but little show'. 'And having arrived were to accept the thing in dumb | Acquiescence'; 'Men I have known fine, are dead in France, in exile, | One my friend is dumb, other friends dead also'; 'Leave dumb the love that filled me'. 'Patriotic tradition and local pastoral were . . . what he began with', as Silkin says; and from that he pushed forward, not only into a realization of the *patria*'s sanctions and restrictions but also into a finely judged equivalent of what Army regulations categorized as 'dumb insolence'. *Severn & Somme* embodies the process. There had to be the finding of some negotiable ground between the ephemeral bravura of 'make | The name of poet terrible in just war' and the enduring witness of 'the silent dead . . . fallen in such a war', 'the noblest cause'. 'Spring. Rouen, May 1917' is a vision of the coinherence of *patria* and rightful patrimony: 'Living and dead, we shall come home at last | To her sweet breast, | England's; by one touch be paid in full'. In that time Gurney asks, rhetorically, even out of his own 'dumb[ness]' 'what music shall not come?' This poem both affirms a conviction and presages a disenchantment. A number of finer later poems, notably 'It is Near Toussaints', are haunted by it. In 'Spring. Rouen, May 1917' the affirmation is made in the form of a question which sets out to be an 'aureate' rhetorical question but turns into a real one, even as it is uttered. The answers to that real question are forthcoming, not only in the direct accusation that England has neglected those whom she should have cherished and cheated those whom she should have paid in full, but also in the awkward factual insistences on just and unjust price, on 'pittance' and the 'unpaid hand', on 'the hours, the wage hours' and 'the vulgar | Infantry—so dull and dirty and so underpaid'.

Belloc wrote, in *The Servile State*, 'It is difficult indeed to dispossess the possessors. It is by no means so difficult . . . to modify the factor of freedom'. Gurney's 'hobby' is at once a transformation of this ambiguous 'factor of freedom' and a recognition that you cannot dispossess the possessors by staking the claims of native genius. It is both creating one's own world and dumbly acquiescing in the fact that it is unlikely ever to be anything but one's own world. The estate of poetry is akin to the condition of those whom Belloc calls 'dispossessed free men'.

Hilaire Belloc, who 'was all our master', is the author (unnamed) of four lines of verse which Gurney quotes in a letter and evidently esteems:

> Of Courtesy, it is not less
> Than Courage of Heart or Holiness,
> Yet in my Walks it seems to me
> That the Grace of God is in Courtesy.

As Gurney says, 'that's true and memorable enough'; but it also shows why, at the same time, Belloc was not good enough and why others whom Gurney admired, Chesterton and Gibson, were not good enough either. With Belloc, as with Sorley, the prosaic insight fails to penetrate the lyric sensibility. Or, rather, the lyric metre and diction rebuff the rhythms and inflexions of the otherwise independent mind. The verse is very lively but it is not alive with sensuous intelligence. Belloc, it must be observed, was Brooke's master too. The author of '1914' knew *The Four Men* 'almost . . . by heart' and his indebtedness is manifest in the fifth sonnet of the sequence. In *The Path to Rome*, Gurney's 'trench companion', there is much said about hardship and labour and something of circumstance. It is characteristic that 'In all these Circumstances' should be the brief running-title for an anecdote about Oxonian pedantry; about the 'great and terrible debate . . . as to whether one should say "under these circumstances" or "in these circumstances"'. Belloc's riposte cuts the knot by proposing '*Quae quum ita sint* as a common formula' at which they all fall to wrangling again 'like kittens in a basket'. That is to say, it is the 'reality of self' which triumphs in Belloc, a selfhood tempered and tested by 'Discipline and Comradeship', 'isolation and despairing fatigue', 'repose, certitude, and, as it were, a premonition of glory'. The 'as it were' betrays the self-satisfied rumination that Belloc's stubborn selfhood so often reposes in; though the exercise of an orthodox lyric sentiment is from time to time most mellifluously done, as in 'Ha'nacker Mill' which Gurney set to music in 1920 or in the song which Brooke almost certainly knew by heart:

> The passer-by shall hear me still,
> A boy that sings on Duncton Hill.

Full of these thoughts and greatly relieved by their metrical expression, I went, through the gathering darkness, southward across the Downs to my home.

The way in which Belloc's style and ethos come together here, in a full close on the phrase 'my home', exemplifies both what Gurney admired and what he had to leave behind. He left it behind because he could not enter into it. With part of his being, I believe, he yearned to as he yearned for the 'golden room' of Gibson and Abercrombie.

> The amazed heart cries angrily out on God.

The heart is 'amazed' and 'cries out' because of the 'men broken', 'horses shot', 'dying in shell-holes both, slain by the mud'; but it is also amazed and angry to find itself crying out from the expectation and idiom of a literary patrimony violently foreclosed upon ('Hungry for beauty', 'pitiful-hearted', 'wending', 'foredone'). In that final line of 'Pain' the push of the denunciation is toward a crying-out *at* God. 'On God' is, in the end, the more acceptable way of putting it. The sonnet, drafted in February 1917, was sent in a letter to Marion Scott. Had the numerous books of verse which Gurney received from her included a poorly-printed pamphlet issued in 1916, he would have seen how compacted in Rosenberg's work amazement and anger had already become. Though Rosenberg's tug-of-war in his poem 'God' was also exerted against the gravitational pull of Abercrombie's epic style, he was clearing his meanings with more certitude than Gurney:

> Who rests in God's mean flattery now? Your wealth
> Is but his cunning to make death more hard.
> Your iron sinews take more pain in breaking.
> And he has made the market for your beauty
> Too poor to buy, although you die to sell.

There is no evidence that Rosenberg's *Moses*, privately printed as were the two previous pamphlets, *Night and Day* (1912) and *Youth* (1915), ever came to the notice of Marion Scott, or of Gurney, and no evidence from Rosenberg's letters that he knew of *Severn & Somme*. The common factor is the admiration both men felt and expressed for Abercrombie and Gibson. One is inclined to say of each of them, as Robert Frost said of Edward Thomas, that 'he was suffering from a life of subordination to his inferiors'. They were not literary hacks, however, and where Thomas had 'about lost patience with the minor poetry it was his business to review', they had their enthusiasms, at some of which the amazed heart now cries out. We once more encounter an Edwardian and Georgian 'reality of circumstance', Edward Thomas's 'centrifugal age, in which principles and aims are numerous, vague, uncertain, confused, and in conflict', in which 'the lack of good criticism, or even of moderately good criticism that has any authority, defrauds many noble and beautiful voices of the ears which expect them.' It is noteworthy that, like Gurney in his numerous amazed and angry cries that England had refused to honour his draft, and like Rosenberg with his emblem of marketed beauty, Thomas associates false taste with social injustice: the noble and beautiful voices have been 'defrauded' of their rightful audience. If Gurney in his later asylum poems comes to sound more and more like a man riding a hobby horse, that is because, in an exemplary way, he is. A man shut away for some fifteen years, reiterating with slightly varying cadence 'I was a war poet, England bound to honour by Her blood', is by that very evidence obsessed, devoted to one idea 'out of proportion to its real importance'. What causes him to 'cry out' is the discovery that the lyric voice does not necessarily square with the facts of experience. There is, of course, nothing unusual in this discovery. What is remarkable is the way in which the squaring up is made the body of the poetry itself.

Both Blunden and Kavanagh have pointed out that the poet who was clearly moved and delighted by the great church-edifices of Gloucester and Tewkesbury came increasingly to associate the 'square shaped' creations of men's minds and hands with 'a sense of rightness and order'. When he writes of the 'square shaping' of Byrd's 'Motetts' (he had bought a volume of them for a shilling in the Faringdon Road), it is possible that he is linking typography, the square breves and semi-breves, the spade-headed minims, of Tudor church music with Byrd's rectitude, his dual fidelity as recusant and craftsman. Recusancy in a general sense appealed to Gurney (though he himself was brought up an Anglican). He saw himself as having 'wrought a square thing out of my stubborn mind', though the stubbornness here is awkwardly ambiguous. Is the mind 'stubborn' because it will yield, or because it will not yield? Belloc and Chesterton, laureates of intractability, were hugely forthcoming and Gibson's *Collected Poems 1905–1925* is a volume of nearly 800 pages. Gurney began with Belloc-like lyric notions: 'At present I am writing a ballad of the Cotswolds, after Belloc's "South Country" ... I find ballad writing very grateful and comforting to the mind ... Someday maybe I'll write music with not less facility'. Some seventeen months later, in February 1917, he writes: 'You see, most of my (always slow) mind is taken up with trying not to resist Things, which means a passive unrhythmical mind and music'. The hobbyist has found his vocation. While metre and rhythm in such poems as 'Tewkesbury' and 'It is

Near Toussaints' seem to hover between standard pentameter and alexandrine, with abrupt stress-clusters making each line a law to itself, the 'slow
spirit' of the sense goes straight on, taking enjambment in its stride, taking
the measure of the 'passive unrhythmical mind and music', the 'trying not to
resist Things', those massive determinisms which he sensed in the energies,
inertias, and attritions of the war and the post-war years.

The reaction of the creative spirit when it first discovers that it has been
taken in, has taken, or mistaken, album trillings for 'wrought art's perfection', is one of rage; and it may take some time to discover that there is a
wrought art's perfection quite over and above the deft management of
aureate cliché. Gurney does discover that; but he prefers for some time to
realize in musical terms his awareness of verbal power. He quotes three lines
of Whitman and immediately relates them to a 'chord on trumpets' which
he scribbles on a treble stave:

He calls 'this chord on trumpets' 'my mind-picture of triumph and restrained
gloriously-trembling exultation'. This is from a letter of late September 1915.
Just over two years later, 23 October 1917, he writes from the trenches that
he 'illicitly walked under the stars, watching Orion and hearing his huge
sustained chord . . . through the night'. Again he scribbles out a patch of stave:

and, immediately afterwards, quotes some verse (four lines of Belloc, seven
of Yeats's 'The Folly of Being Comforted'), adding: 'The great test of Art—
the Arts of Music, Writing, Painting anyway is to be able to see the eyes
kindly and full of calm wisdom that would say these things behind the page'.
What he says is less than what he does. 'The eyes kindly and full of calm
wisdom' is a literary autodidact's philosophizing. What he conceives and
embodies in his scribbled chords is something other than his own fondness
for synaesthetic imagery ('the song Orion sings', 'Music of light', 'Some
silver thread of sound', 'music's gold') and something more than the device,
employed by Belloc in *The Path to Rome* and *The Four Men*, of inserting song

melodies and snatches of tune. I am convinced that it is in these two passages where Gurney strikes his chord that we get close to his creative being. For that which 'strikes a chord' in him, he finds that he can strike a chord. It is like Whitman's 'clef of the universes'. Gurney's chord is a figure or emblem of technique as 'exultation', linking the cosmic architecture of the stars in the night sky to the minute particulars with which man expresses his 'cunning and masterful mind'. 'The attitude towards Bach', he writes around New Year 1916, 'can hardly be called by so cold a word as admiration, it is an enormous and partly incredulous love; a wonder at such a wealth of wonderfulness and such a control'. This 'partly incredulous love' is the positive of which 'The amazed heart cries angrily out on God' is the negative. Gurney's emblem is of control at such a pitch that technical perfection is itself the chord of the 'calm wisdom', that 'foundation stone' of belief in 'simplicity . . . most powerful' which is 'to be desired above all things whatsoever'. As we read Gurney's simple phrases our minds move from that which upholds us ('foundation stone') to that which we look up to ('to be desired above all things whatsoever'):

> What is best of England, going quick from beauty,
> Is manifest, the slow spirit going straight on,
> The dark intention corrected by eyes that see,
> The somehow getting there, the last conception
> Bettered, and something of one's own spirit outshown;
> Grown as oaks grow, done as hard things are done.

These lines are from 'Tewkesbury', belonging to the 1919–22 period, just prior to the poet's committal to Barnwood House asylum, Gloucester. Gurney here returns upon the stubbornness and stumbling of his own autodidacticism, transfiguring the innocent self-absorption of the 'hobby', the good intentions of the barrack-room debating club. 'Somehow', 'something', those mere space-filling words, are 'realized', as a musician 'realizes' a figured bass; 'outshown' is almost 'outshone'—you have to blink your eyes to make sure that it is not 'outshone'; plain speech is wrought from impediment, from inept repetitiousness. 'Tewkesbury', to Gurney, is first and foremost the tower of the noble abbey-church, just as 'Gloucester' is above all the great cathedral and its massive yet delicate tower. These 'fair fashioned' shapes of 'Square stone', appearing to rise so effortlessly yet slowly and painfully con-structed 'by the laboured thought', unite the centuries-old huddle of common

life with the great cosmic architecture visible in the night sky in hard-won
exultant contrast and commingling:

> Square tower, carved upward by the laboured thought,
> The imagined bare concept, how must that soften
> Now to the ivory glow and pride unsought—
> Queenly Andromeda not so exalted often.

Gurney's achievement, seen in this light, is to have composed an architecture of rhythm and phrasing that is at once 'laboured' and 'bare' and
'exalted':

> It is near Toussaints, the living and dead will say:
> 'Have they ended it? What has happened to Gurney?'
> And along the leaf-strewed roads of France many brown shades
> Will go, recalling singing, and a comrade for whom also they
> Had hoped well. His honour them had happier made.
> Curse all that hates good. When I spoke of my breaking
> (Not understood) in London, they imagined of the taking
> Vengeance, and seeing things were different in future.
> (A musician was a cheap, honourable and nice creature.)
> Kept sympathetic silence; heard their packs creaking
> And burst into song—Hilaire Belloc was all our master.
> On the night of all the dead, they will remember me,
> Pray Michael, Nicholas, Maries lost in Novembery
> River-mist in the old City of our dear love, and batter
> At doors about the farms crying 'Our war poet is lost',
> 'Madame—no bon!'—and cry his two names, warningly, sombrely.

This, it could be argued, is the work of a man simultaneously unable to leave
things well alone and too obsessed to attend well to details that need tending.
It is made up of hoarded bits and pieces, 'little bits of jargon', 'poor bare jests'.
In certain details of syntax and rhyme it seems 'amateurish', it has the 'faults or
deficiencies' sometimes found in the work of 'one who cultivates anything as
a pastime': 'remember me . . . Novembery'; 'His honour them had happier
made'. It sounds like a beginner's work, though by this time he is far from
that; the verse carries a heavy burden of echo and obsessed recollection. 'It is
Near Toussaints' recalls 'Toussaints' of *War's Embers*: 'It was the day of all the
dead— | Toussaints'. Belloc had set the last part of *The Four Men* on 'The
Second of November 1902', the inspiration of the 'Duncton Hill' song.
Gurney has conflated La Toussaint, 1 November, and La Fête des Morts,
2 November, but in this, one gathers, he may simply be following French

custom. In 'All Souls' Day 1921' he goes back over the ground of that first 'Toussaints'. 'Merville' is named in both, but he now writes of the 'tolling summons' and 'other land memories' that 'These were of All Souls' Day indeed'. Before even *Severn & Somme* appeared, he had said 'I want badly to write an "All-Hallows Day" and "A Salute", but cannot get time to think, and am not big enough for what I want to say.' In the years that followed he wrote himself into what he wanted to say and attempted also to write himself out of the anger and suffering, in the process of writing it out through an intermittent but reiterative series of Hallow-tide poems. We first heard the theme in any strength in 'Spring. Rouen, May 1917' of *Severn & Somme*: 'We shall come home, | We shall come home again, | Living and dead, one huge victorious host—'. In the 'Toussaints' of *War's Embers*, the 'lines of khaki without end', common yet ominous, march living into a landscape of the dead; unvanquished rather than victorious. In 'It is Near Toussaints', 'along the leaf-strewed roads of France many brown shades | Will go, recalling singing' and it is the same scene, but they are revenants. It is Hallowe'en, 'the night set apart for a universal walking abroad of spirits', 'the night', as Gurney says, 'of all the dead'. The poem uneasily involves the unearthly and the familial, the threatening presences and the decent pieties. It is the mood of 'To the Prussians of England' accosting a remembrance of *patria* and patri-mony, the 'beauty | Of common living', 'the old City of our dear love', the 'house of steadfastness and quiet pride'.

Walt Whitman, who celebrated 'spontaneous songs', 'ecstatic songs', was a dedicated reviser and reworker of his texts, 'returning', as he said, upon his poems, 'considering, lingering long'. Gurney, his disciple in craft as in thought, was also a reviser in that original sense of the word: he looked again or repeatedly at; he looked back or meditated on; he went through again what he had once been through. A quatrain from one of the *War's Embers* poems: 'Where's Gurney now, I wonder, | That smoked a pipe all day; | Sometimes that talked like blazes, | Sometimes had naught to say?', is recalled and retuned: 'Have they ended it? What has happened to Gurney?' That which may strike us as awkwardness is in fact both intensification and opening out, a release from harmless metrical prattle into a 'new rhythmus' as Whitman had called it. The falling trochaic cadences of 'ended . . . happened . . . Gurney' caught in the rising inflection of the two-fold question remind us of Whitman's 'recitative', as in 'This Compost', a poem which Gurney particularly admired: 'Where have you disposed of their carcasses? | Those drunkards and gluttons of so many generations?'

In 'It is Near Toussaints' formal homage is still paid to Belloc, which is fitting. There are things in the poem that chime with a sentence from *The Path to Rome*:

> The mind released itself and was in touch with whatever survives of conquered but immortal Spirits.

As I have tried to show, Belloc could invoke, with some grace and panache, the idea of 'release' from various forms of collectivist secularist constraint. He could not release himself, or those who were constrained by his eloquence, from the limitations of an agreeable fluency. Nevertheless his paradox 'conquered but immortal', like Chesterton's 'adamantine tendernesses', points us towards the centre of Gurney's argument, his indignant vision of 'The rulers of England, lost in corruptions and increases | All mean . . . While the cheated dead cry, unknowing, "Eadem Semper"'. This is like Owen's 'old Lie'; it is also like Belloc's 'divergence' between 'moral phrases' and 'touting and cozening'. '*Madame—no bon!*' is Gurney's retort to 'unknowing' and knowing one's place, and pretty grim at that. Brophy and Partridge have described the typical wartime *estaminet* and its proprietress who 'must have no objection to tobacco smoke and ribald choruses in English and pidgin French'. It is here that Gurney sets the scene of several poems, 'The Estaminet', 'Toasts and Memories', ' "On Rest" ', 'Le Coq Francais', 'Laventie', 'Robecq Again', 'It is Winter'. 'No bon', like 'Tray bong' and 'Na pooh fini' is a bit of the pidgin French that Gurney enjoyed. '*Madame—no bon!*' is, however, something more than the sum-total of these memories. The impassive matriarch of the *estaminet*, gathering to herself Gurney's regal amanuensis, 'La Comptesse Tilda', and the 'Unknown Lady' of *Severn & Somme*, is even so the intolerant *patria*, 'England the Mother', 'darling Mother and stern', now sternly rebuked, sombrely warned, in the 'two names' of the poet and in the name of the 'cheated dead', those 'conquered but immortal Spirits'. Love and 'fierce indignation' may be perilously balanced here, but the balance is held; and the indignation, like the love, is wholly accounted for, not only by the evidence of the 'life' but also, and more importantly, within the perplexed yet open measures of the work. But there would be little point and even less justice in claiming so much for Gurney's indignant vision if one did not believe that, in 'It is Near Toussaints' and others of his finest poems, he had worked his own release from what Gibson cheerily termed 'the manifold | Delights a little net of words may hold' and had discovered, within the texture of diction, syntax, and rhythm, the exact, and exacting, sense of 'stumbling blind through the difficult door', the matching of 'lines and reality'.

The assertion that Gurney 'detested irony' is allowable if we take 'irony' to mean 'sarcasm', 'ridicule', 'dissimulation', 'pretence', any of those thoughts, words, or gestures which he, like Whitman, would deem a betrayal of comradeship. I further concede that he thought Hardy's *The Return of the Native* 'perverse' in its exploitation of 'all those feelings that make one lump the world's experiences'. I could not agree that he rejected a more magnanimous ironic awareness, a sense of the 'contradictory outcome of events as if in mockery of the promise and fitness of things'. The constant witness of his poems and letters attests not only to his angry bewilderment but also to his stubborn grasp of the promise and fitness of things. 'Lump' is demotic; it is also magisterial. Our capacity to endure is both judge and thrall of the mere necessity to endure. It is a form of assent that squares with the adamantine tendernesses of Whitman's 'And often to me they are alive after what custom has served them, but nothing more'. For such poets as Whitman and Gurney there are always two tunes: the tune that is called and what they make of it. And that, in a double sense, is their calling (or their hobby).

26

Isaac Rosenberg, 1890–1918

I saac Rosenberg is a Jewish poet who works within the textures and through the medium of the English language. He is indeed, fully and integrally, a British poet, though I read some significance into the fact that, on one occasion at least, he sought reassurance on the question of his nationality. 'Thanks for the information about my being a British subject' he remarked in a letter to Ernest Lesser. Rosenberg, at that time aged 23, was a student at the Slade School of Art. His citizenship, thus affirmed or reaffirmed, entitled him to compete for the newly established Rome Prize of 1913.

The basic facts behind his inquiry can be briefly stated. He was the child of a young Lithuanian Jew who had arrived in Britain in 1887 or 1888 and of the young wife who had followed him a short time later. Isaac was born in Bristol in 1890, the Rosenbergs' second surviving child (there were to be five more who reached adulthood). When he was 7 the family moved to London, to a succession of small dwellings in the East End.

One of the earliest and still one of the best advocates of Rosenberg's work, the late D. W. Harding, was an academic psychologist; and the emphasis given by his formal training is evident, but not obtrusive, throughout his critical analysis of Rosenberg's poetry and poetics. Harding's emphasis is placed—I think rightly—on the aspects and qualities of Rosenberg's intuitively profound grasp of the English language; and he is to be trusted at points where academic hypothesis has an opportunity (provided it has the ability, as Harding certainly had) to check itself against the nature and structure of what is actually upon the page. Harding writes:

> [Rosenberg's] finest passages are not concerned exclusively either with the strength called out by war or with the suffering: they spring more directly

from the events and express a stage of consciousness appearing before either simple attitude has become differentiated.

I am sufficiently persuaded that experience moves into and through language much as Harding suggests. One cannot come to an equitable valuation of Rosenberg's work without acknowledging his own recognition of the psychology of circumstance, of the interrelatedness of experience and language, or without perceiving the cogency with which he engages his own inwardness and 'outer semblance'.

As critics we have the uncritical habit of referring, ponderously yet airily, to an author's 'individual voice', as if this were a simple and uncontested birthright. And yet, in literature, few things are more difficult to achieve or to describe. One strong indication of the quality of Rosenberg's creative imagination is that it perceives this to be so, within the given nature of things. It is the true nature of the free will to know itself circumscribed, of the abrasive intellect to know itself abraded; of clear-sightedness to recognize its occlusions and self-occlusions, of integrity to have to live with the knowledge of collusion and compromise. In the definitive 'brute' confrontations, the individual voice is that speaking self-realizing speech which can in some way be freed from, or even denied to, the general undifferentiating clamour of things: things material and things of the mind—the alienating power that seventeenth-century moral writers epitomized by the word 'opinion'.

Among the numerous locations and dislocations in which I sense Rosenberg's own acknowledgement of such conditions, we may note the following examples, taken from various letters in chronological sequence: 'the very fibres are torn apart, and application deadened by the fiendish persistence of the coil of circumstance' (1911); 'one conceives one's lot (I suppose it's the same with all people, no matter what the condition) to be terribly tragic' (1911); 'Create our own experience! We can, but we don't' (1911); 'I have thrown over my patrons they were so unbearable, and as I can't do commercial work, and I have no other kind of work to show, it puts me in a fix' (n.d. 1912?); 'when one's only choice is between horrible things you can choose the least horrible' (1915); 'I[,] feeling myself in the prime and vigour of my powers . . . seeing with helpless clear eyes the utter destruction of the railways and avenues of approaches to outer communication cut off' (October 1915); 'I send you here my two latest poems, which I have managed to write, though in the utmost distress of mind, or perhaps because of it' (11 March 1916); 'I am determined that this war, with all its powers for devastation, shall not master my poeting . . . I will not leave a corner of my consciousness covered up, but saturate myself with the strange and extra-ordinary conditions of this life, and it will all refine itself into poetry later on' (Autumn 1916); 'Sometimes I give way and am appalled at the devastation this life seems to have made in my nature . . . I seem to be powerless to compel my will to any direction, and all I do is without energy and interest' (14 February 1918); 'I want it [the "Unicorn"] to symbolize the war and all the devastating forces let loose by an ambitious and unscrupulous will' (8 March 1918).

Reading through these quotations in chronological order, spanning a period from sometime prior to 1911 until a few weeks before his death in action in the Spring of 1918, I am struck by a weight of coherence embedded within the long run of disadvantage and ill luck, yet detached from it. I have, further, the strong impression that all these happenings, in one sense random, in a profounder sense purposeful, are mediated for us through an overall and distinct vision of circumstance and conduct, a strength of purpose that is not diminished by its being at the same time an acknowledgement of enforced weakness, bafflement, and failure.

I would add that a pattern and substance of mind, displayed chronologic-ally here, is also to be recognized as the pattern and substance of Rosenberg's poetry at its characteristic best. The accomplishment, the finished work, the book, the poem as it stands, the particular self-containment, or aloofness, of the work of art is nonetheless always vulnerable to the mass and weight of 'opinion', a form of inertia for which the phrase 'general reading public' seems not merely inadequate but also unjust. In consideration of British and American poetry in the second half of the twentieth century, the quotidian has been, with significant exceptions, overvalued as the authenticating factor in works of the imagination. The poem itself, assessed in this way, becomes the author's promise to pay on demand, to provide real and substantial evidence of a suffering life for which the poem itself is merely a kind of tictac or flyer.

Although it is a stultifying error to suppose that the poem's link with actuality exists only in such simple cause and effect relationships: *I feel, therefore the poem has life*, it needs to be said that, from first to last, Rosenberg is a poet of feeling; and this notwithstanding the fact that a recurrent word, a keyword even, when he talks about his own writing, is 'idea'. I do not mean that he feels strongly about ideas, or that he is a theorist of the emotions, but rather that he feels the ideas and thinks his feelings:

Expression

Call—call—and bruise the air!
Shatter dumb space!
Yea! We will fling this passion everywhere,
Leaving no place

For the superb and grave
Magnificent throng,
The pregnant queens of quietness that brave
And edge our song

Of wonder at the light,
(Our life-leased home)
Of greeting to our housemates. And in might
Our song shall roam

Life's heart, a blossoming fire
Blown bright by thought,
While gleams and fades the infinite desire,
Phantasmed naught.

Can this be caught and caged?
Wings can be clipt
Of eagles, the sun's gaudy measure gauged,
But no sense dipt

In the mystery of sense.
The troubled throng
Of words break out like smother'd fire through dense
And smouldering wrong.

'Expression' was included in Rosenberg's second pamphlet, *Youth*, which places it no later than March or early April 1915. The first thing to be said is that it is all idea and all feeling; in this respect it is already at one with Rosenberg's later and somewhat better-known poems of 1916–18, 'Break of Day in the Trenches', 'Returning, we hear the larks', 'Dead Man's Dump', 'Daughters of War'.

What, one is asked, is 'Expression' about? It is about itself; its syntax, especially in the enjambments of the first three stanzas, is like Donne's in the 'Third Satire' as he seems to hear and envisage someone striving to attain Truth: 'and hee that will | Reach her, about must, and about must goe'; though the vision of itself that Rosenberg's poem enacts is not at all like Donne. The thinking—of which 'Expression' is an active record—is that of a creative imagination certainly influenced by reading Emerson and probably influenced also by reading Nietzsche.

'Expression' is a poem of energy endeavouring to work outwards, struggling not to be turned back upon itself. What it arrives at, in the final three
lines, the most nearly paraphrasable lines of the poem, is essentially the
nexus of circumstance from which the desire to write it has sprung:

> The troubled throng
> Of words break out like smother'd fire through dense
> And smouldering wrong.

The nature of the 'dense and smouldering wrong' is, I believe, sufficiently
documented in the brief extracts from letters which I gave earlier; one of
these in particular calls for repetition here:

> I[,] feeling myself in the prime and vigour of my powers...seeing with
> helpless clear eyes the utter destruction of the railways and avenues of
> approaches to outer communication cut off.

In a sentence which I have not previously quoted Rosenberg adds: 'It is true
I have not been killed or crippled, been a loser in the stocks, or had to
forswear my fatherland, but I have not quite gone free and have a right to say
something'. A few days after writing this, in October 1915, he went to the
recruiting office, was passed fit (despite being in poor health and below
regulation height) and was posted to the 12th (Bantam) Battalion of the
Suffolk Regiment at Bury St Edmunds. In the first of the surviving letters
written after enlistment ('on YMCA notepaper, headed "HM Forces on
Active Service" ') he remarks: 'Besides[,] my being a Jew makes it bad
amongst these wretches. I am looking forward to having a bad time
altogether'. Those four abrupt words 'my being a Jew' focus his attention,
and ours, on a new phase of his imaginative concentration—from now until
his death his writing, particularly in the verse play *Moses* and in the final
lyrics, will identify itself with increasing insistence as Jewish—but the 'dense
| And smouldering wrong' confirmed and contested in the three closing
lines of 'Expression' engages the racial issues with questions and conditions
common to Jew and Gentile alike in the first decade and a half of the last
century: how to exist with decency on the line between respectable poverty
and abject penury; how to claim one's entitlement to speak, and beyond
that, even to be heard when one is so circumscribed.

Wilfred Owen, whose family circumstances were fairly modest and who
would not have been considered suitable officer material in the peacetime
regular army, took his status as a 'gentleman' for granted as he took also

for granted his moral obligation to speak out as a witness on behalf of the inarticulate common soldier. Yet three of the most remarkable British poets of the First World War were members of that mute stratum. One of these was, and indeed is, 22311 Pte. I. Rosenberg, 8 Platoon B Coy, 1st KORL, BEF.

The doctrine of personal responsibility can be taken too far or not far enough. There is little danger at the present time of the majority opinion taking it too far. Granted that caveat, I do not hold Wilfred Owen person-ally responsible for his blankness respecting articulacy among the other ranks. Each phase of culture is characterized, if only in part, by such patches of blankness. Owen, the sincere Shelleyan among his pre-war occupations and preoccupations, was eager in his concern for social welfare and lyrical in his appreciation of beauty found in unlikely places:

> On Sat[urday] being now tired of the West End, I thought a little ugliness would be refreshing; and striking east from the P[ost] O[ffice] walked down Fenchurch St. and so into the Whitechapel High Street, & the Whitechapel Road. Ugliness! I never saw such beauty, in two hours, before that Saturday Night. The Jews are a delightful people, at home, & that night I re-read some Old Testament with a marvellous great sympathy & cordiality!

This Daedalean epiphany occurred on the evening of Saturday, 12 June 1915. Owen's perambulations would have taken him close to Dempsey Street, in which the Rosenbergs lived at number 87. Whitechapel High Street and Whitechapel Road, together with the adjacent Library and Art Gallery, were the meeting-places for Isaac and a circle of friends and acquaintances, a group at once closely- and loosely-knit, which included David Bomberg and Mark Gertler, John Rodker and Joseph Leftwich, Sonia Cohen whose portrait Rosenberg painted, whom Bomberg courted, and who married Rodker: a magnificently unmute throng, notwithstanding Leftwich's memories of their 'mooch[ing] around the streets of White-chapel completely wrapped up in our own misery'.

A surviving letter from Rosenberg to the businessman and novelist Sydney Schiff ('Stephen Hudson') dated or postmarked 8 June 1915, four days before Owen took that epiphanic stroll, shows him occupied in mailing, to various men-of-letters whom he hoped to interest in his work, copies of a privately printed pamphlet of poems, *Youth*, one hundred copies of which seem to have been run off—presumably after hours—by his friend Reuben Cohen, using the printing press of his employer Israel Narodiczky.

This letter to Schiff, though short, is, to use a word of Rosenberg's conjuring, pregnant: pregnant with statement and implication. It has three paragraphs. In the first he states that 'What people call technique is a very real thing, it corresponds to construction and command of form in painting'; then he adds 'My technique in poetry is very clumsy I know'. The tone of magisterial diffidence is entirely characteristic. The second paragraph wonders 'whether Mr. Clutton Brock could get me some Art writing to do for any journals he is connected with'. The final paragraph is one sentence, at once abrupt and distracted (*distrait*):

> I am thinking of enlisting if they will have me, though it is against all my principles of justice—though I would be doing the most criminal thing a man can do—I am so sure my mother would not stand the shock that I don't know what I can do.

In fact and in practice Rosenberg's technique proves more than equal to the forces of distraction—a word by which I mean to invoke: agitated incertitude, not knowing what to do for the best; also chronic absent-mindedness ('My memory, always weak, has become worse since I've been out here'), a form of forgetfulness which is not actually a sign of weakness but of strength—the immense strength of other priorities, such as working on massive and complex poems in your head amid the manifold terrors and routine hard labour of life in the trenches.

Poets during the greater part of the nineteenth century were conventionally expected, and repeatedly enjoined, to teach. Wordsworth's original conception of this role was that the poet's privilege and burden is to teach radically new doctrines of relationship: both to the self and to society, and to the self in its relation and disrelation to society. Owen is perhaps the last true representative of this form of Romantic *paideia*, a continuity unbroken from 1798 to 1918. I risk the word 'true' as being perilously appropriate to the increasingly laboured, increasingly exhausted, line of moral succession. It was at once Owen's strength and weakness that he half-recognized how a radical doctrine of poetic teaching had become diffused, while it had also hardened, into a standing convention of ideals. Owen, in 1917–18, began to teach the hollowness, the rigid carapace, of the ideal, but he did so in forms of eloquence impossible to disengage fully from those of the discredited patrimony. 'All a poet can do to-day is warn. That is why the true Poets must be truthful.' The message of Owen's statement is the necessary eradication of the 'old Lie', but the oratory of his voice is still much like that of Tennyson—although, by 1918, Owen clearly regarded Tennyson as a great liar (recall that Tennyson had lamented the failure of *Idylls of the King* to 'teach men those things', i.e. the modern world's lack of and need for 'reverence and chivalrous feeling').

Far more than Owen, Rosenberg was a poet made and re-made by exposure. I allude here first to Owen's poem of that title—'Exposure'—a late work begun in December 1917 and finished in September 1918, a lament for soldiers as men excluded, shut out of their own homes, deprived, sufferers of unremitting privation; and secondly to Rosenberg's letter, written in the Autumn of 1916 to Laurence Binyon:

> I am determined that this war, with all its powers for devastation, shall not master my poeting; that is, if I am lucky enough to come through all right. I will not leave a corner of my consciousness covered up, but saturate myself with the strange and extraordinary new conditions of this life, and it will all refine itself into poetry later on.

It is one thing to 'determine' a course of action; quite another to fulfil it. Victory in this field can be achieved only through technique (I do not say that technique guarantees success). Rosenberg's technique is in part instinctive, i.e. reading 'exposure' correctly: not as deprivation but as openness to saturation. In part it is associative. I refer here to the close association, at a period crucial to them both, of the young Rosenberg and the young David Bomberg. It was a sparring friendship, begun around 1908 on the pavements of Whitechapel and Stepney and continued at the Whitechapel Library, and subsequently, though not regularly, in the homes of one or other of their group.

The next step in my discussion takes us from Rosenberg's and Bomberg's well-documented association towards much more debatable ground. I claim to associate Rosenberg's discovery of technique in writing with Bomberg's discovery of technique in painting. There is no documentation that I know of to confirm my claim as anything more than speculation. At several points in his monumental study *David Bomberg* (1987), Richard Cork refers to the artist's definition of, sense of, 'mass', a definition which Bomberg did not formally articulate until many years after Rosenberg's death but which Cork finds entirely applicable to work done as early as 1914. I am somewhat puzzled by Cork's own inclination to treat the term 'mass' as if it were interchangeable with the words 'bulk' and 'weight'. I can understand the phrase 'sense of mass' only in terms of relationship, totality even; and certainly my suggestion that we carry over 'sense of mass' to Rosenberg's grasp of word-relations would be meaningless in any other interpretation. You cannot rightly speak of the 'bulk' or 'solidity' of a word in isolation, whereas it makes perfectly good sense so to describe one figure, or one figuration, in a painting.

Siegfried Sassoon described Rosenberg acutely and memorably as having 'modelled words with fierce energy and aspiration', and if my suggestion extends the metaphor it cannot change its dimension. To possess a 'sense of mass' in language would require a sense of contexture, an appreciation of, and an ability to initiate, the changes that single words and phrases undergo when moved from one context to another. As a form of technical experiment this can be traced back at least to Chaucer, but I cannot think of another modern poet writing in English who conducts the experiment more intensively than does Rosenberg. One finds a particular phrase repeated in various places: not so much reused as reforged: a reforging of feeling, with idea, into language. 'Like breath rekindling a smouldering fire' from an early poem becomes the magnificent last stanza of 'Expression': 'The troubled throng | Of words break out like smother'd fire through dense | And smouldering wrong.' The line 'With fierce energy I aspire' in a poem of 1912 finds a new concentration in the Young Hebrew's words in *Moses* (1916): 'Into that fierce unmanageable blood' and again in 'What fierce imaginings their dark souls lit' ('Dead Man's Dump', 1917). Two lines from a poem of 1914 or 1915, 'Pale horses ride before the morning | The secret roots of the sun to tread' are re-energized in 'Chagrin', one of his finest poems: 'We ride, we ride, before the morning | The secret roots of the sun to tread'. Let us call this method: thinking through the phrase or image; to so do is to endeavour to conjure up Rosenberg's gift of verbal interpenetration by means of our own impacted sense. 'Thinking through the phrase or image' signifies that the phrase or image is mediator of the idea. And let us introduce the further sense of 'think through', to resolve by process of thought. These senses are to be understood as working simultaneously not consecutively.

In its revised form 'Midsummer Frost' (which was first published in *Youth*) three new lines appear:

> He heareth the Maytime dances;
> Frees from their airy prison, bright voices,
> To loosen them in his dark imagination.

Although the intrinsic quality of these lines is not high, they present their own paraphrase of what, in Rosenberg's finest work, can only with the greatest difficulty be paraphrased (and rightly so). Asked to find the most succinct description of Rosenberg's 'desire' I would say: *the desire to free his voice*. To free his voice from what? From the condition of being regarded, or disregarded, as an expendable 'young Hebrew', a slave in the vast pool of London labour; subsequently, by simple extension, as an unidentifiable waste item in Field Marshal Haig's ever increasing expenditure of blood and treasure.

In this desire, this practice, the technical, the psychological, and the ethical are entirely at one. Each is authenticated in the other; and the earliest master-statement of such threefold validation is the poem 'Expression'. And 'Expression' itself vindicates the comparative failure of earlier attempts to free the voice: 'My Days'; 'The Present'; 'The Key of the Gates of Heaven' ('A word was the key thereof'); 'Peace' ('With fierce energy I aspire'); 'You and I' ('All our life before was but embryo | Shaping for this birth—this living moment'). 'Vindicate' rather than 'validate': the phrases I have just now quoted have little intrinsic value. It is the necessity of such failures, inseparable from his way of thinking through, that is vindicated by the weight and power of the works written in the last two years of Rosenberg's life.

If the freeing of the voice entails for Rosenberg a virtually incessant reworking of ideas through a remaking of the word-relations, it is equally evident that the integrity of the word requires a process of unmaking. In one of his most beautifully articulated short poems 'A worm fed on the heart of Corinth' (1916), the 'worm' is said to have 'lured her [Helen's] vivid beauty | To his amorphous sleep'. The 'amorphous sleep' may be understood as England's self-hypnosis of wealth and power, the sick romanticism of imperial duty and sacrifice, the poems of Henley and Newbolt, for instance, a code of conduct for professional men of letters as much as for professional men of war: all that is summed up in Wilfred Owen's contemptuous 'Tennyson, it seems was always a great child. So should I have been but for Beaumont Hamel'. In Rosenberg's poem there is found what Bomberg would term a 'sense of mass'. The single phrase on which I have concentrated, 'amorphous sleep', is only part of the total weight of the poem. The sense of 'amorphous' is not fulfilled until the final line 'More amorous than Solomon'. That one can so address the interdependence of these lines—and especially these words, 'amorphous', 'amorous'—is a justification of the entirety of the poet's imaginative grasp, and of the applicability to language of the painterly term 'mass'. The early poems have occasional striking lines, but do not reveal working interdependence of lines; that is to say, they are deficient in, even devoid of, the sense of mass.

Having achieved so much, so strikingly, in so small a compass, in 'A worm fed on the heart of Corinth', what is Rosenberg's direction, where is his mixed sense of potentiality and of restriction, and of potentiality within the restriction, to take him? It is not easy to chart the forwards, or sideways, movement of the work mainly because so much of it survives as major or minor fragments; but also because so much of the dating is uncertain. It is known that, from the completion and publication of the verse-play *Moses* in 1916, Rosenberg's attention had been increasingly devoted to plays in verse, of which two, *The Amulet* (1917) and *The Unicorn* (1918), have come down to us as a loose sequence of substantial fragments. In addition, there are two brief fragmentary drafts of yet another play, to have been called 'Adam' or 'Adam and Lilith'. Included in one of them are these two lines:

> As my thoughts, my pulses, pass
> Hungry to you, to roam your vivid beauty.

Ian Parsons writes that *Adam* was 'abandoned in favour of "The Unicorn" ' and that it came chronologically 'just before the latter play'. Vivien Noakes, while stating that it is 'impossible to date the individual MSS' of *The Amulet* and *Adam*, nonetheless finds it at least 'possible that the surviving drafts of *Adam* were written between *The Amulet* and *The Unicorn*'.

Rosenberg began to work on *The Unicorn* during 'the summer of 1917'. If the projected *Adam* did indeed come 'just before' *The Unicorn*, the surviving brief fragments could possibly have been drafted in the first half of 1917. 'A worm fed on the heart of Corinth' is dated 1916.

The phrase 'to roam your vivid beauty' in the draft for *Adam* is a variant of 'Who lured your vivid beauty' in 'A worm fed on the heart of Corinth'. 'To roam your vivid beauty' is either a vague adumbration of the intense realization still to be achieved of 'Who lured her vivid beauty' or—and this seems more likely—it is a subsequent intentional diffusion, a surrender of the kind of power achieved in the brief, concentrated lyric of 1916.

If I am right in my conjecture, Rosenberg stands as an example—certainly rare if not unique—of a poet who, having attained that which, in our fallibility, we recognize as perfection, takes the elements of that intense achievement and rethinks his way through them, even at the cost of diffusing and dissipating the grasped power. That he would have done so with pain is indicated by his correspondence: 'Now when my things fail to be clear I am sure it is because of the luckless choice of a word or the failure to introduce a word that would flash my idea plain, as it is to my own mind'. That he could, at the same time, be capable of disrupting his own coherences is indicated just as forcefully in his letters. Defending Emerson, and especially Emerson's poetry, he writes:

> Everybody has agreed . . . about the faults and the reason is obvious; the faults are so glaring that nobody can fail to see them. But how many have seen the beauties? . . . And I absolutely disagree that it is blindness or carelessness; it is the brain succumbing to the Herculean attempt to enrich the world of ideas.

There is one characteristic and essential term common to both these letters: the word 'idea'. The poet who strives for the 'word that would flash my idea plain, as it is to my own mind' and who knows very well when he has failed to find that word, is nonetheless pre-eminently the celebrant of this idea. I believe that, for the sake of advancing the idea, Rosenberg would be prepared, though not gladly, to sacrifice finality of phrase. In this respect he is the most significant English heir of Emerson as D. H. Lawrence and Ivor Gurney are the most significant English heirs of Whitman.

It is particularly in their engagement with—which is also a disengagement from—the expectations of a postulated readership that Gurney and Rosenberg, brought up in very different social circumstances, are nonetheless much alike. By 'postulated readership' I mean critically, or entrepreneurially, postulated. The 'common readership', like the 'common standard of taste' is more often than not a confection of literary middlemen. The true common reader is a natural aristocrat of the spirit, and is far more necessary, far more valuable, to a culture such as ours than are the majority of its writers. In the opening line of Gurney's 'War Books' I take 'they' to be the entrepreneurial 'they':

> What did they expect of our toil and our extreme
> Hunger—the perfect drawing of a heart's dream?
> Did they look for a book of wrought art's perfection,
> Who promised no reading, no praise, no publication?

Here Gurney indicates 'perfection', not in the sense of a working ideal for true labourers in the craft, but rather as an imposed limitation, set by an artificial consensus of tastes. In the introduction to the American edition of his (so-called) *New Poems*, D. H. Lawrence argues that a new protean sense of language and form must now be the poet's medium of endeavour; he must not seek to match the 'treasured gem-like lyrics of Shelley and Keats'. This may be a gross misreading of Keats, but it does not misread the demands of the taste-makers of Lawrence's own time, which was also Gurney's and Rosenberg's time. 'Gem-like lyrics' fails to distance Lawrence's opinion sufficiently from, for example, ex-Prime Minister Asquith's presidential address to the English Association in 1919 (with such locutions as 'incomparable lines', 'enduring power of appeal to every successive generation of lovers of poetry', 'sovereign quality of Style', and 'the stamp of immortality'), though it cannot be confused with the table-talk of Edward Marsh, who had, as he once told Rupert Brooke, 'a decided preference for poetry he could read at meals'. For Rosenberg, as for Lawrence and Gurney, the 'perfect' was composed too often of the inessential.

Not every public pronouncement was a simple projection of personal taste and opinion. A. C. Bradley, who in 1911 preceded Asquith as President of the English Association, spoke in his own presidential address of the undue influence exerted by 'the frequent incompetence of readers', 'the partially incompetent lover of poetry'. There are readers, Bradley says, 'who tend to pervert all pathos into sentimentality'. G. K. Chesterton, whom Rosenberg thought 'sly and certainly anti-Jewish', established a context in which to assess the hegemony of 'taste'. In his book on Robert Browning, published in 1903 as part of the popular *English Men of Letters* series, Chesterton observed that Browning belonged by birth

> to the solid and educated middle class—the class which is interested in letters, but not ambitious in them, the class to which poetry is a luxury, but not a necessity.

As it is Chesterton's case that we begin to understand the quality of Browning's individual voice by comprehending the cost to him of establishing a resistance to that culture of 'interest', his kinds of defeat and failure as well as the characteristics of his success, so my own discussion has attempted to take account of the causes and consequences of Rosenberg's battle with circumstance. 'Circumstance' is the material poverty of his life; it is also the cajoling and demanding 'interest' of those whose literary bent is at home with their worldly pull and substance.

Like Browning, Rosenberg was ambitious. Like Browning's his ambition was to release his own voice from the constraints of the conventionally approved voices of poetry. Rosenberg spoke incisively of poetics in terms of the 'expressive line' in painting. The term, which perhaps originates in Blake's 'bounding line', is also very like a capacity which Richard Cork attributes to Bomberg's paintings in 1913–14: the ability to make visible the 'highly energized moment'. That which Rosenberg calls the 'idea' is the 'highly energized moment'. Such a moment either will, or will not, be made 'visible' in the texture of words as it will, or will not, become visible in the painting's texture of pigment. When this is achieved, Rosenberg claims, 'It is nature's consent, her agreement that what we wrest from her we keep'. In similar terms he had written in a letter (undated, but probably July 1916): 'It [the subject of war] should be approached in a colder way [than in Brooke's "begloried sonnets"], more abstract, with less of the million feelings everybody feels; or all these should be concentrated in one distinguished emotion'.

It was perhaps the major weakness of Browning's poetry that it lent itself too easily to a cultic yearning for esoteric interpretation: the proliferation of Browning Societies. A taste for the 'exotic' is not unusual among those for whom art, in Chesterton's phrase, is a luxury, not a necessity. The gifted artist emerging from obscure poverty is especially vulnerable to such a misreading; the gifted Jewish artist emerging from such circumstances into Gentile culture is, if not the most, then among the most vulnerable: it goes with being a 'rootless cosmopolitan'. To be dubbed an exotic is to be at once acknowledged from the centre and retained at the periphery, as one of the licensed 'eccentrics' whom Mill advocated, in the essay *On Liberty*, as a necessary counterforce to democracy's levelling powers.

When, in 1922, due largely to the untiring efforts of his sister Annie, the first posthumous collection of Rosenberg's poems appeared in print, it carried an 'Introductory Memoir' by Laurence Binyon. Binyon, the civilian author of perhaps the most widely known and widely quoted poem of the Great War, 'For the Fallen', was one of the several men of letters to whom Rosenberg, before the outbreak of war, had submitted examples of his early work, hoping for a favourable reception. Binyon indeed responded generously to the 'letter in an untidy hand from an address in Whitechapel', and a meeting took place at Binyon's invitation. The very fact that ten years after that meeting and four years after Rosenberg's death, Binyon, a busy professional man and a perhaps even busier amateur of poetry and the arts, took the trouble to put together a fifty-page tribute, and to lend the publication his considerable name, speaks well for his gifts of human sympathy. When Binyon turns critic, which he does in only one paragraph of the memoir, his emphasis is placed heavily on the 'obscurities, the straining and tormenting of language in the effort to find right expression, the immaturities of style and taste' which, he suggests, do not adequately represent 'the ardent toil, and the continual self-criticism which underlay' the young poet's work.

Considered as criticism of Rosenberg's writing as it existed in 1912, Binyon's emphasis is neither inaccurate nor uncalled-for. But in 1922, with the bulk of the poet's surviving work, including *Moses* (1916), 'Louse Hunting' (1917), 'Dead Man's Dump' (1917), available for assessment, the limitation of Binyon's engagement is all too evident. What we do find, however, is the assurance that 'even as a young boy, Rosenberg cherished the traditions of his race and aspired to become a representative poet of his own nation'. It is of course easily demonstrable that, in the last two years of his life, Rosenberg focused his imagination increasingly upon Jewish themes, Jewish history, the warrior heroes of Israel. He wrote to Sydney Schiff in August 1916: 'Heine, our own Heine, we must say nothing of. I admire him more for always being a Jew at heart than anything else'. Nonetheless, Rosenberg 'aspired to become a representative poet of his own nation' as Donne, Blake, and Keats are representative poets of Rosenberg's own nation—i.e. England (or, if you prefer, Great Britain). If he had aspired to become a representative poet of his own nation, in Binyon's sense, he would have immersed himself in the study of Hebrew, a language which he did not bother to learn. Nor did he show much interest in Yiddish, though both parents were Yiddish speakers, and his Whitechapel friend Joseph Leftwich was a poet and prose-writer in both Yiddish and English; there was still, at that time, a Yiddish theatre in Whitechapel; in 1913 Bomberg made chalk and crayon studies of an audience emotionally involved in a performance: but from these aspects of local culture also, Rosenberg seems to have kept mostly aloof. He would, it is reasonable to think, have wished his work to be recognized as profoundly Jewish, as the testament of a 'young Hebrew' who was also a Levite. He would, I believe, have rejected with anger and scorn any suggestion that his poems, prose-writings, letters, paintings, and drawings could be most appropriately catalogued and shelved under the heading *Judaica*.

One's sense that Binyon's critical imagination is a poorer thing than his sympathy is compounded by a further sense that sympathy itself is less percipient, less effectively sympathetic, where critical imagination is lacking, as I believe it to be lacking in Binyon's pietas, his dutiful endorsement of the 1922 volume *Poems by Isaac Rosenberg*. The key to my belief is an important collection of verse that appeared two years after the Rosenberg volume, in 1924. This was the *Golden Treasury of Modern Lyrics*, designed as a definitive volume in direct line of succession to Palgrave's original *Golden Treasury* of 1861. Its editor was Laurence Binyon. Among Rosenberg's army contemporaries represented in the new treasury one finds the names of Edmund Blunden, Rupert Brooke, Wilfred Gibson, Robert Graves, Robert Nichols, Wilfred Owen, Siegfried Sassoon, Charles Sorley, and Edward Thomas. Rosenberg is neither represented nor referred to. It is as if misfortune can be attended to in its place, provided it keeps its place, which, so far as Rosenberg's work is concerned, it becomes painfully clear, is among the exotica, not within the canon. Binyon enters the usual caveat, a disclaimer of a kind, which editors have in any case by rote: 'Some pieces which should have found a place may have been overlooked; the right things may have been read in the wrong mood; mistakes of judgement are probably inevitable'.

The indicator here is 'mood'. In the judging of works of art the reader's, spectator's, auditor's 'mood' is at best irrelevant, at worst a gross intrusion. The greatest tribute one can pay to a fine work of art—a tribute that one ought to be able to take for granted—is that its qualities reveal one's own 'mood' to be redundant.

It is necessary to state, finally, that during Rosenberg's formative years, there was an exotic genre in vogue. Verse plays were 'in'. Lascelles Abercrombie and Gordon Bottomley, both of whom Rosenberg greatly admired and who took a kindly interest in him, wrote them. Edward Marsh devoted forty-four pages of *Georgian Poetry 1913–1915* to Bottomley's 'King Lear's Wife'. A further forty-four pages of the same volume were taken up by Abercrombie's 'The End of the World'. Wilfred Gibson's *Borderlands and Thoroughfares*, published in 1914, contained three short verse plays. Compared to the *bizarrerie* of such works, the tenor of Rosenberg's *Moses*, *The Unicorn*, and *The Amulet* is markedly classical.

There is little to be gained in arguing questions of eligibility for, or exclusion from, a century's canon. The fact that the idea of such a canon is prevalent, however, requires acknowledgement, because prescription and proscription are agents and effects of power. Moreover, Rosenberg's creative intelligence is one that concerns itself particularly closely with matters of power, both in terms of finding one's voice and in the recognition of those forces of status and circumstance which facilitate the transmission of some voices and threaten others with enforced silence. Rosenberg wrote, in March 1918:

> If I am lucky, and come off undamaged, I mean to pull all my innermost experiences into the 'Unicorn'. I want it to symbolize the war and all the devastating forces let loose by an ambitious and unscrupulous will.

There must surely be more than one canon at any given time: a canon of general acceptance and a canon of intrinsic value. General acceptance presupposes general acceptability. Intrinsic value need not be generally acceptable. I see no reason in theory, however, to prevent a work from taking its rightful place in both canons.

Even now, despite the exemplary textual attention which his work has received, Rosenberg does not have a wide readership; but the intrinsic value of his work was recognized immediately it became known and has been so recognized ever since:

> Living in a wide landscape are the flowers—
> Rosenberg, I only repeat what you were saying—.

These words, by the outstanding British poet of the Second World War, Keith Douglas, serve as a fitting conclusion. Douglas, of course, does not *only* repeat what Rosenberg was saying: the words of his tribute are those of an indebtedness in which there is no mere repetition, no transiency; nothing redundant.

27
Rhetorics of Value and Intrinsic Value

It has never been easy to define the nature of value; nonetheless forms of discourse have been designed and devoted—over many centuries—to such an attempt. Monetary theorists have created cogent descriptions, but individual cogency has not prevented general confusion even over the real nature of *intrinsic value* in relation to coins of the realm: although this term, on first acquaintance, carries a convincing air of authority.

I have deliberately restricted myself, at this point of the discussion, to the noun in the singular. To undertake any assessment of the meaning of value is to risk appearing a fool. To pronounce upon human values may expose one as an ethical charlatan. 'Human values' can, at any time and on any occasion, become vulnerable to the harsh dismissal that Dietrich Bonhoeffer gave to 'cheap grace'.

Two inferences may be drawn from what I have said thus far. It may be wiser to speak in terms of value rather than of values. It may be useful to restrict a discussion of the singular, 'value', to statements regarding the nature of *intrinsic value*. The matter of intrinsic value carries a distinct referential weight in two particular areas or spheres of activity and discourse: coinage, where it can be assayed, and moral philosophy, where it cannot. In most cases the crux of the problem is the intersection of the material and the symbolic, if intersection can be said actually to take place. If there is no intersection there is likely to be hiatus, a 'gap', somewhat in Gillian Rose's sense of *aporia*. The suspect nature of much general discourse on the nature and quality of that mystical entity or aura called 'human values' can be traced to a variety of attempts to claim continuity where none exists. This is particularly the case with the type of value-discourse that is a simple trope of monetary values, and much could be said on this in relation to currency reforms advocated and in part supervised by Isaac Newton and John Locke and in further relation to the symbolic application of monetary value to ethical and aesthetic values by various writers. If asked to name the major proponent of that form of rhetoric in which intrinsic currency value is somehow understood as underpinning and validating intrinsic ethical or aesthetic value, I would reply: John Ruskin, especially in *Unto This Last*, *Munera Pulveris*, and sections of *Fors Clavigera*. As is readily apparent from Letters 12 and 58 of *Fors*, Ruskin's own rhetorical currency can prove less than stable: in the first instance, debased with vituperation; in the second, sounding Puginesque in its insistence on purity of design. In the instance of Letter 12, it is a mark of futility to project an exhausted rage against a largely unspecified and unrealizable enemy whom one chooses to name 'Judas'. There are examples enough of this self-stultifying rhetoric among the major Victorian moralists and their immediate successors: in Thomas Carlyle especially, but also in Matthew Arnold and Ruskin; as, later, in T. S. Eliot, who took his cue from Arnold, and in Ezra Pound, who, to some extent, derived his ethical aesthetics from Ruskin.

The history of ideas is a respectable genre to which I am as indebted as any educated or self-educated man or woman of our time. It has to be said, however, that one cannot profitably debate the substance and issue of intrinsic value from the standpoint of the historian of ideas; the difficulty is revealed to be with the minting and assaying of ideas as themselves; with the transformation of ideas of quality into inherently qualitative statements. In arguments of this kind, direct quotation rather than paraphrase, therefore, must figure prominently within the texture of one's own presentation.

David Hume writes in 'Of Refinement in the Arts':

> Knowledge in the arts of government naturally begets mildness and moderation, by instructing men in the advantages of humane maxims above rigour and severity, which drive subjects into rebellion, and make the return to submission impracticable by cutting off all hopes of pardon.

To set Hume on the arts of government against a characteristic turn of phrase from one of the several sets of Tudor injunctions to the reformed clergy—'that this damnable device of despair may be clearly taken away and firm belief and steadfast hope surely conceived of all their parishioners'—is to detect, even in this small compass, significant differences and similarities. Each quotation tunes its effect by the correspondence between two given but indeterminate values: political value and English word value. In the Edwardian Injunctions of 1547, drawn up and set down with the authority and approval of Archbishop Cranmer and Lord Protector Somerset, 'despair' has a double valency, at once spiritual and temporal: it is doubly 'damnable'. Those who despair are desperate. As Thomas More wrote: 'The deuil is desperate and hath not nor cannot haue faith and trust in gods promises'. A man in despair re-enacts the political as well as the spiritual desperation of the arch-fiend: he is ready for all manner of treasons, plots, and stratagems. Correlatively, a quiet conscience in respect to God, within the terms set by the archbishop, signifies a compliant citizen, obedient to the government of the Lord Protector, mindful of the interests of the commonweal above his own.

That which stays implicated in the words authorized by Cranmer and Somerset is explicated in Hume. His word 'advantages' was understood in 1752 as it was in 1547, as advantages to the ruler rather than to the ruled. Each example is addressing the matter of convenience. In the Tudor injunctions, convenience is spelled out as a magisterial rigour of supervision. The concern manifested in the distribution of such instructions to the parish clergy is less with the diffusion of intrinsic value supposedly emanating from the boy-king—and which his fine profile portrayed on gold coins of fluctuating bullion value seems designed to suggest—than with the threat of contagion by real or imagined evil. Hume's 'Of Refinement in the Arts' is also focused on convenience, which surfaces (supposing there to be depth) in such words as 'diffuse' (vb), 'advantageous', 'naturally begets', 'render', 'beneficial':

> But industry, knowledge, and humanity, are not advantageous in private life alone: They diffuse their beneficial influence on the *public*, and render the government as great and flourishing as they make individuals happy and prosperous.

The significance of the verb 'diffuse' should not be overlooked in this genial sequence of politic salutes to private and public equity. Hume structures his sentences with such economy of syntax as to inhibit our sense of the pervading indeterminacy of his critical terms. We have to recall that diffusion means 'wide and general distribution': this is the substance of the piece, though 'substance' on reflection is not the right word. The grammar floats an insubstantiality—'and render the government as great and flourishing as they make individuals happy and prosperous'. Consider the question of clauses introduced by 'as'. English literary syntax, at the time when Hume was composing his *Essays, Moral, Political, and Literary*, was the beneficiary of various strong and weak forms of the 'as'-clause. The first I will term the clause of simple indemnity: 'as good as gold'; it is a weak form dependent upon a strong sense, at the proverbial level, of intrinsic value. The *Oxford English Dictionary* (*OED*) calls it the *comparative of equality*. The second, which I name the comparative of commonweal, is well demonstrated in the 'King James' rendering of Isaiah 24: 2: 'And it shall be as with the people, so with the priest, as with the seruant, so with his master, as with the maid, so with her mistresse, as with the buyer, so with the seller, as with the lender, so with the borower, as with the taker of vsurie, so with the giuer of vsurie to him'. This is the strong form of the *OED*'s comparative of equality: Isaiah is in fact threatening that the people will be made equal in desolation and destruction, but such threats of 'levelling' would be without effect if there were not the ever-present sense of the hierarchic and stratified commonweal as a divine propriety.

The apocalyptic pseudo-logic of such admonitions in the English of 1611 may be counted—together with the archaisms of *Euphues* that were novelties in Thomas Hobbes's childhood—among the stylistic influences discernible in *Leviathan* even while that monster is swallowing whole the old power of the English prophetic voice:

> For as that stone which by the asperity, and irregularity of Figure, takes more room from others, than it selfe fills . . . is by the builders cast away as unprofitable, and troublesome: so also, a man that by asperity of Nature, will strive to retain those things which to himselfe are superfluous, and to others necessary; and for the stubbornness of his Passions, cannot be corrected, is to be left, or cast out of Society, as combersome thereunto.

No more of that nonsense, observe, concerning the stone that the builders rejected having become the 'head of the corner': though the resonance of that great *sententia* is not without its value to Hobbes. The formulation 'as the stone which . . . so also a man that' is decorative rather than substantial; but Hobbes is skilled at making the inconsequential appear to be of consequence. In this respect he anticipates David Hume, or at least the Hume of *Essays, Moral, Political, and Literary*. I am thinking, for example, of Hume's equivocating use of 'really' when he asserts (in 'Of the Original Contract') the supremacy of 'general opinion' in moral and critical matters: 'in all questions with regard to morals, as well as criticism, there is really no other standard, by which any controversy can ever be decided'. Even so, Hobbes is his master in points of detail, in particular the knack of using fashions of syntax so as to make opinion appear to be genuine ratiocination.

There is, however, more to be said of *Leviathan* even if not—at least for the time being—of Hume's thoughts on matters literary and social. *Leviathan*, whatever else it is or is not, is a tragic elegy on the extinction of intrinsic value. None of Hobbes's opponents understood this, with the possible exception of Clarendon, himself a tragic elegist of no mean power, and except, possibly, Joseph Butler, in the *Fifteen Sermons* of 1726 and the two Dissertations, 'Of Personal Identity' and 'Of the Nature of Virtue' (both 1736). Hobbes's despair, in *Leviathan*, arises from the extinction of personal identity, which he in turn identifies with intrinsic value in the person of the young Royalist Sidney Godolphin, killed in the Civil War. The three sentences from Hobbes's 'A Review and Conclusion' beginning 'Nor is there any repugnancy between fearing the Laws, and not fearing a publique enemy' are among the greatest English examples of 'high sentence'—the equal of Browne's *sententiae* in *Urne Buriall* or Ralegh's in his preface to *The History of the World*. The question that follows is this: if Hobbes is seriously of the opinion that intrinsic value in the English commonweal perished when Godolphin was killed, how does he read his own elegiac tribute to his dead friend? The three sentences end with a splendid *traductio*: 'who hating no man, nor hated of any, was unfortunately slain in the beginning of the late Civill warre, in the Publique quarrell, by an undiscerned and an undiscerning hand'. If it can be granted that such sentences resonate in this way, may we conclude that Hobbes, with his impeccable sense of timing and upstaging, is here upstaging his own pretended cynicism of despair? How far is he implying that the intelligence that created *Leviathan* is the true heir in an untrue world, and witness for an unwitnessing future, to the magnanimity of Godolphin, Falkland, and the Great Tew 'symposium', whatever arguments to the contrary might be drawn from the theses of the work itself?

Nothing that I have so far said with regard to Godolphin's significance, for Hobbes the man as also for his *Leviathan*, adds one iota to the assessment made by Irene Coltman in *Private Men and Public Causes: Philosophy and Politics in the English Civil War* (London: Faber, 1962). We move into the next, and perhaps more contentious, stage of my argument by glancing at the final sentence of her study of Godolphin's posthumous endowment to late seventeenth-century political thought, a sentence that she takes from

Clarendon's *Brief View and Survey*, a bitter attack on Hobbes's abandonment of the spirit and principles of Great Tew: 'I cannot forbear to put him [Hobbes] in mind, that I gave him for an expiation of my own defects, and any trespasses which I may have since committed against him, the Friendship of that great Person'. 'That great Person' is Sidney Godolphin; and 'Friendship' between Hobbes and Godolphin was initiated, so Clarendon avers, by his introducing them to each other at a time when all three were fellow members of the Great Tew symposium. 'Gave him for an expiation': this is a *mea culpa* that does not mitigate—indeed it may exacerbate—the severity of Clarendon's indictment of Hobbes's book. Though 'expiation' is a singularly powerful word, Clarendon cannot be said to surrender any of the indignation to which he clearly feels entitled: the word stands in the guise of a word now foreign to Hobbes, the meaning of which needs to be given him clearly and slowly, even while its implication (tempting old friends to the sin of wrath) is laid at his door. For Clarendon, then, it is as if 'intrinsic value' is something tightly knit that treachery and ingratitude cause to unravel. It is easier to say what 'intrinsic' value is in defeat than in victory. Intrinsic value, for the loser, is sealed into enduring qualities of the life that was; the price paid by the victor is the inevitable lifelong penalty of compromise and corruption. This, I believe, is how writers as different as Andrew Marvell (in the 'Horatian Ode') and Clarendon (in the *Brief View and Survey*) reflected upon these issues.

'Reflection' is a word entirely characteristic of Joseph Butler's *Fifteen Sermons Preached at the Rolls Chapel*. Unlike Clarendon, Hobbes, or Marvell, Butler's experience of the Civil War and the first thirty or so years of its aftermath was gained at second hand. It is clear, however, that for him, as much as for Clarendon and John Bramhall, one of the more dreadful legacies of the mid-century anarchy was the publication and success of *Leviathan*. Nonetheless, where Bramhall and Clarendon struggle to uproot the new, Butler reassesses the tried and tested: for him the essay is an assay; and reflection is at the heart of it. In this he so anticipates the significance that Coleridge attaches to the word *reflection* that the relative sparsity of references to him throughout the *Marginalia*, and elsewhere in Coleridge's writings, is surprising.

There is a significant early letter written by George Eliot in 1842, when she was in her twenty-third year, at a time when even the earliest of her published fiction had still to be written; it is significant as anticipating the kind of self-correcting speculative rumination that characterizes the

authorial commentary in *Middlemarch*. The letter in question is her response
to an acquaintance, an Independent clergyman and professor of theology,
who was attempting to lead her back to the intense Evangelical faith from
which she had recently turned away. She is here commenting on a course
of corrective reading which the Reverend Francis Watts had prescribed
for her:

> You have well stated one of my sources of doubt: still I am aware that *with*
> *adequate evidence* Bishop Butler's little phrase 'for aught we know' must silence
> objections, for, the existence of evil being allowed, and the solution adopted
> that all partial evil is universal good, then as a certain amount of temporal evil
> is to the whole amount of temporal good, so in an infinitely surpassing
> proportion would be the eternal woe of a limited number to the eternal
> bliss of a larger multitude and to *possible* moral results co-extensive with the
> Divine Government.

The two phrases to which I draw particular attention are the quotation of
Butler's own locution 'for aught we know' and Eliot's own words (under-
lined in the autograph) '*with adequate evidence*'. In Butler's *Analogy* (1736), as
Eliot's editor Gordon Haight observes, 'the phrase [for aught we know]
appears repeatedly'. Haight conjectures that the particular instance George
Eliot has in mind occurs in chapter seven of Butler's treatise: 'The natural
government of the world is carried on by general laws. For this there may be
wise and good reasons: the wisest and best, for aught we know to the
contrary'.

Of all George Eliot's writings it is in *Middlemarch*, in the final redirecting
toward redemption of the book's burden of particular and manifold error
and waste, that she stays closest to the substance of Butler's Christian ethics.
Middlemarch is a novel whose general ethos is in the *Analogy*'s 'for aught we
know', while its structuring of plot and character seems determined by
Eliot's own caveat that '*with adequate evidence*' Butler's 'little phrase . . . must
silence objections':

> But the effect of [Dorothea's] being on those around her was incalculably
> diffusive: for the growing good of the world is partly dependent on unhistoric
> acts; and that things are not so ill with you and me as they might have been, is
> half owing to the number who lived faithfully a hidden life, and rest in
> unvisited tombs.

In some mysterious way, then, some 'infinitely surpassing proportion',
nothing of real worth is irretrievably lost. In a novel so powerfully attentive

to humanity's perverse gift for supplanting things of value with things that are worthless, the 'incalculably diffusive' nature of the benefaction is made to seem equal with foresight and moral deliberation.

Eliot saw herself as a meliorist and initially, in such a passage as that with which she concludes *Middlemarch*, may be thought of as carrying some way further Locke's connection of intrinsic value and 'improvement'. As he argues that intrinsic value is only latent, dormant even, in a piece of land until or unless human labour develops it by work of hand—manures it, that is to say—so she seems able, in the closing paragraphs of her novel, to suggest that human worth itself may lie deep and dormant and unrealized if it is not thoroughly worked by the 'manifold wakings of men to labour and endurance'.

I say 'able to suggest' to characterize degrees of relative success and failure. Also, I wish to anticipate that familiar style of incredulity (familiar, I mean, to ancient readers—like myself—of E. P. Thompson's *The New Reasoner*) that one can be so indulgent toward the rhetoric of political quietism. The success may be described as Eliot's capacity to represent an actuality of reflection and endurance by an achieved style that, in its own reflective power and in its demands upon both author's and reader's sustained powers of attention, shows itself the moral equivalent of those very qualities it describes. For the author of *Middlemarch*, intrinsic value is not so much in things, or even in qualities, as in a faculty: the faculty of sustained attention; attention conceived of, moreover, as a redemptive power. Coleridge, who comprehended this faculty better than any of his contemporaries, and whose comprehension is exemplified in the title of a major work, *Aids to Reflection*, left nothing that so embodied this comprehension as do George Eliot's *Middlemarch* and Wordsworth's *The Prelude*. Coleridge's most radically creative ideas and perceptions are sustained, in *The Prelude*, with Wordsworth's ideas and perceptions engrafted upon them, as they are not sustained even in *Aids to Reflection*.

The faculty of attention in George Eliot's work is indisputable: to praise this is not to deny that on major issues, both particular and general, she finds herself attending to a self-projected impasse; nor to deny that, at such points, she is capable of dissolving the frame as calculatingly as an equivocating politician in his memoirs. 'Dissolving' refers back, in the first instance, to the final paragraph of *Middlemarch*, in the second, to the paragraph in Hume's essay 'Of Refinement in the Arts' quoted above. The word the two passages have in common is 'diffusive'. Hume: 'They [industry, knowledge, and humanity] diffuse their beneficial influence on the *public*.' Eliot: 'But the effect of [Dorothea's] being on those around her was incalculably diffusive'. Taken phrase against phrase I would be hard put to say that Eliot is ethically more reliable than Hume. They are both lobbyists: Hume for his own pleasures and satisfactions; Eliot for her self-stabilizing compensations of 'partly dependent' and 'half-owing'—little drawn breaths and exhalations of scruple that compare badly with Keats's 'I have been half in love with easeful Death', a phrase that has the capacity to cut short and cauterize the unlovely aspects of Keats's self-absorption: a failing that he was well able to combat (though it was never easy) in the poems of 1819.

Middlemarch in its entirety, however, compares favourably with Hume's *Essays, Moral, Political, and Literary* in its entirety. Eliot writes with sufficient command of detail (of both plot and style) over some hundreds of pages that the body of her detailed accuracies is able to ride the shock of her special pleading and evasiveness. In this, George Eliot is very like Wordsworth; in both of them quantity, taken overall, enhances quality. There is enough evidence, in context, of stubborn attentiveness over a broad and varied range of a given world that reflective language itself becomes a redemptive agent of the author's self-deceptions, willed and unconscious evasions, ethical sentimentality and political shape-shifting. It is the ability to recognize, and to realize in the arduous process of writing itself, the nature of the redemptive faculty or agency that characterizes the major writer. Judged by these standards, *Middlemarch* is a great work, *Essays, Moral, Political, and Literary* a set of accomplished personal and social amusements.

If Butler's *Fifteen Sermons* is not a great work in the sense that *Middlemarch* is great, it is even so more than an amusement, more than what Joseph Addison meant by it in the *Spectator* of 30 March 1711, recalling how often he 'amus[ed himself] with the Tomb-stones and Inscriptions' in Westminster Abbey. At this date 'to amuse' could mean both 'to divert with pleasant trifles' and 'to engage in sober reflection'. Butler cannot be contained by either definition, whereas a polished amenability to both is a characteristic of many successful sermons and periodical essays of the period. In such a context, Hume's *Essays, Moral, Political, and Literary* can be understood as a collection of urbane and amusing lay-sermons.

From Butler's tenth sermon, 'Upon Self-Deceit':

Truth, and real good sense, and thorough integrity, carry along with them a peculiar consciousness of their own genuineness: there is a feeling belonging to them, which does not accompany their counterfeits, error, folly, half-honesty, partial and slight regards to virtue and right, so far only as they are consistent with that course of gratification which men happen to be set upon.

It is possible to challenge both the premises and delivery of this argument. If we object to Hume's equivocation in his statement that there is 'really' no standard of morality other than that imposed by opinion, should we not also object to Butler's 'Truth, and real good sense, and thorough integrity'? Or to his 'peculiar consciousness' or to that 'feeling' which 'does not accompany ... counterfeits'?

Hume, it is true, was able to record the bishop's approval and general recommendation of the two volumes of Essays, Moral, Political, and Literary when they appeared in 1741 and 1742. The diction employed by both Butler and Hume is the common diction of eighteenth-century rational theology and moral philosophy. One has to fine-tune the language of criticism in order to reveal the distinction between them; but, as the language of criticism ought in any case to be fine-tuned, this requirement should not be unexpected or unwelcome. Distinctions within broadly similar forms of idiom may indicate differences in basic premise. Butler retained a sense of the Fall and its consequences, if not in the deep-set Augustinian sense, then in some form sufficiently marked to differentiate his view from that of Hume and the Deists:

> Lastly, the various miseries of life which lie before us wherever we turn our eyes, the frailty of this mortal state we are passing through, may put us in mind that the present world is not our home; that we are merely strangers in it, as our fathers were.

Butler here is profoundly Pauline (or profoundly 'pseudo-Pauline', since the reference is to Hebrews) as Hume never is. And so, for Butler 'our ignorance, the imperfection of our nature, our virtue and our condition in this world' are intrinsic to our creatureliness: notice, in the words just quoted (from the beginning of Sermon XIV), how 'virtue' is not lacking but is found together with 'our ignorance' and 'the imperfection of our nature'. At the heart of his thinking, that is to say, the author of The Analogy of Religion Natural and Revealed to the Constitution and Course of Nature does not rely on analogy—our own philosophy's resistance to Butler and pre-ferral of Hume rests on the assumption that it does and is thereby outdated as

Hume is not—but on the intervention of incarnated Grace in our carnal perplexity: our 'imbecility or weaknes' as Hooker called the natural condition. It is to be remarked that the phrase 'for aught we know', upon which George Eliot placed emphasis and which Haight confirms as characteristically recurrent throughout Butler's *Analogy*, is found earlier, in the preface to *The Lawes of Ecclesiasticall Politie*, where Hooker remarks that 'the staines and blemishes found in our State' as 'springing from the root of humaine frailtie and corruption, not only are, but have been alwaies more or lesse, yea and (for any thing we know to the contrary) will be to the worlds end complained of, what forme of government soever take place'. In such writing—and here I place Hooker and Butler together—the 'root' is at once our frailty and our conscience. A single root, it yet performs a double function: as aboriginal frailty, it transforms gifts into penalties and is itself further disfigured; as aboriginal grace, it remains within the density of fallen nature, transforming frailty and corruption into redemptive self-knowledge, and is itself finally transfigured. Hooker's name does not feature in the index to the excellent volume of *Joseph Butler's Moral and Religious Thought: Tercentenary Essays*; neither does that of Donald MacKinnon, who gave concentrated attention to Butler's ethics and whose own affirmation that 'the language of repentance is not a kind of bubble on the surface of things' re-established the proper *gravitas* of Butler for the mid-twentieth century. John Henry Newman's name is noted, and rightly; for he several times acknowledged his indebtedness to Butler, referring to him as 'the greatest name in the Anglican Church'. The word 'aboriginal', just introduced, recalls that link by alluding to Newman's phrase for the inheritance of Original Sin: 'the human race is implicated in some terrible aboriginal calamity'. Butler, in what Newman elsewhere calls 'his grave and abstract way', might demur at 'terrible' and 'calamity' but that he grasps the full nature of *implication* cannot be doubted. His strength—and in this he stands in the direct line from Hooker through to Newman—is to comprehend and accept the intrinsic value of our self-realization in and through conscience as stemming directly from the implicated nature of our strength and frailty.

Allusions—or even precise references—to the nature of the intrinsic do not of themselves guarantee intrinsicality. Both this and the subsequent chapter attempt a double task: to offer a succinct natural history of the term 'intrinsic value' and to ask whether there is any way in which intrinsic value can be proven in a context or contexts other than that of the assay office at the Mint. One can put a gold or silver coin to the 'assay'; it is conceivable, though this may be merely a conceit, that one could assay with equivalent precision the intrinsic value of Shakespeare's sixty-sixth sonnet or Keats's 'Ode to a Nightingale'.

Ben Jonson entered in his commonplace book—published posthumously as *Timber, or, Discoveries: Made upon Men and Matter*—ideas given to him by his wide and deep reading, particularly in classical Latin authors and in such Humanist authorities as Erasmus: 'Wheresoever, manners, and fashions are corrupted, Language is, It imitates the publicke riot. The excesse of Feasts, and apparell, are the notes of a sick State; and the wantonnesse of language, of a sick mind'. The intelligence that believes in these words, from where-soever derived, and seals that belief by giving them this cogent stability, affirms also its acceptance of a doctrine of intrinsic value, albeit tacitly. The tacit understanding here is that language does not universally descend into corruption in company with a sick mind, or the mind of a sick state. Jonson had no doubt that his own times were sick; but he never doubted the capacity of language, his own language in particular, to retain its sanity and to guard the sanity of those who gave it their assent. Giving assent to one of Jonson's moral axioms is not necessarily an exercise for the prudent: he requires of his readers the full *yea, yea!* Failing that, I think he would prefer the full *nay, nay!* to 'maybe' or 'just possibly' or 'perhaps'. If you do answer with *yea, yea!*—as I admit that I do—you are henceforward committed to a course of thought and statement that accepts opposition as a part of the common lot, which can hardly avoid controversy, and which will be, or from some points of vantage will appear to be, narrowly constrained and constraining.

Toward, and into, this matter of constraint, however, more than one way of approach is open. Peter Geach has observed that 'if you opt for virtue, you opt for being the sort of man who *needs* to act virtuously ... And if you opt for chastity, then you opt to become the sort of person who *needs* to be chaste'. Geach credits the philosopher Philippa Foot with this neo-Aristotelianism; but she would not have claimed that the retrieval began with her. She could have found it in Butler's *Fifteen Sermons*, in the Third Sermon, 'Upon Human Nature':

> But allowing that mankind hath the rule of right within himself, yet it may be asked, 'What obligations are we under to attend to and follow it?' ... The question ... carries its own answer along with it. Your obligation to obey this law, is its being the law of your nature. That your conscience approves of and attests to such a course of action, is itself alone an obligation.

If I conclude that the condition of language—the language of imaginative attestation—in relation to the conditions laid down by the world is very much as Ben Jonson depicts it; and if I further conclude that a paradigm of ethical self-evaluation and affective acceptance is in being as Bishop Butler describes it; and that this paradigm in its bearing upon the world (as also the world's bearing upon it) is essentially the same today as it was in 1726: then I have put myself in the position of being obligated to speak somewhat as I have spoken throughout this chapter. If I am constrained to choose not to be a part of the 'public riot' and if I abide by Ben Jonson's analogy (health of the State : sickness of the State :: health of language : sickness of language) or if I propose to push the issue deeper than analogy into interrelationship or even interpenetration (State-into-language / language-into-State), then Butler's argument offers more serrations and striations, more toe-hold and hand-hold for the resistant conscience of our imagination, than can be found in the arguments of any other eighteenth-century author—not excluding such a triumph of the moral imagination as Samuel Johnson's *Life of Richard Savage*. My language is in me and is me; even as I, inescapably, am a minuscule part of the general semantics of the nation; and as the nature of the State has involved itself in the nature that is most intimately mine. The nature that is most intimately mine may by some be taken to represent my intrinsic value. If it is so understood, it follows that intrinsic value, thus defined, bears the extrinsic at its heart.

A crucial issue remains. In so framing the matter, do I confuse intrinsic with mediated value? Here again Butler has shown that, in some if not all circumstances, intrinsic and mediated value cannot, may not, be separated. It is my 'obligation to obey this law [in] its being the law of [my] nature'; that is, in and of itself, the intrinsic being that I mediate.

The rest is paradox. For the poem to engage justly with our imperfection, so much the more must the poem approach the nature of its own perfection. It is simply not true to say that the intrinsic value of a line or phrase cannot be assayed and proven in close and particular detail. For the intrinsic value of the entire poem so to be established would require the significant detail to illumine and regulate the whole. I am left with no other course but to say that the great poem moves us to assent as much by the integrity of its final imperfection as by the amazing grace of its detailed perfection. At those points where the intrinsic value of the formal structure, by whatever means, is revealed to us, that value is on the instant mediated.

28

Poetry and Value

Joseph Butler and Gottfried Wilhelm Leibniz had a close acquaintance in common, although they never met. Each was a mentor of Caroline, queen-consort of George II. Leibniz's acquaintance with her was closer and of a longer duration; even so, her devotion to Butler's *Analogy of Religion* was such that he owed his public rise and acclaim to her interest perhaps as much as to his own distinction of intellect and spiritual *savoir-faire*.

Butler and Leibniz were more closely related, however, than such biographical marginalia might indicate. It has been observed of the author of the *Analogy* that his 'metaphysic of personal being as radically active *and* sentient is profoundly pluralistic as well as profoundly relational, and has more affinities with Leibniz (that most Anglican of continental philosophers) than with either Spinoza or Descartes: he is troubled by neither of their characteristic problems—maintaining individual distinctness or genuine interaction, respectively'. We have now to decide what 'profoundly pluralistic' means in this—or any—context; and what, if anything, terms and phrases such as 'radically active *and* sentient', 'profoundly relational', 'maintaining individual distinctness [and] genuine interaction' have to do with the topic of this chapter: 'Poetry and Value'.

It has been noted that there is surprisingly little reference to Butler in Coleridge's philosophical, theological, and political writings, and astonishingly little in the *Marginalia* and *Table Talk*. I came to Coleridge long before I came to Butler and until quite recently if asked with which English thinker I associate the terms 'radically active *and* sentient', 'maintaining individual distinctness [and] genuine interaction', I would have named the author of *Aids to Reflection*, *Biographia Literaria*, 'This Lime-Tree Bower My Prison', and 'Dejection: An Ode'. One of the 'lost' great books of the past two hundred years is *Aids to Reflection* as it might have been if Coleridge had chosen to reflect upon the axioms of Joseph Butler rather than the aphorisms of Archbishop Leighton. But one must avoid sophistication. The fact is that the name of Leibniz features far more prominently than that of Butler in the indices to Coleridge's major works. Butler and Coleridge show strong affinity in areas of thought relating to individual distinctness and genuine interaction because each—Butler by affinity, Coleridge by derivation—shares Leibniz's awareness of particular forms of potentiality and realization, and perhaps also of loss. In my own autodidactic inquiry into the nature of intrinsic value and the questionable relationship of value-theory to the spoken and written word, especially as this is formalized in the art of poetry, they exist as a triumvirate of moral assessors. I should add that, attached as I am to a form of belief in Original Sin, one that is probably not too far removed from the orthodox, I expect my assessors to be in some respects compromised, though this in no way lowers them in my estimation. I should say further that however evasive I may be on the question, the fact that I do have such a strong attachment to Newman's 'terrible aboriginal calamity' makes particularly difficult my attempts to give some kind of priority to the status of intrinsic value as an ethical referent. As we observed in the previous chapter, Hobbes, in *Leviathan*, presents us with an enduring vision of 'inhaerent', or intrinsic, value, but in the person of a dead man and in the body of a vanished society. In this respect, *Leviathan* is a powerfully elegiac work; and when the 'inhaerent'—meaning the 'intrinsic'—is praised in an elegiac context, the term must carry a different kind of inference from the specific weight of the word 'intrinsic' as applied to precious metals employed in the manufacture of coins. I am conscious, also, that what initially draws me to the idea of intrinsic value is a set of expectations and presuppositions that are themselves attached to interest and thereby compromised. I find that I am here presenting two interinvolved—but not indivisible—categories as if each confronted us with issues identical to those of the other: questions relating to the nature of language and questions relating to poetics. The status of language in relation to the speakable and the unspeakable is less problematic than that of poetics so situated: it is this latter ganglion of energy, *technē*, belief, and opinion that I have committed myself to address in this chapter. In the case of Dietrich Bonhoeffer and Helmuth James von Moltke, as their last recorded words indicate, language did not in the end forsake them, nor did they finally surrender language to some existential brute force such as that evoked by Czesław Miłosz in his parable of 'a man threatened with instant death'. We can be reasonably certain that neither Bonhoeffer nor von Moltke would have concluded in his final hours or moments that what '*judge[s]* all poets and philosophers' is the 'very amusing sight' of machine-gun bullets upending cobblestones 'on a street in an embattled city'. Miłosz's observation, like much of the late twentieth-century poetry on which he has made his mark, is suspended between vitalism and nihilism essentially as Bonhoeffer in his *Ethics* foresaw the condition of an overridingly post-Christian world: 'Vitalism ends inevitably in nihilism, in the destruction of all that is natural'. The spirit that motivated Bonhoeffer and von Moltke was grounded in its own recognition of intrinsic value, which was neither the semantic irreducibility of Mallarmé nor the zero-apprehension of Miłosz's man under machine-gun fire. There is a significant similarity between Ezra Pound's belief in the absolute authority of poetics—'all values ultimately come from our [i.e. the poets'] judicial sentences'—and Miłosz's belief in the absolute supremacy of the corrida and its 'moment of truth'. This likeness of opposites stems from the fact that the provenance of both is *symboliste*, or, one might say, Romantic-confrontational. This is not the situation in which Bonhoeffer and von Moltke find themselves and find language adequate to their particular witness. Poetry is ruled out of their form of witness only if one forgets the Psalms and the kenotic hymn of Paul's Epistle to the Philippians. As this essay is inescapably confessional, I am bound to offer myself as a child of our time who, forced to respond to the disputatious 'relevance of poetry after Auschwitz' question, would think immediately of Paul Celan's 'Todesfuge' but only belatedly of the Psalms and the Prophets.

I say 'inescapably confessional', but is there not also something artificial or engineered in the premise and mannerism of modern confession, something at once arbitrary and highly convenient in so presenting the issues as being exclusively Romantic-confrontational? To read Bonhoeffer's *Ethics* or the last letters of Helmuth James von Moltke is to discover that they have more in common with Butler's *Fifteen Sermons* than with the poetics of existential crisis. In his 'Preface' to the second edition (1729) of the sermons Butler writes:

> If the observation [i.e. that benevolence is no more disinterested than any of the common particular Passions] be true, it follows, that self-love and benevolence, virtue and interest are not to be opposed, but only to be distinguished from each other; in the same way as virtue and any other particular affection, love of arts, suppose, are to be distinguished.

Given the climate of confrontation and exclusiveness within which the particular manners and mannerisms of modern poetics have evolved, Butler's suggestion that, in order to distinguish, you do not absolutely have to draw up things *in extremis* or antagonistically comes as a moment of surprising grace; and, indebted as I am to Blake's *The Marriage of Heaven and Hell*, I would nonetheless offer the structure of Butler's comment as a form of critical observation upon the explicit strategies of that powerfully isolationist yet powerfully influential work: 'Without Contraries is no progression. Attraction and Repulsion, Reason and Energy, Love and Hate, are necessary to Human existence'.

There is a contrary view: namely, that in the passage from Butler's 1729 'Preface' we have the grammar of a sceptic and hedonist; and that the impacted antithetical syntax of Blake's sentences reveals the extremes to which a radical moralist must go to disrupt the easy flow of self-serving parlance. It is quite true that there is a marked absence of tension in Butler's argument. It is equally the case that Blake's language of radical opposition does our simple thinking for us less straightforwardly than at first appears. If attraction and repulsion are demonstrably contraries, does it necessarily follow that reason and energy are similarly opposed, on any grounds other than Blake's say so? There is an energy of reason, a reason in energy, which Blake's own work embodies in itself and for itself, and which is not of its own volition demeaned to the level of marketable slogan, though such a process can be forced through by others, as Allen Ginsberg and his British counterparts made evident when they took up Blake half a century ago. In part, what we are attempting to define as 'intrinsic value' is a form of technical integrity that is itself a form of common honesty. Believing, as I have admitted I do, in the radically flawed nature of humanity and of its endeavours entails an acceptance of the fact that, in one way or another, our integrity can be bought; or our honesty can be maimed by some flaw of *technē*; at the same time, however, our cynicism can be defeated, our defeatism thwarted, by processes within the imagination that, as processes, are scarcely to be distinguished from those that discover and betray some flaw in our conceptual structure or hypothesized ideal. There are, indeed, various terms—'discover' and 'betray' are two of them, 'reduce' and 'invent' are others—that in themselves reveal this to be so. They are descriptive of *technē* and also imply moral deductions having to do with technicalities. The supporting evidence is preserved in and by the *Oxford English Dictionary* (*OED*).

Another way of stating the claim is to say that the ethical and the technical are reciprocating forces and that the dimension in which this reciprocation may be demonstrated is the contextual. If context is the arena of attention, it is also the arena of inattention. Crucial nodes of discourse are crucial precisely because they bring attention and inattention together in a specific crux, as here in a passage from an early letter of Leibniz: 'Pilate is condemned. Why? Because he lacks faith. Why does he lack it? Because he lacks the will to attention. Why this? Because he has not understood the necessity of the matter . . . Why has he not understood it? Because the causes of understanding were lacking'.

Leibniz was aware that 'an inevitable necessity . . . would destroy the freedom of the will, so necessary to the morality of action'. Such being the case, Pilate is condemned by a mechanics of inner necessity that has the appearance of intimate mimesis, of being an accurate slow-motion exposure of Pilate's psychological incapacity and moral illogicality in the process of *becoming* 'inevitable necessity', that is to say, 'the necessity of the matter'.

The names of Leibniz and Butler were brought together at this discussion because Butler's method in *Fifteen Sermons* is similar to that aspect of Leibniz's method as revealed in the letter to Magnus Wedderkopf. He appears as a sceptic and a hedonist because he apprehends the mental rhythms of scepticism and hedonism rather as Leibniz apprehends the inertia of Pilate's logical illogic. There is certainly vanity, in more than one sense of the term, in Leibniz's presentation of Pilate's hypothetical thought-process as a psychological, metaphysical, and semantic *fait accompli*; it is perhaps vain of Butler to display before us, in so steady a fashion, the inner workings of self-deceit, cant, and hypocrisy and to show an equal certitude in charting their acceptable opposites. I believe, on the grounds of a close reading of *Fifteen Sermons*, that he recognizes such tendencies as comprising several facets of that human nature within which his own nature is implicated. From evidence both internal and historical, we have a basis from which to project his likely answer to the question, *Where do you stand?*: 'between Ecclesiasticus and Shaftesbury's *Character-istics*'. That, if you like, describes the general terrain within which his moral sensibility moves most freely; but 'freely' does not accurately define Butler's capacity for making distinctions, which although they derive from the standard figures of eloquence, nonetheless attest to a reflectively working mind.

It is manifest [a] great Part of common Language, and of common Behaviour over the World, is formed upon Supposition of . . . a Moral Faculty; whether called Conscience, moral Reason, moral Sense, or divine Reason; whether considered as a Sentiment of the Understanding, or as a Perception of the Heart, or, which seems the Truth, as including both.

It was my recollection of this passage especially—it is from the 'Dissertation of the Nature of Virtue', 1736—that caused me to cavil at Blake's opposing Reason to Energy. Each clause in Butler's sentence is a modifier or qualifier; there is an immediate connection here between his *referral* to a 'Faculty, or practical discerning Power within us' and the demonstration of that power of discernment in the structure of the sentence. It is in the light of this example also that I take further a suggestion made by one of Butler's editors, W. R. Matthews, in 1914:

Perhaps the most original part of Butler's teaching is his treatment of the 'particular passions.' He observes that all desires for particular objects are, in the strict sense, disinterested, since they seek their external object as their end and rest in that.

Considered as 'teaching', there is perhaps not much originality here: it seems thoroughly in line with that form of modified Thomism that Hooker diffused into the body of Anglican thought and that one finds cropping up in various unlikely places. The originality is in the active shaping of the reflective voice; and the quality of that voice itself is effective in conveying to the reader a sense of what it means to take the measure of one's own thought through the common medium of language.

This speculation may be taken a step further by suggesting a modification to the sense in which we understand 'disinterested' in relation both to Butler's intentions and to the nature of language itself. Language, whatever else it is and is not, can be understood historically as a form of seismograph: registering and retaining the myriad shocks of humanity's interested and disinterested passions. One may not be always alert to this characteristic in daily conversation, and it is probably better for us that this is so; but no one could consult the great *OED* and fail to appreciate that the term 'seismograph', crude as it is, at least registers something of that seemingly illimitable capacity. One must conclude that a reflective grasp of language will necessarily involve more than an easy familiarity with the surface conventions for conveying 'intelligence' (i.e. information), conventions that, by and large, do not interfere with one's self-possession or the possessiveness of one's own interested passions. Reflection—certainly as Butler and Coleridge would understand the term—is the faculty or activity that draws the naturally interested sensibility in the direction of disinterestedness. It is not necessary to suppose or suggest that some hypostasized condition of perfect disinterest is attainable within the usages, whether ordinary or extraordinary, of the English language. The particular quality of our humanity describable in terms of poetry and value is best revealed in and through the innumerable registrations of syntax and rhythm, registrations that are common to both prose and poetry and to which as writers and as readers we attend or fail to attend.

Not only Butler but also Coleridge can be associated with Leibniz, particularly if we bear in mind a passage from *Nouveaux Essais sur l'entendement humain* (1703) in which Leibniz challenges Locke's interpretation of the understanding or intellective soul (Leibniz's term for it is 'l'âme'), a passage to which Coleridge returned more than once in his own philosophical writings. Leibniz writes:

> You [*Philalèthe* = Locke, the Lockeans] oppose to me this axiom received by the philosophers, that there is nothing in the soul which does not come from the senses [*que rien n'est dans l'âme qui ne vienne des sens*]. But the soul itself must be excepted and its affections [*Mais il faut excepter l'âme même et ses affections*]. *Nihil est in intellectu quod non fuerit in sensu, excipe: nisi ipse intellectus.*

Coleridge seized on this Leibnizian redirecting of the Aristotelian maxim as if he saw in it the possibility of encrypting the very nature of intrinsic value: such value would be held permanently to attention within the clause itself, *nisi ipse*. Coleridge thus expatiated on his understanding of Leibniz's modifier:

> the act of comparing supposes in the comparing Faculty, certain inherent forms, that is, Modes of reflecting, not referable to the Objects reflected on, but pre-determined by the Constitution and (as it were) mechanism of the Understanding itself.

This is no advance from Butler's discourse on the 'Moral Faculty'. In fact in requiring the locution 'and (as it were) mechanism' Coleridge's definition is retrograde. We should not underrate, even so, the significance of this endeavour, a significance that is enhanced by Coleridge's capacity for attuning conceptual hypotheses to his semantic perceptiveness, his immediate sense of language as mediator in the struggle toward a grasp of intrinsic natures (one of several ways in which he anticipates Hopkins's search for instress and inscape).

Gerard Hopkins's poetry, as also in certain instances his prose, is both material evidence of and expert witness to the precise nature of the activity of reflection that we see adumbrated in Butler and developed by Coleridge. Hopkins simultaneously clarifies and complicates these issues: first, because his mastery of the essential techniques is such that he reduces to a bare minimum the distance between the mediate and the immediate characteristics of language; second, because, in his profoundest theological allegiance, he is totally committed to mediation. At the same time, therefore, he is both innovative, finding radically new ways of compounding the intellective with the sensuous elements of language, and also reactionary: devoted to those beliefs and practices that, in severe opposition to the liberalizing inclinations of the century, concentrated a worshipper's attention upon Mary as Mediatrix and upon the saints as intercessors. Hopkins at Oxford was a pupil of both Walter Pater, for whom intrinsic value was signified— irrespective of context I would say—by the 'hard gem-like flame', and T. H. Green, who felt able to criticize Butler for being 'content to leave the moral nature a cross of unreconciled principles', and whose own sense of intrinsic value was, like that of Locke and George Eliot, inseparable from ideas of improvement, of the moral imperative to bring to fulfilment within society, as much as within the individual life, latent qualities and virtues that would otherwise remain dormant or, worse, in a condition of torpor.

To say that these are artificial distinctions is to evade the issue. The most refined forms of artifice, brought to bear upon the conditions of our natural life, lose something of their artificiality even as they infiltrate and complicate spontaneous activity. Green's objection to Butler's 'cross of unreconciled principles' is brusque and inappropriately theatrical though less so than Ruskin's choice of the name 'Judas' for the national betrayal of the values of a true commonweal by estimating wealth as commodity values, that is to say, assessing national wealth in terms of what is more truly 'illth'.

Ruskin in fact acknowledged that the 'use of substances of intrinsic value as the materials of a currency, is a barbarism' but maintained nonetheless its utility as a 'mechanical check' and as an instrument of exchange with 'foreign nations'. In short, intrinsic value, understood in terms of bullion value, was demanded by the conditions of life: to which Ruskin reacted in the mid- to late nineteenth century very much as Hobbes had understood anarchy and arbitrary force in the mid-seventeenth century. Until recently

I was essentially an adherent of 'intrinsic value' as delineated by Ruskin. I am now much less sure of my position, partly because I am no longer confident that I can discern the point at which Ruskin himself crosses an indeterminate line between, on the one hand, regarding money as 'an expression of right', or entitlement, or as a sign of relations, and, on the other hand, using a monetary trope in which 'intrinsic value' is by sleight of will substituted as the vital referent. In the first instance, Ruskin concedes that, if received as a 'sign', money is '*Always, and necessarily ... imperfect ... but capable of approximate accuracy if rightly ordered*'; in the second instance, the 'expression of right' itself takes on a mysterious intransitive quality that is thereafter to be received—and not questioned—by us as 'intrinsic value'. Any acknowledgement of 'approximate accuracy' is dissolved and Ruskin's real authority of eloquence is devoted, as here in *Munera Pulveris*, to the creation and promulgation of an idea of the intrinsic that is scarcely to be distinguished from the intransitive:

> It does not in the least affect the intrinsic value of the wheat, the air, or the flowers, that men refuse or despise them. Used or not, their own power is in them, and that particular power is in nothing else.

This has an undeniable eloquent beauty; but to what is it applied? Ruskin is devoting the same degree of intensity to his subject that Wordsworth in 'Michael' or 'Resolution and Independence' or 'The Female Vagrant' or Book XII of *The Prelude* devotes to the unrecognized and publicly unfulfilled powers of men and women forced to live in various kinds of straitened circumstance.

What Wordsworth and Ruskin have in common, in these passages at least, is the eloquence of mourning. They are essentially elegists when they write of the intrinsicality of the despised and rejected among the common people and the common things of the earth, as Hobbes was an elegist when he wrote of the 'inhaerent' virtues of the dead Royalist soldier-poet Sidney Godolphin. At such points, Wordsworth and Ruskin seem to spring from common seventeenth- and eighteenth-century roots: from Locke's association of intrinsic value with potentiality for improvement and from the philosophy of individuation made axiomatic in Butler's 'Preface' to *Fifteen Sermons*: 'Everything is what it is, and not another thing'. The crucial difference is that whereas in 1690 (Locke) and 1729 (Butler) the tone is optimistic or at least melioristic, by the first decade of the nineteenth century (*The Prelude*, Book XII) it is, at best, stoical.

The great exception, and the major challenge, to these conclusions is John Henry Newman. It is in Newman's pastoral theology that Butler's teaching finds its nineteenth-century fulfilment. And Newman is no more an elegist—in the central body of his writing—than is Butler. Edward Sillem, the editor of Newman's *Philosophical Notebook*, implies that Newman read Butler in the same spirit as that in which he read St Athanasius and St John Chrysostom, whose writings 'expressed the inner unity of their own minds rather than that of an abstract system'. My reason for choosing this particular observation will be apparent in the general context of our discussion of intrinsic value. If, as is true of Newman (according to Sillem), the intrinsic value, the 'inner unity', is in the mind's conduct and disposition of its own best qualities, there is no arbitrary limit to, or restriction upon, the burgeoning of such estimation. Our notion of intrinsic value does not inevitably make us *laudatores temporis acti*. Our grasp of intrinsic value is transitive in its implications. The elegiac celebration of 'intrinsic value' understands the value as being in some sense isolated from current degradation, and therefore as being inviolate, held securely within the sphere of the intransitive. With Ruskin, more than with Wordsworth, the result is loss of proportion: it is surely disproportionate when Ruskin claims: 'It does not in the least affect the intrinsic value of the wheat, the air, or the flowers, that men refuse or despise them'. Locke would have said, and here he would be cogent as Ruskin is not, that the intrinsic value of a bushel of wheat cannot be isolated from the value of the human labour that contributed to its growth and harvesting. The idea, then, that some other human act, i.e. of 'refusing' the bushel of wheat, preserves a mysterious integrity of its 'own power' within the rejected grain is a sentiment little short of the absurd. One is put in mind of the fate of certain elderly authors who, rescued from oblivion by côteries and the editors of small-circulation journals, are invariably described as having been hitherto 'strangely' or 'unaccountably' neglected. The 'neglect' by some kind of imaginative fiat is simultaneously held to be both their 'documentary claim' to present notice and an intrinsic part of the 'neglected' author's newly proclaimed value. A vicarious solipsism is also a demeaning charity.

The title of this chapter is 'Poetry and Value'. It is time to make explicit a number of conclusions that have been implicit, or in suspension, during the earlier part of this discussion. We need to return to the question 'What is the constitution of the activity we call "reflection"?' In the chapter of 'Prudential Aphorisms', in the second edition of *Aids to Reflection*, Coleridge advised his reader: 'Whether you are reflecting for yourself, or reasoning with another, make it a rule to ask yourself the precise meaning of the word, on which the point in question appears to turn'; and, in the same section of his book, he noted: 'At the utmost [moral philosophers as opposed to "the botanist, the chemist, the anatomist, &c"] have only to rescue words, already existing and familiar, from the false or vague meanings imposed on them by carelessness, or by the clipping and debasing misusage of the market'. He is referring to the misusage of such words as 'happiness', 'duty', 'faith', 'truth', and, by implication, of the word 'reflection' itself. 'Reflection' is not here identifiable as a 'passive attending upon the event' or even as a 'wise passiveness' but in metaphors of, and associations with, energy conceived as a 'co-instantaneous yet reciprocal action' of the individual will and an empowering law; of 'THE WORD, as informing; and THE SPIRIT, as actuating'. Language, that is to say, does not issue from reflection but is an inherent element within the activity of reflection itself; it is an integral part of the body of reflection.

The issue here, for Coleridge as for Butler and Leibniz and, albeit less happily, for Ruskin also, is whether the intrinsicality of value can be, ought to be, made viable in and for the contingent world, the domain of worldly power and circumstance. In each case the answer—in principle—is yes; in practice the resolution is, in varying degrees and for various reasons, less than perfect. The toll is most severe in the case of Ruskin and is the effect of a cause that Coleridge precisely anticipated, in *Aids to Reflection* when defining sophistry: 'For the juggle of sophistry consists, for the greater part, in using a word in one sense in the premiss, and in another sense in the conclusion'. I read this as a prescient description of that flaw in Ruskin's argument, to which I earlier drew attention, and which I now attribute to the term 'intrinsic' occurring in one sense in the premise and in another sense in the conclusion. One may balk at the word 'sophistry', if sophistry can be understood only as intentional juggling to deceive. I do not believe that Ruskin intentionally misleads; nor do I say that we have here the broken or jumbled threads of an inattentive weaver of platitudes. Ruskin's was a great and scrupulous mind. He is overcome, in this particular area of discourse, as we are all overcome, at some time or another in our particular areas of discourse, by a kind of neutral, or indifferent, or disinterested force in the nature of language itself: a force that Coleridge describes incomparably well in the sudden blaze of a sentence at the beginning of *Aids to Reflection*: 'For if words are not THINGS, they are LIVING POWERS, by which the things of most importance to mankind are actuated, combined, and humanized'. As much weighs here upon that plural present indicative of the verb *to be*—the 'verb substantive'—as weighs upon the verbs 'discover', 'betray', 'reduce', 'invent' in other contexts, or upon the locutions *excipe* and *nisi ipse* in Leibniz's modifying of the Aristotelian axiom, *nihil est in intellectu, quod non fuerit in sensu*. And certainly no less weighs upon the grammar of a sentence in Helmuth James von Moltke's farewell letter before his execution in January 1945, rejoicing that, in the end, the Third Reich could find no justification for killing him other than the fact of his Christianity: 'not as a big landowner, not as a nobleman, not as Prussian, not as a German . . . but as a Christian and nothing else'.

Syntax such as we find here, in this context, establishes the *Grundbass* (as we would speak of the ground-bass in a Bach *continuo*) in the midst of the *Abgrund*: the abyss, the deep, in the psalms of penitence and lamentation. I do not say, however, that with von Moltke's words we move into a dimension unique to him and unperceived or unanticipated by such a thinker as Joseph Butler. Coleridge and Newman seem especially able to comprehend and to take further the implications and resonances of certain of Butler's phrases of adumbration. Newman's *An Essay in Aid of a Grammar of Assent* builds upon the sense of Butler's 'full intuitive conviction' as much as upon the distinction between '*mere power and authority*', a distinction that Butler says 'everybody is acquainted with', though he refrains from adding 'but which not everybody understands'. Newman also works to ensure that 'full intuitive conviction' is not confused with or supplanted by 'blind propension'. Coleridge's achievement is to show how 'full intuitive conviction' as well as 'blind propension', the tendency to mistake power for authority, and above all, perhaps, how a sense of 'the moral rule of action interwoven in [our] nature', as Butler calls it, can without arbitrariness of analogy, be extended into the nature of human language itself, in such a way that language becomes, not a simple adjunct or extension of 'the moral rule of action' but rather a faculty of reflective integration.

A poem issues from reflection, particularly but not exclusively from the common bonding of reflection and language; it is not in itself the passing of reflective sentiment through the medium of language. The fact that my description applies only to a minority of poems written in English or any other language, and to the poetry written in Britain during the past fifty years scarcely if at all, does not shake my conviction that the description I have given of how the uncommon work moves within the common dimension of language is substantially accurate.

Alienated Majesty

29

Alienated Majesty:
Ralph W. Emerson

The words 'alienated majesty' are taken from Emerson's essay 'Self-Reliance': 'In every work of genius we recognize our own rejected thoughts: they come back to us with a certain alienated majesty'. Like a number of other sayings by Emerson, the potential value of this axiom seems neither perfectly fulfilled nor completely exhausted by the essay in which it appears. Leaving aside for the moment the evidence of the *Journals*, which witness from and to themselves, we may find that Emerson out of context has a gnostic intelligence ideally embodied in the form of the aphorism; and the reasons for this being so are charted in the *Journals* some twelve months before the anonymous publication of his first collection of essays, *Nature*, in September 1836. The force in Emerson is felt at the point where immediate apperception has yet to attach itself to public obligation; though what precisely is meant by public obligation must itself be carefully considered in the course of this chapter.

'Self-Reliance' formed part of *Essays: First Series* published in 1841. By this time Emerson was already translating himself from the language of self-apprehension into the exemplary speech of public self-awareness. The sense of 'alienation' in 1841 does not sustain the sense it had in 1836; and is none the better for the change. The aphorism with which we began—a sentence from 'Self-Reliance'—starts as a journal entry for 28 November 1836 (two months after the publication of *Nature*) on what Emerson there calls 'the charm which belongs to Alienation or Otherism'. The *Oxford English Dictionary* (*OED*) records 'Otherism' as a 'rare' word, first appearing in 1826, and only in a sense alien to Emerson's: 'Devotion to the interests of others; altruism'. One of the citations is dated 1894 and comes from Henry Drummond's *Lowell Lectures on the Ascent of Man*, originally delivered in

Boston the year before: 'From Self-ism to Other-ism is the supreme transition of history'. To set this against Emerson's journal entries is to see demonstrated on a small scale what the lecturing vogue did to New England thinking inside sixty years. Clearly, Emerson's 'Otherism' is not 'altruism' but what in German is known by two words, *Entfremdung* and *Verfremdung*. The first means *estrangement*, the second is *artistic (especially theatrical) distancing*. It is arguably a prime function of the imagination to grasp both senses at once—a Protean contest even when not Herculean. The natural history of American creative thinking, from Emerson's *Nature* to O'Hara's *Collected Poems* (1971) reveals this to be the case, and does so in an exemplary fashion, for richer, for poorer, for good or ill, that is not equalled or even truly complemented in British literature over the same span of time. Hardy is very like Emerson in the way he can dwarf his own greatness of perception yet ennoble things that life has stunted. The British Jew Isaac Rosenberg (1890–1918) seized what was strongest in Emerson's philosophical *otium* and hammered it into his own negotiations: 'We know our poem by its being the only poem. The world is too full of echoes and we seize on the real voice'. The Victorian Jesuit Gerard Hopkins who conceded, 'I always knew in my heart Walt Whitman's mind to be more like my own than any other man's living' took, both as theologian and theologically disciplined poet, the nature of alienated majesty as his running theme. But Hopkins's alienated majesty is not Emerson's alienated majesty, which is not Whitman's; the difference is the subject of this chapter and the two succeeding ones.

When Emerson wrote, on 28 November 1836, that he saw plainly the charm which belongs to Alienation or Otherism, he did so with two months' experience of being a published author. 'My own book I read with new eyes when a stranger has praised it.' As *Nature* had appeared minus the author's name, a stranger's praise would indeed impart a shock of self-recognition, an instantaneous fusing of vantage and vulnerability perhaps never to be experienced so nakedly again. But even here the immediacy is to some extent diffused and dissipated by the presenting and representing vein within Emerson's creative and critical being. 'My own book I read with new eyes' *must* be the little work entitled *Nature* and yet it *need* not be; the statement is arrived at by way of general representation. 'The very sentiment I expressed yesterday without heed, shall sound memorable to me tomorrow if I hear it from another.' Such phrases as 'the very sentiment', 'shall sound memorable to me tomorrow', could have been culled from an autograph album or a reciter's treasury; their weakness has sufficient weight to nullify 'I read with new eyes'.

The furthest implications of 'alienated majesty' are inseparable from the nearest implications of 'I read with new eyes'. What Emerson most truly means by that second phrase is repeatedly pointed and justified in his early lectures and throughout the *Journals*. In an entry of 24 November 1836, he was especially quick in getting to the quick of Coleridge's critical genius: 'Every opinion he expresses is a canon of criticism that should be writ in steel, & his italics are italics of the mind'; on 14 January 1836 he had observed in a public lecture that Coleridge had 'possessed extreme subtlety of discrimination . . . surpassing all men in the fineness of distinctions he could indicate, touching his mark with a needle's point'.

I do not argue that the pull towards public oratory coarsens the *finesse* preserved by the self-reflections of the *Journals*. There is no qualitative difference between the two estimates of Coleridge, the first from Emerson's public lecture and the second from a journal entry eleven months later; and there are, at first sight, no grounds for disputing the firm conclusion expressed by the editors of his *Early Lectures* that 'All his books were first hammered out on the rostrum. His "low tones that decide," ostensibly disdaining tricks of oratory, are tones of the practiced rhetorician who wrote to be heard'.

On reflection, however, their conclusion can be disputed: 'hammered out' takes too much for granted and elides an ambiguity. 'Hammered out' connotes one thing if you have in mind a farrier and anvil and another if you think of lecturers and lecterns. The quality which Emerson praises in Coleridge is not 'hammering' so much as accuracy in fine measurement, and it is Emerson's ability to match the characteristic which he praises with a descriptive felicity of his own making that is one of his enduring though inconstant strengths. His work is characterized less by his repeated decline into sentiment than by the tenacity with which, in spite of the pressures of taste and opinion, he retained over a long period and in a long succession of cogent ripostes the power to depict how taste, opinion, and influence were constituted and diffused throughout the texture of New England life and culture. That which pulled Emerson away from himself was very like that which pulled William James and Josiah Royce away from themselves: a progressive, even if spasmodic, disdain for a basic hermeneutical fact which Emerson himself had struck upon in his journal entry for 20 June 1835: his instant of recognition that 'There is every degree of remoteness from the line of things in the line of words'. Royce and James are finally estranged from their own deepest intelligence by a failure to recognize the existence of such an *aporia*.

In his book *The Star of Redemption*, published in 1921, the philosopher Franz Rosenzweig states that 'Genius is by no means innate, as current liberal education would have it; on the contrary, it one day takes a person by surprise because it depends on the self and not merely on the personality.' Such a distinction between self and personality—one in which priority is given to self—is now infrequently and insufficiently made. 'Alienation', considered in its negative aspects, which are the only aspects many would ascribe to it, arises from a confusion of the one with the other, or from an inability to hold the one steady against the other. In the lecture-circuit environment of nineteenth-century New England, self and personality were held in constant public and private disequilibrium. I would not say, as the editors of Emerson's *Early Lectures* maintain, 'All his books were first hammered out on the rostrum' but rather that the public rostrum was, of peculiar necessity, the place on which his creative self was both thwarted and abetted by his professional personality. Both sides of the disequilibrium were potent: if either had markedly prevailed his nature would be easier for our strangers' eyes to read.

That Emerson fully realized—or at some level of his being fully intuited—the nature of the case is demonstrated by the fluctuating disenchantment of his journal entries concerning his friendship with Henry Thoreau and his spasms of sympathy for, irritation with, Bronson Alcott. 'I told H. T. that his freedom is in the form, but he does not disclose new matter. I am very familiar with all his thoughts—they are my own quite originally drest.' The adverbial form 'quite', as employed here, has a marked intensity. Emerson entrusts to it a fair weight of his irritated egotistic self which differs significantly from his self-conscious literary personality enamoured of Henry the seducer, the 'good river-god', whose suspect spontaneity Emerson contrives to present only by the most arch of literary mannerisms: 'Henry Thoreau is like the woodgod who solicits the wandering poet & draws him into antres vast & desarts idle, & bereaves him of his memory, & leaves him naked, plaiting vines & with twigs in his hand'.

If Emerson, in these journal entries, is asking himself how far, if at all, rugged spontaneity may be 'merely the tune of the time', it is a question that he is right to ask. The fact that he repeatedly asks it, of himself and of those among his closest intellectual companions as well as of Boston and New

England society in general, is a contributory factor to that stamina without which the creative self cannot maintain its independence from the cultural personality. One recalls, inevitably, Charles Eliot Norton's unsparing description of Emerson in old age:

> his optimistic philosophy has hardened into a creed, with the usual effects of a creed in closing the avenues of truth. He can accept nothing as fact that tells against his dogma. His optimism becomes a bigotry . . . He refuses to believe in disorder or evil.

Norton himself, in 1873, is singing one of the tunes of the time, but to dismiss his observation as an ignoble attack on a once great mind now broken by age would be petty in itself. That element or characteristic which Norton condemns in 1873 is already there in the 1830s. The way in which Emerson in the winter of 1852–3 accurately predicts the historical moment of Whitman's arrival is, as everyone observes, striking, uncanny; but equally striking is the way in which he simultaneously contrives to nullify the perception by speaking as if from the thick of the imperceptive Boston *haut-monde*:

> 'Tis said that the age ends with the poet or successful man, who knots up into himself the genius or idea of his nation . . . So that we ought rather to be thankful that our hero or poet does not hasten to be born in America, but still allows us others to live a little, & warm ourselves at the fire of the sun, for, when he comes, we others must pack our petty trunks, & begone.

The pitch of Emerson's observation is far from that of the mere cultural *bienpensant*. Three years before the appearance of *Leaves of Grass* he senses Whitman coming and estimates both 'the greatness and the cost of him'—as Brecht would say of Shakespeare's Coriolanus. Fifty years after Emerson's journal entry, William James, in *The Varieties of Religious Experience* (1902), is far less able to grasp the meaning either of the greatness or the cost. In the *Varieties*, as in James's letters, or the ethical writings of Josiah Royce, or the correspondence of John Hay, or William Roscoe Thayer's *Life and Letters of John Hay*, poetry has its place; and its place is to be supportive of self-improvement and broad ideas of social progress, or even, on occasion, to excite sensations of empathy with etiolate pathological symptoms. 'As Tennyson writes', James will say; or again, 'As an anarchist poet writes', and again, 'The well-known passage from Walt Whitman is a classical expression of this sporadic type of mystical experience'; and more, 'This primacy, in the faith-state, of vague expansive impulse over direction is well expressed in Walt Whitman's lines'.

Part of the problem is that James, clinical psychologist as he is, has no words to connect him with semantic energy and inertia other than such terms as the verb 'to express'—a limitation which he shares with the human subjects of his clinical case-histories. 'But the more I seek words to express this intimate intercourse [of the person's individual self with God], the more I feel the impossibility of describing the thing by any of our usual images.' Those are the recorded sentiments of one of James's many case-subjects. 'I will again refer to a poem you probably know, "A Grammarian's Funeral" by R. Browning, in Men & Women. It always strengthens my back bone to read it; and I think the Feeling it expresses of throwing upon Eternity the responsibility of making good your onesidedness some how or other . . . is a gallant one, and fit to be trusted if onesided activity is in itself at all respectable.' These are the sentiments of William James himself, from a letter to a friend. Set James's words alongside those of his patient, previously quoted, and we see that the patient has the more genuinely inquiring mind. In *The Varieties of Religious Experience* one encounters strenuous case-work and, running parallel to it, a languid literary sensibility and condescending 'taste' ('poor Bunyan', 'poor Nietzsche', 'poor Margaret Mary Alacoque'). One must conjecture that James supposes the strenuous commitment of his clinical case-work to be capable of infusing its own energy into the languor of sensibility. On such evidence it must be said that he was mistaken and that William Empson's caveat—'The idea that the theorist is not part of the world he examines is one of the deepest sources of error'—applies generally to the work of William James as also to that of Josiah Royce; but not to the writings of Emerson, who recognized, at least sometimes, that he was a part of the world he examined.

At the heart of Emerson's thinking world stands 'Experience', the essay published in 1844, two years after the death of his five-year-old son. 'Experience' reads as if written in a state of what is now called post-traumatic stress disorder and as if its true title were 'Alienation'. To say this is not to deny the piece its power (it may be the most powerful of all Emerson's essays) but to attempt to register something of its unique pitch, the affirmation within its nihilism, the sharp particularity in its general blankness, the massive steadiness of its vertiginous suggestions. What I have termed 'pitch' is set by such phrases as the following: 'The only thing grief has taught me, is to know how shallow it is'; 'We animate what we can, and we see only what we animate'; 'the individual is always mistaken'; 'Life has no memory'; 'Two human beings are like globes, which can touch only in a point, and, whilst they remain in contact, all other points of each of the spheres are inert'; 'A sympathetic person is placed in the dilemma of a swimmer among drowning men'. Those who know the essay will protest on good grounds that these quotations give no indication of the total effect of the piece, in which Emerson is arguing for fraternity, for perception, for sympathy, for duty, decency in conduct, hope; finally for faith. True enough, but he does so in the context of a vision of 'absolute nature' that is as bleak as Melville's. Emerson says here, exactly as he says in other essays and throughout the *Journals*, that 'All writing comes by the grace of God, and all doing and having'; he says here, as he says elsewhere, that 'Every man is an impossibility, until he is born; every thing impossible, until we see a success'. He says essentially the same of genius, 'It is the distinction of genius that it is always inconceivable—once & ever a surprise', in a journal entry of mid-June 1838. To return to the essay 'Experience', 'I can see nothing at last, in success or failure, than more or less of vital force supplied from the Eternal'. The word that Emerson uses for the 'Eternal', in the immediate vicinity of this statement, is 'God'; his faith—against the odds—is not ostentatiously heterodox; but I see very little difference in his mind at this stage between 'God' and 'absolute nature'. If Emerson's God is the archetype of reconciliation, as 'Concord and Boston, the dear old spiritual world' would have it, God also is the arch-alienator of self from personality. 'Experience' is the record of Emerson's realization of this fact: it is the discovery most intimately related to a writer's grasp of her or his own style, as Emerson indicates in 'Experience' and the *Journals*. He writes:

> The middle region of our being is the temperate zone. We may climb into the thin and cold realm of pure geometry and lifeless science, or sink into that of sensation. Between these extremes is the equator of life, of thought, of spirit, of poetry,—a narrow belt.

He does not say—my commentary hazards the suggestion—that this 'narrow belt' is identical with the 'line' that 'is a hair's breadth' and that must be walked by anyone who at any time 'innocently . . . began to be an artist'. For Emerson, it would be the thin line along which his own naked self of apprehension and his performing personality can exist together: 'There is every degree of remoteness from the line of things in the line of words'.

Look again at the precise words with which Emerson praises Coleridge, in his early lecture 'Modern Aspects of Letters', delivered on 14 January 1836:

> I think that the biography of Coleridge is written in that sentence of Plato,
> 'He shall be as a god to me who shall rightly define and divide'. He possessed
> extreme subtlety of discrimination; and of language he was a living dictionary,
> surpassing all men in the fineness of distinctions he could indicate, touching
> his mark with a needle's point.

This is finely said, but even so, you could touch the mark with a needle's
point ten thousand times and achieve nothing more significant than needlepoint. Needlepoint is a form of stitch-work, widely used for chair-covers
and kneelers, in which a design is worked on coarse material in closely-
placed identical stitches of variously coloured wool. According to the *OED*,
the English term in this sense is not recorded prior to 1865, though the skill
was practised long before that date. However, except for a special application of the sense, the caveat may be dismissed as soon as entered. Language,
as Coleridge intends it to be understood, and as Emerson intends Coleridge
to be understood, is not embroidery. There was a great deal of literature in
nineteenth-century America and in Britain that was merely decorative; and
some of it passed at the time for high thought. One of the most telling
aspects of Emerson's criticism of his contemporaries, both in his *Journals* and
in essays such as 'Experience', is that much of the scientific and literary
discourse regarded at the time as creative is in fact merely modish: 'The
grossest ignorance does not disgust like this impudent knowingness', he
writes in 'Experience'; and in the *Journals* he berates his own assent to,
complicity with, furtherance of, 'parrot echoes of the names of literary
notabilities & mediocrities'.

Kay Redfield Jamison has asked—it is for her a rhetorical question—'Do we
diminish artists if we conclude that they are far more likely than most people to
suffer from recurrent attacks of mania and depression, experience volatility of
temperament, lean towards the melancholic, and end their lives through
suicide?' However, we diminish artists when we limit them to the terms of
our own prejudicates, as we find William James limiting them throughout *The
Varieties of Religious Experience*, or as Jamison herself diminishes them in *Touched
with Fire* (1993). James observed that 'the world we recognize officially in
literature and in society is a poetic fiction far handsomer and cleaner and better
than the world that really is'. As an observation by someone enjoying the status
of major thinker this perhaps qualifies for Emerson's epithet: 'impudent
knowingness'. That semantic precision for which, and with which, Emerson
praised Coleridge is secluded by James to his clinical case-work and by Josiah
Royce to his methodology of philosophical logic. The rest is essentially *pot*

pourri, lyric cries, musings, 'very deep insight[s] into the meaning of life', everything, in short, that Boston reserves to the 'realm' of Poetry. In this respect the writings of James the materialist and Royce the absolute idealist are indistinguishable. As a test-case consider Royce's small but significant volume, *William James and Other Essays* (1911), particularly the chapters, which began as occasional addresses, on 'William James and the Philosophy of Life' (The Phi Beta Kappa Oration delivered at Harvard University, June 1911) and 'Loyalty and Insight' (the Commencement Address delivered at Simmons College, Boston, June 1910). It could be argued that James on 'the world that really is', a world less clean than the one 'we recognize officially in literature and in society', like Royce on 'the highest forms of the spiritual life', is doling out an Emersonian largess, the superfluities of what might be called his noetic style, one that he in turn possibly derived from Coleridge's *Confessions of an Inquiring Spirit*.

During the same period (1910–11) in which he put together and published *William James and Other Essays*, Royce was conducting his formidable Harvard Seminar on Comparative Methodology. Sufficient records of these seminars exist (particularly for the 1913–14 series) to suggest that the style of delivery adopted by Royce in his Phi Beta Kappa Oration on James would not have been tolerated at those meetings. It may be protested that, in suggesting a significant contrast between the quality of Royce's 'William James and the Philosophy of Life' and that of his supervisory observations in the Methodology Seminar, one is ignoring or discounting such factors as appropriateness to the occasion, the significance of public decorum and rhetorical propriety. There is, however, no good reason why a Phi Beta Kappa Oration or a college Commencement Address should be devoid of those characteristics of attentive self-scrutiny, of attention to the private discipline of thinking. Indeed 'private discipline of thinking' itself may be questioned on the grounds that it may be understood to mean something that has no bearing upon public matters; an eccentricity, a hobby horse. Our private thoughts have public consequences and obligations. I believe that Emerson and Thoreau understood this and acted upon it in ways that more officially public men, such as John Hay, did not. William Roscoe Thayer's *Life and Letters of John Hay*, while consenting to 'poesy's' drift into the derelict margins of the commonweal, nonetheless assumes— fancifully—that it has the central place in the sphere of civic intelligence that Wordsworth, for one, believed it should and could have.

Emerson's genius, basically and substantially understood, is in the perception of this dislocation of public and private. In 'The Over-Soul':

> The great distinction between teachers sacred or literary,—between poets like Herbert, and poets like Pope,—between philosophers like Spinoza, Kant, and Coleridge, and philosophers like Locke, Paley, Mackintosh, and Stewart,—between men of the world, who are reckoned accomplished talkers, and here and there a fervent mystic, prophesying, half insane under the infinitude of this thought,—is, that one class speak *from within*, or from experience, as parties and possessors of the fact; and the other class, *from without*, as spectators merely, or perhaps as acquainted with the fact on the evidence of third persons.

Yet Emerson overlooks a factor even while he distinguishes Herbert, Spinoza, Coleridge as speakers 'from within' from Pope, Locke, and Paley as speakers 'from without, as spectators merely'. He might better have noted that the exclusion works in two ways and to the total detriment of the commonweal. The 'men of the world' *may* be 'spectators merely' of the visionary power possessing those who have found their 'centre'and through whom 'the Deity will shine'; but the 'spectators' are fully enabled, consciously or unconsciously, to exclude the 'Deity' from the centre of the places of civic power because, in Emerson's terms, the 'Deity' can be persuasively demonstrated by the 'accomplished talkers', the 'men of the world', to be a socially useless and publicly peripheral spirit, since, on such evidence as Emerson produces, such 'Deity' is the gift principally, of 'fervent mystic[s], prophesying, half-insane under the infinitude of [their] thought'. What Emerson does not clearly apprehend is the virtually unlimited tolerance that his 'men of the world' are willing to extend to visionaries of the Emersonian type, turning the visionary himself into a mere spectator of his own isolated intensity. In such circumstances, if you leave out the qualitative dimension of language, it is not possible to distinguish the work of genuine autodidactic intelligence from the effusions of the free-wheeling crank. As Charles Peirce would caustically observe, 'maniacs are original enough, if the quality of the product is nothing'.

In his essay *On Liberty*, originally published in 1859, John Stuart Mill argued that:

> Precisely because the tyranny of opinion is such as to make eccentricity a reproach, it is desirable, in order to break through that tyranny, that people should be eccentric. Eccentricity has always abounded when and where

strength of character has abounded; and the amount of eccentricity in a society has generally been proportional to the amount of genius, mental vigour, and moral courage it contained. That so few now dare to be eccentric, marks the chief danger of the time.

Stated semantically, the difficulty—since Mill liberally enfranchised for the common man and woman forms of self-expression which had always been enjoyed by the idle rich—has been to make a qualitative distinction between the eccentric and the erratic. This latter term derives from the editorial commentary to *The Letters of William James*, in the 1920 edition prepared by his son. The incident recorded here took place in 1889, when James was 48. His son writes:

> The erratics of the philosophical world were significant phenomena, and sometimes interested him most just when they were most 'queer'—when they were perhaps aberrant to the point of being pathological specimens ... He filled the 'Varieties of Religious Experience' with the records of abnormal cases and with accounts of the mental and emotional adventures of people whom the everyday world called cranks and fanatics.

The incident referred to was the occasion of James's testimonial to Charles Eliot Norton, President of Harvard, on behalf of 'a workman in a tack factory ... who has nevertheless gone quite deeply into studies philosophic, mathematical and sociological'. The man, it is recorded, subsequently 'withdrew from the tack factory forever, spent many years in a Mills Hotel working over an unsalable *magnum opus*, and every now and then appealing for funds'.

The phrase 'interested him' (like the verb 'to enjoy' or the noun 'enjoyment') is difficult, perhaps impossible, to separate from the implications of condescension. I find it particularly difficult, in the example of William James and the man from the tack factory, to decide at what point interest becomes a form of goading. If we take *eccentric* in its basic sense of *outside, away from, the centre*, it is arguable that James goaded the tack factory man into an eccentricity which is wholly alien to Mill's utopian vision of orbiting geniuses, but which nonetheless is the reality behind such Liberal scene-setting.

There is more grasp of eccentricity's blessing and curse in a single entry from Emerson's *Journal* than can be found in Mill's panegyric or in James's feckless and meddling condescension: an entry for June 1847, 'American mind a wilderness of capabilities'. Like much else in Emerson that is ponderable, the weight of the idea is carried by its semantic energy.

The word 'wilderness' for a New Englander in 1847 would be characterized chiefly by its ambiguity: a wild uninhabited, uncultivated region awaiting settlement, rich in as yet untamed possibilities for civilization; a wild uninhabited, uncultivated region into which you may venture and be lost forever, a region forever intractable to human settlement. Emerson is a thinker along the thin line that divides fecundity from desolation. I do not think that he would distance his own mind from the perilous ambivalence that he attributes to the 'American mind' as a mid-century phenomenon of the Western hemisphere.

'Alienated majesty' is Emerson's phrase although, as was suggested at the outset of this chapter, the context in which it is found, the essay on 'Self-Reliance', is not one that releases the richest implications of the phrase. 'Self-reliance' is too like 'self-help'. Emerson's vision of alienated majesty more truly belongs close to either side of what I have just called 'the thin line that divides fecundity from desolation'. Desolation for Emerson was both existential and civic. One of the finest passages that he wrote was set down in his journal on 30 January 1842, two days after the death of his little son:

> Mamma, may I have this bell which I have been making, to stand by the side of my bed.
> Yes it may stand there.
> But Mamma I am afraid it will alarm you. It may sound in the middle of the night and it will be heard over the whole town, it will be louder than ten thousand hawks it will be heard across the water, and in all the countries. It will be heard all over the world.
> It will sound like some great glass thing which falls down & breaks all to pieces.

It is as if a dialogue which is begun in order to record the natural delicate fecundity of the child's fancy turns imperceptibly into a soliloquy on the gigantic fragility of life and the happiness of all things depending on the resilience of that finest of all threads, faith in the safekeeping of a beloved child. The thin line which Emerson treads here is that between the uncanny and the fey, the *unheimlich* and the faery: it is the line which Emily Dickinson treads again and again in her poetry and letters. Emerson in this passage is writing as a sleepwalker walks, the shock he has received is so intense that he balances on the narrowest of surfaces in perfect safety. The balance is incited by an uncanniness and is itself truly uncanny. With Dickinson, the line-walking is entirely different; it is a conscious exploit-ation of a double standard. She knows that Amherst society is mildly prurient and that she is herself regarded by these strangely respectable folk as a fey reclusive creature. Returning upon our earlier play with 'needle's point' and needlepoint: let Amherst's domain of sentiment and sensibility be represented by needlepoint (dining-room chair seats and kneelers); Dickinson's Coleridgean ability to touch her mark 'with a needle's point' is, in her best work, uncanny.

But there is always a price to be paid. Dickinson all too often in her lesser writing is merely coy, or faery. Emerson's existential desolation, even at its most poignantly beautiful, resembles Hans Andersen rather than Søren Kierkegaard. There is not the element of *perforce* in his bleakest writing; his eccentricity is the cultivation of *otium*; he is never forced by the ungovernable and the arbitrary to leave the security of the provincial centre. Herman Melville and Charles Peirce suffer an enforced eccentricity; Emerson does not.

Civic desolation, then. In Josiah Royce's last work, posthumously published, *The Hope of the Great Community* (1916), his academic titles are listed as 'Late Alford Professor of Natural Religion, Moral Philosophy and Civil Polity at Harvard University'. Similar but amplified terms might describe the ground of research for these three chapters on alienated majesty, in which our chief concern is with the literature of natural and revealed religion, moral philosophy, and civil polity, both in nineteenth-century New England and in Britain, with particular attention to civil polity as this is encountered not only in the work of Emerson but also in that of Whitman and Hopkins, who took civil polity no less seriously than Emerson did. The domain of civil polity, in all three authors, is where the most substantial rationale may be found for choosing 'alienated majesty' as our subject and title.

30

Alienated Majesty:
Walt Whitman

In *The Star of Redemption*, Franz Rosenzweig observes that 'The language of the revelation of the soul seemed somehow uncanny for the spirit of the [nineteenth] century which recreated everything in its image, as object-ive and worldly'. I am in fact less troubled by the objective and worldly in the work of the age than I am by its confounding of the uncanny with the mere power to enchant: a confusion from which neither Nathaniel Hawthorne nor Henry James was able fully to extricate himself, nor even Herman Melville, if we think of 'Hawthorne and His Mosses'; nor Emily Dickinson in the frailer instances of her poetic genius.

In such a catalogue, the name of Walt Whitman stands as a major exception. He wins his exemption by stratagems and devices which were superficially or even profoundly disturbing to several of those whose names are listed in the previous paragraph. The admirable Thomas Wentworth Higginson—as sterling a character as Joshua Chamberlain—had recom-mended Whitman's poetry to Emily Dickinson but her response was that she had been told 'he was disgraceful'. This is more a riposte than a protest: a ripple of acquired distaste, in keeping with such formal nomenclatures as 'Mount Holyoke Female Seminary'. Emerson's distress went much deeper: he had recognized the greatness of *Leaves of Grass* when it first appeared in 1855. It is well known that while visiting Boston, in March 1860, to see the third edition of *Leaves of Grass* through the press, Whitman walked and talked with Emerson for two hours on the Common; that Emerson urged him to expurgate or at least tone down the 'sex element' in such additional poems as 'Children of Adam'; and that Whitman's response was 'no, no'. It is probably fair to say that as Emily Dickinson's stratagem, when cornered, was female modesty, Whitman's stratagem when cornered was male braggadocio.

The word much favoured by Whitman which links my preamble with his actual practice is 'spontaneous', as in 'Give me to warble spontaneous songs recluse by myself, for my own ears only.' Whitman, on the evidence of the work that he self-consciously committed to us in the 'deathbed' edition of 1891, is one of the least spontaneous warbling poets of modern times. Anyone who has examined the published facsimile of his so-called 'Blue Book', a mass of autograph interlinings, interleavings, and slivers of paper glued into his own copy of the 1860–1 Thayer and Eldridge edition of *Leaves of Grass*, will be in a position to confirm this description of his compositional methods. To this let us add the less obviously demonstrable suggestion that Whitman's homing-in upon the idea of spontaneity is not in itself purely spontaneous. Emerson had urged, in the Phi Beta Kappa Oration of 1837, 'The American Scholar':

> The poet, in utter solitude remembering his spontaneous thoughts and recording them, is found to have recorded that, which men in crowded cities find true for them also. The orator distrusts at first the fitness of his frank confessions ... until he finds that he is the complement of his hearers ... [and that] the deeper he dives into his privatest, secretest presentiment, to his wonder he finds, this is the most acceptable, most public, and universally true. The people delight in it; the better part of every man feels, This is my music, this is myself.

Whitman is *sui generis* only in the sense—though it is the essential and final sense—that what he leaves us is absolutely and uniquely his own. His philosophy of poetry he derives immediately from Emerson, his philosophy of genius he derives directly from Carlyle; and each of these mentors is himself inspired by German writers and the first great generation of English Romantics. Whitman, however, stands out, even from these grand forebears and forerunners by the extent to which he depends upon a self-engendered myth of self-conception. Whitman *is*, as he and none other may conceive himself *to be*.

Be that as it may, Whitman was reviewing Carlyle's *Heroes and Hero Worship*, *Sartor Resartus*, *The French Revolution*, *Past and Present*, and *Chartism* for the *Brooklyn Daily Eagle* in October and November 1846. In 'The Modern Worker', the third book of *Past and Present* (1843), Carlyle wrote: 'Some I do know, who did not call or think themselves "Prophets", far enough from that;

but who were, in very truth, melodious Voices from the eternal Heart of Nature once again; souls forever venerable to all that have a soul'. Place alongside this Whitman's late piece written on hearing news of the death of Thomas Carlyle in February 1881: 'Not for his merely literary merit, (though that was great)—not as "maker of books", but as launching into the self-complacent atmosphere of our days a rasping, questioning, dislocating agitation and shock, is Carlyle's final value'. Whitman is able radically to redefine the tone of that spirit from which his own polemic derives. In his 1881 memorial tribute, he picks up, like an echo across almost half a century, Carlyle's key word 'Prophets' and his phrase 'melodious Voices from the eternal Heart of Nature': 'The word prophecy is much misused [in general parlance]; it seems narrow'd to prediction merely. That is not the main sense of the Hebrew word translated "prophet"; it means one whose mind bubbles up and pours forth as a fountain, from inner, divine spontaneities revealing God'. The word 'spontaneities' recurs here as a term, for Whitman, of prime value, but as significant is the particular way in which he shakes Carlyle free from a pernicious sweetness in his prophetic vocabulary: 'melodious Voices from the eternal Heart of Nature'. 'Melodious Voices' is the equivalent of those early Emersonian locutions—'The very sentiment I expressed yesterday without heed', and so on—which were described in the previous chapter as potentially being 'culled from an autograph album or reciter's treasury'. Whitman does not want Carlyle any further debilitated by a salon-sweetness so alien to his real nature: 'as launching into the self-complacent atmosphere of our days a rasping, questioning, dislocating agitation and shock'. If asked to define in one sentence the particularity of Whitman's inventive genius as a poet my response would be that he redefined and re-expressed the nature of the 'melodious Voice' in terms of a questioning, dislocating agitation and shock, though not a rasping one because Whitman's poetic voice does not rasp; it is truly a 'great melody', more so even than Edmund Burke's prose, out of which, and upon which, Yeats derived and bestowed that memorable phrase.

The comparison is not misplaced. Whitman, contrary to some of his own statements and to what has casually been assumed to be the case, has a tenderness towards the witness and achievement of the past. Even so, it is equally the case that to Whitman the past reveals evidence of what Emerson calls 'alienated majesty', meaning more than anything, perhaps, lost opportunities of greatness, of supreme self-recognition, and self-realization. In one of his editorial pieces for the *Brooklyn Daily Eagle* (18 March 1846), he writes, under the heading 'You Cannot Legislate Men into Virtue!':

> It is amazing, in this age of the world—with the past, and all its causes and
> effects, like beacon lights behind us—that men show such ignorance, not only
> of the province of law, but of the true way to achieve any great reform . . . It
> must work its way through individual minds. It must spread from its own
> beauty, and melt into the hearts of men—not be forced upon them at the
> point of the sword, or by the stave of the officer.

That one amazing phrase, 'like beacon lights behind us', lies close to the
heart of the mystery of Whitman's creative and critical vision, a vision
which may be read in the light of Emerson's own extraordinary locution.
Beacon lights, 'behind us', but presumably still burning nonetheless, are a
type of alienated majesty: at once steadfast and bypassed, urgent and forlorn,
no less unheeded than heeded; course-keepers receding ever deeper into the
chaos of the past. The power of the phrase is enhanced, not diminished, by
our knowledge that Whitman aligns his own genius with 'the law of
successions', a phrase from *Democratic Vistas*:

> Law is the unshakable order of the universe forever; and the law over all, and
> law of laws, is the law of successions; that of the superior law, in time,
> gradually supplanting and overwhelming the inferior one.

Reading deeply and widely in Whitman is partly a technical matter—the
assimilation of our imagination into the characteristic long-line verse paragraphs of the *Leaves of Grass* poems—and partly a matter of his historical
ethics becoming a matter of conviction, for us as well as for him, through
the medium of a language which seems itself to have evolved by the very
process which it describes.

As Whitman himself affirms and protests, in the 1881 memorial tribute to
Carlyle, 'It is time the English-speaking peoples had some true idea about
the verteber of genius, namely power. As if they must always have it cut and
bias'd to the fashion, like a lady's cloak!' The situation and circumstances of
nineteenth-century American writing, however, the alternatives with
which it found itself presented, were less sharply outlined than Whitman
here suggests. In the case of Hawthorne's work, which he would have
known, and Dickinson's, which he would not, we are able to see 'power',
the 'verteber of genius', clearly manifested in their biased cutting of fashions
already known and approved by 'our comfortable reading circles', as Whitman calls them, or even in 'the dear old spiritual world' of Concord and
Boston, as Emerson half humorously describes it. A final and absolute
confrontation of 'that verteber of genius, namely power' with the

entrenched pieties and taboos of an extended provincialism is to be observed in the grotesque, partly self-willed, crushing of Melville and Charles
Peirce but even more by the self-promoting ingenuity with which Whitman, in the twenty-seven years after his notorious dismissal by Secretary
Harlan, contrived to manipulate to his own advantage each subsequent
public confrontation and affront.

> I am the poet of the Body and I am the poet of the Soul,
> The pleasures of heaven are with me and the pains of hell are with me,
> The first I graft and increase upon myself, the latter I translate into a
>   new tongue.

If by 'the latter' Whitman means us to understand 'the pains of hell', he
probably should not be taken at his word. The pains of hell, as these would
be sharply and fully understood in the New England of 1855, were translated into a new tongue by Hawthorne, Dickinson, and Melville. So far as
I am able to discern, Whitman did not believe in the pains of hell. He
believed, like Emerson, in the bifold nature of alienation, of alienation as
both estrangement and artistic distancing.

Throughout the 1840s Whitman, though never a legislator, was a polemicist of legislation, a daily commentator upon the activities of the
legislature. His sense of an entitlement to a 'say' in matters of government
and questions of general concern is evident, not only in his editorial writings
of that period but also in the legislative timbre of Leaves of Grass, particularly
of the long, originally untitled poem which he subsequently decided to call
'Song of Myself'. This legislative tone or timbre seems to have passed easily,
'spontaneously' one could say, from the newspaper editorials into the long
chant-like lines of the 1855 volume of poems. The radical sense of alienation, in both prose and poetry is evidenced in the presence of the gap, the
aporia, between an almost mystical respect for the idea of the law and a
continual accosting of legislature for its persistent shortcomings. The middle
term of the premise, as it is also for Emerson, is ignorance: the alienator of
humanity, whether in the individual spirit or the spirit of the common-
wealth.

In his contributions to the Brooklyn Daily Eagle for the years 1846–7,
Whitman frequently apostrophizes 'the mighty power of this republic', 'the
old fathers of our freedom', 'Jefferson, the great apostle of liberty', 'the great
voice of Jefferson'. 'Surely no people that ever lived', he writes on Thanksgiving Eve, 1847, 'have more cause than we, for thankfulness to God! for a

devout, cheerful, perpetual satisfaction with all those outward influences of government and social organization which are so potent to open the avenues to, or retard, human happiness'.

How would the resonances of that word 'potent' have sounded to Whitman, as he set it down in print, and how, if at all, might the way in which he heard it have influenced the forms of eloquence which he developed in his poetry? These forms Whitman, in spite of the mass of contrary evidence which he bequeathed to his executors and subsequently to us, persisted in oversimplifying—in mid-flight as it were—by the term 'spontaneous'. Or did he oversimplify? Not if we are thinking in terms of political polemic, but yes, possibly, if we think in terms of polemical verse-chant, where additional forces are necessarily engaged, which affect both broadly and minutely the contexture in which the simple is simply rejoiced in, and which can leave the standard affirmations of belief—'the mighty power of this republic' and so on—looking stranded if not useless and wasted.

Politically, there is no question that Whitman regarded spontaneity, in and of itself, as one of the most essential potencies: 'It is true, meanwhile,' (he continues in his *Brooklyn Daily Eagle* contribution on Thanksgiving Eve, 1847) 'that this happiness must proceed from the individual's self—when it is to be positively enjoyed'. This sentence follows, spontaneously yet of necessity, from the preceding statement that government and social organization are 'potent' not only to further but also to 'retard' human happiness. 'Spontaneity' is, in a sense *indifferent*, as all power considered in the abstract is indifferent; and there is some danger in the fact that, to Whitman, happiness, spontaneity, *and* indifferency are equally ciphers of potency, with an exponential range of implications for the political imagination which employed them but did so with a frequently top-heavy weightedness for less agile minds encountering them on the printed page:

> What blurt is this about virtue and about vice?
> Evil propels me and reform of evil propels me, I stand indifferent.

'Indifferent' for Whitman is a term of valency, on a par with spontaneity and happiness. Indifferency is also knit into the 'verteber of genius, namely power', which has for Whitman equal significance in politics, ethics, and rhythmic chant. The dictionary definitions for 'indifferent' restrict rather than enhance our reading of Whitman's usage: 'unbiased', 'impartial', 'disinterested', 'neutral', 'fair', 'just', 'even', 'even-handed', 'unconcerned', 'unmoved', 'careless', 'apathetic', 'insensible', 'undetermined', 'equivocal', 'ambiguous', 'not definitely possessing either of two opposite qualities', 'of no consequence or matter either way', 'unimportant', 'immaterial'.

Such definitions cannot assist us in our reading of Whitman's voice-tone though a grasp of some several dozen sense inflections may lull us into a supposition that they do. The question arising from these two lines from Section 22 of 'Song of Myself' turns on some basic moral questions, e.g. what constitutes vanity or callousness. In the work of major writers we may wish to believe that it is unnecessary to separate questions of moral nature from the textual nature of the work; that the author, in some mysterious way, will have taken care of that, will have ensured by virtue of profound semantic self-questioning and sifting that if the thing sounds right it will also be ethically right. However, there are strong challenges to this assumption. Gerard Hopkins, who though not greater than Whitman can stand comparison with him, wrote in a letter to Robert Bridges: 'I always knew in my heart Walt Whitman's mind to be more like my own than any other man's living. As he is a very great scoundrel this is not a pleasant confession'.

For Hopkins, Whitman's declared 'indifference' as to whether it was virtue or vice, good or evil, that propelled his interest in men and women would make him 'a very great scoundrel'. For Hopkins the issue that held his soul to the test was whether the beauty of the created world draws one towards the love of God or away from it. The fact that Whitman, with his magnificent recreative powers of description which Hopkins would have envied with the sincerest desire of emulation, appeared indifferent to any moral distinction between the sensuous and the sensual, would have struck the self-sacrificial Jesuit as one of the most deadly of sins. Semanticist as he was, I conceive him concluding from the sense-inflections of the word 'indifferent' that though things might well go differently, might go differently and well, no finesse of inflection could redeem Whitman's statement from its damnable alienation of the majesty of God's love.

If this is a fair conjectural construction of Hopkins's case against Whitman, such criticism comes all the more forcibly from one who was comparable to Whitman in the grasp of 'that verteber of genius, namely power', where 'grasp' includes both an understanding of theory and principle and a practical ability to master what Hopkins called 'the naked thew and sinew' of English and English verse-making. Hopkins would argue that swagger is not necessarily strength and that when Whitman swaggers, as he does in these two lines, his weakness shows itself as a characteristic moral provocation. The thought is basically Emerson's (as in 'Self-Reliance'), but Whitman chooses to phrase it in a more braggart fashion. This confrontation—between what Whitman says he stands for and what Hopkins says he will not stand for—is one of the most exemplary in the entire spread of British and American writing across the nineteenth century.

More may be said in defence of Whitman's challenge of indifferency to the *mœurs contemporaines* of New York and New England. Like Henry Thoreau and to some extent Emerson, indifferency was Whitman's way of access to a deeper piety than that which satisfied the *bienpensants* of contemporary religious appearances. All three—Emerson, Thoreau, and Whitman—realized that indifference was vital in itself and vital to the experiment each was conducting on the relationship of language to democratic self-realization. Whitman wrote in one of his *Brooklyn Daily Eagle* pieces (28 December 1846) that 'the depth of radical poetry lies in the hearts of all men, low and high; and we would it were oftener developed than it is by the monotonous customs of our working-day land'. 'Depth of radical poetry' as it sounds here could equally be read as 'depth of radical sentiment'. Whitman is a man of his age as well as a great original; and it may be the case that such writers experience actuality as a form of language, and language as a dimension of actuality, amid which, against which, into which, and for which, one's own personal utterances are to be fed, rejected, tried, and measured. The evidence of Whitman's notebooks bears witness to a form of radical experience which was initially 'poetic' in the quasi-euphemistic sense that is still current, and which, by a sudden leap of the creative faculty, became reconstituted, reconsecrated even, in terms of a language-experiment.

In his introduction to *An American Primer*, a brief but pregnant collection of Whitman's lecture-notes published in 1904 after the poet's death, Horace Traubel remarked:

> In referring to the Primer upon another occasion, Whitman said: 'This subject of language interests me—interests me: I never quite get it out of my mind. I sometimes think the Leaves is only a language experiment—that it is an attempt to give the spirit, the body, the man, new words, new potentialities of speech . . . The new world, the new times, the new peoples, the new vista, need a tongue according . . .'.

The statement closely corresponds to some sentences in the fourth paragraph of 'A Backward Glance o'er Travel'd Roads', the essay which Whitman completed in May 1888, a few days before his sixty-ninth birthday and printed as the introduction to a prose miscellany *November Boughs* in the same year. This essay was itself a synthesis of a number of earlier magazine articles. In it he declares:

> Behind all else that can be said, I consider 'Leaves of Grass' and its theory experimental—as, in the deepest sense, I consider our American republic itself to be, with its theory.

'I think', he adds, 'I have at least enough philosophy not to be too absolutely certain of any thing, or any results'.

Because of the interaction of ideas among Coleridge and Carlyle and Carlylean Emerson and because of the influence of Emerson upon Thoreau and Whitman, it is not surprising to find Whitman referring to *Leaves of Grass* as 'experimental'; nor, considering the same body of interactions, reactions, and influences, is it surprising to hear him refer to the American republic as 'in the deepest sense' experimental. What is surprising is the strong bond of identity that Whitman establishes between 'the depth of radical poetry . . . in the hearts of all men' (the language of democratic sentiment) and the technical business of 'language experiment'.

From this perspective, the question of indifference has implications markedly different from those in Whitman's braggart affectation (as Hopkins would have understood it and condemned it): 'Evil propels me and reform of evil propels me, I stand indifferent'. What is truly focused and sustained in the 1855 *Leaves of Grass* is the experimental question of 'how much liberty society will bear'.

> Apart from the pulling and hauling stands what I am,
> Stands amused, complacent, compassionating, idle, unitary,
> Looks down, is erect, or bends an arm on an impalpable certain rest,
> Looking with side-curved head curious what will come next,
> Both in and out of the game and watching and wondering at it.

I cannot paraphrase the sense of 'an impalpable certain rest' except to say that it is what much of the variegated indifference, in 'Song of Myself' and elsewhere, amounts to: the interinvolvement of seemingly contradictory emotions, conflicts of feelings in phrases that are simultaneously ephemeral and substantial, as in the conjunction of 'impalpable' and 'certain' or equally 'certain rest'. To answer the question 'what does Whitman's "indifferent" mean?', one might do as he does, make a sequence (all these present examples are drawn from the 1855 prose 'Preface' to *Leaves of Grass*). That is to say, 'indifferent', to Whitman, means, besides other things, the sum total of:

'the union always surrounded by blatherers and always calm and impregnable' ('impregnable' having the paradoxical double sense of being able to be impregnated, and securely fortified);

'Of all mankind the great poet is the equable man';

'High up out of the reach he [the poet] stands turning a concentrated light';

'What is past is past';

'These understand the law of perfection in masses and floods . . . that its finish is to each for itself and onward from itself . . . that it is profuse and impartial';

'nothing is finer than silent defiance advancing from new free forms';

'The depths are fathomless and therefore calm. The innocence and nakedness are resumed . . . they are neither modest nor immodest';

'Liberty relies upon itself, invites no one, promises nothing, sits in calmness and light, is positive and composed, and knows no discouragement';

'As they emit themselves facts are showered over with light';

'all the self-denial that stood steady and aloof on wrecks and saw others take the seats of the boats';

'The prudence of the greatest poet . . . divides not the living from the dead or the righteous from the unrighteous';

'The English language . . . is the medium that shall well nigh express the inexpressible' (I include this, understanding him to mean that it will do this out of the indifference of its largess);

'The soul of the nation also does its work. No disguise can pass on it . . . no disguise can conceal from it. It rejects none, it permits all'.

Perhaps, of these thirteen instances, Hopkins (if he read them) would reject one outright as morally outrageous; reflect that two, though not incitement to evil, are perilously ambiguous; set aside seven as matters of indifferency; endorse one as being in the very best traditions of sacrificial self-discipline (his fervent patriotism would recall the sinking of the troopship *Birkenhead*). The observation concerning the English language he could have accepted in the spirit of comradeship, though he might change Whitman's 'well nigh express the inexpressible' to 'well nigh speak the unspeakable'. The final instance, 'As they emit themselves facts are showered over with light', brilliantly tropes the instressing of inscape of Hopkins's theory and prac- tice—think of the poem 'The Starlight Night' and certain passages in the notebooks and journals. 'I always knew in my heart Walt Whitman's mind to be more like my own than any other man's living.'

Desiring above all things to be understood, to be received, the great poet finds that he is not understood, not received. In this experience of the world's intractable nature Whitman and Hopkins were not unalike. It is evident, even from a late poem such as 'Spirit That Form'd This Scene', that Whitman is aware of actual or potential audience-hostility as one among other contingencies that are either mastered, or got round in some uncertain way, or wholly succumbed to. The particular irony of having to stress such a factor in Whitman's case is that, like Wordsworth, he put a great stress on clarity, directness, immediacy of rhetorical and ethical impact. In jottings called 'Rules for Composition', dating probably from the early 1850s, he recommended to himself: 'A perfectly transparent plate-glassy style, artless, with no ornaments, or attempts at ornaments, for their own sake,—they only looking well when like the beauties of the person or character, by nature and intuition, and never lugged in to show off, which nullifies the best of them, no matter when and where'.

If that element we choose to call the paraphrasable philosophical burden of a major poet's work is significant (as it *is*, though more in its nexus of relationships with other elements than is sometimes allowed for), the germ of much of the thought that subsequently burgeons in *Leaves of Grass* may be found by consulting Whitman's early notebooks, as in this entry possibly dating back to 1847:

> The soul or spirit transmutes itself into all matter—into rocks, and can [*illegible*] live the life of a rock—into the sea, and can feel itself the sea— into the oak, or other tree—into an animal, and feel itself a horse, a fish, or a bird—into the earth—into the motions of the sun and stars—.

A highly intelligent autodidact of the nineteenth century could arrive at some such synthesis from a study of Alexander von Humboldt, Wordsworth, Audubon, Agassiz, and various works of ancient philosophy, such as Aristotle's *On Sense and Sensible Objects* or *On Coming-To-Be and Passing Away*. But it is not matters of synthesis, precisely, that are most relevant here; rather a particular form of collocation.

There is a word used often enough by Whitman for us to understand it as a characteristic of his idiom of eloquence. The word is 'inure', formerly 'enure', and like 'indifferent' it has numerous sense-inflections: 'to put into operation or exercise; to carry into act'; 'to bring by use, habit, or continual exercise to a certain condition or state of mind, to the endurance of a certain condition, to the following of a certain kind of life'. Whitman uses 'inure' in the 1855 'Preface' to *Leaves of Grass*; here it celebrates the manifold offerings and offerings-up of humanity throughout history and across all divides of race and nation: 'these singly and wholly inured at their time and inure now and will inure always to the identities from which they sprung or shall spring'. The word haunts Whitman's ear, I believe, because it doubles an active and a passive function. A person who puts, or carries, something 'into act' may necessarily become habituated to the endurance of certain conditions, to the following of a certain kind of life, as an unavoidable consequence of that act. Considered as belonging to a tradition of moral thought, it is a less precisely defined version of Bishop Butler's pronouncement, itself derived from Aristotle, that 'Your obligation to obey this law, is its being the law of your nature'. The fact that it is less clearly defined says much for Whitman's consistency beneath the level of his polemical contradictions. 'Inure' is brought within the circumference (with Whitman always extremely broad) of the 'indifferent'. Whatever the sharpness of our perceptions and preoccupations, as creatures of Nature we both act (inure) and are made to suffer (are inured) indifferently. We become used to that which uses us up. In the third line of Whitman's 'Beginners', one of the finest of his short poems, we are told:

> How they inure to themselves as much as to any—what a paradox
> appears their age.

Beginners are simultaneously begetters, initiators, novices, learners, tyros. Whether as initiates or as tyros they endure the consequences of what they carried into act.

In 'Beginners', as in some other of Whitman's writings, he may have been working his way towards, or into, a rhythm of inurement, less beautifully and consistently realized than the rhythmic syntax of indifference, which had already been mastered in the opening lines of the (then untitled) 1855 'Song of Myself'. But in any case we should expect the rhythm of inurement to be more awkward and occluded; all this is inherent in the accumulated sense-inflections of the verb. The third line of 'Beginners' is itself a working of such rhythm. Even more remarkable is the penultimate line of a poem called 'Thought' (one of five poems, written at various periods, carrying that title; there are three more entitled 'Thoughts'). The 'they' in the line means persons in high places:

> And often to me they are alive after what custom has served them, but
> nothing more.

How powerful this line is, in its well-judged ungainliness, its deadness of step. And yet of course how alive it is in its inertia.

Alienated Majesty:
Gerard M. Hopkins

A mong the numerous consequences of the era of so-called 'protest art' is the irrational embarrassment of the current reaction against the theme of protest, or of political writing in general. Whatever the excesses and affectations of the 1960s and '70s may have done to harm the cause of poetry, there is nonetheless a real connection between it and politics: as real now, if we could disclose its true stratum or vein, as in the Tudor court poetry of Skelton, Surrey, and Wyatt or in the political sonnets of Milton or in the relation that exists between Wordsworth's 'Preface' to *Lyrical Ballads* and his tract *On the Convention of Cintra*, or between Whitman's editorials for the *Brooklyn Daily Eagle*, and other papers, and *Leaves of Grass*. As the word 'politics' has been rendered so suspect, I have opted in these chapters on alienated majesty for the term 'civil polity', gleaned from the title-page of Josiah Royce's last book, *The Hope of the Great Community*, published post-humously in 1916, where the author is referred to as 'Late Alford Professor of Natural Religion, Moral Philosophy and Civil Polity at Harvard University'.

Civil polity—let us make the claim—is poetry's natural habitat. To approach Emerson, Whitman, and Hopkins in terms of this claim is to place particular emphasis upon the nature of 'alienated majesty', Emerson's fine phrase in which he perhaps spoke more profoundly than he knew of the powerfully inhibiting element in New England society. This element simultaneously restricted and enlarged powers of the imagination in Emerson, Whitman, and Dickinson, in Hawthorne, Thoreau, and Melville. Moreover, in all these writers I sense that the alienated majesty is the body and spirit of civil polity itself. The greatest crisis affecting civil polity during their lifetimes was obviously the Civil War, though in Emerson's case the passing of the Fugitive Slave Law by the governing body of the

Commonwealth of Massachusetts in 1851 took more out of him—more even than the death of his son nine years previously and certainly more than was exacted by his sidelines experience of the War itself.

If the life and work of Gerard Hopkins appear at first sight alien to the New England context, that particular frisson may not be altogether inappropriate to the argument, since aliening, alienness, even alienism—as well as self-estrangement, the reverse to the brave face of Emersonian self-reliance—are here being placed under review. Hopkins, however, remains an outsider of a more elusive kind. He comes across as being remarkably whole, even when riven by affliction and desolation; he is the same man in his late poems as he is in his sermons and retreat-notes; his introspection, which is that of the Ignatian *Spiritual Exercises*, is quite other than the introspection of Emerson, Dickinson, or Melville. His rejection of Whitman is fierce but entirely without affectation, which is more than can be said of Dickinson's.

Hopkins was acquainted with Whitman's poetry: a selection, edited by William Rossetti, had appeared in England in 1868; within three years of its appearance Whitman received greetings and praise from Swinburne and Tennyson. In 1874 George Saintsbury reviewed a new British edition of *Leaves of Grass* in the *Academy*, a review which Hopkins read. There is no way, of course, that Whitman could have known anything about Hopkins.

On the face of it, Hopkins represented everything which, in *Democratic Vistas*, Whitman urged American writers and readers to reject: Europe's 'feudal, ecclesiastical, dynastic world', to the idioms of which Hopkins, on first sight, appears to cleave. As a follower of St Ignatius of Loyola and a student of the Ignatian *Spiritual Exercises* he took into his devotional life and language the terms which, in the 1530s, Ignatius, himself a member of the warrior caste, a *caballero*, had written into his book of instructions: 'if anyone would refuse the request of such a king, how he would deserve to be despised by everyone, and considered an unworthy knight' ('The Kingdom of Christ').

> I caught this morning morning's minion, king-
>   dom of daylight's dauphin,

and so on. Moreover, within the immediate context of late-middle Victorian England, Hopkins, when he allowed his mind to attend to politics (which in fact he did fairly frequently) was, except in certain matters

pertaining to Ireland, a thoroughgoing Tory Imperialist: 'I enclose a poem,
the Bugler. I am half inclined to hope the Hero of it may be killed in
Afghanistan', that is, killed heroically defending some vulnerable outpost of
the Empire, the Raj.

At the same time, Whitman recognized power when in its presence,
and he could scarcely have missed its presence in Hopkins's poetry if only
he had read it. A minor *leitmotiv* in these chapters on alienated majesty is
Whitman's 'It is time the English-speaking peoples had some true idea
about the verteber of genius, namely power'. 'Verteber', a form of the
word as given in Noah Webster's *American Dictionary* in 1828 and 1832,
would have appealed to Hopkins, who emphasized the 'naked thew and
sinew' in his observations on the admirable way in which some writers
could use rhythm and syntax; Dryden, in particular, Hopkins admired for
this quality, calling him 'the most masculine of our poets'. Moreover,
Whitman's rejection of Europe and its literature is more qualified by detail
than the brief quotation from *Democratic Vistas* suggests. In a lengthy
footnote within that piece, he points to works of world literature including those by Shakespeare, Cervantes, Milton, and Goethe as providing
'models, combined, adjusted to other standards than America's, but of
priceless value to her and hers'. Nor is *Democratic Vistas*, of 1867–70, the
only place in which we find a greater degree of *finesse* in his treatment of
European literature. In one of his *Brooklyn Daily Eagle* pieces (' "Home"
Literature' of 11 July 1846) he condemns William Cowper for teaching
'blind loyalty to the "divine right of kings" ', a crime for which he would
have condemned the then two-year-old Hopkins had his seer's vision
foreknown several poems and numerous letters, and he also denounces
'Walter Scott . . . Southey, and many others' who 'laugh to scorn the idea
of republican freedom and virtue'. But when he dismisses the 'tinsel
sentimentality of Bulwer', the 'inflated, unnatural, high-life-below-stairs,
"historical" romances of Harrison Ainsworth', not only is Whitman
forthrightly, entirely, correct in his critical judgement, he is also markedly
close in pitch of attention to Hopkins, another fine, albeit informal, critic
of modern letters:

> If anything made me think the age Alexandrine (as they say), an age of
> decadence (a criticism that they sling about between the bursting Yes and
> blustering No, for want of more things to say . . .), well, it would be to see
> how secondrate poetry (and what I mean is, not poetry at all) gets itself put
> about for great poetry.

Or:

> Now [Browning] has got a great deal of what came in with Kingsley and the
> Broad Church school, a way of talking (and making his people talk) with the
> air and spirit of a man bouncing up from the table with his mouth full of bread
> and cheese and saying that he meant to stand no blasted nonsense.

Hopkins disliked what he called 'bluster', as his comic portrayal of Robert
Browning's poetry and Charles Kingsley's muscular Christianity reveals;
and it is likely that he would have seen Whitman as a blusterer also ('I sound
my barbaric yawp over the roofs of the world'); unjustly because, as James
Wright showed, in a beautifully appreciative essay, Whitman is one of the
most delicate of poets, and with a gift of parody and self-parody to equal
Hopkins's. But, of course, we know why Hopkins, while admitting that he
knew his own mind to be 'more like Whitman's than any other man's
living', objected to his American senior. It is because Whitman was 'a very
great scoundrel'; and he was a scoundrel, in Hopkins's eyes, because he
claimed to be 'indifferent' to moral and doctrinal issues which Hopkins took
as matters essential to salvation. Whitman understood or appeared to understand sensuality as good; to Hopkins the line between sensuous and sensual
was as fine-drawn as it had been for Milton, who introduced the word
'sensuous' into English.

To repeat: how Whitman would or would not have responded to the
poetry of Hopkins is entirely a matter for speculation. It is conceivable that
he might have been drawn, as so many readers of Hopkins have in fact been
drawn, into the error of regarding him as a wild nature poet of a power to
rival Keats and Shelley who unfortunately fell among Jesuits and whose gift
was consequently repressed. The contrary opinion needs here to be stated,
that the *Spiritual Exercises* not only saved Hopkins from repression and
despair but also gave to his poetry those distinguishing features which set
the seal of greatness upon it.

Hopkins had dedicated himself to poetry some considerable time before
he realized that he most truly and powerfully desired to dedicate himself to
the service of Christ and the salvation of his own soul. He told Dixon that
he had burnt his early verse 'before I became a Jesuit and resolved to write
no more, as not belonging to my profession, unless it were by the wish of
my superiors'. As to that section of the *Exercises* headed 'A consideration to
obtain information on the matters in which a choice should be made', its
particular significance for his situation may have increased rather than

ALIENATED MAJESTY

diminished during the twenty years in which he was a member of the Society:

> Once an immutable choice has been made there is no further choice, for it cannot be dissolved, as is true with marriage, the priesthood, etc. It should be noted only that if one has not made this choice properly, with due consideration, and without inordinate attachments, he should repent and try to lead a good life in the choice he has made. Since this choice was ill considered and improperly made, it does not seem to be a vocation from God, as many err in believing, wishing to interpret an ill-considered or bad choice as a divine call. For every divine call is always pure and clean without any admixture of flesh or other inordinate attachments.

The suggestion may here be made that a poetic gift, working to the pitch evident even in Hopkins's early work, is always inordinate in its demands. There is a certain poignancy in rereading, in this light, Emerson's words from the essay 'Experience': 'if one remembers how innocently he began to be an artist, he perceives that nature joined with his enemy'. At the age of fifteen Hopkins 'innocently . . . began to be an artist'; but poetry, such as he was to write in his later years, is not an innocent occupation, even when, as in most cases, it escapes being confronted by the demands of a vocation such as his.

Hopkins offered his great ode, 'The Wreck of the Deutschland', composed during the first half of 1876 with the permission and indeed the encouragement of his superior, to the Society, to the English Catholic Church, and to the English people; in the trust, as Norman H. MacKenzie says, that it would 'win over to the truth widening circles of Englishmen'. When it failed to win over even the editor of *The Month*, Hopkins returned, so far as the Society cared or was aware, to the production of 'little presentation pieces which occasion called for'. His genius, henceforth, was in hiding; though not in the half-surreptitious way which he attributes to his bird-watching 'heart' in 'The Windhover'.

This crucial episode reveals, however, the strength of mind with which Hopkins lived according to the rule. He avoided two errors of romantic sentiment. First, there is no evidence that he ever sided with his genius against his vocation. He did not regret having taken vows. Secondly, he made no attempt 'to interpret an ill-considered or bad choice'—what Emerson wryly terms the innocent beginnings of the artist's life—as 'a divine call'.

Here too the line between the understanding and misunderstanding is very thin-drawn; our misunderstanding, not Hopkins's. His early sonnet

'Where art thou friend', of April 1865, has been read as 'in effect a
dedication of his poetry to Christ's service'. Such a sense of dedication, at
that stage in his spiritual life, need not be taken as a misjudgement.
If MacKenzie is right in his 'Note on Missing Poems' it was shortly
thereafter, in the fall of 1865, that Hopkins began to sense that his 'deepening religious devotion was challenging his future as a secular poet'. I
interpret 'secular' as 'pertaining to the world of literary success or fame'
rather than as 'choosing worldly themes or subjects' since Hopkins's poetry
could scarcely ever have been described as 'secular' in the latter sense. The
secular world in the other sense, acknowledged and then put aside, figures
in the generous letter of understanding and comfort addressed to his former
teacher, the Anglican Church historian and minor poet Richard Watson
Dixon, in June 1878:

> It is sad to think what disappointment must many times over have filled your
> heart for the darling children of your mind . . . For disappointment and
> humiliations embitter the heart and make an aching in the very bones. As
> far as I am concerned I say with conviction and put it on record again that you
> have great reason to thank God who has given you so astonishingly clear an
> inward eye to see what is in visible nature and in the heart such a deep insight
> into what is earnest, tender, and pathetic in human life and feeling as your
> poems display.

Such a letter may help clarify our understanding in several ways. First, it
makes evident that the mind and heart which could offer this kind of
consolation in such full measure, and yet measure the rightness of each
phrase, would not at this time (just less than two years after the rejection of
'The Wreck of the Deutschland') be deluded into fancying that public fame
or notoriety as a poet might be construable as an alternative form of 'divine
call'. Secondly, it suggests that Hopkins is able to envisage that talk of poetry
could constitute, when called for (which would not be often), part of the
dutiful, necessary language of charity, and that, in performing this office, he
finds it appropriate to use the commonplaces of natural religion, moral
philosophy, and civil polity. Such phrases as 'a deep insight into what is
earnest, tender, and pathetic' are, taken by themselves, no different from
Josiah Royce's 'very deep insight into the meaning of life'. Here, as in a
myriad other instances around us, it is context that effects the change in
quality. Such language, in Royce's *William James and Other Essays*, is not the
best he can do, merely the best he permitted himself to do, for a Phi Beta
Kappa Oration or Commencement Address.

There are ways of offering up commonplace to the greater glory of God. Hopkins and in his way Whitman can do this; as Lincoln can. Others cannot. What Whitman offers up, in *Drum-Taps*, are phrases that represent the verbal strivings of the common soldiers of the Union army, as they endeavour to bring home the unspeakable nature of what they have been forced to endure and to witness: 'tumultuous now the contest rages', 'a desperate emergency', 'Faces, varieties, postures beyond description', 'I see a sight beyond all the pictures and poems ever made', 'O the bullet could never kill what you really are, dear friend'. Very finely, these half-defeated phrases of common endurance are matched by long lines of great exactitude: 'The glisten of the little steel instruments catching the glint of the torches'; and both the half-articulate and the minutely articulate are imperceptibly combined into a formal generosity of cadence that does duty for them both:

> Comes before me the unknown soldier's grave, comes the inscription
> rude in Virginia's woods,
> *Bold, cautious, true, and my loving comrade.*

'Inscription rude': the rough inscription, that Whitman ensures shall be confronted by his readers although, as his endless revisions to *Leaves of Grass* make clear, he is himself anything but a rough inscriber.

'Comrade' is a key-word for Whitman: his language is comradely with half-dead phrases ('postures beyond description') as it is with the young men who uttered them and are dead. It is his equivalent of Hopkins's dutiful, necessary language of charity.

'Common', the commonness of common soldiers, their common suffering, the commonness of their slang and platitudes, is a key-term in Whitman's polemic of civil polity, in the transcendent commonness of *Democratic Vistas*:

> Grand, common stock! to me the accomplish'd and convincing growth, prophetic of the future; proof undeniable to sharpest sense, of perfect beauty, tenderness and pluck, that never feudal lord, nor Greek, nor Roman breed, yet rival'd.

And this is to be distinguished sharply from what he elsewhere calls 'the mean flat average':

> To-day, in books, in the rivalry of writers, especially novelists, success, (so-call'd), is for him or her who strikes the mean flat average, the sensational

appetite for stimulus, incident, persiflage, &c, and depicts, to the common calibre, sensual, exterior life.

It will readily be observed that between the two phrases 'grand, common stock' and 'the common calibre'—as they occur in context—there stands a *massif* of contrary implications; and yet the bulk of the divide itself is substantially built up around the word *common*. Both examples occur within some thirty pages of the same work, *Democratic Vistas*. That Whitman here perceives, more clearly than most Whitmanites of the succeeding century and a half, that a 'grand common stock' shall not find its destiny realized in the 'common calibre', the 'mean flat average', is an insight which registers itself semantically rather than discursively. It goes some way towards explaining why Whitman, like Emerson and indeed like Hopkins, invested so heavily in the idea of *genius*. 'Genius' was to them as 'intrinsic value' was to Ruskin. Together, 'genius' and 'intrinsic value' are caught, without hope of success, in the crisis of civil polity to which I have attached Emerson's phrase 'alienated majesty'. For Whitman, in the years following Lincoln's assassination and with emancipation betrayed by reconstruction, it was the mean flat average that increasingly alienated the grandeur of the common stock.

'I find within my professional experience now a good deal of matter to write on.' If I did not already know whose words these are, I have no reason to suppose that I could identify the author. They are found in a letter from Hopkins to Robert Bridges (14 August 1879). To the same recipient, Hopkins writes, 'The state of the country is indeed sad, I might say it is heartbreaking, for I am a very great patriot' (16 June 1881). Six months later, he writes to Dixon: 'My Liverpool and Glasgow experience laid upon my mind a conviction, a truly crushing conviction, of the misery of town life to the poor and more than to the poor, of the misery of the poor in general, of the degradation even of our race, of the hollowness of this century's civilisation' (1 December 1881).

Concern for civil polity coexists with Hopkins's ever increasing devotion to the service of Christ and the salvation of his own soul. To understand the nature of this coexistence, the chapter 'Academic Theology and Hopkins's Self-Consciousness' in Walter J. Ong's *Hopkins, the Self, and God* (1986) helps us; as do Christopher Devlin's notes to his edition of *The Sermons and Devotional Writings of Gerard Manley Hopkins* (1959), in which he glosses several passages in Duns Scotus's *Scriptum Oxoniense* to indicate reasons why

Hopkins should care for him so greatly. According to Scotus, 'the self-perfection to which man aspires is in the natural order' although 'the achievement of it requires supernatural aid'. The idea that the kingdom of original justice was not rendered wholly inaccessible by the consequences of the Fall had a particular attractiveness for Hopkins, as did the radical suggestion, also originating with Scotus, that 'God the Son's descent into creation' was 'an act of love which would have taken place in one form or another' whether or not the Fall had taken place. One can see the consequences of this Christology in the foundation and development of Hopkins's theological politics. He was a commonweal man through and through, and if 'Christ's humanity was God's first intention in creating', a far stronger light is thrown upon the idea of humanity's eternal status in the divine polity than if the Incarnation is understood wholly as an act of redemption consequent upon the Fall.

'Now *what was the common weal?* what was the joint and common good of that kingdom?' Hopkins's rhetorical question was raised and answered, by himself, in the presence of the Sunday evening congregation at St Francis Xavier's Church, Liverpool, 18 January 1880, in a sermon on the text 'Thy kingdom come'. Hopkins's answer to his own question was not straight out of Ignatius:

> it was that God should be glorified in man and man glorified in God. Man was created to praise, honour, and serve God, thus fulfilling God's desire in bringing him into being and by so doing to save his soul, thus fulfilling his own desire, the desire of everything that has being. He was created to give God glory and by so doing to win himself glory. This was the good that first commonwealth aimed at, this was its common weal.

The foundation of this declaration is certainly that of *The Spiritual Exercises*, but the final impression and expression have been shaped by Hopkins; as he might have said himself, he has put his own stress on it. I have the feeling, when reading such a passage, that this is something from a very late response to Hobbes: a belated but powerful addition to a sequence which began in the mid-seventeenth century with Bramhall's *A Defence of True Liberty* (1655) and Clarendon's *A Brief View and Survey of the Dangers and Pernicious Errors to Church and State* (1676) and was continued in the first half of the eighteenth century by Bishop Butler's *Fifteen Sermons* of 1726. If there seems something anachronistic, even archaic, in this way of presenting these issues, it should be added that there is something anachronistic, possibly archaic, in anyone's following *The Spiritual Exercises*, set down in the early 1530s, in the midst of a progressive, increasingly secularist age; which is to say that Hopkins was thoroughly committed to his position and knew that his position committed him to appearing, to hostile Liberalism, two or three centuries behind the times.

One of the most grievous losses to modern English poetry is the 'great ode' to Edmund Campion which in September 1881 Hopkins told Bridges he had begun, but which a month later he told Dixon had been 'laid aside'; no trace of it remains. St Edmund Campion (beatified in 1886, canonized in 1970) was one of the English Jesuit martyrs of the reign of Queen Elizabeth I, and Hopkins's ode, described by him as 'something between the *Deutschland* and [Dryden's] *Alexander's Feast*, in sprung rhythm of irregular metre', had been intended as a celebration of the three hundredth anniversary of Campion's martyrdom, 1 December 1881.

The late sonnet 'Tom's Garland: Upon the Unemployed' is so unwieldy largely because Hopkins, in 1888, is attempting to compose a variant upon a mid-seventeenth century political sonnet, such as Milton, or perhaps even Hobbes, might have written. Hopkins offers what he calls a 'crib' for the poem, sent to Bridges in February 1888:

> Must I interpret it ['Tom's Garland']? It means then that, as St. Paul and Plato and Hobbes and everybody says, the commonwealth or well ordered human society is like one man; a body with many members and each its function; some higher, some lower, but all honourable, from the honour which belongs to the whole.

There is little point in objecting that Hopkins has failed to take the individual stress of either St Paul or Plato or Hobbes in so lumping them together, because the added 'and everybody' clearly indicates that the sentence is intended to be read as one of good-humoured exasperation.

Even so, 'Tom's Garland' is to be judged as a passionately serious effort to match navvies' labour with imaginative toil. In terms of consequence and effect this is a far stretch from Coleridge's intention when he wrote, in *The Friend*, of requiring 'the attention of my reader to become my fellow-labourer', though Hopkins's massive strenuosities in this poem may be indirectly derived from that source. We have to say that if, as Ong claims, Hopkins was 'inside his own epoch in history, at home in his own age', 'Tom's Garland' is a strange way of showing this to be the case, or we must add that his at-home-ness produces some strange metaphysical children, or 'darling children of [the] mind' as he expressed it in his letter to Dixon. MacKenzie observes that the poem may have been influenced by Ford Madox Brown's sonnet 'Work' which he wrote to accompany his painting of the same title. MacKenzie adds that Brown's well-known painting 'illustrated Carlyle's teachings on the need for all men to have some work to do, whether with brawn (like the navvies shown excavating in Hampstead) or brain (like two onlookers, Carlyle and the controversial social philosopher F. D. Maurice)'. The problem with the theme of 'alienation' is that, understood purely as a *topos*, it in no way prevents the philosopher who proposes it from being thoroughly at home in the world he trounces and castigates, like that couple of well-to-do loungers in Brown's painting, pleasantly observing the navvies' labour and seemingly entirely satisfied to have matters remain like that. But 'Tom's Garland' is a much stranger piece of work than Brown's painting. There is a likelihood, it has been observed, that Hopkins intended to write a burlesque element into this poem. There would be good precedent for it, in Milton's political sonnets such as 'On the New Forcers of Conscience under the Long Parliament', 'On the Detraction which followed upon my writing Certain Treatises', 'A book was writ of late called *Tetrachordon*', though it must be added that Milton's three sonnets wed terseness to the burlesque. Whereas they are terse and on target, Hopkins is not. In describing his intentions in 'Harry Ploughman', the companion piece to 'Tom's Garland', Hopkins said that he 'wanted the coda for a sonnet which is in some sort "nello stilo satirico o bernesco"', i.e. in the burlesque satirical style, after the manner of the early sixteenth-century Italian poet Francesco Berni, known for his comic and satirical attacks on individuals written in the form of the caudate sonnet. Hopkins added, 'It has a kind of rollic at all events'.

The noun 'rollic' appears to be derived from the verb 'to rollick', 'to frolic, sport, or romp, in a joyous, careless fashion', a dialect word, introduced into polite letters early in the nineteenth century. This verb and its noun and adjective were employed, throughout the century, by a bevy of second-order humourists, notably in the magazines, *Blackwood's Magazine*, *Pall Mall Gazette*, *Macmillan's Magazine*, *Fraser's Magazine*, *The Saturday Review*. An equally significant word applied by Hopkins to 'Tom's Garland' itself as well as to 'Harry Ploughman' is 'robustious'. The *Oxford English Dictionary* states that it was in 'common use during the 17th century. In the 18th it becomes rare, and is described by Johnson (1755) as "now only used in low language, and in a sense of contempt". During the 19th it has been

considerably revived, esp. by archaizing writers'. Both 'rollick' and 'robustious' are more appropriate to Hopkins's own gloss on 'Tom's Garland'
(provided in his letter of 10 February 1888 to Bridges) than they are to the
sonnet itself, which he finally described, in the same letter, as being 'very
pregnant . . . and in point of execution very highly wrought. Too much so,
I am afraid'.

In principle we ought not to object to a sonnet being simultaneously
'robustious' and 'very highly wrought'. Both terms combine well to describe the vernacular artifice of Milton's political sonnets. In principle again,
such a combination could, in Hopkins's case, relate closely to one of his
sharpest creative realizations: the relation of 'monumentality' to 'bidding'.
'Bidding' is Hopkins's term for 'the art or virtue of saying everything right *to*
or *at* the hearer . . . and of discarding everything that does not bid, does not
tell'. Hopkins goes on to make one of his most penetrating observations: 'It
is most difficult to combine this bidding, such a fugitive thing, with a
monumental style'. It is the key to what is right and wrong in his own
poetic method; to what is strong and weak in Keats's poems of 1819–20
('To Autumn', the unfinished 'Hyperion'); and to what, in Wordsworth or
Tennyson, strikes us as noble simplicity rather than mere verbosity or
canting. It allows us to realize the very different factors which assure, on
the one hand, the triumph of Whitman's 'Song of Myself' and the more
limited but real success of Wilfred Owen's half-rhyme and para-rhyme in
his ode 'Insensibility'. Whitman knows that if he can say the objective
details 'right *to* or *at* the hearer', over a sufficiently long span, the bidding
will transform itself into its own form of monumentality. Owen recognizes
that he can at one and the same time annul and confirm our expectations of
customary monumentality:

> But cursed are dullards whom no cannon stuns,
> That they should be as stones.

And he further recognizes that half-rhyme, which sustains order and expectation while maintaining its scepticism of them, also draws bidding
power into the extremities of the lines. The genius of Hopkins's own late
poetry—'That Nature is a Heraclitean Fire and of the comfort of the
Resurrection', 'Thou art indeed just, Lord . . .'—is itself a structural compounding of bidding with monumentality: 'Mine, O thou lord of life, send
my roots rain'.

If civil polity is poetry's natural habitat, there are implications for such poems as 'Tom's Garland', which is markedly political and which, by the final line, has revealed itself as one of the most grotesquely unnatural of nineteenth-century poems. There is a natural explanation for this, but this in itself is part of the problem. 'Tom's Garland' is grotesque as Carlyle in 'Shooting Niagara' is grotesque or as Ruskin is in *The Storm Cloud of the Nineteenth Century*. Ong suggests that 'Hopkins, like Newman, had very little if any of the defensiveness which betrays intellectual insecurity and freezes the mind'. But Hopkins is *not* like Newman, and 'Tom's Garland' is rigid with 'intellectual insecurity', or insecure intellectualism, in every line. Hopkins's own description of Scotus's disrelation to his age—'a kind of feud arose between genius and talent', the genius being Scotus, the talent that of his detractors—is more intimately and painfully true of Emerson and Carlyle. The feud between genius and talent took place within themselves, and the talent was closely attached to projections and self-projections of civic alienation. Alienation—thrown-ness—is real and deadly, but Carlyle is not thrown by any aspect of civil polity and Emerson is brutally thrown by polity perhaps only once, in the passing of the Massachusetts Fugitive Slave Law of 1851. Civil polity, in the form of Emerson's 'communities of opinion', is sufficiently alienating, simply in and of itself, as Emily Dickinson clearly perceived; you do not need to adopt alienated attitudes to excite its attention. Alienated majesty signifies a reality, however, even if not an actuality. In this it resembles intrinsic value with which it has an oblique interrelationship; a direct link, even, in Emerson's essay 'Self-Reliance'. Alienated majesty is tied by a law of opposites to a variety of Emersonian positives—'transcendent destiny', 'the integrity of your own mind', 'intrinsic right', 'the independence of solitude', 'inscrutable possibilities', 'the great and crescive self, rooted in absolute nature', 'the essence of genius'.

It is appropriate to end with a confusion of this term 'genius', at once a word of Romantic elitism and one of the most democratic of attributes. That the word can be associated with democracy is due, in no small part, to the work of Emerson, Whitman, and Hopkins. Democratic does not mean egalitarian. In Whitman's words, 'Great genius and the people of these states must never be demeaned to romances'; as Emerson writes, 'Genius is power; Talent is applicability'. Emerson again, 'The great genius returns to essential man.' Devlin observes of Hopkins that his 'view of genius (at least of poetic genius) was that it was a seeming approach to being a whole specific nature, "so that each poet is like a species in nature and can never recur"'. The issue is held in common by the three writers: it is the endeavour to conceive a uniting of individual genius to the genius of the commonwealth. In the fourth of the sermons preached by Hopkins at St Joseph's, Bedford Leigh (23 November 1879), the Christ presented to us is one who 'by acts of his own human genius' founded 'this Catholic Church . . . its ranks and constitution, its rites and sacraments'. It will be objected that a hierarchical institution cannot be democratic, but what it cannot be, in the world's terms, is egalitarian, even though it teaches equality before God. It may be further objected that these are exactly the terms on which Hopkins must be sharply differentiated from Emerson and Whitman. The burden of these three chapters has been to find that objection unsustainable, insofar as all three writers know democracy to be alienated from its proper majesty by the egalitarian and the mean.

Hopkins writes in his journal of 1872, 'I thought how sadly beauty of inscape was unknown and buried away from simple people and yet how near at hand it was if they had eyes to see it and it could be called out everywhere again'. In such a passage, he unites one of his most essential terms, 'inscape', with civil polity. He is perhaps like Wordsworth and surely like Ruskin, a Tory democrat. I do not believe, however, that he would have quarrelled with Whitman—a democrat but no Tory—when he claimed, of American poets wedded to the American nation, 'of them a bard is to be commensurate with a people'.

Word Value in F. H. Bradley
and T. S. Eliot

In F. H. Bradley's *Appearance and Reality* the word 'somehow' occurs with remarkable frequency. Here are a few instances: 'while it will be certain that the self and its identity *somehow* belong to reality, it will be equally certain that this fact has *somehow* been essentially misapprehended'; 'Now this . . . shows that self-sameness exists as a fact, and that hence *somehow* an identical self must be real'; 'we have somehow together, perhaps, several elements and some relations; and what is the meaning of "together", when once distinctions have been separated?'; 'the mass of relational appearance . . . exists, and existing it must somehow qualify the world, a world the reality of which is discovered only at a level other than its own'; 'Our result so far is this. Everything phenomenal is somehow real'; 'The idea of a being qualified somehow, without any alienation of its "what" from its "that" . . . is a positive idea'; 'That which I desire is not consciously assumed to exist, but still vaguely, somehow and in some strange region, it is felt to be there; and, because it is there, its non-appearance excites painful tension'; and so on.

We are accustomed in our general reading to encounter the word 'somehow' as a term of prevarication, or of deliberate or unintentional absence of clear focus; with speciousness and with inanity. One associates it with dramatized yearning. Tennyson's 'Oh yet we trust that somehow good | Will be the final goal of ill' is a sublime instance; Dorothea Casaubon (née Brooke) employs it in chapter 22 of *Middlemarch*, when she reproves the domain of art, to which she is drawn, for excluding so many from its wealth of meaning and feeling: 'all this immense expense of art, that seems somehow to lie outside life and make it no better for the world, pains one'. It is the gesture also of aspiring pietas, as in Laura Simmons's memorial verses for Professor Josiah Royce, written in 1916 and published in the *Boston Herald* and the *New York Times*:

Somehow, somewhere,
The master-mind moves toward the goal it sought!

Even more than with phrases of inane aspiration, however, we may associate 'somehow' with the tone of planned evasion, 'somehow irrelevant', 'somehow preeminently so', 'yet somehow so magically moving'.

It seems advisable to give some critical account of the frequency with which this word of dubious association occurs in *Appearance and Reality*, particularly in the light of T.S. Eliot's praise of Bradley's style. In 1927 he describes this as being 'perfectly welded with the matter', a style which when set beside Ruskin's is of 'a greater purity and concentration of purpose'; 'Bradley, like Newman, is directly and wholly that which he is'. How is it, then, that a style so composed should take as one of its key-terms a word which lends itself to evasion, prevarication, cop-out, vague aspiration, incompetence, inarticulacy? Eliot uses the word only once in the poems; a few times in the plays. In 'Portrait of a Lady' 'somehow' is a facet of character, as it frequently is in Browning.

In *Knowledge and Experience in the Philosophy of F. H. Bradley*, Eliot himself uses the 'somehow' construction in passages that are glosses on Bradley's argument. Though a sense of the wide range of implication in Bradley's usage is essential to a grasp of his philosophy, no more than a tentative coverage can be given in Eliot's thesis or in this present chapter. It must however be clearly understood that Bradley is by no means unaware of the weight of his key-term and that, moreover, he is ready to use its negative senses in ways that strengthen his own positive case.

The question involves supplementaries, e.g. whether, if there exists something we can call practical knowledge, absolute transcendent knowledge can be real also, and not an adumbration, some infinitely free-ranging chimera. 'And there can be really no such science as the theory of cognition.' And yet, as Eliot observes, 'The intended object is ultimate reality'.

Bradley's 'somehow' is more than a verbal tic or a subterfuge though he is aware that it is frequently no more than these. To attempt to define his positive sense of the term by analogy: an author—a poet, say—seeks the precise word: for minutes, hours, days, it fails to deliver itself; its absence is a felt presence. Suddenly it is here. How? Somehow it has come to be. *Somehow* is whatever protracted or split second activity of the mind makes real the presence of the right word. This *somehow* is the direct opposite of what I have heard described as the '*somehow* of abdication'; instead we are given what may be termed a *somehow* of realization. Here again are the opening sentences of chapter 14 of *Appearance and Reality*:

> Our result so far is this. Everything phenomenal is somehow real; and the absolute must at least be as rich as the relative.

Put another way: the Bradleian *somehow* belongs to an actual syntax of metaphysics; the quality of its action is that in context it rests in its own intelligibility. 'How ... does it embrace, and transcend, and go beyond, the relational form of discursive intelligence?' is a question put by Bradley, 'it' being 'this way of apprehension'.

I would say that we are close here to the notion of an objective correlative, that in the distinction here made between the discursive intelligence and a way, or ways, of apprehension we have also the distinction in Eliot himself between two major modes of his poetic comprehension. To the discursive intelligence belong *The Waste Land* in the form in which Eliot originally presented it to Pound's scrutiny, *Four Quartets* and the plays. With the way of apprehension, the syntax of becoming, we may associate *Ash-Wednesday*, *Sweeney Agonistes*, *Marina*, and—perhaps surprisingly—the two sections of the unfinished *Coriolan*. The very measure in which *Ash-Wednesday* and *Marina* move is the measure of becoming, the 'somehow' of coexistent appearance and reality, in which differences are a part of the 'felt unity', 'felt totality', 'internal felt core' even when they elude categorization, even when no more exists between them than a sensation of belonging, of recognition.

The English poet, critic, and sometime Anglican apologist C. H. Sisson, generalizing in relation to early Eliot, suggests that 'There is an element of pre-vision in poetry, to the extent that it may uncover elements which have not yet begun to operate in the conscious life of the poet, but will do so in time'. Then, criticizing the way in which Eliot uses one of Andrewes's Nativity Sermons in *Journey of the Magi*, Sisson concludes that the incorporation *verbatim* of early seventeenth-century English is a mistake: Andrewes 'was expounding what was accepted. We are looking for an apprehension'. Bradley several times uses the word 'felt': in addition to the 'felt unity', 'felt totality', and 'internal felt core', he refers to 'felt mass', 'felt experience', 'the felt "this" ', 'felt background'. In this light it is possible to see Eliot as a poet whose keenest sense of feeling is apprehension—apprehension being both a disposition to fear (the shadow) and a clear way of perceiving (through shades, gradations). And it is in the evocation of a not clearly defined boundary between apprehension as fear and apprehension as perception that the early Eliot excels as a poet and is in advance of the majority of his contemporaries.

A key-term in our discussion must be 'context', a word implied by Bradley and used by Eliot, though sparingly, in his commentary on Bradley. Context is implied by Bradley's use of the word 'relation': 'Relation pre-supposes quality, and quality relation ... Qualities are nothing without relations'; 'But we have found that the very essence of finite beings is self-contradictory, that their own nature includes relation to others'. Bradley also has words for connections that are not positively relational: 'congeries', for instance, or 'mere coincidence'. A person's 'environment' is and is not his true context:

> His wife possibly, or his child, or, again, some part or feature of his inanimate environment, could not, if destroyed, be so made good by anything else that the man's self would fail to be seriously modified.

It may be the case that Bradley's influence persists into the final stages of Eliot's work. If so, it is in a very restricted sense. The recurrent motif of the plays is the translation of some person or persons from an existence that has become an 'inanimate environment' into the true context of their life. It is, however, no more than a motif because, in *The Confidential Clerk* and *The Elder Statesman* Eliot abstains from the modifying power of language itself, a power that Bradley excels in conveying, and therefore withholds the most immediate instrument of relation from the plays' discoveries. And although if one had not found him already, one might well come to God through reading Bradley's *Appearance and Reality*, the salvation of a piece of writing is not on the same terms as the salvation of an individual soul; and we should not give credit where it is not due. *The Confidential Clerk* and *The Elder Statesman* are in these senses beyond redemption.

The intention here is not to attribute the falling away in Eliot's later work to any article or aspect of his Christian faith and ecclesiology. The causes are prevailingly secular and relate to questions of access. In proposing to consider word value in Bradley and Eliot, we might initially examine several uses of the word 'enjoy' in both writers. First, Bradley:

> For it is in finite selves ... that the good *must* be realized. And, further, to say that perfection must be always the perfection of something else, appears quite inconsistent. For it will mean either that on the whole the good is nothing

whatever, or else that it consists in that which each does or may enjoy, yet not
as good, but as something extraneously added unto him. The good, in other
words, in this case will be not good.

To 'enjoy', as we use it quasi-legally and colloquially, means both to have
unchallenged access to and to derive pleasure from, or, to take pleasure in.
'To enjoy the fruits of one's labours' is to have rightful access to them and to
derive pleasure from them. Bradley's phrase is more complex: it allows right
of access but rebuts easy-come hedonism. Eliot's use of 'enjoy' and 'enjoyment' in *Knowledge and Experience* is also complex; referring to the mere
'physiological process' while tacitly allowing the physiological process as a
latent source of active not contemplative pleasure.

In the essay 'The Perfect Critic' (1920) Eliot writes (with 'end' here
meaning the condition to which it moves) that 'the end of the enjoyment of
poetry is a pure contemplation from which all the accidents of personal
emotion are removed; thus we aim to see the object as it really is and find a
meaning for the words of Arnold'. This stems directly from the words of the
argument in the third chapter of *Knowledge and Experience* and is generous to
Arnold.

At some stage subsequently in Eliot's literary criticism the term 'enjoy' /
'enjoyment' is shown as a different proposition. The accidents of personal
emotion become part of the gusto of the occasion. Though I am not sure
that one could put one's finger on the precise point of change and though
there are some exceptions, the impressionistic spread becomes more marked
and the fineness of distinction is obscured. In a wartime lecture of 1943,
'The Social Function of Poetry', he had spoken of the value of the art 'to the
whole people, whether they read and enjoy poetry or not'. In the BBC talk
'Virgil and the Christian World' (1951) he recalled his first acquaintance, as
a schoolboy, with Homer: 'The obstacle to my enjoyment of the *Iliad*, at
that age, was the behaviour of the people Homer wrote about'. Let us give
some consideration to these excerpts. The last example we might wish to
enjoy as a joke; but what Eliot depicts as a schoolboy obtuseness is a widely
prevalent adult reaction: your enjoyment of a work is ruined if it speaks or
shows things to which you object. Bradley has a good phrase, in *Appearance
and Reality*, about the writer's vulnerability to 'the captious ill-will or sheer
negligence of his reader'. If we could agree that what many readers and
theatre-goers like to think of as their rightful enjoyment *is* the exercise of
captious ill-will and sheer negligence, we might also agree, or at least accept,

that shifts in word value are relatable to questions of author-audience relationship and indeed to the radical question of authorial integrity. 'The Social Function of Poetry', as previously noted, was a lecture given in wartime London; 1943 was the kind of year in which any author might gladly be persuaded that his or her concentration on semantic richness, finesse, emphatic or unemphatic, was a self-withholding from the opportunities and demands of the common struggle.

Such an atmosphere of expectation is strongly felt in chapter 5, 'War Interlude', of E. Martin Browne's *The Making of T. S. Eliot's Plays*. On 22 May 1940, by some irony the day on which there came into force the UK Emergency Powers (Defence) Act, giving the government control over persons and property, Browne asked Eliot 'whether we could possibly do an emergency version of *Murder in the Cathedral*'. He meant a production so cut as to be playable by a company of '5 men and 4 women'. He reiterated, 'It would frankly *be* an emergency version and billed as such; but it would enable us to present the play in a lot of places where it will never otherwise be seen, and to give its most essential values'. Eliot responded, on 5 June, the day on which the German panzers crossed the Somme, 'Of course you may knock *Murder* about as you think best and use it in the . . . repertory for the dur[ation] of the war. I shall be happy to see it serve that purpose'.

In Britain, in May–June 1940, it seemed unnecessary for anyone to gloss what they meant by values and purpose. Put another way, you could rely on people in general to read into certain terms the bulk of their own emotional investment; even Spartan cryptograms like 'Go To It' and 'London Can Take It' would shortly be so invested and enriched. The capacity of ordinary men and women to pour a vast amount of accumulated belief into a set of neutral terms such as 'values' and 'purpose' was the correlative of Churchill's capacity to recirculate Victorian and Edwardian nationalist and imperial clichés so that they seemed both preordained and new minted for the common struggle of each particular day. Lincoln's genius as an orator was not dissimilar. The soul of a beleaguered nation can be upheld by such means; in the circumstances of Britain, 1940, and Gettysburg, 19 November 1863, justly and rightly so. Again, it is a matter of context—by which one means anything from the closest and keenest affinity to the loosest congeries. It is a significant distinction; and the double danger in a seemingly harmless word like 'enjoy' (or 'enjoyment') is first that it appears unambiguous and secondly that it disarms criticism, since only a churl would wish to ruin the hard-won restorative leisure of his fellow men and women.

Some nine years after Dunkirk there was a fracas in Edinburgh, where *The Cocktail Party* was having its opening run during the Festival. The trouble arose from the effectiveness of one line and a half in the last act of the play:

They smear the victims
With a juice that is attractive to the ants.

The impresario Henry Sherek who was providing the financial backing for the production wrote in a memo to E. Martin Browne, 'There is universal distaste and criticism of the juice line. Surely the horror is enough without this? It seems unnecessary to me and why fight *everybody*?' And Browne himself informed the author that the phrases in question 'have, as I prophesied, aroused a general reaction of strong distaste'. Eliot cut the offending sentence. I believe that he was wrong to do so. You might say that it offends by a preciosity of cruelty, but babbling preciosity is part of the environment in the play, an environment which Celia abandons to seek and find her real being, as indeed it is part of Festival 'high culture'. In the mannered flat recital of her body's final context, that travesty of individualism, the mannered values of cocktail-society and Festival first nights receive a disproportionate shock. Enjoyment, as a component of aesthetic status, is put out by the obscene (as Eliot had pointed out as long ago as March 1918, 'Another variety of the pleasant ... is the unpleasant'). Distaste, as here expressed in terms of proscribing, is itself a form of obscenity.

The fact that E. Martin Browne was director for all the plays from *Murder in the Cathedral* on gives an effect of continuity to the circumstances, the circumstances being—or appearing to be—the progressive deterioration of Eliot's creative gifts in direct contact with the cultural phenomena of enjoyment, taste, distaste. In an interview given during the Edinburgh run of *The Cocktail Party* Eliot observed that 'The first and perhaps the only law of the drama is to get the attention of the audience and to keep it. If their interest is kept up to the end, that is the great thing'. At a significant level this is undeniably the case, but a question remains as to the final significance of that significant level. What Eliot calls the 'more poetic side' in his reported remarks is an added factor (I would not call it an added dimension): 'One of the things about poetry is that it does excite different reactions from different people. The main thing is that they should enjoy it; but they get different things out of it'.

In the set of 1950 Chicago lectures, 'The Aims of Education' Eliot speaks of 'ill-regulated emotion amongst the public'; he refers to the 'inevitable' nature of our embroilment in 'undefined defining terms' which are 'a permanent condition of language and of thought' and points to our obligation to find 'the right compromise for ourselves—the puzzle of the balance between those activities in which we participate, and those of which we can only hope to be an appreciative spectator'. Set 'appreciative spectator' against 'ill-regulated emotion amongst the public' and apply both terms to the Edinburgh *contretemps* which had taken place the previous year—1949—and which, on the evidence of his valedictory sentence to the final lecture, may have been in Eliot's mind when he was preparing these four Chicago pieces. 'The Aims of Education', in the phrases just quoted, describes a battle which Eliot had already lost. Those people who felt 'a general reaction of strong distaste' to the sentence taken out of Act III no doubt believed themselves appreciative spectators; but 'strong distaste'—unlike 'taste'—always speaks for unregulated public and private emotion. 'Taste' may be the expression either of an unregulated private emotion or of an educated judgement working so swiftly as to be equivalent to intuition: taste in this sense is a true manifestation of the Bradleian 'somehow'. Eliot is right to alert his Chicago audience to the power of 'undefined defining terms' and ought subsequently to have taken more notice of, or given more notice than he appears to have done, to William Empson's great work, first published in 1951, *The Structure of Complex Words*. Eliot's later critical practice is coarser than his Bradleian theory, though he seems to have believed to the end that no diremption had taken place.

His finest work—the critical theory and practice together with the poetry—reveals the closest and keenest affinity with the Bradleian movement of intelligible apprehension: I mean by this the sense that his best writing gives of being the appreciative participant in a process of its self-enlightenment:

> *If* poetry is a form of 'communication', yet that which is communicated is the poem itself, and only incidentally the experience and the thought which have gone into it. The poem's existence is somewhere between the writer and the reader.

Eliot's 'somewhere between' has affinities with the Bradleian 'somehow', and the reality of a poem such as *Marina* exists somehow and somewhere between the intelligible apprehension, understood as the rudiments of grace, and the briefly unintelligible affrighted apprehension with which Hercules, in the poem's epigraph, comes belatedly to his senses. Eliot brings the Bradleian moment and the Senecan moment into telling affinity.

Telling affinity, however, is not necessarily the same as communication or communicated experience: this is Eliot's argument in the introduction to *The Use of Poetry and the Use of Criticism*. In the first section of *Little Gidding* he declares that: 'the communication | Of the dead is tongued with fire beyond the language of the living', and communication here may mean apprehension, as in *Marina* or in *Ash-Wednesday*. The main burden of *Four Quartets* is devoted to a communication of meaning which is in part a confession that when we speak of communication we are for the most part 'begging the question'. This forces Eliot back upon the negative, the negating, associations of the Bradleian 'somehow': upon mere approximation, the half-adequate, the half-articulate; with the 'periphrastic study', inadequate and otiose repetitions of 'Something I have said before', with 'shabby equipment always deteriorating', the 'shell, a husk of meaning'.

It can be argued that, in *East Coker* and *The Dry Salvages*, Eliot stresses the half-achieved, the shabbiness of poetic presumption, in order that *Little Gidding* may draw up failure somehow into the meaning of love and thereby revoice weary presumption as active and measured oblation. One may question, even so, whether the redemptive shift affects the semantic depth of the verse itself. Let us agree that the truth of the pattern, as Eliot sees it, requires *Little Gidding* to be, not an epiphanic splendour but the faintest apprehension that all shall be well; and that shabbiness therefore remains an essential part of the vision of redemption. There remains the question of address. In writing of this kind the author addresses the topic, addresses himself and addresses either the faintly projected reader or some undefined group of dramatis personae who represent the 'you' of common humanity. The language of the English Litany, of the Catechism, of the General Confession, is appropriate to the intention. The language of ambivalence, of solecism, could be shown as appropriate—or inappropriate—only step by step:

> Whatever we inherit from the fortunate
> We have taken from the defeated
> What they had to leave us—a symbol;
> A symbol perfected in death.

One may question the phrase 'we have taken'. In itself the verb makes us raptors—to take from the defeated is pillage or rape. If the defeated had something to leave us, in what sense can we have taken it—does 'take' here simply mean 'to receive' as in 'take Communion'? What evidence is there elsewhere in *Little Gidding* that 'we', ourselves the defeated, have the strength or the nerve necessary for cultural pillage? The fortunate, we are to suppose, are also the defeated, and the sense here is meant to echo the general idea expressed in 'Tradition and the Individual Talent' (1919):

> Someone said: 'The dead writers are remote from us because we *know* so much more than they did'. Precisely, and they are that which we know.

In *Little Gidding* 'we' are no longer merely of the tribe of writers; 'we' is Everyman, the antithesis to Rimbaud's '*Je* est un autre'. Rimbaud's radical dislocation of language is discreetly but appropriately acknowledged in the awkward syntax of Eliot's 'Precisely, and they are that which we know.' The four lines from *Little Gidding*, however, are at once too cumbered and too loose. Bradley's 'somehow' calls for the 'precisely...', not for the shuffling parataxis.

In *Four Quartets* as opposed to *Ash-Wednesday* and *Marina* Eliot is invested by, and investing in, what is accepted. You can object that he is addressing as a communicant Anglican a nation which is only in a nominal or residual sense Christian. Nevertheless, half a century ago in Britain, particularly in the Britain of 1939–45, it was not difficult to prompt a form of immediate assent from that vast but amorphous body of residual Christian acceptance. As with Eliot's ideal condition of poetry, the people had 'different reactions' to the state religion; they got 'different things out of it'.

One can concur with John Booty's suggestion that 'To read the last three of the *Four Quartets* is to be reminded, time and again, of the trials through which Britain and Eliot went during the 1940's'. My final estimation of the quality of the work differs significantly from his; and I find troubling all such evidence of the seamless way in which the language of *Four Quartets* merges into the faintly rhapsodic language of the Anglican commentaries upon it. The public language of 1939–45 was in part the ubiquitous voice of the BBC as well as the weekly harangues from Pathé newsreels in the local cinema. The voice of *Four Quartets* is also the voice with which, in September 1944, Eliot addressed the Association of Bookmen of Swansea and South Wales at Swansea—a town that had suffered heavy damage in the Blitz of February 1941. It is like—if only partly like—the secular voice of the Sunday evening radio 'Postscripts' given by J. B. Priestley or of one of the better sessions of The BBC Brains Trust. The closest similarity,

accidentally struck, yet somehow of a piece, is that between Priestley's
'Dunkirk' Postscript and Eliot's 'Defence of the Islands' dated '9 vi. 40'.
Priestley, the self-made rich radical, distrusted by many in Parliament and by
some in broadcasting, is completely his own man in a tradition of public
oratory deriving from 'The Charge of the Light Brigade'. In 'The little
holiday steamers made an excursion to hell and came back glorious',
'excursion' is well-chosen: they were excursion steamers. As a historian of
radio has observed, 'Mr. Priestley was not an outstanding popular novelist
for nothing'. His style throws its own light on our examination of such
notions as 'enjoyment'. Like Churchill, in most ways his political opposite,
Priestley relishes recharging the cliché for an immediate purpose. It was
purpose rather than effect that he and Churchill were concentrated upon.
This is in a sense Bradley's 'felt unity', 'felt totality' or, even more to the
point, that same author's 'My Station and Its Duties', being imputed to a
people who comprised in actuality a congeries of ill-regulated emotion. It is
the matter of adequate technique rising to the occasion and somehow
becoming more than adequate. You can say that it has dated, but it has
not, because, paradoxically, it is so much part of the texture of it its time and
belongs there as Tennyson's 'Light Brigade' belongs to 1854, and as Richard
Eurich's painting *The Withdrawal from Dunkerque, 1940* belongs, and as
Eliot's 'Defence of the Islands' does not:

> and the memory of those . . .
> contributing their share to the ages' pavement
> of British bone on the sea floor
>
> and of those who, in man's newest form of gamble
> with death, fight the power of darkness in air
> and fire.

Eliot's duty in 'Defence of the Islands', as he doubtless sees it, is to write
something accessible and appropriate to the occasion: what seems appropriate, to him, is to preach continuity of values; but he does this in a style
wholly bereft of word value.

The public wireless language of the war years was also that of Tommy
Handley and *ITMA*, written and delivered in a style and manner that aped
the spasmodic and the insanely repetitious in the nature of the times. Due to
official and circumstantial ineptitude, tragedy was briefly eclipsed by farce,
or manifested itself as instantaneous farce: a potent hybrid in drama about
which Eliot had written pioneeringly and well. Yet again, if we take

Priestley's and Eliot's words quoted above, words written probably within a few days of each other, the advantage is with Priestley. A highly popular comedienne and singer of the day was named Gracie Fields and one of the south coast excursion steamers was named after her. The *Gracie Fields* was destroyed off Dunkirk. Priestley does the voices in a way that Eliot, sometime advocate of voices, can scarcely have objected to:

> But now—look!—this little steamer, like all her brave and battered sisters, is immortal.

'Little' for pathos (the *Gracie Fields* was in fact one of the newer ships). 'But now—look!—' is two voices in one: interjector in a WEA debate and word-elbowing comedian at the Holborn Empire. 'Battered sisters' because all ships are 'she' and because working females are battered in a variety of ways. 'Immortal' because that too is part of the jargon of entertainment, 'Palm Court' style ('we would now like to present our rendition of Sir Edward Elgar's immortal melody *Salut d'Amour*') and because the only way to survive 1940 was *somehow* to make the cant of 'immortal' melodies (i.e. Britain's mystical stamina) part of, a party to, a real feat of survival.

Though Eliot is no match for Priestley in this vein, it is just conceivable that had he found it possible to continue the *Coriolan* sequence beyond 'Difficulties of a Statesman' and the 'Triumphal March' of 1931, he would have possessed an instrument of great range and resonance with which to engage, as well as his progressive confessional motivation, the inner voice of Cyril Edward Parker and the inner voice of his own rage cut into, and cutting across, the public world of the Jarrow hunger marches, the wicked folly of Munich, the limbo of a 'Phoney War' and the many times blundering sacrificial ordeal of 1940–5. *Coriolan* remains one of the major 'lost' sequences in English poetry of the twentieth century and *Four Quartets* is the poorer for Eliot's having 'lost' it.

His lecture 'Scylla and Charybdis', though written and delivered early in 1952, remained unpublished in English until 1985. Writing here of Valéry's 'Le Cimetière marin' Eliot observes that the poet has put himself into the work 'to the point at which the surrendering of the maximum of [his] being to the poem ends by arriving at the maximum of impersonality'. This is better than the 1919 assertion, 'Poetry is not a turning loose of emotion, but an escape from emotion' because it avoids the loose and baggy implications of the word 'escape'.

Lyndall Gordon has cleverly spotted in Henry James's *Notebook*—an entry for 5 February 1895—the sketch for a projected story which 'seems almost to create Eliot, to forecast him'. Gordon asks how it is possible that James could thus imagine:

> a sensibility so highly developed that it did not as yet exist, but might evolve, particularly in the context of the high-minded New England in which both James and Eliot spent their formative years.

This is somewhat too respectful towards the high-mindedness which combined, in William James and especially in Josiah Royce (who chaired and approved Eliot's doctoral dissertation), a professional academic discipline with an undisciplined public philosophical whimsy and sanctimoniousness. Evidence for this assertion would set the published report of Royce's 1913–14 Harvard seminar on Comparative Methodology against his popular addresses, preserved in *William James and Other Essays on the Philosophy of Life* (New York, 1912) and *The Hope of the Great Community* (New York, 1916). With James's *The Varieties of Religious Experience* one would endeavour to show how his clinical investigation is repeatedly stultified by his confusion of case-study conclusions with the conclusions of a complacent aesthetic and a condescending ethical taste. As late as 1964 Eliot had occasion to observe 'how closely my own prose style was formed on that of Bradley and how little it has changed in all these years'. However, where Bradley's prose style is all of a piece, Eliot's is not. There is a split in Eliot as there is in Royce and in William James. Eliot did not simply decline over the years from acuity and the trenchant into a broad opinionatedness. Analytical finesse and knowing belletrism cohabited in his critical and cultural writings from the first. It pleased him as a beginner to be approved by such people as George Saintsbury, Charles Whibley, Desmond MacCarthy.

Much in late Eliot that is demonstrably bad stems from two interconnected sources: from elements in his intellectual inheritance and from wrong decisions unconsciously and consciously taken. These too were anticipated in earlier work, for example the review of Julien Benda's *La Trahison des clercs* which Eliot contributed to an issue of the *Cambridge Review* on 6 June 1928. He appears to have suited his words with much care and forethought to the timeless quality of the average Cambridge mind. The essay is an attack on several writers, Barrès and Péguy especially, whom Benda has already attacked in his book. Eliot furthers the depreciation exclusively by tone; no evidence is brought forward to justify the accusations. 'I dislike both of these writers as much as M. Benda does.' 'I do not want to enter upon an analysis which would presuppose a knowledge of the work of Barrès and Péguy [*quaere*: presuppose *whose* knowledge?]. I only offer as my opinion, the view that not only the practical judgment but the theoretic judgment of these two writers is poisoned by an excess of sensibility over thought. I have myself found them both quite futile.' 'There is a hopeless confusion in Barrès and Péguy which was bound to vitiate everything they wrote.' This is the style of a clever and ambitious Harvard senior. In June 1928 Eliot was three months short of his fortieth birthday.

And yet, in the concluding paragraph of this same piece we find another definition of the 'good poem' to set in sequence with those of 1919 and 1952:

> A good poem, for instance, is not an outburst of pure feeling, but is the result of a more than common power of controlling and manipulating feeling.

Even here, though, 'manipulating' is questionable. The examples of the verb, in its full range of senses as recorded by the *Oxford English Dictionary* (2nd edn., 1989), belong almost exclusively to the nineteenth century. A citation from the *Athenaeum* (4 June 1892) is exemplary as it stands: 'This manipulating of a language'. It is exemplary because, as it stands, one cannot tell whether the phrase is meant pejoratively or not. This is some indication that the verb situates itself precisely on a fine line dividing praiseworthy dexterity from specious contrivance. The art and practice of poetry keeps also to this fine line.

It is very much to Eliot's credit that he is found, across a span of more than thirty years, returning upon what is for him a crucial description; knowing each time that something basic has failed to clear its own meaning in, or at, his hands. Is it centrally or marginally to his discredit that he is also, on occasion, ambitiously manipulative in what he writes, in how he acts? We seem here to confront an embarrassment: it strikes one as not proper to arrogate to oneself the right to judge statements and issues that are so rawly presented as crucially confessional, penitential. Such compunction is probably not called for, however; one is confronted less by confessional starkness than by aesthetic confusion. 'Aesthetic' here implies assumptions about values which turn into presumptions as to intrinsic value. Eliot's self-laceration in *Four Quartets* over questions of verbal incompetence, matters of his own volition and which he presents to us with an enviable competence, gives not so much a syntax of self-recognition as a stasis of yearning, a yearning which is the negative correlative of a Schopenhauerian and Nietzschean exaltation of music as the supreme art. Eliot in the lecture 'Poetry and Drama' draws his audience's attention to the margins of language, as he apprehends them, to:

> a fringe of indefinite extent, of feeling which we can only detect, so to speak, out of the corner of the eye and can never completely focus... At such moments, we touch the border of those feelings which only music can express.

If Eliot 'apprehends' these margins, such apprehension suggests itself as a travesty of *Ash-Wednesday* and *Marina*. It is understandable that someone imbued with the spirit of Royce's idealism, or perhaps repelled by the irregular stratum of obtuseness that crops up throughout *The Varieties of Religious Experience*, might come to overestimate the significance of 'worn-out... fashion'; it is difficult to understand how or why so dedicated a reader of Bradley as Eliot shows himself to be could drift into the marginal sentimentalities of 'The Music of Poetry' (1942) and 'Poetry and Drama' (1951).

My criticism of Royce relates principally to the 'same vast task of the ages' tone which so closely anticipates the tone of Laura Simmons's memorial verses. That motto-phrase comes from his book *The Problem of Christianity* (1913), which was based on a course of lectures delivered in 1912. There is, needless to say, more substance to those lectures than my highly selective quotation allows to appear. There is, for example, in the closest proximity to the motto-phrase, a judicious comparison and contrast of the complementary virtues and limitations of Christianity and Buddhism, which reads like a proposal for Eliot's poetic line from *The Waste Land* to *Ash-Wednesday*:

> Each [religion] deplores humanity as it is, and means to transform us. The contrast is, therefore, hardly to be defined as a contrast of hope with despair. For each undertakes to overcome the world, and assures us that we can be transformed... Buddhism... has as its goal a certain passionless contemplation, in which the distinction of one individual from another is of no import, so that the self, as *this* self, vanishes. Christianity conceives love as positively active, and dwells upon a hope of immortality.

If an outline proposal for a final statement would suffice, we could say that we have here an adumbration not only of *The Waste Land* and *Ash-Wednesday* but of *Four Quartets* also. Somewhere in the creative mystery, however, passionless contemplation—*apatheia*—blurs into apathy: I mean the apathy to which Eliot refers, in a letter of 1920, as being characteristic of the post-war reading public. It is as if his writing became infected by the public apathy which he had determined to oppose and correct. The bathetic locution 'those feelings which only music can express' is a signature of apathy like the earlier suggestion that poetry needs to be in such 'relation to the speech of its time that the listener or reader can say "that is how I should talk if I could talk poetry" '.

The routine demands made, between 1940 and 1945, upon an author of Eliot's high reputation, for work of an appropriate public significance, are suggested by John Booty's reference to 'the trials through which Britain and Eliot went during the 1940's'. At a distance of sixty years it is now possible—as it was not possible then—to see the state of Britain at that time as something other than the consummation of Randolph Churchill's ideal of Tory Democracy co-acting with that late flowering of progressive Liberalism set out in the Beveridge Report. In that still divided and unequal nation Eliot steeled himself to do what was then called Work of National Importance. In 'The Music of Poetry', though he says that the poet 'must, like the sculptor, be faithful to the material in which he works', Eliot's material is no longer primarily language; it is Christian Thought; or the People as he understands them. And how he understands people is still very much how he understood them in the pub scene of *The Waste Land*, only now, instead of saying 'Well, if Albert won't leave you alone, there it is, I said', they say 'that is how I should talk if I could talk poetry'. This is not enhancement but impoverishment, and the language of *Four Quartets* also is language that has suffered impoverishment. Making it part of the Anglican Lectionary is not going to amend that radical absence.

33

Eros in F. H. Bradley
and T. S. Eliot

Poetry is one of the multifarious forms of self-consciousness. It is a consciousness of self, a consciousness to, and in, itself; and an embarrassment to itself and others. When a radical embarrassment is overcome by the fascination of technique we have various forms of the baroque—none of which can be said to characterize the age we live in. Eros is common to the art of all periods, though I do not propose to consider it in the forms in which it currently finds expression. Eros is the power that can be felt in language when a word or half-finished phrase awaits its consummation. Eros is so palpably present in rhyming verse that at times it seems like a parody of itself; it is less evident in blank verse but is there nonetheless because enjambment thrusts meaning across the line and because the syntactical unit awaits its own fulfilment. Pope is one of the most immediately erotic of poets, F. H. Bradley one of the most directly erotic of modern philosophers. Biography contributes details—Lady Mary Wortley Montagu and Martha Blount in Pope's case; in Bradley's, a woman to whom he was attached, platonically or not, for many years and to whom his books are dedicated. I am less concerned with biographical detail, however, than with pitch of premise and of hypothesis. As when he writes: 'Desire, for me, is a felt whole containing terms and a relation, and pleasure and pain. But it contains beside an indefinite mass of the felt, to call which an object strikes my mind as even ludicrous'. Or again, 'We may be told that the End, because it is that which thought aims at, is therefore itself (mere) thought. This assumes that thought cannot desire a consummation in which it is lost. But does not the river run into the sea, and the self lose itself in love?' And again, 'where desire is unsatisfied, it is not always mere feeling, as against the object, which pervades the soul. The image of the desired, as against present perception, floats or is held before the attention, and the feeling of pain, we may suppose, must sharpen the contrast until at length the difference is seen'. Desire, for Bradley, is thought, sign, attention, and alienation. This is the level, perhaps the only level, at which Eliot can manage Bradley outside the purely conceptual range of his 1916 dissertation *Knowledge and Experience in the Philosophy of F. H. Bradley*:

> Because I do not think
> Because I know I shall not know
> The one veritable transitory power.

Such lines—they are from the beginning of *Ash-Wednesday*—have an attractiveness that owes much to Bradley. They read as by someone who has read the allusions to eros, in *The Principles of Logic, Appearance and Reality, Essays on Truth and Reality*, with close and loving attention, but has changed all affirmations to negations. That is not quite what I meant to say. Eliot does affirm, very beautifully many times, but what he affirms are negations. We who are Bradleians should make much of *Ash-Wednesday* and of *Marina*, and—just possibly—of *Burnt Norton*. There is not much else on which to rejoice. The young Eliot is an inspired flâneur of the erotic; there is no eros in late Eliot, but something indeterminately other, contained in the final play within the convention of an old father's love for a young, redemptive daughter.

When Bradley's second book, *Ethical Studies* (1876), was reprinted in 1927, Eliot reviewed it for the *TLS*, subsequently including his piece as chapter 4 of *For Lancelot Andrewes* (1928). He praised the author's 'scrupulous respect for words, that their meaning should be neither vague nor exaggerated'. Not only can it be said that, in isolation, numerous passages from Bradley's books constitute the most beautiful aphoristic writing in English metaphysics since the *Moral and Religious Aphorisms* of Benjamin Whichcote, published in 1753, but it can also be noted that Bradley's last published work, a posthumous publication, was his collection *Aphorisms* (1930), written 'at various times of his maturer life'. Having said that, one has to correlate the burden of Eliot's suggestion with the significance of one of Bradley's own most ponderable words—'somehow'. It occurs some twenty-six times in *The Principles of Logic*, no less than forty-one in *Essays on Truth and Reality*, and as many as eighty-eight in *Appearance and Reality*. If unspecified, unbounded yearning is one of the energies of eros, then 'somehow' is part of the erotic language. Certainly the demotic would regard it as such. This is not to say that a philosopher is therefore debarred from using it but rather that when a philosopher uses it as often as Bradley does, the effect upon his style is to make it at once something more and something less than that the words shall be 'neither vague nor exaggerated'. There is a stratum of Bradley's style, which makes it peculiarly what it is, and in which Eliot shows no sign of interest, which indeed he misrepresents in his carefully chosen words of praise.

It is difficult to conceive of a more evasive word than 'somehow', and yet Bradley makes it the term of focus for a number of his inquiries into the nature of being. He can use it to imply: something as yet unspecified which shall yield up its specificity to human attentiveness and human expenditure of time; in other words, it is a shorthand form for allotting space to available precision, a bit like *nota bene*, a memorandum for an experiment yet to be conducted. On one occasion he writes that the ' "somehow", as it is, does not satisfy us. It is the name of something which, for us, is not all there, and is not actually contained in our fact'. We might overhastily conclude that a philosopher who commits himself to, draws so heavily upon, a term half-dead from colloquial usage, a word out of the conversational argot, must himself be 'not all there'; and Bradley's has been for some years a shrouded name.

There remains a challenge—to oneself—to bring together Eliot's praise for a grasp and conveyance of meaning 'neither vague nor exaggerated' with Bradley's own sentences as one finds them in his second book, *Ethical Studies* (1876):

> The artist and poet, however obscurely, do feel and believe that beauty, where it is not seen, yet somehow and somewhere is and is real; though not as a mere idea in people's heads, nor yet as anything in the visible world.

> So far religion and morality are the same; though, as we have seen, they are also different. The main difference is that what in morality only is to be, in religion somehow and somewhere really is, and what we are to do is done.

Such passages strain almost hopelessly beyond bearing the conventional understanding of what can be accomplished with verb-tenses within the patterns of ordinary grammar ('somehow and somewhere really is, and what we are to do is done'). It is in this way, in the strangeness of the tense-collocations, that Bradley's prose half-invents the tense-music of *Ash-Wednesday* ('Because I know I shall not know'; 'For what is done, not to be done again'; 'Still is the unspoken word, the Word unheard'). It is there still, though more didactically and less eloquently, in the opening of *Burnt Norton* and again from the same poem's valedictory lines:

> There rises the hidden laughter
> Of children in the foliage
> Quick now, here, now, always——.

In his 1927 essay on Bradley Eliot claims that 'A system of ethics, if thorough, is explicitly or implicitly a system of theology'. This is debatable to say the least, though one might agree that there is a connection that Eliot thought he saw, a powerful one, between Bradley's sceptical idealism and the tradition of belief into which, in 1927, Eliot had so recently been initiated. To quibble somewhat with 'system': I think that once the demands of his Harvard thesis had been met, Eliot's interest in the 'systemic' Bradley was negligible; and that once the obligations of a 1927-mode *TLS* review were behind him, what he had meant there by Bradley's 'great gift of style' became a mere nod of obligation. For the *TLS*, around 1927, having a great gift of style meant writing like Charles Whibley. An association with Charles Whibley seemed to Eliot, the literary journalist, no bad thing; but Eliot the poet is looking for metaphysical données; exemplary moments of peculiar music; and it is just such a peculiar music that is given him by the odd glissades and cornerings of Bradley's prose: 'what in morality only is to be, in religion somehow and somewhere really is, and what we are to do is done'.

There is a trace also of this tense-interest in the long essay on Dante written two years after the Bradley review. Eliot gives in translation (his own, following that by P. H. Wicksteed): 'And my spirit, after so many years since trembling in her presence it had been broken with awe, without further knowledge by my eyes, felt, through hidden power which went out from her, the great strength of the old love'. That which Bradley's strange-sounding English (in the two passages quoted from *Ethical Studies*) and the awkward Wicksteed–Eliot translation of Canto XXX of the *Purgatorio*, have in common is a sense of 'ingathering', 'infolding' all things within and including time. 'In-folded' is the penultimate verb in *Four Quartets*, and it may be that Eliot saw Bradley as, in some way, the philosopher of wasted and redeemed time (though this is not the Bradley of the 1916 dissertation or the 1927 eulogy; it is a Bradley drawn in from somewhere else, from the margins of Eliot's official paideuma).

One is haunted, while reading passages such as the two quoted from *Ethical Studies*, by a notion that the ideas scarcely more than adumbrated there await submission to logical process in such a way that 'somehow' could be endowed with an algebraic letter. In the 'Additional Notes' of 1922 to *The Principles of Logic* (originally of 1883) Bradley claims that 'we have . . . with every idea an assertion that it possesses, so far, the character of Reality, and further is real somehow'. Barring the presence of one word, this is Adam's dream as Keats conceived of it in his letter to Benjamin Bailey (22 November 1817). That one word is 'assertion'. Adam's dream is not an assertion but a beholding. A poem ('the' poem) is positioned at some point between the assertion and the dream. Again, in the same 'Additional Notes' of 1922 Bradley suggests that 'There are no "mere ideas" . . . Logic *must* assume that the ideal is real somehow and somewhere. The idea that did not qualify Reality would certainly fail to be an idea'. Like an idea, or an action, or a person, the poem, coming into being, qualifies Reality, which is not to say that it necessarily gives value to Reality or gives real value. Most poems drain the Reality they qualify, but Reality is not the same as it was before they were written. In this factor stands our main justification for devoting time to the discussion of poetry and other arts. Fragile as it is, the energy so committed is nonetheless a sufficient riposte to the Pragmatist's scepticism, as Bradley frames it, concerning the question whether 'the world of art belongs to the region of the worthless-in-itself'.

I would not recommend Eliot's *Knowledge and Experience in the Philosophy of F. H. Bradley* to anyone seeking a painless, or even a tolerably painful, introduction to that philosopher's meaning and mystery. Nor, as previously suggested, would I direct that person to chapter IV of *For Lancelot Andrewes*. Bradley's memorial in Eliot is in *Ash-Wednesday* and some of the *Ariel Poems* and part, at least, of *Burnt Norton*, and it is an adequate memorial. I wish I could give a less qualified testimonial.

The recognition of the connection between Bradley and Eliot's Christian poetry does not originate with me. Hugh Kenner suggested it in a chapter on Bradley in *The Invisible Poet* (1959), though he does not refer to *Marina*, perhaps the most Bradleian of all Eliot's poems. I say 'most Bradleian' because it takes the 'somehow' / 'somewhere' line of Bradley's idealism as its points of departure and of final non-resolution:

> What seas what shores what grey rocks and what islands
>
> .   .   .   .
>
> And woodthrush calling through the fog
> My daughter.

These opening and closing lines of the poem, not quite exclamations and not quite questions, follow each other, as with a natural undisturbed syntax, as though nothing has intervened; and yet what has intervened is something that Bradley had variously named the 'underlying felt whole', 'felt totality', 'the ambiguous existence of what has been and is about to be'.

That final quotation marks one of the relatively few occasions on which Bradley appears to tolerate ambiguity. In this relative intolerance he is writing against the pull of what, around the time of his death, in 1924, would become the strongest inclination in modern British literary criticism. Laura Riding and Robert Graves's *A Survey of Modernist Poetry*, with its study of syntactical ambiguity in a Shakespeare sonnet, dates from 1927. Empson's *Seven Types of Ambiguity* was first published in 1930.

Eliot's own approach to Bradley, in the 1927 *TLS* review, keeps very much within the older tradition. Saintsbury or Whibley would not have disowned the piece. Eliot writes, as they would happily have done, of Bradley's 'great gift of style', a style that is 'perfectly welded with the matter'. We are still in the pre-war world of secure belletrist assertion; he probably read this in his own mind as the best tribute he could offer to Bradley's generation, men like Royce, under whom he had studied at Harvard in the years 1911–14. It is one of the perennial mysteries to do with Eliot that he could—seemingly—inhabit two worlds simultaneously and apparently without distress: a kind of Boston / Home Counties world of say, 1911, where books are still said to be 'extremely readable in snippets' and a different world typified by the Riding–Graves *A Survey of Modernist Poetry* of 1927.

I have in the past been too ready to accuse the young Eliot of opportunistic toadying; I am more reluctant now. The 1920s were a weird time of slippage and overlap: Saintsbury, Whibley, Riding, and Graves, and of course Eliot. Bradley's great gift to Eliot is that he is at one and the same time (so to speak, reviewing the collected oeuvre), a stately Victorian moralist, as in 'My Station and Its Duties' (Essay V of *Ethical Studies*, 1876) and the speculative philosopher who writes 'But an idea has also another side, its own private being as something which is and happens. And an idea, as content, is alienated from this its own existence as an event'. If you stress alienation you are bound to stress context, as a kind of counterweight. Bradley does place an emphasis on context which he is careful to distinguish from mere 'content', mere 'congeries', though it is not the presentation of context in a form which would most be of use to a literary critic—let us say

someone who wished to take further the approach of Riding and Graves in
their remarks on Shakespeare's Sonnet 129.

If Bradley emphasizes context, he is nonetheless sparing with his usage of
the term itself. What we are looking at, and for, are words that add up to
that definition. It could for instance be called 'context' when Bradley writes:
'For phenomena to exist without inter-connexion and unity, I agree is
impossible'; 'felt totality' is 'context' whereas 'confused coexistence' is not.
As readers of Eliot we may play with the idea that such a sense of 'context'
and the use of the term 'objective correlative' are contextually related; and
as readers of Bradley our concern might equally be with those of his phrases
which possibly influenced Eliot's move towards this significant definition.
In *Essays on Truth and Reality*, for instance, Bradley writes of 'the opposition
of not-self to self', adding that 'even when the correlation of self and not-
self has been objectified, this complex object comes against the self still in
that way which (to be strict) is no relation'. If this is the source of Eliot's
1919 term (in the essay on *Hamlet*) it is richer than anything Eliot made of it;
because, for one thing, it helps to 'place' Hamlet the man—the character,
what you will—as well as Eliot's own problems in handling intractable
material. But there are other *loci* in *Essays on Truth and Reality* which
might equally be seen as the source of Eliot's phrase. There are other
candidates, such as George Santayana's *Interpretations of Poetry and Religion*,
but to say more on this would be to quibble. The heart of Eliot's matter is
undoubtedly Bradley.

That the intensity of Eliot's involvement with Bradley had diminished by
the time of the 1927 review of *Ethical Studies* was Hugh Kenner's opinion,
delivered in 1959, but the suggestion requires some qualification. Late in
life, addressing a Convocation of the University of Leeds in 1961, Eliot
made a penultimate reference to Bradley 'whose works—I might say whose
personality as manifested in his works—affected me profoundly'. His final
estimate was of course the 'Preface' to *Knowledge and Experience in the
Philosophy of F. H. Bradley*, the 1916 dissertation belatedly published in
1964, a year before Eliot's death, in which he writes that he 'can present
this book only as a curiosity of biographical interest, which shows, as my
wife observed at once, how closely my own prose style was formed on that
of Bradley and how little it has changed in all these years'. Observe in
passing how firmly Eliot, once the enemy of personality, has swung the
weight of his own elderly personality in support of that very concept or
entity. But age alone may not have been responsible for the heavy shift in

emphasis. There is a crucial indication, as early as March 1928, that Eliot seriously mishandled a paragraph in Bradley; and this tactical error affected key-passages in the criticism he wrote thereafter.

In the eleventh essay of *Essays on Truth and Reality* Bradley writes:

> Morality and religion can be regarded as means to worldly success or to bodily health. We can say the same thing of pleasure, or again pleasure may be taken not as a means but as the end which all else should subserve. The pursuit of beauty in art may be spoken of as a more or less useful amusement, or as a way perhaps of keeping out of vice. And truth again also undeniably is useful, and is a means and instrument valued for the sake of other purposes. All this is justifiable, but justifiable only when we remember that it is but relative.

The burden of this passage is carried by the significance of the phrases 'can be regarded', 'may be taken', 'may be spoken of', 'undeniably is useful'. Bradley is acknowledging a social tone; he may not be actively hostile to it, but we can be fairly clear that he does not want it regarded as exclusively his.

In the March 1928 'Preface' to the second edition of *The Sacred Wood*, Eliot delivers a series of remarks which must surely be modelled on Bradley's paragraph. He writes:

> Poetry is a superior amusement: I do not mean an amusement for superior people. I call it an amusement *pour distraire les honnêtes gens*, not because that is a true definition, but because if you call it anything else you are likely to call it something still more false. If we think of the nature of amusement, then poetry is not amusing; but if we think of anything else that poetry may seem to be, we are led into far greater difficulties.

As an exercise in *de haut en bas* irony, Eliot's passage is markedly inferior to Bradley's. To write 'Poetry is' followed by 'I do not mean' followed by 'I call it' followed by 'not because that is' is far more self-shackling than to write 'can be regarded', 'may be taken', and so on. Even at its best, Eliot's critical tone was hardly more than an epigone of Bradley's philosophical style and, in the 1928 'Preface' to *The Sacred Wood*, comes very close to parody. And there is more to be said.

Once Eliot has allowed himself to say (even in irony, in jest, even) that poetry 'is' a superior amusement, he has compromised himself and compromised his critical language. Even if you say 'superior amusement' only to save yourself from calling it something worse, you have unnecessarily given hostages to 'the Pragmatist', who was suspected by Bradley of believing that the world of art belongs to the region of the worthless-in-itself.

That body of opinion which focuses upon, solidifies itself around, the sense of an object 'worthless-in-itself' is a power with which you cannot compromise; the price exacted for your recalcitrance is that of alienation. Bradley has a fair amount to say, from a technical philosophical angle of approach, on the question; and since I have called the young Eliot an inspired flâneur of eros, I will add that he is equally an inspired flâneur of alienation. That is what the young Eliot is about: eros and alienation. The deepening failure of Eliot, both as a poet and critic, to focus his powers, I attribute to his increasing inability—and it begins fairly early, in the late 1920s—to contemplate the heavy cost of being, of becoming, radically, irretrievably, alienated.

Even if Bradley's sense of the term is more purely philosophical than is any use to which it will be put in the following assessment of Eliot's creative and critical decline, we perhaps need to investigate a few of his usages and applications as a preliminary to considering alienation as a hazard from which Eliot backed, or bowed, away (the first two come from *Appearance and Reality*, the third from *Essays on Truth and Reality*):

> an idea has . . . its own private being as something which is and happens. And an idea, as content, is alienated from this its own existence as an event.

> For the whole of finite being and knowledge consists vitally in appearance, in the alienation of the two aspects of existence and content.

> No pursuit can justify a lapse from its own code of honour, or a search or a love for alien codes and effects. And thus an immoral spirit in the philosopher is, I presume, certain, unless kept in check, more or less to injure his philosophy. But from the other side the same thing holds of an unusual gift of conscientious or religious feeling.

To take this last instance first: Bradley is essentially concerned with what he calls 'single-mindedness' and with lapses from that form of integrity, lapses which may be induced by excesses of virtue as much as of vice. What that single-mindedness comprises would seem to be the absolute integrity of the idea. In the two excerpts from *Appearance and Reality*, Bradley appears to be debating the alienation of extreme objectification from extreme subjectivism while seeing this condition as a necessary and probably inescapable component in the process of thought—an insight which again could have fed into Eliot's conception of the objective correlative.

And yet it does appear that we have to enter a crucial caveat here, if only to clear our minds of it, and so as not to have it warping everything we say subsequently: that Eliot, the early inspired flâneur of alienation and alienated eros—'On Margate sands | I can connect | Nothing with nothing'—became the purveyor of Christianized angst to *les honnêtes gens*; and this as a consequence merely of a lapse of attention in reading Bradley: 'Poetry is a superior amusement' in place of 'The pursuit of beauty in art may be spoken of as a more or less useful amusement'. Subsequently, in the lecture halls of Harvard, London, Chicago, Swansea, Leeds, Eliot becomes increasingly able to connect everything with everything. He alienated himself more and more from immediate context while ingratiating himself more and more with generalized assumptions of, and about, pleasure: in short, he became a pragmatist. The middle- and late-period lectures and essays—'The Music of Poetry', 'What Is Minor Poetry?', 'The Three Voices of Poetry', 'Goethe as the Sage', 'The Classics and the Man of Letters' could only have been written and delivered by someone reconciled to the discovery that the world of art is the region of the worthless-in-itself and that the overriding reality to be accommodated is what Bradley termed 'the captious ill-will or sheer negligence' of the average reader–auditor.

In his early critical writings Eliot's sense of enjoyment is Bradleian. He writes that Coleridge's 'end [i.e., conclusion, whether intended or not] does not always appear to be the return to the work of art with improved perception and intensified, because more conscious, enjoyment'. 'Enjoyment', here, is still very close to the Bradleian 'realization', 'attention', 'inter-connexion and unity' or even 'consummation'. Eliot writes of Charles Whibley—to whose memory he dedicated *The Use of Poetry and the Use of Criticism*—that he 'has not the austerity of passion which can detect unerringly the transition from work of eternal intensity to work that is merely beautiful and from work that is beautiful to work that is merely charming'. 'Austerity of passion' is a phrase that Eliot would not have begrudged Bradley—he applauded the 'purity and concentration of purpose' in Bradley's style. Such choice of words is, so to speak, hierarchical in intention; and Bradley was well known to be a recalcitrant Tory. He wrote in *Essays on Truth and Reality* that 'Philosophy cannot exist apart from absolute sovereignty, and we have to choose between monarchy and chaos', and phrases of similar resonance occur throughout Bradley's work: 'Within this known region, and not outside, lies all the kingdom hidden by ignorance; and here is the object of all intelligent doubt, and every possibility that is not irrational'. Or:

But as long as, and so far as, any detail, however trifling, essentially belongs to logic, that detail, so far is justified. It is real with the reality of that kingdom in which it owns a place, however mean that place may be, and although we fail satisfactorily to explain its presence and precisely assign its function and standing.

The difference, I would say, between these utterances of Bradley and the tone of Eliot's 'Preface' to *For Lancelot Andrewes*—'classicist in literature, royalist in politics, and anglo-catholic in religion'—is that between a sense of 'eternal intensity' on Bradley's part and a speech that is merely charming, on Eliot's. It is the spirit of the flâneur again. Moreover, tempting as it may be to associate irrevocably Bradley's intensity with English Tory politics, I would add that the younger writer who most powerfully reminds me of the Bradleian hierarchies is Simone Weil who in a 'Spiritual Autobiography' of May 1942 wrote of the adolescent experience of contrasting her own achievements with those of her brilliant brother: 'I did not mind having no visible successes, but what did grieve me was the idea of being excluded from that transcendent kingdom to which only the truly great have access and wherein truth abides'.

What the young, or young-ish, Eliot does is, precisely, to assign function and standing to the superlative, the good, and the mediocre, in the domain of art. His brutish rage against working men who ride 'ten in a compartment to a football match at Swansea' is a self-maiming travesty of Bradley's essay 'My Station and Its Duties'. The brutishness is not excused by, though it is partially explained by, Eliot's early Bradleian stance; Bradley was himself frequently accused of brutality in his dismissals of other thinkers. I have chosen my words with some care, however, and am not proposing that 'brutishness' and 'brutality' are exact synonyms. Bradley is never crass, Eliot is; he operates well below the levels of insensibility to which he consigns his foes. But that is the price we pay, presumably willingly enough, to have his early critical writings, in particular 'The Function of Criticism' (1923), for the pronouncements of accurate assignment: an unerring sense of pitch in distinguishing work of eternal intensity from work that is merely beautiful and from work that is merely charming.

Work of eternal intensity is outside the consensus. If the question is put, 'actual or alleged consensus?', the response must be that the alleged consensus *is* the actual consensus, through the imposition of *force majeure*. The merely beautiful and the merely charming are creatures of the consensus, of *force majeure*.

By consensus I mean the opposite of what Eliot means by 'tradition' in the 1919 essay 'Tradition and the Individual Talent'. 'Eternal intensity' can stand as equivalent of—admittedly it is not so convincing as—Simone Weil's 'transcendent kingdom' and Bradley's 'absolute sovereignty'. Take a further passage from the 'Preface' to the 1928 edition of *The Sacred Wood*:

> It will not do to talk of 'emotion recollected in tranquillity' which is only one poet's [Wordsworth's] account of his own methods; or to call it a 'criticism of life' [Arnold's words], than which no phrase can sound more frigid to anyone who has felt the full surprise and elevation of a new experience of poetry. And certainly poetry is not the inculcation of morals, or the direction of politics; and no more is it religion or an equivalent of religion, except by some monstrous abuse of words.

If you are not willing that poetry should be 'emotion recollected in tranquillity' or 'a criticism of life' or the inculcation of morals or the direction of politics or a form of substitute religion (and Eliot is right to refuse these terms), then you may be reduced to calling it 'a superior amusement'. But if you do find yourself so reduced, it is the outcome of an earlier strategic or tactical error. The remarkable thing about the passage quoted above is the degree to which Eliot recovers or partly recovers from his initial misconstruction or misapplication of Bradley on 'amusement'. The 'full surprise and elevation of a new experience of poetry' is an effective redefinition of older resonances. 'Surprise' is a Wordsworthian sensibility word, and 'elevation' could have been applied with equal conformity to Thomson's *The Seasons* or Tennyson's *Idylls of the King*. And yet their combination and attribution to what Eliot calls 'a new experience of poetry' is itself new. Eliot may or may not have known Herman Melville's phrase 'one shock of recognition' that Edmund Wilson was later to make much of, but recognition is what is being invoked by Eliot, albeit in language less 'made new' than by Melville or by Eliot's contemporary Pound.

Writing in 1919 on 'Swinburne as Critic', and noting Swinburne's remarkable acuity in appreciating the dramatic verse of Shakespeare's contemporaries, Eliot moves on to his own estimate of their achievements: 'they had a quality of sensuous thought, or a thinking through the senses, or of the senses thinking, of which the exact formula remains to be defined'. 'Of which the exact formula remains to be defined' is Eliot's rendering of Bradley's 'somehow'; how he registers Bradley's 'realize', 'realization', is demonstrated by his subsequent homing-in on his own phrase, trimming and tightening it, as in the sentence approving Chapman, in whom 'there is a direct sensuous apprehension of thought, or a recreation of thought into feeling'. How he registers his own 'of which the exact formula remains to be defined' is demonstrated by his subsequently showing that, in Donne's lyrics, 'the most powerful effect is produced by the sudden contrast of associations', e.g. in the line 'A bracelet of bright haire about the bone'.

Eliot said, in effect, that he never ceased to be a Bradleian. I say that in some vital respect he did. The advantage, as in all disputes of this kind, lies with him. My case rests on the fact that at some point the Bradleian 'enjoyment', which is essentially 'realization', comes to be associated, in Eliot's mind, with being pleased; and, moreover, does not rule out the possibility of being pleased in one's rôle as captious, ill-willing, and negligent reader. But the decline (for decline is how I understand it) is not a steady curve on the graph. When, in 'The Three Voices of Poetry' (National Book League lecture, 1953) Eliot says that 'part of our enjoyment of great poetry is the enjoyment of *overhearing* words which are not addressed to us', we seem to be listening to Bradley's *bête noire* John Stuart Mill. However, in a piece delivered three years later ('The Frontiers of Criticism', University of Minnesota, 1956), Eliot can be heard reinvigorating his distinctions: if 'we over-emphasize *enjoyment*, we will tend to fall into the subjective and impressionistic, and our enjoyment will profit us not more than mere amusement and pastime'. But again, Eliot may have forgotten that, a quarter-century earlier, he had announced, in the 'Preface' to the second edition of *The Sacred Wood*, that poetry *is* an 'amusement'. The break was not sudden and the edges were serrated, but in some phase of his human progress Eliot ceased to be a Bradleian purist and became a man-of-letters and a raconteur.

There is a remark by Aldous Huxley which Eliot quotes with approval in his Minnesota lecture 'The Frontiers of Criticism': 'Even a man who is perfectly adjusted to a deranged society can prepare himself, if he so desires, to become adjusted to the Nature of Things'. If Huxley means by this 'adjusted to the Nature of Things by way of Zen', I cannot see in the proposal anything more than a marginal readjustment: as things have worked out, I mean. Commodity will absorb, has absorbed, everything it encounters, not least the Zen poets of San Francisco. As long ago, or as recently, as 1956 Eliot himself can be caught wondering 'whether the weakness of modern criticism is not an uncertainty as to what criticism is for'.

The function of criticism is to serve something that in the first instance cannot be broadly realized. Its duty is to point to the minute particulars, particulars in which the individual judgement of the critic is itself implicated. In my own fashion I am complicating, not restating, the principle of the objective correlative. As we have observed, the principle, though not of Bradley's precise coining, may owe much to his definitions; and the mechanics, even, are very much as he conceived them, mainly in *Essays on Truth and Reality* (1914). Bradley writes there that:

> The 'this' of feeling . . . everywhere, I agree, is positive and unique. But when, passing beyond mere feeling, you have before you what you call 'matter of fact' the case forthwith is altered. The uniqueness has now to be made 'objective'. It has to be contained within the judgement and has to qualify the context of your truth.

Correlatively—and this is characteristic of Bradley and, moreover, adds the essential complicating factor—there is failure and its consequences: 'you have failed to get within the judgement the condition of the judgement. And the accomplishment of this (if it were possible) would involve the essential transformation of your judgement'.

To 'get within the judgement the condition of the judgement' is, so far as I can be said to understand it, the basic essential of all true criticism. And not only criticism. Each true poem is required to bear within it the condition of the judgement that inspired it. Because I see Eliot as the crucial poet and critic of the last century, it is for me a major issue that he increasingly neglected the turn of Bradley's conditional ('would involve'), substituting instead the simple ' "this" of feeling'. When, in the 1961 lecture 'To Criticize the Critic', he says 'about any writer in the field of aesthetics I always incline to ask: "what literary works, paintings, sculpture, architecture and music does this theorist really enjoy?" ', Eliot implies the reality of something more palpable than the tenuosities of the theorist. Eliot's language itself is a congealed nebulosity: what, for instance, is the value of 'really' in 'really enjoy'? The question from which this flaccidity detracts, and which is as old as Plato's *Republic*, was phrased by R. L. Nettleship as 'How do we distinguish one power from another?' How do you distinguish and describe types of potency by using language that is itself impotent? You could say of Eliot's question ('what literary works . . . does this theorist really enjoy?') that it has failed to get within the judgement Bradley's condition of the judgement. William Empson seems to understand the issue, characteristically, when in *The Structure of Complex Words* he writes that 'The idea that the theorist is not part of the world he examines is one of the deepest sources of error, and crops up all over the place'.

To end this chapter with a positive illustration of what has so far been somewhat negatively described, we may turn to Charles Williams, for many years a reader and editor with the Oxford University Press at their London headquarters. Williams was greatly admired by Eliot, though perhaps more as an exemplary Christian than as a writer. Our subject remains eros, alienation, and power, specifically the power of words when arranged in alien and alienating formal patterns on the printed page, and more generally the power that can be conferred by popular attention, that can be withheld by inattention, caprice, or policy or because of the priorities of general and specialist education.

Alice Mary Hadfield, Williams's biographer, has said of him that 'There is no doubt that he had a conviction of [his] genius and an appetite for fame. He knew he ought to be a literary power and he longed to be . . . He did not consent to these longings because he saw so deeply into them and experienced their power so fully'. I begin with biographical conjecture or hypothesis, somewhat against the tilt of my own critical bias—which is for the alien and alienating formal word-pattern before everything—because I want to root the sense of creative isolation and autonomy in a double seam: first in the commonplace actuality of literary ambition thwarted and fame largely denied; second, and more importantly, in the recognition of verbal power rooted in a kind of rift between self-recognition made public (on the one hand) and public non-acceptance (on the other). We are talking about a wounding of spirit that is at the same time a wounding of language, and about language's capacity for self-healing—material of which Søren Kierkegaard was the supreme artificer, especially in *Fear and Trembling*. It is perhaps worth noting that, in his capacity as reader and editor for Oxford University Press during the 1930s, Charles Williams was responsible, together with Alexander Dru, for the introduction of Kierkegaard to British readers.

Williams was a good theologian and, at his best, a great critic both formally and informally of English poetry because he recognized that language is arbitrary, autonomous, at the same time that it is bound, helpless. In this sense he could recognize in it not only an expression of, but a paradigm for, our human nature. As a Christian he would have agreed with the anti-Christian William Empson that the theorist is inextricably part of the world he examines. As a Christian also he would have understood the fundamental dilemma of the poetic craft: that it is simultaneously an imitation of the divine fiat and an act of enormous human self-will. In one of his books of theology he writes that 'poetry can do something that philosophy can not, for poetry is arbitrary and has already turned the formulae of belief into an operation of faith'. 'Arbitrary' itself can mean either discretionary or despotic. Poetry can be in, or out, of grace; and the mind of the maker can imitate either God's commandment or Lucifer's 'instressing of his own inscape' as Hopkins splendidly and humbly described it: 'it was a sounding, as they say, of his own trumpet and a hymn in his own praise'.

All of Williams's profoundest aphorisms (a number of his judgements were set down aphoristically) about the activity of poetry are poised on this edge of recognition: that what may be a declaration of righteousness is nonetheless a hair's breadth away from monstrous assertion. There are statements quoted or paraphrased by Hadfield from still unpublished letters: the 'imagination producing out of actuality a thing satisfying to itself', 'The call of poetry in word and thought is to be final'.

Williams's critical masterpiece is *The English Poetic Mind* of 1932. Among other things he notes there that 'poetry is a thing *sui generis*. It explains itself by existing'; and again, 'the chief impulse of a poet is, not to communicate a thing to others, but to shape a thing, to make an immortality for its own sake'; and again, 'Poetry has to do all its own work; in return it has all its own authority'. He also writes of 'the sense which poetry has of its own vigil before its own approaching greatness'.

It was at this time, from the 1930s to the mid 1940s (Williams died in 1945), that Eliot was falling into a kind of dereliction of the critical imagination. Dereliction: 'the action of leaving or forsaking (with intention not to resume)', 'the condition of being forsaken or abandoned'; 'a morally wrong or reprehensible abandonment or neglect'. It is instructive to read the 'Conclusion' to *The Use of Poetry and the Use of Criticism*, the Charles Eliot Norton Lectures for 1932–3. That middle sense of 'dereliction'—'the condition of being forsaken or abandoned'— is very strong there; those thirteen concluding pages read in the style of a threnos:

> Poetry is of course not to be defined by its uses. If it commemorates a public occasion, or celebrates a festival, or decorates a religious rite, or amuses a crowd, so much the better.

The Charles Eliot Norton Lectures were delivered some twelve to eighteen months after the publication of 'Triumphal March' and 'Difficulties of a Statesman', the two surviving sections of the unfinished *Coriolan* (1936) and the passage just quoted reads like jottings for, or a précis of, 'Triumphal March'. In the preceding chapter it was implied that had Eliot been able to finish *Coriolan*, as a book about the size of *Ash-Wednesday*, the future pattern and direction of his own poetry would have been different. To say this is not to accuse Eliot of wilful dereliction; these things are out of our control, and his inability to complete that sequence was an unwilled dereliction of the creative faculty. In any case, and as if by irony, the years in which Eliot was writing the last three sections of *Four Quartets* were the years of his wartime commitment to cultural work dedicated to the national interest. Nor is one accusing Eliot by pointing to the almost complete obscurity into which Williams's *The English Poetic Mind* fell in 1932 and to the celebrity that was primed and waiting to receive *The Use of Poetry and the Use of Criticism* when that book appeared in 1933. This is a recurring phenomenon of commodity culture and writers favoured by it are not to be too harshly censured for failing to make a personally disadvantageous response. At the same time we notice how Eliot's practice and observation of others' practice, as relatively early as 1933, have already become something of a tragi-comedy of manners:

> Even when two persons of taste like the same poetry, the poetry will be arranged in their minds in slightly different patterns; our individual taste in poetry bears the indelible traces of our individual lives with all their experience pleasurable and painful . . . And it is not merely a matter of individual caprice. Each age demands different things from poetry, though its demands are modified, from time to time, by what some new poet has given.

A sentence such as 'the poetry will be arranged in their minds in slightly different patterns' merely evokes interior decorating done on the cheap. 'Each age demands . . . ' falls on the page with no assurance that Eliot still has in a corner of his mind Pound's phrases from *Hugh Selwyn Mauberley*:

> The age demanded an image
> Of its accelerated grimace,
> Something for the modern stage.

Which is increasingly what Eliot was to provide.

34

A Postscript on
Modernist Poetics

In 'Self-Reliance,' Ralph W. Emerson writes:

> In every work of genius we recognize our own rejected thoughts: they come
> back to us with a certain alienated majesty. Great works of art have no more
> affecting lesson for us than this. They teach us to abide by our spontaneous
> impression with good-humored inflexibility then most when the whole cry
> of voices is on the other side.

Emerson advocates sticking by our own thoughts, publishing our own
thoughts, getting the credit for their being our own thoughts, and all in
good time, before some 'stranger will say with masterly good sense precisely
what we have thought and felt all the time'. Emerson's phrase 'a certain
alienated majesty' is a good one, though his opinion is a shade fatuous.
Emerson's transcendentals have a noxious tendency to translate themselves,
over a century and a half, into the unpleasant realities that surround us. Is it a
legitimate criticism of the Emersonian ethos to frame the objection in these
terms, or should we simply conclude that the best among us may in time
become the victim of posthumous circumstance? On the whole, I think the
criticism stands. Like Carlyle but unlike Whitman or Emily Dickinson,
Emerson lacks that faculty of self-projection into the ludicrous, so that he is
wrong-footed as they are not by the absurd consequences of time and change.

Despite a liking for his phrase my emphasis differs quite radically from
Emerson's. Whenever we have made anything of our own and made it
well—a poem, say—our words come back to us with a certain alienated
majesty. In the act of creation we alienate ourselves from that which we
have created, or, conversely, the genius of language alienates us from itself.
We are no longer masters of a well-considered *curriculum vitae* in free verse,

or blank-verse sonnets, or whatever; the anecdote is no longer the agency of our self-promotion; something recalcitrant has come between us and our expectant and expected satisfaction.

Where F. H. Bradley appears at his richest in suggestion is in the two sentences quoted near the end of the previous chapter:

> you have failed to get within the judgement the condition of the judgement. And the accomplishment of this (if it were possible) would involve the essential transformation of your judgement.

At one essential level the art of making a poem does not differ from the making of an act of criticism: in each case the crucial step requires getting within the judgement the condition of the judgement. Occasionally one can see this happening as if in slow motion; authors' drafts are a way of preserving this effect, though my own insistence on such practice may reverse the customary trend of advice. Rather than saying, 'see how clever this particular leap of the imagination has been', I find myself repeatedly urging, 'how recalcitrant, how obstructive, this material is'.

When Keats, in Book I of the first *Hyperion*, is endeavouring to reveal how poisonous now to the Titan in his decline are the 'spicy wreaths | Of incense' offered up by mortal men, he focuses on the central impression of pollution. Suddenly we find:

> Instead of sweets, his ample palate took
> Savour of poisonous brass and metal sick.

Our question can be put as follows: what is contributed to the quotation by the sudden onset of the word 'savour'? First, it is getting within the judgement the condition of the judgement, 'savour' being so to speak the normative focus of eating or drinking; second, though Hyperion is in one sense helpless, a sufferer, a degree of petulance within the suffering is perhaps suggested by the verb form 'took savour' and by the moment of enjambment in which, presumably, he might have come up with some alternative less satisfyingly wounded.

However we take it, Eliot's recurring commonplace phrase—'the enjoyment of poetry'—seems not to apply to anything that really matters here; the phrase savours more of the question whether or not one should, in lifting the teacup, crook the little finger. Whatever strange relationship we have with the poem, it is not one of enjoyment. It is more like being brushed past, or aside, by an alien being.

If I am not denying, or decrying, human contact between 'the' poem and the reader, then the contact has to be reestablished in some radical, or reverse, order. Karl Rahner's 'The Theology of the Symbol' is useful in this respect (one might as well be matter-of-fact about it: the alien strangeness of the poem does not involve questions of awe, or the reader having to feel inferior, or anything like that). Rahner's 'first statement' is that 'all beings are by their nature symbolic, because they necessarily "express" themselves in order to attain their own nature'. And, further, 'Being expresses itself, because it must realize itself through a plurality in unity'. It has to be said that Rahner's 'self-expression' is not quite what self-expression is taught to be in various creative-writing classes; it is more self-subsistent than they suggest; I am not sure that what is now known as the 'confessional' element is vital to it, which may seem a strange thing to say since Rahner was a priest of the Roman Catholic church. But confessionalism is not exhibitionism, and the so-called 'confessional' movement in post-modern art and literature is mainly a mating-display clumsily performed. What we are talking about has altogether more reserve: 'A being,' says Rahner, 'comes to itself by means of "expression", in so far as it comes to itself at all'. 'The' poem in this sense, but perhaps only in this sense, is one of us. It is one of us because its formal distinctions need to be set and kept. But the great poem comes to itself more entirely than we do and withdraws into itself more effectively than we do.

A telling distinction between inept self-expression on the one hand and, on the other, the preservation of formal distinctions as a necessary part of self-expression, is to be found in the correspondence between the old Yeats and the young actress, poet, exhibitionist, Margot Ruddock. The correspondence was exchanged mainly in the years 1934–7. Margot Ruddock began sending Yeats her poems. They were also lovers, it seems only fair to say; one may entertain certain obligations of a lover. After receipt of one batch, Yeats responded: 'I do not like your recent poems. You do not work at your tecnic ... When your technic is sloppy your matter grows second-hand—there is no difficulty to force you down under the surface—difficulty is our plough'. And she responded, 'Do you know that you have made poetry, my solace and my joy, a bloody grind I hate!' She was probably wrong in attaching what she so much needed—the possession of solace and joy—to the art she had scarcely begun to practise, or not even to practise, if we take Yeats's strictures seriously. It is the being forced down under the surface by the resistance of technique that inaugurates a self-alienating process which, as it drives down into strata that are not normally encountered, may produce alien objects. I do not intend to overdramatize—these are not the 'monsters', the 'chimera[s]' that Bradley conceived of as by-blows of the idealizing imagination. The alien is what we did not expect to find. It may be no more than a sweet bit of functioning: to stay with Bradley, 'When "white", "hard" and "sweet" and the rest coexist in a certain way, that is surely the secret of the thing'. The lump of sugar yields up its secrets, and the poem is the coexistence in a certain way of various elements. In what Yeats says to Margot Ruddock we may find yet another vindication of the Bradleian axiom: the 'condition of the judgement' in this case would be the blade of the plough driving under the surface together with the soil's resistance itself; obedience to that mechanical principle would be—would have been—the essential transformation of Ruddock's judgement; either a finer poem or the realization that she was no poet and that there was no poem there.

What you cannot, in equity, inflict upon the poem is the kind of demand made by a maxim of Charles Peirce's pragmaticism. Peirce writes,

> The elements of every concept enter into logical thought at the gate of perception and make their exit at the gate of purposive action; and whatever cannot show its passports at both those two gates is to be arrested as unauthorized by reason.

Too close to Bunyan for comfort. Probably, old poets are like Ignorance anyway, being shown at the end that there is a way to hell even from the very gates of heaven. I regret finding myself in dissent from Peirce, since I believe he had a greater mind than Bradley's. Even so, it cannot be said that the poem is a concept in Peirce's sense, nor is it logical thought, nor is purposive action quite what it is about.

'For poetry makes nothing happen' is a phrase I would rather have avoided. I nonetheless concede that I may appear to have forced myself upon it. How can I say that poetry is, in all the terms one may want to bring to it, unserious, and yet repudiate Auden on the grounds of insufficient seriousness? I think Auden was responding to the imposition, or imputation, of pseudo-seriousness; he was in a sense addressing Eliot's audience and its immense expectations, or anticipating the immense audience Raymond Williams would have, audiences who certainly expected something to happen as a result of poetry being written by and talked about by famous people with seemingly well-worked out social programmes: *The Use of Poetry and the Use of Criticism, Notes Towards the Definition of Culture, The Idea of a Christian Society, Reading and Criticism, The Long Revolution, Culture and Society 1780–1950*. In this context, Auden's 'For poetry makes nothing happen' is an anticipatory 'caprice' (to use a word Bradley frequently employed). What I find myself opposing is the whole confrontation—commitment versus caprice. Late Auden, like Isherwood, is all caprice: those ignominious last books, *About the House, Thank You, Fog*, and the rest. Alienated majesty is not caprice.

One of the issues in question is whether in a discussion of this kind there exists any form of middle ground, a middle ground, that is, other than the territory of, say, university final examinations in English, a system which, though it may not formally subscribe to Peirce's pragmaticism, has nonetheless set up its two gates: of attested perception and of symbolic purposive action, at the one of which it requires a passport of admission while at the other it issues its own passport of qualification.

The existence or absence of a middle ground is an argument associated in recent years with the late Gillian Rose and with her book *The Broken Middle*. Most definitions of the function of literature in our time assume the existence of a middle ground. I am not convinced that a middle ground is necessary, or that its postulation as a necessity is even required. For as Rose says: 'How to represent the aporia [the no-way, the impasse, the broken middle] between everyone and every "one" is the difficulty'. To return for a moment to the Emerson statement with which we began: despite its crudity, the 'alienated majesty' it invokes nonetheless exists in relation to 'every "one"'. The difficulty which Rose describes arises when the productive or receptive self of every 'one' is idly reduced to a word of convenience representing a generic carrier of preformulated opinion: a truncation which the writer cannot escape even in opposing it and resisting Emerson's 'whole cry of voices... on the other side'.

Gillian Rose writes that 'For Aristotle, "the greatest of aporias" is to know the individuality of individuals, that is, individual substance, unknowable except in universal terms'. It was perhaps this greatest of aporias that Duns Scotus attempted to penetrate with his sense of *haecceitas*, thisness. F. H. Bradley makes much of 'thisness', possibly derived from a knowledge of *haecceitas* (Peirce in this respect was also a Scotist); it figures significantly in Bradley's three major books, *The Principles of Logic*,

Appearance and Reality, and *Essays on Truth and Reality*. 'Thisness, if we like, we may call particularity':

> This detail appears to come to us on compulsion; we seem throughout to perceive it as it is, and in no sense to make or even to alter it. And this detail it is which constitutes thisness.

Even so, for Bradley 'thisness' has a weaker valency than 'this'. 'Thisness' is a perfectly manageable category; the 'this', I take it, comes upon us with something of Peirce's 'Brute Actuality'.

Gerard Hopkins appears to be a stumbling-block to the argument. He is the supreme poet of 'haecceitas'—though in fact he uses the term scarcely at all. 'Haecceitas' for Scotus is the *ultima realitas entis*; it is also the *ultima solitudo*. Hopkins is however no more the poet of creaturely *haecceitas*— though he is that, powerfully—than he is the poet of the Incarnation and of the Resurrection; and the structure of one of his greatest poems is determined by this double gift of Christian eschatology. 'That Nature is a Heraclitean Fire and of the comfort of the Resurrection' is a triple caudated (or 'tailed', or coda-ed) sonnet amounting to twenty-four lines in all. The first fourteen lines delineate aspects of the Heraclitean world, of infinite change, its eternal round of creation and destruction, which is all intricately and beautifully detailed as Hopkins imitates its wondrous thisness:

> Down roughcast, down dazzling whitewash, | wherever an elm arches,
> Shivelights and shadowtackle ín long | lashes lace, lance, and pair.

Roughcast and whitewash are indigenous ways of walling buildings, perhaps a memory of Wales where Hopkins would have seen the shadows and reflections cast by the sun and absorbed or cast back by the dazzling white of barn-sides or farmhouse walls. A 'shivelight' is a splinter of light; 'tackle' is a word for bits of ships' rigging, so 'shadowtackle' is the patterns of branch and twig-work from the nearby trees and bushes rigging the bright walls in the light of the sun. But then the day of the spirit turns dark as man's brevity and destiny are themselves reflected on. Suddenly there bursts in an uncouth anacoluthon: 'Enough! the Resurrection'. It is a great moment, one of the greatest grammatical moments in nineteenth-century English poetry. It has been criticized for its arbitrariness, but arbitrariness is the making of it. The Resurrection is a kind of eschatological anacoluthon; no amount of standard grammar can anticipate or regularize that moment. It is the only alternative to that wonderful patterning of *haeccei-tas*—'the wórld's spléndour and wónder'—that nonetheless in periods of desolation and at the hour of death is also the *ultima solitudo*. It is, let us say, the perfect response to Bradley's objection. Hopkins has got within the judgement the condition of the judgement, and it has involved the essential transformation of his judgement. It is the coming together of faith and what Yeats calls 'technic'. That 'uncouth anacoluthon' is an instance of the supremacy of technique—in the very instant and thereafter abandoned as technique.

The beauty of Hopkins places us under a very great pressure. Explaining the point of that 'Enough! the Resurrection' is not difficult exactly, but it imposes a great strain upon the nerves. It is not generally serviceable; it cannot be extrapolated into a rule or theory: it is one of those once-for-all things. Bradley's eros, if we want a theory of energy that will make a topos out of a technic and that will be answerable across a wide range of expectation, is a much safer bargain. Bradley writes: 'We have the idea of perfection—there is no doubt as to that—and the question is whether perfection also actually exists'. 'There is no doubt as to that'. This is flatter than a flat assertion, and yet a brief flicker lights up the flatness; the momentary uncertainty as to whether 'no doubt' goes with 'perfection' or with 'idea'. If asked for Bradley's basic affirmation of eros this is what I would point to. Disappointing, in a sense; and, if disappointed, we can turn to the concluding pages of *Essays on Truth and Reality* where the erotic element as we understand it is more explicitly considered. The issue perhaps semi-dormantly between us is that I am not asking for a poetry that is descriptive of eros and the erotic; I am claiming for the writing of major poetry the necessity of something I can do no better than call an erotic impulse. The element of eros need not stray outside the semantic field. With Yeats and Margot Ruddock it does, but their exchange of letters is not exemplary for that reason. Rather, when Yeats writes to his carnal lover of the failings of her poetry, the eros of technique strikes through with its own form of alienated majesty. It somehow cuts out the middle ground as Eliot in his own late criticism does not. Like eros, also, language has its arbitrariness.

Among those theologically-minded critics most deeply engaged with the arbitrary nature of poetry, we encounter not only Charles Williams but also Austin Farrer, particularly in his book *The Glass of Vision* (1948). For him the matter of poetry turns on the question of the *ought*. Originating—obviously—from the Kantian concept of moral obligation, the question is effectively engrafted by Farrer upon the body of general semantics and the particular obligations of choice that confront the poet as he works within textures that are only partly of his own choosing. The question, together with Farrer's partial resolution of it (for the resolution cannot be one that is self-per-fected), merits quotation at some length. He aims to show us the 'ought' of moral obligation, the 'ought' of choice and the 'ought' of semantic potential as making together a thing inseparate:

> It is this 'ought' which is at the heart of the riddle. The poet does not know what sort of an 'ought' it is, except that it is the 'ought' with which his craft is concerned, and that he is able to feel and acknowledge it . . . [W]hat he must feel in the 'ought' is the quality of human existence clamouring for expression and, as it were, pressing upon his mind and directing the manipulation of the poetical symbols.

It is possible to quarrel with the phrase 'human existence clamouring for expression', which strikes the ear as too Shelleyan. I would say that the urgency of the 'ought' connects with that which is below or beyond clamour, the 'torpor' as Wordsworth called it, the *vis inertiae*—and I would add that 'human existence clamouring for expression' is not at any time easily separable from cant.

In so stressing 'cant', I appeal to Charles Williams, who says that it is when versifiers use 'language without the intensity it should convey and concentrate that Cant begins to exist'. The issue with Williams's 'intensity' is similar to that which we have with Farrer's 'clamouring': if we are to allow 'intensity' we must also press for 'density', if necessary as heavy as lead.

What we encounter here is the intertwining nature of the arbitrary, the arbitrariness, in the senses of free choice, arrogation of free choice, and the despotic. It is essential to track this dangerous amalgam as it works its way through the field of signs, creating its odd felicities and wreaking havoc.

The arbitrariness of the sexual signalling of compatibility, the arbitrariness of discovering the right word out of a thousand possibilities, constitute the heart of the erotic commonplace. What Charles Williams depicts, in his vision of eros, is that 'profound contrariety' which is as much a part of love's truth as are adamic nuptials. 'But in what sense, then', Williams asks of *Paradise Lost*, 'can there be justification in this poetry? The verse has been raised to its height to deny something which the tremendous power of the verse continually expresses.' He also writes, 'Poetry has to do all its own work; in return it has all its own authority'.

The arbitrary, by a long process of semantic conglomeration, is at once freedom of will and the will obdurate in itself and subject to, and in service to, a greater obduracy ('difficulty is our plough'). There is something in constraint which frees the mind, and something in freedom which constrains it. 'The verse has been raised to its height to deny something which the tremendous power of the verse continually expresses': this does not seem to me to stand as some kind of oxymoron or stultification, but quite the reverse. In such terms one would speak of a 'preoccupation' with the ineradicability of conflict not conceding any diminishment of the real power of that which is opposed. But such words may be part of the self-comforting language of the consensus.

Of the political philosophers, apart from Adorno, or Hannah Arendt in her very late *Lectures on Kant's Political Philosophy* or Gillian Rose in her equally late *The Broken Middle*, I would name Simone Weil's—also late—*L'Enracinement*, as an uncondescending attempt to reduce ('reduce', at least in her case, is not reductive) the intractable nature of poetry to a position of moral influence; to be able to say of it, 'it has connected':

> Simultaneous composition on several planes at once is the law of artistic creation, and wherein, in fact, lies its difficulty.
>
> A poet in the arrangement of words and the choice of each word, must simultaneously bear in mind matters on at least five or six different planes of composition . . . Politics, in their turn, form an art governed by composition on a multiple plane.

Compared to this, Eliot's treatment of Gottfried Benn, in 'The Three Voices of Poetry' (1953), is inane. His discussion of Benn's opinions, eight years after the end of the Second World War, taking as it does Benn's description of lyric 'of the first voice' as being 'addressed to no one' and ignoring as it does Benn's several years of sympathy with, though not membership of, the Nazi Party, ought not to have been accepted as simply another distinguished contribution to pan-European understanding. Of course the lyric is addressed to no one; or, as Charles Williams says, the poetic word is arbitrary. I have no quarrel with Benn on that; and I can perfectly well understand someone in 1933 deluding himself that the Nazi Party would be the saviour of Germany: such a belief would be a manifestation of the perverted eros. What is to be criticized here is Eliot's failing the Bradleian criterion: in speaking of Benn's theory of the lyric he has not got the condition of the judgement within the judgement, and therefore the discussion of Benn's lyric theory remains as nothing more than a point of minor etiquette. Eliot on Benn, in 1953, could have been, ought to have been, at least on the level of *Coriolan*, that last moment but one in Eliot's work in which the Bradleian elements in his thinking might have pushed him through into a style of writing as significant, as truly major, as Yeats's best work in the volume *Last Poems and Two Plays* of June 1939, a volume that contains 'The Statues', 'A Bronze Head', 'High Talk', as well as the play 'The Death of Cuchulain'. In these late writings Yeats is more Bradleian than is Eliot—though I do not think he read Bradley. He did read John McTaggart whom Bradley respected, 'profound McTaggart' as Yeats called him. Yeats is, contestably, more Bradleian than is Eliot because he gets the power both of Bradley's high talk—the high talk of eros—and of the sense of Bradley's word 'mere'. Everything in Bradley is merely itself, or merely less than itself, except when it is 'somehow' raised above itself by the power of eros.

The final stanza of Yeats's 'The Statues' begins with two of the strangest-sounding lines in twentieth-century poetry:

> When Pearse summoned Cuchulain to his side
> What stalked through the Post Office?

The lines allude to the moment on Easter Monday 1916 when Padraic Pearse read the proclamation of the founding of the Irish Republic from the steps in front of the Dublin General Post Office in O'Connell Street. The building was then held by the forces of the Republic until the surrender on 29 April. The writer-patriot who initiated the modern cult of ancient Ireland and her great mythic hero Cuchulain was not Pearse but Standish O'Grady, with his *History of Ireland: The Heroic Period* (1878), and *History of Ireland: Cuculain and His Contemporaries* (1880). Pearse, who was a school-teacher, preached this myth to the boys under his care.

Donal McCartney has written that the 'image of Cuchulainn strapped to a post and shedding his life's blood in the defence of his people while a torpor hung over their minds did much to inspire the blood-sacrifice doctrine of the 1916 leaders'. He adds significantly that the 'cult of a personified Mother Eire, and of her child, "Cuchulainn the Valiant" left deep traces on the phraseology of the 1916 Proclamation. Some of its phrases read as if they were the words of a reincarnated Cuchulainn'. So that, in one version, is how Pearse summoned Cuchulain to his side on the steps of the General Post Office on Easter Monday, 1916: in the language of the Proclamation itself. Yeats clearly knew his modern scholars of the ancient Ireland. There is another projected version in a prose draft that Yeats made for 'The Statues': 'Where are you now. Is it true that you shed the / sun-burn & became pale white; Did you appear / in the Post Office in 1916 is it True that / Pearse called on you by name of Cuchullain / Certainty we have need of you. The vague flood is at its / Height . . . from all four quarters is coming / Come back with all your Pythagorean num- bers'. So what stalks through the Post Office is the spirit of disciplined energy, a force manifest against the 'filthy modern tide | And . . . its formless, spawning fury'. It is in the name of 'intellect . . . calculation, number, measurement' that Yeats accomplishes the considerable feat of bringing together the powerfully disparate presences of Pythagoras, Phidias, and Cuchulain and having the resulting confederacy make sense. The method is one of rhetorical effrontery. If you can succeed with the inherent absurd- ity of the phrase 'What stalked through the Post Office?', it may seem that your other problems are not going to get out of hand. 'The Statues', however, does more than commemorate the inchoate yet fully accoutred eros of Pearse's envisioning; Yeats intensifies it by rawly opposing to such a vision something of the obdurate mundanities of its conversion into fact.

But only something or some thing; of all those mundanities which, once registered, intrude their thingy cackle into Yeats's elevated historicisms, he takes as gift the one location already claimed as sacred by government directive as well as by national sentiment. In addition to the General Post Office, the actual cityscape of the Rising comprised the Marrowbone Lane Distillery, the Mendicity Institute, Watkins Distillery, and the College of Surgeons. Civic topography and hasty tactical planning involved a degree of banality that, in the nineteenth century, only the genius of Dickens and Whitman could imbue with tragic implications and of which, in the twentieth, perhaps only *Ulysses* took the full measure. Carlyle and Arnold knew how to deploy civic absurdities in effective but narrow satiric channels, which Eliot would later exploit in some of his most rancorous criticism.

Yeats's advancing skill in managing the quotidian or pedestrian connota- tions shows here in alignment with another of his finest poems, 'Easter, 1916', written much closer to the event. In it he is at pains to show how ill-suited to heroism the Republicans had seemed in their earlier days in drill-halls, but at the same time he softens the gaucheness with well-selected peri- phrases and adjectives, so that the generalized symbols may appear as minute particulars:

> I have met them at close of day
> Coming with vivid faces
> From counter or desk among grey
> Eighteenth-century houses.

Eliot declared, in an essay published in 1921, that Andrew Marvell 'takes a slight affair, the feeling of a girl for her pet, and gives it a connexion with that inexhaustible and terrible nebula of emotion which surrounds all our exact and practical passions and mingles with them'. It is one of Eliot's most startling sentences, though 'nebula' does more to clarify F. H. Bradley or Henry James or his own best poetry or that of Yeats than it does to particularize the nature of Marvell's wit.

My sense of an affinity between Bradley and some of the poems of Eliot and of Yeats has to do partly with the metaphysical entanglements of their politics and aesthetics (and with a shared species of hierarchical Toryism) and partly with their disposition towards establishing a grammar for the eros of the imagination in forms that abruptly align transient with eternal.

> Nothing in any appearance, so far as that something is in any sense positive, can conceivably be lost; and so much as this seems certain. On the other side, by addition, by resolution, and by reunion in a more concrete totality, the divisions and the conflict of appearances can everywhere be harmonized. And all one-sidednesses, thus transformed, can contribute each its full content to the unbroken and self-complete Reality.

That is Bradley; and what he maintains as a certainty, Yeats invokes as a grand rhetorical question. 'What stalked through the Post Office?' is a way of reopening Bradley's affirmation ('the conflict of appearances can everywhere be harmonized') into a kind of angry wound.

To what degree is Yeats, elsewhere in his later work, like Keats's Hy- perion, satisfyingly wounded, complacently angry, or merely petulant? A crucial text here must be Yeats's introduction, of 1931, to *The Words upon the Window-pane* where he writes of collecting 'materials for my thought and work, for some identification of my beliefs with the nation itself'. The consequence of this willed and wilful identification is that 'Swift haunts me'—he means as the flawed image of an envisioned flawless unity—just as Swift haunts the macabre spirit-ventriloquy of the closing lines of *The Words upon the Window-pane*: 'Perish the day on which I was born!'

The Yeats who here seeks 'an image of the modern mind's discovery of its own permanent form' is like the Bradley who writes of 'the unbroken and self-complete Reality' and the Eliot who desiderates 'the timeless moment': each is angry in his opposition to that which is contrary, 'uneducated vulgar opinion', 'democratic bonhomie' that 'seemed to grin through a horse collar', and the scepticism which Eliot pillories in the loaded 'you' in 'You are not here to verify'.

Yeats's political aesthetics or aesthetical politics is easier to evaluate in more narrowly circumscribed cases. When Yeats chaired the committee to select the design of the new coinage of the Irish Free State, he may have come close to realizing, in the acceptances of educated common opinion, some 'identification' of his beliefs 'with the nation itself'. Conversely and correlatively, when he refuses to applaud the Irish government's installation of the Cuchulain statue in the GPO, he could be taken as saying 'Perish the day on which I born an Irishman':

> No body like his body
> Has modern woman borne,
> But an old man looking back on life
> Imagines it in scorn.
> A statue's there to mark the place,
> By Oliver Sheppard done,
> So ends the tale that the harlot
> Sang to the beggar-man.

Yeats's symbolism in *Wheels and Butterflies,* in *The King of the Great Clock Tower, Commentaries and Poems,* and in *Last Poems and Two Plays* aims to be as rich and throwaway as the phrase he pitches at us in the Old Man's prologue to 'The Death of Cuchulain': 'When they told me I could have my own way, I wrote certain guiding principles on a bit of newspaper'. 'On a bit of newspaper' meaning something immediately to hand, and 'a bit of newspaper' as suggesting the quotidian litter of the rabble. The phrase offers Yeats, who invented or came upon it, an idiom for transfiguring crude juxtaposition, though I am not convinced he knew how to put it to most effective use. What he is looking for in his late writings is a unit comprising antithetical, even mutually repellent, forces, in which the calculated is at one with the spontaneous: integration that is simultaneously diremption; a kind of monad of linguistic energy, a unit of speech itself becoming a Yeatsian form.

However, this hierarchical-vernacular monad does not seem to me characteristic of his last book in its larger attitudes and concentrations. I have singled out 'The Statues' as a poem in which the necessary concentration is achieved; but the book as a whole is characterized more by aloof hauteur on the one side and haughty rabble-rousing on the other; a difference that is complementary rather than antithetical. If in 'The Statues' Yeats is recognizing that the rapturous symmetrical cadences of 'Easter, 1916' no longer suffice, there is no trace of that recognition in the trumpery of the final stanza of 'Three Songs to the One Burden'.

In Chapter 32, I argued that in *Little Gidding* Eliot insists on the condition of shabbiness as an essential part of the vision of redemption, and I further argued that, having granted Eliot his premise, we are nonetheless right to insist that the condition evoked must remain within the poem's own jurisdiction. It should be something that the formal rhetoric reveals in the process of becoming; it cannot be surrendered to the open field of response where indiscrimination and chaotic associativeness hold sway; it cannot be left, in short, to the shabby impositions of the idle reader, who may here be thought of as one thinks of the idle rich in a mood to go slumming.

Conversely, the juridical power of the poem is not found in utterances that are merely grandiose or imposing:

> I must lie down where all the ladders start
> In the foul rag and bone shop of the heart.

This rhetorically self-enamoured couplet is not an improvement on *Little Gidding* and perhaps not even on the cringing platitudes of Eliot's 'Defence of the Islands'. The technical misjudgement in each case has to do with a sense of premature closure: in 'Defence of the Islands' audience expectation forecloses upon the authority proper to the poem; in 'The Circus Animals' Desertion' Yeats, knowing how well the adjective 'foul' and the substantive 'heart' have served him and others in the past, is declaiming automatically. Or, to return once more to the word 'majesty': Eliot relies upon an associative majesty, the *roi fainéant* of publicly accredited sentiment, while Yeats lays claim to some supposed majestic right of his own characteristic jargon in order to ennoble humiliation. What is missing in each case is the awareness of necessary formal alienation.

Eliot's 'Triumphal March' brutally juxtaposes the 'aethereal' aloofness of the conqueror ('the eyes watchful, waiting, perceiving, indifferent') with the raucously populist ('Don't throw away that sausage'). What clearly still fascinates him, as he had been fascinated in his great early work, is the requirement to make incoherencies cohere, without imposing the ruminative, well-modulated voice of a man of letters, a tone which so weakens *Four Quartets*. These are scenarios about language-issues, but they are not in themselves language-experiments. They stand in contrast to Yeats's last poems, among which language-experiments are still to be found, even where they appear at their most visual:

> Belly, shoulder, bum
> Flash fishlike; nymphs and satyrs
> Copulate in the foam.

Yeats wants to hear how 'bum' goes with 'Flash' and 'fishlike' and 'Copulate' with 'foam' and how Shakespeare's sonic triumphalism (Escalus's riposte to Pompey the bawd) can energize senescent disgust even in the density of its rage. He wants to hear himself saying these things for the pleasure that harnessed recalcitrance gives him; and in this he differs from the old Eliot.

Yeats died and Eliot abdicated (I have attempted to account for and to describe the extent of that abdication elsewhere in this book). Each in his own way, throughout the 1920s and 1930s, had fought for the intelligence of poetry within the civic domain in ways that should stand to us now as exemplary. Nonetheless, to have abandoned *Coriolan* and to have completed *The Rock* instead is indicative of a savage defeat. One reads Yeats's last poems and the introduction to *The Words upon the Window-pane* in a different spirit, with the sense that here was a battle much more narrowly lost. But it was lost, even so, and the poems of Yeats and Eliot which give momentary realization to Bradley's 'mere extraordinary fact' as something at once banal and tragic in implication have found few successors in post-war Britain. Instead, we are left with Bradley's 'mere momentary caprice', 'mere speculative refinement', 'mere polemics'.

Auden wrote that 'art is a product of history, not a cause': 'it does not re-enter history as an effective agent'. Though this formulation is preferable to 'Poetry makes nothing happen', I would phrase it differently. A poem re-enters history in a multitude of circumstances, and it may indeed do so as an effective agent, or hostage. Nonetheless, whatever historical effects it may produce, or be made to produce, are as collusive with good and ill or as absurd as those of any other historical entity. Yet the poem—the true poem, the poem that has got within its judgement the condition of the judgement—is not exhausted by the uses to which it is put; it is alienated from its existence as historical event. This intolerable condition, rejected, may lead a poet to a political aesthetics; embraced, to an apolitical one; these twin betrayals—Yeats's 'Three Songs to the One Burden' on the one hand and his 'On being asked for a War Poem' or the late 'Politics' on the other—haunt modernist poetics.

In a successful poem a particular word may instantaneously perform what it desiderates. This is as true of the word 'Savour' in *Hyperion* as it is of 'Slouches' in 'The Second Coming', of 'automatic' in 'She smooths her hair with automatic hand', of 'beauty' in 'to get the beauty of it hot', or of 'beyond me' in 'Living to live in a world of time beyond me'. These conjunctions of word with word *somehow* re-enact the Bradleian moment, the moment of creative eros. The act of composing is itself the instant of composure, even when it is discord that is composed. The magnificent composure is nonetheless an alienated majesty; the alienated majesty is in itself unstinting.

But so much cannot be our final word. 'Alienated majesty' may be no more than 'a broken Coriolanus' or that conjuring of a broken Swift ('Swift beating on his breast in sibylline frenzy blind') who, because Yeats can finally do nothing more to reconcile his genius with the civic imagination, is condemned to sleep 'under the greatest epitaph in history'.

Editorial Note

The *Collected Critical Writings* of Geoffrey Hill reprints three published volumes of Hill's criticism (*The Lords of Limit*, 1984; *The Enemy's Country*, 1991; and *Style and Faith*, 2003), with occasional corrections and revisions. It adds two further collections which Hill likewise conceived of as books: *Inventions of Value* and *Alienated Majesty*. The former collects seven essays that were previously published but not collected; the chapters in the latter were delivered as lectures and have not been published before. While inclusion of an essay or lecture in the *Collected Critical Writings*, even in revised form, does not necessarily indicate that Hill wholly approves it, nor exclusion that he wholly disapproves of it, that is nonetheless the general tendency.

As editor, I have worked from Hill's own copies of his three books of criticism, which he variously marked and annotated; the published versions of the uncollected essays (a few of these he also marked); and typed or word-processed versions of lectures he delivered. In the case of *The Lords of Limit*, *The Enemy's Country*, *Style and Faith*, and the uncollected essays, I have incorporated annotations which corrected errors and made other revisions; when he has given further references, I have usually added these to the notes. In the case of the chapters that comprise *Alienated Majesty*, I have made alterations, mainly stylistic, in changing the lectures to chapters. I have also supplied the references to the first three essays on 'Alienated Majesty'. Hill has read the entire typescript and made further revisions.

THE LORDS OF LIMIT

Chapters 1–9 were collected and published as *The Lords of Limit* (London: Deutsch, 1984; New York: Oxford University Press, 1984).

1. Poetry as 'Menace' and 'Atonement'
Delivered as an inaugural lecture at the University of Leeds in 1977 and published in *The University of Leeds Review*, vol. 21 (1978), pp. 66–88.

2. The Absolute Reasonableness of Robert Southwell
Delivered as the Joseph Bard Memorial Lecture to the Royal Society of Literature, London in 1979.

3. 'The World's Proportion': Jonson's Dramatic Poetry in *Sejanus* and *Catiline*
Jacobean Theatre, ed. John Russell Brown and Bernard Harris, Stratford-upon-Avon Studies, vol. 1 (London: Arnold, 1960), pp. 113–32.

4. 'The True Conduct of Human Judgment': Some Observations on *Cymbeline*
The Morality of Art, ed. D. W. Jefferson (London: Routledge & Kegan Paul, 1969), pp. 18–32.

5. Jonathan Swift: The Poetry of 'Reaction'
The World of Jonathan Swift, ed. Brian Vickers (Oxford: Basil Blackwell, 1968), pp. 195–212.

6. Redeeming the Time
Agenda, vol. 10, no. 4 / vol. 11, no. 1 (Autumn 1972 / Winter 1973), pp. 87–111.

7. 'Perplexed Persistence': The Exemplary Failure of T. H. Green
Poetry Nation (later *PN Review*), no. 4 (1975), pp. 128–45.

8. What Devil Has Got Into John Ransom?
Delivered as the Judith E. Wilson Lecture on Poetry at the University of Cambridge, in 1980; published in *Grand Street*, vol. 2, no. 4 (Summer 1983), pp. 81–103.

9. Our Word Is Our Bond
Agenda, vol. 21, no. 1 (Spring 1983), pp. 13–49.

THE ENEMY'S COUNTRY

Chapters 10 through 14 were delivered as the Clark Lectures at Trinity College, Cambridge in 1986; then published as *The Enemy's Country* (Oxford: Clarendon Press, 1991; Stanford, CA: Stanford University Press, 1991).

STYLE AND FAITH

Chapters 15–21 were collected and published as *Style and Faith* (New York: Counterpoint, 2003).

15. Common Weal, Common Woe
TLS, no. 4490 (21 April 1989), pp. 411–12, 414.

16. Of Diligence and Jeopardy
TLS, no. 4520, (17 November 1989), pp. 1273–76.

17. Keeping to the Middle Way
TLS, no. 4786 (23 December 1994), pp. 3–6.

18. A Pharisee to Pharisees
English, vol. 38, no. 161 (Summer, 1989), pp. 97–113.

19. The Eloquence of Sober Truth
TLS, no. 5019 (11 June 1999), pp. 7–12.

20. The Weight of the Word
TLS, no. 4630 (27 December 1991), pp. 3–6.

21. Dividing Legacies
Agenda, vol. 34, no. 2 (Summer 1996), pp. 9–28.

INVENTIONS OF VALUE

22. Translating Value: Marginal Observations on a Central Question
Translating Life: Studies in Transpositional Aesthetics, ed. Shirley Chew and Alistair Stead (Liverpool: Liverpool University Press, 2000), pp. 199–213.

23. Language, Suffering, and Silence
Delivered at the Annual Convention of the Association of Literary Scholars and Critics in Toronto in 1998. Published in *Literary Imagination*, vol. 1, no. 2 (Fall 1999), pp. 240–55.

24. Tacit Pledges
A. E. Housman: A Reassessment, ed. Alan W. Holden and J. Roy Birch (New York: St Martin's Press, 1999; Basingstoke: Macmillan, 2000), pp. 53–75.

25. Gurney's 'Hobby'
Delivered as the F. W. Bateson Annual Memorial Lecture at Corpus Christi College, Oxford, 1984. Published in *Essays in Criticism*, vol. 34 (1984), pp. 97–128.

26. Isaac Rosenberg, 1890–1918
Warton Lecture on English Poetry, delivered in 1998 at Keble College, Oxford. Published in *The Proceedings of the British Academy*, vol. 101 (Oxford: Oxford University Press, 1999), pp. 209–28.

27. Rhetorics of Value and Intrinsic Value

28. Poetry and Value
Chapters 27 and 28 were delivered as the Tanner Lectures on Human Values in 2000 at Brasenose College, Oxford. Published in *The Tanner Lectures on Human Values*, vol. 22 (Salt Lake City, UT: University of Utah Press, 2001), pp. 253–83.

ALIENATED MAJESTY

29. Alienated Majesty: Ralph W. Emerson

30. Alienated Majesty: Walt Whitman

31. Alienated Majesty: Gerard M. Hopkins
Chapters 29 to 31 were delivered as the Ward-Phillips Lectures in 2000 at the University of Notre Dame.

32. Word Value in F. H. Bradley and T. S. Eliot
Delivered in 2001 as the T. S. Eliot Memorial Lecture in St Louis, MO.

33. Eros in F. H. Bradley and T. S. Eliot

34. A Postscript on Modernist Poetics
Chapters 33 and 34 were given as the Empson Lectures in 2005, delivered at the
University of Cambridge.

Abbreviations

CRS   *Publications of the Catholic Record Society*
ELH   *Journal of English Literary History*
MLQ   *Modern Language Quarterly*
OED²   *Oxford English Dictionary*, 2nd edn., ed. John Simpson and Edmund
       Weiner, 20 vols. (Oxford: Clarendon Press, 1989)
PMLA   *Publications of the Modern Language Association*
REL   *Review of English Literature*
RES   *Review of English Studies*
TES   *Times Educational Supplement*
THES   *Times Higher Educational Supplement*

Notes

PRELIMINARY EPIGRAPHS

Criticism is now...in itself: F. H. Bradley, *Collected Essays*, 2 vols. (Oxford: Clarendon Press, 1935), vol. 1, pp. 45–6 ('The Presuppositions of Critical History', 1874).

Just Criticism...a prophecy: *The Prose of John Clare*, ed. J. W. and Anne Tibble (London: Routledge & Kegan Paul, 1951), p. 218. Clare quotes Alexander Pope, *An Essay on Man*, Epistle 2, l. 136.

A rather different...dead eyes?: *Woodstock: A Moral History*, ed. A. P. Rossiter (London: Chatto and Windus, 1946), pp. 36–7.

THE LORDS OF LIMIT

Epigraphs

O Lords of Limit...light: W. H. Auden, *The English Auden*, ed. Edward Mendelson (New York: Random House, 1977), p. 115.

Quintilian calls him...felicity': Paul Harvey, ed., *The Oxford Companion to Classical Literature*, corr. repr. (Oxford: Clarendon Press, 1940), p. 215. In the preface to his translation of the works of Horace, Christopher Smart writes that he has 'especially attended to what the critics call his *curiosa felicitas*, of which many of my predecessors seems not to have entertained the most remote idea'; see *The Poetical Works of Christopher Smart*, ed. Karina Williamson, 6 vols. (Oxford: Clarendon Press, 1980–96), vol. 5, p. 5.

And for this reason...*Infelicities*: J. L. Austin, *How to Do Things with Words*, 2nd edn., ed. J. O. Urmson and Marina Sbisà (Cambridge, MA: Harvard University Press, 1975), p. 14.

It is always...afraid of?: Iris Murdoch, *The Sovereignty of Good* (London: Routledge, 1970), p. 72 ('On "God" and "Good" ').

...the Igbo believe...Chukwu's house': Chinua Achebe, *Morning Yet on Creation Day* (Garden City, NY: Anchor Press, 1975), p. 166.

1. Poetry as 'menace' and 'atonement'

Thus my noblest...menace: Karl Barth, *The Epistle to the Romans*, tr. Edwyn C. Hoskyns (London: Oxford University Press, 1933), p. 266.

'mighty figures...marble': Michael Meyer, *Ibsen* (Harmondsworth: Penguin, 1974), p. 244.

'a poem . . . box': *Letters on Poetry from W. B. Yeats to Dorothy Wellesley* (London: Oxford University Press, 1940), p. 24.

when the words . . . indescribable: T. S. Eliot, *On Poetry and Poets* (London: Faber and Faber, 1957), p. 98. Cf. R. L. Megroz, who writes of Joseph Conrad that 'only in the immense range of the art of fiction . . . could there have been any lasting prospect for him of the peace which comes of self-realization and self-annihilation'; see *Joseph Conrad's Mind and Method: A Study of Personality in Art* (New York: Russell & Russell, 1964), p. 80 (first pub. 1931).

'instinct' . . . inclination': *OED*², s.v. 'instinct, n.'

'assent' . . . concern oneself': *OED*², s.v. 'assent, n.'

'The poet's job . . . justice': *The Letters of Ezra Pound 1907–1941*, ed. D. D. Paige (London: Faber and Faber, 1951), p. 366.

'the effort . . . verse': William Empson, *Seven Types of Ambiguity*, 3rd edn., revised (London: Chatto and Windus, 1953), p. ix.

'method . . . posed': Erich Auerbach, *Mimesis*, tr. Willard R. Trask (Garden City, NJ: Doubleday, 1957), p. 356.

'a concretion . . . ultimately are': D. M. MacKinnon, *The Problem of Metaphysics* (London: Cambridge University Press, 1974), p. 110.

Those masterful . . . heart: W. B. Yeats, *The Collected Poems of W. B. Yeats*, ed. Richard J. Finneran, new edn. (New York: Macmillan, 1989), pp. 347–8.

'poem . . . sayable': Henry Rago, 'Faith and the Literary Imagination—The Vocation of Poetry', in Nathan A. Scott, ed., *Adversity and Grace: Studies in Recent American Literature* (Chicago: University of Chicago Press, 1969), p. 251.

'Poetry . . . real ones': *The Notebooks of Samuel Taylor Coleridge*, ed. Kathleen Coburn, 5 vols. (New York: Pantheon Books, 1957–2002), vol. 1, part 1, p. 90 (87G.81).

'one . . . philosopher': Hannah Arendt, *Men in Dark Times* (Harmondsworth: Penguin, 1973), pp. 153–4.

'requires . . . success': Frank Kermode, *Modern Essays* (London: Fontana, 1971), p. 95: referring to the theories of Ehrenzweig.

'Surrealism . . . against them': Jean-Paul Sartre, 'Black Orpheus', tr. Arthur Gillette, *Stand*, vol. 6, no. 1, p. 9.

'Her . . . these': Hugh Kenner, *The Pound Era* (London: Faber, 1975), p. 175.

'confession . . . through': Thomas Mann, *The Genesis of a Novel*, tr. Richard and Clare Winston (London: M. Secker and Warburg, 1961), p. 73 ('Bekenntnis und Lebensopfer durch und durch').

' "angelism . . . order': Nathan A. Scott, *The Broken Center: Studies in the Theological Horizon of Modern Literature* (New Haven, CT: Yale University Press, 1966), pp. 53–4.

'does not sell . . . holiness': Jerzy Grotowski, *Towards a Poor Theatre*, ed. Eugenio Barba (London: Methuen, 1975), p. 34 (first pub. 1968).

'the mind's . . . thinking': *The Collected Works of Samuel Taylor Coleridge*, 16 vols. (Princeton, NJ: Princeton University Press, 1969–2002), vol. 7, part 1, p. 124 (*Biographia Literaria*, ed. James Engell and W. Jackson Bate, 2 parts).

'*win*[*ning*] . . . stream': Ibid.

'human . . . intellect': Ibid., p. 141.

'return . . . upon himself': *The Complete Prose Works of Matthew Arnold*, ed. R. H. Super, 11 vols. (Ann Arbor, MI: University of Michigan Press, 1960–77), vol. 3, p. 267. For a different use of the phrase, see Baxter Hathaway, 'The Lucretian "Return upon Ourselves" in Eighteenth-Century Theories of Tragedy', *PMLA* 62:3 (September 1947), pp. 672–89.

'There was . . . himself': Stuart M. Sperry, *Keats the Poet* (Princeton, NJ: Princeton University Press, 1973), p. 252.

'tortuous . . . reader': MacKinnon, *The Problem of Metaphysics*, p. 66.

Not . . . be: *The Poetical Works of Gerard Manley Hopkins*, ed. Norman H. MacKenzie (Oxford: Clarendon Press, 1990), p. 183.

'the coinherence . . . culture': Nathan A. Scott, *The New Orpheus: Essays toward a Christian Poetic* (New York: Sheed and Ward, 1964), p. 161.

'the principal . . . scientism': Ibid., p. 142.

no more than a structure of grammar and syntax: Ibid., p. 160.

'intransitive attention': Nathan A. Scott, *Negative Capability: Studies in the New Literature and the Religious Situation* (New Haven, CT: Yale University Press, 1969), p. 97.

'a calculated . . . meditation': *The New Orpheus*, p. 147; cf. p. 63.

'the world . . . work': Ibid., p. 163.

'makes good . . . experience': Ibid.

'adventure in atonement': Scott, ed., *Adversity and Grace*, p. 50.

'the comedy . . . redemption': Ibid., p. 55.

'the drama . . . reconciliation': Ibid., p. 38.

'the language . . . things': D. M. MacKinnon, *A Study in Ethical Theory* (London: A. & C. Black, 1957), p. 138.

'when the language . . . reduction': Rago, in Scott, ed., *Adversity and Grace*, p. 242.

'the empirical guilty conscience': John H. Rodgers, *The Theology of P. T. Forsyth* (London: Independent Press, 1965), p. 40.

'a saint . . . the soup': G. K. Chesterton, *Charles Dickens* (London: Methuen, 1906), p. 36.

For one . . . mistake: Helen Waddell, *Peter Abelard* (London: Constable, 1939), pp. 23–4.

It is an anxiety . . . form of re-creation: See Matthew Hodgart, 'Misquotation as Re-creation', *Essays in Criticism*, vol. 3 (1953), pp. 28–38 and also Christopher Ricks, *The Force of Poetry* (Oxford: Oxford University Press, 1987), pp. 392–416.

'No man . . . money.': *Boswell's Life of Johnson*, ed. George Birkbeck Hill, rev. L. F. Powell, 6 vols. (Oxford: Clarendon Press, 1934), vol. 3, p. 19.

'numerous . . . literature': Ibid., pp. 19–20.

'necessity': Cf. *The Yale Edition of the Works of Samuel Johnson* (New Haven, CT: Yale University Press, 1958–), vol. 2, p. 494: 'Composition is, for the most part, an effort of slow diligence and steady perseverance, to which the mind is dragged by necessity or resolution' (*The Adventurer*, no. 138, 2 March 1754).

'wreaths of fame and interest': Andrew Marvell, 'The Coronet', l. 16.

'erotic honey': Thomas Mann, *Essays of Three Decades*, tr. H. T. Lowe-Porter (New York: Knopf, 1947), p. 397.

'A knitting editor . . . the other."': Katherine Whitehorn, in *The Observer Review*, 6 Oct. 1968, p. 27.

'anybody . . . courts': Simone Weil, *The Need for Roots*, tr. Arthur Wills (London: Routledge & Paul, 1952), pp. 36–7.

'social and public institution': Donald Davie, in *PN Review*, vol. 5, no. 1 (1977), p. 18.

'the fullness . . . medium': W. K. Wimsatt, *The Verbal Icon* (London: Methuen, 1970), p. 269.

Stephen Spender . . . thought: Stephen Spender, *Eliot* (London: Fontana, 1975), p. 188.

It's harder . . . sinner: T. S. Eliot, *The Elder Statesman* (London: Faber and Faber, 1959), pp. 89–90.

'the point . . . "crime"': Spender, *Eliot*, p. 188.

It may be . . . anxiety: Harry Guntrip, *Psychology for Ministers and Social Workers* (London: Independent Press, 1949), p. 84.

'pathological . . . impotence': Delmore Schwartz, 'T. S. Eliot as the International Hero', in *Selected Essays of Delmore Schwartz*, ed. Donald A. Dike and David H. Zucker (Chicago: University of Chicago Press, 1970), pp. 124–5.

'Claverton . . . gesture': Grover Smith, *T. S. Eliot's Poetry and Plays*, 2nd edn. (Chicago: University of Chicago Press, 1974), p. 248.

'the kind . . . gives': Eliot, *On Poetry and Poets*, p. 18.

the ascetic . . . utility: Ibid., p. 85.

'abstention': W. W. Robson, *Critical Essays* (London: Routledge and Kegan Paul, 1966), p. 49.

'a fringe . . . express': Eliot, *On Poetry and Poets*, pp. 86–7.

'as he grew . . . truthtelling': *New Statesman*, 17 Sept. 1976, p. 376.

'the local . . . shape': Ibid.

'struggle . . . "poetry-lovers"': C. K. Stead, *The New Poetic* (Harmondsworth: Penguin, 1967), p. 189 (first pub. 1964).

'it is not . . . deafness': Jon Silkin, 'Symposium on Poetry', *The Review*, nos. 29–30 (1972), p. 10.

'to take . . . 'usurp': *OED*², s.v. 'assume'.

'Where . . . poets?': Keidrych Rhys, *Poems from the Forces* (London: Routledge & Sons, 1941), p. xiii: 'Where are our war poets? . . . That rhetorical question one has so often heard asked by our Sunday newspapers and public men!'

[Rupert Brooke] . . . attitude: *The Letters of Charles Sorley* (Cambridge: University Press, 1919), p. 263. John H. Johnson, *English Poetry of the First World War* (Princeton, NJ: Princeton University Press, 1964), p. 35, and Jon Silkin, *Out of Battle: The Poetry of the Great War* (London: Oxford University Press, 1972), p. 75, quote and comment upon this letter.

A voice...any other: Quoted in *The Collected Poems of Rupert Brooke*, 2nd edn. (London: Sidgwick & Jackson, 1928), p. clvii.

For we speak...something: Rush Rhees, *Without Answers* (London: Routledge & K. Paul, 1969), p. 150. Cf. Ludwig Wittgenstein, *Culture and Value*, ed. G. H. von Wright, tr. Peter Winch (Chicago: University of Chicago Press, 1980), p. 52.

it is precisely...success: Stephen Prickett, 'True Education Must Create an Accountable Élite', *THES*, 17 June 1977, p. 15.

In silence...the Moon: Coleridge, *Collected Works*, vol. 16, part 1, p. 819 (*Poetical Works: Poems (Reading Text)*, ed. J. C. C. Mays).

Humphry House...beauty': *Coleridge* (London: R. Hart-Davis, 1953), p. 101.

In his loneliness...arrival: Coleridge, *Collected Works*, vol. 16, part 1, p. 393 (*Poems*).

The two...in doubt: Kathleen Coburn, *The Self Conscious Imagination* (London: Oxford University Press, 1974), p. 1.

'prophetic...protesting': Sunday O. Anozie, *Christopher Okigbo* (London: Evans Bros., 1972), p. 181.

'the political...God': Cesare Pavese, *This Business of Living*, tr. A. E. Murch (London: Owen, 1961), p. 103 ('Il corpo politico non muore e non risponde quindi davanti a nessun dio').

'a clear...rebel': Quoted by M. I. Finley, *The Listener*, 5 June 1969, p. 790.

'American...morality': Conor Cruise O'Brien, *The Suspecting Glance: The T. S. Eliot Memorial Lectures delivered at Eliot College in the University of Kent at Canterbury, November 1969* (London: Faber and Faber, 1972), pp. 34–5.

'the famous...appropriate': Ibid., p. 35.

'understood...change': Ibid., p. 47.

'conceptual...judgment': Adrian Cunningham, 'Salvation through Art', in Ian Gregor and Walter Stein, eds., *The Prose for God: Religious and Anti-Religious Aspects of Imaginative Literature* (London: Sheed and Ward, 1973), p. 24.

'strikes....actual': MacKinnon, *A Study in Ethical Theory*, 188.

'the study...science': O'Brien, *The Suspecting Glance*, 90.

'slogans...sages': Ibid., p. 11.

'technically sweet': Robert Oppenheimer, quoted by Robert Jungk, *Brighter Than a Thousand Suns* (Harmondsworth: Penguin, 1960), p. 266.

'one can never...utilitarianism': MacKinnon, *A Study in Ethical Theory*, pp. 5–6.

'the poet...lighter ones': *Conversations with Claude Lévi-Strauss*, ed. G. Charbonnier, tr. John and Doreen Weightman (London: Cape, 1969), p. 111.

'specific gravity...as such': Quoted by C. J. Shebbeare, 'The Atonement and Some Tendencies of Modern Thought', in L. W. Grensted, ed., *The Atonement in History and in Life* (London: SPCK, 1929), p. 302 ('Die Sünde ist das spezifische Gewicht der menschlichen Natur als solcher').

'searching...cosmos': Keith Sagar, *The Art of Ted Hughes* (Cambridge: Cambridge University Press, 1975), p. 4.

'high energy-construct . . . discharge': Charles Olson, 'Projective Verse', in James Scully, ed., *Modern Poets on Modern Poetry* (London: Collins, 1966), p. 272.

'Baudelaire . . . damnation': T. S. Eliot, *Selected Essays*, 2nd edn. (London: Faber and Faber, 1934), p. 391.

'frightful discovery of morality': Ibid., p. 163.

In every age . . . damned: Ibid.

'real poets . . . verse': Alexander Gladkov, *Meetings with Pasternak*, tr. and ed. Max Hayward (London: Collins and Harvill Press, 1977), p. 155.

'somewhat of the opinion . . . work': Charles Péguy, *Basic Verities,* tr. Ann and Julian Green (London: K. Paul, 1943), p. 24.

'the academic . . . pray': H. A. Williams, 'Theology and Self-Awareness' in A. R. Vidler, ed., *Soundings* (Cambridge: Cambridge University Press, 1963), p. 71.

'*Attrition* . . . no more.': Jeremy Taylor, *Vnum Necessarium, or, The Doctrine and Practice of Repentance* (London, 1655), p. 601. Cf. *The Sermons of John Donne,* ed. George R. Potter and Evelyn M. Simpson, 10 vols. (Berkeley, CA: University of California Press, 1953–62) vol. 9, p. 266: 'For, for Contrition, we doe not, we dare not say, as some of them, That Attrition is sufficient'.

'repentance . . . (*meta-noia*)': Martin Jarrett-Kerr, *Our Trespasses: A Study in Christian Penitence* (London: SCM Press, 1948), p. 97.

'sorrow not mingled . . . of God': Taylor, *Vnum Necessarium*, p. 638.

After . . . redemption: Wallace Stevens, *Opus Posthumous* (London: Faber and Faber, 1959), p. 158.

'explicitly . . . poetry': Vincent Buckley, *Poetry and Morality* (London: Chatto and Windus, 1959), p. 41.

'laboriously acquired' . . . clearness': Arthur Symons, *The Symbolist Movement in Literature*, rev. edn. of 1919 (New York: Dutton, 1958), pp. 82, 66, 40.

'must . . . language': Scott, *The Broken Center*, p. 67.

'the effect . . . despair': P. T. Forsyth, *The Principle of Authority* (London: Independent Press, 1952), pp. 7–8.

'The man . . . popular.': Ibid., p. 324.

'spontaneous overflow of powerful feelings': William Wordsworth, *Lyrical Ballads, and Other Poems, 1797–1800*, ed. James Butler and Karen Green (Ithaca, NY: Cornell University Press, 1992), p. 744.

'being fallen into the "they"': Dietrich Bonhoeffer, *No Rusty Swords*, tr. Edwin H. Robertson and John Bowden (London: Fontana, 1970), p. 51: quoting Heidegger.

'word-helotry': George Steiner, 'In Bluebeard's Castle', *The Listener* (15 April 1971), p. 476.

To take . . . to praise: William Empson, *Complete Poems*, ed. John Haffenden (London: Penguin Books, 2000), pp. 76–7 ('Courage means Running', but adopting the 1956 reading 'flat' for 'wise').

2. The Absolute Reasonableness of Robert Southwell

'inhuman ferocity': *Publications of the Catholic Record Society* (London: Catholic Record Society, 1905–), vol. 5: John Hungerford Pollen, ed., *Unpublished*

Documents Relating to the English Martyrs: Vol. I, 1584–1603 (1908), p. 325. Pollen's translation of Southwell's Latin. In subsequent notes, the *Publications of the Catholic Record Society* will be abbreviated as *CRS*.

'Grinding . . . punishments': Robert Southwell, *An Humble Supplication to Her Maiestie*, ed. R. C. Bald (Cambridge: Cambridge University Press, 1953), p. 34

'more fierce and cruell': *CRS*, vol. 5, p. 208: Richard Verstegan's Dispatches.

'to the Reverend . . . Fayth': *An Epistle of Comfort, To The Reverend Priestes, & to the Honorable, Worshipful, & other of the Laye sort restrayned in Durance for the Catholicke Fayth . . . Imprinted at Paris*. According to the *Short Title Catalogue*, 'the imprint is false; printed in Arundel House in London, possibly by John Charlewood in 1587'.

'seeing . . . contemplate': J. R. Roberts, 'The Influence of *The Spiritual Exercises* of St Ignatius on the Nativity Poems of Robert Southwell', *Journal of English and Germanic Philology*, vol. 59 (1960), p. 452; cf. Pierre Janelle, *Robert Southwell the Writer* (Mamaroneck, NY: P. P. Appel, 1971), p. 109 (first pub. 1935).

'almost inevitable martyrdom': *Humble Supplication*, p. xvii. Editorial introduction.

'yearning . . . purpose': A. O. Meyer, *England and the Catholic Church under Queen Elizabeth*, tr. J. R. McKee (London: K. Paul, Trench, Trübner, 1916), pp. 190, 212.

'there is a note . . . methodology': Roberts, 'The Influence of *The Spiritual Exercises*', p. 455; cf. Janelle, *Robert Southwell the Writer*, p. 110.

'bless . . . objects': *CRS*, vol. 5, p. 319: Pollen's translation of Southwell's Latin.

'particularly . . . Preachers': [Richard Challoner], *Memoirs of Missionary Priests* ([London] 1741), p. 42.

'Every priest . . . matter': *CRS*, vol. 5, pp. 318, 316: Pollen's translation of Southwell's Latin.

'English . . . tongue': *The Poems of Robert Southwell, SJ*, ed. James H. McDonald and Nancy Pollard Brown (Oxford: Clarendon Press, 1967), pp. xix–xx.

'an England . . . Puritan': Martz, *The Poetry of Meditation*, p. 9.

'the internal . . . camp': Meyer, *England and the Catholic Church*, p. 171.

'mutual recrimination' . . . laity': John Bossy, *The English Catholic Community 1570–1850* (London: Darton, Longman, and Todd, 1975), p. 32.

'amongst . . . kind': J. C. H. Aveling, *The Handle and the Axe: The Catholic Recusants in England from Reformation to Emancipation* (London: Blond and Briggs, 1976), p. 68.

'special . . . legend': Ibid., pp. 72, 67.

'a cheerful . . . manliness': Janelle, *Robert Southwell the Writer*, p. 3.

'mild . . . temper': Martz, *The Poetry of Meditation*, p. 205.

'in great favour . . . respect': Janelle, *Robert Southwell the Writer*, pp. 109–10.

'Campion's Brag': cf. A. C. Southern, *Elizabethan Recusant Prose 1559–1582* (London: Sands, 1950), pp. 151, 153–6.

'rapidly . . . journey': *Humble Supplication*, p. xvii; Richard Simpson, *Edmund Campion: A Biography*, revised edn. (London: J. Hodges, 1896), p. 225.

'spontaneous effusions': Janelle, *Robert Southwell the Writer*, p. 109.

'well-ordered will': Ibid., p. 111. The phrase is apt; though more recent scholarship doubts Southwell's authorship of the translation from Estella.

'the deliberate...poetry': *The Sermons and Devotional Writings of Gerard Manley Hopkins*, ed. Christopher Devlin (London: Oxford University Press, 1959), p. 118.

'suitable...expression': Janelle, *Robert Southwell the Writer*, p. 153.

accusations and slanders: See Simpson, *Edmund Campion*, pp. 224–5.

The 1591...Ruffians': *Humble Supplication*, pp. xi, 60, 64.

'*miles gloriosus*': Simpson, *Edmund Campion*, pp. 365, 367.

'the most...controversy': Meyer, *England and the Catholic Church*, p. 210.

'the creative art of denigration': Helen C. White, 'Some Continuing Traditions in English Devotional Literature', *PMLA*, vol. 57, no. 2 (1942), p. 966.

'a spirite...devotion': Quoted in Martz, *The Poetry of Meditation*, p. 8; cf. White, 'Some Continuing Traditions', p. 967.

'uncompromising...writings': R. C. Bald, 'Donne and Southwell', in *Humble Supplication*, p. 79.

The title-page...thoroughly contentious: *The Nevv Testament of Iesus Christ, translated faithfvlly into English...Printed at Rhemes...1582*. Note, for example, p. 182: 'Heretikes may by penal lawes be co[m]pelled to the Catholike faith' (annotation to Luke 14: 23).

'Controversy...poets too': Meyer, *England and the Catholic Church*, p. 221.

'Witty...feeling': *CRS*, vol. 5, pp. 90–1.

'a terrible...catholics': Meyer, *England and the Catholic Church*, p. 222.

'caddish': C. C. Martindale, 'Edmund Campion', in Maisie Ward, ed., *The English Way* (London: Sheed and Ward, 1933), p. 240: 'In Elizabeth's time the State became the cad as such'.

'the intimate...fields': David Mathew, 'John Fisher', ibid., p. 208.

'hankered': Bossy, *The English Catholic Community*, p. 11.

'local...instances of this: Christopher Haigh, *Reformation and Resistance in Tudor Lancashire* (Cambridge: Cambridge University Press, 1975), pp. 54, 64, 85, 145.

'savage torpor': William Wordsworth, *Lyrical Ballads, and Other Poems, 1797–1800*, ed. James Butler and Karen Green (Ithaca, NY: Cornell University Press, 1992), p. 746.

'sluggishness...ignorantia': Bossy, *The English Catholic Community*, pp. 102, 223; cf. *CRS*, vol. 39 (1942): *Letters and Memorials of Fr. Robert Persons*, vol. 1, p. 108.

Elizabethan...sank into them: See Aveling, *The Handle and the Axe*, pp. 74, 151–3.

'association...England: Simpson, *Edmund Campion*, 223.

'that wicked...mischief': *CRS*, vol. 5, p. 314. Pollen's translation of Southwell's Latin.

'greene witts...witt': *Humble Supplication*, 18.

'apparell'...Calling': Ibid., p. 8.

'garnished . . . colours': *John Gerard: The Autobiography of an Elizabethan*, tr. Philip Caraman (London: Longmans, Green, 1951), p. 18 n.

Dr William Allen . . . vernacular: Janelle, *Robert Southwell the Writer*, pp. 7–9 and 9 n. 20. T. F. Knox's translation of Latin MS, English College, Rome.

'Southwell . . . Puritans': Ibid., p. 198.

'a thoroughly . . . religion': Ernst Cassirer, *The Platonic Renaissance in England*, tr. James P. Pettegrove ([Edinburgh]: Nelson, 1953), p. 74.

Christopher Morris . . . Elizabeth herself': Christopher Morris, *Political Thought in England: Tyndale to Hooker* (London: Oxford University Press, 1953), pp. 174–5, 126, 195.

'no puritan . . . hatred': Meyer, *England and the Catholic Church*, p. 350.

'contumelious termes': *Humble Supplication*, p. 2.

'a reply . . . scorn': Meyer, *England and the Catholic Church*, p. 351.

Edmund Campion . . . equitie': Southern, *Elizabethan Recusant Prose*, pp. 154–5.

The Proclamation . . . pecuniary summe': *Humble Supplication*, pp. 60–1, 63.

'measure . . . Equity': Ibid., p. 3.

'sound beliefe' . . . disposition: Ibid., p. 14.

'Let it be scanned . . . carrieth.': Ibid.

'For a long time . . . should be': *Selected Historical Essays of F. W. Maitland*, ed. Helen M. Cam (Cambridge: Cambridge University Press, 1957), pp. 133, 131. 'Its' refers to the Court of Chancery which dispensed equity.

'the recourse . . . the law': *OED*², s.v. 'equity'.

'notion . . . law" ': Lon L. Fuller, *Legal Fictions* (Stanford, CA: Stanford University Press, 1967), p. 87.

In the beautiful . . . himself': Robert Southwell, *Marie Magdalens Funeral Teares (1591)*, facsimile edn. (Delmar, NY: Scholars' Facsimiles & Reprints, 1975), pp. 32 and 32 verso.

If equities . . . weightes: *The Collected Poems of S. Robert Southwell SJ*, ed. Peter Davidson (Manchester: Carcanet, 2007), p. 63; cf. Southwell, *Poems*, 75.

'Thogh I were . . . disprove my courses': *Marie Magdalens Funeral Teares*, p. 39 verso; *Marie Magdalens Funeral Teares*, p. 40 verso; *Humble Supplication*, pp. 2–3; Robert Southwell, *Two Letters and Short Rules of a Good Life*, ed. Nancy Pollard Brown (Charlottesville, VA: University Press of Virginia, 1973), pp. 33, 79.

the 'great age . . . dilemma': H. R. Trevor-Roper, *Historical Essays* (London: Macmillan, 1957), p. 92.

'uncanonical': Meyer, *England and the Catholic Church*, p. 79.

'declaration . . . priest': Bossy, *The English Catholic Community*, p. 37.

And for the next . . . scaffold: *CRS*, vol. 5, pp. 8–17.

'in accordance . . . normal reason': Morris, *Political Thought in England*, p. 106.

'Because . . . reason.': Devlin, *Life of Southwell*, p. 287.

Maitland has said . . . divorced from literature': Maitland, *Selected Historical Essays*, p. 125.

'during Shakespeare's... equity': John W. Dickinson, 'Renaissance Equity and *Measure for Measure*' in *Shakespeare Quarterly*, vol. 13 (1962), p. 287; Wilbur Dunkel, 'Law and Equity in *Measure for Measure*', ibid., p. 285.

weighing of justice with equity: For the theme, see Christopher St German, *Doctor and Student*, ed. T. F. T. Plucknett and J. L. Barton (London: Selden Society, 1974), pp. 94–8 (the chapter 'Quid sit equitas' / 'What is equytie') and pp. xliv–li. On St German's indebtedness to Jean Gerson, see J. B. Trapp in *The Yale Edition of the Works of St. Thomas More*, 14 vols. (New Haven, CT: Yale University Press, 1963–85), vol. 9, p. xlvi ('Gerson is a major source, though not specifically acknowledged as such, for [St German's] leading notions of *lex eterna*, equity, and conscience'). For the appeal to equity, see also *The Life of Fisher*, ed. Ronald Bayne (London: Early English Text Society: Oxford University Press, 1921), pp. 56, 57, 60.

As Paul Vinogradoff has shown: *Roman Law in Medieval Europe*, 2nd edn. (Oxford: Clarendon Press, 1929), pp. 55–6, 66; see also p. 106: 'justitia est constans et perpetua voluntas jus suum cuique tribuendi [the definition of justice as given in the Digest]'.

'a work... beauty': Janelle, *Robert Southwell the Writer*, pp. 286–7.

'great plea... silence': R. W. Chambers, *Thomas More*, 2nd edn. (London: Clarendon Press, 1938), p. 336.

'monster... taciturny': *CRS*, vol. 5, p. 283.

'a new kind... one word': Janelle, *Robert Southwell the Writer*, pp. 66–7.

'hinterland': This term was suggested to me by D. W. Harding's brilliant essay, 'The Hinterland of Thought', in *Experience into Words* (London: Penguin, 1974), pp. 176 ff. In fairness to Harding and myself it must be added that I employ it in a different sense.

'wittye crueltye': *Epistle of Comfort*, p. 125 verso, translating St Cyprian.

The executioner... porredge pot: *The Works of Thomas Nashe*, ed. Ronald B. McKerrow, rev. F. P. Wilson, 5 vols. (Oxford: Basil Blackwell, 1958), vol. 2, p. 327.

'the pleasure... description': G. R. Hibbard, *Thomas Nashe: A Critical Introduction* (London: Routledge and Paul, 1962), p. 174.

'the martyr... his mouth"': *CRS*, vol. 5, p. 207.

And as a cunninge... by them: Southwell, *Epistle of Comfort*, p. 203 recto, verso.

'Our teares... felicitye': Ibid., p. 113 recto.

It is a great... our cure: Robert Southwell, *Spiritual Exercises and Devotions*, ed. J.-M. de Buck, tr. P. E. Hallett (London: Sheed & Ward, 1931), p. 59. For Southwell's Latin, see p. 141. Buck considers that the passage may have been copied from 'some spiritual work in vogue at the time'.

'had particular significance for Southwell': McDonald and Brown in Southwell, *Poems*, p. 146.

The modern 'consensus'... Christ: F. V. Filson, *A Commentary on the Gospel According to St. Matthew* (London: A. and C. Black, 1960), p. 138; David Hill, ed., *The Gospel of Matthew* (London: Oliphants, 1972), p. 200; J. C. Fenton, *The*

Gospel of St. Matthew (Harmondsworth: Penguin, 1963), pp. 179–80; *The Gospel According to Matthew in the Revised Standard Version*, ed. H. Benedict Green (London: Oxford University Press, 1975), p. 116. Hopkins reads the text in Southwell's spirit; see Hopkins, *Sermons and Devotional Writings*, p. 96.

'the violence ... patient suffering': Nashe, *Works*, vol. 2, p. 234.

epigraph on the title-page: Given in both Latin and English ('The Kingdom of heauen suffereth violence, and the violent beare it awaye'). Cf. the *Rhemes New Testament*, p. 29: 'And from the dayes of Iohn the Baptist vntil novv, the kingdom of heauen suffereth violence, and the violent beare it avvay' (Matthew 11: 12).

'And though ... *foughte for it*': Southwell, *Epistle of Comfort*, p. 31 verso, 32 recto.

Thy ghostly ... tender love: Southwell, *Collected Poems*, p. 48; cf. *Poems*, p. 55.

'in my judgment ... to God': Luther, *Lectures on Romans*, tr. and ed. Wilhelm Pauck, The Library of Christian Classics, vol. 15 (London: SCM Press, 1961), p. 349.

'if you wish ... fear nothing': *Spiritual and Anabaptist Writers*, ed. George Hunston Williams and Angel M. Mergal, The Library of Christian Classics, vol. 25 (London: SCM Press, 1957), p. 369.

'for the Kingdom ... knives': *The Great Commentary of Cornelius à Lapide*, tr. Thomas W. Mossman, 6 vols. (London: John Hodges, 1891–96), vol. 2, pp. 58, 60 (*St Matthew's Gospel, chaps. X to XXI*).

'tiranical persecution ... thy desire': *Epistle of Comfort*, p. 79 verso; *Marie Magdalens Funeral Teares*, p. 25 recto; *Humble Supplication*, p. 4; *Marie Magdalens Funeral Teares*, p. 58 recto; ibid., p. 7 recto; ibid., p. 38 recto, verso.

'I am urged ... detest': *Two Letters*, p. 56.

as not ... spiritual plane': Southwell, *Triumphs over Death*, quoted in Janelle, *Robert Southwell the Writer*, p. 233. Janelle's comment, p. 232.

'Of the venerable martyr ... butchery': *The Rambler*, NS vol. 8 (1857), p. 114, quoted in Bede Camm, *Forgotten Shrines*, 2nd edn. (London: MacDonald & Evans, 1936), pp. 359 and 361 n.

The 'officers ... George Haydock: *CRS*, vol. 5, pp. 288–9, 57–62.

For Southwell ... emblem: Cf. John Morris, *The Troubles of our Catholic Forefathers related by themselves*, 1st ser. (London: Burns and Oates, 1872), p. 98, on the execution of Fr Cuthbert Maine, 1587: 'a very high gibbet ... and all things else, both fire and knives, set to the show and ready prepared'.

In a letter ... medicines" ': *CRS*, vol. 5, p. 318. Pollen's translation of Southwell's Latin; p. 301, Pollen's note on 'veiled style'.

Then sayd the Angel ... them: *The Holie Bible Faithfvlly Translated into English* (Douai, 1609–10), p. 998.

Remember ... dyed: *Epistle of Comfort*, p. 201 recto.

(indeed ... martyrdom): Ibid., p. 202 verso.

'the reparation ... offences': Maitland, *Selected Historical Essays*, p. 131.

'Transformation': Cf. Janelle, *Robert Southwell the Writer*, 190; Helen C. White, 'Southwell: Metaphysical and Baroque', in *Modern Philology*, vol. 61, no. 3 (1964), p. 161; cf. F. W. Beare, *A Commentary on the Epistle to the Philippians*, 3rd edn. (London: Black, 1973), p. 140: 'Even now [Paul] tells us, the transformation is proceeding within us'.

'translations ... alteratio[n]': Janelle, *Robert Southwell the Writer*, p. 184; *Poems*, pp. xcvi, 135; *Epistle of Comfort*, p. 154 recto.

And this ... glorye: *Epistle of Comfort*, pp. 203 verso, 204 recto.

'[He] will refashion ... from the body': Beare, *Commentary*, p. 138.

Christ's Parousia: Cf. Beare, pp. 138, 140.

There is no reason ... the Crosse: *Epistle of Comfort*, p. 32 recto, verso.

'transfigured ... passion': Ibid., p. 32 recto.

'Calvary's turbulence': W. B. Yeats, *The Collected Poems of W. B. Yeats*, ed. Richard J. Finneran, new edn. (New York: Macmillan, 1989), p. 126 ('The Magi').

'For Thy sake ... nothing': *Spiritual Exercises and Devotions*, p. 104: for Southwell's Latin, see p. 180.

a fair amount of Ovid by heart: Janelle, *Robert Southwell the Writer*, p. 135.

'From bosomes ... tumble thick: *Seneca His Tenne Tragedies translated into Englysh* (London, 1581), p. 33 recto (*Thyestes*), p. 72 recto (*Hippolytus*).

Whye doest ... reason: *Epistle of Comfort*, p. 205 recto.

'masculine perswasive force': 'On his Mistris', John Donne, *The Elegies and the Songs and Sonnets*, ed. Helen Gardner (Oxford: Clarendon Press, 1965), p. 23.

'make ... experience': Ibid., p. xviii

'how well Verse and Vertue suite together': Southwell, *Collected Poems*, p. 1; cf. *Poems*, p. 1.

'Whose measure ... too little have': Southwell, *Collected Poems*, pp. 3, 5, 25; cf. *Poems*, pp. 2, 5, 28.

'Baroque ... transformation': White, 'Southwell: Metaphysical and Baroque', p. 161.

'uneven account' ... 'just measure': Southwell, *Collected Poems*, pp. 66, 65; cf. *Poems*, pp. 79, 77.

'the affections ... God': *Epistle of Comfort*, pp. 191 recto, 190 verso.

'mediocrity' ... behaviour': *OED²*, s.v. 'mediocrity'.

'monotony' ... or pitch': *OED²*, s.v. 'monotony'.

'loathed pleasures' ... 'Cruell Comforts': *Collected Poems*, pp. 44, 36, 36, 47 (cf. *Poems*, pp. 50, 41, 41, 54), *Humble Supplication*, p. 34.

'awestruck' ... man': Roberts, 'The Influence of *The Spiritual Exercises*', p. 454.

This little Babe ... surprise: *Collected Poems*, p. 13 ('New heaven, new warre'); cf. *Poems*, p. 14.

'naïve ... concession': *Agenda*, vol. 13, no. 3 (Autumn 1975), p. 32. For Southwell's phrase see *Marie Magdalens Funeral Teares*, p. A3 verso.

Southwell...Euphuistic style: See Janelle, *Robert Southwell the Writer*, pp. 191–4 and Herbert Thurston, 'Father Southwell the Euphuist?', *The Month*, vol. 83 (1895), p. 243.

'complexity of association': White, 'Southwell: Metaphysical and Baroque', p. 166.

Antonin Artaud...Rodez: Charles Marowitz, *Artaud at Rodez* (London: M. Boyars, 1977), p. 73.

'Excessus' signifies 'ecstasy': Étienne Gilson, *The Mystical Theology of Saint Bernard*, tr. A. H. C. Downs (London: Sheed & Ward, 1940), p. 26. See also E. Gordon Rupp, *The Righteousness of God* (London: Hodder and Stoughton, 1953), p. 143: '"Excessus mentis," [Luther] says, means "either the alienation of mind" or "the rapture of the mind into...faith," and this is really what is meant by "ecstasis"'; and *A Study of Wisdom: Three Tracts by the Author of 'The Cloud of Unknowing'*, tr. Clifton Wolters (Oxford: SIG Press, 1980), p. 21: '"Ibi Benjamin adolescentus in mentis excessu" [Psalm 68: 28, Vulgate] which means in English, "There is Benjamin, the young child, transported out of mind"'.

'solace'...Tower: Janelle, *Robert Southwell the Writer*, p. 68.

'pretty babe...brest': *Collected Poems*, p. 14; cf. *Poems*, p. 15.

'the most hackneyed of all conceits': Janelle, *Robert Southwell the Writer*, p. 168

parody of the Petrarchan tradition: See *Poems*, p. 124.

'exceeding...right': *OED*², s.v. 'excessive'.

'variation...manner': Martz, *The Poetry of Meditation*, pp. 81–3, 364. Puente's work was first published in 1605. John Heighman's English translation was not issued from St Omer until 1619.

St Ignatius...tradition: Janelle, *Robert Southwell the Writer*, p. 109.

'excess...necessity': *Two Letters*, p. 36.

'phancy' and 'self delite': *Collected Poems*, pp. 43–4; cf. *Poems*, p. 50.

'Let vs...therin': *Epistle of Comfort*, p. 37 verso.

'the Jesuit discipline...wildness': Devlin, *Life of Southwell*, p. 85.

I would further suggest...not lost on him: cf. Étienne Gilson, *The Spirit of Mediaeval Philosophy*, tr. A. H. C. Downs (London: Sheed & Ward, 1936), pp. 290–2; Rupp, *The Righteousness of God*, p. 143; Wolters, *Three Tracts*, p. 21.

'I am come hither...poor life': Devlin, *Life of Southwell*, p. 321.

'Loue...loue': *Marie Magdalens Funeral Teares*, p. 52 recto, verso.

3. The World's Proportion

The words...awrie: John Donne, 'The First Anniversary', ll. 302–4. *The Epithalamions Anniversaries and Epicedes*, ed. W. Milgate (Oxford: Clarendon Press, 1978), p. 30.

Jonson...Romans: John Edwin Sandys in *Shakespeare's England*, 2 vols. (Oxford: Clarendon Press, 1916), vol. 1, p. 274.

'Words are the Peoples': *Ben Jonson*, ed. C. H. Herford and Percy Simpson, 11 vols. (Oxford: Clarendon Press, 1925–52), vol. 8, p. 621.

'accurate eye...ordinary speech': Marchette Chute, *Ben Jonson of Westminster* (New York: Dutton, 1953), pp. 85, 74.

the tricks . . . nose: L. C. Knights, 'Ben Jonson, Dramatist' in Boris Ford, ed., *The Age of Shakespeare*. Reprinted with revisions (Harmondsworth: Penguin, 1956), p. 304.

Character writers . . . stock response: See David Nichol Smith, *Characters from the Histories & Memoirs of the Seventeenth Century* (Oxford: Clarendon Press, 1918), pp. 2, 63, 223. Of James I, 'some *Parallel'd* him to *Tiberius* for *Dissimulation*'; of Charles II, 'His person and temper, his vices as well as his fortunes, resemble the character that we have given us of *Tiberius*'; of Strafford, 'in a worde, the Epitaph . . . that Silla wrote for himselfe, may not be unfitly applied to him'. See also *Sir Fulke Greville's Life of Sir Philip Sidney*, ed. Nowell Smith (Oxford: Clarendon Press, 1907), p. 39 (first pub. 1652): 'nor yet like that gallant Libertine *Sylla*'. These polemic analogues share a common field of classical reference with Jonson's two plays.

CICERO . . . infamy?: *Catiline*, IV, ll. 316 ff. *Ben Jonson* vol. 5, p. 508.

We demand . . . stripping us: A. R. Bayley, *The Great Civil War in Dorset 1642–1660* (Taunton: Burnicott and Pearce, 1910), pp. 351–3. For the discovery of this passage I am indebted to Christopher Hill and Edmund Dell, eds., *The Good Old Cause* (London: Lawrence and Wishart, 1949), p. 368. However, their transcript differs from Bayley's in certain details. I have retained Bayley's readings.

'shipwrack'd . . . fortunes': *Catiline*, IV, ll. 413 ff. *Ben Jonson*, vol. 5, p. 511.

CAT. . . . stand for: *Catiline*, I, ll. 409 ff. *Ben Jonson*, vol. 5, p. 448.

'industrie', 'vigilance': *Catiline*, III, l. 33. *Ben Jonson*, vol. 5, p. 469.

'to make . . . choice': *Catiline*, II, l. 373. *Ben Jonson*, vol. 5, p. 467.

PETREIVS . . . world: *Catiline*, V, ll. 11 ff. *Ben Jonson*, vol. 5, p. 527.

altar . . . bower: 'London, 1802', from 'Poems Dedicated to National Independence and Liberty'.

MY LORD . . . magistrate: Dedication to *Catiline*, *Ben Jonson*, vol. 5, p. 431.

I thinke meete . . . can be: *Wilson's Arte of Rhetorique 1560*, ed. G. H. Mair (Oxford: Clarendon Press, 1909), p. 156.

'great melody' . . . 'Whiggery': W. B. Yeats, *The Collected Poems of W. B. Yeats*, ed. Richard J. Finneran, new edn. (New York: Macmillan, 1989), p. 241 ('The Seven Sages').

'masculine' wit: *Catiline*, II, l. 45. *Ben Jonson*, vol. 5, p. 455.

'great states-woman': *Catiline*, II, l. 38. *Ben Jonson*, vol. 5, p. 455.

'shee-*Critick*': *Catiline*, II, l. 45. *Ben Jonson*, vol. 5, p. 455.

play 'the orator': *Catiline*, III, l. 688. *Ben Jonson*, vol. 5, p. 491.

SEM. . . . competitors: *Catiline*, II, ll. 96 ff. *Ben Jonson*, vol. 5, pp. 457–8.

There is the incident . . . pages: *Catiline*, II, ll. 506 ff. *Ben Jonson*, vol. 5, p. 451.

'an outrage to probability': *The Collected Works of Samuel Taylor Coleridge*, 16 vols. (Princeton, NJ: Princeton University Press, 1969–2002), vol. 12, part 3, p. 185 (*Marginalia*, ed. George Whalley, 6 parts).

'men turn'd *furies*': *Catiline*, III, l. 332. *Ben Jonson*, vol. 5, p. 479.

'wishings tast of woman': *Catiline*, III, l. 82. *Ben Jonson*, vol. 5, p. 474.

CET.... dead: *Catiline*, III, ll. 663 ff. *Ben Jonson*, vol. 5, p. 490.

In *Epicoene*... natures: See Edward B. Partridge, *The Broken Compass* (London: Chatto & Windus, 1958), ch. 7.

the noted... world: *Seianus*, I, ll. 216–17, *Ben Jonson*, vol. 4, p. 362.

'needy'... 'sloth': e.g. *Catiline*, I, l. 161, *Ben Jonson*, vol. 5, p. 440; III, l. 715, *Ben Jonson*, vol. 5, p. 492; IV, l. 184, *Ben Jonson*, vol. 5, p. 504; IV, l. 226, *Ben Jonson*, vol. 5, p. 505; I, ll. 205, 211, *Ben Jonson*, vol. 5, p. 441.

'bothe her owne... owne prey': *Catiline*, I, l. 586. *Ben Jonson*, vol. 5, p. 453.

All *Rome*... suffer: *Seianus*, V, l. 256. *Ben Jonson*, vol. 4, p. 446.

CIC.... such: *Catiline*, III, ll. 438 ff. *Ben Jonson*, vol. 5, p. 483.

CAT.... nectar: *Catiline*, I, ll. 102 ff. *Ben Jonson*, vol. 5, p. 438.

SEIANUS... lusts: *Seianus*, III, ll. 598 ff. *Ben Jonson*, vol. 4, pp. 412–13.

SAB.... Rhodes: *Seianus*, IV, ll. 163 ff. *Ben Jonson*, vol. 4, p. 424.

James I's... succinctly enough: See G. P. Gooch, *English Democratic Ideas in the Seventeenth Century*, 2nd edn., rev. H. J. Laski (New York: Harper, 1959), p. 53 (1st edn. pub. 1898, 2nd edn. pub. 1927).

'government exists... accordingly': Louis I. Bredvold, *The Intellectual Milieu of John Dryden* (Ann Arbor, MI: University of Michigan Press, 1934), p. 143.

'originally non-dramatic' nature: U. M. Ellis-Fermor, *The Jacobean Drama* (London: Methuen, 1936), pp. 99–100.

The golden laws... allowing: Herbert J. C. Grierson, *The Poems of John Donne*, 2 vols. (Oxford: Oxford University Press, 1912), vol. 1, pp. 113–16, prints this poem as 'Elegie XVII'. Helen Gardner in her edition of *The Elegies and The Songs and Sonnets* (Oxford: Clarendon Press, 1965) places it among the 'Dubia' (pp. 104–6) and questions the attribution of the poem to Donne 'on internal evidence' (p. xlvi).

'free sword': *Catiline*, I, l. 230. *Ben Jonson*, vol. 5, p. 442.

It could be argued... comment: This statement is affected by Gardner's opinion but I have decided to let it stand. Dramatists frequently fell foul of the censors. *Sejanus* itself, despite Jonson's caution, barely scraped past official disapproval. Fulke Greville destroyed a tragedy in manuscript because he thought it 'apt enough to be construed, or strained to a personating of vices in the present Governors, and government' (Greville, *Life of Sir Philip Sidney*, p. 156).

This *anachronic*... amusing: Coleridge, *Collected Works*, vol. 12, part 3, p. 178 (*Marginalia*).

A meere vpstart... sweat for't: *Catiline*, II, ll. 119 ff. *Ben Jonson*, vol. 5, p. 458. The whole question of the 'new man' is obviously one of the great thorny problems of the era. It cannot be fully discussed here, but see *The Yale Edition of the Works of St Thomas More*, 14 vols. (New Haven, CT: Yale University Press, 1963–85), vol. 12, p. 374 and Charles Till Davis, *Dante and the Idea of Rome* (Oxford: Clarendon Press, 1957), p. 91. The fact remains that Cicero, the *arriviste*, is 'good'; Sejanus, the *arriviste*, 'wicked'; and the necessity to cajole us into the acceptance of this fact influences both action and imagery in the two Roman plays. Cicero is an approved 'new man' but feels some need for self-justification. 'Cecil noted in 1559 that "the wanton bringing up and ignorance of the nobility forces the Prince to advance new men that can serve" ' (quoted in *The Age of Shakespeare*, p. 16). The 'new man' versus the 'wanton' nobility is, essentially, the situation of *Catiline*.

the ladie ARETE . . . gowne: *Cynthias Reuells* I, ll. 89 ff. *Ben Jonson*, vol. 4, p. 38.

we will eate . . . opalls: *The Alchemist*, IV, i. 156 ff. *Ben Jonson*, vol. 5, p. 364.

'kemb'd' . . . 'sleek'd': *Catiline*, I, ll. 561–2. *Ben Jonson*, vol. 5, p. 453.

Hence comes . . . made: *Catiline*, I, ll. 573 ff. *Ben Jonson*, vol. 5, p. 453.

'Twas vertue . . . all men noble: *Catiline*, II, l. 127. *Ben Jonson*, vol. 5, p. 458.

CHOR . . . helme: *Catiline*, III, ll. 60 ff. *Ben Jonson*, vol. 5, p. 470.

he piercing . . . truth: Greville, *Life of Sir Philip Sidney*, p. 36.

We haue . . . for vertue: *Catiline*, II, ll. 131 ff. *Ben Jonson*, vol. 5, p. 458.

He was . . . in others: *Seianus*, I, ll. 124 ff. *Ben Jonson*, vol. 4, p. 359. On Jonson's classical sources in this passage, see also *Sejanus: His Fall*, ed. Philip J. Ayers (Manchester: Manchester University Press, 1999 [1990]), pp. 86–7.

In this . . . Recording Muse: *Absalom and Achitophel*, ll. 817–28. *The Poems of John Dryden*, ed. James Kinsley, 4 vols. (Oxford: Clarendon Press, 1958), vol. 1, p. 238.

NUR[SE] . . . crime: *The New Inne*, V, ll. 56 ff. *Ben Jonson*, vol. 6, p. 486. 'Nurse' is Lady Frampul disguised.

money . . . knaue: *Catiline*, V, l. 299. *Ben Jonson*, vol. 5, p. 536.

In *Catiline* . . . tragedy: Editorial 'Introduction to "Catiline and his Conspiracy" ', *Ben Jonson*, vol. 2, p. 122.

It is not manly . . . punishment: *The Divell is an Asse*, V. viii. 169 ff. *Ben Jonson*, vol. 6, p. 269.

4. 'The True Conduct of Human Judgment'

When Queen Elizabeth . . . masques: E. K. Chambers, in *Shakespeare's England*, 2 vols. (Oxford: Clarendon Press, 1916), vol. 1, p. 105.

especially . . . taste: J. Dover Wilson, prefatory note to *Cymbeline*, ed. J. C. Maxwell (Cambridge: University Press, 1960), p. ix.

'taking rank . . . Yeomen': F. E. Halliday, *The Life of Shakespeare* (London: G. Duckworth, 1961), p. 178.

'since Princes will have such Things': Francis Bacon, *The Essayes or Counsels, Civill and Morall*, ed. Michael Kiernan (Cambridge, MA: Harvard University Press, 1985), p. 117 ('Of Maskes and Triumphs').

It has been suggested . . . 'dual purpose' play: J. M. Nosworthy, *Cymbeline*, Arden edn. (London: Methuen, 1955), p. xvi. This text is used for quotations. Richard Thayer Thornberry, in *Shakespeare and the Blackfriars Tradition* (Ohio State University Dissertation, 1964), rejects the dual purpose theory and regards *Cymbeline* as a play composed specifically for the Globe.

'an unlikely . . . tricks': Harley Granville-Barker, *Prefaces to Shakespeare*, 2nd series, (London: Sidgwick & Jackson, 1944), p. 244.

'to commit ... material': Maxwell in *Cymbeline*, p. xxxix.

the supreme theme ... destiny: Well described by G. Wilson Knight, *The Crown of Life* (London: Oxford University Press, 1947), ch. 4.

Emrys Jones's persuasive essay: Emrys Jones, 'Stuart Cymbeline', in *Essays in Criticism*, vol. 11, no. 1 (1961), pp. 84–99.

'the fulfilment ... people': Ibid., p. 90.

To the medieval chroniclers ... connotations: Robin Moffet, '*Cymbeline* and the Nativity', in *Shakespeare Quarterly*, vol. 13, no. 2 (1962), pp. 207–18.

I felt that Stalingrad ... out: Alan Sillitoe, *Road to Volgograd* (London: Pan, 1966), p. 40.

'magnetized ... spot': Knight, *The Crown of Life*, p. 155.

a kind of interpretative ... incoherent: Jones, 'Stuart Cymbeline', p. 98.

'a central fumbling ... logic': Ibid., p. 97.

'being too close ... audience': Ibid.

Even if it were an established ... play: It is on record that the play was acted at Court in 1634, but that is not quite the same thing.

'officiously' ... ill-judged actions': Jones, 'Stuart Cymbeline', p. 97.

'two supremely excellent human beings': Moffet, '*Cymbeline* and the Nativity', p. 208.

'one of the great women ... world': Mark Van Doren, *Shakespeare* (London: Allen & Unwin, 1941), p. 309.

All I can ... ought to be: Letter quoted by A. M. Eastman and G. B. Harrison, *Shakespeare's Critics* (Ann Arbor, MI: University of Michigan Press, 1964), pp. 172–3.

('My face ... appears'): 'The Good-morrow', 1. 15. John Donne, *The Elegies and The Songs and Sonnets*, ed. Helen Gardner (Oxford: Clarendon Press, 1965), p. 70.

'quite out of character': *Cymbeline*, ed. Nosworthy, p. 17.

'too good to be true': *Cymbeline*, ed. Maxwell, p. xxxix.

'Shakespeare intends ... virtue': *Cymbeline*, ed. Nosworthy, p. 4.

beneath Posthumus' ... embodies: Homer D. Swander, '*Cymbeline* and the "Blameless Hero"', *ELH*, vol. 31 (1964), pp. 259–70 (p. 260).

'the two characters ... actor': Homer D. Swander, '*Cymbeline*: Religious Idea and Dramatic Design', in *Pacific Coast Studies in Shakespeare* (Eugene, OR: University of Oregon Press, 1966), p. 251.

The objection ... the play': F. R. Leavis, *The Common Pursuit* (London: Chatto & Windus, 1952), p. 176.

It is right to point ... at work here: Derek Traversi, *Shakespeare: The Last Phase* (London: Hollis & Carter, 1965), p. 62.

'the puritanical ... *The Tempest*': Knight, *The Crown of Life*, p. 149.

'But quick, and in mine arms': *The Winter's Tale*, iv. iv. 132.

'deep centre': Leavis, *The Common Pursuit*, p. 174.

brauncheth it selfe ... rumors: Francis Bacon, *The Advancement of Learning*, ed. Michael Kiernan (Oxford: Clarendon Press, 2000), p. 26 (*The Oxford Francis Bacon*, vol. 4).

'the sums he gave . . . give': D. Harris Willson, *King James VI and I* (London: Jonathan Cape, 1956), p. 261.

'British toughness' . . . obnoxious: Knight, *The Crown of Life*, 136.

The Britons . . . little world': L. C. Knights, *Drama and Society in the Age of Jonson* (London: Chatto & Windus, 1951), p. 254 n. 3. A reference to *Locrine*.

'the character . . . James I': Jones, 'Stuart Cymbeline', p. 96.

some earlier editors . . . to 'by': Moffet, '*Cymbeline* and the Nativity', p. 215.

fearing him as their Iudge . . . teares to God: *The Political Works of James I*, ed. Charles Howard McIlwain (Cambridge, MA: Harvard University Press, 1918), p. 61.

'the ending of *The Tempest* . . . reticent': David William, '*The Tempest* on the Stage', in John Russell Brown and Bernard Harris, eds., *Jacobean Theatre* (Stratford-upon-Avon Studies, vol. 1) (London: Arnold, 1960), p. 135.

hamartia: A term covering a gamut of flaws from 'simple error' to 'sin'. For a full description see Gerald F. Else, *Aristotle's Poetics: The Argument* (Cambridge, MA: Harvard University Press, 1957), esp. pp. 376–99. One is aware that Shakespeare may not have known the *Poetics*.

If wee present . . . Hodge-podge: I am indebted to the discussion by Robert Weimann in Arnold Kettle, ed., *Shakespeare in a Changing World* (London: Lawrence & Wishart, 1964), pp. 36–7.

sutable . . . together: Thomas Tomkins, *Songs of 3. 4. 5. 6. Parts* (London, 1622) A2 recto.

Their spirit . . . described: Notably by Charles Barber, '*The Winter's Tale* and Jacobean Society', in Kettle, ed., *Shakespeare in a Changing World*, pp. 233–52.

it must be confessed . . . life: Bacon, *Advancement of Learning*, p. 117.

'the Caution . . . Iudgement': Ibid., pp. 117–18.

'there is more Baconism . . . recognized': Barber, '*The Winter's Tale* and Jacobean Society', pp. 247–8.

'Experimentation . . . magic': Hardin Craig, *The Enchanted Glass* (Oxford: Blackwell, 1952), p. 75.

'degenerate Naturall Magicke': Bacon, *Advancement of Learning*, p. 89.

Wilson Knight . . . of her son: *The Crown of Life*, p. 130.

'primal nature . . . aspect': Ibid., p. 159.

'rehabilitated nature': Cf. Basil Willey, *The Seventeenth Century Background* (London: Chatto and Windus, 1953), ch. 2.

'Man had learned . . . animals': Craig, *The Enchanted Glass*, p. 99.

'on occasion . . . heroine': *Cymbeline*, ed. Nosworthy, p. lxii.

'Should not the smoke . . . heavens?': Bernard Harris, '*Cymbeline* and *Henry VIII*', in John Russell Brown and Bernard Harris, eds., *Later Shakespeare* (Stratford-upon-Avon Studies 8) (London: Arnold, 1966), p. 228. Cf. the sacrifice described in Seneca's *Oedipus*, ll. 310–28 (tr. Alexander Neville in 1563 and later reprinted in revised form in *Seneca his Tenne Tragedies*, ed. Thomas Newton, 1581).

'chromatic tunes': See Peter Warlock, *The English Ayre* (London: Oxford University Press, 1926), p. 57. 'Chromatic tunes' is a phrase from a poem set by John Danyel. Warlock analyses the chromaticism of Danyel's setting on pp. 58–61.

'false relation': False relation is one of the key-themes in *Cymbeline*, implying false conjunction and false report. For a description of false relation in Jacobean music, see the essay by Wilfrid Mellers in Boris Ford, ed., *The Age of Shakespeare* (Harmondsworth: Penguin, 1956), p. 394.

Vncertaine certaine...dying last: John Danyel, *Songs for the Lute Viol and Voice* (London, 1606), H ii recto.

'aims at effecting...surprise': Harold S. Wilson, '*Philaster* and *Cymbeline*', in Alan S. Downer, ed., *English Institute Essays 1951* (New York: Columbia University Press, 1952), p. 162.

'the real...compromised': William, '*The Tempest* on the Stage', p. 135.

Cymbeline...'enchanted ground': *Cymbeline*, ed. Nosworthy, p. xlviii.

drenched in flesh...conuersant: Bacon, *Advancement of Learning*, p. 107.

'taste well': Bacon, *Advancement of Learning*, p. 107.

5. Jonathan Swift: the Poetry of 'Reaction'

That he was not 'mad'...authority: Irvin Ehrenpreis, *The Personality of Jonathan Swift* (London: Methuen, 1958), pp. 117–26.

Swift read...Hobbes: Harold Williams, *Dean Swift's Library* (Cambridge: The University Press, 1932), p. 54 and appendix, p. 15.

Sir William Temple...his pupil: Irvin Ehrenpreis, *Swift: The Man, his Works, and the Age*, 3 vols. (London: Methuen, 1962–83), vol. 1, p. 98.

'more than the "great Ministers" had gone': W. B. Yeats, *Explorations* (London: Macmillan, 1962), p. 358.

'occupied so much...leisure': *The Poems of Jonathan Swift*, ed. Harold Williams, 2nd edn., 3 vols. (Oxford: Oxford University Press, 1958), p. 965.

When I saw...your letters: 'The Dean to Tho: Sheridan', 1718. *Poems*, p. 978.

I was t'other day...twenty years past: *The Correspondence of Jonathan Swift*, ed. Harold Williams, 5 vols. (Oxford: Oxford University Press, 1963–5), vol. 5, p. 271.

'taking his ease at the Castle': Ricardo Quintana, *Swift: An Introduction* (London: Oxford University Press, 1955), p. 11.

Swift has been called...wrote': Yeats, *Explorations*, p. 354.

Dr Johnson...Dean of St Patrick's: Samuel Johnson, *The Lives of the Most Eminent English Poets*, ed. Roger Lonsdale, 4 vols. (Oxford: Oxford University Press, 2006), vol. 3, p. 209.

It has been remarked...his life': Ehrenpreis, *Swift: The Man*, vol. 1, pp. 71, 77.

Ireland's ruling caste...population': William Edward Hartpole Lecky, *History of England in the Eighteenth Century*, 3rd edn., 8 vols. (London: Longmans, Green, 1883), vol. 2, p. 221.

When to my House...Parlor Door: *Poems*, p. 1045.

Sheridan's description . . . reciprocating talent: In making this assertion one is obliged to acknowledge, though not to overestimate, Swift's reference to Sheridan's 'bad Verses' (*Correspondence*, vol. 2, p. 307). He had recently been annoyed by the tone of Sheridan's 'The Funeral'.

so successful . . . the other: F. Elrington Ball, *Swift's Verse* (London: J. Murray, 1929), p. 244.

Swift . . . by heart: Though this may be mythical. For a discussion of Swift in relation to Butler see Clarence L. Kulisheck, 'Swift's Octosyllabics and the Hudibrastic Tradition', *Journal of English and Germanic Philology*, vol. 53 (1954), pp. 361–8.

Swift's library . . . often associated: Williams, *Swift's Library*, p. 76: *Paradise Lost*, noted 1715; missing 1745.

'never was one of his Admirers': *The Prose Works of Jonathan Swift*, ed. Herbert Davis, 16 vols. (Oxford: Blackwell, 1939–74), vol. 4, p. 274.

'agony and indignation': *Poems by John Wilmot, Earl of Rochester*, ed. Vivian de Sola Pinto, 2nd edn. (London: Routledge, 1964), p. xxix.

With mouth . . . those two!: *The Works of John Wilmot Earl of Rochester*, ed. Harold Love (Oxford: Oxford University Press, 1999), p. 52 ('Tunbridge Wells', ll. 110–19).

'Stand further . . . Matadore: Swift, 'The Journal of a Modern Lady', 1729. *Poems*, p. 452.

My female Friends . . . *Trumps?*)': 'Verses on the Death of Dr. Swift', 1731. *Poems*, p. 562.

'The Dean . . . the Knave: *Poems*, p. 565.

It is known . . . the description': Henry Craik, *The Life of Jonathan Swift*, 2nd edn., 2 vols. (London: Macmillan, 1894), vol. 1, p. 175; cf. *Poems*, pp. 88–90.

Nor do they trust . . . the Man: *Poems*, p. 450.

'embarrassed . . . situation': *Poems*, p. 684: editorial note.

She railly'd well . . . *a Bite*: *Poems*, pp. 707–8.

You must ask . . . a *bite*': *Correspondence*, vol. 1, p. 40.

The somewhat complex question . . . discussion: See, e.g. A. O. Aldridge, 'Shaftesbury and the Test of Truth', *PMLA*, vol. 60 (1945), pp. 129–56; Peter Dixon, 'Talking Upon Paper', *English Studies*, vol. 46, no. 1 (Feb. 1965), pp. 36–44.

'ironical praise . . . addressed to': Dixon, 'Talking Upon Paper', p. 38. His sources are Steele and Swift. Cf. Swift, *Prose Works*, ed. Davis, vol. 4, p. 91.

So, the pert Dunces . . . Ale: 'To Mr. Delany', 1718. *Poems*, p. 216.

When Swift . . . Raillery': *Poems*, p. 890 n.

His own poem 'The Journal' . . . friends: *Poems*, p. 277.

It may seem that infringements . . . skill: See *Correspondence*, vol. 5, p. 269, Appendix XXIX, for a fine 'free fall' demonstration of raillery of the second type: Swift to Lord Charlemont.

In a letter . . . among us': *Correspondence*, vol. 5, p. 7.

Swift had a tendency to count heads: *Correspondence*, vol. 5, p. 270, Appendix XXX, 'Swift's Friends Classed by their Characters'.

For in your publick . . . to morrow: *Correspondence*, vol. 2, pp. 44–5.

Defeat restores . . . isolation: For a fuller discussion of this theme see Ronald Paulson, 'Swift, Stella and Permanence', *ELH*, vol. 27 (1960), pp. 298–314.

Although critics . . . mature verse: e.g. Herbert Davis, *Jonathan Swift* (New York: Oxford University Press, 1964), pp. 171–2. Davis's argument, originally published in 1931, that Temple's influence distorted Swift's 'natural bent' and that the Pindarics are a temporary diversion rather than a false start, is a suggestive one. It is necessarily qualified by later debate and research into the authorship of doubtful poems in the Christie Book and *The Whimsical Medley*.

Swift's attitude . . . ambiguous: As a 'practical politician' Swift took a shrewd view of the usefulness of anarchy; e.g. *Correspondence*, vol. 2, p. 113: 'I have been long afraid that we were losing the Rabble' (to Charles Ford, 7 August 1714); *Correspondence*, vol. 2, p. 131: 'If any thing witholds the Whigs from the utmost Violence, it will be onely the fear of provoking the Rabble' (to Charles Ford, 27 September 1714).

so-called 'ungenerous' . . . invective: Editorial commentary, *Poems*, pp. 296, 82. Charles Peake, 'Swift's *Satirical Elegy on a Late Famous General*', *REL*, vol. 3 (1962), pp. 80–9, vindicates Swift's method.

KEEPER . . . duly: *Poems*, p. 835.

'uncontrolled outburst': Williams in *Poems*, p. xvi.

Bless us, *Morgan* . . . Pity: *Poems*, p. 837.

The magisterial tone . . . pasturage-tithes: Louis A. Landa, *Swift and the Church of Ireland* (Oxford: Clarendon Press, 1954), p. 135 ff.

It has been said . . . contemporaries': Maurice O. Johnson, *The Sin of Wit: Jonathan Swift as a Poet* (Syracuse, NY: Syracuse University Press, 1950), p. 117.

Attention has been drawn . . . Le Sage: Ehrenpreis, *Personality of Swift*, 43–8.

'On a F[ar]t Let in the House of Commons': Formerly attributed to Prior, but rejected by H. Bunker Wright and Monroe K. Spears, eds., *The Literary Works of Matthew Prior* (Oxford: Clarendon Press, 1959), vol. 2, p. 791. Apparently of mid-seventeenth-century origin.

At last . . . his Ear.): Prior, *Literary Works*, vol. 1, p. 264: 'Paulo Purganti and His Wife'.

My Lord . . . the Flames: 'The Problem', 1699. *Poems*, p. 66.

He found . . . her Face: *Poems*, p. 589.

The catharsis . . . exclamation': Johnson, *The Sin of Wit*, p. 112.

the real importance . . . '*mortal*': See Kathleen Williams, *Jonathan Swift and the Age of Compromise* (Lawrence, KS: University Press of Kansas, 1968), p. 148–53. See also Kathleen M. Williams, ' "Animal Rationis Capax": A Study of Certain Aspects of Swift's Imagery', *ELH*, vol. 21, no. 3 (1954), pp. 193–207.

On Sense and Wit . . . round: *Poems*, p. 593.

'mad, maddened refrain': D. H. Lawrence, *Selected Poems*, ed. Mara Kalnins (London: Dent, 1992), p. 288 (introduction to *Pansies*, 1929).

'the complainants' . . . subjects': Ehrenpreis, *Personality of Swift*, p. 43.

Yet, some Devotion . . . a Thorn: *Poems*, p. 896.

'Perfectly calculated': The phrase happens to be taken from Ricardo Quintana's *Swift: An Introduction*, p. 142. I quote it quite out of context, and it should be read here simply as a representative phrase. I am not trying to short-circuit Quintana's discussion.

The Nymph . . . poison'd: 'A Beautiful Young Nymph Going to Bed', *Poems*, p. 583.

'gnashing insanity': Lawrence, *Selected Poems*, p. 288 (introduction to *Pansies*, 1929).

Johnson . . . remarks . . . affectation': *Johnson on the English Language*, ed. Gwin J. Kolb and Robert DeMaria (New Haven, CT: Yale University Press, 2005), p. 105 (vol. 18 of *The Yale Edition of the Works of Samuel Johnson*).

One recalls . . . 'the ruin to come': Yeats, *Explorations*, p. 350.

Of 'more-pow'r' . . . woman': See Johnson, *The Sin of Wit*, pp. 26–7.

Yes, says the *Steward* . . . all to naught: *Poems*, p. 71.

such as the anonymous 'South Sea Ballad' of 1720: See *Roxburghe Ballads*, vol. 8, part 1 (1897), p. 256.

Swift's Pindaric 'aberration': Ball, *Swift's Verse*, p. 16.

And so say I . . . be civil: 'Mary the Cook-Maid's Letter', 1718. *Poems*, p. 986.

He braced . . . possessed: Lecky, *History of England in the Eighteenth Century*, vol. 2, p. 427.

And thus . . . Buffoonery: *Sensus Communis: An Essay on the Freedom of Wit and Humour* (1709), vol. 1, p. iv; cf. *Characteristicks of Men, Manners, Opinions, Times*, ed. Philip J. Ayres (Oxford: Clarendon Press, 1999), vol. 1, p. 43. See also W. K. Wimsatt, ed., *English Stage Comedy* (New York: Columbia University Press, 1955), p. 5.

6. Redeeming the Time

The smaller . . . possibility: Iris Murdoch, *Sartre: Romantic Rationalist* (London: Bowes & Bowes, 1961), p. 29.

One looks nervously . . . deceived itself: It will be objected that the French experience of the nineteenth century was in many ways different from that of British society. I agree. However, Iris Murdoch's discussion (pp. 26 ff.) places the topic in a general European context of the nineteenth and twentieth centuries. Joyce, Conrad, Woolf, and I. A. Richards are named together with Rimbaud, Mallarmé, Proust, and Sartre.

Henry Adams . . . silence is best': Adams, *The Degradation of the Democratic Dogma* (New York: Capricorn Books, 1958), p. 131.

E. P. Thompson . . . denunciation': Thompson, *The Making of the English Working Class* (Harmondsworth: Penguin, 1968), p. 682 (first pub. 1963).

R. H. Tawney . . . collapsed': Tawney, preface to *Life and Struggles of William Lovett* (London: McGibbon & Kee, 1967), p. xiv (first published 1876).

'involve a wedding . . . attitudes': Charles L. Stevenson, *Ethics and Language* (New Haven, CT: Yale University Press, 1960), p. 210.

by the use ... Newton: Theodore Redpath, 'John Locke and the Rhetoric of the Second Treatise', in Hugh Sykes Davies and George Watson, eds., *The English Mind: Studies in the English Moralists Presented to Basil Willey* (Cambridge: Cambridge University Press, 1964), p. 69.

Here I stand ... THE BILL: Quoted in Cecil Driver, *Tory Radical: The Life of Richard Oastler* (New York: Oxford University Press, 1946), p. 197.

the striking change ... doubt: Ibid.

England has been described ... society: Frederick Engels, *The Condition of the Working Class in England* (London: Granada, 1969), p. 37.

It is true ... the winds: Quoted in Thompson, *The Making of the English Working Class*, p. 586.

canting locution 'polished': See *Boswell's Life of Johnson*, ed. George Birkbeck Hill, rev. L. F. Powell, 6 vols. (Oxford: Clarendon Press, 1971), vol. 1, p. 390: 'But in more polished times there are people to do everything for money' (16 May 1763). Cf. *The Journal of the Rev. John Wesley, A. M.*, ed. Nehemiah Curnock, 8 vols. (London: R. Culley, 1909–16), vol. 1, p. 238: 'the Choctaws, the least polished, that is, the least corrupted, of all the Indian nations' (30 June 1736).

Oastler is not 'compelling' but compelled: See Driver, *Tory Radical*, 197.

Heavy as frost ... doth live: William Wordsworth, *Poems*, ed. John O. Hayden, 2 vols. (New Haven, CT: Yale University Press, 1981), vol. 1, p. 527; cf. William Wordsworth, *Poems in Two Volumes, and Other Poems, 1800–1807*, ed. Jared Curtis (Ithaca, NY: Cornell University Press, 1983), p. 275.

It has been pointed out ... iambic': George Saintsbury, *Historical Manual of English Prosody* (London: Macmillan, 1910), p. 200 n. 1.

'broken-backed': Colin Campbell Clarke, *Romantic Paradox: An Essay on the Poetry of Wordsworth* (London: Routledge & Kegan Paul, 1962), p. 88.

There have been ... embers'): *The Correspondence of Gerard Manley Hopkins and Richard Watson Dixon*, ed. Claude Colleer Abbott (London: Oxford University Press, 1935), pp. 147–8.

Writers on linguistics ... silence.': Seymour Chatman, 'Robert Frost's "Mowing": An Inquiry into Prosodic Structure', *The Kenyon Review*, vol. 18 (1956), p. 422.

But Adam's thoughts ... could have done: George Eliot, *Adam Bede*, ed. John Paterson (Boston: Houghton Mifflin, 1968), p. 170.

'the speech of the landscape': George Eliot, *Impressions of Theophrastus Such*, ed. Nancy Henry (Iowa City, IA: University of Iowa Press, 1994), p. 24.

'affectionate joy ... language': Ibid., p. 22.

'fat central England': Ibid., p. 30.

But I come back ... people's side: *Essays of George Eliot*, ed. Thomas Pinney (London: Routledge and Kegan Paul, 1963), pp. 421–3.

An early critic ... Tory-Democrat': Joseph Jacobs (1895); quoted in *Essays of George Eliot*, ed. Pinney, p. 415.

On 28 January 1810 ... Thomas Poole: *Collected Letters of Samuel Taylor Coleridge*, ed. Earl Leslie Griggs, 6 vols. (Oxford: Clarendon Press, 1956–71), vol. 3, p. 281.

'fixities ... association': *The Collected Works of Samuel Taylor Coleridge*, 16 vols. (Princeton, NJ: Princeton University Press, 1969–2002), vol. 7, part 1, p. 305 (*Biographia Literaria*, ed. James Engell and W. Jackson Bate, 2 parts).

Of Parentheses ... Hortus siccus: *Collected Letters of Coleridge*, vol. 3, p. 282.

For one ... end': Arthur Symons, introduction to *Biographia Literaria*, Everyman edn. (London: J. M. Dent, 1906), p. xi.

'moral copula' ... fatalism': Coleridge, *Collected Works*, vol. 14, part 1, p. 249 (*Table Talk*, ed. Carl Woodring, 2 parts; 11 Sept. 1831); cf. vol. 14, part 1, p. 148 (12 Sept. 1831).

For if words ... humanized: Coleridge, *Collected Works*, vol. 9, p. 10 (*Aids to Reflection*, ed. John Beer).

On some future ... watch-words: Coleridge, *Collected Works*, vol. 7, part 2, p. 143 (*Biographia Literaria*).

'detestable': Coleridge, *Collected Works*, vol. 14, part 1, p. 418 (*Table Talk*; 14 Aug. 1833); cf. vol. 14, part 2, p. 249 (15 Aug. 1833).

The architecture ... economy: *Autobiography of Edward Gibbon as originally edited by Lord Sheffield* (London: Oxford University Press, 1950), pp. 143–4.

By fencing ... prejudice: Ibid., p. 80.

'tendentious ... image': See Redpath, 'John Locke and the Rhetoric of the Second Treatise', pp. 55, 69.

[Chesterfield is] ... wit: Oliver Elton, *A Survey of English Literature: 1730–1780*, 2 vols. (London: E. Arnold, 1928), vol. 1, p. 9.

'words in the best order': Coleridge, *Collected Works*, vol. 14, part 1, p. 90 (*Table Talk*; 25–6 Aug. 1827); cf. vol. 14, part 2, p. 68 (12 July 1827).

'Good Sense': Ibid., vol. 14, part 1, p. 122 (7 May 1830); cf. vol. 14, part 2, p. 85 (9 May 1830).

'very plain language': Ibid., vol. 14, part 1, p. 154 (4 June 1830); cf. vol. 14, part 2, p. 102 (31 May 1830).

'thro' ... words ... general': *Collected Letters of Coleridge*, vol. 3, p. 281.

[Newman's] ... at all: J. M. Cameron, *The Night Battle: Essays* (London: Burns & Oates, 1962), p. 204.

These comments ... Anglican period: Ibid., p. 203.

The structure ... undergoing: Walter E. Houghton, *The Art of Newman's 'Apologia'* (New Haven, CT: Yale University Press, 1945), pp. 51–2. The two sentences under discussion are from pp. 260–1 of the 1913 edition of Newman's work.

John Beer ... arguments': Beer, 'Newman and the Romantic Sensibility', in Davies and Watson, eds., *The English Mind*, p. 215.

I shall endeavor ... done my best: *Collected Letters of Coleridge*, vol. 3, p. 282.

If I may dare ... endure': Coleridge, *Collected Works*, vol. 7, part 1, p. 88 (*Biographia Literaria*).

All that metaphysical . . . common sense: Coleridge, *Collected Works*, vol. 14, part 1, p. 492 (*Table Talk*; 28 June 1834); cf. vol. 14, part 2, p. 293 (28 June 1834).

Mr Roebuck . . . themselves: *The Complete Prose Works of Matthew Arnold*, ed. R. H. Super, 11 vols. (Ann Arbor, MI: University of Michigan Press, 1960–77), vol. 3, p. 274 (*Lectures and Essays in Criticism*).

has any one . . . poor thing!: Ibid., p. 273.

'the superfluous Christian name': Ibid., p. 274.

In 1836 . . . Barraclough!': See C. Aspin, *Lancashire: The First Industrial Society* (Rossendale: Helmshore Local History Society, 1969), p. 117.

Plainly . . . intelligible: *The Letters of Gerard Manley Hopkins to Robert Bridges*, ed. Claude Colleer Abbott (London: Oxford University Press, 1935), pp. 265–6.

Hopkins wrote . . . business': Ibid., p. 284.

'jaded': Ibid., p. 201.

In 1832 . . . the reader': Quoted by Noel Annan, 'John Stuart Mill', in Davies and Watson eds., *The English Mind*, p. 233.

men who speak . . . Sherry: William Wordsworth, *Poems*, vol. 1, p. 879 (Preface to *Lyrical Ballads*, 1802). Cf. *The Prose Works of William Wordsworth*, ed. W. J. B. Owen and Jane Worthington Smyser, 3 vols. (Oxford: Clarendon Press, 1974), vol. 1, p. 139; and William Wordsworth, *Lyrical Ballads and Other Poems, 1797–1800*, ed. James Butler and Karen Green (Ithaca, NY: Cornell University Press, 1992), p. 751.

Mrs Transome . . . ring hollow: George Eliot, *Felix Holt, the Radical*, ed. F. C. Thomson (Oxford: Clarendon Press, 1980), p. 27.

It is, in fact . . . artisans: Andrew Ure, *The Philosophy of Manufactures or, an Exposition of the Scientific, Moral, and Commercial Economy of the Factory System of Great Britain* (London: C. Knight, 1835), p. 23, quoted in Thompson, *The Making of the English Working Class*, p. 396 n. 1.

'a particle . . . alternative': *OED²*, s.v. 'or'.

I cannot express . . . moment: Quoted in F. M. Leventhal, *Respectable Radical: George Howell and Victorian Working Class Politics* (Cambridge, MA: Harvard University Press, 1971), p. 11.

How strange . . . luxury: Huddersfield Committee pamphlet 'Humanity against Tyranny', quoted in Driver, *Tory Radical*, p. 106.

a light that ought . . . world: In *Aids to Reflection*, Coleridge quotes John 1: 9 to describe 'Reason . . . the Power distinctive of Humanity . . . "the Light that lighteth every man" '; see Coleridge, *Collected Works*, vol. 9, p. 235.

F. M. Leventhal . . . status: Leventhal, *Respectable Radical*, p. 12.

Hopkins wrote . . . speech': Hopkins, *Letters to Bridges*, p. 46.

If asked . . . organic time': Hans Meyerhoff, *Time in Literature* (Berkeley, CA: University of California Press, 1955), p. 107; Daniel D. Pearlman, *The Barb of Time* (New York: Oxford University Press, 1969), p. 22.

It is as though . . . cannot: I consider my point to be justified even though the first 11½ lines of the 20-line poem concern working and belonging. What is the key-note of this belonging?—'Little I reck ho!' (l. 9). Tom, in work, may be heedlessly happy but I cannot believe that Hopkins regarded this state as ideal. Little recking could so easily turn to great wrecking (cf. *Letters to Bridges*, pp. 27–8). The verbal texture is lumpy, not sinewy.

'the achieve of, the mastery of the thing': Hopkins, 'The Windhover', l. 8.

'the jading and jar of the cart': Hopkins, *The Wreck of the Deutschland*, stanza 27, l. 2.

In the contemporary . . . end came: Reprinted in the appendix to *Immortal Diamond*, ed. Norman Weyand and Raymond V. Schoder (London: Sheed & Ward, 1949).

A man or a womman . . . OUTE: *The Cloud of Unknowing*, ed. Phyllis Hodgson (London: Oxford University Press, 1958), p. 74 (first pub. 1944). Quoted in modernized form by David Knowles, *The English Mystical Tradition* (London: Burns & Oates, 1961), p. 97: 'A man or a woman, affrighted by any sudden chance of fire, or of a man's death, or whatever else it be, suddenly in the height of his spirit he is driven in haste and in need to cry or to pray for help. Yea, how? Surely not in many words, nor yet in one word of two syllables. And why is that? Because he thinketh it over long tarrying, for to declare the need and the work of his spirit. And therefore he bursteth up hideously with a great spirit, and cryeth but one little word of one syllable: such as is this word FIRE or this word OUT'.

Helen Gardner . . . 'nakid beyng of him': Gardner, in *Essays and Studies*, vol. 22 (1937), p. 106.

Hopkins describes . . . always intoned: *Further Letters of Gerard Manley Hopkins including his Correspondence with Coventry Patmore*, ed. Claude Colleer Abbott, 2nd edn. (London: Oxford University Press, 1956), p. 114.

'manner of utterance . . . speaking': *OED²*, s.v. 'intonation'.

'that unfortunate intonation of Aberdeenshire': Thomas Newte, *A Tour in England and Scotland in 1785* (1791), cited in *OED²*, s.v. 'intonation'.

'An "intonation pattern" . . . phrase.': Chatman, 'Robert Frost's "Mowing" ', p. 422.

'The opening phrase . . . choristers.': *OED²*, s.v. 'intonation'.

In 1859 . . . mankind': *The George Eliot Letters*, ed. Gordon S. Haight, 9 vols. (New Haven, CT: Yale University Press, 1954–78), vol. 3, p. 231.

The medieval . . . England: Quoted in Alfred Thomas, *Hopkins the Jesuit* (London: Oxford University Press, 1969), p. 7 n. 1.

I am surprised . . . Catholicism: *Further Letters of Hopkins*, 93.

Michael Trappes-Lomax . . . stables': Trappes-Lomax, *Pugin: A Mediaeval Victorian* (London: Sheed & Ward, 1932), p. 55.

he complained that . . . Lincoln races': Quoted in Denis Gwynn, *Lord Shrewsbury, Pugin and the Catholic Revival* (London: Hollis and Carter, 1946), p. 15.

Walter J. Ong . . . around him?: Ong, in Weyand and Schoder, eds., *Immortal Diamond*, pp. 100–1.

When D. P. McGuire . . . modern life': Quoted in W. H. Gardner, *Gerard Manley Hopkins: A Study of Poetic Idiosyncrasy in Relation to Poetic Tradition*, 2 vols. (London: M. Secker and Warburg, 1944–9), vol. 2, p. 371.

'We lash ... last!': 'The Wreck of the Deutschland', stanza 8, ll. 2–3.

'christens her wild-worst Best': 'The Wreck of the Deutschland', stanza 24, l. 85.

the Corpus Christi procession: Hopkins, *Letters to Bridges*, p. 149: 'the procession ... represents the process of the Incarnation and the world's redemption'.

In the death-cry ... sacrifice: See E. Margaret Thompson, *The Carthusian Order in England* (London: SPCK, 1930), p. 400.

The copy ... '*Martyrium*': Evelyn Waugh, *Edmund Campion*, 2nd edn. (London: Hollis and Carter, 1947), p. 55. Waugh attributes the French phrase to Canon Didiot.

'ah! bright wings': 'God's Grandeur', l. 14.

'ah my dear': 'The Windhover', l. 13.

' "Some find me ... on drum': Hopkins, *The Wreck of the Deutschland*, stanza 11, ll. 1–3.

'They fought with God's cold—': Ibid., stanza 17, l. 1.

'And wears ... man's smell': Hopkins, 'God's Grandeur', l. 7.

'I did say yes': Hopkins, *The Wreck of the Deutschland*, stanza 2, l. 1.

'Christ, King, Head': Ibid., stanza 28, l. 5.

Extremes meet ... of mine: Hopkins, *Letters to Bridges*, p. 157.

'you cannot eat ... difference': Ibid.

The only good ... voice: Ibid., p. 280.

'recurb' and 'recovery': 'The Wreck of the Deutschland', stanza 32, l. 3.

Hopkins wrote ... enjoyment: Donald Davie, 'Hopkins as a Decadent Critic', in *Purity of Diction in English Verse* (London: Chatto & Windus, 1952), p. 171. I am aware that the *OED* allows, as early as 1631, the use of 'jaded' to suggest 'dull or sated by continual use or indulgence'. But Hopkins, in the *Letters to Bridges*, speaks of his 'life ... of a continually jaded and harassed mind' (221); he writes that he is 'always jaded, I cannot tell why, and my vein shews no signs of ever flowing again' (178); and also refers to his 'flagging and almost spent powers' (170). Matthew Arnold writes of his brother William who died, aged 31, worn out with service in India, as 'jaded' (see 'The Southern Night', l. 58). Milton, in the *Ludlow Mask* of 1634, has Comus, at his most speciously suasive, speak of delights 'to please, and sate the curious taste'. (On pleasures exempt from satiety, see *The Yale Edition of the Works of Samuel Johnson* (New Haven, CT: Yale University Press, 1958–), vol. 2, p. 191 and A. E. Housman, *Collected Poems and Selected Prose*, ed. Christopher Ricks (London: Penguin Books, 1988), p. 274.) I suggest that Arnold and Milton use each word with particular justice, and that to turn one of Hopkins's words against himself, to make him appear like a Victorian Comus, is less than just.

7. 'Perplexed Persistence': The Exemplary Failure of T. H. Green

'his value ... self-contradictory': *Works of Thomas Hill Green*, ed. R. L. Nettleship, 3 vols. (London: Longmans, Green, 1888), vol. 3, p. 104.

'sent ... Truth': Bernard M. G. Reardon, *From Coleridge to Gore: A Century of Religious Thought in Britain* (London: Longman, 1971), p. 305: quoting Henry Scott Holland.

'He would not ... 'but it is true': Green, *Works*, vol. 3, p. clxi.

'Abstract ... nothing': T. H. Green, *Prolegomena to Ethics*, ed. A. C. Bradley, 5th edn. (Oxford: Clarendon Press 1929), p. 33 (1st edn. 1883; 5th edn. 1907).

'true philosophic ... what he is': Green, *Works*, vol. 3, pp. 116–17.

'concrete experience': Green, *Prolegomena to Ethics*, p. 19; I. A. Richards, *Principles of Literary Criticism* (London: Routledge, 2001), p. 71: 'concrete experiences' (first pub. 1924).

'content ... principles': Ibid., vol. 3, p. 104.

'Man reads ... things': Ibid.

'unconditionally ... world': Henry Sidgwick, *Outlines of the History of Ethics*, 5th edn. (London: Macmillan, 1902), pp. 272, 276 (first pub. 1886). The phrases are from Sidgwick's paraphrase and discussion of Kant's philosophy.

the ineluctable fact: I wish to acknowledge my indebtedness, here and elsewhere in this chapter, to D. M. MacKinnon, *A Study in Ethical Theory* (London: A. & C. Black, 1957).

'sways & oscillates' ... *Belief*': *The Collected Works of Samuel Taylor Coleridge*, 16 vols. (Princeton, NJ: Princeton University Press, 1969–2002), vol. 12, part 2, p. 266 (*Marginalia*, ed. George Whalley, 6 parts).

In *Prolegomena* ... as a whole': Green, *Prolegomena*, p. 81.

He further contends ... political life': Ibid., p. 105.

'Thus the "Treatise ... the new': Green, *Works*, vol. 1, p. 3.

'every explanation ... metaphor': Ibid., vol. 3, p. 82.

to which Whitehead draws attention: Alfred North Whitehead, *Symbolism* (London: Cambridge University Press, 1928). The quoted phrases are from pp. 86–7.

'We hold ... allies': *Mill on Bentham and Coleridge*, ed. F. R. Leavis (London: Chatto and Windus, 1971), p. 140 (Mill's essays were first published in 1838 and 1840; Leavis's edn. in 1950).

'call for ... other classes': Alfred Marshall, *Principles of Economics*, 7th edn. (London: Macmillan, 1916), p. 45 (first pub. 1890).

'the language of ethics' ... despot': MacKinnon, *A Study in Ethical Theory*, pp. 185, 65.

'the chasm ... object': John H. Muirhead, *Coleridge as Philosopher* (London: G. Allen & Unwin, 1930), p. 93.

'when every ... language': Green, *Works*, vol. 3, p. 475.

'compound ... healthy-mindedness': Quoted in Melvin Richter, *The Politics of Conscience: T. H. Green and His Age* (London: Weidenfeld and Nicolson, 1964), p. 44.

He deplored, in *Prolegomena* ... chance': Green, *Prolegomena*, p. 288.

'Green . . . with it': H. J. Laski, *The Decline of Liberalism* (London: Oxford University Press, 1940), p. 11 (*L. T. Hobhouse Memorial Trust Lectures*, no. 10).

'one of . . . English literature': *The Complete Prose Works of Matthew Arnold*, ed. R. H. Super, 11 vols. (Ann Arbor, MI: University of Michigan Press, 1960–77), vol. 3, p. 267 ('The Function of Criticism at the Present Time').

'the civilising arts of life': *The Collected Writings of John Maynard Keynes*, 30 vols. (London: Macmillan, 1971–89), vol. 28, p. 368.

'the best . . . grammar': P. T. Forsyth, *Religion in Recent Art* (Manchester: Abel Heywood & Son, 1889), p. 231.

'Oh, how I sympathise . . . criticism': A. and E. M. S[idgwick], *Henry Sidgwick: A Memoir* (London: Macmillan, 1906), p. 177.

'points beyond . . . formal implication': Meyrick Heath Carré, *Phases of Thought in England* (Oxford: Clarendon Press, 1949), p. 368.

which Whitehead has so precisely described: Whitehead, *Symbolism*, p. 88.

' "*Bona fide* . . . interest': *Prolegomena*, p. 403 n. 1.

'Wordsworthian sentiment . . . principle': Richter, *The Politics of Conscience*, pp. 47–8.

Green described . . . poetry': Green, *Works*, vol. 3, p. xviii.

In England . . . really: Ibid., p. 118.

'I like' and 'I don't like': Ibid.

'The natural . . . man': Ibid., p. 119.

'the fixed . . . view': A. C. Bradley, *Oxford Lectures on Poetry*, 2nd edn. (London: Macmillan, 1909), p. 131.

'that perplexed . . . question': Ibid., p. 136.

It is evident . . . do not: Ibid., p. 131.

'Perplexed, and longing to be comforted': William Wordsworth, *Poems*, ed. John O. Hayden, 2 vols. (New Haven, CT: Yale University Press, 1981), vol. 1, p. 555 ('Resolution and Independence', l. 117); cf. William Wordsworth, *Poems in Two Volumes, and Other Poems, 1800–1807*, ed. Jared Curtis (Ithaca, NY: Cornell University Press, 1983), p. 128.

'speaks as from . . . perplexed" ': Leslie Stephen, *Studies of a Biographer*, 2nd edn., 2 vols. (London: Duckworth, 1929), vol. 1, p. 248.

'Yet . . . breath': Bradley, *Oxford Lectures on Poetry*, pp. 136–7.

The ethical . . . is: Hastings Rashdall, *The Theory of Good and Evil*, 2 vols. (Oxford: Clarendon Press, 1907), vol. 1, pp. 216–17. The work is dedicated 'To the memory of my teachers Thomas Hill Green and Henry Sidgwick'.

I had . . . melody: Quoted in Richter, *The Politics of Conscience*, p. 162, alluding to Tennyson, *In Memoriam* XCVI ('Perplext in faith, but pure in deeds, | At last he beat his music out').

Richter says . . . inarticulate': Ibid., pp. 80, 158.

'Few . . . said': Green, *Works*, vol. 3, p. lxii.

'with singular clearness . . . time': John H. Muirhead, *Reflections*, ed. John W. Harvey (London: G. Allen & Unwin, 1942), p. 42.

'almost confounding humility': Ibid.

I . . . written word: Quoted in Richter, *The Politics of Conscience*, 14.

'music', 'perplexing', and 'gleam': Cf. 'Lines Composed a Few Miles above Tintern Abbey' ll. 91 ('The still, sad music of humanity'), 60 ('somewhat of a sad perplexity'), and 148–9 ('these gleams | Of past existence').

Coleridge commenced . . . harmonies': Coleridge, *Collected Works*, vol. 4, part 1, p. 14 (*The Friend*, ed. Barbara E. Rooke, 2 vols).

'the charlatanry of common sense': Green, *Works*, vol. 1, p. 168.

'agreeable sensations and reflections': Ibid., vol. 3, p. 98.

'cultivated opinion' as 'confused': Ibid., p. lxxiv.

'wilfulness' and shallowness: Ibid., p. xliv.

In *Prolegomena* . . . thorough': Green, *Prolegomena*, p. 168.

'Shy . . . phrase': William Wordsworth, *The Thirteen-Book Prelude*, ed. Mark L. Reed, 2 vols. (Ithaca, NY: Cornell University Press, 1991), vol. 1, p. 310.

'the oral channel . . . worked': Hugh Sykes Davies and George Watson, eds., *The English Mind: Studies in the English Moralists Presented to Basil Willey* (Cambridge: Cambridge University Press, 1964), p. 183.

'valuable warnings . . . sins': Richard Chenevix Trench, *On the Study of Words*, 6th edn. (London: J. W. Parker and Son, 1855), p. 42 (first pub. 1851).

'how deep . . . many words': Ibid. I am indebted to Austin Warren, *Rage for Order* (Chicago, IL: University of Chicago Press, 1948), pp. 61, 63; to Hugh Kenner, *The Pound Era* (London: Faber, 1975), pp. 102–5; and to an essay by Darcy O'Brien in *New Blackfriars* (October 1972), pp. 466–70.

'there is no alternative . . . their way': *Prolegomena*, p. 419.

'It may . . . resisting': Ibid., p. 117.

'Success . . . before him': Quoted in Richter, *The Politics of Conscience*, p. 150.

'Those . . . *tilth*': Green, *Works*, vol. 3, p. xviii.

' "Swing" . . . in it" ': Ibid., pp. xxxvii–xxxviii.

'came in with Kingsley . . . blasted nonsense': *The Correspondence of Gerard Manley Hopkins and Richard Watson Dixon*, ed. Claude Colleer Abbott (London: Oxford University Press, 1935), p. 74.

had a theory . . . syllogism: Green, *Works*, vol. 3, p. xxxviii.

'locked . . . case': Elisabeth W. Schneider, *The Dragon in the Gate: Studies in the Poetry of G. M. Hopkins* (Berkeley, CA: University of California Press, 1968), p. 35. Subsequent quotations are from pp. 35–6.

'all the *hooks* . . . metaphor': Coleridge, *Collected Works*, vol. 4, part 1, pp. 20–1 (*The Friend*).

'earnestness' . . . energy': Green, *Works*, vol. 3, pp. 353–4.

Though he had . . . all: Ibid., pp. lxiv–lxv.

'unconscious social insolence': Ibid., p. 460.

'assumption of superiority': Coleridge, *Collected Works*, vol. 4, part 2, p. 277 (*The Friend*).

'the characteristic . . . experience': A. J. M. Milne, *The Social Philosophy of English Idealism* (London: Allen and Unwin, 1962), p. 89.

'weakness . . . filled up': Green, *Works*, vol. 3, p. 91.

'signs of the strain . . . values': Richter, *The Politics of Conscience*, p. 201.

Newman wrote . . . arguments': Newman, *An Essay in Aid of a Grammar of Assent*, ed. I. T. Ker (Oxford: Clarendon Press, 1985), p. 266 (first pub. 1870).

'against mere impulse . . . alike': A. and E. M. Sidgwick, *Henry Sidgwick*, p. 243. (H.S. to Roden Noel, 1871).

Sidgwick's 'law . . . flexible': Ibid.

'to enlighten . . . meditation': *Mill on Bentham and Coleridge*, ed. Leavis, p. 99.

'like a good rider . . . horse': Walter Bagehot, *Collected Works*, ed. Norman St John-Stevas, 15 vols. (London: The Economist, [1966]–1986), vol. 1, p. 213 (in the review essay on Shakespeare, first pub. in 1853).

'the dogmatic . . . *dichotomy*': Muirhead, *Coleridge*, p. 83.

as Richter has claimed: Richter, *The Politics of Conscience*, p. 47.

'unfused . . . conspicuous': Green, *Works*, vol. 3, p. 88.

'The account . . . actualised" ': Ibid., p. 76.

'As the poet . . . place': Ibid., p. 90.

'how the moral intelligence gets into poetry': Allen Tate, *Essays of Four Decades* (London: Oxford University Press, 1970), p. 149, quoting and discussing a phrase of Yvor Winters.

'The new students . . . items appear': Carré, *Phases of Thought in England*, p. 367.

'the form . . . data': Ibid., p. 368.

Not as to the sensual . . . sign: Green, *Works*, vol. 3, p. 273.

Shakespeare, Keats, and Tennyson: E.g. ibid., pp. 90, 273–4.

'the indestructible . . . life': A. and E. M. Sidgwick, *Henry Sidgwick*, p. 541: referring to section cxxiv of the poem.

A pioneering study . . . existentially" ': A. Birch Hoyle, *The Teaching of Karl Barth* (London: Student Christian Movement Press, 1930), p. 226. Cf. A. and E. M. Sidgwick, *Henry Sidgwick*, pp. 539–41; D. G. James, *Henry Sidgwick: Science and Faith in Victorian England* (London: Oxford University Press, 1970), pp. 39–41.

She ceased . . . lay: Wordsworth, *Lyrical Ballads and Other Poems, 1797–1800*, ed. James Butler and Karen Green (Ithaca, NY: Cornell University Press, 1992), p. 58 ('The Female Vagrant'). Cf. William Wordsworth, *Poems*, vol. 1, p. 134 ('Guilt and Sorrow').

the consciousness . . . found it: *Philosophical Remains of Richard Lewis Nettleship*, ed. A. C. Bradley, 2nd edn. (London: Macmillan, 1901), p. 132 (first pub. 1897 as *Philosophical Lectures and Remains of Richard Lewis Nettleship*, 2 vols).

'approach philosophy . . . language': Ibid., pp. li–lii n. 2.

'the "I" . . . feeling': Green, *Works*, vol. 3, p. 104.

As has been . . . transmute them: Ibid., p. 72.

For Green . . . developed': Ibid.

'imperfect . . . progressive': Ibid., p. 73.

'implies . . . self ': Ibid., p. 72.

'[Green] . . . self-sacrifice': Holland, quoted in Reardon, *From Coleridge to Gore*, p. 305 n. 2.

He may 'find . . . repentance: *Prolegomena*, p. 108.

'to the significant . . . imagination': Dorothea Krook, *Three Traditions of Moral Thought* (Cambridge: Cambridge University Press, 1959), p. 10.

'From Coleridge . . . lay writers': William Ralph Inge, *The Platonic Tradition in English Religious Thought* (London: Longmans, Green, 1926), p. 95.

'deep seriousness . . . place': Ibid., p. 90.

'when the poet . . . elements': Green, *Works*, vol. 3, p. 45.

his own argument: Ibid., pp. 104–5.

'I could have done . . . did something: MacKinnon, *A Study in Ethical Theory*, p. 129.

'An Answer to Mr. Hodgson': Green, *Works*, vol. 1, pp. 521–41.

The original subscribers . . . four hundred: Coleridge, *Collected Works*, vol. 4, part 2, p. 407 (*The Friend*).

'to direct his remarks . . . clerisy" ': J. R. de J. Jackson, *Method and Imagination in Coleridge's Criticism* (London: Routledge and K. Paul, 1969), p. 32.

'the attention . . . fellow-labourer': Coleridge, *Collected Works*, vol. 4, part 2, p. 21 (*The Friend*).

'abstruse and laboured': Ibid., vol. 2, p. 442.

'passed through . . . rest': Forsyth, *Religion in Recent Art*, p. 189. Forsyth is not here discussing Green, though he knew Green's work. See John H. Rodgers, *The Theology of P. T. Forsyth* (London: Independent Press, 1965), p. 312.

8. What Devil Has Got into John Ransom?

The question . . . contentious: *The Literary Correspondence of Donald Davidson and Allen Tate* ed. J. T. Fain and T. D. Young (Athens, GA: University of Georgia Press, 1974), p. 344.

'It will seem . . . unfriendship': Quoted in Michael O'Brien, *The Idea of the American South 1920–1941* (Baltimore, MD: Johns Hopkins University Press, 1979), p. 134.

To Allen Tate . . . middle age: Allen Tate, *Memories & Essays, Old and New: 1926–1974* (Manchester: Carcanet, 1976), p. 43.

'meaty and flavorsome': *Davidson–Tate Correspondence*, p. 284.

'John . . . indeed': Ibid., p. 104.

'cruelly polite snobbishness': Ibid., p. 322.

'if . . . art': John Crowe Ransom, *The World's Body* (Baton Rouge, LA: Louisiana State University Press, 1968), p. 211.

'it is common . . . argument': Ransom, *The New Criticism* (Norfolk, CT: New Directions, 1941), p. 295.

'argument . . . argument': Ibid.

'a good poem' . . . self ': *The World's Body*, p. 2.

'vocalism' . . . prose': Ransom, *Beating the Bushes: Selected Essays 1941–1970* (New York: New Directions, 1972), pp. 175–6.

'nothing...manoeuvre': *The World's Body*, p. 347.

Allen Tate declared...his poetry': Quoted in Thomas Daniel Young, *Gentleman in a Dustcoat: A Biography of John Crowe Ransom* (Baton Rouge, LA: Louisiana State University Press, 1976), p. 465.

Ransom's definition: *The World's Body*, p. 348.

'wit...detachment': Ibid., p. 3.

'torture of equilibrium': 'The Equilibrists': John Crowe Ransom, *Selected Poems*, 3rd edn. (London: Eyre & Spottiswoode, 1970), p. 85.

'the supreme equilibrist': Miller Williams, *The Poetry of John Crowe Ransom* (New Brunswick, NJ: Rutgers University Press, 1972), p. 20.

'balance...poetry': Ibid., p. 11.

'Eclogue': *Selected Poems*, p. 15.

'Survey of Literature': Ibid., pp. 68–9.

'nervous strain'...moderns': *The New Criticism*, p. 38.

'an intolerable...surface': Tate, *Memories & Essays*, p. 42.

'an intense sympathy'...serenity': Young, *Gentleman in a Dustcoat*, p. 460.

George Eliot's dictum...life': George Eliot, *Felix Holt, the Radical*, ed. Peter Coveney (Harmondsworth: Penguin, 1972), p. 129.

'an act of will'...'attention': *The World's Body*, p. 236; *The New Criticism*, p. 273.

'The plight...desperate': *The World's Body*, p. 253.

'I am an Anglophile...American': Ransom, *God Without Thunder: An Unorthodox Defence of Orthodoxy* (London: G. Howe, 1931), p. 356.

'John...mystery': *Davidson–Tate Correspondence*, p. 312.

'respect...circumference': *Selected Poems*, p. 59.

'Far...center': Ibid., p. 37.

'It...nature': Ibid., p. 66.

'workmanlike...argument': Ibid., p. 152.

'metaphysical...eccentric': *The New Criticism*, p. 190. Cf. Tate's pejorative use of 'eccentric', *Davidson–Tate Correspondence*, p. 140.

'middling ways': *Selected Poems*, p. 58.

'the three careers...center': Robert Buffington, *The Equilibrist: A Study of John Crowe Ransom's Poems, 1916–1963* (Nashville, TN: Vanderbilt University Press, 1967), p. 2.

'keep...separate': Ibid., p. 1.

'the agony of composition': *The World's Body*, p. 348.

'reliance...judgment': *Memories & Essays*, p. 43.

'calm'...'remorseless': Louis D. Rubin, *The Wary Fugitives: Four Poets and the South* (Baton Rouge, LA: Louisiana State University Press, 1978), pp. 14, 49, 55,

'eccentricities...thesis': Graham Hough, in Thomas Daniel Young, ed., *John Crowe Ransom: Critical Essays and a Bibliography* (Baton Rouge, LA: Louisiana State University Press, 1968), pp. 187–9.

the more literal mind: But see Young, *Gentleman in a Dustcoat*, p. 140.

'no art ... faculties': Quoted in Rubin, *Wary Fugitives*, p. 49.

'the rational power ... Spectre.': S. Foster Damon, *A Blake Dictionary* (London: Thames and Hudson, 1973), pp. 380–2.

logic of 'abstraction': Cf. John M. Bradbury, *The Fugitives: A Critical Account* (Chapel Hill, NC: University of North Carolina Press, 1958), p. 129.

'logical structure' ... 'beautiful poem': *The New Criticism*, p. 53.

'natural ... judgments': Young, *Gentleman in a Dustcoat*, p. 437.

'meditative ... effect: *Beating the Bushes*, pp. 175–6.

'remorseless' ... 'ruthless': Rubin, *Wary Fugitives*, pp. 55–6; Ransom, *God Without Thunder*, p. 127.

'we may hardly ... everybody': *The World's Body*, p. 279.

'the kind of poetry ... adult mind': Ibid., p. viii.

'Images ... darkness': Ibid., pp. 116–17.

took Kant as his mentor: Young, *Gentleman in a Dustcoat*, p. 423.

'perpetually disquieted': *God Without Thunder*, p. 304.

'a man ... "situation" ': *Beating the Bushes*, p. 82.

Kant ... mutilation': *God Without Thunder*, p. 304.

'awkward or ... or fix': *OED*², s.v. 'strait, n.'.

The phrase is William Empson's: William Empson, *Complete Poems*, ed. John Haffenden (London: Penguin Books, 2000), p. 53 ('This Last Pain').

The Kenyon Critics: John Crowe Ransom, ed., *Studies in Modern Literature from the Kenyon Review* (Cleveland, OH: World Pub., 1951).

Ransom published ... still critical: Young, ed., *John Crowe Ransom*, p. 243.

Christopher Norris: *William Empson and the Philosophy of Literary Criticism* (London: Athlone Press, 1978), pp. 124, 213 n. 31.

'gestures not of deference': *Selected Poems*, p. 59.

'Our Two Worthies': Ibid., p. 61.

'obstinate intellectual waywardness': Graham Hough, in Young, ed., *John Crowe Ransom*, p. 189.

'beautiful thing': Young, *Gentleman in a Dustcoat*, p. 478.

'academic standing' ... meat': *Davidson–Tate Correspondence*, p. 87.

'seriously concerned ... efforts': Young, *Gentleman in a Dustcoat*, p. 140.

Rubin's suggestion: Rubin, *Wary Fugitives*, p. 280.

His hypothesis ... modernity': *The World's Body*, pp. 11–12.

amiable unpretentiousness ... 'gentleness': Rubin, *Wary Fugitives*, p. 63; Young, *Gentleman in a Dustcoat*, p. 326.

'self-expression' ... feathered': *Davidson–Tate Correspondence*, p. 172.

'two kinds ... philosophical': *The World's Body*, p. 34.

Schopenhauer's 'knowledge without desire': Ibid., p. 45.

'predatory ... interest': Ibid., p. 38.

'pitch of attention': *The New Criticism*, p. 273.

'the groan...sighs': Robert Graves, *Collected Poems: 1914–1947* (London: Cassell, 1948), p. 23: 'Lost Love'.
As Vivienne Koch...structure: Koch, in Young, ed., *John Crowe Ransom*, p. 127.
'Eclogue': For information on the successive versions of this poem I am indebted to Robert Buffington, *The Equilibrist*, pp. 135–6.
'disparity'...'real logic': *The New Criticism*, p. 242.
F. O. Matthiessen suggested...the meaning': Matthiessen, in Young, ed., *John Crowe Ransom*, p. 85.
'consider...conscience': *The World's Body*, p. 91.
'the confusion...density': *The New Criticism*, p. 79.
'Platonic...monsters': *The World's Body*, p. 225.
'good poet': *The New Criticism*, p. 295.
'good poem': *The World's Body*, p. 2.
'beautiful poem': *The New Criticism*, p. 53.
'an absorbing...mania': *The World's Body*, p. 72.
'a simplified...mania': *The New Criticism*, p. 165.
'great...there': Davidson, quoted in Young, *Gentleman in a Dustcoat*, p. 123.
'obligations'...authorship': *The World's Body*, p. xv.
'In this century...story': Rubin, *Wary Fugitives*, p. 356.
'naturalistic rabble': *God Without Thunder*, p. 349.
'aggressions': *The World's Body*, p. 198 n. 1.
'cold fury': *Beating the Bushes*, p. 112.
'Poetic...technique': *The New Criticism*, p. 79.
'ritual...occasions': Ibid., p. 205.
'It is not...thing.': *The World's Body*, p. 59.
Allen Tate...popular vote': Tate, *Essays of Four Decades* (London: Oxford University Press, 1970), p. 466.
'kind of obliquity': *The World's Body*, p. 32.
'We are creatures...features': *God Without Thunder*, p. 303.
Modern poetry, Tate said...languages': *Davidson-Tate Correspondence*, p. 140.
'shaken'...not as a leaf': *Selected Poems*, p. 125.
Ransom's critics: e.g. Young, *Gentleman in a Dustcoat*, pp. 375–7.
'objectionable...staple': *The New Criticism*, p. 253.
'were agreed...evidences': Ibid., p. 99.
'nature still waits...contingent': *God Without Thunder*, p. 153.
'things...materiality: *The World's Body*, p. 116.
'the world...objects': Ibid., p. 123.
'the vast...contingency': *Beating the Bushes*, p. 107.
'the stubborn...world': *God Without Thunder*, p. 255.
'marvelling...substance': *The World's Body*, p. 142.
'the denser...world': *The New Criticism*, p. 281.
'ontological...poets': Ibid., p. 335.
'stubborn substance': *Beating the Bushes*, p. 61.

'dense natural context': Ibid., p. 109.

F. P. Jarvis ... critical theory: In Young, ed., *John Crowe Ransom*, pp. 206–9.

Bradley embodied ... fact': A. C. Bradley, *Oxford Lectures on Poetry*, 2nd edn. (London, 1909), p. 71.

in a late essay: *Beating the Bushes*, p. 172.

'self-division ... good': Bradley, *Oxford Lectures on Poetry*, p. 71.

Ransom argues here ... so irreconcilable': Quoted in Young, *Gentleman in a Dust-coat*, p. 89.

'[Poetry's] nature ... autonomous': Bradley, *Oxford Lectures on Poetry*, p. 5.

'the artist ... not real': *The World's Body*, p. 198.

'As science ... body': Ibid.

'sly analogy' ... language': *The New Criticism*, p. 79.

'A poem' ... world.': *Beating the Bushes*, p. 75.

Ransom once ... metaphors': *The World's Body*, p. 137.

in one of his last essays: *Beating the Bushes*, p. 174.

'majesty ... contingency': *God Without Thunder*, pp. 333–4.

'Figures ... course': *The World's Body*, p. 133.

'Why ... were': *Selected Poems*, p. 4.

'And ... Remember': Ibid., p. 18.

'No ... fear': Ibid., p. 34.

'A cry ... heart': Ibid., p. 37.

'Honor ... doves': Ibid., p. 85.

'Whose ministers ... saith'' ': Ibid., p. 101.

'until ... again': Ibid., p. 111.

'Conrad ... Conrad!': Ibid., p. 118.

Captain Carpenter: Ibid., pp. 44–6.

In an essay of 1942: *Beating the Bushes*, pp. 70–1.

'monad' ... being': OED^2, s.v. 'monad'.

as the medieval mystics perceived: *The Cloud of Unknowing*, ed. Justin McCann (London: Burns Oates and Washbourne, 1947), p. xvii.

the passage from *Hamlet* ... analysis: *Beating the Bushes*, pp. 136–43.

'realism' ... the fact': Ibid., p. 48.

'a few Axioms': *The Letters of John Keats, 1814–1821*, ed. Hyder Edward Rollins, 2 vols. (Cambridge, MA: Harvard University Press, 1958), vol. 1, p. 238 (letter of 27 Feb. 1818 to John Taylor).

'axioms in philosophy ... our pulses': Ibid., p. 279 (letter of 3 May 1818 to J. H. Reynolds).

'The rhythm ... thought': C. H. Sisson, *English Poetry 1900–1950: An Assessment* (London: Hart-Davis, 1971), p. 30.

'the social issue ... fiction': *Selected Poems*, p. 148.

Robert Buffington: *The Equilibrist*, p. 112.

Raymond Williams's acute analysis: In *The Manchester Guardian*, 9 Dec. 1960, quoted by Martin Jarrett-Kerr, 'The 491 Pitfalls of the Christian Artist', in Nathan

A. Scott, ed., *The Climate of Faith in Modern Literature* (New York: Seabury Press, 1964), p. 203.

'behind . . . language': *The New Criticism*, 79.

'the whole body . . . words': *OED*², s.v. 'language' (the 'language of polite letters' is quoted under 3*b*).

'dull readers . . . affiliations': *The New Criticism*, pp. 102–3.

'those Yale . . . reader': *Beating the Bushes*, pp. 171, 176.

'that terrible . . . strategy': *The World's Body*, p. 272.

'the last . . . poets': *The New Criticism*, p. 275.

'the possibility . . . destruction': *The World's Body*, p. 241.

'are easy . . . for them': *Beating the Bushes*, p. 160.

'more intense . . . known': Ransom, quoted in Young, *Gentleman in a Dustcoat*, p. 402.

'The bad artists' . . . strangely possessed': *The World's Body*, p. 39.

'humble reader': *The New Criticism*, p. 158.

'plain reader' . . . pain': Laura Riding and Robert Graves, *A Survey of Modernist Poetry* (London: Heinemann, 1929), p. 106.

9. Our Word Is Our Bond

And I might mention . . . concerned: J. L. Austin, *Philosophical Papers* (Oxford: Clarendon Press, 1961), pp. 227–8.

'Now for the *Poet* . . . lieth': *The Prose Works of Sir Philip Sidney*, ed. Albert Feuillerat, 4 vols. (Cambridge: Cambridge University Press, 1962), vol. 3, p. 29 (edn. first pub. 1912).

'The Imagination . . . truth.': *The Letters of John Keats 1814–1821*, ed. Hyder Edward Rollins, 2 vols. (Cambridge, MA: Harvard University Press, 1958) vol. 1, p. 185 (letter of 22 Nov. 1817 to Benjamin Bailey).

'The poem . . . about it.': *The Collected Poems of Wallace Stevens* (London: Faber and Faber, 1955), p. 473: 'An Ordinary Evening in New Haven', XII.

'All values . . . judicial sentences': *The Letters of Ezra Pound 1907–1941*, ed. D. D. Paige (London: Faber and Faber, 1951), p. 249 (letter of 8 July 1922 to Felix E. Schelling). Whitman writes in a similar vein in 'Song of the Answerer', 'The maker of poems settles justice, reality, immortality'; see Walt Whitman, *Complete Poetry and Collected Prose*, ed. Justin Kaplan (New York: Library of America, 1982), p. 317.

intellectus agens: Cuthbert Butler, *Western Mysticism*, 3rd edn. (London: Arrow Books, 1960), p. 101 n. 2: 'Intellectus agens dicitur qui facit intelligibilia in potentia esse in actu' (first pub. 1922); *The Sermons and Devotional Writings of Gerard Manley Hopkins*, ed. Christopher Devlin (London: Oxford University Press, 1959), p. 125: 'Here we touch the *intellectus agens* of the Averrhoists and the doctrine of the Hegelians and others'.

recta ratio factibilium: David Levy, 'Faith and Sensibility', in *PN Review*, vol. 4, no. 3 (1977), p. 63: 'The scholastics held that "art is a virtue of the practical intellect, *recta ratio factibilium*" '.

mens rea and *actus reus*: John R. Silber, 'Being and Doing: A Study of Status Responsibility and Voluntary Responsibility', in Marjorie Grene, ed., *The*

Anatomy of Knowledge (London: Routledge and K. Paul, 1969), p. 166: '*mens rea*, the awareness of the wrongfulness or unlawfulness of the conduct, and *actus reus*, the physical manifestation of *mens rea*'.

'boasting . . . carried': Vernon Watkins, *Ballad of the Mari Llwyd and Other Poems*, 2nd edn. (London: Faber and Faber, 1947), p. 89.

'If you are a judge . . . a state of mind.': J. L. Austin, *How to Do Things with Words*, ed. J. O. Urmson (Oxford: Clarendon Press, 1965), p. 88 ('Reprinted lithographically from corrected sheets of the 1963 reprint').

'a performative utterance . . . soliloquy': Ibid., p. 22.

'ordinary language' . . . practical matter': Austin, *Philosophical Papers*, p. 130.

'parasitic . . . medium: Austin, *How to Do Things with Words*, p. 104.

'determined . . . prose': Isaiah Berlin, *Personal Impressions* (London: Hogarth Press, 1980), pp. 101–2.

'accuracy . . . *bond*': Austin, *How to Do Things with Words*, p. 10. According to its official webpage, in 1923 the London Stock Exchange received 'its own Coat of Arms, with the motto "Dictum Meum Pactum" (My Word is My Bond)'.

'controlled interplay': Karl Britton, 'Symbolic Actions and Objects: "The weak pipe and the little drum" ', in *Philosophy*, vol. 54 (1979), p. 289: 'The poem says something that arises from the controlled interplay of just these words'.

Austin's belief . . . 'philosophically unimportant': See Urmson's remark in Austin, *How to Do Things with Words*, p. 5 n. 2.

'there appeared . . . exposition': Berlin, *Personal Impressions*, p. 104.

'the complex and recalcitrant nature of things': Ibid., p. 113.

'even "ordinary" language . . . extinct theories': Austin, *Philosophical Papers*, p. 130.

'considerations . . . may infect statements': Austin, *How to Do Things with Words*, p. 55.

'perfectly neat . . . 'awkward questions': *Works of Thomas Hill Green*, ed. R. L. Nettleship, 3 vols. (London: Longmans, Green, 1888), vol. 3, pp. 108–9.

'distinguished . . . ideas': *Berkeley's Commonplace Book*, ed. G. A. Johnston (London: Faber and Faber, 1930), p. 123 n. 156.

'manifold inextricable labyrinths': *The Works of George Berkeley, Bishop of Cloyne*, ed. A. A. Luce and T. E. Jessop, 9 vols. (London: T. Nelson, 1948–57), vol. 2, p. 35 (introduction to *A Treatise Concerning the Principles of Human Knowledge*).

'inflexible natures . . . of things': *Locke's Conduct of the Understanding*, ed. Thomas Fowler, 5th edn. (Oxford: Clarendon Press, 1901), p. 51: 'For to have right conceptions about them, we must bring our understandings to the inflexible natures and unalterable relations of things, and not endeavour to bring things to any preconceived notions of our own'.

'things themselves' . . . understood': Ibid.

'of excellent use': Berkeley, *Works*, vol. 2, p. 38 (introduction to *A Treatise Concerning the Principles of Human Knowledge*).

powers: I allude to the Coleridgean sense of the word. See *The Collected Works of Samuel Taylor Coleridge*, 16 vols. (Princeton, NJ: Princeton University Press, 1969–2002), vol. 9, p. 10 (*Aids to Reflection*, ed. John Beer).

'impose on the understanding': Berkeley, *Works*, vol. 2, p. 38 (introduction to *A Treatise Concerning the Principles of Human Knowledge*).

'all controversies purely verbal': Ibid., p. 39 (introduction to *A Treatise Concerning the Principles of Human Knowledge*).

mistaking empty words for legitimate concepts: See ibid., p. 141: 'a man cannot be too much upon his guard . . . to prevent his being cheated by the glibness and familiarity of speech into a belief that those words stand for ideas, which, in truth, stand for none at all' ('First Draft of the Introduction to the Principles').

'If it were not for Sin . . . as *Angels* do': Benjamin Whichcote, *Moral and Religious Aphorisms* (London: Elkin Mathews & Marrot, 1930), no. 731, p. 82 (first pub. 1753).

'naked, undisguised ideas': Berkeley, *Works*, vol. 2, p. 40 (introduction to *A Treatise Concerning the Principles of Human Knowledge*).

'stripped of words': *Locke's Conduct of the Understanding*, p. 92.

'controversial relish': George Santayana, *Some Turns of Thought in Modern Philosophy: Five Essays* (Cambridge: Cambridge University Press, 1933), p. 26.

a 'jejune and dry way . . . mathematicians only': *Locke's Conduct of the Understanding*, p. 91.

'the short jejune way . . . ethiques': *Berkeley's Commonplace Book*, p. 17.

'plain unsophisticated arguments' . . . 'plausible discourses': *Locke's Conduct of the Understanding*, pp. 91–2.

'proper sentiments' . . . 'ordinary affairs of life': Donald Davie, *Articulate Energy: An Inquiry into the Syntax of English Poetry* (London: Routledge & Paul, 1955), p. 121, quoting Berkeley: 'In the ordinary affairs of life, any phrases may be retain'd, so long as they excite in us proper sentiments'.

'signs or counters', 'fiduciary symbols': Davie, *Articulate Energy*, 121, quoting Berkeley, and St-John Perse.

carefully-elaborated discourse: Frederick J. Powicke, *The Cambridge Platonists: A Study* (London: J. M. Dent and Sons, 1926), pp. 51–2: '[Whichcote] seems to have introduced a new style. Instead of reading a carefully-elaborated discourse, he spoke from a few notes fluently, easily, and sometimes colloquially'.

Whichcote's 'candor': Ibid., p. 78. See *The Works of the Learned Benjamin Whichcote*, 4 vols. (Aberdeen, 1751), vol. 2, p. 245: 'God expects that the reader of scripture should be of an ingenuous spirit, and use candor, and not lie at the catch'.

Hobbes's 'Perspicuous Words': *Leviathan*, ed. C. B. Macpherson (Harmondsworth: Penguin, 1968), p. 116: 'The Light of humane minds is Perspicuous Words, but by exact definitions first snuffed, and purged from ambiguity'.

The Platonists' concern . . . Divine Reason: Whichcote, *Moral and Religious Aphorisms* no. 633, p. 73: 'Reason is the *first* Participation from God; and Virtue is the *second*' (first pub. 1753).

'speak accurately': Powicke, *The Cambridge Platonists*, p. 73. See *Works of Whichcote*, vol. 2, p. 80.

Hobbes's audacity: Dorothea Krook, *Three Traditions of Moral Thought* (Cambridge: University Press, 1959), p. 106: 'Hobbes adds (with an audacity that Hooker would have found stupefying)'.

'troublesome multiplicity': Powicke, *The Cambridge Platonists*, 74. See *Works of Whichcote*, vol. 2, p. 81: 'And this is fit for you to know to avoid a troublesome multiplicity in religion'.

the world's ineluctable necessity: Krook, *Three Traditions of Moral Thought*, 95: 'The logic of the argument is inescapable . . . for it follows by an ineluctable necessity from [Hobbes's] view of man's nature'.

'real language of men': William Wordsworth, *Poems*, ed. John O. Hayden, 2 vols. (New Haven, CT: Yale University Press, 1981), vol. 1, pp. 867, 883, 888 (Preface to *Lyrical Ballads*, 1802). Cf. *The Prose Works of William Wordsworth*, ed. W. J. B. Owen and Jane Worthington Smyser, 3 vols. (Oxford: Clarendon Press, 1974), vol. 1, pp. 118–19, 143, 150–1; and William Wordsworth, *Lyrical Ballads and Other Poems, 1797–1800*, ed. James Butler and Karen Green (Ithaca, NY: Cornell University Press, 1992), pp. 741, 754, 757.

'native and naked dignity of man': Wordsworth, *Poems*, vol. 1, p. 880 (Preface to *Lyrical Ballads*, 1802). Cf. *Prose Works*, vol. 1, p. 140; *Lyrical Ballads and Other Poems*, p. 752.

'airy useless notions' . . . 'real and substantial knowledge': *Locke's Conduct of the Understanding*, p. 94.

another Lockean idiom: Ibid., p. 95: 'To accustom ourselves in any question proposed, to examine and find out upon what it bottoms'.

'the wisdom of the world': Green, *Works*, vol. 3, p. 233: 'The wisdom of the world . . . represents the mental state of what St Paul calls the carnal or natural man'.

'a sharpened awareness . . . phenomena': Austin, *Philosophical Papers*, p. 130.

'patient accumulation of data about actual usage': Berlin, *Personal Impressions*, p. 113.

'the conduct of meetings and business': Austin, *How to Do Things with Words*, p. 156.

His work . . . H. L. Hart'): John Passmore, *A Hundred Years of Philosophy*, 3rd edn. (Harmondsworth: Penguin, 1968), p. 598.

He requires . . . ideal ones': Austin, *Philosophical Papers*, p. 38.

'mind is incorrigibly poetical' . . . 'many-coloured ideas': Santayana, *Some Turns of Thought in Modern Philosophy*, pp. 22–3.

'taking the sentences . . . the next one': G. J. Warnock, in Isaiah Berlin and others, *Essays on J. L. Austin* (Oxford: Clarendon Press, 1973), p. 36.

'in a peculiar way hollow or void': Austin, *How to Do Things with Words*, p. 22.

Avoid the practice ... other writers: *MHRA Style Book: Notes for Authors and Editors*, ed. A. S. Maney and R. L. Smallwood (Leeds: MHRA, 1971), p. 16.

' "Wherefrom father Ennius ... mould in plaster': Ezra Pound, *Poems and Translations*, ed. Richard Sieburth (New York: Library of America, 2003), pp. 550, 529.

'egocentric naïveties' and 'obtuse assurance': F. R. Leavis, *The Great Tradition* (London: Chatto and Windus, 1948), p. 210: '[Conrad's] irony bears on the egocentric naïveties of moral conviction ... and the obtuse assurance with which habit and self-interest assert absolute rights and wrongs'.

'compacted doctrines': William Empson, *The Structure of Complex Words* (London: Chatto and Windus, 1951), p. 39: 'it is often said ... that a word can become a "compacted doctrine" '.

'philosophers ... to any word': J. L. Austin, *Sense and Sensibilia*, ed. G. J. Warnock (Oxford: Clarendon Press, 1962), p. 62.

'the innumerable ... language': Ibid., p. 73.

Charlotte Brontë retorted: Quoted in Robert Bernard Martin, *The Accents of Persuasion* (London: Faber & Faber, 1966), p. 27.

'turned and picked up ... Salient': John Brophy and Eric Partridge, eds., *Songs and Slang of the British Soldier 1914–1918*, 2nd edn. (London: E. Partridge, 1930), pp. 193–4.

'our chains rattle ... them': Coleridge, *Collected Works*, vol. 7, part 2, p. 143 (*Biographia Literaria*, ed. James Engell and W. Jackson Bate, 2 parts).

'If said by an actor ... soliloquy': Austin, *How to Do Things with Words*, p. 22.

'surveying ... ethical space': Ibid., p. 10.

'noumena' ... 'nous' ... 'sense or meaning': See Coleridge's note on Hooker's *Ecclesiastical Polity*, Book 1, section 2 ('That which doth assign unto each thing the kind, that which doth moderate the force and power, that which doth appoint the form and measure of working, the same we term a *Law*'): 'The Law is Res *noumenon*; the Thing is Res *phænomenon*'. Coleridge, *The Collected Works*, vol. 12, part 2, pp. 1143–4 (*Marginalia*, ed. George Whalley, 6 parts).

'it is ... a Poet by': Sidney, *Prose Works*, vol. 3, p. 11.

This ioyous day ... which the Lord vs taught: *The Poetical Works of Edmund Spenser*, ed. J. C. Smith and Ernest de Selincourt (London: Oxford University Press, 1912), p. 573.

'ye are dearly bought': 1 Corinthians 6: 20, in Tyndale's New Testament (1534): 'For ye are dearly bought'; in the Bishops' Bible (1568): 'For ye are dearely bought'.

Spenser's 'felicity': Cf. *Sermons of M. John Caluin, on the Epistles of S. Paule to Timothie and Titus*, tr. L[aurence] T[omson] (London, 1579), p. 574: 'let vs be content with that that hee will giue vs, and then shall wee want nothing for oure full felicitie'; p. 575: 'let vs learne therefore at this day, to seeke all our felicitie, in giuing our selues to GOD ... let vs also suffer him to possesse vs, and guide vs as his, that we bee no more at our owne libertie, but wholy dedicate to his seruice'.

'felicissime audax'... 'curiosa felicitas': Paul Harvey, ed., *The Oxford Companion to Classical Literature*, corr. repr. (Oxford: Clarendon Press, 1940), p. 215: 'Quintilian calls [Horace] "felicissime audax", and Petronius refers to his "curiosa felicitas" or "studied felicity"'.

'extra-linguistic': G. J. Warnock, in Berlin and others, *Essays*, p. 73.

Pauline cadences: Including Ephesians 4: 8, 'He is gone vp an hye, and hath ledde captivitie captive' (Tyndale New Testament, 1534); 'When he ascended vp on hie, he led captiuitie captiue' (Geneva, 1560); the verse alludes to Psalm 68: 18. In his prologue to Deuteronomy, Tyndale writes that 'as Paule sayeth that we are bought with Christes bloude a[n]d therfore are his servauntes a[n]d not oure awne, a[n]d ought to seke his will and honoure onlye a[n]d serue one another for his sake' (Tyndale Pentateuch, 1530).

'contemplation'... 'beholding the Idaea playne': Spenser, *Amoretti* LXXX, LXXXVIII, *Poetical Works*, pp. 575, 577.

'haste and botching': J. W. Lever, *The Elizabethan Love Sonnet*, 2nd edn. (London: Methuen, 1966), pp. 100-1: 'Whatever Spenser's intentions were, there are unmistakable signs of haste and botching in the little 1595 volume containing *Amoretti* and *Epithalamion*'.

'erected wit'... reaching unto it': Sidney, *Prose Works*, vol. 3, p. 9. Cf. William Tyndale, *The Obedie[n]ce of a Christen Man* ([Antwerp], 1528), p. xxxv verso: 'Because y[t] the will of ma[n] foloweth the witte and is subiecte vnto the witte and as the witte erreth so doith the will: a[n]d as the witte is in captivite: so is the will: nether is it possible that y[e] will shuld be fre where the witte is in bondage'.

Theodore Spencer... the other': Theodore Spencer, 'The Poetry of Sir Philip Sidney', in *ELH*, vol. 12 (1945), p. 253.

'Idea'... things': Sidney, *Prose Works*, vol. 3, pp. 8, 13-14.

'captived... world': Ibid., p. 18.

'For my owne part... Wit': *Sir Fulke Greville's Life of Sir Philip Sidney*, ed. Nowell Smith (Oxford: Clarendon Press, 1907), p. 224 (first pub. 1652)

'"But ah", Desire... food"': *The Poems of Sir Philip Sidney*, ed. William A. Ringler (Oxford: Clarendon Press, 1962), p. 201.

'an erection of those engendering parts': *OED*², s.v. 'erection', citing Hugh Plat, *The Jewell House of Arte and Nature*, 1594.

'dark and disputed matter': Hopkins, *Sermons*, ed. Devlin, p. 150.

problems which the writer 'unconsciously' raises: Ibid., p. 339: 'the problems which GMH, sometimes unconsciously, raises'.

'bearing a part in the conversation': *Locke's Conduct of the Understanding*, p. 98: 'The shame that such dumps cause to well-bred people, when it carries them away from the company, where they should bear a part in the conversation'.

The theologian D. M. MacKinnon: MacKinnon, *The Problem of Metaphysics* (Cambridge: University Press, 1974), pp. 22, 39.

'there is that . . . what they are': Green, *Works*, vol. 3, p. 87.

'primitive purity and shortness': quoted in *Critical Essays of the Seventeenth Century*, ed. J. E. Spingarn, 3 vols. (Oxford: Clarendon Press, 1908–9), vol. 2, pp. 117–18.

'we can know . . . perversely': Austin, *Philosophical Papers*, p. 142.

'providence of wit': Dryden, 'To my Honored Friend Sir Robert Howard on his Excellent Poems', l. 34. *The Poems of John Dryden*, ed. James Kinsley, 4 vols. (Oxford: Clarendon Press, 1958), vol. 1, p. 14.

'concupiscence of witt': Donne, 'The Crosse', l. 58. John Donne, *The Divine Poems*, ed. Helen Gardner (Oxford: Clarendon Press, 1952), pp. 26–8.

'anarchy of witt': Dryden, 'Prologue to Albumazar', l. 17. *Poems*, vol. 1, p. 141.

Cudworth . . . acted with': *A Sermon Preached Before the House of Commons, March 31, 1647*, facsimile edn. (New York: Facsimile Text Society, 1930), p. 27.

Vaughan's 'But living . . . myre': *The Works of Henry Vaughan*, ed. L. C. Martin, 2 vols. (Oxford: Clarendon Press, 1914), vol. 2, pp. 522–3: 'The Night'.

'for if he . . . runne': *Leviathan*, p. 194.

'doctrine of the *Infelicities*': Austin, *How to Do Things with Words*, p. 23; *Philosophical Papers*, pp. 226–7.

entitles his lectures 'Sense and Sensibilia': In his foreword to *Sense and Sensibilia*, p. v, Warnock writes that Austin 'first used the title "Sense and Sensibilia" in Trinity Term of the following year [1948], and this was the title he subsequently retained'.

'not everyone . . . I did': Warnock, in Berlin and others, *Essays*, p. 44.

'liked authority' . . . position': Ibid., p. 33; Berlin, *Personal Impressions*, p. 105.

'learn from the distinctions encapsulated in their ordinary uses': Warnock, in Berlin and others, *Essays*, p. 37.

to drive 'with care': G. W. Pitcher, in ibid., p. 19.

'clumsily . . . clumsily': Austin, *Philosophical Papers*, p. 147.

'without effect' . . . effects': Austin, *How to Do Things with Words*, p. 17.

jurists' 'timorous fiction . . . fact': Ibid., p. 4 n. 2.

'In these discussions . . . Austin': Pitcher, in Berlin and others, *Essays*, p. 21.

'magic circle': Berlin, *Personal Impressions*, p. 115.

'Elegance . . . 'Obscurity': *The Letters of David Hume*, ed. J. Y. T. Greig, 2 vols. (Oxford: Clarendon Press, 1932), vol. 1, p. 17 (letter of March or April 1734).

'most excelle[n]t . . . learning': Sidney, *Prose Works*, vol. 3, p. 21.

Hopkins's ambiguous . . . pieces'): Dark and disputed matter, to my mind. Compare, for example, *The Poetical Works of Gerard Manley Hopkins*, ed. Norman H. MacKenzie (Oxford: Clarendon Press, 1990), p. 148: 'And the azurous hung hills are his wórld-wíelding shoulder' ('Hurrahing in Harvest'); Hopkins, *Sermons*, ed. Devlin, 198: 'Satan, who is the κοσμοκράτωρ, the worldwielder, gave nature all an impulse of motion which should destroy human life'; *The Correspondence of Gerard Manley Hopkins and Richard Watson Dixon*, ed. Claude

Colleer Abbott (London: Oxford University Press, 1935), p. 53: 'In Nature is something that makes, builds up, and breeds … and over against this, also in Nature, something that unmakes or pulls to pieces'. How does Hopkins come, within the space of four years, to apply what is essentially the identical term to both the Saviour and Satan without detecting, so far as I can see, his own 'paradox and problem'?

The man himself … he was: Austin, *Philosophical Papers*, p. 78.

'working the dictionary': Ibid., p. 135. Not as Austin prescribes: 'quite a concise one will do', p. 134.

'overriding': *OED*[2] cites Hallam, *Constitutional History* (1876), vol. 1, part 4, p. 349: 'The unconstitutional and usurped authority of the star-chamber over-rode every personal right'; and Calhoun, *Works* (1874), vol. 3, p. 589: 'The Constitution must override the deeds of cession, whenever they come in conflict'.

'*insouciant* latitude': Austin, *Sense and Sensibilia*, p. 58.

'could not bear … fantasy': in Berlin and others, *Essays*, pp. 43, 27; Berlin, *Personal Impressions*, 101.

'decent and comely order': *Princeton Encyclopedia of Poetry and Poetics*, ed. Alex Preminger, enlarged edn. (London: Macmillan, 1975), p. 870.

'*parasitic*' … joking': Austin, *How to Do Things with Words*, pp. 22, 9.

'spiritual assumption … *bond*': Ibid., p. 10.

'flurried' or 'anxious to get off': Austin, *Philosophical Papers*, p. 132.

'jargon' … ordinary language': Ibid., p. 137.

'superstition … language': Ibid., p. 133.

'clear up … snares us': Ibid., pp. 125, 137, 150.

'cheerfully subscribe … ideals': Ibid., p. 151 n. 1.

'the old Berkeleian … manifold" ': Austin, *Sense and Sensibilia*, p. 61.

'a_2 … clumsily"]': Austin, *Philosophical Papers*, p. 147 and n. 1.

Iris Murdoch … language-world': *The Sovereignty of Good* (London: Routledge, 1970), p. 25.

R. L. Nettleship … results': *Philosophical Remains of Richard Lewis Nettleship*, ed. A. C. Bradley, 2nd edn. (London: Macmillan, 1901), p. 138 (first pub. 1897 as *Philosophical Lectures and Remains of Richard Lewis Nettleship*, 2 vols). But see n. 1: '[There is much conjectural restoration in this paragraph]'.

'drama of reason': *Collected Letters of Samuel Taylor Coleridge*, ed. Earl Leslie Griggs, 6 vols. (Oxford: Clarendon Press, 1956–71), vol. 3, p. 282.

Words … use it: Nettleship, *Philosophical Remains*, pp. 136–7.

'LIVING POWERS': Coleridge, *Collected Works*, vol. 9, p. 10 (*Aids to Reflection*).

'within the process': Green, *Works*, vol. 3, p. 72.

'outside the process … developed': Ibid.

'ecstasy': Ibid., p. 79.

'transparency' of description: G. J. Warnock, *English Philosophy since 1900*, 2nd edn. (London: Oxford University Press, 1969), p. 102: '[Austin's] aim is not merely to describe the workings of language … transparent'.

Kantian 'manifold'... tincture: Green, *Works*, vol. 3, p. 153 ('manifold of sense'), p. 79 ('the world's manifold').

'malicious pleasure': Berlin, *Personal Impressions*, p. 112.

'if the poet says... order': Austin, *Philosophical Papers*, p. 228.

'to a youth... new names': Coleridge, *Collected Works*, vol. 7, part 2, p. 143 (*Biographia Literaria*).

'linguistic phenomenology': Austin, *Philosophical Papers*, p. 130 ('only that is rather a mouthful').

'ontological manoeuvre': John Crowe Ransom, *The World's Body* (Baton Rouge, LA: Louisiana State University Press, 1968), p. 347: 'The critic should regard the poem as nothing short of a desperate ontological or metaphysical manoeuvre'.

R. P. Blackmur... distress': *Language as Gesture: Essays in Poetry* (London: G. Allen & Unwin, 1954), p. 358.

Kenneth Burke's... are one': *A Grammar of Motives* (New York: Prentice-Hall, 1945), p. 491.

'satisfies the desire... *end attained*': A. E. Teale, *Kantian Ethics* (London: Oxford University Press, 1951), p. 209.

'verbal precision'... 'indistinct watch-words': Coleridge, *Collected Works*, vol. 7, part 2, pp. 143–4 (*Biographia Literaria*).

'*Praetendere*... the crime': Austin, *Philosophical Papers*, p. 208.

'Nec te Lar... verba tuae': *The Art of Love and Other Poems*, tr. J. H. Mozley (London: W. Heinemann, 1969), p. 194 (first pub. 1929). If 'crime' is too 'portentous', Mozley's 'weakness' is arguably not emphatic enough.

'the grand name without the grand thing': *The Complete Prose Works of Matthew Arnold*, ed. R. H. Super, 11 vols. (Ann Arbor, MI: University of Michigan Press, 1960–77), vol. 3, p. 280 ('The Function of Criticism at the Present Time').

'that rather woolly word "imply" ': Austin, *Philosophical Papers*, p. 224.

'issued in ordinary circumstances': Austin, *How to Do Things with Words*, p. 22.

'the density... density': John Crowe Ransom, *The New Criticism* (Norfolk, CT: New Directions, 1941), p. 79.

Those invocations: Hopkins, *Poetical Works*, pp. 124, 128, 123.

'Dim sadness... name': Wordsworth, *Poems*, vol. 1, p. 552 ('Resolution and Independence'); cf. William Wordsworth, *Poems, in Two Volumes, and Other Poems, 1800–1807*, ed. Jared Curtis (Ithaca, NY: Cornell University Press, 1983), p. 124.

'A pleasurable... love': Wordsworth, *Poems*, vol. 1, p. 457 ('Michael'); cf. Wordsworth, *Lyrical Ballads and Other Poems*, 255.

'dogged in den': Hopkins, *Poetical Works*, 121 ('The Wreck of the Deutschland').

'dear and dogged man': Ibid., p. 171 ('Ribblesdale'). In the autograph of 'Ribblesdale' sent to Dixon on 29 June 1883, Hopkins writes 'doggèd'; see Hopkins, *Letters to Dixon*, 108.

'heavy bodies': *The Note-Books and Papers of Gerard Manley Hopkins*, ed. Humphry House (London: Oxford University Press, 1937), p. 223: 'We may think of words as heavy bodies... Now every visible palpable body has a centre of gravity . . . The centre of gravity is like the accent of stress, the highspot like the accent of pitch'.

'most recondite and difficult': Hopkins, *Sermons*, ed. Devlin, 200.

'a dogged veracity': *Boswell's Life of Johnson*, vol. 3, p. 378; cf. vol. 1, p. 203 ('a man may write at any time if he will set himself doggedly to it') and vol. 5, p. 40. For instances of 'dogged' in the twentieth century, compare Schoenberg, who 'claimed as his only virtue' a 'dogged persistence and refusal to give up' (Malcolm MacDonald, *Schoenberg* (London: Dent, 1976), p. 62) and Wyndham Lewis's claim that Passchendaele was prepared by a 'perfect combination' of the 'appetite of the Teuton for this odd game called war' and 'British "doggedness" in the gentle art of "muddling through" ' (*Blasting & Bombardiering* (London: Eyre & Spottiswoode, 1937), p. 160). In September 1916 Captain Harry Yoxall described his battalion: 'not brilliant but hardworking and dogged' (quoted in Malcolm Brown, *Tommy Goes to War* (London: J. M. Dent, 1978), p. 196).

'ordinary . . . beliefs': Austin, *How to Do Things with Words*, p. 22; Green, *Works*, vol. 3, pp. 117, lxxiv; Berlin, *Personal Impressions*, p. 101.

'the audible . . . company': *Locke's Conduct of the Understanding*, p. 98.

'*bona fide* perplexity': Green, *Prolegomena to Ethics*, ed. A. C. Bradley, 5th edn. (Oxford: 1907), p. 403 (1st edn. 1883).

'paradoxes and problems': Donne, *Iuuenilia: or Certaine Paradoxes and Problemes* (London, 1633). See Donne, *Paradoxes and Problems*, ed. Helen Peters (Oxford: Clarendon Press, 1980).

'impudently': J. B. Leishman, *The Monarch of Wit* (London: Hutchinson's University Library, 1951), p. 56: 'Such are the impudent paradoxes . . . of Ovid's *Amores* . . . Donne seems to have been the first to perceive what novel, surprising and shocking effects might be produced by exploiting the . . . *Amores*'.

'I did best . . . my subject': 'You know my uttermost when it was best, and even then I did best when I had least truth for my subject'. Quoted in John Donne, *The Divine Poems*, p. xxxvii.

'to lay him . . . wantonnesse': John Donne, *Devotions upon Emergent Occasions*, ed. Anthony Raspa (Montreal: McGill-Queen's University Press, 1975), p. 16.

'Or . . . that?': Ibid., p. 63.

'*Fevers* . . . destruction': Ibid., p. 63.

Marlowe's Faustus: R. C. Bald, *John Donne: A Life* (Oxford: Clarendon Press, 1970), p. 73: 'Marlowe seems to have made the deepest impression on [Donne] . . . and it has been shown that recollections of the damnation of Faustus returned to haunt his imagination in after years'.

'thinking experience': A. J. M. Milne, *The Social Philosophy of English Idealism* (London: Allen & Unwin, 1962), p. 89.

'*Noble* parts . . . *misery*': Donne, *Devotions*, ed. Raspa, p. 64.

Nygren . . . "*bent upon itself*" ': Anders Nygren, *Agape and Eros*, Part II, vol. 2, tr. Philip S. Watson (London: SPCK, 1939), pp. 267–8 n. 3.

'hazardous course' . . . purposes': OED^2, s.v. 'compromise', *v* 8; 4; *sb* 5 *fig*.

the dyer's hand ... infected hand: Shakespeare, Sonnet 110. *OED*², s.v. 'infect' *v*: 'ad. L *infect-*, ppl. stem of *inficĕre* to dip in, stain'. See also *Oxford Latin Dictionary*, s.v. 'inficio', 'To immerse in a pigment, dye'. In his commentary on Horace's Ode 3.5, Kenneth Quinn writes that 'the comparison of the soldier's training to the dyeing of cloth goes back to Plato'; see *Horace: The Odes* (Basingstoke: Macmillan, 1980), p. 254. On 'infection', cf. *The Institution of Christian Religion* (London, 1561), p. 50 recto: 'man at his fyrst creation was farre other than his posteritie euer sins, whiche takyng their beginnyng from hym beyng corrupted, hath from him receiued an infection [*labem*] deriued to them as it were by inheritaunce' (Calvin's *Institutes* 1.5.8, in Thomas Norton's translation).

'curva voluntas': Augustine, *Enarrationes in Psalmos*, 3 vols. (Turnhout: Brepols, 1956), vol. 1, p. 505 (*Corpus Christianorum, Series Latina*, vols. 38–40): on Psalm 44: 17. Another edition of the text is to appear in the *Corpus Scriptorum Ecclesiasticorum Latinorum* as vol. 93, part 1b. Cf. Augustine, *Expositions of the Psalms*, tr. Maria Boulding, 6 vols. (Hyde Park, NY: New City Press, 2000–4), vol. 1, p. 294 (*The Works of Saint Augustine: A Translation for the Twenty-first Century*, vol. 16 of Part III).

'Actuality ... resistance': *Collected Papers of Charles Sanders Peirce*, ed. Charles Harts-horne, Paul Weiss, and Arthur W. Burks, 8 vols. (Cambridge, MA: Harvard University Press, 1931–58), vol. 1, p. 7. Cf. Charles S. Peirce, *The Essential Peirce*, 2 vols, ed. Peirce Edition Project (Bloomington, IN, 1992–8) vol. 2, p. 435 ('the Brute Actuality of things and facts', in 'A Neglected Argument for the Reality of God').

'we must consider ... speech-act': Austin, *How to Do Things with Words*, p. 52.

'saying ... customers': Warnock, in Berlin and others, *Essays*, p. 83.

As Warnock notes: Ibid. See Austin, *How to Do Things with Words*, p. 57; *Philosophical Papers*, pp. 229–30.

'When I asked ... no words came out': Julien Cornell, *The Trial of Ezra Pound: A Documented Account of the Treason Case by the Defendant's Lawyer* (London: Faber, 1967), p. 32.

'self-stultifying procedures': Austin, *How to Do Things with Words*, p. 51: 'Just as the purpose of assertion is defeated by an internal contradiction (in which we assimilate and contrast *at once* and so stultify the whole procedure), the purpose of a contract is defeated if we say "I promise and I ought not" '. Cf. Cornell, *The Trial of Ezra Pound*, 41: 'While the doctors are agreed that he is to this extent mentally abnormal ... I think it may fairly be said that any man of his genius would be regarded by a psychiatrist as abnormal'.

('A ... of course'): Cornell, *The Trial of Ezra Pound*, p. 166.

'All four experts ... state.': Ibid., p. 45.

'the key ... Confucius': Ibid., p. 157.

'peculiar ... law': Ibid., p. 46.

'was imprisoned ... fact': Ibid., p. vii.

'there is ... opposition': Donald Hall, *Remembering Poets: Reminiscences and Opinions* (New York: Harper & Row, 1978), p. 242.

'that stupid suburban prejudice': Ibid., p. 185: Pound in conversation with Allen Ginsberg.

'insufficient desperation': Richard Reid, 'Ezra Pound Asking', in *Agenda*, vol. 17, nos. 3–4. vol. 18, no. 1 (3 issues) (Autumn–Winter–Spring 1979/80), pp. 171–86 (p. 172): 'Yet to charge Pound with banality would be to understate the disturbing quality of this text, its insufficient desperation'.

'solid entities': Empson, *Complex Words*, p. 39: 'A word may become a sort of solid entity, able to direct opinion'.

'compacted doctrines': Ibid.

T. H. Green argued ... itself': Green, *Works*, vol. 3, p. 116.

'act of attention' ... purpose': Nettleship, *Philosophical Remains*, pp. 135, 392.

'I guess I was off base all along': Hall, *Remembering Poets*, p. 148.

In a note ... fatiguing: Cornell, *The Trial of Ezra Pound*, p. 73.

sounds magisterially Shelleyan: As Pound himself remarked, *Letters*, p. 249: '(This arrogance is not mine but Shelley's, and it is absolutely true ...)'.

logopoeia: *Literary Essays of Ezra Pound*, ed. T. S. Eliot (London: Faber and Faber, 1954), p. 25: 'LOGOPOEIA, "the dance of the intellect among words"'.

Christopher Ricks's redefinition: In conversation with me.

'The poet's job ... justice': Pound, *Letters*, p. 366.

'the cultivation ... law': Coleridge, *Collected Works*, vol. 7, part 2, p. 144 (*Biographia Literaria*).

'Fact is richer than diction': Austin, *Philosophical Papers*, p. 143.

'I certainly omitted ... open to me': Pound, *Letters*, pp. 310–11.

And now ... Fama volet': J. P. Sullivan, *Ezra Pound and Sextus Propertius: A Study in Creative Translation* (London: Faber and Faber, 1965), pp. 170–1.

('Near ... book-stall'): Pound, *Poems and Translations*, p. 529.

'imbecility': Pound, *Letters*, p. 310: 'faced with the infinite and ineffable imbecility of the British Empire ... faced with the infinite and ineffable imbecility of the Roman Empire'.

'exemplary instances ... vocabulary': Nathan A. Scott, *The Poetry of Civic Virtue* (Philadelphia: Fortress Press, 1976), pp. x, 123, 135.

'redeeming ... absurdity': Ibid., pp. 102, 97.

'absolute closures of possibility': Ibid., p. 66.

'foundational' ... 'primal reality': Ibid., p. 4.

'wanting the precept ... what is': Sidney, *Prose Works*, vol. 3, p. 14.

'dark and disputed ... field': Hopkins, *Sermons*, pp. 149–51.

'*the doing* be ... so-and-so': Ibid.

'hantle of howlers': Edwin Morgan, *Essays* (Cheadle: Carcanet Press, 1974), pp. 255–76.

'Caesar ... misagony': Ibid., pp. 259–63.

'are hardly . . . imagination': Ibid., p. 259.

'It may seem . . . mind': Ibid., p. 260.

'the self unqualified in volition': Silber, 'Being and Doing', in Grene, ed., *The Anatomy of Knowledge*, p. 206.

'murky . . . actuality': Morgan, *Essays*, pp. 263, 258.

first-grade . . . pun': Ibid., p. 257.

'ideas of guilt . . . interesting': Murdoch, *The Sovereignty of Good*, p. 68.

'Verbalism . . . skill.': Pound, *Literary Essays*, p. 283.

'a sloppy and slobbering world': Pound, *Letters*, p. 378.

'the transition . . . Pound: C. H. Sisson, *English Poetry 1900–1950: An Assessment* (London: Hart-Davis, 1971), p. 102.

'I never . . . God damn it': Cornell, *The Trial of Ezra Pound*, p. 192.

'the tyro . . . dangerous': Pound, *Literary Essays*, p. 283.

'the finest wrought': Ibid.

'the crime . . . writing': Cornell, *The Trial of Ezra Pound*, p. 195.

'*by his being . . . his signature*': Austin, *How to Do Things with Words*, p. 60.

'a verdictive . . . exercitives': Ibid., p. 152.

'Now comes . . . incompetent person': Cornell, *The Trial of Ezra Pound*, p. 61.

'And when . . . finished with the subject.': Pound, *Letters*, p. 347.

THE ENEMY'S COUNTRY

Epigraphs

Deeds, it seems...a Poet: John Dryden, *The Works of John Dryden*, ed. Edward Niles Hooker, H. T. Swedenberg, and Vinton A. Dearing, 20 vols. (Berkeley, CA: University of California Press, 1956–2000), vol. 1, p. 109.

You cannot...upon him: Ezra Pound, *Selected Prose 1909–1965* (New York: New Directions, 1973), p. 114.

A Note on the Title

'Thou art...enemies countrey': Thomas Nashe, *The Works of Thomas Nashe*, ed. Ronald B. McKerrow, rev. F. P. Wilson, 5 vols. (Oxford: B. Blackwell, 1966), vol. 1, p. 258

'the vast field...Enemy's country': *Sir William Davenant's Gondibert*, ed. David F. Gladish (Oxford: Clarendon Press, 1971), p. 24.

'A learned poetry...of ignorance': Hugh MacDiarmid, *The Complete Poems of Hugh MacDiarmid*, ed. Michael Grieve and W. R. Aitken, 2 vols. (Harmondsworth: Penguin, 1985), vol. 2, p. 1030 ('The Kind of Poetry I Want').

'all the artists...but intellectuals': John Berryman, *The Freedom of the Poet* (New York: Farrar, Straus & Giroux, 1976), p. 215.

'tossing'...'edit and annotate': W. B. Yeats, *The Collected Poems of W. B. Yeats*, ed. Richard J. Finneran, new edn. (New York: Macmillan Books, 1989), pp. 140–1 ('The Scholars').

Opinion': Cf. Fulke Greville, *Workes Written in His Youth* (London, 1633), p. 244: 'Who like an Idoll doth apparel'd sit | In all the glories of Opinions art' (*Caelica*, sonnet 96); *Poems and Dramas of Fulke Greville*, ed. Geoffrey Bullough, 2 vols. (Edinburgh: Oliver and Boyd, [1938]), vol. 1, p. 143.

'his much honor'd friend M. Hobbes': Davenant, *Gondibert*, p. 3.

'not by common...Prospect': Ibid., p. 24.

'Words, contexture, and other circumstances of Language': Thomas Hobbes, *Humane Nature, or The Fundamental Elements of Policies* (London, 1650), p. 51.

'covenants of mutuall trust': Thomas Hobbes, *Leviathan*, ed. C. B. Macpherson (Harmondsworth: Penguin, 1968), p. 196.

'covenants extorted by feare': Ibid., p. 198.

'justice of manners and justice of actions': Ibid., p. 207.

'submission to arbitrement': Ibid., p. 213.

10. Unhappy Circumstances

Aubrey records...worke': *Aubrey's 'Brief Lives'*, ed. Andrew Clark, 2 vols. (Oxford: Clarendon Press, 1898), vol. 1, pp. 340–1. On 'turn and wind', see OED^2, s.v. 'turn', 64 a.

When Hobbes...the rest': *Leviathan*, ed. C. B. Macpherson (Harmondsworth: Penguin, 1968), p. 209.

The Art of Complaisance...Conversation: See George Etherege, *The Man of Mode*, ed. John Barnard (London: E. Benn, 1979), pp. xxxiii–xxxiv (editor's introduction);

Paul Hammond, *John Oldham and the Renewal of Classical Culture* (Cambridge: Cambridge University Press, 1983), p. 205.

accommodated in the word 'compleasance' itself: See Walter W. Skeat, *A Concise Etymological Dictionary of the English Language*, 2nd rev. edn. (Oxford: Clarendon Press, 1885), p. 355: 'Please ... L. *placere*, to please. Allied to *placare*, to appease'. Cf. ibid., s.vv. 'complacent', 'complaisant', 'placable'.

The intimate relationship of power with appeasement, of pre-emption with flexibility and obligingness, is evident in the word, as was sometimes recognized by writers after Hobbes. The author of 'A Letter of Advice to a Young Poet' (1721) advises a friend to lay down his pen unless he 'can disguise [his] Religion as well-bred Men do their Learning, in Complaisance to Company'; see Jonathan Swift, *Irish Tracts and Sermons 1720–1723*, ed. Herbert Davis and Louis Landa (Oxford: Basil Blackwell, 1963), p. 328. David Hume in 'Of the Standard of Taste' (1757) writes that 'where a man is confident of the rectitude of that moral standard, by which he judges, he ... will not pervert the sentiments of his heart for a moment, in complaisance to any writer whatsoever'; see David Hume, *Essays, Moral, Political and Literary*, ed. Eugene F. Miller, rev. edn. (Indianapolis, IN: Liberty Fund, 1985), p. 247.

This relationship is characteristic in numerous instances of English style: whether in Sir Robert Howard's genial subjective coerciveness on matters of taste (discussed in Ch. 13, p. 227) or in the way in which Professors Bradbury and Bigsby take possession of 'our' and 'ours' ('Accordingly, this continuing series is an endeavour to look at some of the most important writers of our time'; 'Our wish is that, in their very variety of approach and emphasis, these books will stimulate interest in and understanding of the vitality of a living literature which, because it is contemporary, is especially ours'.—'General Editors' Preface' to the series 'Contemporary Writers' (London, 1982–)). 'Especially ours' elides the indeterminate commonality of 'our time' with the elusive determination 'our wish'. It is 'our wish' to oblige the clichés of current conversation ('we live in a major creative time', 'the works of major post-war writers'); it is also 'our' wish to present such authors as Margaret Drabble and John Le Carré as 'most important writers'. '*Our*' time must here mean '*your* time made placable to *our* cultural scenario'. If they truly meant 'our time' they would have to take account of e.g. *my* time. Margaret Drabble and John Le Carré do not figure among the most important writers of my time, but my scepticism, and the views of those who might share my scepticism, are effectively excluded from consideration by being included in the complacent locution. This appeal to the supposed consensus seems to me in direct conflict with Dr Johnson's meaning when he wrote that Gray's 'Elegy' 'abounds with images which find a mirrour in every mind, and with sentiments to which every bosom returns an echo', though Bradbury and Bigsby doubtless 'rejoice to concur with the common reader' according to their understanding of that term. To the suggestion that Johnson's statement is itself merely a matter of opinion delivered with aplomb I would reply that his priorities strike me as being right and that he avoids blurring or eliding the implications of his words. For Johnson it is the *poem* that establishes and maintains the tone; the sensibility of the 'common reader' may be judged by his or her capacity to echo or reflect its intrinsic qualities. The fact that, in the case of Gray's 'Elegy', so many common readers have manifested this capability is a tribute to the poem itself rather than to 'the spirit of contemporary criticism'.

It was observed ... obliging': In the sermon preached at her funeral. See Aubrey, *Brief Lives*, vol. 1, p. 119; and see Hammond, *John Oldham and the Renewal of Classical Culture*, 205.

'patience ... domination: Barnard, in Etherege, *The Man of Mode*, p. xxxiv.

Etherege's ... change it': Etherege, *The Man of Mode*, p. 91.

In Hobbes's terms ... *Intractable*': Hobbes, *Leviathan*, p. 210.

'An Ode ... aloofe': *Ben Jonson*, ed. C. H. Herford and Percy Simpson, 11 vols. (Oxford: Clarendon Press, 1925–52), vol. 8, pp. 174–5.

Harriet's depiction ... 'poignancy': Etherege, *The Man of Mode*, pp. 142 and xxxviii (editor's introduction).

'the mind must be thought sufficiently at ease': Samuel Johnson, *The Lives of the Poets*, 4 vols., ed. Roger Lonsdale (Oxford: Clarendon Press, 2006), vol. 1, p. 215.

the author of the 'Epilogue' ... Rochester: See Charles E. Ward, *The Life of John Dryden* (Chapel Hill, NC: University of North Carolina, 1961), pp. 83, 109, 114.

by 1697 ... John Dennis: See Ward, *Life of John Dryden*, pp. 240, 250–1, on Dryden's 'refusal to compromise'; and see George McFadden, *Dryden the Public Writer 1660–1685* (Princeton, NJ: Princeton University Press, 1978), p. 91: 'As for Dryden, he chose to be loyal to James when he clearly perceived it to be ruinous', p. 132: 'Mulgrave's ... steady adherence to the cause of the Duke of York'. I am indebted to Ian Jack for an opinion.

how to relate *otium* to *negotium*: Hobbes states the problem plainly: 'The rules of *just* and *unjust* sufficiently demonstrated, and from principles evident to the meanest capacity, have not been wanting; and notwithstanding the obscurity of their author, have shined, not only in this, but also in foreign countries, to men of good education. But they are few, in respect of the rest of men, whereof many cannot read: many, though they can, have no leisure; and of them that have leisure, the greatest part have their minds wholly employed and taken up by their private businesses or pleasures'; see *Behemoth*, ed. Ferdinand Tönnies, 2nd edn. (London: Frank Cass, 1969), p. 39.

(etymologically impacted ... paronomasia): See the *Oxford Latin Dictionary* (Oxford: Clarendon Press, 1982), p. 1168: 'negōtium ... [neg- (NEQVE) + OTIVM]'.

that 'vacation ... ease': *A Discourse of the Common Weal of this Realm of England* (written *c*.1552), ed. Elizabeth Lamond (Cambridge: Cambridge University Press, 1893), p. 10; *Sir William Davenant's Gondibert*, ed. David F. Gladish (Oxford: Clarendon Press, 1971), p. 24.

Francis Meres . . . Horace: *Elizabethan Critical Essays*, ed. G. Gregory Smith, 2 vols. (Oxford: Clarendon Press, 1904), vol. 2, p. 313.

('Aoniae iucunda per otia ripae'): John Milton, *Complete Shorter Poems*, ed. John Carey, 2nd edn. (London: Longman, 1997), p. 157.

('Yet ease and leasure . . . men'): *Complete Prose Works of John Milton*, 8 vols. (New Haven, CT: Yale University Press, 1953–82), vol. 1, p. 804: 'Not such a lazy life is implied here as modern usage would suggest. Ease simply meant freedom from physical labor; leisure, freedom and opportunity for study' (editorial note by R. A. Haug). See also: 'So that being now quiet from State-Adversaries and publick Contests, he had leisure again for his own Studies and private Designs' (Edward Phillips, *The Life of Mr John Milton* (1694), in *The Early Lives of Milton*, ed. Helen Darbishire (London: Constable, 1932), p. 72).

Dryden's letters . . . epilogues: e.g. *The Letters of John Dryden*, ed. Charles E. Ward (Durham, NC: Duke University Press, 1942), pp. 13, 23, 113; *The Prologues and Epilogues of John Dryden: A Critical Edition* by William Bradford Gardner (New York: Columbia University Press, 1951), pp. 23, 32, 91, 102–3.

'by incoherent . . . neglect': John Locke, *An Essay Concerning Human Understanding*, ed. Peter H. Nidditch (Oxford: Clarendon Press, 1975), p. 7.

'The only . . . worry': *Impact: Essays on Ignorance and the Decline of American Civilization* by Ezra Pound, ed. Noel Stock (Chicago, IL: H. Regnery, 1960), p. 218. See also Ezra Pound, *Gaudier-Brzeska: A Memoir*, new edn. (Hessle: Marvell Press, 1960), pp. 64–5. Cf. *The Letters of Wyndham Lewis*, ed. W. K. Rose (London: Methuen, 1963), pp. 340–1. See also 'Whoever is not in the possession of leisure can hardly be said to possess independence. They talk of the *dignity of work*. Bosh. True Work is the *necessity* of poor humanity's earthly condition. The dignity is in leisure. Besides, 99 hundredths of all the *work* done in the world is either foolish and unnecessary, or harmful and wicked' (Herman Melville, in a letter of 5 September 1877, cited in Jay Leyda, *The Melville Log: A Documentary Life of Herman Melville 1819–1891*, 2 vols. (New York: Harcourt, Brace, 1951), vol. 2, p. 765).

Dryden and Pound . . . society of his day: And one may add George McFadden's observation: 'Throughout his whole life [Dryden's] record clearly shows a pattern of generous encouragement to younger writers, beyond a parallel in our literature until Ezra Pound came along' (*Dryden the Public Writer*, p. 149).

'platitude . . . aridity': Ezra Pound, *Selected Prose 1909–1965*, ed. William Cookson (London: Faber, 1973), p. 361; Ezra Pound, *Literary Essays*, ed. T. S. Eliot (London: Faber and Faber, 1954), p. 70.

('you cannot . . . him'): Ezra Pound, *Patria Mia* (Chicago, IL: R. F. Seymour, 1950), p. 47. Cf. Hobbes, *Behemoth*, p. 38: 'But *wise*, as I define it, is he that knows how to bring his business to pass (without the assistance of knavery and ignoble shifts) by the sole strength of his good contrivance'.

His 'choice . . . his 'technic': e.g. 'Postscript to the Reader [of Virgil's *Aeneis*]', in *The Poems of John Dryden*, ed. James Kinsley, 4 vols. (Oxford: Clarendon Press,

1958), p. 1424; Pound, *Literary Essays*, p. 115; *Ah, Sweet Dancer: W. B. Yeats, Margot Ruddock*, ed. Roger McHugh (London: Macmillan, 1970), p. 81.

Hobbes's definition . . . thing': Hobbes, *Leviathan*, pp. 151, 295. See the excellent discussion in C. B. Macpherson, *The Political Theory of Possessive Individualism: Hobbes to Locke* (Oxford: Clarendon Press, 1962), pp. 219–20.

The state . . . hands': John Clapham, *The Bank of England: A History*, 2 vols. (Cambridge: University Press, 1944), vol. 1, pp. 26, 35–6; W. Marston Acres, *The Bank of England from Within, 1694–1900*, 2 vols. (London: Oxford University Press, 1931), vol. 1, p. 66; Dryden, *Letters*, p. 170 n. 4.

the virtues of '*labor*' . . . richness: Virgil, *The Eclogues and Georgics*, ed. R. D. Williams (London: Macmillan, 1979), pp. 144 n. 199, 136–7 nn. 43–70, 139–40 nn. 118–46.

'*improbus*': Ibid., p. 141 nn. 145–6.

'quid meruere . . . labores?': Ovid, *Metamorphoses*, tr. Frank Justus Miller, 2 vols. (London: W. Heinemann, 1916), vol. 2, p. 372.

the word 'silly': *OED*², s.vv. 'seely' and 'silly'.

Those are Davenant's phrases: Davenant, *Gondibert*, p. 24.

'hominumque boumque labores': Virgil, *Eclogues and Georgics*, ed. Williams, pp. 32, 140 nn. 118–21: 'the hard toil of men and oxen alike'.

'durum genus': Ibid., pp. 30, 137 n. 63: 'an aetiological explanation of why men are hardy'. I am indebted to Katy Ricks for her advice.

('hiems curasque resolvit'): Ibid., p. 36. I owe the point about Dryden's reworking of these lines to David Ricks.

('aut oculis . . . talpae'): Ibid., pp. 33, 143 nn. 181–3.

Mildmay Fane . . . *negotium*': Mildmay Fane, second earl of Westmorland, *Otia Sacra (1648)* facsimile edn., ed. Donald M. Friedman (Delmar, NY: Scholars' Facsimiles & Reprints 1975), p. viii (editor's introduction).

'Rimes' . . . times': Ibid., p. 174.

('Bidding me . . . surfet'): Ibid., pp. 8, 15, 25, 26, 33, 34. There is a proper use for pleonasm, as Milton for example demonstrates in Satan's speeches in *Paradise Regain'd*.

'a very just . . . display': Johnson, *Lives of the Poets*, vol. 1, p. 215.

'Few things . . . do': Letter to the Reverend Dr Wetherell, 12 Mar. 1776. *Boswell's Life of Johnson*, ed. George Birkbeck Hill, revised edn., 6 vols. (Oxford: Clarendon Press, 1934), vol. 2, p. 424.

'frigid tranquillity' . . . empty sounds.': *Johnson on the English Language*, ed. Gwin J. Kolb and Robert DeMaria (New Haven, CT: Yale University Press, 2005), p. 113 (vol. 18 of *The Yale Edition of The Works of Samuel Johnson*).

'just as a man's language . . . limitation': Laurence Binyon, *The Flight of the Dragon* (London: J. Murray, 1911), p. 14, quoted in Pound, *Pavannes and Divagations* (Norfolk, CT: New Directions, 1958), p. 149. Pound's rendering differs very slightly from the source. I have retained Binyon's wording.

the 'subjective element': Binyon, *The Flight of the Dragon*, p. 14.

'the "statesman . . . idiom': *ABC of Reading* (London: Faber and Faber, 1951), p. 34.

his indignation . . . cloth: Johnson, *Lives of the Poets*, vol. 4, p. 183.

'Business' is . . . fulfilment: Herbert, in 'Employment (II)', writes 'Life is a businesse, not good cheer; | Ever in warres'; this is followed in the next stanza by 'Oh that I were an Orenge-tree | That busie plant!' (*The Works of George Herbert*, ed. F. E. Hutchinson (Oxford: Clarendon Press, 1959), p. 79).

Consider two quotations: 'that little fancy and liberty I once enjoy'd, is now fetter'd in business of more unpleasant Natures' (Sir Robert Howard, *The Great Favourite, Or, The Duke of Lerma* (London, 1668), facsimile edn. (New York: Garland, 1975), A2 verso); 'the Multiplicity, the Cares, and the Vexations of your Imployment, have betray'd you from your self, and given you up into the Possession of the Publick. You are Robb'd of your Privacy and Friends, and scarce any hour of your Life you can call your own' (Dryden, 'The Epistle Dedicatory' to *All for Love* (13: 8)).

Contrast with them two further quotations: 'I often had occasion to remark, Johnson loved business, loved to have his wisdom actually operate on real life', Boswell, *Life of Johnson*, vol. 2, p. 441 (20 March 1776); cf. vol. 4, pp. 86–7. 'I have been to hear the Lord Chief Justice sum up [in the Tichborne case] . . . It is interesting to see that there is no other way, in the long run at least, for carrying on important things than the way of carrying on the unimportant ones. Business must be businesslike. The day of judgment however will be dramatic throughout', Gerard M. Hopkins, *Further Letters*, ed. Claude Colleer Abbott, 2nd edn. (London: Oxford University Press, 1956), p. 60 (24 Feb. 1874).

Professor Sir Walter Raleigh wittily observed 'I lead the life of a defaulting debtor . . . chivied by people who behave as if they had lent me money' (*The Letters of Sir Walter Raleigh: 1879–1922*, ed. Lady Raleigh, 2 vols. (London: Methuen, 1926), vol. 1, p. xviii). How far is it true that to have one's 'wisdom actually operate on real life' is at the same time to 'betray . . . you from your self'? To what extent is there validity in the suggestion that to be thus betrayed 'from your self' is a necessary 'real life' corrective to a Romantic absolutist aesthetic (e.g. *The Letters of Ezra Pound: 1907–1941*, ed. D. D. Paige (London: Faber and Faber, 1951), p. 249)? Or suppose someone to say, 'When will you be giving us another volume of your verses, Mr X?' Is the particular relish of the word 'give' its being at once a 'little fancy' and a demand-note? Mr X might justly bridle at being so chivvied by brisk assumptions about *otium*. Judged by Johnson's and Hopkins's standards, however, his understandable resentment and self-pity could appear merely otiose. It is further to be remarked that Crashaw's anonymous panegyrist precludes our dithering on either side of the question: 'hee made his skill in Poetry, Musicke, Drawing, Limming, graving . . . to bee but his subservient recreations for vacant houres, not the grand businesse of his soule ('The Preface to the Reader', *Steps to the Temple* (1646), in Richard Crashaw, *The Poems, English, Latin, and Greek*, ed. L. C. Martin (Oxford: Clarendon Press, 1927), p. 76). This too may be taken as a necessary corrective to some of the other arguments cited here (including, of course, my own). Calvin provides a more forceful corrective or challenge, in his belief, as John T. McNeill puts it, that 'every man in all circumstances' has his business with God (*negotium cum Deo*); see *Institutes of the Christian Religion*, ed. John T. McNeill, tr. Ford Lewis Battles, 2 vols. (Philadelphia, PA: Westminster Press, 1960), vol. 1, p. 212 n. 2.

'desidiosa . . . negotium': I am indebted to Miriam T. Griffin, *Seneca: A Philosopher in Politics* (Oxford: Clarendon Press, 1976), esp. pp. 315–66, 'The Philosopher on Political Participation'. The two phrases which I quote appear on p. 318. The Senecan oxymoron can still be heard, in the last decade of the eighteenth century, in Arthur Murphy's 'translation, or rather imitation' of Johnson's Latin poem composed 'after revising and enlarging the English . . . Dictionary': 'He curs'd the industry, inertly strong, | In creeping toil that could persist so long'. See *An Essay on the Life and Genius of Samuel Johnson LL.D.* by Arthur Murphy Esq. (London, 1792), pp. 82–5.

'Although the Management . . . way': Samuel Butler, *Prose Observations*, ed. Hugh de Quehen (Oxford: Clarendon Press, 1979), p. 194.

the '*Amphion*' . . . Spaniards: *The Poems and Letters of Andrew Marvell*, ed. H. M. Margoliouth, 3rd edn., rev. Pierre Legouis and E. E. Duncan-Jones, 2 vols. (Oxford: Clarendon Press, 1971), vol. 1, pp. 109, 123.

'Resistless genious': Marvell, *The Poems and Letters*, vol. 1, p. 124.

'royal prerogative of Genius': Samuel T. Coleridge, *Marginalia*, ed. George Whalley, 6 parts (Princeton, NJ: Princeton University Press, 1980–2001), part 2, p. 781 (vol. 12 of the Bollingen *Collected Works of Samuel Taylor Coleridge*).

'barbaric genius': George Santayana, *The Life of Reason*, 1-vol. edn. (New York: Scribner, 1954), p. 311 (first pub. 1905–6).

'Genius . . . Caliban': Wyndham Lewis, *The Art of Being Ruled* (London: Chatto and Windus, 1926), pp. 247–9. 'We compose ourselves into a militant league of hatred against the "creative" monster, the inventive brute. Genius has become for us Caliban: what *we* have become, to make this possible, we do not care to consider'.

the '*daimon*' . . . kind': *The Letters of D. H. Lawrence*, ed. Aldous Huxley (New York: Viking Press, 1932), pp. xv, xxix (editor's introduction).

'A happy . . . Nature': 'Preface of the Translator, with a Parallel, of *Poetry* and *Painting*', *De Arte Graphica. The Art of Painting, by C. A. Du Fresnoy, With Remarks, Translated into English . . . by Mr. Dryden* (London, 1695), p. xxxiv.

'No, my Lord . . . immortality': *The Letters of John Wilmot, Earl of Rochester*, ed. Jeremy Treglown (Oxford: Basil Blackwell, 1980), p. 234. See also p. 206 for a note on Blount.

jure natalium: Until the nineteenth century, the public orator of the University of Cambridge had 'the right, often exercised, of presenting noblemen or their sons for the complete degree of Master of Arts, *jure natalium*, and without examination'; see A. G. Hyde, *George Herbert and His Times* (New York: Putnam's, 1906), p. 65.

'*Naturall Power* . . . Luck.': Hobbes, *Leviathan*, p. 150; cf. Macpherson, *Political Theory of Possessive Individualism*, p. 35.

'whom I . . . Tewkesbury': *The Tragedy of Richard III*, I. ii. 240–1 (*F*1).

'You must . . . serues': *Marlowe's Edward II*, ed. William Dinsmore Briggs (London: D. Nutt, 1914), p. 31. Contrast Mycetes' speech ('I might command you to be slain for this') in *Tamburlaine*, p. 57 of *The Plays of Christopher Marlowe*, ed. Roma Gill (London: Oxford University Press, 1971); Mycetes, 'the witless King' (p. 70), himself an otiosity.

'Qual . . . morto': *Dante's Inferno*, tr. Laurence Binyon (London: Macmillan, 1933), p. 156.

'I am my selfe alone': *The Third Part of Henry the Sixt*, v. vi. 83 (*F*1).

'What . . . dead': Pound, *The Spirit of Romance* (London: J. M. Dent, 1910), p. 123.

drafts of the 'Malatesta Cantos': See Daniel Bornstein, 'The Poet as Historian: Researching the Malatesta Cantos', *Paideuma*, vol. 10 (1981), pp. 282–91, at 291. See also Michael F. Harper, 'Truth and Calliope: Ezra Pound's Malatesta', *PMLA*, vol. 96, no. 1 (1981), pp. 86–103. The fullest examination of these cantos in relation to their drafts and to their sources was made by Lawrence S. Rainey, *Ezra Pound and the Monument of Culture: Text, History, and the Malatesta Cantos* (Chicago, IL: University of Chicago Press, 1991).

'I . . . how it is': Pound, *Make it New* (London: Faber and Faber, 1934), pp. 150–1.

'Capo . . . end'): *Dante's Inferno*, pp. 326–7.

'still gleams . . . acts': Ezra Pound, *Selected Prose 1909–1965*, p. 169.

'The Italian . . . personality': *Pavannes and Divagations*, p. 12.

'Stone . . . Fellow': Clarendon, *The History of the Rebellion and Civil Wars in England*, 3 vols. (Oxford, 1702–4), vol. 1, p. 191.

'*We* . . . *businesse*': Aubrey, *Brief Lives*, vol. 1, p. 156: from the funeral sermon.

'vicious . . . Phrase': Thomas Sprat, 'History of the Royal Society', in J. E. Spingarn, ed., *Critical Essays of the Seventeenth Century*, 3 vols. (Oxford: Clarendon Press, 1908), vol. 2, p. 117.

'the ambitious . . . conceaved': Davenant, *Gondibert*, p. 52 ('The Answer of Mr Hobbes').

'our stubborne language': 'An Elegie upon the death of the Deane of Pauls, Dr Iohn Donne', in *The Poems of Thomas Carew*, ed. Rhodes Dunlap (Oxford: Clarendon Press, 1970), p. 73 (first pub. 1949).

'Poesy . . . Nature)': Davenant, *Gondibert*, p. 40.

'The comprehensive . . . Line': Spingarn, ed., *Critical Essays of the Seventeenth Century*, vol. 2, p. 298.

'vultum clausum': See *Characters from the Histories and Memoirs of the Seventeenth Century*, ed. David Nichol Smith (Oxford: Clarendon Press, 1918), p. 153.

'*viso* . . . Milton: *Reliquiae Wottonianae* (London, 1651), p. 435. Although in this edition the recipient is not named, it was no secret. Wotton's letter had been made public in Milton's *Poems* of 1645. The date of the letter is 13 Apr. 1638 and Wotton is here repeating advice he had given to an unknown recipient in (possibly) 1636. See *The Life and Letters of Sir Henry Wotton* by Logan Pearsall Smith, 2 vols. (Oxford: Clarendon Press, 1907), vol. 2, pp. 364, 381.

'as free ... stranger': Izaac Walton, *The Compleat Angler 1653–1676*, ed. Jonquil
Bevan (Oxford: Clarendon Press, 1983), p. 63; cf. p 174.

'not play[ing] ... life': Aubrey, *Brief Lives*, vol. 2, pp. 53–4 ('He had not a generall
acquaintance').

'To be admitted ... Service.': Robert Gould, *Poems Chiefly Consisting of Satyrs and
Satyrical Epistles* (London, 1688/9), A4 verso.

His poems ... Estate': Eugene Hulse Sloane, *Robert Gould: Seventeenth Century Satirist*
(Philadelphia, PA, 1940), pp. 12–15 (Ph.D. thesis, University of Pennsylvania,
1938).

Ezra Pound ... *Epitaphios Bionos*: Pound, *ABC of Reading*, pp. 147–53; see also
Hammond, *John Oldham and the Renewal of Classical Culture*, pp. 36–41.

His praise ... exhausted quite': *The Poems of John Oldham*, ed. Harold F. Brooks and
Raman Selden (Oxford: Clarendon Press, 1987), p. 316, 'To the Memory
of ... Mr. Harman Atwood'.

'inspiration' ... word': Davenant, *Gondibert*, p. 22.

'Bagpipe': Hobbes in ibid., p. 49.

'Poetique Rage': *The Poems of John Oldham*, 70 ('Poetic Rage' / 'guilty Age');
Remains of Mr. John Oldham in Verse and Prose (London, 1684), A[1] verso:
Thomas Flatman, 'On the Death of Mr. John Oldham. A Pindarique Pastoral
Ode' ('frantick Age' / 'poëtick Rage').

'durum ... share': Virgil, *Eclogues and Georgics*, ed. Williams, p. 35. The English
rendering is taken from *Virgil*, tr. H. Rushton Fairclough, 2 vols. (Cambridge,
MA: Harvard University Press, 1978), vol. 1, p. 99 (first pub. 1908).

'whom he had never seen': Ward, *Life of John Dryden*, p. 253.

Keats ... Pernambuca': Keats's note to *King Lear*, quoted in Caroline F. E. Spur-
geon, *Keats's Shakespeare: A Descriptive Study* (London: Oxford University
Press, 1928), p. 51.

'They stood ... fall': 'Eleanora' was published in 1692. Gould, in 1688/9, had
written to, and of, 'Eleanora's' husband: 'Neither are these Showres of Liberality rain'd only on your Domesticks; Strangers, as well as they, have their share'
(Gould, *Poems*, A4 verso).

'For, we are fallen ... people.': *The State of Innocence and Fall of Man: An Opera.
Written in Heroique Verse ... by John Dryden* (London, 1677), b1 verso.

'Interests ... other': Aubrey, *Brief Lives*, vol. 2, p. 72. 'Was not the most magnificent
of all replies to Hobbes Milton's *Paradise Lost*?' (Marjorie Hope Nicolson,
'Milton and Hobbes', *Studies in Philology*, vol. 23, no. 4 (1926), p. 411). The
cogency of this challenge is not diminished by a recognition of complementary
elements, as in 'Christ's almost Hobbesian exaggeration of the aristocratic
element in the Aristotelian magnanimous man's renunciation of the world' at
Paradise Regain'd, vol. 3, pp. 47–51. See Carey's note in Milton, *Complete Shorter
Poems*, p. 465.

The legislative style ... Abdiel: *Paradise Lost*, v. 805–907. Abdiel's 'flame of zeale' is
supremely 'reason'd'; Satan's 'fury' is a cheating 'passion'. It could equally well

be said that Dryden's legislative style, like Thomas Sprat's 'Reason set out in plain, undeceiving expressions', is one man's offering towards those unattainable 'united indeavors of some publick minds . . . conversant both in Letters and business' which the proposer for erecting an English Academy envisaged as a 'brave . . . undertaking' in '*Civil History*' and a moral lesson in 'obedience' (see Spingarn, *Critical Essays of the Seventeenth Century*, vol. 2, pp. 112, 114–15).

'Princes . . . Heroes)': Davenant, *Gondibert*, p. 45: 'The Answer of Mr Hobbes'.

11. The Tartar's Bow and the Bow of Ulysses

'Tuneful . . . Song': *Milton's Sonnets*, ed. E. A. J. Honigmann (London: Macmillan, 1966), p. xiii.

'with . . . accent': Ibid.

'humor' . . . exigencies': Ibid.; see also *OED*[2], s.v. 'humour, humor, *v*', citing Milton's phrase.

'a . . . style': Honigmann, *Milton's Sonnets*, p. 131.

('Thou . . . Quire'): Honigmann, *Milton's Sonnets*, p. xiii.

Milton's drafts . . . tongue': John Milton, *Poems, Reproduced in Facsimile from the Manuscript in Trinity College, Cambridge* (Menston: Scolar Press, 1970), pp. 43, 45; Honigmann, *Milton's Sonnets*, p. 126.

'declamatory' . . . no more than this: For a full discussion see Ian Spink, *English Song: Dowland to Purcell* (London: Batsford, 1974), esp. part 1, ch. 2, 'The New Men and the New Music', and part 2, ch. 1, 'Henry Lawes' "tunefull and well measur'd song"'. See also Honigmann, *Milton's Sonnets*, pp. 127–8; *Selected Songs of Thomas Campion*, ed. W. H. Auden (Boston: David Godine, 1973), p. 17. I am indebted to Richard Luckett for his advice.

It will . . . 'intolerable': See Richard Peters, *Hobbes* (Harmondsworth: Penguin, 1956), p. 17.

'intolerable wrestle . . . meanings': T. S. Eliot, *Four Quartets* (London: Faber and Faber, 1944), p. 17.

Bacon . . . Customes'): *The Twoo Bookes of the Proficience and Advancement of Learning* (London, 1605), facsimile edn. (Amsterdam: Theatrum Orbis Terrarum, 1970), The second Booke, 57, 56 verso. For Bacon's conflation of the Tartar's bow with the Parthian bow, see *The Advancement of Learning*, ed. Michael Kiernan (Oxford: Clarendon Press, 2000), p. 311 (*The Oxford Francis Bacon*, vol. 4).

'attamen . . . sufficiunt': *The Works of Francis Bacon*, ed. James Spedding, Robert Leslie Ellis, and Douglas Denon Heath, 7 vols., new edn. (London: Longmans, 1870), vol. 1, p. 646; vol. 4, p. 434, 'yet all is not enough'.

'retro . . . retorqueant': Ibid. ('they shoot back at the understanding from which they proceeded').

'inseparable . . . life': Bacon, *The Twoo Bookes*, The second Booke, p. 57.

'collective body of assumptions': Simon Patrick, *A Brief Account of the New Sect of Latitude-Men* (1662), introduction by T. A. Birrell, (Los Angeles, CA: William Andrews Clarke Memorial Library, 1963), p. iv: Birrell's phrase.

Sir Robert Howard's ... others': *The Great Favourite Or, The Duke of Lerma* (London, 1668), facsimile edn. (New York: Garland, 1975), A4 verso, A3.

'prouidently towards the *Future*': Thomas Hobbes, *Eight Bookes of the Peloponnesian Warre Written by Thucydides* (London, 1629): first page of 'To the Readers'.

'certain fortuitous Concretions ... sentence': Citations given by OED^2, s.v. 'contexture'.

Puttenham says ... man': George Puttenham, *The Arte of English Poesie*, ed. Gladys Doidge Willcock and Alice Walker (Cambridge: Cambridge University Press, 1936), p. 197.

intrinsic perplexities: As recognized also by Sidney, who referred to 'a slidingnesse of language' in the *New Arcadia* (see *The Prose Works of Sir Philip Sidney*, ed. Albert Feuillerat, 4 vols. (Cambridge: Cambridge University Press, 1962), vol. 1, p. 319 and *The Countess of Pembroke's Arcadia (The New Arcadia)*, ed. Victor Skretkowicz (Oxford: Clarendon Press, 1987), p. 288).

When Chaucer ... Nicholas': *The Works of Geoffrey Chaucer*, ed. F. N. Robinson, 2nd edn. (London: Oxford University Press, 1957), pp. 44 (l. 2779), p. 48 (l. 3204).

'Measure' ... short': Puttenham, *The Arte of English Poesie*, p. 67.

In Skelton's ... merry': John Skelton, *Magnyfycence*, ed. Robert Lee Ramsay (London: Oxford University Press, 1958), pp. 4–5 ('wylde Insolence', 'I ponder ... wrought'), p. liii ('so-called tumbling verse'), p. lxviii ('macaronic hexameter'), p. xiii ('a notable shortcoming ... is the character-drawing'), pp. 22–3 ('To passe ... perylous thynge'), p. 1 ('A goodly ... merry'). First published by the Early English Text Society, Extra Series, 98, in 1908. See also p. xlii: 'It would seem that Skelton prided himself especially on the invention and delineation of this little group of typical evil courtiers [i.e. Counterfet Countence, Crafty Conueyaunce, Clokyd Colusyon, Courtly Abusyon]'. Robert S. Kinsman suggests, in his introduction to *John Skelton: Poems* (Oxford: Clarendon Press, 1969), that 'Skelton ... seeks metrically to distinguish the characters of his play' (p. x). In the quoted passage I adopt Ramsay's punctuation and capitals but retain Rastell's (?) unindented line-setting.

'conformity ... measure': OED^2, s.v. 'number, *n.*', 14a.

Wyatt's ... deserued: The editorial problems presented by Wyatt's poems are notorious. See the full discussion of textual questions in H. A. Mason's *Editing Wyatt* (Cambridge: Cambridge Quarterly, 1972) and *Sir Thomas Wyatt: A Literary Portrait* (Bristol: Bristol Classical Press, 1986). My reading is indebted to Richard Harrier, *The Canon of ... Wyatt's Poetry* (Cambridge, MA: Harvard University Press, 1975), pp. 131–2 (I have removed the MS contractions from 'serued', 'deserued'). Harrier transcribes from the Egerton MS; Mason argues for the superiority of the Devonshire text's markedly different reading of the final line. See also Kenneth Muir, ed., *The Life and Letters of Sir Thomas Wyatt* (Liverpool: Liverpool University Press, 1963), pp. 146, 164, 166; William Tydeman, ed., *English Poetry 1400–1580* (London: Heinemann Educational, 1970), pp. 220, 19.

'haughty ... serfs': *The Ancrene Riwle (The Corpus MS: Ancrene Wisse)*, tr. M. B. Salu (London: Burns & Oates, 1955), p. 158. In Middle English: '& þolieð ofte danger of swuch oðerhwile þe mahte beon ower þreal', *Ancrene Wisse, Parts Six and Seven*, ed. Geoffrey Shepherd (London: Nelson, 1959), p. 7.

'newfangleness': In Chaucer, e.g. 'The Squire's Tale', l. 610: 'Men loven of proper kynde newefangelnesse, | As briddes doon that men in cages fede'.

In Arcites' death-speech: See Nevill Coghill, 'Chaucer's Idea of What is Noble', *English Association Presidential Address* (London: English Association, 1971), p. 13. Coghill observes that in these lines Chaucer is free from the influence of Boccaccio, the author to whom 'The Knight's Tale' is elsewhere much indebted.

'a figure . . . away': *The Garden of Eloquence (1593)* by Henry Peacham, facsimile edn. (Gainesville, FL: Scholars' Facsimiles & Reprints, 1954), p. 56.

Puttenham . . . 'reproue': Puttenham, *The Arte of English Poesie*, pp. 202–3. But Puttenham appears to conflate '*Prosonomasia*, or the Nicknamer' (a 'by-name geuen in sport', as 'Errans mus' for 'Erasmus') with *paronomasia* (*OED²*: 'after παρονομάζειν to alter slightly in naming', 'play upon words which sound alike', 'a pun'). The compiler of the 1589 'table' or index complicates matters further by referring to '*Paronomasia, or the nicknamer*' (see p. 312). Angel Day, in *The English Secretorie* (1586), also 'confused' the two terms (see *OED²*, s.v. 'prosonomasia'). Thomas More offers an example of 'lepida paranomasia' in referring to Luther as 'pater, potator Lutherus'; see *Responsio ad Lutherum*, ed. John M. Headley, 2 parts (New Haven, CT: Yale University Press, 1969), part 1, p. 314 (vol. 5 of *The Complete Works of St. Thomas More*).

'vnkyndly': *Tottel's Miscellany (1557–1587)*, ed. Hyder Edward Rollins, 2 vols. (Cambridge, MA: Harvard University Press, 1929), vol. 1, p. 39 (no. 52).

The seventh chapter . . . courtiers': Puttenham, *The Arte of English Poesie*, pp. 154–5.

'ornament poeticall': Ibid., p. 137.

'spacious . . . diuision': I allude to Troilus' speech on the defection of Cressida, in Shakespeare's play (v. ii. 137–60, at 150), to which later reference is made (text as First Folio [*F*1]).

'I doute not . . . iudgmente': Wyatt, *Life and Letters*, p. 189.

'but one . . . chaynged': Ibid., p. 197.

'[W]hat . . . thynges?': Ibid., p. 203.

Puttenham . . . interpretation of words: Puttenham, *The Arte of English Poesie*, pp. xxxviii, xviii.

'real . . . suffering': William Wordsworth, *Poems*, ed. John O. Hayden, 2 vols. (New Haven, CT: Yale University Press, 1981), vol. 1, p. 878 (Preface to *Lyrical Ballads*, 1802). Cf. *The Prose Works of William Wordsworth*, ed. W. J. B. Owen and Jane Worthington Smyser, 3 vols. (Oxford: Clarendon Press, 1974), vol. 1, p. 138; and William Wordsworth, *Lyrical Ballads and Other Poems, 1797–1800*, ed. James Butler and Karen Green (Ithaca, NY: Cornell University Press, 1992), p. 751.

'figures rhethoricall': Puttenham, *The Arte of English Poesie*, p. 196. Note p. 154, where Puttenham warns that figures draw common utterance 'from plainnesse and simplicitie to a certaine doublenesse, whereby our talk is the more guilefull & abusing'.

'practisis' and 'trafiques': Wyatt, *Life and Letters*, pp. 127–8.

'DISPUTANDI . . . CHURCH': *Reliquiae Wottonianae* (London, 1651), Ac8 verso.

'morall Images, and Examples': *Sir Fulke Greville's Life of Sir Philip Sidney*, ed. Nowell Smith (Oxford: Clarendon Press, 1907), p. 223.

'the "fleering . . . nose" ': Puttenham, *The Arte of English Poesie*, p. lxxxii.

'fain[ing]': *The Works of Thomas Nashe*, ed. Ronald B. McKerrow, corr. repr., 5 vols. (Oxford: B. Blackwell, 1966), vol. 1, p. 183.

'Ovt . . . selfe?': Ibid.

'iesting': Ibid., p. 209.

'Cum autem . . . rebel'): Bacon, *Works*, vol. 1, p. 645; vol. 4, p. 433.

'You . . . time': Joyce Rathbone, 'A Pianist as Violinist', *Tempo: A Quarterly Review of Modern Music*, 123 (1977), pp. 14–22, at p. 21.

Two . . . alone: *The Poems and Letters of Andrew Marvell*, ed. H. M. Margoliouth, 3rd edn., rev. Pierre Legouis and E. E. Duncan-Jones, 2 vols. (Oxford: Clarendon Press, 1971), vol. 1, p. 53.

'pushed beyond . . . reasonable': OED^2, s.v. 'strained'.

'dissections . . . Word: *Essays in Divinity* by John Donne, ed. Evelyn M. Simpson (Oxford: Clarendon Press, 1952), p. 57. There is a beautiful enactment of the pains of cribration in Newman's letter to his sister Jemima, 29 Jan. 1838. It is of course true that 'Newman customarily used little dashes, to do duty for a comma, a semi-colon or a full stop, when he was writing informally and at speed' (*A Packet of Letters: A Selection from the Correspondence of John Henry Newman*, ed. Joyce Sugg (Oxford: Clarendon Press, 1983), p. xxi, editor's introduction) but in this letter the customary device is made a parody of itself and of the various pressures which make it necessary. The plethoric 'little dash' suggests both unremitting activity and continuous agitation ('—I put it by—I take it up—I begin to correct again—it will not do—alterations multiply— pages are re-written—little lines sneak in and crawl about—') while taking comic advantage of both; it is as if the 'dashes' were themselves dashing away with the smoothing-iron. The charm of the passage is chiefly due to the fact that Newman does, after all, most effectively reduce the 'business' to 'a very homely undertaking': 'washing a sponge of the sea gravel and sea smell' (p. 43).

'this examination . . . Saviours': *The Sermons of John Donne*, ed. George R. Potter and Evelyn M. Simpson, 10 vols. (Berkeley, CA: University of California Press, 1953–62), vol. 10, p. 247.

In a letter . . . power: The sermon 'Preached to the King, at White-Hall, the first of April, 1627': Donne, *Sermons*, vol. 7, pp. 39–40, 393. R. C. Bald, *John Donne: A Life* (London: Clarendon Press, 1970), p. 525 n. 1, suggests that, as a result of the trouble caused by this sermon, it may have become Donne's habit thereafter 'to write out his Court sermons in full'.

If I say . . . speech: One observes that 'heft' itself may sustain a subtle tuning, as in Whitman's 'Hefts of the moving world at innocent gambols silently rising, freshly exuding' ('Song of Myself', l. 553) or Emily Dickinson's 'There's a certain Slant of light, | Winter Afternoons—| That oppresses, like the Heft |

Of Cathedral Tunes—' (*The Poems of Emily Dickinson*, ed. R. W. Franklin (Cambridge, MA: Belknap Press, 1999), p. 142). One observes further that received tuning-words may be satirically subjected to violent hefts, as in Nashe's 'Hence, double diligence, thou mean'st deceit' (*Svmmers Last Will and Testament*, 1163; see *Works*, vol. 3, p. 270) or in Jonson's 'the *Senate's* brainlesse diligence' (*Seianus*, III. 472; see *Ben Jonson*, ed. C. H. Herford and Percy Simpson, 11 vols. (Oxford: Clarendon Press, 1925–52), vol. 4, p. 408). Anthony Lane draws my attention to a passage in C. S. Peirce (see *Collected Papers of Charles Sanders Peirce*, ed. C. Hartshorne, P. Weiss, et al., 8 vols. (Cambridge, MA: Harvard University Press, 1931–58), vol. 6, p. 217): 'It is not in perceiving its qualities that they know it, but in hefting its insistency then and there, which Duns called its *haecceitas*—or, if he didn't, it was this that he was groping after'. I understand 'its . . . its . . . its' to refer to 'every correlate of an existential relation' posited in a previous sentence. Although 'hefting' strikes one as having been chosen with a degree of expressive care, 'It is not . . .' and 'it was this . . .' appear as lax and intrusive locutions in a statement which lays a heavy semantic burden on 'it'. Metaphysically deft and resonant ('hefting its insistency then and there'), syntactically both strained and slack, Peirce's sentence embodies the positive and negative aspects of word-hefting.

'such . . . as may serve . . . are so': John Locke, *An Essay Concerning Human Understanding*, ed. Peter H. Nidditch (Oxford: Clarendon Press, 1975), pp. 476, 492.

'unsteady . . . Notions': Ibid., p. 492.

'being true . . . uncertaine': *The Works of George Herbert*, ed. F. E. Hutchinson (Oxford: Clarendon Press, 1941), pp. 264–5.

'just occasion': Ibid., p. 265.

'divine vertue': Ibid., p. 267.

'Since . . . Musique': John Donne, *The Divine Poems*, ed. Helen Gardner (Oxford: Clarendon Press, 1952), p. 50.

'I am . . . sit': Ibid., p. 44.

'I returned . . . patronage of you': *Poems and Letters*, vol. 2, p. 81.

In the lyric dialogues . . . 1650s: See e.g. Donald M. Friedman, *Marvell's Pastoral Art* (Berkeley, CA: University of California Press, 1970), pp. 2, 33 n. 11.

'busie Companies of Men': *Poems and Letters*, vol. 1, p. 51. Compare 'the busie humm of men' in Milton's 'L'Allegro', l. 118.

'really . . . you': Ibid., vol. 2, p. 42.

'precious Time' . . . *Colen*' etc.): Ibid., vol. 2, pp. 323–5.

'*Civill* . . . House': John Donne, *Sermons*, vol. 3, p. 361, 'Preached at Saint Pauls upon Christmasse day, 1621'; *The Diary of Samuel Pepys*, ed. Robert Latham and William Matthews, 11 vols. (London: Bell, 1970–83), vol. 7, p. 24; Marvell, *Poems and Letters*, vol. 2, pp. 52, 44, 23.

'The Ballast . . . businesse': *Poems and Letters*, vol. 2, pp. 33, 61.

as Sir Henry Wotton observes . . . tacite': *The Life and Letters of Sir Henry Wotton*, ed. Logan Pearsall Smith, 2 vols. (Oxford: Clarendon Press 1907), vol. 2, p. 15.

'My L: Mordants ... Chatham': *Poems and Letters*, vol. 2, pp. 53, 60.

'You are not ignorant of our Business with you': *Amboyna, A Tragedy ... Written by John Dryden* (London, 1673), p. 54.

'my Tanger=Boates business': Pepys, *Diary*, vol. 7, p. 24. See also vol. 6, pp. 146, 172, 286; vol. 11, pp. 278–9.

'For the *Moral ... Poet*': Du Fresnoy, *De Arte Graphica. The Art of Painting*, tr. Dryden, p. xix ('Preface of the Translator').

''tis your business ... here': Dryden, *Poems*, ed. Kinsley, 39.

'Thus fell ... innocence': *Characters from the Histories and Memoirs of the Seventeenth Century*, ed. David Nichol Smith (Oxford: Clarendon Press, 1918), p. 86.

'For, this life ... businesse': Donne, *Sermons*, vol. 8, p. 53.

('Make you ... will'): Epistle to the Hebrews, 13: 21 (as 1611).

'Domestique ... practice': Greville, *Life of Sir Philip Sidney*, pp. 185, 211. The 'ideal' model for the integration of 'domestic affairs' with the common weal is given in book 11, ch. 3, of More's *Utopia*: 'Therfore matters of greate weyghte and importaunce be brought to the electyon house of the syphograuntes, whyche open the matter to their familyes; and afterwarde, when they haue consulted among them selfes, they shewe their deuyse to the cowncell' (*The Utopia of Sir Thomas More*, ed. J. H. Lupton (Oxford: Clarendon Press, 1895), p. 137). For the cohabitation of ideal and unideal in the Tudor Court see E. W. Ives's discussion, *Anne Boleyn* (Oxford: Blackwell, 1986), ch. 1: 'More himself was well aware that in the real world of the Renaissance court, the best that morality and honesty could hope to achieve was compromise. How difficult that was, his own future career would show' (p. 9). For a figurative application see Milton, *The Tenure of Kings and Magistrates*: 'to dispose and *oeconomize* in the Land which God hath giv'n them, as Maisters of Family in thir own house and free inheritance' (John Milton, *Selected Prose*, ed. C. A. Patrides (Harmondsworth: Penguin, 1974), p. 280).

'Poetical ... not 'reall'': Greville, *Life of Sir Philip Sidney*, p. 46.

'safe ... duty': Ibid., p. 126. Dryden's poetic and dramatic 'interest in the limits of maxims' has been suggested by Alan Fisher: 'The maxims of rational control are true, they are wise, and they apply—but there is no *power* in them: they cannot save one from the forces of life'. See Phillip Harth, Alan Fisher, and Ralph Cohen, *New Homage to John Dryden* (Los Angeles, CA: William Andrews Clark Memorial Library, 1983), pp. 38, 42.

'buisinesses and other accidents': Wotton, *Life and Letters*, vol. 2, p. 96; collated with the original manuscript held in the Public Record Office, London (SP99, Bundle 21, fo. 124).

'insolent' ... 'devourers': *The Odyssey*, tr. A. T. Murray, 2 vols. (London: W. Heinemann, 1919), vol. 2, pp. 275, 267.

'aptnesse' and 'cunnynge': Roger Ascham, *English Works*, ed. William Aldis Wright (Cambridge: Cambridge University Press, 1904), p. 62.

'I never ... *Cleopatra*': Du Fresnoy, *De Arte Graphica. The Art of Painting*, tr. Dryden, p. liv.

'*Con Amore* ... it selfe': *Of the Elements of Architecture: The Second Part*. In *Reliquiae Wottonianae*, 1651; see p. 274.

'Instantly ... not': Ralph W. Emerson, *Essays and Lectures*, ed. Joel Porte (New York: Viking Press, 1983), p. 60 ('The American Scholar').

12. Caveats Enough in their Own Walks

An apophthegm of Cicero: See *Cicero's Letters to Atticus*, ed. D. R. Shackleton Bailey, 7 vols. (Cambridge: University Press, 1965–70), vol. 1, pp. 198–9.

Bacon ... Pound: It also appears in Jonathan Swift, *A Discourse on the Contests and Dissentions Between the Nobles and the Commons of Athens and Rome*, ed. Frank H. Ellis (Oxford: Clarendon Press, 1967), p. 126.

'learned men' ... walkes': *The Twoo Bookes of the Proficience and Advancement of Learning* (London, 1605), facsimile edn. (Amsterdam: Theatrum Orbis Terrarum, 1970), The first Booke, p. 14.

'did believe ... indulgent': *Characters from the Histories and Memoirs of the Seventeenth Century*, ed. David Nichol Smith (Oxford: Clarendon Press, 1918), p. 95.

'the common practice of men': Ibid., p. 94.

He wrote frequently ... of the whole Businesse': *The Life and Letters of Sir Henry Wotton*, ed. Logan Pearsall Smith, 2 vols. (Oxford: Clarendon Press 1907), collated, as indicated, with the original manuscripts held in the Public Record Office and in the British Library: vol. 2, p. 42 (PRO, SP84, vol. 70, fo. 58), vol. 2, p. 50 (SP84, vol. 70, fo. 122), vol. 2, p. 56 (BL Stowe MS175, fo. 71).

'one maine knott in the whole businesse': Wotton, *Life and Letters*, vol. 2, p. 191; cf. *Letters and Dispatches from Sir Henry Wotton to James I and his Ministers in the Years MDC XVII–XX* (London: Roxburghe Club, 1850), p. 223.

'tyme to knit knotts': Ibid., vol. 2, p. 96 (PRO, SP99, Bundle 21, fol. 124).

'ballance' ... duty': *Sir Fulke Greville's Life of Sir Philip Sidney*, ed. Nowell Smith (Oxford: Clarendon Press, 1907), p. 126.

'holding a meane ... equiuocation': Wotton, *Life and Letters*, vol. 2, p. 251 (SP99, Bundle 24, fo. 190 verso).

'*Policie*' ... 'most immersed': Bacon, *Twoo Bookes*, The second Booke, p. 64.

'that which taketh ... Generalities': Ibid., p. 64.

'*Macciauell* ... do': Ibid., The second Booke, p. 77.

The ancient ... renown: *The Annals of Tacitus*, ed. Henry Furneaux, 2nd edn., rev. H. F. Pelham and C. D. Fisher, 2 vols. (Oxford: Clarendon Press, 1896–1907), vol. 1, pp. 529–31

Seneca ... proscripsit': Seneca, *Moral Essays*, tr. John W. Basore, 3 vols. (London: Heinemann, 1932), vol. 2, pp. 90–1: 'in which he himself proscribed for all time the agents of proscription' (I have changed Basore's 'sponsors' to 'agents').

'the wit ... thereby': Bacon, *Twoo Bookes*, The first Booke, p. 20.

'diligent ... creatures': Ibid., The first Booke, p. 22.

'Every . . . season': Ecclesiastes 3: 11, 'He hath made euery thing beautifull in his time' (King James Bible).

Bacon . . . pleasure: See The first Booke, p. 4.

Clarendon . . . eare': *Characters*, p. 95.

Aubrey . . . 'bussinesse': *Aubrey's Brief Lives*, ed. Oliver Lawson Dick (Harmondsworth: Penguin, 1972), p. 233. Andrew Clark 'suppressed' this phrase in his edition (Oxford: Clarendon Press, 1898), p. 2 vols: see vol. 1, p. 188.

'convivium . . . theologicum': *Characters*, p. 92.

Aldrovandus . . . fishes: Second edition, 'much enlarged' (London, 1655), p. 178. This was the first appearance of the passage. See Izaac Walton, *The Compleat Angler 1653–1676*, ed. Jonquil Bevan (Oxford: Clarendon Press, 1983), pp. 272–3, for the 1676 reading, which differs in small details.

George Wither's . . . matter': *The Hymnes and Songs of the Chvrch . . . Translated, and Composed by G.W.* (London, 1623), A2, A2 verso.

'Comeliness': Patrick Collinson, in *Godly People: Essays on English Protestantism and Puritanism* (London: The Hambledon Press, 1983), p. 534, quotes a Puritan in 1642 indicating that he was not a noncomformist in 'things of small matter, not touching . . . conscience but Comelynesse'.

'To this . . . *mediocrity*': *The Sermons of John Donne*, ed. George R. Potter and Evelyn M. Simpson, 10 vols. (Berkeley, CA: University of California Press, 1953–62), vol. 8, pp. 88–9. It was a familiar reproach that the disguised Jesuit mission-priests went about in costly ostentatious attire. Southwell defended the practice, as being framed 'to the necessity of our daies'. 'It is noe sure Argument of inward vanity to be vaine in shew, sith a modest and an humble mynd may be shrowded vnder the glorious and Courtly Robes of a virtuous *Hester*', in *An Humble Supplication to Her Maiestie by Robert Southwell*, ed. R. C. Bald (Cambridge: Cambridge University Press, 1953), p. 8, 8 n. 2, 9 (*An Humble Supplication* was published in 1591).

'generous . . . men': *Characters*, 77.

Wither . . . easier way: Wither, *Hymnes and Songs*, A3 verso.

Walton's . . . what it may seem: An impression substantiated by the textual history of this very phrase: 'the most honest, ingenious, and harmless Art of Angling', 1653; 'the most *honest, ingenuous, quiet,* and *harmless* art of *Angling*', 1676. See Walton, *The Compleat Angler*, ed. Bevan, pp. 69, 193. See further, p. 654.

The Life . . . Wottonianae: David Novarr, *The Making of Walton's 'Lives'* (Ithaca, NY: Cornell University Press, 1958), ch. 5, provides a useful commentary on significant verbal changes in the three editions of *Reliquiae* issued during Walton's lifetime.

'Old fashioned Poetry, but choicely good': It may be worth noting that Walton also uses 'choicely good' to commend carps' tongues as a delicacy: Walton, *The Compleat Angler*, ed. Bevan, 130.

In the third edition of 1661: p. 76.

But 'strong lines' . . . obscurity': *Sir William Davenant's Gondibert*, ed. David F. Gladish (Oxford: Clarendon Press, 1971), p. 52, 'The Answer of Mr Hobbes'. See also

George Williamson, *Seventeenth Century Contexts* (London: Faber and Faber, 1960), pp. 120–31.

'At this...bite': *Wotton*, ed. Smith, vol. 2, p. 20; cf *Letters of Sir Henry Wotton to Sir Edmund Bacon* (London, 1661), p. 162. One may add: 'having in the meane tyme like the fishermen of thease lagune only prepared owre netts and owre hookes to catche somewhat heereafter', vol. 2, pp. 97–8 (SP99, Bundle 21, fo. 141).

added to the second edition: Walton, *The Compleat Angler*, ed. Bevan, 49.

as though floating...maxims: The kind of *tone* I have in mind is 'Per il che si ha a notare che gli uomini si debbono o vezzeggiare o spegnere', Englished by Dacres as 'for it is to be noted, that men must either be dallied and flatterd withall, or else be quite crusht'. See *Il Principe*, ed. L. Arthur Burd (Oxford: Clarendon Press, 1891), pp. 188–9 and *The Prince*, tr. Edward Dacres (London: A. Moring, 1929), p. 9 (Dacres' translation first pub. 1640).

'reciprocall...duties': Greville, *Life of Sir Philip Sidney*, p. 180.

'To come...power': *King Lear*, I. i. p. 170 (*Q1–2*: 'betweene').

('Huddled...Convenience'): *The Metaphysical Poets*, ed. Helen Gardner, rev. edn. (Harmondsworth: Penguin, 1966), p. 222.

'But Fate...betwixt': *The Poems and Letters of Andrew Marvell*, ed. H. M. Margoliouth, 3rd edn., rev. Pierre Legouis and E. E. Duncan-Jones, 2 vols. (Oxford: Clarendon Press, 1971), vol. 1, p. 39.

'the various movements...different Passions': *The Works of John Dryden*, ed. Edward Niles Hooker, H. T. Swedenberg, Jr., and Vinton A. Dearing, 20 vols. (Berkeley, CA, 1956–2000), vol. 17, p. 30 (*An Essay of Dramatick Poesie*).

'Nor did...spent': Cf. Walton, *Compleat Angler*, ed. Bevan, p. 76.

'*Legatus est...causa*': Samuel Johnson, in *Idler*, no. 30 (11 Nov. 1758), refers to 'Sir Henry Wotton's jocular definition'; see *The Yale Edition of the Works of Samuel Johnson* (New Haven, CT: Yale University Press, 1958–), vol. 2, p. 94.

Pound's...translate': *Literary Essays of Ezra Pound*, ed. T. S. Eliot (London: Faber & Faber, 1954), p. 25.

Bacon's caveat...really are: Bacon, *The Twoo Bookes*, The first Booke, p. 19. I also quote Spedding's gloss (vol. 3, p. 285 n. 1) on Bacon's augmented Latin version (vol. 1, p. 452): 'delicias et lauticias'.

'And you must Fish for him with a strong Line': 3rd edn. (1661), p. 127.

'box where...lie': *The Works of George Herbert*, ed. F. E. Hutchinson (Oxford: Clarendon Press, 1941), p. 88 ('Vertue', l. 10).

According to Walton's marginal note: See Novarr, *The Making of Walton's 'Lives'*, p. 160.

'stretched sinews'...'art': *The Works of George Herbert*, p. 41 ('Easter', ll. 11, 7–8).

'crabbed...syntax': John Donne, *The Satires, Epigrams and Verse Letters*, ed. W. Milgate (Oxford: Clarendon Press, 1967), p. 228 (editorial commentary).

Donne engineers...self-purification: Ibid., p. 223 (editorial commentary).

As Walton observed...this voyage': Donne's wounded ambition and Walton's brisk parenthetical tact are equally concerned with Donne's self-blighted career, the disgrace and loss of worldly prospects incurred by his secret marriage to Ann More. See R. C. Bald, *John Donne: A Life* (London: Clarendon Press, 1970), pp. 128, 145–6.

'the painfull . . . Vertue': Davenant, *Gondibert*, p. 14.

Such words . . . circumstances: In the 'Preface' to *The Elements of Architecture* Wotton expands upon the sentiment of the letter from Venice: 'I have born abroad some part of his [the King's] *civil* Service; yet when I came home, and was again resolved into mine own simplicity, I found it fitter for my *Penne* (at least in this first publique adventure) to deale with these plain *Compilements*, and tractable *Materials*; then with the *Laberynths* and *Mysteries* of *Courts* and *States*' (*Reliquiae Wottonianae* (1651), p. 198).

The Rt Hon. H. H. Asquith . . . Bohemia"': *Sir Henry Wotton, with Some General Reflections on Style in English Poetry* (Oxford: Oxford University Press, 1919), pp. 3, 7, 8, 6 (English Association Pamphlets, no. 44).

written . . . remembered: *Wotton*, ed. Smith, vol. 1, pp. 170–1.

'ordinary . . . Life': John Locke, *An Essay Concerning Human Understanding*, ed. Peter H. Nidditch (Oxford: Clarendon Press, 1975), p. 492.

written in 1619 or 1620 . . . Petrarch: Asquith, *Sir Henry Wotton*, p. 7, suggests 1619; for 1620 see Wotton, *Life and Letters*, vol. 1; pp. 171–1 n. 1; vol. 2, p. 415.

'forraign imployments . . . Nation': Walton, *Compleat Angler*, ed. Bevan, 76.

You meaner *Beauties* . . . shall rise?: This is a notoriously 'eclectic' text. I accept the argument, and adopt the reading, of J. B. Leishman, ' "You meaner Beauties of the Night": A Study in Transmission and Transmogrification', *The Library*, vol. 26, nos. 2–3 (1945), p. 99–121.

'Thy worth . . . the throng': John Milton, 'To Mr. H. Lawes, on his Aires', l. 5.

'Jewell of Diamonds . . . pleas'd he should call her': These revisions are noted in Novarr, *The Making of Walton's 'Lives'*, pp. 175–7.

Wotton . . . practice of the time: Wotton, *Life and Letters*, vol. 1, p. 174 n. 3.

'great dexteritie . . . conceyte': Ibid., vol. 1, p. 354 (SP99, Bundle 3, fo. 108).

'rich Iewel . . . deare': 1. v. 46–7.

'points of conuenience . . . *stato*': Bacon, *The Twoo Bookes*, The first Booke, p. 9.

Machiavelli's . . . e le cose': Machiavelli, *Il Principe*, pp. 190, 246, 361.

'affayres of the world': Machiavelli, *The Prince*, p. 48.

'A peece . . . curiositie': Wotton, *Life and Letters*, vol. 2, p. 147; *Letters and Dispatches*, 24.

('I call . . . occupation'): Wotton, *Life and Letters*, vol. 1, p. 351 (SP99, Bundle 3, fo. 88).

'how wholeheartedly . . . profession': Ibid., vol. 1, p. 66.

'enter'd into . . . matter': Letters to Lord Zouch, 8 May 1592, 21 Apr. 1591 (*Reliquiae Wottonianae*, The Fourth Edition (London, 1685), pp. 651, 649).

Among Plutarch's: *Moralia*: *Plutarch's Moralia*, tr. Frank Cole Babbitt, 14 vols. (London: W. Heinemann, 1927–69), vol. 2, pp. 4–41 ('How to Profit by one's Enemies').

Of the Benefit . . . Enemies: *The Works of Henry Vaughan*, ed. L. C. Martin, 2 vols. (Oxford: Clarendon Press, 1914), vol. 1, pp. 97–108.

'Where our ... our selves.': Ibid., p. 103.

'vitious unfolding ... errours': Ibid., p. 104.

'so ingenuous: Thus, in editions of 1651 (c2) and 1654 (47); 'so ingenious', 1672 (c6). See above, p. 651.

Pliny the Elder's discourse: In *Nat. Hist.* 34. 9–19.

'quas ne victor quidem abolevit': *Annals*, ed. Furneaux, vol. 1, p. 532. See also Tacitus, *Histories / Annals*, tr. Clifford H. Moore and John Jackson, 4 vols. (London: W. Heinemann, 1937), vol. 3, pp. 62–3.

exercised in discreet privacy: *Annals*, ed. Furneaux, vol. 2, pp. 436–7. See also Pliny, *Letters*, tr. William Melmoth, 2 vols. (London: W. Heinemann, 1915), vol. 1, pp. 58–61.

'adulatio' and 'avaritia': *Annals*, ed. Furneaux, vol. 1, pp. 180, 182. See also *The Annals of Tacitus*, ed. F. R. D. Goodyear, 2 vols. (Cambridge: University Press, 1972), vol. 1, p. 97.

It is a piece of unassimilated matter lodged in the body politic: I here repeat a phrase from Ch. 9, p. 152.

flagitia: *Annals*, ed. Furneaux, vol. 1, p. 652. See also *Histories / Annals*, vol. 3, pp. 238–9.

'verba ... permodesto': *Annals*, ed. Furneaux, vol. 1, p. 189. See also Goodyear, vol. 1, pp. 139–40.

'words ... reueng'd': *Ben Jonson*, vol. 4, p. 407, l. 445.

'meta-theology' ... divines': John Donne, *Essays in Divinity*, ed. Evelyn M. Simpson (Oxford: Clarendon Press, 1952), pp. 59, 129 (Simpson's notes). In the *OED* (1933), s.v. 'metatheology', Donne's usage (*ante* 1615) is the sole citation. In the second edition (1989), Donne remains the single example of this sense (*a*). However, there is now a sense (*b*) = the philosophical study of the nature of religious language or statements. The *OED*² gives three citations for the second sense (1957, 1959, 1967), and records the derivations 'meta-theologian' (1967) and 'meta-theological' (1969). It is perhaps necessary to remark that, when I speak of 'meta-poetry', I do not mean 'the philosophical study of the nature of poetic language or statements'.

'mis-interpretable ... Ostentation': John Donne, *Essays in Divinity*, p. 59.

There is a letter ... resist them': John Donne, *Paradoxes and Problems*, ed. Helen Peters (Oxford: Clarendon Press, 1980), pp. xxv–xxvi and xxv n. 2 ('General Introduction'); Bald, *John Donne: A Life*, p. 121 and n.1; John Donne, *Selected Prose*, chosen by Evelyn Simpson, ed. Helen Gardner and Timothy Healy (Oxford: Clarendon Press, 1967), p. 111.

('When thou hast done ... not done'): John Donne, *The Divine Poems*, ed. Helen Gardner (Oxford: Clarendon Press, 1952), p. 51.

'they have beene written ... [truth]': Donne, *Selected Prose*, p. 111.

('But what thynge ... suche thynges'): *The Life and Letters of Sir Thomas Wyatt*, ed. Kenneth Muir (Liverpool: Liverpool University Press, 1963), p. 203.

('There is nothing . . . peruert'): *The Works of Thomas Nashe*, ed. Ronald B. McKerrow, corrected reprint, 5 vols. (Oxford: B. Blackwell, 1966), vol. 1, p. 154.

'the short and sure precepts of good example': William Cornwallis, *Discourses upon Seneca the Tragedian (1601)*, facsimile edn. (Gainesville, FL: Scholars' Facsimiles & Reprints, 1952), G4 recto.

13. Dryden's Prize-Song

'to judge rightly . . . performance': Samuel Johnson, *The Lives of the Poets*, 4 vols, ed. Roger Lonsdale (Oxford: Clarendon Press, 2006), vol. 2, pp. 119–20.

'intelligence at bay': Ezra Pound, *Selected Prose 1909–1965*, ed. William Cookson (London: Faber, 1973), p. 386.

''tis not necessary . . . Taste': Robert Howard, *The Great Favourite, Or, The Duke of Lerma* (London, 1668), A3 ('To the Reader'). See Hoyt Trowbridge, 'The Place of Rules in Dryden's Criticism', *Modern Philology*, vol. 44 (1946–7), pp. 84–96, esp. pp. 86–7. Wittgenstein's searching remarks on taste are translated in *Culture and Value*, tr. Peter Winch (Chicago, IL: University of Chicago Press, 1980), pp. 59–60.

chaos of the individual mind: Cf. Thomas Hobbes, *English Works*, ed. William Molesworth, 11 vols. (London: J. Bohn, 1839–45), vol. 1, p. xiii: 'if you will be a philosopher in good earnest, let your reason move upon the deep of your own cogitations and experience; those things that lie in confusion must be set asunder, distinguished, and every one stamped with its own name set in order; that is to say, your method must resemble that of creation'.

Ruskin . . . value: *The Works of John Ruskin*, ed. E. T. Cook and Alexander Wedderburn, 38 vols. (London: George Allen, 1903–12). See e.g. vol. 17, p. 164; vol. 18, p. 391; vol. 27, p. 217.

Pound . . . egotism': *Selected Prose*, p. 34.

'graded . . . word': Pound, *Guide to Kulchur* (London: P. Owen, 1960), p. 317 (first pub. 1938).

'literature . . . meaning': *ABC of Reading* (London: Faber and Faber, 1951), p. 28.

'voudriez vous . . . legions?': *Les Essais de Michel de Montaigne*, ed. Pierre Villey (Paris: PUF, 1965), p. 921: livre III, ch. vii, 'De l'incommodité de la grandeur'.

'Neither . . . disallowed': *The Twoo Bookes of the Proficience and Advancement of Learning* (London, 1605), facsimile edn. (Amsterdam: Theatrum Orbis Terrarum, 1970), The first Booke, p. 17. The anecdote is also mentioned by Clarendon, *A Brief View and Survey of the Dangerous and Pernicious Errors to Church and State in Mr Hobbes's Book Entitled Leviathan* (London, 1676), p. 5.

in Florio's English version of it: *The Essayes of Michael Lord of Montaigne*, tr. John Florio, 3 vols. (London: G. Richards, 1908), vol. 3, p. 190 (first pub. 1603).

'brute' . . . 'actuality': *Collected Papers of Charles Sanders Peirce*, ed. Charles Hartshorne, Paul Weiss, and Arthur W. Burks, 8 vols. (Cambridge, MA: Harvard University Press, 1931–58), vol. 1, p. 7 ('Actuality is something brute'; from the Lowell Lectures of 1903). See also *Semiotic and Significs: The Peirce-Welby Correspondence*, ed. C. S. Hardwick (Bloomington, IN: Indiana University

Press, 1977), p. 26 (letter of 12 Oct. 1904) and cf. Charles S. Peirce, *The Essential Peirce*, 2 vols, ed. Peirce Edition Project (Bloomington, IN: Indiana University Press, 1992–8), vol. 2, p. 435 ('the Brute Actuality of things and facts', in 'A Neglected Argument for the Reality of God').

'nothing...manœuvre': John Crowe Ransom, *The World's Body* (Baton Rouge, LA: Lousiana State University Press, 1968), p. 211 (first pub. 1938).

'the necessity...audience': Edward Pechter, *Dryden's Classical Theory of Literature* (Cambridge: Cambridge University Press, 1975), p. 106.

'Voulez-vous...fictions?': Nicolas Boileau-Despréaux, *Œuvres complètes*, ed. François Escal (Paris: Gallimard, 1966), pp. 158, 169, 174, 182 (*L'Art poétique*). Cf. Pechter, *Classical Theory of Literature*, pp. 67–8.

Joel Spingarn's notion: *Critical Essays of the Seventeenth Century*, 3 vols. (Oxford: Clarendon Press, 1908), vol. 1, p. xciii.

'admirable...Spectateurs': François Hédelin, abbé d'Aubignac, *La Pratique du théâtre*, ed. Pierre Martino (Algiers: J. Carbonel, 1927), p. 38.

'La tourbe...d'inconstance': Montaigne, *Les Essais*, p. 624: livre XI, ch. xvi, 'De la gloire'.

'au peuple...à contenter': Ibid., p. 918.

'N'offrez...plaire': Boileau, *Œuvres complètes*, p. 159.

Montaigne...'la tourbe': Peter Burke, *Montaigne* (New York: Oxford University Press, 1981), pp. 4–6; Frieda S. Brown, *Religious and Political Conservatism in the 'Essais' of Montaigne* (Geneva: Droz, 1963), p. 75.

Dryden...freedom: George McFadden, *Dryden the Public Writer 1660–1685* (Princeton, NJ: Princeton University Press, 1978), p. 43.

'Les autres...moy mesme': Montaigne, *Les Essais*, pp. 657–8: livre III, ch. xvii, 'De la praesumption'.

'to write...honour: Allardyce Nicoll, *A History of English Drama 1660–1900*, 6 vols. (Cambridge: Cambridge University Press, 1952), vol. 1, p. 328 (vol. 1 is the 4th edn. of *Restoration Drama, 1660–1700*); Charles E. Ward, *The Life of John Dryden* (Chapel Hill, NC: University of North Carolina Press, 1961), p. 57.

In the end...'good measure': Ward, *The Life of John Dryden*, p. 302.

'Que toûjours...Rime': Boileau, *Œuvres complètes*, p. 157. Charles S. Peirce calls *bon sens* 'a pretty phrase for ineradicable prejudice'. See *Values in a Universe of Chance: Selected Writings of Charles S. Peirce (1839–1914)*, ed. Philip P. Wiener (Stanford, CA: Stanford University Press, 1958), p. 269.

One hears...'shuffling': e.g. Dustin Griffin, 'Dryden's "Oldham" and the Perils of Writing', *MLQ*, vol. 37 (1976), p. 146; Ruth Salvaggio, *Dryden's Dualities* (Victoria, BC: University of Victoria, 1983), pp. 60, 61, 66; Nicholas Jose, 'Dryden and Other Selves', *The Critical Review*, vol. 25 (1983), p. 111.

'the chorus...close quarters': *OED²*, s.v. 'bay, *n.*⁴'.

an attack by the Earl of Rochester: See Ward, *Life of John Dryden*, pp. 109, 126.

Jean Segrais: See 'The Dedication of the Aeneis', in Dryden, *Poems*, ed. Kinsley, pp. 1051–2, 2046.

Davenant's argument...labour': *Sir William Davenant's Gondibert*, ed. David F. Gladish (Oxford: Clarendon Press, 1971), pp. 24, 22.

''Tis not...Bubbles': *The Spanish Fryar: Or, The Double Discovery...Written by Mr. Dryden* (London, 1695), A2 verso ('The Epistle Dedicatory').

Rochester's...sneers: See Ward, *Life of John Dryden*, p. 182; Mark van Doren, *John Dryden: A Study of his Poetry*, 3rd edn. (New York: H. Holt, 1946), p. 28.

'prevailing...procedure': *OED*², s.v. 'genius', 3*c*.

Eliot...'nebula': T. S. Eliot, *Homage to John Dryden: Three Essays on Poetry of the Seventeenth Century* (London: Hogarth Press, 1924), pp. 22, 23; T. S. Eliot, *John Dryden, Poet, Dramatist, Critic* (New York: Terence & Elsa Holliday, 1932), p. 34.

Auden...say': *A Choice of Dryden's Verse* (London: Faber, 1973), p. 9.

One of Dryden's...Marcellus: Anon., 'Damon, an Eclogue on the untimely Death of Mr. Oldham', in *Remains of Mr. John Oldham in Verse and Prose* (London, 1684), A5 verso. Noted by Griffin, 'Dryden's "Oldham" and the Perils of Writing', p. 148 n. 35.

'blooming Ripeness'...Habitude': *The Poems of John Oldham*, pp. 292–3.

'Rich...Knave': Ibid., pp. 199, 224.

In November 1684...fifty-fourth year: He was born on 9 Aug. 1631.

and had been Poet Laureate...Rochester: See Ward, *Life of John Dryden*, pp. 56, 186; *Poems*, ed. Kinsley, p. 1955; Paul Hammond, *John Oldham and the Renewal of Classical Culture* (Cambridge: Cambridge University Press, 1983), pp. 19, 29–30.

It has been suggested...emotions: Thomas H. Fujimura, 'The Personal Element in Dryden's Poetry', *PMLA*, vol. 89 (1974), pp. 1007–23 at 1010.

'capricious...hatred': Ward, *Life of John Dryden*, p. 83.

Dryden...afterwards: See the letter from Rochester in the country to Henry Savile in London, spring 1676: 'You write me word that I'm out of favour with a certain poet whom I have ever admired for the disproportion of him and his attributes'. Treglown associates this remark with Dryden's anger at Rochester's gibes in 'An Allusion to Horace' written in the winter of 1675–6. *The Letters of John Wilmot, Earl of Rochester*, ed. Jeremy Treglown (Oxford: Basil Blackwell, 1980), pp. 119–20; Dryden's letter to Rochester some three years earlier (April–May 1673) had been entirely amiable. 'The reasons for Rochester's change are far from clear, though possibly the Earl of Mulgrave's patronage of Dryden, from 1674 or 1675 onwards, contributed to Rochester's disaffection': *The Letters of John Dryden*, ed. Charles E. Ward (Durham, NC: Duke University Press, 1942), p. 145 (editorial commentary).

At about...satire: Hammond, *John Oldham and the Renewal of Classical Culture*, pp. 30, 63–5.

Oldham's *Satyrs*...print: For the date 1680–1 see *The Poems of John Oldham*, p. xxxiii; on the other points see pp. xlvii, civ n. 81. See also Hammond, *John Oldham and the Renewal of Classical Culture*, pp. 86, 218; Ward, *Life of John Dryden*, p. 167.

and other poets...1682: *Poems*, ed. Kinsley, pp. 1913–14.

'indulgent': Dryden's word for Aeneas, v. 470; discussed by Griffin, 'Dryden's "Oldham" and the Perils of Writing', pp. 138–9.

'Thus *Nisus* fell ... race together into death: Twelve or thirteen years before the publication, in 1697, of the *Aeneis* Dryden had translated the Nisus and Euryalus episodes from books v and ix. These were included in *Sylvae* (1685). It is therefore highly probable that the composition of 'To the Memory of Mr Oldham' (1684) coincided with Dryden's work on these passages, which are the ground upon which the elegy builds its solemn descant. See *Poems*, ed. Kinsley, pp. 1180–4 and 1294–307, for collation of 1685 and 1697. See also Hammond, *John Oldham and the Renewal of Classical Culture*, pp. 208–16.

The Latin ... 'sed ... ': See *The Aeneid of Virgil*, ed. R. D. Williams, 2 vols. (London, 1972–3), vol. 1, p. 107 (5. 332–2).

('venerande ... ambo'): Ibid., vol. 2, pp. 58, 64 (9. 276, 446).

('sed nox ... umbra'): Ibid., vol. 1, p. 152 (6. 866).

'sed pronus ... cruore': Ibid., vol. 1, p. 107 (5. 332–3).

Our own ... mid-nineteenth century: *The Penguin Dictionary of Historical Slang*, ed. Eric Partridge, abridged by Jacqueline Simpson (Harmondsworth: Penguin, 1972), p. 831. Even so, it would be astonishing if the colloquialism were not in earlier use. Richard Luckett draws my attention to *The Diary of Samuel Pepys*, ed. Robert Latham and William Matthews, 11 vols. (London: Bell, 1970–83), vol. 1, p. 261: 'as if a man should shit in his hat and then clap it upon his head', which seems in the right vein.

Dryden's feeling about the general run of his worldly luck: See McFadden, *Dryden the Public Writer 1660–1685*, p. 143: 'One of the most attractive traits in Dryden is his élan, his good spirits, and his lack of defensiveness; anxiety about his income is perhaps the only breach in his confident, cheerful approach to literature and the world. He probably was dissatisfied with himself for being so awkward at the game of success, for missing many opportunities that had been the making of several of his friends and dozens of his acquaintances'.

Oldham himself ... Argument': *The Poems of John Oldham*, p. 89. The punctuation of this transcript differs very slightly from that of the original text. Cf. *Some New Pieces Never Before Publisht*, by the Author of the *Satyrs upon the Jesuites* (London, 1681), 'Advertisement', a2 verso.

Robert Gould ... verses: In Oldham, *Remains* (London, 1687).

Gould's tribute ... 1687: Hammond, *John Oldham and the Renewal of Classical Culture*, p. 208.

The Laureat ... in print: Eugene Hulse Sloane, *Robert Gould: Seventeenth Century Satirist* (Philadelphia, PA, 1940), pp. 24, 121 (Ph.D. thesis, University of Pennsylvania, 1938).

Bunyan's ... Mr *Save-all*: John Bunyan, *The Pilgrim's Progress from this World to That which is to Come*, ed. James Blanton Wharey, 2nd edn., rev. Roger Sharrock, corr. repr. (Oxford: Oxford University Press, 1967), p. 101.

Dryden anticipates Bunyan: But only in print. *The Pilgrim's Progress* was first published in the following year (1678). It is likely, however, that Bunyan had completed the work by 1672. See the edition by N. H. Keeble (Oxford: Oxford University Press, 1984), p. 264.

'my Lord *Turn-about*...Mr. *Any-thing*': *The Pilgrim's Progress*, ed. Wharey and Sharrock, p. 99.

Such absurdities...arbitrary: Compare the placing of the expletive in Pound's 'Et Faim Saillir Les Loups des Boys' in Ezra Pound, *Poems and Translations*, ed. Richard Sieburth (New York: Library of America, 2003), p. 1178.

'good sense, at all events': Samuel T. Coleridge, *Table Talk*, ed. Carl Woodring, 2 parts (Princeton, NJ: Princeton University Press, 1990), part 2, p. 85 (vol. 14 of the Bollingen *Collected Works of Samuel Taylor Coleridge*): 'Poetry is certainly something more than good sense, but it must be good sense, at all events; just as a palace is more than a house, but it must be a house, at least'. Cf. part 1, p. 122.

'And often to me...nothing more': Walt Whitman, *Complete Poetry and Collected Prose*, ed. Justin Kaplan (New York: Library of America, 1982), p. 513 ('Thought').

Pound observed...ruins': David Anderson, 'Breaking the Silence: The Interview of Vanni Ronsisvalle and Pier Paolo Pasolini with Ezra Pound in 1968', *Paideuma*, vol. 10 (1981), pp. 331–45, at 336.

'Malice'...false': Samuel Butler, *Prose Observations*, ed. Hugh de Quehen (Oxford: Clarendon Press, 1979), p. 60.

'running the difficult middle course': Cf. Steven N. Zwicker, *Politics and Language in Dryden's Poetry* (Princeton, NJ: Princeton University Press, 1984), esp. ch. 4, 'Politics and Religion: the "Middle Way"'.

14. 'Envoi (1919)'

In 'Hugh Selwyn Mauberley' as it appears in Ezra Pound, *Personae: The Shorter Poems*, ed. Lea Baechler and A. Walton Litz (New York: New Directions, 1990), 'Envoi (1919)' is distinguished from the other poems of the sequence by being printed in italic type. This distinction was not made in the first edition issued in April 1920 by the Ovid Press. All eighteen poems are there printed in roman type, each with a decorative initial designed by Edward Wadsworth. In the table of contents of that volume 'Envoi (1919)' is emphatically distinguished from the twelve poems of 'Part I' and the five of 'Part II'; it is printed in capitals, centred between two ruled lines. In the text, however, 'Envoi (1919)' is not set off in any way; there are no blank pages separating it from Parts I and II; no differentiation of typeface. One may reasonably hesitate to impute emblematic significance to typography or other details of book-production which may have been simple expediencies. Even so, in the years following the work's first appearance, 'Envoi (1919)'—'this lovely little poem' as Leavis called it in *New Bearings in English Poetry* (Harmondsworth:

Penguin, 1963 [1932]), p. 123, 'the masterpiece of the sequence' according to Pound's biographer Charles Norman (*Ezra Pound*, rev. edn. (New York: Funk & Wagnall's 1969 [1960]), p. 222)—has many times been singled out for close and admiring attention.

It stands in opposition to (as some have said) or (as others have more recently argued) in apposition to 'Medallion', the eighteenth and final poem of the sequence. The earliest admirers of *Mauberley* established a way of looking at these two poems. 'Envoi (1919)' makes manifest the virtues of seventeenth-century English song, of the true voice of feeling matched by felicitous accuracy of diction and rhythm. 'Medallion' emanates from a more etiolated *virtù*, from principles and qualities in themselves preferable to the unprincipled and tasteless products of the market-place but vitiated by an atrophied aestheticism, an introverted refinement which is a lesser thing than felicitous accuracy declaring its intrinsic value 'in action'. This interpretation, culminating in 1955 with John J. Espey's book-length study of the sequence (*Ezra Pound's 'Mauberley': A Study in Composition* (London: Faber, 1955)), was challenged by Thomas E. Connolly in his review of Espey's thesis ('Further Notes on Mauberley' *Accent*, vol. 16, no. 1 (Winter 1956), pp. 59–67, at 60, 63). Unable to accept 'Envoi (1919)' as Pound's brilliant self-affirming, self-vindicating lyric of farewell to an England incapable of comprehending such beauty and such *virtù*, he assigned its authorship to 'H. S. Mauberley', and this view of the poem's 'limitedness' was further emphasized by A. L. French in an essay published nine years later (' "Olympian Apathein": Pound's *Hugh Selwyn Mauberley* and Modern Poetry', *Essays in Criticism*, vol. 15 (1965), p. 441); though the limitations were there claimed as Pound's not H. S. Mauberley's. That is to say: what Pound had proclaimed as his strength was rather to be seen as the outcome of a 'disabling' misjudgement. A third opinion, originating, in 1973, in an essay by J. Brantley Berryman (' "Medallion": Pound's Poem', *Paideuma*, vol. 2 (1973), pp. 391–8), is that 'Medallion', as much as 'Envoi (1919)', is to be understood as a successfully affirmative and definitive poem by Pound, unmodified by irony, and that each represents a particular mode which he had already described and advocated and which he is here putting into effect as forms having equal validity, equally opposed to the weak stridencies of English life and letters in the period immediately following the end of the First World War. 'Envoi (1919)' embodies the lyricism which Pound calls 'melopoeia' ('Marianne Moore and Mina Loy' (1918), in *Selected Prose 1909–1965*, ed. William Cookson (London: Faber, 1973), p. 394), while 'Medallion' displays the qualities of imagism or 'phanopoeia' (ibid.; see the discussion by Berryman cited above and also F. A. B. Jenner, ' "Medallion": Some Questions', *Paideuma*, vol. 8 (1979), pp. 153 ff.). The crucial challenge in each case is how to make momentary grace endure and indeed triumph over the vicissitudes of time and of mortal indifference or hostility.

'To Thomas Campion... 1928: *Literary Essays of Ezra Pound*, ed. T. S. Eliot (London: Faber and Faber 1954), pp. 155–7; Hugh Kenner, *The Pound Era* (London: Faber, 1975), pp. 393–4 (first pub. 1971).

'Chaque pièce... médaillon': Quoted by Berryman, '"Medallion"': Pound's Poem', p. 397.

as Pound suggested... did not: *Literary Essays*, pp. 285–9, at p. 285.

Among the English poets... neatness': Ibid., pp. 363, 368.

'The eyes turn topaz.': Ezra Pound, *Poems and Translations*, ed. Richard Sieburth (New York: Library of America, 2003), p. 563.

'interpretative crisis': Jenner, '"Medallion"': Some Questions', p. 154.

'strategic position': *Selected Prose*, p. 26.

'the incessant... city': 'Gaudier-Brzeska Vortex', in *Gaudier-Brzeska: A Memoir*, by Ezra Pound, new edn. (Hessle: Marvell Press, 1960), p. 24 (first published in 1916). See also Ezra Pound, *Guide to Kulchur* (London: P. Owen, 1960), p. 67 (first published in 1938).

'destroys... *HSM*': Jenner, '"Medallion"': Some Questions', p. 156.

'Part II... eye on': French, 'Olympian Apathein', p. 442.

'Villon... fact': *The Spirit of Romance* (London: J. M. Dent, 1910), p. 187.

'lords... world': *Selected Prose*, p. 160.

'sublimity... sense': *Literary Essays*, p. 327.

'gross silence': *Impact: Essays on Ignorance and the Decline of American Civilization*, ed. Noel Stock (Chicago, IL: H. Regnery, 1960), p. 163.

'Mauberley... novel': *The Letters of Ezra Pound 1907–1941*, ed. D. D. Paige (London: Faber and Faber, 1951), p. 248.

'*étude* in ephemera': *Literary Essays*, p. 323.

'he does... all his own': Ibid., p. 300.

'the domination... Henry James's style': Ibid., p. 296.

'goes bail for the nation': *Patria Mia* (Chicago, IL: R. F. Seymour, 1950), p. 64.

'catalogues... crudity': *Spirit of Romance*, p. 163; *Selected Prose*, p. 115.

'disgusting... his own': *Pavannes and Divagations* (Norfolk, CT: New Directions, 1958), p. 149.

'the most... opened': *Selected Prose*, p. 373.

'shot himself... values': *Letters*, p. 374; see also Bryant Knox, 'Allen Upward and Ezra Pound', *Paideuma*, vol. 3 (1974), pp. 71–83; A. D. Moody, 'Pound's Allen Upward', ibid., vol. 4 (1975), pp. 55–70.

'forced levity... spirit': See Moody, 'Pound's Allen Upward', p. 63.

'the old combattant': *The Cantos of Ezra Pound*, 4th edn. (London: Faber, 1987), p. 437.

'you could call... respect him': *Impact*, p. 163.

'to free... affects': *Selected Prose*, p. 330.

'Hoping... so': *The Complete Poetical Works of Thomas Hardy*, ed. Samuel Hynes, 5 vols. (Oxford: Clarendon Press, 1982–95), vol. 2, p. 206 ('The Oxen'); cf. *The Complete Poems of Thomas Hardy*, ed. James Gibson (London: Macmillan, 1976), p. 468.

'This difference... commonplace': *Selected Prose*, p. 41.

'capacious... observation': *Literary Essays*, pp. 311, 295.

'The passion... cry.': Ibid., p. 296.

'In the gloom . . . against it': *Cantos*, p. 51.

'the ἀνάγκη . . . necessity': *Literary Essays*, p. 300.

'the aimless . . . humanity': *Spirit of Romance*, p. 124.

'the violent . . . wallow': Ibid., pp. 123–4.

'famous . . . arts': Carroll F. Terrell, *A Companion to the Cantos of Ezra Pound*, 2 vols. (Berkeley, CA: University of California Press, 1980–4), vol. 1, p. 37.

'against . . . notch': *Guide to Kulchur*, p. 159.

'*templum aedificavit*': Canto 8: *Cantos*, p. 32.

'The suicide . . . depression': *Cantos*, p. 625. See Knox, 'Allen Upward and Ezra Pound'.

('nox . . . dies'): See J. P. Sullivan, *Ezra Pound and Propertius: A Study in Creative Translation* (London: Faber and Faber, 1965), p. 142.

('When thou . . . vnder ground'): *Campion's Works*, ed. Percival Vivian (Oxford: Clarendon Press, 1909), pp. 17, 358.

and Waller . . . rare'): *Poems, &c* (London, 1645), pp. 48–9:

> Goe lovely rose,
> Tell her that wasts her time and me,
>   That now she knowes
> When I resemble her to thee
>   How sweet and fair she seems to be.
>
> Tell her thats young,
> And shuns to have her grace[s] spy'd
>   That hadst thou sprung
> In desarts where no men abide,
>   Thou must have uncommended dy'd.
>
> Small is the worth
> Of beauty from the light retir'd;
>   Bid her come forth,
> Suffer her selfe to be desir'd,
>   And not blush so to be admir'd.
>
> Then dye that she,
> The common fate of all things rare
>   May read in thee
> How small a part of time they share,
>   That are so wondrous sweet and fair.

The title-page states that 'All the Lyrick Poems in this Booke were set by Mr HENRY LAVVES'.

'Time is the evil': *Cantos*, pp. 147, 444.

'Rhythm . . . TIME': *ABC of Reading*, pp. 198, 202.

But Pound . . . inscription: e.g. 'Two kinds of banks have existed: The MONTE DEI PASCHI and the devils'; 'Our poetry and our prose have suffered incalculably whenever we have cut ourselves off from the French' (*Selected Prose*, pp. 240, 354).

'coercions', 'personal tyranny': Ibid., pp. 159, 160.

'anyone . . . middle': *Cantos*, p. 59.

('Law . . . pivot': *Cantos*, p. 269; see Robert Schultz, 'A Detailed Chronology of Ezra Pound's London Years, 1908–1920. Part One', *Paideuma*, vol. 11 (1982), pp. 456–72, at p. 466.

'Kung . . . meaning'): *Guide to Kulchur*, p. 18.

'life-long, unchangeable passion': *Selected Prose*, p. 159.

'prominent . . . discard': Ibid., pp. 408, 431.

'Provincialism . . . uniformity': Ibid., p. 160.

'a soft . . . verbiage': *Literary Essays*, p. 185; *Guide to Kulchur*, p. 324.

'the preciseness . . . precise': *Spirit of Romance*, pp. 92, 93.

'substance . . . light': Ibid., p. 160. In *A Drunk Man Looks at the Thistle* (1926), Hugh MacDiarmid, who, despite extreme political differences, admired Pound and described himself as being 'in some ways greatly influenced by' him, was drawn to these same lines by Dante. See *The Complete Poems of Hugh MacDiarmid*, ed. Michael Grieve and W. R. Aitken, 2 vols. (Harmondsworth: Penguin, 1985), vol. 1, pp. 153–4; Hugh MacDiarmid, *The Company I've Kept: Essays in Autobiography* (London: Hutchinson, 1966), p. 170; and Hugh MacDiarmid, *A Drunk Man Looks at the Thistle*, ed. Kenneth Buthlay (Edinburgh: Scottish Academic Press, 1987), p. 164.

'The style . . . revelation': *Patria Mia*, p. 42.

'new, nickel-plated, triumphant': Ibid., pp. 48–9.

'pianola', 'kinema', 'steam yacht': *Poems and Translations*, pp. 550, 550, 554.

'courteous, tawdry, quiet old': *Patria Mia*, p. 49.

'The traditional . . . seem': *Selected Prose*, p. 331.

'derivative convention': See David Anderson, 'A Language to Translate Into: The Pre-Elizabethan Idiom of Pound's Later Cavalcanti Translations', *Studies in Medievalism*, vol. 2, no. 1 (Fall 1982), p. 10.

born out of their due time: See *Spirit of Romance*, p. 99: 'Both Dante and Shakespear were men "born in their due time"'; *Selected Prose*, p. 26: 'To be born a troubadour in Provence in the twelfth century was to be born, you would say, "in one's due time"'.

a genus . . . aligned himself: As—arguably—did T. S. Eliot. See 'Baudelaire in our Time', in *For Lancelot Andrewes* (London: Faber & Gwyer, 1928), pp. 86–99, esp. p. 97: 'The important fact about Baudelaire is that he was essentially a Christian, born out of his due time, and a classicist, born out of his due time'. See also Thomas Hardy, 'In Tenebris II': 'Till I think I am one born out of due time, who has no calling here', in *Complete Poetical Works*, vol. 1, p. 208; cf. *Complete Poems*, p. 168. The allusion is to 1 Corinthians 15: 8, in the King James

Version of 1611: 'And last of all he was seene of me also, as of †one borne out of due time [†or, an abortiue'.

'The English . . . days': *Poems and Translations*, p. 553. See Connolly, 'Further Notes on Mauberley', p. 63.

'*motz el son*': *Selected Prose*, p. 37; *Literary Essays*, p. 170.

practised for the last time in England by Campion and Lawes: Cf. 'Even the deified Purcell is not up to Lawes' (First Book of Ayres, especially) in these matters': *Ezra Pound and Music*, ed. R. Murray Schafer (London: Faber and Faber, 1978), p. 104 (written in 1918).

'hardness' and '*logopoeia*': *Literary Essays*, pp. 285, 33.

'Envoi (1919)' . . . the 'book' will have: Eva Hesse, 'Books Behind the Cantos (Part I)', *Paideuma*, vol. 1 (1972), pp. 138–51, bears on this.

'you use . . . irony': 'Ezra Pound, Letters to Natalie Barney', ed. Richard Sieburth, *Paideuma*, 5 (1976), pp. 279–295, at p. 282.

the 'not quite it' and the 'not quite not it': *Selected Prose*, p. 31.

'the one adjective . . . Murano': *Pavannes and Divagations*, pp. 5–6.

Madison Cawein: See *Poetry: A Magazine of Verse*, vol. 1, no. 4 (Jan. 1913), pp. 104–5.

Arthur Upson: See *The Collected Poems of Arthur Upson*, ed. Richard Burton, 2 vols. (Minneapolis, MN: E. D. Brooks, 1909), vol. 2, pp. 168, 166.

The first issues . . . *Verse*: See *The Little Book of Modern Verse*, ed. Jessie B. Rittenhouse (New York: Houghton Mifflin, 1913), pp. 181–2.

Pound met . . . 1917: See *Literary Essays*, pp. 431–40; *Ezra Pound and Music*, pp. 35–50, 183–6. See also Donald Gallup, *Ezra Pound: A Bibliography of Ezra Pound* (Charlottesville, VA: University Press of Virginia, 1983), pp. 237, 243, 244, 257.

'mak[ing] it new': 'Make it New' is the Confucian axiom (*xin ri ri xin*, from the *Da xue*) used by Ezra Pound as the title of a collection of his essays, *Make it New* (London: Faber and Faber, 1934), and translated by him in *Confucius: The Great Digest & Unwobbling Pivot* (London: P. Owen, 1952), p. 36. See also Pound's Canto LIII.

'once been . . . democracy': *Literary Essays*, p. 436.

'the vortex of pattern': Ibid., p. 434.

'impressionist or "emotional" music': Ibid.

'This old music . . . concentration.': Ibid., p. 433.

('Out of the conquered Past . . . Death'): *The Little Book of Modern Verse*, 20th impression (March 1923), p. 181.

'constant affinity . . . Lovelace': *The Younger American Poets*, by Jessie B. Rittenhouse (Freeport, NY: Books for Libraries 1968), p. 29, 35 (first pub. 1904).

('at my grates no Althea'): *Cantos*, p. 519.

'olde . . . writers': *Literary Essays*, p. 395; cf. Gallup *Ezra Pound: A Bibliography*, p. 253 (c727).

'the "sweet . . . tone': *Literary Essays*, p. 323.

'worn smooth . . . singing': *Guide to Kulchur*, p. 281.

'you cannot call . . . upon him': *Patria Mia*, p. 31.

those claims . . . poetry: e.g. 'All values ultimately come from our judicial sentences' (*Letters*, 249); 'The tyro can not play about with such things, the game is too dangerous' (*Literary Essays*, p. 283).

'By what . . . beauty': *Selected Prose*, p. 47.

'An Anachronism . . . knowledge': *Pavannes and Divagations*, pp. 89–90.

'the naivest . . . sense': Ibid., p. 8.

'Till change . . . alone': *Poems and Translations*, p. 557.

'What thou . . . from thee': *Cantos*, p. 521.

'Beauty . . . another': *Literary Essays*, p. 241.

'Beauty . . . accusation': *Selected Prose*, p. 116.

' "beauty . . . Beardsley': *Cantos*, p. 444.

of 'conflicts . . . passéism': *Pound / Joyce: The Letters of Ezra Pound to James Joyce, with Pound's Essays on Joyce*, ed. Forrest Reed (London: Faber, 1968), p. 113 (editorial commentary).

the 'archaizing . . . collections': Donald Davie, 'The Universe of Ezra Pound', *Paideuma*, vol. 1 (1972), pp. 263–9, at p. 268.

'mellifluous archaism': *Pound / Joyce*, p. 122.

'sheer poetic . . . poetry': *Spirit of Romance*, pp. 150, 160, 234.

'tones clear as brown amber': *Literary Essays*, p. 433.

parochial: *Patria Mia*, p. 64: 'being born an American is no excuse for being content with a parochial standard'.

'the beautiful . . . τὸ καλόν': See John Espey, 'The Inheritance of τὸ καλόν', in *New Approaches to Ezra Pound*, ed. Eva Hesse (London: Faber, 1969), pp. 319–30. See Patrides's commentary on Masson's translation of Milton's letter to Charles Diodati (23 Sept. 1637): 'The Latin original provides here a Greek phrase which specifies "the beautiful" as τὸ καλόν, which Milton realized implies both an aesthetic and a moral judgement' (Milton, *Selected Prose*, ed. C. A. Patrides (Harmondsworth: Penguin, 1974), p. 361).

when reading Coleridge: Espey, 'The Inheritance of τὸ καλόν', p. 319.

'We see . . . market place': Pound, *Poems and Translations*, p. 550.

a letter of William James: *The Letters of William James*, ed. Henry James, 2 vols. (London: Longmans, Green, 1920), vol. 2, p. 117.

the brusque note to . . . Elkin Mathews: *Pound / Joyce*, p. 286; dated 2 June 1916. Mathews feared that a prosecution might be brought against certain poems in *Lustra*.

'quicksand . . . concealers': *Impact*, p. 163.

('pli selon pli'): *Cantos*, p. 15; *Companion to the Cantos*, vol. 1, p. 13 n. 21.

'a vortex . . . odds': *Selected Prose*, p. 386.

'Prince . . . Conteurs': See Richard Sieburth, 'Ezra Pound, Letters to Natalie Barney', p. 280.

'the great . . . benignity': *Literary Essays*, pp. 322, 295.

'*collage* . . . misreadings': Hugh Kenner, *The Poetry of Ezra Pound* (London: Faber, 1951), p. 151.

'bravura' . . . powers': *OED*², s.v. 'bravura'.

'Can a man . . . Beddoes has done so': Pound, *Selected Prose*, p. 351.

'The archaism has its use': Sieburth, 'Ezra Pound, Letters to Natalie Barney', p. 282.

'beauty of the means': Ibid., p. 41.

'Labour . . . very slowly': *Pavannes and Divagations*, pp. 219–20.

Pound also . . . ever since': *Letters*, p. 340; Kenner, *The Pound Era*, p. 330. See also *Cantos*, p. 572 (Canto 87). See also the commentary in Terrell, *A Companion to the Cantos*, vol. 1, pp. 198–9: 'As opposed to art, where "Slowness is beauty" . . . usurers are in a hurry: "Time is money!" '.

'strongly marked time': Yeats to Lady Gregory, 10 Dec. 1909 (*The Letters of W. B. Yeats*, ed. Allan Wade (London: R. Hart-Davis, 1954), p. 543).

'He reads it . . . majestical': Allen Ginsberg, 'Allen Verbatim', *Paideuma*, vol. 3 (1974), pp. 253–73, at p. 263.

'Rhythm . . . very slow': David Gordon, ' "Root / Br. / By Product" in Pound's Confucian Ode 166', *Paideuma*, vol. 3 (1974), pp. 13–32, at p. 25.

Pound's theory . . . frequencies': *Guide to Kulchur*, p. 73.

Pound reads . . . anything else: See R. Murray Schafer, 'The Developing Theories of Absolute Rhythm and Great Bass', *Paideuma*, vol. 2 (1973), pp. 23–35: 'Hugh Kenner has suggested that the term *absolute rhythm* may have been stimulated by Rémy de Gourmont's *Le Latin mystique* (Paris, 1892). Although the precise expression does not appear there, the idea may indeed have been suggested by certain remarks in that book' (p. 25).

'delli occhi . . . tardi e gravi': *Dante's Purgatorio*, tr. Laurence Binyon (London: Macmillan, 1938), pp. 66–7; *Dante's Inferno*, tr. Laurence Binyon (London: Macmillan, 1933), pp. 44–5. See also *Spirit of Romance*, p. 118 'I Vecchii' ('Mœurs Contemporains', VII; *Poems and Translations*, p. 525) and Canto 7 (*Cantos*, p. 24).

'The massive head . . . incision': *Literary Essays*, p. 295.

that 'quality . . . things': David Gordon with Carroll F. Terrell, 'Meeting E. P. and then . . .' *Paideuma*, vol. 3 (1974), pp. 343–60, at p. 351.

'inevitable . . . field': *Guide to Kulchur*, pp. 105–6. Pound thought he saw such qualities in Mussolini! Here as elsewhere one clings grimly to the sense of his own dictum: 'you could call [him] a damn fool *and* respect him' (*Impact*, p. 163).

'I wrote . . . twenty-five years': Quoted by Knox, 'Allen Upward and Ezra Pound', p. 79.

('prose kinema'): Pound, *Poems and Translations*, p. 550.

'Professionals . . . taken out': *Pound/Joyce*, p. 51. For Wittgenstein's remarks on tempo, see *Culture and Value*, tr. Peter Winch (Chicago, IL: University of Chicago Press, 1980), pp. 57, 75.

the 1939 disc . . . 'Envoi (1919)': For information on Pound's several recordings see Gallup, *Ezra Pound: A Bibliography*, pp. 443–6.

'full . . . unswerving': *Gaudier-Brzeska*, p. 99. Pound says that these 'are the sort of phrases that arise in the literary mind in the presence of Epstein's sculpture'. Pound claims, on the following page, that 'there are two types of mind which the mediocre world hates most'. One is 'this mind of the slow gestation, whose absoluteness terrifies "the man in the street" '. The other 'follows the lightning for model'.

'perhaps . . . imperfections': *Literary Essays*, p. 442.

'consummation of métier': Ibid., p. 170.

'melody . . . the soul': Ibid., p. 442.

' "absolute . . . expressed': Ibid., p. 9. See also *Gaudier-Brzeska*, p. 84: 'I said in the preface to my *Guido Cavalcanti* that I believed in an absolute rhythm'. What he actually wrote in that introduction was: 'When we know more of overtones we will see that the tempo of every masterpiece is absolute, and is exactly set by some further law of rhythmic accord'. See Schafer, 'The Developing Theories of Absolute Rhythm and Great Bass', p. 25.

'on his one and only visit': Jessie B. Rittenhouse, *My House of Life: An Autobiography* (Boston: Houghton Mifflin, 1934), pp. 228–9. Rittenhouse recalls that 'he was about to sail for England, being unable longer to "bear the brunt of America" '. This would date the meeting as very early in 1911. See Schultz, 'A Detailed Chronology', p. 461.

Though she found . . . the Rittenhouse ethos: Rittenhouse's review appeared on pp. 575–8 of *The Bookman: A Magazine of Literature and Life*, vol. 46, no. 5 (Jan. 1918). Her review also contained appraisals of *The Chinese Nightingale* by Vachel Lindsay and *Asphalt*, by Orrick Johns. My attention was drawn to this review by Vittoria Mondolfo, 'An Annotated Bibliography of Criticism of Ezra Pound 1918–1924', *Paideuma*, vol. 5 (1976), pp. 303–22, at p. 304.

'charm . . . thing': From Rittenhouse's comments on Orrick Johns; see note above.

('See, they return . . . Wavering!'): Pound, *Poems and Translations*, p. 244. On the use of 'systema graeca' in the poem, see *Ezra Pound and Dorothy Shakespeare: Their Letters 1909–1914*, ed. Omar Pound and A. Walton Litz (New York: New Directions, 1984), p. 218; and also D. S. Carne-Ross, 'Jocasta's Divine Head: English with a Foreign Accent', *Arion*, 3rd ser. vol. 1, no. 1 (1990), pp. 135–6.

'reflective' . . . feel of the thing': See Sally M. Gall, 'Pound and the Modern Melic Tradition: Towards a Demystification of "Absolute Rhythm" ', *Paideuma*, vol. 8 (1979), p. 35–45, at p. 37.

'The Coming of War: Actaeon': *Poems and Translations*, p. 285.

'To break . . . heave': *Cantos*, p. 518.

the nine . . . disguise: Hugh Witemeyer, *The Poetry of Ezra Pound: Forms and Renewal, 1908–1920* (Berkeley, CA: University of California Press, 1969), p. 193.

'detail . . . justice': *Letters*, p. 366.

('Wrong . . . acorn'): *Poems and Translations*, p. 549.

'poetry . . . music': *Selected Prose*, p. 394.

'good verbalism' . . . "usage" ': *Literary Essays*, p. 283; *ABC of Reading*, p. 37.

'the utterance . . . despair': *Selected Prose*, p. 394.

'done cantos...done about it': *Pound/Joyce*, p. 163.

'canorous lyric measures': Leavis's phrase, in *New Bearings in English Poetry*, pp. 122–3.

'a dance...characters': *Selected Prose*, p. 394; the 1918 definition. Cf. Pound's subsequent definition, where 'intellect' replaces 'intelligence'. See *Literary Essays*, p. 25.

When Pound...Generation': See W. B. Yeats, *Autobiographies*, ed. William H. O'Donnell and Douglas N. Archibald (New York: Scribner, 1999), p. 255 (first pub. 1926).

'I said...difficult" ': Ibid., p. 333.

'noble courage': W. B. Yeats, *Memoirs*, ed. Denis Donoghue (London: Macmillan, 1972), p. 92.

'spirit of mockery': Yeats, *Autobiographies*, p. 333.

STYLE AND FAITH

Epigraphs

Knowledge cannot ... when we are come thither: *The Sermons of John Donne*, ed. George R. Potter and Evelyn M. Simpson, 10 vols. (Berkeley, CA: University of California Press, 1953–62), vol. 3, p. 359.

If it were not for Sin ... *Angels* do: Benjamin Whichcote, *Moral and Religious Aphorisms*, 1753 (London: Elkin Matthews & Marrot, 1930), no. 731.

Preface

'The Hebrew word *bachan* ... spectator': John Calvin, *Commentary on the Book of Psalms*, tr. from the original Latin and collated with the author's French version by the Revd. James Anderson, reprint edn., 5 vols. (Grand Rapids, MI: Eerdmans, 1949), vol. 1, p. 165.

The Holy Ghost ... style too: *The Sermons of John Donne*, vol. 5, p. 287.

15. Common Weal, Common Woe

Joseph Wright's *English Dialect Dictionary*: See James Milroy, *The Language of Gerard Manley Hopkins* (London: André Deutsch, 1977), p. 39. (*The English Dialect Dictionary, being the complete vocabulary of all dialect words still in use, or known to have been in use during the last two hundred years*, was published, in six vols., by Henry Frowde (Oxford: Clarendon Press) from 1898 to 1905.)

'with the heyday of English philology': Milroy, *The Language of Gerard Manley Hopkins*, p. 49.

when the proposal ... February 1884: See *OED*[2], vol. 1, pp. xxxv–lvi ('The History of the Oxford English Dictionary'); see esp. pp. xxxv, xxxvi, xlii.

'almost exactly ... date': K. M. Elisabeth Murray, *Caught in the Web of Words: James A. H. Murray and the 'Oxford English Dictionary', with a preface by R. W. Burchfield (New Haven, CT: Yale University Press, 1977), p. 312.*

'the Oxford ... indicated': *Dictionary of National Biography*, ed. Leslie Stephen and Sidney Lee, repr. edn., 22 vols. (London: Smith, Elder & Co., 1909), vol. 19, p. 1120.

'still common in Ireland': Richard Chenevix Trench, *English Past and Present*, 1855, 10th edn., rev. (London: Macmillan, 1877), p. 202.

'accepted ... indifferent': K. M. Elisabeth Murray, *Caught in the Web of Words*, p. 195.

'The Signification (*Sematology*)': Thus in the 'Corrected Reissue' of the 1884–1928 *OED* (1933), 12 vols., vol. 1, p. xxxi.

'The Signification, or *senses*': *OED*[2] (1989), vol. 1, p. xxviii.

Murray had conceded ... most difficult duties': See *OED*, 'Corrected Reissue' (1933), vol. 1, p. xxxi.

'So also *pitch* ... than nothing and not-being': *The Sermons and Devotional Writings of Gerard Manley Hopkins*, ed. Christopher Devlin (London: Oxford University Press, 1959), p. 151.

'the peculiar meaning ... word': Peter Milward, *A Commentary on G. M. Hopkins' 'The Wreck of the Deutschland'* (Tokyo: The Hokuseido Press, 1968), p. 86.

'though this scarcely . . . definition which will': Norman H. MacKenzie, *A Reader's Guide to Gerard Manley Hopkins* (London: Thames & Hudson, 1981), p. 34.

'a Dictionary . . . language': *OED²* (1989), vol. 1, p. xxxvi, col. 1.

'short dictionaries . . . actually need help': William Empson, *The Structure of Complex Words*, 1951, 3rd edn. (London: Chatto and Windus, 1977), p. 396.

'the interactions . . . included': Ibid., p. 391.

'straddle': Ibid., p. 394.

'going together': Ibid., p. 392.

'long . . . significations': *OED*, 'Corrected Reissue' (1933), vol. 1, p. xxxi.

'that was not . . . universally practised in those parts': *The History of the Rebellion and Civil Wars in England, by Edward Earl of Clarendon: Also, his Life, Written by Himself*, 2 vols. (Oxford: Oxford University Press, 1843), vol. 1, p. 533.

'he had a memory . . . dexterity and addresse': *Characters from the Histories and Memoirs of the Seventeenth Century*, ed. D. Nichol Smith (Oxford: Clarendon Press, 1918), p. 94.

'Ther neede no more be sayd . . . dexterity': Ibid., p. 153.

'the common practice of men': Ibid., p. 94.

'temper and spirit': *Clarendon: Selections*, ed. G. Huehns (London: Oxford University Press, 1955), p. 374.

'posture of affairs': Ibid., p. 375.

In the original text . . . five sentences: See Sir Thomas Elyot, *The Boke Named the Gouernour*, 1531 (London: J. M. Dent, 1937), p. 2.

Some quotations . . . pencil: 'The Completion of the Oxford English Dictionary 1884–1928', *The Periodical*, vol. 13, no. 143 (15 Feb. 1928), p. 16.

Murray . . . photographs: K. M. Elisabeth Murray, *Caught in the Web of Words*, frontispiece and *passim*.

'For if words . . . POWERS': *The Collected Works of Samuel Taylor Coleridge*, 16 vols. (Princeton, NJ: Princeton University Press, 1969–2002) vol. 9, p. 10 (*Aids to Reflection*, ed. John Beer).

'Parts of speech . . . human mind': Ralph W. Emerson, *Nature*, 1836, in *Emerson: Essays and Lectures*, ed. Joel Porte (New York: The Library of America, 1983), p. 24.

'iron determination . . . work': K. M. Elisabeth Murray, *Caught in the Web of Words*, p. 289.

'the creative . . . embrace': Coleridge, *Collected Works*, vol. 7, part 2, p. 26 (*Biographia Literaria*, ed. James Engell and W. Jackson Bate).

'diverging . . . faculties': Ibid.

'famous quotations': K. M. Elisabeth Murray, *Caught in the Web of Words*, p. 223.

'crack-jaw . . . surgical words': Ibid., pp. 221–2.

'acknowledge . . . times': Ibid., p. 223.

'to every man . . . *all* English': *OED*, 'Corrected Reissue' (1933), vol. 1, p. xxvii.

'in the interest of English Literature': K. M. Elisabeth Murray, *Caught in the Web of Words*, p. 158.

'He held ... time': Ibid., p. 24.

'superfluous quotations': Ibid., 274.

the need ... authors: *OED*, 'Corrected Reissue' (1933), vol. 1, p. xxxii.

'of an unusually ... nature': *The Periodical*, vol. 13, no. 143 (15 Feb. 1928), p. 12.

'Bradley knew Shelley ... rich poetry': *The Collected Papers of Henry Bradley, With a Memoir by Robert Bridges*, 1928 (College Park, MD: McGrath Publishing Company, 1970), p. 24.

'the author ... few Germans can': Ibid., p. 34.

'tact' ... William Sotheby: *Collected Letters of Samuel Taylor Coleridge*, ed. Earl Leslie Griggs, 5 vols. (Oxford: Clarendon Press, 1966), vol. 2, p. 444.

When *The Times* ... literary masterpiece': K. M. Elisabeth Murray, *Caught in the Web of Words*, p. 224.

T. H. Green's phrase: *Works of Thomas Hill Green*, ed. R. L. Nettleship, 3 vols., 5th impression (London: Longmans, Green, 1906), vol. 3, p. 400.

'willed contrivance' ... readers': Eric Griffiths, *The Printed Voice of Victorian Poetry* (Oxford: Clarendon Press, 1989), pp. 275–6.

'the Brute Actuality of things and facts': Charles S. Peirce, *The Essential Peirce*, 2 vols., ed. Peirce Edition Project (Bloomington, IN: Indiana University Press, 1992–8), vol. 2, p. 435 ('A Neglected Argument for the Reality of God').

'a simultaneous ... contrivance': Griffiths, *Printed Voice of Victorian Poetry*, p. 275.

'this double character ... words': Ibid., p. 276.

'man of science' ... human speech': K. M. Elisabeth Murray, *Caught in the Web of Words*, pp. 292–3.

'I am not ... newspaper.': Ibid., p. 292.

'men who speak ... not understand': William Wordsworth, *Poems*, ed. John O. Hayden, 2 vols. (New Haven, CT: Yale University Press, 1981), vol. 1, p. 879 (Preface to *Lyrical Ballads*, 1802). Cf. *The Prose Works of William Wordsworth*, ed. W. J. B. Owen and Jane Worthington Smyser, 3 vols. (Oxford: Clarendon Press, 1974), vol. 1, p. 139; and William Wordsworth, *Lyrical Ballads and Other Poems, 1797–1800*, ed. James Butler and Karen Green (Ithaca, NY: Cornell University Press, 1992), p. 751.

'unfortunately slain ... hand': Thomas Hobbes, *Leviathan*, 1651, ed. C. B. Macpherson (Harmondsworth: Penguin Books, 1968), p. 718.

'give us ... permit': 'Direction to Readers for the Dictionary' in K. M. Elisabeth Murray, *Caught in the Web of Words*, p. 348 (Appendix II).

'the volunteer sub-editors ... loss of time': 'The Completion of the Oxford English Dictionary 1884–1928', *The Periodical*, vol. 13, no. 143 (15 Feb. 1928), p. 8.

'handling and reducing ... slips': *OED*, 'Corrected Reissue' (1933), vol. 1, p. xvi.

'practical utility ... direction': Ibid., p. xxvii.

'hee unobserv'd ... privat returnd': This is the final line of *Paradise Regain'd*.

'who every one ... before the Judge': John Bunyan, *The Pilgrim's Progress*, 1678, ed. N. H. Keeble (London: Oxford University Press, 1984), p. 79.

'the knavery . . . haunt': Hobbes, *Leviathan*, p. 92.

'timorous, and supperstitious': Ibid.

'exact . . . ambiguity': Ibid., p. 116.

'Perspicuous Words': Ibid.

'juggling . . . knavery': Ibid., p. 176.

'the run of thought . . . different things': *The Journals and Papers of Gerard Manley Hopkins*, ed. Humphry House and Graham Storey (London: Oxford University Press, 1959), p. 119.

'that the scripture . . . english tonge': William Tyndale, *The Obedience of a Christen Man and How Christen Rulers Ought to Governe*, Antwerp, 1528; facsimile edn. (Amsterdam: Theatrum Orbis Terrarum / Norwood, NJ: Walter J. Johnson, 1977), f. xii recto.

'The love . . . direction': Trench, *English Past and Present*, p. 3.

'devoted . . . tradition': *The Collected Papers of Henry Bradley*, p. 51.

'it is the privilege . . . possessed by it': Coleridge, *Collected Works*, vol. 10, p.13 (*On the Constitution of the Church and State*, ed. John Colmer).

'an interesting . . . institutions': Ibid., p. lxi.

'bringing . . . them all': *OED²*, s.v. 'conception'.

'die experienced . . . vollied glare': Herman Melville, 'The March into Virginia, Ending in the First Manassas (July, 1861)', in *Battle-Pieces and Aspects of the War*, 1866 (New York: Da Capo, 1995), pp. 22–3.

'Every fact . . . never cease to be true': K. M. Elisabeth Murray, *Caught in the Web of Words*, pp. 187, 366 n. 57.

'Cannon . . . thunder'd': Alfred, Lord Tennyson, 'The Charge of the Light Brigade', *Tennyson: A Selected Edition*, ed. Christopher Ricks (Berkeley, CA: University of California Press, 1989), p. 509.

'the elixir . . . thousand years': *Johnson on the English Language*, ed. Gwin J. Kolb and Robert DeMoria (New Haven, CT: Yale University Press, 2005), p. 105.

'the recognition . . . Queen Victoria': K. M. Elisabeth Murray, *Caught in the Web of Words*, p. 289.

'a single item . . . debit side': *OED²*, s.v. 'assets, 3'.

'national benefits': Coleridge, *Collected Works*, vol. 10, pp. 71–2.

as Peter Milward says: Milward, *A Commentary on 'The Wreck of the Deutschland'*, p. 106.

'terrible aboriginal calamity': John Henry Cardinal Newman, *Apologia Pro Vita Sua*, ed. Martin J. Svaglic (Oxford: Clarendon Press, 1967), pp. 217–18 (first pub. 1864).

16. Of Diligence and Jeopardy

the Wallis edition: *The New Testament, Translated by William Tyndale 1534: A Reprint of the Edition of 1534 with the Translator's Prefaces and Notes and the Variants of the Edition of 1525*, edited for the Royal Society of Literature by N. Hardy Wallis, with an introduction by the Right Honourable Francis Foot (Cambridge: Cambridge University Press, 1938).

'forme and pressure': *Hamlet*, III, ii. 24.

Tyndale's Erasmian reply ... than hee did': See S. L. Greenslade, *The Work of William Tindale*, with an Essay on Tindale and the English Language by G. D. Bone (London and Glasgow: Blackie and Son, n.d. [1938]), p. 61.

as A. W. Pollard argues: See *The Holy Bible: An exact reprint in Roman type, page for page, of the Authorized Version published in the year 1611*, with an introduction by Alfred W. Pollard (Oxford: Oxford University Press, 1985), p. 10 (originally publ. 1911).

Fry's 1862 reprint of Tyndale's New Testament: *The first New Testament printed in the English language (1525 or 1526), translated from the Greek by William Tyndale*, reproduced in facsimile from the copy in the Baptist College, Bristol, with an introduction by Francis Fry (Bristol: Printed for the Editor, 1862).

'The Prophete Jonas': *'The Prophete Jonas', with an introduction before teachinge to understonde him and the right use also of all the Scripture, etc. etc., by William Tyndale*, reproduced in facsimile, 'to which is added Coverdale's version of Jonah', with an introduction by Francis Fry (London: Willis and Sotheran, 1863).

Mombert's ... Pentateuch: *William Tyndale's Five Books of Moses, called The Pentateuch, 1530*, ed. J. I. Mombert, 1884 (Carbondale, IL: Southern Illinois University Press, 1967).

'does not give the *letter* in facsimile': Ibid., p. cii.

'the ready use ... ends to be served': Ibid., p. lxvii.

'in order to clarify the text': *New Testament* (1534), ed. Wallis, p. xv.

'large body ... students': Ibid., p. xiii.

'dedicated ... 450 years': *Tyndale's New Testament, translated from the Greek by William Tyndale in 1534.* A modern-spelling edition, with an introduction by David Daniell (New Haven, CT: Yale University Press, 1989), p. xxx.

'the processe ... the 'texte': *The Pentateuch*, ed. Mombert, p. 3.

'the imperfection ... accuracy': Ibid., p. vii

'It is uncomfortable ... glossing': *Tyndale's New Testament*, ed. Daniell, p. xxxi.

'There is ... across the world': Ibid., p. vii.

'Count it ... fynnesshed': *The New Testament: The Text of the Worms Edition of 1526, in original spelling, as translated by William Tyndale*, edited for the Tyndale Society by W. R. Cooper, with a preface by David Daniell (London: The British Library, 2000), p. 554.

'Lyke as a sicke man ... an whole man': *New Testament* (1534), ed. Wallis, p. 310 (translating Luther, 'Vorrede auff die Epistel S. Pauli an die Römer', at VII, 2).

'the doctrine ... unbelievable': Paul Rigby, *Original Sin in Augustine's Confessions* (Ottawa: University of Ottawa Press, 1987), p. 1.

'there is ... unreality': St Augustine, *Enchiridion, or Manual to Laurentius concerning Faith, Hope and Charity*, tr., with an introduction and notes, by Ernest Evans (London: The Society for Promoting Christian Knowledge, 1953), p. xxiii.

'gredie to do euell': *New Testament* (1534), ed. Wallis, p. 326.

'without faith', 'with oute ... God': *The Pentateuch*, ed. Mombert, p. 385; *New Testament* (1534), ed. Wallis, p. 302.

'when a man...cannot': St Augustine, *The Problem of Free Choice [De Libero Arbitrio]*, tr. Mark Pontifex (Westminster, MD: Newman Press, 1955), p. 192.

'le mal...le serf-arbitre': Paul Ricoeur, *Le Conflit des interprétations: Essais d'herméneutique* (Paris: Éditions du Seuil, 1969), p. 281.

'grace and apostleshyppe': *New Testament* (1534), ed. Wallis, p. 319.

'terrible curving in on itself': *Luther's Works, Volume 25: Lectures on Romans*, 1515–16, ed. Jaroslav Pelikan, Hilton C. Oswald, and Helmut T. Lehmann (St Louis, MO: Concordia Publishing House, 1972), p. 346 ('curvitas nimia valde').

'We never...salvation': Paul Ricoeur, ' "Original Sin": A Study in Meaning', tr. Peter McCormick, in *The Conflict of Interpretations: Essays in Hermeneutics*, ed. Don Ihde (Evanston, IL: Northwestern University Press, 1974), p. 286.

'the involuntariness...voluntary': Ibid.

'all the synne...frailte': Tyndale, '*The Prophete Jonas*', A iiii recto ('W.T. Vnto the Christian Reader').

'ouermoch...vnchristenlye': *The Pentateuch*, ed. Mombert, p. 396.

'the dampnacion...ceremonies': *New Testament* (1534), ed. Wallis, p. 399.

the 'Idolatrie...imaginacion': *The Pentateuch*, ed. Mombert, p. 165.

'dyed in the faith': Ibid., p. 293.

(though the anonymous...not be his): See Erasmus, *Enchiridion militis Christiani: An English Version*, ed. A. M. O'Donnell (Oxford: Oxford University Press for the Early English Text Society, 1981), pp. xlix–liii.

'some affections...doutfull': Ibid., p. 68.

'These affections...resemble': Ibid.

'after so lo[n]ge...teachi[n]ge': William Tyndale, *The Obedience of a Christen Man and How Christen Rulers Ought to Governe*, Antwerp, 1528; facsimile edn. (Amsterdam: Theatrum Orbis Terrarum, 1977), p. xxiii.

'yf christes...yf we be not all perfecte yᵉ fyrst daye': Ibid., p. xxiii verso. I would wish to indicate a few details, in the introduction to the present volume, which strike me as being 'not all perfecte'. These objections become, in my usage, matters of mere 'worldly busynesse' and perhaps do an injustice to the editor whose argument, if I read aright its 'True Christianity always releases' (*Tyndale's New Testament*, ed. Daniell, p. xxviii) (that is, as a statement, not a paraphrase), is able to give to Tyndale's doctrine a degree of assent which my own argument lacks. It is equally the case, however, that Tyndale, in his 1526 colophon 'To the Reder', invited correction of 'ought...oversene thorowe negligence' (*New Testament* [1526], ed. W. R. Cooper, p. 554), and these suggestions could perhaps be offered and received in that spirit. There appears to be no authority for *Enchiridion militis Christi* (pp. viii, xvii) as the title of Erasmus's book; the final word should be *Christiani*. The 'Translators to the Reader' preface of the 1611 Bible is not really 'difficult to find' (p. x); it is included in the Oxford University Press 'Exact Reprint in Roman Type' of 1833 which was reproduced and reissued in 1985. It is not strictly true to say that 'Black letter was the standard, indeed the only, printing type from Gutenberg and Caxton until the later sixteenth century' (p. xiv). In Tyndale's Pentateuch (1530) only Genesis and Numbers are printed in blackletter; the three remaining books are in roman. In the revised edition (1534) Genesis itself is reset in roman.

'The ring of Establishment authority': *Tyndale's New Testament*, ed. Daniell, p. xxiv.

'in their new ... English': Ibid., p. viii.

'Tyndale was not a committee': Ibid., p. xxviii.

'Tyndale's ... history', etc.: Ibid., p. vii.

'has a short ... works': Ibid., p. xxxii.

'the significance ... craftsman': Ibid., p. xxiii.

'the excellence ... praised': Norman Davis, *William Tyndale's English of Controversy*, The Chambers Memorial Lecture delivered at The University College, London, 4 March 4, 1971 (London: H. K. Lewis for The University College, 1971), p. 3.

'the Apostle ... Bible': *The Pentateuch*, ed. Mombert, p. vii.

'Tyndale spoke for all humanity': *Tyndale's New Testament*, ed. Daniell, p. xxviii.

'bloudy ... heritike': Tyndale, *Obedience*, pp. xxiiii, xxiii verso.

'when all ... person': *The Pentateuch*, ed. Mombert, p. 161.

'goodly lawes of loue': Ibid., p. 164.

'the edyfyi[n]ge ... believe)': *New Testament* (1526), ed. W. R. Cooper, p. 555.

'Latin-inspired ... classes': *Tyndale's New Testament*, ed. Daniell, p. xxviii.

'If literature ... importance': John Davy Hayward, *Prose Literature since 1939*, Arts in Britain, Pamphlet no. 5 (London: Longmans, Green & Co. for The British Council, 1947), p. 47.

'The Authorised Version ... trouble"': Ibid., p. xxviii.

'incomparable ... gentlemen': *Donne's Sermons: Selected Passages*, with an Essay by Logan Pearsall Smith (Oxford: Clarendon Press, 1919), p. xxxvi (editor's introduction).

('The opinions ... British Council'): standard official disclaimer.

'Cleaue vnto ... storye': *The Pentateuch*, ed. Mombert, p. 162.

'The litterall sense is spirituall': Tyndale, *Obedience*, p. cxxxiiii verso.

'Sublime ... perfection': *Tyndale's New Testament*, ed. Daniell, pp. xiv, ix, x.

'committees ... ears': Ibid., p. viii.

'the vivid ... Hebrews show': Ibid., pp. xviii, viii, xvii, xvii, xx, xxvii.

'wonderful ... reasoning': Ibid., pp. xxi, xxiii.

('accessible Tyndale'): Ibid., p. xxvii.

'the laye people': *The Pentateuch*, ed. Mombert, p. 3.

'impossible ... tonge': Ibid.

'a boke ... handes': Ibid., p. 517.

'I thynke ... brede of the soule': *New Testament* (1534), ed. Wallis, p. 293.

'the old punctuation ... clause': G. D. Bone in Greenslade, *The Work of William Tindale*, p. 61.

('the moare ... it is'): *New Testament* (1534), ed. Wallis, p. 293.

'Tyndale understood ... along': *Tyndale's New Testament*, ed. Daniell, p. xxi.

'dragged through ... sorrows': St Augustine, *Enchiridion*, p. 24.

'led, through...sufferings': *St. Augustine: Confessions and Enchiridion*, tr. and ed. Albert C. Outler (London: SCM Press, 1955), p. 354.

'uncovered': *Tyndale's New Testament*, ed. Daniell, p. vii.

Leviticus 18...every instance: See *The Pentateuch*, ed. Mombert, pp. 350–2.

'With modernised...it once was': *Tyndale's New Testament*, ed. Daniell, p. vii.

'The ne- | we...Nouember': *Historical Catalogue of Printed Editions of the English Bible 1525–1961*, rev. and expanded from the edn. of T. H. Darlow and H. F. Moule, 1903, ed. A. S. Herbert (London: British and Foreign Bible Society, 1968), p. 6.

'There is no...Pater': G. D. Bone in Greenslade, *The Work of William Tindale*, pp. 67–8.

'writing...wanted': Davis, *William Tyndale's English of Controversy*, p. 23.

('though we read...nothinge at all'): *The Pentateuch*, ed. Mombert, p. 7 ('A prologe shewinge the vse of the scripture').

('It is not...oure eyes'): Ibid.

'ydle...wordes': Ibid.

'in manye...playne ynough etc': *New Testament* (1534), ed. Wallis, p. 3.

'equitie...dealing': A. C. Southern, ed., *Elizabethan Recusant Prose 1559–1582* (London: Sands and Co., n.d. [1950]), p. 154; Robert Southwell, *An Humble Supplication to Her Majesty*, 1591, ed. R. C. Bald (Cambridge: Cambridge University Press, 1953), p. 3.

'to put...another': *OED*[2], s.v. 'apply'.

'that we maye...sores': *The Pentateuch*, ed. Mombert, p. 7.

'brethren...fayth': *New Testament* (1534), ed. Wallis, p. 3.

'the weake stomackes': Ibid.

'that since...we live in': 'A "New Look" for the Good Book', press release issued by the REB Office, Oxford University Press, 8 June 1989.

'bloudy': Tyndale, *Obedience*, f. xxiv.

'think tank': REB press release, 8 June 1989.

'even...tirantes': Tyndale, *'The Prophete Jonas'*, A iii verso.

'process...text': See *The Pentateuch*, ed. Mombert, p. 3.

'terreble...tre[m]bled at': Ibid., p. 521.

('for then wee...damnacion'): *The First and Second Prayer Books of Edward VI*, with an introduction by the Right Reverend E. C. S. Gibson, Bishop of Gloucester (London: Dent / Everyman's Library, 1910), p. 215.

'When my wife...worthily': REB Press Release, 8 June 1989.

'leatherex...blocking': 'The Design of the Revised English Bible', press release issued by the REB Office, Oxford University Press, 29 June 1989.

'yf wee receyue...unworthely': *First and Second Prayer Books of Edward VI*, p. 215.

'yf they...ordinaunces': *The Pentateuch*, ed. Mombert, p. 517.

'The Kingdom...country': Karl Barth, *The Epistle to the Romans*, 1918, tr. E. C. Hoskyns, 6th edn. (London: Oxford University Press, 1933), p. 263.

'The Gospel...plead': Ibid., p. 38.

'If the Bible's...their congregations': REB press release, 8 June 1989.

'The revision...possible': *The Revised English Bible with Apocrypha* (Oxford and Cambridge: at the University Presses, 1989), Introduction to the New Testament, p. iv.

'The translators . . . all the time': Ibid., p. iii.

'Fields . . . Benjamin': Ibid., p. 687 (Jeremiah 32: 44).

'each sentence . . . uppermost': G. D. Bone in Greenslade, *The Work of William Tindale*, p. 61.

'kepe myne ordinaunces': *The Pentateuch*, ed. Mombert, p. 354.

'guiding principle . . . English': REB, Introduction to the Old Testament, p. xvii.

'He was a prisoner . . . territory': Gordon Rupp, 'Sermon preached at the Commemoration of Benefactors', *Emmanuel College* [Cambridge] *Magazine, Quatercentenary Issue 1584: 1984* (Cambridge: Printed for the College, 1984), p. 24.

'was a great . . . melt away': Ibid.

'Me[n] shal bye . . . Beniamin': *The Geneva Bible*, a facsimile of the 1560 edn. (Madison, WI: University of Wisconsin Press, 1969).

'archaisms . . . terms': REB, Introduction to the New Testament, p. iv.

'field at Anathoth': Jeremiah 32: 8–9.

'the processe . . . texte': *The Pentateuch*, ed. Mombert, p. 4.

'it is read . . . out loud': REB press release, 8 June 1989, p. 3.

'a living tool': Ibid.

'the circumstances before and after': *New Testament* (1534), ed. Wallis, p. 3 ('W. T. Vnto the Reader').

'Conscientious . . . Bible': REB press release, 8 June 1989.

'For to every man . . . business': *OED* (1933), vol. 1, p. xxvii.

'For the domain . . . business': *OED*² (1989), vol. 1, p. xxiv.

'historical principles': The original title was *A New English Dictionary on Historical Principles*.

('the office . . . another'): Charles Dickens, *Great Expectations*, ed. Margaret Cardwell (Oxford: Clarendon Press, 1993), p. 208.

'The Joint Committee . . . Mary Stewart': REB press release, 8 June 1989, p. 3.

'due humility': D. Coggan, 'Preface to the Revised English Bible', *The Revised English Bible with Apocrypha* (Oxford and Cambridge: at the University Presses, 1989), p. ix.

'intelligibility': Ibid., p. viii.

'wide range . . . backgrounds': Ibid.

'bycause . . . besyed': Erasmus, *Enchiridion militis Christiani*, pp. 14–15.

'temporall . . . princes': Ibid.

'the besynesse of the world': Ibid.

'fluent . . . appearance': REB press release, 8 June 1989.

'it is better . . . ma[n]': Tyndale, *Obedience*, p. xxxiii verso.

'bondage . . . inuencions': *New Testament* (1534), ed. Wallis, p. 457.

'The Gospel . . . own sake': Barth, *The Epistle to the Romans*, pp. 38–9.

'captiuite of ceremonies': *New Testament* (1534), ed. Wallis, p. 399.

'affirmation of resurrection': Barth, *The Epistle to the Romans*, p. 39.

17. Keeping to the Middle Way

Robert Burton: Burton's *Anatomy of Melancholy* was first published in Oxford in 1621. Cited here is the Clarendon Edition, based on a complete collation of the six seventeenth-century editions and published in 6 vols. by the Clarendon Press, Oxford, 1989–2001. Vols. 1–3 (Text) were edited by Thomas C. Faulkner, Nicholas K. Kiessling, and Rhonda L. Blair, with an introduction by J. B. Bamborough; vols. 4–6 (Commentary, together with biobibliographical and topical indexes) were edited by J. B. Bamborough and Martin Dodsworth.

'Divine' and as 'schollar': Burton, *Anatomy*, vol. 1, pp. 20, 11.

It is most true . . . workes: Ibid., p. 13.

'tug between two interests': William Empson, *The Structure of Complex Words*, 3rd edn. (London: Chatto and Windus, 1977), p. 2.

'unrighteous subtleties': Burton, *Anatomy*, vol. 3, p. 351.

'mad pranks': Ibid., p. 343.

Ramist 'fad': Walter J. Ong, *Ramus, Method, and the Decay of Dialogue: From the Art of Discourse to the Art of Reason* (Cambridge, MA: Harvard University Press, 1958), p. 315.

Though Burton . . . the work itself: See Burton, *Anatomy*, vol. 1, p. 11.

although Ramus . . . once: Ibid., vol. 6, p. 409: *Biobibliography*, RAMUS.

'Divines use . . . commonly best': Burton, *Anatomy*, vol. 1, p. 11.

'the composition . . . Schollar': Ibid.

a priest of the Ecclesia Anglicana: Ibid., vol. 1, p. 20.

no taste for 'controversie': Ibid., vol. 1, p. 21 ff.

Jewel's *Apologie* . . . Hooker's *Ecclesiastical Politie*: John Jewel, Bishop of Salisbury, *An Apologie, or aunswer in defence of the Church of England . . . Newly set forth in Latine, and nowe translated into Englishe*, London, 1562 (Amsterdam: Theatrum Orbis Terrarum, 1972); John Whitgift, *Answer to the Admonition* (1572); Richard Hooker, *Of the Lawes of Ecclesiasticall Politie* (1593). On Hooker's debt to Whitgift's writings, see *Studies in Richard Hooker: Essays Preliminary to an Edition of His Works*, ed. W. Speed Hill (Cleveland, OH: Case Western Reserve University, 1972), p. 16.

'The *medium* is best': Burton, *Anatomy*, vol. 3, p. 394.

'sobriety . . . God': Ibid., p. 361.

'keepe . . . diligence': Ibid., p. 434 (Proverbs 4: 23).

Tertullian's *regula* . . . *irreformabilis*: Tertullian, *De virginibus velandis*, cited (in English) by Hooker in *Lawes*, bk. 3, ch. 10, section 7: '*The rule of faith*, saith Tertullian, *is but one and that a lone immoveable, and impossible to be framed or cast anew*'. *The Folger Library Edition of the Works of Richard Hooker*, ed. W. Speed Hill, 7 vols. (Cambridge, MA and Tempe, AZ: Harvard University Press and MRTS, 1977–98), vol. 1, p. 244; see also the Commentary, vol. 6, pp. 554 and 586.

Though Hooker . . . like circumstances': Hooker, *Works*, vol. 1, pp. 244–5.

'oftentimes . . . Mercy': John Donne, *Essays in Divinity*, ed. Helen Gardner (Oxford: Clarendon Press, 1952), p. 91.

number of substantial . . . *Trybulacion*: Cf. the index in Burton, *Anatomy*, vol. 6, p. 389.

'an horrour . . . paynfull deth': *The Yale Edition of the Works of St. Thomas More*, 14 vols. (New Haven, CT: Yale University Press, 1963–85), vol. 12, pp. 277, 281 (*A Dialogue of Comfort Against Tribulation*).

J. R. Knott . . . detail: John R. Knott, *Discourses of Martyrdom in English Literature, 1563–1694* (Cambridge: Cambridge University Press, 1993), pp. 80 n. 105, 46 n. 45.

Warren Wooden: Warren W. Wooden, *John Foxe* (Boston, MA: Twayne Publishers, 1983).

'persecucion for the fayth': More, *Works*, vol. 12, p. 292.

'No greater . . . religion': Burton, *Anatomy*, vol. 3, p. 366.

'It is incredible . . . these many yeares': Ibid.

('even all those . . . true regenerate man'): Ibid., p. 29.

'loose . . . in all kingdomes': Ibid., p. 396.

'absorbed . . . thinking': John Donne, *The Divine Poems*, ed. Helen Gardner (Oxford: Clarendon Press, 1952; reprinted from corrected sheets, 1959), p. xxi n. 1.

Hooker . . . distempered affections': Hooker, *Works*, vol. 1, p. 302.

'inordinate melancholies . . . dejections of spirit': *The Sermons of John Donne*, ed. George R. Potter and Evelyn M. Simpson, 10 vols. (Berkeley, CA: University of California Press, 1953–62), vol. 5, pp. 283–4.

Burton . . . to divert it: Burton, *Anatomy*, vol. 3, pp. 351, 427.

'we are naturally . . . impediment or let': Hooker, *Works*, vol. 1, pp. 96–7.

('our manifolde sinnes and wickednes'): *The Prayer-Book of Queen Elizabeth*, 1559 (London: Griffin Farran & Co., 1890), p. 42.

Publica . . . oratio: Cyprian, *Opera*, vol. 3A, ed. M. Simonetti and C. Moreschini (Turnholt: Brepols, 1976), p. 93 ('De dominica oratione').

('the love . . . dulie ordered'): Hooker, *Works*, vol. 2, p. 113.

('to thintent . . . co[m]mon profit'): Jewel, *Apologie*, p. 17 recto.

'ye multitude of idle cerimones': Ibid., p. 16 verso.

'common advise . . . publiquely don': Hooker, *Works*, vol. 2, p. 116.

'anie blinde . . . common prayer': Ibid.

'all the good . . . the new': Jewel, *Apologie*, p. 17 recto.

'*the vulgar sort amongst you*': Hooker, *Works*, vol. 1, p. 14.

'the gullish commonalty': Burton, *Anatomy*, vol. 3, p. 351.

'may appere . . . *Res plebeia*': Sir Thomas Elyot, *The Boke Named the Gouernour*, 1531 (London: Dent / Everyman's Library, n.d. [1907]), p. 2.

to appease . . . appeasyng of the same': *The First and Second Prayer Books of Edward VI* (London: Dent / Everyman's Library, 1910), p. 5.

I [the melancholic] am . . . restored in good time: Burton, *Anatomy*, vol. 3, p. 441.

Calvin's magnanimity: *The Institution of Christian Religion*, Written in Latine by M. John Calvine and translated into English according to the authors last edition by Thomas Norton (London: Vautrollier, for Toy, 1578), pp. 100–100 verso [II: 2, 15].

'Of marveilous . . . threescore yeares with them': Hooker, *Works*, vol. 1, p. 76.

'diligent observuer . . . vulgar folly': Ibid., vol. 2, p. 18.

'It is a wonder . . . further into the dark]': Burton, *Anatomy*, vol. 3, pp. 355–6.

'Apparitions...Darknesse': See Hobbes, *Leviathan*, ed. C. B. Macpherson (Harmondsworth: Penguin Books, 1968), pp. 91-3.

'mu[n]grel *Democratia*': *The Works of Thomas Nashe*, ed. R. B. McKerrow, 5 vols., rev. F. P. Wilson (Oxford: Blackwell, 1966), vol. 3, p. 168.

'For that which is common...no mans': Burton, *Anatomy*, vol. 1, p. 88.

'That which is...despised': Nashe, *Works*, vol. 2, p. 166.

'Sheepe demolish...&c': Burton, *Anatomy*, vol. 1, p. 55.

More's protest in *Utopia*: *The Utopia of Sir Thomas More*, ed. J. H. Lupton (Oxford: Clarendon Press, 1895), pp. 51-6.

'vnder-hand cloaking...pretences': Nashe, *Works*, vol. 1, p. 220.

'pretences...poore': Donne, *Sermons*, vol. 3, p. 363.

'censorys'...commyn wele': Thomas Starkey, *A Dialogue Between Pole and Lupset*, ed. T. F. Mayer (London: Royal Historical Society, 1989), pp. 103, 136.

'to translate...action': Alistair Fox and John Guy, *Reassessing the Henrician Age: Humanism, Politics, and Reform, 1500-1550* (Oxford: Blackwell, 1986), p. 51.

'to insist...motes in the Sun': Burton, *Anatomy*, vol. 1, p. 55.

'that as *Salust*...fingers ends': Ibid., p. 79. The ascription to Sallust is—on the scholarly authority—incorrect. See Burton, *Anatomy*, vol. 4, p. 122 (Commentary).

'not only...salvation': William Randolf Mueller, *The Anatomy of Robert Burton's England* (Berkeley, CA: University of California Press, 1952), p. 33.

Commune bonum: Nashe, *Works*, vol. 3, p. 168.

Bonum simplex of Augustine: Donne, *Sermons*, vol. 5, p. 274.

When I behold...of the one or of the other: Hooker, *Works*, vol. 2, p. 342.

'our narrow...looks farther': Donne, *Sermons*, vol. 8, p. 274.

'*spiritus vertiginis*...not that I do so': Ibid., vol. 10, p. 56.

'spirituall wantonnesse': Ibid., vol. 3, p. 353.

'a spirituall drunkennesse...themselves': Burton, *Anatomy*, vol. 1, p. 65.

'great fruitfulness': *Collected Works of Erasmus* (Toronto: University of Toronto Press, 1974-), vol. 24, p. 284 ('Literary and Educational Writings 2').

'increase'...even the 'sumptuous': Nashe, *Works*, vol. 3, pp. 145, 148-9, 171.

'profligated...'bankerupt': Ibid., vol. 3, pp. 168, 149.

'generous high-mindedness': *Collected Works of Erasmus*, vol. 24, p. 284.

'how affluent...neuer mentions it': Nashe, *Works*, vol. 3, p. 6.

'it is the function...the truest': Cited in *The Yale Edition of the Works of St. Thomas More*, vol. 13, pp. lxxix-lxxx.

'exuberant fertility and abundance': Ibid.

(as Burton said of Lucian): See Burton, *Anatomy*, vol. 3, p. 374.

'ferall vices': Ibid., vol. 1, p. 84.

'whole catalogue...any thing': Nashe, *Works*, vol. 3, pp. 178, 212.

'gallantry...preferred': Burton, *Anatomy*, vol. 1, pp. 5, 54.

'boiles of the common-wealth': Ibid., p. 76.

'expert...poore': Donne, *Sermons*, vol. 6, p. 304.

'rubbish menialty': Nashe, *Works*, vol. 3, p. 183.

'the more ignorant . . . people)': Hobbes, *Leviathan*, p. 175.

'dirty people of no name': Edward Hyde (Edward, Earl of Clarendon), *A Brief View and Survey of . . . Mr. Hobbes His Leviathan* (London, 1674), in *Early Responses to Hobbes*, edited by G. A. J. Rogers, 6 vols. (London: Routledge / Thoemmes Press, 1996), p. 320.

'I am one of the Common People': Thomas Hobbes, *A Dialogue between a Philosopher and a Student*, ed. Alan Cromartie (Oxford: Clarendon Press, 2005), p. 17 (vol. 11 of *The Clarendon Edition of the Works of Thomas Hobbes*). See Keith Thomas, 'Social Origins of Hobbes's Political Thought', in *Hobbes Studies*, ed. K. C. Brown (Oxford: Blackwell, 1965), p. 200.

'my fathers house . . . in the Land': John Bunyan, *Grace Abounding to the Chief of Sinners*, 1666, ed. Roger Sharrock (Oxford: Clarendon Press, 1962), p. 5.

'Grace . . . to the flesh': Ibid.

'the brilliant . . . energy': Wyndham Lewis, *Time and Western Man* (London: Chatto and Windus, 1927), p. 123.

'*Mundus furiosus*': Burton, *Anatomy*, vol. 1, p. 45.

ataxia: Ibid., p. 68.

'so many . . . whirlegigs': Nashe, *Works*, vol. 3, p. 178.

'king of fishes': Ibid., p. 149.

'light friskin of . . . witte': Ibid., p. 151.

'extemporean stile': Burton, *Anatomy*, vol. 1, p. 17.

'intelligence at bay': Ezra Pound, 'Rémy de Gourmont', in Ezra Pound, *Selected Prose, 1909–1965*, ed. William Cookson (London: Faber, 1973), p. 386.

'may wee not . . . *hipocritis*': Nashe, *Works*, vol. 1, p. 22.

'I cannot forbid . . . idle text': Ibid., pp. 154–5.

'melancholy men . . . *excutiat*': Burton, *Anatomy*, vol. 1, p. 24.

'CAVETE FAELICES': Ibid., vol. 3, p. 446.

'expertus . . . satis': Ibid., vol. 1, p. 14; vol. 2, p. 8; vol. 3, p. 395.

'fleshly minded . . . vpon him': Nashe, *Works*, vol. 1, pp. 201–202.

'We [devils] . . . burne them': Ibid., vol. 1, p. 218.

'Their [pagan philosophers'] . . . Hell fire': Burton, *Anatomy*, vol. 1, p. 30.

'naked to the worlds mercy': Ibid., p. 34.

'wandering . . . absurdities': Hobbes, *Leviathan*, p. 117.

'Patience . . . of the minde': Sir William Cornwallis, *Discourses upon Seneca the Tragedian*, London, 1601; a facsimile reproduction, ed. R. H. Bowers (Gainesville, FL: Scholars' Facsimiles & Reprints, 1952), p. H4 recto.

'In summe . . . past cause': Hobbes, *Leviathan*, p. 96.

'*effudi . . . meus*': Burton, *Anatomy*, vol. 1, p.17.

'For if . . . let them runne': Hobbes, *Leviathan*, p. 194.

'God speaks . . . *soluta*': Donne, *Sermons*, vol. 2, p. 50.

'For he . . . mans life': Burton, *Anatomy*, vol. 3, pp. 409, 422.

stultus and its cognates: Ibid., vol. 1, e.g., pp. 12, 25, 26, 28, 29, 31, 31, 32, 34, 41, 48, 54, 56, 57, 58, 60, 62, 63, 65, 99, 100, 101, 102, 103, 104, 105, 111.

'close & couert dealing': More, *Works*, vol. 2, pp. xcvi, 82.

'What they call . . . like a foole': Cited in *OED*², s.v. 'stultiloquy'

'We must make . . . in this kinde': Burton, *Anatomy*, vol. 3, pp. 424, 443, 416.

'extemporean . . . affected': Ibid., vol. 1, p. 12.

Be not solitary, be not idle: Ibid., vol. 3, p. 445.

This likewise . . . to enjoy it: Ibid., vol. 3, p. 334.

'endlesse . . . abruptlie': Nashe, *Works*, vol. 1, p. 245.

'praecipitate, ambitious age': Burton, *Anatomy*, vol. 1, p. 9.

'Be styll . . . I am God': Psalm 46: 10 (*Geneva Bible*, 1560).

If any man . . . *rise and walke*: Burton, *Anatomy*, vol. 3, p. 444.

'confused company . . . speake': Ibid., p. 471.

'smatterer': Ibid.

'accurate musicke . . . phantasie': Ibid., p. 443.

'equall musick . . . equall possession': Donne, *Sermons*, vol. 8, p. 191.

'by . . . steppes . . . knowledge': Hooker, *Works*, vol. 1, p. 74.

'the name . . . ambition': Donne, *Sermons*, vol. 8, pp. 184–5.

'whether it be . . . in you': Hooker, *Works*, vol. 1, p. 51.

'We must make . . . *ex vi morbi*': Burton, *Anatomy*, vol. 3, p. 424.

'things doubtfull': Hooker, *Works*, vol. 1, p. 50.

'a rule . . . our faith': Donne, *Sermons*, vol. 7, p. 262.

('inordinate melancholies . . . sinfull melancholy'): Donne, *Sermons*, vol. 5, pp. 283–4, p. 295; vol. 4, pp. 328, 329; vol. 7, p. 269; vol. 3, p. 270.

He confesses . . . occasion: See *John Donne: Biathanatos*, ed. E. W. Sullivan (Newark, DE: University of Delaware Press, 1984), p. 29.

'*Cupio dissolvi* . . . be with Christ': Donne, *Sermons*, vol. 7, p. 445, referring to Philippians 1: 23.

Seale then . . . Everlasting night: Donne, *The Divine Poems*, pp. 48–9.

a commonplace found in More's *Utopia*: *The Utopia of Sir Thomas More*, p. 290.

It is, however, necessary . . . English translations: In the 1611 New Testament, the phrases 'euerlasting life' and 'life euerlasting' occur fourteen times. The most powerful common application may have been that of John 6: 40, used in the Order for the Burial of the Dead in the first Edwardian Prayer Book of 1549 (but dropped from the revised forms), closely followed by the 'euerlasting lyfe', 'lyfe euerlasting' from the Ministration of Baptism and the Solemnization of Matrimony in the 1549, 1552, and 1559 Prayer Books.

'first, last, everlasting day': 'The Anniversarie,' in John Donne, *The Elegies* and *The Songs and Sonnets*, ed. Helen Gardner (Oxford: Clarendon Press, 1966), p. 71.

'most fearefull . . . Malediction': John Donne, *Devotions upon Emergent Occasions*, ed. Anthony Raspa (Montreal: McGill-Queen's University Press, 1975), pp. 79–80.

The Gentils . . . very Essence: Donne, *Sermons*, vol. 7, p. 272.

Nox est . . . dormienda: Catullus, 5.6.

Nox tibi . . . dies: Propertius, 2.15.24.

'turns from . . . associative magic': Donne, *Sermons on the Psalms and Gospels*, ed. E. M. Simpson (Berkeley, CA: University of California Press, 1967), p. 26 (editor's introduction).

'A Nocturnall upon S. Lucies Day': Donne, *Elegies* and *Songs and Sonnets*, pp. 84–5.

'Others commend . . . harpe': Burton, *Anatomy*, vol. 3, p. 443.

ad sanam mentem: Ibid., p. 424.

'fierce with darke keeping': Francis Bacon, *The Twoo Bookes of the Proficience and Advancement of Learning*, London, 1605; facsimile edn. (Amsterdam: Theatrum Orbis Terrarum, 1970), *The first booke*, p. 21 recto.

'The power . . . glorie': Hooker, *Works*, vol. 2, p. 425.

'darke texts needs notes': John Donne, *The Satires, Epigrams, and Verse Letters*. ed. W. Milgate (Oxford: Clarendon Press, 1967), p. 92.

'rescu[ed] from degradation': Edgar Wind, *Pagan Mysteries in the Renaissance* (London: Faber, 1958), p. 174.

'Man receaued . . . able': Calvin, *Institution*, p. 68 verso (I: 15, 8).

Euer since *Euah* . . . tempted and tempting: Nashe, *Works*, vol. 2, p. 136.

'I am . . . contagious': Donne, *Sermons*, vol. 9, p. 311.

'our selves . . . destruction': Donne, *Devotions upon Emergent Occasions*, p. 63.

'melancholy . . . 'tis all one': Burton, *Anatomy*, vol. 1, p. 25.

'the whole . . . induction': Ibid., p. 65.

Thy soule . . . expect and tarry: Ibid., vol. 3, p. 442.

'depart[ing] . . . treasured up': Donne, *Sermons*, vol. 5, p. 289.

the 'harmonie . . . the other': Bacon, *Twoo Bookes*, p. 20.

18. A Pharisee to Pharisees

The text of 'The Night' used in this study is that of *The Works of Henry Vaughan*, ed. L. C. Martin, 2 vols. (Oxford: Clarendon Press, 1914), pp. 522–3. The poem is as follows:

John 2.3 [3.2]

Through that pure *Virgin-shrine*,
That sacred vail drawn o'r thy glorious noon
That men might look and live as Glo-worms shine,
     And face the Moon:
     Wise *Nicodemus* saw such light   5
     As made him know his God by night.

     Most blest believer he!
Who in that land of darkness and blinde eyes
Thy long expected healing wings could see,
     When thou didst rise,   10
     And what can never more be done,
     Did at mid-night speak with the Sun!

O who will tell me, where
He found thee at that dead and silent hour!
What hallow'd solitary ground did bear   15
         So rare a flower,
    Within whose sacred leafs did lie
    The fulness of the Deity.

         No mercy-seat of gold,
No dead and dusty *Cherub*, nor carv'd stone,   20
But his own living works did my Lord hold
         And lodge alone;
    Where *trees* and *herbs* did watch and peep
    And wonder, while the *Jews* did sleep.

         Dear night! this worlds defeat;   25
The stop to busie fools; cares check and curb;
The day of Spirits; my souls calm retreat
         Which none disturb!
    Christs progress, and his prayer time;
    The hours to which high Heaven doth chime.   30

         Gods silent, searching flight:
When my Lords head is fill'd with dew, and all
His locks are wet with the clear drops of night;
         His still, soft call;
    His knocking time; The souls dumb watch,   35
    When Spirits their fair kinred catch.

         Were all my loud, evil days
Calm and unhaunted as is thy dark Tent,
Whose peace but by some *Angels* wing or voice
         Is seldom rent;   40
    Then I in Heaven all the long year
    Would keep, and never wander here.

         But living where the Sun
Doth all things wake, and where all mix and tyre
Themselves and others, I consent and run   45
         To ev'ry myre,
    And by this worlds ill-guiding light,
    Erre more then I can do by night.

         There is in God (some say)
A deep, but dazling darkness; As men here   50
Say it is late and dusky, because they
         See not all clear;
    O for that night! where I in him
    Might live invisible and dim.

Therefore he came under cover of darkness: See Edwyn Clement Hoskyns, *The Fourth Gospel*, ed. Francis Noel Davey, 2 vols. (London: Faber, 1940), vol. 1, p. 226: 'darkness and night are in the Fourth Gospel sinister words . . . Nicodemus occupies a dangerous position betwixt and between; and this is suggested from the very beginning of the narrative'. See also Richard Ollard, *Clarendon and His Friends* (London: Oxford University Press, 1987), p. 69: in the spring of 1642 Edward Hyde deemed it prudent to visit Charles I 'only in the dark . . . upon emergent occasions'.

Like representatives . . . chop-logic upon it: See Jonathan F. S. Post, *Henry Vaughan: The Unfolding Vision* (Princeton, NJ: Princeton University Press, 1982), pp. 202–3: 'Vaughan unfolds and develops a complex parallel between the Pharisee Nicodemus and himself that both establishes their "kinred" (l. 36) connections and underscores their basic differences'. My suggestion is that we, as glossers and glozers, approach Vaughan's poem like well-meaning Pharisees. We may or may not see the light.

'to words and rhythms': Frank Kermode, 'The Private Imagery of Henry Vaughan', *RES*, new series, vol. 1 (1950), p. 206.

'his own . . . limited wisdom': Post, *Henry Vaughan*, p. 203.

a 'bookish poet': Kermode, 'Private Imagery', p. 206.

'the academic . . . a man to pray': H. A. Williams, 'Theology and Self-Awareness', in *Soundings*, ed. A. R. Vidler (Cambridge: Cambridge University Press, 1963), p. 71.

'refuses . . . corrupt times': Post, *Henry Vaughan*, p. 208.

Vaughan's embroilment . . . apocalyptic signs: Ibid., pp. 188–9.

'quickens to a palpable ecstasy': E. C. Pettet, *Of Paradise and Light: A Study of Vaughan's 'Silex Scintillans'* (Cambridge: Cambridge University Press, 1960), p. 149.

'blest Mosaic thorn': *Hymns and Spiritual Songs for the Fasts and Festivals of the Church of England*, 1765, XXXII, in *The Poetical Works of Christopher Smart*, ed. Karina Williamson, 6 vols. (Oxford: Clarendon Press, 1980–96), vol. 2, p. 89.

'Others might expound . . . the text.': M. M. Mahood, *Poetry and Humanism*, 2nd edn., 1950 (New York: W. W. Norton, 1970), p. 255.

In *Abr'hams* Tent . . . shady *Even*: Vaughan, *Works*, vol. 1, p. 404.

'One of the largest . . . magnetism': Mahood, *Poetry and Humanism*, pp. 271–2.

'active commerce . . . existence': Ibid.

'By 1650 . . . vanished.': Louis L. Martz, *The Paradise Within: Studies in Vaughan, Traherne and Milton* (New Haven, CT: Yale University Press, 1964), p. 13 n. 8.

'The logical . . . *Olives*.': Kermode, 'Private Imagery', p. 223.

'in these times . . . triall': Vaughan, *Works*, p. 149.

'The *Sonne* . . . *Olives*': Ibid., p. 138.

I write . . . presence of darknes: Ibid., p. 217.

'recreates . . . reality': S. L. Bethell, *The Cultural Revolution of the Seventeenth Century*, (London: Dennis Dobson, 1951), p. 134.

Auden . . . angst: W. H. Auden, *New Year Letter* (London: Faber, 1941), pp. 35, 108.

'making our last . . . Nativity': Sir Thomas Browne, *The Major Works*, ed. C. A. Patrides (Harmondsworth: Penguin Books, 1977), p. 284.

'rhyming' in a sense . . . sounds: Alice Goodman drew my attention to this.

'the creation . . . coincidence': Sigurd Burckhardt, 'The Poet as Fool and Priest', *ELH*, vol. 23, 1956, p. 281; cf. Sigurd Burckhardt, *Shakespearean Meanings* (Princeton, NJ: Princeton University Press, 1968), pp. 24-5.

'union . . . extremes': Mahood, *Poetry and Humanism*, p. 279.

'committed . . . hermeticism': Kermode, 'Private Imagery', p. 208; see also Browne, *Major Works*, pp. 30, 103 n. 28.

'the troublesom . . . Rimeing': in the prefatory note added in 1668 to *Paradise Lost*.

'*tagge his Verses*': *Aubrey's Brief Lives*, ed. Oliver Lawson Dick (Harmondsworth: Penguin Books, 1972), p. 364.

'the childish . . . riming': *Campion's Works*, ed. Percival Vivian (Oxford: Clarendon Press, 1909), p. 37.

His own lyrics . . . contention: e.g. ibid., pp. 11, 13, 16, 17, 20, 22, 132, 140, 165, 172, 185 ['loue' : 'moue']; 12, 14, 15, 22, 132, 161, 165, 168, 186 ['loue' : 'proue']. And there are further instances.

'pretty knack': See *OED*², s.v. 'tag, v.¹': 'It shows a pretty knack at tagging verses' (James Russell Lowell).

'like cleare springs . . . 'Rose-cheekt *Lawra*': *Campion's Works*, pp. 50-1.

Changing shapes . . . loue: Ibid., p. 234.

'the light–darkness . . . Vaughan': Bethell, *Cultural Revolution*, p. 157.

But in Vaughan . . . ('The Water-fall'): Vaughan, *Works*, pp. 7, 39, 398, 419, 423, 425-6, 434, 438-9, 449, 451-2, 466, 481, 488, 502, 511, 517, 519, 521, 524, 528, 529, 537.

to 'compose' . . . by authority': Senses given in *OED*², s.v. 'compose'.

'manufactured . . . has gone': Pettet, *Of Paradise and Light*, p. 153.

'despite . . . into rapture': Post, *Henry Vaughan*, p. 207.

'Lux est umbra Dei': Browne, *Major Works*, pp. 71, 314 n. 50.

'adumbration': Ibid.

'a thorough-going intellectual': Alan Rudrum, 'Some Remarks on Henry Vaughan's Secular Poems', in *Poetry Wales*, vol. 11, no. 2: *A Special Issue on Henry Vaughan*, p. 49.

'*Servus inutilis: peccator maximus*': Vaughan's epitaph (1695), on his tombstone in Llansantffraed, Brecon. See F. E. Hutchinson, *Henry Vaughan: A Life and Interpretation* (Oxford: Clarendon Press, 1947), p. 240.

'contingency': senses and dates of occurrence given in *OED*².

'Dionysian': *Henry Vaughan: The Complete Poems*, ed. Alan Rudrum (New Haven, CT: Yale University Press, 1981), p. 629 (editorial commentary).

'detached . . . with either': Post, *Henry Vaughan*, p. 209.

'conversion . . . experience': Kermode, 'Private Imagery', p. 206; see also Pettet, *Of Paradise and Light*, pp. 16-17.

'No one read . . . imagination': Post, *Henry Vaughan*, p. 111.

'shining ring...intimated': Pettet, *Of Paradise and Light*, p. 5.

light–darkness eschatology: In *Olor Iscanus* (1651), in his translation of 'Casimirus, Lib. 4. Ode 15', Vaughan employs 'light' : '*night*' at 11.13–14 where Sarbiewski's Latin does not require it. G. Hils, in his translation of the same ode, is both closer to the text and rather more surprising in his English word-finding, though one cannot make large claims for his skill. See Vaughan, *Works*, vol. I, p. 88; Mathias Casimire Sarbiewski, *The Odes of Casimire*, tr. G. Hils (London, 1646); repr. edn. (Los Angeles, CA: The Augustan Reprint Society [Publication no. 44], 1953), pp. 76–7. The point I wish to make is that Vaughan's 'light' : '*night*' is here mechanical, not metaphysical, and that 'The Night' regenerates the mere tag of 'Lib. 4, Ode 15' as well as the pretty conceit of 'To Amoret'.

'Christian theology...theology sweeps above it': Walter J. Ong, *The Barbarian Within and Other Fugitive Essays and Studies* (New York: Macmillan, 1962), p. 104. See also Thomas Vaughan, *Lumen de lumine* ('When I seriously consider the system or fabric of this world I find it to be a certain series, a link or chain which is extended...from that which is beneath all apprehension to that which is above all apprehension'), in *The Works of Thomas Vaughan*, ed. Arthur Edward Waite (London: Theosophical Publishing House, 1919), p. 269. This passage is quoted in M. M. Mahood's admirable essay in her *Poetry and Humanism*, pp. 279–80.

19. The Eloquence of Sober Truth

Early Responses to Hobbes: The 6 vols. boxed as *Early Responses to Hobbes* are reproduced in facsimile from their original editions, and each work is paged individually. They are here given their complete titles and listed by date of publication: John Bramhall, Bishop of Derry, *A Defence of True Liberty from Antecedent and Extrinsicall Necessity* (1655); George Lawson, *The Political Part of Mr Hobbs his Leviathan* (1657); William Lucy, Bishop of St David's, *Observations, Censures, and Confutations of Notorious Errours in Mr. Hobbs his Leviathan and other books* (1663); John Eachard, *Mr Hobb's State of Nature considered* (1672); Edward Hyde (Edward, Earl of Clarendon), *A Brief View and Survey of the Dangerous and Pernicious errors to Church and state in Mr Hobbes's Leviathan* (1674); and Thomas Tenison, *The Creed of Mr Hobbes Examined* (1670), bound with pamphlets by Robert Filmer, Seth Ward, Pierre Bayle et al. (1652–1738).

'a mighty...words': George Watson, 'The Reader in Clarendon's *History of the Rebellion*', *RES*, New Series, vol. 25, no. 100 (1974), p. 398.

'this our imbecillitie': *The Folger Library Edition of the Works of Richard Hooker*, ed. W. Speed Hill, 7 vols. (Cambridge, MA / Tempe, AZ: Harvard University Press / MRTS, 1977–8), vol. 4, p. 103.

'peaceful and lofty sentences': A. P. D'Entrèves, *The Medieval Contribution to Political Thought* (London: Oxford University Press, 1939), p. 89.

'diligent and distinct consideration': Hooker, *Works*, vol. 4, p. 101.

'subtiltie of Satan': Ibid., vol. 5, p. 78 ('A Learned and Comfortable Sermon of the
    Certaintie and Perpetuitie of Faith in the Elect', 1585).
'works of nature'...performed': Ibid., vol. 1, p. 67.
'admirable dexteritie of wit': Ibid., p. 3.
cannot be taken...respect: See W. P. J. Cargill Thompson, 'The Philosopher of
    the "Politic Society"', in *Studies in Richard Hooker: Essays Preliminary to an
    Edition of His Works*, ed. W. Speed Hill (Cleveland, OH: Case Western Reserve
    University, 1972), pp. 14–15.
when Hooker...mince words: Hooker, *Works*, vol. 1, p. 76. See also *Studies in
    Richard Hooker*, ed. W. Speed Hill, p. 175.
'[his] attitude...censure': Egil Grislis, 'The Hermeneutical Problem in Hooker', in
    Studies in Richard Hooker, ed. W. Speed Hill, p. 203.
Conscious as Hyde...if not his confusion: See Richard Ollard, *Clarendon and His
    Friends* (Oxford: Oxford University Press, 1988), pp. 111–12.
'may [not] loose...virtue': See Watson, 'The Reader in Clarendon's *History of the
    Rebellion*', p. 403.
'seasonably and appositely': *Characters from the Histories and Memoirs of the Seventeenth
    Century*, ed. D. Nichol Smith (Oxford: Clarendon Press, 1918), p. 94.
'cozen and deceave': Ibid., p. 153.
The Earl of Strafford...'pride': See *Clarendon: Selections from 'The History of the
    Rebellion and Civil Wars' and 'The Life by Himself'*, ed. G. Huehns (London:
    Oxford University Press, 1955), p. 147.
'the late...Rebellion': Clarendon, *Brief View*, pp. 56, 54.
'made his Defence...eloquence': *Clarendon: Selections*, p. 137 (capitals as in first
    edition, 1702, vol. 1, p. 173).
'deceitfull men...particulars': Bramhall, *Defence*, p. 19.
a precedent...deliberation: Ibid., p. 47.
When he writ...all this night: Lucy, *Observations*, p. 6.
In Bramhall's...between them: See Bramhall, *Defence*, p. 14.
'changeth shapes in...particular': Ibid., p. 104.
the common errors...desperation: See ibid., pp. 3, 7, 71, 74.
'descend...question': Ibid., pp. 19, 139.
'take every word...Objections': Lucy, *Observations*, p. 308.
'genuine sense': Bramhall, *Defence*, p. 40.
'rip up...business': Ibid., p. 158.
'voluntary'...genuine sense: Ibid., pp. 37–48.
'explicitly...loci': Walter J. Ong, *Ramus, Method, and the Decay of Dialogue: From
    the Art of Discourse to the Art of Reason* (Cambridge, MA: Harvard University
    Press, 1958), p. 315.
Burton's...the indeterminate: See Robert Burton, *The Anatomy of Melancholy*, ed.
    T. C. Faulkner et al., 6 vols. (Oxford: Clarendon Press, 1989–2001), vol. 3,
    p. 458; *The Countesse of Pembrokes Arcadia, written by Sir Philippe Sidnei*, facsimile

reproduction of the 1891 photographic facsimile of the original 1590 edition (Kent, OH: Kent State University Press, 1970), bk. 1, ch. 5.

'affections . . . in the other': Bramhall, *Defence*, p. 4.

'inhaerent' 'vertue': Thomas Hobbes, *Leviathan*, 1651, ed. C. B. Macpherson (Harmondsworth: Penguin Books, 1968), p. 75.

'this controversy . . . praedetermined to one': Bramhall, *Defence*, p. 41.

'meer Logomachy': Ibid., p. 130.

'true morall liberty . . . between us': Ibid., p. 212.

'unfortunately . . . hand': Hobbes, *Leviathan*, p. 718.

Hobbes's . . . Clarendon: E.g. Sidney, *Arcadia*, p. 269; Walter Ralegh, *The History of the World*, ed. C. A. Patrides (London: Macmillan, 1971), pp. 56–7 (on the character of Henry VIII); *Clarendon: Selections*, pp. 54–5 (on the character of Lord Falkland), pp. 200, 229 (on European reactions to the execution of Charles I).

'tautology' and 'wresting': E.g. Lucy, *Observations*, pp. 354–5, 357, 365; Clarendon, *Brief View*, pp. 73, 75, 107.

'meer animosity', 'antipathy': Bramhall, *Defence*, pp. 229, 200.

'melancholy', 'desperate imaginations': Clarendon, *Brief View*, p. 179.

'very far from . . . *thoughts*': Ibid., p. 12.

'terms of Art . . . the key': Ibid., pp. 21–2.

to make 'Animadversions upon': Lucy, *Observations*, facsimile title page (1663); Clarendon, *Brief View*, pp. 2, 5, 16, 59, 204, 231.

'Conster . . . no otherwise': Hooker, *Works*, vol. 5, p. 165 ('A Learned Discourse of Justification', 1586).

Ong stresses . . . argument: See Walter J. Ong, *The Presence of the Word* (New Haven, CT: Yale University Press, 1967), p. 87.

One would add . . . period: See Jean Mohl, *John Milton and His Commonplace Book* (New York: Ungar, 1969).

'this present . . . braine': Hooker, *Works*, vol. 1, p. 83.

'Sophisters . . . multitude': Bramhall, *Defence*, p. 249; see also pp. 157–8 ('Innovators and seditious Oratours, who are the true causes of the present troubles of Europe').

'Shakespeare': See *Coriolanus*, Act II, Scene iii ('many-headed Multitude').

But how far . . . 1640s?: See John Ripley, *'Coriolanus' on Stage in England and America, 1609–1994* (Madison, WI: Farleigh Dickinson University Press, 1998), p. 343. Ripley finds no record of performance between 1609 and 1681 (an adaptation by Nahum Tate).

'many-headed multitude': Sidney, *Arcadia*, p. 220.

From Horace's first *Epistle*: *OED*², s.v. 'many-headed'.

'natural ability or capacity': Ibid., s.v. 'genius'.

'form . . . and model': *Clarendon: Selections*, pp. 65–6.

'Sudden Glory . . . a signe of Pusillanimity': Hobbes, *Leviathan*, p. 125.

his own negative . . . timidity: See *OED*², s.v. 'pusillanimity'.

'The Light...ambiguity': Hobbes, *Leviathan*, p. 116.

even...bad odour: See *OED*², s.v. 'snuff, vb'.

'crafty ambitious persons'...purposes: Hobbes, *Leviathan*, pp. 91–3.

'our Senses...true Religion: Ibid., p. 409. I have received enlightenment on this passage from an unpublished essay by Dr Steve Bishop.

'for if...let them runne': Hobbes, *Leviathan*, p. 194.

'the Holy Ghost...of language': *The Sermons of John Donne*, ed. George R. Potter and Evelyn M. Simpson, 10 vols. (Berkeley, CA: University of California Press, 1953–62), vol. 6, p. 55.

'to please...innocently': Hobbes, *Leviathan*, pp. 101–2.

But living...myre: *The Works of Henry Vaughan*, ed. L. C. Martin, 2 vols. (Oxford: Clarendon Press, 1914), vol. 2, pp. 522–3.

Wilt thou...their doore?: John Donne, *The Divine Poems*, ed. Helen Gardner (Oxford: Clarendon Press, 1952; repr. from corrected sheets, 1959), p. 51.

'even as thou...mercy of thee': *The Two Liturgies AD 1549 and AD 1552; with Other Documents Set Forth by Authority in the Reign of King Edward VI*, ed. J. Ketley (Cambridge, at the University Press, 1844), p. 471 (spelling regularized to the standard of 1844).

'result...typography': Ong, *The Presence of the Word*, p. 86.

(the first recorded...*The Alchemist*, 1610): See *OED*², s.v. 'register'.

'subdue...transported with': *Clarendon: Selections*, p. 19.

'uncharitableness' and 'ignorance': Ibid., p. 51; Clarendon, *Brief View*, p. 91, taking up a phrase in Hobbes, *Leviathan*, p. 272.

'heat and animosity'...'heat and passion': Clarendon, *Selections*, p. 106.

'where that...dust and heat': John Milton, *Selected Prose*, ed. C. A. Patrides (Harmondsworth: Penguin, 1974), p. 213.

'the incomparable *Grotius*': Clarendon, *Brief View*, p. 141.

'all the general...and knowing': *The Analytical Didactic of Comenius*, tr. Vladimir Jelinek (Chicago, IL: University of Chicago Press, 1953), p. 97; cf. Jan Amos Comenius, *Novissima linguarum methodus* (Geneva: Droz, 2005), p. 158.

'exquisite reasons...demonstrative': Milton, *Selected Prose*, p. 211.

'Rules of Arithmetic...experiment': Clarendon, *Brief View*, p. 79.

'Etymologie': Clarendon, *Brief View*, pp. 182, 204; Lucy, *Observations*, pp. 64, 280.

('the ambiguous...free'): Bramhall, *Defence*, p. 16.

'mist of words...his Structure': Clarendon, *Brief View*, p. 26.

'the Liberty...monstrous Soveraign': Ibid., pp. 55, 56.

'Property...precious term': Ibid., p. 56.

'Occupancy' is 'a sacred title': Lucy, *Observations*, p. 440.

'Lands and Goods': Clarendon, *Brief View*, p. 107.

the Copies...King and People: Ibid., p. 110.

vindicate (a verb he favoured): Ibid., pp. 37, 45, 223. See also p. 108, 'vindications', p. 244, 'vindicator'. See also *Selections*, ed. Huehns, pp. 1, 6, 8.

'exercise...understanding': Clarendon, *Brief View*, pp. 16, 46, 185–6, 230.

('such inestimable . . . no name'): Ibid., pp. 319–20.

'a proper . . . speaking': Ibid., p. 37.

'vindicate . . . oppress it': Ibid.

'reflexion . . . purpose': Ibid., p. 11.

the vision of the suffering servant: See Isaiah 53: 2–5; Philippians 2: 7–8.

'private': Clarendon, *Brief View*, e.g. pp. 77, 79, 100, 105.

'ordain'd . . . acceptation': Ibid., p. 22.

'that common . . . human life': Ibid., p. 29.

'all the customes of the Nations': Ibid., pp. 76–7.

'enormities . . . Tradition': Ibid., p. 302.

Bramhall equates 'custome' . . . 'habits': See Bramhall, *Defence*, p. 177.

'old truth . . . ancestors': Ibid., p. 195.

For Lucy . . . '*custome*': See Lucy, *Observations*, p. 75.

it is not . . . made legall: Robert Filmer, *Observations Concerning the Originall of Government* (in *Early Responses to Hobbes: Pamphlets*), p. 31 [actually 33].

'Disputes . . . stand for': John Locke, *An Essay Concerning Human Understanding*, ed. P. H. Nidditch (Oxford: Clarendon Press, 1975), pp. 511–12.

The original sense . . . include each other: *OED*², s.v. 'reduce'.

'the end . . . the Hearer': Locke, *Essay*, p. 405.

W. D. J. Carghill Thompson's . . . myth-making: See Thompson, 'The Philosopher of the "Politic Society" ', in W. Speed Hill, ed., *Studies in Richard Hooker*, p. 40.

'For as much . . . Person': Bramhall, *Defence*, p. 47.

'of such questions . . . circumstances': Hooker, *Works*, vol. 1, p. 14.

'And also the same . . . circumstances': *The Institution of Christian Religion, Written in Latine by M. John Calvine, and Translated into English according to the authors last edition, by Thomas Norton* (London: Thomas Vautrollier for Humfrey Toy, 1578), p. 623 verso [IV: 20, 8].

Archbishop Whitgift . . . 1572–3: See V. J. K. Brook, *Whitgift and the English Church* (London: English Universities Press, 1957), pp. 33, 42–4.

More recently . . . pamphlets themselves: Ibid., p. 127.

The *Ecclesiastical Polity* . . . humility: Ibid., p. 152.

'The Church . . . proportionable': Hooker, *Works*, vol. 1, p. 23.

where *T.H.* demands . . . respectively: Bramhall, *Defence*, p. 22.

The 'Schole-men' . . . etymology: Ibid., pp. 29, 152, 156, 158, 172–3, 198, 200, 226, 236.

('afterward . . . *confidence*'): Lucy, *Observations*, p. 130.

Hooker's 'proportionable' . . . 'respectively': Hooker, *Works*, vol. 1, p. 23; Lucy, *Observations*, p. 130; Bramhall, *Defence*, p. 22.

John Newton of Olney: See *An Authentic Narrative of some Remarkable and Interesting Particulars in the Life of John Newton* [1764] (New York: Evert Duyckinck, 1806), e.g. pp. 59–60, 92.

B[ishop Butler] . . . a very horrid thing!: *The Rise of Methodism: A Source Book*, ed. R. M. Cameron (New York: Philosophical Library, 1954), pp. 287–8.

'indeterminate . . . what good I can': Ibid., pp. 288–9.

'a change of form... substance': Gerald Bray, *Documents of the English Reformation* (Minneapolis, MN: Fortress Press, 1994), p. 113.

'Elizabethan assumptions... normal reason': Christopher Morris, *Political Thought in England: Tyndale to Hooker* (London: Oxford University Press, 1953), p. 106.

At times... *traductio*: Followed particularly by Clarendon, *Brief View*, e.g. pp. 108, 166, 174, 231, 253. See also Bramhall, *Defence*, pp. 7, 71.

'comfortable places... despair': Bray, *Documents*, p. 339.

'ridiculous men'... (Bancroft): Brook, *Whitgift*, p. 146.

'common persons'... (Whitgift): Ibid., p. 90.

'the common... (Hooker): Hooker, *Works*, vol. 1, pp. 14–15.

'the many headed multitude'... (Bramhall... et al.): Bramhall, *Defence*, p. 249.

'dirty people...' (Clarendon): Clarendon, *Brief View*, p. 320.

'secret corner-meetings...' (Hooker... Hobbes): Hooker, *Works*, vol. 1, p. 47.

'desperate cause... Oratours': Bramhall, *Defence*, pp. 7, 71, 158, 249.

'acts of rage... Doctrines': Clarendon, *Brief View*, pp. 108, 179, 272.

'Stone Dead hath no Fellow': *Clarendon: Selections*, p. 141; John Simpson and Jennifer Speake, eds., *The Concise Oxford Dictionary of Proverbs*, 2nd edn. (Oxford: Oxford University Press, 1992), p. 242.

'Extremely beautiful... *fido inganno*': Torquato Tasso, *Discourses on the Heroic Poem*, tr. Mariella Cavalchini and Irene Samuel (Oxford: Clarendon Press, 1973), p. 178.

Cleare dishonoure... to warke: Henry Parker, Lord Morley, *Tryumphes of Fraunces Petrarcke*, ed. D. D. Carnicelli (Cambridge, MA: Harvard University Press, 1971), p. 107.

'tacitly'... conjuring: See Clarendon, *Brief View*, pp. 122, 140; Bramhall, *Defence*, p. 133 ('a politick deafness').

'turne and tranlace... sundry shapes': George Puttenham, *The Arte of English Poesie*, ed. G. D. Willcock and A. Walker (Cambridge: Cambridge University Press, 1936), p. 203.

Sir Thomas Wyatt... 1530s: See Kenneth Muir, *Life and Letters of Sir Thomas Wyatt* (Liverpool: Liverpool University Press, 1963), pp. 189, 197, 203; see also Ch. 11 above, pp. 197–200.

'The prophet... faith': Hooker, *Works*, vol. 5, p. 76.

poysonous sugar... royall tytle: Sidney, *Arcadia*, pp. 228, 228 verso.

That saying... such presumption: Clarendon, *Brief View*, p. 15.

'Antiphilus... flatterie': Sidney, *Arcadia*, p. 227 verso.

The type of exemplary... Clarendon and Swift: See Clarendon, *Brief View*, p. 15; Jonathan Swift, *A Discourse of the Contests and Dissentions Between the Nobles and the Commons in Athens and Rome*, ed. F. H. Ellis (Oxford: Clarendon Press, 1967), pp. 90, 92, 93, 97–8.

as C. A. Patrides discerned: See Milton, *Selected Prose*, p. 196 (editorial note).

'The end then... God aright': Ibid., p. 182.

'sober truth': Clarendon, *Brief View*, p. 15.

'plain dealing': Ibid., p. 289, and cf. p. 282.

'pretending . . . perspicuity': Clarendon, *Brief View*, p. 289; see also p. 282.

'an irreparable loss . . . quarrel': Ibid., p. 320.

Locke's 'Substances': See Locke, *Essay*, pp. 520–1.

'not what the words . . . praedetermined to one': Bramhall, *Defence*, p. 41.

'man . . . creature': Ibid., p. 107.

intention: *OED*², various senses. For analyses of motive and intention, see, e.g. Bramhall, *Defence*, pp. 19, 37, 74; Lucy, *Observations*, p. 205; Robert Filmer, *Observations on Milton* (in *Early Responses to Hobbes: Pamphlets*), p. 18; Robert Filmer, *Observations on Grotius* (in *Early Responses to Hobbes*), p. 27; Clarendon, *Brief View*, pp. 235–6, 272 [actually 262].

'They who . . . publick good': Milton, *Selected Prose*, p. 196.

Tyndale's *Obedience of a Christen Man*: *The Work of William Tyndale*, ed. G. E. Duffield (Appleford: Sutton Courtenay Press, 1964), p. xxxiii; quotes part of a letter from Thomas Cromwell's agent Stephen Vaughan, who reported Tyndale's willingness to 'suffer what pain or torture, yea, what death his grace will' provided that the king would 'grant only a bare text of the scripture to be put forth among his people'.

Clarendon's 'Epistle . . . Majesty': Clarendon, *Brief View,* six unnumbered prefatory pages.

20. The Weight of the Word

'interesting . . . of more interest than': Isabel Rivers, *Reason, Grace and Sentiment: A Study of the Language of Religion and Ethics in England 1660–1780. Volume I: Whichcote to Wesley* (Cambridge: Cambridge University Press, 1991), e.g. pp. 13, 17, 49, 50, 56, 57, 61, 71, 80, 99, 148, 168, 179, 210, 213, 226, 239.

'the Interest of *Sects* . . . Religion': Ibid., pp. 70–1, 82, 102, 170–1, 190.

'very interesting' . . . 'extraordinarily interesting': Ibid., pp. 115, 117, 161, 162, 168, 195.

has 'not taken . . . scholars': Ibid., p. 4.

Campion's 'Brag': See A. C. Southern, ed., *Elizabethan Recusant Prose 1559–1582* (London: Sands and Co., n.d. [1950]), pp. 153–5.

'a *Preacher* . . . Parish': Rivers, *Reason*, p. 50.

'I design . . . understood': Ibid., p. 215.

'plain and natural Method': Ibid., p. 34.

'require . . . Study': Ibid., p. 19.

My subject is . . . ascertained: Ibid., pp. 2–3.

'do justice . . . subject': Ibid., p. xii.

('For Locke's . . . Volume II'): Ibid., p. 48 n. 98.

'fitted . . . worldly state': Ibid., p. 58.

This only . . . *Disbelief*, etc.: John Locke, *An Essay Concerning Human Understanding*, 1690, ed. P. H. Nidditch (Oxford: Clarendon Press, 1975), p. 663.

'Propositions . . . Religion)': Ibid., p. 712.

'unwary . . . Understandings': Ibid.

'riveted . . . pull'd out again': Ibid.

'essentially . . . grace': Rivers, *Reason*, p. 1.

'Without perplexing . . . speculations': Edward Stillingfleet (1662), cited in *OED*[2], s.v. 'nice'.

'To stand upon nice . . . useless': Benjamin Whichcote, *Moral and Religious Aphorisms*, 1753 (London: Elkin Matthews & Marrot, 1930), no. 1008.

'I have ever thought . . . forgotten': Rivers, *Reason*, pp. 70–1.

'It is not . . . by us': William Law, *The Collected Works of the Reverend William Law*, 9 volumes, London: for J. Richardson, 1762; reprint edn. (Setley: G. Moreton, 1892–93), vol. vi, p. 73.

'the way . . . austere': Jeremy Taylor, *The Great Exemplar* (London, 1649), cited in *OED*[2], s.v. 'nice'.

'He . . . perplexes . . . Love': *The Poems of John Dryden*, ed. James Kinsley, 4 vols. (Oxford: Clarendon Press, 1958), vol. 2, p. 604.

'the love of Complacencie and Acceptation': Richard Baxter, *Of Saving Faith* (London, 1658), cited in *OED*[2], s.v. 'complacency'.

'arbitrary . . . vain': Isaac Barrow, *Works* (London, 1689), cited in *OED*[2], s.v. 'complacence'.

'by wickedness . . . his own': Whichcote, *Aphorisms*, no. 642.

'Compleasance . . . *to the rest*': Thomas Hobbes, *Leviathan*, ed. C. B. Macpherson (Harmondsworth: Penguin Books, 1968), p. 209.

('familiar Toad'): Alexander Pope, 'An Epistle from Mr. Pope to Dr. Arbuthnot', line 319. See *The Poems of Alexander Pope*, ed. John Butt (New Haven: Yale University Press, 1963), p. 608.

('the silent . . . Heart'): Law, *Works*, vol. 7, p. 133.

'Accomplishment . . . World': Ibid., p. 142.

'*Form* . . . the Air': Ibid., p. 119.

('*since Almighty* . . . *Questions*'): Izaac Walton, *The Lives of John Donne, Sir Henry Wotton*, etc., The World's Classics (London: Oxford University Press, 1927), p. 295.

'mere Nonconformist': Baxter, quoted in *The Reverend Richard Baxter under the Cross (1662–1691)*, Frederick J. Powicke (London: Jonathan Cape, 1927), p. 71.

'*singular Dexterity*' . . . '*Garb and phrase*': [Barnabas Oley], 'A Prefatory View of the Life and Vertues of the Authour, and Excellencies of This Book', in George Herbert, *Remains* (1652), b10 recto; repr. in facsimile (Menston: Scolar Press, 1970).

Barrow's use of the 'co-prefix': Rivers, *Reason*, pp. 77–8.

'pertinently . . . properly': Ibid., p. 125.

'If any Expressions . . . Latitude': Isaac Watts, *Hymns and Spiritual Songs 1704–48: A Critical Edition*, ed. S. L. Bishop (London: Faith Press, 1962), p. liii.

'I hope . . . uncharitable spirit': cited in Rivers, *Reason*, p. 179.

'I take "language" . . . include': Ibid., p. 3.

'virtuously . . . epicure': Isaac Barrow, cited in ibid., p. 78.

'*pertly* . . . fortunate': *The Notebooks of Samuel Taylor Coleridge 1794–1804*, ed. Kathleen Coburn, Bollingen Series L, 2 vols. (New York: Pantheon Books, 1957), vol. 1 (Text), no. 1655.

'He was to stand ... Face': Isaac Barrow, *Of Civil Contentment, Patience and Resignation to the Will of God, In Several Sermons* (London: for Round, Tonson, and Taylor, 1714), p. 232.

Set against Foxe ... Ridley: *Foxe's Book of Martyrs*, ed. and abridged by G. A. Williamson (London: Secker and Warburg, 1965), pp. 132–7, 219–28, 290–312.

'physical sensibility' ... 'literature or art': *OED*², s.v. 'sensation'.

('to confirm ... Suffering'): Rivers, *Reason*, p. 105.

'was recognised ... puritans': Ibid., p. 53.

'corrections ... wrong-headed: Ibid., p. 76.

All *general* privations ... hell!: Edmund Burke, *A Philosophical Enquiry into the Origin of our Ideas of the Sublime and Beautiful*, ed. J. T. Boulton (London: Routledge, 1958), p. 71.

'When the Principles ... religious': Whichcote, *Aphorisms*, no. 28.

'The *State* ... Will': Ibid., no. 853.

'There is no ... Righteousness': Ibid., no. 902.

'an exact ... devotion': Law, *Works*, vol. 4, p. 162.

'*lively* ... *spirit*': Ibid., p. 133.

'relentless ... principles': *A Burning and a Shining Light: English Spirituality in the Age of Wesley*, ed. David Lyle Jeffrey (Grand Rapids, MI: Eerdmans, 1987), p. 120.

To proceed ... devotion: Law, *Works*, vol. 4, p. 136.

'To live ... Virtue': Whichcote, *Aphorisms*, no. 250.

'Our Happiness ... without': Ibid., no. 857.

'due or proportionate ... qualities': *OED*², s.v. 'temper'.

'A *wise* ... more': Whichcote, *Aphorisms*, no. 250.

In vain ... Devotion dies: Watts, *Hymns and Spiritual Songs*, p. 194 (Book II: 34).

'But what ... call for that?': John Donne, *Devotions upon Emergent Occasions*, ed. Anthony Raspa (Montreal: McGill-Queen's University Press, 1975), p. 63 (Twelfth Meditation).

Serious Call: William Law, *A Serious Call to a Devout and Holy Life*, 1728, 2nd edn., corr. (London: for William Innys, 1732), p. 244.

'He saw ... baptize it': Owen Chadwick, *Michael Ramsey: A Life* (Oxford: Clarendon Press, 1990), p. 42.

Then shall ... my relief: *The Works of George Herbert*, ed. F. E. Hutchinson (Oxford: Clarendon Press, 1941), p. 90.

'Of this blest ... in heaven': Chadwick, *Michael Ramsey*, p. 398.

'in a sense most true': Herbert, *Works*, pp. 167–8.

'subject ... moral prose': Rivers, *Reason*, p. 2.

Addison's two *Spectator* papers: Nos. 453 (9 Aug. 1712) and 465 (23 Aug. 1712) of *The Spectator*, ed. Donald F. Bond, 5 vols. (Oxford: Clarendon Press, 1965), vol. 4, pp. 94–8 and 141–5. The 'ode' appears on pp. 144–5.

'There is not ... gratitude': Ibid., p. 222.

'In our retirements ... serious': Ibid., p. 272.

'If gratitude ... Maker?': Ibid., p. 222.

696 NOTES TO PP. 359-63

'O how...declare...?': Ibid., p. 224 (hymn, verse 2).

'piece of divine poetry': Ibid., p. 223.

Burnet's distinction...sublime': See *Characters from the Histories and Memoirs of the Seventeenth Century*, ed. D. Nichol Smith (Oxford: Clarendon Press, 1918), p. 252.

'states of mind'...'disclaimer': Rivers, *Reason*, pp. 84, 236, 152, 176.

'peculiar edge'...'thoughts': Ibid., p. 115.

'consideration...Sampson': Ibid., p. 146.

'meditation...act': Ibid.

'the communication...practises it': Barrow, cited in Rivers, *Reason*, p. 78.

'it is a sign...excellency': Rivers, *Reason*, p. 114.

('Blest...Heaven!'): *Representative Verse of Charles Wesley*, ed. Frank Baker (London: Epworth Press, 1962), p. 3 ('Christ the Friend of Sinners').

'tasting how gracious the Lord is': Rivers, *Reason*, p. 128.

'appeal...criticism': Ibid., p. 241.

'the philosophical...all men': John and Charles Wesley, *Selected Prayers, Hymns, Journal Notes, Sermons, Letters and Treatises*, ed. Frank Whaling (New York: Paulist Press, 1981), p. 31.

'Take care...long received': Letter to Dorothy Furly, 15 September 1762. See *The Letters of the Rev. John Wesley, A.M.*, ed. John Telford, 8 vols. (London: The Epworth Press, 1931), vol. 4, p. 189.

Now, even now...purple wave: *The Eucharistic Hymns of John and Charles Wesley*, ed. J. Ernest Rattenbury (London: The Epworth Press, 1948), p. 204.

'For then...he sank': *The Poems of William Cowper*, ed. John D. Baird and Charles Ryskamp (Oxford: Clarendon Press, 1980-95), vol. 1, p. 215.

'Original sin...Christianity': Rivers, *Reason*, p. 227.

'natural "pondus"...principle': Ibid., p. 162.

'good books...world': Ibid., p. 116.

'certain impulsion...downward': Hobbes, cited in *Jonathan Edwards: Representative Selections*, ed. Clarence H. Faust, and Thomas H. Johnson (New York: Hill & Wang, 1962), p. lxxii. Cf. Hobbes, *De Cive: English Version*, ed. Howard Warrender (Oxford: Clarendon Press, 1983), p. 47 and *De Cive: Latin Version*, ed. Howard Warrender (Oxford: Clarendon Press, 1983), p. 94.

'as it were heavy as lead': Ibid., p. 162.

'*the Divine...the Same*': Hobbs's *Tripos in Three Discourses* (London: for Matt Gilliflower, Henry Rogers, 1684), p. 254.

'the imperfection...avoid it': *William Tyndale's Five Books of Moses, called The Pentateuch*, 1530, ed. J. I. Mombert, 1884 (Carbondale, IL: Southern Illinois University Press, 1967), p. vii.

'idle heart in hearing': Rivers, *Reason*, p. 115.

'*private* interest': *Jonathan Edwards*, p. 360.

Ruskin's 'intrinsic value': *The Works of John Ruskin*, ed. E. T. Cook and Alexander Wedderburn, 39 vols. (1903-12), vol. 17, p. 153 (*Munera Pulveris*); see also vol. 27, p. 217 (*Fors Clavigera*).

'cold . . . preaching': Rivers, *Reason*, p. 175.

'arbitrary signs': Ibid., p. 125.

'tone . . . solutions': Ibid., p. 179.

'intrinsic Malignity': Whichcote, *Aphorisms*, nos. 486, 918.

'internal . . . body': *Jonathan Edwards*, p. 362.

'There is nothing . . . hath': Whichcote, *Aphorisms*, no. 457.

'there are . . . insoluble': Rivers, *Reason*, p. 38; see also p. 43.

Charles Wesley: A Reader. Ed. John R. Tyson (Oxford and New York: Oxford University Press, 1989).

The Unpublished Poetry of Charles Wesley: Ed. S. T. Kimbrough, Jr., and Oliver A. Beckerlegge, 3 vols. (Nashville, TN: Abingdon Press, 1988–93).

'Intrinsic Goodness': Whichcote, *Aphorisms*, no. 540.

21. Dividing Legacies

'we have . . . than the latter': T. S. Eliot, *The Varieties of Metaphysical Poetry: The Clark Lectures at Trinity College, Cambridge, 1926, and the Turnbull Lectures at the Johns Hopkins University, 1933*, ed. Ronald Schuchard (London: Faber & Faber, 1993; New York: Harcourt Brace Jovanovich, 1994), p. 199.

'What many of you . . . Strafford': Ibid., p. 224.

'Dante and his School . . . Middleton Murry: Ibid., pp. 6–7, 10–11 (Editor's Introduction).

As is usually the case . . . on 14 April: Ibid., p. 7.

It also appears . . . from its true centre: Ibid., p. 10 (Editor's Introduction).

'The style . . . not English prose': Ibid., p. 224 n.

It has to be said that . . . gravity: Ibid., pp. 58–9.

'To read . . . his own thinking': John Donne, *The Divine Poems*, ed. Helen Gardner (Oxford: Clarendon Press, 1952; reprinted from corrected sheets, 1959), p. xxi n. 1.

the *via media* . . . parlance: See particularly 'John Bramhall' (1927), in T. S. Eliot, *Selected Essays*, 2nd edn. (London: Faber, 1934), pp. 344–52.

'points of triangulation': Eliot, *Varieties of Metaphysical Poetry*, p. 61.

'curious blend . . . his own work': 'Francis Herbert Bradley' (1927), in Eliot, *Selected Essays*, p. 406.

'the increasing . . . metaphysical inquiry': F. H. Bradley, *Essays on Truth and Reality*, 1914 (Oxford: Clarendon Press, 1950), p. vi (Preface).

'there has been . . . incredible': Ibid.

'*echt metaphysisch*' . . . detail can match: Eliot, *Varieties of Metaphysical Poetry*, p. 48.

'On Our Knowledge . . . Imaginary': Ibid., pp. 55 n., 88 n.

'as a pupil . . . how to say it': T. S. Eliot, *Knowledge and Experience in the Philosophy of F. H. Bradley* (London: Faber, 1964), p. 9.

('ideas may be . . . the real world'): Bradley, *Essays*, p. 29.

'the most arduous . . . record exists': Hugh Kenner, *The Invisible Poet: T. S. Eliot* (London: Faber, 1960), p. 81.

attacked... 'civilised class': *The Letters of T. S. Eliot, Volume I: 1898–1922*, ed. Valerie Eliot (London: Faber, 1988), pp. 369–70.

Schuchard notes... reciprocated the sympathy: Eliot, *Varieties of Metaphysical Poetry*, pp. 29–30.

rhetorical tribute ... classical *apatheia*: I say 'rhetorical tribute to precedent' because *apatheia* is a stoic virtue or quality. Housman claimed that he was neither Stoic nor Epicurean but Cyrenaic. See *The Letters of A. E. Housman*, ed. Archie Burnett, 2 vols. (Oxford: Oxford University Press, 2007), vol. 2, p. 329.

There are only two ways... an event: *Letters of T. S. Eliot*, vol. 1, p. 285.

'Please let us be ... before': Ibid., p. 285.

Woods had written ... for that degree: Ibid., p. 143.

'extraordinary power' ... literary opinion: G. Wilson Knight, 'T. S. Eliot, Some Literary Impressions', in *T. S. Eliot: The Man and His Work*, ed. Allen Tate, 1966 (Harmondsworth: Penguin Books, 1971), p. 246.

'shrewd enough... truly belong': Peter Ackroyd, *T. S. Eliot* (London: Hamish Hamilton, 1984), p. 330.

'only after... on his own account': Richard Wollheim, 'Eliot and F. H. Bradley: An Account', in *Eliot in Perspective: A Symposium*, ed. Graham Martin (London: Macmillan, 1970), p. 190.

'Conflict... Jesuitism': Eliot, *Varieties of Metaphysical Poetry*, p. 89.

'For you can hardly ... to his mind': Ibid.

'psychologism' ... Donne's style of thought: Ibid.

'idealism ... other ways': *OED*², s.v. 'psychologism'.

'The *fourth point*... fruit from this': *The Spiritual Exercises of St. Ignatius*, tr. Anthony Mottola (New York: Image Books, 1964), p. 72.

'Eliot's most elusive poem': Kenner, *The Invisible Poet*, p. 234.

'waking up... make of it all': Denis Donoghue, *The Old Moderns: Essays on Literature and Theory* (New York: Knopf, 1994), p. 119.

'the origin... non-active suggestion': Bradley, *Essays*, p. 22; see also Eliot, *Varieties of Metaphysical Poetry*, p. 88 n.

That Eliot himself... January 1933: Eliot, *Varieties of Metaphysical Poetry*, pp. 64, 65 (editor's notes); pp. 257, 259.

'the subject... modern problems': Ibid., p. 224 n.

'If in some game... "Ah, Souldier" ': Christopher Ricks, *T. S. Eliot and Prejudice* (London: Faber, 1988), pp. 159–60. The bibliographical information and the Shakespeare quotation are also given by Ricks.

misquotations and 'minor mistranscriptions': Eliot, *Varieties of Metaphysical Poetry*, pp. 33–6 (editor's note on text and editorial principles). A clutch of misquotations is corrected on pp. 52 n., 56 n.; see also 89 n. For Schuchard's term 'minor mistranscriptions', see, e.g. pp. 103 n., 108 n., 116 n., 124 n., 134 n.

Shakespeare's 'gnomic utterance' ... Ripeness is all: Ibid., pp. 52 n., 53 n. See also pp. 35–6 for editorial references to Frank Kermode (1975) and Christopher Ricks (1977) on creative misquotation.

'the finding . . . upon instinct': Quoted in John Passmore, *A Hundred Years of Philosophy*, 2nd edn., 1957 (Harmondsworth: Penguin Books, 1966), p. 61 n. I acknowledge a general indebtedness over many years to Passmore's invaluable book.

'Tradition' . . . 'The Metaphysical Poets': These essays, first published separately in 1919, 1921, and 1923, appear together in Eliot, *Selected Essays*, and elsewhere, as also in *Selected Prose of T. S. Eliot*, ed. Frank Kermode (New York: Harcourt Brace Jovanovich, 1975), pp. 37–76.

'rigorous metaphysician': Passmore, *A Hundred Years of Philosophy*, p. 60.

'painfully obscure work': Wollheim, 'Eliot and F. H. Bradley', p. 170. This should not be read as Wollheim's final opinion of the quality of Eliot's dissertation.

'that there is . . . adequate explanations': *Josiah Royce's Seminar 1913–1914, as Recorded in the Notebooks of Harry T. Costello*, ed. Grover Smith (New Brunswick, NJ: Rutgers University Press, 1963), p. 42. Eliot was a member of the seminar, to which he presented a paper on 9 Dec. 1913. Royce quoted, or paraphrased, Peirce's observation at the seminar held on 28 Oct. 1913. Costello's notes do not reveal whether or not Eliot was present at that meeting.

In really great . . . not visible: Eliot, *Knowledge and Experience*, p. 75.

'My Station and Its Duties': F. H. Bradley, *Ethical Studies*, 2nd edn., rev., 1876 (Oxford: Clarendon Press, 1927), pp. 160–213.

'believed upon instinct': Passmore, *A Hundred Years of Philosophy*, p. 61 n.

We . . . have experience . . . my known world: Bradley, *Essays*, pp. 159–60.

Eliot's discovery . . . Aquinas: Text as in Dante Alighieri, *La Divina Commedia*, ed. and ann. C. H. Grandgent, rev. Charles S. Singleton, 1933 (Cambridge, MA: Harvard University Press, 1972), p. 930 (*Paradiso* c. 33, l. 144). For my reference to Aquinas, see ibid., p. 930 n. 144.

'Hooker's philosophy . . . than Donne's': Eliot, *Varieties of Metaphysical Poetry*, p. 68 n.

'the intellectual . . . Catholic Church': Ibid., p. 224 n.

'what many of you . . . unjust of me': Ibid., pp. 224, 190.

To meet with Hooker . . . formal ratiocination: *The Folger Library Edition of the Works of Richard Hooker*, ed. W. Speed Hill, 7 vols. (Cambridge, MA and Tempe, AZ: Harvard University Press / MRTS, 1977–8), vol. 1, p. 61 (sense 1); vol. 1, p. 84 (sense 2); vol. 1, p. 86 (sense 3); vol. 1, p. 14 (sense 4); vol. 1. p. 81 (sense 5); vol. 2, p. 16 (sense 6); vol. 1, p. 127 (sense 7).

Of similar significance . . . 'for common utilities sake': Ibid., vol. 1, p. 83; vol. 1, p. 84; vol. 1, p.183; vol. 1, p.185; vol. 1, p.190; vol. 1, p.190; vol. 1, p. 96; vol. 2, p. 17; vol. 2, p. 37; vol. 2, p. 46.

'extraordinarily . . . imagination': Eliot, *Varieties of Metaphysical Poetry*, pp. 81 and 82 n. 41.

'I attempted . . . conceits': Ibid., p. 138.

'teasing the idea' . . . soul and body which we knew': Ibid., pp. 85, 132, 155.

'the only . . . personality of Donne': Ibid., p. 155.

'the publication . . . poetic mind': Ibid., pp. 1–2.

'probably . . . labour': Eliot, *Selected Essays*, p. 30.

In 'The Love Song... voice praying: *The Complete Poems and Plays of T. S. Eliot* (London: Faber, 1969), pp. 13–17 ('Prufrock'), p. 192 ('Little Gidding').

'posture... delegated' to us by Shakespeare: Ricks, *T. S. Eliot and Prejudice*, pp. 161–2.

It is supposed... carefully excluded: *The Prose Works of William Wordsworth*, ed. W. J. B. Owen and Jane Worthington Smyser, 3 vols. (Oxford: Clarendon Press, 1974), vol. 1, p. 122. Cf. William Wordsworth, *Poems*, ed. John O. Hayden, 2 vols. (New Haven, CT: Yale University Press, 1981), vol. 1, p. 868; and William Wordsworth, *Lyrical Ballads and Other Poems, 1797–1800*, ed. James Butler and Karen Green (Ithaca, NY: Cornell University Press, 1992), p. 742.

'antagonism... common humanity': Ricks, *T. S. Eliot and Prejudice*, p. 255.

Whitman... *Drum-Taps*: e.g. in 'A March in the Ranks Hard-Prest, and the Road Unknown', lines 7, 12–14, in *Whitman: Poetry and Prose*, ed. Justin Kaplan (New York: The Library of America, 1982), p. 440.

'apathy... abuse': *Letters of T. S. Eliot*, vol. 1, p. 369.

The residual beneficiaries... torpor: Ibid., p. 370. By 'Anglican literary "spirituality"' I have especially in mind the prevailing sentiment which takes *Four Quartets* to be not only in the contemplative tradition but also in the canon and which bases its own *bienpensant* soliloquies on that misapprehension. I take, as an exemplary instance of a prevalent type, John Booty's *Meditating on Four Quartets* (Cambridge, MA: Cowley Press, 1983). My criticism is not directed at the work of prayer of the contemplative orders.

I anticipate... human condition': See Christopher Ricks, 'Philip Larkin', in *The Force of Poetry* (Oxford: Oxford University Press, 1984), pp. 274–84; e.g.: 'Larkin's classical temper shows its mettle when he deplores modernism, whether in jazz, poetry, or painting: "I dislike such things not because they are new, but because they are irresponsible exploitations of technique in contradiction of human life as we know it. This is my essential criticism of modernism, whether perpetrated by Parker, Pound or Picasso; it helps us neither to enjoy nor endure"' (p. 278). The 'temper' here is not 'classical' but postprandial. It is no more 'classical' to 'deplore' modernism than it is to invoke the wit and wisdom of Dr Johnson. Johnson was knowledgeable and skilled in the tragic-comedy of spleen: in this he recollects a classical line of wit and anticipates important facets of modernism's comedy—as in Beckett, Wyndham Lewis, and early Eliot. The locution 'shows its mettle' ('quality of disposition or temperament') could be read as punning escape-clause, as meaning 'shows itself for what it is', but I do not associate this kind of covert mechanism with the broad integrity of Ricks's critical practice. It is clear, I think, that we are to read 'spirit' as 'courage', and that he believes Larkin to possess an inherent virtue of reactionary personality which turns even 'his greatest soft sell' (p. 279) into an awareness of 'destination', which in turn 'itself arrives at one of Larkin's greatest destinations, the end of "The Whitsun Weddings"' (p. 280). If I cannot accept 'greatest destinations' it is because I am conscious of being urged to an acceptance of a patrimony that is nowhere proven. In rejecting the Larkin package I am made to reject Wilfred Owen too, and Blunden, and Gray, in addition to which I am beneficiary of Dr Johnson's tacit approval. I must conclude that there is a tone that Larkin represents which is stronger even than Ricks's acute sense of pitch; what Larkin represents is an assumption, a narrow English possessiveness, with regard to 'good sense' and 'generous common humanity'. 'Good sense', so propertied, so keen to admit others, at a price, to its proprieties, strikes me as mere *bienséance*. During his lifetime Larkin was granted endless credit by the bank of Opinion, and the rage which in some quarters greeted his posthumously published *Letters* was that of people who consider themselves betrayed by one of their own kind. In fact Larkin betrayed no one, least of all himself. What he is seen to be in the letters he was and is in the poems. The notion of accessibility of his work acknowledged the ease with which readers could overlay it with transparencies of their own preference. Mill, who condescended to Wordsworth's poetry, allowed it the major significance of reflecting Mill's own love of mountains, thereby rescuing Mill from depression. Mill's intellectual heirs ('a person's taste is as much his own peculiar concern as his opinion or his purse') found it convenient to suppose that Larkin's peculiar concern as a poet was exactly conformable to their pursed opinions ('human life as we know it'). *The Waste Land*, at its first appearance, could only be understood exegetically; that is its remaining strength. *Four Quartets*, from its existence as an entity, was granted the major significance of reflecting Anglican empathy, a tendency that finds exemplary utterance in Booty's 'Whether fully conscious of the fact or not, Eliot seems to have here the right order for our time' (*Meditating on Four Quartets*, p. 60).

INVENTIONS OF VALUE

22. Translating Value

'intrinsic'...poetic worth': A. C. Bradley, *Oxford Lectures on Poetry*, 2nd edn. (London: Macmillan, 1909), pp. 4–5 ('Poetry for Poetry's Sake').

'may be directly...useless sound': I. A. Richards, *Principles of Literary Criticism* (London: Routledge, 2001), p. 67 (first pub. 1924).

Ruskin's 'intrinsic value': *The Works of John Ruskin*, ed. E. T. Cook and Alexander Wedderburn, 39 vols. (1903–12), vol. 17, p. 153 (*Munera Pulveris*); see also vol. 27, p. 217 (*Fors Clavigera*).

'mind free from all *prejudice*': David Hume, *Essays Moral, Political, and Literary*, ed. Eugene F. Miller (Indianapolis, IN: Liberty Fund, rev. edn., 1988), p. 239 ('Of the Standard of Taste').

'a delicate taste of wit or beauty': Ibid., p. 236.

'a due attention to the object': Ibid., p. 232.

'absurd and ridiculous': Ibid., p. 231.

'personal values' ... hostile to literature': Christopher Ricks, *Essays in Appreciation* (Oxford: Clarendon Press, 1996), p. 317.

'the taste model ... too simple': James Griffin, *Value Judgment* (Oxford: Oxford University Press, 1996), p. 22.

'Those finer emotions ... nature': Hume, *Essays*, p. 233.

'the Polite Wit': *Monsieur Pascall's Thoughts, Meditations and Prayers*, tr. Joseph Walker (London, 1688), p. 235.

'the refin'd wit': Ibid., p. 236.

'the nimbly discerning mind': *Pascal's Pensées*, tr. H. F. Stewart (New York: Pantheon Books, 1950), p. 495.

('The good or ill ... disposal'): Hume, *Essays*, p. 5 ('Of the Delicacy of Taste and Passion').

'Philosophers ... *attained*': Ibid.

It is natural ... another: Ibid., p. 229.

beliefs 'wrought into' human nature: Thomas Hobbes, *Leviathan*, ed. C. B. Macpherson (Harmondsworth: Penguin, 1968), p. 180.

Wordsworth esteemed Hume among the very worst of critics: William Wordsworth, *Poems*, ed. John O. Hayden, 2 vols. (Harmondsworth: Penguin, 1977), vol. 2, p. 934 ('Essay, Supplementary to the Preface'). Cf. William Wordsworth, *The Prose Works of William Wordsworth*, ed. W. J. B. Owen and Jane Worthington Smyser, 3 vols. (Oxford: Clarendon Press, 1974), vol. 3, p. 71.

It is supposed...excluded: *Wordsworth's Preface to 'Lyrical Ballads'*, ed. W. J. B. Owen (Copenhagen: Rosenkilde and Bagger, 1957), p. 114. Cf. *Poems*, vol. 1, p. 868 and *Prose Works*, vol. 1, p. 122.

'But the ignorance...enemies': Wordsworth, *Poems*, vol. 2, p. 923; cf. *Prose Works*, vol. 3, p. 62.

'opponents whom I internally despise': Wordsworth, *Poems*, vol. 2, p. 924; cf. *Prose Works*, vol. 3, p. 62.

'who talk . . . pleasure': *Wordsworth's Preface*, p. 122; cf. *Poems*, vol. 1, p. 879 and *Prose Works*, vol. 1, p. 139.

'transport' . . . prudence and discretion': Hume, *Essays,* p. 4.

'the perfection of the man . . . united': Ibid., p. 236.

'to fix and ascertain': Ibid., p. 230.

'the common sentiments of human nature': Ibid., p. 232.

Then . . . open it: John Bunyan, *The Pilgrim's Progress*, ed. N. H. Keeble (Oxford: Clarendon Press, 1984), pp. 96, 274–5.

'many meanings can have *one word*': Sigurd Burckhardt, 'The Poet as Fool and Priest' in *ELH*, vol. 23, no. 4 (December 1956), p. 287; repr. in Sigurd Burckhard, *Shakespearean Meanings* (Princeton, NJ: Princeton University Press, 1968), p. 32.

'Donne is really . . . applied': Walter J. Ong, *The Barbarian Within, and Other Fugitive Essays and Studies* (New York: Macmillan, 1962), p. 64.

'their Soule . . . ends': Robert Burton, *The Anatomy of Melancholy*, ed. Thomas C. Faulkner et al., 6 vols. (Oxford: Clarendon Press, 1989–4), vol. 1, p. 79.

'in the fineness . . . point': *The Early Lectures of Ralph Waldo Emerson*, ed. Stephen E. Whicher and Robert E. Spiller, 3 vols. (Cambridge, MA: Belknap Press, 1959–72), vol. 1, p. 378.

'when one has halted . . . *here*, and *here*': A. E. Housman, *Selected Prose*, ed. John Carter (Cambridge: Cambridge University Press, 1962), p. 27. Housman quotes from Arnold's 'Memorial Verses' to Goethe.

'A landmark only!' . . . landmark?: Ruskin, *Works*, vol. 34, p. 571.

'the tripper from Manchester or Birmingham': Ibid., p. 571.

'blasphemed the name . . . and openly': Ibid., p. 40.

'plague-wind': Ibid., pp. 9, 31, 32, 33, 34, 35, 36, 38, 39, 42, 59, 67, 78.

'plague-cloud': Ibid., pp. 28, 30, 38, 40, 51, 64, 70, 71, 72.

'as if it were made of dead men's souls': Ibid., p. 33.

'illth': Ruskin, Ibid., vol. 17, p. 89 (*Unto This Last*) and p. 168 (*Munera Pulveris*).

'Mr Ruskin is . . . significance': John Ruskin, *Unto This Last & Other Essays on Art and Political Economy* (London: Dent, 1907), p. xi.

'inhaerent': Hobbes, *Leviathan*, p. 75.

'an undiscerned, and an undiscerning hand': Ibid., p. 718.

'durable admiration . . . envy': Hume, *Essays*, p. 233.

'Used or not . . . else': Ruskin, *Works*, vol. 17, p. 153 (*Unto This Last*).

'Everything costs . . . pay it': *Letters of John Ruskin to Charles Eliot Norton*, 2 vols. (Cambridge, MA: Houghton Mifflin, 1904), vol. 1, p. 243.

drawn their term out of the language of the despised Scholastics: See *Locke on Money*, ed. P. H. Kelley, 2 vols. (Oxford: Clarendon Press, 1991), vol. 1, p. 87 n. 2.

And you will . . . bargain: Ruskin, *Works*, vol. 27, p. 217. Letter 12 is dated 'December 1871'; the passage quoted here continues by invoking the joylessness of Christmas (and 'still less Easter') for Judas. See also ibid., vol. 18, p. 414 (*The Crown of Wild Olive*).

Carlyle 'spoiled Ruskin's style for him': *The Correspondence of Gerard Manley Hopkins and Richard Watson Dixon*, ed. Claude Colleer Abbott (London: Oxford University Press, 1935), pp. 51–2.

eloquent tribute: See, e.g. *Works*, vol. 28, p. 22, and Ruskin's index to *Fors Clavigera*, s.v. 'Carlyle' (*Works*, vol. 29, p. 619).

'master': Ibid., vols. 14, p. 288; 24, p. 347; and 34, p. 355.

'the same natural . . . any thing': John Locke, *Two Treatises of Government*, ed. Peter Laslett (Cambridge: Cambridge University Press, 1988), p. 298.

'I should best . . . value': Ruskin, *Works*, vol. 28, p. 19.

'I will make . . . advice': Ibid., p. 19.

Locke's attitude . . . was 'unusually harsh': Neal Wood, *John Locke and Agrarian Capitalism* (Berkeley, CA: University of California Press, 1984), pp. 106–7.

'the longing . . . literature itself': Ricks, *Essays in Appreciation*, p. 319.

'moral existence' . . . moral life at all': Lionel Trilling, *A Gathering of Fugitives* (Boston, MA: Beacon Press, 1956), p. 39.

There is . . . found it so: William Wordsworth, *Lyrical Ballads and Other Poems, 1797–1800*, ed. James Butler and Karen Green (Ithaca, NY: Cornell University Press, 1992), p. 267. Cf. Wordsworth, *Poems*, vol. 1, p. 467.

'good sense . . . of life': Hume, *Essays*, p. 247.

'a thing subject . . . associations': Wordsworth, *Poems*, vol. 2, p. 947; cf. *Prose Works*, vol. 3, p. 82.

a quibble for which he did not choose to stoop aside: My allusion is to Johnson, on Shakespeare's quibbles; see his 'Preface to Shakespeare', 1765.

the term 'pitch', which elsewhere I have distinguished from 'tone': See Ch. 21, p. 375.

'where words . . . perfect pitch': Jon Stallworthy, *Between the Lines: Yeats' Poetry in the Making* (Oxford: Clarendon Press, 1963), p. 6.

A poet who . . . depth: Geoffrey Hill, 'The Conscious Mind's Intelligible Structure', *Agenda*, vol. 9, no. 4 and vol. 10, no. 1 (Autumn/Winter, 1971/2), p. 21.

'Nothing else . . . of my own': Gerard M. Hopkins, *The Sermons and Devotional Writings of Gerard Manley Hopkins*, ed. Christopher Devlin (London: Oxford University Press, 1959), p. 123.

'does not distinguish . . . [this-ness]': Hopkins, *Sermons and Devotional Writings*, p. 293.

'A politician . . . purchase': Edmund Burke, *Reflections on the Revolution in France*, ed. Conor Cruise O'Brien (Harmondsworth: Penguin, 1986), p. 267.

'Our Senses . . . true Religion': Hobbes, p. 409.

'The dream insisted . . . by the road': Cited in Gerard M. Hopkins, *The Journals and Papers of Gerard Manley Hopkins*, ed. Humphry House and Graham Storey (London: Oxford University Press, 1959), pp. 413–14; cf. Ruskin, *Works*, vol. 6, p. 38.

'Not imposed outwards . . . strong feeling': Hopkins, *Journals and Papers*, p. 215.

I see . . . but worse: Text as given in *Gerard Manley Hopkins*, ed. Catherine Phillips (Oxford: Oxford University Press, 1986), p. 166. *The Poetical Works of Gerard Manley Hopkins*, ed. Norman H. MacKenzie (Oxford: Clarendon Press, 1990), pp. 181–2, gives variorum readings. MacKenzie states (p. xliii) that 'some famous poems . . . were in fact left without a finalized text', 'I wake and feel the fell of dark' was one of these. MacKenzie adds (p. 449) that the 'bracketed' MS reading 'As I am mine, their sweating selves; but worse' was added 'perhaps to reduce any suggestion that [GMH] felt worse than the lost'. I cannot see that the 'suggestion', even if only tenuously present, could have been theologically tolerable to Hopkins, once he had noticed it. The grammar of his self-correction strikes me as being powerfully characteristic.

23.   Language, Suffering, and Silence

maximum period: Peter Hoffmann, *The History of the German Resistance, 1933–1945*, tr. Richard Barry (Cambridge, MA: MIT Press, 1979), p. 514.

her children . . . give evidence: Gerard M. Hopkins, *The Poetical Works of Gerard Manley Hopkins*, ed. Norman H. MacKenzie (Oxford: Clarendon Press, 1990), p. 358.

'to save . . . consciences': Gerard M. Hopkins, *The Sermons and Devotional Writings of Gerard Manley Hopkins*, ed. Christopher Devlin (London: Oxford University Press, 1959), p. 279.

'remain[ed] as dumb as a tree-stump': Pierre Janelle, *Robert Southwell the Writer* (London: Sheed & Ward, 1935), pp. 66–7. The source of this information was Robert Cecil, subsequently Secretary of State.

'monster' of 'strange taciturnity': *Unpublished Documents Relating to the English Martyrs*, ed. John Hungerford Pollen (London: Catholic Record Society, 1908), p. 283 (*CRS*, vol. 5).

'for this . . . punishe me': R. W. Chambers, 'Introduction', in Nicholas Harpsfield, *The Life and Death of Sr Thomas Moore, Knight, Sometymes Lord High Chancellor of England*, ed. E. V. Hitchcock, published for the Early English Text Society (London: Oxford University Press, 1932).

'with pacience and mekenesse' . . . feithe': *The Imitation of Christ: The First English Translation of the 'Imitatio Christi'*, ed. B. J. H. Biggs (Oxford: Oxford University Press, 1997), p. 111.

'Paul's defence . . . Acts 26': Ibid., p. 198.

'great plea for the liberty of silence': R. W. Chambers, *Thomas More*, 2nd edn. (London: J. Cape, 1938), p. 336.

'esteemed very light . . . commendable fame': Harpsfield, *Life*, p. 189.

'Christ . . . place': John Donne, *The Sermons of John Donne*, ed. George R. Potter and Evelyn M. Simpson, 10 vols. (Berkeley, CA: University of California Press, 1953–62), vol. 4, p. 341.

So whosoever . . . speechlesse: Ibid., vol. 5, p. 233.

'Jesus not only...theological statement': Christa K. Dixon, *Negro Spirituals: From Bible to Folk Song* (Philadelphia, PA: Fortress Press, 1976), p. 74.

'The story...resistance': Arthur C. Jones, *Wade in the Water: The Wisdom of the Spirituals* (Maryknoll, NY: Orbis Books, 1993), pp. 31–2.

'black folks...humanity': James H. Cone, *The Spirituals and the Blues* (New York: Seabury Press, 1972), p. 52.

'the silent adjustments...enormously complicated': Ludwig Wittgenstein, *Tractatus Logico-Philosophicus*, tr. C. K. Ogden (London: Routledge & Kegan Paul, 1981), pp. 62–3 ('die stillschweigenden Abmachungen zum Verständnis der Umgangssprache sind enorm kompliziert').

I'll tell you...way: Cone, *Spirituals and Blues*, pp. 42, 150.

'[Christ] made himselfe...likenesse of men': Philippians 2 : 7.

'business on both sides of the road': Wordsworth, 'A Letter to the Bishop of Llandaff' (written in 1793; first printed in 1876) in William Wordsworth, *Poetry and Prose*, ed. W. M. Merchant (Cambridge, MA: Harvard University Press, 1970), p. 99. Cf. William Wordsworth, *The Prose Works of William Wordsworth*, ed. W. J. B. Owen and Jane Worthington Smyser, 3 vols. (Oxford: Clarendon Press, 1974), vol. 1, p. 49.

'The wonders...ornament': Isaac Watts, *Horae Lyricae: Poems Chiefly of the Lyric Kind in Three Books* (Exeter: H. Ranlet, 1795), p. xii.

a matter of social fact: *Religious Folk-Songs of the Negro as Sung at Hampton Institute*, ed. R. Nathaniel Dett (Hampton, VA: Hampton Institute Press, 1927), 'Introduction' and pp. 255, 260, 263.

'awoke and found it truth': *The Letters of John Keats*, ed. Hyder Edward Rollins, 2 vols. (Cambridge, MA: Harvard University Press, 1965), vol. 1, p. 285.

men for contemplation...souls: William Wordsworth, *The Thirteen-Book Prelude*, ed. Mark L. Reed, 2 vols. (Ithaca, NY: Cornell University Press, 1991), vol. 1, pp. 310–11.

'among the walks of homely life': Wordsworth, *Thirteen-Book Prelude*, vol. 1, p. 310 (l. 265).

looking into...uninitiated: *Religious Folk-Songs*, p. 262.

'must go back and be with them': Wilfred Owen, *Collected Letters*, ed. Harold Owen and John Bell (London: Oxford University Press, 1967), p. 521.

I came...the first: Letter of 4 Oct. 1918, ibid., p. 580.

'I write for myself'...'confusing answer': Kanan Makiya, *Cruelty and Silence: War, Tyranny, Uprising, and the Arab World* (New York: W. W. Norton, 1993), pp. 238–9.

'Though we be...right': Second letter to John Frith, in *The Work of William Tyndale*, ed. G. E. Duffield (Appleford: Sutton Courtenay, 1964), pp. 397–8.

'To confess...rightness': Ezra Pound, *Drafts & Fragments of Cantos CX–CXVII* (New York: New Directions, 1968), p. 27.

cor curvum in se ipsum: Martin Luther, *Luthers Werke: Schriften* (Weimarer Ausgabe), 58 vols. (Weimar: H. Böhlau, 1883), vol. 56, p. 304: 'Natura nostra vitio primi peccati tam profunda est in seipsam incurua'; p. 305: '[cor hominis] ita curuum in se, Vt nullus hominum, quantumlibet sanctus (seclusa tentatione), scire possit'.

detortae in infima voluntatis: Augustine, *St. Augustine's Confessions with an English Translation by William Watts, 1631*, 2 vols. (Cambridge, MA: Harvard University Press, 1912), vol. 1, pp. 382–3.

semper peccator . . . semper justus: *Luthers Werke*, vol. 56, p. 442. Cf. Gordon Rupp, *The Righteousness of God: Luther Studies* (London: Hodder & Stoughton, 1953), pp. 179, 183, 255.

mocked his spiritual impertinence: Thomas More, *The Complete Works of St. Thomas More*, 15 vols. (New Haven, CT: Yale University Press, 1963–97), vol. 8 (in 3 parts), parts 1, p. 420, and 3, p. 1419; W. A. Clebsch, *England's Earliest Protestants 1520–1535* (New Haven, CT: Yale University Press, 1964), pp. 112–13, 288.

'terrible aboriginal calamity': John Henry Cardinal Newman, *Apologia Pro Vita Sua*, ed. Martin J. Svaglic (Oxford: Clarendon Press, 1967), p. 218.

'People in our rank . . . same thing': William Wordsworth, *The Letters of William and Dorothy Wordsworth*, ed. Ernest de Selincourt and Chester L. Shaver, 2nd edn., 8 vols. (Oxford: Clarendon Press, 1967–93), vol. 1, p. 355 (letter to John Wilson, 7 June 1802); cf. Wordsworth, *Poetry and Prose*, p. 843.

'expresses . . . oppressed': *Young Poets of Germany: An Anthology*, ed. Uwe-Michael Gutzschhahn, tr. Raymond Hargreaves (London: Forest Books, 1994), p. 163. This is a publisher's advertisement, *not* an integral part of the original German text or of the English translation.

'in which . . . to be done': Matthew Arnold, *The Poems of Matthew Arnold*, ed. Kenneth Allott (London: Longmans, Green & Co., 1965), p. 592.

'a representation . . . enjoyment': Ibid., p. 592.

'I have rejected . . . poetry': *The Oxford Book of Modern Verse, 1892–1935*, ed. W. B. Yeats (Oxford: Oxford University Press, 1936), p. xxxiv.

('About suffering . . . Old Masters'): W. H. Auden, *The English Auden*, ed. Edward Mendelson (New York: Random House, 1977), p. 237.

'poetry makes . . . mouth': Ibid., p. 242.

The work . . . philosophers: Czesław Miłosz, *The Captive Mind*, tr. Jane Zielonko (Harmondsworth: Penguin, 1980), p. 41.

To the reasonable question . . . possibly threatening: This paragraph incorporates several phrases from my uncollected essay, 'The Conscious Mind's Intelligible Structure', *Agenda*, vol. 9, no. 4, and vol. 10, no. 1 (Autumn/Winter 1971/2), pp. 14–23.

the Proustian '*moments privilégiés*': For a discussion of Proust and *moments privilégiés*, see Roger Shattuck, *Proust's Binoculars* (New York: Random House, 1963), pp. 69–74.

'The right art . . . enjoyment': Arnold, *Poems*, p. 592.

For poetry . . . tamper: Auden, *The English Auden*, p. 242.

I have ... sacrifice of time: Gerard M. Hopkins, *The Letters of Gerard Manley Hopkins to Robert Bridges*, ed. Claude Colleer Abbott (London: Oxford University Press, 1935), pp. 60–3.

'bicker': *The Poems of Tennyson*, ed. Christopher Ricks, 2nd edn., 3 vols. (Berkeley, CA: University of California Press, 1987), vol. 2, p. 500 ('The Brook', l. 26).

To lift up ... live: Hopkins, *Sermons and Devotional Writings*, p. 241.

24.   Tacit Pledges

It is no mere ... of each: F. H. Bradley, *Ethical Studies* (1876), 2nd edn. (Oxford: Clarendon Press, 1927), p. 184.

'What Balfour did ... of the two': A. E. Housman, *The Letters of A. E. Housman*, ed. Archie Burnett, 2 vols. (Oxford: Clarendon Press, 2007), vol. 1, p. 527.

'Class is ... that it is': Ibid., vol. 2, p. 247.

'we ... standard of convention': A. E. Housman, 'Introductory Lecture delivered before the Faculties of Arts and Laws and of Science in University College, London, October 3, 1892', in *Collected Poems and Selected Prose*, ed. Christopher Ricks (London: Penguin, 1989), p. 268.

'the amount ... to analyse it': 'The Application of Thought to Textual Criticism', 4 Aug. 1921, ibid., p. 328.

'There is ... commodities': Ibid., p. 421.

'eloquence ... *overheard*': 'Thoughts on Poetry and its Varieties' (1833), in *Collected Works of John Stuart Mill*, 33 vols. (Toronto: University of Toronto Press, 1963–91), vol. 1, p. 348.

persistent harping ... the emotions: *Autobiography* (1873), ibid., vol. 1, pp. 150–3.

licensed eccentricities ... democratic majority: *On Liberty* (1859), ibid., vol. 18, p. 269; cf. *On Liberty*, ed. Gertrude Himmelfarb (Harmondsworth: Penguin, 1985), p. 132.

'somewhat self-satisfied dislike of life': A paper read to the Literary Society, Marlborough College, 15 May 1913, in *The Letters of Charles Sorley with a Chapter of Biography* (Cambridge: Cambridge University Press, 1919), p. 49.

'it was ... for him': Letter of 6 March 1914, ibid., p. 108.

'He is ... life intolerable': Ibid., p. 263.

'the Great War ... imagination': Housman, *Letters*, vol. 2, p. 392.

'Illic Jacet': *Last Poems* IV; see A. E. Housman, *The Poems of A. E. Housman*, ed. Archie Burnett (Oxford: Oxford University Press, 1997), pp. 74–5.

'when ... Flanders': *Alfred Edward Housman 26 March 1859–30 April 1936* [Special Issue of *The Bromsgrovian*] (Bromsgrove: Bromsgrove School, 1936), p. 29.

'the universal maintaining medium': Bradley, *Ethical Studies*, p. 185.

George Herbert Housman ... Boer War: See in John Pugh, *Bromsgrove and the Housmans* (Bromsgrove: The Housman Society, 1974), pp. lxvii–lxxiii (Appendix E: George Herbert Housman).

'The Olive': *Additional Poems* XXIII, in Housman, *Poems,* p. 162.

'on the conclusion of the peace': Ibid., p. 482.

'Astronomy': *Last Poems* XVII, ibid., p. 86.

'Farewell to a name and a number': *More Poems* XL, ibid., p. 139; cf. Housman, *Collected Poems and Selected Prose*, p. 186.

So ceases . . . dear to me: *More Poems* XL, in Housman, *Collected Poems and Selected Prose,* p. 186. Cf. Housman, *Poems*, p. 139.

'And trains all night groan on the rail': *A Shropshire Lad* IX, in Housman, *Poems*, p. 13.

'Where I lodge a little while': *A Shropshire Lad* XII, ibid., p. 16.

'The lover of the grave': *A Shropshire Lad* XVI, ibid., p. 19.

'the strengthless dead': *A Shropshire Lad* XIX, ibid., p. 21.

'the coloured counties': *A Shropshire Lad* XXI, ibid., p. 22.

'the truceless armies': *A Shropshire Lad* XXVIII, ibid., p. 25.

'Sleepy with the flow of streams': *A Shropshire Lad* XXXV, ibid., p. 36.

'The moon stands blank above': *A Shropshire Lad* XXXVI, ibid., p. 36.

'cloud-led shadows': *A Shropshire Lad* XLII, ibid., p. 43.

'The felon-quarried stone': *A Shropshire Lad* LIX, ibid., p. 61.

'All desired and timely things': *Last Poems* XXIV, ibid., p. 92.

'The pine lets fall its cone': *Last Poems* XL, ibid., p. 107.

'The upshot beam would fade': *Last Poems* XLI, ibid., p. 109.

'lying about the world': *More Poems* IX, ibid., p. 120.

'silent hills indenting | The orange band of eve': *More Poems* XXXIII, ibid., p. 135.

'When the bells justle in the tower': *Additional Poems* IX, ibid., p. 152.

'the intellectually surprising . . . correct word': I give this as quoted in *The Collected Poems of Sidney Keyes*, ed. Michael Meyer (London: Routledge, 1945), p. 117.

topographically accurate: Robin Shaw, *Housman's Places* (Bromsgrove: The Housman Society, 1995), p. 115.

'The lover of the grave . . . for love': *A Shropshire Lad* XVI, in Housman, *Poems*, p. 19.

'in the fields where . . . about the world': *More Poems* IX, ibid., p. 120.

('the town . . . universal'): Pugh, p. 167.

'found himself . . . measured them': Henry James, *The Tragic Muse* (Harmondsworth: Penguin, 1978), p. 199. The allusion is to *Hamlet*.

'dare not speak its name': Lord Alfred Douglas, 'Two Loves'.

When . . . tacit pledge: Richard Perceval Graves, *A. E. Housman: The Scholar Poet* (New York: Charles Scribner's Sons, 1980), p. 113; cf. Douglas Kerr, *Wilfred Owen's Voices: Language and Community* (Oxford: Clarendon Press, 1993), p. 182, referring to Owen's 'recent contact with the "secret men" of the embattled homosexual community in London'.

'Because I liked . . . stiff and dry': Housman, *Poems*, pp. 132–3.

'The financial expert . . . under hedges" ': Housman, *Letters*, vol. 2, pp. 111–12.

'unprintable': *The Letters of A. E. Housman*, ed. Henry Maas (Cambridge, MA: Cambridge University Press, 1971), p. 276 n.

'figleaf . . . 'let himself go': Laurence Housman, quoted in Graves, *Housman*, p. 101.

We'll . . . no more: Housman, *Poems*, p. 70.

'the stanza . . . delight': Housman, *Collected Poems and Selected Prose*, p. 367.

When I shall . . . out of mind: *A Shropshire Lad* LXIII, in Housman, *Poems*, p. 65.

For nature . . . mine or no: *Last Poems* XL, ibid., p. 107.

'amusing my self . . . Inscriptions': *The Spectator*, ed. Donald F. Bond, 5 vols. (Oxford: Clarendon Press, 1965), vol. 1, p. 109 (no. 26: 30 March 1711).

What though . . . divine': *The Spectator*, vol. 4, p. 145 (no. 465: 23 Aug. 1712).

'For My Funeral': *More Poems* XLVII, in Housman, *Poems*, pp. 145, 461; Graves, pp. 265–6.

Cyrenaic casuistry: Housman, *Letters*, ed. Burnett, vol. 2, p. 329: 'I respect the Epicureans more than the Stoics, but I am myself a Cyrenaic'.

an anecdote . . . lavatory: Graves, *Housman*, p. 249.

'Idealists . . . human being': *Philosophical Investigations*, tr. G. E. M. Anscombe, 3rd edn. (New York: Macmillan, 1969), p. 122e.

'self-complacency': A. E. Housman, *Selected Prose*, ed. John Carter (Cambridge: Cambridge University Press, 1962), p. 42.

'to read attentively . . . self-will': Ibid., p. 51.

Lucida tela diei . . . and here: Ibid., p. 27. Housman quotes from Arnold's 'Memorial Verses' to Goethe.

'it is by the same . . . commit suicide: F. H. Bradley, *Appearance and Reality*, 2nd edn. (Oxford: Clarendon Press, 1930), pp. 224–5 (first pub. 1893).

'the most prolific . . . Terence Hearsay collection': Graves, *Housman*, p. 107.

'under pain . . . subjectivity': cited by *OED²*, s.v. 'solipsism'.

its cognate 'solipsistic' . . . by William James: *OED²*, s.v. 'solipsistic'.

'Our bodies . . . our minds': Housman, *Collected Poems and Selected Prose*, p. 432.

'a remarkable . . . earthinesss': Sorley, *Letters*, p. 51.

Durkheim: Émile Durkheim, *Le Suicide: Étude de sociologie* (Paris: F. Alcan, 1897).

'answers to nothing real': Housman, *Collected Poems and Selected Prose*, p. 367.

If Bradley . . . Mill's philosophy: Bradley, *Ethical Studies*, pp. 85–141 ('Pleasure for Pleasure's Sake').

'philosophical' or 'practical' hedonism: Graves, *Housman*, p. 249: 'Housman was a philosophical hedonist'. Cf. *Letters*, ed. Burnett, vol. 2, p. 329: 'I am myself a Cyrenaic'; the doctrine of Aristippus of Cyrene, who established the Cyrenaic school, was that of 'practical hedonism' (*OED²*).

'the one . . . diffuseness': Mill, *Collected Works*, vol. 1, p. 499.

'Poetry . . . poet's mind': Ibid., p. 348.

'this stuff': Housman, *Collected Poems and Selected Prose*, p. 370.

'I take . . . with me': Percy Withers, *A Buried Life: Personal Recollections of A. E. Housman* (London: Jonathan Cape, 1940), p. 102.

Housman is diametrically opposed by the poetry of Thomas Hardy: But cf. Housman, *Letters*, ed. Burnett, vol. 2, p. 330. 'For Hardy I felt affection, and high admiration for some of his novels and a few of his poems'.

an entry in Wittgenstein's *Notebooks 1914–1916*: Ludwig Wittgenstein, *Notebooks 1914–1916*, ed. G. H. von Wright and G. E. M. Anscombe, 2nd edn. (Chicago, IL: University of Chicago Press, 1979), p. 82e.

Here we see ... with it: Ludwig Wittgenstein, *Tractatus Logico-Philosophicus*, tr. C. K. Ogden (London: Routledge, 1981), pp. 152–3.

I could not ... never seen: *The Complete Poetical Works of Thomas Hardy*, ed. Samuel Hynes, 5 vols. (Oxford: Clarendon Press, 1982–95), vol. 3, p. 215; cf. *The Complete Poems of Thomas Hardy*, ed. James Gibson (London: Macmillan, 1976), p. 878.

'Her strong enchantments failing': *Last Poems* III, in Housman, *Poems*, p. 74.

'When the eye of day is shut': *Last Poems* XXXIII, ibid., p. 101.

Her strong enchantments ... to-day: *Last Poems* III, ibid., p. 74.

'The queen ... Evil': Ibid., p. 374.

'the portrayal ... vanquished': Housman, *Collected Poems and Selected Prose,* p. 486 (the words are Katharine Symons's).

'Poetry': *The Poems of Wilfred Owen*, ed. Jon Stallworthy (London: Hogarth Press, 1985), p. 192.

'truth to which Solipsism has blindly borne witness': Bradley, *Appearance and Reality*, p. 229.

My way ... focus: Ibid.

'Disabled': Owen, *Poems*, pp. 152–4.

And round ... girl's: *A Shropshire Lad* XIX, in Housman, *Poems*, p. 21.

ἀμενηνός: Homer, *Odyssey* 11.29 (νεκύων ἀμενηνὰ κάρηνα).

'The shades ... a shade': F. H. Bradley, *Aphorisms* (Oxford: Clarendon Press, 1920), no. 98 (unpaginated).

'We know that ... truth': Quoted as epigraph, Hugh Lloyd-Jones, *Blood for the Ghosts: Classical Influences in the Nineteenth and Twentieth Centuries* (London: Duckworth, 1982). This contains two useful essays on Housman as classical scholar. Either Wilamowitz or his translator had in mind Arnold's sonnet to Shakespeare.

'many books': Wilfred Owen, *Collected Letters*, ed. Harold Owen and John Bell (London: Oxford University Press, 1967), pp. 581–2 ('But one day I will write Deceased over many books').

'Poetry': Cf. Owen, *Poems*, p. 123 ('poets' tearful fooling', 'Insensibility', l. 8); p. 155 ('(That's for your poetry book)', 'A Terre' l. 10); p. 192 ('Above all I am not concerned with Poetry', 'Preface').

Heart, you ... with shot: Ibid., p. 143 ('Greater Love', ll. 19–20).

I have just ... I mean: Owen, *Collected Letters*, pp. 484–5.

'I think ... of poetry': Housman, *Collected Poems and Selected Prose*, p. 352.

by way of Bridges's *Shorter Poems*: Housman, *Letters,* ed. Burnett, vol. 1, p. 434 and vol. 2, p. 181.

'expressionless' men: Owen, *Collected Letters*, p. 422: 'The men are just as Bairnsfather has them—expressionless lumps' (letter of 4 Jan. 1917). Bruce Bairnsfather did not depict the British private soldier as 'expressionless', a fact which can be demonstrated by spending ten minutes or so with *Fragments from France*, 1917. 'In Dixie-Land: "Well, Friday—'ow's Crusoe?" ', to take one example, shows eight tommies, each with a distinct, strongly realized, facial expression, each one a delineated 'character'. If there are 'expressionless' stereotypes in Bairnsfather, they are more likely to be officers: vacant 'silly ass' faces for subalterns, Blimpish for general staff. It is nonetheless true that Bairnsfather has evolved an English comedy of humours as artificial in its way as *Jorrocks's Jaunts*. Owen requires 'the men' to be 'expressionless lumps' to establish the moral ground upon which his war poems are based: the conviction that he alone can give a terrible inarticulacy its voice (cf. *Collected Letters*, p. 521, letter of 31 Dec. 1917).

editorial in Horatio Bottomley's *John Bull*: See Owen, *Collected Letters*, pp. 468 n. 2, 568, 585 n. 2.

If you could . . . mori: Owen, *Poems*, p. 117.

'famous Latin tag': Owen, *Collected Letters*, p. 500.

'abrupt': Quinn in Horace, *The Odes*, ed. Kenneth Quinn (London: Macmillan Educational, 1984), p. 244.

'the most difficult . . . Roman Odes': Pasquali quoted in Horace, *The Odes*, ed. Quinn, p. 244.

'mysterious avoidance': Quinn in Horace, *The Odes*, p. 244.

'particular sought pitch and accent': Henry James, *The Art of the Novel* (New York: Charles Scribner's Sons, [1908]), p. 81.

'straight measure': Ibid., p. 79.

'*usurping* consciousness': Ibid., p. 90.

'displacement': Ibid., p. 86.

'indispensable centre': Ibid., p. 84.

slights poetry . . . recovery of his spirits: See Mill, *Collected Works*, vol. 1, pp. 150–3, 344–5, 348–9, 403.

'the general tendency . . . mankind': Mill, *Collected Works*, vol. 18, p. 268; cf. *On Liberty*, pp. 130–1.

'atmosphere . . . breathe freely': Ibid., p. 267; cf. *On Liberty*, p. 129.

'I do not . . . as poetry': F. H. Bradley, *Essays on Truth and Reality* (Oxford: Clarendon Press, 1914), p. 468 n. 1.

'Solipsism . . . a truth': T. S. Eliot, *Knowledge and Experience in the Philosophy of F. H. Bradley* (London: Faber, 1964), p. 141.

the entertainment is Eliot's: When Eliot, in 'Little Gidding', predicts 'the hedges | White again, in May, with voluptuary sweetness', how far is the Bradleian 'voluptuary' (cf. Bradley, *Ethical Studies*, p. 270 n.) an implicit condescension to Wordsworthian 'sensations sweet' as particularized by the Victorian and Georgian lyric style, for instance in Housman's set pieces ('The hawthorn sprinkled up and down | Should charge the land with snow', *A Shropshire Lad* XXXIX, 'under blanching mays', *Last Poems* XL)? For Geoffrey Grigson, *The Englishman's Flora* (London: Phoenix House, 1958), pp. 166–71, the may can be over-sweet, indeed fulsome: 'The stale, sweet scent from the trimethylamine the flowers contain, makes them suggestive of sex . . . Trimethylamine is an ingredient of the smell of putrefaction' (p. 168). In John Amphlett and Carleton Rea's exemplary *The Botany of Worcestershire* (Birmingham: Cornish Bros, 1909), pp. 140–1, this is a specificity that goes unrecorded though they note that 'into the usages and rejoicings of the country-side the plant has entered largely'. Housman's art brings the hawthorn particularly into his necessitarian returns upon the usages and rejoicings of the Worcestershire ('Shropshire') countryside: 'In valleys green and still | Where lovers wander maying', *Last Poems* VII; 'the flowers | Stream from the hawthorn on the wind away', *Last Poems* IX. If such verses are a form of parody on 'usages and rejoicings', the intelligence that dictates them is not at all remote from the decent sensibilities of Amphlett and Rea ('Orchis . . . From an untranslatable word, referring to the double tuberous root', p. 348). I am pondering here the affinity between one style of closed meanings and another and debating, as I have throughout the chapter, the nature of the pressure which social *mores* impose upon the individual voice. These are mutual overhearings and tacit understandings, within Mill's range of assumptions though not with his particular emphasis. The true genius in these restricted circumstances is Edward FitzGerald's refusing blancmange at a wedding breakfast, 'Ugh! Congealed bridesmaid' (the anecdote is recounted by Robert Bernard Martin, *With Friends Possessed: A Life of Edward FitzGerald* (New York: Atheneum, 1985), p. 193). Housman's table-talk can be both witty and suggestive, but not with this kind of purchase on chance and possibility. His set lyric melancholy ('The garland briefer than a girl's') seems at times as vulnerable to FitzGerald's peculiar felicities of entertainment as to Sorley's suggestion of a 'somewhat self-satisfied dislike of life' (see p. 408, above). But then again one might say that FitzGerald, in the language and cadences of the *Rubáiyát*, seems at times vulnerable to the quality and scope of intelligence at work in his letters and conversation; and that there is nothing in Sorley's verse to match the grasp of expectation and circumstance shown in his remarks on the occasion of Brooke's death (see p. 408, above). It is appropriate to recall here Housman's own words concerning the fitting of our judgement not to the truth of things but to the standard of convention (see p. 407, above).

'no character . . . "hero"': James, *Art of the Novel*, p. 90.

'understanding . . . degree': *OED*[2], s.v. 'intelligence', sense 2.

A worm . . . Solomon: Isaac Rosenberg, *The Poems and Plays of Isaac Rosenberg*, ed. Vivien Noakes (Oxford: Oxford University Press, 2004), p. 126. I have deleted the full stop after 'sung'.

'invisible worm . . . night': William Blake, *Songs of Innocence and of Experience*, ed. Andrew Lincoln (Princeton, NJ: Princeton University Press, 1991), plate 39: 'The Sick Rose' (unpaginated).

'packed with material . . . work': Shaw, *Housman's Places*, back cover.

'quality . . . imaginings': Cited in *OED*[2], s.v. 'amorphous'.

'What is best . . . straight on': *Collected Poems of Ivor Gurney*, ed. P. J. Kavanagh (Oxford: Oxford University Press, 1982), p. 129 ('Tewkesbury').

'delighted . . . readers': Shaw, *Housman's Places*, back cover.

25. Gurney's 'Hobby'

'they will not say much . . . was needed': Ivor Gurney, *War Letters: A Selection*, ed. R. K. R. Thornton (Manchester: Carcanet, 1983), p. 211. See also p. 180.

'Strange Service', 'Pain', and 'Servitude': Ivor Gurney, *Collected Poems of Ivor Gurney*,
    ed. P. J. Kavanagh (Oxford: Oxford University Press, 1982), pp. 31, 36, 37.

'larger and finer . . . my bow': Ibid., p. 211.

'pursued merely . . . importance': *OED²*, s.v. 'hobby' 5. See also T. S. Eliot, *The Sacred
    Wood* (London: Methuen & Co., 1967), pp. 39–40 ('to George Wyndham [literature]
    was a hobby').

As a musician . . . Royal College of Music: Michael Hurd, *The Ordeal of Ivor Gurney*
    (Oxford: Oxford University Press, 1978), p. 140: 'he had failed his FRCO
    examination'. This was in 1921, by which time he was already afflicted. His
    professional training had been interrupted by war service. See also Gurney, *War
    Letters*, p. 97 on his 'job', namely composing: 'Once I could not write away
    from the piano; that [Gurney's setting of a Masefield poem] was written in the
    front line. Indeed I am becoming fit for my job—by which, as you know, I do
    not mean fighting' (24 August 1916).

'Sleep', a setting . . . twentieth century': Hurd, pp. 38, 182, 209; I. A. Copley, *The
    Music of Peter Warlock: A Critical Survey* (London: D. Dobson, 1979), p. 102.

In a letter . . . thesis: Gurney, *War Letters*, p. 53.

'like a flood': Ibid., p. 40.

'in the manner of Walt Whitman': P. J. Kavanagh, in Gurney, *Collected Poems*, p. 244.

'Walt Whitman . . . *Ironical* work)': Ibid., p. 244.

'detested irony': Kavanagh, in ibid., p. 9.

'electrical waves': 'There were, as well, delusions of being persecuted by electrical
    waves', Kavanagh, in ibid.

'Compree no grub?': Gurney, *War Letters*, p. 109.

'Bide a wee, s'il vous plait': Ibid.

'My dear Howler': Ibid., pp. 51, 56, 111, 143, 156, 164, 181.

'Erbert Owls': Ibid., p. 220.

'the great . . . British Museum': Ibid., p. 164.

La Comptesse Tilda: Ibid., p. 234.

'Dear houses . . . asleep': Ibid.

'There's a bit . . . two months': Ibid., p. 230.

'No more . . . 'Blighty': Gurney, *Collected Poems*, p. 170 ('Farewell').

Donald Davie . . . distinct styles': 'Gurney's Flood', *London Review of Books*, vol. 5,
    no. 2 (Feb. 1983), p. 7.

'the intricacies . . . subject': Kavanagh, in Gurney, *Collected Poems*, p. 12.

'looks to have . . . texture': Ibid., p. 113 ('Schubert').

'true . . . Azure': Ibid., p. 114 ('Imitation').

'The Artist . . . blood.': Gurney, *War Letters*, p. 219.

'little bits of jargon': Ibid., p. 57.

'grub, Fritz, and Blighty': Ibid., p. 147.

'poor bare jests . . . my number's up"': Ibid., pp. 216–17.

'When on a sudden . . . home!': Gurney, *Collected Poems*, p. 56.

I saw a scrawl . . . at that: Gurney, *War Letters*, pp. 104–5.

'were written . . . an officer)': Ibid., p. 130.

'the accumulative weight . . . one large': Ibid.

'disturbed by multitudinous things': Hilaire Belloc, *The Servile State* (London: T. N. Foulis, 1912), p. 127.

'all that human . . . differentiation': Ibid.

'the silhouettes . . . certain lights': Kavanagh, in Gurney, *Collected Poems*, p. 13.

'all the beauties of . . . Gloucestershire': Davie, 'Gurney's Flood', p. 6.

'exalted spiritual': Gurney, *War Letters*, p. 130.

('And infinitely far that star Capella'): Gurney, *Collected Poems*, p. 103 ('Fragment').

'Faces infinitely grimed in': Ibid., p. 87 ('Canadians').

'Infinite lovely chatter of Bucks accent': Ibid., p. 102 ('The Silent One').

'Everyday things . . . Infinitely delighted': Ibid., p. 115 ('Looking Out').

'one of my . . . brothers': Ibid., p. 188 ('The Coin').

'occasional bathetic . . . intentional': Kavanagh, ibid., p. 13.

'nothing . . . and fine beauty': Ibid., p. 83 ('Near Vermand').

'England, terrible . . . pleased": Ivor Gurney, *Severn & Somme* (London: Sidgwick & Jackson, 1917), p. 69 ('England the Mother'); cf. Ivor Gurney, *Severn & Somme and War's Embers* (Manchester: Carcanet, 1997), p. 51.

'astonishing creative pride': Hurd, *Ordeal*, p. 35.

'For the English Police . . . Yard': Gurney, *Collected Poems*, p. 265.

'the great honour of song': Ibid., p. 192 ('The Last of the Book').

'A favourite occupation . . . importance.': *OED*², s.v. 'hobby' 5.

'competitive or bureaucratic toil': G. K. Chesterton, *What's Wrong with the World*, 3rd edn. (New York: Dodd, Mead, & Co., 1910), p. 127.

'universal duty': Ibid.

'Woman . . . twenty hobbies': Ibid., p. 128.

'The Emancipation of Domesticity': See Jay P. Corrin, *G. K. Chesterton & Hilaire Belloc: The Battle Against Modernity* (Athens, OH: Ohio University Press, 1981), pp. 30–31.

('Out of the heart's . . . worst anger'): Gurney, *Collected Poems*, p. 196 ('War Books').

'Do as you please': Gurney, *War Letters*, p. 115.

'punctuate as you please': Ibid., p. 141.

'The grammar . . . to say.': Ibid.

'There is no time . . . gets destroyed': Ibid., p. 127.

'Neither he . . . modern technique.': Ibid., p. 211.

'craft': Ibid., p. 243.

'method': Ibid., p. 161.

'scrupulousness': Ibid., p. 160.

'care': Ibid.

'respect . . . materials': Ibid., p. 219.

'It seems to me . . . faint praise': Ibid., p. 183.

'I say . . . things whatsoever': Ibid., p. 120.

'corporate life and mutual obligations': Belloc, *The Servile State*, p. 74.

'common life which once nourished [the] social sense': Ibid.

'the dearness of common things': Gurney, *Collected Poems*, p. 119 ('The Dearness of Common Things').

'beauty | Of common living': Ivor Gurney, *War's Embers and Other Verses* (London: Sidgwick & Jackson, 1919), p. 24 ('Camps'); cf. *Severn & Somme and War's Embers*, p. 63.

'the common goodness . . . day after day': Gurney, *Collected Poems*, p. 167 ('While I Write').

'the day's | Common wonder': Ibid., p. 256 ('Girl, Girl, Why Look You So White?').

'the commonness of the tale': Ibid., p. 173 ('Butchers and Tombs').

'To be signallers . . . common infantry': Ibid., p. 175 ('Signallers').

'Casual and common is the wonder grown—': Ibid., p. 106 ('Longford Dawns').

'a Common Private makes but little show': Gurney, *Severn & Somme*, p. 8; cf. *Severn & Somme and War's Embers*, p. 20.

'How England . . . vast endurance': Gurney, *Collected Poems*, p. 94 ('Mist on Meadows').

'inertia and custom': Belloc, *The Servile State*, p. 110.

'instinct' and 'tradition': Ibid., pp. 122–3.

what Lionel Trilling . . . circumstance': Lionel Trilling, *The Opposing Self: Nine Essays in Criticism* (New York: Viking Press, 1955), p. 41.

'intended to be a sort of counterblast against': Gurney, *War Letters*, p. 130.

dedicated 'To the Memory of Rupert Brooke': Gurney, *Severn & Somme*, p. 65; cf. *Severn & Somme and War's Embers*, p. 49.

'begloried sonnets': Isaac Rosenberg, *The Collected Works of Isaac Rosenberg*, ed. Ian Parsons (New York: Oxford University Press, 1979), p. 237.

'as simple as ordinary talk': Rosenberg, *Collected Works*, p. 239.

'after the English manner': Gurney, *Severn and Somme*, p. 13 ('To Certain Comrades'); cf. *Severn & Somme and War's Embers*, p. 21.

'radiant shining': Gurney, *Severn & Somme*, p. 64 ('Requiem: Pour out your bounty'); cf. *Severn & Somme and War's Embers*, p. 49.

'a gathered . . . under the night': Rupert Brooke, *The Collected Poems of Rupert Brooke: With a Memoir*, 22nd impression (New York: Dodd, Mead, & Co., 1936), p. 147.

'heavy servitude': Gurney, *Severn & Somme*, p. 67 ('Servitude'); cf. *Severn & Somme and War's Embers*, p. 50.

'The boys who . . . speak to': *Severn & Somme*, p. 34 ('Scots'); cf. *Severn & Somme and War's Embers*, p. 31.

'Mind you take . . . loss.': Christopher Hassall, *Rupert Brooke: A Biography* (London: Faber & Faber, 1964), p. 496.

'England's royal grace and dignity': Gurney, *Severn & Somme*, p. 55 ('Spring. Rouen, May 1917'); cf. *Severn & Somme and War's Embers*, p. 44.

'These sonnets . . . in them.': Quoted in Hassall, *Rupert Brooke*, p. 503n. 1.

'Most of the book . . . with me': Gurney, *Severn & Somme*, p. 8; cf. *Severn & Somme and War's Embers*, pp. 19–20.

Gurney's tone here is . . . derivative: Cf. Hilaire Belloc, *The Four Men: A Farrago* (London: T. Nelson and Sons, 1912), p. 8: '"You may call me Myself," I answered, "for that is the name I shall give to my own person and my own soul"' and Walt Whitman, *Leaves of Grass*, 'Song of Myself'.

'I never was famous . . . show': Gurney, *Severn & Somme*, p. 8; cf. *Severn & Somme and War's Embers*, p. 20.

Gurney's second volume . . . the same year: Gurney, *Collected Poems*, pp. 24–5; 'Chronology'; cf. Hurd, *Ordeal*, pp. 115–44.

'aflame with anger': Blunden, in *Poems by Ivor Gurney . . . with a Memoir by Edmund Blunden* (London: Hutchinson, 1954), p. 13.

'he began . . . had served': Hurd, *Ordeal*, p. 145.

'(I was a war poet . . . Her blood)': Gurney, *Collected Poems*, p. 251 ('O Tan-Faced Prairie Boy').

'Who, first war poet . . . to Duty)': Ibid., p. 257 ('Watching Music').

'boys bemocked at': Gurney, *Severn & Somme*, p. 69 ('England the Mother'); cf. *Severn & Somme and War's Embers*, p. 51.

Jon Silkin . . . 'enormous social forces': Jon Silkin, *Out of Battle: The Poetry of the Great War* (London: Oxford University Press, 1972), pp. 120–9 (123).

('But still . . . of pride'): Gurney, *War's Embers*, p. 41 ('To his Love'); cf. *Severn & Somme and War's Embers*, p. 76.

'"Nobly" is not merely . . . the aureate direction': Silkin, *Out of Battle*, p. 123.

'I've been collecting . . . these purple seas': *The Letters of Rupert Brooke*, ed. Geoffrey Keynes (New York: John Day Co., 1968), p. 677.

'Of the "golden phrases" . . . remain.': Brooke, *Collected Poems*, xclvii.

'red-gold waves of hair': G. Wilson Knight, 'Rupert Brooke' in *Neglected Powers: Essays on Nineteenth and Twentieth Century Literature* (New York: Barnes & Noble, 1971), p. 294. This challenging essay takes a more whole-hearted view than I do of Brooke's importance.

'*embodiment* of poetry': Ibid.

'some inner, spiritual, reality': Ibid.

'golden hours', 'misty gold' . . . crying flames': Brooke, *Collected Poems*, pp. 6, 11 (twice), 22, 33, 84, 97, 103, 143, 132.

'a great little book': Gurney, *Severn & Somme*, p. 7; cf. *Severn & Somme and War's Embers*, p. 19.

'simple act of . . . communication': *Letters from America by Rupert Brooke with a Preface by Henry James* (London: Sidgwick & Jackson, 1916), p. xxi.

'golden sky' . . . gold glow': W. W. Gibson, *Friends* (London: E. Matthews, 1916), pp. 11 (twice), 17 (twice), 18 (twice), 31, 32, 35 (twice), 36 (twice), 37 (twice).

'her golden voice . . . deafer': Brooke, *Collected Poems*, p. 69.

'carried off' . . . 'by half-laughing at it': F. W. Bateson, *English Poetry and the English Language*, 3rd edn. (Oxford: Clarendon Press, 1973), pp. 88–9.
'Bask in . . . gold flame': Gurney, *Collected Poems*, p. 168 ('It Is Winter').
'Let me . . . night quiet—': Ibid., p. 170 ('Prelude').
'homely songs of gold': Ibid., p. 177 ('The New Poet').
'O warmth! O golden light!': Ibid., p. 184 ('Snow').
'lamp shadows . . . on gold': Ibid., p. 200 ('The Elements').
'lit with gold . . . the room': Ibid., p. 256 ('Watching Music').
'dark with firelight's gold power': Ibid., p. 257 ('Watching Music').
'Golden firelight . . . the nerve': Ibid., p. 183 ('Bach—Under Torment').
'every form of touting . . . with it': Belloc, *The Servile State*, pp. 90–1.
'disappointed men . . . friendly again': Gurney, *Collected Poems*, p. 87 ('First Time In').
O for some . . . joy-crowned: Ibid., p. 158 ('The Golden Age').
'the moral strain . . . unstable thing': Belloc, *The Servile State*, p. 86.
'curious originality': Blunden, in *Poems by Ivor Gurney*, p. 13.
'peculiar unconventionality . . . to traditions': Blunden, in ibid., p. 19.
'We shall enter unsurprised into our own': Gurney, *Collected Poems*, p. 52 ('The Old City—Gloucester').
'has always desired . . . from the home': Chesterton, *What's Wrong with the World*, p. 74.
'a great house . . . free movement': Gurney, *War Letters*, p. 207.
'at one point, in May 1920 . . . impossibility': Hurd, *Ordeal*, p. 140.
'Many songs . . . to work': Gurney, *Collected Poems*, p. 269.
('Hedging . . . was good'): Ibid., p. 269.
('Working in strict discipline, music, or strict rhyme'): Ibid., p. 271.
'Did they look . . . nor publication?': Ibid., p. 196 ('War Books').
The pages . . . glad gorilla . . . : Ibid., pp. 180–1 ('Masterpiece'; ellipses in original).
'this remarkable character . . . world had seen': Frank Swinnerton, *The Georgian Literary Scene*, rev. edn. (London: J. M. Dent & Sons, 1938), p. 188.
'the economic conditions . . . *force majeure*': *R. H. Tawney's Commonplace Book*, ed. J. M. Winter and D. M. Joslin (Cambridge: Cambridge University Press, 1972), p. 74.
'words of routine': Walt Whitman, *Complete Poetry and Collected Prose*, ed. Justin Kaplan (New York: Library of America, 1982), p. 236 ('Song of Myself', stanza 42, l. 33).
'Above all I am not concerned with Poetry': Wilfred Owen, *The Poems of Wilfred Owen*, ed. Jon Stallworthy (New York: Norton, 1986), p. 192 ('Preface').
'(That's for your poetry book)': Ibid., p. 155 ('A Terre').
Marsh's several acts of generosity: See Marcia Allentuck, 'Isaac Rosenberg and Gordon Bottomley: Unremarked Documents in the Houghton Library', *Harvard Library Bulletin*, vol. 23, no. 3 (July 1975), pp. 252–70 (esp. 258–9).
'in modern society . . . human superior': Tawney, *Commonplace Book*, p. 74.
'like a king . . . . . . of promise': Osbert Sitwell, 'A Short Character of Sir Edmund Gosse' in *Horizon*, vol. 5, no. 28 (April 1942), p. 245.

'Ere he has scorned his Father's patrimony': Gurney, *Severn & Somme*, p. 32 ('Acquiescence'); cf. *Severn & Somme and War's Embers*, p. 30.

patrimony ... an unhonoured draft: Davie, 'Gurney's Flood', p. 7.

We'll have ... England's life: Gurney, *Collected Poems*, p. 52 ('To the Prussians of England').

growth ... 'in Prussia and in England': Belloc, *The Servile State*, p. 188.

'sincerely attempted to introduce German efficiency': Chesterton, *What's Wrong with the World*, p. 6.

'My dear lady ... and why not?': Gurney, *War Letters*, p. 186.

'that half cynical nobility ... complain much': Ibid., p. 40.

'stoical fatalism': Ibid., p. 106.

to whom he dedicated three poems in *War's Embers*: 'Toasts and Memories', 'Recompense', and ' "On Rest" '.

'of which I do not think ... most folk': Ivor Gurney, *Collected Letters*, ed. R. K. R. Thornton (Manchester: Carcanet, 1991), p. 526.

'Marsh did not ... manuscript': Hurd, *Ordeal*, p. 144.

'Some men ... their own world': Gurney, *War Letters*, p. 220.

'This dumbness ... in oneself.': Ibid., p. 246.

Till the politest ... seen. Ivor Gurney, *Collected Poems*, ed. P. J. Kavanagh (Manchester: Carcanet, 2004), p. 250 ('The Silent One').

'conduct demanded ... intolerable': Charles Sorley, *Letters of Charles Sorley* (Cambridge: University Press, 1919), p. 263.

'So be merry, so be dead': Charles Sorley, *Marlborough and Other Poems*, 3rd edn. (Cambridge: Cambridge University Press, 1916), p. 58.

'And the blind fight the blind': Ibid., p. 56.

'Who sent us forth? Who brings us home again?': Ibid., p. 47.

'It is easy to be dead': Ibid., p. 69.

'higher vision': W. R. Sorley, *Moral Values and the Idea of God* (Cambridge: Cambridge University Press, 1918), p. 255.

'the license of a poet': Ibid., p. 476.

'a confusion of values': Ibid., p. 34.

'And having arrived ... Acquiescence': Gurney, *Collected Poems*, p. 176 ('To Y').

'Men I have known ... dead also': Ibid., p. 201 ('December 30th').

'Leave dumb the love that filled me': *Severn & Somme*, p. 41 ('The Estaminet'); cf. *Severn & Somme and War's Embers*, p. 36.

'Patriotic tradition ... began with': Silkin, p. 124.

'dumb insolence': *Songs and Slang of the British Soldier: 1914–1918*, ed. John Brophy and Eric Partridge, 2nd edn. (London: Eric Partridge at the Scholartis Press, 1930), p. 120.

'make ... just war': Gurney, *Collected Poems*, p. 31 ('To the Poet before Battle').

'the silent dead ... fallen in such a war': Gurney, *Severn & Somme*, p. 63 ('Requiem: Nor grief nor tears'); cf. *Severn & Somme and War's Embers*, p. 49.

'the noblest cause': Gurney, *Severn & Somme*, p. 64 ('Requiem: Pour out your bounty'); cf. *Severn & Somme and War's Embers*, p. 49.

'Living and dead ... not come?': Gurney, *Severn & Somme*, pp. 53–6 (55); cf. *Severn & Somme and War's Embers*, pp. 42–5 (44–5).

'pittance': Gurney, *Collected Poems*, p. 147 ('Swift and Slow').

'unpaid hand': Ibid., p. 110 ('We Who Praise Poets').

'the hours, the wage hours': Ibid., p. 127 ('Kilns').

'the vulgar ... so underpaid': Ibid., p. 175 ('Signallers').

'It is difficult ... factor of freedom': Belloc, *The Servile State*, p. 124.

'dispossessed free men': Ibid., p. 82.

'was all our master': Gurney, *Collected Poems*, p. 171 ('It is Near Toussaints').

Gurney quotes ... evidently esteems: Gurney, *War Letters*, p. 226.

Of Courtesy ... in Courtesy: Hilaire Belloc, *Verses* (London: Duckworth, 1910), p. 20. The text differs from that given in Gurney's transcription.

'that's true and memorable enough': Gurney, *War Letters*, p. 226.

'almost ... by heart' ... of the sequence: Hassall, *Rupert Brooke*, pp. 482–3.

'trench companion': Gurney, *Severn & Somme*, p. 7; cf. *Severn & Somme and War's Embers*, p. 19.

'great and terrible debate ... kittens in a basket': Belloc, *The Path to Rome* (London: G. Allen, 1902), pp. 194–5.

'Discipline and Comradeship': Ibid., p. 15.

'isolation and despairing fatigue': Ibid., p. 364.

'repose, certitude ... of glory': Ibid., p. 328.

The passer-by ... my home: Belloc, *The Four Men*, p. 310.

The amazed heart cries angrily out on God: Gurney, *Collected Poems*, p. 36 ('Pain').

'men broken' ... 'foredone': Ibid.

letter to Marion Scott: Gurney, *War Letters*, pp. 127–8.

Who rests ... die to sell: Isaac Rosenberg, *Poems and Plays*, ed. Vivien Noakes (Oxford: Oxford University Press, 2004), p. 117.

admiration ... for Abercrombie and Gibson: Gurney's initial enthusiasm for Abercrombie subsequently waned. See *War Letters*, pp. 84, 158.

'he was suffering ... inferiors': Quoted in William Cooke, *Edward Thomas: A Critical Biography 1878–1917* (London: Faber, 1970), p. 184.

'about lost patience ... to review': Quoted in ibid.

'centrifugal age ... ears which expect them': *A Language Not To Be Betrayed: Selected Prose of Edward Thomas*, ed. Edna Longley (Manchester: Carcanet Press, 1981), p. 66.

'square shaped': Gurney, *Collected Poems*, p. 122 ('Had I a Song').

'a sense of rightness and order': Kavanagh, ibid., p. 15.

'square shaping': Ibid., p. 258 ('The Motetts of William Byrd').

'wrought a square thing out of my stubborn mind': Ibid., p. 119 ('The Sea Borders').

'At present ... less facility': Gurney, *War Letters*, p. 36.

'You see ... music': Ibid., p. 126.

'slow spirit': Gurney, *Collected Poems*, p. 129 ('Tewkesbury').

'this chord of trumpets ... exultation': Gurney, *War Letters*, p. 40.

'illicitly walked ... the page': Ibid., p. 226.

'the song Orion sings': Gurney, *Severn & Somme*, p. 50 ('Winter Beauty'); cf. *Severn & Somme and War's Embers*, p. 41.

'Music of light': Gurney, *War's Embers*, p. 20 ('Fire in the Dusk'); cf. *Severn & Somme and War's Embers*, p. 61.

'Some silver thread of sound': Gurney, *War's Embers*, p. 48 ('Old Martinmas Eve'); cf. *Severn & Somme and War's Embers*, p. 78.

'music's gold': Gurney, *Collected Poems*, p. 257 ('Watching Music').

device ... snatches of tune: e.g. *The Path to Rome*, pp. 259, 440; *The Four Men*, title-page, dedication, pp. 86, 92, 112.

'clef of the universes': Whitman, p. 400 ('On the Beach at Night Alone'). Cf. 'a kind of common triad of the New England homestead', Charles Ives, *Essays before a Sonata and Other Writings*, ed. Howard Boatwright (London: Calder and Boyars, 1969), p. 47.

'cunning and masterful mind': Gurney, *War Letters*, p. 180.

'The attitude towards Bach ... such a control': Ibid., p. 51.

What is best ... are done: Gurney, *Collected Poems*, p. 129 ('Tewkesbury').

'fair fashioned': Ibid., p. 51 ('Old City—Gloucester').

'Square stone': Ibid, p. 129 ('Tewkesbury').

Square tower ... exalted often: Ibid., p. 120 ('Andromeda over Tewkesbury').

It is Near Toussaints ... sombrely: Ibid., p. 171 ('It Is Near Toussaints').

'faults or deficiencies ... as a pastime': *OED*[2], s.v. 'amateurish' and 'amateur'. Cf. D. H. Lawrence, *The Letters of D. H. Lawrence*, ed. James T. Boulton, 8 vols. (Cambridge: Cambridge University Press, 1979–2000), vol. 2, p. 43 ('Don't be an amateur—it is so damnable. Take the thing seriously, your writing').

'It was ... Toussaints': Gurney, *War's Embers*, p. 36 ('Toussaints'); cf. *Severn & Somme and War's Embers*, p. 71.

last part ... on 'The Second of November 1902': Belloc, *The Four Men*, pp. 297–310.

'tolling summons' ... indeed': Gurney, *Collected Poems*, p. 125 ('All Souls' Day 1921').

'I want badly ... to say': Gurney, *War Letters,* p. 116.

'We shall come ... victorious host—': Gurney, *Severn & Somme*, p. 55; cf. *Severn & Somme and War's Embers*, p. 44.

'lines of khaki without end': Gurney, *War's Embers*, p. 36 ('Toussaints'); cf. *Severn & Somme and War's Embers*, p. 71.

'the night ... of spirits': *OED*[2], s.v. 'Hallow-e'en', citing *Chambers' Book of Days* (1864).

'house of steadfastness and quiet pride': *War's Embers*, p. 16 ('The Farm'); cf. *Severn & Somme and War's Embers*, p. 59.

'spontaneous songs': Whitman, *Complete Poetry and Collected Prose*, p. 446 ('Give Me the Splendid Silent Sun').

'ecstatic songs': Ibid., p. 171 ('Beginning My Studies').

'returning'...long': Ibid., p. 165 ('As I Ponder'd in Silence').

'Where's Gurney now...to say?': *War's Embers*, p. 31 ('Toasts and Memories'); cf. *Severn & Somme and War's Embers*, p. 67.

'new rhythmus': Whitman, *Complete Poetry and Collected Prose*, p. 530 ('Proud Music of the Storm').

Whitman's 'recitative': Ibid., p. 168 ('To Thee Old Cause'); p. 401 ('Song for All Seas, All Ships'); p. 521 ('The Ox-Tamer'); p. 583 ('To a Locomotive in Winter').

'This Compost', a poem...admired: Cf. Gurney, *War Letters*, pp. 41, 91, 93.

'Where have...many generations?': Whitman, *Complete Poetry and Collected Prose*, p. 495 ('This Compost').

The mind released...Spirits: Belloc, *The Path to Rome*, pp. 431–2.

Chesterton's 'adamantine tendernesses': Chesterton, *What's Wrong with the World*, p. 283.

'The rulers of England..."Eadem Semper"': Gurney, *Collected Poems*, p. 249 ('What's in Time').

'old Lie': Owen, *Poems*, ed. Stallworthy, p. 117 ('Dulce et Decorum Est').

'must have...pidgin French': *Songs and Slang of the British Soldier*, p. 122.

'The Estaminet': Gurney, *Severn & Somme*, p. 40; cf. *Severn & Somme and War's Embers*, p. 34.

'Toasts and Memories': Gurney, *War's Embers*, p. 30; cf. *Severn & Somme and War's Embers*, p. 66.

'"On Rest"': Gurney, *War's Embers*, p. 67; cf. *Severn & Somme and War's Embers*, p. 89.

'Le Coq Français': Gurney, *War's Embers*, p. 80; cf. *Severn & Somme and War's Embers*, p. 97.

'Laventie': Gurney, *Collected Poems*, p. 77.

'Robecq Again': Ibid., p. 111.

'It is Winter': Ibid., p. 168.

'No bon': Gurney, *War Letters*, p. 109.

'Tray bong': Ibid., p. 75.

'Na pooh fini': Ibid., p. 109.

Gurney's regal amanuensis: Ibid., p. 219.

'Unknown Lady': Gurney, *Severn & Somme*, p. 35 ('To an Unknown Lady'); cf. *Severn & Somme and War's Embers*, pp. 31–2.

'darling Mother and stern': Gurney, *Severn & Somme*, p. 69 ('England the Mother'); cf. *Severn & Somme and War's Embers*, p. 51.

'fierce indignation': Gurney, *Collected Poems*, p. 149 ('Sonnet—September 1922').

'the manifold...may hold': Gibson, *Friends*, p. 13.

'stumbling blind through the difficult door': Gurney, *Collected Poems*, p. 146 ('The Not-Returning').

'lines and reality': Ibid., p. 218 ('Where the Mire').

'sarcasm'...'pretence': *OED²*, s.v. 'irony', senses 1, 3.

'perverse' ... world's experiences': Gurney, *War Letters*, p. 40.

'contradictory outcome ... of things': *OED*², s.v. 'irony', sense 2 *fig*.

'And often ... nothing more': Whitman, *Complete Poetry and Collected Prose*, p. 513 ('Thought').

26. Isaac Rosenberg, 1890–1918

'Thanks for ... British subject': Isaac Rosenberg, *The Collected Works of Isaac Rosenberg: Poetry, Prose, Letters, Paintings and Drawings*, ed. Ian Parsons (London: Chatto and Windus, 1979). Ernest Lesser was Honorary Secretary of the Jewish Education Aid Society (ibid., p. 195 n. 4). In the event, Rosenberg was unsuccessful (ibid., p. 198).

[Rosenberg's] finest ... differentiated: D. W. Harding, *Experience Into Words* (London: Chatto and Windus, 1963), p. 94. The chapter on Rosenberg was originally published as an essay in *Scrutiny* in 1935.

'outer semblance': Rosenberg, *Collected Works*, p. xxv. The words 'Isaac Rosenberg his outer semblance?' are scribbled on a fine self-portrait—a rapid pencil-sketch—done in the trenches.

'the very fibres ... circumstance': Ibid., p. 181.

'one conceives ... terribly tragic': Ibid.

'Create ... we don't: Ibid., p. 182.

'I have thrown ... in a fix': Ibid., p. 197.

'when one's ... least horrible': Ibid., p. 215.

'I[,] feeling ... cut off': Ibid., p. 218.

'I send ... of it': Ibid., p. 230.

'I am determined ... later on': Ibid., p. 248.

'Sometimes I ... energy and interest': Ibid., p. 268.

'I want ... unscrupulous will': Ibid., p. 270.

recurrent word ... 'idea': Ibid., pp. 183, 184, 190, 191, 198, 199, 201, 203, 210 (twice), 238, 239 (twice), 242, 255 (twice), 257, 262 (twice), 265 (three occurrences), 266, 268, 287, 289, 290, 291 (twice), 292 (twice), 293, 295, 298, 303. I have omitted a few colloquial uses.

Expression: Isaac Rosenberg, *The Poems and Plays of Isaac Rosenberg*, ed. Vivien Noakes (Oxford: Oxford University Press, 2004), pp. 95–6. Noakes dates the poem to 'Late 1914 or early 1915' (ibid., p. 340).

'and hee ... must goe': John Donne, *The Satires, Epigrams and Verse Letters*, ed. W. Milgate (Oxford: Clarendon Press, 1967), p. 13.

not at all like Donne: Rosenberg, *Collected Works*, pp. 180–1, 183, 198, 221, 223, 265, 288 (for Rosenberg's knowledge, and appreciation, of Donne), 208, 266, 288–9 (for Emerson).

Nietzsche: Ibid., p. 301 (the only reference to Nietzsche in *Collected Works*). Rosenberg could have read Nietzsche in English translation from 1909 on, in a four-volume selection published by Unwin in 1909 and in 'the first complete and authorized English translation', ed. Oscar Levy, 18 vols. (Edinburgh: Foulis, 1909–13). A. R. Orage, *Friedrich Nietzsche: The Dionysian Spirit of the*

Age was published by Foulis (London and Edinburgh) in 1906. Joseph Cohen, *Journey to the Trenches: The Life of Isaac Rosenberg* (London: Robson Books, 1975), p. 84, states that Rosenberg 'read widely, ranging outside literature to Darwin and Nietzsche'.

'It is true . . . say something': Rosenberg, *Collected Works*, p. 218.

'Besides[,] my being . . . altogether': Ibid., p. 219.

Wilfred Owen . . . inarticulate common soldier: See Wilfred Owen, *Collected Letters*, ed. Harold Owen and John Bell (London: Oxford University Press, 1967), pp. 422 ('The men are . . . expressionless lumps'), 521 ('it was a blindfold look, and without expression'), 562 ('I see to it that he is dumb').

8 Platoon B Coy . . . BEF: *Collected Works*, p. 271, Army address as of 7 March 1918. There were several changes of address during Rosenberg's two years at the Front.

On Sat[urday] . . . cordiality!: Owen, *Collected Letters*, p. 341; cf. 338, Cohen, *Journey to the Trenches*, p. 119 makes the connection.

'mooch[ing] around . . . misery': Richard Cork, *David Bomberg* (New Haven: Yale University Press, 1987), p. 20.

Youth . . . Narodiczky: Rosenberg, *Collected Works*, p. xiii (editorial note on printing-date of *Youth*); 231 (editorial note on Reuben Cohen); p. 212 (editorial note on Israel Narodiczky).

'What people . . . painting': Ibid., p. 216.

'My technique . . . I know': Ibid.

'whether Mr. Clutton Brock . . . connected with': Ibid.

I am thinking . . . I can do: Ibid.

('My memory . . . out here'): Ibid., p. 258.

working on massive and complex poems in your head: Ibid., pp. 222–3, 224, 226, 230, 232, 237, 238, 249, 252, 268–9, 272; see esp. p. 231: 'I have been working on "Moses"—in my mind, I mean—and it was through my absentmindedness while full of that that I forgot certain orders, and am now undergoing a rotten and unjust punishment'; p. 235: 'I know my faults are legion; a good many must be put down to the rotten conditions I wrote it [*Moses*] in—the whole thing was written in barracks, and I suppose you know what an ordinary soldier's life is like'; p. 257: 'We are more busy now than when I last wrote, but I generally manage to knock something up if my brain means to, and I am sketching out a little play ["The Unicorn"]. My great fear is that I may lose what I've written, which can happen here so easily. I send home any bit I write, for safety, but that can easily get lost in transmission'.

'All a poet . . . truthful.': *The Poems of Wilfred Owen*, ed. Jon Stallworthy (London: Hogarth Press, 1985), p. 192 ('Preface').

'old Lie': Ibid., p. 117 ('Dulce et Decorum Est').

Tennyson . . . a great liar: See, e.g. Owen, *Collected Letters*, p. 482.

'teach men . . . chivalrous feeling': *Alfred Lord Tennyson: A Memoir by his Son*, new edn., 2 vols. (New York: Macmillan, 1911), vol. 2, p. 337.

'Exposure': Owen, *Poems*, pp. 162–3.

I am determined . . . later on: Rosenberg, *Collected Works*, p. 248.

artist's definition of . . . 'mass': Cork, *David Bomberg*, pp. 75, 83.

'modelled words with fierce energy and aspiration': Sassoon in Rosenberg, *Collected Works*, p. ix. This edition reprints Sassoon's 'Foreword' from the original *Collected Works*, ed. Gordon Bottomley and Denys Harding (London: Chatto and Windus, 1937), pp. ix–x.

'Like breath . . . fire': Rosenberg, *Poems and Plays*, p. 15 ('My days are but the tombs of buried hours'). Noakes gives the date as 'unknown', while Parsons (in Rosenberg, *Collected Works*, p. 10) gives a date of '1911'. 'Expression' is dated by Noakes as 'Late 1914 or early 1915'.

'With fierce energy I aspire': Rosenberg, *Poems and Plays*, p. 63 ('Peace', l. 5; for date, see ibid., p. 324).

'Into that . . . blood': Ibid., p. 200 (l. 317).

'What fierce . . . souls lit': Ibid., p. 139 (l. 20).

'Pale horses . . . tread': Ibid., p. 102 ('At Night', ll. 13–14).

'We ride . . . tread': Ibid., pp. 104–5 (ll. 21–2). While Parsons dates 'At Night' to 1914 and 'Chagrin' to 1915–16 (in Rosenberg, *Collected Works*, pp. 61, 95), Noakes dates both poems to '1914 or 1915' (in Rosenberg, *Poems and Plays*, pp. 342, 344).

He heareth . . . imagination: Rosenberg, *Poems and Plays*, p. 74 (ll. 21–3). Both versions are printed in Rosenberg, *Collected Works*, pp. 85–7.

('A word was the key thereof'): Rosenberg, *Poems and Plays*, p. 33 (l. 9).

('With fierce energy I aspire'): Ibid., p. 63 (l. 5).

('All . . . living moment'): Ibid., p. 38 (l. 28).

'lured her . . . sleep': Ibid., p. 126 (ll. 5–6). The source for this poem is undoubtedly Blake's 'The Sick Rose'.

'Tennyson . . . Beaumont Hamel': Owen, *Collected Letters*, p. 482.

'More amorous than Solomon': Rosenberg, *Poems and Plays*, p. 126.

the dating . . . uncertain: Despite the efforts of both Parsons in Rosenberg, *Collected Works* and Noakes in Rosenberg, *Poems and Plays*.

two brief fragmentary drafts: Parsons in Rosenberg, *Collected Works*, p. 177 includes a single 31-line fragment which he edited for legibility; Noakes in Rosenberg, *Poems and Plays*, pp. 242–6 transcribes the two pieces of paper bearing Rosenberg's lines intended for *Adam*.

As my thoughts . . . beauty: Rosenberg, *Collected Works*, p. 177. Cf. Rosenberg, *Poems and Plays*, pp. 242–4: 'As my thoughts my pulses pass | Hungry to you, to roam your vivid be['. The phrase 'roaming your vivid beauty' appears on p. 245.

'abandoned . . . latter play': Parsons in Rosenberg, *Collected Works*, p. 177.

'impossible . . . *The Unicorn*': Noakes in Rosenberg, *Poems and Plays*, p. 404.

'the summer of 1917': Noakes in Rosenberg, *Poems and Plays*, p. 407.

'Now when my . . . mind': Rosenberg, *Collected Works*, p. 260.

Everybody has agreed . . . ideas: Ibid., p. 266. It is as if Rosenberg realizes his own
    struggle in the process of describing Emerson's.
What did they . . . no publication?: Ivor Gurney, *Collected Poems of Ivor Gurney*, ed.
    P. J. Kavanagh (Oxford: Oxford University Press, 1982), p. 196.
'treasured . . . Keats': *Phoenix: The Posthumous Papers of D. H. Lawrence* (London:
    Heinemann, 1936), p. 218.
'incomparable lines': H. H. Asquith, *Sir Henry Wotton, with Some General Reflections
    on Style in English Poetry* (London: Heinemann, 1919), p. 6.
'enduring power . . . of poetry': Ibid., p. 7.
'sovereign quality of Style': Ibid.
'the stamp of immortality': Ibid., p. 9.
'a decided preference . . . meals': *The Prose of Rupert Brooke*, ed. Christopher Hassall
    (London: Sidgwick and Jackson, 1956), p. xxv.
'the frequent incompetence of readers': A. C. Bradley, *The Uses of Poetry* (Oxford:
    University Press, 1912), p. 11.
'the partially incompetent lover of poetry': Ibid., p. 9.
'who tend . . . sentimentality': Ibid.
'sly and certainly anti-Jewish': Rosenberg, *Collected Works*, p. 244.
to the solid . . . necessity: G. K. Chesterton, *Robert Browning* (London: Macmillan,
    1903), p. 3.
'expressive line': Rosenberg, *Collected Works*, p. 295.
'bounding line': *The Prophetic Writings of William Blake*, ed. D. J. Sloss and J. P. R.
    Wallis, 2 vols. (Oxford: Clarendon Press, 1926), vol. 2, p. 326: 'How do we
    distinguish one face or countenance from another, but by the bounding line
    and its infinite inflexions and movements?' (from *A Descriptive Catalogue*, 1809,
    p. 64).
'highly energized moment': Cork, *David Bomberg*, p. 67.
'It is nature's . . . keep': Rosenberg, *Collected Works* (1979), p. 296 (from Rosenberg's
    major statement on the nature of expression-making, the lecture 'Art', printed
    in *South African Women in Council*, Dec. 1914 and Jan. 1915).
'It [the subject of war] . . . emotion': Ibid., p. 237.
'eccentrics' whom Mill advocated: See *On Liberty* (1859), in *Collected Works of John
    Stuart Mill*, 33 vols. (Toronto: University of Toronto Press, 1963–91), vol. 18,
    p. 269: 'Precisely because the tyranny of opinion is such as to make eccentricity
    a reproach, it is desirable, in order to break through the tyranny, that people
    should be eccentric'.
'Introductory Memoir' by Laurence Binyon: *Poems by Isaac Rosenberg*, ed. Gordon
    Bottomley (London: Heinemann, 1922), pp. 1–50.
'letter in an . . . Binyon's invitation: Ibid., pp. 1–3.
fifty-page tribute: The fact that pp. 12–50 of the 'Introductory Memoir' consist of
    extracts from Rosenberg's correspondence, with a minimal linking commentary,
    does not detract from one's sense of the considerable burden of compilation
    which Binyon willingly undertook.

'obscurities, the straining . . . underlay': Binyon in *Poems by Isaac Rosenberg*, p. 11.
'even as a young boy . . . nation': Binyon, ibid., p. 9.
'Heine . . . anything else': Rosenberg, *Collected Works* (1979), p. 242.
Hebrew . . . to learn: Cohen, *Journey to the Trenches*, pp. 18, 27.
Joseph Leftwich . . . in both Yiddish and English: *The Golden Peacock: An Anthology of Yiddish Poetry*, ed. Joseph Leftwich (Cambridge, MA: Sci-art Publishers, 1939), p. lv ('Foreword'): 'Rosenberg did not know much Yiddish, certainly he could not write it and he did not easily express himself in it, though his parents were Yiddish-speaking. And if he showed any interest in Yiddish, it was only to ask me to translate one or two of his poems into Yiddish (as I did) so that he could show them to his father who might in that way grasp better what he was trying to do. His father also wrote poetry in Hebrew and Yiddish'.
Bomberg made . . . studies of an audience: Cork, *David Bomberg*, pp. 43 (plates 48, 49), 44–5. Seven years later he produced an oil painting, *Ghetto Theatre*, in a significantly different spirit: pp. 135–6 and plate 177.
Rosenberg . . . kept mostly aloof: Cohen, *Journey to the Trenches*, p. 96, states that in late 1913 Rosenberg and Mark Gertler took Edward Marsh to see 'a Yiddish play . . . in the crowded theatre in Whitechapel'.
who was also a Levite: Ibid., p. 174, quotes from 'a prose poem' by the poet's father mourning the death of 'my dear son, Isaac, the Levite'. Leftwich, p. 719, prints his own English translation of another poem, 'To the Memory of My Son Isaac'.
'Some pieces . . . inevitable': *The Golden Treasury of Modern Lyrics*, selected and arranged by Laurence Binyon (New York: Macmillan, 1925), p. vi.
If I am lucky . . . unscrupulous will: Rosenberg, *Collected Works*, p. 270.
Living in a wide . . . saying—: Keith Douglas, *Complete Poems*, ed. Desmond Graham, 3rd edn. (London: Faber and Faber, 1998), p. 108. I do not intend, in calling Douglas 'the outstanding British poet of the Second World War', to slight Sidney Keyes, whose potential for greatness I discuss in 'Sidney Keyes in Historical Perspective', pp. 398–418 of Tim Kendall, *The Oxford Handbook of British and Irish War Poetry* (Oxford: Oxford University Press, 2007).

27. Rhetorics of Value and Intrinsic Value
'cheap grace': Dietrich Bonhoeffer, *The Cost of Discipleship*, tr. R. H. Fuller (London: SCM Press, 1948), pp. 37–49 (from *Nachfolge*, 1937).
Gillian Rose's sense of *aporia*: Gillian Rose, *Mourning Becomes the Law* (Cambridge: Cambridge University Press, 1996), pp. 8, 10. For further discussion, see Ch. 34, pp. 569 and 573.
'human values': Chapters 27 and 28 were originally delivered as 'Tanner Lectures on Human Values'.
currency reforms advocated . . . by Isaac Newton and John Locke: See *The Correspondence of Isaac Newton*, 7 vols. (Cambridge: Cambridge University Press for the Royal Society, 1959–77), vols. 4–7; *Locke on Money*, ed. P. H. Kelly, 2 vols. (Oxford: Clarendon Press, 1991).

'Judas': See Letter 12 of *Fors Clavigera* in *The Works of John Ruskin*, ed. E. T. Cook
   and Alexander Wedderburn, 39 vols. (1903–12), vol. 27, p. 217. See also
   Ch. 22, p. 389.

Ezra Pound . . . derived his ethical aesthetics from Ruskin: Hugh Witemeyer,
   'Ruskin and the Signed Capital in Canto 45', *Paideuma*, vol. 4, no. 1 (Spring
   1975), pp. 85–8, acknowledging Hugh Kenner, *The Pound Era* (Berkeley:
   University of California Press, 1971), pp. 323–6; Guy Davenport, *The
   Geography of the Imagination* (San Francisco, CA: North Point Press, 1981),
   pp. 44–8.

Knowledge in the arts . . . pardon: David Hume, 'Of Refinement in the Arts' in
   Essays, Moral, Political, and Literary, ed. Eugene F. Miller (Indianapolis, IN:
   Liberty Fund, 1985), pp. 273–4.

'that this damnable device . . . parishioners': Gerald Bray, *Documents of the English
   Reformation* (Minneapolis, MN: Fortress Press, 1994), p. 253.

Edwardian Injunctions of 1547 . . . Somerset: Ibid., p. 247.

'The deuil . . . gods promises': Thomas More, cited in *OED*², s.v. 'desperate'
   (sense 1).

But industry . . . prosperous: Hume, *Essays*, p. 272.

'wide and general distribution': *OED*², s.v. 'diffusion'.

For as that stone . . . thereunto: *Leviathan*, ed. C. B. Macpherson (Harmondsworth:
   Penguin Books, 1968), p. 209.

'head of the corner': Matthew 21: 42, Mark 12: 10, Luke 20: 17, Acts 4: 11, 1 Peter
   2: 7 (King James Bible, 1611).

'in all questions . . . decided': Hume, *Essays*, p. 486.

'Nor is there . . . publique enemy': Hobbes, *Leviathan*, p. 78.

'who hating . . . hand': Ibid., p. 718.

'I cannot forbear . . . Person': Edward Hyde, Earl of Clarendon, *A Brief View and
   Survey* . . . (London, 1676; photofacsimile reprint, London: Routledge Thoemmes
   Press, 1996), p. 320.

relative sparsity of references . . . the *Marginalia*: See George Whalley in Samuel
   T. Coleridge, *Collected Works*, 16 vols. (Princeton, NJ: Princeton University
   Press, 1969–2002), vol. 12, part 1, p. 867: 'considering . . . that in Feb. 1801
   [Coleridge] regarded Butler as one of "the three greatest, nay, only three *great*
   Metaphysicians which this Country *has* produced" . . . it is surprising how few
   references [he] makes to Joseph Butler' (Whalley is the editor of part one of the
   Marginalia, in six parts, comprising vol. 12 of the *Collected Works*).

You have well . . . Divine Government: George Eliot, *Letters of George Eliot*, ed.
   Gordon S. Haight, 9 vols. (New Haven, CT: Yale University Press, 1954–78),
   vol. 1, p. 135.

'The natural government . . . contrary': Ibid., p. 135 n. 9.

But the effect . . . unvisited tombs: George Eliot, *Middlemarch*, ed. David Carroll
   (Oxford: Oxford University Press, 1988), p. 682.

Eliot saw herself as a meliorist: *OED²*, s.v. 'meliorist', quoting J. W. Cross: 'In her general attitude to life, George Eliot was neither optimist nor pessimist. She held to a middle term, which she invented for herself, of *meliorist*'.

Locke's connection of intrinsic value and 'improvement': John Locke, *Two Treatises of Government*, ed. Peter Laslett (Cambridge: Cambridge University Press, 1988), p. 298.

'manifold wakings of men to labour and endurance': Eliot, *Middlemarch*, p. 644.

'I have been half in love with easeful Death': John Keats, *The Poems of John Keats*, ed. Jack Stillinger (Cambridge, MA: Belknap, 1982), p. 281. See F. R. Leavis, *Revaluation* (London: Chatto & Windus, 1956), p. 249.

'amus[ed himself]...Inscriptions': *The Spectator*, ed. Donald F. Bond, 5 vols. (Oxford: Clarendon Press, 1965), vol. 1, p. 109 (no. 26: Friday, 30 March 1711).

Truth...set upon: *Fifteen Sermons Preached at the Rolls Chapel*, ed. W. R. Matthews (London: G. Bell, 1949), p. 159.

bishop's approval...*Essays, Moral, Political, and Literary*: *Dictionary of National Biography*, ed. Leslie Stephen and Sidney Lee, 24 vols. (London: Oxford University Press, 1921–7) vol. 10, p. 217.

Lastly, the various...fathers were: Butler, *Fifteen Sermons*, p. 106.

reference is to Hebrews: Hebrews 11: 13 ('they were strangers and pilgrims on the earth').

'our ignorance...in this world': Butler, *Fifteen Sermons*, p. 217.

'imbecility or weaknes': Richard Hooker, *The Folger Library Edition of the Works of Richard Hooker*, ed. W. Speed Hill, 7 vols. (Cambridge, MA and Tempe, AZ: Belknap Press and MRTS, 1977–1998), vol. 5, p. 173 (*Tractates and Sermons*).

'the staines and blemishes...take place': Hooker, *Works*, vol. 1, pp. 15–16.

Hooker's name does not feature in the index to the excellent volume: Christopher Cunliffe, ed., *Joseph Butler's Moral and Religious Thought: Tercentenary Essays* (Oxford: Clarendon Press, 1992).

'the language of repentance...things': D. M. MacKinnon, *A Study in Ethical Theory* (London: A. & C. Black, 1957), p. 138.

'greatest name in the Anglican Church': Quoted in *Joseph Butler's Moral and Religious Thought*, p. 8.

'the human race...aboriginal calamity': John Henry Cardinal Newman, *Apologia Pro Vita Sua*, ed. Martin J. Svaglic (Oxford: Clarendon Press, 1967), p. 218.

'his grave and abstract way': Ibid., p. 463 ('Answer in Detail to Mr Kingsley's Accusations').

'Wheresoever...of a sick mind': *Ben Jonson*, ed. C. H. Herford, Percy Simpson, and Evelyn Simpson, 11 vols. (Oxford: Clarendon Press, 1925–52), vol. 8, p. 593.

'if you opt for virtue...chaste': Peter Geach, *God and the Soul* (New York: Schocken Books, 1969), p. 123.

But allowing...obligation: Butler, *Fifteen Sermons*, p. 64.

28.   Poetry and Value

'metaphysic of personal being...respectively': Christopher Cunliffe, ed., *Joseph Butler's Moral and Religious Thought: Tercentenary Essays* (Oxford: Clarendon Press, 1992), p. 146.

if Coleridge had chosen to reflect upon the axioms of Joseph Butler: William Hazlitt, in the essay 'My First Acquaintance with Poets', records Coleridge's praise of Butler's *Fifteen Sermons Preached at the Rolls Chapel*. This was noted by John Beer on p. lxxxix of his edition of Coleridge's *Aids to Reflection* (1993), vol. 9 of the *Collected Works of Samuel Taylor Coleridge*, 16 vols. (Princeton, NJ: Princeton University Press, 1969–2002). On the surprisingly few references to Butler in Coleridge's writings, see Ch. 27, p. 470.

'terrible aboriginal calamity': John Henry Cardinal Newman, *Apologia Pro Vita Sua*, ed. Martin J. Svaglic (Oxford: Clarendon Press, 1967), p. 218.

'inhaerent': Thomas Hobbes, *Leviathan*, ed. C. B. Macpherson (Harmondsworth: Penguin, 1968) p. 75. See Ch. 27, pp. 468–9; see also Ch. 22, p. 388.

'a man threatened...embattled city': Czesław Miłosz, *The Captive Mind*, tr. Jane Zielonko (Harmondsworth: Penguin Books, 1980), p. 41. For further discussion, see Ch. 23, pp. 402–3.

'Vitalism ends...natural': Dietrich Bonhoeffer, *Ethics*, tr. Reinhard Krauss, Charles C. West, and Douglas W. Stott (Minneapolis, MN: Fortress Press, 2005), p. 178; this is vol. 6 of *Dietrich Bonhoeffer Works*. Cf. Bonhoeffer, *Ethik*, ed. Ilse Tödt, Heinz Eduard Tödt, Ernst Feil, and Clifford Green (Munich: Christian Kaiser Verlag, 1992), p. 17 (vol. 6 of *Dietrich Bonhoeffer Werke*): 'Vitalismus endet zwangsläufig im Nihilismus, im Zerbrechen alles Natürlichen'.

'all values...sentences': Letter to Felix E. Schelling, 8 July 1922 in *The Letters of Ezra Pound*, ed. D. D. Paige (New York: Harcourt Brace, 1950), p. 181.

If the observation...distinguished: Joseph Butler, *Fifteen Sermons Preached at the Rolls Chapel*, ed. W. R. Matthews (London: Bell, 1969), p. 23.

'Without Contraries...existence': William Blake, *The Early Illuminated Books* (Princeton, NJ: Princeton University Press, 1993), p. 145.

'Pilate...lacking': Gottfried Wilhelm Leibniz, *Philosophical Papers and Letters*, ed. Leroy E. Loemker (Dordrecht: D. Reidel, 1969), p. 146.

'an inevitable necessity...action': Gottfried Wilhelm Leibniz, *Theodicy: Essays on the Goodness of God, the Freedom of Man, and the Origin of Evil*, tr. E. M. Huggard (London: Routledge & K. Paul, 1952), p. 57.

It is manifest...both: *The Analogy of Religion...to Which Are Added Two Brief Dissertations*, 5th edn. (London: Robert Horsfield, 1765), p. 452.

'Faculty, or practical discerning Power within us': Ibid., p. 453.

Perhaps the most original...in that: Matthews in Butler, *Fifteen Sermons*, pp. xxii–xxiii.

a passage to which Coleridge returned more than once: Notably in Coleridge, *Collected Works*, vol. 7, part 1, p. 141 (*Biographia Literaria*, ch. 9, first paragraph); vol. 9, p. 79 (*Aids to Reflection*, Aphorism 6); and vol. 13, p. 226 (*Logic*, ch. 12, second paragraph).

You . . . *nisi ipse intellectus.*: Gottfried Wilhelm Leibniz, *Nouveaux Essais*, ed. Jacques Brunschwig (Paris: GF-Flammarion, 1990), p. 88.

Aristotelian maxim: On the early history of the maxim, see Paul F. Cranefield, 'On the Origin of the Phrase *Nihil est in intellectu quod non prius fuerit in sensu*', *Journal of the History of Medicine and Allied Sciences*, vol. 25, no. 1 (Jan. 1970), pp. 77–80.

the act of comparing . . . Understanding itself: Coleridge, *Collected Works*, vol. 9, p. 225 (*Aids to Reflection*).

'hard gem-like flame': Walter Pater, *The Renaissance: Studies in Art and Poetry: The 1893 Text*, ed. Donald L. Hill (Berkeley, CA: University of California Press, 1980), p. 189.

'content to leave . . . principles': T. H. Green, *Works*, 3 vols. (London: Longmans Green, 1888), vol. 3, p. 104.

'Judas': See Letter 12 of *Fors Clavigera* in *The Works of John Ruskin*, ed. E. T. Cook and Alexander Wedderburn, 39 vols. (1903–12), vol. 27, p. 217. See also chapter 22, p. 389.

'illth': Ruskin, *Works*, vol. 17, p. 89 (*Unto This Last*) and p. 168 (*Munera Pulveris*). On Ruskin's 'illth', see also Ch. 22, p. 388.

the 'use of substances . . . is a barbarism': Ruskin, *Works*, vol. 17, p. 159.

'mechanical check' . . . 'foreign nations': Ibid.

'an expression of right': Ibid., p. 192.

'*Always* . . . rightly ordered': Ibid., p. 158 n. 1.

It does not . . . nothing else: Ibid., p. 153.

'Everything is what it is, and not another thing': *Fifteen Sermons*, p. 23.

'expressed . . . abstract system': John H. Newman, *The Philosophical Notebook*, ed. Edward J. Sillem, 2 vols. (Louvain: Nauwelaerts, 1969–70), vol. 1, p. 94.

'Whether . . . appears to turn': Coleridge, *Collected Works*, vol. 9, p. 47 (*Aids to Reflection*).

'At the utmost . . . misusage of the market': Ibid.

'passive attending upon the event': T. S. Eliot, *Selected Essays* (London: Faber, 1934), p. 21 ('Tradition and the Individual Talent').

'wise passiveness': William Wordsworth, *Poems*, ed. John O. Hayden, 2 vols. (Harmondsworth: Penguin, 1977), vol. 1, p. 356 ('Expostulation and Reply').

'co-instantaneous yet reciprocal action': Coleridge, *Collected Works*, vol. 9, p. 75 (*Aids to Reflection*).

'THE WORD . . . actuating': Ibid., p. 77.

'For the juggle . . . conclusion': Ibid., p. 46.

'For if . . . humanized': Ibid., p. 10.

'verb substantive': See, e.g. Coleridge, *Collected Works*, vol. 13, pp. lxv–lxvi, 16, 18–19, 80, 82, 89–90, 132 (*Logic*).

'not as . . . nothing else': Helmut James von Moltke, *Letters to Freya: 1939–1945*, tr. Beate Ruhm von Oppen (New York: Knopf, 1990), p. 410; cf. Helmut James von Moltke, *Briefe an Freya, 1939–1945*, ed. B. R. von Oppen (Munich: Beck,

1988), p. 60: 'nicht als Grossgrundbesitzer, nicht als Adliger, nicht als Preusse, nicht als Deutscher... sondern als Christ und als gar nichts anderes'.

'full intuitive conviction': Butler, *Fifteen Sermons*, p. 12.

'mere power and authority': Ibid., p. 57.

'everybody is acquainted with': Ibid.

'blind propension': Ibid., p. 197.

'the moral rule... nature': Ibid., p. 255.

ALIENATED MAJESTY

29. Alienated Majesty: Ralph W. Emerson

'In every . . . alienated majesty': Ralph W. Emerson, *Essays and Lectures*, ed. Joel Porte (New York: Viking, 1983), p. 259 ('Self-Reliance'); cf. *Collected Works of Ralph Waldo Emerson*, 6 vols. to date (Cambridge, MA: Belknap Press, 1971–), vol. 2, p. 27.

'the charm . . . Otherism': *Emerson in His Journals*, ed. Joel Porte (Cambridge, MA: Belknap Press, 1982), p. 155 (28 Nov. 1836). I have followed here and subsequently the dates given by Porte, which are sometimes conjectural, as well as his text, which has been lightly regularized. Cf. Ralph W. Emerson, *Journals and Miscellaneous Notebooks*, 16 vols., ed. William H. Gilman et al. (Cambridge, MA: Belknap Press, 1960–82), vol. 5, p. 254.

'We know . . . voice': Isaac Rosenberg, *The Collected Works of Isaac Rosenberg: Poetry, Prose, Letters, Paintings, and Drawings*, ed., intro., and notes by Ian Parsons, foreword by Siegfried Sassoon (New York: Oxford University Press, 1979), p. 288.

'I always knew . . . living': Gerard M. Hopkins, *The Letters of Gerard Manley Hopkins to Robert Bridges*, ed. Claude Colleer Abbott, rev. impression (London: Oxford University Press, 1955), p. 155 (18 Oct. 1882).

'My own book . . . praised it.': *Emerson in His Journals*, p. 155 (28 Nov. 1836); cf. *Journals and Miscellaneous Notebooks*, vol. 5, p. 254.

'The very sentiment . . . another.': *Emerson in His Journals*, p. 155 (28 Nov. 1836); cf. *Journals and Miscellaneous Notebooks*, vol. 5, p. 254.

'Every opinion . . . the mind': *Emerson in His Journals*, p. 155 (24 Nov. 1836); cf. *Journals and Miscellaneous Notebooks*, vol. 5, p. 252.

'possessed . . . needle's point': Ralph W. Emerson, 'Modern Aspects of Letters,' in *The Early Lectures of Ralph Waldo Emerson*, 3 vols., ed. Stephen E. Whicher and Robert E. Spiller (Cambridge, MA: Harvard University Press, 1959–72), vol. 1, p. 378.

'All his books . . . heard': Emerson, *The Early Lectures*, vol. 1, p. v. The phrase 'low tones that decide' appears in Emerson's poem 'Uriel' (l. 15).

'There is every degree . . . line of words': *Emerson in His Journals*, p. 140 (20 June 1835); cf. *Journals and Miscellaneous Notebooks*, vol. 5, p. 51.

'Genius . . . personality': Franz Rosenzweig, *The Star of Redemption*, tr. William W. Hallo (New York: Holt, Rinehart, and Winston, 1971), p. 149.

'I told H.T. . . . drest.': *Emerson in His Journals*, p. 264 (placed after Sept.? 1841); cf. *The Journals and Miscellaneous Notebooks*, vol. 8, p. 96.

'good river-god': *Emerson in His Journals*, p. 254 (6 June 1841); cf. *The Journals and Miscellaneous Notebooks*, vol. 7, p. 454.

'Henry Thoreau . . . his hand': *Emerson in His Journals*, p. 391 (July–Aug. 1848); cf. *The Journals and Miscellaneous Notebooks*, vol. 10, p. 344. The allusion is to *Othello*, Act I, scene iii.

'merely the tune of the time': *Emerson in His Journals*, p. 126 (19–20 Aug. 1834); *The Journals and Miscellaneous Notebooks*, vol. 4, p. 315.

his optimistic philosophy...evil: Charles Eliot Norton, *Letters of Charles Eliot Norton*, 2 vols., ed. Sara Norton and M. A. DeWolfe Howe (Boston, MA: Houghton Mifflin, 1913), vol. 1, p. 503 (15 May 1873).

'Tis said...begone: *Emerson in His Journals*, pp. 441–2 (Winter? 1852–3); cf. *The Journals and Miscellaneous Notebooks*, vol. 13, p. 120.

'the greatness and the cost of him': Bertolt Brecht, *Brecht on Theatre: The Development of an Aesthetic*, ed. and tr. John Willett (New York: Hill and Wang, 1964), p. 263.

'As Tennyson writes': William James, *The Varieties of Religious Experience* (Cambridge, MA: Harvard University Press, 1985), p. 304 (first pub. 1902).

'As an anarchist poet writes': Ibid., p. 256.

'The well-known passage...mystical experience': Ibid., p. 314.

'This primacy...lines': Ibid., p. 398 n. 16.

'But the more...images.': Ibid., p. 63.

'I will again...respectable.': William James, *The Correspondence of William James*, 12 vols., ed. Ignas K. Skrupskelis and Elizabeth M. Berkeley, assisted by Bernice Grohskopf and Wilma Bradbeer (Charlottesville, VA: University Press of Virginia, 1995), vol. 4, p. 248 (Jan. 1868).

'poor Bunyan': James, *Varieties of Religious Experience*, p. 132.

'poor Nietzsche': Ibid., p. 297.

'poor Margaret Mary Alacoque': Ibid., p. 328.

'The idea...error': William Empson, *The Structure of Complex Words*, 3rd edn. (London: Penguin, 1977), p. xii ('Comment for Second Edition (1951)'; first pub. 1951).

'The only thing...it is': Emerson, *Essays and Lectures*, p. 472; cf. *Collected Works*, vol. 3, p. 29.

'We animate what...animate': Emerson, *Essays and Lectures*, p. 473; cf. *Collected Works*, vol. 3, p. 30.

'the individual is always mistaken': Emerson, *Essays and Lectures*, p. 484; cf. *Collected Works*, vol. 3, p. 40.

'Life has no memory': Emerson, *Essays and Lectures*, p. 484; cf. *Collected Works*, vol. 3, p. 40.

'Two human beings...inert': Emerson, *Essays and Lectures*, p. 488; cf. *Collected Works*, vol. 3, p. 44.

'A sympathetic person...men': Emerson, *Essays and Lectures*, p. 490; cf. *Collected Works*, vol. 3, pp. 46–7.

'absolute nature': Emerson, *Essays and Lectures*, p. 487; cf. *Collected Works*, vol. 3, p. 44.

'All writing...doing and having': Emerson, *Essays and Lectures*, p. 483; cf. *Collected Works*, vol. 3, p. 40.

'Every man...success': Emerson, *Essays and Lectures*, p. 483; cf. *Collected Works*, vol. 3, p. 40.

'It is the distinction...a surprise': *Emerson in His Journals*, p. 187; cf. *Journals and Miscellaneous Notebooks*, vol. 7, p. 17.

'I can see nothing...the Eternal': Emerson, *Essays and Lectures*, p. 483; cf. *Collected Works*, vol. 3, p. 40.

'Concord and Boston...world': Emerson, *Essays and Lectures*, p. 480; cf. *Collected Works*, vol. 3, p. 36.

The middle region...belt: Emerson, *Essays and Lectures*, p. 480; cf. *Collected Works*, vol. 3, p. 36.

the 'line'...breadth': Emerson, *Essays and Lectures*, p. 482; cf. *Collected Works*, vol. 3, p. 39.

'innocently...an artist': Emerson, *Essays and Lectures*, p. 482; cf. *Collected Works*, vol. 3, p. 38.

I think...needle's point: *Early Lectures*, vol. 1, p. 378. Emerson alludes to Plato, *Phaedrus*, 266b.

'The grossest ignorance...knowingness': Emerson, *Essays and Lectures*, p. 475; cf. *Collected Works*, vol. 3, p. 31.

'parrot echoes...mediocrities': *Emerson in His Journals* 408 (Nov.–Dec. 1849); cf. *Journals and Miscellaneous Notebooks*, vol. 11, p. 192.

'Do we diminish...suicide?': Kay Jamison, *Touched with Fire: Manic-Depressive Illness and the Artistic Temperament* (New York: Free Press, 1993), p. 259.

'the world we recognize...really is': James, *Varieties of Religious Experience*, pp. 80–1.

'very deep insight[s]...life': Josiah Royce, *William James and Other Essays on the Philosophy of Life* (Freeport, NY: Books for Libraries, 1969) 52 (repr. of 1911 edn.).

'the highest forms of the spiritual life': Royce, *William James*, p. 22.

Royce...Comparative Methodology: See Grover Smith, ed., *Josiah Royce's Seminar, 1913–1914: As Recorded in the Notebooks of Harry T. Costello* (New Brunswick, NJ: Rutgers University Press, 1963).

'poesy's' drift...common weal: See, e.g. William Roscoe Thayer, *The Life and Letters of John Hay*, 2 vols. (Boston, MA: Houghton Mifflin, 1915), vol. 1, pp. 52–73.

The great distinction...persons: Emerson, *Essays and Lectures*, p. 395; cf. *Collected Works*, vol. 2, p. 170.

their 'centre'...will shine': Emerson, *Essays and Lectures*, p. 395 ('If he have found his centre, the Deity will shine through him'); cf. *Collected Works*, vol. 2, pp. 169–70 ('The Over-Soul').

'maniacs are...nothing': Charles S. Peirce, *Charles Sanders Peirce: Contributions to The Nation*, 3 vols., ed. Kenneth Laine Ketner and James Edward Cook (Lubbock, TX: Texas Tech Press, 1975), vol. 1, p. 141.

Precisely because...the time: John S. Mill, *On Liberty*, ed. David Bromwich and George Kateb (New Haven, CT: Yale University Press, 2003), p. 131.

The erratics...fanatics: William James, *The Letters of William James*, 2 vols., ed. Henry James (Boston, MA: Atlantic Monthly Press, 1920), vol. 1, pp. 292–3.

'a workman...for funds': James, *Letters of William James*, vol. 1, pp. 292–3.

'American mind . . . of capabilities': *Emerson in His Journals*, p. 372; cf. *Journals and Miscellaneous Notebooks* 10:77.

Mamma, may I . . . pieces: *Emerson in His Journals*, p. 277; cf. *Journals and Miscellaneous Notebooks*, vol. 8, p. 166.

30. Alienated Majesty: Walt Whitman

'The language . . . worldly': Franz Rosenzweig, *The Star of Redemption*, tr. William W. Hallo (New York: Holt, Rinehart, and Winston 1971), p. 200.

'he was disgraceful': Emily Dickinson, *The Letters of Emily Dickinson*, 3 vols., ed. Thomas H. Johnson and Theodora Ward (Cambridge, MA: Belknap Press, 1958), vol. 2, p. 404 (25 Apr. 1862).

Emerson's distress . . . in 1855: Ralph W. Emerson, *Selected Letters*, ed. Joel Myerson (New York: Columbia University Press, 1997), pp. 383–4; cf. *The Letters of Ralph Waldo Emerson*, 10 vols., ed. Ralph L. Rusk et al. (New York: Columbia University Press, 1939–95), vol. 4, p. 520–1.

Whitman walked . . . 'no, no': Walt Whitman, *Complete Poetry and Collected Prose*, ed. Justin Kaplan (New York: Viking Press, 1982), pp. 914–15 (*Specimen Days*); cf. Walt Whitman, *Prose Works (1892)*, 2 vols., ed. Floyd Stovall (New York: New York University Press, 1963–4), vol. 1, pp. 281–2 and Horace Traubel, *With Walt Whitman in Camden*, 9 vols. (Boston, MA, etc.: Small, Maynard, etc., 1906–96), vol. 1, pp. 50–1, 151; vol. 3, pp. 439–40.

'Give me to warble . . . only': 'Give Me the Splendid Silent Sun', l. 10. Whitman, *Complete Poetry and Collected Prose*, p. 446; Walt Whitman, *Leaves of Grass: A Textual Variorum of the Printed Poems*, 3 vols., ed. Sculley Bradley et al. (New York: New York University Press, 1980), vol. 2, p. 498.

'Blue Book' . . . compositional methods: *Walt Whitman's Blue Book: The 1860–61 Leaves of Grass Containing His Manuscript Additions and Revisions*, 2 vols., textual analysis by Arthur Golden (New York: New York Public Library, 1968).

The poet . . . this is myself: Ralph W. Emerson, *Essays and Lectures*, ed. Joel Porte (New York: Viking, 1983), pp. 64–5; cf. *Collected Works of Ralph Waldo Emerson*, 6 vols. to date (Cambridge, MA: Belknap Press, 1971–), vol. 1, p. 63.

'Some I do know . . . soul': Thomas Carlyle, *Past and Present*, ed. Chris R. Vanden Bossche, Joel J. Brattin, and D.J. Trela (Berkeley, CA: University of California Press, 2005), p. 232 (first pub. 1843).

'Not for his . . . final value': Whitman, *Complete Poetry and Collected Prose*, p. 887 (*Specimen Days*); cf. Whitman, *Prose Works (1892)*, vol. 1, p. 250.

'The word prophecy . . . revealing God': Whitman, *Complete Poetry and Collected Prose*, p. 887 (*Specimen Days*); cf. Whitman, *Prose Works (1892)*, vol. 1, p. 250.

'The very sentiment . . . heed': *Emerson in His Journals*, ed. Joel Porte (Cambridge, MA: Belknap Press, 1982), p. 155 (28 Nov. 1836); cf. Ralph W. Emerson, *Journals and Miscellaneous Notebooks*, 16 vols., ed. William H. Gilman et al. (Cambridge, MA: Belknap Press, 1960–82), vol. 5, p. 254.

'great melody': W. B. Yeats, *The Collected Poems of W. B. Yeats*, ed. Richard J. Finneran, new edn. (New York: Macmillan, 1989), p. 241 ('The Seven Sages', l. 16).

'alienated majesty': Ralph W. Emerson, *Essays and Lectures*, p. 259 ('Self-Reliance');
cf. *Collected Works of Ralph Waldo Emerson*, vol. 2, p. 27.

It is amazing . . . the officer: Walt Whitman, *The Journalism*, 2 vols., ed. Herbert
Bergman et al. (New York: P. Lang, 1998–2003), vol. 1, p. 290; cf. Walt
Whitman, *The Gathering of the Forces*, 2 vols., ed. Cleveland Rodgers and John
Black (New York: G. P. Putnam's Sons, 1920), vol. 1, p. 60.

Law is . . . inferior one: Whitman, *Complete Poetry and Collected Prose*, p. 948; cf.
Whitman, *Prose Works (1892)*, vol. 2, p. 380.

'It is time . . . lady's cloak!': Whitman, *Complete Poetry and Collected Prose*, p. 887
(*Specimen Days*); cf. Whitman, *Prose Works (1892)*, vol. 1, p. 250.

'our comfortable reading circles': Whitman, *Complete Poetry and Collected Prose*,
p. 887 (*Specimen Days*); cf. Whitman, *Prose Works (1892)*, vol. 1, p. 250.

'the dear old spiritual world': Emerson, *Essays and Lectures*, p. 480 ('Experience');
cf. *Collected Works*, vol. 3, p. 36.

I am the poet . . . new tongue: Whitman, 'Song of Myself', ll. 422–4 (section 21);
cf. *Complete Poetry and Collected Prose*, p. 207 and *Leaves of Grass*, vol. 1, p. 26.

'mighty power of this republic': Whitman, *Journalism*, vol. 2, p. 254 (22 Apr. 1847);
cf. Whitman, *Gathering of the Forces*, vol. 1, p. 201.

'the old fathers of our freedom': Whitman, *Journalism*, vol. 2, p. 254 (22 Apr. 1847);
cf. Whitman, *Gathering of the Forces*, vol. 1, p. 201.

'Jefferson, the great apostle of liberty': Whitman, *Journalism*, vol. 2, p. 223
(11 Mar. 1847); cf. Whitman, *Gathering of the Forces*, vol. 1, p. 199.

'the great voice of Jefferson': Whitman, *Journalism*, vol. 2, p. 320 (1 Sept. 1847); cf.
Whitman, *Gathering of the Forces*, vol. 1, p. 212.

'Surely no people . . . human happiness': Whitman, *Journalism*, vol. 2, p. 362
(24 Nov. 1847); cf. Whitman, *Gathering of the Forces*, vol. 2, pp. 173–4.

'It is true . . . positively enjoyed': Whitman, *Journalism*, vol. 2, p. 362 (24 Nov. 1847);
cf. Whitman, *Gathering of the Forces*, vol. 2, p. 174.

What blurt . . . indifferent: Whitman, 'Song of Myself', ll. 464–4 (section 22);
cf. *Complete Poetry and Collected Prose*, p. 209 and *Leaves of Grass*, vol. 1, p. 29.

The dictionary . . . 'immaterial': *OED²*, s.v. 'indifferent'.

'I always knew . . . confession': Gerard M. Hopkins, *The Letters of Gerard Manley
Hopkins to Robert Bridges*, ed. Claude Colleer Abbott, rev. impression (London:
Oxford University Press, 1955), p. 155 (18 Oct. 1882).

'the naked thew and sinew': Hopkins, *Letters to Bridges*, pp. 267–8 (6 Nov. 1887).

'the depth of radical poetry . . . land': Whitman, *Journalism*, vol. 2, p. 161;
cf. Whitman, *Gathering of the Forces*, vol. 2, p. 146.

In referring . . . tongue according . . . ': Walt Whitman, *An American Primer*, ed.
Horace Traubel (Philadelphia, PA: R. West, 1980), pp. viii–ix.

Behind all else . . . results: Whitman, *Prose Works (1892)*, vol. 2, p. 713; cf. *Complete
Poetry and Collected Prose*, p. 657.

'how much liberty society will bear': Whitman, *Journalism*, vol. 2, p. 79
(8 Oct. 1846); cf. Whitman, *Gathering of the Forces*, vol. 2, p. 12 ('There must

be continual additions in our great experiment of how much liberty society will bear').

Apart from . . . at it: Whitman, 'Song of Myself', ll. 75–9 (section 4); cf. *Complete Poetry and Collected Prose*, p. 191 and *Leaves of Grass*, vol. 1, p. 5.

'the union . . . impregnable': Whitman, *Complete Poetry and Collected Prose*, p. 8; cf. *Prose Works (1892)*, vol. 2, p. 742.

'Of all mankind . . . man': Whitman, *Complete Poetry and Collected Prose*, p. 8; cf. *Prose Works (1892)*, vol. 2, p. 743.

'High up . . . concentrated light': Whitman, *Complete Poetry and Collected Prose*, p. 9; cf. *Prose Works (1892)*, vol. 2, p. 437.

'What is past is past': Whitman, *Complete Poetry and Collected Prose*, p. 9; cf. *Prose Works (1892)*, vol. 2, p. 438.

'These understand . . . impartial': Whitman, *Complete Poetry and Collected Prose*, p. 12 (ellipses in original); cf. *Prose Works (1892)*, vol. 2, p. 442.

'nothing is finer . . . forms': Whitman, *Complete Poetry and Collected Prose*, p. 14; cf. *Prose Works (1892)*, vol. 2, p. 445.

'The depths . . . immodest': Whitman, *Complete Poetry and Collected Prose*, pp. 15–16 (ellipsis in original); cf. *Prose Works (1892)*, vol. 2, p. 447.

'Liberty relies . . . no discouragement': Whitman, *Complete Poetry and Collected Prose*, p. 17; cf. *Prose Works (1892)*, vol. 2, p. 744.

'As they emit . . . light': Whitman, *Complete Poetry and Collected Prose*, p. 18; cf. *Prose Works (1892)*, vol. 2, p. 449.

'all the self-denial . . . the boats': Whitman, *Complete Poetry and Collected Prose*, p. 22; cf. *Prose Works (1892)*, vol. 2, p. 747.

'The prudence . . . unrighteous': Whitman, *Complete Poetry and Collected Prose*, p. 23; cf. *Prose Works (1892)*, vol. 2, p. 454.

'The English language . . . inexpressible': Whitman, *Complete Poetry and Collected Prose*, p. 25; cf. *Prose Works (1892)*, vol. 2, pp. 456–7.

'The soul . . . it permits all': Whitman, *Complete Poetry and Collected Prose*, p. 26 (ellipsis in original); cf. *Prose Works (1892)*, vol. 2, p. 458.

'A perfectly transparent . . . when and where': Walt Whitman, *Notebooks and Unpublished Prose Manuscripts*, 6 vols., ed. Edward Grier (New York: New York University Press, 1984), vol. 1, p. 101.

The soul or spirit . . . sun and stars—: Whitman, *Notebooks and Unpublished Prose Manuscripts*, vol. 1, p. 57.

'to put into . . . kind of life': *OED*[2], s.v. 'enure' and 'inure'.

'these singly . . . shall spring': Whitman, *Complete Poetry and Collected Prose*, p. 23; cf. *Prose Works (1892)*, vol. 2, p. 747.

'Your obligation . . . your nature': Joseph Butler, 2 vols., *Works*, ed. W. E. Gladstone (Oxford: Clarendon Press, 1896), vol. 2, p. 71 (Sermon III of *Fifteen Sermons*); cf. Joseph Butler, *Fifteen Sermons*, ed. W. R. Matthews (London: G. Bell, 1914), p. 64.

How they . . . their age: 'Beginners', l. 3; cf. Whitman, *Complete Poetry and Collected Prose*, p. 171 and *Leaves of Grass*, vol. 2, p. 434. In 'Beginners' the successive phrases 'How they are...', 'How they inure...', 'How all times...' contrive to suggest both the plain demonstrative adverb (*this is how things are*) and an exclamation (*in what a way!*) and, I believe, a muffled question (*how is it that...?*) The passionate statements that things *are* so contain the implicit question 'why do they *have* to be so?' In this poem, Whitman's language is wrought to such a pitch ('provides for', 'inure', 'purchase') and the rhythms are so handled that the polemical statement and the metaphysical question are co-inherent. In seven lines Whitman has composed both a manifesto and a shock of recognition.

And often to me...nothing more: 'Thought' ('Of persons arrived...'), l. 7; cf. Whitman, *Complete Poetry and Collected Prose*, p. 513 and *Leaves of Grass*, vol. 2, p. 424.

31. Alienated Majesty: Gerard M. Hopkins

'alienated majesty': Ralph W. Emerson, *Essays and Lectures*, ed. Joel Porte (New York: Viking, 1983), p. 259 ('Self-Reliance'); cf. *Collected Works of Ralph Waldo Emerson*, 6 vols. to date (Cambridge, MA: Belknap Press, 1971–), vol. 2, p. 27.

'feudal, ecclesiastical, dynastic world': Walt Whitman, *Complete Poetry and Collected Prose*, ed. Justin Kaplan (New York: Viking, 1982), p. 933; cf. Walt Whitman, *Prose Works (1892)*, 2 vols., ed. Floyd Stovall (New York: New York University Press, 1963–4), vol. 2, p. 366.

'if anyone would refuse...unworthy knight': *The Spiritual Exercises of St. Ignatius*, tr. Anthony Mottola (Garden City, NJ: Image Books, 1964), p. 67.

I caught...daylight's dauphin: Gerard M. Hopkins, 'The Windhover', ll. 1–2; cf. *The Poetical Works of Gerard Manley Hopkins*, ed. Norman H. MacKenzie (Oxford: Oxford University Press, 1990), p. 144.

'I enclose a poem...Afghanistan': Gerard M. Hopkins, *The Letters of Gerard Manley Hopkins to Robert Bridges*, ed. Claude Colleer Abbott, rev. impression (London: Oxford University Press, 1955), p. 92 (8 Oct. 1879).

'It is time...namely power': Whitman, *Complete Poetry and Collected Prose*, p. 887 (*Specimen Days*); cf. Whitman, *Prose Works (1892)*, vol. 1, p. 250.

'naked thew and sinew': Hopkins, *Letters to Bridges*, pp. 267–8 (6 Nov. 1887).

'the most masculine of our poets': Ibid.

'models...to her and hers': Whitman, *Complete Poetry and Collected Prose*, p. 959; cf. Whitman, *Prose Works (1892)*, vol. 2, p. 393.

'blind loyalty...Ainsworth': Walt Whitman, *The Journalism*, 2 vols., ed. Herbert Bergman et al. (New York: P. Lang, 1998–2003), vol. 1, p. 463; cf. Walt Whitman, *The Gathering of the Forces*, 2 vols., ed. Cleveland Rodgers and John Black (New York: G. P. Putnam's Sons, 1920), vol. 2, pp. 243–4.

If anything...great poetry: Hopkins, *Letters to Bridges*, p. 275 (25 May 1888).

Now [Browning]...no blasted nonsense: Gerard M. Hopkins, *The Correspondence of Gerard Manley Hopkins and Richard Watson Dixon*, ed. Claude Colleer Abbott (London: Oxford University Press, 1955), p. 74 (12 Oct. 1881).

('I sound ... world'): Whitman, 'Song of Myself', l. 1333 (section 52); cf. *Complete Poetry and Collected Prose*, p. 247 and Walt Whitman, *Leaves of Grass: A Textual Variorum of the Printed Poems*, 3 vols., ed. Sculley Bradley et al. (New York: New York University Press, 1980), vol. 1, p. 82.

Whitman ... most delicate of poets: See James Wright, 'The Delicacy of Walt Whitman', *Collected Prose*, ed. Anne Wright (Ann Arbor, MI: University of Michigan Press, 1983), pp. 3–22.

'more like Whitman's ... great scoundrel': Hopkins, *Letters to Bridges*, p. 155 (18 Oct. 1882).

'before I became ... superiors': Hopkins, *Correspondence of Hopkins and Dixon*, p. 14 (5 Oct. 1878).

Once an immutable choice ... inordinate attachments: Ignatius of Loyola, *Spiritual Exercises*, pp. 83–4.

'if one remembers ... with his enemy': Emerson, *Essays and Lectures*, p. 482; cf. *Collected Works*, vol. 3, p. 38.

'win over ... Englishmen': MacKenzie in Hopkins, *Poetical Works*, p. 320.

'little presentation ... called for': Hopkins, *Correspondence of Hopkins and Dixon*, p. 14 (5 Oct. 1878).

'heart' in 'The Windhover': Hopkins, 'The Windhover', ll. 7–8 ('My heart in hiding | Stirred for a bird'); cf. *Poetical Works*, p. 144.

'in effect ... Christ's service': MacKenzie in Hopkins, *Poetical Works*, p. 270.

his 'deepening ... secular poet': MacKenzie in Hopkins, *Poetical Works*, p. 282.

It is sad to think ... your poems display: Hopkins, *Correspondence of Hopkins and Dixon*, pp. 8–9 (13 June 1878).

'very deep ... life': Josiah Royce, *William James and Other Essays on the Philosophy of Life* (New York: Macmillan, 1969), p. 52 (repr. of 1911 edn.).

'tumultuous now the contest rages': Whitman, 'The Artilleryman's Vision', l. 9; cf. *Complete Poetry and Collected Prose*, p. 450 and *Leaves of Grass*, vol. 2, p. 506.

'a desperate emergency': Whitman, 'I Saw Old General at Bay', l. 4; cf. *Complete Poetry and Collected Prose*, p. 450 and *Leaves of Grass*, vol. 2, p. 521.

'Faces, varieties ... description': Whitman, 'A March in the Ranks Hard-Prest, and the Road Unknown', l. 14; cf. *Complete Poetry and Collected Prose*, p. 440 and *Leaves of Grass*, vol. 2, p. 494.

'I see ... ever made': Whitman, 'A March in the Ranks Hard-Prest, and the Road Unknown', l. 7; cf. *Complete Poetry and Collected Prose*, p. 440 and *Leaves of Grass*, vol. 2, p. 494.

'O the bullet ... dear friend': Whitman, 'How Solemn as One by One', l. 7; cf. *Complete Poetry and Collected Prose*, p. 454 and *Leaves of Grass*, vol. 2, p. 554.

'The glisten ... the torches': Whitman, 'A March in the Ranks Hard-Prest, and the Road Unknown', l. 19; cf. *Complete Poetry and Collected Prose*, p. 440 and *Leaves of Grass*, vol. 2, p. 494.

Comes before me...*comrade*: Whitman, 'As Toilsome I Wander'd Virginia's Woods', ll. 11–12; cf. *Complete Poetry and Collected Prose*, p. 442 and *Leaves of Grass*, vol. 2, p. 510.

Grand, common stock...yet rival'd: Whitman, *Complete Poetry and Collected Prose* 946; cf. Whitman, *Prose Works (1892)*, vol. 2, p. 379.

To-day, in books...exterior life: Whitman, *Complete Poetry and Collected Prose*, pp. 974–5; cf. Whitman, *Prose Works (1892)*, vol. 2, p. 408.

'I find within...write on.': Hopkins, *Letters to Bridges*, p. 86.

'The state of the country...great patriot': Hopkins, *Letters to Bridges*, p. 131.

'My Liverpool and Glasgow...century's civilisation': Hopkins, *Correspondence of Hopkins and Dixon*, p. 97.

'the self-perfection...supernatural aid': Christopher Devlin, in *The Sermons and Devotional Writings of Gerard Manley Hopkins*, ed. Christopher Devlin (London: Oxford University Press, 1959), p. 340.

'God the Son's descent...one form or another': Devlin in Hopkins, *Sermons and Devotional Writings*, p. 109.

'Christ's humanity...in creating': Devlin in Hopkins, *Sermons and Devotional Writings*, p. 296.

'Now what was...kingdom?': Hopkins, *Sermons and Devotional Writings*, p. 59.

it was...common weal: Ibid.

'great ode': Hopkins, *Letters to Bridges*, p. 135 (16 Sept. 1881).

but which...'laid aside': Hopkins, *Correspondence of Hopkins and Dixon*, p. 76 (23 Oct. 1881).

'something between...irregular metre': Hopkins, *Letters to Bridges*, p. 136 (16 Sept. 1881).

'crib': Hopkins, *Letters to Bridges*, p. 272 (10 Feb. 1888).

Must I interpret it...to the whole: Hopkins, *Letters to Bridges*, pp. 272–3 (10 Feb. 1888).

'the attention...my fellow-labourer': Samuel Taylor Coleridge, *Collected Works*, 16 vols. (Princeton, NJ: Princeton University Press, 1969–2002), vol. 4, part 1, p. 21 (*The Friend*, ed. Barbara E. Rooke, 2 parts).

'inside...own age': Walter J. Ong, *Hopkins, the Self, and God* (Toronto: University of Toronto Press, 1986), p. 90.

'illustrated...F. D. Maurice)': MacKenzie in Hopkins, *Poetical Works*, p. 485.

'wanted the coda...at all events': Hopkins, *Letters to Bridges*, p. 266 (6 Nov. 1887).

'to frolic...careless fashion': *OED²*, s.v. 'rollick, *v*.' The citations to the magazines are found in this entry and under 'rollick, *n*.'

word applied by Hopkins...'robustious': Hopkins, *Correspondence of Hopkins and Dixon*, p. 153 (2 Dec. 1887).

'common use...archaizing writers': *OED²*, s.v. 'robustious'.

'very pregnant...I am afraid': Hopkins, *Letters to Bridges*, p. 274 (10 Feb. 1888).

'the art or virtue...monumental style': Hopkins, *Letters to Bridges*, p. 160 (4 Nov. 1882).

But cursed . . . as stones: Wilfred Owen, 'Insensibility', ll. 50–1; cf. *The Poems of Wilfred Owen*, ed. Jon Stallworthy (New York: Norton, 1986), p. 123.

'Mine, O thou lord of life, send my roots rain': Hopkins, 'Thou art indeed just, Lord . . . ', l. 14; cf. *Poetical Works of Gerard Manley Hopkins*, p. 201.

'Hopkins . . . freezes the mind': Ong, *Hopkins, the Self, and God*, p. 92.

'a kind . . . talent': Gerard M. Hopkins, *Further Letters of Gerard Manley Hopkins*, ed. Claude Colleer Abbott, 2nd edn. (London: Oxford University Press, 1956), p. 349 (letter to Coventry Patmore, 3 Jan. 1884).

'communities of opinion': Emerson, *Essays and Lectures*, p. 264 ('Self-Reliance'); cf. *Collected Works*, vol. 2, p. 32.

'transcendent destiny': Emerson, *Essays and Lectures*, p. 260 ('Self-Reliance'); cf. *Collected Works*, vol. 2, p. 28.

'the integrity of your own mind': Emerson, *Essays and Lectures*, p. 261 ('Self-Reliance'); cf. *Collected Works*, vol. 2, p. 230.

'intrinsic right': Emerson, *Essays and Lectures*, p. 263 ('Self-Reliance'); cf. *Collected Works*, vol. 2, p. 31.

'the independence of solitude': Emerson, *Essays and Lectures*, p. 263 ('Self-Reliance'); cf. *Collected Works*, vol. 2, p. 31.

'inscrutable possibilities': Emerson, *Essays and Lectures*, p. 475 ('Experience'); cf. *Collected Works*, vol. 3, p. 32.

'the great . . . absolute nature': Emerson, *Essays and Lectures*, p. 487 ('Experience'); cf. *Collected Works*, vol. 3, p. 44.

'the essence of genius': Emerson, *Essays and Lectures*, p. 269 ('Self-Reliance'); cf. *Collected Works*, vol. 2, p. 37.

'Great genius . . . demeaned to romances': Whitman, *Complete Poetry and Collected Prose*, p. 19; Whitman, *Prose Works (1892)*, vol. 2, p. 451.

'Genius . . . applicability': *Emerson in His Journals*, ed. Joel Porte (Cambridge, MA: Belknap, 1982), p. 304 (Mar.–Apr. 1843); cf. Ralph W. Emerson, *Journals and Miscellaneous Notebooks*, 16 vols., ed. William H. Gilman et al. (Cambridge, MA: Belknap, 1960–82), vol. 8, p. 373.

'The great . . . essential man': Emerson, *Essays and Lectures*, p. 280 ('Self-Reliance'); cf. *Collected Works*, vol. 2, p. 49.

'view of genius . . . can never recur" ': Devlin in Hopkins, *Sermons and Devotional Writings*, p. 278.

'by acts . . . rites and sacraments': Hopkins, *Sermons and Devotional Writings*, p. 37.

'I thought . . . everywhere again': Gerard M. Hopkins, *The Journals and Papers of Gerard Manley Hopkins*, ed. Humphry House and Graham Storey (London: Oxford University Press, 1959), p. 221.

'of them . . . a people': Whitman, *Complete Poetry and Collected Prose* 7 ('Preface' to *Leaves of Grass* [1855]); cf. *Prose Works (1892)*, vol. 2, p. 741.

32.   Word Value in F. H. Bradley and T. S. Eliot

'somehow': For further discussion of 'somehow' in the work of Bradley, see Ch. 33, pp. 549–50.

'while it will be ... painful tension': F.H. Bradley, *Appearance and Reality*, 2nd edn. (Oxford: Oxford University Press, 1930), pp. 89–90, 97, 106–7, 125, 127, 216, 326. For a more comprehensive list, see note to Ch. 33, p. 748.

'Oh yet we trust ... goal of ill': Alfred Tennyson, *Tennyson: A Selected Edition*, ed. Christopher Ricks (Berkeley, CA: University of California Press, 1989), p. 396 (*In Memoriam*, LIV. 1–2).

'all this immense ... pains one': George Eliot, *Middlemarch*, ed. David Carroll (Oxford: Oxford University Press, 1986), p. 214 (Book II, ch. 22).

Somehow ... goal it sought: In Josiah Royce, *The Hope of the Great Community* (New York: Macmillan 1916), p. vii (dedicatory verses, 'Josiah Royce, 1855–1916').

'somehow irrelevant ... so magically moving': Listed by Christopher Ricks in a review of Leslie Fiedler, *What Was Literature?* (New York: Simon & Schuster, 1982); see Christopher Ricks, *Reviewery* (New York: Handsel, 2001), p. 180.

'perfectly welded ... wholly that which he is': T. S. Eliot, *Selected Essays*, 2nd edn. (New York: Harcourt, Brace, 1964), p. 395 (first pub. 1932, enlarged edn. 1960; 'Francis Herbert Bradley').

Eliot himself uses ... Bradley's argument: T. S. Eliot, *Knowledge and Experience in the Philosophy of F.H. Bradley* (London: Faber and Faber, 1964), pp. 85, 111, 128, 148, 167.

It must however ... own positive case: See, e.g. F. H. Bradley, *Essays on Truth and Reality* (Oxford: Clarendon Press, 1914), p. 330: 'But the notion of a psychical subject, standing opposed to the object and then transcended somehow in knowledge, must be rejected as illusory'. See also pp. 40, 41–2 n. 1, 110, 313 ('and hence the "somehow", as it is, does not satisfy us'), and 354.

'And there can be ... theory of cognition.': Bradley, *Appearance and Reality*, p. 65.

'The intended object is ultimate reality': Eliot, *Knowledge and Experience*, p. 86.

Our result so far ... as rich as the relative: Bradley, *Appearance and Reality*, p. 127.

'How ... discursive intelligence?': Bradley, *Appearance and Reality*, p. 93.

'this way of apprehension': Ibid.

an objective correlative: See e.g. Bradley, *Appearance and Reality* 96 and *Essays on Truth and Reality*, pp. 119 n. 1, 195, 247, 264, 278, 326, 417. For Eliot's use of the term, see T. S. Eliot, *Selected Essays*, pp. 124–5 ('Hamlet and His Problems').

'felt unity': Bradley, *Appearance and Reality*, p. 95.

'felt totality': Ibid., pp. 95, 204.

'internal felt core': Ibid., p. 79.

'There is an element ... do so in time': C. H. Sisson, *English Poetry 1900–1950: An Assessment* (London: Hart-Davis, 1971), p. 129.

'was expounding ... apprehension': Sisson, *English Poetry 1900–1950*, p. 144.

'felt mass': Bradley, *Appearance and Reality*, p. 95.

'felt experience': Ibid., p. 199.

'the felt "this"': Ibid., p. 228.

'felt background': Ibid., p. 95, 461.

'context': On 'context' in Bradley and Eliot, see further Ch. 33, pp. 553–4.

'Relation presupposes . . . without relations': Bradley, *Appearance and Reality*, p. 21.

'But we have found . . . relation to others': Ibid., p. 370.

'congeries': Ibid., pp. 66, 157, 228.

'mere coincidence': Ibid., p. 208.

His wife . . . seriously modified: Ibid., p. 67.

'enjoy': See further the discussion of Eliot on poetry as amusement in Ch. 33, pp. 555–7 and 560–1.

For it is in finite . . . will be not good: Bradley, *Appearance and Reality*, p. 375; for other uses of 'enjoy' see pp. 10 and 19.

'physiological process': Eliot, *Knowledge and Experience*, p. 70.

'the end of the enjoyment . . . words of Arnold': T. S. Eliot, *The Sacred Wood: Essays on Poetry and Criticism*, 7th edn. (London: Methuen, 1950), pp. 14–15 (first pub. 1920).

third chapter of *Knowledge and Experience*: See esp. Eliot, *Knowledge and Experience*, p. 70 (and see also Eliot's note on p. 106).

there are some exceptions: Such as Eliot's warning against over-emphasizing enjoyment, in *On Poetry and Poets* (New York: Farrar, Straus, & Cudahy, 1957), p. 131 ('The Frontiers of Criticism'); this passage is discussed in Ch. 33, p. 560.

'to the whole . . . poetry or not': Eliot, *On Poetry and Poets*, p. 12.

'The obstacle . . . wrote about': Ibid., p. 139.

'the captious . . . his reader': Bradley, *Appearance and Reality*, p. 171.

On 22 May 1940 . . . property: *Chronology of the Second World War* (London: Royal Institute of International Affairs, 1947), p. 22.

'whether we could . . . *Cathedral*': E. Martin Browne, *The Making of T. S. Eliot's Plays* (Cambridge: Cambridge University Press, 1969), p. 153.

'It would frankly . . . essential values': Ibid.

5 June . . . crossed the Somme: *Chronology of the Second World War*, p. 23.

'Of course you may . . . serve that purpose': Browne, *The Making of T. S. Eliot's Plays*, p. 154.

'Go To It' and 'London Can Take It': See Asa Briggs, *The History of Broadcasting in the United Kingdom*, 5 vols., rev. edn. (Oxford: Oxford University Press, 1995), vol. 3, p. 199 (vol. 3: *The War of Words*); and Anthony Aldgate and Jeffrey Richards, *Britain Can Take It: The British Cinema in the Second World War* (Oxford: B. Blackwell, 1986), p. 220.

Lincoln's genius . . . 19 November 1863: See Abraham Lincoln, *Speeches and Writings 1859–1865*, ed. Don E. Fehrenbacher (New York: Viking, 1989), p. 536.

They smear . . . to the ants: Quoted in Browne, *The Making of T. S. Eliot's Plays*, p. 226.

'There is universal distaste . . . *everybody*?': Ibid.

'have . . . strong distaste': Ibid.

'Another variety . . . unpleasant': *The Egoist*, March 1918, p. 43, in a review of *Georgian Poetry, 1916–1917*; he was referring to Rupert Brooke's sonnet on sea-sickness. (I am indebted to Christopher Ricks for this reference.)

'The first . . . the great thing': Browne, *The Making of T. S. Eliot's Plays*, p. 236.

'more poetic side': Ibid.

'One of the things . . . out of it': Ibid.

'ill-regulated . . . language and of thought': T. S. Eliot, *To Criticize the Critic and Other Writings* (London: Faber and Faber, 1965), pp. 70–1.

'the right compromise . . . appreciative spectator': Ibid., p. 82.

valedictory sentence to the final lecture: Ibid., p. 124 ('though you may have been thinking of your next cocktail party').

William Empson's . . . *Complex Words*: Empson is noted in passing in Eliot's 1951 lecture, 'The Frontiers of Criticism'; see Eliot, *On Poetry and Poets*, p. 125.

Eliot's later . . . no diremption had taken place: In 1961, before an audience at the University of Leeds, he recalled 'F. H. Bradley, whose works—I might say whose personality as manifested in his works—affected me profoundly'; see Eliot, *To Criticize the Critic*, p. 20 ('To Criticize the Critic').

If poetry . . . the writer and the reader: T. S. Eliot, *The Use of Poetry and the Use of Criticism* (Cambridge, MA: Harvard University Press, 1933), p. 30 ('Introduction').

'the communication . . . the living': T. S. Eliot, *The Complete Poems and Plays of T. S. Eliot* (London: Faber and Faber, 1969), p. 192 ('Little Gidding', I, ll. 52–3).

'begging the question': See Eliot, *The Use of Poetry and the Use of Criticism*, p. 30 ('if it is communication, for the word may beg the question').

'periphrastic study': Eliot, *The Complete Poems and Plays*, p. 179 ('East Coker', II, l. 19).

'Something I have said before': Ibid., p. 181 ('East Coker', III, l. 35).

'shabby equipment always deteriorating': Ibid., p. 182 ('East Coker', V, l. 9).

'shell, a husk of meaning': Ibid., p. 192 ('Little Gidding', I, l. 32).

Whatever . . . in death: Ibid., p. 196 ('Little Gidding', III, ll. 43–6).

Someone said . . . which we know: Eliot, *The Sacred Wood*, p. 52 ('Tradition and the Individual Talent'); cf. Eliot, *Selected Essays*, p. 6.

'*Je* est un autre': Arthur Rimbaud, *Œuvres complètes*, ed. Rolland de Renéville and Jules Mouquet (Paris: Gallimard, 1963), pp. 268, 270 (letters to George Izambard of 13 May 1871 and to Paul Demeny of 15 May 1871).

Nevertheless, half a century ago . . . residual Christian acceptance: There is some documentation of this in Briggs, *The History of Broadcasting in the United Kingdom*, vol. 3, pp. 570–4, 'Politics, Religion and Society'; see also pp. 21 and 112. The index to vol. 3 (*The War of Words*) may also be consulted under 'Big Ben Minute'; 'Canterbury, Archbishop of'; 'Central Religious Advisory Committee'; 'Christmas Broadcasts'. Ogilvie, the first wartime Director-General of the BBC, approved the introduction (4 Dec. 1939) of 'a new daily wartime rhythm into broadcasting . . . with the new early morning prayers *Lift Up Your Hearts* and the new daily physical exercises *Up in the Morning Early*'. See also W. R. Matthews, *Saint Paul's Cathedral in Wartime 1939–1945* (London: Hutchinson, 1946), p. 32: 'About this time I was visited by an eminent psychologist and a well-known business man who . . . had evolved a formula, "It all depends on me" . . . The formula was doubtless excellent, up to a point, but seemed to me to be one-sided when viewed in the light of Christian faith and I, therefore, took the opportunity of a broadcast to add to it, "and I depend on God". It was encouraging to find that this enlarged watchword was taken up all over the country'.

'To read . . . 1940's': John Booty, *Meditating on Four Quartets* (Cambridge, MA: Cowley Publications, 1983), p. 8.

The public language . . . local cinema: Fully documented in Briggs, *The History of Broadcasting in the United Kingdom*, vol. 3 (*The War of Words*) and Aldgate and Richards, *Britain Can Take It*.

Eliot addressed the Association . . . at Swansea: His topic was 'What is Minor Poetry?', reprinted in Eliot, *On Poetry and Poets*, pp. 34–51. For a brief account of the Swansea blitz, see the British Information Services, *Front Line: The Official Story of the Civil Defense of Britain* (New York: Macmillan, 1943), pp. 85, 89, and 111.

Priestley's 'Dunkirk' . . . 'Defence of the Islands': On Priestley, see Briggs, *The History of Broadcasting in the United Kingdom*, vol. 3, p. 196 and Derek Parker, *Radio: The Great Years* (Newton Abbot: David & Charles, 1977), pp. 104–6. Eliot's 'Occasional Poem' originally appeared as a poster designed by E. McKnight Kauffer for the British Pavilion at the New York World's Fair in 1940; see Donald Gallup, *T. S. Eliot: A Bibliography*, rev. edn. (London: Faber & Faber, 1969), p. 345. It next appeared as the preface to Monroe Wheeler, ed., *Britain at War* (New York: Museum of Modern Art, 1941) and should, if possible, be read in the context of that volume. It appears in Eliot, *The Complete Poems and Plays*, p. 201.

'Mr. Priestley . . . nothing': Parker, *Radio*, p. 104.

'My Station and Its Duties': Reprinted in F. H. Bradley, *Ethical Studies*, 2nd edn. (Oxford: Clarendon Press, 1927), pp. 160–213.

and the memory . . . and fire: Eliot, *The Complete Poems and Plays*, p. 201.

Tommy Handley and *ITMA*: See Briggs, *The History of Broadcasting in the United Kingdom*, vol. 3, pp. 511–13 (*ITMA*, an acronym of 'It's That Man Again', was a popular radio programme of the 1940s.)

a potent hybrid . . . pioneeringly and well: Eliot, *The Sacred Wood*, p. 92 ('Notes on the Blank Verse of Christopher Marlowe').

A highly popular . . . Gracie Fields: See Briggs, *The History of Broadcasting in the United Kingdom*, vol. 3, pp. 99, 112, 119, 124, 135, and 273 (vol. 3: *The War of Words*).

But now—look! . . . immortal: Parker, *Radio*, p. 104.

had he found it possible . . . of 1931: A. D. Moody, suggests that the sequence 'was left unfinished because the impulse went into the choruses of *The Rock*, which Eliot was commissioned to write in 1933'; see A. D. Moody, *Thomas Stearns Eliot: Poet* (Cambridge: Cambridge University Press, 1979), p. 165. It is a good point but I think the problems and issues are more deeply seated (or buried) than that.

His lecture 'Scylla and Charybdis': It first appeared in *Agenda*, vol. 23, nos. 1–2 (Spring–Summer 1985), the 'T. S. Eliot Special Issue'. Repr. in William Cookson, ed., *Agenda: An Anthology. The First Four Decades (1959–1993)* (Manchester: Carcanet, 1994), pp. 285–99.

'to the point...maximum of impersonality': Eliot in Cookson, *Agenda: An Anthology* 298.

'Poetry...emotion': Eliot, *The Sacred Wood*, p. 58 ('Tradition and the Individual Talent'); see also Eliot, *Selected Essays*, p. 10.

a sensibility...spent their formative years: Lyndall Gordon, *T. S. Eliot: An Imperfect Life* (New York: Norton, 1998), p. 401.

Royce's...Comparative Methodology: See Grover Smith, ed., *Josiah Royce's Seminar, 1913–1914: As Recorded in the Notebooks of Harry T. Costello* (New Brunswick, NJ: Rutgers University Press, 1963). See further Ch. 29, p. 501.

With James's...condescending ethical taste: See Ch. 29, pp. 497–8, 500, 503.

'how closely...all these years': Eliot, *Knowledge and Experience*, pp. 10–11.

Analytical finesse...Desmond MacCarthy: For further discussion, see Ch. 33, p. 553.

'I dislike both...everything they wrote.': Eliot's review was reprinted in Eric Homberger, William Janeway, and Simon Schama, eds., *The Cambridge Mind: Ninety Years of the Cambridge Review, 1879–1969* (Boston: Little, Brown, 1971); see pp. 225, 226, and 229.

A good poem...manipulating feeling: Eliot in Homberger, Janeway, and Schama, *The Cambridge Mind*, p. 231.

a fringe...can express: Eliot, *On Poetry and Poets*, p. 93.

'worn-out...fashion': Eliot, *The Complete Poems and Plays*, p. 179 ('East Coker', II, l. 19).

'same vast task of the ages': Josiah Royce, *The Problem of Christianity* (Chicago, IL: University of Chicago Press, 1968), p. 192 (first pub. 1913).

Each [religion]...immortality: Royce, *The Problem of Christianity*, p. 192.

in a letter of 1920: T. S. Eliot, *The Letters of T. S. Eliot*, 1 vol. to date, ed. Valerie Eliot (London: Faber and Faber, 1988–), vol. 1, pp. 369–70.

'relation to...could talk poetry"': Eliot, *On Poetry and Poets*, pp. 23–4 ('The Music of Poetry', 1942).

Beveridge Report: See Briggs, *The History of Broadcasting in the United Kingdom*, vol. 3, pp. 547–56 (vol. 3: *The War of Words*).

'must, like the sculptor...works': Eliot, *On Poetry and Poets*, p. 24.

'Well, if Albert...I said': Eliot, *The Complete Poems and Plays*, p. 66 (*The Waste Land*, II, l. 163).

33. Eros in F. H. Bradley and T. S. Eliot

'Desire...ludicrous': F. H. Bradley, *Essays on Truth and Reality* (Oxford: Clarendon Press, 1914), p. 197.

'We may be told...in love?': F. H. Bradley, *Appearance and Reality*, 2nd edn. (Oxford: Clarendon Press, 1930), p. 153.

'where desire...is seen': F. H. Bradley, *The Principles of Logic*, 2 vols., 2nd edn. rev. (London: Oxford University Press, 1922), vol. 1, p. 32.

Because...power: T. S. Eliot, *The Complete Poems and Plays of T. S. Eliot* (London: Faber, 1969), p. 89 ('Ash-Wednesday', I, ll. 11–13).

'scrupulous...exaggerated': T. S. Eliot, *For Lancelot Andrewes: Essays on Style and Order* (London: Faber & Gwyer, 1928), p. 85 ('Francis Herbert Bradley').

'at various times of his maturer life': F. H. Bradley, *Aphorisms* (Oxford: Clarendon Press, 1930) prefatory remark (unpaginated).

'somehow': On Bradley and 'somehow,' see also Ch. 32, pp. 532–4.

twenty-six times...*Logic*: Bradley, *The Principles of Logic*, vol. 1, pp. 34, 54, 118, 138, 148, 237 (three times), 272, 316, 318, and 388; and vol. 2, pp. 400, 404, 434, 465, 491, 505, 581, 628, 634, 635 (twice), 654, 677, and 710.

no less than...*Truth and Reality*: Bradley, *Essays on Truth and Reality*, pp. 6, 15, 35, 40, 41 n. 1, 42n. 1 (twice), 45, 77, 110, 121, 139, 140, 206, 222, 248, 249, 251, 252, 269, 270, 271 (twice), 271 n. 1, 273, 277 (twice), 302 (four), 313 (twice), 326 (twice), 330, 350 n. 1, 354, 368, 442, 464.

and as many...*Appearance and Reality*: Bradley, *Appearance and Reality*, pp. xvi, xvii, 1, 9 (twice), 10, 13, 16, 18, 26, 27 (twice), 34, 35, 36, 37, 42, 53, 54, 62, 65, 73, 90 (twice), 94, 97, 105, 106, 123 (twice), 124, 125 (twice), 126, 127, 137, 140, 141 (twice), 160 (twice), 164, 177, 180, 181, 183, 193, 194, 213, 215, 216, 237, 243, 249, 281, 282, 283, 284 (twice), 285, 326 (twice), 328, 340, 348, 350, 373, 376, 379, 386, 430, 468, 497, 499 (twice), 504 (twice), 510 (twice), 524, 547, 549 (twice), 559 (twice), 560, 561, 561 n. 1.

'"somehow"...in our fact': Bradley, *Essays on Truth and Reality*, p. 313.

The artist...visible world: F. H. Bradley, *Ethical Studies*, 2nd edn. (Oxford, 1927), p. 320.

So far...is done: Ibid., p. 334.

('Because I...Word unheard'): Eliot, *The Complete Poems and Plays* (London, 1969), pp. 89, 90, and 96 ('Ash-Wednesday' I, l 12; I, l 32; and V, l 4.).

There rises...here, now, always—: Eliot, *The Complete Poems and Plays*, p. 176.

'A system...theology': Eliot, *For Lancelot Andrewes*, p. 83.

'great gift of style': Ibid., p. 69.

'And my spirit...the old love': T. S. Eliot, *Selected Essays*, 2nd edn. (New York: Harcourt, Brace, 1964) p. 224 (first pub. 1932, enlarged edn. 1960).

'Ingathering': Cf. Eliot, *Selected Essays*, p. 228 (from the translation of *Paradiso*, Canto XVIII).

'In-folded': Eliot, *The Complete Poems and Plays*, p. 198.

'we have...real somehow': Bradley, *The Principles of Logic*, vol. 1, p. 237.

Adam's Dream...1817: John Keats, *The Letters of John Keats 1814–1821*, ed. Hyder Edward Rollins, 2 vols. (Cambridge, MA: Harvard University Press, 1958), vol. 1, p. 185 ('The Imagination may be compared to Adam's dream—he awoke and found it truth').

'There are no . . . an idea': Bradley, *The Principles of Logic*, vol. 1, p. 237.

'the world of art . . . worthless-in-itself': Bradley, *Essays on Truth and Reality*, p. 128.

Hugh Kenner . . . chapter on Bradley: Hugh Kenner, *The Invisible Poet: T. S. Eliot* (London: Methuen, 1965), pp. 35–9.

What seas . . . My daughter: T. S. Eliot, *The Complete Poems and Plays*, pp. 109–10.

'underlying felt whole': Bradley, *Essays on Truth and Reality*, p. 31.

'felt totality': Bradley, *Appearance and Reality*, pp. 95, 204.

'ambiguous existence . . . about to be': Bradley, *Essays on Truth and Reality*, p. 31.

'great gift . . . matter': Eliot, *For Lancelot Andrewes*, p. 69.

'extremely readable in snippets': Ibid.

too ready to accuse . . . toadying: See Ch. 21, p. 369.

'But an idea . . . event': Bradley, *Appearance and Reality*, p. 165.

'content': Ibid., p. 208.

'congeries': Ibid., pp. 66, 157, 228; *Essays on Truth and Reality*, p. 270; *The Principles of Logic*, vol. 1, pp. 5, 7, 8.

Riding and Graves . . . Sonnet 129: Laura Riding and Robert Graves, *A Survey of Modernist Poetry* (London: Heinemann, 1929), pp. 59–82.

Bradley emphasizes context: See Ch. 32, p. 535.

sparing with . . . term itself: An instance occurs at Bradley, *Appearance and Reality*, p. 156.

'For phenomena . . . impossible': Ibid., p. 188.

'confused coexistence': Bradley, Ibid., p. 204.

we may play . . . 'objective correlative': See Ch. 32, p. 534.

'the opposition . . . no relation': Bradley, *Essays on Truth and Reality*, pp. 416–17.

But there other . . . phrase: Ibid., pp. 194–5, 247, 264, 278, 326.

Kenner's opinion: Kenner, *The Invisible Poet*, p. 39.

'whose works . . . profoundly': T. S. Eliot, *To Criticize the Critic and Other Writings*, (London: Faber and Faber, 1965), p. 20.

'can present . . . these years': T. S. Eliot, *Knowledge and Experience in the Philosophy of F.H. Bradley* (London: Faber, 1964), pp. 10–11.

Morality and religion . . . relative: Bradley, *Essays on Truth and Reality*, p. 346.

Poetry . . . difficulties: T. S. Eliot, 'Preface to the 1928 Edition', *The Sacred Wood: Essays on Poetry and Criticism*, 7th edn. (London: Methuen, 1950), pp. viii–ix (first pub. 1920).

an idea . . . an event: Bradley, *Appearance and Reality*, p. 165.

For the whole . . . content: Ibid., p. 397.

No pursuit . . . feeling: Bradley, *Essays on Truth and Reality*, pp. 14–15.

'On Margate . . . nothing': Eliot, *The Complete Poems and Plays*, p. 70 (*The Waste Land*, III, ll. 300–2).

'the captious . . . negligence': Bradley, *Appearance and Reality*, p. 171.

'end . . . enjoyment': Eliot, *The Sacred Wood*, p. 13.

'realization': Bradley, *Appearance and Reality*, p. 366.

'attention': Ibid., p. 400.

'inter-connexion and unity': Ibid., p. 188.

'consummation': Ibid., p. 152.

'has not . . . charming': Eliot, *The Sacred Wood*, p. 37.

'purity . . . purpose': Eliot, *For Lancelot Andrewes*, p. 70 ('Francis Herbert Bradley').

'Philosophy . . . chaos': Bradley, *Essays on Truth and Reality*, p. 381.

'Within . . . not irrational': Bradley, *Appearance and Reality*, p. 458; see also p. 432.

But as long as . . . standing: Bradley, *The Principles of Logic*, vol. 1, p. 617; see also p. 704.

'classicist . . . religion': Eliot, *For Lancelot Andrewes*, p. ix.

'I did not mind . . . abides': Simone Weil, *Waiting for God*, tr. Emma Craufurd (New York: Harper and Row, 1973), p. 64.

'ten in a compartment . . . Swansea': Eliot, *Selected Essays*, p. 16 ('The Function of Criticism').

It will not do . . . abuse of words: Eliot, *The Sacred Wood*, p. ix.

'one shock of recognition': Herman Melville, 'Hawthorne and his Mosses': 'For genius, all over the world, stands hand in hand, and one shock of recognition runs the whole circle round'. See Edmund Wilson, *The Shock of Recognition: The Development of Literature in the United States Recorded by the Men Who Made It* (Garden City, NY: Doubleday, Doran, 1943), p. 199.

'made new': 'Make It New' is the Confucian axiom (*xin ri ri xin*, from the *Da xue*) used by Ezra Pound as the title of a collection of his essays, *Make It New* (London: Faber and Faber, 1934), and translated by him in *Confucius: The Great Digest & Unwobbling Pivot* (London: P. Owen, 1952), p. 36. See also Pound's Canto LIII.

'they had . . . defined': Eliot, *The Sacred Wood*, p. 23.

'there is . . . into feeling': Eliot, *Selected Essays*, p. 246 ('The Metaphysical Poets').

'the most powerful . . . associations': Ibid., p. 243 ('The Metaphysical Poets').

'A bracelet . . . the bone': Eliot is discussing line 6 of Donne's 'The Relique'.

Bradleian 'enjoyment': For a discussion of 'enjoy' in Bradley and Eliot, see Ch. 32, pp. 535–7.

'part of our . . . not addressed to us': T. S. Eliot, *On Poetry and Poets* (New York: Farrar, Straus, & Cudahy, 1957), p. 109.

John Stuart Mill: See 'Thoughts on Poetry and Its Varieties' (1833), in *Collected Works of John Stuart Mill*, 33 vols. (Toronto: University of Toronto Press, 1963–91), vol. 1, p. 348. 'Poetry and eloquence are both alike the expression or utterance of feeling. But if we may be excused the antithesis, we should say that eloquence is *heard*, poetry is *overheard*'.

'we over-emphasize . . . and pastime': Eliot, *On Poetry and Poets*, p. 131.

'Even a man . . . Nature of Things': Quoted in Eliot, *On Poetry and Poets*, p. 116 ('The Frontiers of Criticism').

'whether . . . criticism is for': Ibid.

The 'this' . . . of your truth: Bradley, *Essays on Truth and Reality*, p. 264.

'you have failed . . . your judgement': Ibid., p. 265.

'about any writer . . . enjoy?" ': Eliot, *To Criticize the Critic*, p. 20.

'How do we . . . another?': R. L. Nettleship, *Lectures on the Republic of Plato* (London: Macmillan, 1925), p. 192.

'The idea . . . the place': William Empson, *The Structure of Complex Words*, 3rd edn. (London: Penguin, 1977), p. xii ('Comment for Second Edition (1951)'; first pub. 1951).

Williams was . . . a writer: See Eliot's review of Charles Williams, *The Descent of the Dove* (London: Longmans, Green, 1939) in *New Statesman and Nation*, vol. 18, no. 459 (9 Dec. 1939), pp. 864, 866; his introduction to Charles Williams, *All Hallows' Eve* (New York: Pellegrini & Cudahy, 1948); and his obituary of Williams, in the *Times* (17 May 1945).

'There is no doubt . . . fully': Alice Mary Hadfield, *An Introduction to Charles Williams* (London: R. Hale, 1959), p. 80.

'poetry can do . . . operation of faith': Charles Williams, *The Descent of the Dove: A Short History of the Holy Spirit in the Church* (London: Longmans, Green, 1939), p. 123.

'instressing . . . own praise': Gerard M. Hopkins, *Sermons and Devotional Writings*, ed. Christopher Devlin (London: Oxford University Press, 1959), p. 201.

'imagination . . . itself': Williams, quoted in Alice Mary Hadfield, *Charles Williams: An Exploration of His Life and Work* (New York: Oxford University Press, 1983), p. 114.

'The call . . . final': Williams, paraphrased in Hadfield, *Charles Williams*, p. 133.

'poetry . . . existing': Charles Williams, *The English Poetic Mind* (Oxford: Clarendon Press, 1932), p. vii.

'the chief . . . sake': Ibid., p. 5.

'Poetry . . . authority': Ibid., p. 167.

'the sense . . . approaching greatness': Ibid., p. 198.

'the action . . . or neglect': *OED*², s.v. 'dereliction'.

Poetry . . . the better: T. S. Eliot, *The Use of Poetry and the Use of Criticism* (Cambridge, MA: Harvard University Press, 1933), p. 155.

In the preceding chapter . . . would have been different: See Ch. 32, p. 543.

Even when . . . given: Eliot, *The Use of Poetry and the Use of Criticism*, p. 141.

The age . . . modern stage: Ezra Pound, *Personae*, ed. Lea Baechler and A. Walton Litz (New York: New Directions, 1990), p. 186 (*Hugh Selwyn Mauberley*, II, ll. 1–3). Cf. Pound, *Poems and Translations*, ed. Richard Sieburth (New York: Library of America, 2003), p. 549.

34.   A Postscript on Modernist Poetics

In every . . . other side: Ralph W. Emerson, *Essays and Lectures*, ed. Joel Porte (New York: Viking, 1983), p. 259 ('Self-Reliance'); cf. *Collected Works of Ralph Waldo Emerson*, 6 vols. to date (Cambridge, MA: Belknap Press, 1971–), vol. 2, p. 27.

'stranger . . . time': Emerson, *Essays and Lectures*, p. 259; cf. *Collected Works*, vol. 2, p. 227.

you have failed...your judgement: F. H. Bradley, *Essays on Truth and Reality* (Oxford: Clarendon Press, 1914), p. 265.

'spicy wreaths | Of incense': John Keats, *The Poems of John Keats*, ed. Jack Stillinger (Cambridge MA: Harvard University Press, 1982), p. 252 (*Hyperion*, I, ll. 186–7).

Instead of sweets...and metal sick: Keats, *Poems*, p. 252 (*Hyperion*, I, ll. 188–9).

'The Theology of the Symbol': Karl Rahner, *Theological Investigations*, 23 vols. (publishers vary, 1961–2), vol. 4, pp. 221–52 (vol. 4 is entitled 'More Recent Writings', tr. Kevin Smyth).

'first statement'... nature': Ibid., p. 224.

'Being...in unity': Ibid., p. 229.

'A being...at all': Ibid., p. 230.

'I do not...our plough': W. B. Yeats, *Ah, Sweet Dancer* (London: Macmillan, 1970), p. 81.

'Do you...I hate!': Ibid., p. 88.

'monsters': F. H. Bradley, *Appearance and Reality*, 2nd edn. (Oxford: Clarendon Press, 1930), p. 43.

'chimera[s]': Ibid., p. 73.

'When "white"...thing': Ibid., p. 16.

The elements...by reason: Charles S. Peirce, *The Essential Peirce*, 2 vols., ed. Peirce Edition Project (Bloomington, IN: Indiana University Press, 1992–8), vol. 2, p. 241.

Ignorance: See John Bunyan, *The Pilgrim's Progress*, ed. James Blanton Wharey, rev. Roger Sharrock (Oxford: Oxford University Press, 1960), p. 163.

'For poetry...happen': W. H. Auden, *The English Auden*, ed. Edward Mendelson (New York: Random House, 1977), p. 242 ('In Memory of W. B. Yeats', stanza 2, l. 5).

'How to...is the difficulty': Gillian Rose, *The Broken Middle* (Oxford: Blackwell, 1992), p. 155.

'For Aristotle...terms': Ibid., p. 116.

'Thisness...particularity': F. H. Bradley, *The Principles of Logic*, 2nd edn., rev. 2 vols. (London: Oxford University Press, 1922), vol. 1, p. 65.

This detail...constitutes thisness: Ibid.

the 'this': On 'the "this" of feeling' (Bradley, *Essays on Truth and Reality*, p. 264), see Ch. 33, p. 561.

'Brute Actuality': Peirce, *The Essential Peirce*, vol. 2, p. 435 ('the Brute Actuality of things and facts', in 'A Neglected Argument for the Reality of God').

He is...scarcely at all: Gerard M. Hopkins, *Sermons and Devotional Writings*, ed. Christopher Devlin (London: Oxford University Press, 1959), p. 151 ('Is not this pitch or whatever we call it Scotus's *ecceitas*?'); see the note on pp. 293–4.

ultima realitas entis: Hopkins, *Sermons and Devotional Writings*, p. 283.

ultima solitudo: Ibid.

Down roughcast...and pair: Gerard M. Hopkins, *Poetical Works*, ed. Norman H. MacKenzie (Oxford: Clarendon Press, 1990), p. 198 ('That Nature is a Heraclitean Fire and of the comfort of the Resurrection', ll. 3–4).

'Enough! the Resurrection': Hopkins, *Complete Poetical Works*, p. 198 ('That Nature is a Heraclitean Fire and of the comfort of the Resurrection', l. 16).

'the wórld's . . . wónder': Ibid., p. 120 (*The Wreck of the Deutschland*, l. 38).

'We have . . . actually exists': Bradley, *Appearance and Reality*, p. 131.

the arbitrary nature of poetry . . . Charles Williams: See further Ch. 33, pp. 562–3.

It is this . . . poetical symbols: Austin M. Farrer, *The Glass of Vision* (London: Dacre Press, 1948), p. 122.

'torpor': In the Preface to *Lyrical Ballads* (1800); see *Lyrical Ballads, and Other Poems, 1797–1800*, ed. James Butler and Karen Green (Ithaca, NY: Cornell University Press, 1992), p. 746.

'language without . . . to exist': Charles Williams, quoted in Alice Mary Hadfield, *Charles Williams: An Exploration of His Life and Work* (New York: Oxford University Press, 1983), p. 122.

as heavy as lead: See Ch. 20, p. 362.

'profound contrariety': Charles Williams, *The Descent of the Dove* (London: Longmans, Green, 1939), p. 87.

'But in what . . . expresses.': Charles Williams, *The English Poetic Mind* (Oxford: Clarendon Press, 1932), p. 126.

'Poetry . . . own authority': Ibid., p. 167.

Simultaneous . . . multiple plane: Simone Weil, *The Need for Roots*, tr. Arthur Wills (Boston: Beacon Press, 1952), p. 207.

'of the first voice' . . . no one': T. S. Eliot, *On Poetry and Poets* (New York: Farrar, Straus, & Cudahy, 1957), p. 106.

'profound McTaggart': W. B. Yeats, *The Collected Poems of W. B. Yeats*, ed. Richard J. Finneran, new edn. (New York: Macmillan, 1989), p. 340 ('A Bronze Head', l. 13).

Bradley's word 'mere': In *Appearance and Reality* I counted 700 instances of 'mere' in the book's 570 pages and have almost certainly missed others.

When Pearse . . . Post Office: Yeats, *Collected Poems*, p. 337 ('The Statues', ll. 25–6).

not Pearse but Standish O'Grady: See Raymond J. Porter, *P. H. Pearse* (New York: Twayne, 1973), p. 19.

'image . . . leaders': Donal McCartney in *1916: The Easter Rising*, ed. O. Dudley Edwards and Fergus Pyle (London: MacGibbon & Kee, 1968), p. 45 ('Gaelic Ideological Origins of 1916').

'cult . . . reincarnated Cuchulainn': Ibid.

'Where are you . . . numbers': Quoted in Jon Stallworthy, *Vision and Revision in Yeats's Last Poems* (Oxford: Clarendon Press, 1969), p. 126. See also W. B. Yeats, *The Poems*, ed. Daniel Albright (London: Dent, 1992), p. 822 (which appears to mistranscribe Stallworthy's 'Certainty' as 'Certainly').

'filthy modern . . . fury': Yeats, *Collected Poems*, p. 337 ('The Statues', ll. 29–30).

'intellect . . . measurement': Ibid. (ll. 26–7).

the actual . . . College of Surgeons: See *The Irish Uprising 1916–1922*, ed. Goddard Lieberson (New York: Macmillan 1966), pp. 34–5.

I have met . . . houses: Yeats, *Collected Poems*, p. 180 ('Easter, 1916', ll. 1–4).

'takes a slight . . . with them': T. S. Eliot, *Selected Essays*, 2nd edn. (New York: Harcourt, Brace, 1964), p. 259 (first pub. 1932, enlarged edn. 1960; 'Andrew Marvell').

Nothing . . . Reality: Bradley, *Principles of Logic*, vol. 2, p. 673.

'materials for . . . nation itself': W. B. Yeats, *The Variorum Edition of the Plays of W. B. Yeats*, ed. Russell K. Alspach and Catharine C. Alspach (New York: Macmillan, 1969), pp. 957–8; cf. W. B. Yeats, *Wheels and Butterflies* (New York: Macmillan, 1935), p. 7.

'Swift haunts me': Yeats, *Variorum Edition of the Plays*, p. 958; cf. Yeats, *Wheels and Butterflies*, p. 7.

'Perish the day on which I was born!': Yeats, *Variorum Edition of the Plays*, p. 956; cf. Yeats, *Wheels and Butterflies*, p. 56.

'the timeless moment': T. S. Eliot, *The Complete Poems and Plays of T. S. Eliot* (London: Faber and Faber, 1969), p. 192 ('Little Gidding', I. 54).

'uneducated vulgar opinion': F. H. Bradley, *Ethical Studies*, 2nd edn. (Oxford: Clarendon Press, 1927), p. 169.

'democratic bonhomie' . . . horse collar': W. B. Yeats, The *Variorum Edition of the Poems of W. B. Yeats*, ed. Peter Allt and Russell K. Alspach (New York: Macmillan, 1965), p. 835; cf. Yeats, *The King of the Great Clock Tower, Commentaries and Poems* (New York: Macmillan, 1935), p. 30.

'You are not here to verify': Eliot, *Complete Poems and Plays*, p. 192 ('Little Gidding,' I. 45).

No body . . . beggar-man: Yeats, *Variorum Edition of the Plays*, p. 1063; cf. Yeats, *Last Poems and Two Plays* (Dublin: Cuala Press, 1939), p. 47.

'When they . . . newspaper': Yeats, *Variorum Edition of the Plays*, p. 1051; cf. *Last Poems and Two Plays*, p. 32.

I must lie down . . . the heart: Yeats, *Collected Poems*, p. 348 ('The Circus Animals' Desertion', ll. 39–40).

served him and others: e.g. 'A meteor of the burning heart', Yeats, *Collected Poems*, p. 14 ('The Indian to his Love'); 'O heart, O troubled heart', *Collected Poems*, p. 194 ('The Tower'); 'Had de Valera eaten Parnell's heart', *Collected Poems*, p. 280 ('Parnell's Funeral'); 'lie | With a foul witch', *Collected Poems*, p. 121 ('The Witch'); 'the foul ditch where they lie', *Collected Poems*, p. 184 ('On a Political Prisoner'). Cf. Alexander Pope, *The Rape of the Lock*, Canto 1, l. 100: 'They shift the moving Toyshop of their Heart'.

('the eyes watchful, waiting, perceiving, indifferent'): Eliot, *Complete Poems and Plays*, p. 127 ('Triumphal March', l. 31).

('Don't throw away that sausage'): Ibid., p. 128 ('Triumphal March', l. 46).

Belly, shoulder . . . in the foam: Yeats, *Collected Poems*, p. 338 ('News for the Delphic Oracle', ll. 34–6).

(Escalus's riposte to Pompey the bawd): Shakespeare, *Measure for Measure*, II, i: 'Truth, and your bum is the greatest thing about you, so that in the beastliest sence, you are *Pompey* the Great'.

completed *The Rock* instead: See A. D. Moody, *Thomas Stearns Eliot: Poet* (Cambridge: Cambridge University Press, 1979), p. 165

'mere extraordinary fact': Bradley, *Appearance and Reality*, p. 98.

'mere momentary caprice': Ibid., p. 331. For further uses of 'caprice' in Bradley, see *Essays on Truth and Reality*, pp. 11, 16, 50, 51, 52, 55, 56, and 67; and *Ethical Studies*, pp. 122, 152, 174, 176, 190, and 198.

'mere speculative refinement': Bradley, *Appearance and Reality* p. 342.

'mere polemics': Ibid., p. xi.

'art is a product . . . effective agent': W. H. Auden, *Prose, Volume II: 1939–1948*, ed. Edward Mendelson (Princeton, NJ: Princeton University Press, 2002), p. 7 ('The Public v. the Late Mr William Butler Yeats').

'Three Songs to the One Burden': Yeats, *Collected Poems*, pp. 328–30.

'On being asked for a War Poem': Ibid., pp. 155–6.

'Politics': Yeats, *Collected Poems*, p. 348.

'Slouches': Ibid., p. 187 ('The Second Coming', l. 22).

'She smooths . . . hand': Eliot, *Complete Poems and Plays*, p. 69 (*The Waste Land*, l. 255); cf. Eliot, *The Annotated Waste Land with Eliot's Contemporary Prose*, ed. Lawrence Rainey (New Haven, CT: Yale University Press, 2005), p. 65.

'to get the . . . it hot': Eliot, *Complete Poems and Plays*, p. 66 (*The Waste Land*, l. 167); cf. *The Annotated Waste Land*, p. 62.

'Living to live . . . beyond me': Eliot, *Complete Poems and Plays*, p. 110 (*Marina*, l. 30).

'a broken Coriolanus': Eliot, *Complete Poems and Plays*, p. 74 (*The Waste Land*, l. 416); cf. *The Annotated Waste Land*, p. 70.

('Swift beating . . . frenzy blind'): Yeats, *Collected Poems*, p. 237 ('Blood and the Moon').

sleep 'under the greatest epitaph in history': Yeats, *Variorum Edition of the Plays*, p. 942; cf. Yeats, *Wheels and Butterflies*, p. 40.

Index

subjective/subjectivity (*cont.*)
  'element' (Pound) 183
  self-interrogation 154–5
  and solipsism 415, 417
subjectivism
  and Bradley, F. H. 556
  and Owen 420
  and Pound 246
Suckling, John
  'Love's Feast' 49
suffering
  of Christ 152
  and silence 394–406
  youthful 173
surrealism 6
Swan, Richard 187
Swift, Jonathan 71–87, 636
  and Addison 76
  and anarchy 72, 80, 606
  'An Apology to the Lady Carteret' 72
  'Baucis and Philemon' 76
  'A Beautiful Young Nymph Going
    to Bed' 84
  'Cadenus and Vanessa' 77–8
  'Cassinus and Peter' 82
  'The Character of Sir Robert
    Walpole' 80
  *A Compleat Collection of Genteel and
    Ingenious Conversation* 76
  correspondence 72, 73, 79
  and decency 83
  and democracy 85
  'A Description of a City Shower' 74
  friendships 72–4, 79
  health of 71–2
  'The Humble Petition of Frances
    Harris' 85
  and invective 80–1
  and Ireland 73–4
  'The Journal' 79
  'The Journal of a Modern Lady' 77
  'Lady Acheson Weary of the Dean' 72
  'The Legion Club' 81
  A Modest Proposal 84–5
  'On the Death of a Late Famous
    General' 80
  'A Panegyric on the Dean, in the
    Person of a Lady in the
    North' 83–4

  Pindaric(s) 80, 86
  and politics 71, 72, 73, 80, 85, 86
  *A Proposal for Correcting, Improving and
    Ascertaining the English Tongue* 76
  and raillery 78–9, 80–1
  and reaction 71, 77
  and satire 75, 76, 77
  scatological humour 82
  and Sheridan 74, 76, 79, 605
  'Strephon and Chloe' 82–3
  and taste 77
  and Temple 606
  'To Mr. Delany' 80
  and Unity of Being 79–80
  'Vanbrug's House' 76
  'Verses on the Death of Dr.
    Swift' 72, 76
Swinburne, Algernon Charles 41,
  519, 559
Swinnerton, Frank 435
Sylvester, R. S. 309
symbol(s)
  and Eliot, T. S. 540
  Farrer on 572
  and feeling 416
  fiduciary 149, 161
  Rahner on 567
  and value 465–6
  words as 158
  and Yeats 576, 577
symbolism 18–19, 106–7, 111, 365,
  396, 480
Symons, Arthur
  The Symbolist Movement in Literature 18
Symons, Clement 409, 418
Symons, Katharine E. 408–9, 410
sympathy
  and Binyon 462
  and economics 111
  and Emerson 496, 499
syntax 100, 400, 484, 489
  and the 'as'-clause 467–8
  and Blake 481
  and Bradley, F. H. 534
  as contingency 326
  and Donne 216, 451
  and Dryden 231, 242
  and Eliot, T. S. 371, 534, 541,
    545–6, 552–3

Index of Biblical Passages